THE POLITICAL ECONOMY OF THE WORLD TRADING SYSTEM

Third Edition

THE POLITICAL ECONOMY OF THE WORLD TRADING SYSTEM

THE WTO AND BEYOND

Third Edition

BERNARD M. HOEKMAN

and

MICHEL M. KOSTECKI

OXFORD

UNIVERSITY PRESS

OXFORD
UNIVERSITY PRESS

Great Clarendon Street, Oxford OX2 6DP

Oxford University Press is a department of the University of Oxford.
It furthers the University's objective of excellence in research, scholarship,
and education by publishing worldwide in

Oxford New York

Auckland Cape Town Dar es Salaam Hong Kong Karachi
Kuala Lumpur Madrid Melbourne Mexico City Nairobi
New Delhi Shanghai Taipei Toronto

With offices in

Argentina Austria Brazil Chile Czech Republic France Greece
Guatemala Hungary Italy Japan Poland Portugal Singapore
South Korea Switzerland Thailand Turkey Ukraine Vietnam

Oxford is a registered trade mark of Oxford University Press
in the UK and in certain other countries

Published in the United States
by Oxford University Press Inc., New York

© Bernard M. Hoekman and Michel M. Kostecki 2009

British Library Cataloguing in Publication Data

Data available

Library of Congress Cataloging in Publication Data

Data available

Library of Congress Control Number: 2009934133

Typeset by SPI Publisher Services, Pondicherry, India
Printed in Great Britain
on acid-free paper by
CPI Antony Rowe, Chippenham Wiltshire

ISBN 978–0–19–955376–1 (Hbk.)
978–0–19–955377–8 (Pbk.)

1 3 5 7 9 10 8 6 4 2

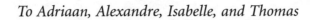

To Adriaan, Alexandre, Isabelle, and Thomas

PREFACE

STARTING as an obscure trade agreement, unknown to most citizens of participating countries, by the early 1990s the General Agreement on Tariffs and Trade (GATT) had become a prominent institution. The Uruguay Round of multilateral trade negotiations, held during 1986–93, played an important role in raising its profile, catapulting it into the public consciousness for the first time in its history. The Uruguay Round led to the creation of the World Trade Organization (WTO), and expanded the coverage of the multilateral trading system to include trade in services and intellectual property rights. Since its formation the visibility of the WTO has grown further, reflecting both negotiations to expand its coverage in the Doha Round and the large number of dispute settlement cases that are handled by the organization every year.

At the time the first edition of this book was written (1993–4), no readily accessible, yet comprehensive, introduction to the economics and politics of the trading system existed. Information about the operation of the GATT was not easy to obtain. Many documents were confidential, with access restricted to government officials. The situation changed dramatically subsequent to the establishment of the WTO and the concurrent emergence of the Internet. Most WTO documents and reports can now be downloaded freely from the WTO home page (www.wto.org). Greatly expanded coverage of the institution in the press and dedicated newsletters—both print and online—makes it much easier than in the past to remain up-to-date with respect to WTO-related events.

The greater press coverage and extensive monitoring of the WTO by nongovernmental entities reflects the public interest in the institution. The WTO is frequently at the centre of trade conflicts between members that concern large groups of people as well as specific industries. Examples are disputes between the US and the European Union (EU) on the use of genetically modified organisms and hormones in consumer products, the tax regimes that apply to revenues earned from foreign sales, and the trade effects of environmental policies. Suggestions to expand the reach of the WTO are hotly debated in policy circles and strongly supported or opposed by a variety of interest groups.

The objective of this third edition remains unchanged: to offer a self-contained introduction to the political economy of the multilateral trading system. A substantial legal literature on the WTO and its case law now exists, as well as a rapidly expanding body of work that focuses on the negotiating process. This book complements the legal and process-oriented literature on the WTO by providing a self-contained treatment of the policy, economic and development-related aspects of the trading system, as well as the basic 'rules of the game'. The focus is on understanding the forces that drive processes and outcomes and the incentives for governments to abide by negotiated agreements.

Governments are not the social welfare-maximizing entities they are often assumed to be in introductory economics textbooks. Policies reflect pressures by domestic interest groups and the preferences of governments and domestic political institutions, as well as actions of other governments, who in turn are responding to their own interest groups. A political economy approach helps to understand how the WTO functions, why the post-war GATT was very successful in reducing tariffs, and why it has proven much more difficult to expand the reach of multilateral disciplines to other domestic policies that have an impact on trade.

There have been major developments in the trading system since the second edition was completed in 2000. The membership of the WTO has expanded to 153, and now includes China. The rapid economic expansion and trade growth achieved by China and other major emerging markets such as Brazil and India is changing the balance of power in global trade relations. Developing countries are increasingly prominent players in the organization. The number of preferential trade agreements continues to grow, and has expanded rapidly in Asia, a region that 10 years ago was not much engaged in this agenda. The difficulty of concluding the Doha Round raises important questions about the structure and modalities of multilateral cooperation on trade.

In this third edition we discuss these developments in some depth. All chapters have been revised extensively and updated to the end of 2008. A significant amount of new material has been added on dispute settlement cases throughout the book, a number of which have been of major significance both in terms of clarifying WTO disciplines and in terms of economic impacts. New material has also been added on agricultural trade policy, trade in services, the increasing use of contingent protection by developing countries, preferential trade agreements (reciprocal and nonreciprocal), the changing 'balance of power' in the institution and the world economy as a result of the rapid growth of China and other emerging markets—which has increased the prominence of economic development concerns in WTO discussions, led to numerous new coalitions between countries and an increase in the number of contingent protection measures imposed by developing countries, as well as the emergence of 'aid for trade' assistance on the agenda of the WTO—the difficulties of extending the WTO to cover 'behind the border' policy areas such as investment, competition and procurement policies, and the re-emergence of environment-trade policy questions (global climate change).

This edition also attempts to take into account much of the relevant academic literature that has been published since the late 1990s. In the pre-WTO period, the study of the trading system was a bit of a niche field, whether in economics, political science (international relations) or international public law. One effect of the increased popular interest in the institution (in part a result of the dispute settlement case load and in part reflecting controversial negotiations) and the expansion of its substantive coverage and membership has been a veritable explosion of papers that analyse the rationale for multilateral trade cooperation, coalition formation, the process of WTO negotiation and the economics (and political economy) of proposed rules. This body of work has done much to improve our understanding of 'how the WTO works'.

Many new boxes and examples have been incorporated into the text to relate the operation of the trading system to the real-world economic interests that underpin and are affected by it. The Annex (Annex 2) providing a brief synthesis of basic economic concepts and the effects of trade policy instruments has been extended to include a brief treatment of the welfare effects of trade in services, trade preferences and preference erosion, and discrimination in government procurement. As in previous editions, short guides to more specialized works are included at the end of each chapter and there is an extensive and up-to-date bibliography.

We owe a substantial intellectual debt to those who have written on various aspects of the multilateral trade regime, to many members of the WTO Secretariat, both past and present, as well as to numerous trade negotiators, government officials and scholars. Some of the material used in this book draws on joint work with a large number of friends and colleagues, including Kym Anderson, Chad Bown, Simon Evenett, Kishore Gawande, Joe Francois, Peter Holmes, Henrik Horn, Robert Howse, Mike Leidy, Patrick Low, Will Martin, Aaditya Mattoo, Petros Mavroidis, Patrick Messerlin, Richard Newfarmer, Alessandro Nicita, Marcelo Olarreaga, Carlos Primo Braga, Susan Prowse, Jayanta Roy, Kamal Saggi, Joel Trachtman, David Vines and Alan Winters.

We are particularly indebted to Chad Bown, Henrik Horn, Patrick Low, Petros Mavroidis, John Odell and Kamal Saggi for reading and commenting on drafts of parts of this third edition, and to Francis Ng, Karen McCusker, Maria-Rosa Perrin, Müslüm Yilmaz, Mark Koulen, Roy Santana, Jean-Pierre Lapalme, Hans-Peter Werner, Olivier Naray and Reza Etemad-Sajadi for assistance, providing data and helping to update tables, figures and other material.

We are also grateful to Marco Bronckers, Rashad Cassim, Bill Davey, Alan Deardorff, Ishac Diwan, Alice Enders, Philip English, Simon Evenett, Mike Finger, Gary Horlick, Henrik Horn, Bob Hudec, Marion Jansen, Serafino Marchese, Will Martin, Keith Maskus, Aaditya Mattoo, Patrick Messerlin, Costas Michalopoulos, Marcelo Olarreaga, Pier Carlo Padoan, David Palmeter, Carmen Pont-Viera, Garry Pursell, Frieder Roessler, André Sapir, Maurice Schiff, Richard Snape,

T. N. Srinivasan, Bob Staiger, Bob Stern, Alan Sykes, David Tarr, Diana Tussie, John Whalley, John Wilson, Alan Winters, Jamel Zarrouk and B. K. Zutshi for comments, discussions and suggestions that helped improve this or previous editions.

None of the above is responsible for the views expressed in this book or any errors and inaccuracies, nor should anything said in this book be attributed to our current or past employers. That responsibility is ours alone.

B.M.H.
M.M.K.

CONTENTS

LIST OF FIGURES

LIST OF TABLES

LIST OF ABBREVIATIONS

AB	Appellate Body
ACP	African, Caribbean and Pacific
ACWL	Advisory Centre on WTO Law
AD	antidumping
AGOA	African Growth and Opportunity Act
AITIC	Agency for International Trade Information and Cooperation
AMS	Aggregate Measure of Support
AoA	Agreement on Agriculture
APEC	Asian-Pacific Economic Cooperation
ASEAN	Association of South-East Asian Nations
ATC	Agreement on Textiles and Clothing
AVE	*ad valorem* equivalents
BATNA	best alternative to a negotiated agreement
BIS	Bank for International Settlements
BIT	bilateral investment treaty
BOP	balance-of-payments
BPO	business process outsourcing
BTN	Brussels Tariff Nomenclature
CAFTA	Central America Free Trade Agreement
CAP	Common Agricultural Policy
CBD	Convention on Biological Diversity
CBEA	Caribbean Banana Exporters Association
CCCN	Customs Cooperation Council Nomenclature
CER	Closer Economic Relations
c.i.f.	cost, insurance and freight
CMEA	Council of Mutual Economic Assistance
COMESA	Common Market for Eastern and Southern Africa

CRTA	Committee on Regional Trade Agreements
CSI	Coalition of Service Industries
CTE	Committee on Trade and the Environment
CTH	change in tariff heading
CTS	Consolidated Tariff Schedules
CUTS	Consumer Unity and Trust Society
CVDs	countervailing duties
CWB	Canadian Wheat Board
DDA	Doha Development Agenda
DFID	Department for International Development
DISC	Domestic International Sales Corporation
DR–CAFTA	Dominican Republic–Central America Free Trade Agreement
DS	dispute settlement
DSB	Dispute Settlement Body
DSP	dispute settlement procedure
DSU	Dispute Settlement Understanding
DUP	directly unproductive profit-seeking
EBA	Everything But Arms
EBRD	European Bank for Reconstruction and Development
ECOSOC	United Nations Economic and Social Council
EEC	European Economic Community
EFTA	European Free Trade Association
EIF	Enhanced Integrated Framework
EPA	Economic Partnership Agreement
EPZ	export processing zone
ERP	effective rate of protection
ESM	emergency safeguard mechanism
EU	European Union
EUROBIT	European Association of Manufacturers of Business Machines and Information Technology Industry
FATS	foreign affiliate trade in services
FAO	Food and Agriculture Organization
FDA	Food and Drug Administration
FDI	foreign direct investment

FIRA	Foreign Investment Review Act
f.o.b.	free-on-board
FOGS	Functioning of the GATT System
FSC	Foreign Sales Corporations
FTA	free trade agreement
GATS	General Agreement on Trade in Services
GATT	General Agreement on Tariffs and Trade
GDP	gross domestic product
GI	geographical indication
GMO	genetically modified organisms
GPA	Government Procurement Agreement
GSM	Global System for Mobile communications
GSP	generalized system of preferences
HACCP	Hazard Analysis Critical Control Point
HS	Harmonized Commodity Description and Coding System
IBRD	International Bank for Reconstruction and Development
ICC	International Chamber of Commerce
ICITO	Interim Commission for the International Trade Organization
ICT	information and communication technology
ICTSD	International Centre for Trade and Sustainable Development
IDB	Integrated Database
IF	Integrated Framework
IFIA	International Federation of Inspection Agencies
ILEAP	International Lawyers and Economists Against Poverty
ILO	International Labor Office
IMF	International Monetary Fund
IPR	intellectual property rights
ISO	International Organization for Standardization
IT	information technology
ITA	Information Technology Agreement
ITC	International Trade Centre
ITO	International Trade Organization
ITU	International Telecommunications Union
JITAP	Joint Integrated Trade Assistance Programme

JOBS	Jumpstart Our Business Strength
LAN	local area network
LCA	Liverpool Cotton Association
LDC	least developed country
LTA	Long-Term Arrangement
MAI	Multilateral Agreement on Investment
MAS	mutually agreed solution
MEA	multilateral environmental agreement
MFA	Multifibre Arrangement
MFN	most favoured nation
MRAs	mutual recognition agreements
MRL	maximum residual limit
MTNs	multilateral trade negotiations
NAFTA	North American Free Trade Agreement
NAMA	nonagricultural market access
NES	national environmental standards
NGO	nongovernmental organization
NRA	nominal rate of assistance
NRP	nominal rate of protection
NTB	nontariff barrier
NTM	nontariff measure
OECD	Organization for Economic Cooperation and Development
OTC	Organization for Trade Cooperation
OTDS	Overall Trade Distorting Support
OTRI	Overall Trade Restrictiveness Index
PAFTA	Pan-Arab Free Trade Agreement
PhRMA	Pharmaceutical Research and Manufacturers of America
PPM	production process method
PSE	Producer Support Estimate
PSI	pre-shipment inspection
PTA	preferential trade agreement
QRs	quantitative restrictions
RAM	recently acceded member
R&D	research and development

ROO	rules of origin
SACU	Southern African Customs Union
SADC	Southern African Development Community
SBTC	skill-biased technical change
SCM	subsidies and countervailing measures
SDT	special and differential treatment
SG	safeguard
SGS	Société Générale de Surveillance
SITC	Standard International Trade Classification
SME	small- and medium-sized enterprise
SPS	sanitary and phytosanitary
SSG	special safeguard
SSM	special safeguard mechanism
STDF	Standards and Trade Development Facility
STE	state-trading enterprise
SVE	small and vulnerable economies
TABD	Transatlantic Business Dialogue
TACD	Transatlantic Consumer Dialogue
TBR	Trade Barrier Regulation
TBT	Technical Barriers to Trade
TED	turtle exclusion device
TMB	Textiles Monitoring Body
TPRB	Trade Policy Review Body
TPRM	Trade Policy Review Mechanism
TRAINS	Trade Analysis and Information System
TRIMs	Trade-Related Investment Measures
TRIPS	Trade-related Intellectual Property Rights
TRQ	tariff rate quota
TRS	technical regulations and standards
TWN	Third World Network
UL	Underwriters Laboratories
UN	United Nations
UNCTAD	United Nations Conference on Trade and Development
UNDP	United Nations Development Programme

UNEP	United Nations Environment Programme
USSR	Union of Soviet Socialist Republics
USTR	United States Trade Representative
VAT	value added tax
VER	voluntary export restraint
WCO	World Customs Organization
WHO	World Health Organization
WIPO	World Intellectual Property Organization
WITS	World Integrated Trade Solution
WTO	World Trade Organization

INTRODUCTION

ESTABLISHED in 1995, the World Trade Organization (WTO) administers the trade agreements negotiated by its members, in particular the General Agreement on Tariffs and Trade (GATT), the General Agreement on Trade in Services (GATS), and the Agreement on Trade-related Intellectual Property Rights (TRIPS). The value of total world trade in goods and services, including payments for intellectual property was some US$16 trillion (thousand billion) in 2007. The WTO's rules and principles establish a legal framework for much of this exchange.

The WTO builds upon the organizational structure that had developed under GATT auspices. At its creation in 1947, the GATT was essentially a tariff agreement. Over time, as average tariff levels fell as a result of periodic rounds of negotiations, the focus expanded to cover nontariff barriers (NTBs) and domestic policies with an impact on trade. A complex patchwork of policy-specific agreements emerged. Participation in the GATT expanded steadily. By the end of the Uruguay Round (1994), 128 countries had joined the GATT. Since the entry into force of the WTO in 1995, another two dozen countries acceded, bringing the total to 153 as of 2008. Suggestions made during the Uruguay Round negotiations that 'GATT is dead' and more recent criticisms of the WTO sit oddly with these signs of popularity.

The underlying philosophy of the WTO—as was the case for the GATT that preceded it—is that open markets, transparency and nondiscriminatory trade policies are conducive to the national welfare of all countries. A rationale for the way the organization works—through reciprocal negotiations that define enforceable commitments and mutually agreed rules of the game for trade-related policies—is that the prospect of better access to export markets helps governments overcome political constraints that prevent the adoption of more efficient trade policies.

Although there are many similarities with the GATT, the WTO differs in a number of important respects from the institution that preceded it. These differences have potentially important implications for the functioning of the trading system, in particular for developing economies. The GATT was a rather flexible institution. Bargaining and deal-making lay at its core, with significant opportunities for countries to 'opt out' of specific disciplines. This is much less the case today. The WTO rules apply to all members, and are subject to binding dispute settlement procedures. This is attractive to groups seeking to introduce multilateral disciplines on a variety of subjects—ranging from the environment and labour standards to competition and investment policies to animal rights. But it is a source of concern to groups who perceive the (proposed) multilateral rules to be inappropriate or worry that the adoption of specific rules may affect detrimentally the ability of governments to regulate domestic activities and deal with market failures in ways that they deem most appropriate.

Almost from the start of its existence the WTO attracted a significant amount of critical attention. Public concerns are to some extent a reflection of the increasing speed at which global integration is occurring. Between 1900 and 2000 the value of international trade doubled. The cross-border flow of foreign direct investment (FDI) expanded even more rapidly, growing 10 times faster than world production. Since 2000, trade and FDI flows have continued to grow at a blistering pace, with world trade doubling once again and the stock of outward FDI passing the $13.5 trillion mark in 2007—accounting for some 10 per cent of world output (UNCTAD, 2008). In the post 2000 period, the growth rates of developing country trade have significantly exceeded those of high-income countries, helping to sustain high rates of economic growth and reductions in poverty rates. These positive trends coincided with more liberal trade policies and market-oriented reforms. Only one employee in ten is currently working in countries that are largely separated from the world market, compared to two-thirds some three decades ago (Dicken, 1998). Multinational corporations have assumed a much greater role in the world economy. In 2006, some 75 million people were employed by foreign affiliates of multinational companies, a threefold increase compared to 1990, with much of the growth in developing countries. One-third of all affiliates of multinational companies are located in China, although most of these tend to be small in scale or joint ventures (UNCTAD, 2007).

The high and sustained rates of growth in trade and cross-border investment flows have been beneficial from a global economic point of view, with the increase in developing countries' market shares improving the global distribution of income and economic activity. Developing countries as a group now account for 35 per cent of world trade, up from only 20 per cent in the early 1990s. The most impressive performer has been the Chinese economy, more than tripling its share in world exports between 1990 and 2007 and on track to become the largest exporter of goods in 2008 (WTO, 2008). 'Fear of China' is common among producers of manufactures around the globe, not least in other developing countries, as is 'fear of India' among producers in rich countries of what used to be nontradable services supplied to businesses and households. The absence of significant across-the-board imposition of protectionist measures in importing countries is as much a testimony to the success of the trading system as is the observed growth in trade it has helped generate. Whether the open global trading system that now exists can be sustained depends on how effective societies will be in undertaking and facilitating the adjustments that are needed to accommodate the economic expansion of developing countries. To some extent those adjustments may imply the use of trade policies that are permitted by WTO rules—such as antidumping, which has been increasingly used by many countries—but mostly they require domestic policies that target the affected groups directly.

The need for liberalization is greatest in agriculture where policies in rich countries impose significant negative spillovers of many developing countries—a central issue in the Doha Development Agenda (DDA), and the one that is largely responsible for the slow progress of the negotiations. As important as managing adjustment, is for countries that have seen their trade shares increase greatly to play a more prominent role in contributing to the public good of an open multilateral trading system. This implies a greater willingness to lock in liberalization through the WTO and accede to requests for fuller reciprocity in trade negotiations. Such fuller participation in the WTO by the emerging market economies is one of the major challenges confronting the multilateral trading system. Without greater reciprocity, pressures will grow for protection in importing countries that are being forced to adjust as their domestic industries contract as a result of competition from (more) efficient exporters. Increasingly this is a services agenda, intermediated by foreign direct and portfolio investment (including sovereign wealth funds).

The growth of developing country trade since the mid-1990s is both an example of the importance of the WTO and the challenge confronting the organization. New trade powers need to be accommodated and integrated into the system, which requires greater attention to be given to addressing the concerns of low-income countries that are lagging behind. The enormous heterogeneity of the WTO membership—which can no longer be characterized by a North–South divide—complicates the needed agreement on where the boundaries of the institution lie. Views differ significantly on what the objectives of the WTO are or should be.

A number of the ministerial meetings of the WTO post-1995 were accompanied by demonstrations by groups spanning the nongovernmental organization (NGO) community, farmers and labour unions seeking to limit or to expand the reach of multilateral disciplines. High-profile and sometimes violent street protests during the 1999 Seattle WTO ministerial helped scuttle efforts to launch the so-called millennium round and marred ministerial meetings in Cancun (2003) and Hong Kong (2005). In Cancun, a Korean farmer committed suicide in front of TV cameras for the world to see. Many citizens of member countries have a very limited and often skewed understanding of what the WTO is and does, and what it is not and does not do. The extent of the disconnect that emerged in the late 1990s is exemplified by a 1999 Swiss TV programme in which a small boy is scared to go to sleep because 'there is a WTO under my bed'. Although opposition to the GATT and the Uruguay Round was quite intense at times—giving rise to posters representing the institution as a 'GATTzilla' (referring to the cartoon monster Godzilla)—it never reached the point where a TV producer could feel comfortable assuming it impacted on the fears of children. Matters have improved substantially since 2000 as a result of an active outreach effort by the WTO Secretariat, but NGO concern and opposition remains prominent, as illustrated by a steady drumbeat of WTO criticism at the World Social Forum—a rival convention to the WTO-friendly World Economic Forum held annually in Davos, Switzerland.

Although efforts to liberalize trade have always been opposed—sometimes very vocally—by domestic groups who stand to lose from greater competition (for example farmers in high-income countries), the terms of the debate surrounding the WTO now extend well beyond the traditional trade liberalization agenda. Understanding how the WTO works, its strengths and weaknesses, and what might be done to make the institution a more effective tool of multilateral cooperation is vital. Many of the WTO's critics continue to have serious misconceptions about the organization, while many of those who are seeking to expand the WTO's mandate often appear to ignore basic principles of economics and risk the continued viability of an institution that has played a key role in sustaining the open economic system, which has helped raise per capita incomes in much of the world to levels never seen before in history. At the same time, some of the criticism reflects deeply held beliefs and concerns. Some of the subjects that are a bone of contention cannot or should not be dealt with by the WTO and claims of sins of commission or omission are therefore often inappropriate. But some matters can and should be laid at the door of the WTO.

Our goal in this book is to provide a succinct description of the principles, rules and procedures of the multilateral trading system, as well as a political economy-informed discussion of how it functions. This book does not provide a detailed negotiating history—who did what and when—although the results of negotiations and ministerial meetings are discussed at some length, including the subjects that were on the table in the DDA. Being an introduction, this book cannot be more than a starting point. Guides to further reading are provided at the end of every chapter. Readers interested in pursuing specific subjects in greater depth should consult the works recommended there as well as the bibliography.

The book is organized into five parts. Part I provides a brief historical overview of the evolution of the multilateral trading system, major developments in world trade and introduces the basic functions of the trade regime (Chapter 1). Part II deals with the WTO as an institution. Chapter 2 describes the organizational structure of the WTO, its scope and functions. Chapter 3 discusses WTO enforcement and dispute settlement provisions, and summarizes the case load to date. Chapter 4 analyses the role of the WTO as a forum for negotiations. Special attention is given to the concept of reciprocity, as this is a key element of multilateral trade negotiations (MTNs).

Part III discusses the core disciplines of the WTO, which are contained in three multilateral agreements. Chapter 5 describes the GATT rules for merchandise trade—disciplines on tariffs, quotas, subsidies, customs procedures and product standards, among others. In each instance we discuss the political economy rationale underlying the rules, using cases and examples drawn from practice to illustrate their relevance and operation. Chapter 6 turns to the major sector-specific agreements that have been negotiated under GATT auspices, the three most important being the Uruguay Round Agreements on Agriculture and on Textiles and Clothing, as well as the Information Technology Agreement (ITA). Both sectors have a long history of protectionism in many countries, and both continue to have higher levels of protection in many countries than other sectors. Chapters 7 and 8 discuss the two major additions that were made to the trading system in the Uruguay Round: disciplines on policies affecting trade in services as embodied in the GATS, and the agreement on TRIPS respectively.

In Part IV, we describe and assess the major 'holes and loopholes' in the WTO. The various mechanisms allowing for the re-imposition of trade barriers are discussed in Chapter 9, which summarizes the rules on—and the economics of—the use of instruments of contingent protection. These have been very important in dealing with domestic political pressures for (re-)imposition of protection. Although often abused to the detriment of both national and global welfare, recent research has shown that they can also play a constructive political function by helping governments that decide to undertake far-reaching liberalization to implement and sustain economy-wide policy reforms. Chapter 10 deals with one of the most important exceptions to the most favoured nation (MFN) rule allowed by the WTO: preferential trade agreements (PTAs). Almost all WTO members are participants in one or more PTAs, raising serious questions about the practical relevance of the WTO nondiscrimination principle. Since the creation of the WTO the number of PTAs has increased steadily, as have nonreciprocal duty-free access schemes for least developed countries (LDCs). As a result, multilateralization of preferential trade is one of the major challenges confronting the WTO. Chapter 11 discusses the provisions of the WTO allowing for the negotiation of so-called plurilateral agreements, which apply only to those members that sign them. The most important of these is currently the Agreement on Government Procurement. The use of such agreements may well increase in the future, as it allows for subsets of members to move forward in areas where consensus cannot be obtained.

Part V addresses recent trends and challenges confronting the WTO. Chapter 12 discusses the evolving role of developing countries and former centrally planned economies in the multilateral trading system, and the concerns that these countries have regarding its operation. Chapter 13 deals with a number of subjects that are likely to be on the negotiating agenda for some time to come, including competition (antitrust) policy, labour standards, investment and environmental policies. Chapter 14 turns to the question of governance of the trading system, the role of NGOs and the importance of ensuring domestic transparency of trade and investment policies.

The concluding chapter briefly summarizes some of the major themes that emerge from previous chapters and discusses possible futures for the WTO and the challenge of sustaining international cooperation in the trade area post-Doha.

The volume includes two annexes. Annex 1 provides a listing of WTO members and some of the key characteristics that help determine their influence and participation in the institution. Annex 2 summarizes the economics of major trade policy instruments. It covers tariffs, quotas, trade in services, subsidies, externalities and market failure, price discrimination (dumping), FDI, trade preferences, preferential public procurement and rent seeking. Although the discussion in the volume is mostly nontechnical, we hope inclusion of the material in Annex 2 will assist students of international relations, economics and business, as well as the interested reader, to relate basic economic concepts and analytical frameworks to the trade policy instruments that are the subject of WTO disciplines.

CHAPTER 1

THE TRADING SYSTEM IN PERSPECTIVE

ECONOMIC theory suggests that countries should pursue liberal trade policies and exchange goods and services on the basis of their comparative advantage. In practice, however, most nations actively intervene in international trade. Since 1947, the GATT has been the major focal point for industrialized country governments seeking to lower trade barriers. Progress towards liberalization of trade was fitful at times, often involving two steps forward and one step back. Nonetheless, recurring MTNs and the positive demonstration effects of the success of outward-oriented development strategies aimed at integration into the world economy resulted in a steady decline in the average level of protection in most countries. The processes and disciplines of the GATT helped governments to liberalize trade and to resist pressures for protection. This in turn helped foster ever-greater integration of the global economy through trade. The extent to which world trade has grown since the 1950s is truly phenomenal, especially when put in historical perspective. The volume of trade increased 27-fold between 1950 and 2006, three times more than the growth in global gross domestic product (GDP) (WTO, 2007). The GATT and, since 1995, the WTO played an important role in creating the multilateral framework that has supported this trade expansion.

1.1. TRADE, GROWTH AND GLOBAL INTEGRATION

The value of global trade in goods and services passed the US$15 trillion (thousand billion) mark in 2006. At US$12.5 trillion, trade in goods accounted for the lion's share of global flows, followed by trade in commercial services, which had grown to US$2.7 trillion in 2006 (WTO, 2007). Reported data on trade in knowledge, as measured by payments of royalties for use of trademarks, patents and so forth, added up to some US$140 billion in 2006. As data on both trade in services and the arms-length exchange of knowledge are incomplete (we return to this in the chapters on services and intellectual property), the US$15 trillion figure is an underestimate of the value of total cross-border flows of goods and services.

With only a few exceptions, notably in 2009 as a result of the global financial crisis and recession, trade has grown more rapidly than output each year since 1950 (Figure 1.1). The more rapid growth of trade as compared to GDP—by a factor of 2 during the post-1990 period—has resulted in rising merchandise trade-to-GDP or openness ratios for all regions (Figure 1.2).

Trade growth has been driven by a mix of technological and policy changes that reduced trade costs. These in turn have generated changes in the organization of production, stimulating a great increase in so-called vertical specialization, with

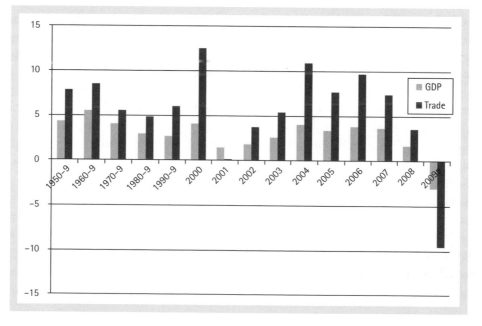

Fig. 1.1. Growth in the volume of world merchandise trade and GDP (per cent)

Source: WTO.

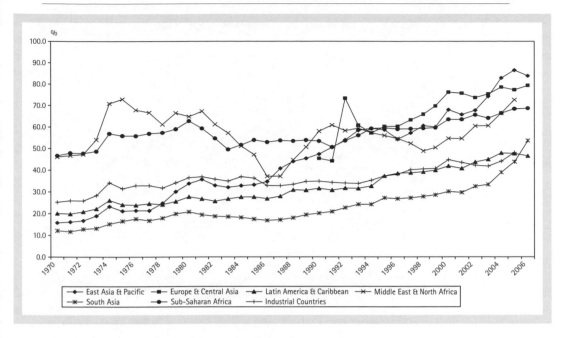

Fig. 1.2. Trade openness (ratio of trade to GDP), 1970–2006

Source: World Bank, World Development Indicators.

firms concentrating on (specializing in) specific bits of the production chain for a product. All these changes are inter-related, with policy reforms helping to stimulate technological change, and technological and managerial changes in turn putting pressure on policies. As discussed later in this book, the GATT played at best a marginal role in the trade policy reform process in developing countries—its impact was largely restricted to Organization for Economic Cooperation and Development (OECD) countries, as these were the nations that participated most actively in the institution. Developing countries began to liberalize their trade unilaterally during the 1980s and 1990s, supported by the international financial organizations, in particular the World Bank and the International Monetary Fund (IMF). The significance of the trading system for developing country members' policies only began to rise after the creation of the WTO in 1995.

Starting with average tariffs in the 20–30 per cent range around 1950 (WTO, 2007), complemented by a variety of NTBs that were often more binding (including quantitative restrictions and exchange controls), over time and in large part through recurring MTNs, average levels of protection of industrialized countries were lowered. As of 2006, the average uniform tariff equivalent of OECD merchandise trade policies was only 4 per cent (Kee, Nicita and Olarreaga, 2008), mostly reflecting protection of agriculture. Imports of many manufactures are

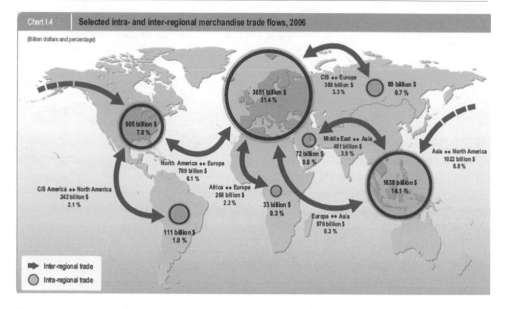

Fig. 1.3. Inter- and intra-regional trade flows, US$ billion and per cent, 2006

Source: WTO (2007).

now duty-free. In contrast to developed economies, most developing economies maintained relatively high barriers to trade for much of the post-Second World War period. Only in the 1980s did many low-income countries start to liberalize their trade. These differences in policy stances help in understanding the prevailing patterns of trade.

Global trade flows are dominated by exchanges within and between the three major regions of the global economy (the so-called triad): Europe, North America and East Asia. In 2006, intra-East Asia and intra-North American trade—represented by the circles in Figure 1.3—accounted for 53 per cent of world trade and about two-thirds of the total merchandise trade of the three regions. Trade in goods between members of the EU accounts for about one-third of global merchandise trade. Some 40 per cent of all developing country exports are destined for other developing countries.

All 49 LDCs[1] together accounted for only 1 per cent of world trade in 2006, reflecting the small size of their economies and very low per capita incomes. Their share has actually fallen over time—it stood at 1.7 per cent in 1970. South Asia and

---

[1] A country is defined as an LDC on the basis of a set of criteria applied by the United Nations Economic and Social Council (ECOSOC). The list is reviewed every three years to determine whether countries should be added or graduated from the list. In December 2007 Cape Verde was graduated, reducing the number of LDCs to 49. The next country to graduate will be the Maldives (in 2011).

Sub-Saharan Africa (including South Africa) together represent some 5 per cent of world trade; Latin America (excluding Mexico) another 3.6 per cent. The low trade shares of many of the poorest countries is in part a reflection of the very rapid increase in trade of East Asian countries, as well as the sustained growth in trade between high-income countries. In absolute terms most developing countries have seen the value of trade increase over time. The weaker relative trade performance of many developing countries has implied that the interests of individual developing countries are increasingly distinct, with some having benefitted greatly from the open global trade regime, but many others not perceiving significant benefits associated with WTO membership. As a result, the institution has become more concerned with the question of how to enhance the benefits of membership and assist poor countries in harnessing potential trade opportunities.

Developing countries have increasingly become producers and traders of manufactures. The share of manufactures in total exports of developing countries increased from just 30 per cent in 1980 to some 70 per cent in 2005—almost as high as in high-income countries (Figure 1.4). A substantial proportion of this global trade in manufactures, especially between OECD countries, comprises intra-industry trade—the exchange of similar, differentiated products. Intra-industry trade ratios are frequently above 60 per cent for OECD countries. Since the 1990s they have risen to similar levels for dynamic developing and transition economies. The corollary of the great increase in the share of manufactures in developing country exports is a fall in the share of agriculture and natural resource products. Of course, there are substantial variations in the share of manufactures in exports across countries and regions. Sub-Saharan African countries remain heavily dependent on (specialized in) natural resources and agriculture—e.g. oil, cocoa, cotton or coffee—as do many countries in Latin America (e.g. beef, sugar, grains) and the Middle East (oil). For the world as a whole, however, trade in merchandise is

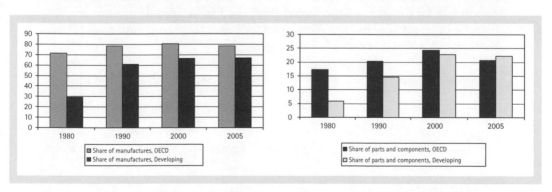

Fig. 1.4. Share of manufactures and parts and components in total exports, 1980–2005

Source: UN Comtrade database.

mostly trade in manufactured products. Agricultural products accounted for only 8 per cent of world trade in 2006—with the three largest exporters being developed economies: the EU, the US and Canada.

The rapid increase in the share of trade in manufactures, and within this, trade in components and parts, is one striking illustration of the process of globalization of production (Box 1.1). Among developing countries, East Asian economies took the lead in specializing in labour-intensive manufactures. Initially concentrating on simple products such as garments and footwear, these countries now produce a

Box 1.1. Changes in Global Production Sharing

The geographic fragmentation of manufacturing processes has long been a feature of world trade. One of its earlier forms involved the production of primary commodities in developing (and some developed) countries, shipment of these goods to (largely) industrial nations for further processing, and then the re-exportation (in part) of the processed product back to the primary commodity producer or third countries. For example, tin ore might be mined in Thailand or Malaysia, shipped to Japan for refinement and further manufacture and re-export. Such production sharing trade flows were based in part on comparative advantage, but policies—such as tariff escalation (tariffs that increase with the degree of processing of a good)—also contributed to this pattern of exchange.

The magnitude of such traditional production sharing trade has been eclipsed by international exchange of manufactured parts and components. A comparison of the value of East Asian trade in traditional inputs—agricultural raw materials, ores, minerals and nonferrous metals and unprocessed foodstuffs like cocoa and coffee beans—with manufactured components reveals that in 1984, Asian imports of traditional inputs were more than double those of manufactured components. By 1996, component imports were US$67 billion higher. Ten years later, at $781.8 billion, imports of components were over three times larger than traditional inputs. At 15.1 per cent, the average annual growth rate for component imports over this period was almost double that of traditional products. A similar pattern is observed for East Asian exports during this period, the ratio rising from 2 to over 8 (see Box Table).

Trade flow and product	Value (US$ bn)			Growth (%)
	1984	1996	2006	1984–2006
Imports				
Traditional inputs	39.2	98.9	247.4	7.9
Manufactured components	17.9	165.6	781.8	15.1
Exports				
Traditional inputs	17.0	27.6	110.0	8.2
Manufactured components	33.0	177.8	942.4	13.1

Source: 1984 and 1996, Ng and Yeats (1999). 2006 data provided by Francis Ng.

diversified mix of manufactured goods and participate very intensively in the process of global production sharing. East Asian global exports of components grew at an annual rate of 15 per cent during 1984–2006, more than four percentage points above the growth rate for all trade. Exports of components to other East Asian markets grew even faster (about 21 per cent per year). As a result, the share of all parts and components exports destined for regional markets almost doubled from 25 to 46 per cent. The corresponding figures for Latin America, for example, were only 17 per cent and 14 per cent respectively (Aminian, Fung and Ng, 2007). This illustrates another phenomenon—the increasing pace of regionalization of dynamic economies. The 2008–9 global recession revealed that fragmentation of production increases the sensitivity of trade to income: as demand fell, trade fell much faster. Regional vertical specialization did not insulate countries from the business cycle.

Although potentially incompatible with the process of globalization of production if associated with formal preferential trade agreements that create red tape such as restrictive rules of origin (see Chapter 10), the East Asian experience illustrates that regional integration reinforces the process of globalization if driven by market forces and complemented by openness to trade with the rest of the world. Trade expansion and the growth in production sharing have played an important role in the reorientation and expansion of trade between Central and Western Europe, and have also been increasing for a number of Latin American and North African countries, although in these regions the share of intra-industry trade is much lower than it is for East Asia and Central Europe.

An implication of the rising share of manufactures in global trade is that the factor content of trade has changed. As recently as the late 1980s many developing country exports were predominantly natural resource and unskilled-labour intensive. In all regions with the exception of the Middle East, a counterpart of the increase in production and exports of manufactures has been greater use of technology and skilled labour (human capital). Overall the skill-intensity of production and trade has been rising in both developed and developing countries, including in Sub-Saharan Africa (Table 1.1). This does not fit the prediction of the standard trade model where international exchange is driven by differences in factor prices that in turn are a reflection of differences in endowments of countries.

The 'standard' prediction from endowment-based theories of comparative advantage (Heckscher-Ohlin) is that as OECD countries have a more educated and skilled labour force, they should specialize in products that use such factors relatively intensively. The relative prices of goods that use less skilled labour more intensively should then fall as trade is liberalized (and those of skilled goods increase), which in turn should reduce the relative wages of the factors used in producing these goods domestically. At the same time, as unskilled labour-intensive activities are downsized and relative wages fall, there should be an

Table 1.1. Factor intensity of merchandise exports, 1988 and 2006

	Natural resources		Unskilled labour		Technology		Human capital	
	1988	2006	1988	2006	1988	2006	1988	2006
Industrial countries	24.4	23.1	9.4	7.3	38.9	44.6	27.3	25.0
Developing countries:								
East Asia & Pacific	29.0	15.1	29.2	17.3	23.4	50.6	18.5	16.9
Europe & Central Asia	59.4	46.5	15.1	10.3	14.0	20.7	11.5	22.5
Latin America & Caribbean	67.7	54.6	5.7	5.1	13.1	21.6	13.5	18.7
Middle East & North Africa	77.3	85.6	5.3	2.9	13.5	8.8	4.0	2.8
South Asia	51.0	42.5	35.1	24.5	8.0	16.8	6.0	16.2
Sub-Saharan Africa	74.0	72.3	19.5	4.2	1.9	11.7	4.6	11.8

Source: UN Comtrade and World Bank.

expansion in the demand for such labour in all parts of the economy. Conversely, developing countries should specialize in goods that use less skilled labour more intensively, as that is a factor with which they are well endowed, implying that liberalization should boost unskilled wages. It turns out that neither the product price effects nor the economy-wide expansion in unskilled labour intensity is observed in the data. Indeed, a large literature has concluded that the observed rise in the capital and skill-intensity of production and trade is mainly a reflection of technical change that is 'biased' towards (benefits) the more skilled. Skill-biased technical change (SBTC) is one explanation for the declining share of unskilled labour in total exports of almost all countries.

The increasing fragmentation or splintering of the production chain has been driven in part by technological changes that have lowered the costs of communication and transport, as well as by rapid growth in FDI flows. The latter in turn are in part also a result of the information and communication technology (ICT) revolution, which greatly facilitates control and communications and the far-reaching liberalization of policies towards FDI in developing countries, as well as other policy reforms that have improved the investment climate (Figure 1.5). Although data suggest that starting in 2005, policies towards FDI may have started to become somewhat more restrictive on the margin, the dominant trend has been for governments to take action to reduce barriers to FDI. The response to both technological changes and policy reforms was spectacular. The global value of stocks of FDI rose sixfold between 1990 and 2006, substantially faster than the growth in trade, which increased 'only' 35 times over the same period. As discussed in Chapter 7, much of this FDI is associated with services and is in part a response to decisions by many governments around the world to privatize state-owned utilities (such as telecommunications) and to open access to foreign provision of

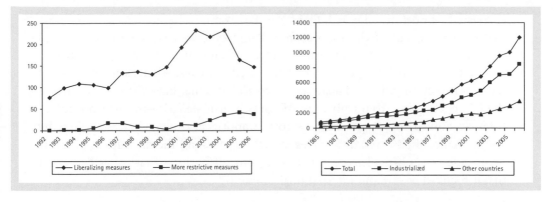

Fig. 1.5. Changes in FDI policies (number of measures per year) and value of FDI stocks, US\$ million

Source: UNCTAD (2007).

services. However, much of it is in natural resources and manufacturing and related activities—such as energy services and distribution.

Foreign direct investment in manufacturing-related activities may be either horizontal or vertical in nature. Vertical FDI involves the establishment of facilities that specialize in specific parts of the production chain, with location of affiliates depending on the comparative advantage (comparative costs) of the host country. Horizontal FDI entails a firm essentially replicating plants that produce similar goods, implying that FDI and trade are substitutes for the parent firm. An example of horizontal FDI is the creation of Japanese car factories in the US the 1980s and 1990s, driven by protectionist American trade policies (so-called tariff jumping FDI). An example of vertical FDI would be BMW setting up a plant in South Africa to produce car seats that are incorporated into the cars it makes in Germany and other parts of the world. Vertical FDI often entails outsourcing energy- or labour-intensive parts of the production process to affiliates in countries that are well endowed with the required inputs. In principle such production could also be outsourced to unaffiliated firms located in such countries, but these may not exist or, if they do, lack the capacity to satisfy the required production standards. There may also be concerns regarding the ability to enforce contracts or potential leakage of technology that induce multinational firms to keep production 'in-house'. The relative importance of horizontal and vertical FDI varies depending on many factors. On average horizontal FDI tends to be relatively more important for developed countries, reflecting their similarity in factor endowments. Vertical FDI tends to be relatively more important for North–South FDI flows.

Of the US\$12 + trillion global trade in goods, a significant share is intra-firm, involving flows between affiliates and parent firms. In the case of the US, some 45 per cent of total merchandise imports are intra-firm. Such trade is highly correlated—by definition—with FDI flows. For example, Bernard et al. (2007) note that only 2 per cent of US imports from Bangladesh in 2000 were intra-firm, as compared to 75 per cent of imports from Ireland and Japan. In the case of Ireland the trade is driven by exports from US-owned affiliates, whereas in the case of Japan it reflects imports by Japanese-owned affiliates that have been established in the US. US imports from China are still mostly arms-length—intra-firm transactions accounted for 18 per cent of total imports in 2000. Understanding the determinants of observed differences in FDI inflows, and the magnitude of intra-firm trade versus arms-length outsourcing and offshoring of tasks has become a major focus of research in international economics.

Global integration and growth

The expansion of trade and FDI are just two dimensions of the multifaceted process of global integration that has been occurring in recent decades. Cross-border trade and investment flows have been a major engine of the process— 'machines' that allow countries to transform one set of goods and services into another set that they value more highly. The increase in trade openness and cross-border investment is beneficial to the world as a whole. Empirical research by economists has shown a significant positive relationship between openness and economic growth (e.g. Greenaway, Morgan and Wright, 2002). Figure 1.6 charts the association between trade and growth by looking at a sample of 72 developing countries, divided into two groups: 'globalizers'—the 24 countries that saw the greatest increase in their ratio of trade to GDP between the mid-1970s and mid-1990s—and 'nonglobalizers'. Globalizers grew faster than both the nonglobalizers and the industrial countries over the period considered.

In a widely cited article, Sachs and Warner (1995) conclude that open developing countries grew by an average of 3.5 percentage points faster than a comparator group of closed economies. The sustained rise in post-Second World War European export–output ratios (compared to the pre-war period) was associated with a sustained increase in the average growth rate (Ben-David and Loewey, 1997). Sustained economic growth is critical in lowering poverty rates. East Asia, the developing region that has relied on trade the most intensively as part of its development strategy, has seen a number of countries catch up with the industrialized nations in terms of per capita income and significantly reduce the number of people living in poverty.

There is a vigorous academic debate on the relationship between openness and growth. For example, Dani Rodrik has argued that data and methodological weaknesses do not allow strong conclusions to be drawn (Rodrik, 1997; Rodriguez and Rodrik, 2001). Sceptics agree there is a positive association between openness and growth, but are not convinced the direction of causality is correct: they argue

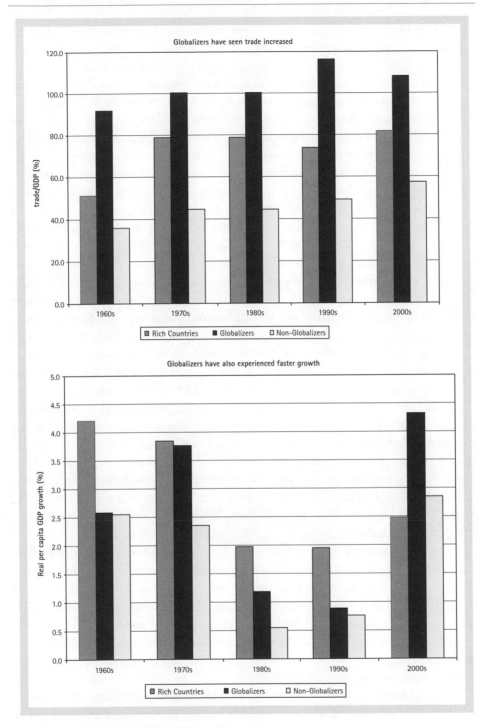

Fig. 1.6. Trade and growth go hand in hand

Source: Updated data, following Dollar and Kraay (2004).

that it may be it is growth that leads to openness rather than the other way around. One approach to disentangling causality is to examine the effects of those dimensions of openness that cannot be influenced by policy—that is, factors that are truly exogenous. Finding such factors is not easy. Examples are population, land area, borders and distances between countries. However, as noted by Winters (2004), such variables could have indirect effects on growth. Thus, geography may influence health, endowments or institutions, any one of which could affect growth directly as well as via trade performance.

While the technical academic debate continues, Frankel and Rose (2002) have shown that openness does indeed play a role even after allowing for geography and its possible indirect effects, while Wacziarg and Welch (2008) demonstrate that even if the cross-country evidence was not robust over the 1990s, if one takes countries' histories individually, the dates of trade liberalization do characterize breaks in investment and GDP growth rates. Specifically, for the 1950–98 period, they find that countries that liberalized their trade (raising their trade-to-GDP ratio by an average of 5 percentage points) enjoyed on average 1.5 percentage points higher growth in GDP per year compared with their pre-reform growth rate.

Because of the methodological problems that affect cross-country empirical analysis of the effects of trade liberalization, research has also focused on the *indirect* channels through which openness can affect growth (Winters, 2004). For example, liberalization will increase the variety of imports available to firms and households, allowing for a better match with the preferred characteristics of goods that are sought by buyers. Opening may also increase the variety of exports through greater specialization of production aimed for the world market. Both can contribute to productivity growth and, hence, aggregate growth. Feenstra and Kee (2004) show for a sample of 34 countries that more than 50 per cent of country productivity differences in the 1982–97 period can be explained by the differences in industry export variety.

Openness is also an important channel for the diffusion of knowledge. The research and development that is embodied in imported goods—especially capital goods—offers a specific mechanism through which the total factor productivity of an economy can be increased. More open economies tend to be more innovative, because of greater trade in knowledge (a greater quantity and variety of information, ideas and technologies associated with product and process innovations), and because greater competition spurs innovation, leading to higher rates of capital accumulation and productivity growth.

Empirical research has found that more productive firms are innately better at exporting, so that opening an economy leads to their growth and the demise of the least-productive firms. In the short run greater openness to trade and FDI will imply that local firms lose market share to foreign producers, impeding them from exploiting economies of scale and thus lowering their productivity. As less efficient firms are forced to shut down, survivors will lower their cost base and/or upgrade their production processes. Over time, therefore, the average productivity of domestic firms will increase.

The existence of such competition effects has been documented by many empirical studies. Pavcnik (2002) is a representative example focusing on the trade liberalization undertaken in Chile. This involved the abolition of most NTBs and a reduction of import tariffs from over 100 per cent for some products to a uniform rate of 11 per cent across all industries. Using firm-level panel data, Pavcnik found that the productivity of plants in the import-competing sectors grew 3–10 per cent more than in the nontraded goods sector, which suggests that the exposure to international competition forced previously shielded plants to improve their performance. Exiting plants were on average 8 per cent less productive than plants that continued to operate.

Thus, openness leads to better exploitation of comparative advantage in terms not only of industries but also of firms within each industry. As noted by Anderson and Winters (2008), if the more productive firms are also foreign owned—as often will be the case given that foreign firms must be efficient enough for FDI to be worth the extra fixed costs involved in establishment abroad—then being open to FDI multiplies the gains from trade openness. Lower productivity firms may also gain, as the fixed costs of investing in newly opened foreign markets may become justifiable as a result of the prospect of larger sales volumes that come with exporting. Lower foreign tariffs should induce these firms to simultaneously export and invest in productivity improvements. In short, trade liberalization—both at home and abroad—can lead not just to a one-off increase in productivity and efficiency gains but also to higher rates of capital accumulation and productivity growth in the reforming economy because of the way reform energizes entrepreneurs.

No country has developed without being open and engaging with the world economy. Those that did not—such as India and China earlier in the twentieth century—paid a very high price in terms of continued poverty and low growth. Indeed, the importance of openness for growth is perhaps best illustrated by the experience of these two countries in the 1990s: liberalization and its associated integration into the world economy was associated in both cases with very significantly higher and sustained growth rates.

Managing global integration

Globalization, like any major technological change, gives rise to adjustment costs. It opens countries to exogenous shocks such as the 2008–9 global recession, which had major implications for trade because of the greater specialization in tasks. Global integration has cultural and social ramifications as well as economic dimensions, and these must be recognized and managed. On the other hand, there is an enormous opportunity for continuing to use global integration to reduce poverty, hunger and economic injustice. Attenuating the negative effects of integration in instances where there are cross-border spillovers and assisting disadvantaged groups within and across countries is an important task for governments. The gains from trade generate additional resources that can be used by governments to assist in achieving such noneconomic objectives.

Trade liberalization is not a panacea that will automatically generate large growth benefits. Ben-David and Papell (1998) examine the post-Second World War growth path of 74 countries and conclude that 46 experienced a significant slowdown in economic growth rates during the period, even though openness ratios were rising. Relatively few countries have been able to attain and sustain growth rates that were high enough to result in convergence with the per capita income levels of industrialized nations. Indeed, country groups with the largest income gaps in 1960 have not shown any 'catch-up' convergence. Income gaps between many countries appear to be increasing rather than decreasing. Reasons for this are complex, but one common factor that characterizes incidences of convergence is the intensity (depth) of trade integration. Countries that trade intensively with each other tend to exhibit a relatively high incidence of income convergence (Ben-David and Loewey, 1997).

Of course, there is much more to growth than trade and trade policy. Greater trade integration is associated with faster growth, but complementary measures are needed to realize its full potential—including management of fiscal and monetary policy, public investment in human capital (education) and infrastructure, and the quality of public and private sector governance and contract enforcement. Of particular importance is that the overall policy regime is not biased against exports—which includes ensuring a competitive real exchange rate. For example, the magnitude of the beneficial knowledge spillovers from trade and inward FDI discussed above depends importantly on skill levels in importing countries and the ability to absorb and adapt the technologies. Much also depends on geography. Small landlocked countries surrounded by other low-income countries will inherently face much greater challenges than countries that are in close proximity to large industrialized economies.

Thus, for trade reforms to promote growth through improved price incentives, other policies are needed to ensure that investment flows into internationally competitive sectors and that weak or corrupt institutions do not undercut the positive incentives. For liberal trade policies to have a sustained effect on growth, they must be combined with other policies that encourage investment, allow effective conflict resolution and promote human capital accumulation. Competition policy, broadly defined to include the labour market and the regulation of entry, is particularly important: firms must be able to enter new areas and to exit declining, unprofitable activities. Research by Bolaky and Freund (2008) shows that increased openness to trade is associated with a *lower* standard of living in economies with high barriers to the creation of new firms and restrictive labour market regulation that inhibits hiring. This is because such policies may prevent the expansion of the most productive firms by inhibiting the downsizing or exit of less profitable industries. As discussed at greater length in Chapter 7, policies affecting the performance of service sectors are also important in this regard—the availability, quality and cost of services are a key determinant of the competitiveness of firms.

Despite the fact that the term globalization is used incessantly, the world economy still is far from being integrated. Science, technology and a growing component of cultural life have become genuinely borderless. Advances in telecommunications and informatics industries and steadily decreasing transportation costs reduce the tyranny of distance. English has become the first second-language of the world. That said, borders continue to exist. Intranational transactions in goods and services continue to be a multiple of international transactions for all countries. This holds even for tradable goods. Many researchers have found that the so-called border effect is a robust feature of the world economy. Even in the case of what should be markets that are highly integrated—such as Canada and the US; or individual members of the EU, where governments have abolished trade barriers—bilateral trade is much less than equivalent trade within each country.[2]

Although barriers to trade and investment have been declining, for many sectors and activities policy continues to discriminate against foreign producers. Most glaringly, the global economy remains characterized by severe restrictions on the international movement of labour and highly distorting agricultural support policies in OECD countries. There are few signs that government policies are becoming significantly more welcoming towards liberalization of the temporary movement of service providers, let alone reducing barriers to labour mobility more generally. The unwillingness to liberalize trade in agricultural products was a major factor impeding more rapid progress in the Doha Round negotiations. Truly global industries such as electronics and aerospace coexist with a large set of industries that retain a regional or purely national character. Many of these are services that despite advances in technology remain effectively nontradable, and thus require FDI for international provision to occur.

---

[2] The classic paper in this area is McCallum (1995), who found that trade between Canadian provinces was some 20 times larger than trade between Canada and the United States. Subsequent research suggests that estimates of the border effect and 'home bias' are very sensitive to the accuracy of the characterization of internal trade costs and depend on the size of countries—the larger the country the lower the border effect. Most analysts find 'border effects' in the range of 5 to 15. Although these large effects cannot be attributed to the existence of a border alone, they do provide a measure of the extent to which markets are not integrated.

1.2. TRADE POLICY AND TRADE AGREEMENTS

International trade has been a feature of the world economy for millennia. The volume and pattern of whatever trade has taken place has largely been determined by trade costs. Such costs are in part physical—starting with the technical feasibility of transporting a good from A to B and, if feasible, the cost of doing so—and in part 'financial'—a function of the taxes or tribute that must be paid to those with the power to levy them, and the probability of complete expropriation (through theft and piracy) or loss (due to breakage, spoilage or natural calamities).

Technology and power have been the major forces determining trade flows over time, defining at any point in time the ability of regions to exploit their comparative advantages. Technological and institutional innovations that reduced transaction costs have had enormous impacts on what can be and is traded. Major innovations included 'hard science' inventions such as the sailing ship, the steam engine, development of railroads, aircraft, container shipping and refrigeration, as well as 'soft' inventions such as mechanisms to extend credit to traders and the development of contracts and procedures to enforce them.

As stressed by Findlay and O'Rourke in their excellent survey of the history of world trade since the Middle Ages, the exercise of power has had equally important impacts on trade:

> ...the greatest expansions of world trade have tended to come not from the bloodless tâtonnement of some fictional Walrasian auctioneer but from the barrel of a Maxim gun, the edge of a scimitar or the ferocity of nomadic horsemen. When trade required more workers, [these] could always be enslaved. When trade required more profits, these could be earned via plunder or violently imposed monopolies. For much of [history] trade can *only* be understood as being the outcome of some military or political equilibrium between contending powers...Politics thus determined trade, but trade also helped to determine politics, by influencing the capacities and incentives facing states.
> (Findlay and O'Rourke, 2007: xviii–xix)

From a historical perspective the policy stance advocated by many economists—unilateral free trade—has been applied relatively rarely, most notably by Great Britain in the second half of the nineteenth century. As free trade has been the exception rather than the rule, it is not surprising that trade agreements between sovereign states have frequently been used to overcome barriers to trade. Even in the case of imperial expansion and the pursuit of formal or informal empires by metropolitan powers, trade agreements sometimes were an important instrument. Examples in the nineteenth century were trade treaties negotiated between Britain and Latin American countries such as Brazil and Argentina (Gallagher and

Robinson, 1953). Sometimes trade agreements have been a key element in the process of economic integration of independent territories—a noteworthy example was the German customs union (the Zollverein), which was a key building block of what is now the Federal Republic of Germany.[3]

A characteristic of colonial expansion was the application of metropolitan systems of law and protection of property rights to 'associated' territories—indeed, a defining characteristic of an empire is that control extends beyond foreign to domestic policy (Doyle, 1986). This was a fundamental dimension of the Roman Empire and helped create the pre-conditions for a single, integrated economy. Piracy was suppressed, roads built, and with sea and land routes substantially secure, commerce spread throughout the Mediterranean. The pottery, bronze, wine and oil of Italy were exchanged for African grain and eastern spices. Economies of scale led to large productive enterprises scattered throughout what was otherwise an overwhelmingly agricultural world (Gibbon, 1776).

The Iberian, Dutch and English empires of the sixteenth century and thereafter were of a different character in that the depth of integration was less. More important were discriminatory trade policies that sought to monopolize trade or to restrict competition. For example, not able to compete with more efficient Dutch shipping technology and constituting a less attractive market for some colonial products, seventeenth century England imposed trade restrictions on its colonies. The trade of American colonies was often subjected to exclusivity requirements— through a ban on trade with other states or through mandatory use of metropolitan shipping services—and regulated through restrictions on colonial production. Often, regulations prohibited local processing of goods or production of goods that could compete with output produced by the colonial power (Davies, 1997).

Trade relations between European powers and Asian territories initially tended to be less dictated by the former, reflecting more powerful local states. The latter produced goods (such as spices) that were sought after in European markets, forming a natural basis for trade. Often European traders sought to obtain agreement on (or to impose) extra-territorial application of home country law to commercial transactions and the protection of property rights. Local rulers who sought to limit the impact of a foreign presence on their control of society frequently were willing to accept such extra-territoriality. One form this took was through establishment of so-called treaty ports. Examples were Macao, Nagasaki and Goa. These served as an 'air lock' between international commercial relations and the control of civil society more generally:

---

[3] Keller and Shiue (2007) analyse the impact of removing borders between German states participating in the Zollverein. They conclude that this had a significant impact in integrating markets (as measured by convergence in prices of grains), but that much of the integration was also due to changes in technology—specifically the introduction of railroads connecting the various states.

From St. Paul's claim of civis Romanus sum against the subordinate patrimonial kingdom of Herod and the steelyard of the Hanse in London to the immunities of European settlers in Alexandria, Tunis, Constantinople and Shanghai, foreign powers have demanded extra-territorial application of their law over their nationals (both natural and legal persons). The outcome has often been the establishment of a regulated treaty port.   (Doyle, 1986: 202)

Trade cannot prosper without legal security of property rights and mechanisms to enforce contracts. One lesson from international trade relations between states throughout history is that traders will seek to ensure that such mechanisms are applied. This can be achieved through a variety of means—full-fledged integration into a formal empire being the most far-reaching one; and free trade agreements and treaty ports between sovereign states being alternative solutions.[4] At an even broader and more general level history clearly shows that geopolitical stability matters critically for trade—political turmoil and major conflicts are associated with a decline in trade. Periods of hegemonic dominance have been associated with trade expansion because of the associated decline in uncertainty and trade costs, as the hegemonic power controlling a specific set of trade routes or region provided the peace and security as well as the institutional infrastructure needed to enforce contracts and protect property rights. In more recent times, this infrastructure has been provided in part through explicit cooperation between states, the GATT/WTO being one important vehicle for such cooperation.

From the perspective of exporters it is of little import what motivates a government to restrict trade. What matters is to induce governments to lower trade barriers. Abstracting from the exercise of military force or the threat thereof, formal trade agreements generally are the tool that is used to do so. As mentioned, the alternative—convincing governments to adopt a unilateral free trade stance—has only rarely been observed, making moves by countries to voluntarily pursue unilateral trade liberalization in recent decades somewhat exceptional in historical perspective.[5] As already mentioned, a major exception in the nineteenth century was Great Britain. It repealed its so-called Corn Laws in 1846 (which restricted imports of wheat and other grains and had been imposed in 1815 at the end of the Napoleonic wars) and moved to essentially a unilateral free trade stance at home

---

[4] There is an interesting literature exploring the emergence and maintenance of legal norms in the absence of central authority. A conclusion that emerges from these studies is that the threat of ostracizing a member of a club who is reliant on repeated interaction with other members can have a powerful impact as an enforcement device. Government involvement in contract enforcement is not necessarily required. Milgrom, North and Weingast (1990) and Greif (1993) discuss historical examples. Similar dynamics have been shown to prevail in modern Sub-Saharan Africa—see Fafchamps (2004).

[5] Many countries and colonies had low tariffs in the nineteenth century, but this was essentially imposed on them by the hegemonic/colonizing powers (Bairoch, 1989).

and in the overseas territories it controlled. This free trade policy applied to all sources of supply, not just British goods.[6]

Other major powers also liberalized trade during this period, but did so through the negotiation of trade treaties. The conclusion of the Cobden–Chevalier Treaty between Britain and France in 1860 created the equivalent of a free trade zone between the two countries and was followed by a series of trade agreements. During 1862–7, France concluded commercial treaties with virtually every major trading power in Europe (with the exception of Russia) as well as with the United States. All these treaties included a most-favoured-nation clause, following the lead of the Cobden–Chevalier agreement. As in each case the countries involved also negotiated treaties with each other and Great Britain, the trade concessions granted were multilateralized. As of the late 1860s, France was at the centre of an impressive network of trade agreements that substantially reduced protectionist trade barriers throughout Europe (Curzon, 1965). Average tariffs in Europe fell to some 9–12 per cent in the mid-1870s as a result of these treaties (Bairoch, 1989).

A key outlier during this period was the United States, which maintained high tariffs on manufactures to support its industry. Much of this industry was located in the North of the country, which implied that the agricultural sector— concentrated in the South—effectively was obliged to transfer a share of its income to the North as it was forced to pay more for machinery and consumer goods. This is an example of trade diversion that can be associated with the formation of a customs union—see Chapter 10 and Annex 2. A doubling of average tariffs in 1861 to 47 per cent helped set off the civil war: an objective of the South was to escape tariffs through secession from the Union (Adams, 1993: 330).

The nineteenth century was the period during which much of the intellectual debate about free trade emerged. There were two clear camps. Those in favour of free trade included Adam Smith (*The Wealth of Nations*, 1776) and David Ricardo (*On the Principles of Political Economy and Taxation*, 1817). Others argued that trade barriers were required to support infant industries. Influential contributions here were Alexander Hamilton's *Report on the Subject of Manufactures* (1791) and Friedrich List's *National System of Political Economy* (1841). The ideas of Smith and Ricardo on the benefits of free trade and the principle of comparative advantage provided the intellectual support for the free trade movement in Europe— both on the European continent and in Britain. Writings by Hamilton and List constituted a source of inspiration for those who favoured protection of infant manufacturing industry in the United States and Germany respectively. As is often the case, there was a time lag between the development of the theories and government action inspired by them. The British free trade movement emerged

---

[6] British industry helped enforce this free trade stance. For example, when the British government in India attempted to impose a small revenue tariff in 1853–4, the British textile industry ensured that an equivalent excise tax was levied on Indian textiles (Doyle, 1986: 264).

half a century after the publication of Smith's works. Full-fledged US infant industry protectionism materialized a quarter of a century after the publication of Hamilton's Report.

Despite the rise of infant industry protection in the major powers during the latter part of the nineteenth century, the global economy became significantly more integrated. Global trade expanded much faster than global output, driven by major reductions in transport costs as a result of technical changes (railroads, steamships), increased demand for commodities such as cotton, and large-scale migration into the Americas. This expansion in trade and factor flows generated significant adjustment pressures. In the case of Britain, for example, the rapid growth in New World agricultural production and exports led a large decline in the profitability of British agriculture. Real land rents fell by over 50 per cent between 1870 and 1913 (Findlay and O'Rourke, 2007: 396). Although industrialists benefitted greatly from both the rise in industrial output and the increased demand derived from export opportunities, and producers of inputs in trading partners profited from demand for their goods, British and European agricultural interests lost. The resulting lobbying for protection led to gradually increasing protection of agriculture on the European continent. Average tariffs rose from essentially 0 to 20/40 per cent between 1880 and 1910 in countries such as France and Germany. However, Great Britain maintained its free trade stance until the outbreak of the First World War.

After the First World War, restrictive trade policies became the norm. To some extent this was in response to the United States, which was unwilling to participate in efforts during the 1920s to re-establish a more open global economy following the disruption to trade that had been caused by the war and war-time policies. As the US economy moved from recession to depression following the 1929 stock market crash and subsequent monetary policies, the US Congress adopted the infamous Smoot-Hawley Tariff Act, raising average US tariffs on dutiable imports from 38 to 52 per cent. This led US trading partners to impose retaliatory trade restrictions and engage in rounds of competitive devaluation of their currencies. A domino effect resulted, as trade flows were diverted to relatively unprotected markets, forcing down prices, giving rise to protectionist pressures there, and thus leading to higher trade barriers.

At the end of the Second World War, statesmen such as Presidents Roosevelt and Truman and, particularly, Cordell Hull, the US Secretary of State, were deeply influenced by the lessons of the post-First World War period. They perceived the need for establishing cooperative mechanisms to avoid both competitive devaluation and the excessive use of trade barriers to guarantee the national market to domestic producers (Gardner, 1969). The negative consequences of the beggarthy-neighbour policies of the early 1930s were still very vivid in 1945. They inspired the US willingness to pursue the type of international cooperation it had spurned in the 1920s and early 1930s and actively support multilateral liberalization efforts, including efforts to negotiate the International Trade Organization (ITO) and the GATT. In the Anglo-American view, the post-war international economic system was to be constructed in such a way as to remove the economic causes of friction that were believed to have been at the origin of the Second World War. An important element in this vision was the establishment of a stable world economy that would provide all trading nations with nondiscriminatory access to markets, supplies and investment opportunities.[7] There was a strong perception that there was a positive correlation between trade and peace, and, as important, between nondiscrimination and good foreign relations (Bailey, 1932).[8] In the US, the Reciprocal Trade Agreements Act of 1934 had already initiated a shift to a more liberal trade policy stance through the adoption of the unconditional MFN principle, albeit firmly grounded in the principle of reciprocity. This policy was extended after the Second World War and incorporated into the draft charter of the ITO and the GATT.

1.3. FUNCTIONS OF THE MULTILATERAL TRADING SYSTEM

Multilateral cooperation among sovereign nations often occurs through the creation of institutions. Because a central authority is absent in international relations, political scientists have developed the concept of a regime, defined as 'sets of implicit or explicit principles, norms, rules and decision-making procedures around which expectations converge in a given area of international relations' (Krasner, 1983: 2). The principles and procedures imply obligations, even though these are not enforceable through a hierarchical legal system. Regimes reflect patterns of cooperation over time among members that are based on the existence of shared interests. The multilateral trading system is a good example of a regime.

Two viewpoints are helpful in understanding the role of the trading system. The first is to regard it as a mechanism for the exchange of trade policy commitments. The second is to consider it as a mechanism through which the resulting code of conduct in implemented and enforced, that is, to focus on the result of the

---

[7] Although there were major differences between the US and the UK regarding the latter's insistence that the system of Commonwealth preferences be maintained.

[8] The academic literature on the relationship between trade and the probability of war has argued that this may go either way. For example, two countries that are on opposing sides of the globe and do not trade at all are less likely to go to war than two neighbouring states that trade a lot. However, Mansfield (1994) has concluded that, controlling for such factors, there is a robust negative relationship between the volume of trade between country pairs and the probability of a war between them.

exchange. Much of this book focuses on the outcome of negotiations and the disciplines that members agree to apply. What follows first briefly discusses the system as a forum for exchange, a subject that is explored in greater depth in Chapter 4. We then summarize the main elements of the system as a code of conduct: the nondiscrimination rule (MFN and national treatment), transparency, enforcement and flexibility (as exemplified by a variety of safety valves and vagueness in some disciplines).

The system as a market

The WTO is a forum for the exchange of liberalization commitments. That is, it is a market. Bargaining and negotiation are the main instruments used to reduce barriers to trade and agree to rules of behaviour. Multilateral trade negotiations are mechanisms through which governments exchange market access and other policy commitments.

In any country the structure of protection at any point in time is the result of the interaction between the demands expressed by various interest groups in society and the responses by governments and legislatures. Attempts to alter this equilibrium and move towards a national welfare-increasing reduction in protection will generate opposition by those groups that expect to lose from liberalization. Such losses are usually concentrated in import-competing industries, while the gainers—consumers of the products concerned—tend to be much more diffuse. This gives rise to a political economy problem. Those facing losses have a much greater individual incentive to organize and invest in lobbying against liberalization than those that gain from reform have to lobby for liberalization (Olson, 1965). Individual gains are relatively small and dispersed among a large number of voters, while losers are more concentrated. This is the main reason why trade restrictions are imposed in the first place.[9]

A MTN can solve this problem by confronting those who gain from protection with another lobby that may be equally powerful: the set of firms that benefit from greater access to foreign markets. Similarly, through reciprocally reducing trade barriers, the prisoners' dilemma that confronts large countries can be overcome, again improving world welfare. Moreover, by encompassing many products, a MTN can generate some automatic compensation for those who lose protection for their sector by lowering the average price of consumption and investment goods by providing access to cheaper imports.

A MTN is akin to a market in the sense that countries come together to exchange market access commitments on a reciprocal basis. It is a barter market. In contrast to the markets one finds in city squares, countries do not have access to a medium

---

[9] In developing countries without an effective tax administration, tariffs frequently have an important revenue rationale as well.

of exchange: they do not have money with which to buy, and against which to sell, trade policies. Instead they have to exchange apples against oranges: tariff reductions for iron against foreign market access commitments for cloth. This makes the trade negotiation market relatively inefficient, and is one of the reasons that MTNs can be a tortuous process.

Why do countries use trade policy?

To understand the role of the WTO as a market for the exchange of trade policies it is useful to first consider the rationale for trade restrictions. Motivations for activist trade policy can be divided into a number of types. First, revenue: governments need income, and taxing trade is often the easiest method of collecting it. Taxation of trade for revenue purposes has been a hardy perennial throughout recorded history, and remains important for many developing countries. Of course, those who are subject to the tax have an incentive to lobby for exemptions and invest resources to induce the authorities to lower the tax burden. Taxes imposed by rulers can constitute an important motivation for conquest or, more peacefully, for cooperation, such as the negotiation of tax treaties. Tax policy can have important effects on trade patterns. For example, in the fourth century BC, Rhodes was a major commercial power in the Eastern Mediterranean, controlling the neighbouring seas and with a vibrant port. Rhodes charged a two per cent tax on the value of cargo carried on all ships entering its harbour, including transit cargo. To divert shipping, Roman traders lobbied for the creation of a free port in Delos. Once established, trade rapidly shifted away from Rhodes, and the port lost most of its harbour tax revenues. This tax competition proved very costly from a social welfare point-of-view: Rhodes used part of its tax proceeds to police the sea-lanes and prevent piracy. Without the revenue, these activities declined, piracy increased significantly and trade became more costly (Adams, 1993: 83–4).

Another motivation for trade policy is to improve the terms of trade—the ratio of the prices they get for their exports and the prices they pay for imports. This rationale applies only to countries that have the power to influence world market prices because of their economic size or market power. Such 'large' countries can use trade policy either to reduce the prices of imports and/or to increase the prices of exports. (Large countries that use trade policy for revenue purposes will *ipso facto* affect the terms of trade as well.) Economic theories that allow for imperfect competition, product differentiation and increasing returns to scale have potentially expanded the number of situations under which countries can in practice affect their terms of trade. Thus, a country does not have to be 'large' in an absolute sense to be able to affect its terms of trade for a given product.

A third motivation is mercantilist—a belief that imports are bad and exports are good. This belief is generally based on the observation that imports must be paid for and thus imply the transfer of foreign exchange abroad (historically specie—gold or silver), whereas exports bring in foreign exchange. The objective of mercantilist policy is a trade surplus—ensuring that the value of exports exceeds the value of imports. Mercantilism is often driven by nationalism, the perception being that trade surpluses and political power are closely linked. Mercantilist policy therefore tends to favour direct promotion of exports and restrictions on imports through tariffs, quotas, prohibitions or state monopolies. The policy makes no economic sense. Starting with philosophers and economic thinkers such as David Hume, Adam Smith, John Stuart Mill and David Ricardo, it has been pointed out that imports are desirable and that exports are simply a way to pay for imports. Moreover, a trade surplus will have macroeconomic effects that will act to push the balance of payments back into equilibrium.[10] The theory of comparative advantage and gains from free trade was developed largely in reaction to mercantilist thought and practice.

Fourth, trade barriers frequently have been used as instruments for agricultural and industrial development. This was an important factor in the latter part of the nineteenth century, with continental European powers and the United States pursuing activist trade policies to protect infant industries. French colonies relied heavily on discriminatory trade policies such as tariff walls against the rest of the world, keeping British goods out of these markets. With France, Germany and the United States becoming increasingly industrialized, British trade dominance was eroded and British goods came to be diverted away from traditional export markets, initially the newly industrializing markets, and subsequently rest-of-the-world colonial territories. These policies eventually helped induce Britain to abandon the free trade policy it had adopted in the mid-1850s and begin to pursue preferential trade regimes with its own territories. This in turn led to the adoption of a system of imperial preferences that became a major bone of contention between the UK and the US in the negotiations on the GATT and ITO.

Finally, trade policy is a source of rents for specific groups in society. Protectionist policies have the effect of redistributing income from consumers of the affected goods to those that produce them or to those that control the right to import. By imposing barriers to trade, some segments of society gain at the expense of other groups. It is for this reason that protectionism can constitute good politics. It is a mechanism through which interest groups can be rewarded for political support in relatively nontransparent ways. Groups seeking protection from

---

[10] The fallacy of mercantilist thought regarding the need for a positive balance of trade inspired David Hume to develop his famous 'price–specie flow' mechanism. This illustrated the point that trade surpluses and associated inflow of specie would drive up prices and result in a loss of export competitiveness.

Box 1.2. Political economy drivers of trade policy

Economists have developed two broad types of analytical frameworks to reflect the fact that policy is endogenous—the result of a political process in which groups seek to maximize their utility or welfare. Both proceed by embedding either a voting or lobbying model of the political process into an economic model. The former often focus on the 'median voter', whose preferences will determine outcomes in two-party elections. The latter start from the presumption that interest groups will lobby politicians for specific policies that benefit them, and offer political (and financial) support for their election conditional on their preferred policies being pursued. These models help to understand why countries adopt policies that do not maximize national welfare: policies may not be economically efficient, but they are 'politically' efficient—they emerge as the equilibrium outcome of a specific political process.

There is strong empirical support for the view that trade policy formation is driven by political economy forces. However, empirical research on the political economy of trade policy has long had only a tenuous connection with underlying theoretical frameworks that generated clear predictions that could be tested. This changed with the development of a formal theoretical political economy framework by Grossman and Helpman (1994, 2002). This allows for formation of lobbies and is based on the simple precept of a government that maximizes a weighted sum of welfare (W) and lobbying contributions (C): $G = aW + C$, where a is the weight the government puts on a dollar of welfare relative to a dollar of contributions from special interests. Free trade would be the efficient outcome if the government maximized welfare, that is, if the objective function G admitted only W. In order to induce the government to set positive tariffs government must be compensated, via contributions, for the loss in consumer welfare weighted by a. A tariff t_i on good i raises its price p_i above the world market price, while an import subsidy lowers it. Assuming that individuals own capital that is specific to a sector, increasing the price of the good produced by that sector raises the return to the specific capital used to produce it. Owners of sector-specific capital in an import-competing sector thus have a strong incentive to politically organize and offer the government contributions in return for a tariff—with higher tariffs eliciting a higher 'payment (contribution). The Grossman-Helpman model yields a precise testable implication about the cross-sector pattern of protection and has generated a cottage industry of empirical applications and tests.

The model predicts that in politically organized import-competing sectors (those that form lobbies) trade protection is positively related to the ratio of domestic production to imports. The intuition here is that large domestic sectors make the largest lobbying contributions, while the lower the import volume, the lower the social cost of protection, thus diluting the opposition of consumers to tariffs for that sector. Thus, the model predicts there is a tradeoff between additional profits for specific factors employed in an industry and consumer surplus. Empirical studies find strong support for this prediction, but also conclude that governments appear to place great weight on social welfare: estimates of the a parameter are invariably very high, implying a weight on welfare that is 50–100 times greater than the weight given to lobbying contributions (Gawande and Krishna, 2004). Potential explanations for this are that there is likely to be substantial uncertainty about whether protection will in fact be delivered, thus lowering the effective impact of contributions, and that the Grossman-Helpman model does not take into account that many goods are inputs into the production of other goods, as a result of which lobbies work against each other (Gawande, Krishna and Olarreaga, 2005; Gawande and Hoekman, 2006).

import competition or the right to control imports often offer political support to the government (or to challengers in elections) as a quid pro quo (Box 1.2). Government officials may benefit directly from trade restrictions by capturing the rents associated with control over goods that can be sold in domestic markets at prices above their world market rate (cost).

It is often difficult to distinguish between the motivations for restricting trade. For example, trade policies that are part of an industrial policy may create rents and affect the terms of trade. There are similarities between mercantilism and infant industry protection—both have strong nationalistic connotations, and both rest on weak economic foundations (the economics of infant industry protection is discussed further in Chapters 5 and 9). However, in principle a major difference is that infant industry protection can (and should) be pursued in a nondiscriminatory manner. Given the objective of protecting local economic activity, this is most efficiently done in a nondiscriminatory way if governments decide to use trade policy instruments. Mercantilism in contrast is essentially bilateral in nature—what matters is the bilateral trade balance.

Historically, revenue considerations have figured almost universally—even free trade Britain imposed significant revenue tariffs. One implication is that one cannot necessarily determine from the average tariff or the magnitude of tariff revenue collections how high trade barriers are. What matters is the difference in the extent to which domestic and foreign products are taxed. If this difference is small, a country can be characterized as maintaining a liberal trade policy, even if tariffs are imposed.

Impacts of trade policy on welfare

From a national welfare perspective, the utility of trade policy depends largely on the market power of a country. A small country that cannot influence prices on world markets will generally lose from imposing trade barriers. Protection gives rise to both production and consumption distortions: producers confront artificially high domestic prices that encourage them to produce 'too much' of the protected products, while consumers consume 'too little'. Producers gain at the expense of consumers, and the deadweight losses associated with the transfer from the latter to the former imply that overall welfare is reduced. The elimination of these distortions is, therefore, a major source of the gains from liberalization (Box 1.3). Trade liberalization helps nations to realize a more efficient utilization of their resources (production capacities). Trade liberalization has two essential effects. First, it brings about a reallocation of resources towards those activities in which the country has comparative advantage. The economy becomes more productive on average as those industries in which the country has a comparative advantage expand by drawing resources from previously protected or subsidized industries

Box 1.3. Gains from specialization

The central concept underlying trade is opportunity cost. Producing (consuming) something comes at the cost of not producing (consuming) something else. An important economic theorem states that there are gains from trade associated with minimizing opportunity costs through the division of labour (specialization). Consider a simple example. Suppose the people of Plains, who are good at raising animals (say cows), must also spend time growing wheat (at which they are less good than raising cows). Each hour spent growing wheat has a high opportunity cost in terms of cows forgone, but there is no choice but to devote the time required to grow wheat. Suppose the people of Agria are good at farming, but do not have much aptitude for raising cows. Agria will then have a high opportunity cost in terms of time not spent farming. If these two countries/groups of people could trade with each other, they could concentrate on what each one does best. Economists say that they would specialize according to their comparative advantage. This will ensure that total output produced expands in both regions, and that each is able to consume more wheat and beef and milk than would be possible without trade.

The decision what to specialize in depends on what one does best compared with the other things that could (or would have to) be done. The people of Plains might be better farmers than those in Agria, in that for every hour invested in farming they get a larger harvest. However, as long as an hour spent by the people in Plains on farming has a higher cost in terms of forgone cows than does an hour spent on farming in Agria, Plains should specialize in cows. What matters is not *absolute*, but *comparative* advantage. International trade provides nations with the opportunity to specialize in production according to their comparative advantage. A country may be better at everything than another country in absolute terms, but by definition it cannot have a comparative advantage in everything.

(which either grow more slowly or contract following liberalization). Second, trade liberalization expands the consumption opportunities of countries, as more efficient production generates greater income and increased opportunities to buy goods and services from other countries (see Annex 2 for a graphical illustration and brief discussion of the standard mechanics of the gains from trade and the effects of trade policies).

The inter-industry reallocation and adjustment process that is the basis of the standard theory of comparative advantage and the gains from trade is replicated *within* industries as well: the more productive domestic firms in an industry expand by drawing resources from less productive firms that contract or go out of business. Recent theoretical developments and empirical analysis have emphasized the importance of recognizing that there is much heterogeneity of firm performance and efficiency/productivity within industries, and that this is a significant source of the welfare gains from trade liberalization (Melitz, 2003). Many empirical studies have shown that much if not most of the adjustment associated with trade reform involves shifting of resources within an industry rather than across industries (Hoekman and Winters, 2007). Recognition of the heterogeneity of firms within and across industries helps to understand this empirical observation, and helps to understand why trade liberalization is important for economic growth over time. As the more efficient firms expand and the less efficient ones contract and either exit or are taken over, the overall productivity of the economy increases. If there are scale economies and imperfect competition, liberalization will allow more efficient firms to further reduce unit costs as their market expands.

Recent theorizing that stresses heterogeneity of firms also helps to explain why some firms in an industry export while others only sell on the domestic market (Tybout, 2003). It also provides a much better understanding of the forces that result in intra-industry trade. If there are fixed costs associated with contesting international markets, only the more efficient firms will be able to export their products, and different firms will specialize in different varieties of (differentiated) products. Thus, liberalization, by allowing the more efficient firms to expand, not only will promote the overall export performance of an economy, but also much of the resulting trade will be of the intra-industry type. Consumers gain not just because of the elimination of the traditional production and consumption distortions but also because they get access to a much wider range of (differentiated) goods and services—many of which may not be produced at all in autarky.

As a result of the technological changes discussed previously and the resulting increase in scope to separate in time and space the various productive tasks along a value chain, including not just goods (components) but also services such as design, marketing and back-office administrative transactions processing, liberal trade policies allow firms to exploit factor cost differences across countries for specific tasks. Given that gains from liberalization are larger, the greater the variance of rates of protection across tasks, and that protection of some tasks or activities—e.g. services—is low or nonexistent (see Chapter 7), technological changes that permit trade in tasks increase the gains from liberalization of trade in goods, even if tariffs are relatively low (Anderson and Winters, 2008).

Motivations for international cooperation

In contrast to small countries, large countries may be able to change the terms of trade—the price of their exports relative to the price of imports—in their favour by restricting trade. However, for the world as a whole the imposition of trade restrictions by one or more countries can only reduce welfare. Large countries thus may find themselves in a so-called Prisoners' Dilemma situation: it is in each country's interest to impose restrictions, but the result of such individually rational behaviour is inefficient (see Chapter 4). All countries end up in a situation where their welfare is lower than if they applied free trade policies.[11] Both small and large countries, therefore, have an incentive to cooperate and agree to reduce or abolish trade barriers. Trade and trade liberalization is a positive-sum game.

Although basic trade theory suggests that small countries that are price-takers on world markets and that want to maximize their wealth should not impose trade barriers, a major reason why free trade is rarely observed is that some groups in a society will gain from protection (at the expense of others). As costs of liberalization generally are concentrated in specific industries, usually those that have invested resources in (lobbied for) protection, they will oppose liberalization. Potential losers are concentrated and often already organized—as organization will have been required in order to obtain the protection in the first place. The overall benefits of a liberal trade regime are in the aggregate usually greater than losses accruing to those who gained from protection. However, these benefits accrue to a large and diffuse set of agents. On an individual or household level basis, the benefits of liberalization are in most cases small, creating only weak incentives for the potential winners to organize themselves politically. In principle, the losers can be compensated, as the removal of the inefficiencies caused by protectionist policy will, once the economy has adjusted, increase total output and consumption by more than the (transitional) losses incurred by those who must change the economic activity they are engaged in. Actually compensating the losers is not always easy, however, and in practice occurs only rarely, and, if so, is generally partial.

One reason for this is that compensation is difficult—governments may not have the instruments needed. Trade integration may affect the redistributive capacity of governments by changing the structure of the economy and, therefore, the tax base, and by affecting the distribution of political power. The capacity and willingness to provide for domestic redistribution and compensation cannot be analyzed separately from the decision to open the country to trade and foreign direct investment flows (Verdier, 2005). This suggests that policymakers may need to provide insurance mechanisms in order to secure national welfare gains. To minimize distortions, any such instruments should not involve manipulation of relative factor and goods prices (which, of course, is exactly what trade policies do). Examples of such instruments are lump-sum, one-off payments and mechanisms that provide insurance against declines in the value of key assets such as land and human capital. The latter is particularly important in rural communities as land values may be a primary base for local tax revenues, and thus the provision of public goods and services.

---

[11] That is, large countries need to take into account the possibility of retaliation. Another problem is that if tariffs are not set at the optimal level, large countries may easily lose from activist trade policy—even if other countries pursue free trade.

The imbalance in the strength of political forces favouring and opposing liberalization provides a possible rationale for the pursuit of reciprocal trade negotiations. Rather trivially, although a (small) country will benefit from liberalizing its trade, it is even better if trading partners do the same. More important from a political economy perspective is that by making liberalization conditional on greater access to foreign markets, the total gains of liberalization increase and in the process liberalization becomes more feasible politically. Being able to point to reciprocal, sector-specific export gains may be critical in mobilizing domestic political support for liberalization at home. By obtaining a reduction in foreign import barriers as a quid pro quo for a reduction in domestic trade restrictions, specific export-oriented domestic interests that will gain from liberalization have an incentive to support it in domestic political markets. This political economy rationale for reciprocal negotiations is now generally accepted as a basic explanation for the existence of trade agreements and the WTO.

Economists often stress the importance of the terms of trade in providing a theoretically consistent rationale for the formation of trade agreements. The argument is that countries negotiate away the negative terms-of-trade externalities that would be created by the imposition of trade restrictions in partner countries (Bagwell and Staiger, 2002). Questions can be raised regarding the empirical relevance of this explanation for small countries that cannot affect world prices (in the terms of trade sense). Part of the answer may be that most products that are traded are differentiated, potentially giving small countries some market power (as what matters is not the size of the country, but the degree to which the product(s) of the country are substitutable and the number and cost of alternative suppliers of substitutes). However, for low-income countries that export mostly commodities the empirical relevance of such product differentiation-based market power is likely to be very limited. More important, governments of a small country may want to be a member of the WTO because its exporters will benefit from the low tariffs that large WTO member countries negotiate reciprocally with one another but must then extend to all other members under the MFN rule.

This explanation can only be partial, however, because it does not explain why large countries want small countries to join the WTO. It may be that in practice large countries simply do not care, as small countries cannot affect the terms of trade. An implication is that trade agreements will tend to reflect the concerns of large countries, and that reciprocal exchanges of trade policy commitments will be concentrated among large countries. To a significant extent this is indeed what occurs. However, at the same time large countries have supported expansion of the membership of the WTO, and negotiated bilateral trade treaties and preferential access arrangements with small countries. This is difficult to square with the terms-of-trade explanation for trade agreements, suggesting other motivations must be relevant as well.

The term-of-trade rationale has also been criticized in the specific context of the WTO because the GATT does not discipline the use of export taxes, which can be used to affect the terms of trade (Ethier, 2001b, 2004; Regan, 2006). If terms-of-trade considerations were indeed the sole driver of trade agreements, governments would want to discipline all border policies that can influence the terms of trade. In the WTO this is not the case. Nor can terms-of-trade theories explain why small country governments negotiate limits on their own use of import tariffs and other policies when joining trade agreements.

Another strand of economic theory (e.g. Tumlir, 1985; Staiger and Tabellini, 1987; Maggi and Rodriguez-Clare, 1998, 2008) provides an alternative rationale: trade agreements may offer a mechanism to governments that want to commit to a set of policies that may not be (politically) feasible to adopt or maintain. This line of theory has trade agreements serving as a lock-in mechanism or anchor for trade and related policy reforms. By committing to certain rules that bind policies, a government can make its reforms more credible: officials can tell interest groups seeking the (re-)imposition of trade policies that doing so will violate their commitments and generate retaliation by trading partners.

This rationale for trade agreements is conditional on agreements being enforced. In practice, agreements may not be enforced against small countries because the incentives for trading partners to invest the required resources may be too weak, that is, costs exceed expected benefits. If this is the case—as is suggested by the evidence summarized in Chapter 3—this weakens the commitment explanation for cooperation, making it conditional on there being a terms-of-trade externality needed to induce compliance (generate the credibility). In addition, the large number of holes and loopholes that are embodied in the WTO weaken the credibility-cum-commitment that is implied by membership—as governments still have great leeway to (re-)impose protection. As is often pointed out in the economic literature on the WTO, it is an incomplete contract.

A third perspective on the rationale of trade agreements has been developed by Ethier (2004, 2007), who categorically rejects the 'real world' validity of terms-of-trade driven explanations. Ethier stresses that WTO members retain access to instruments through which they can affect their terms of trade, starting with export taxes—which, as mentioned, are not subject to disciplines. Instead, Ethier stresses domestic political economy dynamics, and builds on—is consistent with—a long tradition that starts from the premise that governments seek to maximize political support: their concern is to get re-elected or to remain in power. This in turn implies that they will respond to and seek to satisfy the domestic constituencies that they need to stay in power. Taking as given that governments are conservative in the sense that they put greater weight on prospective losses for groups in society than on the expected gains from liberalization (which is realistic as losers can be identified and will mobilize whereas many of the beneficiaries of greater exports do not know who they are), governments have incentives to impose or maintain protection because this raises the incomes of the groups from which they derive political support. If foreign governments could be induced to liberalize, however, that provides a direct gain for existing exporters. This in turn changes the government's incentives as it affects the balance of political support. A more liberal stance becomes optimal as the government will benefit from reducing import tariffs on a quid pro quo basis (see also Grossman and Helpman, 2002).

An interesting distinct feature of Ethier's analysis is that it provides an explanation for *gradual* liberalization: trade reforms generate higher levels of political support if spread out over time. Gradualism is a standard feature of virtually all trade agreements, in that they tend to be implemented in stages. Usually this is explained on the basis of adjustment costs. Ethier (2004) offers another motivation for gradualism: it has a political support rationale.

Although the formal theoretical frameworks that have been developed by economists in recent years have helped clarify the possible rationales for trade agreements, the economic literature can only offer a partial perspective. Complementary explanations for the formation of trade agreements have been offered in the international relations and political science literature. These disciplines place more emphasis on the role of power, on domestic political considerations and the structure of institutions, and on 'noneconomic' objectives and values such as the avoidance of war and ideology. The stress on power and foreign policy considerations is clearly historically relevant given the impact of the exercise of power on trade flows (Findlay and O'Rourke, 2007). In practice, as stressed by the WTO (2007), the huge differences between countries and their underlying interests imply that there can be no single, formal 'grand theory' of the GATT/WTO.

In our view, although the terms-of-trade (market access-cum-cost shifting) framework is elegant and generates important insights into the factors that will support trade agreements, it is too abstract to help understand the actual process of multilateral cooperation on trade. The genesis of the GATT reveals rather unambiguously that terms-of-trade considerations did not drive negotiations or determine the final outcome (Curzon, 1965; Jackson, 1969; Dam, 1970). In practice, the political economy-based frameworks provide greater insights into the design and mechanics of cooperation in the GATT/WTO.

Reciprocity

For a nation to negotiate, it is necessary that the expected gain from doing so is greater than the gain available from unilateral liberalization. By obtaining reciprocal concessions, these gains are ensured (Box 1.4). More technically, what reciprocity in trade negotiations does is to help to offset the externalities (economic inefficiencies) that are imposed by countries as they implement trade policies,

---

Box 1.4. Political economy forces and reciprocal liberalization

---

Hillman and Moser (1996) argue that a useful way to understand the role of reciprocity is to start from the premise that import-competing industries have property rights to their home markets, a right that has been acquired as a result of past lobbying or political support granted to governments. In the same way that protection can be explained as the outcome of a political process where governments seek to maximize political support—taking into account the fact that tariffs are often used for revenue purposes and tend to persist after alternative tax bases are developed—reciprocal liberalization can be explained as the outcome of a political process. In this case the interests of the domestic right-holders (the import-competing industries) are balanced with those of domestic export industries seeking equivalent rights in foreign markets (and lower input costs). If the latter group offers enough political support, erosion of the former group's rights may prove politically rational. For a discussion of the resulting dynamics in the context of US trade policy, see, for example, Destler (2005) and Devereaux, Lawrence and Watkins (2006).

Whatever is offered by one country (the *demandeur*) in a MTN as a quid pro quo for a demand by a trading partner must be of interest to the government asked to alter its policies. Thus, to be effective the offer must help meet the objectives of influential foreign lobbies that will then push for the desired change in policy in their country. Alternatively, offers might be designed to help the government compensate groups that are likely to lose significantly from a reduction in protection. Options here include a gradual reduction in the level of protection and acceptance of safeguard mechanisms—as discussed below, two 'principles' that characterize the WTO.

Although export interests are the primary players in supporting liberalization in the MTN context, other groups favouring liberalization may also play a role. Examples include consumer or economic-development lobbies (the effect of development aid is frequently offset by protection against developing country exports, an example of incoherent policies to which we return in Chapter 12). To mobilize such groups they must be aware of the detrimental impact of trade policies on their objectives, and these impacts must be large enough to induce them to organize. The provision of information on the effects of protectionist policies is, therefore, of great importance. Indeed, the need for such information is quite independent of the MTN process, given that in many instances a unilateral change in policy would be welfare-improving. The main point, however, is that what counts is political support. If consumer and other groups favouring a liberal trade policy do not mobilize and exercise political influence, they generally will be irrelevant.

generally driven by a desire to respond to interest groups that seek protection and have supported the election (or selection) of a given government. In effect, by insisting on reciprocity countries may be able to ensure that their 'terms of trade' are not affected detrimentally as a result of own liberalization, in the process counterbalancing the resistance by losing lobbies with the support generated by those that benefit.

Reciprocity in trade negotiations comes in many guises. It may be diffuse or specific (Keohane, 1984). If specific, it may be expressed in quantitative or qualitative terms, and may apply to levels or to changes in protection (Winters, 1987a). Although the GATT and the GATS have as underlying goals a broad balance of market-access commitments, by requiring reciprocity, nations attempt to minimize free riding. In the case of bilateral negotiations, this is done by a suitable choice of products on which concessions are offered and sought; in the case of multilateral across-the-board negotiations, it is done by a suitable choice of products to be exempted from liberalization (see Chapter 4).

Generally, nations are quite successful in minimizing free riding. For example, internalization, defined by Finger (1974, 1979) as the sum of all imports originating in countries with whom a country exchanges concessions as a percentage of total imports of goods on which concessions are made, was about 90 per cent for the US in the Dillon (1960–1) and Kennedy (1964–7) Rounds. Allen (1979), focusing explicitly on bilateral bargains made in the Kennedy Round, showed that there was a relationship between the size of concessions made on commodity tariffs and the degree of bargaining power a country had on a commodity vis-à-vis its major trading partners. Thus, reciprocity is in part a function of the weight a country can bring to bear in a negotiation.

Reciprocity also applies when countries accede to the WTO. Given that new members obtain all the benefits in terms of market access that have resulted from earlier negotiating rounds, existing members invariably demand that potential entrants pay an 'admission fee'. In practice this implies not only that upon joining the WTO a country's trade regime must conform with the rules of the GATT, GATS and TRIPS, but also that the government will be asked to liberalize access to its market. Accession modalities are discussed further in Chapter 2.

For reciprocity to work it is important that lobbies favouring open markets do not have other means of getting what they want. Finger (1991) has pointed out that large countries increasingly negotiate increased market access for their exporting firms bilaterally. Such bilateral alternatives weaken the power of reciprocity in the multilateral context, as they reduce the incentives for export interests to support liberalization during MTNs. If true, this would constitute a major systemic downside of regional integration. As discussed in Chapter 10, other analysts take an opposite view and argue that PTAs may create political economy forces that generate support for expanding preferential liberalization to nonmembers and thus eventual multilateralization (Ethier, 2004; Baldwin, 2006a).

A code of conduct for trade policy

The trade policy exchange market (MTNs) generates specific commitments by the participants. These commitments pertain to market access—specific liberalization promises—and to certain rules of the game that all agree to abide by. The WTO encompasses a complex set of specific legal obligations regulating trade policies of member states. These are embodied in the GATT, the GATS and the TRIPS agreement. The rules and principles of the WTO constrain the freedom of governments to use specific trade policy instruments, and are largely motivated by a desire to constrain the ability of signatories to re-impose protection through the 'back door'.

As mentioned previously, one view of the role of the WTO is that is analogous to a mast to which governments can tie themselves to escape the siren-like calls of various pressure groups (Roessler, 1985). It is a mechanism through which the political market failure that is inherent in many societies—both industrialized and developing—can be corrected, at least in part, because reneging on liberalization commitments requires compensation of affected trading partners. However, much depends on the will of governments to tie themselves to the mast and on the strength of the rope used. WTO rules and disciplines—discussed at length in later chapters—embody many holes and loopholes that governments can invoke if they desire to. Much also depends on whether it makes economic sense to tie oneself to the mast. A necessary condition is that abiding by the rules is in the national interest of members. As discussed subsequently, a number of existing WTO rules arguably do not meet this test.

The WTO embodies a rule-oriented approach to multilateral cooperation. This contrasts with what can be characterized as a results-oriented or managed-trade approach—agreements on trade flows, market share or international prices. The WTO establishes a framework for trade. It does not define or specify outcomes. Four principles are of particular importance in understanding both the pre-1994 GATT and the WTO code of conduct: (1) nondiscrimination; (2) transparency (3) accountability; and (4) flexibility. Each of these is discussed at length in subsequent chapters; what follows briefly summarizes the main features of each.

Nondiscrimination: MFN and national treatment

The principle of nondiscrimination has two components, the MFN rule and the national treatment principle. Both components are embedded in the main WTO rules on goods, services and intellectual property. However, their precise scope and nature differ across these three areas, especially national treatment (see later chapters). The MFN rule requires that a product made in one member country be treated no less favourably than a 'like' (very similar) good that originates in any other country. Thus, if the best treatment granted a trading partner supplying a specific product is a 5 per cent tariff, then this rate must be applied immediately and unconditionally to the imports of this good originating in all WTO members.

Most favoured nation applies unconditionally. It cannot be made conditional on considerations of reciprocity, which is a principle that applies in negotiations, not in the application of negotiated rules. However, exceptions are made for the formation of free trade areas or customs unions and preferential treatment of developing countries. Upon accession of a new member, an existing member may also invoke the WTO's nonapplication clause (Article XIII). These exceptions to MFN are discussed in subsequent chapters.

Most favoured nation is a fundamental rule for the WTO for a number of reasons. It ensures that deals that are struck between two countries to lower tariffs are not 'undone' subsequently by one of the parties offering better terms to another country. That is, MFN is an instrument that helps make reciprocity 'work' (Bagwell and Staiger, 2002, 2004). It provides insurance against so-called concession diversion (Schwartz and Sykes, 1997; Ethier, 2004). Most favoured nation also reduces overall negotiating costs—once a negotiation has been concluded with one country, the results extend to all. This obviates the need for other countries to initiate discussions to obtain similar treatment. Instead, negotiations can be limited to the principal suppliers of specific products. Most favoured nation also provides smaller countries with a guarantee that larger countries will not exploit their market power by raising tariffs against them in periods when times are bad and domestic industries are clamouring for protection, or alternatively, give specific countries preferential treatment for foreign policy reasons. Most favoured nation raises the costs of lobbying for protection by ensuring that all exporters to a market will be affected by an increase in protection. Most favoured nation therefore helps in the enforcement of multilateral rules by raising the costs to a country of defecting from the trade regime to which it committed itself in an earlier MTN or upon accession. If it desires to raise trade barriers it must apply the new policies to all WTO members. This increases the political cost of reneging on prior commitments because it implies higher economic costs for importers, who then have stronger incentives to object to the policy change. Finally, from a consumer welfare perspective, if policy does not discriminate between foreign suppliers, importers and consumers will continue to have an incentive to source from the lowest cost foreign supplier.

The national treatment rule is the second leg of the nondiscrimination principle. It requires that foreign goods—once they have satisfied whatever border measures apply—be treated no less favourably than like or directly competitive goods produced domestically in terms of internal (indirect) taxation (Article III: 2 GATT). That is, goods of foreign origin circulating in the country should be subject to the same taxes and charges that apply to identical goods of domestic origin. A similar obligation applies to nontax policies (regulations) (Article III: 4 GATT). In both cases, the obligation is to provide treatment 'no less favourable'. A government is free to discriminate in favour of foreign products (against domestic goods) if it desires, subject, of course, to the MFN rule—all foreign products must be given the same treatment.

National treatment is a virtually all-encompassing discipline. The potential reach of the national treatment provisions in WTO agreements is far-reaching: they span virtually *all* governmental policies that affect the conditions for sale and distribution, widely interpreted, of imported products (Horn and Mavroidis, 2004). Moreover, the rule is not limited to explicitly discriminatory measures, but also spans any policy that *indirectly* has the effect of discriminating against imports. The rationale for national treatment is to preclude the use of domestic regulatory or tax policies to nullify a negotiated tariff concession. The reach of the principle is, therefore, limited to the impact of specific policies on (very) specific products, with much depending on whether domestic and imported products are 'like' each other.

The provision has, not surprisingly, given rise to a substantial number of disputes and case law, which is discussed in Chapter 5.

Although the nondiscrimination rules are invariably regarded as fundamental and defining principles for the trading system, the theoretical rationale for MFN remains a matter of debate and research by economists. Although it is clear that the policymakers who designed the GATT placed great weight and importance on the principle of nondiscrimination—strongly influenced by the inter-war experience—exactly how MFN helps to sustain cooperation and what its role is in moving countries to adopt lower tariffs than they otherwise would is less clear. Much of the literature on this question—which is surveyed in WTO (2007) and Horn and Mavroidis (2001)—has tended to focus on analysing situations where countries are symmetric. More recent analyses that allow for the types of asymmetry that characterize actual trade relationships may help in deepening the understanding of the role played by nondiscrimination (Box 1.5).

Transparency: information and communication

Ensuring that commitments are implemented requires access to information on the trade regimes that are maintained by members. Numerous mechanisms are incorporated into the agreements administered by the WTO to facilitate communication between members on the policy areas covered by agreements. A large number of specialized committees, working parties, working groups and councils meet regularly in Geneva. These interactions allow for the exchange of information and views, concerns and disagreements to be aired, and potential conflicts to be defused in an efficient manner.

World Trade Organization members are required to publish their trade regulations, to establish and maintain institutions allowing for the review of administrative decisions affecting trade, to respond to requests for information by other members, and to notify changes in trade policies to the WTO. These internal transparency requirements are supplemented by multilateral surveillance of trade policies by WTO members, facilitated by periodic country-specific reports (Trade Policy Reviews) that are prepared by the secretariat and discussed by the WTO Council—the so-called Trade Policy Review Mechanism (see Chapter 2). This external surveillance also fosters transparency, both for citizens of the countries

Box 1.5. Understanding the role of MFN

Economic first principles suggest that the optimal tariff policy of a country is likely to be discriminatory. One reason already alluded to for this is whether or not a country can affect the terms of trade. Another is whether or not the government imposes tariffs to collect revenue. In both cases, according to the so-called Ramsey pricing rule (Ramsey, 1927), the level of the tariff should be higher on producers (consumers) that have less elastic supply (demand). If the demand for a good is uniformly less elastic than that for another good, the optimal tax rate is higher for the first good due to the lower deadweight loss from taxing it rather than the second good. If the first good is totally inelastic there is no deadweight loss from taxing it, and the first best can be reached by taxing just this good. Broda, Limão and Weinstein (2006) provide evidence that countries that are not bound by the GATT/WTO systematically set higher tariffs on goods that are supplied inelastically, and that those that can affect the terms of trade do indeed levy higher tariffs, as predicted by the theory.

The various potential reasons motivating the use of MFN mentioned in the text taken together suggest that MFN is important in supporting the use of trade agreements by governments. Given the myriad differences across countries, it is quite unlikely that the nondiscrimination rule affects all countries in a similar fashion. Research has begun to emerge that puts country heterogeneity at centre stage. Saggi and Sengul (2008) argue that useful insights regarding the role of the GATT/WTO system in world trade can be achieved by formally analysing GATT as a club whose only requirement is that members grant MFN to each other. They show that the desirability of such an MFN club from a country's perspective depends on how its production cost compares to others. In their model, receiving MFN from others is of greater value to countries that have relatively lower costs of production. In related work, Saggi (2009) concludes that adoption of MFN by a country hurts the smaller exporter to its market while benefitting the larger one. Thus, the application of MFN by a country does not necessarily benefit all of its trading partners.

Saggi and Yildiz (2005) note that when market structure is asymmetric across countries, MFN does not necessarily dominate tariff discrimination even from a world welfare perspective An intriguing result of their analysis is that a high-cost country may choose to join an MFN club even though its welfare as a member is lower relative to a world in which no such club exists (i.e. a scenario where all countries pursue tariff discrimination). This result obtains because the fate of a high-cost country as a nonmember can be even worse than that as a member. This result may shed some light on the role played by special and differential treatment (SDT) in the multilateral trading system (discussed in Chapter 12). Saggi and Sengul (2008) suggest that such exceptions to MFN may be necessary to undo some of the adverse distributional effects of an MFN club on high-cost members. In their analysis the adoption of SDT helps ensure that the MFN club benefits all members.

concerned and for trading partners. It reduces the scope for countries to circumvent their obligations, thereby reducing uncertainty regarding the prevailing policy stance.

Transparency is a basic pillar of the WTO. It is a legal obligation, embedded in Article X GATT and Article III GATS. Transparency is important for several reasons. It reduces the pressure on the dispute settlement system, as measures can be discussed in the appropriate WTO body. Frequently, such discussions can address perceptions by a member that a specific policy violates the WTO—many potential disputes are defused in informal meetings in Geneva. Transparency is also vital in terms of ensuring 'ownership' of the WTO institution—if citizens do not know what the organization does it will have less legitimacy and political support for it may erode. The Trade Policy Reviews are a unique source of information that can be used by civil society to assess what the implications are of the overall trade policies that are pursued by a government. From an economic perspective, transparency can also help reduce trade-policy-related uncertainty. Countries with policy regimes that are perceived by investors as unstable are generally associated with higher capital costs—investors will demand a risk premium on funds invested in such countries to take into account the probability of losses due to policy reversals. Such premia can be high. Mechanisms to improve transparency can help lower risk perceptions by reducing uncertainty. World Trade Organization membership itself, with the associated commitments on trade policies that are subject to binding dispute settlement, can also have this effect.

Accountability: enforceable commitments

Liberalization commitments and agreements to abide by rules of the game will have little value if they cannot be enforced. The nondiscrimination rules play an important role in ensuring that market access commitments are implemented and maintained. The tariff commitments made by WTO members in a MTN and upon accession are enumerated in schedules (lists) of concessions. These schedules establish so-called ceiling bindings—the member concerned cannot raise tariffs above bound levels without negotiating compensation with the principal suppliers of the products concerned. The MFN rule then ensures that such compensation—usually reductions in other tariffs—extends to all WTO members, raising the cost of reneging. Once tariff commitments are bound, it is important that other, nontariff, measures that can hollow out the value of the tariff concession are not used. A number of GATT provisions, including a ban on the use of quantitative restrictions on imports and exports and the rules on subsidies, essentially serve this purpose (see Chapter 5).

If a country perceives that actions taken by another government have the effect of nullifying or impairing negotiated market access commitments or the disciplines of the WTO, it may bring this to the attention of the government involved and ask that the policy be brought into conformity with its obligations. If satisfaction is not obtained, WTO dispute settlement procedures may be invoked. These involve the establishment of a panel of impartial experts who are charged with determining whether a contested measure violates a member's commitments under the WTO. Because the WTO is an inter-governmental agreement, private parties do not have legal standing before the WTO's dispute settlement body. Only governments have the right to bring cases. The existence of dispute settlement procedures precludes the use of unilateral retaliation. For small countries in particular, recourse to a multilateral body is vital, as unilateral actions will be ineffective and thus not be credible. More generally, small countries have a great stake in a rule-based international system, as this constrains the likelihood of being confronted with bilateral pressure from large trading powers to change policies that are not to their liking.

Flexibility: calibrated commitments and (conditional) safety valves

A final principle characterizing the WTO is flexibility. This manifests itself in a number of forms. One is that governments may, if they desire, re-impose trade restrictions in specified circumstances. There are three types of provisions in this connection: articles allowing for the use of trade measures to attain noneconomic objectives, articles aimed at ensuring 'fair competition', and provisions allowing for intervention in trade for economic reasons. The first include provisions allowing for policies to protect public health or national security, and to protect industries that are seriously injured by competition from imports. The underlying idea in the latter case is generally that governments must be able to use trade policy instruments when competition from imports becomes so vigorous that domestic competing industries confront major adjustment pressures, with consequent political and social problems. The second type of measures include the right to impose countervailing duties on imports that have been subsidized and antidumping duties on imports that have been dumped—sold at a price that is below that charged in the home market. The objective of 'fair competition' is often in direct conflict with market access, as the instrument used by governments to attain 'fairness' is usually a trade barrier. Such barriers are, however, perfectly legal and permitted as long as they satisfy the criteria laid down in the relevant WTO provisions. Finally, the third type of 'safety valve' allows for actions to be taken if there are serious balance-of-payments difficulties, or if a government desires to support an infant industry.

1.4. FROM GATT TO WTO

The General Agreement on Tariffs and Trade was not formally an international organization (that is, a legal entity in its own right), but an inter-governmental treaty. As a result, instead of member states, GATT had contracting parties.

This changed with the establishment of the WTO, which is an international organization that administers multilateral agreements pertaining to trade in goods (GATT, 1994*a*, as well as numerous issue-specific agreements on antidumping, subsidies, import licensing, and so forth), trade in services (GATS), and trade-related aspects of intellectual property rights (TRIPS). To reflect the fact that the WTO is an organization, in this book we will generally use the terms 'contracting parties' to refer to signatories of the pre-1994 GATT, and 'members' to refer to signatories of the WTO. We also make a distinction between the GATT 1947 (the old GATT) and the GATT 1994 that is embodied in the WTO. The old GATT was both a set of rules and an institution; the new GATT is just one of three multilateral agreements that are overseen by the WTO.

The WTO applies to agreements between nation-states and customs territories that address government policies. The WTO deals predominantly with the actions of governments, establishing disciplines on trade policy instruments such as tariffs, quotas, subsidies or state trading. Thus, the WTO is a regulator of regulatory actions taken by governments that affect trade and the conditions of competition facing imported products on domestic markets. In this it is no different from the old GATT.

A fundamental perception of the founders of the GATT was that multilateral institutions facilitating cooperation between countries were important not only for economic reasons, but also that the resulting increase in interdependence between countries would help to reduce the risk of war (Meade, 1940; Hull, 1948; Penrose, 1953; Hirschman, 1969). The expected increase in real incomes following trade liberalization and nondiscriminatory access to markets was expected to reduce the scope for political conflicts. The increase in transparency and the availability of a forum in which to discuss potential or actual trade conflicts was expected to reduce the probability of these spilling over into other domains. The Preamble of the GATT 1947 states that its objectives include raising standards of living, ensuring full employment and a large and steadily growing volume of real income and effective demand, developing the full use of the resources of the world and expanding the production and exchange of goods (GATT, 1994*a*: 486). It goes on to say that reciprocal and mutually advantageous arrangements involving a substantial reduction of tariffs and other barriers to trade, as well as the elimination of discriminatory treatment in international trade, will contribute to the realization of these objectives. Nowhere is any mention made of free trade as an ultimate goal. This continues to be the case under the WTO.

The GATT emerged from the negotiations to create an ITO after the Second World War. The negotiations on the charter of such an organization, although concluded successfully in Havana in 1948, did not lead to the establishment of the ITO because the US Congress was expected to refuse to ratify the agreement. The GATT was negotiated in 1947 between 23 countries—12 developed and 11 developing—before the ITO negotiations were concluded.[12] The countries involved in the 1947 exchange of tariff reductions were anxious that implementation of liberalization not be conditional upon the conclusion of the ITO talks. Therefore, they created the GATT as an interim agreement. As the ITO never came into being, the GATT was the only concrete result of the ITO negotiations.

Although the GATT incorporated the provisions of the commercial policy chapter of the ITO, having been conceived as a temporary trade agreement, it lacked an institutional structure. In the first years of its operation it did not even exist as an entity except once or twice a year when formal meetings of the contracting parties were held (Curzon and Curzon, 1973). Its organizational structure emerged only gradually. Although major decisions were taken at the sessions of the CONTRACTING PARTIES,[13] it rapidly became obvious that a standing body was needed. An inter-sessional committee was formed in 1951 to organize voting by airmail or telegraphic ballot on issues relating to import restrictions justified for balance-of-payments reasons. This committee was replaced in 1960 by a Council of Representatives, which was given broader powers and responsibilities for day-to-day management. Throughout the 1947–94 period, the GATT secretariat was formally known as the Interim Commission for the International Trade Organization (ICITO), created during the negotiations on the ITO. It was technically a United Nations (UN) body, as the ITO negotiations occurred under UN auspices. Because the ITO never came into existence, the formal relationship between the GATT (a treaty) and the UN was always tenuous.

Over the more than four decades of its existence, the GATT system expanded to include many more countries. It evolved into a de facto world trade organization, but one that was increasingly fragmented as 'side agreements' or codes were negotiated among subsets of countries. Its fairly complex and carefully crafted basic legal text was extended or modified by numerous supplementary provisions, special arrangements, interpretations, waivers, reports by dispute settlement panels and council decisions. As of the early 1990s, a well-oiled GATT machine existed, helping contracting parties manage developments in the trading system, including through surveillance of trade policies and assisting conflict resolution through consultations, negotiations, mediation and dispute settlement.

Some of the major milestones are summarized in Table 1.2. The early years of the GATT were dominated by accession negotiations, a review session in the mid-1950s

---

[12] The founding parties to the GATT were Australia, Belgium, Brazil, Burma, Canada, Ceylon, Chile, China, Cuba, Czechoslovakia, France, India, Lebanon, Luxembourg, Netherlands, New Zealand, Norway, Pakistan, Southern Rhodesia, Syria, South Africa, the United Kingdom and the United States. China, Lebanon and Syria subsequently withdrew.

[13] The term CONTRACTING PARTIES, in capital letters, was used to denote joint actions taken by all signatories to the agreement.

Table 1.2. From GATT to WTO: a chronology

Date	Event
1947	Tariff negotiations between 23 founding parties to the GATT concluded.
1948	GATT provisionally enters into force on 1 Jan. 1948. Delegations from 53 countries sign the Havana Charter establishing an ITO in March 1948.
1949	Annecy round of tariff negotiations.
1950	China withdraws from the GATT. The US Administration abandons efforts to seek Congressional ratification of the ITO.
1951	Torquay round of tariff negotiations. Germany (Federal Republic) accedes.
1955	A review session modifies numerous provisions of the GATT. A move to transform GATT into a formal international organization (an Organization for Trade Cooperation— OTC) fails. The US is granted a waiver from GATT disciplines for certain agricultural policies. Japan accedes to the GATT.
1956	Fourth round of multilateral negotiations held in Geneva.
1957	Creation of the European Economic Community.
1960	A council of representatives is created to manage day to day activities. The Dillon Round is launched.
1961	Dillon Round concluded. The 'Short-Term Arrangement' permitting quota restrictions on exports of cotton textiles agreed as an exception to GATT rules.
1962	The Short-Term becomes the Long-Term Arrangement on Cotton Textiles.
1964	The Kennedy Round begins.
1965	Part IV (on Trade and Development) is added to the GATT, establishing new guidelines for trade policies of—and towards—developing countries. A Committee on Trade and Development is created to monitor implementation.
1967	Kennedy Round concludes.
1973	The Tokyo Round starts.
1974	The Agreement Regarding International Trade in Textiles, better known as the Multifibre Arrangement (MFA) enters into force, replacing the Long-Term Agreement. The MFA restricts export growth to six per cent per year. It is negotiated in 1977 and 1982 and extended in 1986, 1991 and 1992.
1979	Tokyo Round concludes. Includes a set of 'codes of conduct' on a variety of trade policy areas that countries can decide to sign on a voluntary basis. Most codes predominantly attract OECD membership.
1982	A GATT ministerial meeting—the first in almost a decade—fails to agree on an agenda for a new round.
1986	After lengthy preparatory work, including national studies on trade in services, the Uruguay Round is launched in Punta del Este, Uruguay.
1990	A ministerial meeting in Brussels fails to conclude the Uruguay Round. Canada formally introduces a proposal to create a Multilateral Trade Organization that would cover the GATT, the GATS and other multilateral instruments agreed in the Uruguay Round.
1993	In June the US Congress grants fast-track authority to the US Administration—under which it cannot propose amendments to the outcome of negotiations—setting a 15 December deadline for the Uruguay Round to be concluded. Three years after the scheduled end of negotiations, the Uruguay Round is concluded on 15 December in Geneva as a 'Single Undertaking'.
1994	In Marrakech, on 15 April, ministers sign the Final Act establishing the WTO and embodying the results of the Uruguay Round.
1995	The WTO enters into force on 1 January. Financial services agreement concluded but US does not sign.

(cont.)

Table 1.2. (*Continued*)

Date	Event
1996	Maritime services talks collapse. The first WTO ministerial conference hosted by Singapore creates working groups on trade and investment, trade and competition policy, transparency in public procurement and trade facilitation. Integrated Framework for Trade-related Technical Assistance created.
1997	Forty governments agree to eliminate tariffs on computer and telecommunication products by the year 2000 (the Information Technology Agreement). Negotiations on an Agreement on Basic Telecommunications and a Financial Services Agreement are concluded under GATS auspices.
1998	The second WTO ministerial conference commemorating the fiftieth anniversary of the multilateral trading system takes place on 18–20 May in Geneva.
1999	Ministerial meeting in Seattle fails to launch a new round.
2000	Negotiations start on the so-called built-in agenda determined at the end of the Uruguay Round—agriculture and services.
2001	China accedes to the WTO. A new round is launched in Doha, Qatar, the Doha Development Agenda, spanning trade in agriculture, manufactures, and services. EU puts in place the 'Everything But Arms' initiative granting LDCs duty and quota free access to its markets.
2003	Establishment of the 'G20' group of developing countries. The 'mid-term' review Ministerial meeting in Cancun collapses amid disagreement on whether to launch negotiations on the four so-called Singapore issues, as well as differences on agriculture—including an African Heads of State call for accelerated reductions in cotton subsidies. General Council Decision allowing WTO members to grant compulsory licences to import pharmaceutical products if there is insufficient local manufacturing capacity.
2004	In July a negotiating framework is agreed that includes only one of the four Singapore issues—trade facilitation, paving the way for continued negotiations. EU expands to encompass 25 member states.
2005	The final stage of the Uruguay Round Agreement on Textiles and Clothing is implemented, abolishing remaining quantitative restrictions on imports imposed by WTO members. Ministerial meeting in Hong Kong makes little progress beyond agreement to abolish export subsidies, agreement on duty- and quota-free market access for LDCs. TRIPS Agreement amended to formalize 2003 decision on compulsory licensing—the first ever amendment to the WTO; Aid for Trade taskforce established.
2006	The inability of the major protagonists to make concessions leads the Director General to suspend the Doha negotiations in mid year.
2007	Vietnam becomes the hundred-and-fiftieth member of the WTO. Expiry of US Trade Promotion Authority in June reduces prospects of timely conclusion of Doha talks. Deadline for conclusion of Economic Partnership Agreements between EU and ACP countries expires.
2008	The EU concludes a series of EPAs with ACP countries. In July another mini-Ministerial effort to agree on negotiating modalities for the Doha Round fails. In December, the Director-General of the WTO decides not to call for a Ministerial meeting to push forward Doha negotiations, citing a lack of demonstration.
2009	WTO launches an initiative to monitor and report on the use by Members of trade-related policy responses to the global financial crisis and recession. Ministerial conference planned for November 2009—the first in four years.

that led to modifications to the treaty, and the creation of the European Economic Community (EEC) in 1957. In 1962, derogations from the GATT rules in the area of trade in cotton textiles were negotiated. This developed into successive Multifibre Arrangements (MFA-I through MFA-IV; see Chapter 6)—a complex system of managed trade that was inconsistent with the basic principles of the GATT, but that benefitted producers in OECD countries as well as many of the developing countries that were granted a minimum level of guaranteed access to rich country markets. Starting in the mid-1960s, recurring rounds of MTNs gradually expanded the scope of the GATT to a larger number of nontariff policies. Until the Uruguay Round, effectively no progress was made on liberalization of trade in agricultural products and textiles and clothing. The deal that finally subjected these sectors to multilateral disciplines included agreement on the creation of the GATS, TRIPS and the WTO itself.

There are many similarities between the old GATT and the WTO. The basic principles remain the same. The WTO continues to operate by consensus and continues to be member-driven. However, a number of major changes did occur. Most obviously, the coverage of the WTO is much greater. Moreover, in contrast to the old GATT, the WTO agreement is much more of a 'single undertaking'— most of its provisions apply to all members. Thus, the WTO has many more implications for developing countries than did the GATT, where participation was more à la carte as well as being limited to trade in goods. In the dispute settlement area, the process became more 'legalistic' with the creation of a standing Appellate Body. Finally, much greater transparency and surveillance functions were granted to the secretariat through the creation of the Trade Policy Review Mechanism.

1.5. CHALLENGES FOR GLOBAL COOPERATION ON TRADE

The GATT proved a very successful instrument through which industrialized countries gradually lowered and bound their tariffs. The idea that a rule-based approach is superior to an outcome- or results-based trading system steadily gained adherents during the GATT years. Whereas many governments in the 1960s and 1970s were engaged in efforts to manage trade—through central planning, barter, or commodity agreements—this approach proved unsuccessful. Commodity agreements were difficult to enforce and generally failed. Central planning and centralized trade proved to be an unsuccessful system of economic management and was abandoned following the dissolution of the Council of Mutual

Economic Assistance (CMEA) and the Union of Soviet Socialist Republics (USSR), and the opening of the Chinese economy to international trade and private sector participation.

Over time the agenda of MTNs grew to include various nontariff policies. In part this reflected the expansion in use of instruments that circumvented GATT disciplines—voluntary export restraint agreements being an important example (Nogues, Olechowski and Winters, 1986). In the 1990s, the focus of attention began to turn to domestic regulatory regimes. However, tariffs have not become irrelevant. In OECD countries, tariffs on agricultural products are a multiple of those applied to manufactures, and within manufacturing, there are tariff peaks exceeding 15 per cent on many labour-intensive products in which developing countries have a comparative advantage. Developing countries tend to have barriers against imports of manufactures that are much higher than those prevailing in OECD countries. They also have high rates of protection on imports of many agricultural goods. Barriers to trade in services are more difficult to measure, but the consensus view is that these tend to be higher than those prevailing for trade in goods.

Although a significant tariff negotiating agenda still exists, future MTNs will revolve increasingly around nontariff measures (NTMs) and domestic policies that are deemed to have an impact on trade. Table 1.3 reports a measure of the overall level of trade restrictiveness implied by policies. The Overall Trade Restrictiveness Index (OTRI) is defined and calculated as the uniform tariff equivalent of observed policies on a country's imports. That is, they represent the tariff that would be needed to generate the actual level of trade reported for a country in 2006. The OTRI captures all policies on which information is reported by the United Nations Conference on Trade and Development (UNCTAD) (*ad valorem* tariffs, specific duties and NTMs such as price control measures, quantitative restrictions, monopolistic measures and technical regulations and mandatory product standards). As many NTMs are not necessarily protectionist in intent or effect, the OTRI is not

Table 1.3. Overall trade restrictiveness index, 2006 (per cent)

	Total Trade	Agriculture	Manufacturing
High Income (tariffs only)	7.0	43.1	4.3
	2.1	12.4	1.4
Upper Middle Income (tariffs only)	13.0	29.3	11.8
	4.6	6.6	4.5
Lower Middle Income (tariffs only)	11.8	26.5	10.6
	6.5	11.5	6.0
Low Income (tariffs only)	17.7	26.6	16.7
	10.8	15.3	10.4

Source: World Bank and IMF (2008).

necessarily a good measure of the level of protection that a government seeks to provide domestic industry. However, it is a good measure of the level of trade restrictions that are implied by policy, whatever the intent. Table 1.3 also reports the OTRI using only tariff data (including the *ad valorem* equivalent of specific duties). The data reveal that there is still a significant tariff negotiating agenda confronting WTO members, especially in agriculture, but that NTMs account for a major share of the overall level of trade restrictiveness.

This has implications for international cooperation: the interface between trade policy and economic policy more generally defined has become increasingly blurred. Agreeing on the elimination or reduction of NTMs is more difficult than negotiating downward the levels of tariffs. One reason for this is that it is much less obvious that specific NTMs are detrimental to a country's welfare. For example, attitudes towards environmental quality or product safety differ across countries, and this may be reflected in differences in environmental or product standards or in targeted subsidy programmes. Economic theory suggests that under certain conditions intervention will be called for (see Annex 2). Negotiations on regulatory issues, therefore, may be zero-sum games (some countries may lose), in contrast to tariff reductions, which are positive-sum (all countries gain, even though certain groups in each country will lose unless they are compensated). Another problem, again in contrast to tariffs, is that it can be difficult to agree on what constitutes a NTM. Even if agreement is reached on what types of policies are trade-distorting, incrementally reducing their negative impact may not be feasible. For many NTMs, all that may be possible is to agree to apply basic principles of transparency, national treatment, and MFN, and to seek to adopt procedural rules. However, pressures for harmonization of policies have been mounting. Although the GATT traditionally shied away from attempts to agree on common policies, differences in nontrade policies—regarding the environment, labour standards or antitrust—are increasingly leading to claims that these result in unfair competition and should be countervailed. A major challenge for WTO members is to deal with these pressures.

Experience has amply demonstrated that calls for protection and incentives to renege on liberalization commitments will inevitably arise. The Uruguay Round negotiations were a response to the managed trade and new protectionism that had proliferated during the late 1970s and early 1980s. The extensive recourse made by OECD governments to trade-distorting NTMs (antidumping, export restraint agreements, subsidies) was in part driven by exogenous shocks. These included the collapse of the Bretton Woods system of fixed exchange rates, and successive price hikes for crude oil imposed by the OPEC cartel, which helped give rise to stagflation (a mix of rising prices, weak output growth and rising unemployment). Matters were compounded by international political developments such as *détente* that reduced the primacy of foreign policy considerations in maintaining cooperation in trade.

As in the inter-war period, trade restrictions formed part of an inappropriate policy response to structural adjustment pressures, which were augmented by the emergence of East Asian countries as competitive suppliers of labour-intensive manufactures. The difference with the inter-war period was that multilateral cooperation did not break down. Although GATT rules were frequently ignored and circumvented, more often than not the letter, if not the spirit, of the rules of the game was honoured. The explosion of grey area measures, especially voluntary export restraints (VERs), constituted a major challenge to the system, but as discussed at greater length in subsequent chapters, VERs emerged in large part because of GATT disciplines on the use of emergency protection. The launch and successful completion of the Uruguay Round revealed that the major trading nations were willing to maintain multilateral cooperation and strengthen disciplines regarding the use of NTMs. The system proved robust during the 1997–8 financial crises—there was no significant increase in protectionism in East Asia or the OECD. Greater use of protectionist policies was observed in the 2008–9 global recession, but most countries did not significantly raise trade barriers. Those that invoked trade policy tended to use contingent protection mechanisms permitted by the WTO (antidumping, safeguards).

The World Trade Organization members confront a very different world from that existing in the immediate post-Second World War period. Although the US continues to be the dominant economy of the world, it is no longer a public-spirited hegemon willing to tolerate free riding and deviations from multilateral rules by trading partners for foreign policy reasons. Many of the trade disputes and the recourse to NTMs that emerged in the 1980s were in part a reflection of what Bhagwati (1991) has called the diminished giant syndrome of the US. Since then, the relative decline of the US in economic terms has continued, with the expansion of the EU to encompass 27 countries as of 2008, and the very rapid growth of China. The world economy is ever more multipolar. Instead of one dominant economic and political power (the US), there are now at least three major players— the EU, the US and China. None of the three can be relied upon to take up the type of leadership role provided by the US at the end of the Second World War. At the same time, the WTO as an international organization cannot take the lead—it is a membership-driven (controlled) institution, with a secretariat that has no power to self-initiate action or to make decisions. At the end of the day what matters is the continued willingness of WTO members to abide by the negotiated rules of the game, and to use the multilateral institution as a mechanism to liberalize trade further and pursue cooperation in areas that give rise to disputes and friction. This requires there to be clear-cut gains for all members—something that is becoming more difficult to achieve as talks confront thorny issues of domestic regulation. However, much still needs to be done on the 'traditional' agenda—the potential gains from further liberalization of trade in goods and services are still very large, for both OECD countries and for developing economies.

1.6. FURTHER READING

Ronald Findlay and Kevin O'Rourke, *Power and Plenty: Trade, War and the World Economy in the Second Millennium* (Princeton: Princeton University Press, 2007) is a fascinating, highly informative account of global trade and its determinants for most of recorded history. *Against the Tide: An Intellectual History of Free Trade* (Princeton: Princeton University Press, 1996), by Douglas Irwin, is a masterful tour de force that is required reading for anyone with an interest in the case that has been made for and against free trade. David Mansfield, *Power, Trade and War* (Princeton: Princeton University Press, 1994) is a careful empirical analysis of the relationship between an open international system, bilateral trade flows and the probability of war.

For an appraisal and history of negotiations of the Havana Charter and the General Agreement on Tariffs and Trade, see William Brown, *The United States and the Restoration of World Trade* (Washington, DC: The Brookings Institution, 1950); and William Diebold, *The End of the ITO* (Princeton: Princeton University Press, 1952). Richard Gardner, *Sterling-Dollar Diplomacy: The Origins and the Prospects of Our International Economic Order* (New York: McGraw-Hill, 1969, 2nd edn) is an excellent discussion of the motivations and processes underlying the construction of the post-war international economic institutions, including the GATT. An early study of the GATT system that continues to be well worth reading is Gerard Curzon's *Multilateral Trade Diplomacy* (London: Michael Joseph, 1965).

There is a large literature on the political economy of trade policy decisions and institutional design issues. I. M. Destler, *American Trade Politics* (Washington, DC: Institute for International Economics, 2005), now in its fourth edition is a classic and regularly updated book on the politics of US trade policy. Arye Hillman, *The Political Economy of Protectionism* (New York: Harwood, 1989) surveys the economic literature.

Robert Keohane, 'Reciprocity in International Relations', *International Organization*, 40 (1986): 1–27, discusses the notion of reciprocity from a political science and international relations perspective. L. Alan Winters, 'Reciprocity', in M. Finger and A. Olechowski (eds), *The Uruguay Round: A Handbook* (Washington, DC: The World Bank, 1987) does so from the perspective of an economist. S. H. Bailey, 'The Political Aspect of Discrimination in International Economic Relations', *Economica*, 12 (1932): 96–115, is an often-cited contemporary assessment of the costs of discrimination in trade.

Those interested in the theoretical framework underpinning the terms-of-trade view of the rationale for the WTO can do no better than consult Kyle Bagwell and Robert Staiger, *The Economics of the World Trading System* (Boston: MIT Press, 2002). For a theoretical analysis of the WTO that combines the terms-of-trade rationale with a political commitment motivation on the part of governments, see

Andres Rodriguez-Clare, 'A Political Economy Theory of Trade Agreements', *American Economic Review*, 97 (4) (2007): 1374–406. The various theories that have been developed to explain the role of the WTO by economists, political scientists and legal scholars are surveyed and summarized in WTO, *World Trade Report 2007* (Geneva: WTO, 2007).

A clear and accessible introduction to the legal and institutional aspects of the world trading system is presented in John H. Jackson, *The World Trading System: Law and Policy in International Relations* (Cambridge: MIT Press, 1997). John Croome, *Reshaping the World Trading System* (Leiden: Kluwer, 1999) is a detailed negotiating history of the Uruguay Round, written by a GATT insider. The prevalence of NTBs at the beginning of the 1980s is documented and quantified in Julio Nogues, Andrej Olechowski and L. Alan Winters, 'The Extent of Nontariff Barriers to Industrial Countries Exports', *World Bank Economic Review*, 1 (1986): 181–99. Patrick Low, *Trading Free: The GATT and US Trade Policy* (New York: Twentieth Century Fund, 1993) discusses the evolution of US trade policy thinking in the 1980s, the use of contingent protection and US attitudes towards the GATT.

Gilbert Winham, 'GATT and the International Trade Regime', *International Journal*, 15 (1990): 786–822, is a leading political scientist's view of the GATT and its role in international relations. Frieder Roessler, 'The Scope, Limits and Function of the GATT Legal System', *The World Economy*, 8 (1985): 287–98, discusses the role of GATT rules as constraints on governments. Alan Deardorff, 'An Economist's Overview of the World Trade Organization', in G. Flake and F. Myeong-Hwa Lowe-Lee (eds), *The Emerging WTO System and Perspectives From East Asia* (Washington, DC: Korea Economic Institute of America, 1996) provides an insightful and accessible economist's view of the WTO, emphasizing the importance of the institution as a forum for communication and information exchange.

A special issue of *The World Economy* (volume 23, April 2000) 'Developing Countries and the Next Round of WTO Negotiations' reviews many of the issues that were to figure on the agenda of the Doha Development Agenda. Bernard Hoekman, Aaditya Mattoo and Philip English (eds), *Development, Trade and the WTO: A Handbook* (Washington, DC: The World Bank, 2002) is a compilation of short papers that describe the WTO and the subjects on the Doha negotiating agenda. Donna Lee and Rorden Wilkinson (eds), *The WTO after Hong Kong: Progress In, and Prospects For, the Doha Development Agenda* (London: Routledge, 2007) provides an international relations perspective on the Doha negotiations, including discussions of coalitions and negotiating strategies. The UN Millennium Project Taskforce on trade report, 'Trade for Development' (New York: United Nations Development Programme, 2005) is a comprehensive analysis of the issues on the Doha agenda and their importance from an economic development perspective.

CHAPTER 2

THE WORLD TRADE ORGANIZATION

THE World Trade Organization was established on 1 January 1995. The WTO builds on the organizational structure of the GATT and its secretariat—to a significant extent it formalizes and extends the structure that had gradually evolved over a period of some 50 years. The Punta del Este Ministerial Declaration launching the Uruguay Round did not call for the creation of a WTO. In principle, it was not necessary to create an international organization to implement the outcome of the negotiations. The Canadian suggestion to establish a Multilateral Trade Organization in 1990—subsequently supported by the EU—was therefore something of a surprise.[1] The proposal was motivated by a desire to create a single institutional framework for world trade (Croome, 1999). This would encompass the modified GATT, the new agreements on services (GATS) and intellectual property (TRIPS), as well as all other agreements and arrangements concluded under the auspices of the Uruguay Round. The US initially opposed the idea, but after negotiations on the substance of the new organization, agreed to the framework that currently exists, including the name change.[2]

At Punta del Este it had been agreed that the negotiations were to be a 'single undertaking'. With the proposal to create the WTO, the concept of a single undertaking was redefined to mean that all GATT contracting parties had to become a WTO member. There was no alternative—remaining a member of GATT 1947 would have

[1] For convenience, in this book we use the acronym EU to denote both the European Union and the European Communities. The latter is formally the correct appellation in WTO contexts.

[2] The choice of name was somewhat ironic given the attention that was being given to intellectual property rights, as the acronym WTO was already in use by the World Tourism Organization, a Madrid-based special agency of the UN.

no value given that it was an institutional entity that was effectively going to disappear. Developing countries therefore all joined the WTO, something that was not on the agenda at all when negotiations started in 1986. Although the US Congress remained suspicious of any limitations to its powers on trade policy, it also decided to join the new organization. During the ratification debate it became clear that the establishment of the WTO would not do much to change the status quo as far as the exercise of national sovereignty was concerned, as the GATT 1947 was a binding international treaty. However, the GATT was not an international organization, whereas the WTO is. Thus, WTO has the legal personality to sign agreements with states— which it used to negotiate and sign a headquarters agreement with Switzerland.

The establishment of the WTO was a significant event. Attempts to put the GATT on a more secure organizational footing had been made periodically since the failure of the US Congress to ratify the ITO. During a 1955 meeting to review the GATT, a number of contracting parties proposed establishment of an Organization for Trade Cooperation. This proposal was much less elaborate than the ITO but it also failed to win the approval of the US Congress (Jackson, 1990). The issue of providing an institutional framework for international trade reappeared again in the ECOSOC in 1963, based on a suggestion by a group of experts to create a new UN agency with universal membership and substantial powers in the sphere of international trade (Kostecki, 1979). The idea was that this body would implement recommendations of UNCTAD as well as other relevant policy decisions taken by organs of the UN. The proposal envisaged that the GATT would become the new agency's Committee on Tariffs. The proposal did not meet with much interest among the major trading nations. However, the 1964 UN General Assembly resolution establishing UNCTAD provided that it should be concerned with matters relating to the elaboration of a comprehensive trade organization. Nothing concrete came of this—despite lengthy discussions about the need for a New International Economic Order during the 1970s—in large part because of the widely differing views held by industrialized market economies and much of the developing world regarding the appropriate basis for international trade. With the creation of the WTO, an international trade organization emerged that is firmly based on GATT principles—reciprocity and nondiscrimination.

2.1. Scope, Functions and Structure of the WTO

The Marrakech Agreement establishing the WTO charges the organization with providing the common institutional framework for the conduct of trade relations among its members in matters for which agreements and associated legal obligations apply (Article II). Four Annexes to the WTO define the substantive rights and obligations of members. Annex 1 has three parts: Annex 1A entitled 'Multilateral Agreements on Trade in Goods', contains the GATT 1994 (the GATT 1947 as augmented by a large number of Understandings and supplementary Agreements negotiated in the Uruguay Round); Annex 1B, which contains the GATS; and Annex 1C, the Agreement on TRIPS. Annex 2 contains the Understanding on Rules and Procedures Governing the Settlement of Disputes—the WTO's common dispute settlement mechanism. Annex 3 contains the Trade Policy Review Mechanism (TPRM), an instrument for surveillance of members' trade policies. Finally, Annex 4—entitled 'Plurilateral Trade Agreements'—consists of agreements that bind only signatories. Together, Annexes 1–3 embody the Multilateral Trade Agreements. Article II WTO specifies that all the agreements contained in Annexes 1, 2 and 3 are an integral part of the WTO Agreement, and are binding on all members. All of these instruments are discussed further below or in the rest of this book.

The WTO has a number of functions. It is charged with facilitating the implementation and operation of the Multilateral Trade Agreements, providing a forum for negotiations, administering the dispute settlement mechanism, providing multilateral surveillance of trade policies, and cooperating with the World Bank and the IMF to achieve greater coherence in global economic policymaking (Article III WTO). The WTO is headed by a ministerial conference of all members, meeting at least once every two years (Figure 2.1). More frequent participation by trade ministers than occurred under the old GATT—where a decade could pass between ministerial meetings—was intended to strengthen the political guidance of the WTO and enhance the prominence and credibility of its rules in domestic political arenas.

Experience suggests that ministerial conferences often are not a very effective use of the time of ministers, especially those from smaller trading nations. This is because in negotiations the controversial issues require agreement between the major players. The latter may take a significant amount of time to strike a deal among each other, thereby marginalizing the potential for participation by ministers of smaller countries at a ministerial conference. Excluded from the main negotiating fora where the major players and a selected subset of other countries were trying to hammer out compromises at the Seattle ministerial meeting in late 1999, many ministers spent much of the time 'on call' or dealing with bilateral issues. Although procedural improvements and innovations were implemented to enhance transparency and participation at ministerial conferences—discussed below and in Chapter 14—the 'endgame' negotiations cannot involve 150+ negotiators.

In an effort to reduce transaction costs and limit the agenda of ministerial conferences, during the Doha Round increasing use has come to be made of so-called mini-ministerial meetings, involving a subset of WTO members. Although such meetings do not have a good track record in dealing with technical matters or substantive disagreements between major players, they played an important role in

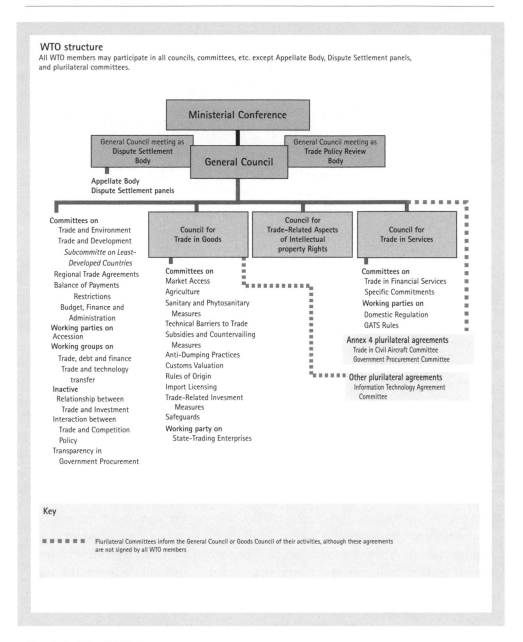

Fig. 2.1. The WTO structure

Source: WTO.

raising the political profile of WTO talks in member countries and getting countries with similar interests to converge on common positions. Many of the mini-ministerials involved countries that were members of regional groupings or specific negotiating coalitions.

Between meetings of the ministerial conference, the WTO is managed by a General Council at the level of officials. The General Council meets about 12 times a year. On average, some 70 per cent of all WTO members take part in Council meetings, usually represented by delegations based in Geneva. The General Council turns itself, as needed, into a body to adjudicate trade disputes (the Dispute Settlement Body—DSB) and to review trade policies of the member countries (the Trade Policy Review Body—TPRB).

Three subsidiary councils operate under the general guidance of the General Council (Figure 2.1): the Council for Trade in Goods; the Council for Trade in Services; and the Council for Trade-Related Aspects of Intellectual Property Rights. Separate committees deal with specific subject areas, such as trade and development; surveillance of trade restrictions actions taken for balance-of-payment purposes; surveillance of regional trade agreements; trade-environment linkages; and the WTO's finances and administration. Additional committees, subcommittees and working groups and working parties deal with matters covered by the GATT, GATS or TRIPS Agreement. Committees functioning under auspices of the Council on Trade in Goods exist on subsidies, antidumping and countervailing measures, technical barriers to trade (product standards), import licensing, customs valuation, market access, agriculture, sanitary and phytosanitary measures, trade-related investment measures, rules of origin and safeguards. In addition, working groups have been established to deal with notifications, state-trading enterprises, and to study the relationship between trade and investment, between trade and competition policy and transparency in government procurement.

Similarly, specific committees address matters relating to the GATS or TRIPS. Committees also exist to administer the Plurilateral Agreements—which apply only to those members that sign them (see Chapter 11). Given their nature, these are not under the guidance of the General Council but operate within the general framework of the WTO and inform the Council of their activities. There is currently one de facto 'plurilateral' committee that administers an agreement among a subset of WTO members that is subject to the MFN rule—the Information Technology Agreement. This is a so-called zero-for-zero agreement under which signatories agreed to remove barriers to trade on information technology products. Given that these products are covered by the GATT, this committee reports to the General Council. All WTO members may participate in all councils, committees, and so forth, except the Appellate Body, dispute settlement panels, the Textiles Monitoring Body, and committees dealing with plurilateral agreements.

All councils, committees, subcommittees, bodies, standing groups, working parties and negotiating groups are chaired by a WTO member, with the exception of the Trade Negotiations Council, the body that oversees MTNs. This is now chaired by the Director-General of the WTO. Generally only the more important trading nations (less than half of the membership) regularly send representatives to most meetings. Participation reflects a mix of national interests and resource constraints. Least developed countries in particular tend not to be represented at many meetings, in part because they may have no delegation based in Geneva (see Annex 1) but more generally because they do not have the capacity or the interest to engage in all of the subjects that are dealt with by the WTO. All of the fora, plus working parties on accession (averaging close to 30 during 1995–2008), dispute settlement panels (370+ as of 2008), meetings of regional groups, heads of delegations, and numerous ad hoc and informal groups add up to 1,200+ events a year at or around the WTO headquarters in Geneva. Most WTO business is conducted in English, but many official WTO meetings require French and Spanish interpretation—all three are official languages.

The main actors in day-to-day activities are officials that are affiliated with the delegations of members. The WTO—as was the GATT 1947—therefore can be regarded as a network organization (Blackhurst, 1998). The WTO Secretariat is the hub of a very large and dispersed network comprising official representatives of members based in Geneva and their colleagues located in capitals. Ministries of trade, foreign affairs, finance, telecommunications, transport and agriculture, as well as specialized bodies such as customs authorities, central banks, health and safety standards administrations, environmental protection agencies, national patent and trademark agencies, and so on, all tend to have staff that deal with WTO matters and provide inputs into WTO activities. All these officials in turn are likely to work with and respond to national business and nongovernmental groups that have a stake in specific policies covered by the WTO or that seek to have additional measures put on the table. The operation of the WTO, therefore, depends on the collective input of thousands of civil servants and government officials that deal with trade issues in each member country. Initiatives to launch MTNs and settle disputes—the two highest profile activities of the WTO—are the sole responsibility of WTO members themselves, not the secretariat.

The member-driven nature of the organization puts a considerable strain on the delegations in Geneva. Many countries have no more than one or two persons dealing with WTO matters; some have no representation in Geneva at all. Active players in WTO fora tend to have large delegations, although officials will often also cover meetings at UNCTAD, the World Intellectual Property Organization (WIPO), the International Labor Office (ILO), the World Health Organization, the Economic Commission for Europe and other international organizations located in Geneva.

The WTO Secretariat, which has its offices at the Centre William Rappard in Geneva is relatively small—standing at some 600 people, about one-third of whom are translators and support staff. This figure does not include the 22 staff members and judges of the WTO Appellate Body, which is independent of the WTO Secretariat but is housed in the same building. The secretariat's role is to provide members with technical and logistical support, including organizing meetings of governing bodies and preparing background documentation when requested by committees or the Council. It has very little formal power to take initiatives. For example, the Director-General has no authority to initiate dispute settlement proceedings against a member, no matter how blatantly it may have violated WTO rules. Nor can the secretariat interpret WTO law or pass judgement on the conformity of a member's policy with WTO rules. This is the sole prerogative of members, although a key task of the secretariat is to facilitate dispute resolution by supporting the work of panels. There is also little scope for the WTO Director-General to determine the topics to be put on the WTO agenda. The general situation was well described at an informal meeting during the Uruguay Round, where a diplomat addressing the Director-General noted: 'Sir, there is a difference between you and me; I am a Contracting Party and you are a Contracted Party'.

The secretariat plays an important role in reducing transaction costs by distributing information and enhancing transparency by undertaking periodic reviews of member trade policies. The latter is one of the few areas where the secretariat has been given a mandate to undertake action on its own responsibility. A significant proportion of WTO staff time is dedicated to participation in workshops and seminars in developing country members, an area of activity that expanded greatly after 2000. Even though the mandate of the WTO Secretariat is formally limited, staff can have substantial influence as a result of institutional memory and expertise. The less knowledgeable and assertive is a chairman of a given working party or committee, the stronger the influence of the secretariat is likely to be. The Director-General, the head of the WTO Secretariat, is in some sense the guardian of the collective interest of the member states. The WTO's rules and procedures allow the Director-General to act as a broker in many situations. Historically the head of the secretariat has often played a major role in encouraging and cajoling countries to maintain and strengthen multilateral cooperation in trade (Box 2.1).

Finances and budget

The financial contributions to the budget of the WTO are based on GATT 1947 practice. The WTO's income comes from assessed contributions calculated on the basis of each member's share in the total trade of all WTO members, computed as a three-year average of the most recent trade figures (if this share is less than 0.015 per cent, a minimum contribution is assessed). In 2008, the nine largest trading nations contributed close to two-thirds of the total administrative budget. The EU contribution is assessed separately for each of its member states, and includes intra-EU trade. This makes the EU by far the largest contributor to the budget, accounting for over 40 per cent of the total. The WTO Appellate Body has a budget that is independent of the WTO's.

Box 2.1. The Director-General, 1948–2008

The first Director-General of the GATT (or Secretary-General as the post was called in the early days of the GATT), Sir Eric Wyndham White, was a charismatic figure who managed the GATT for over 20 years. The very survival and functioning of the GATT and its secretariat in the post-war period was to a large extent the result of his creativity and experience (Curzon, 1973). In 1968 he was followed by Professor Olivier Long—a distinguished Swiss diplomat, academic and lawyer—who was the man at the wheel during the Tokyo Round. Long was followed in 1980 by Ambassador Arthur Dunkel, a Swiss trade official. A skilful mediator, he managed the launching of the Uruguay Round, playing a central role at almost every turning point and crisis that affected the negotiations. Through quiet and tenacious diplomacy he made an important contribution to the final package of the Uruguay Round, which was largely based on the so-called Dunkel Draft of 1991. As noted by Rubens Ricupero (1998), Dunkel was not to set foot on the 'Promised Land', and it fell to the next DG, Peter Sutherland, to finalize the negotiations in 1993 and to usher in the WTO at the 1994 ministerial meeting in Marrakech.

The appointment of Sutherland, a former EU Commissioner, marked a change in the type of person chosen by members to run the secretariat. Whereas the Director-General previously had always been an official, with the creation of the WTO the job has come to be filled by politicians. The higher public profile of the WTO also caused the selection process to become more difficult. In 1995, Peter Sutherland was succeeded by Renato Ruggiero. A former Trade Minister of Italy, Ruggiero was a controversial appointment, opposed by the US and many developing countries preferring a non-European candidate. As a compromise Mr. Ruggiero was given only a four-year mandate, rather than the regular five-year term, and it was understood that his successor would not be a European.

Upon his departure in early 1999, drawn-out and fractious consultations among members failed to arrive at a consensus on the selection of his successor. Out of an original field of four candidates, two from developing and two from OECD countries, members split between two candidates, both of whom lobbied hard for the job: the Right Honourable Mike Moore, a former Prime Minister of New Zealand, and H. E. Dr Supachai Panatchpakdi, a former Deputy Prime Minister of Thailand, In the end, a compromise deal was struck under which it was agreed that each candidate would become Director-General—sequentially—for a shortened, nonrenewable term of three years each. The process was widely regarded as the most contentious and divisive in the history of the GATT/WTO up to that point, and a symptom that the governance of the trading system needed to be improved.

Mr Moore started his term in 1999 and oversaw the contentious Seattle meeting as well as the ministerial that launched the Doha Round. Dr Supachai Panatchpakdi, the first DG from a developing country, served his three-year term beginning in 2002, and played a key role in the 2003 Cancun ministerial. In September 2005, following a process in which a number of candidates lobbied actively for the job, Pascal Lamy, a French national who had been the European Commissioner for Trade until 2004, was appointed as DG with a four-year term. The three other candidates competing for the post were all from developing countries: Carlos Pérez del Castillo of Uruguay, Jaya Krishna Cuttaree of Mauritius and Luiz Felipe de Seixas Corrêa of Brazil. In 2009, Mr Lamy was reappointed for another four-year term.

In addition to regular budget contributions, WTO members provide additional grants for specific purposes such as technical assistance or training of officials from developing countries. During the Doha Round, members agreed to create a special trust fund in which all grants for technical assistance would be placed by donors, with the Secretariat reporting to the WTO Committee on Trade and Development on the use of funds. At the time of writing the trust fund had an annual budget of some CHF25 million, equivalent to some 10 per cent of the WTO budget. In 2008, the budget of the WTO Secretariat was CHF180 million; with another CHF44 million for the Appellate Body and its secretariat. EU Member States and the European Commission have contributed around two-thirds of the total funding for the Doha Development Agenda Global Trust Fund since it was first set up in 2002. With an annual budget of CHF24 million (ca. €15 million), the Fund is the WTO's main multilateral technical assistance and training programme, organized and managed by the WTO's Institute for Training and Technical Assistance. Its activities are mainly geared towards officials from developing and transition economies (including countries in accession), with priority given to LDCs.

2.2 DECISION-MAKING

Most decision-making in the WTO is based on bargaining and consultation. As was the case under the GATT 1947, consensus is the modus operandi of the institution. Unlike the World Bank or the IMF, the WTO does not have an executive body or board comprising a subset of members, some of whom represent a number of countries. Such executive boards facilitate decision-making by concentrating discussions among a smaller but representative group of members. The closest the GATT ever came to such a forum was the Consultative Group of Eighteen (CG18), which was established in 1975. It ceased meeting in 1985, and never substituted for the GATT Council of Representatives (Blackhurst, 1998).

Even in cases where GATT rules called for a formal vote—such as on the granting of waivers of GATT obligations to a country (Article XXV GATT)—negotiation and consultations would seek to establish a consensus text before a formal vote was held (Jackson, 1997). Consensus was facilitated by another GATT tradition—not to allow progress to be frustrated by one party's obstinacy—unless it happened to be one of the major trading powers. Decision-making by consensus is a useful device to ensure that only decisions on which there is no major opposition—and consequently that have good chances of being implemented—are made. This is important because the WTO has few means of forcing unwilling governments to implement decisions.

Consensus in GATT/WTO practice does not imply unanimity. Instead it signifies that no delegation participating in a General Council or ministerial conference has a fundamental objection on a specific matter. Those that are not present—or abstain—do not count. However, exactly what is implied by consensus remains somewhat unclear. For example, in the Doha ministerial meeting, India insisted on 'explicit consensus' for launching negotiations on new subjects such as competition policy. What this meant, and how it differs from 'normal' consensus, was never defined.

Achieving consensus can be a complex process, in part because it may require issue linkages and logrolling. Consensus reinforces conservative tendencies in the system. Proposals for change can be adopted only if unopposed—creating the potential for paralysis. At the end of the 2003 Cancun ministerial conference, Mr Pascal Lamy—at that time the EU trade commissioner—blamed the consensus principle for the Conference's failure, noting that it greatly complicated the process of obtaining agreement (*Financial Times*, 16 September 2003). Offsetting the inherent complexity and cost associated with consensus is that once it has been achieved the decisions that are taken should have substantial legitimacy. The consensus practice is of value to smaller countries as it enhances their negotiating leverage—especially if they are able to form a coalition—in the informal consultations and bargaining that precede decision-making. It is in this connection that the quality of a country's delegation can be significant in determining its effective influence.

Achieving consensus among 150+ countries is clearly not a simple matter. World Trade Organization members have developed various mechanisms to limit the number of countries in specific deliberations. The first and most important device is to initially involve only 'principals'. To some extent this is a natural process—a country that has no agricultural sector is unlikely to be interested in discussions centring on the reduction of agricultural trade barriers. In general the EU and the US tend to be part of most groups that form to discuss a specific topic. They are supplemented by countries that have a principal supplying interest in a product, and the major (potential) importers whose policies are the subject of interest because they offer large markets. Most of the poorer members have generally taken a back seat in WTO deliberations. Another mechanism is coalition formation. A group of influential emerging economies, including Argentina, Brazil, Mexico, Egypt, India, South Africa, the ASEAN members and more recently China, actively participate in WTO fora. Many of these countries coalesced in the G20, a coalition that had great influence in the Doha Round. A third mechanism is to appoint chairpersons that have established a reputation for objectivity and neutrality, and who represent countries that do not have a major stake in the subject at hand. The chairpersons of WTO negotiating groups play an important role in helping negotiators define possible compromises, clarifying the interests of the parties involved and identifying potential solutions (Odell, 2005). They often are nationals of smaller nations.

In the Tokyo Round, contentious matters on which deals had to be struck were often thrashed out in the so-called Green Room, a conference room adjacent to the Director-General's office. Green Room meetings were part of a consultative process through which the major countries and a representative set of developing countries—a total of 20 or so delegations—tried to hammer out the outlines of acceptable proposals or negotiating agendas. Such meetings generally involved the active participation and input of the Director-General. A convention has since emerged to call such meetings Green Room gatherings, no matter where they are held. Once a deal has emerged among the principals, it is submitted to the general WTO membership. Although amendments may be made, these are usually marginal given that those that are most affected by—and have the greatest interest in—the subject are all on board.

The Green Room process has great potential to lead to controversial outcomes if countries with strong interests in a subject are excluded or not kept informed and consulted on proposed deals. This became a contentious issue during the Seattle ministerial meeting. Many developing countries that were excluded from critical Green Room meetings where attempts were being made to negotiate compromise texts of a draft agenda for a new MTN felt that they were not being kept informed of developments and were not being granted the opportunity to defend their views. After the Seattle Conference a large number of African and Latin American WTO members denounced what they considered the 'exclusive and nondemocratic negotiating structure' of ministerial meetings (Sutherland, Sewell and Weiner, 2001).

As discussed further in Chapter 14, proposals have been made periodically to formalize the Green Room process by creating an executive committee to manage the WTO agenda, based on shares in world trade (Schott and Buurman, 1994; Pedersen, 2006). To date, no progress in this direction has proven possible in the WTO. Although there was widespread dissatisfaction with the organization of the Seattle and Cancun ministerial conferences, subsequent discussions on 'internal transparency and effective participation of members' revealed that there was no serious interest among most of the membership to explore the merits of creating an executive body.[3] On the contrary, the Doha Declaration emphasized the collective responsibility of ensuring the effective participation of all members (WT/MIN(01)/DEC/1, para. 10). To some extent the problem is addressed by the consensus principle, which requires that all members be on board before a proposal or agreement can be adopted. Efforts to enhance the transparency of the Green

---

[3] See WT/GC/M/57, paras. 132–70.

process and consult with the rest of the membership—as was done during the Doha Round through the vehicle of 'friends of the chair' and ministers acting as 'facilitators' for specific subjects to build a bridge between insiders and outsiders— helped attenuate perceptions of effective exclusion. However, although transparency, consultation and consensus provide some reassurance to countries that they will be able to reject deals that are not in their interest, it does not ensure that those who want a seat at the table where deals are hammered will get one. The outlines of the deal that led to the launch of the Doha Round in Qatar were negotiated in a nine-hour Green Room meeting among 22 ministers, with no consultation or briefing of other members during the meeting (Pedersen, 2006).

Voting and influence

Recourse to voting may be made if a consensus cannot be reached. Article X WTO specifies when voting is called for (see Table 2.1). If required, voting is based on the principle of 'one-member-one vote'. This distinguishes the WTO from the IMF and World Bank, where weighted voting is extensively used. Unanimity is required for amendments relating to general principles such as MFN or national treatment. Interpretation of the provisions of the WTO agreements and decisions on waivers of a member's obligations require approval by a three-quarters majority vote. A two-thirds majority vote is sufficient for amendments relating to issues other than general principles mentioned above. Where not otherwise specified and where consensus cannot be reached a simple majority vote is in principle sufficient. As matters requiring a majority vote situation by design will not be central to the functioning of the WTO, this is not likely to lead to conflicts. In all cases, in contrast to the consensus practice, if voting occurs the majority required is relative to all WTO members; not with respect to those members that happen to be present at a particular meeting.

Table 2.1. Decision-making in the WTO

Decision Rule	Type of Issue
Unanimity	Amendments concerning general principles such as nondiscrimination
Three-quarters majority	Interpretations of the provisions of the WTO and waivers of WTO disciplines for members
Two-thirds majority	Amendments to the WTO relating to issues other than general principles; accession
Consensus	Where not otherwise specified

A member is not bound by any amendment that passes a vote if it is opposed to it, and the change is such as to alter its rights and obligations (Article X WTO). The ministerial conference may decide to ask a member that does not accept an amendment to withdraw from the WTO, or grant it a waiver. As the major traders must remain part of the WTO for it to retain its value, it is difficult to imagine them being asked to withdraw. Large players therefore cannot be forced to adopt changes they are unwilling to accept voluntarily. In practice voting rarely occurs. World Trade Organization members decided in 1995 not to apply provisions allowing for a vote in the case of accessions and requests for waivers, but to continue to proceed on the basis of consensus (WT/L/93). Legislative amendments are quite rare, as in practice changes to agreements occur as part of broader multilateral rounds. To date there has been only one formal amendment to a WTO agreement (TRIPS—see Chapter 8).

A country's influence in the WTO depends largely on its share in world trade and the size of its market (GDP). A country's trade-policy stance is irrelevant: free traders do not have any more say in the WTO than countries with highly protectionist regimes. The major players are therefore the major trading powers—the EU, the US and more recently China. The EU, through the Brussels-based European Commission, is a major player both because a number of EU member states are among the largest trading nations, and because individual member states no longer have full sovereignty over trade policy: this has been delegated to the European Commission.[4] Historically, countries that accord great importance to multilateralism—such as Australia, Canada, the Nordic countries, Switzerland—have been active in the WTO. For specific policy issues, the level of influence is also determined by the importance of the matter for the country. For example, Argentina, a relatively small trading nation, is an important grain exporter and has more influence on decisions concerning international trade in grains than on a topic such as telecommunications. Issues that arise are often product-specific. What matters then is the country's share of world trade in the product involved, and the importance of the products concerned in total exports of the country. This product-specificity explains much of the bilateral or plurilateral nature of the interactions that take place in the WTO.

Of the top 20 traders as measured by shares in world exports and imports, only one—Russia—is not yet a WTO member at the time of writing (Table 2.2). There is a close correlation between the top 20 and who's who in the WTO. Although industrialized market economies have historically dominated the list, in recent years a number of developing countries have become major traders. While this is in

---

[4] As EU Member States still have sovereignty over many dimensions of services regulation and intellectual property law, individual EU members each have a vote in the WTO if recourse is made to voting. The 'payment' for this is that each member pays dues to the WTO based on its total trade, including intra-EU.

Table 2.2. Top 20 traders, 2007 (US$ billion and percentage)

Rank	Exporters	Value	Share	Rank	Importers	Value	Share
1	Extra-EU (27) exports	1,695	16.5	1	United States	2,017	19.0
2	China	1,218	11.8	2	Extra-EU (27) imports	1,949	18.4
3	United States	1,163	11.3	3	China	956	9.0
4	Japan	713	6.9	4	Japan	621	5.9
5	Canada	418	4.1	5	Canada	390	3.7
6	Korea, Republic of	372	3.6	6	Hong Kong, China	371	3.5
7	Russia	355	3.5	7	—retained imports	96	0.9
8	Hong Kong, China	350	3.4	8	Korea, Republic of	357	3.4
	—domestic exports	19	0.2	9	Mexico	297	2.8
	—re-exports	331	3.2		Singapore	263	2.5
9	Singapore	299	2.9		—retained imports	120	1.1
	domestic exports	156	1.5	10	Russian Federation	223	2.1
	re-exports	143	1.4	11	Taipei, Chinese	220	2.1
10	Mexico	272	2.6	12	India	217	2.0
11	Taipei, Chinese	246	2.4	13	Turkey	170	1.6
12	Saudi Arabia	229	2.2	14	Australia	165	1.6
13	Malaysia	176	1.7	15	Switzerland	161	1.5
14	Switzerland	172	1.7	16	Malaysia	147	1.4
15	Brazil	161	1.6	17	Thailand	141	1.3
16	United Arab Emirates	154	1.5	18	Brazil	127	1.2
17	Thailand	152	1.5	19	United Arab Emirates	121	1.1
18	India	145	1.4	20	Saudi Arabia	94	0.9
19	Australia	141	1.4				
20	Norway	139	1.4				

Notes: Trade of EU states is not reported separately as the EU operates as a bloc in the WTO. Retained imports are defined as imports less re-exports.

Source: WTO.

part due to the fact that the EU now spans 27 countries, all of the developing countries listed in Table 2.2 are important trading nations. Countries such as Brazil and India have traditionally exerted substantial influence both because of their economic size and because they have often acted as spokespersons for other developing countries.

Although small developing economies by definition are not major traders, they can be—and have been—influential in the WTO. In part this is the result of the consensus principle and the tendency for small countries to cooperate and establish joint positions on issues. Small countries can also act as honest brokers between larger players. A case in point was the role played by HE. Ali Mchumo, the Tanzanian Ambassador to the WTO, who was chairman of the WTO General Council during 1999 and in that capacity played a significant role in the difficult process of selecting a new Director-General.

2.3. TRANSPARENCY: NOTIFICATION
AND SURVEILLANCE

Transparency at both the multilateral (WTO) and national level is essential to reduce uncertainty and enforce agreements. Efforts to increase transparency of members' trade policies takes up a good portion of WTO resources. The approach is inspired by what Jagdish Bhagwati has called the Dracula principle: problems may disappear once light is thrown on them (Bhagwati, 1988). The transparency provisions of the WTO relate to both the acts of the WTO itself, and the actions of its members. As far as the WTO itself is concerned, WTO decisions and other major WTO documents are published on the WTO website. After years of debate, pursuant to a 2002 Decision of the General Council, most WTO documents are either immediately available to the public or more rapidly de-restricted (WT/L/452, 16 May 2002).[5] Older decisions and documentation are published in a series entitled *Basic Instruments and Selected Documents* (*BISD*). The secretariat also prepares regular newsletters and publishes ad hoc studies on aspects of the multi-lateral trading system.

Turning to transparency of members' trade-related policies, the WTO requires that all national trade laws and regulations be published. Article X of the GATT, Article III of the GATS and Article 63 of the TRIPS Agreement all call for relevant laws of general application, judicial decisions and administrative rulings to be made public. There are over 200 notification requirements embodied in the various WTO agreements and mandated by ministerial and General Council decisions. All of these require the existence of appropriate bodies or agencies in members that have the responsibility to implement them. For example, WTO members must provide a consolidated notification, including all changes in laws, regulations, policy statements or public notices, to the secretariat each year. So-called enquiry points must be created to provide—on request—relevant documents regarding health and product standards, as well as all relevant measures of general application which pertain to or affect the operation of the GATS. The antidumping and subsidies agreements require that national authorities motivate decisions in anti-dumping and countervailing duty cases and provide data on actions taken. World

---

[5] One set of documents that have traditionally not been published are the results of tariff re-negotiations (see Chapter 9). Moreover, access to the WTO integrated database with tariff line level information is restricted to participating governments. Only data at the six-digit level or higher is publically available. As the 'devil is generally in the details' when it come to trade measures, this policy impedes the ability of think-tanks and NGOs to undertake detailed analysis of national trade policies. Negotiating documents—so-called Jobs—are restricted to members. However, one result of the interest in WTO activities is that many restricted documents are quickly leaked to the press or NGOs. A good source is *Inside US Trade*.

Trade Organization members are also required to notify any quantitative restrictions that they maintain or modify.

In February 1995, the Council for Trade in Goods established a Working Group on Notification Obligations and Procedures with the mandate to review the notification obligations and procedures. As a result of recommendations by the group, the notification obligations under GATT 1947 relating to import licensing procedures were eliminated in 1998. To assist members navigate and comply with the many notification obligations, the secretariat is required to provide a listing of notification requirements and members' compliance on an ongoing basis and circulate this semi-annually to all members.

As noted previously, the WTO also has important surveillance activities. The membership as a whole periodically reviews trade policy and foreign trade regimes of members (Box 2.2). The purpose of the TPRM is to contribute to improved adherence by WTO members to the rules and disciplines they have signed on to and achieve greater transparency in, and understanding of, prevailing trade policies and practices (WTO, 1994: Annex IIIA).

Numerous WTO bodies have transparency and information exchange functions. Many committees that oversee the functioning of specific agreements review the relevant policies of members at intervals varying between three months and two to three years. Matters of interest to developing countries are discussed in the Committee on Trade and Development. Created in 1965 to oversee a new addendum to the GATT—Part IV, dealing with trade and development—this committee devotes much of its time to discussion of implementation of provisions calling for special and differential treatment of developing countries. It also is responsible for surveillance of regional integration arrangements between developing countries. Multilateral surveillance of trade restrictions for balance-of-payments purposes takes place in the Committee on Balance of Payments Restrictions. Traditionally a largely ceremonial undertaking, discussions and decisions taken by this committee became significantly tougher after the establishment of the WTO (see Chapter 9). The Textiles Monitoring Body (TMB) was responsible for surveillance of all measures taken under the Uruguay Agreement on Textiles and Clothing (ATC), as well as monitoring compliance with the agreed programme to liberalize trade in textiles and clothing, which was implemented prior to 2005 (Chapter 6).

Although it is often argued by NGOs that one of the major failings of the WTO is a lack of transparency of its operations, great progress has been made on this front in comparison to the GATT 1947 situation. The best illustration is the WTO Internet homepage, which provides access to much of the documentation that is prepared by and submitted to the WTO—documents that under GATT procedures were 'restricted' and not made available to the public. In addition, cooperation between other international organizations with a mandate to focus on trade has greatly expanded public access to data on trade flows and trade policies. An

Box 2.2. The Trade Policy Review Mechanism

The WTO's Trade Policy Review Mechanism (TPRM), established during the Uruguay Round, builds on a 1979 GATT Understanding on Notification, Consultation, Dispute Settlement and Surveillance, under which contracting parties agreed to conduct a regular and systematic review of developments in the trading system. The objective of the TPRM is to examine the impact of trade policies and practices of members on the trading system, and to contribute to improved adherence to WTO rules through greater transparency. The legal compatibility of any particular measure with WTO disciplines is not examined, this being left for members to ascertain.

The TPRM was originally motivated in part by concerns that the only available review of global trade policies at the time was one produced by the US (Keesing, 1998). Although the TPRM suffers from some important limitations—discussed below—it is an important element of the WTO because it fosters transparency and enhances communication, thereby strengthening the multilateral trading system.

Country-specific reviews are conducted on rotational basis. The frequency of review is a function of a member's share in world trade. The four largest players—the EU, the US, Japan and Canada—are subject to review by the WTO General Council every two years. In principle, the next 16 largest traders are subjected to reviews every four years, and the remaining members are reviewed every six years. A longer periodicity may be established for LDCs. The TPRM is based on a report prepared by the government concerned and a report by the WTO Trade Policies Review Division. Trade Policy Review reports are supplemented by an annual report by the Director-General that provides an overview of developments in the international trading environment.

By subjecting the largest OECD markets to periodic review, the TPRM shifts the balance of power in the WTO, ever so slightly, in favour of the developing countries, by ensuring that the trade policies of the major traders are subject to regular public peer review (Francois, 2001). Equally important, the TPRM also provides domestic interest groups with information necessary to determine the costs and benefits of national trade policies. The working documents of the country reviews are freely available from the WTO website and printed copies of the TPRM publications (which include the full policy statement by the government, the government report, a detailed report written independently by the WTO Secretariat, and the detailed discussions and questions raised during the review) are available for sale from the WTO Secretariat or from the copublisher of the documentation.

A shortcoming of the reports is that they are not very analytical in the sense of determining the economic effects of various national policies—how large are the implied transfers, and who benefits and loses from the prevailing policies. This task is left for national stakeholders to undertake (think-tanks, policy institutes). To do it they need to be aware of the reports, and have ready access to the data that underlie the reports. It is not clear to what extent TPRM reports inform domestic policy debates and influence policy reforms. The secretariat is limited in what it can do as far as engaging in a policy dialogue with members, both in Geneva and in-country. Bolstering partnerships with national research institutes and think-tanks could do much to enhance the impact of the reports at the national level.

example is the World Integrated Trade Solution (WITS)—a software package and data retrieval tool that integrates data collected by UNCTAD, the ITC, the UN and the WTO, and that is now widely used to analyse the effects of the trade policies and trade negotiations. World Integrated Trade Solution is a joint venture between UNCTAD and the World Bank.

It is a truism that to reduce protection, the groups that are negatively affected need to be aware of the costs of such policies (Finger, 1982). Transparency of policies and their effects is a key input into any process of improving policies and sustaining an open trading system. Monitoring and constructive engagement in the WTO requires data. The same is true if countries are to enforce their rights through the Dispute Settlement Understanding (DSU). The public good of information is currently underprovided by the multilateral trading system—a major weakness that reduces its value to the citizens of its members. Large lacunae in the available databases exist on a variety of relevant policies affecting international integration. Even in the area where information is the best—barriers to goods trade—the focus of data collection (and thus analysis) is mostly on statutory MFN tariffs. Data on the types of nontariff policies that are often used by countries—such as subsidies for specific industries and excessively burdensome product standards—are not collected on a comprehensive and regular basis by the WTO or any other organization. Matters are much worse when it comes to information on policies affecting services trade, foreign investment and the movement of people. Services now account for over 40 per cent of international transactions, although data limitations imply there is substantial uncertainty on the real magnitude of the flow (see Chapter 7). Even less is known about the origin and destination of services trade and investment flows and the policies affecting these.

An effort to begin to remedy these gaps is urgently needed. The lack of data makes it difficult to examine the relationship between policies and performance and to identify priorities for domestic reform and international cooperation in key areas such as services. Better data on underlying policies are a pre-condition for better policy advice and understanding of the process of globalization. Comprehensive data are also needed for the more 'pedestrian' but critically important objective of monitoring policies. The lack of comprehensive and up-to-date data on policies affecting cross-border trade, finance and investment became an urgent matter in 2008–9 when concerns arose about the possible negative spillover effects of policy responses to the crisis. Absence of such information impeded effective monitoring of the extent to which to support policies discriminated against foreign products and suppliers.

The WTO Secretariat is an obvious candidate to take on the task of compiling comprehensive data on trade policies—going beyond applied and bound tariffs, to include bilateral preferences, nontariff measures (antidumping, subsidies, standards, rules of origin), services and investment policies, as well as data on bilateral flows of services trade, FDI and the sales of foreign affiliates. However, to make this happen WTO members must grant the secretariat the needed independence—and the resources—to do the job, and agree to make the data public, available from the web free of charge in a format that lends itself to analysis. Realizing these conditions will require political will and high-level commitment. Although much has been done to improve access and transparency to WTO documents, to date there has been limited investment in data collection and reporting and working with other organizations to fill data gaps.

2.4. ACCESSION (ARTICLE XII WTO)

Article XII WTO states that membership is open to any state or separate customs territory possessing full autonomy in the conduct of its external commercial relations. Accession terms must be agreed between the applicant and the WTO members. Accession normally follows a number of stages, negotiations usually being the final substantive phase. Summarizing, the procedure involved is that the government communicates its desire to join the WTO by writing a letter to this effect to the WTO Director-General. In practice, it will usually have requested observer status before this point. The General Council then establishes a working party consisting of interested countries to examine the application. The establishment of the working party requires consensus. Thus, any WTO member can oppose the launch of accession talks, and some have exercised that option. For example, starting with its first request in 1996, the formation of a working party on Iran was repeatedly blocked by the United States until 2005, when it dropped its opposition in support of European efforts to persuade Iran to renounce its suspected attempts to develop nuclear weapon capability.

The government seeking accession must submit a detailed memorandum describing its trade regime. On the basis of this memorandum, members of the working party will discuss and clarify the functioning of the trade regime with the applicant, usually through specific questions that are based upon the memorandum. World Trade Organization inconsistent measures will have to be removed, or be subjected to negotiated special provisions. The information requirements associated with the WTO's examination of the applicant's trade regime are significant, spanning all the policies covered by the WTO agreements, including reporting on tariff revenue collection, support provided to industries, the regulatory regime applied to goods and services, etc. Of course, collecting and reporting the information of the trade regime is just the first step. What will often take much longer is the process of understanding WTO requirements, identifying where reforms are needed to bring the trade regime into compliance with WTO rules, and designing and implementing these changes.

A key aspect of this ostensibly multilateral proceeding is its bilateral component. Accession negotiations are held between the acceding government and all members interested in enhancing their access to the markets of the country seeking membership. As part of the accession process, the newcomer negotiates schedules of tariff concessions and specific commitments on trade in services with each interested WTO member. Once bilateral market access negotiations are concluded, the report of the working party is sent to the General Council. A draft Decision and Protocol of Accession is attached to the report, as is the negotiated tariff schedule. Accession of a new member must be approved by a two-thirds majority of existing members. Any existing WTO member may invoke a nonapplication clause (Article XIII WTO) that allows it not to apply its WTO commitments to the new member. If invoked, the new member may do the same (that is, 'retaliate in kind'). Once a country has acceded, the Protocol of Accession is legally binding.

Each WTO member has the right to present specific demands to the applicant country, both with respect to tariff and nontariff issues. Not all WTO members make use of this prerogative—most either play no role or confine themselves to passive participation in the accession working party meetings—but all have the opportunity to seek redress for the alleged shortcomings of the applicant country's trade regime. As of October 2008, 25 countries (including Russia) were involved in the process of WTO accession. Between 1995 and October 2008, 26 countries acceded, including important trading nations such as China, China Taipei, Vietnam and Ukraine, as well as numerous former centrally planned economies and other developing countries.[6]

Until the 1990s, the requirement that the applicant's trade regime conform to GATT law was far from a demand that the newcomer be a paragon of liberal trade virtues. New members were required to comply with a limited set of rules. Negotiations tended to be tempered by pragmatism and flexibility. This changed significantly under the WTO—conditions imposed for accession became much more stringent. Aspirant members of the WTO are likely to be requested to bind their whole tariff schedule at, or close to, applied rates. The country seeking accession will usually also have to liberalize access to its markets much more

---

[6] As of end 2008 the following countries were in the accession queue: Afghanistan, Algeria, Andorra, Azerbaijan, Bahamas, Belarus, Bhutan, Bosnia and Herzegovina, Comoros, Ethiopia, Iran, Iraq, Kazakhstan, Lao People's Democratic Republic, Lebanon, Libya, Montenegro, Russian Federation, Samoa, Sao Tomé and Principe, Serbia, Seychelles, Sudan, Tajikistan, Uzbekistan, Vanuatu and Yemen. All have observer status in the WTO. Observer governments that have not yet applied to join WTO include Equatorial Guinea and the Holy See (Vatican). The 24 countries that joined the WTO between 1995 and mid-2008 are: Ecuador, Bulgaria, Mongolia, Panama, Kyrgyzstan, Latvia, Estonia, Jordan, Georgia, Albania, Oman, Croatia, Lithuania, Moldova, China, Chinese Taipei, Armenia, Cambodia, Nepal, Saudi Arabia, Vietnam, Tonga, Ukraine and Cape Verde (in chronological order).

than was the case in the past. Average applied rates significantly higher than 10 per cent are unlikely to be accepted.

The conditions imposed on applicant countries are often seen by them as excessively burdensome. Progress in expanding WTO membership has consequently been slow—most accessions take several years. Some, including Algeria, China and Saudi Arabia, spanned more than a decade, and Russia's accession efforts have taken over 15 years at the time of writing. The Chinese and Russian accession experiences are discussed in Chapter 12, as are those of several LDCs.

There are several reasons why accession is considerably more burdensome than it used to be under the GATT. First, and most obviously, the coverage of the WTO is substantially more far-reaching than was the GATT. Second, a change occurred in the attitude of major trading powers, especially the United States. Before the end of the Cold War and the collapse of the Soviet Union in the late 1980s, the US was willing to tolerate trade policies that were detrimental to its export interests for the sake of foreign policy objectives. In the 1990s, the pursuit of national economic interests became more dominant. Third, the large trading powers increasingly perceived accession to the WTO as a major step in a country's integration into the world economy and as a way of encouraging the acceding government to abandon interventionist economic policies in favour of more open and market-oriented approaches. That perspective was particularly important in accession negotiations of countries such as China and Vietnam and continues to be in the case of Russia. In a related vein, there appears to be a tendency to exploit incumbent market power and seek commitments from acceding countries that go beyond the letter of the WTO law. For example, a number of transition economies have been asked to make commitments and report progress on privatization of state-owned enterprises—a matter on which the WTO is silent.[7]

The bottom line is that a country that desires to enter the WTO is a *demandeur*. It must negotiate with incumbent club members, and more often than not will have little bargaining power. The accession process is asymmetric—the acceding country cannot negotiate additional benefits in excess of those already embodied in existing WTO agreements, whereas the WTO members may, and do, ask for more than the status quo. Indeed, sometimes applicants are asked to do more than incumbent countries have committed themselves to. An example is tariff bindings, where the current rule of thumb appears to be that bindings should be comprehensive and not be higher than double the average import-weighted average applying in OECD countries (some 10 per cent). This compares to an average bound rate of incumbent developing countries of 20 per cent or so for those

---

[7] As discussed in Chapter 5, ownership of firms is not of concern to WTO members. What matters is their behaviour. Members may use state-trading enterprises, but such firms may not use their market power to circumvent tariff bindings and related commitments, or engage in discrimination (violate the MFN rule).

tariff lines that are bound. (As discussed further in Chapter 5, many tariff lines remain unbound.) Other examples of asymmetries are demands for abolition of agricultural subsidies, more comprehensive service sector commitments than many existing members have made, and making accession conditional on implementation of required reforms (as opposed to allowing a gradual transition path). A noteworthy feature of the post-1995 (WTO) period is that accession candidates have sometimes been asked to make commitments in policy areas that are not subject to WTO disciplines (see Chapter 12).

2.5. THE WTO AND OTHER INTERNATIONAL ORGANIZATIONS

Numerous other international organizations in addition to the WTO play a role in fostering multilateral cooperation on trade and international exchange more generally. Examples are the International Monetary Fund (IMF), the International Bank for Reconstruction and Development (IBRD), the various UN bodies such as UNCTAD, UNDP, the UN Economic Commissions, as well as specialized organizations such as the Bank for International Settlements (BIS), World Customs Organization (WCO), the International Telecommunications Union (ITU) or the World Intellectual Property Organization (WIPO).

The relationship between GATT 1947 and these organizations was largely informal. The only exception was the IMF: Article XV GATT calls for the contracting parties to cooperate and consult with the IMF on matters relating to foreign exchange reserves, the balance of payments and exchange rate issues. Article XV GATT states that the contracting parties and the IMF 'may pursue a coordinated policy with regard to exchange questions' and that contracting parties 'shall not, by exchange action, frustrate the intent of the provisions of the GATT'. The IMF had a formal role in the GATT Balance-of-Payments Committee, responsible for determining whether a country had a balance-of-payments problem (see Chapters 5 and 9).

This state of affairs changed with the creation of the WTO. Article III:5 WTO states that the WTO is to cooperate with the IMF and the World Bank 'to achieve greater coherence in global economic policy making'. Formal agreements were negotiated between the WTO and the Bank and Fund (Nogues, 1998; Winters, 2000). These aim at strengthening interagency relations through promotion of cooperation and collaboration. The agreements give the WTO Secretariat the right to be present at meetings of the Executive Boards of the Bretton Woods institutions, and grant the Bretton Woods institutions observer status at formal WTO meetings. The staff of the three organizations is frequently in touch at the technical level. Periodic joint meetings are held, and technical assistance efforts are coordinated in the context of the so-called Enhanced Integrated Framework for LDCs (see Chapter 12).[8] Moreover, the WTO Secretariat concluded numerous Memoranda of Understanding with other organizations involved in trade-related technical assistance and support to negotiators in the Doha Round, and conducted joint capacity building with other organizations.

Other international bodies that have links with the WTO include the International Organization for Standardization (ISO), the Brussels-based World Customs Organization (WCO), the World Intellectual Property Organization (WIPO), the Codex Alimentarius Commission (a subsidiary of the UN's Food and Agriculture Organization—FAO), and the International Office of Epizootics. The WTO cooperates with WIPO (through the TRIPS Agreement), the ISO (because of the WTO disciplines on product standards), the ITU (telecommunications, e-commerce), and the WCO (which develops rules of origin and classifications of goods). International governmental organizations are invited to attend the WTO ministerial conferences. For example, more than 80 such organizations were represented in Hong Kong in 2005.

In principle, other international organizations can obtain formal observer status. Requests to this effect need to be approved by the General Council. Such status applies to specific WTO agreements and WTO bodies, such as the General Council, the Trade Policy Review Mechanism, the Committee on Technical Barriers to Trade, etc. As of 2008, only FAO, IMF, OECD, UN, UNCTAD, World Bank and WIPO had been given observer status in the General Council. (As a joint venture 'daughter institution' the International Trade Centre (ITC) also has observer status.) Other bodies have dozens of observer organizations.

The General Agreement on Tariffs and Trade 1947 and UNCTAD were frequently looked on as rival organizations, as they had similar areas of interest, but differed greatly in terms of their functions, operations and underlying ideology. The WTO and UNCTAD cooperate in a joint venture, the ITC—dating back to 1964—which provides export promotion and marketing assistance and related training and consulting services to developing countries. The WTO works more closely with UNCTAD and the ITC than was the case under the old GATT. For example, starting in 2006 the three entities started to publish an annual set of country tariff profiles—a summary of protection levels, main trade partners and trends in trade. Both ITC and UNCTAD provide services that are complementary to the WTO, including activities aimed at strengthening negotiation capacity of developing countries and technical assistance in the area of trade facilitation and customs procedures. The ITC also provides assistance on export promotion and

---

[8] Chapter 14 briefly discusses the topic of coherence of international policymaking.

market analysis, and works with UNCTAD to provide trade flow data and information on trade and investment policies.

2.6. NONGOVERNMENTAL ACTORS AND THE WTO

The WTO is an inter-governmental organization. Only government representatives have legal standing. The private sector and NGOs do not have direct access to WTO meetings and negotiating fora. If such groups have concerns or desires that they would like to see addressed, they must convince their governments to take up the issue. Given that the WTO is a trade organization, it should be no surprise that the interest groups which have historically been listened to most by governments are firms and industry associations. As discussed earlier, the main players on the domestic political front are import competing and export-oriented industries. In contrast to organizations such as the OECD, where business groups have observer status and participate in some meetings, or the ILO, which has a tripartite governing structure—employer groups, labour unions and governments—the WTO has not allowed nongovernmental entities to participate in its work. Interaction with NGOs has been limited to organizations that are directly concerned with issues that are addressed by the WTO. The first formal arrangements for cooperation were concluded with the International Federation of Inspection Agencies, in connection with pre-shipment inspection (see Chapter 5).

Numerous NGOs, especially those representing environmental interests and labour groups have become very active in national and international debates on the WTO. They are particularly interested in enhancing their access to the dispute settlement process and WTO meetings more generally. Their concerns relate in part to transparency of process, reflecting a perception that governments have 'sold out' to multinational business, seeking to conclude agreements that are detrimental to the environment and to workers. Some would argue that these concerns are misconceived given that the WTO is arguably the most democratic international organization extant, in that it operates by consensus and, if voting occurs, it is on the basis on one-member-one-vote. Others argue that there are valid concerns relating to the perceived legitimacy of the WTO, and that without action to bring the critics on board and address their worries, the WTO will find it difficult to pursue its mandate.

Matters such as environment and labour standards, food safety regulation, intellectual property and consumer protection, business ethics and corruption are all issues that concern the citizens of all WTO members. Numerous pressure groups and political organizations want to include labour and environment in future trade talks and demand that new trade deals contain a 'social clause'. There is an obvious temptation to use the WTO system as an instrument to enforce norms and rules in such nontrade areas. If worded along the lines of 'thou shall adopt my norms' this can be zero-sum.

In principle, encouraging greater participation of single-issue NGOs, the business community and consumer protection groups in debates on the future WTO agenda would be useful to ensure new inflow of ideas and the maintenance of the communication channels with various pressure groups. The challenge of achieving this in a balanced fashion is nontrivial. A distinction needs to be made between enhancing the two-way flow of information, opportunities to observe or voice views at meetings, and giving nongovernmental bodies a seat at the negotiating or decision-making table. The fact that the WTO is an inter-governmental organization in which only governments have standing makes the latter impossible. But it should prove feasible to encourage greater involvement of business organizations and NGOs in the daily operations of the WTO. For example, the European Communities has suggested that NGOs and parliamentarians from the reviewed WTO country be permitted to observe the meetings of the TPRB and that an open meeting at senior official or ministerial level combined with a symposium for dialogue with civil society be held every year (WT/GC/W/412, 6 October 2000). The United States has proposed that some council and committee meetings be open to NGOs and that they should be allowed to make submissions to certain WTO bodies (WT/GC/W/413/Rev. 1, 13 October 2000). The US also supported an EU proposal to open the TPRB meetings to the public, e.g. by webcasting.

A step in the direction of greater WTO openness towards civil society was reached in March 2002 when the WTO Secretariat decided to organize special workshops where both critics and supporters would participate. This morphed into an annual 'Geneva week' public forum where NGOs and other organizations, as well as members, organize and participate in seminars and workshops on trade subjects that are of interest to them. Another breakthrough was when NGOs were invited to attend (but not to speak at) the plenary sessions of the ministerial conferences in Singapore (December 1996) and subsequent ministerial conferences. About 2,100 NGO representatives participated in the plenary session of the 2005 Hong Kong ministerial conference, up from some 1,580 registered for the plenary session in Cancun (2003).

Another important step was made by the Appellate Body in the shrimp-turtles litigation (see Chapter 3 below), with the decision to accept an amicus brief by a NGO. In a subsequent case involving the US and the EU (British Steel—DS/138), it decided that it had the discretion to accept such briefs. Many WTO members, especially developing countries, object strongly to these decisions, which gave rise to repeated criticisms in the debate in the WTO Dispute Settlement Body on these reports. However, given the negative consensus rule that prevails in the WTO regarding panel and Appellate Body reports, there is little that can be done by members absent to ensure a general re-negotiation of the rules in this area (see Chapter 3). A step towards greater transparency of dispute settlement proceedings was made in the Hormones case—discussed in Chapter 3—with the parties agreeing to broadcast part of the proceedings (see Chapter 14).

2.7. CONCLUSION

The WTO grew out of the GATT 1947, which successfully developed and oversaw global trading rules in the period after the Second World War. The creation of the WTO can be seen as the fulfilment of the vision of the participants at the Bretton Woods conference in 1944, albeit half a century later. Although the WTO is very similar to the old GATT in terms of day-to-day operations and general approach, it is a very different animal. The WTO is less 'diplomatic' and more 'legalistic' than the GATT was. This is perhaps best illustrated by the great expansion in the coverage of its disciplines, the associated increase in dispute settlement cases, and the large number of formal notification requirements. The long accession queue and the intense interest in the operation of the system that can be observed on the part of NGOs as well as business illustrate the importance that is accorded to the institution by civil society. Much of this interest (and concern) is sparked by the WTO's dispute settlement procedures, by the mechanics of the negotiating process that generate the rules of the game, and the substance of the rules themselves. These are subjects of subsequent chapters.

2.8. FURTHER READING

For an influential contemporary discussion of the design of a successor organization to the GATT 1947, see John H. Jackson, *Restructuring the GATT System* (London: Pinter Publishers, 1990). Major players in the Uruguay Round negotiations give their views on the dynamics and process in Jagdish Bhagwati and Mathias Hirsch (eds), *The Uruguay Round and Beyond: Essays in Honor of Arthur Dunkel* (Ann Arbor: University of Michigan Press, 1998). An informative history of the Uruguay Round negotiations is presented in John Croome, *Reshaping the Trading System* (Deventer: Kluwer, 1999). For an analysis of the WTO as a network organization see Richard Blackhurst, 'The Capacity of the WTO to Fulfill Its

Mandate', in A. Krueger (ed.), *The WTO as an International Organization* (Chicago: University of Chicago Press, 1998). Michael Trebilcock and Robert Howse, *The Regulation of International Trade* (London: Routledge, 2006) is a comprehensive treatment of WTO rules. They also compare WTO disciplines with those that apply in the EU and NAFTA. M. Matsushita, M. Schoenbaum and P. Mavroidis, *The World Trade Organization: Law, Practice and Policy* (Oxford: Oxford University Press, 2006) is a comprehensive legal review of the WTO. Amrita Narlikar, *The World Trade Organization: A Very Short Introduction* (Oxford: Oxford University Press, 2005) delivers exactly what the title promises.

Official GATT and WTO documents are published annually by the secretariat in a series called 'Basic Instruments and Selected Documents'. Most WTO documents can be downloaded from the WTO homepage (www.wto.org). The WTO website also offers general information and training material. The WTO Annual Report provides an overview of major developments in trade, trade policy and WTO activities, as well as basic statistics on trade flows and trends. Of particular interest is the WTO *World Trade Report*, which provides an in-depth treatment of a specific trade policy topic each year. The 2007 edition of this report provides an excellent comprehensive discussion of the literature on and experience of the multilateral trading system since it was established in 1948. The Trade Policy Reviews published by the WTO Secretariat are a valuable source of information on the trade and related policies maintained by individual WTO members.

CHAPTER 3

DISPUTE SETTLEMENT AND ENFORCEMENT OF RULES

In contrast to most international organizations that rely on diplomatic means to resolve conflicts, WTO dispute settlement (DS) procedures are elaborate and legally binding. This chapter first briefly presents a number of conceptual considerations that help to understand the role and nature of the WTO dispute settlement system. We then describe the major features of the system and discuss its operation to date as reflected in the case load between 1995 and 2007. The chapter concludes with a discussion of systemic questions and proposals that have been made to make the system more effective, both in the context of a review of the DS system by WTO members themselves and by the academic community, practitioners, NGOs and the business community.

3.1. THE RATIONALE FOR A DISPUTE SETTLEMENT BODY

Effective enforcement of negotiated commitments is a pre-condition for the trading system to work. Because the WTO is an inter-governmental agreement, it must be what economists call 'self-enforcing'. There is no supra-national body that can impose rulings and enforce judgements. Instead, compliance with a negotiated agreement must come about because not doing so will result in a situation that is worse than the one that prevails if governments stick to their deals. Insofar as a government judges that defection is in its interest at a given point in time, cooperation can only be maintained if there is a credible threat by other WTO members that reverting back to a noncooperative policy stance will be punished by retaliation. This (threat of) retaliation must generate expected costs that are larger than the short-term gain from violating an agreement. In the WTO retaliation is exercised by the country or countries that are injured by the adoption of a policy that violates a prior agreement. They must enforce the terms of a deal themselves.

This immediately raises the question of why a Dispute Settlement Body (DSB) is needed. This is less obvious than it may appear. For example, Hungerford (1991) argues that a DSB may create incentives for members of a trade agreement to deliberately generate a dispute because they know it will be resolved. One rationale for the creation of a DSB is to reduce the prevalence of opportunism and use of (unilateral) retaliation by creating a presumption that action by a country to change the negotiated terms of a deal will result in compensation. The DS mechanism provides an objective forum in which the facts of a matter can be determined (through an exchange of information and independent evaluation) and where as a result 'excessive' retaliation (an immediate 'tit-for-tat' response) can be avoided (Bagwell and Staiger, 2002).

Simple theoretical analyses of DS mechanisms assume that enforcement of a specific negotiated contract occurs in a situation of certainty: violations are observed and are unambiguous. In practice, however, there will often be uncertainty regarding whether or not a certain policy measure violates the WTO. As will be seen repeatedly in subsequent chapters, the disciplines of many WTO agreements are often fuzzy, ambiguous or simply not defined. As a result there can easily be legitimate uncertainty regarding the appropriate interpretations of a provision in a specific context. For example, a measure that appears to violate a tariff binding or a negotiated commitment may in fact be permitted because it is a legal domestic tax that is collected at the border. Disputes then may involve disagreements in how to interpret a provision. Over time a body of case law reduces the associated uncertainty. Thus, the DSB can help address one form of contractual incompleteness that is inherent in the WTO—the vagueness of many of its disciplines—by interpreting the contract, filling gaps on specific matters where the treaty is silent, or, granting exceptions and thereby modifying certain aspects of a discipline. The latter implies that a dispute may serve as a mechanism to facilitate a form of 'efficient breach' of an agreement (Lawrence, 2003).

Thus, by spelling out more clearly what the applicable disciplines are, the DSB serves to reduce uncertainty regarding the legitimacy of certain types of measures, in the process reducing the use of unilateral retaliation against perceived violations of an agreement that are in fact due to exogenous shocks to demand or supply and not driven by policy. More generally, the DSB can counteract the moral hazard problem that is likely to arise as a result of each WTO member interpreting vague provisions in a manner that suits its interests. Moreover, by providing a forum in which deviations can be publicized, other WTO members may be brought into the picture who also have an incentive to see cooperation sustained (Maggi, 1999). Finally, the DSB can help identify where negotiations are needed to clarify disciplines.

It is often stressed by economists that the WTO is an 'incomplete contract'. This implies that it does not (and cannot) specify what is permitted of governments in every state of the world. Instead, the WTO contains only a few specific, unambiguous disciplines (the most obvious being the tariff bindings). Other fundamental disciplines—such as national treatment—will require interpretation to determine if and how they have been violated in a specific instance. That is, a dispute may be needed to determine the ambit of the discipline in a specific, contested circumstance and the relevant facts. Horn and Mavroidis (2007) argue that the role of the DSB is to ease a coordination problem confronting WTO members by specifying an agreed-upon procedure for adjudication. Through the creation of the DSB, WTO members can circumvent the problem of agreeing on the specifics of the contract by agreeing to let a third party—panels and the Appellate Body (AB)—adjudicate on their behalf. In effect, the resulting rulings are accepted by the parties as an acceptable outcome of a negotiation they never completed or they generate new negotiations to clarify the applicable law.

For the DSB to play a role in 'completing' the WTO contract, and, in particular, to address instances of vagueness in language, rulings need to establish a precedent. In principle, dispute resolution under the WTO does not formally establish a precedent in that panels are not required to conform to the reasoning of prior panels or AB rulings, nor is the latter legally bound to follow its own prior case law. It is often argued that this approach has its roots in the GATT tradition of 'negotiated' dispute settlements where finding a pragmatic solution to a trade conflict was more important than legal consistency (Hudec, 1993), but it arguably has its roots in international law more generally. The fact that any resolution to a dispute did not create a precedent facilitated adoption of the panel reports by the council: every contracting party was reading panel reports with the 'skeletons in their closets' in the back of their minds (Mavroidis, 2007). In practice, however, given similar factual issues, there is a very high likelihood that WTO panels will follow AB rulings. The AB has made clear that its rulings should be applied by subsequent panels. For example, in 2007 a panel went against AB rulings that zeroing in antidumping (see Chapter 9) was WTO-inconsistent. The AB overturned the panel, stating that panels are expected to follow previously adopted AB reports addressing the same issue. It noted that failure to do so would undermine the development of a coherent and predictable body of jurisprudence.

The objective of DS in the WTO is to maintain the balance of negotiated concessions. This explains why the remedy in WTO dispute settlement is *prospective*: the offending member is called upon to bring its measures into compliance. Whether this is enough of an incentive is a question to which we return below—many commentators argue it is not and would prefer to see a system that offers affected countries compensation for injury incurred as well as the standard WTO remedy, that is, *retrospective* measures. Prospects for this are not bright, in part because it would change the nature of the WTO. The relatively weak enforcement mechanisms in the WTO reflect the incomplete nature of the WTO contract: there is presumably a reason why governments signed a deal that is fuzzy in a particular area. For example, this may reflect trade costs—see Horn, Maggi and Staiger (2006)—which in practice are still quite significant (see Anderson and van Wincoop, 2004). The result will be that governments will not want to subject themselves to a process where they are subject to penalties that they deem inappropriate given the absence of *ex ante* specificity on the rules that will apply. This may be so in particular for countries that expect to be both complainants and respondents over time—likely to be the case for any large player. As noted by Ethier (2001*a*), this gives countries an incentive to agree to remedies that are limited in scope—that is, to design the DS mechanism to weaken remedies rather than strengthen them. Given that in any dispute the complainant has a clear incentive to push for maximalist remedies (the equivalent of criminal versus civil damages in a domestic setting), *ex ante*—that is, in designing the agreement, before any disputes have been brought—the participants in a trade negotiation may conclude that they are better off if DS is delegated to a third party that is constrained to recommend a remedy focused on maintaining the original balance of concessions. Strong enforcement can have the perverse effect of inducing countries to make fewer commitments in the first place, resulting in an outcome that is inferior to one where there is weaker enforcement—in that the expected benefits of cooperation are higher (Lawrence, 2003).

3.2. WTO Dispute Settlement Procedures

World Trade Organization dispute settlement procedures may be initiated whenever a member desires. This requires that the member claim that an action by another member has 'nullified or impaired' a concession that was negotiated previously (such as a tariff binding) or breaks a WTO rule and 'impairs the attainment of an objective' of the WTO. In the case of goods, complaints may take three forms (Article XXIII GATT). The first is a violation complaint, which consists of a claim that one or more disciplines or negotiated commitments have been violated. Second, members may bring a 'nonviolation' complaint: this allows a government to argue that a measure nullifies a previously granted concession even though no specific rules are violated (Article XXIII: 1*b*). The third possibility is a so-called situation complaint, under which a member may argue that 'any other situation' not captured by the violation or nonviolation options has led to nullification or impairment of a negotiated benefit. (The latter is of very little practical significance.) Both GATS and TRIPS allow for both violation and non-violation complaints, although in the case of TRIPS WTO members have agreed not to invoke the nonviolation provision until the TRIPS Council has determined the scope and modalities for such complaints. Article 64 TRIPS calls for this to be done within five years of the creation of the WTO, but as agreement proved impossible, members have periodically agreed to extend the moratorium, most recently at the 2005 Hong Kong ministerial meeting.

In theory, nonviolation cases could be important to the functioning of the system as they provide a way for members to contest the effects of policies that reduce the value of negotiated concessions but that are not subject to WTO disciplines. Countries such as the US have a tradition of using unilateral trade actions to defend their commercial interests in such instances. Section 301 of the Trade Act of 1974, as amended, allows (and sometimes requires) the US Government to take unilateral retaliatory actions against alleged unfair trading practices of partner countries. In principle, a nonviolation dispute is the WTO instrument to pursue such cases—although in practice they are very rare and hardly ever successful.

Disputes arising under any WTO agreement are dealt with by the DSB, which has the authority to establish panels, adopt panel reports, scrutinize implementation of recommendations and authorize retaliatory measures if the losing party to a dispute does not abide by the panel's recommendations. The DSB is essentially the WTO Council—it simply changes name when it considers disputes. The rules of the game are laid out in the Uruguay Round Dispute Settlement Understanding (DSU). The DSU covers all disputes arising under WTO agreements—that is, relating to GATT, GATS and TRIPS. The same procedures are used for settling disputes across all issues—there is a unified dispute settlement mechanism. However, some of the specific Uruguay Round agreements discussed in Chapter 5 contain special DS provisions. If these procedures differ from the general WTO provisions, the special procedures apply.

The use of WTO dispute settlement mechanisms is mandatory in all instances where a dispute concerns matters on which agreements have been concluded. If a member decides to pursue a dispute it must submit the case to the WTO adjudicating bodies (Article 23.2 DSU). It may not go ahead and retaliate. Article 23 DSU was important for many countries because it was aimed at disciplining the US use of 'aggressive unilateralism' (Bhagwati and Patrick, 1990). Only if a member does not comply with the outcome of the process, and the DSB authorizes retaliation may instruments such as Section 301 be used to retaliate. Even then, the magnitude of the retaliatory measures that may be imposed must first be determined by the WTO (Box 3.1).

Box 3.1. Settlement of disputes

Stage I: Consultations. Members must initially attempt to solve their disputes through bilateral consultations. The good offices and conciliation by the WTO Director-General may also be sought. The goal of the consultation stage is to enable the disputing parties to understand the factual situation and the legal claims and hopefully to settle the matter bilaterally. The objective of the DS process is to facilitate a settlement—Article 3.7 DSU specifies that a 'solution mutually acceptable to the parties to a dispute and consistent with the covered agreements is clearly to be preferred' to the formation of a panel. At any stage in the DS process the parties may reach an informal settlement (this is termed a mutually agreed solution (MAS) in WTO speak). Parties may also invoke mediation (Article 5 DSU).

Stage II: Request for a panel. If parties are not able to settle their dispute through consultations within 60 days, the establishment of a panel may be requested. Other WTO members may join as co-complainants if the original complainant accepts them (Article 4:11 DSU). The DSB establishes a panel, drafts terms of reference and determines its composition. Drawing on a large roster of potential panellists (who have all been nominated by WTO members), the WTO Secretariat suggests the names of three or four potential panellists to the parties to the dispute. Parties have the right to object to a proposed panellist. Panellists serve in their individual capacity, may not be subjected to government instructions, and tend to be members of delegations or retired civil servants knowledgeable in trade matters. They may also include academic scholars. The WTO Secretariat provides administrative support and generally prepares the background documentation regarding the facts of the case.

Stage III: The panel at work. The panel usually goes through the following steps in pursuing its mandate to perform an objective assessment of the facts and the applicability of and conformity with the relevant WTO agreements: (1) examination of facts and arguments; (2) meetings with the parties and interested third parties (those with a 'substantial interest' in a dispute (Article 10 DSU); (3) interim review—descriptive and interim reports are sent to the parties, who may request a review meeting with the panel; (4) drafting of conclusions and recommendations; and (5) issuing of their report to the parties and circulation to the DSB. Panels have power of discovery: they may seek information and technical advice from any appropriate body or person (Article 13 DSU), and issue questionnaires to the parties in a case. Panels are supposed to conclude their work within 6 months, and exceptionally, 9 months. In practice the average is slightly over one year.

Stage IV: Adoption decision or appeal. The panel report must be adopted by the DSB within 60 days, unless a consensus exists not to adopt, or a party appeals the findings of the panel. Appeals are supposed to be limited to issues of law or the legal interpretation developed by the panel, although in practice this restriction is not necessarily a binding one. An Appellate Body, composed of seven persons who are broadly representative of the WTO's membership, deals with such appeals. Appeal proceedings should not exceed 60 days and must be completed within 90 days. The AB is limited to judging matters of law and the legal consistency of panel reports. It has some discretion in key areas—for example in determining who has the burden of proof, a question on which it has reversed panels. The AB report is final and is adopted by the DSB.

Stage V: Implementation. If it is impracticable to comply immediately, the offending country is given a 'reasonable period of time' to do so (Article 21.3 DSU). The length of this

(cont.)

Box 3.1. (Continued)

period can, at the request of the parties, be determined through binding arbitration. If the respondent fails to act within this period, parties are to negotiate compensation pending full implementation (Article 22.2 DSU). If this cannot be agreed, the complainant may request authorization from the DSB to suspend equivalent concessions against the offending country (that is, to retaliate). This authorization is automatic (as a consensus is needed to refuse it).

The magnitude of the retaliation is determined by the DSB, generally on the recommendation of the original panel. Arbitration may be sought on the level of suspension, the procedures and principles of retaliation (Article 22.6). Retaliation is intended to be temporary, until such time as a member has brought its measures into compliance—the basic objective of the DSU. In principle, retaliation occurs under the same agreement, but the choice of sector/product is left to the discretion of the WTO member. If retaliation is not feasible under the same agreement that was invoked in the dispute, a member may ask the DSB for authorization to suspend concessions under another agreement.

If there is disagreement whether the respondent has brought its measures into compliance, recourse is to be made to the DS procedures. That is, the process starts again, using where possible the original panel, but subject to an accelerated time frame (90 days) (Article 21.5). As discussed below, such Article 21.5 compliance panels have played a prominent role in a number of key cases brought to the WTO. One reason is that panels rarely make specific recommendations: it is left to the WTO member concerned to bring its measures into compliance.

Dispute settlement under GATT and WTO

Dispute settlement under the GATT was based on the consensus principle. This ensured that both parties to a dispute had to agree on the outcome, increasing the likelihood of implementation. It also created opportunities for parties to a dispute to block either the initiation or the completion of the process. This could be achieved through refusal of one of the parties to a dispute to agree to the formation of a panel, to delay the appointment of a panel or to refuse to adopt the panel report. In the 1980s and early 1990s, a growing number of fractious trade disputes that could not be resolved gave rise to concerns regarding the effectiveness of GATT dispute settlement procedures. These disputes reflected the intensification of competition resulting from changing patterns of comparative advantage, as well as vaguely worded GATT provisions and differences in their interpretation in key areas such as subsidies and agriculture. A number of the disputes that were brought to the GATT in the 1980s were essentially attempts by contracting parties to more clearly define GATT provisions—they substituted for negotiations. It is therefore not surprising that they were controversial.

In practice, GATT contracting parties made only limited use of the consensus rule to block dispute settlement. Legal research has concluded that the GATT dispute mechanism worked much better than was generally recognized. Of some 278 complaints considered under general DS provisions between 1948 and 1994, 110 led to legal rulings by panels, the others being settled before a report was produced. Of the 88 cases where the panel found a violation had occurred, the majority were adopted. Moreover, many of those not adopted did lead to a satisfactory outcome. Hudec (1993) found that overall, over the life of the GATT 1947, the success rate of cases addressed by GATT—that is, disputes settled—was well over 90 per cent. After 1980, the rate of nonadoption of panel reports increased significantly, reflecting the fact that many of the contested issues were in areas where the rules were not clear or that were the subject of ongoing negotiations during the Uruguay Round.

The success of a system that could so easily be blocked by one party to a dispute can be explained in large part by self-interest. Losing parties knew that at some point in the future they would bring cases themselves. If they were to block disputes or adoption of reports this would greatly reduce the value of negotiated commitments. The GATT (and the WTO) is a repeated game (see Chapter 4)—parties know they will interact over an indefinite time horizon. As noted by Hudec (1993), other factors were that GATT contracting parties 'owned' the agreements and that the disciplines of the GATT generally made good economic sense. In many cases, officials of countries that lost a case had an interest in enforcing GATT rules because it helped them adopt more efficient instruments of trade policy.

Compared to the GATT 1947, dispute settlement under the WTO was strengthened by eliminating the possibility of blocking the formation of a panel and the adoption of panel reports, introducing time limits for the various stages of panel proceedings, defining standard terms of reference for panels, creation of an appeals process and automaticity of approval for retaliation in cases of noncompliance with a panel recommendation. Under the WTO, adoption of panel reports can only be blocked by a 'negative consensus', that is, all WTO members must agree that the panel report is fundamentally flawed, a highly improbable event. To counterbalance the removal of the blocking option for losing parties, Uruguay Round negotiators created a new standing Appellate Body. This entity—essentially an appeals court—can be asked to consider challenges regarding the legal interpretations of a panel. It comprises seven members, appointed for four years, renewable once. Thus, one outcome of the Uruguay Round was to shift towards a two-stage process, under which panels become akin to lower level courts, albeit a court with constantly changing composition, as panellists (judges) are drawn from a roster and are appointed on a case-by-case basis. Box 3.1 summarizes the various stages involved in settling disputes.

Although virtually all disputes go through some or all of the stages laid out in Box 3.1, the DSU also provides for the option of binding arbitration (Article 25 DSU). This requires mutual agreement by the parties and is binding—no appeal is possible to the AB. However, in case of noncompliance with the outcome of the arbitration, the parties may ask for a compliance panel to be established and/or request authorization to retaliate. As of 2008, Article 25 had been invoked only once, in a copyright dispute brought by the EU against the US (see Chapter 8).

Why the strengthening and legalization of the DS system if it worked pretty well? One reason was the use of Section 301 and its variants by the US (Bhagwati and Irwin, 1987). The US insisted that a quid pro quo for agreeing to Article 23 DSU-type disciplines was a strong DSU with more teeth.

3.3. OPERATION OF THE SYSTEM

Many considered that the strengthening of GATT dispute settlement procedures was one of the major results of the Uruguay Round—especially for developing countries. The expectation was that small players would have greater incentives to bring cases (Schott and Buurman, 1994; Croome, 1999). The experience appears to support the optimistic expectations. Over 160 requests for consultations were brought to the WTO in its first five years of operation; three times more on a per annum basis than under the GATT. In the first ten years of the WTO more cases were brought than during the 46 GATT years. Developing countries are more often involved than in the past—acting as a complainant in 33 per cent of all cases and targeted as a respondent in 27 per cent of all cases through end 2006. Developing countries have successfully contested actions by large players (examples included some of the first cases brought to the WTO: a Costa Rican claim against US restrictions on cotton textiles and a case brought by Venezuela and Brazil contesting US gasoline regulations). Developing countries also increasingly contest each other's policies. Disputes between developing countries giving rise to requests for consultations and panels span all regions. Examples have included Brazil–Philippines (desiccated coconut); Guatemala–Mexico (antidumping actions on cement), India–Turkey (textiles), Indonesia–Argentina (safeguards for footwear), India–South Africa (antidumping duties on pharmaceuticals), Colombia–Nicaragua (import charges), Costa Rica–Trinidad and Tobago (antidumping on spaghetti), and Thailand–Turkey (textiles). However, LDCs have made very limited use of DS procedures. As of end 2008, only one LDC has initiated a case (Bangladesh against India—an antidumping dispute that resulted in a MAS in favour of Bangladesh).[1] No LDCs have been involved as a respondent.

---

[1] This case is discussed in Taslim (2006), who describes the strategy pursued by the Bangladeshi producer of batteries who was affected by Indian antidumping. Taslim argues that assistance by the Advisory Centre on WTO Law (discussed below) was important in documenting that India was most likely violating WTO rules and that the decision to bring the matter to the WTO was a key factor in inducing the Indian government to withdraw the measure.

The more frequent use of DS relative to the GATT years is in part simply a reflection of the expansion in the coverage of multilateral disciplines and the larger membership of the WTO. Many of the claims that are brought to the WTO could not have been brought under GATT as they deal with sectors where new disciplines were negotiated in the Uruguay Round (such as agriculture, textiles and clothing, services and intellectual property protection). The increasing use of antidumping by developing countries against other developing economies is also a factor.

Notwithstanding a number of high-profile cases that were not resolved—some of which are discussed below—the DSU works rather well. Most cases are settled bilaterally or are resolved with the losing party implementing the panel or AB report. The AB has often corrected aspects of a panel's reasoning, but reversed the findings of the panel relatively infrequently. Over time, the tendency to reverse panel decisions has diminished due to the fact that panels have more jurisprudence at their disposal to base decisions on.

The DS process takes a long time, especially if it goes through all the stages described in Box 3.1. On average, consultations, the panel stage and appeal to the AB take almost two years (Table 3.1). Implementation will take another year or so on average, and if recourse is needed to an Article 21.5 compliance panel a complainant is looking at another seven months. Thus, this is not a venue for rapid resolution of disputes, something that has discouraged many businesses from petitioning their governments to invoke the WTO dispute settlement system. That said, it is important to bear in mind that many disputes do not go through all these stages. Indeed, many never result in the formation of a panel. Moreover, relative to the GATT era, WTO cases actually take less time—by between two and five months—despite many more disputes brought forward (Grinols and Perrielli, 2006).

What follows summarizes the operation of the system in the 1995–2006 period using a database and methodology developed by Horn and Mavroidis (2008a, b).

Table 3.1. Average duration of dispute settlement processes, 1995–2006

Proceeding	Average Duration
Consultations	210.2 days
Panel	406.4 days
Appellate Body	89.3 days
Reasonable period of time for implementation if set by arbitrator	12 months
Reasonable period of time for implementation when agreed bilaterally	9.5 months
Compliance panel	225.9 days
Appellate Body (compliance cases)	87.7 days

Source: Horn and Mavroidis (2008b).

The focus is on bilateral disputes, where *bilateral* refers to a dyad of WTO members (complainant, defendant). This is done to disaggregate multiple complaints, where more than one WTO member challenges a practice. Thus, if four WTO members bring the same complaint against another WTO member, this is counted as four bilateral disputes—even if there is only one panel formed to address the complaints (as is often done). In many disputes there are also countries that file a Request to Join in Consultations. Whether they have an interest in supporting the defendant or the complainant(s) is often unclear and not specified in the request. In practice, however, countries that request to join in consultations generally are on the complaining side, and that is assumed in the descriptive statistics presented below.[2] During 1995–2006 there were 965 bilateral disputes, as compared to 'only' 351 formal requests for consultations under the DSU. Although this number may appear large, relative to the number of potentially contestable policy measures it is actually very small—given 150 + WTO members that each trade hundreds or thousands of products with each other. Thus, it is not clear how representative the sample of actually observed disputes is.

The EU and the US are respondents twice as often as they are complainants, and are involved in the lion's share of all disputes (Table 3.2). The EU and the US complained 266 times, accounting for 28 per cent of the 965 bilateral disputes. In terms of activity, other industrialized and high-income countries (including three high-income WTO Members that are (self-)classified as developing in the WTO: Hong Kong, South Korea and Singapore) lead with 369 bilateral complaints (38 per cent of the total), followed by developing countries (non-LDCs), with 322 bilateral disputes (33 per cent). Least developed countries complained or joined the complainant only eight times and account for less than 1 per cent of all bilateral disputes. The EU and the US are the most frequent target of challenges (541 times or 56 per cent of all bilateral disputes). Developing and other industrialized countries follow with 256 (27 per cent) and 165 (17 per cent) respectively. To date, LDCs have never been challenged.

In 60 per cent of all the bilateral disputes through the end of 2006, participants did not initiate the original complaint but joined at a later stage. The EU and US tend to initiate fewer cases against developing countries than they join at a later stage, and the same is true of developing country complaints against the EU or US. Both groups tend to disproportionately launch cases against other members of the same group.

The majority of disputes have involved GATT rules and disciplines (Table 3.3). Alleged violation of MFN and national treatment (Articles I and III of the GATT) account for almost one-third of the GATT disputes. Other often invoked GATT disciplines in disputes are the ban on the use of quantitative restrictions (Article XI

---

[2] The same is true of participation by third parties, i.e. countries that are not acting as complainants but participate to reserve their rights in a dispute. Busch and Reinhardt (2006a) conclude that 70 per cent of third parties intervene in support of the complainant.

Table 3.2. Who targets who? Bilateral disputes, 1995–2006

	Complainant	Respondent			Total
		G2	IND	DEV	
G2	EU	49	32	54	135
	US	41	46	44	131
	G2 total	90	78	98	266 (28%)
IND	Australia	23	9	12	44
	Canada	44	16	19	79
	Japan	44	9	21	74
	Korea	17	3	7	27
	Mexico	28	2	14	44
	New Zealand	17	4	7	28
	Norway	11	1	0	12
	Switzerland	6	4	11	21
	Other	24	9	7	40
	IND total	214	57	98	369 (38%)
DEV	Argentina	14	1	7	22
	Brazil	18	6	3	27
	Chile	10	2	6	18
	Colombia	11	0	5	16
	Costa Rica	5	0	5	10
	Ecuador	10	1	0	11
	Guatemala	9	2	6	17
	Honduras	10	0	3	13
	India	34	4	3	41
	Thailand	14	6	3	23
	Other	95	8	21	124
	DEV total	230	30	62	322 (33%)
LDC*	LDCs	7	0	1	8 (0.8%)
	Grand total (% of all cases)	541 (56%)	165 (17%)	259 (27%)	965 (100%)

* Involves one complaint by Bangladesh against India and requests to join in consultations by Congo, Madagascar and Malawi.

Source: Horn and Mavroidis (2008*a*).

GATT), claims of violation of tariff bindings (Article II) and lack of transparency (Article X). Of the 351 cases under the DSU through end 2006, only 144 led to a panel report. The difference in these numbers reflects cases that were settled, dropped or remained pending. The consultation process and more generally the role and effectiveness of the system in getting WTO members to settle cases 'out of court' is an important and relatively neglected dimension of the WTO dispute settlement process (Davey, 2005). The distribution of these 144 cases is reported in Table 3.4. The data reveal a similar pattern as shown in Table 3.2. The EU and US tend to contest actions by each other and other industrialized countries, while

Table 3.3. WTO Agreements invoked in requests for consultations

Agreement Invoked in Dispute	Share of Total (%)
GATT	36.0
Antidumping	9.5
Subsidies and countervailing measures	9.3
Agriculture	7.5
Safeguards	4.5
Import licensing	4.4
Technical barriers to trade	4.4
WTO	4.4
Sanitary and phytosanitary measures	4.0
TRIPS	3.3
TRIMS	3.1
Agreement on Textiles and Clothing	2.1
GATS	1.9
Customs valuation	1.6
DSU	1.5
Rules of origin	0.7
Other	1.6
ALL	99.8

Source: Horn and Mavroidis (2008*b*).

other industrialized and developing nations tend to bring more cases against the EU and the US.

In these 144 disputes it is not at all straightforward to determine who won and who lost. A major problem in assessing outcomes is that some policy measures (and thus some claims) will be more important than others to the claimants. It is very difficult if not impossible for outside observers to determine what 'really mattered' and what did not. For instance, there have been several high profile

Table 3.4. Bilateral disputes considered by panels and claims won (number and per cent)

Complainant	G2	Respondent		TOT
		IND	DEV	
G2	20 (62%)	22 (63%)	13 (90%)	55 (65%)
IND	35 (55%)	5 (95%)	7 (51%)	47 (56%)
DEV	33 (61%)	4 (23%)	5 (70%)	42 (58%)
TOT	88 (58%)	31 (57%)	25 (67%)	144 (59%)

Note: Numbers in parentheses are the average share of claims won by complainant group.

Source: Hoekman, Horn and Mavroidis (2008).

disputes where the defendant 'won' the case in that the panel and/or AB accepted many of the arguments made, but lost on the particular application. In some situations, being found to have violated a WTO agreement or commitment may actually be the preferred outcome for a government if it sees this as helpful in pursuing a policy reform that is opposed by a powerful domestic constituency. Or, the objective may simply have been to raise the political profile of a policy matter, perhaps as part of a strategy to place the subject on the agenda of a MTN. Thus, 'losing' a case may actually imply winning it as far as the complainant is concerned.

This problem also affects efforts taken by legal scholars—inspired by Hudec (1993)—to assess whether governments comply. Hudec argued that compliance is the appropriate measure of the outcome of a case. Although this has the advantage of being an objective measure that is comparable across cases, it is not necessarily a good measure of the outcome of a dispute for the reason just noted. Even if the variable of interest is held to be implementation, this can occur on either substantive or procedural grounds. For example, if a complainant loses on all substantive claims but nonetheless wins the case because the respondent did not notify the measure, this will not change anything—notification will make no difference in economic terms. Although obviously important, implementation as the benchmark is not necessarily the most appropriate indicator of outcomes given the absence of information regarding the 'true' underlying objectives of the parties to a dispute.

One dimension of disputes that can be readily observed and measured is the number of legal claims that are made—defined as a factual matter and the legal provision that it allegedly violates. Although the economic and legal significance of specific claims will vary significantly, a measure of who wins and who loses can be calculated as the share of claims that panels determine to have violated the WTO. Hoekman, Horn and Mavroidis (2008) undertake this exercise, classifying outcomes into three groups: (1) claims where the complainant prevailed; (2) claims where the defendant prevailed; and (3) a residual group of claims where the outcome is unclear. (Although in principle a panel should either find for or against a claim by a complainant, the third category is needed because claims may not be addressed by a panel as result of the exercise of judicial economy.)

The majority of claims made in the disputes relate to the three contingent protection-related disciplines of the WTO: the agreements on antidumping (AD), subsidies and countervailing measures (SCM) and safeguards (SG) (Table 3.5). This is not surprising given that in absolute terms the case law on these three instruments constitutes almost 25 per cent of all disputes (Horn and Mavroidis, 2008b). In part this is simply a reflection of the significant increase in the use of these three instruments (Chapter 9).[3] Another reason that may explain

[3] The high share of SG claims is somewhat misleading in that they do not imply these types of cases have come to be an important share of all DS. The high number of claims instead reflects similar

Table 3.5. Distribution of legal claims across WTO provisions

Provision/Agreement	Number of Claims
Antidumping (AD)	615
Agreement on Textiles and Clothing (ATC)	13
Agreement on Agriculture (AA)	46
DSU:3.7 (Determination of utility of a dispute)	16
GATS	30
GATT:II (Tariff bindings)	23
GATT:III (National Treatment)	88
GATT:VI (Antidumping)	69
GATT:X (Transparency)	46
GATT:XI (Quantitative restrictions)	19
GATT:XIII (Nondiscriminatory use of QRs)	10
GATT:XIX (Emergency protection)	69
GATT:XX (Exceptions)	25
Subsidies and Countervailing Measures (SCM)	269
Safeguards (SG)	580
Sanitary & Phytosanitary Measures (SPS)	285
Technical Barriers to Trade (TBT)	14
TRIPS	61
WTO:XVI.4 (Conformity of laws)	30

why the majority of claims occur for these three instruments is the fact that detailed procedural requirements are laid out for actions under each to be WTO-compliant. Many of these requirements are not expressed in precise language. For example, a number of AD disputes concern a provision requiring the investigating authorities to publish the essence of their findings (Article 12 AD Agreement). However, it does not spell out exactly what must be published.

The shares of all claims that are substantiated by panels across the 144 cases are reported in Table 3.4. Hoekman, Horn and Mavroidis (2008) find that developing countries tend to put forward a significantly greater number of claims than high-income WTO members. But if the focus is on the share of claims 'won', the data suggest that outcomes are broadly similar across industrialized and developing countries, despite the differences in 'capacity' and 'administrative sophistication' that presumably exist across the groups. Although capacity constraints of various

(identical) cases being brought by multiple WTO members. More specifically, the US steel safeguard cases alone (WT/DS248-254, 258–9) represent almost 80 per cent of the total number of SG claims made. This compares to the 15 per cent share of the US in the total number of safeguard actions imposed during the 1995–2005 period (Bown, 2006). A similar point can be made in respect of disputes concerning the use of sanitary and phytosanitary (SPS) measures. Of the 286 claims made in respect of the SPS agreement, over 90 per cent pertain to the *EC—Approval and Marketing of Biotech Products* disputes, which involved three complainants (WT/DS 291/292/293).

types certainly may constrain the use of the DS system, the data suggest that *conditional* on a case being brought that leads to the formation of a panel, the success rate as measured by share of claims 'won' is similar. Understanding the reasons for this finding requires further research, but may well reflect the fact that the developing countries that make most use of the system are generally either large or middle-income. The participation constraint for these countries may be much less than it is for low-income countries. In addition, initiatives such as the Advisory Centre on WTO Law (ACWL)—discussed below—may have helped to level the playing field with regard to access to legal expertise.

Legal scholars that have assessed whether WTO members comply with rulings have concluded that implementation rates are relatively high. Davey (2005) calculates that about 80 per cent of cases are resolved, with only 20 per cent ending up going back to the panel for compliance-related disagreements, including requests to retaliate. Many of those eventually are resolved as they often concern measures that require legislative action, which may not be possible within the time set by the DSB for implementation. The contentious disputes mostly have been between OECD members and are concentrated in the area of subsidies and countervailing measures and sanitary and phytosanitary measures—that is, they pertain to instruments of domestic regulatory policy on which there are substantive differences between WTO members and, as a consequence, rules that are 'fuzzier' than in other areas.

Perhaps the most telling statistic regarding the effectiveness of the system is that in only 5 per cent of the 351 cases arising during 1995–2006 did a WTO member request authorization to retaliate. It is noteworthy that to date retaliation has only been implemented by OECD countries although several developing countries have been authorized to retaliate. This may be a reflection of the fact that there is good compliance by countries in cases brought and won by developing countries. However, it is more likely that developing countries recognize that they cannot affect the behaviour of large trading nations and that undertaking retaliation for noncompliance simply imposes costs on their citizens.

The process at work

Many of the specific disputes brought to the WTO will be discussed in subsequent chapters as they help both to understand the specific rules and disciplines of the WTO and provide insight into how the trading system works. What follows provides a flavour of the DS process, presenting some examples of cases that were successfully resolved, with the losing party implementing the recommendations of the panel/AB, and some examples of 'failure'. As mentioned, 'failure' may reflect ambiguity in language or nonacceptance of an effort by the adjudicating bodies to clarify WTO law (or 'fill gaps'), or it may reflect an assessment by the losing party that the original terms of a negotiated deal need to be rebalanced. In the latter situation any consequent retaliation may be regarded as the cost that must be incurred for the required rebalancing to occur.

Two (random) examples of successes are *Japan—Alcoholic Beverages* and *EC—Sardines.* In the former, one of the first cases brought to the WTO in 1995, Canada, the EU and the US complained that the Japanese tax system on alcoholic beverages was discriminatory, in the sense that the tax imposed on *sochu* (a beverage produced predominantly in Japan) was less than that on whisky, vodka and other predominantly 'Western' drinks. Thus, the allegation was that Japan was violating the national treatment rule (Article III GATT). In such cases, as discussed further in Chapter 5, the complainant must show that the products compete for the same market (are 'like' products) and that the tax scheme favours the domestic subset of competing products. The WTO case law has determined that there is no need to show that trade flows have been affected. Given the wide differential in tax rates for *sochu* and competing imports, the panel found that Japan had treated imported alcoholic beverages worse than domestic competing (like) products, and thus violated national treatment. The AB upheld the panel's findings, and Japan agreed to remove the tax differential. Because this took longer than the agreed reasonable period of time for implementation, Japan also paid temporary compensation in the form of lowering tariffs on imports of the affected products until it could revise its system of indirect taxation of alcoholic beverages.

EC—Sardines concerned an EU decision that only the species of fish found in Atlantic and Mediterranean waters (Sardina pilchardus walbaum) could be marketed in the EU as sardines. The consequence was that Sardinops sagax—its Pacific Ocean relative—had to be called 'pilchards' or 'sprats'. Peru contested the measure, arguing that the EU was ignoring an international standard promulgated by the Codex Alimentarius Commission (see Chapter 5) under which the types of fish exported by Peru could legitimately be named 'sardines'. The panel sided with Peru, arguing that the existence of the international standard implied that the EU needed to provide a justification for the adoption of its new idiosyncratic norm, and had not done so. The EU motivated its new rules on the basis of consumer protection—arguing that they were needed to avoid confusing consumers. An amicus curiae brief submitted by the UK Consumers Organization—the largest in Europe—that the new EU regulation 'clearly acts against the economic and information interests of Europe's consumers' did not help the European Commission convince the panel that the measure was in fact justified on the basis of protecting consumer interests (Shaffer, 2006. 195).

On appeal, the AB interpreted the relevant WTO rules in this area—discussed in Chapter 5—by ruling that the burden of proof in these types of cases should be reversed, thus overturning the panel, which had argued that it was the EU that needed to justify its action, given the existence of an international standard. However, it agreed that the case made by Peru was compelling. The ruling regarding burden of proof is an example of the interpretive/clarifying role that is one of the theoretical rationales for the creation of the DSB mentioned previously. The EU agreed to modify its legislation in order to conform to the AB ruling, although a good case can be—and has been—made that the reasoning of the ruling was quite weak in that Peru did not offer much in the way of proof.

Problem cases often involve disputes where members attempt to use the system to contest policies in areas where there are strongly diverging regulatory approaches and preferences, especially in the area of public health and safety. Cases involving regulatory differences also revealed the existence of implementation-related weaknesses, in particular reliance on retaliation as the instrument for dealing with situations where a losing party simply cannot implement the recommendations of the panel because of domestic political constraints. Such cases suggest the appropriate solution is to clarify and rebalance the terms of the treaty (i.e. renegotiate). What follows discusses a number of major cases that illustrate the types of problems that emerged. These involved the EU import regime for bananas, an EU ban on the use of growth and other hormones in beef and a nonviolation dispute between the US and Japan over the Japanese distribution system for film. *Bananas* is one of the longest running WTO disputes and revolves around one of the key disciplines of the WTO: nondiscrimination. It also helped to identify problems with DSU provisions on retaliation and was the first case to invoke provisions of the GATS. *Hormones* is a noteworthy dispute because it deals with a type of conflict that may become more prevalent in the future and that involves scientific judgements as to whether measures are justified ('necessary'). *Kodak–Fuji* is of interest because it deals with a new issue—competition policy—and to date has been the only major nonviolation dispute under the WTO.

EC—Bananas

The EU import regime for bananas has long been a bone of contention because of EU preferences for bananas produced by African, Caribbean and Pacific (ACP) countries. As a result Caribbean producers have traditionally had a substantial share of the EU market, to the detriment of Central and South American countries. Preferences for bananas in the EU are long standing. They caused problems between France and Germany during the negotiations leading to the creation of the EEC in 1957—Germany had a free trade regime for bananas and imported from Latin American countries, whereas France maintained high barriers to support producers in overseas territories and former colonies (Messerlin, 2001). The UK and Spain had similar preferences. These differences led to the imposition of intra-EU trade barriers, basically reserving the UK, French and Spanish markets for ex-colonies. The policies were a very inefficient means of assisting ex-colonies—every dollar transferred cost EU consumers US$5, of which US$3 went to distributors and

US$1 was wasted (Borrell, 1996). Economists have often argued that the preferences were bad policy—it would have been much more efficient to simply have made an income transfer to the preferred countries.

In 1993, the EU adopted a complex import licensing and distribution system for the EU as a whole, as part of its effort to create a single market. The common market organization that was imposed was based on historical trading relationships, and was designed to continue to provide preferential access for ACP countries (signatories of the Lomé Convention). It involved two tariff quotas (one for historical ACP suppliers and one for other growers. Out-of-quota imports were subject to high specific tariffs. Operators traditionally exporting bananas from former British and French Caribbean colonies were granted 30 per cent of all import licences for noncountry-specific quotas. These licences could be used to import ACP bananas or could be sold to firms desiring to import from Latin America. In the latter case, which often occurred, the quota allocation system resulted in a transfer of rents from the (mostly US-based) firms buying the licences to those granted the quota rights. Borrell (1996) estimated that the new EU-wide regime was worse than the national ones it replaced: total costs to EU consumers were some US$2 billion, whereas ACP suppliers obtained US$150 million—a cost per consumer of over US$13 for each dollar transferred.

Latin American producers brought two cases to the GATT contesting the national systems (1992) and the new common EU regime (1993). They won both. As a result, the EU concluded a Banana Framework Agreement with four countries (Costa Rica, Colombia, Nicaragua and Venezuela) in 1994 under which they were allocated specific quotas with the understanding that they would not bring a case to the WTO before 2002. In 1996, four Latin American producers left out of this agreement (Ecuador, Guatemala, Honduras and Mexico) contested the EU import regime in the WTO. They were joined by the United States, which participated on behalf of US multinational fruit firms, such as Chiquita, that were major players in the global distribution of bananas. The US was only able to come into this dispute because of the GATS. Under the GATT, the US was not able to participate as a complainant as it does not produce bananas. With the adoption of the GATS, which covers distribution services, the US could claim that the EU had violated the nondiscrimination rule for access to distribution services.

In this third bananas dispute the EU lost again (see Box 3.2). Failure to comply with the DSB ruling eventually led to the imposition of retaliatory measures by the US. The US retaliation included a provision allowing for a so-called carousel approach: a different set of exports from the EU were to be subjected to retaliatory tariffs of up to 100 per cent in each six-month period. This procedure was designed to maximize the political 'pain' of the retaliation. In this it was successful—as illustrated by lobbying by the UK cashmere products industry against the threatened imposition of tariffs on their goods (*Financial Times*, 26 August 2000: 5).

Box 3.2. The Never-Ending Bananas Case: *EC–Bananas III*

In 1996, Ecuador, Guatemala, Honduras, Mexico and the US contested the new EU banana regime at the WTO, claiming it discriminated against their producers and banana marketing companies. The object of attack was not so much the tariff preferences that were granted to ACP countries—for which the EU had obtained a waiver, which was extended in 2000 to the end of 2007 (see Chapter 12)—but the allocation of quotas. The WTO panel report, published in June 1997, found the EU banana import regime in violation of WTO nondiscrimination and market access rules. The dual tariff rate quota regime was found inconsistent with GATT Article XIII (requiring nondiscrimination in allocation of QRs), and the 30 per cent allocation of import licences to traditional sellers of ACP bananas was deemed inconsistent with GATS nondiscrimination rules (which applied to distribution services). On appeal, the AB endorsed most of the panel's conclusions.

During 1998 the EU revised its regime. It continued to maintain two tariff rate quotas, but assigned import quotas for non-ACP bananas on the basis of historical market shares and abolished the operator categories for allocation of licences. Consultations on the WTO-consistency of the new measures were inconclusive. Just before the January 1999 deadline for implementation, the US sought authorization to retaliate. To this the EU responded that the US should first obtain a panel finding under Article 21.5 DSU that the new mechanism did not conform to WTO rules. Ecuador then requested such a compliance panel. Concurrently, the US sought authorization from the DSB to retaliate against the EU in the amount of US$520 million, to which the EU responded with a request for arbitration to determine the appropriate level of retaliation.

The compliance panel found that the new EU measures were not fully compatible with the WTO. The same panel determined the level of nullification suffered by the US to be equivalent to US$191.4 million, well below the US$520 million requested by the United States. The US was authorized to raise duties against the EU by that amount and did so. Towards the end of 1999, Ecuador also sought and obtained authorization to retaliate. The Ecuadorian request was a multiple first in the history of the trading system: the first request for retaliation by a developing country, and the first time approval for so-called cross-retaliation was sought. Ecuador argued that its merchandise imports from the EU were too small to allow full retaliation (set at US$200 million by the arbitrators) to occur against imports of EU goods. It obtained authorization to suspend concessions under other agreements, including TRIPS, after having exhausted the possibilities for retaliating against imports of EU consumer goods (the panel concluded that retaliation against imports of intermediates and machinery would be 'ineffective'—that is, too costly for the economy). This use of cross-retaliation was not foreseen by negotiators in the Uruguay Round, who had envisaged the need for cross-retaliation as an instrument to enforce the TRIPS agreement (developing countries not being major exporters of intellectual property intensive goods), not as a vehicle for developing country retaliation.

In the event, in contrast to the US, Ecuador never implemented retaliatory actions. In April 2001 the EU notified a MAS with the US and Ecuador. Under the MAS, the US suspended retaliation, the US and Ecuador agreed to support the EU in its request for a

(cont.)

Box 3.2. (*Continued*)

---

tariff-only regime for bananas by 2006. In January 2006 the EU put in place the new regime, which set a tariff of €176 per metric tonne and gave ACP countries a duty-free quota of 775,000 tonnes until the end of 2007, when the ACP waiver would expire. (New Economic Partnership Agreements with ACP nations that conformed to GATT rules were intended to be put in place before the waiver expired.) The level of the specific tariff was influenced by two WTO arbitration decisions, the first requested by Latin American producers, the second by the EU. The first was in reaction to the EU's proposed €230/tonne duty in early 2005, which the arbitrators determined was too high to maintain market shares of the Latin American producers. The next offer of €187/tonne was also subjected to arbitration, and again deemed too high.

In the Doha Round efforts centred on the conclusion of a Bananas Agreement that would improve access for Latin American producers to the EU. As of July 2008, the proposal on the table was for the EU to reduce the tariff to €150 per tonne on January 2009, to be lowered gradually to €116 by 2015. Negotiations on the level of tariff were complemented by continued recourse to the DSB: in early 2007 Ecuador requested another Article 21.5 compliance panel, contesting the legality of the EU's annual duty-free tariff quota of 775,000 tonnes for ACP bananas, for which the waiver for ACP preferences had expired. The US followed suit. The panel found in 2008 that the post-2007 preferences violated MFN. Although the saga is not yet over, the significant changes that the EU has made to its trade relations with ACP countries (GATT-legal Economic Partnership Agreements, EPAs) suggests this dispute may finally be put to rest in the not too distant future, probably along the lines of a draft deal concluded between the EU and the MFN suppliers in July 2008, which fell through when Doha was suspended.

The *Bananas* case illustrated that disagreements between parties on the adequacy of implementing measures have the potential to give rise to a recurring series of disputes dealing with essentially the same issue. It also revealed the weakness of the ultimate enforcement threat that is available. Retaliation by Ecuador is unlikely to induce the EU to change its policies—Latin American banana producers are essentially dependent on the threat of US retaliation. In many cases, however, the US will not be a party to a dispute. And even if it is, the *Bananas* case revealed that US retaliation is not sufficient to bring a dispute to rapid closure. That said, *Bananas* also reveals that the process 'works' even if it is (very) slow and frustrating for the exporters concerned. This dimension of the case was not without its benefits either, as it allowed ACP countries more time to adjust. It should be noted that this case is a rather extreme and special one in that it affected many developing countries. It was not the more standard situation where the matter revolved around the interests of domestic producers—there are no major EU-based producers. Essentially the dispute was a conflict *between* developing countries, with major distributors such as Chiquita taking the side of the Latin American countries that produced many (most) of the bananas that they sold.

Although the preferential access regime for the ACP countries was financed by EU consumers, they were not a factor in the case, nor were there significant industrial processors that might have an interest in getting lower prices. This dispute ended up being part of a broader attack by nonpreferred developing countries on the EU regime of preferences for ACP countries. A later dispute regarding the EU regime for sugar was similar in nature, although in the case of sugar there were both large EU producers and large industrial users and processors, which changes the political economy significantly (see Chapters 6 and 12).

EC—Hormones

Another difficult case that again was directed at an EU policy concerned a ban on the use of hormones in beef, which led to a ban on imports of US and Canadian beef as producers in these countries use hormones to accelerate the growth of cattle. This dispute dates back to the late 1980s, when the EU imposed a ban on six specific hormones, some or all of which are used in North America. US producers have used hormones for decades, in quantities that have been deemed safe for human consumption by the US public health authorities. The EU ban led the US to impose retaliatory measures under Section 301 of its trade law, levying additional tariffs on $100 million of European exports. The EU contested this action, seeking the formation of a GATT panel. The US blocked this, arguing that the matter was clear-cut and that the EU should remove the ban.

After the entry into force of the WTO, in April 1996, the US requested the establishment of a panel. Canada followed suit with a case of its own. Both argued that the EU prohibition on the use of hormones restricted exports of meat, and was inconsistent with, among other things, the provisions of the WTO agreement on sanitary and phytosanitary measures (SPS—see Chapter 5). The SPS agreement was negotiated in part to establish disciplines in this area. In 1997, a panel found that the EU ban was inconsistent with requirements that members base their regulations on international standards where these exist (Article 3.1 of the SPS agreement), have a scientific justification for using national norms if they decide not to follow international standards (Article 3.3 SPS), base their policies on risk assessment procedures that take into account techniques developed by the relevant international organizations (Article 5.1 SPS) and avoid the use of arbitrary or unjustifiable distinctions which result in discrimination or a disguised restriction on international trade (Article 5.5 SPS).

The AB upheld the panel's finding that the EU import prohibition was inconsistent with Articles 3.3 and 5.1 of the SPS agreement, but reversed the finding that the import prohibition was inconsistent with Articles 3.1 and 5.5. As in the EC—Sardines dispute discussed above, it also reversed the burden of proof in disputes under the SPS agreement, ruling that it is up to the complainant to demonstrate that there is no scientific basis for a measure (as opposed to forcing the respondent to demonstrate the scientific basis for its regime). In this case, as in others, the AB revealed that it is more inclined to allow governments to argue that measures are justified to meet national objectives than panels are.

The time period for implementation was set at 15 months through arbitration. Just before the expiration of this period, the EU informed the DSB that it was unable to comply. Political constraints reflecting a strong lobby in the EU that opposed the use of hormones in meat production made it impossible. In June 1999, the complainants sought authorization from the DSB to retaliate on imports worth US$202 million and C$75 million respectively. The EU requested arbitration on this, and, as in *EC—Bananas*, the original panel subsequently determined the appropriate levels to be much lower, at US$116.8 million, and C$11.3 million respectively. The DSB authorized retaliation in these amounts, which both Canada and the US implemented.

In 2003, the EU notified the WTO that it had put in place the required risk assessment mechanisms and had determined that all the hormones posed a health risk. As a result it continued to ban the use of one of the hormones on a permanent basis, and imposed provisional bans on the other five. Canada and the US argued this did not constitute compliance and continued to impose their retaliatory measures. The EU then contested the legality of these countermeasures in February 2005, arguing it had brought its measures into compliance. The panel based its report in part on evidence from a group of scientific experts it had constituted. It ruled that the EU was still in violation of its WTO obligations: the EU had not shown there was a scientific basis for the measures—the studies by the EU were general, not specific to the residual hormones in meat. The panel also found the US in violation of the DSU, arguing that continued retaliation post-2003 required another panel to approve it. This raises a general question: who can say the EU is complying? Where is the burden of proof? The EU appealed. In November 2008, the Appellate Body ruled that it had not been established that the SPS inconsistent measures were removed, but also that Canada and the US were in violation of the WTO by continuing to impose retaliation. The AB recommended that the DSB request the parties to initiate Article 21.5 DSU proceedings to determine whether the EU had indeed removed the inconsistent measure and whether the US retaliatory measures remained legally valid. Thus, the case continues—over ten years since the initial filing and some 20 years after the ban was imposed.

The *Hormones* case is an example of the type of dispute that may become more frequent, that is, cases dealing with differences in regulatory regimes and attitudes towards risk. It is also a noteworthy dispute because there is widespread agreement in the scientific community that hormones are *not* a significant human health risk, notwithstanding the views of the EU body that undertook the risk assessment. The same was true in the more recent case regarding EU policy towards use of genetically modified organisms (GMOs), where experts consulted by the European Commission were of the view that the relevant biotech technologies did not pose a significant risk. In that sense the *Hormones* case should have been relatively easy, compared to one where there are substantial disagreements among technical experts and health professionals. Although a case can be made that the EU ban can be justified through invocation of the precautionary principle (under the SPS agreement), the primary reason that hormones are prohibited in the EU has little to do with public safety and much to do with consumer preferences (fear). European Union agricultural policy is also a factor: the EU does not desire farmers to use techniques that expand output and further increase the cost of the common agricultural policy (Messerlin, 2001).

Nonviolation disputes as an alternative?

Disputes that revolve around differences in public attitudes to risk will always be difficult if not impossible to resolve satisfactorily. In principle, regulatory diversity may be the appropriate outcome. As discussed above, there is a provision in the GATT/WTO that recognizes that governments will never be able to write a complete contract and that there will be instances where the pursuit of domestic policy objectives may have adverse consequences for another WTO member, nullifying a negotiated concession. Nonviolation disputes are a potentially important avenue for countries to raise such situations with trading partners.

Given that by definition the measure that is the subject of complaint will be WTO legal, a member cannot be required to change it. The most that can be expected is compensation in another area. Article 26 of the DSU states that:

where a measure has been found to nullify or impair benefits under, or impede the attainment of objectives, of the relevant covered agreement without violation thereof, there is no obligation to withdraw the measure. However, in such cases, the panel or the AB shall recommend that the member concerned make a mutually satisfactory adjustment... compensation may be part of a mutually satisfactory adjustment as final settlement of the dispute.

Under the GATT, nonviolation cases were largely restricted to subsidy-related cases, reflecting in part the weakness of GATT rules on subsidies and the direct substitutability with a tariff in terms of providing assistance to domestic import-competing producers. In 1996 the US brought a nonviolation case against Japan. The *Kodak–Fuji* dispute illustrated that government measures not subject to WTO rules can in principle be challenged and that nonviolation cases can be used as a transparency device. The panel generated an immense amount of data and information, much of which helped Japan support its case that there was nothing special about the Japanese film market (Box 3.3).

Another case with a nonviolation dimension that was brought to the WTO concerned asbestos. In December 1996, the French government banned the manufacture and sale of asbestos as a health measure. Canada contested the import ban as a violation of the Agreement on Technical Barriers to Trade (because it was not based on international standards), and a violation of the GATT prohibition on

Box 3.3. The *Kodak–Fuji* case and Article XXIII nonviolation disputes

The US has argued for many years that Japanese corporate groups *(Keiretsu)* undermine market access for foreign suppliers by buying predominantly from each other and retaining close vertical linkages between manufacturers, wholesalers and retailers. Kodak, for example, claimed that its access to the Japanese film market was made harder by Fuji's control of film wholesalers. In 1996 the US requested consultations with Japan concerning Japan's laws, regulations and requirements affecting the distribution and sale of imported consumer photographic film and paper. The US claimed that Japanese government measures resulted in less favourable treatment of imported film and paper (a violation of national treatment), were inconsistent with GATT transparency requirements, and nullified and impaired benefits accruing to the US (a nonviolation claim).

A panel was established in October 1996. It found that the US had not demonstrated that the Japanese measures nullified or impaired, benefits accruing to the US within the meaning of GATT Article XXIII: 1*b*, that the Japanese distribution measures accorded less favourable treatment to imported photographic film and paper, or that Japan had failed to publish administrative rulings of general application in violation of GATT transparency requirements (Article X: 1). The 1998 panel report was not appealed.

The panel's decision (over 500 pages long) is very detailed. The panel agreed to treat all the measures attacked by the US (a victory for the US), including decisions of the Japanese competition authorities (the Fair Trade Commission), as possible grounds for complaint (see Hoekman and Mavroidis, 1994). However, the panel noted that the US was only entitled to contest Japanese government measures and not market structures that might have arisen from them. On examining the facts, it concluded that the measures did not reduce market access. Thus, there was no nullification or impairment. The panel did not see anything in Japanese distribution structures that excluded foreigners as a result of public policy, even on a wide interpretation of this term. In particular they concluded that single-brand wholesale distribution is the common market structure—indeed the norm—in major national film markets, including the US.

Kodak had cited a series of government measures including allegations of informal administrative guidance and industrial policy tools that were applied by Japanese firms themselves and served to nullify the opening up of the Japanese film market to outsiders. There were also a number of guidelines on what constituted fair and unfair competition that allegedly deprived Kodak of marketing tools that were of special importance to it as an outsider. Kodak charged that Fuji had a stranglehold on the distribution system that excluded its access to film wholesaling networks, forcing Kodak to sell directly to retailers. A key allegation was therefore the existence of an anticompetitive vertical relationship between Fuji and its primary distributors. Japan argued that Fuji's control of wholesale networks was irrelevant as most of the retailers they served also bought imported film and that Kodak's distribution system amounted to the creation of a wholesale system of its own.

Source: WTO (www.wto.org) and Holmes (1998).

quotas (see Chapter 5). Canada also asked the panel to consider the measures under the nonviolation provision of the WTO if it concluded that no violation had occurred. France (the EU) justified the import ban under Article XX*b* GATT, which allows for import restrictions if necessary to protect human health (see Chapter 9), and asked the panel to reject the applicability of nonviolation as the measure in question was subject to WTO rules. The panel concluded that there was a violation of Article III GATT (because there was discriminatory treatment of chrysotile fibre products exported by Canada) but that this was justified under Article XX GATT. The panel also concluded that a nonviolation case could be brought. The panel and the AB rejected the EU argument that nonviolation cases could only pertain to measures that are not subject to WTO rules. But Canada's nonviolation petition was rejected on the basis that Canada had not established that it suffered nullification or impairment of a benefit.

Although the AB ruling in *EC—Asbestos* appears to create substantial scope to bring nonviolation cases, there are good reasons to doubt that there will be much use made of the provision. A successful case must demonstrate that the targeted WTO member has imposed a policy measure subsequent to the negotiation of a tariff concession, that this could not have been foreseen at the time it was negotiated and that the measure reduced the value of the concession. In principle these conditions do not appear to be very constraining, although much depends on how the burden of proof will be allocated and defined. More important is that the remedy that would need to be employed—compensation—is unlikely to be paid by a WTO member in the absence of a compelling case that there was in fact intent to circumvent a WTO commitment. In the case of a subsidy such a case may be made relatively easily, but this is not so for regulatory instruments (Mavroidis, 2007).

3.4. SYSTEMIC ISSUES AND QUESTIONS

A number of important characteristics of WTO dispute settlement procedures are briefly discussed in what follows. Many of these have been the subject of debate by WTO members, NGOs and scholars, and almost all were raised in the review of the DSU that was mandated by a Uruguay Round ministerial decision. The review could not be concluded in the time frame envisaged by negotiators (1 January 1999), reflecting disagreements between WTO members on the various proposals put forward and the requirement that there be consensus for amending the DSU (Article X WTO—see Chapter 2). The review became part of the Doha Round agenda, although not formally part of the single undertaking. Whether changes will be made to the DSU in the near future appears unlikely, given a general sense that the system—warts and all—is functioning reasonably well.

Governments as filters

Export industries must petition their governments to bring cases to the WTO—first bilaterally through consultations, then to a panel. Only governments have legal standing to bring disputes in the WTO. Thus, export interests must operate through a government filter. If there is a high perceived probability that the government will not be willing to bring the dispute to the WTO, cases may not be brought forward. Governments may not want to go to the WTO for fear of stimulating counterclaims (the 'glass house' syndrome) or because they do not think the payoffs will be high enough—e.g. because there is little trade at stake or because they have other more important issues to settle with the country in question. Developing country governments may be unwilling to bring cases if they fear this will have detrimental consequences in nontrade areas (for example, continued aid flows or defence cooperation).

It is of course a legitimate function of government to determine priorities and to make the tradeoffs it deems most beneficial for the nation as a whole. Nonetheless, if concerns that bringing a case would endanger the relationship with a major trading partner are indeed a factor, to some extent this nullifies the market access rationale for the WTO. It also undermines the establishment of a rule-based as opposed to a power-based system of trade relations.

One option to address this potential problem is to give export interests direct access to the WTO. Levy and Srinivasan (1996) develop a simple model that explores the possible consequences of such 'privatization', and conclude that this is a bad idea. They show that if a government maximizes national welfare it may have good reasons not to pursue a trade case because the expected national return is negative (due to issue linkage by the partner). Removing a government's discretion to decide whether to prosecute a case can also make it more difficult to make commitments in trade negotiations. The Levy and Srinivasan analysis illustrates the importance of full information—governments must be able to determine as accurately as possible what the cost to the economy is of not prosecuting a case. As discussed in Section 3.5, an implication of their analysis is that it is important there be domestic mechanisms to ensure that the appropriate tradeoffs are made, and that the private sector be able to access instruments through which violations can be addressed directly in the domestic courts.

What determines use of the dispute settlement system?

Research investigating the determinants of use of the DSU by WTO members has concluded, not surprisingly, that trade interests are a key variable. Horn, Mavroidis and Nordström (2005) were among the first to explore this question empirically. In order to assess whether participation as complainants is somehow biased to the disadvantage of developing countries, they hypothesize that in an unbiased situation complaints by WTO members (use of the DSU) should be proportional to the number of potentially illegal trade policy measures they encounter. This in turn will be a function of the volume, pattern and composition of their trade. Assuming that countries are similar in terms of the expected frequency with which they violate WTO commitments, Horn, Mavroidis and Nordström conclude that the distribution of bilateral disputes across members during the first four years of the WTO is fairly well predicted by their share in world trade, extent of product diversification and number of partners they trade with, in particular if one disregards very small trade values in the calculation of the un-biased benchmark.

A subsequent analysis by Francois, Horn and Kaunitz (2008) using more comprehensive empirical techniques and data for the whole period 1995–2006 confirms this finding: 'fundamental' factors such as trade volume, composition and per capita income explain participation quite well. Indeed, they conclude that developing countries are over-represented in their use of the DSU. Bown (2005) analyses the determinants of DS strategies in 116 cases involving import restrictions during 1995–2001, distinguishing between exporters that are harmed by an import restriction and those that are not because they were exempted or produce substitutes that are not affected by the measure. Bown distinguishes between four possible strategies: WTO members can bring a case (complain), participate as co-complainants, invoke their third party rights, or do nothing. He finds that size of exports is positively related to the propensity to complain and to participation as a third party.

Thus, trade interest seems to matter: returns on investment in DS procedures are higher when large trade volumes are affected. However, other factors also affect participation. Possible variables include the legal 'endowment' of a country, the ability to credibly threaten retaliation, the organization of domestic polities, a government's administrative efficiency/capacity, the degree of concentration in the affected industry (the higher the concentration, the more likely it is that a firm will petition the government), and the strength of nontrade relationships (national security, dependence on aid, joint membership in a PTA, etc.). The last set of factors is often captured under the heading of asymmetries in 'power'. There is no consensus among analysts regarding the relative importance of these variables. It does not appear that asymmetry in size (power) is a major source of bias in the sense of large traders not being targeted—as noted above the case load to date reveals that the EU and US are very frequently respondents in cases brought by developing nations.

There appears to be more evidence that legal capacity matters, in that constraints in the ability to fight/bring disputes results in fewer cases being brought by developing countries (e.g. Guzman and Simmons, 2005; Busch, Reinhardt and Shaffer, 2008). Retaliation (and retaliatory capacity) also seems to matter. Reinhardt (2000) finds that a dispute in a given year between a country-pair increases the probability of a dispute in the opposite direction the subsequent year by a factor of 55. Bown (2004*a*, *b*) shows that the threat (ability) to retaliate by a complainant has a positive impact in terms of 'helping' respondents implement agreements. In related work, Bloningen and Bown (2003) find that the threat of a retaliatory antidumping action makes it more likely that a WTO member will exclude that country from an AD investigation and less likely that there will be a positive finding of material injury caused by firms originating in the country that can credibly threaten retaliation.

Third parties and amicus curiae briefs

World Trade Organization members can participate in disputes as third parties. (By participating as a third party a WTO member reserves its rights in a dispute and can make submissions to the panel.) Developing countries make the most frequent use of the opportunity to become a third party to a dispute (Horn and Mavroidis, 2008*a*). In the DSU review, a number of proposals were made to allow easier access to any country to participate in disputes, including in the consultations stage. The DSU limits participation by third parties in consultations to members that have a substantial trade interest (Article 4.11 DSU).

Busch and Reinhardt (2006*a*, *b*) argue that if the objective of the DSU is settlement of disputes, widening access for third parties to participate may have detrimental effects, making it more difficult to negotiate a MAS. Thus, the apparent advantages on greater inclusion and 'multilateralization' of disputes may come at the cost of fewer early settlements and more disputes. This matters because early settlements tend to be 'better' not just in the sense of generating compliance at lower cost but result in greater concessions than if a case is litigated (Busch and Reinhardt, 2001). These authors also note that insofar as greater involvement of third parties occurs on both sides of a dispute, the net effect on the probability of win or loss declines—making extended participation less effective.

However, there is an important potential role of third parties in ensuring MFN—that is, precluding the parties from agreeing to a MAS that re-allocates market share away from third parties. Busch and Reinhardt only identify the 'costs' of allowing third parties into the DSU process without assessing this potential benefit (Bown, 2004*c*). Although governments are the players of the DS game, private parties can participate to a limited extent through so-called *amicus curiae* briefs. Multiple decisions by the AB have ruled that such briefs may be considered by panels—as they have the power to seek information and advice, and are free to ignore any brief sent to them. Many WTO members oppose consideration by panels of such briefs because the WTO is government-to-government, and briefs come from nonstate actors. The rulings by the AB on this matter are regarded as an example of the adjudicating bodies over-stepping their mandate. The briefs have proven to be useful in a number of disputes. For example, in the *EC—Sardines* dispute the brief submitted by the UK Consumers Organization was an important piece of evidence that the EU claim that the contested measure was justified on the basis of consumer protection was spurious. This issue was the subject of a number of proposals in the DSU review, but has now been overtaken by practice. Whether any panel has been influenced by an amicus curiae brief is difficult to determine.

Remedies

A government found to be in violation of the WTO is generally told to bring its measures into compliance with the rules. How to do this is left to the discretion of the losing party. The most panels can do is to make specific suggestions regarding the way a losing party can bring its measures into conformity *if* they are requested to do so. If panels limit themselves to standard recommendations to bring measures into compliance, disagreement between the parties on the adequacy of the implementing measures taken by the losing party may preclude the complainant from obtaining authorization to take countermeasures. Another panel will first have to rule on the adequacy of the implementing measures. This 'sequencing problem'—does a member first have to go through a compliance panel before it can ask for and impose retaliation?—first became a matter of conflict in the *Bananas* case. Over time it has been addressed through bilateral agreements between disputants that established a focal point for subsequent practice: an Article 21.5 compliance panel will first review implementation before a WTO member requests authorization to retaliate under Article 22.

The standard remedies generally obtained in the WTO context may not provide enough incentives to the private sector to pursue a dispute. The length of time it can take for the process to run its course is substantial—some three years if appeals and implementation periods are taken into account (the latter can extend to 15 months) (Table 3.1). This is a long time for affected exporters, especially for countries that do not have a diversified export base and may find it difficult (and costly) to find alternative markets. Standard remedies that require a member to bring its measures into compliance with WTO obligations do not involve any compensation for damages incurred, let alone additional financial penalties. This reduces the attractiveness of using the system. If damages or financial compensation could be obtained, the time cost as well as the resource costs associated with the system would become much less important.

In principle, there is nothing to prevent countries from seeking compensation—the fact that complainants do not customarily request compensation is rooted in the history of the GATT. Before and during the Uruguay Round, a number of panels recommended that antidumping and countervailing duties collected by contracting parties in cases where GATT rules had been breached should be given back to the importers who had paid them. Such restitution—which is still far from true compensation for damages incurred—was resisted at the time, and most of these panel cases were not adopted. The first ruling, a 1981 case between Finland and New Zealand (transformers), was adopted, and New Zealand issued a refund. In six subsequent cases refunds were not accepted by the losing party. World Trade Organization members have been unwilling to go down the compensation track, due to uncertainty regarding the possible repercussions (potential liability). Some countries have also argued that their legal systems prohibit compensation. Historically, developing countries have favoured the introduction of rules in the trading system that would allow for claims for monetary damages to be paid to developing countries in instances where illegal measures are imposed against them by industrialized nations. Not surprisingly, GATT contracting parties always rejected this. 'Money damages, said the developed countries, were simply outside the realm of the possible. In effect, they were saying, GATT was never meant to be taken seriously' (Hudec, 2002).

In February 2000, a precedent was set by a panel in a case involving illegal export subsidies granted by Australia to a manufacturer of automotive leather. The panel recommended not only that Australia cease applying this measure, but also that the beneficiary of the subsidy be required to reimburse the funds (the case involved A\$30 million, or about US\$19 million). This was a first for the WTO.[4] The panel report was adopted by the DSB. (Interestingly, the plaintiff (the US) had not requested this remedy; it does not support compensation.) This dispute remains the only instance of retroactive remedies as of 2008; in all other cases standard remedies were applied.

The DSU review generated a number of proposals by developing countries for retroactive remedies, including payment of legal costs by the losing party. But there appeared to be general agreement that the objective of the system should be compliance. Proposals for retroactive measures, trade or monetary compensation, were all limited to situations where a WTO member does not implement a panel or AB recommendation. That is, they were proposed in order to address some of the problems with retaliation as an enforcement device, and not as a remedy in and of themselves.

Enforcement capacity and problems with retaliation

There are asymmetric incentives for countries to deviate from the WTO, as the ultimate threat that can be made against a member that does not comply with a panel recommendation is retaliation. Small countries cannot credibly threaten this because raising import barriers will have little impact on the target market while

---

[4] This had always been possible in principle—what was required was that the panel interpret the relevant language requiring withdrawal of the subsidy as applying as of the date that the subsidy was first applied, rather than as of the date it is found to be illegal (Hoekman and Mavroidis, 1996).

being costly in welfare terms. This of course is simply a reflection of reality and not a function of the WTO. But the result is that in practice there is a lot of 'free riding' by developing countries—relying on other countries to bring disputes and enforce decisions. A possible way out of this dilemma is for small trading nations affected by a dispute to form alliances and retaliate as a group whenever one of the members is affected. More generally, one can conceive of the rules being enforced through retaliation by all WTO members, not just affected members. Both options would reduce the costs to the retaliators, while increasing the cost to the transgressor. However, although multiple parties may bring a joint complaint, only countries with a trade interest may do so. Those not affected cannot participate.

Applying the nondiscrimination principle to retaliation, that is, collective retaliation, has been a standard recommendation by economists for many years. It has always been resisted by WTO members on the basis that the objective of retaliation is not to punish but to maintain a balance of rights and obligations (the reciprocal bargain; Hudec, 1987). A practical problem with collective retaliation is that it implies a direct intrusion in sovereignty—in effect a multilateral institution (the WTO) would be requiring its members to raise tariffs. This helps explain why proposals along these lines—and a number of countries made them in the DSU review, as did observers (Pauwelyn, 2005)—have not had much traction.

Thus, pressure to comply with panel rulings involving small economies is largely moral in nature, although the Ecuador case illustrates the potential that exists under the WTO to expand the threat of retaliation. In practice the system has worked rather well, in that recourse to retaliation has rarely been required to enforce multilateral DS decisions. This is largely a reflection of the repeated nature of the WTO game and the resulting value that governments attach to maintaining a (reasonably) good reputation. Nonetheless, asymmetry in enforcement ability can affect the incentives to use the system.

A number of suggestions have been made in the DSU review and in the literature to address both the asymmetric retaliation capacity constraint and the economic inefficiency/costs of raising tariffs. An innovative proposal to address both problems was suggested by Mexico in 2003: permit WTO members to trade their rights for retaliation in instances where a losing party refuses to implement a panel (or AB) report. Bagwell, Mavroidis and Staiger (2006) analyse the economics of this proposal. They conclude that it makes sense from the perspective of developing countries if the noncomplying party can also bid. They stress that their analysis does not imply that introducing the possibility of tradable remedies into the WTO system is necessarily a good idea given the likely political ramifications of a government imposing WTO-sanctioned retaliatory tariffs against other governments with whom it has no unresolved WTO dispute. However, they note that similar observations can be made about any attempt to bring multilateral elements into WTO dispute resolutions for the purpose of helping small and developing countries take part more effectively in the WTO system.

A basic problem with retaliation is that it involves raising barriers to trade, which is generally detrimental to the interests of the country that does so, and to overall world welfare. Preferable from an economic perspective would be to encourage use of the provisions in the WTO for renegotiating concessions (Mavroidis, 2000). This would ensure that the net impact of dispute resolution would lead towards more liberal trade, rather than create mechanisms through which trade barriers are raised, as re-negotiation involves compensating affected members by reducing other trade barriers. A similar approach can also be adopted to replace retaliation: instead of raising barriers against imports from the country that is not complying, it would be much better if that country were to reduce barriers to trade in an amount that would re-balance the initial level of negotiated concessions. Alternatively, a country that is not in a position to comply with a ruling could offer monetary compensation. In the DSU review a number of developing countries made proposals to this effect—including Ecuador. Assuming that there is agreement on the magnitude of the appropriate level of compensation—determined through the existing WTO process—the question is how to make this incentive compatible.

Economists have suggested two possible approaches. Lawrence (2003) has focused on trade compensation and proposed adoption of what he terms contingent liberalization commitments. In a MTN, each WTO member would designate sectors or methods for liberalization in the event they should fail to comply with DSB findings. This would make retaliation redundant, thus improving global welfare, and level the playing field by addressing the problem of symmetric capacity to retaliate. He argues that by pre-announcing the sectors in which liberalization might take place, the system would create a domestic constituency in each country that would lobby for compliance, motivated by the prospects of losing their protection. The proposal also implies no loss in sovereignty—the countries determine the choice of sectors themselves.

Another approach centres on financial compensation. One practical advantage of this approach relative to trade compensation is that it does not need to be applied on a MFN basis. Financial compensation can be bilateral, as part of a MAS. From the perspective of a petitioning business or industry, money compensation is attractive in that it may create an additional incentive to petition its government to initiate DS cases. Limão and Saggi (2008a) show that a system of monetary fines that is supported by the threat of tariff retaliation is more efficient than one based on retaliation alone, but note that if the ultimate threat to enforce compensation payments is to raise tariffs, nothing will have been achieved. In order to make a system of monetary compensation 'work' without the threat of retaliation, agreement is needed *ex ante* to contribute to a multilateral 'escrow account' (in effect, each WTO member would post a bond). If this can be achieved, Limão and Saggi show that the threat of retaliation is not needed any longer. In subsequent research, Limão and Saggi (2008b) show that small countries may not need to post a bond to maintain cooperation. As is true for the Lawrence (2003) proposal, this would benefit the smaller WTO members that cannot use the threat of retaliation. Bronckers and van den Broek (2005) argue that financial payments between governments to address 'contract violations' are not that uncommon. Examples can be found even in the trade area, in particular bilateral trade agreements. Thus, free trade agreements (FTAs) between the US and Australia, Chile and Singapore, as well as the Dominican Republic–Central America Free Trade Agreement (DR–CAFTA) provide for fines (monetary compensation) when intellectual property rights (IPRs) are violated. The US Congress has established a US$50 million fund to pay such compensation when required (this fund was used to pay financial compensation to the EU in the *US—Copyright* case—see Chapter 8).

Resource constraints and costs of dispute settlement

A consequence of the increasing complexity and coverage of the WTO, as well as the shift towards a more 'legalistic' and less diplomatic approach towards DS implies that relative to the GATT-1947 there is much greater need for legal expertise and capacity. The WTO and its various agreements add up to over 25,000 pages of documentation; the case law that has emerged over time adds another 25,000 pages (Busch, Reinhardt and Shaffer, 2008). Clearly this puts a premium on legal expertise. Industrialized nations are well equipped with legal talent, are well briefed by export interests, and have a worldwide network of commercial and diplomatic representation that feeds their governments with relevant data. Developing countries, in contrast, have limited national expertise available and find it difficult to collect the type of information that is required to bring or defend WTO cases. Although to some extent countries can buy legal expertise,[5] they need to be able to make effective use of it, which is very much a function of in-house capacity in governments and the business community. In general, governments are more likely to bring in outside counsel when being challenged than in defending their market access rights. The result must be that there are a significant number of 'missing cases'—especially in light of the fact that an average DS case can easily cost US$500,000 or more, and as noted above, take two to three years to resolve (Bown and Hoekman, 2005).

Article 27:2 DSU calls for technical assistance to be provided to developing countries by the WTO Secretariat. The secretariat's ability to satisfy this mandate

---

[5] Until the third *Bananas* case (see Box 3.2), countries were impeded from bringing nongovernment, private legal counsel before the panel. The Appellate Body decision in this case to allow representation by private lawyers removed this constraint as far as the Appellate Body was concerned. A subsequent panel then decided there were no provisions in the WTO or the DSU that prevented a WTO member from determining the composition of its delegation to panel meetings (Palmeter and Mavroidis, 2004).

is very constrained. To date, legal technical assistance services have been limited to two outside experts on a part-time basis. The adequacy of the assistance on offer is further reduced by the DSU requirement that it can only be provided *after* a member has decided to submit a dispute to the WTO. Thus, assistance in evaluating whether practices are inconsistent and determining what might be winning cases cannot be given. Consequently, the services of the experts are mostly used when developing countries are respondents.

The ability of developing countries to use the DSU improved with the creation of the Advisory Center on WTO Law (ACWL), one of the few concrete results achieved by the 1999 Seattle ministerial meeting. The Centre was established in Geneva in 2001. In addition to more general legal advice on WTO matters, it offers support to complainants, respondents and third parties in DS proceedings at subsidized rates to developing countries and economies in transition. Its membership, with the exception of the LDCs, contributes to an 'Endowment Fund', with the majority of contributions coming from a number of OECD countries. (The European Commission, the US and Japan do not contribute.) A 'Roster of External Legal Counsel' of private sector attorneys willing to provide counsel to LDCs and other ACWL members is available if a conflict of interest arises so that ACWL cannot provide services through its own attorneys.

Although the ACWL provides legal assistance, it does not have the resources or the mandate to work with developing country exporters or the trade industry associations that are the key part of the public–private partnership framework (Bown and Hoekman, 2005). Indeed, much of its activities concern matters of general WTO law, advice on the consistency of national measures with WTO obligations and training. During 2005–7, only 21 per cent of the opinions provided by the ACWL dealt with a specific dispute. Between 2001 and 2007, the ACWL assisted Members with 29 disputes. Of the 22 cases where the Centre advised a developing country complainant, half had another developing country as the respondent. In four of these cases a law firm from the roster mentioned above advised the party concerned.

The ACWL is a laudatory example of an international initiative to address the problem of limited legal capacity that many developing countries confront. Many proposals have been made that would complement this effort to augment the access to legal expertise by reducing the need for it. Examples include putting in place a 'fast track' DS mechanism for smaller disputes—what Nordstrom and Shaffer (2007) call a small claims procedure, under which disputes involving only a small value of trade would be dealt with by a standing body of panellists on an expedited time frame with decisions not subject to appeal and remedies that include payment of damages, i.e. binding arbitration. Other possibilities that have been proposed include an ombudsman or 'special prosecutor'. This office would be granted the mandate to identify and contest potential WTO violations on behalf of developing countries, using information drawn from private sources, the

TPRM, the business and financial press, etc. Such outsourcing of enforcement could help address both the resource constraints and the incentive problems (fear of cross-issue linkage) that may impede developing country governments from pursuing cases. Although cases brought by the special prosecutor could not be backed by the threat of retaliation (as they are not brought by or on behalf of a government), findings against a WTO member would lead to moral pressure to bring measures into conformity (Hoekman and Mavroidis, 2000).

There is also another aspect to resource costs and constraints: the ability of panels and the AB to deal with very complex, technical/scientific cases such as *EC—Biotech*. As argued by Howse and Horn (2008), in such disputes the task is truly Herculean. The *EC—Biotech* panel report's table of contents runs over almost 40 pages, the main body comprises over 1,000 pages, not counting numerous appendices and addenda. The *EC—Biotech* panel enumerates numerous difficulties it had to deal with, including the fact that the parties submitted over 3,100 documents, some very long, with a resulting lack of coherence of argumentation. Given the inherent complexity of the legal, conceptual and scientific questions panels will be confronted with in such cases, one must ask whether the system should be asked to bear the burden of having to decide on matters that are viewed by members as inherently political in nature.

Settlements

A noteworthy feature of the WTO system is its success in encouraging bilateral settlement of trade conflicts. The presumption underlying the system is that the best way to settle trade disputes is through an out-of-court agreement among the parties concerned. The 60-day consultation period (Box 3.1) is in large part intended for that purpose. Although often regarded as a positive dimension of how the WTO works, a high number of settlements can also be seen as a negative. For example, if there is a high degree of distrust in the likely outcome of the DSU process, countries may use the threat of the DSU and the associated uncertainty of what the outcome may be as an instrument to induce countries to settle. However, the majority view among observers is that settlements are in fact an integral, and positive, dimension of the way that the WTO deals with disputes.

Frequently, bilateral negotiations and a search for a compromise continue in spite of the initiation of DS proceedings. Many cases never reach the panel stage, although precise numbers are very hard to come by. The nature of settlements is such that both parties are presumably satisfied with the outcome. Although there is a reporting requirement—parties should notify the secretariat regarding the out-come of settlements (Article 3.6 DSU)—compliance is rather patchy. The main examples of known settlements are instances where deals are struck after a panel is requested. An illustrative example was a dispute between India and the US over textile import quotas. The US rescinded the contested quotas before the panel could start its work. There is general dissatisfaction regarding the way Article 3.6 DSU has been implemented.

Arguments have been made that if settlements are found not to have been applied on a MFN basis, retroactive remedies should be made possible, and that provisions be created requiring multilateral clearance of settlements before they enter into force (Hoekman and Mavroidis, 2000). In the DSU review a number of proposals along these lines were put forward. Opponents to efforts to making settlements more transparent note that this may result in fewer settlements and put greater stress on the DS system. This is one illustration of the tension that emerged in the course of the DSU review between those favouring stronger rules and those preferring to retain or expand the diplomatic element in dispute resolution (Zimmerman, 2006).

Asymmetric enforcement incentives

Much attention has been devoted in the literature to the hurdles confronting low-income countries in participating as complainants or interested third parties in disputes related to their export market access interests. This ignores an important dimension of the DS process: developing countries are rarely challenged as respondents. As it is unlikely that poor countries are in full compliance with their trade liberalization commitments, a failure to enforce WTO rules reduces the value of participation in such agreements for these countries. This is not just because of the welfare losses associated with import protection, but also because of the resulting diminished incentives for countries to make WTO commitments and externality costs imposed on other (developing) countries.

The lack of challenges may reflect the limited number of market access commitments that many developing countries have made in the WTO and the various special and differential treatment provisions they can invoke. Their small markets can easily imply that the potential gains to foreign exporters in terms of increased market access resulting from winning a case are too small to compensate for the cost of litigation. Moreover, litigation may be politically expensive—many governments may prefer not to be seen as 'picking on' a poor country for WTO violations. Whatever the reason, it should be a matter of concern that even if a poor country wants to make full use of the WTO as a commitment mechanism, the DS system makes enforcement unlikely. This in turn implies that developing countries are not realizing the full economic benefits of WTO membership, which may help explain why commitments by developing countries are more limited than those of industrialized economies (Bown and Hoekman, 2008). One implication of no enforcement vis-à-vis poor countries is that the incentives to invest in negotiating commitments are reduced.

The problems and failures with reliance on formal DS procedures to enforce WTO commitments of low-income countries imply a need to consider alternative mechanisms that induce compliance. In order to be effective, any such mechanism must target domestic constituencies and the membership of the WTO as a whole. As we discuss below, domestic transparency and information mechanisms are critical to prevent capture of policies by interest groups, to give losers as well as winners a greater voice in policy formation and help address the economic problems associated with the weak incentives for enforcement created by current DS procedures.

Stronger rules or more discretion?

As discussed at length by Zimmerman (2006), the DSU review revealed rather deep differences in view between WTO members on the question of whether to move the DS system further in the direction of a judicial model with specific, binding rules and enforcement mechanisms, or whether it was preferable to move back in the direction of the GATT period when dispute resolution was more diplomatic in nature. The former group was in favour of proposals such as the establishment of a permanent panel body (i.e. a true first instance court); a nonrenewable, six-year term for AB judges; explicit multilateral review of each MAS; and additional rights for third parties in disputes. In part the positions taken reflected concerns relating to recent or ongoing disputes. But the issue is a fundamental one that goes to the heart of the question with which this chapter started: what is the purpose of the DSB? Scholars such as Barfield (2001) take the view that it is necessary to move away from further 'legalism', and that re-introducing some elements of discretion is needed to preserve political support for the multilateral trading system in major countries such as the United States. Moves in this direction were opposed by the 2004 report of the Consultative Board to the DG of the WTO (Sutherland et al., 2004), as well as many commentators. Aside from political concerns, this is a split that tends to divide the economists and the lawyers. Economists tend to take the view that as the WTO is an incomplete contract, one cannot and should not expect strong enforcement. Many legal scholars and practitioners tend to take a more 'constitutional' or normative view: 'rules are rules' and they should therefore be enforced (e.g. Pauwelyn, 2005).

From a practical perspective, neither approach gives much guidance as to how to address the issue of 'judicial activism'. The fact of the matter is that no set of rules will ever be unambiguous. The role of the DSB is to interpret the disciplines. As a result it is virtually impossible to preclude 'gap filling' by judges even if that will not be to the liking of WTO members—especially those that are on the losing end of a dispute. The disputes concerning the use of 'zeroing' by the US in antidumping investigations is a good example (see Chapter 9). The solution to disagreements as to the validity of DS findings that involve gap filling is to legislate—either negotiate more specific disciplines or agree that governments are unconstrained in certain dimensions. Absent such clarity, some gap filling is an unavoidable corollary of the incomplete nature of the WTO contract.

3.5. Domestic Dimensions of Enforcement

Greater domestic transparency and mechanisms allowing the use of national enforcement mechanisms could do much to increase the relevance of the WTO for the private sector. There are three dimensions of enforcement at the domestic level: generating the information required to defend WTO rights; in large countries, allocating countermeasures over target industries; and creating institutions that reduce the need to rely on WTO dispute resolution. The latter is crucial if domestic constituencies are to be able to hold governments accountable for the outcome of international negotiations and to increase their 'ownership'.

Upstream links in the WTO dispute settlement chain

Different countries have different institutional arrangements through which firms and other actors interact with their governments and seek to defend their trade interests. In general, a firm has two options in contesting foreign government policies that restrict its ability to contest a market. It can petition the foreign government, either through direct lobbying or through its legal system if a WTO obligation has been violated. Or, it can lobby its own government to take up the issue with the foreign government in question and initiate WTO dispute settlement if a solution is not forthcoming. From the firm's perspective the second route often is not attractive. It must convince its government that the case is worth bringing. This may require considerable resources—a collective action problem must be overcome to bring enough firms in the industry on board. Even if the evidence has been collected, a country may not have the legal and administrative capacity to take action. Finally, if a case is pursued, the outcome (remedy) may not do much to address the concerns of the firm. Thus, many violations are unlikely to be addressed through the WTO.

This is not necessarily bad. High entry barriers or thresholds may be beneficial in ensuring that only major cases are brought to the WTO, ones that cannot be resolved through alternative, private mechanisms. It is difficult to make a judgement, however, because the available data on the prevalence and effect of discriminatory policies (whether or not these violate the WTO) are limited. If there are too few cases, an inefficient outcome for individual firms and for the trading system as a whole may result. The problem is similar to that of the production of a public good, where without cooperation underprovision is likely to result. Solutions to the problem require increasing the net benefits to firms of collecting data on potentially WTO-illegal policies, and increasing (reducing) the expected payoffs (costs) of launching a dispute. Both goals require establishing mechanisms to facilitate private sector cooperation, within and across countries to compile information on—and assess the prospects for dealing—with potential violations.

Cooperation in collection, dissemination and analysis of information

Figure 3.1, drawn from Bown and Hoekman (2005), illustrates the various steps necessary to achieve economically successful litigation in the WTO. First, the private sector must do the pre-litigation economic and legal research necessary to establish the legal merits and economic benefits to pursuing a case. Then it engages its domestic government under the relevant domestic statutory provisions, such as Section 301 and Industry Advisory Committees in the US and the Article 133/Trade Barrier Regulation (TBR) in the EU. Given government willingness to pursue the complaint, the private sector's attorneys and consultants will assist in the preparation of the legal briefs and evidence. Finally, the private sector may also help induce foreign compliance with rulings by identifying the most effective foreign political targets when retaliation is authorized by the DSU, or through a public relations campaign abroad and working with interest groups there who stand to gain from implementation.

Public–private partnerships are critical in pursuing WTO litigation (Shaffer, 2003). In developing countries there are at least three barriers that prevent such partnerships from materializing. One is that exporting interests find it more difficult to organize, perhaps because of the small value or low profit margin earned on the exports—costs outweigh expected returns. A second concern is that even if exporters do overcome barriers to collective organization, they lack the institutional 'entry' routes to engage their government. A third potential constraint is lack of capacity in the private sector.

A problem with the ACWL mentioned above is that it focuses only on the 'downstream' dimension of enforcement, not on the 'upstream' collection of information or the identification of possible violations. One option to deal with the information problem is for the private sector to cooperate and to create mechanisms through which data on trade (and investment) barriers are collected and analysed. This could be realized through periodic surveys of multinationals,

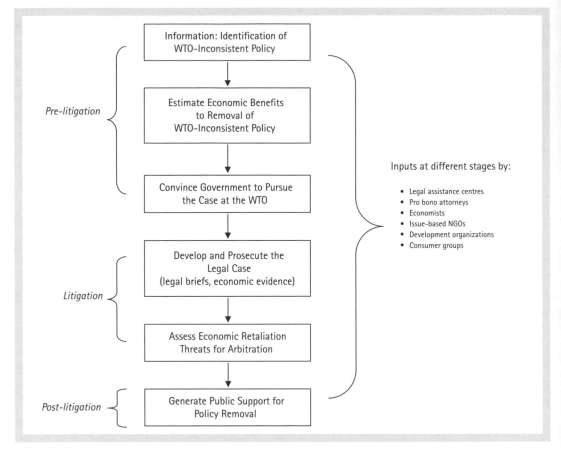

Fig. 3.1. Engaging private sector support to defend market access interests

national firms that produce for export, trade associations and consumer organizations. Such a survey would generate a 'user perspective' on the WTO system,
providing information on problems perceived from a managerial perspective.
The data collected could be used to assess the status quo on export markets,
and help identify potential enforcement cases. An independent 'transparency'
body could coordinate national efforts and assist in identifying potential WTO
violations and possible joint actions, as well as generate publicity. The 2009 Global
Trade Alert, a network of think-tanks that monitor and assess the impacts of trade-
related policies around the world is a recent example of such a body. Although
conceived as a financial crisis response initiative, its activities would be beneficial in
normal times as well.

Many fora already exist through which businesses cooperate and coordinate
their position vis-à-vis government policies. The most prominent international
body is the International Chamber of Commerce (ICC) located in Paris. The ICC

has consultative status in the United Nations system, maintains a close working relationship with the WTO, and is the most visible avenue for international business to express its views on international policy matters. Other entities include the Business and Industry Advisory Committee, which provides business input into the deliberations of the OECD, and the Alliance for Global Business. In many countries there are similar institutions, as well as numerous industry-specific bodies. Although business associations have become more aware of the potential payoff of investing resources to reduce barriers to trade and investment, they have done relatively little to systematically compile information that would help policy-makers identify the key constraints to competition and provide an input into better enforcement of WTO agreements.

Analysis of the information that is compiled must be undertaken if it is to be useful for enforcement purposes. Bown and Hoekman (2005) catalogue and examine a number of different proposals to reduce the costs associated with the extended litigation process characterized in Figure 3.1, and the likely impact of each proposal on reducing the magnitude and altering the scope of the 'missing' developing country caseload. Using the private–public partnership model as a guiding framework, they identify a number of useful roles for various self-interested and altruistic groups—including legal service centres, NGOs, development organizations, international trade litigators, economists, consumer organizations and importers, and law schools—in the enforcement process. These groups may assist with needed information-generation and increased transparency, if they are willing to invest in technological (legal and economic) upgrading—as part of their overall pro bono activities—so as to contribute to the provision of these services to help poor countries use the formal WTO dispute settlement process.

Using national mechanisms to enforce WTO commitments

World Trade Organization rules and commitments are valuable in part because they provide assurances that a given trade policy stance will be maintained. For the potential of instruments such as the TPRM and other transparency devices such as reporting and publication requirements, as well as the DSU, to be fully realized, domestic stakeholders should be able to invoke WTO law and obligations in domestic courts or specialized fora. In many countries this is not the case. Greater access to domestic enforcement mechanism could help enhance the relevance of the WTO. Perhaps the most straightforward way to facilitate domestic enforcement of multilateral obligations is through the creation of 'challenge' mechanisms allowing private parties to contest perceived WTO-inconsistent policies by the government before domestic courts or specialized tribunals. A first step in this direction was made at the WTO level in the (plurilateral) Government Procurement Agreement (GPA)—see Chapter 11. The GPA requires signatories to give private parties access to national mechanisms that allow them to contest actions by procuring entities that violate the agreement. In effect, the 'challenge' mechanisms required by the GPA imply that private parties may invoke its provisions before domestic courts (see Hoekman and Mavroidis, 1997). The TRIPS agreement also requires that WTO members have national enforcement mechanisms in place.

3.6. CONCLUSION

The DS mechanism is one of the unique features of the WTO. Although controversial cases frequently lead to tensions between WTO members, the system has to date worked rather well. The AB has played more of role than might have been expected, taking a rather proactive stance with respect to panel reports and the appropriate interpretation of WTO disciplines. The negative consensus rule for nonadoption of panel reports has reduced the scope for overt politicization of the process. Although a number of disputes have generated controversy, these are the exceptions, not the rule. Most disputes are either 'run-of-the-mill' and are resolved smoothly or deal with recurring problems that negotiators have been struggling with for years. *Bananas* is an example; as are some of the antidumping cases, an area characterized by some 30 years of periodic efforts to write down a more specific set of disciplines (see Chapter 9). Here disputes are in part the continuation of negotiations in another forum.

A more serious problem that has emerged is symptomatic of a more general source of conflict that has become more prominent over time. It concerns fundamental differences between governments regarding domestic regulatory regimes and attitudes towards risk. Huge complexity confronts panels and the AB when asked to deal with some of the disputes that may arise. Differences between societies regarding the amount of risk they are willing to tolerate—for example, the production and consumption of GMOs—are very difficult to address. Efforts to introduce scientific principles into WTO rules may not do much to facilitate DS—this was illustrated in *Hormones*, an issue where there was much more of a scientific consensus than what prevails in an area such as biotechnology and the regulation of genetically modified organisms and their use (discussed in Chapter 5).

The incentive for governments to negotiate and abide by international trade agreements depends in part on the effectiveness of enforcement provisions. Enforcement is particularly important for developing countries, as they will rarely be able to exert credible threats against large trading entities that do not abide by the negotiated rules of the game. Domestic enforcement is a vital dimension in enhancing the relevance of multilateral commitments to domestic stakeholders. In most countries, including high-income nations, domestic interests are restricted in their ability to contest actions by government agencies that may be violating WTO commitments. Civil society has a strong interest in seeking to maximize the extent to which individuals can invoke international treaty obligations in national legal systems. This will remove a number of layers of uncertainty and complexity associated with inducing governments to bring a case to the WTO. Strengthening national enforcement mechanisms can help make the WTO a more relevant instrument from an economic development perspective by increasing the 'owner-ship' of negotiated commitments. The easiest way of making WTO commitments enforceable nationally is to expand on the 'challenge' mechanisms that have been introduced in the GPA (see Chapter 11).

The private sector plays a key role in enforcement. If it does not have an incentive to collect, compile and transmit information on measures that violate the WTO, cases will not be brought. Giving private interests standing in domestic fora via a general challenge procedure could enhance incentives to defend their rights. But private sector participation is also vital in order to ensure that countries can defend their rights at the WTO level. This upstream dimension of enforcement is as important as the efficacy of the downstream panel and AB process. The value of legal assistance to developing countries is heavily dependent on firms bringing cases to their governments and getting a receptive hearing.

As stressed by Lawrence (2003), because the DS system accomplishes several functions, most reforms that would improve performance in one dimension may worsen it in another. Eliminating the provision for retaliatory increases of tariffs in cases of noncompliance would avoid the welfare costs of protectionist policies, but attenuate incentives for compliance. Stronger enforcement instruments—such as collective retaliation—may result in more compliance, but at the cost of reducing the prospects for more ambitious cooperation. Agreeing to replace retaliation with compensation is clearly welfare enhancing in principle, but difficult to implement in a credible manner. However, a number of proposals have been made that could, with political will, be feasible. An example is the compensation fund idea, which would improve on the status quo for small developing countries in particular. Monetary compensation has been introduced in a number of free trade agreements. The decision by the US Congress to authorize a US$50 million fund to finance such claims illustrates that movement in this direction is possible.

There is a consensus among WTO members that DS should remain the pre-rogative of governments. Giving private actors such as NGOs direct access to the WTO is unlikely to improve the process or the outcomes. While business, con-sumer and other groups should have access to mechanisms that allow them to have a voice in the formation of national positions in WTO negotiations and trade policy more generally, a good case can be made that this should not extend to direct access to the WTO for reasons identified by Levy and Srinivasan (1996) and Busch and Reinhardt (2006*a*, *b*). More fundamentally, it will be very difficult to determine who speaks for (is representative of) of civil society as a whole. Wolf (1999) argues that organizations (NGOs) 'can only represent themselves. If NGOs were indeed representative of the wishes and desires of the electorate, those who embrace their ideas would be in power. Self-evidently, they are not'. Problems of representativeness are obviously compounded at the global (WTO) level.

Finally, it is important to recognize that although the DS mechanism attracts much attention in the press and in the academic literature dealing with the WTO, especially (not surprisingly) legal scholars and practitioners, DS is the last resort for WTO members to settle a conflict. As stressed in Chapter 1 and in other chapters in this book, the committee structure and the associated frequent interaction between government officials responsible for a given policy area that is covered by the WTO and the notification, publication and transparency requirements play an important role in defusing potential disputes before they occur. This dimension of the WTO tends to be ignored because it is much less visible.

3.7. FURTHER READING

World Trade Organization dispute settlement procedures are discussed in detail by David Palmeter and Petros C. Mavroidis, *Dispute Settlement in the World Trade Organization: Practice and Procedure* (Cambridge: Cambridge University Press, 2004). Mitsuo Matsushita, Petros C. Mavroidis and Thomas Schoenbaum provide a complete overview of WTO disciplines in the broader context of international economic public law in *The WTO Law and Practice* (Oxford: Oxford University Press, 2006). John Jackson, Bill Davey and Alan Sykes, *Cases, Materials and Texts on Legal Problems of International Economic Relations* (West Publishers, 2008) pull together a mostly legally centred set of documents and writings on WTO cases and agreements.

An exhaustive analysis of DS in the GATT era can be found in Robert Hudec, *Enforcing International Trade Law: The Evolution of the GATT Legal System* (New York: Buttersworth, 1993). World Trade Organization panel and AB reports can be downloaded from the WTO homepage. T. N. Srinivasan, 'The Dispute Settlement Mechanism of the WTO: A Brief History and an Evaluation from Economic, Contractarian and Legal Perspectives,' *The World Economy*, 30 (2007): 1033–68, provides a comprehensive overview and evaluation of DS system.

Economists have begun to devote more attention to formally modelling the DSU and to better understand the relationship between the structure and content of the WTO and its enforcement mechanisms. Some of this work has been inspired and informed by a major American Law Institute project that reviews the WTO case law on an annual basis as a joint venture between leading legal scholars and economists. The case assessments are published in the *World Trade Review* as well as in an annual volume edited by Henrik Horn and Petros Mavroidis published by Cambridge University Press. Horn and Mavroidis have also constructed a database describing various aspects of the DS system. The dataset can be freely downloaded (at www. worldbank.org/trade/wtodisputes). The dataset covers exhaustively all stages of DS proceedings, from the moment when consultations are requested to the eventual implementation of the panel/AB rulings (or, if not yet finalized, the last stage of the DS process that has been officially reported). The dataset contains several hundred variables and was the basis for the descriptive statistics reported in Section 3.2.

Abram Chayes and Antonia Handler Chayes, *The New Sovereignty: Compliance with International Regulatory Agreements* (Boston: Harvard University Press, 1995) discuss alternative approaches to enforcement of international treaties, arguing that in many, if not most, instances noncompliance with agreements is not deliberate, implying that coercive enforcement through the threat of sanctions (retaliation) is inappropriate.

Jagdish Bhagwati, 'Aggressive Unilateralism: An Overview', in J. Bhagwati and H. Patrick (eds), *Aggressive Unilateralism: America's Trade Policy and the World Trading System* (New York: Harvester-Wheatsheaf, 1990) and Marco Bronckers, 'Private Participation in the Enforcement of WTO Law: The New EC Trade Barriers Regulation', *Common Market Law Review*, 33 (1996): 299–318, discuss the use of unilateral 'enforcement' mechanisms by the US and EU, respectively, before the creation of the WTO. Greg Shaffer discusses the interaction between private interests and government bodies in WTO dispute settlement in the EU and US in *Defending Interests: Public–Private Partnerships in WTO Litigation* (Washington, DC: Brookings, 2003).

Robert Hudec, 'The Role of the GATT Secretariat in the Evolution of the WTO Dispute Settlement Procedure', in Jagdish Bhagwati and Mathias Hirsch (eds), *The Uruguay Round and Beyond: Essays in Honor of Arthur Dunkel* (Ann Arbor: University of Michigan Press, 1998) is a characteristically readable account of the evolution of the role the GATT (and now WTO) secretariat has played in the settlement of disputes.

Robert Lawrence, *Crimes and Punishment: Retaliation Under the WTO* (Washington, DC: Peterson Institute for International Economics, 2003) provides an excellent review of practice from a US perspective and the pros and cons of many of the proposals that have been made to make retaliation more effective or to replace it with another mechanism. Claude Barfield, *Free Trade, Sovereignty and Democracy* (Washington, DC: American Enterprise Institute, 2001) makes the case for greater discretion in the DS system. Thomas Zimmerman, *Negotiating the Review of the WTO Dispute Settlement Understanding* (London: Cameron May, 2006) presents a comprehensive discussion and balanced assessment of the proposals made as part of the DSU review, both before and during the Doha Round.

The websites of the major industrialized countries are often excellent sources of data on the state of play of disputes they are involved in—generally much more informative than the material available on the WTO site, which tends to be limited to a narrow legal scope. An example is the annual compilation of the status of WTO disputes provided in *WTO Dispute Settlement: One-Page Case Summaries* (Geneva: WTO; also downloadable from the WTO homepage), which limits reporting to the rulings of WTO adjudicating bodies on the main legal claims made. No information is provided on the economic stakes involved or the actual status of the various disputes—e.g. whether they are settled, ongoing, retaliation is being applied, etc.

NEGOTIATING FORUM

NEGOTIATION is the driving force of the multilateral trading system. Negotiations are used to agree on rules and procedures, to periodically reduce trade barriers, in instances when new countries want to join the club, and to resolve trade conflicts. The WTO is a negotiating forum in which disciplines on trade policies may be agreed upon, against the background of the provisions of the various agreements already concluded. Negotiations take place in permanent and ad hoc bodies, and are often informal. Although the WTO is a multilateral institution, it relies very strongly on bilateral and plurilateral interactions among members. Whatever agreement emerges is multilateralized through the MFN rule.

The negotiations occur between countries that vary enormously in terms of their size and wealth. The fundamentally skewed distribution of power in the trade world is a key factor that affects both process and outcomes. The reality is that the trade giants have less to lose from walking away from a specific negotiation than do small countries, and that this influences the parameters of the deals that are struck. However, a major change since the mid-1990s is that the weaker players have been getting much better prepared and organized as negotiating coalitions. A general consequence is that reaching agreement has become more difficult, as these negotiating groups are less willing—if at all—to acquiesce to deals that they perceive to be insufficiently beneficial to them.

The discussion in this chapter centres primarily on MTNs and the problems that confront negotiators seeking to obtain agreement, the 'modalities' that are used, and the reasons why outcomes do not maximize national welfare. Issues relating to transparency and participation in WTO processes are discussed in Chapter 14. Although more detailed analysis of the outcomes of the various MTNs is left for subsequent chapters, it is useful to start with an overview of the major negotiating rounds that have been held since 1948.

4.1. OVERVIEW OF NEGOTIATING ROUNDS

To date, nine rounds of MTNs have been held under GATT auspices. These include Geneva (1947), Annecy (1949), Torquay (1951), another negotiation in Geneva in 1956, the Dillon Round (1960–1), the Kennedy Round (1964–7), the Tokyo Round (1973–9), the Uruguay Round (1986–94) and the Doha Round (2001) (Table 4.1). The first five rounds dealt almost exclusively with tariffs. Starting with the Kennedy Round, attention began to shift towards nontariff policies and to the problem of trade in agricultural products. Although the Kennedy Round dealt only with nontariff measures that were already covered by the GATT, the Tokyo Round addressed policies that were not subject to GATT disciplines (the foremost examples being product standards and government procurement). This trend was continued in the Uruguay Round, which included trade in services, intellectual property and rules of origin—all matters on which the GATT had very little to say. The Doha Round expanded the agenda further to include trade facilitation, geographical indications, investment and competition policies, and transparency in government procurement.

The rounds get their names from the places at which they were launched or the people who were influential in launching them. With the exception of the early sets of negotiations held in Annecy (France) and Torquay (United Kingdom), the actual negotiations occurred in Geneva, where the secretariat is based.

The early rounds

The first round of multilateral tariff negotiations was the Geneva round of 1947, which led to the creation of the General Agreement. Some 45,000 tariff concessions covering about half of world trade were exchanged by the 23 countries involved. Two MTNs were held relatively soon after the creation of the GATT, and largely consisted of accession negotiations. The first took place in Annecy (France) in 1949, at which time nine countries joined the GATT. A second followed in Torquay (UK) in 1951, with four more countries acceding. This brought GATT membership to a total of 32, as four countries had ceased to participate by 1950. Three of these countries—China, Lebanon and Syria—were original contracting parties, whereas the fourth—Liberia—had joined during the Annecy negotiation. A third round followed in Geneva during 1955–6, by which time Japan had also acceded, bringing

Table 4.1. Trade rounds and selected ministerial meetings, 1947–2007

Name of Round or Meeting	Period and Number of Parties	Subjects and Modalities	Outcome
Geneva	1947 23 countries	Tariffs: item-by-item offer-request negotiations	Concessions on 45,000 tariff lines; US cut its average bound tariff on industrial products by 26 per cent
Annecy	1949 29 countries	Tariffs: item-by-item offer-request negotiations	5,000 tariff concessions; nine accessions
Torquay	1950–1 32 countries	Tariffs: item-by-item offer-request negotiations	8,700 tariff concessions; four accessions; US cut its average bound tariff on industrial products by 3 per cent
Geneva	1955–6 33 countries	Tariffs: item-by-item offer-request negotiations	Modest reductions; US cut its average bound tariff by 4 per cent
Dillon Round	1960–1 39 countries	Tariffs: item-by-item offer-request negotiations, motivated in part by need to rebalance concessions following creation of the EEC	4,400 concessions exchanged; EEC proposal for a 20 per cent linear cut in manufactures tariffs rejected; US cut its average bound tariff by 3 per cent
Kennedy Round	1963–7 74 countries	Tariffs: formula approach (linear cut) and item-by-item talks. Nontariff measures: antidumping, customs valuation	Average tariffs reduced by 37 per cent; some 33,000 tariff lines bound; agreements on customs valuation and antidumping
Tokyo Round	1973–9 99 countries	Tariffs: formula approach with exceptions. Nontariff measures: antidumping, customs valuation, subsidies and countervail, government procurement, import licensing, product standards, safeguards, special and differential treatment of developing countries	Average tariffs reduced by 33 per cent to a 6 per cent on average for OECD manufactures imports; voluntary codes of conduct agreed for all nontariff issues except safeguards
Uruguay Round	1986–94 103 countries in 1986 117 as of end 1993	Tariffs: formula approach and item-by-item negotiations. Nontariff measures: all Tokyo issues, plus services, intellectual property, pre-shipment inspection, rules of origin, trade-related investment measures, dispute settlement, transparency and surveillance of trade policies	Average tariffs reduced by 38 per cent on average. Agriculture and textiles and clothing subjected to rules; creation of WTO; new agreements on services and TRIPS; majority of Tokyo Round codes extended to all WTO members

(cont.)

Table 4.1. (Continued)

Name of Round or Meeting	Period and Number of Parties	Subjects and Modalities	Outcome
Doha Round	2001 150+countries	Liberalization of trade in agricultural and industrial products, and services; protection of intellectual property (geographical indications), disciplines on the so-called Singapore issues (competition, investment, government procurement and trade facilitation), WTO rules (e.g. antidumping, regional integration) and trade and environment	Agreement to create a transparency mechanism for PTAs and to mobilize and monitor the provision of additional 'aid for trade' by high-income countries. Market access and rule-making outcomes unknown at time of writing
Major ministerial meetings:			
Geneva	1982	Launch of new MTN (sought by US)	Failure to agree on a MTN; establishment of a work programme on services
Punta del Este	1986	Launch of Uruguay Round	Agreement to negotiate on services and intellectual property as well as goods
Brussels	1990	Planned conclusion of the Uruguay Round	Failure to agree on agriculture; in the end negotiations only concluded in December 1993
Singapore	1996 130 members	Proposals to discuss labour standards, as well as competition and investment policy, procurement and trade facilitation (the last 4 subjects became known as the 'Singapore issues'); elimination of barriers to trade in information technology products; pursue negotiations on basic telecom and financial services	Information Technology Agreement (ITA) agreed. Creation of working groups on the four Singapore issues. Labour standards rejected as a subject for negotiation. Creation of the Integrated Framework for trade–related technical assistance
Seattle	1999 135 members	Launch of a new MTN. Major issues included developing country concerns on Uruguay Round implementation, modalities of agricultural liberalization, proposals to negotiate on competition, investment, trade–environment, and labour standards	Failure to agree on a MTN or on a work programme. Members pursue only the 'built-in' agenda inherited from the Uruguay Round

Doha	2001	Launch of new MTN–Doha Development Round	Agreement to negotiate on tariffs and NTMs, trade in agricultural products, services and rules; conditional agreement to launch negotiations in 2003 on the Singapore issues
Cancún	2003	Mid-term review of the Doha Round. Key decision meeting to consider launch of negotiation on Singapore issues and demand by African countries to prioritize removal of cotton subsidies in OECD nations	Breakdown of the conference. No agreement on Singapore issues; Formation of the G20, an alliance of 22 developing countries, including Brazil, China and India
Hong Kong	2005 148 members	Advancing the Doha Development Agenda	Agreement in principle to phase out agricultural export subsidies by the end of 2013 and to grant tariff free access for at least 97% of LDC exports (tariff lines); Creation of taskforce on Aid for Trade
Geneva	2008	'Mini-ministerial' to agree on negotiating formulae/modalities proposed by chairs of Doha Round agriculture and nonagricultural market access groups	Failure to agree on specifics of a special safeguard mechanism for agricultural commodities

Note: Data on average cuts in bound tariffs are from WTO (2007).

the total number of contracting parties to 33. None of these rounds had as large an impact in terms of reductions in average tariffs as the 1947 meeting did. Indeed, the outcomes were rather minor. For example, the average cut in US tariffs achieved in 1947 was 21.1 per cent, whereas cuts in the next three rounds were only 1.9, 3.0 and 3.5 per cent respectively (Baldwin, 1986: 193). By the mid-1950s, the weighted-average tariff of the main industrialized nations had been reduced to some 15 per cent.

The Dillon Round (1960–1)

Following the establishment of the EEC in 1957, a series of large-scale tariff negoti-ations were held under GATT auspices. As discussed at greater length in Chapter 10, WTO rules require that a customs union or free trade area cover substantially all trade and does not result in a higher average level of protection against nonmembers. Nonmember countries that are negatively affected by the formation of a customs union (because some participating countries adopt higher tariffs) have the right to compensation. Bilateral compensation negotiations with the EEC were supplemented by a round of more general, multilateral tariff negotiations. A total of 34 nations participated. The Dillon Round—named after the US Under-Secretary of State who proposed the talks—yielded relatively modest results, with only 4,400 tariff conces-sions exchanged. No concessions were granted on agricultural and many other sensitive products, notwithstanding that these were the products where effective tariffs and trade barriers more generally were expected to rise as a result of the formation of the EEC (and more specifically the Common Agricultural Policy).

The Kennedy Round (1963–7)

Named after President John Kennedy, some 46 nations participated in the launch of the Kennedy Round, although membership of the GATT had reached 74 by the end of the round, reflecting accession of many former colonies as independent states. A new tariff negotiating method (an across-the-board formula approach) for indus-trial products was adopted, resulting in an average tariff reduction of 35 per cent for trade in such products. Product-by-product negotiations on agricultural trade were less successful. The Kennedy Round was the first MTN to go beyond tariffs and deal with certain NTMs. It resulted, in particular, in the conclusion of an Antidumping Code (see Chapter 9), and an agreement on US customs valuation procedures for certain products (see Chapter 5). The Kennedy Round was also the first to include a centrally planned economy—Poland—which acceded to the GATT at the end of the round, and included efforts that led to the formal inclusion of preferential treatment in favour of the developing countries. This was embodied in a new Part IV of the General Agreement in 1965 (see Chapter 12).

The Tokyo Round (1973–9)

Ninety-nine countries, representing nine-tenths of world trade, participated in this MTN, named after the city where the negotiations were launched. Tariffs were reduced on thousands of industrial and agricultural products, and some 33,000 additional tariff lines were bound. The total value of trade affected by tariff commitments was in the range of US$300 billion, measured in 1981 imports. As a result, the average import weighted tariff on manufactured products maintained by industrialized nations declined to about 6 per cent. This represented a reduction of 34 per cent (measured in terms of tariff revenue), comparable with the magnitude of tariff reduction achieved in the Kennedy Round. The Tokyo Round also led to the adoption of a range of specific new disciplines. These included the legalization of preferential tariff and nontariff treatment in favour of developing countries and among developing countries (the so-called Enabling Clause, see Chapter 12) and a number of 'codes of conduct' dealing with NTMs or specific products.

Codes were negotiated on subsidies and countervailing measures, technical barriers to trade (product standards), government procurement, customs valuation, import licensing procedures, antidumping (a revision of a Kennedy Round code), bovine meat, dairy products and civil aircraft. The use of codes was partly driven by the fact that developing countries objected to expansion of GATT disciplines, implying that the two-thirds majority required to amend the GATT could not be attained. By negotiating a code, like-minded countries were able to agree to new, legally binding commitments, without having all GATT contracting parties on board. At the same time, it was often argued that this weakened the system, as it allowed countries to pick and choose among disciplines that pertained to subjects covered by the GATT (the term 'GATT à la carte' was often used to describe the code approach).

The Uruguay Round (1986–94)

This MTN—named after the country that hosted the ministerial meeting that established its agenda in 1986—continued the trend of widening the negotiating agenda, increasing the number of participating countries, and taking longer to conclude. In addition to policies affecting trade in goods, trade policy measures affecting investment, trade in services, and intellectual property rights were put on the table. The Uruguay Round led to further liberalization of international trade, including not only tariff reductions but also the elimination of tariffs for certain product groups (so-called zero-for-zero agreements), the reintegration of agricultural trade and textiles and clothing into the trading system, and the expansion of GATT disciplines. The GATT 1994 embodies a series of agreements on specific policies—many of them re-negotiations of Tokyo Round codes (see Chapters 5 and 11). Creation of a new GATT allowed contracting parties to bypass the need to formally amend the GATT 1947, and ensure at the same time that the results of the round were a Single Undertaking that applied to all. The WTO was established to oversee the functioning of the GATT, the GATS and the Agreement on TRIPS. The average tariff on manufactured products of industrial countries, weighted by the volume of trade in the products concerned, fell from 6.4 per cent to 4.0 per cent, a cut of almost 40 per cent. This compares to a weighted-average duty of 20–25 per cent before the creation of GATT (1947), and around 15 per cent at the time of the Dillon Round (the early 1960s) (WTO, 2007).

Major WTO meetings, 1996–9

At the first ministerial meeting of the WTO in Singapore in December 1996, the agenda was intended to centre largely on defining a work programme for the WTO. In contrast to the stocktaking exercises that tended to characterize GATT ministerial meetings, the Singapore ministerial became a negotiating session. High-income countries sought to put government procurement, trade facilitation, competition and investment policy on the WTO agenda, with a minority (led by the US and France) also seeking to introduce the topic of labour standards. During 1996, Asian-Pacific Economic Cooperation (APEC) countries and the EU had been developing an agreement to eliminate trade barriers on information technology products. A proposal to this effect was also put on the table in Singapore. It came as something of a surprise to non-APEC developing countries—some objected to being presented with a precooked deal on essentially a 'take it or leave it' basis—but in the end an ITA was concluded among 40 members (see Chapter 6). This is not a Plurilateral Agreement as defined by the WTO, but an example of a zero-for-zero agreement under which signatories agree to abolish tariffs on a set of commodities on a MFN basis. Developing countries managed to keep labour standards off the WTO agenda. Members agreed to create working groups to discuss and study the relationship between trade and competition and investment policy disciplines, transparency in government procurement, and trade facilitation.

A number of the Uruguay Round agreements—most notably on agriculture and services—embodied a built-in negotiating agenda, calling for new efforts to reduce trade barriers within five years of the entry into force of the WTO. In the case of both services and agriculture, the outcome of negotiations was largely restricted to the creation of a framework that would allow progressive liberalization in the future. Other agreements contained review provisions. To increase the scope for beneficial tradeoffs across issues and strengthen the trading system, a number of governments (led by the EU) argued that rather than pursue only the built-in agenda, it was preferable to expand the agenda to include merchandise tariffs more generally, as well as new issues. That is, they sought to launch a full-fledged round of negotiations. The Geneva ministerial meeting of 1998 provided the mandate to undertake work to prepare for the launching of a new round at its next meeting, scheduled for the end of November 1999 in Seattle. The Seattle ministerial turned out to be a fiasco and failed to launch a new round. Domestic US politics played a key role, with a Democratic administration confronting a Presidential election unwilling to resist efforts by US labour groups to introduce labour standards into the WTO (Box 4.1). Strong differences on the scope of agricultural liberalization between the EU on the one hand and the US and other agricultural exporters on the other were also important, as was the unwillingness of many developing countries to consider accepting agenda items that were being pushed by several high-income countries—most notably labour standards.

Box 4.1. The WTO and the streets of Seattle

The protests in the streets of Seattle during the 1999 ministerial meeting involved an improbable alliance of some 30,000 union activists, environmentalists and religious groups that opposed the process of globalization and were concerned about specific dimensions of the WTO. The protesters ranted against everything from genetically modified crops and child labour to the US embargo on Cuba and the need to protect turtles. A unifying factor was distrust of the WTO system, even though most demonstrators had only a very limited knowledge of the WTO. An important push in the preparation of what some considered as the most important civil disobedience action in the US since the 1960s was given by professional activists of the Direct Action Network. Websites catalogued the official protesting organizations using encrypted email exchanges among a network of affiliated groups.

The collapse of the Seattle talks was variously blamed on the ineffective and non-transparent decision-making process ill-suited for an organization with such a large membership, the complexity of the agenda proposed for consideration, as well as inevitable differences in basic values and culture of the participants. Developing countries strongly opposed discussing trade and labour standards and thought that too little attention was given to their interests. For many of them, the failure of Seattle was a 'blessing in disguise'. For some developed country governments, the street demonstrations were seen as a reflection of the strong links that existed between trade on one hand and the environment, workers' rights and child welfare on the other. Many in the public saw it as a beginning of a new area of 'people over profits', or 'globalization with a human face'. Whatever the perception, Seattle left the WTO bruised and polarized.

Seattle was perceived by many developing countries as a rich country effort to distort the WTO agenda. In their view, NGOs and other lobby groups based in high-income nations with interests that differed substantially from those of people living in poor nations managed to hijack the meeting. Many saw Seattle as a calculated move to shelter advanced country labour-intensive industries from competition from low-income economies. The Indian mass media noted on a number of occasions that the NGOs agitators in the streets of Seattle were displaying arrogance and disdain for poor countries (Reddy, 2000).

A major contributing factor was that the meeting was badly prepared and badly managed. Efforts to whittle down proposals into a single negotiating text only started eight weeks before the Seattle meeting. The Chairman of the WTO General Council and the Director-General did not manage to get key delegations to bridge enough of their differences. Thus, the text that went to Seattle constituted a hodgepodge of issues that no-one thought was adequate for a ministerial conference (Odell, 2002). At Seattle, there was widespread dissatisfaction concerning the role of the chair of the conference (United States Trade Representative (USTR), Charlene Barshefsky), who was widely perceived to be pursuing a US agenda as opposed to making good faith efforts to attain consensus on a balanced agenda. Small countries in particular perceived themselves to be left in the cold, not having access to the negotiating fora where potential deals were being thrashed out. In the end, ministers simply ran out of time—they came close to agreeing on a negotiating agenda, but could not extend the conference because the venue had been booked for a convention of optometrists.

The Doha Round (2001–)

Several factors help to explain why, only two years after the Seattle debacle, a new round of trade negotiations could be launched. First, there was increasing convergence between many low-income country governments and numerous vocal NGOs that the WTO was not a balanced and 'fair' agreement (Panagariya, 2002). New research suggesting that the net benefits for many developing countries resulting from the Uruguay Round were limited—and could even be negative once the effects of TRIPS were considered—played a significant role in this regard (e.g. Finger and Schuler, 2000). Developing countries saw a new round of trade talks as an opportunity to make trade rules 'more fair' and rebalance the deal that had been struck in the Uruguay Round, including through an expansion of domestic 'policy space'.

Developed countries felt that provisions in the Uruguay Round agreements on agriculture and services to initiate new negotiations on these subjects in 2000 would be easier to satisfy in the context of a broader round, as this would allow for cross-issue linkages and tradeoffs. Some also saw a new round as a way to make up—at least partly—for their failure to finalize a Multilateral Agreement on Investment (MAI) in the mid-1990s and to push the frontiers of the WTO by including new disciplines on subjects such as competition policy. Last but not least, there was a strong sense among many OECD policymakers, especially in the US, that the launch of multilateral talks aimed at increasing economic opportunities in developing countries should be part of the response to the 11 September 2001 terrorist attacks on New York and Washington, DC.

The deal that was reached in Doha to launch a MTN papered over deep fault lines and differences in strategic objectives of the participating governments. The negotiating agenda included such diverse subjects as market access, improving existing WTO rules, new disciplines concerning the Singapore issues, implementation of existing agreements and a renewed emphasis on 'special and differential treatment' (SDT) for developing countries. 'Development' was made a prominent objective of the negotiations—as reflected in the formal name of the round: the Doha Development Agenda (DDA). The emphasis on 'development' was in part a reflection of the post-Uruguay Round hangover and the debacle in Seattle, but was also much influenced by the arguments and views of leaders such as Robert Zoellick (then USTR) and James Wolfensohn (then President of the World Bank) that a response to the recent terrorist attacks on the United States required a multipronged response, including greater efforts to integrate the world economy as this would help stimulate economic growth and reduce poverty. As recalled by Zedillo (2007), Zoellick launched a series of articles and speeches less than ten days after 9/11 that were part of a strategy to convince the US Congress of the need to grant Trade Promotion Authority and launch a new round of multilateral trade negotiations. Zoellick argued that:

The international market economy—of which trade and the WTO are vital parts—offers an antidote to this violent rejectionism. Trade is about more than economic efficiency; it reflects a system of values: openness, peaceful exchange, opportunity, inclusiveness and integration, mutual gains through interchange, freedom of choice, appreciation of differences, governance through agreed rules, and a hope for betterment for all peoples and lands.[1]

The effort was successful in mobilizing support for a new MTN but at the cost of what many regarded as overloaded agenda that, driven by a desire to avoid a repetition of Seattle, ended up accommodating a very wide range of preferences— and perhaps most importantly, giving the Round an objective that it was not equipped to deliver.

As in previous rounds, the main protagonists were the US and the EU among the OECD countries, and India and Brazil among developing WTO members. However, Doha differed from previous MTNs in that smaller and poorer countries were much better prepared and organized, forming a variety of coalitions both in the preparation for and during the negotiations. Influential coalitions included the so-called Like Minded Group of developing countries, the LDC group and the Africa Group, all of which pushed for greater attention to be paid to their difficulties in implementation of WTO commitments and for more SDT and nonreciprocity in negotiations. A variety of 'G-x' groups, where 'x' indicates a number of countries participating in the initial launch of the group, played key roles. The most prominent was the G20, a group of countries led by Brazil and India that also included China and South Africa. The G20 had a fluctuating

---

[1] 'The WTO and New Global Trade Negotiations: What's at Stake,' speech delivered at the Council of Foreign Relations, Washington, DC. Cited in Zedillo (2007).

membership, with some governments leaving—sometimes as the result of pressure (inducements) offered by the US (the departure of several Central American countries following the formation of the Central American Free Trade Agreement (CAFTA), being an example)—and others joining. Other groups included the G90—comprising almost the totality of developing countries in the WTO—and the G11, a group of developing countries that were active in the nonagricultural market access talks (Narlikar and Tussie, 2004).

Numerous developing country governments were not convinced that negotiations on the Singapore issues were in their interest. A last minute compromise in Doha was that negotiations on these issues would not start immediately, but would only commence after the 2003 WTO ministerial meeting in Cancun if there was an 'explicit consensus' on the modalities for such negotiations. The main *demandeurs* for negotiations on Singapore issues were the EU, Japan and Korea. Three groups of developing countries—the African Union, the LDCs and the ACP group—had all decided in 2003 not to support the launching of negotiations on any of the Singapore issues. Many of these countries argued that these would generate minor benefits at best, that they could give rise to high implementation costs and divert negotiating resources and political focus away from the market access concerns of major interest to them. Although numerous middle-income economies, including most of Latin America, did not have serious objections to launching negotiations on the Singapore subjects, it became clear at Cancun (2003) that an 'explicit consensus' could not be reached.

The Singapore issues were not the only cause of that failure. The North–South divide in the area of agriculture was deep. Developed countries' farm support policies were a major bone of contention, as was the unwillingness of the US to address demands by West African cotton producers to reduce production subsidies as a priority issue (see Chapter 6). Also important were procedural innovations that had been introduced to enhance the transparency of decision-making processes in ministerial meetings. In Cancun there was an extensive process of consultation and briefings by the Chair of the conference and the 'facilitators' he had appointed. These took up a substantial amount of time and delayed the launch of substantive negotiations on the subjects that were on the agenda—for which there consequently was less time. The Cancun endgame was also hampered by the fact that Ministers who had been appointed to coordinate the work of larger constituencies did not have a clear negotiating mandate. In turn, this reflected a failure on the part of the preparatory process to result in a common understanding of what the negotiating set was (the range of potential concessions and tradeoffs (Pedersen, 2006).

A July 2004 'Framework Agreement' retained only trade facilitation among the Singapore issues for negotiations, the other three being removed from the negotiating table. Negotiations on trade facilitation were to focus on expediting the movement, release and clearance of goods, including goods in transit, with commitments by developing countries linked to implementation capacity and the provision of trade-related technical assistance. The Framework Agreement also specified that LDCs were not expected to make any market access concessions and sketched out negotiating modalities for the key areas of market access for both agricultural and nonagricultural products. Formulas were to be used to reduce trade barriers in both areas, and export subsidies in agriculture were to be prohibited by a specific date to be agreed upon. With most Singapore issues off the table, the post-2003 Doha Round centred on tariffs to a much greater extent than did the Uruguay Round.[2] Conversely, services figured much less prominently than in the Uruguay Round, in part because of a desire by negotiators to first determine what the contours of a possible deal could be for trade in agricultural and industrial products. A major challenge was to deal with the remaining tariff peaks. As average tariff rates in most developed countries are currently low, the main payoff from both a development and an economic efficiency perspective would come from reducing the dispersion in tariff protection. That signified that the highest tariffs should be lowered more than the average. A straightforward way of doing this is to apply a nonlinear tariff reduction formula to tariff negotiations.

The Doha Round participants agreed to make tariff-cutting formulas a core negotiating modality, with eventual emergence of variants of the so-called Swiss formula—first used in the Tokyo Round (1973–9)—as the basis for negotiations. As discussed below (Section 4.4), the formula generates nonlinear cuts, with higher proportional reductions for higher tariffs. It was decided that (at least) two coefficients would be used, one for developed countries and another for developing nations, such that developed countries would reduce their tariffs proportionally more in accordance with the notion of SDT. Limited exemptions would be accepted to allow higher levels of protection for a subset of 'special' and 'sensitive' products. Given that the major developing country negotiating groups spanned a differentiated set of economies, insistence on undifferentiated SDT for all participants made it harder to agree on a coefficient, and focused attention on defining criteria for exempting products from the formula.

Divergence of views on the specification of the formulas and the magnitude of allowable exceptions could not be sufficiently narrowed during 2004–8. At the time of writing (May 2009) the prospects for an imminent conclusion of the Doha Round appear dim, after yet another mini-Ministerial meeting held in late July 2008 ended in failure to agree on the contours of a deal and the decision by the Director-General of the WTO in December 2009 not to call for a WTO ministerial meeting— reflecting his assessment that the political will to make the necessary compromises was lacking. One reason for the lack of enthusiasm to negotiate was the June 2007 expiry of US Trade Promotion Authority—a provision previously called 'Fast Track'

---

[2] Although competition, investment and procurement were taken off the Doha agenda, these subjects continued to be pursued by the EU and US in PTAs with developing countries.

that precludes the US Congress from introducing amendments to a multilaterally negotiated deal. This removed an important focal point for a timely conclusion of the talks. The political calendar of a number of major players implied that Doha was unlikely to conclude before 2010. Elections in the US and India in 2008 and 2009, respectively, meant that these countries were not able to fully engage in negotiations.

Despite the torturous negotiations, the Doha Round was able to address several development-related issues that had become prominent during the first years following the creation of the WTO. Thus, in a Declaration on the TRIPS Agreement and Public Health, developing countries without the capacity to produce pharmaceuticals were permitted to import generics from countries that do have capacity under compulsory licensing arrangements (Chapter 8). A consensus also emerged around the notion that trade negotiations should be complemented by assistance for developing countries, both to deal with implementation costs associated with specific WTO rules, and, more generally, to bolster the competitiveness of domestic firms through actions to reduce the costs of trade and doing business (Chapter 12). Insofar as the Doha Round will lead development agencies to focus more on the trade agenda and trade constraints in developing countries this should be counted as a positive result.

A number of factors help to understand the slow pace of the Doha Round. First of all, the changing nature of the 'power balance' in the WTO: many developing countries had become bigger traders and their weight in the organization had been increasing steadily, especially with the accession of China in 2001. The major developing countries were not prepared to accept a deal that would not result in deep reforms in agricultural policies of the EU, Japan and the US, and many smaller developing nations were concerned that they would suffer losses from the erosion of trade preferences following trade liberalization initiated by larger WTO members. Second, the Doha Round coincided with a boom in international trade, partly driven by trade liberalization undertaken unilaterally by many countries, including the major emerging markets. In general, traders may have perceived the probability of governments increasing tariffs to be low—in turn implying that there was little value in governments agreeing to lower their average tariff bindings. Research suggests that the uniform tariff equivalent of applied tariffs for industrial products in 2006 was less than 5 per cent in high-income countries and about 10–15 per cent in developing economies (Kee, Nicita and Olarreaga, 2008). The relatively low levels of applied tariffs in many countries signify that there is less to play for. This translates into fewer export interests having an incentive to invest (political) resources in engaging in trade talks and providing the political support that is needed for their own liberalization. As most protection is now concentrated in farming, matters are complicated further by the fact that this sector is of significant export interest to only a subset of WTO members. Less than 10 per cent of world trade is in agricultural products. Trade volumes would be higher if rates of protection were lowered; however, it is trade in other merchandise that dominates, and much of this trade is relatively free of barriers to trade.

As multilateral trade negotiations are barter exchanges (Section 4.2), concessions in agriculture by OECD countries need to be balanced by concessions on the part of the agricultural exporting nations that will benefit in mercantilist, export volume terms. Although average levels of protection have fallen in these economies, there are still significant barriers to trade. The low prevailing averages mask relatively high tariff peaks in many countries. In services, despite significant liberalization of trade and investment in recent years, numerous barriers also persist. Finally, it is important to remember that the bargaining coin of the WTO is policy bindings—the levels of protection that a government commits itself not to exceed. These bindings are valuable even if a specific commitment does not imply much, if any, reduction in applied levels of protection, as they create greater certainty that past liberalization will not be easily reversed.

Consequently, even with the narrow market access (tariff) agenda that dominated the Doha Round after 2004, a deal should have been feasible, with 'payment' for OECD agricultural liberalization taking the form of traditional market access liberalization by major developing countries. In practice, however, neither side was willing to offer enough in terms of liberalization and bindings to induce the other to move enough to allow a deal to be struck. This in turn suggests that the major players—and the trade constituencies that drive the political trade policy formation process—perceived their best alternative to a negotiated agreement to dominate an outcome under which they would have had to make additional concessions in order to get more liberalization from their major partners. An alternative perspective would stress that the greater participation and mobilization of developing countries precluded what in their eyes would be an unbalanced deal.

Getting to yes was made even more difficult as world food prices began to rise rapidly in 2007–8, caused in part by steep increases in the price of oil that induced farmers in the EU and the US to allocate more output to the production of bio-fuels, and a number of major suppliers of food staples and inputs such as fertilizer sought to limit domestic price increases through the use of export restrictions. This behaviour bolstered the arguments of those opposing freeing trade in agricultural products and the view that countries need to be able to use trade policies to increase incentives for their farmers to produce agricultural commodities in times when world prices are low. The presumption that it makes economic sense to specialize according to comparative advantage—and thus to allow agriculture to shrink if other countries are more efficient producers—is conditional on world markets clearing without government intervention in times of both shortage and times of plenty. If countries cannot buy at any price, or the world market for a commodity is very thin (e.g., rice), it may make sense to 'self-insure' by encouraging domestic production.

Although prospects for a rapid conclusion of the Doha round remain cloudy, the global recession that hit the world economy in 2008–9 may, perhaps counterintuitively, bolster the probability of a successful conclusion of the round in 2010. The 2008 financial crisis and the global downturn that it led to gave rise to a variety of policy responses by governments in both industrialized and developing countries.

Countries that had the capacity to do pursued monetary easing and implemented fiscal stimulus policies. This helped to lower interest rates and provided support for demand for goods and services. Notwithstanding the rapid policy responses, the credit crunch and desire (need) on the part of households and banks to rebuild balance sheets led to a major contraction in overall demand and thus aggregate demand (income). Reductions in GDP had a multiplier effect on trade: for every percentage point fall in income, trade dropped by four percentage points. This high elasticity between changes in income and trade is a reflection of the process of vertical specialization and fragmentation discussed in Chapter 1.

Some countries responded to the decline in economic activity in 2008–9 with measures to restrict imports and/or to promote exports. There was a market rise in the use of antidumping by some countries—such as Argentina and India (see Chapter 9)—and some countries that had the 'policy space' to do so, raised applied tariffs. Others resorted to greater use of nontariff measures such as licensing. A noteworthy feature of the trade policy responses to the financial crisis was that countries that were not WTO members were among those that increased protection the most (e.g., Russia, the Ukraine). Most WTO members took measures that conformed with the letter of WTO law and national commitments, if not the spirit. This was reflected in actions by several WTO members to limit expenditures financed under fiscal stimulus packages to domestically produced goods and services (e.g., Australia, China, the US); the resumption of export subsidies for dairy products by the EU (followed by the US several weeks later); and the increase in contingent protection. Raising tariffs within ceiling bindings was of course also permitted under WTO rules.

These developments illustrated the value of WTO disciplines, both the national treatment rule—which most countries appeared to comply with—and the specific tariff and other commitments of WTO members. The behaviour of WTO members demonstrated that rules and specific commitments matter. Many had argued that the proposed Doha modalities and exceptions implied the round was not worth much—as applied levels of protection would not drop enough. This ignores the value of constraining the ability of governments to re-impose protection. The trade-related policy responses to the crisis by governments made clear that looking at MTNs through the lens of reductions in applied levels of protection is too narrow a view.

4.2. MULTILATERAL TRADE LIBERALIZATION

As discussed in Chapter 1, an important rationale for small economies to engage in reciprocal, multilateral negotiations to liberalize trade (access to markets) is political. It allows governments to offset opposition to liberalization on the part of import-competing industries by mobilizing political support by export interests through the prospect of greater access to foreign markets. It also allows large countries, which in principle can affect their terms of trade (the prices they get or pay for their exports or imports respectively) and thus may benefit from trade barriers to reach higher levels of real income (welfare) by agreeing to mutual disarmament. In the terminology of game theory, large countries are often trapped in an inefficient, noncooperative equilibrium, whereas small ones may be the hostages of vested interest groups.

Multilateral trade negotiations can usefully be viewed and analysed with the help of game theory and game-theoretic concepts. Game theory is the branch of mathematics that analyses situations where actions by agents (players) are interdependent. Outcomes depend on how the game (the interaction) is structured (the rules of the game), the information available to the players, and the way that players form expectations about the actions of other players. There are two basic types of games, cooperative and noncooperative. The first type assumes that outcomes of games are efficient in the sense that gains from trade are maximized, and what is at issue is the distribution of the possible gains across players. Cooperative games assume that a binding enforcement mechanism exists and that defection by players from the cooperative solution can be observed by other players. Noncooperative games emerge in settings where there is no central enforcement mechanism and where there is no presumption that outcomes will be Pareto-optimal. A Pareto-optimal situation is one where no party can be made better off without another party being made worse off. The fact that trade policymakers are driven as much by (internal) political as economic concerns affects their choice criteria and thus decision outcomes. From an internal political perspective, a Pareto-optimal outcome is one where no party can be made better off without another party knowing that it is being made worse off. Information is important, therefore, in ensuring that political and economic notions of optimality do not diverge too much.

A MTN is an effort to set the rules of the noncooperative international trade game. Countries get together and seek to agree on the type of game they will play in the future. While MTNs are attempts to coordinate, the outcome of negotiations will rarely be Pareto-optimal. Perhaps the most appropriate way of looking at MTNs is to regard them as institution-setting exercises. Various situations can be identified that may give rise to the creation of institutions. One very well-known case is the Prisoners' Dilemma, where players choosing individually rational strategies end up in an equilibrium that is not efficient (Box 4.2).

While a convenient illustration, the Prisoners' Dilemma is a very special and narrow game, in that there is only a single outcome that makes both players better off, and there are only two players. For practical situations of trade negotiations, there are usually many possible outcomes that make all countries better off and are Pareto-superior to the status quo. If players interact over time and are able to communicate

Box 4.2. The Prisoners' Dilemma in trade policy

The Prisoners' Dilemma is illustrated in the payoff matrix below. The equilibrium outcome of the game has both countries imposing trade restrictions (not cooperating), each obtaining a payoff of zero. It is inferior to the Pareto-optimal free trade solution, where each party obtains a payoff of $P - c > 0$, where P is the benefit of obtaining access to the partner country's market, c are the net costs of opening up its own market, and $P > c$. Such costs consist of political variables, augmented by the possible decline in the terms of trade for certain products.* Noncooperation occurs because it is in each country's interest to impose protection, independent of what the other country does. Whatever policy stance is taken by country B, country A will maximize its payoff by choosing a protectionist stance, and vice versa for country B. For example, if B chooses free trade, A's payoff is highest under protection, as $P > P - c$. If B chooses protection, A again will prefer protection, as $-c < 0$. As each country has the same incentive structure, they end up in the noncooperative, inefficient outcome where each earns a payoff of zero. If the countries cooperated and both implemented free trade, they would each obtain $P - c > 0$. In instances such as these, where individually rational behaviour by governments is not efficient, the creation of an institution can help solve the dilemma by fostering cooperation.

		Country B	
		Free Trade	Protection
Country A			
	Protection	$P - c, P - c$	$-c, P$
	Free trade	$P, -c$	$0, 0$

Note: *$P > c > 0$. This specific formulation of the dilemma is drawn from Garrett (1992). Technically, the outcome resulting from noncooperative behaviour is often assumed to be a Nash equilibrium, under which each nation acts to maximize its objectives taking as given the actions of all other nations. The Prisoners' Dilemma is an example of such a situation.

and make credible commitments, the cooperation problem noted above can be regarded as a subset of a more general class of bargaining situations. In the latter, even if countries at any point in time cannot improve upon their joint welfare, there may be possibilities to achieve outcomes that are superior to these equilibria if countries are willing and able to trade across issues—that is, expand the agenda. Conversely, there may be situations where cooperation is not necessary because individually rational strategies lead to a Pareto-optimal outcome. This is the case, for example, in a world where countries cannot affect their terms of trade, markets are perfectly competitive, there are no distortions or rent-seeking interest groups, and governments believe in laissez-faire. In principle no cooperation problem then exists as the government has no incentive to diverge from free trade. Alternatively, and more realistically, a dominant country (a hegemon) may exist that enforces cooperation. Conybeare (1987) discusses these and alternative possibilities in greater depth.

In practice, of course, there are rent-seeking groups in each country, governments do not believe in laissez-faire, and markets are imperfect. In pursuing national objectives, a country may reduce the welfare of other countries by imposing a negative externality on them. An externality arises when a government does not take into account the impact of its actions on other countries, be they good or bad. The economic literature on externalities has focused on two ways to address the problem. One calls for a central authority to impose targeted taxes or subsidies that result in internalization of the externalities. The other postulates that agents will attempt to bargain their way to a Pareto-optimal situation. The first approach is not very relevant in an international context, as no supranational entity exists that has the power to levy the required taxes (assuming these can be calculated in the first place). At the heart of the second approach lies the so-called Coase theorem (named after Ronald Coase, a Nobel Prize winner in economics): given the existence of enforceable property rights and in the absence of transaction costs, externalities will be bargained away such that a Pareto-optimal outcome results. That is, the market—bargaining—will ensure efficiency. In general, for bargaining over rules of behaviour to be possible, it is necessary that players expect to interact with each other over an indefinite time horizon. This creates incentives to cooperate because agreements can be enforced through the threat of retaliation.

The Coase theorem assumes agents have perfect information regarding the economic setting in which they operate and that they can interact costlessly. This includes information on their own and on other parties' utility functions (preferences) and cost functions. In practice these assumptions often will be violated. Thus, usually there can be no certainty that a specific bargaining procedure will lead to an efficient outcome. Bargaining can only solve an externality problem if the external effects are the only cause of market failure, and this is not the case if there is imperfect information. However, if institutions exist that allow competitive bidding for property rights, an efficient reallocation of such rights may be achieved in a world of incomplete information (Samuelson, 1985).

In international affairs, reallocation of, or bidding for, property rights may not appear to be very practical at first glance. Nevertheless, property rights do exist, implicitly defined by rules of sovereignty. That is, nation-states that create externalities implicitly have the right to impose them. The existence of these rights allows negotiations to take place, while the (mutual) negative spillovers created by national trade policies are the inducement for countries to pursue them. Because countries interact continuously, agreements are in principle enforceable as long as defectors can be identified and singled out for retaliation. The WTO puts great emphasis on transparency of procedure and mutual surveillance, which facilitates the identification of violators. Subject to certain conditions, affected countries have the right to retaliate if no or inadequate compensation is offered by the nation violating its WTO obligations (see Chapter 3).

To a large extent MTNs comprise barter, that is, trades occur in a setting where there is no generally accepted medium of exchange (money). Barter is possible when there are (enforced) property rights, marginal valuations of goods differ, and potential transactors can meet each other. Any introductory textbook of economics will explain that barter is inefficient, and that this is one of the historical reasons for the creation of money as a medium of exchange. However, in international relations there is no money and nations are stuck with barter. Three kinds of inefficiencies may arise:

(1) the market (total supply) may not offer any goods a trader is interested in obtaining;
(2) a trader who has something another wants has no interest in what the other has to offer, but is interested in the goods of a third party; and
(3) it may not be possible to equate the trader's marginal valuations of goods.

If the first possibility occurs, trade will not be possible and the status quo will be maintained. If the second possibility occurs, trade will only be feasible if a set of potential trades exists such that all members have something that another wants. In this context, economists sometimes speak of barter's need for a double coincidence of wants. Even if this condition is met, trade will only occur if marginal valuations can be (approximately) equated. This is the third potential problem mentioned above. Trade may not take place, for example, because goods are indivisible.

All these problems affect MTNs—the marketplace where potential traders meet. To ensure that they do not come for nothing (that is, that there is something to trade), a great deal of care is taken to establish an agenda beforehand. This agenda will have some items of interest for all the parties willing to trade. Prior to a MTN, national authorities, industries and bureaucracies will be engaged in a domestic negotiation to determine interests, priorities and possible tradeoffs. It is this work by potential participants that leads eventually to the establishment of the agenda of the MTN.

Establishing the agenda of a MTN is a negotiation in itself. Prior to the launching of the Uruguay Round it took a failed ministerial meeting (in 1982) and five years of work in a GATT Senior Officials Group and elsewhere to prepare the agenda that was eventually mostly embodied in the 1986 Punta del Este Declaration. The problem of defining an agenda also dominated several WTO ministerial conferences. At the 1996 Singapore ministerial conference a number of industrialized nations pushed for the inclusion of workers' rights (labour standards), environmental norms, foreign investment policies and competition law as topics to be put on the WTO work programme. Many developing WTO members vehemently opposed mixing trade policy discussions with issues of labour standards and in the event it was decided that workers' rights was a topic for the ILO, not the WTO.

These issues returned to the fore at the second WTO ministerial meeting (held in Geneva in 1998), which were accompanied by street protests and small-scale riots as various NGOs expressed their displeasure over a perceived lack of legitimacy of, and access to, the institution. Both the Singapore and Geneva meetings were not intended to launch MTNs, but were events that could eventually lead to defining a negotiating agenda. They illustrate the pre-negotiation-type of manoeuvring that eventually helps to define a negotiating agenda. The third WTO ministerial meeting, held in Seattle in late 1999, was formally aimed at launching a new MTN, but it proved impossible to converge and delegates went home frustrated. As discussed above, the debate over Singapore issues re-emerged in subsequent ministerial conferences in Doha and Cancun, with only the issue of trade facilitation accepted for inclusion on the agenda of the Doha Round.

For analytical purposes any trade negotiation can be decomposed into four stages: catalyst, pre-negotiation, negotiation and post-negotiation (Leidy and Hoekman, 1993). In the catalyst stage there is a 'visionary'. This could be an interest group or a government. The implied policy vision is the catalyst, defining in broad terms the issues to be negotiated. In the pre-negotiation phase, informal discussions (negotiations) take place on the possible agenda for the formal negotiations. The agenda constrains the parameters of the formal negotiation that will follow. In the negotiation stage, formal government-to-government bargaining takes place, with interest-group participation. Subject to the implicit parameters established by the agenda, interests groups lobby negotiators, and preferences for policy packages change. Ultimately, depending on bargaining strategies, tactics and time constraints, a formal draft of an agreement may emerge. The final stage of a MTN is the post-negotiation, implementation stage, which determines how the agreements are embodied in a country's laws and procedures and enforced by its administration, judiciary and legislature. There will frequently be an imperfect correspondence between what was negotiated and what is implemented, making it very important how effective surveillance and dispute-settlement procedures are, and how precisely worded the formal agreement is.

It is often assumed in theoretical treatments of negotiations that countries are unitary actors that seek to maximize national welfare. This is rarely the case. Governments that participate in trade negotiations presumably recognize the potential welfare improvements that can be realized by mutual disarmament, that is, liberalization. But governments are subject to lobbying by import-competing interests, as well as other groups that may favour or oppose liberalization. Even governments that seek to maximize national income must take into account political realities that constrain what is feasible. Political constraints arising from interest group interactions play a role both in terms of setting the agenda for negotiations and during the negotiations themselves. The lobbying pressure that may be exerted for and against trade agreements can be—and sometimes must be—substantial (Box 4.3). This lobbying is not just restricted to domestic interest groups—foreign

Box 4.3. Lobbying for NAFTA

One of the more impressive lobbying campaigns seen in Washington, DC, during the 1990s was directed at obtaining congressional approval of the North American Free Trade Agreement (NAFTA). The Mexican authorities strongly supported the NAFTA deal and adopted a proactive strategy to promote the agreement among the members of the US Congress and the American public at large. The high-level group of lobbyists running the campaign included lawyers, trade policy consultants and communication specialists. The public relations team included former high-ranking US government officials and politicians. To generate public support for NAFTA, a number of public relations firms were retained to develop brochures identifying the advantages of the arrangement, organize a pro-NAFTA publicity campaign, produce a TV series, monitor and react to media coverage, and assist Mexican officials in organizing lecture tours in support of the NAFTA agreement. Numerous congressional lobbyists worked on Capitol Hill to ensure congressional support for NAFTA. Many congressmen and their staff were invited to visit Mexico during the campaign. Moreover, a number of large US enterprises, the US Chamber of Commerce and the National Association of Manufacturers grouped together under the umbrella of 'USA–NAFTA' to actively support Congressional ratification.

Opponents did the same. A coalition of NGOs and labour unions opposed NAFTA. Although these groups shaped the formal outcome—e.g. causing the inclusion of specific side agreements on labour and environmental policies—they did not manage to block NAFTA. Without the strong pro-NAFTA lobbying effort there might not have been an agreement.

Lobbying is not simply a one-way private sector exercise. In the US the most important lobbyist of congress is the President. The campaign for NAFTA ultimately was successful because of active engagement by the Clinton White House in the endgame, with the President personally speaking to key legislators. More generally, the politicians and bureaucracy design the specific proposal that helps determine who will be for and against. This explains why two side agreements (on labour and environment) were concluded: they were necessary to win over Democratic critics in congress.

lobbies can also be influential. For example, Gawande, Krishna and Robbins (2004) find that controlling for other determinants of policy, foreign lobbying in the US has an impact on policy, resulting in lower tariffs and NTBs.

Theoretical analyses also tend to pay insufficient attention to features of negotiations that can have major implications for the outcomes and the strategies that are pursued by participants. As stressed by Odell (2002, 2006), a bounded rationality framework is needed to understand trade negotiations, in which it is recognized that negotiators have incomplete information, as well as values, biases and memories of what happened in the last MTN. These play an important role in negotiations, and negotiation analysis therefore needs to consider the fog of initial partisan biases, distrust and incomplete information that makes agreement more difficult to reach.

Issue linkage and the expanding ambit of the WTO

The agenda that is established will determine a set of possible policy packages that could emerge as outcomes or solutions to the negotiation. Not all of the possible packages will be feasible. A necessary condition for the adoption of a package by all participants is that it improves on the status quo ante, or on whatever is expected to be the status quo if negotiations fail (the so-called threat or no agreement point, also called the best alternative to no agreement—the BATNA). Referring to Figure 4.1, the status quo is represented by point X_A. Assume for simplicity there are two parties to the negotiation, and that the vertical and horizontal axes measure the objective function (outcomes) for the governments (abstracting from lobbying for the moment). All possible outcomes that lie to the left or below the dotted lines radiating out from the threat point are not feasible, as they imply less than the status quo for at least one party. Any negotiated outcome within the area spanned by the dashed lines through X_A is a Pareto improvement—both governments gain.

In the figure, there are many possible positive Pareto-improving outcomes. Some policy packages are clearly better for both parties than others. Thus, those packages that form the frontier (x_2 to x_5) dominate all the others for at least one party. The points on the frontier are all Pareto-optimal: if any one of these points is chosen, there are no other packages that make both parties better off. The more possible outcomes there are, the more continuous the frontier will be. In the limit, if what is on the table is perfectly divisible (such as a tariff), the negotiation frontier is a line with an infinite number of Pareto-optimal outcomes. In the more realistic case of a multi-issue

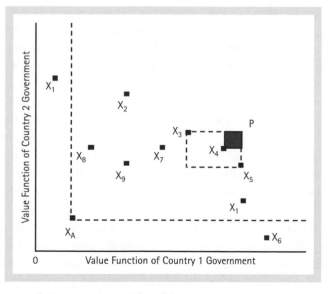

Fig. 4.1. The negotiation space and feasible outcomes

negotiation with many nontariff policies, there will be a large number of feasible policy packages, but moving along the frontier will imply discontinuous jumps from one Pareto-optimal point to another. The location of these various policy packages may change over time, as the result of lobbying pressure, learning and linkage strategies.

The shape of the frontier is not constant. Lobbying pressure affects the effective preferences that ultimately drive negotiations. In the absence of lobbying activity— that is, in the absence of political constraints in a certain area—most governments' notional preferences can be assumed to represent the social welfare. Lobbies, however, will generally inform negotiators of the implied political costs and payoffs of taking certain positions. Once the government has determined the relative political importance of the groups involved, the options available to satisfy their desires, and the costs of these options, the government's effective preferences may well differ from its initial (unlobbied) preferences. As a result the set of feasible policy packages may shrink.

Trades in a MTN occur both within and across issues. Intra-issue trade is exemplified by tariff negotiations. Countries make bids and offers on the level of specific tariffs, or the average tariff level. In principle, if there are enough issues, cross-issue trade may allow agreement if within-issue trade proves insufficient to generate an improvement on the status quo for all concerned. For example, agreement on a definition of subsidies could be made contingent on agreement that stricter rules be imposed on emergency protection against imports. Linkages play a fundamental role in fostering agreement because they allow side-payments to be made.

In terms of achieving an agreement, issue linkage can play two roles in MTNs (Hoekman, 1989). First, it can be used to achieve reciprocity. That is, it allows a distribution constraint to be met: a balance of benefits and concessions. Linkage is actively used in MTNs to achieve reciprocity. Second, linkage may be used to increase potential gains from trade. In this case linkage is an instrument that allows a more efficient outcome to be attained. As noted earlier, MTNs deal with bargaining problems, that is, the issue is to choose a Pareto-optimal outcome out of a set of many possible such outcomes. Agreement may not occur for procedural reasons, or it may be the case that no better solution exists. Sometimes, this may be the result of not being able to link issues, or of attempting to link the wrong issues. For example, powerful nations may attempt to impose linkages on weaker ones. In this case mutual gain is clearly not the objective. Often, such strategies may be counterproductive, especially if attempted by nations that are open to retaliation.

The problem facing negotiators is generally twofold: when and what to link. The need for linkage depends on whether there are sufficient mutual gains to be achieved by cooperating within a given issue area, and whether these gains are distributed relatively symmetrically. If gains are too small, or are distributed too asymmetrically, cross-issue linkage quickly becomes necessary. The need to redefine issues and propose linkages

Box 4.4. Integrative versus distributive bargaining and the WTO

The nature of negotiations in the WTO system varies depending on the issues involved and the countries concerned. Negotiation theory makes a useful distinction between distributive bargaining ('win–lose' or zero-sum games) and integrative bargaining ('win–win' or positive-sum games). Parties engaged in distributive bargaining usually determine their respective target points (desired outcomes) and resistance or threat points (the minimal acceptable outcome). The latter determines when to 'walk away' or to reject the offer. For an agreement to occur there must be a positive settlement range—a set of target points such that the parties can attain a settlement that exceeds the resistance points (Raiffa, 1983). A bargainer must determine an opponent's resistance points through questioning or other tactics. During the negotiation process, participants are likely to modify their perception of how realistic their target points are. A good example of a purely distributive bargaining game in the GATT setting was the negotiation between GATT contracting parties and Switzerland that took place in the mid-1990s regarding the magnitude of the subsidy that Switzerland would grant to keep the organization in Geneva. There was a competing offer from Germany to host the organization in Bonn, where the move of many government departments to Berlin had led to a large amount of suitable vacant office space and meeting room facilities, which allowed the bargaining to occur.

The WTO negotiations are a mix of distributive and integrative bargaining (Odell, 2007). The end result (if successful) is generally integrative (positive sum) in that everyone gains—otherwise they would not agree. Uncertainty or lack of information combined with the large asymmetry in 'power' between WTO members can, however, result in the outcome of a MTN not being in the interest of a particular country. This is sometimes alleged to have been the case as a result of the inclusion of TRIPs in the Uruguay Round (see Chapter 8). But the single undertaking and consensus rules in principle provide mechanisms to reduce the probability of this arising.

Although the final result is integrative (joint gain), in the process of getting to that outcome there is generally a lot of distributive behaviour and tactics: actions by one party to claim value from another or to defend against such claiming. This can take place even when the parties are haggling over the division of the gains from a deal that will benefit all to some degree. The approach of the Like-Minded Group at the Doha ministerial meeting in 2001 is an example of distributive bargaining, as was the strategy of the Cairns Group (Narlikar and Odell, 2006). The former sought to make the launch of a MTN conditional on first addressing implementation concerns of developing countries (see Chapter 12); the latter sought to define the ultimate outcome of the agricultural negotiations before the talks commenced. Odell (2009) compares the Seattle and Doha meetings and gives numerous examples of distributive moves by different parties. Any ministerial stalemates will be characterized by extensive distributive behaviour—with members delaying concessions, arguing the terms of a deal are too skewed for them to accept, that developing countries are not conceding enough market access and by doing so are shooting themselves in the foot, implicitly threatening to do business outside the WTO, etc. These are all attempts to move the agreement point more in their own direction at the expense of others.

explains why MTNs usually require more creativity than simple distributive ('win-lose') bargaining of the type that arises between a buyer and a seller of a car (Box 4.4).

The Uruguay Round agreements on TRIPS, agriculture or textiles would have been considerably different—perhaps nonexistent—if no cross-issue linkages had been made. The question of what to link is equivalent to the question of what to trade and can be answered using the basic microeconomic theory of exchange. The necessary conditions for fruitful issue linkage are that marginal valuations of different agenda items differ across nations, and proposed linkages (trades) result in outcomes that make all parties better off than the status quo ante. For linkage to be feasible, parties must agree on the nature of the set of Pareto-optimal outcomes. The less information parties have about the policies being negotiated, the fuzzier the Pareto-optimal set will be (Tollison and Willett, 1979). The same applies if there is disagreement among the parties regarding the effect of alternative proposals. In general, linkage offers will be determined on a political level based on various criteria: nations will attempt to offer concessions on those subjects they care least about in return for gains on those they care most about. How much a government cares about a subject is likely to be as much a function of the strength of different domestic interest groups as of the relative costs and benefits to the nation as a whole. As producer groups tend to have more concentrated interests than consumers—who are affected by everything on the table—the former tend to be much better informed than the latter (Downs, 1954). This is one of the factors skewing the outcome of negotiations.

Issue linkages can be thought of as replacing any two possible policy packages with one that represents a weighted average of the elements of the two. Lobbying efforts might be directed toward achieving linkage for several reasons. As noted earlier, linkage can create a region of mutual advantage where previously none existed, or can expand the set of mutually beneficial agreements. Consider, for example, the set of possible policy packages $\{x_1, \ldots, x_{10}\}$ displayed in Figure 4.1, and assume that the initial placement of these points corresponds to the unlobbied preferences of negotiators. Assume further that x_4 is now the status quo point.

In this case there is no room for agreement without issue linkage. Issue linkage serves to produce a new possible policy package whose value to negotiators, *ceteris paribus*, must fall strictly within the dashed box connecting the linked policy packages. If, for example, proposals x_3 and x_5 were linked, the linked package might fall within the shaded region in Figure 4.1. If so, the issue linkage makes agreement possible. Although such linkage might be pursued directly by unlobbied governments, interest groups may also pursue issue linkage strategically to move a favoured set of policies to the negotiation frontier. Alternatively, they might seek to block consideration of unfavoured policies. Strong supporters of the status quo might even find it efficient to pursue linkage strategies to empty the effective negotiation set, that is, let negotiations break down.

Historically, GATT contracting parties tended to constrain themselves to trade-offs within subject areas, due to their practice of establishing separate negotiating groups for each issue. In the Doha Round, eight negotiating groups were established in 2002 to work on the main agenda items: agriculture, trade and development, nonagricultural market access, WTO rules, services, dispute settlement, intellectual property rights, and trade and environment. Attempts to link across issues generally are made at the beginning and at the end of a MTN. In the initial, pre-negotiation phase of a MTN, cross-issue tradeoffs occur so as to achieve a balanced negotiating agenda (Winham, 1986). It is only in the final stage of a MTN that positions on issues are completely mapped out and the need for linkage in terms of achieving overall agreement becomes clear. Such tradeoffs tend to be made at a high political level under substantial time pressure. The modus operandi of the Uruguay Round in this connection was the rule that nothing is agreed upon until everything is agreed upon. The same was true in the Doha Round.

As was mentioned in Chapter 2, the chairpersons of WTO negotiating groups play an important role in helping negotiators define potential packages and compromises, as well as to clarify the national interests of the parties involved and identify potential solutions that promote either agreement or modification of its terms (Odell, 2005).

Coalition formation and the nondiscrimination rule

The type of agreement that is likely to emerge from attempts by a group of nations to cooperate will be a function of the number of countries involved, the number of issues and the extent to which nonparticipants can be excluded from the benefits of an agreement. Intuitively, the feasibility of achieving agreement among a given group of nations in part will be a function of their identity. This, for example, is likely to influence the choice of agenda and may determine the set of feasible issue linkages. Not only the identity of nations, but also the absolute number of participants may be important. Generally, as the number of participants goes up, so will transaction costs. Thus, there will also be a tradeoff between the number and types of players and the possibility of achieving comprehensive agreement. The problem then is determining the optimal choice of issues relative to parties in a negotiation. This by no means trivial problem is made even more difficult once the possibilities for coalition formation are taken into account.

The formation of coalitions or clubs of like-minded countries is a possible way to circumvent free-rider problems and increase negotiating leverage. Limiting the number of parties in a negotiation can also be efficient in terms of generating agreement because of reduced transaction costs. This is not necessarily an argument for excluding nonparticipants from the benefits of an agreement. The primary rationale for exclusion is that it can act as an incentive mechanism to induce participation in the MTN. But the benefits of the WTO have the characteristics of a public good: adding members to the club does not detract from the benefits accruing to existing members. Indeed, the contrary is more likely—implying that efficiency is maximized if all nations are included. Frequently, differences in opinion are deep enough to prohibit consensus from emerging. If it is difficult for those in favour of a proposal to internalize the benefits of implementing it (limit free riding by those not in favour), the MFN rule may lead to a breakdown of the discussions. However, if the benefits resulting from an agreement between a group of like-minded countries are so large that free riding by others is not a constraint, the countries involved may agree to form a club. An important example of such 'privileged groups' (Olson, 1965) were the codes negotiated between a subset of GATT contracting parties during the Tokyo Round. In most instances the signatories applied them on a MFN basis.

Countries that are like-minded on an issue may also form coalitions so as to maximize their joint bargaining power. Among the various types of coalitions that may arise in the context of a MTN, one can distinguish between agenda moving, proposal making, blocking and negotiating coalitions (Hamilton and Whalley, 1989). The first three of these are the most common in MTNs, as they require only a limited amount of coordination between coalition members because there is no need to arrive at a common position. In the Uruguay Round, the Cairns group—a coalition of 14 agricultural exporters—was an example of a proposal-making coalition that became a blocking coalition at the 1990 Brussels ministerial meeting (see Chapter 6). Brazil, a Cairns member, took the initiative in August 2003 to form a new Group of 20, limited to developing countries and including China and India.

The G20's immediate aim was to block a joint proposal on agriculture by the EU and US at the Cancun ministerial meeting, which it was successful in doing. Major developing countries often acted as an agenda-moving coalition as regards TRIPS, services and Trade-Related Investment Measures (TRIMs) in the Uruguay Round. African countries provide an example of a blocking coalition during the Seattle ministerial meeting. Being excluded from most Green Room negotiations, African countries issued a public statement to the effect that they would not adopt the proposed final ministerial declaration. In the Doha Round a large coalition of 90 developing countries (the 'G90') successfully blocked the effort by proponents to launch negotiations on three of the four Singapore issues. Negotiating coalitions hammer out a common position and thereafter speak with one voice. The major example of such a coalition is the EU. On specific issues, even large groups of developing countries may be able to act to defend their views. An example is a coalition representing some 110 members ('G110') who jointly insisted on the adoption of a specific date for ending farm export subsidies at the December 2005 ministerial in Hong Kong (Odell, 2007).

Coalition formation is a relevant strategy for both small and large countries. For the latter, the main incentive is likely to be a reduction in transactions costs, and perhaps concern over free riding in certain instances. For small countries the primary attraction is likely to be the potential increase in negotiating power and increased 'visibility'. As in the case of issue linkage, coalition formation in MTNs can also be used by lobbies in an attempt to shift the location of policy packages in the preference ordering of their governments. Returning to Figure 4.1, consider an interest group in Country 2 for whom the policy package x_5 is the worst possible outcome. Assume that Country 2 is the EU, Country 1 is the US, the lobby is the EU film industry and x_5 implies far-reaching liberalization that will greatly benefit the US industry. The EU film industry can attempt to remove x_5 from the feasible set in several ways. First, it can lobby for the status quo at home. A small increase in the value of the status quo to its negotiators is sufficient to eliminate x_5 from the effective feasible set. Alternatively, if x_{10} does not contain the offensive provision on film market liberalization, and is thus ranked higher from the EU film lobby's perspective, it could throw its weight behind domestic and foreign groups supporting package x_{10}. If successful, as reflected in a move of x_{10} to the northwest, it may remove x_5 from consideration. Finally, the industry can also attempt to produce a vertical drop in the valuation of x_5 by its government by directly lobbying against it.

4.3. INTEREST GROUPS AND LOBBYING ACTIVITY

The forgoing conceptual discussion of the incentives and effects of interest group lobbying helps us to understand why negotiations often end up with agreements that are complex and difficult to comprehend for an outsider. Often, the details of the disciplines that are negotiated are incomprehensible without an understanding of the forces that brought an issue to the table. Essentially, all trade negotiations are multilevel, involving both domestic bargaining among interest groups, and negotiations between governments that represent these national interests. In the international relations literature this dimension of international negotiation has been described as a 'two-level' game (Putnam, 1988). In the case of the EU the game is at least three-level, as there are national groups, the EU member states, the European Commission and the WTO level where the EU seeks to speak with one voice.

Industry associations and large enterprises have a strong interest in taking a proactive stand at both the national and the international level. As firms do not have direct access to the WTO (except through amicus briefs in the case of disputes), they must exercise influence through their governments. Business interests play a major role in the design and enforcement of trade rules (Box 4.5). Financial institutions such as American Express, Citibank and American Insurance Group played a very active role in the Uruguay Round and in the horse trading that occurred during the 1997 negotiations on financial services (Chapter 7). In the

---

Box 4.5. Interest groups and the WTO Bananas case

Lobbying activity played both a major role in the design and evolution of the EU bananas regime—which was aimed at giving ex-European colonies (ACP countries) preferential access to the EU market—as well as in the numerous disputes that were brought to the GATT and the WTO. Players included:

- Importers of ACP bananas—three firms (Geest, Fyffes and Jamaica Producers), allied with the Caribbean Banana Exporters Association (CBEA) and its London lobbying office, that became the principal beneficiaries of the modified EU regime put in place in 1993.
- Producers of Latin American ('dollar') bananas—Dole Foods, Chiquita and Del Monte control 70 per cent of global imports and lobbied actively against the proposed 1993 EU regime. Chiquita was the major force behind the US decision to bring the matter to the WTO in 1995–6.
- Importers of dollar bananas—distributors lobbied and litigated against the 1993 regime in German courts and in the EU.
- Caribbean ACP producers—used the CBEA to lobby in favour of ACP preferences and inclusion of Banana Protocols in the Lomé and Cotonou Conventions.

Source: Porges (2000).

Doha Round business groups were much less active and prominent. Instead, the most effective business pressure groups were those lobbying against trade liberalization, such as cotton producers in the US, EU farmers and pharmaceutical producers in developed countries. Instead of business, NGOs were more visible and active, at times teaming up with governments to push for specific outcomes. An example was a joint effort between African governments (led by South Africa) and development NGOs to allow countries without production capacity to import drugs from other countries under compulsory licensing provisions (Chapter 8).

Lobbying is part of the decision-making process in most countries, as it is a useful mechanism for policymakers to obtain information. In many countries lobbying is regulated in that there are laws on 'if, when and how' political preferences may be organized and expressed in the trade policy area. Both Western democracies and one-party states regulate interest group participation but they do it differently. The former do it by allowing stable and enduring interest groups to compete nonviolently through a democratic process for various trade policy options. The latter do it by channelling participation through a hegemonic political institution, which may limit diversity of opinions and restrain trade policy choice. Business–government dialogue on trade policy in developing countries is progressively evolving due to growing pro-business attitudes, strengthening export orientation, growth of the private sector and a more proactive stance by business. To some extent these trends have been supported by technical assistance by bodies such as the Geneva-based International Trade Centre as well as the great increase in inward FDI into developing countries.

The emerging new approach to advocacy in trade policy puts greater emphasis on a structured and formal consultation process and less on bureaucracy-dominated decision-making. More transparency means that policy proposals are subject to public scrutiny through open hearings, public debate and Internet sites. Coalition building is facilitated by networks and online Internet communities that encourage greater participation by smaller business organizations (Kostecki, 2007).

Hundreds of legislative initiatives are required to manage foreign trade systems, agricultural policies, technical standards, intellectual property regimes and other issues of interest to traders and producers located in WTO members. All such legislation is influenced by interest group lobbying. This applies as much to the EU and other OECD countries as to the US. In the EU, the role of lobbying in shaping trade policy is strongly felt. There are hundreds of European and international federations, as well as hundreds of multinational firms with direct representation in Brussels. Numerous management consulting and public relations firms maintain offices close to the EU Commission and are actively involved in efforts to shape EU trade policy. In 2008, there were about 2,700 international and special interest groups represented in Brussels. Around 70 per cent were industry lobbyists, 10 per cent worked for NGOs such as Greenpeace or Oxfam, whereas the rest served as information liaison for various regions, municipalities and other public institutions. The large number of lobbyists reflects the reality that two-thirds of all legislative decisions for the EU are made in Brussels and it is in that city that lobbyists have ready access to the 732 members of the European Parliament and its committee meetings. The laborious process of internal negotiations to arrive at a common stand on issues such as agriculture, IPRs and services liberalization during the Uruguay Round illustrate the importance for stakeholders to have effective representation in Brussels as well as in their home market.

More generally, framing tactics by NGOs—especially when working together with groups of developing countries—can have a major influence on the agenda and on negotiations. The adoption of the TRIPS and public health declaration at the Doha ministerial in 2001—despite strong US opposition—is an example (see Chapter 8).

4.4. RECIPROCITY AND THE MECHANICS OF NEGOTIATIONS

A fundamental concept applying to WTO negotiations is reciprocity. Loosely defined, reciprocity is the practice of making an action conditional upon an action by a counterpart. Reciprocity has ruled trade liberalization by OECD countries in the post-GATT period. Reciprocal trade liberalization was also the central pillar of

the 1934 US initiative for tariff reduction—the Reciprocal Trade Agreements Act—
following the disastrous tariff wars induced by the passage of the 1930 Smoot-Hawley
Act.[3]

Article XXVIII *bis* of the GATT (entitled Tariff Negotiations) states that:

negotiations on a reciprocal and mutually advantageous basis, directed to the substantial
reduction of the general level of tariffs and other charges on imports and exports . . . are of
great importance to the expansion of international trade. The CONTRACTING PARTIES
may therefore sponsor such negotiations from time to time. Negotiations under this Article
may be carried out on a selective product-by-product basis or by the application of such
multilateral procedures as may be accepted by the contracting parties concerned. Such
negotiations may be directed towards the reduction of duties, the binding of duties at then
existing levels, or undertakings that individual duties or average duties of specified categories of products shall not exceed specified levels. The binding against increase of low
duties or of a duty-free treatment, shall, in principle, be recognized as a concession
equivalent in value to the reduction of high duties.

Note that this provision accords equivalence to commitments to lower applied
duties and to commitments to bind tariffs that have already been lowered. Although
historically the focus of negotiations has been on reducing applied levels of protection
(improving market access) and this is generally given greater weight by the business
community and negotiators, the drafters of the GATT accorded equal importance to
binding of policy. Unfortunately, the value of binding is often discounted in public
debates and discussion, which tends to focus on the extent to which a negotiation
results in additional reductions in applied tariffs and other trade-distorting policies.

Reciprocity implies the exchange of a reduction in the level of protection in one
country in return for an equivalent reduction in the level of protection of another
country. Reciprocity criteria or formulae used by participants in negotiations are
left to them to agree on. Until recently, developing countries have not been
required to offer reciprocal concessions or to bind their tariff rates (see Chapters
5 and 12). Reciprocity may be intra- or inter-issue. An intra-issue criterion provides
for the exchange of concessions of an identical nature (tariff concessions against
tariff concessions for a given product or group of products). An inter-issue formula
provides for the exchange of concessions of a dissimilar nature (such as tariff
concessions against removal of quotas). Reciprocity criteria may be product
specific—as in so-called item-by-item negotiations—or more general in nature.
Examples of the latter are so-called across-the-board trade barrier reductions,
which tend to take the form of a formula: an x per cent reduction in average tariffs,
or a y per cent reduction in the dispersion of tariffs. Item-by-item and across-the-
board approaches can be applied to tariffs and nontariff measures, although in the
latter case quantification tends to be much more difficult. Formula approaches in

---

[3] Oye (1992), Low (1993), and Rhodes (1993) analyse the role of reciprocity in US trade relations.

the case of NTMs tend to take the form of general rules, such transparency and nondiscrimination, or agreements to ban the use of specific policy instruments.

Reciprocity criteria for tariffs

When considering a reciprocal package or balance of offers, negotiators might be expected to take into account factors such as the effect of reduction in trade barriers on future trade flows, domestic production, employment and incomes. Although expected economic impacts certainly affect negotiating positions, the criteria or focal points used by negotiators to evaluate offers usually have little relationship, if any, to what economic theory would suggest as reasonable yardsticks. The approaches that have been used are best characterized as providing negotiators with a focal point, that is, something tangible enabling parties to set objectives, evaluate the position of others, assess negotiating progress and identify acceptable compromises. In the case of talks during the GATT period, the focal point was generally nothing more than a measure that took into account the relative size of different countries and was simple to calculate—in practice trade volumes and notional tariff revenue impacts.

Tariff revenue was often used to assess reciprocity, calculated as the reduction in a tariff multiplied by the volume of imports of that product. For example, if imports of a product are US$10 million and the applicable tariff rate is reduced from 50 per cent to 35 per cent, the concession would equal 15 per cent of 10 million, or US$1.5 million. A related method that has been used can be referred to as 'percentage equivalents'. For example, a 50 per cent equivalent reduction would signify that a 50 per cent tariff cut was made with respect to US$1 million worth of imports. A tariff cut of 25 per cent for a product line in which the value of imports is US$2 million is equal to one '50 per cent equivalent'. The general formula is:

$$E = [M \times dT]/50$$

where M is the value of imports and dT is the percentage tariff cut. These methods of assessing reciprocal concessions were often used in the earlier MTNs when trade between two negotiating countries was not bilaterally balanced in a specific product.

Another method is the average cut. Generally, weighted averages rather than simple averages are used in this connection. Suppose that country A imports US$20 million worth of cotton shirts and US$30 million worth of cotton trousers. During trade negotiations it agrees to reduce its tariff on cotton shirts by 5 per cent and its tariff on cotton trousers by 10 per cent. The weighted-average cut in import tariffs for cotton imports by country A is then:

$$E = (0.05 \times \$20 \text{ million} + 0.1 \times \$30 \text{ million})/(\$20 \text{ million} + \$30 \text{ million}) = 8.$$

The average tariff cut by country *A* in the cotton sector is thus 8 per cent. Average cuts do not always provide a satisfactory indication of the magnitude of trade liberalization. For example, if a country's tariff is so high as to be prohibitive (no imports come in at all), there will be nothing to weigh the tariff cut by for the product concerned. Use of the formula will then give a biased picture of the extent of tariff cuts. The more restrictive a given import tariff, the less satisfactory is the use of this type of weighted tariff cut average to calculate the value of concessions. Because of such problems, tariff cuts are sometimes weighted by domestic consumption or production of the products involved, or by the global value of trade in the products.

Reciprocity formulae may be general (across-the-board) or specific (item-by-item). Negotiations conducted on an item-by-item basis rely on a specific reciprocity formula, that is, tariff reduction relating to one product line is exchanged for tariff reduction on another product line. Negotiations conducted on an across-the-board basis rely on a general reciprocity formula. Table 4.2 lists some of the major techniques that have been used in the GATT context.

The process of negotiations on specific concessions in much of the GATT period was essentially bilateral. That is, two contracting parties presented each other with request and offer lists, and negotiations centred on achieving a bilaterally balanced exchange of concessions. However, this network of bilateral negotiations subsequently acquires a multilateral dimension because specific tariff concessions once negotiated bilaterally are generalized through the MFN clause. In practice the large

Table 4.2. Negotiating techniques and formulae

Technique	Major Characteristics
Item-by-item or request-offer	Bilateral negotiations based on requests and offers. Main technique used until Kennedy Round; widely used in subsequent rounds and accession talks
Linear cut	Across-the-board negotiating technique involving an identical percentage reduction in barriers across all sectors. Used in Kennedy Round (formula: $T_2 = rT_1$, where T_2 is the reduced tariff, T_1 is the initial tariff, and r is a coefficient ranging between 0 and 1
Harmonization formula (nonlinear cut)	Aimed at moving the tariff structure of members towards greater uniformity, cutting tariff peaks proportionally more than lower tariffs. In Tokyo Round the so-called Swiss formula was used: $T_2 = RT_1/R + T_1$, where R is a coefficient (set at 14 or 16). The Doha Round negotiations on nonagricultural market access also revolved around a Swiss formula
Zero-for-zero negotiations	Complete abolition of tariffs for a sector or group of commodities

players (the US, the EU) negotiate with virtually everyone, whereas smaller players will negotiate primarily with WTO members that are principal suppliers or constitute important markets. The market opening granted by one country is frequently balanced against tariff reductions made by a number of trading partners simultaneously. The rationale underlying this is that a generalization of bilaterally negotiated concessions though MFN may create free rider problems. Any reduction in trade barriers will also benefit other countries that supply the relevant products, and these countries may not have offered reciprocal concessions. The principle of nondiscrimination clashes here with the principle of reciprocity. Under a MFN clause, no conditionality (discrimination) may be introduced once a concession has been granted. However, conditionality (which is the very essence of reciprocity) may be introduced in the negotiating process. Two general techniques have been conceived to deal with the free rider issue. They are the principal supplier rule and the practice of balancing concessions in exchange for so-called initial negotiating rights.

Under the so-called principal supplier rule, requests for tariff reductions or bindings ('concessions') on a particular product are normally made by, and only by, the principal (largest) suppliers of a product. This limits free riding, as the concessions granted by an importing country (A) to the principal supplier (B) of a product must be balanced by concessions from that principal supplier (B) on products for which A is in turn a principal supplier. The principal supplier mechanism was a long standing US practice, this being the method used in the negotiation of the network of reciprocal trade agreements starting in the 1930s (Jackson, 1969: 219). It was important especially in the early years of the GATT because there were only a few dozen countries participating.

The principal supplier rule effectively reinforces the bilateral character of trade negotiations conducted on a product-by-product basis. Under an unconditional MFN clause governments have few incentives to grant a trade concession to countries that are not its principal suppliers. Granting a concession to a small supplier implies giving away the concession to the principal supplier, as the latter will benefit from it due to the MFN rule. The principal supplier is the trading nation which benefits the most from a concession and is thus probably prepared to offer more reciprocal trade liberalization than a smaller supplier would be prepared or able to do.

Multilateral product-by-product negotiations based on the principal supplier rule rely on multilateral balancing to attain reciprocity. Assume that country A is the principal supplier of good 1 to country B, and that B is the principal supplier of good 2 to A. Assume further that B imports US$500 million from A, whereas A imports only US$250 million from B. Although an exchange is certainly possible, because trade flows are unbalanced, B may demand that A reduce its tariff by twice as much as B. If A is unwilling to do this, and the reciprocity rule used requires equality in cuts as measured, for example, by tariff revenues, negotiations may break down. Involving another country, C, may allow A and B to circumvent their problem. If country C is the principal supplier of good 3 to A, exporting US$500 million, and is also the principal supplier of good 4 to country B, with exports of US$250 million, and in turn imports goods worth US$250 and US$500 million, respectively, from A and B, negotiations are balanced. This is, of course, a stylized example. In practice many goods are involved, and precise balancing is impossible to achieve. The main point is that by involving many countries, more trades are possible given the principal supplier constraint.

Although the principal supplier rule reduces the role of smaller supplier countries in multilateral tariff negotiations, it does not eliminate them as players. One factor leading to the involvement of smaller countries is the need for endgame or last-minute balancing. At the end of the bilateral phase of a round, negotiators know that their country is not only required to grant the benefits of concessions to other countries but also that it is entitled to the benefits of concessions negotiated between other trading nations. At this stage the negotiators attempt to strike a balance in the global effect of concessions. To achieve that objective they may seek to reshuffle previously made requests and offers. A country that finds out that one of its concessions indirectly benefitted another country that refused to grant a reciprocal concession always has the possibility to withdraw the original concession. Thus, the granting of concessions to principal suppliers is often made conditional upon obtaining supplementary balancing concessions from a number of other (smaller) suppliers of the product concerned.

The use of the principal supplier rule with multilateral balancing reflected an explicit attempt by trading nations to form privileged groups. The aim is that the share of the costs and benefits of a product-specific liberalization internalized by club members (principal suppliers) is sufficiently large so that free riding by third parties is no longer a source of concern. The practice of supplementary balancing probably resulted in greater trade liberalization than would have taken place under the strict bilateralism that characterized the pre-GATT trading system. The MFN clause induces requests for concessions from smaller suppliers that would not be players under a conditional MFN approach. The fact that the concession-granting country is able to 'sell' its concession to more than one country allows it to obtain greater compensation than under a system of bilateral bargaining. Greater compensation also implies that more can be offered in terms of market opening (Dam, 1970).

The item-by-item, principal supplier approach was the main technique used in the first five MTNs (up to the Dillon round). Being product-specific, the approach allowed negotiators to be very specific, facilitating use of the trade (revenue) impacts as a metric to evaluate the overall balance of concessions. The extent of liberalization using this approach will be a function of the level of the tariff classification at which commitments are made. Thus, a commitment to lower tariffs at the four-digit level of classification of a product group is more significant than one at the eight-digit level (because there are many more products covered at the more aggregate four-digit level). This advantage is offset by the fact that item-by-item, principal supplier negotiations are resource-intensive. They also are not very effective in reducing barriers where there are no principal suppliers. They also can be micromanaged in a way that allows the MFN obligation to be effectively circumvented.

An example of the latter is provided by a 1904 trade agreement between Germany and Switzerland. Germany committed itself to reducing its tariffs on 'large dapple mountain cattle reared at a spot at least 300 meters above sea level and having at least one month grazing each year at a spot at least 800 meters above sea level' (Curzon, 1965: 60). This has become a classic illustration of the use of creative tariff line definition by trade negotiators to avoid MFN—clearly the provision will not apply to Argentine or Dutch beef! Similar examples can be identified in GATT negotiations (Finger, 1979).

Over time, as the number of participants rose, increasing the complexity of item-by-item negotiations while at the same time reducing their utility (as free riding became less of an issue) attempts were made to shift towards an across-the-board approach. The Kennedy Round saw the introduction of a formula approach to tariff reduction. Underlying this shift was not only the expansion of GATT membership, but also the fact that the US Congress approved of the approach (having earlier rejected it as infringing on its sovereignty). European Economic Community concerns that its average industrial tariffs were lower than those of the US and Japan also played a role (Jackson, 1969).

Across-the-board tariff negotiations in GATT have relied on two basic approaches (focal points): either a uniform percentage cut or a more complex formula that reduces tariffs in a nonuniform way. The percentage cut approach has generally been based on all participants applying the same rate of tariff reduction to all product lines—a so-called linear cut. It was used during the Kennedy Round, with developed countries agreeing to reduce their tariffs on industrial products by 50 per cent, with the exception of a list of 'sensitive' products, some of which were subject to item-by-item negotiations. As tariffs on many of the sensitive items were reduced by only a small percentage or totally excluded from liberalization, the average tariff reduction in the Kennedy Round was only 35 per cent.

The linear approach maximizes the number of tariff lines brought to the bargaining table and is likely to lead to the exchange of a greater amount of concessions than item-by-item negotiations. The average cut approach tends to be preferred by countries with high import tariffs as any equal-percentage tariff cut will still leave the high-tariff country with higher tariffs in the end than other nations that started from a lower tariff level. On the basis of the simple tariff revenue reciprocity metric, negotiators can (and do) treat reductions in low tariffs or the total elimination of low tariffs as equivalent to cuts of higher tariffs as long as there is balance in terms of affected volumes or revenues. From the perspective of economic welfare and efficiency of resource allocation this is completely wrong, as the welfare cost of protection rises with the square of the tariff (see Annex 2).[4] A linear cut will not affect the structure of protection in a country, allowing tariff escalation and differences in rates of effective protection across activities to persist.

Export interests clearly would prefer to see governments adopt approaches that result in high-tariff nations making higher percentage cuts than low-tariff nations. Formulas that result in nonuniform, nonlinear reductions in tariffs will do exactly that. There are very many options in this respect. One possibility discussed in the Tokyo Round was to cut each tariff by a percentage equal to its initial level. Thus, a 60 per cent tariff would be reduced by 60 per cent, whereas a 10 per cent tariff would be reduced by 10 per cent. The EEC suggested that this approach be repeated four times, with tariffs over 50 per cent initially not being reduced below 13 per cent. Another proposition made by the US was to employ the formula $X = 1.5T_1 + 50$, where X is the percentage with which tariffs were to be cut. This formula was to apply to all tariffs below 6.67 per cent, all others being reduced by 60 per cent. This meant that a 6 per cent tariff would fall by $(1.5 \times 6) + 50$, or 59 per cent, whereas a 2 per cent tariff would be cut by 53 per cent. This is an example of a symbolic harmonization formula, as high tariffs are only subject to a linear cut.

Yet another approach, suggested by Switzerland, was to use the formula $T_2 = rT_1/(r + T_1)$. This formula reduced high tariff rates much more than low ones, the ultimate result depending on the value of r that is chosen. In the event, the value of r that was chosen by countries ranged between 14 and 16. Thus, a 14 per cent tariff would be reduced by 50 per cent, tariffs below (above) 14 per cent being reduced less (more) than 50 per cent. As discussed in Section 4.1, in the Doha Round WTO members agreed to use tariff-harmonizing formulas to reduce tariffs in both agriculture and the nonagricultural market access negotiations. A number of variants of the Swiss formula were proposed as the basis of the Doha nonagricultural market access (NAMA) negotiations.

A general problem affecting across-the-board formula approaches is that agreement must be obtained on which formula to use and on the extent to which exceptions to the use of the rule will be permitted for certain products. The larger the scope for exceptions, the less useful it becomes to invest substantial negotiating resources in achieving agreement on the use of a general rule. The shift to a general formula approach in the Kennedy and Tokyo Rounds, although a significant change, did not lead to the demise of item-by-item talks. This was because the exceptions turned out to be rather significant at the end of the day in both negotiations, as the inclusion of a product on the exclusion list by one country

---

[4] This approach is still alive and well, as reflected in the use of predicted losses in aggregate tariff revenue as a measure of what was 'on the table' in the Doha Round (although the motivation of this exercise was not to assess welfare effects but the 'equivalence' of what was being proposed for NAMA and for agriculture). See http://www.wto.org/english/news_e/sppl_e/sppl97_e.htm

tended to lead to the reciprocal addition of products to the list of other countries. In the Uruguay Round, negotiators did not use a formula approach, instead reverting to item-by-item (and sector-by-sector) negotiations.

In the Doha Round, the problem of agreeing on how to treat exceptions became a major subject of negotiation, inseparable from the more general problem of agreeing on the specifics of the formula to be applied. The proposal on the table in mid-2008 was for the coefficient r in the Swiss formula to be between 7 and 9 for industrial countries, with no flexibility for individual products. For developing countries, the coefficient would be based on a sliding scale with a coefficient range of $x = [19–21]$, $y = [21–23]$ or $z = [23–26]$ depending upon the extent of flexibility to deviate from the formula chosen. Countries choosing $x = [19–21]$ as the coefficient could choose to keep 6–7 per cent of tariffs unbound on products covering no more than 6–9 per cent of imports or to make half-of-formula cuts in 12–14 per cent of tariff lines on products covering no more than 12–19 per cent of imports. With a $y = [21–23]$ coefficient, 5 per cent of lines and imports would be allowed no cuts, or 10 per cent lines and imports with half-of-formula cuts. Those choosing $z = [23–26]$ would have no flexibilities at all. Least developed countries were only expected to increase their levels of binding coverage (Martin and Mattoo, 2008).

Whatever approach is used, item-by-item or across-the-board formulas, there are three aspects of the reciprocity concept as practiced in GATT that should be emphasized. First, reciprocity is traditionally measured in terms of incremental rather than absolute trade flows or market access conditions. One dollar of additional market access in one country is exchanged for one dollar of additional market opening in another country. Although all negotiators will contend that export opportunities gained are greater than import opening conceded, even though logically this cannot be true for all countries at the same time (Curzon and Curzon, 1976), the bargaining reflects a balance of perceived advantages at the margin rather than in terms of full equality of market access. Obviously, the complete picture with regard to market access conditions is never absent from negotiators' perspectives. However, it is the balance of incremental reductions that remains the centre of attention when evaluating reciprocity. Jagdish Bhagwati, using a mathematical analogy, has termed this criterion 'first-difference' reciprocity: what effectively is attempted is to equate changes in policy (their 'first derivatives'), not absolute levels (Bhagwati, 1991). Ernest Preeg, an American negotiator commenting on the Kennedy Round and preceding negotiations, describes in detail how negotiators tried to strike a rough balance between the estimated increases in the value of imports and the forecast rise in the value of exports resulting from the tariff concessions (Preeg, 1970).

Second, tariff concessions in MTNs involve tariff *bindings* and not necessarily a reduction in applied barriers. A country may reduce applied tariff levels, but as long as it does not bind these the liberalization is essentially not considered to be a concession in the WTO context. For example, in the Uruguay Round many developing countries requested recognition of autonomous liberalization that had been undertaken during the 1980s, but had a hard time, in spite of initial general assurances incorporated in ministerial declarations, of getting this accepted by negotiating partners unless they were willing to bind this liberalization. Similarly, often the applied tariff rate on a product is less than the bound MFN rate contained in a country's GATT schedule. Again, no credit is obtained from applying lower than bound rates. What matters is the level at which tariff rates are bound. As discussed in Chapter 1, tariff bindings are fundamental in the GATT context, because it is only on the basis of claims that bindings have been violated that a member can initiate dispute settlement procedures.

Third, the extent to which negotiations affect real incomes or other measures of economic welfare is not used in assessing reciprocity. Reasons for this go beyond the enormous technical difficulties that would be associated with agreeing on how to assess such impacts *ex ante*. More important, because governments will have different objectives, a narrowly economic focus to assess reciprocity would be inappropriate in any event. However, from a normative point of view policymakers should be concerned with welfare effects of policy and therefore understand what the general economic implications are of specific negotiating modalities. This is not necessarily the case in practice—in the case of trade policy and negotiations 'do it yourself economics' is often the norm (Henderson, 1986).

As mentioned previously, some of the approaches used in negotiations will by definition have smaller beneficial impacts in economic efficiency terms than others—for example, by leaving unaffected the structure of protection and allowing tariff escalation and dispersion to persist. This is not to argue that negotiators do not understand economics—the use of 'suboptimal' reciprocity criteria and focal points largely reflects political economy realities that in turn affect objectives and negotiating tactics. Long standing efforts by exporting nations to prioritize reductions in tariff escalation and tariff peaks are completely aligned with what economic analysis would identify as a priority from a welfare perspective.

Nominal and effective protection

The dispersion in rates of import protection that tend to prevail in most countries—of which tariff escalation is an example—have led economists to develop a distinction between the nominal rate of protection (NRP) and the effective rate of protection (ERP). The NRP for a product can be measured as the proportional increase in the producer price of a good relative to free trade (trade undistorted by protection). The ERP differs from the NRP by taking into account the magnitude of protection provided to the raw materials and intermediate inputs used to produce a good. The ERP is a better measure of the extent to which activities are protected than the NRP because it incorporates information on the structure of production. The higher are the barriers on imported inputs, the lower the ERP will be for goods that use these inputs, and vice versa (Box 4.6).

The WTO focuses only on nominal rates of protection (tariffs). There are no obligations with respect to effective rates. This does not mean that negotiators do not understand the concept. Return to the first example on steel in Box 4.6. In this

---

Box 4.6. Nominal and effective rate of protection

The nominal rate of protection (NRP) can be defined as

$$NRP = (P - P^*)/P^*$$

where P is the domestic tariff-inclusive price of a good, and P^* is the free trade price. As the latter cannot be observed in practice, most empirical studies take the world price as a measure of P^*. The effective rate of protection (ERP) can be defined as the proportional increase in value added per unit of a good produced in a country relative to value added under free trade (no protection). The magnitude of the ERP depends not only on the nominal tariff on the final product concerned, but also on the tariffs applied to the inputs used, and the importance of those inputs in the value of the final product.

A simple formula for calculating the ERP is

$$ERP = (V - V^*)/V^*$$

where V is the domestic value added per unit of the final good (including the tariffs on that good and on its inputs), and V^* is valued added under free trade. Value added per unit in turn is defined as the gross value of output minus the cost of inputs used in production: $V = t_f P_f - t_i P_i X$, where t_f and t_i are the so-called tariff factors (which equal 1 plus the tariff rate) on the final good and inputs, respectively, P_f and P_i are the prices, and X is the amount of input used to produce a unit of the final good. Value added at free trade prices is the same, except that tariffs in this case do not exist so that the tariff factor $t = 1$.

For example, suppose one ton of steel is worth US$1,000 on the world market. To produce it a factory has to buy one ton of iron ore at a world price of US$600. Assume for simplicity that nothing more is needed for steel production. Under these circumstances the value added per ton of steel in our factory will be US$400. If a 20 per cent nominal tariff rate is imposed on steel imports and no tariff on iron ore, the effective rate of protection in those circumstances will be

$$(1,200 - 600)/400 = 1.5 \text{ or } 50 \text{ per cent.}$$

The ERP in this example is more than double the 20 per cent NRP on steel. If no tariff is imposed on steel but a nominal tariff of 33 per cent is imposed on imports of iron ore, the ERP would be

$$\{(600 + 200) - 1,000\}/400 = -0.5 \text{ or } -50 \text{ per cent.}$$

This example illustrates that an NRP of zero does not necessarily imply that trade is undistorted. As another example, assume that cocoa beans account for 95 per cent of the production cost of cocoa butter. The imposition of a 5 per cent nominal tariff rate on cocoa butter would then imply an effective rate of protection for the cocoa butter industry of 100 per cent.

case the incentives for exporters of steel to reduce the 20 per cent tariff are greater than is suggested by the nominal rate. The fact that the ERP for most products tends to be higher than the NRP (because governments prefer to protect activities that generate higher value added) explains why tariff negotiations continue to be at the centre stage of MTNs, even though average tariffs have fallen significantly since the GATT was created. An average tariff on highly processed goods of only 10 per cent can hide an ERP that is much higher. Interest groups care about the ERP, not the NRP. Although lobbying efforts centre on influencing nominal rates of protection, much of the political manoeuvring that occurs in the domestic trade policy arena is driven by the impact of such protection on the ERP.

At the multilateral level, in MTNs the focus of attention is often more generally on the dispersion of tariffs. Attempts to reduce dispersion—the difference between the highest and lowest rates—through nonlinear tariff reduction formulas will have the effect of reducing differences in the ERP for specific goods. Bringing down the highest tariffs will have the greatest positive impacts on welfare.

RECIPROCITY CRITERIA FOR NONTARIFF MEASURES

Negotiations focused on disciplining the use of NTMs are considerably more complex than tariff talks because the measures concerned may be motivated by nontrade objectives and only incidentally restrict imports (examples include sanitary controls, labelling requirements and product standards). A first difficulty is therefore in determining (agreeing) what measures constitute a barrier to trade and which are legitimate instruments of government regulation. Given that this difficulty is overcome, negotiators confront a challenge in defining a focal point to achieve reciprocity in NTM negotiations. The problem is twofold: the set of potential trades is of a much lower dimension than in the case of tariff negotiations, and it is much more difficult to translate proposals into a common metric.

NTMs are 'lumpier' than tariffs, in that it is often difficult if not impossible to negotiate marginal changes in policies. That is, the equivalent of offering to reduce a tariff by 5 or 10 or 50 per cent does not exist. As a result gains from trade become more difficult to realize, and cross-issue linkages become more important in achieving agreement. The valuation issue is fundamental. In the context of tariff negotiations, it is relatively straightforward to agree how to value requests and offers, although the criteria used may have little economic meaning. A metric for NTM negotiations is much more difficult to establish. In some areas negotiators have been creative in overcoming the problem. For example, as discussed in Chapter 6, in the agricultural setting it was agreed to convert various types of government intervention into an aggregate measure of support. But many of the NTMs that have appeared on the agendas of recent MTNs are not easily expressed in terms of a simple quantitative metric. This makes it more difficult for negotiators to determine whether they have achieved reciprocity. This is the case especially when the focus is on agreeing on rules. Often it may not be feasible to make marginal changes in proposed rules without making the rule irrelevant. Instead, proposed deals involve accepting rule x for policy A in return for rule y for policy B, that is, engage in issue linkage. It then becomes very important to have a clear idea of the economic implications of alternative rules. This requires substantial analysis of the likely effects on both domestic constituents and on the multilateral trading system. It is not surprising therefore that the approach taken is often one of adopting basic principles such as transparency and nondiscrimination, rather than seeking changes in the substance of regulations.

In most NTM negotiations the focus is not on principal suppliers or the change in protection, but on specific measures or rules the implementation of which are assumed to increase market access, or on easily quantified variables that are not necessarily related to trade. For example, participants in the negotiations on an agreement on government procurement (see Chapter 11) focused on the size of the contracts to be covered and the entities to be included (on the basis of past procurement activity). This allowed a balance to be achieved in terms of the percentage of total procurement to be covered by an agreement.

Rules of thumb to assess welfare impacts

Assessing the impact of current policies and the likely consequences of changes in policies for economic welfare is an important task for policymakers. At the end of the day, the end result of a negotiation should be to increase national welfare. Although the process will reflect the self-interested behaviour of numerous interest groups, so that governments will never end up with an outcome that maximizes welfare, if the gains that accrue to some groups are not sufficient to offset the losses of other groups, agreements will be inefficient. Indeed, they may not be feasible to implement.

Officials who are concerned with ensuring that the outcome of negotiations improves the welfare of society, as opposed to the interests of the best organized and powerful interest groups, can use a number of rules of thumb. One such rule is that proposals should reduce the dispersion in effective rates of protection across industries. Another rule of thumb is that across-the-board formulas are preferable to request-offer approaches as they make lobbying for exceptions more transparent and more costly. In terms of tariff reduction formulas, these two rules of thumb suggest that linear reductions (a proportional cut) are inferior to a nonlinear approach, although either of these approaches is superior to request–offer bargaining.

As mentioned, a nonlinear approach need not involve a Swiss-type formula. A 'concertina' approach is an alternative, under which the highest tariffs rates are reduced first and/or more (Corden, 1974). This was the proposed modality in the Doha agricultural negotiations. The proposal on the table in mid-2008 was to use a tiered formula that would require proportional cuts in tariffs, with the cut increasing when moving between each of four progressively higher bands (Chapter 6). This has the economically desirable feature of making larger cuts in the higher—and hence more costly—tariffs. As was the case in the Uruguay round, cuts by developing countries in each band would have been two-thirds those of the industrial countries. The two rules of thumb need to be applied in tandem. Achieving this in practice is very difficult as a result of lobbying for exclusions and exceptions to the formula.

When it comes to NTMs, as discussed at greater length in subsequent chapters, a rule of thumb is that a uniform rule is likely to be desirable for all countries in only certain circumstances. This is particularly the case for domestic regulatory policies once the focus goes beyond basic principles such as national treatment and MFN. In this area, rules that centre on ensuring transparency and due process are unambiguously beneficial, but efforts to impose uniform substantive disciplines may easily be detrimental to some countries.

4.5. A Typology of Key Aspects of Trade Negotiations

We conclude this chapter with a typology of various aspects of MTNs, drawing upon the discussion in the foregoing sections and relating it to basic concepts used in the contemporary theory of negotiations.

MTNs are multi-issue barter exchanges

Barter implies that MTNs involve the exchange of concessions (liberalization/binding commitments). Participants formulate requests (what they want in terms of liberalization by trading partners) and offers (what they are ready to liberalize themselves). As in any type of market situation, every trader (negotiator) will attempt to get as much as possible in exchange for as little as necessary. How a balanced package or outcome is defined will differ from case to case, depending on what is being traded and the objectives of the negotiators. The lack of a fungible medium of exchange requires trade negotiations to have an agenda that allows all the traders to trade something and in so doing improve upon the status quo. Setting the agenda is therefore very important for a successful outcome. Multilateral trade negotiations are usually preceded by an intensive preparation process during which possible issues are identified, preferences are established, issues are ranked, initial positions are formulated and a proposal is made with respect to the contents of the negotiating agenda.

The process that led to the establishment of the negotiating agenda for the Uruguay Round took five years, starting with the preparation for the 1982 ministerial meeting, which failed to result in agreement to launch a new MTN. It only ended with the 1986 ministerial meeting in Punta del Este, Uruguay, where agreement was finally reached on the agenda of the Uruguay Round. The efforts to launch a new MTN at the 1999 Seattle ministerial failed, largely due to disagreements over what should be included on the agenda. At the next ministerial conference in Doha 2001, a new round was launched, with a multidimensional agenda that encompassed no fewer than 19 technical subjects, each reflecting major differences between participating nations that would have to be bridged during the round. In addition, in response to pressure by developing nations the conference adopted a separate decision on 12 implementation-related issues and a special declaration interpreting the TRIPS agreement on questions of public health (Odell, 2007).

For any given agenda, there are virtually hundreds of economic, legal and political issues that must be resolved. Each participant, in evaluating possible final outcomes, must carefully consider the tradeoffs it is ready to accept and instruct its delegation accordingly. The main advantage of dealing with a broad range of issues is that it greatly increases the scope for cooperative behaviour. When it is possible to determine jointly several negotiating issues, trade officials have an opportunity to considerably enlarge the pie before dividing it. The larger is the range of issues considered, the better the chances are that negotiators will act as cooperative problem solvers.

The fact that trade negotiations are barter exchanges makes it more difficult to reveal true preferences and enhances the scope for employing tactics intended to increase a country's potential payoff. Impasses, threats of deadlock and collapse and last-minute deals are part of the repertoire of a competent negotiator. When impasses occur, negotiators must attempt to turn to other issues or modify the formulation of issues in search for some alternative terms of possible agreement. Every good negotiating team must maintain a consistent, coordinated position in all areas of negotiations, be able to rank its requests and offers across all issue areas, and be as well informed as possible about the positions of its negotiating partners. This is difficult, of course. In practice MTNs do not result in Pareto-optimal outcomes because offers are often made on a contingent basis to allow obtaining further concessions from its trading partners. Withdrawal of such contingent offers at the end of the day may lead to the unravelling of a carefully constructed, balanced package as well as significantly reduce the overall welfare payoffs of a deal (Baldwin, 1986).

MTNs are multistage games

Each MTN has a number of stages, starting with a country or leader acting as a catalyst, initiating the pre-negotiations that lead to the establishment of the agenda, followed by the MTN itself, which is followed in turn by the post-negotiation, implementation stage. The negotiation period, in turn, usually has distinct stages as well. There is generally a learning period, during which participants signal their preferences on the various issues on the agenda, determine the options that exist for forming coalitions of various kinds, and simply engage in fact-finding regarding the various policy options that exist. This is followed by a period of substantive negotiations, with players demanding concessions and responding to the demands of others, thereby mapping out the set of feasible solutions. In this stage, many tentative agreements may be reached, but these are conditional upon the final outcome. The fact that the negotiating process evolves in stages may induce negotiating teams to follow a 'nice guy, bad guy' approach. Negotiators first adopt an aggressive style when the initial positions are determined. This may involve taking strongly held stances in an adversarial manner. At a later stage in the negotiating process, a new negotiating team replaces the 'bad guy' and pursues a more cooperative tack. The final stage generally starts close to what is perceived to be the deadline for conclusion of substantive talks. In the past this often has been the date the negotiating authority of the US delegation expires, reflecting the predominance of the US in much of the GATT period. Since the formation of the WTO, the rapid growth of large countries such as China, India, Brazil and the steady expansion of EU membership has reduced the relative importance of the US.

MTNs are multiplayer games

Multilateral trade negotiations are games with many players. The complexity of multiparty negotiations greatly exceeds those involving only two players. Coalitions may form and each participant must explore what options are available in this connection, and what the implications are of others forming coalitions. Various types of coalitions can be distinguished, ranging from informal and ad hoc, session or issue-specific to formal, multi-issue coalitions. The former tend to be much more prevalent than the latter, as it is generally difficult to agree to negotiate as a bloc. The multiparty nature of MTNs greatly increases complexity of the negotiations. The negotiators are not only engaged in transmitting their country's requests, offers and negotiating positions, but are also continuously involved in gathering and transmitting information. One of the more important tasks of trade negotiators is to provide feedback on the preferences and interests of negotiating partners, and feel out to what extent negotiating positions are hard or soft. Such information will help their government in strategy formulation, including the pursuit of possible coalitions. All these tasks have become more important as the number of countries participating actively in WTO negotiations has grown.

MTNs take time and are repeated games

In MTNs, negotiators bargain together over a substantial period of time, and know that they will meet each other repeatedly. The repeated nature of the interaction fosters cooperation by ensuring that if deals made at one point in time are not implemented (or reneged upon), not only will recourse to dispute settlement procedures be feasible, but also future deals may be impeded. History matters in repeated games: actions or positions taken will have an effect on negotiating stances of trading partners in future interactions. Learning will occur, and participants are given an incentive to invest resources in establishing a reputation. Reputation is important in terms of generating trust on the part of negotiating partners that agreements will be implemented, and may also help in exploiting the fact that MTNs have deadlines. As noted earlier, last-minute balancing of concessions is a frequent practice in negotiations where initial bargaining takes place essentially on a bilateral basis. The fact that agreements reached on specific issues at intermediate stages of the negotiating process are conditional upon the overall outcome on all the issues increases pressure on negotiators as the deadline for conclusion of the talks is approached. Skilful negotiators prepare for the endgame confrontations of a MTN by explicitly seeking to link issues in a way that makes threats possible and credible.

Sequencing of issues may be an important part of getting to yes. At the Doha ministerial in 2001 a series of deadlines were agreed for a number of issues, sequenced in a way that key areas of concern to developing countries would be dealt with first. Thus, the subject of strengthening special and differential treatment provisions and dealing with Uruguay Round implementation issues was to be addressed by July 2002; followed by TRIPS and public health (December 2002), agricultural negotiating modalities (March 2003), and nonagricultural negotiating modalities (July 2003). This, in principle, was to lead up to the main decision to be made in the Cancun ministerial, agreeing on whether and how to launch negotiations on the so-called Singapore issues. According to developing country negotiators, this sequence was carefully designed to ensure that developing countries would have full information on the balance of the negotiations, allowing an informed decision to be made on Singapore issues (Ismail, 2007). In the event, only one of the major issues of concern to developing countries was settled before Cancun—TRIPS and public health—and then only after a nine-month delay and rancorous discussion that ultimately only resulted in adding a chairperson's clarification to a text negotiated the previous December. This helps to explain why in Cancun no agreement was obtained to launch negotiations on the Singapore issues.

Governments are not monolithic

Governments represent numerous interests. Participants in MTNs may spend less time negotiating with trading partners than they do internally. There are often large differences within a country on the issues that appear on the agenda—differences among provinces or states, differences between various government departments, as well as differences between consumer, producer and other interest groups. One major actor in the WTO, the EU, is a composite player, which further complicates matters. It now comprises 27 countries, each of which simultaneously needs to internalize the preferences of relevant domestic interest groups on topics on the agenda and agree with its 26 partners on the common position to be taken in the MTN on each these topics.

The implication of this is that lobbying is part and parcel of the process. Both the pre-negotiation stage and the MTN itself involve substantial interaction between governments (negotiators) and interest groups. The extent to which domestic industries (industry associations or major companies) influence the process varies, depending on the country and issue involved. The influence of trade-policy lobbies is particularly important and transparent in the US, which has institutionalized such interactions through a complex system of general and sector-specific advisory bodies. Foreign lobbies may also target a government, and a government may use pressure from other countries to help them overcome political resistance by groups at home. Diversity of internal preferences is another element that can give rise to the formation of (implicit) coalitions as well as attempts to link issues.

Feasible solutions are defined by power and threat points

Negotiating processes and outcomes are influenced by the importance of agreement on an issue for the major players. This depends on the status quo on an issue (the BATNA or threat point associated with breakdown of talks). When there is enough on the table—or the BATNA is bad—negotiators may play games, but they know that they finally have to agree. Conversely, if these conditions are not satisfied the probability of failure increases because the associated costs are low. Care will generally be taken to only initiate negotiations if there is an agenda that offers the possibility of significant gains for all concerned.

In general, *demandeurs* on a topic will have to offer enough to substantially improve upon the status quo for those asked to change their policies, which may not be possible if countries are small. Threatening to block a package deal then becomes an important instrument to pursue key objectives. While size matters— there is little that small countries can do to induce the trading powers to remove policies that affect them detrimentally—in the context of MTNs small players can threaten to block agreement. The resistance by the US to discuss removal of the federal subsidies to the 25,000 US cotton farmers—at US$4.2 billion in 2004–5 larger than the GNP of Burkina Faso, one of the African cotton-producing nations that sought to make this a priority—contributed to the failure of the 2003 WTO ministerial meeting in Cancun.

Generally the threat point or BATNA—the likely implication of a failure to reach agreement—will play an important role in determining the outcome of a MTN. This may be much worse than the status quo ante. The US, for example, has made extensive use of threats before and during MTNs. In the 1980s, for example, the US unilateral trade policy instruments (Section 301, Super 301 and Special 301—see Chapter 8) against alleged unreasonable ('unfair') trade practices in areas such as IPRs that were not subject to GATT discipline at the time (Bhagwati and Patrick, 1990). Preferential trade agreements may also, at least partly, be driven by a desire to put pressure on countries to make progress in the multilateral trade talks. Alternatively, the willingness of a major trading power to conclude a preferential trade agreement may be partly conditional on the positions that potential partners take in the WTO.

Negotiators may strike symbolic or unenforceable deals

The outcomes of MTNs generally comprise a mix of best endeavour-type agreements and legally binding (enforceable) commitments. There are many shades between the two extremes of pro-forma talks that result in promises and substantive negotiations that result in binding disciplines. A prominent example of GATT negotiations that led to a symbolic, 'best endeavour' deal was the adoption of Part IV of the GATT on Trade and Development during the Kennedy Round and the Tokyo Round 'Enabling Clause' calling for special and differential treatment in favour of developing countries (Chapter 12). The decision to call the Doha Round the Doha Development Agenda was largely symbolic, responding to calls by many protagonists to make the WTO more supportive of the economic development of its poorer members. Although symbolic deals and best endeavour commitments are not enforceable, they have had an impact on the trading system. The balance of rights and obligations of WTO members frequently extends well beyond legally binding commitments. Symbolic agreements may become a significant element of that balance. Symbolic deals also have another important function. When an agreement is required for political reasons, but substantive deals are not feasible, a symbolic agreement that incorporates a zone of ambiguity can have value for participants by allowing a deal to be struck. This helps explain why negotiated agreements may be difficult to understand, allow for easy re-imposition of protection, or appear to contain commitments 'made of rubber'.

Equity may matter more than economic efficiency

In an investigation of the distributional and efficiency implications of the tariff proposals made during the Tokyo Round, Chan (1985) concluded that the Swiss formula that was adopted is best explained by solution concepts that emphasize fairness considerations. He found that the Swiss proposal distributed the gains from liberalization across players in proportion to the weight (contribution) of each player rather than maximizing the sum of gains across countries, independent of distribution. Allen (1979) and Baldwin and Clarke (1987) obtained similar results for the Kennedy and Tokyo Rounds respectively. These findings are intuitive as they reflect reciprocity. Thus, outcomes can be expected to reward players proportionately. Brown and Whalley (1980) analyse the efficiency implications of the various formulas that were proposed in the Tokyo Round. They show that countries proposing a particular formula would have gained less in welfare terms from implementing it than they would have gained from implementing the formulas proposed by trading partners. This is because own formulas tended to limit the reduction of barriers in politically sensitive sectors, where the economic gains from reform are greatest. The same is true of the proposals made in the Doha Round to reform policies affecting agricultural and nonagricultural market access.

4.6. FURTHER READING

Useful background reading on international negotiations is provided by Fred Ikle, *How Nations Negotiate* (New York: Harper and Row, 1964). Howard Raiffa, *The Art and Science of Negotiation* (Cambridge, MA: Harvard University Press, 1983) discusses negotiations and bargaining in general. A practical guide is presented in William Zartman and Maureen Berman, *The Practical Negotiator* (New Haven: Yale University Press, 1982). John Odell, *Negotiating the World Economy* (Cornell University Press, 2000) provides a comprehensive analysis of major economic negotiations conducted by the US since the Second World War. John McMillan, 'A Game-Theoretic View of International Trade Negotiations', in John Whalley (ed.), *Rules, Power and Credibility* (London: University of Western Ontario, 1988) explores the applicability of game theory to MTNs.

Gerard Curzon, *Multilateral Commercial Diplomacy* (London: Michael Joseph, 1965) provides a classic reference dealing with the early years of the GATT and its politics and economics. One of the best treatises on the Kennedy Round is Ernest Preeg, *Traders and Diplomats: An Analysis of the Kennedy Round under the General Agreement on Tariffs and Trade* (Washington, DC: Brookings Institution, 1970). A comprehensive and interesting account and analysis of the Tokyo Round is offered by Gilbert Winham, *International Trade and the Tokyo Round Negotiations* (Princeton: Princeton University Press, 1986). The pre-negotiation dynamics and process of the Uruguay Round is discussed by the same author in 'The Pre-negotiation Phase of the Uruguay Round', in Janice Stein (ed.), *Getting to the Table* (London: Johns Hopkins Press, 1989). L. Alan Winters, 'The Road to Uruguay,' *Economic Journal*, 100 (1990): 1288–303, gives a short review of the issues that were put on the Uruguay Round and their GATT history. Jeffrey Schott and Johanna Buurman, *The Uruguay Round: An Assessment* (Washington, DC: Institute for International Economics, 1994) offer a summary of the outcome of the negotiations. Will Martin and Alan Winters (eds), *The Uruguay Round and the Developing Countries* (Cambridge: Cambridge University Press, 1996) is a collection of papers analysing the outcome of the Uruguay Round from an economic perspective.

Thomas Hertel and L. Alan Winters (eds), *Poverty and the WTO: Impacts of the Doha Development Agenda* (Basingstoke, UK: Palgrave Macmillan, 2006) focus on the potential impacts of global trade reforms on poverty and income distribution within countries. Kym Anderson and Will Martin (eds), *Agricultural Trade Reform and the Doha Development Agenda* (Basingstoke, UK: Palgrave Macmillan, 2006) analyse the potential economic consequences of agricultural liberalization and the specific aspects of the Doha talks on agriculture.

Robert Baldwin, 'Toward More Efficient Procedures for Multilateral Trade Negotiations', *Aussenwirtschaft*, 41 (1986): 379–94, offers an accessible review of GATT negotiating techniques and problems. The contributions by Robert Baldwin and Alan Winters in J. M. Finger and A. Olechowski (eds), *The Uruguay: A Handbook for the Multilateral Trade Negotiations* (Washington, DC: The World Bank, 1987) provide succinct treatments of GATT negotiating techniques and principles. Fred Brown and John Whalley assess the welfare implications of the alternative formulas to reduce tariffs that were proposed in the Tokyo Round in 'General Equilibrium Evaluations of Tariff-Cutting Proposals in the Tokyo Round and Comparisons with More Extensive Liberalization of World Trade', *Economic Journal* (December 1980): 838–68.

Recent contributions using a political economy approach to understand the WTO negotiating process have focused on the strategic interactions and coalition building. Miles Kahler and John Odell 'Developing Country Coalition-Building and International Trade Negotiations', in John Whalley (ed.), *Developing Countries and the Global Trading System* (Ann Arbor, MI: Michigan University Press, 1989) analyse developing country involvement in international trade negotiations in the

1980s. Amrita Narlikar, *International Trade and Developing Countries* (London: Routledge, 2003) is a comprehensive analysis that covers the more recent period. The problems confronting bargaining coalitions in WTO are discussed by Amrita Narlikar and Diana Tussie in 'The G20 at the Cancun Ministerial: Developing Countries and their Evolving Coalition in the WTO', *The World Economy*, 27(7) (2004): 947–66. A useful review of the literature on political economy of coalition-building is presented by T. Sandler and K. Hartley in 'Economics of Alliances: The Lessons for Collective Action', *Journal of Economic Literature*, 39 (3) (2001): 869–96.

Robert Tollison and Thomas Willett, 'An Economic Theory of Mutually Advantageous Issue Linkages in International Negotiations', *International Organization*, 33 (1979): 425–49, and James Sebenius, 'Negotiation Arithmetic: Adding and Subtracting Issues and Parties', *International Organization*, 37 (1983): 281–316, discuss the strategy of issue linkage in international negotiations. Mancur Olson, *The Logic of Collective Action: Public Goods and the Theory of Groups* (Cambridge, MA: Harvard University Press, 1965) and Thomas Schelling, *Micromotives and Macro-Behavior* (New York: W.W. Norton, 1978) discuss necessary conditions and incentives for the formation of coalitions or clubs. Giorgio Basevi, F. Delbono and M. Mariotti analyse the complexities for MTNs that involve coalitions, focusing specifically on the EU, in 'Bargaining with a Composite Player: An Application to the Uruguay Round of GATT Negotiations', *Journal of International Comparative Economics*, 3 (1995): 161–74. John Odell discusses the implications of the distribution of trade power in 'Growing Power Meets Frustration in the Doha Round's First Four Years', in Larry Crump and S. Javed Maswood (eds), *Developing Countries and Global Trade Negotiations*, 7–40 (Routledge, 2007).

Jagdish Bhagwati and Hugh Patrick (eds), *Aggressive Unilateralism: America's 301 Trade Policy and the World Trading System* (Ann Arbor: University of Michigan Press, 1990) provide an informative and thoughtful collection of papers exploring the use of Section 301 by the US. Kenneth Oye, *Economic Discrimination and Political Exchange: World Political Economy in the 1930s and 1980s* (Princeton: Princeton University Press, 1992) discusses the role of reciprocal trade bargaining by the US. John Odell provides a detailed analysis of the preparatory process leading up to the Seattle and Doha ministerial meetings in 'Breaking Deadlocks in International Institutional Negotiations: The WTO, Seattle and Doha,' *International Studies Quarterly* (2009).

A compilation of short papers that describe the WTO and the subjects that were on the Doha negotiating agenda is available from B. Hoekman, A. Mattoo and P. English (eds), *Development, Trade and the WTO: A Handbook* (Washington, DC: The World Bank, 2002). UN Millennium Project, *Trade for Development*, (Task Force on Trade, New York: United Nations Development Programme, 2004) includes a comprehensive analysis of the issues on the Doha agenda and their importance from a perspective of economic development. Donna Lee and Rorden

NEGOTIATING FORUM 183

Wilkinson (eds), *The WTO After Hong Kong: Progress In, and Prospects For, the Doha Development Agenda* (London: Routledge, 2007) provide an international relations perspective on the Doha negotiations, including discussions of coalitions and negotiating strategies.

The WTO homepage is a primary source of information on developments in the negotiations. Another very useful online source the ICTSD website is (www.ictsd.org).

CHAPTER 5

TRADE IN GOODS

GOVERNMENTS pursue trade policies for a variety of reasons, including as a means to raise revenue, to protect specific industries (whether infant, strategic, senile or other), to shift the terms of trade, to attain certain foreign policy or security goals, or simply to restrict the consumption of specific goods. Whatever the underlying objective, an active trade policy redistributes income by transferring resources to specific industries and the factors of production employed there, generally at the expense of domestic consumers and taxpayers. It usually does so in an inefficient and nontransparent manner, and for precisely that reason tends to be supported by interest groups that lobby for import restrictions.

The GATT regulates the use of trade policies by WTO members. It does not address the basic question of whether governments should use domestic or trade policies to achieve particular objectives. That is, the issue of efficiency is not addressed directly. The premise is that inefficient instruments such as trade policy must be accepted, and that the best that can be achieved is to discipline the use of different *types* of trade policies and the *level* of the associated trade restrictions. Thus, although countries are free to use trade policies, the GATT generally encourages them to use fewer trade-distorting measures. General Agreement on Tariffs and Trade rules are mostly consistent with what economic theory would recommend in many circumstances, but only in the sense of moving governments to use second- rather than third-best instruments. The objective is to avoid the worst by accepting some bad in government intervention in trade.

Three broad categories of trade policy instruments can be distinguished: measures that affect quantities, restricting the volume or value of transactions; those that directly affect prices, involving the imposition of a monetary charge (tax) on foreign suppliers; and those that indirectly affect quantities or prices. Virtually any policy or action by a government may have an effect on trade (see Deardorff and

Stern, 1998, for a discussion of the many types of policies that have an effect on trade). As noted in Chapter 3, this is explicitly recognized in the GATT, in that dispute settlement procedures allow for so-called nonviolation complaints to be brought. Any policy—whether or not it is prohibited under GATT—can be contested if it acts to deny a benefit under the WTO.

This chapter summarizes the main GATT disciplines relating to specific instruments of trade control. For convenience, Table 5.1 lists the major articles of the GATT. Articles dealing with contingent protection (Articles VI, XII, XVIII and XIX) and general exceptions (Articles XX and XXI) are discussed in Chapter 9.

5.1. Tariffs: Articles I and II

Article I GATT requires that a product made in one member country be treated no less favourably than a 'like' (very similar) good that originates in any other country. Because the initial set of contracting parties to the GATT was quite small (only 23 countries), the benchmark for MFN is the best treatment offered to any country, including countries that may not be a member of the GATT. Similar wording now applies under the WTO.

Most favoured nation applies to all measures applied or enforced at the border as well as to domestic policies covered by the national treatment rule (Article III). To determine if discrimination between suppliers occurs it is necessary to compare apples to apples. The question of how to determine whether products are 'like' each other has been a major area of case law on national treatment. In the case of MFN matters are simpler in that recourse can be and is made to the tariff classification that is used by WTO members: products that are classified under the same heading should be treated the same. We discuss the methods used by countries to classify goods later in this subsection.

The primary focus of both Article I and Article II is tariffs. The customs tariff is in principle the only instrument of protection allowed under the GATT for nonagricultural products, given that quantitative restrictions (QRs) are prohibited by Article XI and domestic measures are subject to the national treatment rule (Article III). The preference for tariffs is consistent with economic theory. Reasons why tariffs are preferable to QRs include the following (see also Annex 2):

- Tariffs maintain an automatic link between domestic and foreign prices, ensuring that the most efficient supplier continues to be able to serve the market. This link is cut with quotas.

Table 5.1. Major GATT articles

Article	Summary
I	General MFN requirement.
II	Tariff commitments (schedules of bindings).
III	National treatment.
V	Freedom of transit of goods.
VI	Allows antidumping and countervailing duties. Superseded by the GATT 1994 Agreement on Antidumping, and the Agreement on Subsidies and Countervailing Measures.
VII	Requires that valuation of goods for customs purposes be based on actual value. Superseded by the GATT 1994 Agreement on the Implementation of Article VII.
VIII	Requires that fees connected with import/export formalities reflect actual costs of services rendered.
IX	Reaffirms MFN for labelling requirements and calls for cooperation to prevent abuse of trade names.
X	Obligation to publish trade laws and regulations; complemented by the WTO's Trade Policy Review Mechanism and numerous notification requirements in specific WTO agreements.
XI	Requires elimination of quantitative restrictions.
XII	Permits trade restrictions if necessary to safeguard the balance of payments.
XIII	Requires that quotas, if used, be administered in a nondiscriminatory manner.
XV	Contracting parties to refrain from using foreign exchange arrangements to frustrate the intent of the provisions of the GATT. Calls for the CONTRACTING PARTIES and the IMF to cooperate and consult with regard to exchange arrangements and restrictions that are in the jurisdiction of the IMF.
XVI	Notification and consultation requirements for subsidies. Export subsidies in principle not to be used after 1958 if they result in under-cutting of domestic producers; may not result in a 'more than equitable share' of world markets. Superseded by the WTO Agreement on Subsidies and Countervailing Measures.
XVII	Requires that state trading enterprises comply with MFN.
XVIII	Allows developing countries to restrict trade to promote infant industries and to protect the balance-of-payments (imposing weaker conditionality than Article XII).
XIX	Allows for emergency action to restrict imports of particular products if these cause serious injury to the domestic industry. Complemented by the WTO Agreement on Safeguards.
XX	General exceptions provision—allows trade restrictions if necessary to attain noneconomic objectives (health, safety).
XXI	Allows trade to be restricted if necessary for national security reasons.
XXII	Requires consultations between parties involved in trade disputes.
XXIII	GATT's main dispute settlement provision, providing for violation and nonviolation complaints. Complemented by the WTO Understanding on Rules and Procedures Governing the Settlement of Disputes (DSU).
XXIV	Sets out the conditions under which the formation of free trade areas or customs unions is permitted.
XXVIII	Allows for renegotiation of tariff concessions.
XXVIII bis	Calls for periodic MTNs to reduce tariffs.
XXXIII	Allows for accession. Superseded by Art. XII WTO.
Part IV	Calls for more favourable and differential treatment of developing countries.

- It is easy to ensure nondiscrimination between foreign sources of supply using tariffs; under a quota this is much more difficult. Quota allocation is often based on arbitrary decisions of officials.
- Tariffs are transparent. Once established, every trader knows the price of market access for specific products. This is not the case under a quota, where the conditions of market access may depend on timing (for example, under a first-come, first-served allocation scheme), past performance (if quotas are allocated based on historical utilization rates) or corruption (bribery of the officials responsible for licensing).
- Tariffs are also more transparent in that the level of nominal protection under tariff is easily calculated, whereas its estimation is more complex under a quota.
- Tariffs generate revenue for the government, whereas under quotas the tariff equivalent may go to the exporters or to intermediaries, depending on how the quotas are allocated. In most cases, governments do not receive the created rents—the extra revenue per unit sold that is due the price-increasing effect of restricting supply is transferred to those who have the quota rights. This is a major incentive for lobbying and rent seeking.
- Tariffs are also more efficient because they reduce lobbying incentives. Tariffs benefit the whole industry producing the protected good, reducing the returns for individual firms to lobby for protection. If quotas are an option, traders may seek individual quota allocations that are as large as possible, inducing socially wasteful lobbying.

Governments may levy tariffs on imports and exports, but import tariffs are by far the more important in practice. Customs tariffs may be:

(1) *ad valorem* (a percentage of the value of imported products);
(2) specific (a given amount of money per physical unit, say US$1.5 per litre of wine);
(3) a combination of the two (e.g. 5 per cent *ad valorem* plus US$1 per litre of wine).

The GATT does not favour one type of tariff over another.[1] In practice, most tariffs are *ad valorem*. Each may have advantages in specific situations. *Ad valorem* rates are more transparent, and are indexed. If the nominal value of a product increases (because of inflation for example), then tariff revenue will keep pace with price increases. Specific tariffs have the advantage of not requiring customs authorities to determine the value of imports when entering the country, and are by definition not sensitive to changes in the value of goods.

---

[1] WTO members may switch from *ad valorem* to specific duties if they desire, as long as this does not result in a violation of a tariff binding.

Product classification

For the GATT machinery to work it is necessary that traders know how their products will be classified for customs purposes, and that members have a common understanding regarding what goes where. Tariff commitments are made at the so-called tariff line level, which are often country-specific, even though most countries use internationally developed systems to classify imports. The main coding systems used for classification purposes during the first 40 years of the GATT era were the Brussels Tariff Nomenclature (BTN) and its successor the Customs Cooperation Council Nomenclature (CCCN). In the late 1980s, countries switched to the Harmonized Commodity Description and Coding System (HS). All these systems were developed by the Customs Cooperation Council in Brussels—which became the World Customs Organization in 1994.[2] The HS allows for a greater range of product classification than its predecessors and is also used for reporting of trade statistics (Box 5.1). More than 200 countries and economies, representing 98 per cent of world trade used the HS in 2008.

The use of the HS by WTO members is important to traders as it reduces uncertainty regarding the treatment of their goods by customs authorities. Knowing how products will be classified allows producers to finetune their production process and tailor and package their products in a way that minimizes the expected duty burden (Box 5.2.). The tariff structure of many countries is quite differentiated—close substitutes may be subject to widely varying tariffs, providing potential opportunities for producers to arbitrage across product (sub)headings.

WTO disciplines for tariffs

There are two basic rules for tariffs. First, tariffs and other policies may not discriminate between foreign products (Article I). Second, they must be bound (Article II). The main exceptions to the MFN rule are if countries are members of preferential trade agreements (Chapter 10), provide tariff preferences in favour of developing countries (Chapter 12) or confront imports from a nonmember country.

---

[2] The genesis of the WCO began with a 1947 Study Group created by 13 European governments with the mandate to examine the possibility of establishing one or more inter-European Customs Unions based on the newly negotiated GATT. In 1948, the Study Group set up two committees—an Economic Committee and a Customs Committee. The Economic Committee was the predecessor of the Organization for Economic Cooperation and Development (OECD); the Customs Committee became the Customs Cooperation Council (CCC). The WCO is now a global organization with 173 members.

Box 5.1. The Harmonized Commodity Description and Coding System (HS)

The Harmonized System provides a legal structure and product typology for the purpose of tariff classification. It comprises 1,241 headings grouped into 96 chapters (in turn subdivided into 21 sections). The system's 5,000 subheadings are identified by a six-digit code, each of which is carefully defined and described, with rules to ensure uniform application. The first four digits indicate a product group or family. The fifth and sixth digits designate specific product lines. For instance, 8470.10 is the code for 'electronic calculators capable of operating without an external source of electronic power and pocket size data recording, reproducing and displaying machines with calculating functions', whereas 8470 is the code for electronic calculating machines as a group. The HS is implemented through an international convention that requires signatories to apply it in a uniform fashion at the six-digit level. Beyond the six-digit level, countries may introduce national idiosyncrasies in their coding systems, as long as these are subclassifications of the applicable six-digit category (Article 3.3 HS). Given that such subclassifications are left to the discretion of countries, they can, in principle, be challenged before the WTO, although this has not occurred so far.

The HS nomenclature builds on an earlier standard, the CCCN, and incorporates certain aspects of the tariff schedules of the United States and Canada. The HS came into effect in 1988, and is used not only for customs purposes, but also for collection of trade statistics and associated transactions (such as transport and insurance). Before the adoption of the HS, countries tended to use the Standard International Trade Classification (SITC) for statistical purposes—developed under UN auspices. This differed substantially from the CCCN. The use of one classification system for both customs and statistical purposes greatly facilitates analysis and monitoring of tariff revenue collection and trade flows.

Source: WCO, *The 2007 Harmonized System, Explanatory Notes* (at http://www.wcoomd.org).

Most favoured nation implies that WTO members must extend any advantage immediately and unconditionally to all WTO members. Unconditional means 'no strings attached'. For example, a country cannot condition a tariff on exporting countries satisfying a specific labour standard (that is, impose a higher rate on countries that do not satisfy whatever criterion is imposed) even if domestic producers are subject to it. However, if a country offers *preferential* access—that is, better than MFN—as is permitted for developing countries, this may be conditioned on the satisfaction of certain criteria (see Chapter 12). Disputes can be brought to the WTO alleging not just *de jure* violation of MFN, but also de facto violation.[3] Moreover, a complainant need not show actual trade effects. It suffices

---

[3] In *Canada—Autos*, a WTO dispute settlement panel was asked to consider whether a measure that limits the benefits of an import duty exemption to a certain class of domestic importers without imposing any restrictions regarding the origin of the imported goods constitutes a de facto violation of MFN. The panel and the AB found against Canada, arguing that the extensive intrafirm trade in automotive products between Canada and the US implied that the Canadian duty exemption scheme was likely to benefit imports from the US.

Box 5.2. Product strategy and customs classification

Average customs tariffs on agricultural products tend to be substantially higher than on industrial goods. Product classification by customs consequently may have important implications for an exporter's competitive position in a given market. In such cases managers will analyse the differences between product duty rates in order to adjust their product strategy. Three examples:

• The Canadian Dehydrators Association exports alfalfa feed products all over the world. It monitors any modifications in customs rates for particular feed product lines in order to modify its export product mix to minimize import charges. One option that is used is to mix dehydrated alfalfa products with other types of feed (such as grains) in order to benefit from lower customs rates.
• An East European company exporting food ingredients to Japan used to mix its powder milk with fat and then separate it again in Japan. It did this to pay lower customs duties on 'frozen cheese' rather than higher duties levied on powder milk and on animal fats when exported separately.
• A US sugar refinery imports 'stuffed molasses', a syrup with a high sugar content, to produce a liquid sugar product for sale to ice-cream and confectionery companies, allowing it to avoid high duties on sugar.

Source: Kostecki (2001).

that a WTO member creates more favourable competitive opportunities for some countries that are not extended to others.

World Trade Organization members may not raise tariffs above the levels they have bound in their schedules. The tariff concessions made by members upon accession or in periodic MTNs are expressed in the form of tariff bindings inscribed in each member's tariff schedule (Article II). By binding its tariff, a member undertakes not to impose a duty on a specific product that is higher than the bound rate. A binding may be identical to the currently applied rate; it may comprise a so-called ceiling rate that is higher than the applied rate; or it may consist of a pre-commitment, a negotiated rate that is lower than the currently applied rate. The last possibility often arises after a MTN has been completed, with the negotiated rate entering into force at a specified future date. Tariff binding does not preclude levying a tax at the border that is equivalent to an internal tax as long as national treatment is satisfied, i.e. governments can collect applicable excise or other indirect taxes at the border (Article III:1a). For example, in *India—Additional Duties on Imports*, a 2008 panel report found that additional duties imposed on US imports were equivalent to internal taxes imposed by Indian States and thus legal. (Note that the burden of proof in such cases is put on the complainant.)

A tariff binding establishes a benchmark for the conditions of market access that a country commits itself to. Any measure taken or supported by a government that has the effect of nullifying or impairing the concession implied by its tariff bindings justifies complaint by trading partners. There is no need to show an impact on trade. Thus, the binding not only restricts the possibility of raising tariffs, but also limits the possibility of using measures that have an equivalent effect, such as indirect taxation (however, as discussed in Chapter 9, there are various ways around this constraint).

World Trade Organization members have agreed to apply the HS at the six-digit level of disaggregation. Thus, up to that level tariff classifications are identical. Beyond the six-digit level—that is, for finer degrees of differentiation—countries are free to define subcategories of products. Although the HS helps to make the customs environment more predictable, it is important to note that WTO members sometimes bind their tariffs at the 10 or 12 digit level of disaggregation. At this level, classification is country-specific. However, members may not impose tariffs at a finer level of disaggregation that exceed the binding that has been made at a more aggregated level.

To a significant extent the tariff schedules determine the relevance of GATT rules. Formally, the product coverage of the GATT for each member is determined by a positive list approach. Each member includes in its schedule the products (tariff lines) on which it is willing to make tariff commitments. These schedules form an integral part of the GATT. The comprehensiveness of tariff bindings for members has traditionally varied considerably. For most industrialized market economies, the share of bound tariffs in the total number of tariff lines has always been high for manufactured goods. The coverage of bindings for most developing countries has historically been very low or nonexistent, and usually limited to ceiling bindings that are significantly higher than applied rates.

Many contracting parties joined GATT 1947 after becoming independent in the late 1950s or in the 1960s. Such former colonies were allowed to accede to GATT without tariff negotiations. Developing countries were also granted special and differential treatment, allowing them not to offer concessions in MTNs (see Chapter 12). This implied that only nondiscrimination disciplines applied, as countries are free to raise tariffs if there are no ceiling bindings. During the Uruguay Round an attempt was made to expand the coverage of bindings by requiring all WTO members to submit tariff schedules. In contrast to GATT 1947, WTO membership requires a schedule of commitments. Moreover, all WTO members are obliged to bind 100 per cent of their agricultural tariff lines—a major change in comparison with GATT 1947, under which agriculture had largely become exempt from disciplines (Chapter 6). Although there are no rules concerning the product coverage of tariff schedules for nonagricultural goods, developing country participation as measured by the scope of tariff bindings increased substantially during the Uruguay Round. This reflected a realization on their part that greater participation in the multilateral trading system was beneficial, as well as significant unilateral liberalization undertaken by many countries since the early 1980s. The share of industrial tariff lines bound by developing countries increased from 22 to 72 per cent (Table 5.2).

Table 5.2. Tariff bindings for industrial products, pre- and post-
Uruguay Round

Country Group	Number of Lines	Percentage of Tariff Lines Bound	
		Pre-Uruguay	Post-Uruguay
Developed countries	86,968	78	99
Developing countries*	157,805	22	72
Transition economies	18,962	73	98

Note: *Data span 26 countries accounting for 80 per cent of the total trade of countries participating.
Source: GATT (1994c).

Binding coverage was above 95 per cent of tariff lines in developed and transition economies in 2007, but developing-country tariffs are either not bound or bound at relatively high levels. Low binding coverage is particularly prevalent for Asian countries (averaging 40 per cent). There is also considerable variation in the share of bound duty-free tariff lines. For developed countries this ranges from 17 per cent for Switzerland to close to 50 per cent for Japan. The share of lines with bound zero duties in developing countries is very low (Bacchetta and Bora, 2004).

Most developing country bindings relate to 'ceilings' (maximum rates), not applied tariffs. Ceiling rates are less valuable than if applied rates were inscribed, but do have value, as they establish an upper bound on the downside risk confronted by traders and investors (Francois and Martin, 2004). The difference between the average applied and bound rate is a measure of what has been called the binding overhang. The greater this difference, the deeper the average tariff cut that must be realized in a MTN for the outcome to imply actual liberalization. It is often not realized that the focus of MTNs is on tariff bindings, not on applied rates. An implication is that a claim that a MTN reduced average tariffs by, say, 30 per cent does not necessarily imply that applied tariffs have fallen by that extent.

Of the 153 members of the WTO, most have scheduled tariff bindings that are far above applied tariff rates. Only eight members have mostly bound their tariffs at applied levels: the EU, the US, Japan and Canada (the Quad), plus China, Chinese Taipei (Taiwan), Hong Kong and Macao. These eight 'full' members account for 67 per cent of world trade and 78 per cent of global GDP (Table 5.3). Although most trade is therefore fully subject to WTO rules, these statistics also imply that one-third of global trade is not 'secure' in that the governments concerned can significantly increase tariffs if they desire without violating tariff bindings. On average, the majority of WTO members can raise applied tariffs threefold if they wish

Table 5.3. Average applied and bound tariff levels, 2008

WTO Members	Global Import Share	Global GDP Share	Simple Average Tariff				Import Weighted Tariff			
			Industry		Agriculture		Industry		Agriculture	
			Bound	Applied	Bound	Applied	Bound	Applied	Bound	Applied
Eight large 'full' members	67.1	78.1	4.1	3.9	13.1	13.4	3.6	3.4	11.4	11.8
26 largest other members	26.2	17.5	27.6	7.9	65.8	19	21.5	7.1	60.2	22.8
All other members	2.0	4.4	34.3	9.9	62.3	17	26.5	9.6	49.7	19.8

Source: Messerlin (2008a).

without incurring any penalties. Least developed countries have even greater 'head-room' to raise tariffs. A post-Cancun Decision of the General Council called for LDCs with a binding coverage less than 35 per cent, while exempt from making tariff reductions, to bind 100 per cent of their tariff lines at the average applying for all developing countries.

Why don't countries bind tariffs at applied rates? In many cases it simply reflects the mercantilism underlying the GATT (that is, a perception that bindings are negotiating chips). In addition, finance ministries may be opposed to losing a revenue raising tool. The latter consideration is particularly important for low-income countries that are dependent on taxation of foreign trade for revenue. Finally, countries with overvalued exchange rates and resulting foreign exchange shortages and rationing often have no wish to be subjected to GATT surveillance in instances where measures are required to safeguard the balance of payments (see Chapter 9).

In a MTN context, a country must determine what the cost–benefit ratio is of binding or not binding at applied rates. One source of benefit is the quid pro quo that may be realized in terms of improved access to foreign markets. This is the benefit that most often appears to be uppermost in the minds of policymakers. However, this is arguably not the key dimension of the tradeoff, especially for small countries with little if any negotiating power. More important is to take into account that binding at or below applied rates can be a powerful tool with which to signal to investors that the government is serious about reducing uncertainty regarding its future trade policy stance. This can have substantial payoffs in terms of reducing risk premia demanded by investors and stimulating capital inflows.

Tariff-related disputes

Numerous disputes have been brought over the years relating to allegations of violations of tariff bindings. These disputes have also clarified the rules of the game. An example is a 1997 case brought by the US against the EU, which had reclassified for tariff purposes certain local area network (LAN) adapter equipment and personal computers with multimedia capability. The US alleged that this violated EU tariff bindings (Article II:1 GATT). The panel found against the EU. On appeal, the Appellate Body (AB) reversed the panel's conclusion, ruling that the US had not satisfied the burden of proof and that the panel should have examined the HS in interpreting the EU tariff commitments. But the AB did not come to a clear conclusion regarding the matter because it may not rule on factual dimensions of a case, but only on the legal reasoning of the panel. The EU eventually abolished tariffs on the products concerned as a result of the Information Technology Agreement (see Chapter 11).

A 2003 case, also against the EU (*EC—Chicken Cuts*), illustrates the type of classification disputes that may arise. The EU had bound its tariffs on meat, 'salted, in brine, dried or smoked' at an *ad valorem* 15.4 per cent. Tariffs on fresh, chilled or frozen poultry were specific, at €102.4 per 100 kilograms, which implied an *ad valorem* equivalent between 40 and 60 per cent. Thai and Brazilian firms had been exporting frozen chicken cuts treated with salt under the salted meat tariff heading until 2002 when the EU instructed customs to classify chicken into the lower tariff item only if salt was added for the purpose of long-term preservation. The complainants argued that it was irrelevant what the purpose of the salt was. The AB found against the EU—on the basis of arguments that have been contested in the literature (Howse and Horn, 2008).

Other fees and charges on imports

World Trade Organization members are constrained regarding the use of fees and specific import taxes that have an effect equivalent to tariffs. Examples include taxes on foreign exchange transactions, service fees affecting importers and special import surcharges. Such para-tariffs as they are sometimes called used to be particularly important in developing countries. Data for a sample of 41 developing countries in the early 1980s indicated that at least one-third of revenue from import taxation was generated by para-tariffs. Such measures were frequently subject to arbitrary implementation and were nontransparent (Kostecki and Tymowski, 1985). They were often driven by specific interest groups that had successfully lobbied for earmarked taxes to finance their activities. Para-tariffs continue to be used today. For example, in 2004 an industrial development surcharge and supplementary duties accounted for some 38 per cent of the overall average level of protection in Bangladesh (World Bank, 2004). In such cases the average statutory customs duty will give a misleading picture of the actual structure of protection, especially if the para-tariffs vary by good or sector.

In contrast to GATT 1947, the GATT 1994 requires that the nature and level of other duties or charges be listed by tariff line in each WTO member's schedule. Allowance is made for the imposition of fees or other charges, as long as these are commensurate with the cost of services rendered (Article II:2c). Article VIII (on fees and formalities related to trade) requires that all such service fees must 'be limited in amount to the approximate cost of services rendered and shall not represent an indirect protection to domestic products or a taxation of imports or exports for fiscal purposes' (Article VIII:1). Examples of such fees include consular transactions, licensing, statistical services, documentation, certification, inspection, quarantine, sanitation and fumigation. Article VIII applies irrespective of whether a country has bound its tariffs. The requirement that service fees be cost-based aims to prevent circumvention of tariff bindings.

In a 1988 GATT dispute concerning the imposition of a uniform *ad valorem* customs user fee by the US, the panel concluded that such fees must be service-specific (GATT, 1994*b*: 251). Imposing an average fee equal to the total cost of customs administration divided by the total value of imports was not acceptable. Although the US altered its customs user fee to conform to these findings, other countries continued to maintain *ad valorem* fees that were inconsistent with the GATT. In part this was because service fees in existence on the date of a country's accession to GATT were grandfathered and thus immune from scrutiny. Developing countries also had greater leeway than industrialized countries, as their tariffs often were not bound. As of the mid-1990s, some developing countries continued to maintain customs user fees of 5 per cent *ad valorem* or higher (Messerlin and Zarrouk, 2000). After 2001, terrorist threats contributed to increases in customs user fees in a number of countries. For example, the US Customs and Border Protection increased certain charges by 10 per cent in 2007 to cover the costs of stricter border controls.

With the establishment of the WTO, in principle all grandfathered policies that are inconsistent with WTO rules had to be abolished. It is likely that over time WTO members will be less tolerant of fees on imports that are not cost-based. The issue arose several times in the WTO. For example, in 1998 the EU contested a US Harbor Maintenance Tax (a 0.125 *ad valorem* duty on imports) as a violation of among others, Articles II and VIII, as well as the Uruguay Round Understanding on the Interpretation of Article II:1*b* (WT/DS118). This Understanding is quite important from a transparency perspective, as it requires members to notify *all* the duties and charges that apply in connection with importation of goods. The case led to a MAS, based on a US commitment to alter its legislation.[4] In *Argentina—Textiles and Apparel* (WT/DS56) the US contested a system of minimum specific import duties and a statistical services tax in Argentina. In its 1998 ruling, the AB found both measures to be inconsistent with Article II:1*b* GATT as they resulted in customs levies in excess of those provided in Argentina's schedule.

Tariff peaks and escalation

The structure of tariffs maintained by WTO members varies considerably in OECD countries. High tariffs are particularly frequent for agricultural imports. In the EU, about one-quarter of post-Uruguay Round imports of manufactured goods is

---

[4] The tax initially applied to exports as well but this was declared to be unconstitutional by the US Supreme Court in 1998 because it was a tax and not a user fee (the US constitution prohibits the use of export taxes). The result of exempting exports was that the tax not only was inconsistent with WTO rules—not being a cost-based user fee—but also violated the national treatment principle.

duty-free, and some 40 per cent are subjected to tariffs below 5 per cent. Tariffs above 25 per cent are imposed on a negligible share of imports of manufactures. In the US, duty-free imports account for some 80 per cent of the total; a tariff rate of more than 10 per cent is imposed on less than 3 per cent of imports. Developed countries' tariffs show important dispersion in bound tariff rates and significant peaks especially in products such as textiles, clothing and leather goods. These three product categories have the lowest share of bound duty-free lines across countries, the highest tariff averages and the most lines with peaks (Bacchetta and Bora, 2004).

World Trade Organization members are free to determine the structure of their tariff regimes. Many countries tend to impose a structure that taxes inputs and unprocessed products less than finished goods. Such tariff escalation has been a problem for developing countries seeking to process commodities before they are exported. The more escalated is the tariff structure maintained in export markets, the greater the difficulty for such countries to generate value-added at home, as the low tariffs on raw materials (usually duty-free) provide an incentive not to process commodities before they are exported. A group of products where tariff escalation has often been a source of particular concern to developing countries are natural resource-based products, defined in GATT to include nonferrous metals and minerals, forestry products and fish and fishery products.

Escalation is a feature of almost all tariff structures. The exceptions are the few economies that essentially have a free trade stance (e.g. Hong Kong) or have implemented a uniform tariff, that is, apply the same tariff to imports of all goods (examples include Bolivia, Chile, the Kyrgyz Republic and Estonia before it acceded to the EU). At the product level, tariff escalation may occur even if the overall structure exhibits little or no escalation. This is often the case for textiles and clothing and leather products, where inputs—cotton, yarn, raw hides—tend to have lower duties than does the finished product.

There are good economic arguments against escalation. A uniform tariff structure ensures that all activities are treated equally, leaving it to the market to determine what activities are profitable to undertake. Uniformity also has important benefits in terms of incentives for rent seeking, as it sends a signal to firms that there will be no exemptions and that it will not pay to lobby for either higher or lower tariffs. Thus, a uniform rate saves on lobbying costs, and induces less corruption and social waste. Lobbying is unattractive because efforts to increase the tariff will affect virtually the whole economy, and solicit opposition by users of imported inputs. Indeed, a uniform tariff, because it puts pressure on industries that are dependent on imports, creates incentives for lobbying in favour of reducing the average rate. In the case of Chile, which maintained an 11 per cent tariff for some years, a decision was made to gradually lower it to 6 per cent, starting in 1998.

Another advantage of a uniform tariff is that it lowers transaction costs—there is no scope to argue about how products should be classified for customs duty calculation purposes. Uniformity also tends to make it easier for the government to monitor the performance of customs agencies—given data on the value of imports it is easy to calculate how much revenue should have been collected. A uniform tariff is more difficult for countries to maintain in MTNs, if these take the form of bid-offer negotiations. All a government can do is to make offers of formula cuts. As a result of this 'constraint'—which is really an advantage from an economic perspective—statements have been made in the WTO Council opposing the use of uniform tariffs. This is an example of putting the cart before the horse: the desire to use a certain negotiating technique potentially impeding the use of an efficient trade policy by WTO members.

In addition to deliberate tariff escalation, dispersion in the structure of tariffs often results from duty exemption programmes. Exemptions may be granted to enterprises that engage in certain 'favoured' activities—a frequent example is foreign investors, who are often granted tax holidays and duty exemption for imported inputs and capital equipment. The welfare effect of such discrimination is ambiguous, but is likely to be negative as it will distort resource allocation incentives and may generate socially wasteful lobbying. This is not the case for duty exemptions granted to firms and industries that produce for export. Exporting firms must be able to import inputs, including machinery, at world prices. Otherwise they will be impeded in their ability to compete on international markets. To ensure that this is not the case many countries have implemented duty drawback or temporary duty-free admission schemes for inputs used in export production as part of their customs procedures. Although such mechanisms are an important tool of export development if they function efficiently, from a political economy viewpoint they suffer from the problem that they reduce the incentives for exporters to support general import liberalization. In general, non-export-related duty exemptions are a costly policy instrument as they can encourage corrution and rent seeking, reduce revenue collected by customs, and distort economic incentives.

The Doha ministerial declaration stipulated that special attention be paid to reducing tariff peaks and escalation. This motivated the use of a nonlinear formula approach, with flexibility for developing countries (see Chapter 4).

5.2. NATIONAL TREATMENT: ARTICLE III

The national treatment rule is the second leg of the nondiscrimination principle. It requires that foreign goods—once they have paid tariffs and satisfied whatever border measures apply—be treated no less favourably than like or directly competitive goods produced domestically in terms of internal (indirect) taxation (Article III:2 GATT). That is, goods of foreign origin circulating in the country must be subject to the same taxes and charges that apply to identical goods of domestic origin. A similar obligation applies to nontax policies (regulations) (Article III:4 GATT). In both cases, members are to provide treatment 'no less favourable' to foreign products as they accord to domestic goods. Although Article III distinguishes between fiscal and nonfiscal measures, the AB increasingly takes the view that Article III.1 GATT discourages the protectionist use of domestic legislation no matter the type of policy involved (Mavroidis, 2007).

National treatment is a general obligation in the GATT, although not in the GATS (see Chapter 7). Its role is to ensure that liberalization commitments are not offset through the imposition of domestic taxes or other regulatory measures. By requiring that foreign products be treated no less favourably than domestically produced competing products, foreign suppliers obtain greater certainty regarding the regulatory environment in which they must operate. The purpose of Article III GATT is to constrain circumvention of tariff bindings through the discriminatory application of domestic policies (Box 5.3). The importance of Article III has increased over time as tariff levels have fallen. Especially in high-income countries, tariffs are now quite low on average, and NTMs increasingly determine the conditions of competition on markets. Some 30 per cent of all tariff lines in OECD countries are subject to NTMs of some kind—not taking into account indirect taxes (Figure 5.1). Many of the NTMs in use today are subject to specific WTO disciplines that are the subject of the remainder of this chapter and subsequent ones. All are subject to the national treatment rule.

Article III:8 GATT excludes subsidies and government procurement from the reach of national treatment. In the case of purchases by government entities, the carve-out from national treatment is only for goods that are not resold. Subsidies are regulated by the WTO Agreement on Subsidies and Countervailing Measures (discussed later in this chapter), whereas procurement is the subject of a plurilateral Agreement on Government Procurement (discussed in Chapter 11). The reason both of these policy areas were excluded from Article III was that the initial GATT contracting parties wanted to be able to use these instruments to favour domestic industries.

The national treatment principle has often been invoked in dispute settlement cases brought to the GATT. It was the basis for the first case brought against China. In its Accession Protocol China bound tariffs on cars at 25 per cent and on parts at 10 per cent. In 2005, China imposed a tax of 25 per cent on cars assembled in China from imported parts. The 2008 WTO panel ruling held that this was a discriminatory internal tax. Even if not regarded as an internal tax it clearly violated the tariff binding. National treatment is a very wide-ranging rule. The obligation applies whether or not a specific tariff commitment was made, and whether or not a tariff is bound. It covers taxes as well as other domestic regulatory measures: *any and all* policies must be applied in a

Box 5.3. The rationale for the National Treatment Principle

The standard theoretical rationale offered for the national treatment rule in the literature is that it prevents 'concession erosion' through indirect taxation or other policies that discriminate against imported goods once they have entered a customs territory. The principle is very far-reaching, which can give rise to tensions. There may be good reasons for governments to adopt regulatory measures that discriminate between foreign and domestic products—for example, if foreign firms are much more efficient and the market is imperfectly competitive higher tax rates on the foreign firm(s) may induce them to lower prices charged to consumers. The national treatment rule precludes the use of domestic tax policy to offset such domestic market distortions. However, it will only rarely be the case that differential taxation of foreign and domestic goods is the optimal instrument to offset domestic distortions. In the example just mentioned, the problem can be addressed more directly through the imposition of tariffs on the foreign products. But as noted by Horn (2006), in practice governments may not be able to negotiate tariffs that internalize whatever distortions occur at the border. If so, the national treatment rule will prevent them from using domestic policies instead—thus potentially reducing welfare.

Saggi and Sara (2008) argue that quality differentials across countries may have important implications for the effects of national treatment. They note that while the notion of likeness of products is central in the application of the rule, a practical problem is that competing products from different countries are often differentiated from one another. Are a Toyota Camry and a Ford Taurus—two cars that contest the same segment of the US market—like products? Although very similar cars, they are not of identical quality and both are inferior to a higher end competitor such as a BMW. Even for relatively homogenous goods, national origin itself can serve as a signal of quality and therefore a source of product differentiation. Motivated by such considerations, Saggi and Sara analyse when and why heterogeneous countries producing differentiated goods find it in their mutual interest to abide by national treatment. In their model, discrimination against the foreign product is in each country's interest. By definition, a national treatment agreement between the two countries rules out such 'beggar-thy-neighbour' tax discrimination. They find that if market size is equal across countries, the high-quality country benefits from national treatment, but the low-quality country loses. On the other hand, when market size differs across countries, national treatment can make both countries better off relative to tax discrimination. Thus, asymmetry in market size helps counterbalance the quality differences across countries, but only when the quality gap between goods is not too large. This result corresponds quite well with the emphasis put on the 'likeness' criterion in the WTO.

nondiscriminatory fashion to like domestic and foreign products. It is irrelevant whether a policy actually hurts an exporter (has an impact on trade). What matters is discrimination per se.

For a violation of Article III GATT to occur, a complainant must establish that a WTO member has intervened through regulatory means so as to afford protection

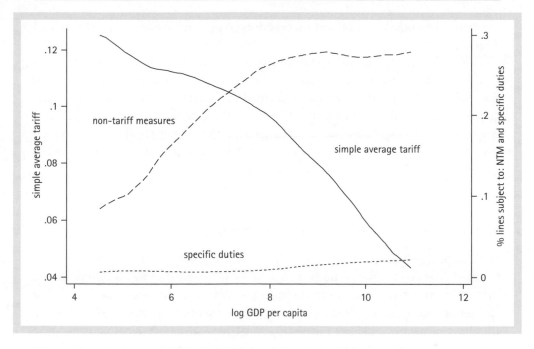

Figure 5.1. Average tariffs and NTMs and per capita income, 2006

Source: Hoekman and Nicita (2008).

to domestic competing (like) products.[5] General Agreement on Tariffs and Trade/ WTO case law has clarified that for likeness to be determined: (1) demand-side factors are relevant; (2) economic criteria may be used; and (3) all like products have to be directly competitive or substitutable. In the GATT years criteria to establish the likeness of goods or that a product was directly competitive or substitutable included whether end-uses in a given market were similar and the product's properties, nature and quality. In the WTO era greater use has begun to be made of economic criteria such as the cross-price elasticity of demand in determining likeness.

For products to be 'like' they have to share some properties beyond what two directly competitive or substitutable products share. So far, WTO case law has offered one such extra property: customs classification. Two products that fall under the same HS classification are considered to be like. However, this is not necessarily sufficient. In the *EC—Asbestos* dispute, for example, the AB found that asbestos-containing construction material and asbestos-free construction material are unlike products for the purposes of Article III.4 GATT, even though from an economic end-use perspective they fulfill exactly the same need. Thus, physical

[5] What follows draws on Hoekman and Mavroidis (2007).

characteristics may be an important criterion (Horn and Weiler, 2004; Howse and Tuerk, 2006).[6]

The WTO agreements on Technical Barriers to Trade (TBT) and Sanitary and Phytosanitary Measures (discussed later in this chapter) address specific types of domestic regulation. If a measure is deemed to violate national treatment but is covered by one of these agreements, the rules of the specific agreement apply. There is a hierarchy of these agreements: the SPS agreement, if applicable to a product, dominates the TBT agreement, while the TBT agreement dominates the more general GATT disciplines (see Mavroidis, 2007).

Regulation 'so as to afford protection'

With respect to fiscal policies, Article III.2 GATT requires that foreign products not be taxed in excess of like domestic products so as to afford protection to domestic directly competitive or substitutable products. World Trade Organization case law has defined the term 'excess' as a nonzero difference in tax rates. But for a measure to afford protection, the tax differential must have an effect. That is, it must be more than *de minimis*, which can only be determined on a case-by-case basis. When it comes to nonfiscal measures, Article III.4 GATT requires that imported products not be treated less favourably than domestic like products. Even if two products are 'like', for a measure to be inconsistent with Article III:4 a complaining member must establish that 'like' imported products are accorded less favourable treatment than 'like' domestic products.

To establish whether a regulation operates in a protectionist manner, a successful complainant does not have to show either protective effects or protective intent. Trade effects and/or regulatory intent do not matter when determining whether a domestic policy measure has the effect of affording protection. Moreover, likeness or direct comparability/substitutability may be established through various means or criteria. The resulting broad reach and flexibility can result in panels and the AB outlawing legislation that may not have protectionist effects or intent.

An example of the type of ambiguity that may arise was a case involving a Chilean law that distinguished between three categories of alcoholic beverages: drinks with less than 35 per cent alcoholic content; drinks between 35 per cent and

---

[6] In this dispute the AB reversed the panel on its determination of likeness by introducing the construct of a 'reasonable consumer', which allowed them to apply available econometric data to a counterfactual situation where this 'consumer' had not been confronted with a choice between asbestos- and nonasbestos-containing products. A result of this approach was that it provided grounds for certain groups to argue that the result of this case is that the WTO applies to production and processing methods (PPMs)—see below.

39 per cent; and drinks with alcoholic content above 39 per cent. The products in the first category were taxed at 27 per cent *ad valorem* and those in the third one at 47 per cent *ad valorem*. The complaining parties argued that some imported products of slightly more than 39 per cent were directly comparable to Chilean products of less than 35 per cent and that the tax differential operated so as to afford protection. Chile responded that the majority of the affected products were domestic and that no protection could therefore result. The AB dismissed the relevance of this fact, arguing equality of competitive conditions for *all* directly competitive or substitutable imported products was required in relation to domestic products, and not just the treatment of imported products within a particular fiscal category. What mattered in particular was the cumulative consequence of the policy: that approximately 75 per cent of all domestic production of the distilled alcoholic beverages at issue fell under the lowest tax rate, whereas approximately 95 per cent of the directly competitive or substitutable imported products were subject to the highest tax rate.

Many countries maintain tax systems under which tariffs paid on imported goods that are used in the production of exports are rebated to the exporter. Many countries also maintain value added tax (VAT) systems under which tax paid on imports are rebated on export. Such drawback systems are permitted by GATT as they do not violate national treatment: what matters for national treatment is whether foreign and domestic like goods are treated the same when sold on the domestic market. However, the VAT and other tax rebates may constitute actionable subsidies if they do more than return actual taxes paid.

5.3. QUANTITATIVE RESTRICTIONS, EXCHANGE RATES AND IMPORT LICENSING

General Agreement on Tariffs and Trade rules on QRs were written when the use of such measures was widespread. During the GATT years QRs were particularly prevalent in trade in agricultural products, textiles and clothing, and steel. Over time, the relative importance of QRs declined substantially. Notwithstanding the reduction in the use of QRs, the GATT provisions banning their use continue to be a frequently invoked basis for dispute settlement. Many of these cases concern developing countries; they also often concern measures that are argued to have an effect that is equivalent to a quantitative restriction.

The economic case against the use of quotas was summarized earlier. A quota cuts the link between domestic and foreign prices, is generally discriminatory, may not allow the changing pattern of comparative advantage over time to be reflected in imports, is less transparent, and more open to administrative abuse and corruption. For all these reasons interest groups seeking protection tend to prefer QRs to tariffs. Another motivation for the use of QRs by governments is that if the associated licences are allocated to exporters they offer some automatic compensation (see Annex 2).

WTO disciplines

Articles XI–XIV of the GATT provide the legal framework addressing QRs. Article XI prohibits them in principle, except for agricultural commodities if concurrent measures are taken to restrict domestic production (Chapter 6). Article XII provides another exception, allowing QRs to be used for balance-of-payments (BOP) reasons. If this is done, Article XIII requires that such quotas in principle apply on a nondiscriminatory basis, whereas Article XIV allows for a request that the Council waives this requirement. These provisions are complemented by the Agreement of Safeguards, which bans the use of VERs, a specific type of QR that is applied by the exporting country rather than the importer (see Annex 2).

The basic obligation imposed on members in Article XI:1 is to refrain from introducing or maintaining QRs, whether on imports or exports. Quantitative restrictions are banned not so much because of economic considerations— although the ban is certainly consistent with economic first principles—but to prevent governments from circumventing tariff bindings. Article XIII requires that if QRs are used they abide by the MFN principle. The economic rationale for this is that a global quota is more efficient than selective QRs. Under a global quota traders (importers) are left free to determine from where to source. The direction of trade (sourcing of imports) will then be responsive to changes in prices, quality and transportation costs. From the standard reciprocity perspective—maintaining a balance of concessions—the MFN rule disciplines the country-specific allocation of quota rights, which can easily imply de facto discrimination. Country-specific allocations are usually based on historical market shares, the idea being to reduce all exporters' market access rights proportionally.

World Trade Organization case law has defined QRs broadly to include any measure that is equivalent. For example, a GATT-era panel report, *Japan— Semiconductors* held that if a government provides incentives for private parties to act in a manner inconsistent with Article XI GATT, such behaviour is GATT-inconsistent. In the semiconductor case, Japanese firms raised prices (which led to reduced exports) as a result of incentives (including administrative guidance and monitoring of costs and prices) by the Japanese government. Thus, the term 'QR' covers anything that might operate as a QR, irrespective of whether the subject of the challenged activity is the state or the private sector. However, for the behaviour by firms to be subject to Article XI GATT, they must be attributable to an action by a government that creates an incentive to cut back imports or exports. Moreover, to attack such de facto QRs a successful legal challenge requires the complainant to demonstrate a causal link between the contested measure and a reduction in trade. In the case of *de jure* QRs, the need to document trade effects is less: what matters is that competitive opportunities of imported products have been affected.

In *Argentina—Hides and Leather* (WT/DS155), the EU held that the presence of representatives of the domestic leather (tanning) industry in Argentine customs sufficed to establish a QR, as it was in their interest to seek to restrict exports of hides. The panel rejected this claim, arguing that the presence of representatives of the domestic industry did not suffice for establishing a violation of Article XI GATT. The panel held that the burden of proof was on the EU to provide evidence that the result was to reduce or restrict exports of hides. Surveillance by competitors could not be shown to be a QR.

Despite the general prohibition on QRs, they were widely used during the GATT years by governments to protect domestic import-competing industries. In the Uruguay Round disciplines in this area were strengthened, with the outlawing of VERs, the tariffication of agricultural quotas and the agreement to phase out textile and clothing quotas administered under the auspices of the MFA (see Chapters 6 and 9). Formal QRs were used especially in the agricultural context by industrialized countries and for BOP purposes by developing countries. A very popular form of QR—used increasingly in the 1970s and 1980s—was the VER, often negotiated as 'undertakings' agreed to by exporters to reduce supply or raise prices in the context of antidumping investigations. Following the ban on VERs and agricultural QRs in the Uruguay Round tariff quotas have become much more important in agriculture (Chapter 6).

Examples of disputes where policies were found to violate WTO rules on QRs include *Canada—Periodicals* (an import ban); *EC—Poultry* (tariff rate quotas); *India—Quantitative Restrictions* (QRs for balance-of-payments purposes); *India—Autos* (a trade balancing requirement); *Dominican Republic—Cigarettes* (a requirement for importers to post a bond operated as a QR); and *Brazil—Retreaded Tires* (import prohibition).

Foreign exchange arrangements and restrictions

Article XV calls on contracting parties not to use exchange rates to frustrate the intent of the provisions of the GATT (Article XV:4). It also requires that the CONTRACTING PARTIES consult fully with the IMF on monetary reserves, balances of payments or foreign exchange arrangements. In such consultations, the CONTRACTING PARTIES are to accept findings of statistical and other facts presented by the Fund and the determination of the Fund as to whether action by a contracting party in exchange matters is in accordance with the Articles of Agreement of the IMF (see Box 5.4). These disciplines were drafted at a time when exchange rates were fixed. The IMF's mission was to monitor exchange rates and assist countries dealing with balance-of-payments problems through the provision of loans to finance deficits and provide breathing room for countries to adjust to an external shock. As countries shifted to systems of (managed) floating exchange rates, the main role of the IMF continued to revolve around surveillance and provision of assistance to members to deal with macroeconomic imbalances.

A country can use the exchange rate to achieve trade policy objectives. Indeed, by undervaluing the exchange rate, the same effect can be achieved as a combination of import barriers and export subsidies. This was recognized by the drafters of the GATT and explains the inclusion of Article XV. The existence of the IMF helps understand why the GATT disciplines are not very specific: it was left to the IMF to address exchange rate misalignments. It is not surprising therefore that there have been no disputes under the GATT or the WTO regarding the level of exchange rates.

Substantial progress was made to eliminate exchange restrictions in the decades following the creation of the GATT. The IMF actively promoted current account convertibility through consultations, technical assistance, programme conditionality and research showing the benefits of such liberalization. Domestic factors also

---

Box 5.4. What's an exchange restriction? *Dominican Republic—Cigarettes*

In a 2004/5 dispute involving two developing countries a WTO panel considered, among others, the definition of exchange restrictions. Responding to Honduras' complaint, the Dominican Republic argued that a foreign exchange fee charged on certain import transactions was an exchange measure within Article XV: 9(a) of the GATT and thus justified even if otherwise inconsistent with GATT Article II. It argued that the fee 'is prescribed by monetary authorities, not by trade or customs authorities; it applies to exchange actions, not to import transactions as such; and it is a charge on foreign exchange transactions imposed through the banking system, not a charge on import transactions levied by customs authorities' (WT/DS302). The panel rejected the above defence under Article XV:9 on the grounds that 'since Article XV:9 of the GATT exempts exchange measures that are applied in accordance with [IMF] Articles, from obligations under other Articles of the GATT, the guiding principle that the IMF prescribed as the criterion for the determination of what constitutes an "exchange restriction" should be respected by this Panel'. Thus, the panel asked the IMF for a legal opinion as to whether the Dominican Republic measure was an 'exchange restriction', and the IMF replied that in its current form, as a fee charged on importation rather than all foreign currency transactions, the measure was not an 'exchange restriction'. The panel followed the IMF's opinion and found that the fee in question was not an exchange measure justified by Article XV:9(a) of the GATT; the AB essentially upheld the panel's finding (DS202 and Howse, 2008).

played a role, for example the rise of the private sector in developing countries, which generally had an interest in dismantling foreign exchange restrictions and controls. Most important was the recognition of the inefficiencies associated with maintaining fixed exchange rates and the need for greater exchange rate flexibility to maintain balance-of-payments equilibrium.

Exchange rates have often been the source of economic tension between trading partners. Countries that are running large current account deficits—that import much more than they export—frequently claim that surplus countries are 'unfairly' manipulating the exchange rate so as to give their exporters a competitive advantage— increasing the domestic prices of imports and reducing the foreign currency denominated export prices. In the 1980s such claims were frequently made against Japan and the Asian 'tigers'; in the 2000s it was the turn of China to bear the brunt of such complaints. Given that the IMF cannot force governments to adjust exchange rates—it can only advise—there have been suggestions that the WTO members should agree to stronger rules in this area that can be enforced through the DSU.

Mattoo and Subramanian (2008a) argue that if there is a clear finding of undervaluation and this is clearly due to government action, this should be regarded as fully equivalent to a violation of import tariff bindings and the ban on export subsidies. They recognize that undervaluation can result from a number of factors, including fiscal and monetary policies, policies related to capital flows, taxes and subsidies, and intervention in foreign exchange markets, but argue there is a clear hierarchy of policy actions in terms of proximate causation. Prolonged one-way intervention in foreign exchange markets by the central bank or by government and quasi-government agencies, redenomination of domestic debt into foreign currency, and extensive forward market operations are policy actions that can clearly be identified as causes of undervaluation. In such cases, they propose that the IMF—as is already the case when members invoke the GATT balance-of-payments articles (see Chapter 9)—assess whether the member's exchange rate was misaligned and whether it was a consequence of clear government action if a dispute is brought to the WTO.

Import licensing

Quantitative restrictions are generally enforced by means of licences. A separate Agreement on Import Licensing Procedures, which applies to all WTO members, aims to strengthen general GATT obligations in this domain. The agreement resembles closely the code on licensing that was negotiated in the Tokyo Round. It aims to enhance transparency of licensing systems and calls for publication of licence requirements, the length of licence validity and the right of appeal of decisions.

Licensing can become a source of disputes when the allocation of quota rights is perceived to be biased and to violate the GATT nondiscrimination principles. Traditionally, licences tend to be allocated on the basis of historical market shares. An alternative would be to auction off the licences to the highest bidder. The latter approach has the economic advantages of generating revenue for the government and reducing the resource allocation distortions generated by quota systems, but the political disadvantage of eliminating discretion (patronage possibilities) and the opportunity for powerful vested interests to obtain quota rents. The WTO rules on import licensing played a major role in the *Bananas* case discussed earlier, which revolved to a great extent around the procedures used by the EU to allocate import licences (see Chapter 3).

5.4. Customs Clearance—Related Provisions

Customs clearance requires the valuation and classification of imports for purposes such as levying tariffs, determining origin, enforcing foreign exchange controls and collecting statistics. Customs procedures may become NTBs if officials incorrectly classify goods or assign goods a value greater than appropriate. An agreement to reduce and bind tariffs would be practically meaningless without a set of rules concerning valuation and classification of imported goods. Arbitrary customs procedures could then be used to ensure that a government collects as much revenue as desired, independent of the formally negotiated tariff schedule. Import-competing industries might also bribe officials to harass importers. To reduce the likelihood that a country's published tariff schedule is not representative of the nominal tariffs that are actually applied, GATT establishes certain rules and principles regarding customs valuation.

Valuation

The provisions on customs valuation contained in the GATT 1947 (Article VII) were not very precise, basically requiring that goods be valued on the basis of their actual value. Before the launch of the Tokyo Round (1973), a number of contracting parties, led by the EEC, felt that certain national valuation practices were restricting international trade. US methods were a major bone of contention, in particular the so-called American Selling Price criterion, which established the value of some imported goods on the basis of the selling price of similar domestically produced goods. Although this clearly violated GATT rules, the US was able to employ this method because it had grandfathered the practice when acceding to GATT. Largely motivated by US practices, in the Tokyo Round a Customs Valuation Code was negotiated which supplemented GATT's valuation provisions and outlawed practices such as the American Selling Price. As was the case with all the Tokyo Round codes, participation was voluntary, and most developing countries did not sign the agreement. The US did sign the agreement and reformed its valuation practices to comply with it.

With the creation of the WTO, the Tokyo Round code became the Agreement on Customs Valuation (formally the Agreement on Implementation of Article VII of GATT). It binds all WTO members. The main impact of the customs valuation agreement was on developing countries, as valuation practices often did not conform to the provisions of the agreement. Separate disciplines were also added on pre-shipment inspection—the practice of requiring the inspection of goods in the country of production before they are shipped—and on rules of origin.

The customs valuation agreement seeks to establish uniform, transparent and fair standards for the valuation of imported goods for customs purposes. The agreement outlaws the use of arbitrary or fictitious customs values. In principle, valuation should be based on the transaction or invoice value of the goods—the price actually paid or payable for the goods (subject to adjustments for freight and other charges). The invoice value method should be applied when:

(1) there are no special restrictions on the disposal or use of goods;
(2) the buyer and seller are not related;
(3) no proceeds of the subsequent sales accrue to the exporter; and
(4) the sale or price is not subject to special conditions that cannot be quantified.

The agreement does not prescribe a uniform system regarding shipping, insurance and handling charges. A country may opt for a cost, insurance and freight (c.i.f.), a cost and freight or a free-on-board (f.o.b.) valuation basis. If customs authorities have reasons to believe that the transaction value is inaccurate, they are required to proceed sequentially through five alternative valuation options:

(1) the value of identical goods;
(2) the value of similar goods;
(3) the so-called deductive method;
(4) the computed value method; and
(5) an unspecified 'if all else fails' method.[7]

---

[7] The *deductive* value method consists of the unit price at which a significant quantity of imported goods is sold to unrelated persons, subject to deductions for commissions, profit margins, transport and insurance costs. The *computed* method consists of summing the cost or value of materials and other inputs employed in producing the imported goods, and adding an amount for profit and general expenses equal to that applied in sales of similar goods by other producers.

It is only when the customs value cannot be determined under one of these options that the next option in the sequence can be used. However, an importer may request that the computed method be used in preference to the deductive method. In many instances, refusal to accept the invoice price will be connected to there being a relationship between buyer and seller. The mere fact of such a relationship is not sufficient grounds for the authorities to reject the invoice price. What matters is that the relationship influences the price. If the value is questioned by customs, the burden of proof is on the importer.

Reflecting fears voiced during the Tokyo Round regarding fraudulent invoicing, especially between related parties, a Protocol to the code gave developing country signatories somewhat greater regulatory flexibility in their customs procedures. Also, technical assistance in implementing code procedures was promised. Despite this, developing country participation in the code remained limited. Fears of reduced tariff revenue as a result of underinvoicing, a wish to maintain discretion in valuing imports, or the administrative burden of implementing code provisions were among the major concerns. In the Uruguay Round, a number of developing countries put forward the view that the need to accept declared values was the main factor prohibiting greater participation in the code. Consequently, they proposed that the agreement be amended to allow more scope for rejecting transactions (invoice) values.

In recognition of developing country implementation concerns, in the Uruguay Round developing countries that were not party to the code were given the right to delay implementing its provisions until 1 January 2000. Application of the computed value method could be delayed for an additional three years, and reservations could be registered in respect of any of the provisions of the agreement if other members consent. Developing countries that valued goods on the basis of officially established minimum values could request approval to retain such practices on a limited and transitional basis, subject to the terms and conditions required by the other members. Requests for such derogations require approval from the WTO Council. An annex to the agreement allows developing countries to request extension of transition periods.

During 1999, in the run-up to the Seattle ministerial meeting, over 40 developing countries requested and obtained extensions of Uruguay Round implementation deadlines. They argued that their customs systems did not yet allow a switch to invoice-based valuation. A problem with using a transactions-based valuation system that puts the burden on customs authorities to query invoice values is that mechanisms and tools must be available for the authorities to determine whether declared values are reasonable. Most OECD countries have sophisticated computer-based systems and risk-assessment techniques that allow them to identify suspect claims, and access to databases that allow them to roughly determine the market value of most commodities that pass the frontier. This is not the case for many developing countries, notwithstanding the technical assistance efforts in this area by organizations such as the WCO, UNCTAD and the IMF. Implementation in developing countries involves much more than issuing a decree that valuation is to conform to WTO rules. Customs administrations need to be automated, infrastructure improved, staff trained, and so forth. This generally takes a significant amount of time and requires the investment of substantial resources. Even Canada, a developed country with ample resources, took five years to complete implementation of the valuation agreement (Staples, 2002).

There have been relatively few dispute settlement cases relating to valuation. One was a case brought by the EU in 1996 against Mexico, claiming that Mexico applied c.i.f. value as the basis of customs valuation of imports originating in non-NAFTA countries, and f.o.b. value for imports originating in NAFTA countries. This was argued to raise the valuation basis for imports, although in practice it should not result in discrimination if intra-NAFTA flows are duty-free.[8] In 2000, the US consulted with Romania in respect of the use of arbitrary minimum and maximum import prices for such products as meat, eggs, fruits and vegetables, clothing, footwear and certain distilled spirits. The dispute was resolved rapidly as a result of Romania changing its regime, which it was obliged to do in any event in the context of its effort to converge to EU norms. In 2003, Guatemala requested consultations with Mexico concerning certain customs rules, procedures and administrative practices that impose officially established prices for customs valuation in Mexico. It also contested Mexico's practice of requiring a deposit or bond to guarantee the observance of these officially established prices. As a result of consultations a MAS concerning footwear and brushes, two areas that were severely affected by the measures, was agreed in 2005.

The Singapore ministerial conference gave the WTO the mandate to take a more comprehensive look at trade facilitation including issues related to customs valuation. This work was conducted in the Doha Round Negotiating Group on Trade Facilitation in cooperation with several other international organizations (TN/TF/1). These negotiations are discussed further in Chapter 13.

Rules of origin

A rule of origin is a criterion used by customs authorities to determine the nationality of a product or a producer. Rules of origin are necessary when there is a desire to discriminate between sources of supply. The WTO has no rules regarding rules of origin. The only multilateral convention dealing with rules of origin is the 1974 International Convention on the Simplification and Harmonization of Customs Procedures (known as the Kyoto Convention), negotiated

---

[8] This case was brought under Article XXIV:5b, that is, the GATT provision dealing with free trade areas, not the valuation agreement.

under the auspices of, and administered by, the WCO in Brussels. This convention, which was revised after lengthy negotiations in 1998, provides a short list of products that should be considered to originate in a country because they are wholly produced or obtained there, that is contain no imported materials. These are largely natural resource-based products extracted or obtained from the territory of the country concerned. Where two or more countries are involved in the production of a product, the Convention states that the origin of the product is the one where the last substantial transformation took place, that is the country in which significant manufacturing or processing occurred most recently. Significant or substantial is defined as sufficient to give the product its essential character.

Various criteria can be used to determine if a substantial transformation occurred. These include a change in tariff heading (CTH), the use of specific processing operations which do (or do not) imply substantial transformation, a test based on the value of additional materials embodied in the transformed product, or the amount of value added in the last country where the good was transformed. Under a CTH the value added may be high or low for a given product, so that a value-added criterion may or may not lead to the same result as a CTH test. Different rules of origin may therefore vary widely in their economic effects. If written in ways that make it difficult to satisfy them, rules of origin can be effective protectionist devices. Thus, the setting of rules of origin may be accompanied by rent-seeking activities, as import-competing lobbies have an incentive to either try and make the rules as restrictive as possible, or to influence the way they are applied. Restrictive rules are particularly important in the context of the negotiation and implementation of preferential trade agreements (see Chapters 10 and 12).

In the application of MFN trade policy the problem is often vaguely defined criteria that generate uncertainty by giving discretion to the importing authorities to determine if a particular rule has been met. The more discretion officials have in this area, the greater the incentive to lobby. Such problems are especially prevalent under value-added criteria, as enforcement of such rules requires detailed investigations of the financial accounts of exporting firms. Box 5.5 gives an example of the operation of rules of origin in one of the major nonpreferential trade policy areas where they are important—antidumping.

In contrast to GATT 1947, the WTO includes an agreement on rules of origin. The WTO Agreement on Rules of Origin aims to foster the harmonization of the rules used by members. The agreement calls for a work programme to be undertaken by a Technical Committee, in conjunction with the WCO, to develop a classification system regarding the changes in tariff subheadings based on the Harmonized System that constitute a substantial transformation. In cases where the HS nomenclature does not allow substantial transformation to be determined by a CTH test, the Technical Committee is to provide guidance regarding the use of

Box 5.5. Origin rules and antidumping

One area where the application of rules of origin is an issue is in the enforcement of antidumping (AD) actions. A European case illustrates how rules of origin can be used to achieve the objectives of a specific lobby. In the mid-1980s, the EU imposed a 20 per cent AD duty on 12 Japanese exporters of photocopiers. In 1988, three years after the AD duty was imposed, a so-called anticircumvention case was brought by the EU industry. It claimed that Japanese exporters had circumvented the AD duty by establishing assembly operations inside the EU that imported most of the parts of photocopiers from Japan, adding very little local value. What is relevant here is not the mechanics of AD—discussed in Chapter 9—but the role of origin rules. The aim of AD is to protect a domestic industry that is injured by dumping. But, in a world where companies establish alliances with—and equity stakes in—rival enterprises, establishing which firms constitute the domestic industry is not always easy. In the photocopier AD investigation, Canon (Japan) subsidiaries located in the EU were regarded as foreign firms, while a Xerox (US) affiliate was treated as a European firm. Similarly, in the follow-up anticircumvention case, the Canon subsidiaries were investigated to determine how much local (EU) value was added in the production process. What is interesting about this case is not only that the composition of the domestic industry was determined arbitrarily, but also that a number of the firms who petitioned Brussels for protection had value-added performances that were *lower* than those of the Japanese firms. These EU firms were basically in the business of importing and distributing photocopiers. They did not produce them. Some even had formal connections with Japanese companies. The AD case was therefore not about dumping, or to protect a national industry, but simply part of a strategy used by individual multinational firms competing for market share. The lack of clearly defined rules of origin introduced one of the elements of discretion that made the strategy attractive to petitioning firms.

Source: Messerlin and Noguchi (1991).

supplementary tests such as value-added criteria. The harmonization programme was to be completed in July 1998 but the Technical Committee was unable to meet this deadline due to the complexity of the task.

The results of the technical review undertaken by the WCO were submitted to the WTO by the revised deadline of November 1999, but as of mid-2008 the harmonization work programme had yet to be completed by the Committee on Rules of Origin. This reflected differences in views between members regarding the specifics of some of the rules, the costs associated with adopting a common set of nonpreferential rules, while at the same time countries remain free to adopt idiosyncratic *preferential* rules of origin, and the extent of discretion that should be left to importing countries regarding the criterion to be applied in instances where no agreement on a common rule exists.

The economic impact of a rule of origin depends on the specific criterion that is used and on the degree of uniformity with which the rule is applied. Rules of origin have been problematical mostly in the context of PTAs. The harmonized set of WCO rules of origin, assuming they are ever adopted by WTO members, will not apply to preferential trade. This is not an oversight. Many countries do not want constraints imposed on their policy freedom with regard to the implementation of PTAs or their unilateral trade preference programmes for developing countries. As discussed further in Chapters 10 and 12, rules of origin are a major instrument for 'fine tuning' the effective scope of preferential liberalization at the product level. First principles would suggest that preferential and nonpreferential rules should be the same and that rules of origin should be simple to administer and transparent. Currently, this remains far from being the case.

Pre-shipment inspection: outsourcing customs

Trade facilitation is a key instrument for countries seeking to reduce transaction costs for traders associated with customs clearance and related regulatory enforcement. Many countries have pursued alternative mechanisms—on either a transitional or longer term basis—to facilitate trade while ensuring that revenue and other objectives are attained. One instrument that may be used to address classification, origin and valuation problems and more generally reduce customs-related compliance costs is pre-shipment inspection (PSI).

As the name suggests, PSI consists of inspection of goods by specialized firms before they are shipped to the country of importation. Governments of importing countries usually decide to engage the services of PSI firms in order to reduce the scope for exporters and importers to engage in either overinvoicing or underinvoicing of imports.[9] Overinvoicing may occur in contexts where there are foreign exchange controls, this being a classic way to transfer capital outside the country. Underinvoicing is usually driven by tax evasion considerations: by under-reporting the value of an imported item, traders may seek to reduce their tax obligation (partially evade applicable tariffs).

Governments use PSI in large part because national customs administrations are not able to undertake the required activities. This may reflect a lack of institutional capacity, or problems related to rent-seeking and corruption. Government-mandated PSI should be distinguished from PSI services that are required as part of a contract between buyers and sellers of a product. Most firms that are internationally active in providing inspection services provide pre-shipment certification and inspection of goods because buyers require it. Such services focus on the specifications and quality of goods, not their value. Government-mandated PSI is predominantly concerned with the determination of the quantity and value of goods

---

[9] PSI may have nonrevenue objectives as well. An example would be to ensure that imports meet national (or international) standards of safety or quality.

imported into their territories, and tends to be motivated by a desire to reduce revenue leakage for the government and control fraud.

Pre-shipment inspection became an issue for GATT in the 1980s because exporters objected to some of the methods used by inspection firms (Low, 1995). Under the WTO agreement on PSI, countries that use PSI agencies must ensure that such activities are carried out in an objective, transparent and nondiscriminatory manner. Verification of contract prices must be based on a comparison with the price(s) of identical or similar goods offered for export from the same country of exportation around the same time. In doing this, PSI entities are to allow for the terms of the sales contract and generally applicable adjusting factors pertaining to the transaction. The selling price of locally produced goods, the export price of other producers, the cost of production or arbitrary prices may not be used for price verification purposes.

The PSI agreement requires that WTO members who use PSI establish appeals procedures. Complaints may also be brought to an Independent Entity, established under Article 5 of the PSI agreement. Through 2008 only two cases have been brought to the entity. In 1996, a working party on PSI was established by the General Council, with a mandate to review the agreement (as provided for under Article 6 of the PSI agreement). The working party consulted with the International Federation of Inspection Agencies (IFIA), the ICC and a firm of PSI auditors. Overall, the experience with the PSI agreement appeared to have been positive. Problems that were identified included across-the-board, 100 per cent inspection requirements, delays in shipments caused by inspectors being unavailable or failing to arrive for scheduled inspections, or inspectors allegedly having little knowledge of the products concerned.

In 2008 more than 36 developing countries used PSI services, including Argentina, Bangladesh, India, Indonesia, Kenya, Liberia, Mexico, Mozambique, Nigeria, Paraguay, Peru, Philippines, Uzbekistan and Zimbabwe (www.Cotecna.com). Data submitted to the PSI committee in 2008 by the International Federation of Inspection Agencies showed a marked reduction in traditional PSI programmes. The trend resulted from a considerable shift towards modern forms of shipment inspection that are considerably less intrusive for exporters (G/VAL/W/63/Rev.10).

Pre-shipment inspection is not a panacea. As discussed by Low (1995), PSI companies have been found to have engaged in bribery to obtain contracts, and circumvention of PSI by traders through exploitation of loopholes in the system (for example, minimum value thresholds) have reduced the effectiveness of these systems in a number of countries. A lack of *ex post* checking of revenues collected against the reports issued by PSI agencies to Ministries of Finance also reduces the usefulness of PSI for countries that use it, especially taking into account that the costs of PSI for governments can be significant. Pre-shipment inspection firms frequently charge a fee of up to 1 per cent of the value of goods inspected.[10] The prevailing consensus in the trade and development community is that PSI may be helpful in the short term but that in the longer run what is required is serious customs reform and institutional strengthening to allow a government to manage the process itself. The potential downsides of PSI have been considerably reduced over the last decade as a result of new approaches and tools, such as the security label and the electronic transmission of results. These innovations permit achieval of higher cost-effectiveness and speed up the flow of information to customs authorities, ensure documentary security and reduce delays in the importation process.

5.5. Subsidies

Subsidies, and measures to counter their impact on trade, frequently gave rise to disputes in the GATT era. This section discusses the WTO rules on subsidies; disciplines on countervailing subsidization are discussed in Chapter 9. Subsidization may benefit import-competing or export industries. If subsidization distorts trade (expands or reduces trade above or below the free trade level) it may work to offset market-opening commitments negotiated in a MTN. From a rule-making and public policy perspective, a problem that arises is that subsidies may be a desirable form of government intervention. Tax-subsidy schemes may be required to bring marginal private costs or benefits into alignment with marginal social costs or benefits. The need for this arises when externalities (market failures) cause social and private costs and benefits to diverge. Usually this implies that private agents are not given an incentive to take into account the costs or benefits of their actions on others in the economy (for an overview of the theory, see Bhagwati, 1971, and the summary in Annex 2).

Tax-subsidy schemes may be an appropriate means of offsetting externalities or distortions associated with overvalued exchange rates or labour market rigidities if these problems cannot be dealt with directly. They may also be used to redistribute income. Aside from their efficiency advantages—in contrast to measures imposed at the border, which distort both producer and consumer incentives, a subsidy can target either consumers or producers—subsidies are superior from a governance viewpoint. This is because they are more 'visible' to taxpayers—and the Ministry of Finance—than trade policies. As a result, subsidies can be expected to be subject to

---

[10] This practice has given rise to discussions in the PSI Committee concerning the consistency of such fees with Articles II and VIII GATT (discussed above). Proposals have been made that flat fees would be more appropriate.

greater critical political scrutiny than tariffs. Necessary conditions for a more efficient allocation of resources to result from intervention are that the problem has been diagnosed correctly and the policy used is targeted appropriately. In practice, governments are prone to fail as often, if not more, than markets— especially if account is taken of the incentives of interest groups to lobby for a subsidy or a tax exemption.

Governments invariably pursue policies that affect the allocation of productive resources and the distribution of income. Such policies may have an impact on the pattern of international trade and investment, and may give rise to frictions and disputes between countries. Many of the measures of a subsidy nature maintained by governments come under the heading of industrial policy. For present purposes industrial policy can be defined to encompass all actions undertaken by governments that have an effect on the structure of production in an economy. This effect may be intended or not, and can be achieved through a variety of policy instruments, of which subsidies are just one. Others include price controls, import restrictions, tax incentives and government procurement policies.

All industrial policies are forms of public assistance or taxation of domestic industries. Theoretically, they can be expressed in terms of a direct subsidy equivalent, which may be greater or less than zero, negative subsidy equivalents implying a burden (tax) instead of a benefit. More generally, the appropriate measure is the effective benefit of government assistance to a firm or the economy as a whole. It may well be that other policies maintained by the government outweigh any direct support given to a firm or sector. Such general equilibrium measures of the net or 'effective' support that is implied by policy are rarely considered by governments explicitly.

The approach taken in the WTO Agreement on Subsidies and Countervailing Measures (SCM) is to focus on subsidies narrowly defined. Loosely speaking, subsidies are defined as policies that directly impact on the government budget and that affect the production of goods. The types of subsidies used by governments to support economic activities include direct payments or grants, tax concessions, soft loans, and government guarantees and equity participation. They may be firm- or industry-specific or generally available. Examples of the latter include regional and activity-specific subsidies (such as the promotion of research and development); subsidies that focus on firms of a particular size (micro or small and medium-sized enterprises); as well as measures aimed at assisting adjustment of industries, protection of the environment, or achievement of cultural objectives.

Many subsidies that are sector-specific may have an economy-wide objective. Examples include subsidies to sectors such as health, education, transportation and communications. Conversely, subsidies that are economy-wide in scope may effectively be industry-specific. An example is the pursuit of an environmental objective the attainment of which requires taxes or subsidies that affect primarily specific sectors such as the chemical or the automotive industry. As of the late 1980s, government subsidies to industry (excluding public services and agriculture) in OECD countries averaged about 2 per cent of the value of industrial output (OECD, 1993). Between two-fifths and three-fifths of these subsidies went to specific sectors, much of it for declining industries such as steel, shipbuilding and mining. Of the service sectors, available statistics showed that rail transport was often highly subsidized, with rates of support varying between 15 per cent and 180 per cent of total value added. The magnitude of subsidies varies greatly across countries, but a general rule of thumb is that the larger the share of government in GDP, the more prevalent are subsidy programmes, both direct financial grants and implicit subsidy schemes that operate through the tax system.

More recent data from reliable sources that allow for cross-country comparisons are available for only a limited number of sectors (agriculture, coal, fisheries). Data on subsidies in service industries are particularly limited. Using national statistical sources for 69 countries the WTO Secretariat documented that aggregate subsidies comprised some US$300 billion in 2003, of which developed countries accounted for over 80 per cent (WTO, 2006). The average ratio of national subsidies to GDP was in the range of 1.4 per cent for developed countries and about 0.6 per cent for developing countries. In the time period assessed there appeared to be a tendency to redirect subsidies towards 'horizontal objectives' and to reduce subsidies in the agricultural sector. For those countries reporting subsidies to the WTO, the report revealed significant omissions—and most WTO members do not report their subsidies (Table 5.4). This is an area where the principle of transparency appears to attract mostly lip service—with the exceptions of the EU, Brazil and Korea.

WTO rules on subsidies

The disciplines in the SCM agreement relating to subsidies have a twofold objective. First, to establish rules to avoid or reduce adverse effects on members, and, more specifically to prevent the use of subsidies to nullify or impair concessions. Second, to regulate the use of countervailing duties (CVDs) by members seeking to offset the injurious effects on their domestic firms of foreign subsidization of products. The latter dimension of WTO rules is discussed in Chapter 9. As discussed further in Chapter 7, there are no subsidy disciplines for services. Special rules apply to agriculture, where there is greater flexibility to use export subsidies and disciplines are imposed in the form of an Aggregate Measure of Support. These disciplines are discussed in Chapter 6.

The GATT 1947 was quite permissive regarding the use of subsidies. This continues to be the case under the WTO, with the difference that the WTO more clearly defines what is covered by multilateral disciplines: any measure that has a

Table 5.4. Subsidies in selected countries (US$ billion, 1998–2002 average)

Country	National Accounts Data	WTO Notifications
Canada	7.7	0.9
EU (15)	109.0	96.3
Australia	4.7	0.3
Japan	34.3	4.2
Norway	4.1	2.9
Switzerland	10.8	0.7
United States	43.5	16.3
Brazil	2.0	1.7
India	12.2	–
Republic of Korea	1.0	1.3
South Africa	0.9	–

Source: WTO, World Trade Report (2006).

cost to the government budget and is specific. The large measure of subsidy freedom makes the WTO quite different from deep regional integration agreements such as the EU, where strict disciplines are imposed on the use of subsidies and CVDs cannot be used by member states on imports from partner countries. Instead, subsidization is subject to explicit rules and EU competition disciplines. If these are violated, countries can be brought before the European Court of Justice.

The reason for the difference is that the objective of the WTO is not deep integration. The WTO subsidy rules attempt to strike a balance between the need to agree on minimum standards regarding the subsidies that may not be used because they distort trade, and ensuring that measures used by importing countries to offset the effects of foreign subsidy programmes are not abused. The SCM agreement distinguishes between three categories of subsidies: nonactionable, prohibited and actionable. Nonactionable subsidies are by definition permitted and cannot be contested. They span all nonspecific subsidies—those that do not primarily benefit a specific firm, industry or group of industries. Nonspecificity requires that allocation criteria are neutral, nondiscriminatory and horizontal (that is do not target or benefit some sectors more than others). Specific subsidies are either prohibited outright or are actionable.

Attempts under the auspices of GATT 1947 to deal with the subsidy issue suffered major difficulties. The term subsidy was not defined in the GATT 1947, and agreement on a definition proved elusive. It also proved difficult to determine what types of subsidies distorted trade. These difficulties led to many disputes and panels in the 1970s and 1980s (many of the cases involved agriculture). Progress was made on both fronts during the Uruguay Round. First, agreement was reached on a definition. A subsidy is deemed to exist if there is a financial contribution by a government (or public body). This in turn may involve an actual or potential direct transfer of funds (such as grants, loans, equity infusions or loan guarantees), forgoing government revenue (tax concessions or credits), or the provision or purchase of products other than general infrastructure. Government funding of a private body to carry out a function that would normally be vested in the government and any form of income or price support is also covered by the definition. This definition is embodied in the SCM Agreement and applies to nonagricultural products (as mentioned, there are separate disciplines for agricultural production and trade—see Chapter 6).

A consequence of the way subsidies are defined in the SCM agreement is that de facto subsidization, resulting from, for example, differential taxation, regulatory policies or the imposition of import duties, is not considered a subsidy. Insofar as these instruments raise concerns they need to be—and often are—addressed by other WTO agreements. Duty drawback schemes and rebates of VAT on exports are not considered to be subsidies as long as the magnitude of the rebate does not exceed the level of taxes applying to products sold on the domestic market.

Subsidies that are contingent, formally or in effect on export performance or on the use of domestic over imported goods are prohibited (Article 3 SCM) (except for LDCs and certain developing countries—see below). Thus, export subsidies and local content incentives may not be used by WTO members. One justification for this strong form of constraint is that both types of measure by definition have a direct impact on trade. Other subsidies will have a more indirect impact on trade, if they have an effect at all.

An illustrative list of export subsidies, attached to the SCM agreement, mentions the provision of products or services (including transportation) for use in export production on terms more favourable than for domestically consumed goods. It also lists export credits and guarantees or insurance at a cost that does not cover long-term operating costs and losses of the insurer (except if a member applies the provisions of the OECD agreement on export credits). A case brought against the US in 1998 clarified that tax concessions on export income also constitute an export subsidy. A necessary condition is that the government, or an institution under its control, provides the subsidy. All export subsidies are deemed specific, whether targeted or not. If WTO members are found to be using export subsidies by a dispute settlement panel, the remedy will generally be a requirement that the measures be removed within a three-month period.

The third category, actionable subsidies, are specific measures that are permitted but may, if they create adverse effects on a WTO member, give rise to consultations, invocation of dispute settlement procedures, or the imposition of countervailing duties by an importing country. For SCM disciplines to kick in (to be actionable) a subsidy must be specific *and* confer a benefit to the recipient(s) *and* have adverse effects on a trading partner. Criteria to determine specificity are laid out in Article 2 SCM. This article states that if a government establishes objective eligibility criteria or conditions that are neutral, do not favour certain enterprises, are economic in nature and horizontal in application (such as number of employees or size of enterprise), and are spelled out in legislation or regulations, a subsidy will not be deemed to be specific if eligibility is automatic and the criteria are strictly adhered to.

Part IV of the SCM agreement made several *specific* subsidies nonactionable if they satisfied certain criteria. These included research and development (R&D) subsidies, aid to disadvantaged regions, and subsidies to facilitate the adaptation of plants to new environmental regulations. However, this part of the agreement was of limited duration: it was to lapse after five years unless WTO members extended them (Article 31 SCM). They did not do so and thus these provisions expired in 2000. As a result there are at present only two types of specific subsidy categories distinguished by the SCM agreement: prohibited and actionable.

Adverse effects include injury to a domestic industry, nullification or impairment of tariff concessions, or serious prejudice or threat thereof to the country's interests. Serious prejudice is defined to exist if the total *ad valorem* subsidization of a product exceeds 5 per cent, the subsidies are used to cover operating losses of a firm or industry or debt relief is granted for government-held liabilities. Serious prejudice *may* arise if the subsidy reduces exports of WTO members, results in significant price undercutting or increases the world market share of the subsidizing country in a primary product. If actionable subsidies have an adverse effect, a government may request consultations with the subsidizing member and ask for a panel if the matter is not settled within 60 days. Article 31 SCM, which as mentioned earlier specified that certain specific subsidies were nonactionable for five years, also reversed the burden of proof on serious prejudice for a period of five years. This was a significant trade discipline—as it greatly facilitated bringing a case —but was allowed to lapse. As also reflected in the limited compliance with reporting of subsidies, the fall into abeyance of this dimension of Article 31 was symptomatic of the generally less than serious attitude towards dealing with subsidies that prevails in the WTO.

The focus of the WTO disciplines (and dispute settlement) in cases where there is prejudice is on the amount of the assistance given, not on the extent to which a subsidy harms trading partners (competitors). This makes little sense from an economic perspective, although it has the advantage of being straightforward to calculate. Subsidy case law developed under the WTO has moved somewhat towards more stringent remedies, in that instead of requiring simply the abolition of an illegal measure, some panels have required re-payment of the subsidy by the firms that benefitted. This is not necessarily a step in the right direction from an economic perspective, as it ignores the effect of the subsidy. In some cases a subsidy may have no injurious effect; in others the damage caused may be a multiple of the subsidy.

In the Doha round it was agreed that the negotiations would clarify and improve disciplines under the SCM Agreement 'while preserving the basic concepts, principles and effectiveness' of the agreement and its instruments and objectives, and taking into account the needs of developing countries and LDCs. Fishery subsidies emerged as a priority area of concern for many developing countries. Debate also focused on whether to extend the list of prohibited subsidies and on the type of payments that should be covered. The US argued that an extension of the prohibited subsidy list was an obvious next step in deepening subsidy disciplines. The EU preferred to put emphasis on strengthening rules prohibiting subsidies that are contingent on the use of domestic inputs (local content) (Article 3.1b SCM). The EU also aimed to loosen rules on export credits, driven primarily by its interest in the aircraft industry. Proposals from developing countries such as India and Brazil aimed at relaxing the disciplines on subsidies, reflecting a perception that government financing was an important means to achieve export growth and/or greater diversification. The overall gist of the SDT proposals in the SCM discussions was the extent to which developing WTO members should be allowed more room to use subsidies. One suggested option was to remove the time frame for seeking an extension to use export subsidies and raise the threshold for being forced to eliminate them (Chapter 12). An important decision taken at the 2005 ministerial meeting in Hong Kong was a conditional agreement to eliminate export subsidies for agricultural products by 2013 (see Chapter 6).

Developing countries and WTO subsidy disciplines

Under the GATT, developing countries were free to use export subsidies. World Trade Organization members are required to notify their subsidy programmes to the WTO Secretariat each year, giving information on the type of subsidy, the amounts involved, the policy objective and intended duration, as well as statistics allowing their trade effects to be determined. Any member may cross-notify alleged subsidies of other countries that the latter have not notified. A number of special provisions for developing and transition economies are included in Article 27 of the SCM agreement. Developing country members listed in an annex (all LDCs and 20 countries that had a GNP per capita below US$1,000) are exempted from the prohibition on export subsidies.[11] Once GNP per capita exceeds US$1,000, nonconforming subsidies must be eliminated within eight years. Developing country WTO members not listed in the annex were to phase out their export subsidies

---

[11] This spanned the following developing countries: Bolivia, Cameroon, Congo, Côte d'Ivoire, Dominican Republic, Egypt, Ghana, Guatemala, Guyana, India, Indonesia, Kenya, Morocco, Nicaragua, Nigeria, Pakistan, Philippines, Senegal, Sri Lanka and Zimbabwe. Market exchange rates are used, not purchasing power parities.

over an eight-year period, starting from January 1995 (Article 27:4 SCM). The prohibition on subsidies contingent on the use of domestic goods (local content) did not apply to developing countries for a period of five years (eight years for LDCs), and further extension could be requested. If granted, annual consultations with the SCM Committee must be held to determine the necessity of maintaining the subsidies. Developing countries that have become competitive in a product—defined as having a global market share of 3.25 per cent—must phase out any export subsidies over a two-year period.

Although the traditional difference in subsidy disciplines applying to industrialized and developing countries was narrowed substantially in the Uruguay Round, especially as regards export subsidies, it proved controversial to implement these provisions. In 2007, the SCM Committee issued a decision, subsequently endorsed by the General Council, extending the temporary exemption for export subsidy disciplines for a number of developing countries that should have abolished such subsidies in 2002. The 2007 General Council decision extends the exemption through the end of 2013, with a two-year phase-out period—the same end date agreed in Hong Kong for the elimination of agricultural export subsidies.[12] In practice this decision implies that other developing countries falling under the $1,000 per capita threshold will also have until 2015 before the export disciplines will bite. Thus, a total of 88 WTO developing country members will not be affected by export subsidy disciplines until 2015 at the earliest.

Many countries, both developing and developed, pursue export promotion programmes. These may involve assistance with penetrating new markets through organization of trade fairs, general advertising campaigns that aim at 'selling' the country and enhancing the visibility of export products, and maintenance of commercial attachés in embassies and consulates. During the 1990s, an increasing number of countries implemented so-called matching grant schemes that subsidize a proportion of the cost of improving production facilities, obtaining ISO 9000 certification of management systems, and exploring new export markets. Such schemes could be regarded as export subsidies if the provision of the grant element is made conditional upon exports.

By far the most important source of concern for developing countries was the prospect that WTO rules would constrain their ability to use export processing zones (EPZs) and similar special economic zones as an instrument to overcome investment disincentives caused by weak business environments. Virtually all developing countries have put in place such zones. Often part of the package of incentives offered to investors are tax exemptions and direct subsidies of varying types. Insofar as economic activity in the zone is directed at exports such support is

[12] The countries concerned are Antigua and Barbuda, Barbados, Belize, Costa Rica, Dominica, Dominican Republic, El Salvador, Fiji, Grenada, Guatemala, Jamaica, Jordan, Mauritius, Panama, Papua New Guinea, St Kitts and Nevis, St Lucia, St Vincent and the Grenadines, and Uruguay.

clearly linked to (conditional on) exports and could therefore fall foul of the ban on export subsidies. The extension of exemptions of export subsidy disciplines through 2015 was largely driven by such concerns.

Special and differential treatment proposals in the Doha Round aimed at allowing developing countries more room to use subsidies (especially in terms of SCM Articles 3 and 27). For example, a proposal to modify SCM Article 27.4 aimed to remove the time frame for seeking an extension to use export subsidies and to raise the threshold for having to eliminate the subsidy. Among developing countries, Brazil wished to focus the Doha Round negotiations on the treatment of export credit guarantees and the interpretation of de facto export subsidies. Some developing countries also supported the view that uniform disciplines on all subsidies would not address the specific problems associated with the fisheries industry. Work on developing specific rules for the latter sector progressed at a slow pace, even though there was a broad agreement that disciplines in the fisheries sector should be strengthened including through the prohibition of certain types of subsidies that resulted in overfishing and overcapacity.

Whether there is a good economic case for these subsidies is of the course the key question from a policy perspective. The answer depends on whether this instrument offsets distortions created by market failures or other government policies. There are possible economic rationales for a more lenient stance for developing countries. Subsidies may be beneficial in stimulating economic development if there are externalities to firms operating in export markets. These may arise through the beneficial effects of learning by doing. Marketing experts have argued that quality upgrading and export marketing of nontraditional products by firms has positive spillover effects on other potential exporters in a developing country, potentially justifying an export subsidy. Export subsidies may also be the appropriate instrument to offset an anti-export bias resulting from an overvalued exchange rate or high rates of protection in cases where first best policies are not available (devaluation or a market determined exchange rate and trade liberalization). Export subsidy programmes may also have an important political dimension as they can give credibility to a government's commitment to maintain an export-oriented strategy, thus encouraging investment of resources and entrepreneurial energies in the development of foreign markets (Bhagwati, 1988).

If the source of the problem is policy-induced, the case for a subsidy is very much a second-best one—the appropriate action is to target the source of the problem. More often than not subsidy policies are driven by rent-seeking interest groups, not by a clearly identified market failure. The stricter disciplines that were negotiated in the Uruguay Round are therefore likely to be beneficial. Even if export subsidies are optimal from a national perspective, they are likely to be distortionary for the world as a whole, can easily be captured by private interests seeking rents and are difficult to target at a well-defined distortion or market failure.

Summing up, the adoption of a 'green–orange–red light' approach towards subsidies in the Uruguay Round was important. The approach is both pragmatic and sensible from an economic perspective. Ensuring that subsidies that are not firm or sector-specific are in principle unconstrained is appropriate as such subsidies are most likely to be used in the pursuit of noneconomic objectives or in efforts to offset market failures. It ensures freedom for governments to use subsidy instruments in many of the cases where there may be a good rationale for it, and reduces the scope for other countries to second-guess the motivation underlying the use of such instruments. Production subsidies can be the most efficient way to offset externalities, but are more often used to redistribute income. If so, they are likely to distort the operation of markets, but in ways that are very difficult to address. Clearly such subsidies can have detrimental effects on foreign countries, and allowance is therefore made for actions to be taken against their trade effects. But the WTO makes no attempt to get involved in questioning government objectives or to determine whether the policy instrument is necessary or effective or appropriate. The focus is only on the effect of the subsidy. This greatly reduces the scope for disputes, as the focus of attention centres primarily on whether a contested measure is an export subsidy. Export subsidies clearly distort trade and will have direct negative effects on some WTO members. Although economists often remark upon the asymmetry in the WTO regarding the use of trade policies—outlawing export subsidies but permitting tariffs—this is simply a reflection of the mercantilist underpinnings of the institution.

Subsidy disputes under the WTO

There have been a number of major subsidy-related disputes in the WTO. Almost all involved export subsidies. Major cases included disputes between Brazil and Canada regarding export subsidies for civil aircraft production (Brazilian and Canadian firms are major producers of regional and corporate jets), a case brought by the EU against the US Foreign Sales Corporation (FSC) legislation (under which US firms could reduce taxes on export income by funnelling revenues through offshore tax shelters), a number of cases by the US alleging that certain provisions of the corporate tax law of a number of European countries constituted de facto export subsidies, two disputes brought by Brazil and other WTO members against the EU export subsidy regime on sugar and US export subsidies for cotton, and finally, two disputes between the EU and US regarding their respective subsidy programmes for civil aircraft (Boeing-Airbus). The agricultural disputes are discussed in Chapter 6.

In 1996, Canada brought a complaint against Brazil's export financing programme for aircraft (WT/DS46), claiming that subsidies granted under Brazil's

Programa de Financiamento às Exportações to foreign purchasers of Embraer aircraft were illegal export subsidies. A 1999 panel report found that Brazil's measures were prohibited export subsidies. On appeal, the AB mostly upheld the findings of the panel. Upon the initial request for consultations by Canada, Brazil responded by counterattacking. In March 1997 it contested what it perceived as illegal export subsidies granted to the Canadian civil aircraft industry with a request for consultations, followed by a request for a panel in July 1998. This panel also concluded that certain of Canada's measures were inconsistent with the SCM Agreement, but rejected Brazil's claim that the Canadian measures constituted an export subsidy. The DSB adopted both reports in August 1999. In both cases the complainants perceived that the losing party did not comply with the rulings and requested the DSB to reconvene the original panels to assess implementation.

The panel on Brazil found it had not complied. Canada requested authorization to retaliate on C$700 million of imports from Brazil. This reflected Canada's calculation of the value of the subsidy granted to Embraer. Canada noted that the damage to its industry was C$4.7 billion, but that it did not seek to use this as the basis of countermeasures. Indeed, both parties agreed that retaliation should be based on the amount of the subsidy, not damage incurred, a practice that has been followed subsequently. Brazil argued that C$700 million was a gross overestimate of the effective magnitude of the subsidy, which in its view should be based on the lost sales by Canada (number of aircraft) multiplied by the per unit (illegal) subsidy on each of these sales. Although the arbitrators rejected this argument, they concluded that the amount of the subsidy and thus the level of authorized countermeasures was C$344 million (WT/DS46/ARB).

In January 2001, Brazil brought another case, Canada—Aircraft Credits and Guarantees (WT/DS222), claiming that Canada was providing export credits and loan guarantees to support exports of aircraft and that these were illegal export subsidies. The panel rejected some of Brazil's claims but upheld the argument that financing provided to a number of airlines buying Canadian aircraft constituted prohibited export subsidies. In May 2002, on the grounds that Canada had failed to implement the recommendations of the DSB within the 90-day time period allocated, Brazil requested authorization to retaliate for an amount of US$3.36 billion. Canada objected to this, the DSB referred the matter to arbitration (under Article 22.6 DSU and Article 4.10 SCM), and the arbitrator determined that Brazil could suspend concessions equal to US$247.8 million. A noteworthy feature of the award was that although it was less than one-tenth of what Brazil had requested, it was 20 per cent higher than the amount of the subsidy calculated by the arbitrator. This was motivated on the basis that a punitive adjustment was justified by Canada's repeated assertions that it would not comply with the panel ruling. This was the first, and to date only, instance of punitive damages awarded in a WTO dispute (Mavroidis, 2007).

These bilateral tit-for-tat cases illustrate a phenomenon that was often hypothe-sized to exist by observers during the GATT years and used to explain the limited number of subsidy disputes—governments are wary of bringing cases because they worry about retaliation. This has been called the 'glass house' effect—if people live in glass houses, they will be concerned about throwing the first stone. As many governments engage in subsidy practices of one kind or another, the glass house effect can be quite strong. The Brazil–Canada disputes illustrate that it may not be a good idea to throw stones if you are living in a glass house! They also illustrate that if the parties to a dispute of this type do not use the WTO process as a way to negotiate a MAS, the outcome can easily be worse than the status quo ante.

This observation also applies to a follow-on case. In 2004, following the termin-ation of a 1992 agreement with the EU on trade in large civil aircraft, the US brought a dispute against EU subsidization of Airbus Industrie—the immediate trigger being the provision of large-scale launch aid for the A380 double-decker jumbo jet. The EU immediately retaliated by bringing its own complaint against the US, alleging major indirect subsidization of Boeing through military contracts, as well as other forms of illegal support. The conflict between the two sides is discussed further in Chapter 11 in the context of the plurilateral Agreement on Trade in Civil Aircraft. This dispute is an example of a case that is both extremely complex factually and politically very sensitive, and that will most probably have to be resolved bilaterally—ideally through agreement that involves more specific disciplines on the future use of subsidies.

As noted earlier, tax systems often result in de facto subsidies. This was illus-trated in a case brought by the EU against the US tax treatment of so-called Foreign Sales Corporations (FSC) in late 1997 (WT/DS108). Under the FSC system, any US firm whose exports have at least 50 per cent US content can set up a FSC, a shell company that is established in a tax haven. More than 90 per cent of FSCs are located in the Virgin Islands, Barbados and Guam (*Financial Times*, 25 February 2000: 7). The US firm 'sells' its exports to the FSC, which then 'exports' them, 'subcontracting' the actual transactions involved back to the US company. Up to 65 per cent of the FSC's profits are exempt from US tax, reducing the US firm's tax burden by anywhere from 15 to 30 per cent (ibid.).

The EU argued that provisions of the US tax code violated the SCM Agreement, as they were conditional on exports. In October 1999 a panel found that the FSC scheme was a prohibited subsidy. On appeal, the AB supported the findings of the panel, and rejected arguments by the US that the FSC was permitted under a 1981 understanding that related to a 1976 GATT dispute concerning the forerunner of the FSC, the so-called Domestic International Sales Corporation (DISC) provi-sions of the pre-1984 US tax code. The DISC allowed US firms to defer taxes on export income. The FSC was adopted in 1984 because the DISC had been found to be inconsistent with GATT subsidy rules. The FSC case was particularly noteworthy because it involved huge sums of money (some US$4 billion in revenue foregone by the US Treasury) and required the US to revise its legislation. The US indicated it would do so and in late 2000 passed the FSC Repeal and Extraterritorial Income Exclusion Act.

In 2001, a compliance panel report concluded that the amended FSC legislation still constituted a prohibited subsidy (violated Article 3 SCM). Arbitration then determined that the EU was permitted to retaliate in the amount of US$4 billion. The EU proceeded to do so in a staggered fashion: it initially imposed an additional duty of 5 per cent on 1,608 US products, which was to rise automatically by one percentage point each month until it reached a ceiling of 17 per cent in March 2005.[13] In 2004 the US made another effort to bring its legislation in compliance by passing the American Jumpstart Our Business Strength (JOBS) Creation Act. The JOBS Act repealed the existing legislation with a complex set of tax provisions and exemptions that were aimed at assisting US-based manufacturing enterprises. The JOBS Act overall was expected to reduce federal tax revenues by approximately $8.5 billion over ten years—in other words it would result in US industry obtaining more in the way of support than the amount of the export subsidy determined by the arbitrator (Atkins, 2005). Thus, the no doubt unintended consequence of bringing the case was that overall US firms now get more 'assistance' (pay less tax), although this is no longer conditional on exports. In 2005 the EU asked for another Article 21:5 compliance panel, which again found that the US was not in compliance, largely as a result of certain transitional arrangements that were included in the legislation.

As in the Brazil–Canada aircraft disputes, after the EU brought the FSC case, the US retaliated by claiming that EU member states had very similar provisions in their tax codes, and brought cases against Belgium, France, Greece, Ireland and the Netherlands (it had done the same in the GATT-1947 era DISC case—see GATT 1994b). In each instance the US held that the income tax laws of these countries granted de facto export subsidies. The US claimed that France allowed firms to deduct certain start-up expenses of its foreign operations through a tax-deductible reserve account, Ireland granted certain trading entities special tax rates on income from export sales, Greece gave exporters special annual tax deductions calculated as a percentage of export income, the Netherlands allowed exporters to establish a special fund for export income, and Belgium granted corporations an index-linked income tax exemption for recruitment of export managers.

---

[13] Product categories affected included precious stones and metals, articles of jewellery, agricultural products (e.g. soybeans, linseed, sunflower seed, orange juice, horse meat), wood products, toys, sporting equipment, board games, textile and apparel products, refrigeration equipment, heavy machinery (engines, boilers, refrigerators), construction equipment and paper products. The choice of these products was based on two criteria: dependency on the US as a source was low (accounting for no more than 20 per cent of total EU imports), and the EU is an exporter of the items concerned (EU Delegation to the USA, Press Release 32/04, 2004).

A final noteworthy subsidy case concerned a 1998 US complaint regarding Australian subsidies granted to producers and exporters of automotive leather. These involved preferential government loans on noncommercial terms and grants. The panel found that the government loan to the firm was not a subsidy contingent upon export performance, but that the payments under the grant contract were illegal export subsidies, and should be withdrawn within 90 days. The report was adopted in June 1999. In September 1999, Australia informed the DSB that it had implemented the panel recommendations. The US contested this and requested that the original panel be reconvened. The parties reached an agreement that Australia would not raise any procedural objection to the reestablishment of the panel, and that the US would not request authorization to retaliate. This agreement was inspired by what had happened in *Bananas* (see Chapter 3). In January 2000, the review panel determined that Australia had failed to withdraw the prohibited subsidies within 90 days, and thus was not in compliance with the recommendations made by the DSB. The panel recommended not only that Australia cease applying this measure, but also that the beneficiary of the subsidy be required to reimburse the funds (the case involved about US$19 million). This was a first in the history of the WTO (although a number of unadopted panel reports had recommended reimbursement of illegal antidumping duties under GATT 1947—see Palmeter and Mavroidis, 2004). However, as discussed in Chapter 3, this has never been repeated.

5.6. State Trading Enterprises

State trading has been poorly attended to in the history of GATT, in part because it was considered a relatively minor aspect of policy among the original signatories of the GATT. It was also most prevalent in agriculture and services—sectors that remained largely outside the purview of multilateral discipline until the Uruguay Round. General Agreement on Tariffs and Trade provisions establishing rules of behaviour for state-trading enterprises (STEs) therefore played only a minor role. This situation changed with the introduction of services into the WTO, the prospective accession to the WTO of many economies in transition, and the conclusion of the Agreement on Agriculture. The prominence of state trading as a policy issue consequently increased. State trading also became a higher profile issue with the emergence of competition policy as a subject of discussion. In effect, state trading is part of a much bigger complex of policy questions to do with the conditions of competition in markets.

There are numerous reasons why governments might be concerned about the existence and behaviour of STEs when negotiating commitments to liberalize trade. Most obviously, if an entity is a monopoly, controls essential facilities or has significant power to affect downstream activities such as distribution, trade policy may be irrelevant in market access terms. Even with zero tariffs, no formal quotas and full national treatment, STEs may be able to foreclose the market to potential foreign entrants. More generally, a firm with exclusive rights may be able to control the price at which it sources from domestic suppliers and distributes imported goods. If prices paid for inputs are below market clearing levels, the entity will effectively enjoy a subsidy that may reduce market access opportunities for foreign goods. Similarly, the entity may be able to impose high mark-ups on imported goods, thereby reducing domestic demand for foreign products. In all these situations the activities of STEs will have an effect equivalent to a tax (tariff) or subsidy (Lloyd, 1982).

Although the rules of the GATT/WTO assume that economic transactions in members are driven by the decisions of enterprises operating in a market environment, GATT contracting parties were unconstrained regarding the ownership of productive assets or the regulation of domestic production. However, it was recognized that enterprises granted exclusive trading rights and privileges could restrict trade and circumvent liberalization commitments in a number of ways. First, STEs could circumvent the MFN principle by discriminating among trading partners in their purchasing and selling decisions. Second, they could limit or expand above the free trade level quantities of imports or exports in contravention of the GATT Article XI prohibition on QRs. Third, they might impose price mark-ups that exceed bound tariff levels. Fourth, they could contravene the national treatment principle by discriminating against imported products in matters affecting, for example, the internal conditions of distribution or sale. Fifth, STEs might engage in nontransparent cross-subsidization activities or benefit from various forms of assistance from governments that distort competition. Finally, STEs might affect competition on export markets if their exclusive privileges allow them to undercut other suppliers.

General Agreement on Tariffs and Trade disciplines on the behaviour of STEs aim to ensure that such entities act in a market-conforming manner. However, the relevant provision of the GATT (Article XVII) gave no clear definition of what constitutes state trading, and a wide range of interpretations of what was meant by state trading was revealed in the notifications that member countries made to the GATT. In the 1970s, the Communist authorities of Czechoslovakia submitted a list of their foreign trade organizations engaging in export and import transactions, whereas Poland and Hungary notified that they did not maintain STEs (Kostecki, 1982).

In the Uruguay Round a working definition of a STE was negotiated: 'Governmental and nongovernmental enterprises, including marketing boards, which have been granted exclusive or special rights or privileges, including statutory or constitutional powers, in the exercise of which they influence through their purchases or sales the level or direction of imports or exports'. Note that there is no mention of ownership—STEs may be fully privately owned. What matters is not ownership, but exclusivity or special privilege. The right of members to maintain or establish STEs or to offer exclusive privileges is not prejudged.

The basic obligation imposed by Article XVII is that members should ensure that STEs not act in a manner inconsistent with the general principle of nondiscrimination (MFN). Three qualitatively different disciplines apply to STEs, depending on the type of entity involved. First, as far as import monopolies are concerned, upon request of trading partners that have a substantial trade in the product concerned, information is to be provided on the import mark-up on the product during a recent representative period, or, if not feasible, the resale price (Article XVII:4b). Second, in their purchases or sales involving either imports or exports, state-owned enterprises, marketing boards and enterprises granted exclusive privileges are to act in a nondiscriminatory manner (Article XVII:1a). Firms granted exclusive privileges are to make purchases or sales solely in accordance with commercial considerations. Third, governments must ensure that enterprises in their jurisdiction are not prevented from acting in accordance with the nondiscrimination principle (Article XVII:1c).

The margins charged by STEs (their mark-ups) must be scheduled similarly to tariffs (Article II:4). Once bound, mark-ups may not exceed the resulting tariff equivalent. Although tariff commitments have been numerous, commitments regarding STEs have been rare. In 1952 Italy undertook not to exceed a 15 per cent mark-up on wheat and rye imported by the Italian government or its agencies. France made a similar commitment regarding wheat imports by the Office National Interprofessionel des Cereals, and undertook a minimum import commitment with respect to lead, tobacco and cigarettes imported by France's tobacco monopoly from countries other than those of the French Union. Both concessions lapsed with the formation of the EEC.

In the Uruguay Round it was agreed to bolster disciplines on—and surveillance of—STEs. The Council for Trade in Goods established a working party on STEs in February 1995. Governments were required to notify all STEs for review by the working party, with the exception of imports intended for consumption by government bodies or STEs themselves. Notifications are to be made independent of whether imports or exports have in fact taken place. Any WTO member that believes another member has not adequately met its notification obligation may raise the matter bilaterally. If not resolved, a counternotification may be made, for consideration by the working party. The working party reports annually to the Council for Trade in Goods.

In the pursuit of its mandate, the working party developed a new questionnaire on state trading. A draft Illustrative List of State Trading Relationships and Activities was approved in July 1999 and adopted by the Council for Trade in Goods in October of that year. Most of the work of the working party is transparency-related. A total of 58 WTO members notified the existence of STEs as of 1995. In October 2006 the working party reviewed a total of 17 notifications, some of which dated back to 2002.

Little is known about the effect of STEs on trade. Indeed, no comprehensive data are available about the extent of STEs. Even if data were available on the prevalence of STEs, information is needed on their behaviour, as what is of concern is not state trading itself, but the magnitude of the trade distortions that are associated with STEs. The current notification process does not generate these types of data. In order to obtain a sense of the potential magnitude of the problem, the extent of public ownership of industry can be used as a proxy. Entities with a majority state-owned equity share accounted for 13 per cent of GDP in a sample of 65 developing countries in the late 1980s and early 1990s, as compared to 6 per cent in a group of 10 OECD members (Schmitz, 1996). In OECD countries, state-owned enterprises are largely found in services. Such entities may have both formal exclusive rights and de facto exclusivity (such as monopoly control of bottleneck or essential facilities in the case of telecommunications).[14]

Since the mid-1990s, government ownership and control of enterprises engaging in trade in goods has declined substantially. A rigorous assessment is difficult in the absence of systematic data on state enterprises. But privatization has reduced the role of state in many countries. This was certainly the case in the transition economies of Eastern Europe and in Russia. China, when acceding to the WTO, agreed to considerably reduce its state-trading operations in industrial goods and to eliminate import monopolies maintained by STEs for agricultural goods such as wheat, rice and corn. Similar commitments were undertaken by Vietnam and have been requested from Russia with respect to the energy sector.

Some 75 per cent of STEs notified to WTO operate in the agricultural sector. Both disputes and the Doha Round negotiations illustrate that agricultural state trading is the primary concern of WTO members. One reflection of this was a concern to tighten disciplines on the provision of food aid and 'parallel' export support such as export credit schemes and food aid. The US in particular also sought to tighten disciplines on the operation of agricultural STEs such as marketing boards (see below).

State trading and (former) centrally planned economies

The presumption that WTO members are market economies has required in the past that nonmarket economies make additional commitments upon accession. Given that tariff concessions by centrally planned economies were meaningless or

---

[14] Article XVII applies only to STEs involved in merchandise trade. Services are the subject of the GATS—see Chapter 7.

of limited value, GATT contracting parties negotiated global import commitments with Poland and Romania when these countries sought to become members of GATT in 1967 and 1971 respectively. These commitments were included in their protocols of accession. Poland agreed to 'increase the total value of its imports from the territories of contracting parties by not less than seven per cent per annum'. General Agreement on Tariffs and Trade contracting parties were permitted to seek 'agreements on Polish targets for imports from the territories of the contracting parties as a whole in the following year'. The Romanian arrangement stated that Romania firmly intended 'to increase its imports from GATT contracting parties as a whole at a rate not smaller than the growth of total Romanian imports provided for in its Five-Year Plan'. This was equivalent to a promise not to decrease the GATT share of imports in total imports of Romania. Inflation and a depreciation of the US dollar vis-à-vis European currencies made these commitments meaningless in the late 1970s, and too burdensome in the 1980s (Kostecki, 1979).

In the case of Hungary, which acceded in 1973, it was concluded that tariff concessions were meaningful, and no voluntary import expansion was negotiated. In all three cases, however, special safeguard provisions were included in the Protocols of Accession allowing for discriminatory actions to be taken against imports from the acceding country. During the 1990s, all three East European countries re-negotiated their Protocols after the collapse of the CMEA (also referred to as COMECON). These re-negotiations, as well as the more recent accession negotiations of economies in transition, revealed that WTO members desire assurances that substantial progress will be achieved towards privatizing enterprises and establishing a market-based regulatory environment—see Chapters 2 and 12.

Dealing with STEs

There are many types of exclusivity arrangements that could have an effect on trade. They range from total monopoly or monopsony control, under which an entity is granted a monopoly right to import or export, to situations where an entity is obliged to compete with domestic buyers on both the domestic and foreign market. Governments may allow certain enterprises (STEs) to affect trade flows through the pursuit of regulatory controls that create (or permit) the exercise of market power. They may also pursue policies that have effects analogous to direct subsidies. More generally, any enterprise with a dominant position may exercise its market power and distort competition, independent of any action by government to support its activities. The question therefore arises where the line should be drawn between STEs, however defined, and regulatory policy more generally (Kostecki, 1982). As it stands, Article XVII is worded quite broadly and potentially covers a wide range of activities.

The sources of market access problems arising from state trading include the explicit privileges granted by governments and de facto obstacles arising incidentally from government policies, which aim at objectives other than the insulation of privileged suppliers. These impediments to competition can be dealt with in a number of different ways.[15] First, behavioural disciplines could be further developed applying to formal privileges granted to those STEs that governments regard as non-negotiable and wish to continue to maintain. This behavioural approach can be complemented by efforts to introduce greater economic content into WTO rules by adopting a set of regulatory principles that seek to ensure that STEs will operate in an efficient and least-trade distorting manner. These could be complemented by provisions relating to domestic enforcement mechanisms. An alternative is to pursue negotiations to eliminate state trading. This is the revealed-preferred approach in WTO accession negotiations, where the emphasis is on assuring full trading rights of enterprises and privatization commitments. Although straightforward in principle, this approach is inherently limited in the sense that governments will differ regarding the extent to which they are willing to negotiate away their rights to grant exclusive rights and privileges in the pursuit of noneconomic objectives. Moreover, insofar as the commitments made by accession candidates do not reflect specific disciplines that are embodied in a WTO agreement, they cannot be enforced.

The issue of addressing de facto exclusivity is best seen as a more general matter. To the extent that STE-like behaviour is facilitated by other government interventions, these should be the focus of attention. Where government policy is not the root of the problem, competition policy questions enter the picture. These, however, should be addressed in the broader context of the current debate on trade and competition. It is important that the 'STE issue' be defined as narrowly as possible in order to ensure that multilateral rules are targeted at those areas that cannot be addressed through the application of general WTO rules and disciplines.

There have been very few formal disputes concerning STEs, although the operation of agricultural marketing boards has long been a matter of concern for the US in particular. In 2003, the US challenged the practices of the Canadian Wheat Board (CWB), claiming unfair and burdensome requirements imposed on imports by the Canadian grain handling system and discrimination resulting from the operation of certain aspects of the Canadian rail transportation system. A major element of the US argument was that Article XVII required a STE to operate solely in accordance with commercial considerations and that the Canadian government therefore should ensure that the CWB do so. The panel concluded that the primary obligation imposed by Article XVII was that a STE operate in conformity with the MFN principle (Article XVII:1(a)), and that the language in Article XVII:1(b)

---

[15] What follows draws on Hoekman and Low (1998).

relating to operating on the basis of commercial considerations were examples of behaviour that, if not observed, could indicate that the nondiscrimination requirement had not been met. That is, operating on the basis of commercial considerations is not an independent obligation imposed by Article XVII. The panel agreed with the US that Canada's grain distribution system violated Article III GATT (national treatment), but that the CWB conformed with Article XVII. This conclusion, endorsed by the Appellate Body, was consistent with a long history of WTO rulings that additional regulatory hurdles cannot be placed only on foreign products. The finding that the distribution activities of STEs must comply with national treatment was also previously stressed in a GATT era dispute between the US and Canada regarding the latter's Foreign Investment Review Act ('FIRA') (BISD 30S/140, 1984).

The case against the CWB was part of a long running conflict between the US and Canada. In response to the loss, the US promised 'to continue through the WTO negotiations to aggressively pursue reform of the WTO rules on state trading in an effort to create an effective regime to address the unfair monopolistic practices of state trading enterprises'(USTR, 2004). In the Doha Round the US obtained support from other WTO members for a proposal to limit monopolistic strategies of export STEs and ban special privileges for export STEs. This area of the Doha negotiations is closely linked to the agricultural talks and the efforts to eliminate export subsidies. However, from an economic perspective, there may be good reasons to organize trade in agricultural commodities through entities like the CWB. As discussed further in Hoekman and Trachtman (2008), the CWB appears to operate rather effectively to exploit quality differences in wheat on world markets in a way that a private entity would also seek to do. Moreover, the CWB pursues equity as well as efficiency objectives, so that imposing a purely 'commercial behaviour' test as the benchmark is inappropriate from an economic as well as a legal perspective.

Countertrade and the WTO

Countertrade arrangements involve exporters and importers negotiating reciprocal deliveries in partial or full settlement of specific exchanges. Examples are counterpurchase, offset, buyback, advance purchase and barter (Banks, 1983). Countertrade is a special case of a linked transaction providing for reciprocal buying and selling. This type of reciprocal arrangement may occur in home markets and in international trade. The motivation for countertrade in the international context includes circumvention of foreign exchange and credit controls, hiding price cuts, satisfying governmentally imposed local content or offset requirements and surmounting barriers to otherwise closed markets. The quantitative importance of countertrade has diminished as a result of market-oriented reforms in transition economies and many developing countries. With the exception of the Government Procurement Agreement (see Chapter 11), there is no reference to countertrade in the WTO. Countertrade is a business practice and as such is not of direct concern to the WTO. What matters is if countertrade regulations adopted by governments imply discrimination or a lack of transparency. But in such cases the relevant provisions of the GATT apply.

5.7. TECHNICAL REGULATIONS AND PRODUCT STANDARDS

Product standards, technical regulations and certification systems are essential to the functioning of modern economies. Product standards are usually voluntary, generally being defined by industry or nongovernmental standardization bodies such as the American National Standards Institute, the British Standards Institution, the Deutsches Institut für Normung and the Association Francaise de Normalisation. Standards have been defined as documents 'established by consensus and approved by a recognized body, that provide, for common and repeated use, rules, guidelines or characteristics for activities or their results, aimed at the achievement of the optimum degree of order in a given context' (ISO/IEC Guide 2, 1991). Technical regulations in contrast are legally binding, and are usually imposed to safeguard public or animal health, or the environment. In most industrialized economies the number of standards greatly exceeds the number of technical regulations. Certification systems comprise the procedures to establish that products or production processes conform to the relevant standard or regulation.

The use of product standards is under the direct control of firms and industries. Most standards are market-driven, and firms desiring to export to or sell in a market have strong incentives to satisfy prevailing standards, be it to ensure compatibility or interconnection, or to signal that products meet minimum quality norms. In the case of technical product regulations there is no choice. Firms must comply and confront legal sanctions if they do not. In the case of both standards and technical regulations, the underlying norms are often determined through a cooperative international process that occurs under the auspices of specialized international bodies that allow for inputs by affected industries. A major player in this field is the International Organization for Standardization (ISO), which is located in Geneva, Switzerland. Whether or not to make norms developed by ISO technical committees mandatory is up to governments.

Technical product regulations are generally intended to deal with specific market failures. Possible rationales for technical regulations and standards (TRS) include information asymmetries, uncertainty, market power and externalities in production or consumption. Many standards have the characteristic of a public good in that use by one agent does not reduce other agents' consumption possibilities (Kindleberger, 1983). Frequently, the greater the use made of such standards, the greater the potential gains to users in terms of reduced transaction costs—there are so-called network externalities. Examples include standards of measurement and conventions such as driving on one side of the road.

In the public goods situation there is a clear-cut case for harmonization, as a common standard is in the interest of all users. Achieving agreement on a specific standard can be difficult, as different groups may have different preferences. Because of free rider problems, government intervention may be required to achieve a common standard. Most standards tend to be impure public goods, in that they benefit a specific, identifiable group (usually an industry and its customers). Although government intervention is not necessary, there remains a need for interested parties to cooperate, and to the extent that there are costs to developing a standard, there may be an incentive to free ride.

Although standards may help achieve technical efficiency, they may also allow incumbent firms in an industry to increase their market power. Standards are one of the possible instruments through which a firm or a group of firms can raise their rivals' costs. Assuming there are costs to meet the standard, its existence may reduce the contestability of a market because potential entrants find it less attractive to compete or to enter. The greater are the barriers to entry, the greater will be the profit-enhancing effect of the standard, all other things equal. Thus, standardization may well be employed strategically by firms or groups of firms that aim to create rents (excess profits).

There are numerous examples of such 'standards-setting' competitions: famous cases include the battle between the Betamax and the VHS standard for video cassettes in the 1980s (which was won by the latter), and more recently, between competing consortia of firms supporting the Blue Ray or the HD standards for high definition TV content, won by Blue Ray (owned by Sony—not, incidentally, the loser of the 1980s fight, from which it had drawn the appropriate lessons by ensuring that major content providers supported its technology). Another example is the Global System for Mobile communications (GSM) standard for mobile telephony. Insofar as the standards are voluntary there is no need to lobby governments in order to obtain the rents because the standards are set by industry groups. What matters is winning the competition if there is one; and, ideally, not having to compete. Government agencies responsible for determining technical regulations can expect to be lobbied by potentially affected parties and may be captured by them.

Because TRS can raise unit costs of production they may inhibit international trade. In general, if TRS differ across countries this will segment markets, even if identical norms are applied in each country to domestic and foreign goods (i.e. the national treatment rule is satisfied). Prices for similar goods of uniform quality will then not be equal across countries, as the different standards inhibit arbitrage. Research stimulated by the EU Single Market programme in the mid-1980s illustrated how significant such TRS-induced market segmentation can be. A typical example was building tiles where voluntary industry standards differed by EU country. Spain was found to be the lowest cost producer of such tiles, average prices being between 40 and over 100 per cent lower than prices charged by producers in other countries such as Germany, France and the Netherlands (Groupe-Mac, 1988). Such price differences were maintained as the result of a combination of differing standards and government procurement regulations. In France, nonstandard tiles could not be used in public works (about 40 per cent of the market), and private firms were hesitant to use nonstandard tiles because insurance companies tended to require that buildings meet industry standards. In Italy, pasta purity laws required that pasta be made of durum wheat, a high-quality type of wheat produced in the south of the country. This increased the cost of pasta in comparison to other EU countries, where pasta tended to consist of a mix of wheat qualities. Thus, a lack of uniform or mutually recognized TRS may have a significant impact on trade.

There is a vigorous debate in the literature whether a 'standards-as-barriers' view of the world is the more accurate one, or whether it is more accurate to take a 'standards-as-catalyst' perspective (Jaffee and Henson, 2004; Anders and Caswell, 2007). Standards and technical regulations can either facilitate or block trade. They can impose additional variable or fixed costs on exporters to the extent that it is necessary to alter production processes to adapt products for export. Moreover, certification requirements to demonstrate compliance can raise trade costs. On the other hand, standards can also reduce trade costs for enterprises. Adoption of common norms or international standards can help firms realize economies of scale and eliminate the need for redundant testing and certification.

The net impact of product standards on trade will depend on the relative magnitude of these effects. The empirical evidence is limited in this area, primarily due to the cost and complexities associated with collecting reliable data and constructing indicators on standards in different sectors across countries. Disdier et al. (2007), using WTO TBT and SPS notifications, find that standards have negative trade impacts, in particular for exports from developing countries to OECD countries. Otsuki, Wilson and Sewadeh (2001), Peterson and Orden (2007) and Wilson and Otsuki (2004) are examples that come to the same conclusion. Wilson and Otsuki (2004) use firm level data on standards and find that in Sub-Saharan Africa, firms invest on average 7.6 per cent of sales in order to comply with foreign standards. Their data also show that experiences differ greatly from one firm or country to another: the range of investment costs reported by firms runs from close to zero to over 100 per cent of annual sales. For firms in countries such as Kenya and Uganda average investment compliance costs as a share of sales can approach 10 per cent, whereas the average in other regions rarely exceeds 4 per cent. Case studies focusing on the costs and benefits of health and safety standards come to similar conclusions: the costs are often nontrivial. Maskus, Otsuki and Wilson (2005) find that a 1 per cent increase in investment to meet compliance costs raises variable (per unit) production costs by between 0.06 and 0.13 per cent—a small amount, but statistically significant. But the lump-sum fixed costs of compliance are nontrivial: averaging US$425,000 per firm in their sample, or about 4.7 per cent of value added.

Those taking a standards-as-catalyst view stress that the overall gains from making the associated investments can be significant (Jaffee and Henson, 2004). Moenius (2004) concludes that country-specific standards tend to promote trade in manufactures, whereas they have a negative impact on trade in homogeneous products such as commodities and agricultural products. This finding is consistent with the interpretation that higher information costs in manufactures can be mitigated with harmonized standards. Anders and Caswell (2007) study the effect of a 1997 introduction of a mandatory Hazard Analysis Critical Control Point (HACCP) standard for seafood by the United States. They concluded that this had a negative overall effect on exporters to the US, with developed country exporters as a group gaining and developing country exporters losing. However, when they focused the analysis at the country level, per capita income level of the exporter was not statistically significant: what mattered was scale. The leading seafood exporters gained market share after the HACCP was mandated; whereas most of the smaller exporters faced losses or stagnant sales. This phenomenon is also stressed by Maskus, Wilson and Otsuki (2001) and Jaffee and Henson (2004): tighter standards result in a shake out of the industry. More efficient suppliers benefit, less efficient ones may be forced out of the market altogether.

Maertens and Swinnen (2009) note that an assessment of the effects of (tighter) standards needs to go beyond a focus on firm-level impacts. In the case of Senegal they show that tougher EU standards were accompanied by an *increase* in exports, and that this led to rising rural incomes and poverty reduction. The standards had an impact on market structure, inducing a shift from smallholder contract farming to integrated estate production. This in turn changed the channels through which poor households benefitted from expanding trade opportunities: through labour markets (wage income) instead of product markets (profits and prices of output sold).

Finally, there are also spillovers associated with specific standards or decisions to tighten standards. Debaere (2005) has shown how a shift in EU policy to zero tolerance of antibiotics had a major adverse effect on Thai exports of shrimp to the EU, much of which was diverted to the US market, which resulted in the launch of a series of US antidumping actions—not just against Thailand but also other exporters such as Vietnam. Peterson and Orden (2005) also conclude that raising US standards on poultry had trade deflection effects.

Thus, TRS can either facilitate or block trade. They can impose additional variable or fixed costs on exporters due to a need to alter production processes to adapt products, and certification requirements to demonstrate compliance can raise trade costs. On the other hand, TRS can also reduce trade costs for firms when produced to international norms for multiple markets. The net impact of product standards on trade will depend on the relative magnitude of these effects. The characteristic of TRS that they are in principle welfare-enhancing distinguishes them from many of the other policies that are subject to WTO rules. However, the above discussion also reveals that TRS may be captured by a subset of firms in an industry and be used as an instrument to create market power. Even if they do not, they will impose costs on firms in trading partners. This tension between the welfare-increasing potential of TRS and their possible trade-impeding effects is, of course, one that arises with any domestic regulatory policy. Because standards have been dealt with under the GATT for many years already, WTO disciplines in this area are of interest not only in their own right, but also for what they suggest about the feasibility of dealing with regulation-related trade tensions more generally.

WTO rules

The WTO does not require that members have product standards. Nor does the WTO develop or write standards. The GATT 1994 Agreement on Technical Barriers to Trade (TBT) aims to ensure that mandatory technical regulations, voluntary standards, and testing and certification of products do not constitute unnecessary barriers to trade. There is a close relationship between the TBT agreement, the national treatment requirement and Article XX GATT (which allows for measures to restrict trade if necessary to protect public health or safety—see Chapter 9). The link with national treatment (Article III GATT) is that 'like' products produced in foreign countries may be subjected to a variety of conformity assessment requirements that can be construed to be discriminatory but may be necessary to ensure compliance with prevailing regulations. The link with Article XX is that both parts of the GATT deal with measures taken by governments to safeguard public health and safety, among other things. Indeed, the preamble of the TBT agreement repeats language found in Article XX:

Recognizing that no country should be prevented from taking measures necessary... for the protection of human... life or health... subject to the requirement that they are not applied in a manner which would constitute a means of arbitrary or unjustifiable discrimination between countries where the same conditions prevail or a disguised restriction on international trade...

The TBT agreement is complemented by a stand alone agreement dealing with sanitary and phytosanitary measures (discussed in the next section).

The TBT agreement embodies disciplines on the adoption of TRS in member countries, and on conformity assessment, testing and certification procedures. It also has a variety of transparency provisions. Two tests are imposed in determining whether a specific regulation raises a legitimate trade concern: does it have a discriminatory trade impact, and whether this is necessary to achieve the objective of the government. The basic rules are that central government bodies do not discriminate (as defined by the MFN and national treatment rules) and do not adopt TRS that are more trade-restrictive than necessary to meet legitimate objectives—which may include national security, the prevention of deceptive practices, the protection of human health or safety, animal or plant life and health, and the environment. Necessity in this context means that WTO members are free to pursue any objective they deem appropriate but at the same time must select an instrument that minimizes possible negative effects on international trade. Necessity does not oblige WTO members to use what economists would call 'first best' (i.e. the most efficient) policies. Instead the focus is on trade effects. In most circumstances, however, a norm that minimizes trade effects is likely to more efficient than one that does not, unless the source of the externality is at the border.

The 'least trade restrictiveness' criterion is a reflection of a basic objective of the agreement: to facilitate trade. A unique feature of the agreement is that it encourages the use of harmonization as a way of reducing TRS-related trade costs (Article 2.4). Relevant international standards developed by bodies such as the ISO—if they exist—must be used as the basis for technical regulations, except if this would be inappropriate because of climatic, geographical or technological factors. In a rather controversial decision, the AB in *EC—Sardines* held that if a country does not use international norms when these exist, it is up to the complaining party to show that the international standard would be ineffective or inappropriate to achieve the objective of the government imposing an idiosyncratic norm. This reversal of the burden of proof greatly increases the scope for governments to diverge from international standards.

In *EC—Asbestos* the AB defined a technical regulation as any measure that applies to an identifiable products or group of products, specifies technical characteristics for these products (e.g. relating to composition and characteristics such as flammability, texture, density, toxicity, etc.) *and* is mandatory. Technical regulations based on product requirements should be worded in terms of performance rather than design or descriptive characteristics. A Code of Good Practice applies regarding the preparation, adoption and application of voluntary standards.

An implication of the definition of a technical regulation is that production and processing methods (PPMs) are only covered by the TBT agreement if they have a direct bearing on the physical characteristics of the product(s). Increasingly certification systems that deal with management processes and systems such as ISO 9000 and ISO 1400 are being used by firms to signal quality and a commitment to social responsibility and as a requirement of purchasers to engage in a trade relationship with exporters. Such standards are not covered by the TBT agreement. The same applies to labels and certification marks insofar as these are limited to the way a product was produced as opposed to its content or physical characteristics.

Conformity assessment procedures are also subject to nondiscrimination. Here again, relevant guides or recommendations issued by international standardizing bodies are to be used if they exist, except if inappropriate for national security reasons or deemed inadequate to safeguard health and safety. In principle, WTO members are to join and use international systems for conformity assessment. The results of conformity assessment procedures undertaken in exporting countries must be accepted if consultations determine these are equivalent to domestic ones. Accreditation on the basis of relevant guides or recommendations issued by international standardizing bodies is to be taken into account as an indication of adequate technical competence of the foreign entity. Members are encouraged to negotiate mutual recognition agreements (MRAs) for conformity assessment procedures, and to apply the nondiscrimination principle when permitting participation of foreign certification bodies in their conformity assessment procedures.

A third component of the disciplines is transparency-related, and builds upon the principle of publication of trade regulations contained in Article X GATT. Each member must notify the WTO when it plans to adopt a TRS that does not conform to an international standard, allow reasonable time for other members to comment, as well as a reasonable period of time for exporters to adapt to new requirements. Moreover, Members must establish a national enquiry point where traders may obtain documents and answers regarding:

(1) technical regulations adopted or proposed by bodies that have legal power to enforce them;
(2) standards adopted or proposed by central or local government bodies, or by regional standardizing bodies; and
(3) conformity assessment procedures, existing or proposed, applied by enforcing bodies.

Best efforts are to be made to ensure that enquiry points are also able to respond to inquiries regarding standards adopted or proposed by nongovernmental standardizing bodies such as industry associations, as well as conformity assessment procedures operated by such bodies. The WTO Secretariat is to establish an information system under which national standards bodies or enquiry points transmit to the ISO Information Centre in Geneva the notifications required under the Code of Good Practice for the preparation, adoption and application of standards.

The agreement is subject to review every three years. The fourth review was completed in November 2006. In general, members are of the view that it has worked smoothly. The committee dealing with the agreement has held regular meetings, and successfully managed issues raised by WTO members. The TBT Agreement was not subject to negotiation in the Doha Round. However, implementation concerns became an element of the broader set of concerns of developing countries in the post-Uruguay Round period. Issues that were raised included the use of eco-labels and certification systems, the growth in environmental, health and safety standards, and capacity constraints that affected their participation in standards-setting bodies. Without adequate infrastructure to deal with these standards and regulations, business firms in developing countries could see their exports restricted, not because of an unwillingness to comply, but due to an inability to identify relevant requirements, implement the necessary institutional and proced-ural changes, or prove compliance in a credible fashion.

TBT disputes

There have been relatively few disputes under the agreement. The TBT agreement was first invoked in a 1996 case brought by Venezuela and Brazil against US standards for reformulated and conventional gasoline. However, the panel found against the US on the basis of Articles I and III GATT, and did not rule on the basis of the allegations regarding the TBT agreement. The two major disputes in this area were *EC—Asbestos* (WT/DS135/R) and *EC—Sardines* (WT/DS/231). As mentioned in Chapter 3, the asbestos dispute involved an argument by Canada that a French ban on the manufacture, importation and sale of asbestos violated the TBT agreement because it was not necessary, and was not based on international standards. The EU argued that the asbestos ban was not a technical regulation in the sense of the TBT agreement. In considering these arguments, the panel deter-mined that a measure constitutes a 'technical regulation' if it affects one or more given products, specifies the technical characteristics of the product(s) that allow them to be marketed in the territory of the member imposing the measure, and is mandatory. The panel concluded that the general prohibition on marketing asbes-tos and asbestos-containing products did not satisfy this definition.

The AB rejected the panel's approach of separating the measure into a ban and the exceptions, and reversed the panel's interpretation. It concluded that the ban as an 'integrated whole' was a technical regulation in the sense of the TBT Agreement (Annex 1.1), as it applied to an identifiable product or group of products, the document introducing the ban laid down one or more product characteristics, and the compliance with these product characteristics was mandatory (WTO, 2008). However, the AB declared itself unable to complete the legal analysis of Canada's TBT claims as it lacked an 'adequate basis' upon which to examine them.

The *EC—Sardines* case has already been discussed in Chapter 3. The relevance of this case is that it was the first time that a panel has found a WTO member to be in violation of its obligations under the TBT Agreement. The AB agreed with the panel that the EC regulation on the common marketing of sardines was a 'technical regulation' within the meaning of Annex 1.1 TBT as it fulfilled the three criteria laid down in the *EC—Asbestos* report.

Reducing transactions costs: harmonization and mutual recognition

Standards are increasingly important in the world economy. A sectoral analysis of the total number of published technical standards as of 2004 concluded that standards are most prevalent in the telecommunications, audio and video engineering, construction materials and building, and electrical engineering industries. For each of these sectors, the total number of standards published exceeded 30,000. Low-technology industries, such as clothing, mining, paper and glass and ceramic industries reported a considerably smaller number of standards—below 6,000 (WTO, 2005). Data collected in UNCTAD's Trade Analysis and Information System (TRAINS) include the number of tariff lines affected by government-mandated technical regulations. The share of imports covered by such regulations varied from 46.2 per cent for Brazil (in 2001) and 31.9 per cent for the United States (in 1999) to surprisingly low estimates of 2.9 per cent for Japan and less than 1 per cent for the EU. This illustrates a general problem concerning NTMs: available data are very incomplete. In the case of the EU for example, TRAINS does not include any standards that are put in place by the EU member states. If these are included, the share of tariff lines rises above the US level (Kee, Nicita and Olarreaga, 2008).

Another set of estimates based on 2001 data suggest that close to 88 per cent of the value of world trade is in products that are potentially affected by environmentally related NTMs, including TBT measures (Fontagné, von Kirchbach and Mimouni, 2005). Over 60 per cent of US exports were subject to health, safety and related standards in their destination markets in the late 1990s. Government-issued certificates were required for 45 per cent of exports to the EU, private, third-party certification was accepted for 15 per cent, and manufacturers self-certification sufficed for the rest (Wilson, 1998).Within the EU, some 75 per cent of the value of intra-EU trade in goods was subject to mandatory TRS in the 1990s. Certification in regulated sectors may involve frequent and redundant sampling of products and testing for conformity to standards. Some products may be subjected to 100 per cent testing—this can effectively block imports if applied only to foreign firms. Unter (1998) estimates that redundant testing and conformity assessment procedures faced by Hewlett Packard increased sixfold between 1990 and 1997.

The GATT rules are helpful for traders in ensuring nondiscrimination and enhancing transparency of TRS, but clearly more is required if transaction costs are to be reduced significantly. There are two major policy options: harmonization and mutual recognition. Harmonization may involve unilateral adoption by one country of another's set of rules, or negotiation of a common set of disciplines—the international standardization that is encouraged by the TBT agreement. Examples abound of unilateral harmonization to the standard of another country. These are often driven by market size disparities: in 1992 Canada adopted US auto emission standards to ensure that its auto makers could realize economies of scale by avoiding separate production lines for the home and US markets. Switzerland adopted the EU TRS regime to ensure that Swiss goods could enter and circulate in the EU on the same basis as EU-produced goods (Messerlin, 1998). Many developing countries use TRS regimes initially developed in Europe or the US, often by maintaining systems inherited from a colonial past or military occupation. Others have deliberately adopted foreign norms. South Korea imported many German and US product standards in the 1950s as part of a strategy to upgrade the quality of industrial production and foster exports. Unilateral recognition of foreign regulatory regimes can be a complement to adopting the standards of a trading partner or international norms. Thus, foreign certification for certain imports may be accepted as proof of safety. For example, the Underwriters Laboratories (UL) mark is accepted in many countries.

Harmonization of standards—adoption of international norms where these exist, or convergence towards the norms applying in major markets such as the EU or US—is one avenue through which to potentially reduce the trade costs associated with product standards. Such benefits could be enhanced insofar as the transatlantic initiative results in greater common EU–US standards, by creating a larger market where the same standards apply or partner norms are accepted as equivalent. If, as a result, fixed costs of compliance can be spread over more sales, third countries will benefit from convergence. Baldwin (2000) notes that cooperation on standards will have fewer adverse effects—if any—on third parties than would arise from the preferential removal of tariffs. Insiders may benefit from lower costs as a result of mutual recognition or the adoption of common standards, but this is also likely to benefit outsiders.

Chen and Mattoo (2008) investigate whether EU harmonization of technical regulations help or hinder third countries, focusing on Harmonization Directives issued by the European Commission that lay down common, mandatory regulations that apply in all EU member states for specific sectors. Chen and Mattoo find that these directives increase trade between EU countries but not necessarily with the rest of the world. Harmonization of standards may actually reduce the exports of excluded countries, especially in markets that have raised the stringency of standards. Among excluded countries, developing countries may be the worst sufferers as their firms are likely to be less well equipped to comply with stricter standards.

Czubala, Shepherd and Wilson (2007) focus on voluntary standards promulgated by the European Committee for Standardization, using a database on EU standards for textiles and clothing to examine the impact of EU standards on African exports of textiles and clothing. Their analysis shows that (nonharmonized)

EU standards tend to hold back African exports. Their findings are consistent with the idea that capacity constraints in Africa can make it difficult for firms to adapt products to meet multiple standards. By contrast, in instances where the EU has adopted the standards developed by the ISO, there is a much weaker negative impact on African exports to the EU.

Shepherd (2007) analyses the impacts of harmonization on the range of products exported by a country's trading partners. Market-specific fixed costs of exporting are used to model product standards. Numerical simulations show that international harmonization can promote penetration of new markets in third countries (i.e. those that do not harmonize), provided that compliance costs do not increase too much as a result of harmonization. Using the same database as Czubala et al. (2007), Shepherd finds that more product standards tend to reduce partner country export variety, whereas international harmonization acts weakly in the opposite direction. A 10 per cent increase in the number of EU standards is associated with a 6 per cent decline in the range of product varieties (tariff lines) exported by the EU's trading partners. A similar increase in the proportion of EU standards that are internationally harmonized produces a small but significant effect (0.2 per cent) in the opposite direction. The data suggest that the strength of this harmonization effect may be up to 50 per cent greater for low-income countries, which is consistent with the existence of constraints to product or process adaptation in developing countries.

Harmonization to facilitate trade has been pursued most intensively by the EU. The European experience suggests that this is unlikely to be a productive strategy as agreement is very difficult to obtain under a consensus rule. A better approach is mutual recognition, under which countries agree to recognize (accept as equivalent) each other's standards and conformity assessment procedures. Mutual recognition agreements are a cooperative mechanism through which the transaction costs associated with conformity assessment systems to establish compliance with standards can be reduced (Box 5.6). Mutual recognition agreements may require some degree of harmonization of either standards or test procedures, especially in areas where mandatory standards or regulations apply, to ensure that the underlying norms satisfy basic minimum standards. As a result, MRAs are not a panacea (Pelkmans, 2007).

Mutual recognition proved a powerful tool for increasing competition in European market. What about effects on excluded countries? Chen and Mattoo (2008) find that MRAs of conformity assessment promote the trade of *both* covered and excluded countries. As both Baldwin (2000) and Chen and Mattoo (2008) note, the impact on third parties of MRAs depends on whether 'restrictive rules of origin' apply, i.e. whether the goods must be produced in the territory of a party to a MRA, and whether a harmonized norm is accepted as being identical in an importing country. Some MRAs impose restrictive origin rules, e.g. agreements between the EU and Australia and New Zealand (Hoekman and Winters, 2007). This implies

Box 5.6. EU–US mutual recognition agreements for conformity assessment

US and EU trade talks on mutual recognition of conformity assessment began in 1992 and aimed at achieving agreement that product test results, inspections and certifications performed by independent entities would be accepted in both markets. In particular, the EU sought assurance that US testing laboratories and product certification bodies were competent to test for compliance with the essential requirements specified in EU directives. The EU also wanted European firms to be able to test and certify to corresponding US regulatory requirements. The US sought to eliminate the perceived discriminatory effects of the EU's new approach to technical regulations, which mandated product certification by approved European bodies — imposing duplicate testing costs on exporters. The EU's increasingly community-wide approach to standardization gave US firms an incentive to negotiate MRAs, as these would lower the costs of accessing the EU market as a whole.

Significant differences in European and US testing and certification systems made agreement difficult. The European system relies less on self-declaration of conformity by enterprises than the US system, and more on mandatory third-party testing and certification. Under the EU's global approach to conformity assessment, only recognized testing, certification and marking institutions are able to issue certification marks. As of the end of 1997, member states had only certified 600 such bodies to the Commission (out of a total of over 10,000, ranging from large multinationals such as Société Générale de Surveillance (SGS), Inchcape or Bureau Veritas to small in-house testing facilities). Virtually all were European (Messerlin, 1998). Another obstacle concerned the extent to which certification and inspection agencies of one country are willing and legally permitted to devolve authority for testing and inspection to the other country's regulators. It was eventually agreed that the EU would accept that the US Food and Drug Administration (FDA) was an independent agency that could not be overruled.

The EU–US MRA, which entered into force in 1998, covered in 2008 such sectors as telecommunications terminal equipment, electromagnetic compatibility, electrical safety, recreational craft, medical devices and pharmaceutical Good Manufacturing Practices. As the legal and mandatory product requirements of the importing party must always be fulfilled, the MRA did not call for a harmonization of product or conformity assessment requirements between the EU and US. Each country maintained its own legislation and regulatory requirements and remained free to set its health, safety and environmental protection levels as it deemed necessary, as long as they complied with international obligations. The MRA must thus evolve with changes in EU and US regulations and is therefore modified from time to time. The agreement addresses acceptance of test data, laboratory accreditation and final product certification.

As of 2000, certifications performed anywhere by a facility recognized under the MRA in the US or Europe are accepted, and manufacturers now have a wider choice of testing laboratories. The agreement also introduced a joint curriculum for training of European and American inspectors. The treaty was expected to eliminate duplicative product testing on an estimated $60 billion worth of traded goods (Semerjian and Beary, 2001). The MRA on telecommunications and information technology products alone could save consumers and manufacturers approximately US$1.4 billion, implying that the frictional costs abolished were equivalent to a 5 per cent tax on the goods traded (Wilson, 1998). Although this is a significant cost reduction, the MRAs are regarded as a second best solution by US industry, which would prefer to rely much more on supplier self-certification instead of third-party conformity assessment.

that nonmembers cannot benefit from the MRA by having their goods tested in MRA countries.

The extant research on product standards suggests that efforts to reduce multiplicity in standards through regional or international harmonization may help reduce overall costs for developing countries. Much also depends on the specifics of the norms that apply—if these are more difficult for developing countries to attain, the result may be trade diversion. Financial or capacity constraints might make it difficult for developing country exporters to comply with the new standards. Finally, the norms may simply be inappropriate for the circumstances prevailing in the developing country.

A question for WTO members, and developing countries in particular, is whether mutual recognition is a viable option to pursue in the multilateral context. The process relies heavily on mutual trust in the competence and ability of the institutions responsible for enforcing mandatory standards and a willingness to be flexible in setting minimum standards. Even if developing countries adopt European, American or international (e.g. ISO) standards, significant institutional strengthening is likely to be required for partner countries to be willing to accept 'home country supervision'. One result of an unwillingness of OECD countries to recognize developing country standards regimes could be a hollowing out of the MFN principle. The potential for recognition to reduce transaction costs and increase the real incomes of WTO members can be significant. The EU now requires third-party testing, certification or quality system registration for certain regulated sectors by organizations certified to the Commission by the member states as technically competent. The requirement that these assessments be undertaken by EU-certified bodies raised the costs of testing and certification to non-EU manufacturers in many sectors and was a prime motivation for EU–US MRA negotiations in the 1990s (Box 5.6).

The publication and notification requirements of the TBT Agreement, in conjunction with the national enquiry points have an important role to play in fostering transparency. They help ensure that traders can readily determine the regulatory situation that prevails in markets to which they want to export. The number of TBT notifications received by the WTO Secretariat during the 1995–2004 period averaged about 610 per year. About 40 per cent concerned measures to protect human health or safety. Other reasons frequently given for notified new measures were prevention of deceptive practices and consumer information and labelling. This suggests that many of the TRS are concerned with solving consumer—producer information asymmetry problems (WTO, 2005).

An important effort has been made by the TBT Committee to increase transparency in the identification and prioritization of technical assistance needs. In particular, the members were encouraged to make use of the Format for the Voluntary Notification of Specific Technical Assistance Needs and Responses and to exchange experiences concerning technical assistance and to identify good practices in this regard (WTO, 2007). A weakness of the TBT Agreement is that language on voluntary product standards developed by industry associations is largely of a best-endeavours nature. This reflects the fact that WTO disciplines focus on government actions—not the private sector. An important challenge confronting WTO members is to explore avenues for reducing the transactions costs incurred by traders due to differences in TRS and, perhaps more importantly, the excess costs incurred due to redundant testing and certification requirements.

A top–down approach aiming at eliminating TRS-related trade conflicts through harmonization or mutual recognition will be difficult in the WTO context. To date it has only proven possible to a limited extent in the EU and between a few OECD countries. Extending this model to a group of 153-plus economies will be difficult. Initiatives using a bottom–up approach to enforcement are likely to be more fruitful. That is, the emphasis might more productively centre on certification activities and an expansion of the role of the private sector in such activities. In addition to PSI-type models, greater acceptance of the supplier's declaration of conformity could be encouraged (Wilson, 1998). Moreover, given the importance that is accorded to the role of competent international standards-setting bodies in defining standards, an important issue for WTO members and civil society in member countries is to ensure that the process through which TRS are developed allows for participation by affected stakeholders. To date, the major players in standards-setting bodies have been industry and subsets of the scientific community, with relatively little participation by developing countries.

Finally, consideration needs to be given to the implications of the burden of proof that is currently imposed on nonmembers of a MRA that seek to accede. This burden can be quite high and give rise to situations where countries that satisfy technical requirements are nonetheless excluded for political or other reasons. A major policy issue is therefore to ensure that the MFN rule does not get circumvented through the negotiation of MRAs. A necessary condition for this is that nonmembers have the opportunity to join such agreements.

5.8. SANITARY AND PHYTOSANITARY MEASURES

Sanitary and phytosanitary (SPS) measures are requirements imposed by governments to ensure the safety of products for human or animal consumption, or to protect the environment (plant life). Most governments establish minimum standards that products, plants or animals must meet in order to be allowed to enter their territory. Usually these norms will apply equally to foreign and domestically produced goods, plants or animals. However, as is the case with TRS more generally, differences in norms may act to restrict trade. Such differences became increasingly prominent during the 1980s, with many countries alleging that import-competing industries or lobbies were using SPS measures to restrict trade.

The economic considerations discussed above that arise with respect to TBT also apply to SPS. One qualitative difference is that SPS measures tend to be more diverse across countries than product standards for manufactures, as the market-place creates strong incentives for products to be compatible where this benefits consumers. Another difference is that there is more scope for 'abuse,' as the norms can be defined so strictly as to ensure that no import ever satisfies them. For example, a country with a large sheep industry but no cows may try to prohibit imports of beef to protect sheep farmers by imposing a health-based SPS measure requiring that beef have a fat content that is very costly to attain (say, less than 1 per cent). Alternatively, if it has a beef industry and could consequently be subjected to a claim of violating national treatment, it might require that the drip content of frozen beef be less than 1 per cent—that is, once unfrozen, no more than 1 per cent liquid is allowed in each carcass. This would be a very difficult standard to meet. Or it could impose a very short shelf-life requirement. It could also use a SPS measure to encourage local processing in cases where it has bound its tariffs. Thus, beef for retail sale might be required to have no more than 3 per cent fat, but beef for further processing could have any fat content. Abuses may also occur in the enforcement of SPS measures. Even if a country uses internationally accepted SPS measures for a product, governments will still inspect imports to ascertain whether they satisfy health requirements. Such inspections may be used as a mechanism to reject imports of politically sensitive goods, even if they meet all health and safety requirements (Box 5.7).

A final very important qualitative difference is that SPS questions give rise to much greater public concern and debate than do TBT-related matters. This is because they pertain to the natural environment, the food that people consume, the technologies that are used to produce food, and to human, plant and animal health. As a result, attitudes to risk and trust in science and scientists play a role in public policy formation in this area in ways that do not arise in the TBT arena.

WTO rules and disputes

The Agreement on the Application of Sanitary and Phytosanitary Measures was negotiated as part of the Uruguay Round Agreement on Agriculture (discussed in the next chapter). It is basically an elaboration of GATT Article XX(b), one of the clauses of the GATT General Exceptions clause, which allows members to impose measures necessary to protect human, animal, or plant life and health, as long as the measure does not result in unjustifiable discrimination between countries or

Box 5.7. International trade and SPS restrictions

Two long running disputes in the 1980s helped motivate negotiators in the Uruguay Round to seek an agreement on SPS measures: Japanese sanitary rules on imports of apples and the EU ban on the use of hormonal substances in livestock and meat products.

Japan formally opened its apple market to foreign competition in 1971. In practice market access continued to be restricted in the decades that followed on the grounds that most imports were not sufficiently protected against pests and plant diseases that could harm Japan's orchards. Apple exporters argued that Japan's phytosanitary regulations were far more stringent than any other country's, and constituted back-door protectionism (GATT Activities, 1987). US trade officials cited Japan's apple import regulations as an unfair trade barrier and regularly raised the issue in bilateral discussions, driven by Congressional representatives from the state of Washington—a major producer. After years of tension, Japanese authorities finally gave in to the external pressure, declaring that certain US orchards had taken adequate measures to eliminate viruses and moths.

In January 1988, the EU banned the use of hormonal substances in the process of fattening animals intended for slaughter and human consumption. This ban affected US exports of meat to the EU, and caused a trade dispute to develop. The US argued that the ban had no scientific foundation—as the use of hormones by US producers was well within safe margins as determined by a variety of scientific agencies—and therefore constituted an unjustifiable trade barrier. According to the US, the ban—if fully implemented—would reduce exports by US$115 million per year. The dispute was brought to the GATT, with the US choosing to invoke the procedures of the TBT Agreement, this being the only relevant instrument at the time. The EU considered that because the ban was aimed at protecting health and concerned production and processing methods—which were not covered by the TBT agreement—the US did not have a case. The US threatened to increase tariffs on certain European goods if the prohibition on importation and sale of meat treated with hormones was implemented. The EU in turn brought the issue of retaliatory measures by the US before the GATT Council (GATT Activities, 1987 and 1988). (For an account of more recent developments regarding the hormones dispute see Chapter 3, Section 3.3).

These examples illustrate why an agreement on SPS measures was considered essential for the trading system. Governments expected that the scope for protectionist abuse of food safety and animal or plant health regulations would be considerably reduced as a result of the agreement, both by establishing clearer rules of the game and providing a better basis for dispute settlement. Both the apple and the hormone cases were brought to the WTO.

acts as a disguised restriction on trade. The agreement applies to all SPS measures that may affect international trade. It applies even if there is no domestic production.

A SPS measure is defined as any measure applied to protect human, animal or plant health from risks arising from the establishment or spread of pests and diseases; from additives or contaminants in foodstuffs; or to prevent other damage from the establishment or spread of pests. Sanitary and phytosanitary measures include all relevant regulations and procedures, including product criteria; processes and production methods; testing, inspection, certification and approval procedures; quarantine treatments; provisions on relevant statistical procedures and risk assessment methods; and packaging and labelling requirements directly related to food safety. As in the case of TRS, there is no requirement that members adopt SPS measures. Nor does the WTO draft SPS norms. The WTO simply establishes disciplines if members implement SPS measures. A difference with the TBT agreement, however, is that the distinction between (mandatory) technical regulations and (voluntary) standards is not made: all SPS measures are covered equally.

The SPS Agreement is *lex specialis* to the TBT Agreement—that is, its more specific provisions apply on matters that are also covered under the latter agreement. The basic rules are that SPS measures are not more trade restrictive than necessary to achieve their objectives, do not unjustifiably discriminate between WTO members and do not constitute a disguised restriction on international trade. They should be based on international standards, guidelines or recommendations, if these exist. If tougher standards are imposed, they must be justified with scientific evidence. In contrast to the TBT agreement, the SPS agreement identifies an indicative list of bodies that promulgate international SPS standards—including the Codex Alimentarius Commission, the International Office of Epizootics and the International Plant Protection Convention.

A crucial provision in the agreement that distinguishes it from the TBT disciplines is that SPS measures must be based on scientific principles (Article 2.2), including an assessment of the risks to human, animal or plant life or health, taking into account risk assessment techniques developed by relevant international organizations (Article 5.1). Only if there is no relevant scientific evidence may governments invoke the so-called precautionary principle. The risk assessment must identify the diseases a member wants to prevent in its territory, the potential biological and economic consequences associated with such diseases, and an evaluation of the likelihood of entry, establishment or spread of these diseases (Article 5.3). In the assessment of risks, available scientific evidence must be considered, as well as relevant processes and production methods; inspection, sampling and testing methods, and the prevalence of specific diseases or pests and environmental conditions (Article 5.2).

The agreement also embodies a recognition element. World Trade Organization members must accept the SPS measures of other members as equivalent—even if they differ from their own—if the exporting country can demonstrate that its SPS measures achieve the desired level of protection (Article 4). Negotiations to achieve bilateral or multilateral agreements on recognition of the equivalence of specified SPS measures are encouraged. Conformity assessment procedures and fees are to conform to MFN and national treatment, procedures and criteria should be published, confidentiality respected, and an appeals procedure established.

The Committee on Sanitary and Phytosanitary Measures may grant developing countries specified, time-limited exceptions in whole or in part from meeting the requirements of the agreement. Least developed countries were able to delay application of the provisions of the agreement until mid-2000. The Committee was charged with the development of a procedure to monitor the process of international harmonization and the use of international standards, and the establishment of a list of international standards and guidelines relating to SPS measures that have a major impact on trade.

As under the TBT agreement, an enquiry point must exist to respond to SPS-related queries from trading partners and to provide relevant documents. If the content of a proposed SPS regulation is not substantially the same as that of an international norm and is likely to have a significant effect on trade, the WTO Secretariat must be notified. This must include a description of the regulation's product coverage and a brief indication of the objective and rationale of the proposed regulation.

Scott (2006) notes that the notification requirements and the SPS Committee have had a major role in defusing potential conflicts and that interactions between members in the regular committee meetings have led to agreed elaborations of certain aspects of the agreement. Particularly important, the *ex ante* review and discussion of specific measures, their rationale and possible (or actual) impact on trade have resulted in a number of instances where a WTO member revises a proposed SPS norm or assists developing country trading partners adapt to new regulations. As stressed in Chapter 2, the numerous WTO committees play an important role in supporting cooperation and defusing potential conflicts. In the case of the SPS Committee, between 1995 and 2005, over 200 specific trade concerns were raised in committee deliberations, about half by developing countries (G/SPS/GEN/204/Rev.5). Around half of the issues raised were resolved (Scott, 2006).

In contrast to the TBT agreement, there have been a number of high profile SPS disputes. This reflects both the fact that SPS measures are more frequently the basis on which governments restrict trade and differences between major traders in the way they regulate. In addition to *EC—Hormones* (discussed in Chapter 3), through 2008 four disputes concerned the question of sufficient scientific evidence (Article 2.2), one referred to harmonization (Article 3), seven dealt with risk assessment (Article 5.1), three referred to discrimination and disguised restrictions (Article 5.5), four dealt with alternative measures and the requirement that SPS measures not be 'more trade restrictions than necessary' (Article 5.6), two concerned provisional application (Article 5.7), and two control inspection and approval procedures (Article 8 and Annex C).

As mentioned in Box 5.7, the first SPS-related dispute (in 1997) concerned Japanese testing requirements for agricultural products. In that case the US complained that for agricultural products for which quarantine was required, Japan prohibited the importation of each variety until the quarantine treatment (fumigation) had been tested for that variety, even though the treatment had proven effective for other varieties of the same product. The products concerned included apples, nectarines, cherries and walnuts. The US argued Japan's measures did not have a scientific justification and were more trade restrictive than necessary. The panel agreed with the US on the first count, but not the second. A footnote to the relevant provision (Article 5.6 SPS) specifies that a measure is 'too' restrictive if another SPS measure exists that is reasonably available (taking into account technical and economic feasibility), achieves the desired level of protection, and is significantly less trade restrictive than the measure that is the subject of dispute. The panel found that only the first and last of these conditions had been demonstrated. The panel also noted that by not having published the testing requirements for any of the products at issue, Japan had violated the transparency provisions of the SPS Agreement.

This case illustrated the importance of being able to document the scientific basis for measures (Article 2.2.) and that these are based on an appropriate risk assessment (Article 5.1). It also sent a clear signal that countries could win cases where these conditions are not met. A dispute brought by Canada in the same year against an Australian prohibition on the importation of untreated fresh, chilled or frozen salmon further clarified the reach of the SPS agreement. The ban was motivated on the basis of preventing the entry of pests and diseases into Australia. Here again it was concluded that the prohibition was not scientifically justified and was not based on an appropriate risk assessment. The panel also found that the measure violated the 'consistency requirement' of the SPS agreement (Article 5.5), which specifies that in comparable situations the same SPS standards should apply. It concluded that Australia had imposed more stringent norms for adult, wild, ocean-caught Pacific salmon and applied lower standards for whole, frozen herring for use as bait and live ornamental finfish. These arbitrary distinctions were found to result in discrimination and act as a disguised restriction on international trade.

In October 1998, the AB reversed the panel's finding that the measure was more trade restrictive than required because the panel had focused on Australia's heat-treatment requirement, rather than the SPS measure at issue (the import prohibition). In considering whether the import ban was excessive, the AB concluded that it was not able to come to a determination given absence of information in the panel report on the relative risks of alternative regulatory options (WT/DS/18/AB/R). In 1999 Australia published an 'Import Risk Analysis' that considered the health risk associated with the importation of fresh, chilled and frozen salmon. Australia also modified its legislation on the quarantine of imports by allowing permits to be issued to release nonheated salmon from Australian quarantine facilities in cases where the product was in a 'consumer-ready form' (defined as skinless fillets of any size, skin-on fillets or steaks of less than 450g or products further processed). Under the new measures, Canadian salmon was required to be eviscerated, headed, gilled, washed, inspected, graded and come from a population for which there is a documented health surveillance system. Additional certification was required for Atlantic salmon. Canada considered that Australia's new fish import policies were still inconsistent with WTO disciplines because they were, *inter alia*, unnecessarily trade restrictive and there was no scientific foundation for limiting exemptions from quarantine to products in 'consumer-ready form'. A new panel agreed with Canada on both counts in early 2008. Canada and Australia subsequently concluded a MAS that included removal of the consumer-ready requirements.

Few issues raise as many concerns about food safety and environmental impact as does the use of biotechnology and GMOs. Public debates on this matter in most EU countries have revealed that many people are not convinced that these technologies should be used for food production. As a result, the EU has put in place a complex, multilevel and multi-actor process for approval of GMOs, complemented by traceability and labelling requirements. In contrast to the EU, the US and several other major agricultural exporters have moved much faster than the EU in adopting GMOs, with the result that an increasing share of their maize, soybean and other agricultural output use these new technologies. The more restrictive regulatory regime in the EU therefore became a market access concern. In 2004, the US, Argentina and Canada brought a dispute against the EU regime pertaining to GMOs. There were two main claims. The first concerned the elaborate system put in place by the EU for firms to obtain pre-marketing approval for GMOs. The complainants held that this process was not being implemented: there was de facto moratorium on the approval of new GMOs. The second complaint concerned the fact that a number of EU member states prohibited the use of GMOs that *had* been approved by the EU certification process. The prohibitions were responses to public opposition to the free circulation of GMOs, and governments justified their bans on the basis of the principle of precaution.

The three complainants argued that the moratorium and bans violated the SPS agreement because there was no scientific justification. In May 2006, the panel issued a complex ruling that took issue with many aspects of the EU's regulation of GMOs. The ruling did not question the sovereign right of any WTO member to put into place strict bio-safety legislation to regulate GMOs, or to reject an application related to a GMO. Instead, the EU was taken to task for not applying its own rules properly (Ching and Lin, 2006; WTO, 2008). In effect, the EU had ceased to accept requests for approvals because the matter had become so politically sensitive, and for the same reason had been unwilling to confront the member states that were imposing a national ban. Subsequent to the ruling, the EU began to approve new GMOs and to take action against recalcitrant EU member states.

Another SPS-related ruling in 2005 considered that Japan's SPS measures regarding fire blight for imports of apples from the United States was not justified. As a result, Japan issued a new phytosanitary protocol that complies with the WTO ruling. This resulted in fewer restrictions on imports of apples from the United States by reducing annual inspections from three to one; lowering the required buffer zone from 500 to 10 metres and eliminating the requirement that crates be disinfected. Japanese apple imports from the US increased substantially following the panel ruling (Calvin and Krissoff, 2005; WTO, 2008).

SPS and domestic regulation

The WTO disciplines on SPS measures are valuable because they establish mechanisms to contest arbitrary and unjustified decisions by Customs, Health, Veterinary or Agricultural authorities to reject goods on the basis of noncompliance with standards. They are process-oriented. No attempt is made in the WTO to agree to the substantive content of SPS measures or to define minimum standards. This is left to the relevant international bodies that address standards-related matters, and countries are encouraged to adopt internationally developed—and therefore consensus-based—standards. This makes it important that all WTO members—including developing countries—have the capacity to participate in the fora that develop SPS norms, which affect their industries and consumers. As under the TBT agreement, developing countries need to strengthen SPS-related institutions, including risk assessment and management mechanisms, and to develop mechanisms to reduce transaction costs. The private sector can play a role in this connection through pre-shipment inspection and related certification programmes.

There is significant scope on paper to pursue harmonization towards international standards as a way to facilitate trade. Despite the fact that there are numerous international norms in the SPS area, countries often tend to diverge from them in ways that do nothing more than raise costs and segment markets, with no benefit in terms of public health or safety. Table 5.5 provides an example for two agricultural products, reporting data on the maximum residual limit (MRL) for an insecticide (chlorpyrifos) permitted by countries for fresh vegetables, garlic, onions and spinach. In two cases there is a Codex standard; in two others there is not. The national norms diverge significantly, for reasons that are very unlikely to reflect a substantive health-related rationale. Confronted with this type of situation, exporters have an incentive to try and attain the highest standard as this gives them access to all markets. This may be costly and unnecessary to achieve a specific safety standard. Adoption of uniform (international) standards would remove one source of friction that can impede trade. Of course, the data also reveal that even if there is an international norm many countries will adopt a tighter standard. Making adoption of international standards mandatory will no doubt be difficult to achieve and there are good arguments against such an approach.

Table 5.5. Maximum residue limits for Chlorpyrifos (parts per million)

	Vegetables	Garlic	Onions	Spinach
Japan	0.11	0.01	0.05	0.01
EU	0.1	0.05	0.2	0.05
US	0.76	0.5	0.5	0.05
Australia	0.1	0.01	0.01	0.01
Korea	0.35	0.5	0.5	0.01
Malaysia	0.38	0.5	0.2	n.a.
Philippines	0.48	0.5	0.2	n.a.
New Zealand	0.2	0.01	n.a.	0.01
Thailand	0.48	0.5	n.a.	1
CODEX	0.52	n.a.	0.2	n.a.

Source: Chen, Yang and Findlay, 2008.

World Trade Organization members remain free to define their technical regulations, but must notify diverging national standards and are required to motivate them. Nonconforming standards can be challenged. In the case of SPS measures—where such motivation requires scientific evidence—much depends on how such evidence is evaluated by WTO dispute settlement panels. The *EC—Hormones* case illustrates that even if the science is relatively unambiguous it may be difficult to induce countries to change their SPS regimes (see Chapter 3). In many cases the science will not be clear-cut, providing scope for fundamental disagreements that revolve around differences in risk attitudes of societies.

The WTO case law to date suggests that appeals to the 'precautionary principle' may be difficult to sustain (although the EU did not do so in *Hormones*). Insistence by countries that significant leeway be granted to governments on the basis of the 'precautionary principle' may then lead to situations where governments cannot comply with DSB rulings and are forced to accept retaliation. Such outcomes are clearly not beneficial to the trading system. International cooperation outside the WTO in fora that focus more directly on the substantive public policy and scientific issues is needed. In the case of GMOs such a forum exists in the Cartagena Protocol on Bio-safety.

The precise nature and limits of the disciplines embodied in the SPS agreement are difficult to discern from a reading of its text as there are many fuzzy provisions. The attempt to use scientific standards as the objective basis by which regulations should be judged does not necessarily do much to address consumer fears. Panel and AB decisions can easily be seen as constraining the freedom of member states to respond to the concerns of their citizens by adopting narrow conceptions of risk analysis and a view of the relationship between science and policy that force policymakers to adhere closely to the conclusions of scientific bodies without leaving sufficient latitude for extra-scientific considerations (Philbrick, 2008).

The area of health and safety norms is clearly one where WTO members must strike a balance in ensuring that the rules are clear and protect market access and permitting governments to intervene in instances where they perceive a need to do so to attain noneconomic objectives. In the GATT era governments were free to determine the public policy justification for SPS measures—the focus of disciplines was on nondiscrimination and on minimizing the trade effects of measures. With the introduction of scientific principles and risk assessment as criteria in the SPS agreement, the WTO became more intrusive and judgemental with respect to social preferences of WTO members.

The reversal of the burden of proof by the AB—requiring the complainant to show that the international norm is sufficient—is an illustration of how the AB has interpreted the balance between right to regulate and the additional disciplines imposed by the SPS agreement. One may argue that the result is that too much discretion is given to governments to diverge from international norms. The burden of proof has also been applied in other contexts in a rather arbitrary manner. For example, in a 2005 dispute brought by the EU against the US, the EU argued that its completion of studies and risk assessments for the use of hormones in meat implied that it had come into compliance with the ruling of the AB in the *EC—Hormones* case, and that continued retaliation by the US was therefore illegal. In mid-2008 the panel ruled that continued retaliation by the US violated the DSU, implying that the US should have requested a new panel to determine if the EU was now indeed in compliance. However, the panel also ruled that the EU still did not satisfy the requirements of the SPS Agreement and rejected the EU claim that it was in compliance simply because it had now undertaken a risk assessment.

The end result of the case law is aptly summarized by Trebilcock and Soloway (2002), who argue that WTO rulings in SPS cases 'are not anchored in a coherent conception of an ideal risk regulation process nor in the appropriate scope and limits of supra-national quasi-judicial review of [SPS] measures. Many aspects of the AB's decisions involve elaborate exercises in semantic "shadow boxing" with panel decisions and convoluted parsing of the wording of the SPS agreement'.

In the Doha Round the substantive rules of the SPS Agreement were not up for negotiation. However, EU arguments in favour of recognizing the multifunctional role of agriculture, and attempts to link trade in agricultural products with environmental concerns and objectives, consumer protection and human, plant and animal health all have a link to the SPS agreement. Some countries agree with the EU position and consider that SPS issues should be clarified through an understanding that would assuage concerns of consumers. Others consider that the matter should be discussed in the SPS and TBT Committees rather than be negotiated.

One dimension of the SPS agenda was on the Doha Round agenda: addressing calls by developing countries that they be granted more effective special and differential treatment and that their implementation concerns be addressed. Developing countries sought more time to comply with other countries' new SPS measures, to ensure a longer 'reasonable interval' between publication of a country's new SPS measure and its entry into force, and put into practice the principle that governments should accept that different measures used by other governments can be equivalent to their own measures for providing the same level of health protection for food, animals and plants. Calls were also made to reinforce the review of the SPS Agreement, encourage developing country participation in setting international SPS standards and improve financial and technical assistance concerning SPS issues.

In April 2003 the SPS committee adopted a principle of applying special and differential treatment for developing countries. This was based on a Canadian proposal whereby members agreed to consultations whenever a developing country identifies a problem with a SPS measure. In 2004 the committee also dealt with the equivalence issue. Equivalence is the mutual acceptance of another member's standards that although different in process have the same effect. The objective is to help developing nations prove that their products are as safe as those in developed nations and to speed up recognition of equivalence of SPS measures for products previously traded or those for which information already exists. In 2002, the World Bank initiated a programme to enhance the capacity of developing WTO members to participate in negotiations and implement standards. The Standards and Trade Development Facility (STDF) included the WTO, the World Health Organization (WHO), FAO, the World Organization for Animal Health (OIE) and the Codex Alimentarius. The principal objectives of the STDF are to increase participation of developing countries in forming international standards and facilitate the implementation of existing requirements.

5.9. TRADE-RELATED INVESTMENT MEASURES

The value of sales by foreign affiliates of multinational firms now exceeds global exports of goods and services. The observed growth in foreign direct investment (FDI) is a consequence of many changes in the world economy, including the decline in communication and transportation costs, and, importantly, liberalization of FDI regimes in many countries. Perceptions about multinational firms and their effects on host countries have undergone a transformation. Most countries are now quite eager to attract FDI; many offer financial incentives to attract FDI and have concluded bilateral investment treaties (BITs). There were close to

2,500 BITs in force in 2006 , compared to some 400 at the beginning of 1990 (Dolzer and Schreuer, 2008). On the other hand, many countries continue to subject multinationals to performance requirements. For example, multinationals may have to comply with trade-related investment measures (TRIMs) such as local content, export or technology transfer requirements. In fact, it is not unusual to find investment incentives being offered in conjunction with performance requirements and other restrictions on FDI, perhaps to partially offset the negative impact of the latter on the likelihood of investment by multinationals. The specific type of policy used often depends on whether FDI is resource-seeking, domestic market-oriented or export-oriented (Caves, 2007). The schizophrenic nature of policy stances reflects the guarded optimism with which many countries continue to view the entry of multinational firms into their markets.

Trade-related investment measures are policies used by governments with a view to forcing foreign investors to meet certain performance standards. Trade-related investment measures often involve discrimination against imports by creating incentives (additional to tariffs imposed at the border) to source from domestic producers. The most prevalent TRIMs are local content requirements—a condition that a minimum proportion of inputs used by an investor be of domestic origin. In most circumstances such measures are inefficient. This is because they either act like a tariff on intermediate goods (this is the case for a local content requirement, where manufacturers are forced to use high cost local inputs) or as a QR (this is the case with a so-called trade-balancing requirement, which acts to restrict imports to a certain quantity). A local content requirement, although equivalent to a tariff, is inferior in welfare terms because the government does not collect any tariff revenue.

An economic case for TRIMs requires there to be domestic distortions or externalities from FDI. Absent such market failures, the optimal FDI policy is no policy at all—governments should allow for unfettered market transactions. Thus, under perfect competition, domestic content rules lower welfare by raising the price of domestic inputs: the resulting benefits to input suppliers are outweighed by the costs incurred by final goods producers (Grossman, 1981). As multinational firms typically arise in oligopolistic industries, the presence of imperfect competition in the host economy is an obvious potential rationale for intervention. Analyses of content protection and export performance requirements under conditions of imperfect competition illustrate that the welfare effects of such policies may be positive (Rodrik, 1987). However, the standard normative prescription applies: more efficient instruments can be identified to address the underlying distortions. For example, in the case of welfare-reducing anticompetitive practices resulting from market power or collusion, vigorous competition policies are called for, whereas domestic policy distortions such as tariffs should be removed at the source. This approach is implicit in the WTO, which not only aims at progressive liberalization of trade, but also prohibits the use of most TRIMs.

Trade-related investment measures were initially one of the more controversial topics on the agenda of the Uruguay Round negotiations. Many developing countries were of the view that attempting to agree to broad-ranging multilateral disciplines on policies affecting investment went far beyond the scope of the GATT, and that the GATT was not necessarily the appropriate forum to address investment-related policies. Certain OECD countries, the US in particular, were of the view that policies distorting investment flows could have a significant impact on trade flows, and should be subject to multilateral trade disciplines. At the start of the Uruguay Round, the US sought to negotiate rules for a long list of TRIMs, including investment-related measures such as remittance policies, ownership limitations and investment incentives. In the end, the TRIMs agreement that emerged was not very ambitious. It basically prohibits measures that are inconsistent with the GATT national treatment principle (Article III) and the ban on the use of QRs (Article XI). The agreement includes a list of prohibited measures (including local content, trade-balancing, foreign exchange-balancing and domestic sales requirements) and requires that all policies not in conformity with the agreement be notified within 90 days of entry into force of the agreement. All such measures must be eliminated within two, five or seven years, for industrialized, developing and least developed countries respectively. However, Article 5.3 of the TRIMs Agreement provides for extension of such transition periods, based on specific requests. In such cases individual members need to provide the Council for Trade in Goods with justification based on their specific trade, financial and development needs (see below).

The listed prohibited measures were already illegal under the GATT. What the TRIMs agreement essentially does is to reaffirm that GATT rules apply in this area. Although this was a point of view that was long held and defended by most OECD countries, it had been resisted by developing countries. The agreement prohibits both mandatory measures and those 'with which compliance is necessary to obtain an advantage' (such as a tax concession or subsidy). Noteworthy is that export performance requirements were not included in the illustrative list. This is somewhat inconsistent with the GATT's prohibition on the use of export subsidies, as the two instruments are very similar in effect.

Although the TRIMs agreement does not go beyond existing GATT rules, these disciplines are quite powerful. The most important TRIMs-related dispute settlement at the time of writing, the 1996 case brought by the EU, Japan and the US against provisions of Indonesia's National Car Programme, may be indicative of the future. Under the contested programme, the government granted 'National Car' company status to Indonesian companies that met specified criteria as to ownership of facilities, use of trademarks and technology. National Car companies were required to meet increasing local content requirements over a three-year period; if requirements were met, they benefitted from exemption from the prevailing luxury tax on sales of cars and exemption from import duties on parts and components. National Cars manufactured in a foreign country that fulfilled the local content requirements were also exempt from import duties and luxury tax. Such imported National Cars were deemed to comply with the 20 per cent local content requirement for the end of the first production year if the value of 'counterpurchased' Indonesian parts and components accounted for at least 25 per cent of the value of the imported cars (WTO, 1998*b*). The panel found that this programme violated the national treatment rule. A major reason Indonesia was targeted was that the policy measures were introduced after the entry into force of the TRIMs agreement. A number of countries apply similar policies were sheltered by the transition period agreed in the Uruguay Round, a number of which have been extended on a case-by-case basis.

In many cases, surveys show that TRIMs require firms to take actions that they would have taken anyway. For example, a policy that requires firms to export is inconsequential if firms were going to export even in the absence of such a require-ment. Surveys by the US Department of Commerce for 1977 and 1982 indicated that only 6 per cent of all the overseas affiliates of US firms felt constrained by TRIMs such as local content requirements, although a far greater percentage operated in sectors where TRIMs existed. In other words, TRIMs often failed to bind (UNCTC, 1991). However, the surveys did not take into account that TRIMs may carry efficiency consequences for the world by discouraging FDI in the first place.

The available empirical evidence suggests that local content and related policies are costly to the economy. A compelling discussion of the evidence illustrating how counterproductive and damaging domestic content requirements and joint venture requirements can be for host country development is provided by Moran (2002). Moreover, domestic content requirements often do not achieve the desired backward and forward linkages, encourage inefficient foreign entry, and create potential prob-lems for future liberalization if those who enter lobby against a change in regime. Governments constrained in eliminating costly status quo trade-related policies that aim at industrial development because protected industries are able to prevent their abolition may be assisted by an international agreement to overcome this resistance. In practice, transition periods will be important in phasing out WTO illegal pro-grammes, as investment decisions will have been taken in the past on the basis of prevailing policies. One example of a phase-out policy is described in Box 5.8.

It was agreed in the Uruguay Round that the agreement be reviewed in the year 2000, at which time it might be complemented by provisions on competition and investment policy. In the course of this review process, the Council for Trade in Goods was to consider whether the agreement should be complemented with provisions on investment policy and competition policy. As mentioned earlier, the Singapore ministerial conference established working groups to study the relationship between Trade and Investment on the one hand and Trade and Competition Policy on the other. If negotiations had been launched in the Doha Round, this would have opened the prospect of stronger multilateral disciplines for

Box 5.8. South African TRIMs in the automotive sector

South Africa has long had a trade policy designed to support the development of a local car industry. Eight production facilities operated in the country as of the late 1990s, producing 38 models, with an average production run of 37,000 units, a very low amount compared to international best practice. Until the mid-1980s, tariffs on cars were very high, ranging up to 100 per cent or more, and car assemblers were subject to require-ments and incentives to source locally. Local content requirements aimed to reduce screwdriver assembly operations that would otherwise be profitable because tariffs on parts and components were well below those on cars. Starting in 1989, a decision was taken to increase competition in the sector. A tariff reduction programme was designed and announced, and an export incentive scheme was created in order to encourage plants to attain greater scale economies. This involved the granting of (tradable) import credits on the basis of realized export volumes—in effect, net foreign exchange earnings counted towards the minimum (50 per cent) local content requirement. In 1995 all local content requirements were abolished and further reductions in tariffs were announced (going beyond the nation's WTO commitments), with an ultimate aim to attain a maximum rate of 40 per cent for vehicles and 30 per cent for parts in 2002.

The South African phase-out strategy of TRIMs in the car sector is interesting in that it sought to balance economic and social policies. The negative impact on the compon-ents sector of elimination of local content requirements and the concurrent gradual reduction of tariffs on components was offset in part by the incentive programme to encourage exports of automotive products. This increased demand for high-quality local output. Although the programme distorts incentives—for example, car companies have an incentive to procure high-value components in which the country may not have the greatest comparative advantage to maximize import credits—the programme led to a significant expansion of automotive exports such as leather seat covers, tyres, and exhaust systems, in the process facilitating adjustment to a policy environment without TRIMs.

Source: Black (1999).

TRIMs. However, no progress proved possible on competition and investment policies, and the TRIMs review did not result in additional provisions. decision by the members. However, it became clear very rapidly that not much could be accomplished in that respect. The working groups' work and the TRIMs review dragged on and not much happened in terms of additional provisions. Developing countries resisted any attempts to extend the scope of the TRIMs Agreement to include a broader definition of investment, re-establishment rights or additional restrictions on nontrade-related performance requirements. Developing countries took the opportunity of the TRIMs review to press for amendment of the treaty to reinforce its development dimension. For example, a joint Brazil-India submission called for expanding the 'policy space' to use certain TRIMs. The OECD countries generally considered that a 'watering-down' of TRIMs disciplines would set a bad precedent and argued that extensions of Uruguay Round transition periods offered enough flexibility. At the same time, however, these developing countries continued to sign bilateral investment treaties.

Developing countries were to have implemented the TRIMs Agreement and eliminated their relevant regulations by 1 January 2000. However, 26 such countries gave notice that at that time they still had a range of TRIMs-incompatible policies in existence and that they intended to maintain many of them. Most of the policies related to the auto industry or the food industry and involved local content requirements. The second most frequently notified type of TRIMs was foreign exchange balancing requirements (Bora, 2001). Developing countries have argued that the process for negotiating extensions to the duration of transition periods should be undertaken through a multilateral framework. In contrast, the EU, Japan and the US held that requests for deadline extensions should only be considered on a 'case-by-case' basis. The bilateral nature of the process caused concern among developing countries that high-income members could use the threat of rejecting requests for an extension as bargaining leverage. Disagreements over extension procedures were partly resolved in July 2000 by a decision that the council chair would oversee multilateral negotiations.

Developing countries did not represent a common front on all TRIMs issues. Given their rather open capital markets, higher income levels, and interest in agricultural trade liberalization, countries in Latin America were not particularly opposed to negotiation of TRIMs. Opposition came from countries in Asia and Africa that sought to maintain the freedom to limit the extent of foreign ownership and production within their economies. Other factors behind objections to a multilateral agreement on investment included asymmetries in the obligations to be undertaken and in the distribution of benefits, limited capacity to negotiate, and limited resources for implementation.

The positions on TRIMs taken by many developing countries in the Doha Round included a push for: (1) unlimited extensions of transitional periods under TRIMs Article 5.2; (2) an exemption from disciplines on the two performance requirements listed in the TRIMs Annex (local content and trade balancing); (3) a ban on extending the list of restricted policies; and (4) agreement that the Council for Trade in Goods automatically would grant extensions of transitional periods under TRIMs Article 5.3 to all developing and least developed countries that request them.

5.10. CONCLUSION

Despite the complexities of the various agreements, the GATT is basically a simple agreement. The key disciplines are nondiscrimination (national treatment and MFN), tariff bindings, the prohibition on QRs, and a variety of disciplines that aim to prevent circumvention of the nondiscrimination principle and negotiated market access commitments. The incentive for interest groups—especially import-competing industries—to lobby for protection and government support cannot be regulated away. Such pressures will always arise. The core GATT rules establish powerful disciplines that substantially reduce the uncertainty regarding the conditions of competition that confront foreign products on markets. Nondiscrimination is a recurring theme in panel and AB decisions, even in cases where Article XX is invoked (see also Chapter 9).

Recent theoretical advances such as Horn, Maggi and Staiger (2006) provide a better understanding why there is more stress on border barriers and less on domestic policy, why GATT permits ceiling bindings instead of requiring full binding at applied levels, and why there are provisions allowing for contingent protection—which are discussed in Chapter 9. Their theoretical framework, as is the case for much of the literature is premised on the assumption that the rationale for trade agreements revolves around the terms of trade. Others, most notably Ethier (2004, 2007), explain the key characteristics of the GATT on the basis of domestic political economy forces and the need for governments to generate political support to get elected and stay in power. Both frameworks do much to deepen our understanding of the GATT and increase the respect one must have for the small visionary group of people who were primarily responsible for drafting the GATT (see Irwin, Mavroidis and Sykes, 2008, on the genesis of the GATT).

Over time, the GATT edifice was expanded to include stronger disciplines on NTMs, thus increasing the scope to bring complaints that WTO commitments are being violated. The contestability of markets can be affected by many policies—subsidies; product standards; customs procedures; and so forth. Many of these are now addressed in the GATT. The rules often make economic sense in that they encourage transparency and push governments to use more rather than less efficient instruments (tariffs, not quotas; least trade restrictive measures). Although the coverage of the GATT expanded steadily to encompass almost all trade policies, a few have so far been left untouched. One policy area where GATT imposes virtually no disciplines is with respect to export taxes. This reflects the mercantilist bias of the system, although a factor may also be that the US Constitution bans the use of export taxes. Under GATT rules, members remain free to impose such taxes, despite the fact that export taxes can be equivalent to import duties. As discussed further in Chapter 13, if WTO members initiate discussions on competition policies, export taxes will also have to be put on the table. More generally, where to draw the line between what should be permitted and remain unconstrained and what deserves to be regulated multilaterally is a question that will become ever more prominent. The subsidy, TBT and SPS issues discussed in this chapter illustrate that this is not just a question that pertains to the 'new' trade agenda discussed in subsequent chapters (services, intellectual property, competition, investment and so forth).

5.11. FURTHER READING

There is no textbook that looks at the economics of all of the policies addressed by the GATT. W. Max Corden, *Trade Policy and Economic Welfare* (Oxford: Oxford University Press, 1997) is a classic text. Another recommended resource on the economics of trade policy is Neil Vousden, *The Economics of Trade Protection* (Cambridge: Cambridge University Press, 1990). Petros Mavroidis, *Trade in Goods* (Oxford: Oxford University Press, 2007) is an up-to-date, comprehensive legal treatment of the GATT. The contributions in B. Hoekman, A. Mattoo and P. English (eds), *Development, Trade and the WTO: A Handbook* (Washington, DC: The World Bank, 2002) provide a series of short, accessible chapters on the content, history and economics of GATT rules.

Based on the WTO Consolidated Tariff Schedules (CTS) database and national sources, Mohamed Bechir, Sébastien Jean and David Laborde provide a global assessment of the gaps between bound and applied MFN tariffs and the effects of reducing this binding overhang in 'Binding Overhang and Tariff-Cutting Formulas,' *Review of World Economics*, 142 (2) (2006). Protection unconstrained by rules is likely to vary substantially over time. In 'Commercial Policy Variability, Bindings and Market Access,' *European Economic Review*, 48 (3) (2004): 665–79, Joe Francois and Will Martin show how rules-based disciplines, such as WTO tariff bindings and bindings on market access in services, constrain this variability. They examine the theoretical effects of such constraints on the expected cost of protection and offer a formalization of the concept of 'market access' that focuses not just on the average level of protection but on the variability of tariffs. The 'World Tariff Profiles' jointly published by WTO, UNCTAD and ITC provides detailed data on bound and applied tariffs of the WTO member countries.

For an overview of the issue of standards in international trade see: 'Trade Standards and the WTO: The Economics of Standards and Trade' in *World Trade Report 2005* (Geneva: WTO; available at http://www.wto.org/english/res_e/booksp_e/anrep_e/wtr05-2b_e.pdf) Alan Deardorff and Robert Stern, *Measurement of Nontariff Barriers* (Ann Arbor: University of Michigan, 1998) is an excellent discussion of the economic impact of different NTMs and how to measure their impact.

The WCO website (www.wcoomd.org) provides information on best practices in customs clearance and the various instruments and tools that have been developed to facilitate trade. For a comprehensive discussion and analysis of government-mandated PSI, the best source remains Patrick Low, *Pre-shipment Inspection Services*, Discussion Paper 278 (Washington, DC: The World Bank, 1995). Rules of origin systems are discussed from a legal and institutional perspective in Edwin Vermulst, Paul Waer and Jacques Bourgeois (eds), *Rules of Origin in International Trade: A Comparative Study* (Ann Arbor: University of Michigan Press, 1994). The economics of rules of origin are the subject of the contributions in O. Cadot, A. Estevadeordal, A. Suwa Eisenmann and T. Verdier (eds), *The Origin of Goods* (Oxford: Oxford University Press, 2006). The economics of subsidies and alternative approaches to disciplining their use are explored in some detail by Richard Snape in 'International Regulation of Subsidies', *The World Economy*, 14 (1991): 139–64, and in the 2006 edition of the *World Trade Report* (Geneva: WTO).

Michel Kostecki, *State Trading in International Markets* (London: Macmillan, 1982) explores the role of state trading in global trade as of the early 1980s. Approaches towards STEs are discussed in the contributions to Thomas Cottier and Petros C. Mavroidis (eds), *State Trading in the Twenty-first Century* (Ann Arbor: University of Michigan Press, 1998). The relevance of the legal rules for countertrade is discussed in Frieder Roessler, 'Countertrade and the GATT Legal System', *Journal of World Trade Law*, 19 (1985): 604–14. The US case against the Canadian Wheat Board is analysed in B. Hoekman and J. Trachtman, 'Canada-Wheat: Discrimination, Non-Commercial Considerations, and the Right to Regulate through State Trading Enterprises,' *World Trade Review* 7 (1) (2008): 45–66.

Alan Sykes, *Product Standards for Internationally Integrated Goods Markets* (Washington, DC: Brookings Institution, 1995) is a recommended reading on standards and standardization in the context of trade and trade policy. Keith Maskus and John S. Wilson (eds), *Quantifying the Impact of Technical Barriers to Trade* (Ann Arbor: University of Michigan Press, 2001) bring together a collection of papers that explore the economic impacts of product standards. Michael Trebilcock and Julie Soloway provide a critical assessment of the role of the Appellate Body in SPS dispute settlement cases in 'International Trade Policy and Domestic Food Regulation: The Case for Substantial Deference by the WTO Dispute Settlement Body Under the SPS Agreement', (University of Toronto, mimeo, 2006). The effect of SPS measures on trade of developing countries is discussed in Steven Jaffee and Spencer Henson, 'Standards and Agro-Food Exports from Developing Countries,' World Bank Policy Research Paper 3348 (Washington, DC, 2004). Procedures related to conformity assessment and certification procedures are described in ISO, *Certification and Related Activities* (Geneva: ISO, 1999).

A good overview of TRIMs issues in the Doha Round from a developing country perspective is provided in Douglas Brooks, Emma Fan and Lea Sumulong, 'Foreign Direct Investment: Trends, TRIMs, and WTO Negotiations,' *Asian Development Review*, 20 (1) (2003). Theodore Moran, *Foreign Direct Investment and Development*, (Washington, DC: Institute for International Economics, 1998) surveys the literature and the experience with TRIMs.

CHAPTER 6

SECTOR-SPECIFIC MULTILATERAL TRADE AGREEMENTS

THE GATT was conceived as a general agreement that would apply to all merchandise trade. In principle, therefore, GATT rules on nondiscrimination, transparency, tariff bindings and so forth, apply to all sectors. In practice, however, industry-specific pressures for protection in major trading nations created strong incentives for governments to grant 'special' treatment to 'special' sectors. This chapter focuses on two key sectors where pressures for protection proved too strong for the trading system to handle—agriculture, and textiles and clothing. Over time these sectors were gradually removed from the reach of many GATT 1947 disciplines. It was only during the Uruguay Round that it proved possible to reintegrate them into the trading system. However, progress on agriculture since then proved very difficult to achieve.

This chapter also discusses the Information Technology Agreement (ITA). Although negotiated among a subset of WTO members during 1996, the ITA is applied on a MFN basis. The ITA is noteworthy in that it is sometimes regarded as proof that single sector agreements are feasible in the WTO context, and it illustrates that it may not be necessary to engage in broader negotiating rounds and cross-issue linkage to achieve liberalization of trade. We argue below that the ITA experience does not support this line of reasoning.

6.1. AGRICULTURE

Poor agrarian economies frequently tax agriculture relative to other tradable sectors. As nations become richer, their policy regimes change from taxing to assisting farmers (Lindert, 1991). The post-1950 period saw substantial growth in agricultural protection and insulation in the advanced industrial economies and its spread to newly industrializing economies (Johnson, 1973). That tendency accelerated in the 1980s to the point where some protectionist countries went beyond self-sufficiency to generate surpluses. These could only be disposed of with the help of export subsidies. This led to serious budgetary pressures and increasing opposition to the cost of agricultural support policies. It also led traditional agricultural-exporting countries to insist that MTNs focus on reducing agricultural protection.

Historically, agricultural trade policy has tended to be been driven by short run phenomena. Food crises led to export controls, whereas gluts led to import barriers. Protectionist measures in agriculture of a permanent nature became increasingly prevalent at the end of the nineteenth century (Findlay and O'Rourke, 2007: 396 ff) and have been a persistent feature of global trade policy ever since. One cause of the protectionist policies that emerged in the late nineteenth century was the steady expansion of American production and the resulting fall in world prices. Although some nations reacted to the resulting change in incentives by adjusting—for example, the Netherlands became more specialized in livestock as the price of feed grains fell—others, including France, Germany and Austria-Hungary, reacted by protecting existing producers and subsidizing exports if domestic output exceeded consumption. Between the First and Second World Wars agricultural protection and domestic market regulation increased further. After the Second World War, agricultural ministries in OECD countries exempted agriculture from key GATT disciplines and recurrent MTNs. The US led the way with its request for a waiver in 1955. With the creation of the EEC and its Common Agricultural Policy (CAP) in 1957, European countries also insisted on special treatment for this sector.

The CAP is the pre-eminent example of how farmers can be insulated from foreign competition. It provided for an intervention or support price at which the Community guaranteed to purchase the agricultural output from farmers, and a threshold price (above the internal support price) below which no imports were allowed. In order to isolate the EU market from international competition, a variable levy equal to the margin between the threshold price and the lowest representative offer price on world markets was imposed on imports. Moreover, a restitution amounting to the difference between the average world price and the internal EU price was granted to European exporters. The programme was extremely costly. Domestic support to agricultural producers averaged more than US$92 billion per year in the EU during 1986–90. However, the EU was not alone.

Domestic support in Japan and the US over the same period averaged US$35 and US$24 billion respectively. In Japan, rice was produced at a cost four times that of competitive producers elsewhere. The same applied to Swiss meat and butter. Budgetary support in the US, the EU and Japan accounted for some 15 per cent of government spending; a figure comparable to what was spent on education. In the post-1990 period the EU, Japan, the US and other OECD nations continued to support farmers, collectively transferring some US$300 billion a year to farmers. This was done through a variety of instruments, but mostly through border protection.

Patterns of intervention in agriculture

Why do governments intervene in agriculture? And why are the policies that are observed so different across countries? Rationales for intervention include: (1) to stabilize and increase farm incomes; (2) to guarantee food security; (3) to improve the balance of payments; (4) to support the development of other sectors of the economy; and (5) to increase agricultural output (Fitchett, 1987). These reasons are in part noneconomic or driven by special interest politics. The political influence of the agricultural sector is substantial in many countries. Agriculture produces food, and food is often very political. President Nyerere of Tanzania once said that if he needed shoes and apartheid South Africa was the only place to get them he would go shoeless, but if he needed corn and the only source available was apartheid South Africa he would buy there. Food shortages can lead to riots, revolutions and wars.

There is a striking difference between the way agriculture is treated in poor and rich countries. In many developing countries, policies tax agriculture and subsidize food consumption of the urban population. In industrialized countries exactly the opposite pattern can be observed: an urban population that is taxed to support farm production and incomes. But in both cases, governments use subsidies, trade barriers, state trading and public purchasing to regulate production and trade (Box 6.1).

Relative to other sectors of the economy, as of the early 1990s agriculture in many industrialized countries was regulated, subsidized and insulated from market forces to an exceptional degree. Production quotas, state purchasing and distribution, subsidies and administered pricing often worked at cross-purposes. In the EU, support programmes were so effective in stimulating output that they had to be complemented by production quotas and incentives to take land out of production (so-called set asides). Matters were not much better in many developing countries. Marketing boards—monopoly buyers and distributors of food—were often established that set prices for farm products below world market levels in a deliberate attempt to lower the cost of subsidizing the prices of basic foodstuffs for the urban

Box 6.1. Why poor countries tax and rich countries subsidize agriculture

Average rates of protection for industries tend to decline across countries as capital-labour ratios increase. Industrialized countries with large capital stocks—both physical plant and equipment and human capital—relative to labour are more open to trade than countries with large stocks of labour relative to capital (mostly developing countries) (Rodrik, 1995). However, rich countries tend to be much more protectionist towards agriculture (supporting domestic production and closing off markets against import competition). In contrast, poor countries tend to promote imports, either explicitly through import subsidies, or implicitly by taxing domestic production.

Anderson and Hayami (1986) argue that this can be explained as follows. In a poor country, food accounts for a large share of total household consumption, whereas in rich countries food accounts for only a small share of expenditure. Moreover, agriculture is the main source of employment in a poor country, whereas it typically accounts for less than 5 per cent of the labour force in a rich one. In poor countries agriculture is also much less capital-intensive than in rich ones. These stylized facts do much to explain the different policy stances that are observed. If agriculture is protected in a poor nation, the resulting increases in food prices have a large impact on the demand for labour (given the size of the agricultural sector) and thus on economy-wide wages (because labour is mobile). The wage rise will be offset to a greater or lesser extent by the rise in food prices, food being so important in consumption. At the same time the wage increase puts upward pressure on the price of nontradables (services) and has a negative impact on industry by lowering profits. As the gains per farmer of protection are low, and the loss per industrialist is high, the latter will be induced to invest resources to oppose agricultural support policies. Supporting agricultural production in a poor country therefore may not make political sense. The converse applies to rich nations, where agricultural support has much less of an impact on wages (the sector being small), on the prices of nontradables and on industrial profits.

A simulation model developed by Anderson (1995) that incorporates these basic differences between poor and rich countries reveals that a 10 per cent rise in the relative price of manufactures in a poor nation (that is, a tax on agriculture) will reduce farm incomes by only 2 per cent, whereas raising those of industrialists by 45 per cent. In contrast, a 10 per cent tax on industry in a rich country (that is, a policy of supporting agriculture) raises incomes of farmers by over 20 per cent, but reduces those of industrialists by only 3 per cent. These differences in costs and benefits for different groups in society—in conjunction with the differences in sizes of the various groups—help explain why farmers in rich countries are willing to invest substantial resources to obtain and maintain protection, and why industrialists and urban populations in developing countries are able to benefit at the expense of farmers.

Honma (1993) empirically investigates whether agricultural protection is determined according to the Anderson-Hayami (1986) framework of endogenous protection. Using panel data on 14 industrial countries between 1955 and 1987, Honma finds that the nominal rate of protection: (1) declines the higher the ratio of labour productivity in agriculture to that in industry; (2) rises as the share in agriculture increases to 4.5 per cent and falls beyond thereafter; and (3) increases as the terms of trade of agricultural products (relative to manufactured goods) decline. He also concludes that the EU is an outlier, with higher levels of support than similar countries. One reason for this may be the role that the CAP played in the formation of the EEC and the role it has had in sustaining European cooperation (Messerlin, 2001).

population or to tax tradable commodities and generate revenue for the government. The result was often a drop in agricultural output, migration to the cities and rising imports of food. This pattern was complemented by the effect of OECD countries' food aid, which further reduced the incentive to adopt a more economically rational agricultural policy.

As a consequence of agricultural intervention, countries with no comparative advantage in agriculture not only became major producers but also net exporters. Production support policies had to be complemented by export subsidies to allow surpluses to be sold. These in turn led to numerous trade conflicts. As farm surpluses were dumped at subsidized prices in international markets, agricultural trade increasingly became managed trade. During the 1986–90 period, OECD economies annually subsidized exports averaging 48.2 million tons of wheat, 19.5 million tons of coarse grains, 1.8 million tons of sugar, 1.2 million tons of beef and 1.2 million tons of cheese and butter. Average annual export subsidies in the EU during 1986–90 were more than US$13 billion, with most of the money allocated to exports of bovine meat, wheat and coarse grains, butter and other milk products (GATT, 1994c). The loss of developing country export revenue resulting from agricultural protectionism in the US, the EU and Japan was significant. For sugar and beef alone, it was estimated to be the equivalent of about half of total international development aid (World Bank, 1986). Policies in developing countries tended to make the situation worse for farmers as they often discouraged farm production through a variety of agricultural and nonagricultural policies. The former included state control of inputs and prices, the latter included high import barriers for manufactures and overvalued exchange rates, both of which reduced the incentive to invest in agriculture (Krueger, Schiff and Valdes, 1988).

A 2008 World Bank research project has generated annual time series estimates of rates and values of assistance/taxation over the past half century for around 75 countries—together accounting for 90 per cent of global population, GDP and agricultural production. For each country, nominal rates of assistance (NRAs)[1] are calculated for key products (Anderson, 2008). The growth of agricultural production support in high-income countries began to reverse in the 1990s, although if 'decoupled' income support for farmers is included, the rate of support has not declined substantially since the Uruguay Round was completed (Figure 6.1). Until recently developing country governments effectively taxed their farmers, imposing an effective tax rate on the order of 20 per cent from the mid-1950s to the mid-1980s. Since then it has diminished, and, on average, become slightly positive.

The US dollar value of the gross subsidy equivalents of the NRAs are shown in Table 6.1. These estimates suggest that, from the mid-1950s through to the

---

[1] The NRA includes the effects of both farm output and farm input price distortions and is expressed as a percentage of total farm production valued at undistorted prices.

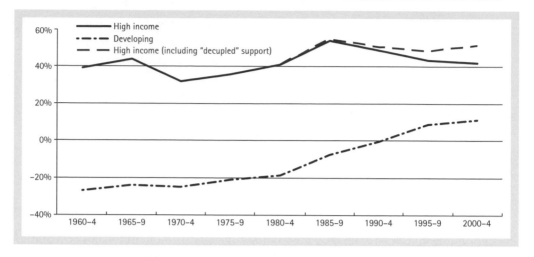

Fig. 6.1. Nominal Rate of Assistance to farmers, high-income and developing countries, 1955 to 2004 (per cent)

Note: Averaged using weights based on the gross value of agricultural production at undistorted prices. High income includes Republic of Korea and Taiwan, Province of China.

Source: Anderson and Valenzuela (2008).

mid-1970s, assistance to farmers in high-income countries almost exactly offset taxation of farmers in developing countries. Until the late 1980s, farmers in developing countries were at a double disadvantage in terms of competitiveness: farmers in OECD countries benefitted from significant levels of support, whereas agricultural production in developing countries tended to be taxed. Since the early 1980s, the gradual decline in taxation of farmers in developing countries and the growth in

Table 6.1. Gross subsidy equivalents of assistance to farmers by region, 1955–2004 (*current US$ billion per year*)

Country Groups	1960–4	1965–9	1970–4	1975–9	1980–4	1985–9	1990–4	1995–9	2000–4
High-income	30.3	43.1	49.0	96.4	133.0	174.1	216.3	200.2	190.9
Developing	−18.7	−21.9	−46.7	−69.0	−92.0	−35.8	0.8	47.9	65.2
Africa	−0.6	−1.3	−3.3	−5.9	−4.0	1.5	−6.3	−6.0	−7.9
Asia	−17.5	−19.0	−37.8	−55.1	−70.8	−28.9	−1.8	27.1	48.0
Latin America	−0.3	−0.7	−4.9	−6.7	−10.4	−9.3	4.7	6.5	5.3
European Transition	−0.2	−0.9	−0.6	−1.3	−6.8	0.8	4.2	20.3	19.7

Note: 'High-income countries' is a subset of OECD countries (Western Europe, Japan, United States, Canada, Australia, New Zealand and Republic of Korea) and Taiwan, Province of China for the periods after 1995.

Source: Anderson and Valenzuela (2008).

assistance to high-income country farmers have combined to see the net global transfer to farmers increase to more than US$250 billion per year. Regionally, outside the high-income group, it is Asia where the payments are largest on aggregate. On a per farmer basis, however, they are now largest in Europe's transition economies. In Africa, meanwhile, farmers still confront discrimination relative to other forms of economic activity.

The data on gross subsidy equivalents of support to farmers show that the overall level of assistance in high-income countries has been virtually constant for the last 15 years, and has been rising in developing countries, perhaps in part as a response to the example set by high-income nations. The high level of production support in high-income countries distorts domestic and world market prices and is detrimental to producers in developing countries and consumers in the high-income countries themselves. Historical policies in many developing countries of taxing agriculture have also been detrimental to farmers, and the more recent trend towards a more neutral policy stance for agriculture relative to other sectors of activity is a positive development from an economic policy perspective.

An important question confronting voters and exporters in foreign countries is how best to try and change the political equilibrium in countries that protect agriculture. The work by Anderson and Hayami mentioned earlier suggests that the observed patterns of intervention can be explained by economic 'fundamentals' such as the share of agriculture in output, per capita incomes, etc. But these factors simply help to understand the forces that lead to agricultural taxation or support over time in the absence of countervailing pressures. Analysis of the political economy forces that generate a given set of policies can help policymakers and other groups seeking to change a given equilibrium. An interesting finding of the empirical literature on this subject is that matters may not be as bad as they could be, in that governments appear to put a much higher value on economic welfare than on assisting farm groups (that is, on responding to political contributions made by such groups) (Box 6.2).

From GATT 1947 to the WTO

The rules applying to agricultural trade under GATT 1947 were weaker than those for manufactured goods because many nations regarded agriculture as a sector of economic activity that deserves special treatment. This attitude manifested itself during the post-war negotiations on the ITO in US insistence that the ITO not affect its agricultural policies. Although the ITO was never ratified, GATT rules on agriculture were in part written to fit existing US agricultural policies. Disciplines for agriculture differed in two major respects from those on trade in manufactures. First, quotas were allowed for agricultural commodities if concurrent measures were taken to restrict domestic production or used to remove a temporary

Box 6.2. Empirical political economy research on agricultural protection

Empirical research on agricultural protection is plentiful (see, for example, the survey by de Gorter and Swinnen, 2002). The literature tends to find that support increases under adverse market conditions for the farming industry; that countries with a comparative disadvantage in agriculture have greater protection (supporting the view that losers from liberalization organize politically), and that a high budget share for food consumption reduces protection. Gardner's (1987) is a classic study in this literature. Gardner assumes governments maximize the weighted sum of consumer surplus (C) and producer rents (R): $W = C + \theta R$. In turn, C and R are functions of farm output quantities (i.e. policy therefore targets production). Unlike Grossman and Helpman (1994) who provide microfoundations for their objective function by including a formal model of the lobbying process, Gardner attributes the value of the parameter θ to the forces that determine lobbying effectiveness. These were measured for 17 farm commodities by the number of producers, their geographical dispersion, the return to agricultural support (determined by output per farm) and the stability of the industry (variability of production patterns) for the period 1912–80. Gardner found that the lower the demand elasticity of a commodity, the greater the level of intervention. This is consistent with the intuition that it is most efficient to tax commodities with the lowest price elasticities of demand, and is the basis for Gardner's conclusion that interventions in US agriculture have been relatively efficient.

Gawande and Hoekman (2006) apply the Grossman-Helpman model—discussed in Chapter 1—to agricultural protection in the US. As is the case for applications of this model to trade in manufactures, their estimates of the government preference (or weight) on welfare is very high: government places at least 40 times as much weight on a dollar of welfare as on a dollar of political contributions (lobbying) by farm interests. That is, the US government is approximately a welfare-maximizer.

These results suggest that things are not as bad as they could be—or as bad as economic models of endogenous protection predict they should be. However, the results are difficult to square with the fact that the deadweight losses of agricultural protection are many billions of dollars. One way of reconciling the estimates with political reality is to recognize that government is not a singular entity with the power to supply protection with certainty. In practice the legislative process leading to protection is uncertain. Contributions are made *before* the award of protection or subsidy, not on delivery of protection or subsidy. Lobbies also make contributions to political agents who cannot guarantee a specific outcome. These real-world dimensions should reduce lobbying contributions, reflecting the much lower probability of success. A unitary government view of the world leads to the conclusion that the low tariffs are due to a welfare-loving government, when in reality it is a self-interested government that delivers tariffs in response to (lower) contributions under uncertainty.

domestic surplus (Article XI GATT). Quantitative restrictions could also be used to deal with shortages of food or other essential exportables. Second, export subsidies on primary products were permitted, as long as these did not lead to more than 'an equitable share' of world trade for the subsidizing country. What equitable meant in practice was not clear, however, and differences in interpretation led to a number of GATT disputes. Over time, more flexibility in the use of QRs and other NTBs in the agricultural sector was introduced through special waivers (starting with the US in 1955); in protocols of accession (for example, Switzerland); through limited tariff bindings on agricultural imports (opening the way for the use of variable levies under the CAP); by allowing residual grandfathered restrictions on imports of agricultural goods to be maintained; and through a proliferation of various 'grey area measures' such as VERs and 'orderly marketing arrangements'.

By accepting—implicitly or explicitly—the notion that agriculture is unique, it proved to be virtually impossible to make cross-sectoral linkages or tradeoffs in MTNs. The establishment of separate negotiating groups for agriculture, staffed 'by civil servants experienced in the defense of domestic farm-support policies... [was] a way of avoiding a tradeoff between agriculture and industry' (Josling, 1977: 11). Problems were compounded by the commodity-specific approach that was pursued in MTN talks on agriculture.

Throughout the 1960s and 1970s, agricultural discussions between the two major players—the EU and the US—were based on two totally different conceptions. The EU favoured the development of a system to manage world trade so as to facilitate the functioning of the CAP. The US, in contrast, supported by countries such as Australia, Canada and New Zealand, sought significant liberalization, while safe-guarding national policies that protected powerful agricultural interests (such as dairy and sugar producers). As a result, very little progress was made in the Kennedy and Tokyo Rounds on agriculture. In both MTNs, the basic premise of the EU was that the CAP was non-negotiable, and that the focus of discussions should be on stabilizing world agricultural markets. The Community proposed that international commodity agreements be negotiated for products such as cereals, rice, sugar and dairy. The US in contrast emphasized the need to expand agricultural trade and to end the special status of agriculture in the GATT (which was somewhat ironic given that the US had started the process of hollowing out multilateral disciplines for agriculture).

In the Tokyo Round these incompatible positions blocked the negotiations for a long time. The deadlock was broken only after the Carter Administration was inaugurated and Robert Strauss was appointed as Special Trade Representative (in 1977). President Carter put greater weight on the successful conclusion of the round than his predecessor and was willing to give in on agriculture. Subsequent bilateral bid-offer negotiations resulted in the reduction of certain tariffs and an increase in various quotas, but did little to achieve general US objectives.

Two sectoral agreements were negotiated: an Agreement on Bovine Meat and an International Dairy Arrangement. Neither was far-reaching. The agreement on meat ostensibly was aimed at increasing trade and the stability of the world market. It implied no binding obligations, however, and in practice had little effect, if any. The dairy agreement was more substantive in that it set minimum prices for major dairy products. However, these prices proved to be unenforceable in practice.

A number of disputes occurred regarding circumvention of the minimum prices by certain signatories (especially the EU), which led the United States to withdraw from the agreement in February 1985. Both arrangements were brought into the WTO as Plurilateral Agreements in 1994, but were dissolved in 1999 (see Chapter 11).

In the early 1980s a constituency emerged in the EU that favoured a reduction in agricultural support. Agricultural subsidies were a significant burden for heavily strained government treasuries, and became increasingly difficult to defend as the ideological balance swung towards greater reliance on markets, competition and deregulation. Two successive oil shocks had led to large fiscal deficits, compounding the pressure on government finances. A decision by the US to engage in a subsidy war with the EU in the 1980s—partly driven by a decline in international food prices, which raised opposition to EU export subsidization—also helped to increase the financial pressure. At the same time, agricultural disputes became more intense, and further enhanced the incentive for dealing with agriculture in the GATT.

These factors allowed the ministerial meeting that launched the Uruguay Round to put agriculture on the table in a comprehensive manner for the first time. The Punta del Este negotiating mandate broke new ground in that there was an explicit reference to liberalization, with all policies affecting agricultural trade to be discussed, including domestic and export subsidies. This contrasted with the Kennedy and Tokyo Round ministerial declarations, which emphasized the status of agriculture as a special (unique) sector and were oriented towards the negotiation of commodity-specific agreements. However, as the negotiations commenced, it rapidly became clear that discussions would continue to be dominated by transatlantic ping pong between the two largest agricultural traders—the EU and the US—which together accounted for about 40 per cent of international trade in food. Any agreement required a deal that they could live with. But they were by no means the only players. Other significant actors included the European Free Trade Association (EFTA) countries and Japan (with highly protectionist systems and basically in the EU camp) and a group of 14 agricultural exporters that sought significant liberalization. This coalition was called the Cairns Group (after the Australian city where the group was formed) and was an ally of the US. It included Argentina, Australia, Brazil, Canada, Chile, Colombia, Fiji, Hungary, Indonesia, Malaysia, New Zealand, the Philippines, Thailand and Uruguay.

The Cairns Group objective was to gradually attain free trade in agricultural commodities, eliminate production distortions, and ensure that binding undertakings to this effect were made. The US initially sought the complete liberalization of trade in agriculture. It was particularly concerned about export subsidies, and sought their rapid and unconditional elimination. The US also insisted on the need to introduce a clear-cut separation between income support for agricultural producers and policies that affected the level of farm production. Income support could be accepted, but only if decoupled from production. The EU initially proposed that negotiations first concentrate on emergency measures for certain sectors, including cereals, sugar and dairy products, to remove structural disequilibria on world markets, followed by liberalization of trade and a reduction of support policies. The EU argued that the goal should not be free trade, but achieving stability on world agricultural markets. It proposed to follow a bid-offer process for specific products along the lines of previous MTNs. It also argued that existing zero (or low) tariff bindings on oilseeds led to severe distortions in the EU market and sought to negotiate a 'rebalancing' of its agricultural protection to make it more uniform. This desire for rebalancing became one of the more contentious issues of the negotiations.[2] Japan supported the idea of a freeze on export subsidy expenditures as a short run step, to be followed by a gradual phase-out, but suggested that domestic subsidies be permitted to maintain a minimum (unspecified) level of self-sufficiency for national security reasons.

Bridging the gap between the EU and the US-Cairns positions proved extremely difficult, not only because of fundamental, substantive differences, but also because of the negotiating strategies that were pursued. Although clearly unacceptable to the EU, for the first two years of the Uruguay Round the US insisted the objective should be the total elimination of trade-distorting support policies within ten years. The resulting standoff led to the breakdown of the Montreal mid-term review of the round in December 1988. After a four-month period of informal consultations it was agreed that the long run objective in the agricultural area was to be progressive reduction in agricultural support, not elimination. This compromise allowed negotiations to continue. In the final phase of the round, discussions remained very contentious, with serious differences of opinion emerging within the EU as well as between the EU and other GATT contracting parties.

At the December 1990 ministerial meeting that was supposed to conclude the round, no agreement could be achieved on agriculture, leading to a breakdown of talks on all the issues on the agenda. In effect, the EU refused to accept the compromise text that was proposed by the chairman of the negotiating group— which would have averaged a cut of about 25 per cent in bound protection levels— as going too far in disciplining export subsidies and the use of specific policies. The proposal would have had significant implications for the CAP—the reform of which was under active discussion at the time. The EU needed to settle its internal debates on agriculture first—in particular to placate the French, who opposed any

---

[2] In earlier MTNs predating the formation of the European Community, a number of European countries bound tariffs on cotton, soybeans (oil, meal and seeds), vegetables and canned fruit at low or zero levels. When these countries joined the EEC, these bindings were incorporated into the common external tariff of the Community. As the CAP led to higher prices of grains, European producers began to import large quantities of soybeans and related products, on which tariff bindings were low. This was a major source of irritation for the EU Commission, which unsuccessfully attempted to close this 'gap in the CAP' in subsequent years.

significant move towards meeting US-Cairns Group demands. Latin American members of the Cairns Group played a major role in opposing any significant weakening of the chairman's proposed text. Argentina, supported by Brazil, made it clear that they would refuse to accept the proposed deal, and stood ready to scuttle the Uruguay Round over the issue (Ricupero, 1998).

An agreement between the EU and the US was eventually reached, after much brinkmanship, with the so-called Blair House Accord in November 1992. By that time internal CAP reform proposals had been developed by the European Commission, allowing a deal to be struck. The EU obtained agreement that its compensation payment policies—under which farmers were paid to take land out of production—would not be included in the definition of the Aggregate Measure of Support (discussed below). It was also agreed that this measure would not be product-specific, and that the extent of liberalization would be limited to a cut of about one-sixth over six years, or less than 3 per cent per year. Although French farmers in particular continued to oppose the deal, the Commission contained this by arguing that the agreement did not go beyond the internally agreed reform of the CAP.

The Uruguay Round Agreement on Agriculture

The Agreement on Agriculture (AoA) that emerged from the Uruguay Round has four main parts dealing with export competition, market access, domestic support and SPS measures (the latter is discussed in Chapter 5).

Export competition. All existing export subsidies had to be scheduled and bound. No new export subsidies were permitted, i.e. any subsidies not scheduled became illegal. By 2000 scheduled export subsidies were to be reduced by 36 per cent in value terms and 21 per cent in volume terms, relative to a 1986–90 base period, in both cases on a commodity-by-commodity basis. For some commodities only the agreed 21 per cent cut in the *volume* of subsidized exports was actually achieved, because international food prices in the late 1990s were higher than in the late 1980s, so that exportable surpluses could be disposed of with lower subsidy outlays.

Market access. On market access it was agreed that NTBs would immediately be converted into tariffs and that industrial countries reduce these tariffs by an average of 36 per cent over six years (24 per cent for developing countries). All agricultural tariffs were bound, an advance over the situation applying to other merchandise tariff lines (see Chapter 5). In practice the cut in tariff bindings could be less than one-sixth as a *weighted* average, as each tariff item needed to be reduced by only 15 per cent of the claimed 1986–8 tariff equivalents (10 per cent for developing countries). There was also considerable scope to concentrate tariff reductions in commodity groups with relatively little effect on trade (Josling, 1994).

The tariff bindings that were implemented by WTO members were in many cases far higher than the actual tariff equivalents of NTBs that applied in the 1986–8 base period. The EU, for example, set bindings about 60 per cent above the actual tariff equivalents of the CAP in the late 1980s, whereas the US set bindings about 45 per cent higher (Ingco, 1996). Many developing countries chose to bind their tariffs on agricultural imports at more than 50 per cent and some as high as 150 per cent— far above the tariff equivalents of restrictions actually in place in the early 1990s. This 'dirty' tariffication implied that actual tariffs at the beginning of the twenty-first century provided no less protection than did the NTBs of the late 1980s.

The so-called binding overhang that resulted was significant. Binding tariffs at such high levels allowed countries to set the actual tariff below the ceiling but to vary it so as to stabilize the domestic market, analogous to the earlier EU system of variable import levies and export subsidies. Such 'made to measure' tariffs (Corden, 1974) are often driven by the seasonal calendar—high rates of protection are imposed during periods when locally produced commodities are available. The high bindings implied that the reduction in fluctuations in international food markets that tariffication was expected to deliver would not necessarily be attained (Goldin and van den Mensbrugghe, 1996).

In recognition of the fact that applied tariffs for some products were set at prohibitive levels, minimum market access commitments were negotiated. These required that the share of imports in domestic consumption for products subject to prohibitive import restrictions increase to at least 5 per cent by 2000 (8 per cent in the case of rice in Japan in lieu of tariffication, less in the case of developing countries).[3] The vehicle used to ensure this minimum market access is generally a tariff rate quota (TRQ), under which a certain volume of imports (the quota) enters at a lower tariff, and out-of-quota imports are subject to a much higher tariff. Special safeguard mechanisms are available to protect domestic producers if imports exceed specific trigger quantities or are priced below trigger price levels. There is also scope to minimize the impact of those imports on the domestic market. For example, a country's required rice imports could be of low feed quality or could be re-exported as food aid.

The market access rules formally introduce scope for discriminating in the allocation of TRQs between countries. The administration of such quotas tends to legitimize a role for state trading agencies. When such agencies have selling rights on the domestic market in addition to a monopoly on imports of farm products, they can charge excessive mark-ups and thereby distort domestic prices easily and relatively covertly—just as such agencies can hide export subsidies if they

---

[3] Countries seeking to delay tariffication were permitted to do so for six years (ten for developing countries) if imports were below 3 per cent of domestic consumption in the 1986–8 base period, no export subsidies were granted and measures to restrict output were implemented. In such cases the minimum market access requirement was higher, increasing from 4 per cent in 1995 to 8 per cent in 2000.

are given that monopoly. Elements of quantitative management of both export and import trade in farm products were therefore legitimized under the WTO.

Domestic support. The third major element of the agreement is a set of disciplines on domestic production support to agriculture. Negotiators defined three categories of subsidies and other types of support, the so-called Green, Amber and Blue 'boxes'. The first comprises instruments that are permitted and unconstrained; the latter two include policies that affect production. The agreement requires high income countries to reduce an Aggregate Measure of Support (AMS) by 20 per cent by 2000 (again relative to a 1986–8 base period). The policies covered by the AMS are considered to distort production and trade and constitute what is often called the Amber Box. This is defined in Article 6 AoA, and includes measures to support prices and subsidies that are tied to, are conditional on, or affect agricultural output. *De minimis* supports are allowed (no more than 5% of agricultural production for developed countries, 10% for developing countries), but the 30 WTO members that had subsidies exceeding *de minimis* levels at the beginning of the post-Uruguay Round reform period were to reduce them by 20 per cent.

World Trade Organization members were required to calculate and enter their base period AMS in their schedules, as well as the 'final bound commitment level' for the AMS. The AMS includes expenditures on domestic subsidies as well as market price support policies such as administered prices, and therefore captures both border and nonborder policies. In principle it covers all support policies that affect trade. However, EU compensation payments and US deficiency payments were excluded from the AMS. Instead, they were put into in a separate 'Blue Box' that was a key component of the Blair House deal between the US and the EU mentioned above. Any support that in principle would be included in the Amber Box is mapped to the Blue Box if it requires farmers to limit output. In contrast to the tariff reduction obligations, which apply at the tariff line, the AMS reduction requirements pertain to the agricultural sector as a whole.[4] That is, the AMS is aggregated over commodities and programmes.

Given the goal of reducing the trade-distorting effects of agricultural policies, the AMS excludes instruments that in principle have minimal effects on production and trade. These so-called Green Box support instruments are defined in Annex 2 AoA. They span subsidies that do not distort trade, are fiscal in nature (are financed by the government budget) and do not involve price support. Green Box measures include programmes that support agriculture generally and do not involve direct transfers to farmers; income transfers that are decoupled from production; and

---

[4] There is a similarity between the AMS and the *montant de soutien* concept, which was introduced by the EU during the Kennedy Round (see Evans, 1972). The *montant de soutien* was defined as the difference between the world price of a product and the price received by a domestic producer. In other words, it was the nominal rate of protection taking into account all instruments affecting producer prices. However, in the Kennedy Round the intention was that support measures would be calculated per commodity.

policies that contribute less than 5 per cent of the value of production. There are no restrictions on the use of Green Box measures.

A so-called peace clause was negotiated regarding the use of countervailing duties and dispute settlement actions to contest the effects of subsidies: members agreed to refrain from new CVD actions for a six-year period and disputes until the end of 2003 (Article 13 AoA). The latter ensured that agricultural subsidies could not give rise to claims of serious prejudice under the SCM Agreement (see Chapter 5) during the implementation period. With expiry of the peace clause in 2004, WTO members can initiate dispute settlement proceedings claiming that subsidy programmes have caused serious prejudice. Before 2004 they needed to make a case that the specific (and very restrictive) conditions laid out in Article 13 had been satisfied. With the expiry of the peace clause all agricultural subsidies—whether they are Green Box, Amber Box, Blue Box or export subsides—can be challenged if a WTO member deems to have suffered serious prejudice or adverse effects as a result.

Developing countries only needed to reduce tariffs, support and export subsidies by two-thirds of the levels mentioned earlier, and had until 2005 to implement this. They were also exempted from the tariffication requirement for products that are primary staples in traditional diets, as long as imports are at least 4 per cent of consumption by 2005. Only production support that exceeds 10 per cent was subject to AMS reduction. Input subsidies for low-income farmers are permitted, as are generally available investment subsidies and export subsidies related to export marketing and internal distribution and transport. It is unclear what the tariff reductions imply in terms of effective liberalization of developing country agricultural markets, as they were not committed to use a particular base year for tariffication. In effect developing countries were granted the freedom to impose tariffs at whatever level they chose to.

The AoA was expected to reduce agricultural protection by about one-fifth or more in industrialized and emerging market economies. An aggregate measure of protection compiled by the OECD Secretariat—the Producer Support Estimates (PSE)—reveal that direct payments and agricultural market price support policies fell in some OECD countries after 1999–2001—e.g. Japan and the US—but increased in the EU, Republic of Korea and a number of other countries (Figure 6.2). All in all, total support to farmers in OECD countries did not decline much (Figure 6.1; Table 6.1), in part as a result of the dirty tariffication that occurred. Anderson, Martin and van den Mensbrugghe (2006) estimate that abolition of agricultural tariffs, subsidies and domestic support programmes would boost global welfare by nearly US$300 billion per year by 2015. Developing countries would receive around half of the global gains from completely freeing all merchandise trade, two-thirds of which would come from global agricultural liberalization. Thus, the level of post-Uruguay Round protection remained high. What the AoA did was somewhat similar to the GATS (Chapter 7) in that the main achievement

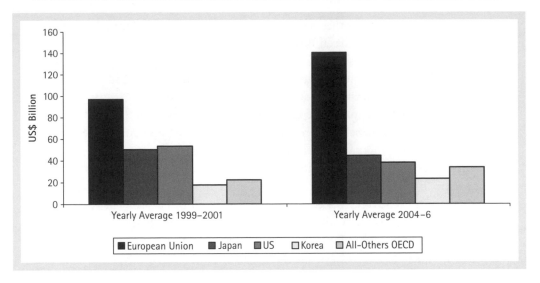

Fig. 6.2. Producer support estimates for OECD members, 1999–2006

Source: http://www.oecd.org/document/0/0,3343,en_2649_33773_39508672_1_1_1_1,00.html

was that agriculture was brought into the fold and a structure was created for future negotiations to lower applied levels of protection.

The Doha Round: pursuing the built-in agenda

Article 20 AoA called for new negotiations to be launched in 2000. These were duly started and subsequently morphed into the Doha Round. Pressure to continue liberalization was strong. Agricultural exporters continued to push for the elimination of trade-distorting farm policies. As, if not more, important, the planned expansion of EU membership required further reform of the CAP, as the status quo regime was not financially sustainable if it were to be extended to Central European countries. Even in the absence of additional liberalization, locking in such reforms through the WTO would be of great value.

The agenda for negotiations on agricultural trade liberalization was conceptually straightforward, centring on the 'three pillars' of agricultural interventions (export competition, market access and domestic support), improving provisions for special and differential treatment for developing countries, and clarifying the scope to pursue noneconomic (nontrade) objectives—e.g. EU arguments that agricultural support programmes were 'multifunctional.'[5]

---

[5] The WTO website provides an excellent overview and detailed information on the state of play and the process of the Doha negotiations on agriculture.

Much of the negotiations focused on agreeing on so-called modalities to reduce bound tariffs and support programmes. These modalities were supposed to establish a framework for WTO members to make commitments on the three pillars on a 'formula' basis. Rather than pursue request-offer negotiations, members agreed to establish specific targets for reductions in export subsidies, domestic support and cuts in tariffs. The talks were characterized by a North–South divide. Developed countries' farm subsidies were major bones of contention, in part because in addition to the traditional set of interventionist OECD countries the US became a target for demands by exporters to open up its market and reduce support. A prominent focal point was US cotton policy, which was detrimental to West African producers. US resistance to making this a priority area for reform played an important role in souring the atmosphere.

The Doha Declaration had envisaged that countries would submit comprehensive draft commitments, based on the 'modalities' in 2003 at the Cancun ministerial conference. A joint EU/US paper drafted at the urging of a mini-ministerial meeting in Montreal in July 2003, proposed a framework for agricultural modalities. With slight modifications, this became the basis of the text on agriculture in the first draft declaration issued on the eve of the Cancun ministerial. This draft was widely seen as enshrining the more protectionist elements of both the US (e.g. maintaining ample scope for countercyclical subsidy payments) and the EU (e.g. maintaining significant barriers to imports). In response Brazil organized a group of developing countries that united around the common cause of reducing trade-distorting policies maintained by the EU and US.

The resulting G20 negotiating group—which included Argentina, Brazil, Chile, China, Egypt, India, Mexico, Nigeria, Pakistan, Philippines, South Africa and Thailand—became a powerful force in the Doha agricultural talks. The creation of the G20 led to a sharp reduction in the visibility and influence of the Cairns Group, as its developing country members were also in either the G20 (Argentina, Brazil, Chile, South Africa) and/or the G33 (e.g. Indonesia, Philippines) and the US ceased to be aligned with other traditional exporters. The G20 comprised a mix of countries with a much broader set of objectives than increasing exports (the main focal point of the Cairns Group). The bargaining coalitions that emerged during the Doha Round were more diverse than those that operated during the Uruguay Round. In addition to the G20—which became a key negotiating group—the G33, a group of developing countries with 'defensive' interests (many were net importers and sought to limit liberalization and expand SDT provisions), played a prominent role.[6] Another defensive group was the G10, comprising countries that provided high levels of support to agriculture (non-EU European countries, Israel, Japan, Korea and Taiwan).

---

[6] Members included many Caribbean and Sub-Saharan African countries, as well as India, Indonesia, Korea, Pakistan, Peru, Philippines, Turkey and Venezuela.

Preferences of the countries associated with each group were by no means always aligned. The G20 included India, which was also a member of the G33. The inclusion of both Brazil—a major exporter with strong interest in liberalization of global agriculture—and India (which sought to maintain significant freedom to intervene in agriculture) meant that the G20 had to balance the offensive and defensive interests of its members. The result was that G20 negotiating positions tended to be 'in the centre'—in effect, already incorporating a deal between members with different preferences and concerns. Constantini and colleagues (2007) use cluster analysis techniques to analyse the internal 'coherence' of the various bargaining coalitions, exploring to what extent they bring together countries with similar structural features (GDP per capita, openness, FDI stocks, human development, food security indicators, share of agriculture in exports, output and employment, level of trade protection). They conclude that the G20 brings together countries that have similar structures, helping to explain the robustness of the group during the negotiations.

Disagreements on the specification of the modalities and the magnitude of allowable exceptions for specific products could not be overcome during 2002–8. Negotiations repeatedly missed deadlines. Despite talks among small subsets of 'representative' WTO members to agree on modalities, progress proved elusive. An example was talks between the so-called five interested parties—Australia and Brazil, representing export interests; the EU and India, representing the 'defensive' interests; and the US (with both offensive and defensive interests)—which did not manage to identify a package of mutually acceptable reforms. The extent of the difficulties were illustrated by the inability to deal with technical issues such as how to go about converting specific tariffs (taxes that are based on volume rather than the value of imported products) into *ad valorem* equivalents. Although these were important, the fact that ministers were asked to deal with such questions illustrated how deep the differences were in this area (Box 6.3).

The 2005 ministerial meeting in Hong Kong did not lead to any major breakthroughs, with the exception of (conditional) agreement to eliminate export subsidies for agricultural products by 2013. As of mid-2006, the contours of a possible agreement finally began to emerge. It was described as a 20–20–20 package by the Director-General of the WTO. Under this proposal the EU would cut its bound agricultural tariffs by an estimated 54 per cent (following a proposal made by the G20), the US would bind its total trade-distorting agricultural subsidies at a maximum of US$20 billion, and developing countries would agree to a maximum tariff on manufactures of 20 per cent. A deal along the lines of the 20–20–20 package would have implied a significant reduction in not only tariff bindings but also applied policies. Negotiators could not agree on a specific compromise, however. Exporters sought deeper cuts in EU tariffs and both the G20 and the EU wanted the US to accept a lower ceiling on its domestic farm subsidies.

Box 6.3. Doha disagreements on *ad valorem* equivalents

In April 2005 the Chairman of the special session of the Committee on Agriculture (the Doha negotiating group) suspended talks as a result of disagreement on how to convert specific tariffs into *ad valorem* equivalents (AVEs). This was needed in order to be able to apply a formula for tariff reductions. The problem revolved around what source of data to use to calculate the AVEs in instances where calculations based on the WTO's Integrated Database (IDB) differed significantly from those resulting from use of the UN Comtrade database. Members had agreed that in such cases, more processed products would use the IDB, whereas more basic commodities would be based on UN Comtrade. Rather than just agreeing to split the difference—i.e. use the average of the two estimates—a more complicated two-stage approach was proposed: (1) a determination if the unit import value for a product in the two databases differed by more than 40 per cent (if not the IDB would used); and, if so (2) a comparison would be made between the AVEs using the two sources, with the IDB used if the difference was less than 20 percentage points. The question was what to do with those products where the difference in AVE estimates was greater than 20 points.

Members had agreed that in such cases the adjustment for commodities should be 25 per cent IDB and 75 per cent Comtrade (as the latter was regarded as having better coverage of processed products), and that the calculation for processed products would be on a 50–50 basis. Switzerland argued that this would favour food exporters, whereas some African countries were of the view that this would put commodities higher up in the band to which the tariff-cutting formula would apply, and thus disadvantage African food exporters.

The issue on which talks broke down was whether the base for the above adjustment should be the unit values or the estimated AVEs. The EU reportedly shifted towards the latter whereas most members thought they had converged to the former. The end result was that this very technical matter was put before ministers at a mini-ministerial meeting in Paris in May 2005. This is not the type of question that ministers should be dealing with. These types of technical issues are matters for negotiators to resolve, working with the WTO Secretariat. The episode illustrated how dysfunctional the talks had become—and that the Secretariat was not able to play the role that it should.

Despite efforts in early 2007 to resuscitate the process, which led to a high-profile meeting between four of the major protagonists (EU, US, Brazil and India) in Potsdam in June, agreement remained elusive. Developing countries remained disappointed by the US offer on agricultural subsidies and the EU unwillingness to open its agricultural markets more. Conversely, the EU and the US were unsatisfied by what they regarded as inadequate offers by Brazil and India on industrial tariffs.

In mid-2008 a draft text issued by the chairperson of the Agriculture negotiating group as a basis for further discussion laid out the most specific and comprehensive blueprint for global liberalization since the negotiations began in 2001, with bracketed ranges for key numeric parameters. What follows briefly describes what was on the table, drawing on the excellent summary by Martin and Mattoo (2008).

Export competition. In the course of the 2000s export subsidies became much less of a problem than in preceding years because world prices of agricultural commodities were relatively high. As a result there was much less need for export subsidies to be used to dump surpluses on global markets. The magnitude of export subsidies is determined by the gap between domestic and world prices. Export subsidies are used when high tariffs raise the domestic price of commodities as a result of which domestic output expands. If there are also domestic production support programmes this output expansion will be greater, potentially impacting world prices through an artificially increased global supply.

Unfortunately, the available data on export subsidies are limited. World Trade Organization members do not notify export subsidies in a comprehensive and timely basis—the situation is similar to that pertaining to notification of nonagricultural subsidies (see Chapter 5).

The July 2004 Framework Agreement had already spelled out in some detail how liberalization was to occur: export subsidies were to be eliminated by a 'credible' date (set at 2013 at Hong Kong), with reductions to be implemented in annual installments during a transition period. Although abolition of all export subsidies would have only a small immediate overall effect given high world prices, a ban would be of significant value in ruling out future recourse to such subsidies in periods with low prices.

The elimination of export subsidies is best seen as a key *consequence* of reducing the gap between domestic and world prices created by border barriers and domestic support programmes. Eliminating export support without reducing tariffs and domestic support would simply result in putting world agriculture in the situation (no export subsidies, high tariffs and domestic support) faced by manufacturing at the dawn of the GATT in the late 1940s. That in itself would be an achievement, but from an economic perspective is likely to have a limited impact (Hoekman and Messerlin, 2006). What matters is a substantial reduction in border protection (Box 6.4).

As part of the Doha Round discussions on export subsidies, the EU, supported by a number of Cairns Group / G20 members, linked elimination of export subsidies to all existing 'equivalent' forms of export subsidization: specifically the subsidy component of official export credits, the activities of STEs and food aid. One interpretation of this linkage is that it was largely tactical. Although the EU is by far the largest user of export subsidies, a number of traditional export-oriented and pro-liberalization countries make use of these alternative instruments. Although the objective in the case of STEs and food aid is generally not to subsidize exports, they may have that effect. Thus, for example, the US grants both export credits and food aid, and Canada has made long standing use of STEs for specific commodities. Alternatively, the focus on equivalent disciplines for alternative instruments

---

Box 6.4. The three pillars: what matters most?

Of the three pillars, most attention centred on domestic support and export subsidies, with major campaigns by NGOs such as Oxfam lampooning the extent to which EU, US and Japanese farmers were coddled. Creative use was made of the detailed data on agricultural protection that had been compiled by organizations such as the OECD. One oft-cited example of the Oxfam critique of EU protection was that the amount spent on the average cow in the EU was enough to fly it around the world in business class. Another was that more was spent on each cow than the annual per capita income of many households in Africa.

However, economic research suggested that what really mattered most from the perspective of farmers in developing countries was border protection in the EU and other OECD nations. Subsidies are expensive and may be inequitable, but analysis concluded that subsidies had a much smaller impact on world prices than tariffs and TRQs. Domestic support in the OECD involves huge income transfers from OECD taxpayers to OECD farmers, but their impact on (developing country) agriculture exporters is smaller than the impact of tariff barriers in both developed and developing countries. Hoekman, Ng and Olarreaga (2004) and Anderson, Martin and Valenzuela (2006) estimated that border barriers accounted for 80–90 per cent of the impact on world prices and thus welfare. In large part this is because of high tariff peaks in OECD and developing countries in products subject to domestic support or export subsidies: for a given amount of domestic production, tariffs lead to lower levels of domestic consumption than domestic subsidies, and therefore lower world prices (Snape, 1987). Anderson, Martin and van den Mensbrugghe (2006), consistent with other studies done at the time, concluded that reductions in agricultural tariffs would deliver 12 times the gains that would be achieved by abolishing export subsidies and trade-distorting domestic support to agriculture.

---

that may give rise to export subsidies can be perceived as a necessary step to ensure that governments do not engage in 're-instrumentation' following a WTO ban on export subsidies on farm products.

Is this a significant issue? Here again there is very limited information. Calculating the subsidy component of an export credit requires data on the amount of the credit, its terms—maturity, interest rate structure, etc.—the credit worthiness / risk profile of the borrower/recipient, etc. The counterfactual will be difficult to determine—would a bank or other financial services provider have provided finance and, if so, at what price? Inherently there will be a subjective element to any assessment of the export subsidy equivalent associated with export credits, the operation of STEs and food aid.

One estimate of export subsidy equivalents of export credits by OECD (2001) for affected products in Australia, Canada, the EU and the US during 1995–8 suggested that these did not exceed 7 per cent for any of the instruments considered. In terms of the overall impact, the share of total agricultural exports to which these instruments apply is small—ranging from less than 2 per cent for the EU to around 5 per cent for Canada and the US. It was highest for Australia (15 per cent). Bulk cereals accounted for almost half of the total subsidy element of export credits granted. When used in a simulation model to assess the impact of these programmes on prices, it was found that US export and domestic prices would be only 2 and 1 per cent higher, respectively, following a ban on export credits. Moreover, the bulk of export credits apply to intra-OECD trade—in the case of the US, South Korea and Mexico are the major recipients. It would appear therefore that these are of second-order importance compared to export subsidies proper (which in turn are second order compared to market price support).

Domestic support. Here the focus was on introduction of a number of additional constraints and reductions in bound levels of support. The AMS was to be reduced using a tiered formula. It would cut EU support by 70 per cent; by 60 per cent in members with intermediate levels of support (including the US); and 45 per cent in other members. A new Overall Trade Distorting Support (OTDS) measure—defined as the sum of the AMS, *de minimis* support, and Blue Box instruments—was to be cut by between 75 and 85 per cent in the EU; 66 to 73 per cent in the US; and 50 to 60 per cent in smaller industrial economies. Permitted Blue Box support would be limited to 2.5 per cent (5 per cent) of the value of agricultural production for developed (developing) members. Product-specific limits would also be introduced on the AMS and the Blue Box, with the allowed level of support to cotton reduced very sharply and under an accelerated timetable (cotton is discussed in more detail below). Projections by Blandford and Josling (2008) suggest that the draft 2008 modalities would not constrain total AMS or OTDS in the US under realistic price projections. However, the product-specific AMS and Blue Box commitments would probably constrain products of particular importance to many developing countries such as sugar, peanuts and cotton. In Europe, the 2008 modalities proposals would lower the OTDS below projected, unconstrained levels of support.

Market access. The method proposed on market access was a 'concertina' approach (see Corden, 1974) under which the highest tariffs rates are reduced more. The proposal was to use a tiered formula that would require proportional cuts in tariffs, with the cut increasing when moving between each of four progressively higher bands (Table 6.2). The proposal would have permitted developed countries to classify 4–6 per cent of tariff lines as sensitive, whereas developing countries could exclude an additional 33 per cent (compared to industrialized economies) and be able to self-designate 'special products' on which they could make smaller-than-formula cuts. Proposals on the number of such special products ranged between 8 and 20 per cent of all agricultural tariff lines. The end result would be to undo much of the harmonization of the basic formula (Martin and Mattoo, 2008).

Table 6.2. Proposed formula for cuts in bound agricultural tariff, July 2008 (%)

Tariff Band	Developed Countries		Developing Countries	
	Range	Cut	Range	Cut
A	0–20	50	0–30	33.3
B	20–50	57	30–80	38
C	50–75	64	80–130	42.7
D	>75	66–73	>130	44–48.6

Source: Martin and Mattoo (2008).

Application of this proposal would have reduced average bound agricultural tariffs by nearly half, from 40.3 to 20.7. World average applied tariffs would be cut by nearly 40 per cent, from 14.5 to 8.9 per cent. Flexibilities for sensitive and special products would significantly attenuate the impact of the formula: the world average bound rate drops by just over a quarter, and the average applied tariff would fall by one-fifth, from 14.5 to 11.8 per cent. In the high-income country group, the formulae with flexibilities would cut four percentage points off applied tariffs, from 15 to 11 per cent, and reduce average bound tariffs from 40 to 30 per cent. In developing countries, taking into account likely flexibilities for sensitive and special products and the large gap between bound and applied rates (40 percentage points on average), the cuts in developing country applied tariffs would be very small—only 1.9 percentage points. Even more than for OECD countries the main effect therefore would have been to lower average levels of bound tariffs: from 54 per cent on average to 45 per cent.

After the Uruguay Round, OECD countries became intensive users of TRQs. As mentioned previously, under a TRQ, there is an out-of-quota tariff that applies to imports above a specified quota quantity. Volumes below the quota limit pay a lower in-quota tariff. Understanding the impact of TRQs is critical to predicting the outcome of attempts to liberalize trade in agricultural products. For example, reducing out-of-quota tariffs will increase imports only if the current demand for imports exceeds the quota amount such that the out-of-quota tariff is operational. If imports are less than the quota level, reductions in out-of-quota tariffs will be ineffective. On the other hand, marginal expansion of the TRQs will be ineffective if imports are greater than the TRQ—the only effect will be to increase the volume of imports on which scarcity rents are earned. If imports are less than the TRQ, expanding the quota will also be ineffective. Only reductions in in-quota-tariffs will stimulate greater imports in this case. Thus, reductions in out-of-quota tariffs may be the most effective instrument for achieving market liberalization in the majority of cases.

Special safeguards

Unlike with normal safeguards (discussed in Chapter 9), the special safeguard (SSG) mechanism included in the AoA permits the automatic imposition of higher duties if import volumes rise above or prices fall below a certain level.[7] It is not necessary to demonstrate that serious injury is being caused to the domestic industry. The SSG can only be used on products that were tariffed in the Uruguay Round by governments that reserved the right to do so in their schedules of commitments. Only 39 countries—17 developed and 22 developing—did so. Safeguards must take the form of temporary duties that may not last more than one year. Tariffs are limited to an additional 33 per cent of the applicable bound rate if the trigger is an import volume surge. Alternatively, if the trigger is a significant reduction in price, the SSG is determined by the difference between the import and the trigger price.

During 1995–2004 only 6 of the 22 developing countries eligible to use the programme actually utilized it, for just 163 tariff lines (Hufbauer and Adler, 2008). Many developing countries that did not use NTMs to distort agricultural trade during the Uruguay Round did not have to engage in the tariffication process and therefore did not have access to the SSG. The right to use the SSG was intended to lapse if there was no agreement in the negotiations to continue the 'reform process' initiated in the Uruguay Round (Articles 5.9 and 20 AOA).

The Doha Round generated numerous proposals regarding the SSG, ranging from keeping it unchanged, revising it to exempt products from developing countries, to abolishing it. Many developing countries proposed that only they be allowed to use special safeguards. This led to proposals to create a new special safeguard mechanism (SSM) that would permit developing countries to raise tariffs temporarily to deal with agricultural import surges. (This rationale for the SSM should be distinguished from protecting farmers in general. The latter objective was addressed by inclusion of provisions allowing developing countries to make smaller or no tariff cuts for 'special products'.) Agreeing on the criteria for a SSM proved to be difficult, with some countries, especially the US, opposing suggestions by the advocates of a flexible SSM—the G33 and its allies—that the SSM should be easy to use, with low thresholds for the import volume trigger, and allow for tariffs above pre-Doha Round bound rates. The US and other agricultural exporters argued that the SSM should not result in tariff increases above pre-Doha Round levels, that it should be limited to a period following liberalization of trade, and not affect the balance of rights and obligations negotiated in the Uruguay Round.

---

[7] The abbreviation SSG comes from the notation used in the tariff schedules of WTO members to indicate that a tariff line could be subject to the special safeguard.

The 2008 draft modalities envisaged a special safeguard mechanism with a volume and a price trigger that would be applicable to all agricultural products. The proposal was that import duties of up to 25 percentage points could be imposed if imports exceeded 110 per cent of a three-year moving average. A price-based measure to restrict imports could then be invoked if the price of imports dropped below 85 per cent of a three-year moving average of import prices, with a duty of up to 85 per cent of the gap between prevailing import prices and the three-year moving average. One matter of contention was whether the combination of the special safeguard duty and the applied tariff rate would be permitted to exceed the pre-Doha bound tariff rate levels (Martin and Mattoo, 2008).

No agreement proved possible on the SSM—which became the proximate cause for yet another breakdown of the Doha talks in July 2008. Five main issue areas were in contention in the SSM debate (Hufbauer and Adler, 2008). First, coverage: all agricultural goods or only a subset? Some countries argued that the SSM should not be available for 'special products' that were exempted from the formula cuts. Second, the type of triggers to be used; the thresholds to apply; and whether there should be a single criterion or alternative triggers that would be conditional on the level of commitment that a country had made. Third, whether SSM tariffs could exceed pre-Doha bound rates and, whether this should be subject to limits. The US wanted higher trigger thresholds for SSM tariffs that exceeded pre-Doha bound rates. Fourth, whether SSM tariffs should be conditional on an injury test of some type. A final issue was whether there should be time limits for SSM actions, as for the SSG.

Measures such as the SSM are essentially motivated by a desire on the part of governments to insulate markets against external shocks—specifically, reductions in world prices that generate import surges. A SSM provides protection and insulation to domestic markets, while reducing market access and increasing the instability of world markets if used by importers accounting for a significant fraction of imports. It was somewhat ironic that while the debates on the design of the SMM were raging in mid-2008 the problem was not low agricultural prices, but the opposite. Governments were taking whatever actions they could to lower consumer prices. In general, the type of SSM that was proposed in the Doha Round might act as a price-insulating measure for developing countries, but as with any trade policy it would generate distributional effects—in this case raising the prices for net consumers of agricultural commodities in the countries using a SSM.

Economists have also pointed to the likely negative spillovers created by SSM-type instruments: any price-insulating effect will likely be diminished by the consequent increase in volatility of world markets for products in which developing countries account for a large share of world production (Ivanic and Martin, 2008). In general, it is unclear why governments should not want to use general safeguards to address import surges if they deem this to be necessary. A major advantage of the general safeguard provision in the GATT is that it requires governments to assess the economy-wide implications of taking action. This is very desirable and helpful from a policy perspective. Arguments sometimes heard that the general WTO safeguard provision cannot be used to respond rapidly are incorrect—as discussed in Chapter 9, measures can be imposed provisionally.

Net food-importing countries

Agricultural liberalization, especially moves towards elimination of export subsidies, may increase world prices of food products, and thus have a negative effect on net food-importing developing countries. During both the Uruguay and Doha Rounds a number of countries expressed concerns regarding the impact of liberalization on food security. The main worry was that global liberalization of agricultural trade could give rise to adverse terms of trade effects.

During the Uruguay Round it was noted that institutions such as the IMF and World Bank had instruments available to finance short-term needs should world prices of food increase significantly. Developed country WTO members also committed themselves to continue to provide food aid, as well as technical and financial assistance, all least developed and the 18 developing countries that were classified as net food-importers. Specific recommendations were adopted at the 1996 Singapore ministerial meeting regarding negotiations on international food aid commitment levels and related concessionality guidelines. In response, the Food Aid Committee decided in December 1997 to extend the life of the Food Aid Convention through June 1999 and to open the Convention for re-negotiation.

Research suggests that the impact of global liberalization on net food importers would be limited, because reforms will be spread out over multiple years and price increases will be offset to some degree by an increase in domestic supply that will be stimulated by higher prices. Trade policy is not the appropriate instrument if the objective is food security. Instead, the key need is to have the foreign exchange (and access to credit) to be able to buy food in times of scarcity. Having the domestic ability to produce food is not required—countries should only specialize in food production if they have a comparative advantage in this activity. A necessary condition for this piece of advice to be appropriate is that countries have access to global markets—that is, can buy supplies. This may not be the case in times of severe global shortage. In 2008, following a steep and rapid rise in food prices, a number of exporting countries imposed export restrictions (taxes or bans). For a brief period, reportedly some countries could not buy staple commodities such as rice at any price. This suggests that disciplining the use of export restrictions should be an important objective of net importers. The WTO only imposes weak disciplines on the use of export restrictions, and efforts in the early part of the Doha Round to put this matter on the negotiating table failed.

The reason for the high prices that emerged in 2007 had nothing to do with liberalization—the main fear expressed by net importers in the MTNs—but with global economic developments: the boom in China and other emerging markets up to early 2008, and the resulting rise in oil and other commodity prices. Energy price increases in turn led to greatly increased production of bio-fuels in the US that used maize and other cereals as feedstock, further driving up food prices (Mitchell, 2008). This episode illustrated that liberalization was not a potential problem—it was the lack of global liberalization that had severe implications for net importers. If trade had been free in agricultural products and bio-fuels, Brazil and other major sugar-producing countries could have exported much more efficiently produced ethanol to the US and EU than these countries could supply themselves, without the associated additional negative impacts of diverting food production towards bio-fuel production.

The increase in global food prices had deep roots in decades of trade-distorting policies that encouraged inefficient agricultural production in rich countries (most recently in the 2000s in the form of bio-fuels), led to recurrent dumping of surpluses on global markets, and discouraged efficient production in developing countries (World Bank and IMF, 2008). In turn, as discussed above, developing countries have often taxed their farmers. Overall, the result was declining agricultural prices, overproduction in high-income countries, underproduction in poor countries, thinner global agricultural markets, more volatility, and lower overall reserve supply capacity and food security. Matters were compounded by the use of export controls by Argentina, Ukraine, Russia and Kazakhstan for wheat, and Vietnam, India and China for rice. These restrictions were imposed in an effort to decouple domestic from global markets and rein in domestic food prices. Such export restrictions went beyond food—China, for example, imposed export taxes on fertilizer in an effort to reduce input prices for domestic farmers. Fertilizer costs had increased in line with oil prices; the reduction in supply caused by export taxes increased prices in importing countries further. The result was to put pressure on farmers in low-income countries that are credit-constrained—reducing planting areas and future yields.

Export restrictions tend to: (1) distort prices and the allocation of resources, therefore impeding investment and the supply-side response; (2) prevent local farmers from receiving the higher world market price for their production; (3) displace local production to crops that are not subject to export restrictions, therefore aggravating food security and price concerns; and (4) exacerbate the rise and fluctuations of global food prices, therefore creating a vicious incentive for trading partners to follow suit, curb exports and hoard (Chauffour, 2008). Moreover, by signalling that global markets cannot be relied upon to function, export controls create incentives for importing countries to subsidize domestic production and emulate the types of policies pursued in many high-income OECD countries.

Trade policy is therefore part of the problem. Export restrictions can help stabilize domestic prices in the exporting country but at a significant cost in terms of greater world price volatility and higher average prices for net importers. As trade liberalization generally takes a long period of time to be negotiated and implemented, there is, in principle, ample opportunity for governments to develop or strengthen safety-net programmes and complementary policies to maintain real incomes of the poor. Such time does not exist in instances where there are acute shortages that are exacerbated by 'beggar thy neighbour' export restrictions. But in such situations trade policies are useless for net importing countries—governments will want to lower tariffs, not raise them.

The food price increases that occurred in 2007–8—and the response by food exporters—revealed that an exclusive focus on liberalization on the import side and reducing domestic support is too narrow. Export restrictions and export taxes also needed to be on the WTO negotiating agenda. Current disciplines are weak—Article XI GATT is permissive for agriculture export restraints, and export taxes are unconstrained (see Chapter 5). The fact that these measures were not on the table was not because no proposals to this effect had been put forward. Efforts by Japan and the EU to do so in the Doha Round were rebuffed by a number of developing countries such as Argentina. The 2008 draft modalities only required members to notify the WTO of restrictions or bans 90 days after they were imposed and that these measures were not to exceed one year.

Major agricultural subsidy disputes

We conclude this chapter with a discussion of two major agricultural subsidy disputes. One concerned US cotton subsidies, the other the EU policy set affecting sugar. These cases illustrate the complexity of policy in this area, the extent to which policies create distortions that affect negatively developing countries, and the scope that the WTO offers to attack support programmes that exceed what is permitted (has been scheduled).

Cotton. In the mid-2000s the US was the world's second-largest cotton producer (after China) and the world's leading exporter. The US provided substantial support to its 25,000 cotton producers: averaging some US$3 billion a year in 2005–7 (as subsidies are a function of prices, the amount rises with declines in world prices in any given year). Chinese subsidies were about US$1 billion in 2002 (Baffes, 2005). Economists have estimated the effects variously, with the average estimated negative impact on world prices being in the 6–14 per cent range (Alston, Sumner and Buncke, 2007). The negative spillover is particularly detrimental to other cotton producers, including four West African countries: Benin, Burkina Faso, Chad and Mali. In the Doha Round these countries were known as the Cotton 4 or C-4). In Benin, Burkina Faso and Mali, cotton accounts for roughly

5 per cent of GDP, with between 200,000 to 300,000 households involved in production. In Benin and Mali, cotton accounts for one-third of total exports; for Burkina Faso the figure is 75 per cent. Sumner (2006) estimated that removing cotton subsidies, as part of freeing all merchandise trade, would expand cotton exports from Sub-Saharan Africa by 75 per cent. The developing countries' share of global cotton exports, meanwhile, would rise from 56 to 85 per cent by 2015. Removal of US cotton subsidies was estimated to increase household incomes of cotton producers by 2.3 to 8.8 per cent, enough to support the expenditure on food for one million people in the four countries concerned (Alston, Sumner and Buncke, 2007).

The West African countries formed a coalition in the Doha Round. They pushed for the abolition of export and other trade-distorting subsidies granted to cotton producers in the US, EU and China, and that their cotton farmers be compensated during the transition period in which subsidies were to be phased out. This was a first for the multilateral trading system: LDCs coming forward with a specific demand. The West African proposal attracted much support from other developing countries, as well as the donor community in several OECD nations (Lee, 2007).

The US strongly resisted, arguing that agricultural policies needed to be addressed horizontally as part of an overall agreement on agriculture and not on a product-specific basis. It also argued that African countries should focus on diversifying their economies away from a reliance on cotton towards producing textiles, which could then be granted preferential market access to the US under the African Growth and Opportunity Act. At the Cancun ministerial the second draft of the ministerial text called on the WTO Director-General to consult with the international agencies, including the Bretton Woods institutions, to redirect their programmes and resources to assist these countries to diversify out of cotton; the same draft was deafeningly silent on price-depressing subsidies in the US, China and elsewhere. The lack of willingness to address the African demands on cotton was a factor that strengthened the resolve of African delegations more generally to hold firm on their opposition to accept to launch negotiations on the Singapore issues.

From a visibility standpoint, the Cotton 4 gained considerably from tabling their initiative—the direct link between policies in the most powerful trading economies and their anti-development consequences in depressing incomes of the world's poorest emerged with worldwide notoriety. However, the proposal for 'special treatment' or 'early harvest' met resistance from developed and developing countries alike, and gained only limited support within the WTO membership. Moreover, the proposal for compensation was difficult for trade ministers to address.

In 2002 Brazil had initiated a WTO dispute settlement case against the US cotton programme (*US—Upland Cotton*, WT/DS267). In September 2004, a WTO panel ruled against the United States, as did the Appellate Body in March 2005. The panel/AB ruled that: US cotton subsidies had exceeded the 1992 benchmark year level of subsidy commitments; the direct payments made under US farm programmes were not covered by the Green Box as they were not fully decoupled income support (because payments were accompanied with planting restrictions); so-called Step 2 programme payments that compensated US exporters and cotton mills for the difference between domestic and world prices were prohibited subsidies; US export credit guarantees were prohibited export subsidies; and US domestic support measures that were 'contingent on market price levels' had resulted in excess cotton production and exports that, in turn, reduced world prices (led to price suppression) and as a result caused 'serious prejudice' to Brazil. The AB recommended removal of the 'prohibited subsidies' by July 2005 and the serious prejudice resulting from 'actionable subsidies' by September 2005.

Following nonimplementation by the US, Brazil sought authorization to retaliate against US$4 billion of US exports based on the magnitude of the subsidies granted by the US. It also requested authorization to cross-retaliate in other areas (i.e. TRIPS). The US in turn requested WTO arbitration, which was suspended following a mid-2005 agreement between the parties. In February 2006, the US Congress approved a bill that repealed the Step 2 subsidy programme for upland cotton. As these export subsidies accounted for about 10 per cent of total subsidies to the US cotton industry, Brazil requested a compliance panel to determine whether the US cotton programme continued to violate WTO rules. In December 2007, the panel ruled that the US was still not in compliance; the AB agreed in its June 2008 report (see Schnepf, 2008).

This was an important case on a number of dimensions. Together with the sugar case discussed below, it signalled that developing countries could and would use the dispute settlement mechanism to contest agricultural support policies if they violated the WTO. It also illustrated that the SCM agreement has a broad reach and that arguments can be brought to the WTO that subsidy programmes cause price suppression on world markets. The case was also important in revealing that the distinction between Green and Amber categories of subsidies may not be very useful from a 'legal certainty' perspective—a number of programmes that had been assumed to be in the Green Box were found to be contestable. More importantly, the case illustrates that it is only when there is intense and focused scrutiny of a set of policies that it may become clear whether a programme satisfies the Green Box legal criteria (economists will argue that the separation is simply not possible to make, as in 'general equilibrium' any policy can have an indirect effect on output). Although certain aspects of the reasoning and approach used by the panel and AB can be criticized—e.g. whether and to what extent US policies suppressed world prices, a question on which economists disagree (Sapir and Trachtman, 2008)—much of the information that emerged as a result of the case was certainly not common knowledge. The case, as do others, reveal the limits of the Trade Policy Review Mechanism and other transparency and notification requirements of the WTO: what is needed is analysis of the effects of policies—not just to determine economic impacts but also whether they violate WTO disciplines.

Sugar. Trade protection for sugar production has been a longstanding feature of the international economy, dating back to at least the 1800s (Mitchell, 2005). It has been greatest in countries of the northern hemisphere that produce sugar beets, which is twice as expensive to produce as sugar produced from cane. Over the years, high protection lowered consumption, reduced imports and led to surplus production that was dumped on the world market supported by export subsidies. As world market prices fell and producers confronted subsidized competition from beet sugar, all governments of sugar-producing countries confronted calls for protection.

The EU, Japan and the US all impose high levels of support. Since the early 1970s, US sugar imports declined from more than five million tons per year to about one million tons per year. Japan's sugar imports fell from 2.5 to 1.5 million tons between 1980 and 2000. The EU was a net importer of about 2.5 million tons of sugar in the early 1970s, compared to net exports of about five million tons in the early 2000s. In 1999–2001, the value of gross receipts of sugar producers in the EU was more than double the value of their output measured at world prices. In this period, total OECD support for sugar was equivalent to about half of global exports (US$6.35 billion compared to US$11.6 billion), similar in value to the total exports of sugar of all developing countries (US$6.5 billion). The EU accounted for 43 per cent of the US$6.35 billion in OECD support for sugar. Much of this support was provided through very high border protection—around 90 per cent for the EU. Its support policies resulted in the EU becoming the second largest exporter in the world (after Brazil), accounting for 12 per cent of world exports. At the same time, the EU was also the world's fourth-largest importer, an idiosyncrasy that reflected the preferential access granted to African, Caribbean and Pacific (ACP) countries under the Sugar Protocol of the Cotonon Convention between the EU and ACP states, the successor to the earlier Lomé Convention. The end result of the interventions in the major countries was that they became self-sufficient and effectively closed to competition.

The decline in import demand for sugar by the EU and the US depressed world prices and adversely affected more efficient producers in developing countries such as Brazil and a number of African economies. Estimates indicate that world prices could have been 40 per cent higher in the absence of the protection of sugar in OECD nations (Mitchell, 2005). High protection led to the emergence of high fructose corn syrup as a substitute for sugar in the US and Japan, which came to account for 40–50 per cent of sweetener use in these countries. Developed in the 1960s, corn syrups were profitable because of high sugar prices, and over time became cheaper than beet sugar. As is often the case, the protectionist policy led to a market reaction that undermined the original objective—leading to pressure in the EU for controls to be imposed on corn syrup production.

In 2002, Australia, Brazil and Thailand launched a dispute against EU sugar.[8] In *EC—Sugar*, the complainants argued that the EU violated its WTO export subsidy commitment levels, in part through de facto cross-subsidization of exports as a result of guaranteeing high annual intervention (support) prices for a given quantity of EU sugar, and in part as the result of re-exporting an amount of sugar equivalent to what it imported from ACP countries on a preferential basis.

The EU policy regime for sugar complemented high intervention or support prices for sugar with production quotas. These were of two types: so-called quota A and quota B. The sum of A and B quotas determined the maximum amount of sugar that could be sold in the EU market in a given year. All excess production had to be exported. Production of A and B sugar benefitted from the high intervention price in the EU; excess production—so-called C sugar in EU jargon—did not. There is no physical difference between these various categories: there is one world price for sugar, be it A, B or C sugar. The producer price for A sugar was greater than the producer price received for B sugar. Both were less than the basic intervention or support price as a result of a levy that was used to finance the export subsidies needed to sell excess production on the world market.

In addition to (part of) the B quota, the EU also exported an amount of sugar equal to what it imported from ACP countries under its preferential access programme (the Cotonou Convention). This equalled some 1.3 million tons, rising to up to 1.6 million tons in some years. Given that EU production exceeded consumption at the intervention price, in effect all the ACP sugar was 're-sold' on the world market. That is, the effects of the ACP sugar protocol imports on the EU market were 'sterilized' by exporting the amount imported. As the ACP sugar was bought at the intervention price, the export sales incurred a significant loss, which was absorbed by the EU budget (taxpayers). These costs are clearly export subsidies, and were recognized as such by the panel and the EU.

A key question in the dispute revolved around what producers do with the rents, in particular whether they use them to cross-subsidize production and exports of C sugar. De Gorter, Just and Kropp (2008) show that cross-subsidization is possible for a variety of permutations of production costs, world price levels and support prices implied by a quota level B. Article 9.1(c) AoA requires that payments on the export of an agricultural product be 'financed by virtue of governmental action', a condition that was met in this case. The panel argued that the EU policy was 'a governmental action' that allowed the cross-subsidiza-tion to be 'financed' by EU exporters. This is consistent with economic analysis. Note that the panel finding does not expand the scope to argue more generally that

---

[8] What follows draws on Hoekman and Howse (2008).

policies support cross-subsidization. A pre-condition for such a case is specific subsidy disciplines. These have only been negotiated for agriculture in the WTO.

A second key issue concerned the total volume of sugar exports. For a WTO member to be able to grant an agricultural export subsidy it must be scheduled and be subject to reduction commitments to ensure that the percentage reductions in budgetary outlays and quantities specified in Article 9.2(b)(iv) AoA are achieved by the end of the implementation period. The EU scheduled: (1) a 'base quantity level' of 1,612,000 tons, to be progressively reduced to 1,273,500 tons in 2000 as the 'final quantity commitment level' for sugar; and (2) a 'base outlay level' of €779.9 million, to be progressively reduced to €499.1 million in 2000.

In 2001 the EU exported 4.1 million tons. The excess over what was permitted comprised 1.3 million metric tons of ACP sugar and 1.5 million tons of C sugar. The EU claimed that, by virtue of Footnote 1 to its Schedule, the total ceiling it had bound itself to achieve was not 1,273,500 tons but this amount plus a maximum of an additional 1.6 million tons. Footnote 1 reads as follows: 'Does not include exports of sugar of ACP and Indian origin on which the Community is not making any reduction commitments. The average of export in the period 1986 to 1990 amounted to 1,6 mio t.' The EU essentially argued that the purpose of the footnote was to allow it to meet its commitments in the body of its schedule while continuing to subsidize exports of sugar of ACP and Indian origin up to 1.6 million tons. The panel and AB rejected this argument and ruled against the EU. As discussed further in Chapter 12, this case had major implications for the ACP countries that had benefitted from preferential access to the EU.

How important is agriculture?

The deadlock over agriculture in the Doha Round raises the question of what the opportunity cost was of putting agriculture so much at the centre of the Doha Round. As noted in Chapter 1, agriculture accounts for only a small share of global trade and an even smaller share of the GDP of the rich countries—less than 5 per cent. The political economy factors discussed above imply that in rich countries there is simply not a significant constituency that feels strongly about the transfers that are made to farmers. At the end of the day food is too small a share of the consumption basket and expenditures of most households. Moreover, many groups in OECD countries actively support agricultural support programmes on the basis of equity or re-distributional grounds, or see it as a matter of national (food) security. The reaction of net exporters in 2008 to the rapid escalation of world food prices bolstered the views of those who argued that countries should have domestic food production capacity. Many developing countries went into the Doha Round ambivalent about global agricultural liberalization because they feared they might lose as a result of rising prices as the global price suppressing effects of OECD protection was removed. Although this would benefit their farmers, the historical pattern of taxation of the farm sector in many low-income countries indicates that farmers weigh less heavily than do urban consumers of food. (Although simulation models generally concluded that the overall impact on prices from liberalization would be limited on an annual basis—given that the results of the MTN would be implemented over many years—this never appeared to have much of an impact on those arguing that a Doha Round would be bad for net importers.)

Agriculture is very important for countries with a comparative advantage in the sector, many of which are developing countries (Hertel and Keeney, 2006). Many of the poorest people in developing countries depend on agriculture and higher prices can therefore have major implications for poverty reduction (Hertel and Winters, 2006). The problem is that many of the groups concerned are in countries that are not major markets and which therefore have little to offer in a MTN. Incentives were skewed further by the fact that a large number of the poorest countries were not going to make any market access concessions (see Chapter 12): they essentially removed themselves from the quid pro quo bargaining game altogether. They did not need to bargain because they had duty-free, quota-free access to major markets such as the EU (under its Everything But Arms, EBA, initiative) and a number of other OECD countries. But most important from a development and poverty reduction perspective is that what matters most is to enhance productivity and reduce trade and transactions costs for the countries concerned. This is a domestic policy reform and investment agenda, and only indirectly a function of the policies of OECD countries (Chapter 12).

The Doha Round experience raises questions as to whether MTNs are capable of generating significant additional liberalization or whether they may not be better used as a mechanism to lock in national reforms that have resulted from a domestic political process. The issue linkage literature discussed in Chapter 4 suggests that it makes sense—and indeed, will be necessary—to link agriculture to a broader agenda. The empirical question is whether the resulting negotiating set has enough in it to induce movement on agriculture.

Paarlberg (1997) has argued against issue linkages when it comes to agriculture. In his view the Uruguay Round neither facilitated nor motivated agricultural liberalization beyond what had been decided in the EU through the MacSharry reforms of 1992 and the domestic US reforms of 1990 and 1995–6. Before the Uruguay Round, Runge and von Witzke (1990) predicted that EU expansion to include Eastern European countries of Poland and Slovenia would be the source of demand for liberalizing the CAP. Budgetary pressures, linkages with new issues such as the environmental consequences of the CAP and the emergence of interest groups around these issues, and the long-term decline in the power of agricultural lobbies through attrition in the number of people working the land did force a rethinking of institutions such as unanimity in voting for policy changes (that existed in the EU before the 1992 reforms).

These analysts suggest that the basic driver of reform in this sector must be national (and, increasingly, as countries pursue regional integration of markets, regional). Doha suggests that aggressive attempts to force multilateral liberalization may not have much success—in the end, what was on the table was a significant package of additional binding of past and ongoing national reforms, but little in the way of additionality once flexibilities and sensitivities are taken into account. International pressure through MTNs may play a useful role in helping to push along domestic reforms that are already being considered, but the experience to date in the WTO suggests that issue linkage is very difficult to operationalize in practice. From this perspective the Uruguay Round outcome may have been an outlier in generating an agricultural deal because the formation of the WTO created a take-it-or-leave-it situation. In the Doha Round the threat of exclusion did not exist.

Matters were compounded by what was arguably an excessive focus on reduction of applied levels of protection. If this is not achieved and the MTN breaks down, this has a high opportunity cost: it comes at the expense of not achieving greater lock-in of national/regional policy reforms. History illustrates that a focus on locking-in policy reforms can be very valuable when the economic situation deteriorates and pressures for protection rise as was the case in 2008–9. The emphasis that was put in the Doha Round on actual liberalization of agricultural trade may therefore have been an example of letting the best become the enemy of the good—as the opportunity costs of nonagreement were significant, including absence of progress on NAMA and services, which together account for more than 95 per cent of the trade of most countries.

6.2. TEXTILES AND CLOTHING

Starting in the late 1950s trade policies towards textiles and clothing imports were gradually exempted from many GATT 1947 disciplines. Being labour-intensive and requiring relatively low technology inputs, the production of textiles and clothing is an activity in which many developing countries have a comparative advantage. Indeed, for a large number of countries this sector is the entry point into the production of manufactures. As domestic industries in high-income nations came under pressure from cheaper imports, initially from Japan, and subsequently from other Asian countries, they successfully lobbied for trade restrictions. Bilateral, discriminatory trade restrictions steadily expanded in terms of product and country coverage, and by the early 1990s a global web of QRs existed.

Protectionism was driven by a desire to maintain employment of unskilled or semi-skilled workers. Textile and clothing industries were often regionally concentrated, and accounted for a substantial share of total manufacturing employment in many OECD countries in the 1960s. Trade protection slowed down the adjustment process in OECD countries, but did not stop it. Total employment in the sector declined steadily over time. Trade policy therefore can be seen as attenuating pressure from imports, giving industries more time to adjust (downsize, improve productivity). The policy came at a high economic cost, however, and one that was inequitably distributed. The price-increasing effect of protection impacted especially hard on lower income groups. For example, estimates for Canada revealed that in relative terms the burden of protection was four times higher for low-income consumers than for higher income groups (UNCTAD, 1994).

It was on the occasion of Japan's accession to GATT in 1955, at that time still a developing economy and a major exporter of textiles and clothing, that the concept of market disruption was first extensively discussed in the GATT. The first step towards formalization of a system of managed trade in this sector was the Short-Term Arrangement on Cotton Textiles, introduced during the Dillon Round (1961). This rapidly evolved into a Long-Term Arrangement (1962), which in turn led to four successive Multifibre Arrangements (1974–94) (Table 6.3). The discriminatory character of the MFA was progressively intensified and country and product coverage considerably extended. Initially limited to cotton fabrics, over time wool, man-made fibres, vegetable fibres and silk blends were added. By 1994, MFA-IV had 45 signatories, including 31 developing and Central and Eastern European countries that exported textiles and clothing, and eight importers. Among these, Austria, Canada, the EU, Finland, Norway and the United States applied restrictions, whereas Japan and Switzerland did not.[9] Exporters were subject to bilaterally agreed quantitative export restrictions or unilaterally imposed import restraints. As textiles and clothing accounted for about 45 per cent of total OECD imports from developing countries in the early 1980s, it was the MFA and not MFN that was the cornerstone of the institutional framework for North–South trade.

Determining the impact of the MFA is quite complex. Although it was clearly very detrimental to the most efficient suppliers (such as China), to some extent the losses imposed on developing country exporters were reduced because the quotas were generally enforced by the exporters themselves. Insofar as the quota was

---

[9] On the export side, MFA-IV covered Argentina, Bangladesh, Brazil, China, Colombia, Costa Rica, Czech Republic, Dominican Republic, Egypt, El Salvador, Fiji, Guatemala, Honduras, Hong Kong, Hungary, India, Indonesia, Jamaica, Kenya, Macao, Malaysia, Mexico, Oman, Pakistan, Panama, Peru, Philippines, Poland, Republic of Korea, Romania, Singapore, Slovakia, Slovenia, Sri Lanka, Thailand, Turkey and Uruguay.

Table 6.3. A chronology of managed trade in textiles and clothing

Date	Event
1955	Japan introduces 'voluntary' export restraints (VERs) on cotton textiles shipped to the US. Restraints are continued in 1956.
1956–60	The UK imposes VERs on cotton textiles from Hong Kong, India and Pakistan.
1961	The US textile and clothing industry makes its support for the 1962 Trade Act and the Kennedy Round conditional on interim restrictions to deal with 'market disruption' caused by surges of imports from low-cost countries. The Short-Term Arrangement on Cotton Textiles is negotiated in July 1961.
1962	The Long-Term Arrangement regarding International Trade in Cotton Textiles (LTA) imposes a 5 per cent growth limit on imports of cotton products and places an important portion of the North–South trade in textiles under a managed trade regime.
1967	The LTA is extended for three years.
1970	The LTA is extended for another three years.
1973	To gain the support of the textile industry for the 1974 Trade Act (granting negotiating authority to participate in the Tokyo Round). The US Administration persuades major developing-country garment exporters to accept a Multifibre Arrangement (MFA). The MFA limits the growth of textile and clothing imports to 6 per cent per annum.
1974	A Textile Surveillance Body is created to supervise the implementation of the MFA under the auspices of the GATT textile committee, which is composed of the parties to the arrangement.
1977	An extension is agreed for a five-year period (MFA-II), including a provision for 'jointly agreed reasonable departures' from MFA rules under special circumstances.
1982	MFA-III is negotiated, extending the arrangement for five more years. The 'reasonable departure' clause is dropped.
1985	Developing countries covered by the MFA establish an International Textile and Clothing Bureau to promote the elimination of the arrangement and the return of trade in textiles and clothing to the GATT.
1986	The MFA is extended until 1991 (MFA-IV).
1991	The MFA is extended again until 1994.
1995	The Uruguay Round Agreement on Textiles and Clothing (ATC) sets out the rules for a transition process, which is expected to result in 2005 in the full integration of textiles and clothing into the GATT system.
2005	The ATC provides for its own termination on 1 January 2005.

binding, this implies that rents were being transferred to the exporters that had obtained licences to export (see Annex 2). Estimates of the magnitude of these quota rents are difficult to obtain as few countries auctioned off the quota licences or established markets in which quota allocations could be traded. An exception was Hong Kong, where quota prices for constrained items such as dresses, woven parkas, knitted pullovers and cotton sweaters ranged from US$6 to US$40 per dozen in 1996–7 (Spinanger, 1999).

The MFA created strong incentives for geographic diversification of textile and clothing production. For example, as Hong Kong became more constrained by QRs, Chinese investors established production facilities in other countries such as Mauritius, which then became significant exporters. During the MFA years, a pattern of 'quota-hopping' FDI emerged as newly constrained firms set up shop in markets that were not (yet) constrained. A number of developing countries therefore benefitted from the quota regime by obtaining a 'guaranteed' market in the US or the EU. Such countries were often higher cost suppliers than large producers such as China, and confronted the prospect of increasing competition if the MFA were to be abolished.

Another effect of the MFA was that it created incentives for quality upgrading. Given that the VERs constrained quantities (number of shits, etc.), suppliers that were restricted could earn more if they could increase the unit values of the products they shipped. Harrigan and Barrows (2006), in a study of the effects of the removal of MFA restrictions as a result of the ATC (see below), estimate that the average price of textile and clothing imports by the US from all exporters fell significantly in product categories that had been subject to restrictions.

Bringing textiles and clothing into the fold

As in the case of agriculture, it was only in the Uruguay Round that textiles and clothing were seriously discussed in a MTN. The reasons were not the same, however. In agriculture, important factors were the financial burden of agricultural support programmes and the trade tensions that these programmes had caused. In textiles and clothing there was no pressure from OECD Finance Ministries. Although consumer organizations in high-income countries undoubtedly did not welcome the cost-increasing effect of the MFA, their voice was barely heard. The main common element was pressure from exporters, in particular those countries that perceived they would do better under a more competitive (less managed) trade regime. An implicit link was established between the demands by the US and the EU to address issues such as services and TRIPS in the Uruguay Round, and the desire of many developing countries to see an improvement in the market access conditions for their manufactured exports, in particular clothing.

Not surprisingly, negotiations were quite difficult. Major areas of disagreement concerned the application of general GATT rules, the modalities of phasing out of MFA restrictions, the duration of the transitional period and its product coverage, and the need for special safeguards. However, these areas were all addressed without the type of brinkmanship that characterized the agricultural negotiations. The ATC stipulates that the MFA was to be phased out over a ten-year period (1995–2004) and that standard GATT rules prohibiting the use of QRs and VERs (see Chapter 9) would apply. Products covered by the ATC were to be integrated into GATT in four stages. In 1995, at least 16 per cent of HS categories that were subject to MFA restrictions in 1990 were to be 'integrated'—i.e. no longer be subject to QRs. In 1998 (stage two) another 17 per cent of tariff lines would be integrated, followed by a further 18 per cent in 2002 (stage three) and the remaining 49 per cent by the end of 2004.

The ATC implementation strategy followed by the US and the EU complied with the letter, if not the spirit of the agreement. Very few textile or clothing categories that are important for developing countries were liberalized in the first stages of the MFA abolition (Spinanger, 1999). The EU and the US carefully chose to liberalize categories where imports were either already unrestricted or were relatively capital-intensive. Virtually all of the liberalization of the politically sensitive items was left for the final stage—the end of 2004. Not surprisingly, this gave rise to concerns on the part of developing country exporters regarding the implementation of the agreement.

Supervision of the implementation of the agreement was in the hands of a Textiles Monitoring Body (TMB), comprising an independent chairperson and 10 individuals who were broadly representative of the WTO membership, balancing export and import interests. Textiles Monitoring Body members rotated periodically and were expected to act on a personal basis. The TMB had a conciliatory and semi-judicial role. It examined all measures taken under the ATC, and their conformity with the agreement's rules and programmes for integration and liberalization. Matters on which agreement could not be reached could be brought to WTO dispute settlement. As noted in Chapter 3, a number of textile-related disputes were brought to the WTO after 1995. Indeed, one of the first cases to be brought by a developing country (Costa Rica) concerned US restrictions on this sector.

Implementation of the ATC resulted not only in the abolition of QRs, but also in the demise of the special, bilateral safeguard measures permitted under the agreement. The ATC contained a special safeguard clause in Article 6, which could be invoked during the implementation period of the ATC (that is, up to 2004) for products being integrated into the WTO. Under the ATC, safeguard actions could be discriminatory, were subject to a less stringent injury criterion and did not require compensation of affected exporters. Actions could be taken if imports of a product increased so much as to cause serious damage, or threat thereof, to the domestic industry producing like (or directly competitive) products. Damage indicators included standard economic variables such as output, productivity, capacity utilization, inventories, market share, exports, wages, employment, domestic prices, profits and investment (Article 6.3 ATC). Transitional ATC safeguard actions could be applied on a discriminatory basis, in contrast to measures taken under the Agreement on Safeguards. They required demonstration of a sharp and substantial increase in imports, actual or imminent, from the targeted countries. Measures were not to exceed three years duration or until the product is integrated into GATT 1994, whichever came first.

Over 30 safeguard actions under the ATC were taken between 1995 and 2002, mostly by the US against developing country textile exporters but also by developing countries against each other (for example, Brazil was an active user). The measures were reviewed by the TMB, and many were rescinded. Three ATC safeguard actions led to WTO disputes, all involving the US. In all three cases, the panels, supported by the AB, concluded that the US had violated the provisions of the ATC.[10] The panels signalled that the transitional safeguards in ATC were to be regarded as exceptional instruments and that members invoking this provision of the ATC had to be in full compliance with the various criteria laid out in the agreement. As from the end of 2004, safeguard measures on trade in textiles must be compatible with WTO rules—that is, be applied on a nondiscriminatory basis and conform to other WTO rules.

The back-loaded nature of ATC implementation created the possibility that importing countries might not remove all QRs by 2004. To reduce the probability of this occurring, the ATC required that quotas grow substantially over the ten-year transition. This ensured that import-competing industries would gradually be subjected to more competition. Quotas were to grow by 16 per cent in stage one, 25 per cent in stage two and 27 per cent in stage three. Thus, a 6 per cent permitted growth rate in 1994, became 7 per cent per year during 1995–7; 8.7 per cent during 1998–2001; and 11 per cent per year during 2002–4.

The ATC was implemented as scheduled at the end of 2004, albeit in a rather messy way, with continued restrictions being imposed on China in particular. China's protocol of accession allows WTO members to take product-specific safeguard actions on the basis of 'market disruption' rather than the more constraining 'serious injury' criterion required by the WTO for regular safeguards for a 12-year period (until 2013). In principle, the impact of the elimination of QRs in this sector depends on how constrained the most efficient exporters were. Because of the 'voluntary' nature of the restrictions, the restrictiveness of the MFA (and later ATC) has been measured in the literature as an export tax equivalent: the implicit tax on exports that is associated with the quantitative limit imposed by the importing country. These taxes were on the order of 20–50 per cent for China, and, in the case of the US, were estimated to have *increased* during the ATC implementation period (Francois and Wörz, 2007). The reason was the huge increase in export potential of China as a result of sustained high growth in that country. The export potential greatly surpassed ATC quota growth rates, resulting in policy becoming more restrictive over time.

Under the ATC, policy was more restrictive towards China than other exporters. China's QRs were more likely to be binding; grew at a slower rate; and were subject

---

[10] United States: Restrictions on Imports of Cotton and Man-Made Fibre Underwear from Costa Rica, WT/DS24/AB/R (10 February 1997); United States: Measures Affecting Imports of Shirts and Blouses from India, WT/DS33/AB/R (25 April 1997) and US-Cotton Yarn from Pakistan (WT/DS/192).

to greater constraints in terms of the ability to shift QRs across product categories and time (Brambilla, Kandelwal and Schott, 2007). Francois and Wörz (2007) conclude that as measured by export tax equivalents, the US did not implement the ATC as envisaged by negotiators, because protection increased between 1996 and 2004 for 15 of the exporting countries that were subject to restrictions. In contrast, Canada implemented the ATC according to plan—export tax equivalents had dropped to zero by 2004. In the EU, the average tax equivalent for clothing fell from 13 to 3.6 per cent between 1996 and 2004, except for China, which still confronted an equivalent tax of 19.4 per cent in 2004.

The implication of removing what were still high export tax equivalents at the end of 2004 was clear: large export surges. Chinese exports to the US increased by 39 per cent in 2005, with exports of formerly quota constrained items rising by 270 per cent (Brambilla, Kandelwal and Schott, 2007). In response the EU and the US re-imposed restrictions in the form of negotiated export growth quotas with China. Dayaratna-Banda and Whalley (2007) argue that the result of implementation of the ATC was to shift from a general quota regime affecting all (competitive) developing countries to one where the major markets targeted restrictions on the major supplier—China. Once the provisions of China's accession protocol have expired, WTO members will have to limit themselves to standard instruments of contingent protection to protect domestic producers. As discussed in Chapter 9, China is already the primary target of antidumping actions.

The demise of the MFA was a major achievement, not least because the agreement to reintegrate this sector into the GATT reflected a major change in the negotiating strategy of developing countries. They insisted that progress in this area was a quid pro quo for the TRIPS agreement and the GATS. Full liberalization of trade was not achieved, of course. Tariffs remain much higher on textile and clothing products than most other manufactures. In the Uruguay Round the trade-weighted tariff average in developed countries for these products fell to 12.1 per cent, down from 15 per cent. Access conditions for developing countries continue to differ as a result of PTAs with, and unilateral preference programmes of, OECD countries. These create incentives for so-called outward processing trade and related investments in this sector by providing duty- and quota-free access for products that satisfy the applicable rules of origin (see also Chapters 10 and 12).

A major motivation for these preferential access regimes on the part of developing countries is to attenuate the competitive impacts of China and other more efficient exporters becoming less constrained by QRs. The MFA and the ATC created rents for suppliers that were not constrained. As the ATC was implemented, less efficient suppliers saw market shares erode as a result of greater competitive pressure. This was particularly marked for Sub-Saharan African countries, which confront especially high trade costs. Countries such as Lesotho that had increased exports of clothing to the US fourfold between 2000 and 2004, driven by liberal rules of origin and duty-free access under the African Growth and Opportunity

Act, saw exports decline by 43 per cent in items for which China was constrained in 2005 (Brambilla, Kandelwal and Schott, 2007).

6.3. THE INFORMATION TECHNOLOGY AGREEMENT

Both the agreements on agriculture and on textiles and clothing are multilateral agreements—they apply to all WTO members. Both are sector-specific and the objective in both cases is to (re)integrate these sectors into the WTO. They differ in that the ATC was a time-bound agreement that expired in 2005. As mentioned in Chapter 4, another type of agreement that may be negotiated under the WTO involves the elimination of barriers for subsets of products. These so-called zero-for-zero agreements became prominent in the Uruguay Round, and continue to be strongly supported by industry groups. Examples of sectoral zero-for-zero agreements concluded in the Uruguay Round—under which subsets of (mostly) OECD countries agreed to eliminate tariffs, either immediately or following a transition path—included deals on agricultural, construction and medical equipment, beer, furniture, paper, pharmaceuticals and toys (Mann and Liu, 2009).

The most prominent example of a zero-for-zero deal that was incorporated into the WTO is the Ministerial Declaration on Trade in Information Technology Products, generally called the Information Technology Agreement (ITA), concluded in 1997 by 39 countries accounting for 90 per cent of world information technology (IT) trade. Participants agreed to eliminate tariffs over a three-year period on almost all IT products on a MFN basis. The major product categories covered by the agreement include computers, parts and accessories, telecommunication equipment (including modems, pagers and fax machines), semi-conductors, semi-conductor manufacturing equipment, and certain software and scientific instruments. Consumer electronics are excluded. Tariffs were cut in four equal installments, with developing country signatories having until 2005 to eliminate tariffs on certain items. Other duties and charges were to be abolished upon the entry into force of the agreement.

The ITA was driven by a coalition of IT firms and industry associations that sought to eliminate barriers to trade in their products and used a variety of international non-WTO mechanisms to build a constituency for liberalization. The ITA was the first liberalization agreement concluded after the Uruguay Round (the agreements on finance and telecoms concluded in 1997 were not stand-alone but continuations of Uruguay Round negotiations that could not be brought to closure during the round). At the time the agreement was concluded, some observers noted that such issue-specific, targeted agreements illustrated that the WTO, in contrast to the GATT, could make progress on liberalization without launching a round. It also suggested that 'privileged groups' of the kind discussed in Chapter 4 could be constructed, that is, deals involving enough players with an interest on an issue to allow free riding by nonparticipants to be discounted.

A closer look at the ITA negotiating history suggests that there is little reason to believe that it will (or should) be a model for future liberalization initiatives under WTO auspices. Discussions on the coverage of the agreement were contentious, and numerous linkage strategies were employed by participants in efforts to ensure that a 'balance of concessions' would be attained. The IT 'sector' spans many different products, and much of the negotiation involved discussions regarding the coverage of the agreement. The EU insisted that trading partners offer concessions on market access for alcoholic beverages as a condition for signing the ITA. Developing countries attempted to obtain concessions on textiles, although at the end of the day their negotiating leverage proved insufficient.[11]

The product coverage of the ITA ended up reflecting primarily the interests of the Quad. It deals only with a subset of the policies affecting trade in the IT products selected: the ITA is a tariff-only agreement. It proved impossible to address any nontariff policies affecting market access. Consumer electronics—products of greater interest to developing countries as suppliers than to the Quad—were not included under the ITA. The ITA is therefore a rather unbalanced agreement from a developing country perspective. Elimination of tariffs on the products included under the ITA will be of benefit to consumers in developing country signatories (including foreign investors), but no quid pro quo was obtained. Standard reciprocity and 'internalization' considerations of the type discussed in earlier chapters were important in the ITA. However, given that any deal would have to be applied on a MFN basis, the US insisted that the ITA signatories must cover at least 90 per cent of total production of the IT products included under the agreement.

The ITA was to a large extent the brainchild of major IT companies in the EU and US. These firms and their industry associations—the US Information Technology Industry Council, the European Association of Manufacturers of Business Machines and Information Technology Industry (EUROBIT) and the Japanese Electronic Development Association—were prime movers behind the initiative to eliminate tariffs on their products. They jointly developed recommendations for the February 1995 G7 ministerial conference on a Global Information Society, proposing that tariffs on the building blocks of the infrastructure of such a society be abolished by 2000. Industry groups continued to push the idea in the context of other fora, especially the Transatlantic Business Dialogue (TABD) and APEC. This

---

[11] At the time, some were calling the ITA the Information, Textiles and Alcohol Agreement (Fliess and Sauvé, 1998: 62).

constellation of interests was successful at the end of the day in abolishing tariffs on much of their output, but this success came at a cost. It essentially involved taking care of the concerns of a set of large and powerful enterprises in mostly OECD countries. These firms will in future have less of an incentive to support more general liberalization of their home markets.

The Declaration calls for periodic review of the product coverage of the ITA. The first such review took place very soon after the ITA was agreed. The associated talks and subsequent reviews are often described as working towards an 'ITA-2'. To date, no agreement has proved possible on extending the product coverage and going beyond tariffs to cover disciplines on NTMs. Extension of product coverage has been contentious because of disagreements on where to draw the boundary between an 'IT product' and other electronic products. Problems have also arisen on how to classify products that use new technologies and that were not explicitly listed in the original ITA schedules of signatories.

Disagreements between ITA members on such classification issues led to a formal dispute in the WTO in May 2008. The US and Japan contested decisions by the EU to impose tariffs on products such as cable boxes that can access the internet, certain flat panel LCD monitors, and computer printers that can also scan and fax documents. These tariffs created an inducement for export companies to assemble the final product inside the EU. The tariffs averaged 10 per cent, and were supported by new EU member countries such as Poland that had attracted substantial FDI in the affected high-tech sectors.

6.4. CONCLUSION

If GATT was perceived to lack teeth, it was in part due to the de facto exclusion of trade in agriculture and textiles and clothing from the reach of its disciplines. The agreements reached in the Uruguay Round therefore constituted a significant step forward in the process of reasserting the relevance of the general principles of nondiscrimination and open markets. Without these agreements the WTO would have been much less credible as an organization.

The examples of both agriculture and clothing have much to teach about the political economy of multilateral liberalization and negotiation. The agriculture case illustrates that if domestic lobbies are strong and can mobilize the support of other groups (who may be primarily driven by quite different objectives, including noneconomic reasons), multilateral cooperation can break down. Standard reciprocity does not work in the sense that intrasectoral tradeoffs are not feasible. The domestic interests seeking better access to foreign markets could be and were satisfied through negotiations that were limited to manufactures. The potential gains from trade in policies affecting market access for manufactures were more than large enough to allow significant progress to be made in reducing barriers to trade in manufactures. No linkage was required with agriculture, and US attempts to impose such linkages in recurrent MTNs failed because they were not credible. The cost of total breakdown of a MTN because of lack of agreement on agriculture was simply too great.

Progress was made in the late 1980s on agriculture because new interest groups appeared that sought to control agricultural support programmes. In the case of the EU, these included finance ministries. The adoption of the Maastricht treaty, which set targets for government deficits and public debt in the run-up towards European Monetary Union and the prospect of future enlargement of the EU maintained serious pressure on agricultural expenditure. The emergence of environmental lobbies also played a role. An increasing awareness of the environmental downside of intensive and polluting farming encouraged by existing production support policies helped to undercut support for production-increasing policies. Last but not least, the emergence of the Cairns Group was an important factor. It was less inclined than the US to compromise, as the issue was vital to export interests of the group, and therefore could act as both a proposal making and a blocking coalition.

Although internal political dynamics played an important role in reintegrating agricultural trade policies into the GATT/WTO, the power of the agricultural lobby remains very strong. Tariff protection remains formidable in many WTO members. Noneconomic considerations continue to play a major role in domestic and international discussions on agriculture. The AoA states that 'nontrade concerns' must be taken into account in future efforts to liberalize trade in this sector. The preamble to the agreement identifies food security, protection of the environment and ensuring the viability of rural areas as examples of objectives that may be realized through agricultural policies. The 'multifunctionality' of agriculture is frequently used by the EU and other WTO members as a justification for agricultural intervention. Where to draw the line regarding the 'legitimacy' of agricultural policies is an ongoing source of debate. However, there is no compelling rationale for permitting the use of trade measures to attain noneconomic objectives.

The Doha Round made clear how hard it is to use a MTN to generate significant additional liberalization of agriculture. The differences in interests across and within countries are great, and putting together a package of tradeoffs within the sector that was acceptable to the major players proved very difficult. The issue linkage literature discussed in Chapter 4 suggests that in such situations it is necessary to link agriculture to a broader agenda. With the removal of the Singapore issues in 2004, such linkage was largely limited to concessions by the major agricultural exporters on manufactures and/or services. In principle a good case can be made that there should have been enough on the table. In mid-2008 negotiators had come close to a deal on agriculture and NAMA modalities, but at the end of the day agricultural sensitivities led to yet another breakdown of talks—specifically the design of a special safeguard mechanism for agricultural imports.

The focus of the WTO is on policy bindings—the maximum level of protection that can be accorded to goods or services. Although what matters for exporters are applied levels of protection, this is not the focus of WTO negotiations. For many developing countries applied trade policies are much more liberal than is implied by their commitments in the WTO. As a result, deep 'liberalization' commitments associated with a specific formula to cut tariffs may not do much, if anything, to lower applied rates of protection. The extent of the 'binding overhang' is significant. For Brazil, for example, the import-weighted average tariff for agricultural merchandise is 40 per cent, compared to an applied average MFN rate of 10 per cent. Similar ratios prevail for other countries.

An important determinant of the perceived value of such bindings is what traders expect to happen in the future—is it likely that governments will raise tariffs above applied levels? Absent tariff bindings that are at, or close to, applied rates, under the WTO rules they are free to do so. If the expected probability of 'backsliding' is low, negotiators will be either (1) pressured to seek very deep cuts in bindings so as to reduce actual levels of protection; or (2) not pressured much insofar as exporters confront relatively low applied tariff barriers and see only a limited net benefit associated with further reductions (given the costs they need to expend to lobby for the cuts to be achieved) (Hoekman and Vines, 2007). Deep cuts in bindings may be resisted by negotiators as 'giving up too much'—in the Brazil case just mentioned to get close to the current applied average tariff, the cut in bound tariffs would have to be some 75 per cent. This is hard to sell politically at home—it appears to be a lot, even though such a cut would not do much to reduce actual levels of protection. The insistence by developing countries that they make less deep liberalization commitments than high-income countries makes it more difficult to agree on a level of reduction that would be meaningful in terms of actual liberalization. In principle there should be a feasible deal that links agriculture, manufactures and services, but the experience to date suggests that such a deal may need to put much greater emphasis on the value of binding unilateral (and regional) liberalization.

A different story applies in textiles and clothing. Here there were also powerful lobbies in OECD countries that were successful in obtaining protection. But there were no direct budgetary implications that created pressure to abolish such protection. Although regressive in income distribution terms, protection of textiles and clothing was not subject to strong opposition from consumer groups, in part because competition was not choked off completely as exporters diversified across developing country locations and firms in the domestic industry improved their productivity or exited. The explanation for the agreement to integrate textiles and clothing into the GATT in this case is more in line with standard reciprocal negotiating dynamics. Developing countries insisted on liberalization as a quid pro quo for agreeing to accept the TRIPS and GATS agreements. This gave the lobbies in the US and the EU, who sought disciplines on services policies and stronger enforcement of intellectual property law, an incentive to confront the domestic clothing industry. This industry had in any event become smaller, more specialized and itself increasingly engaged in international production. The lower quality garments industry had declined substantially in size in both the US and the EU in the 1980s, reducing its political clout. Here there is also much less scope to raise 'multifunctionality' concerns and argue that trade policies are required to meet noneconomic objectives. Nonetheless, liberalization will occur slowly. Textile and clothing tariffs continue to offer domestic industries levels of protection that greatly exceed those applying to other manufacturing industries. Moreover, import-competing industries are very well aware of the existence of antidumping and safeguard instruments.

6.5. FURTHER READING

T. Warley, 'Western Trade in Agricultural Products', in *International Economic Relations in the Western World 1959–71* (London: Royal Institute of International Affairs, 1976) provides a historical overview of agricultural policies and trade of OECD countries. L. Alan Winters, 'The Political Economy of the Agricultural Policy of Industrialized Countries', *European Review of Agricultural Economics*, 14 (1987): 285–304, discusses the question of why farmers have been able to obtain high levels of protection. The same author, in 'The So-called Noneconomic Objectives of Agricultural Support', *OECD Economic Studies*, 13 (1989): 238–66, critically addresses the rationales that have been offered for such policies. Anne Krueger, Maurice Schiff and Alberto Valdes, 'Agricultural Incentives in Developing Countries: Measuring the Effect of Sectoral and Economy-wide Policies', *World Bank Economic Review*, 2 (3) (1988): 255–72, analyse the effects of agricultural and nonagricultural policies on farmer's incentives in developing countries.

Tim Josling, Stefan Tangermann and T. Warley, *Agriculture in the GATT* (London: Macmillan, 1996) provide a comprehensive treatment of 40 years of discussions and negotiations on agriculture in the GATT, and include a summary evaluation of the Uruguay Round Agreement on Agriculture. Richard Higgott and Andrew Cooper, 'Middle Power Leadership and Coalition Building: Australia, the Cairns Group and the Uruguay Round', *International Organization*, 49 (1990): 589–32, discuss the formation and operation of the Cairns Group. Tim Josling, 'Agriculture in the Next WTO Round', in Jeffrey Schott (ed.), *The WTO After Seattle*

(Washington, DC: Institute for International Economics, 2000) discusses the agenda going into the Doha Round.

Kym Anderson and Will Martin (eds), *Agricultural Trade Reform and the Doha Development Agenda* (Basingstoke and Washington, DC: Palgrave Macmillan and the World Bank, 2006) collect a set of papers that analyse from an economic perspective what was being negotiated in the Doha Round. Kimberly Elliott, *Delivering on Doha: Farm Trade and the Poor* (Washington, DC: Petersen Institute for International Economics, 2006) gives a well-written accessible overview of the issues, challenges and impacts of agricultural policies and the approaches that were proposed to reduce support levels in the Doha Round.

Carl Hamilton (ed.), *Textiles Trade and the Developing Countries: Eliminating the Multifibre Arrangement in the 1990s* (Washington, DC: The World Bank, 1990) presents a set of papers that analyse and describe the workings of the MFA. Irene Trela and John Whalley's contribution to that volume provides quantitative estimates of the economic impact of the MFA. Craig Giesse and Martin Lewin give a detailed review of the history of the MFA in 'The Multifibre Arrangement: Temporary Protection Run Amuck', *Law and Policy in International Business*, 19 (1987): 51–170. Another good source is Vinod Aggarwal, *Liberal Protectionism: The International Politics of Organized Textile Trade* (Berkeley: University of California Press, 1985). O. G. Dayaratna and John Whalley, 'After the Multifibre Arrangement, the China Containment Agreements,' *Asia-Pacific Trade and Investment Review*, 3 (1) (2007): 29–54, discuss the period leading up to and immediately after the implementation of the ATC.

The negotiating history of the ITA is described in detail in Barbara Fliess and Pierre Sauvé, 'Of Chips, Floppy Disks and Great Timing: Assessing the WTO Information Technology Agreement' (Paris: Institut Français des Relations Internationales, 1998).

CHAPTER 7

TRADE IN
SERVICES

SERVICES—which include activities as disparate as transport of goods and people, financial intermediation, communications, distribution, hotels and restaurants, education, healthcare, construction and accounting—are vital to the functioning of any economy. Even in the lowest income countries, services generate at least 40 per cent of GDP. Services account for 70 per cent or more of economic activity in high-income countries. Common explanations for the rise in the share of services in output and employment as countries become richer include increasing specialization and exchange of services through the market ('outsourcing'), with an associated increase in variety and quality that may raise productivity of firms and welfare of final consumers, in turn increasing demand for purchased services and the fact that the scope for (labour) productivity improvements in the provision of many services is less than in agriculture and manufacturing. The latter implies that over time the (real) costs of these services will rise relative to merchandise, as will their share of employment (Baumol, 1967; Fuchs, 1968).

Services are essential inputs into the production of all industries. Service sector policies therefore can have a major effect on economic performance. Starting in the 1980s, many countries began to undertake regulatory reforms to increase the contestability of service markets. In part these reforms were driven by changes in technologies that allowed competition to emerge in markets that were traditionally regarded as natural monopolies. Service sector reforms were also supported by manufacturing and agricultural interests. In order to benefit from the process of globalization with its attendant 'splintering' or 'fragmentation' of the production chain (see Chapter 1), enterprises must have access to efficient service inputs. As nations reduce tariffs and other barriers to trade, effective rates of protection for manufacturing industries may become negative if they continue to be confronted with input prices that are higher than they would be if services markets were contestable. It is therefore not surprising that liberalization and regulatory reform of service markets began to emerge as a high-profile policy issue in the 1980s. Nor is it surprising that governments started to focus on policies affecting trade and investment in services, as service suppliers started to recognize the existence of a rapidly growing international market.

The initiative to consider rules for trade in services was launched by the US in the early 1980s. The US perceived it had a comparative advantage in services, and sought to link further liberalization of 'old trade' to progress in liberalizing trade in services. An initial attempt to put services on the GATT negotiating agenda was made by the US during the 1982 GATT ministerial meeting. This attempt met with vigorous resistance on the part of many contracting parties and agreement could not be reached to negotiate in this area. However, the meeting did result in establishing a GATT work programme on services, with the major countries agreeing to undertake national studies of their services sectors with a view to documenting status quo policies and better understanding the potential implications of applying GATT-type rules to trade in services. This helped to generate a spate of research on an issue that had been virtually ignored by trade economists.

A major result of the Uruguay Round was the creation of the General Agreement on Trade in Services (GATS). By establishing rules and disciplines on policies affecting access to service markets, the GATS greatly extended the coverage of the multilateral trading system. This chapter starts with brief overviews of global trade flows in services, the barriers that restrict such trade and the economics of service sector protection and liberalization. This is followed by a summary of the main elements of the GATS and its operation to date, as well as efforts during the Doha Round to expand the coverage of the agreement. The chapter ends with a brief assessment of the usefulness of the GATS as an instrument for the pursuit of service sector reform and suggestions for further reading.

7.1. CONCEPTUAL AND EMPIRICAL QUESTIONS

Liberalizing trade in services was long thought to be an oxymoron, as historically many services have been nontradable. If trade occurred, the services tended to be embodied in goods, information flows or in people. Although trade in some services such as transportation has always been significant, technological changes have made an increasing number of services and tasks more tradable, resulting in a rapid expansion in trade.

Trade in services differs from trade in goods because services tend to be intangible and nonstorable (Box 7.1). Proximity between providers and demanders is often required for exchange to be feasible (Bhagwati, 1984; Sampson and Snape, 1985). Although more and more transactions may occur across borders (using telecommunications media), permitting provider and demander to be in different geographic locations, many services continue to require that provider and consumer be in the same place at the same time. This constraint can be satisfied through physical movement of consumers to the location of service providers (an example is tourism), or via the entry of service providers into the territory of a consumer (for example, management consulting). In a statistical sense all the above transactions comprise trade and are registered as such in the balance of payments as long as the movements of consumers and providers are short term, generally defined as lasting less than one year. They all involve exchanges between the resident of one country and that of another.

Establishment of a commercial presence in a country—engaging in foreign direct investment (FDI)—is another way of contesting services markets. If cross-border, long-distance exchange or temporary physical movement of either provider or consumer does not suffice for an exchange to be feasible, firms can only sell their services in foreign markets by establishing a long-term physical presence. In national accounts statistics the sales of the foreign affiliates or branches do not

Box 7.1. Services are different

Services have unique characteristics that differentiate them from manufactured products in international trade. The characteristics most frequently noted include:

- Intangibility—services are difficult to touch. To paraphrase the newspaper *The Economist*, services are products you cannot drop on your foot. Consequently, international transactions in services are often difficult to monitor, measure and tax.
- Nonstorability—it is often impossible to store services in inventory; services are typically produced and consumed at the same time. This implies that not only is it more difficult to trade services across space, but it is also difficult to trade across time.
- Heterogeneity—services are often nonstandardized and highly tailored to the needs of customers. There is therefore a considerable degree of variation in what is effectively supplied across international borders. The extent of product differentiation is very great.
- Joint production—services are typically produced with some input by the demander. That is, customers participate in the production process, providing critical information or feedback to providers that partly determines the latter's efficiency and productivity (in business school parlance, services are often a high-touch industry).

These characteristics help explain why a different approach was taken towards the design of multilateral disciplines for trade in services as compared to goods.

represent trade. However, as discussed below, in the WTO it does. As of the early 1990s, some 50 per cent of the global stock of FDI involved services activities, up from only 25 per cent in 1970. It rose to 60 per cent as of 2005, with the global stock of FDI exceeding the US$10 trillion mark (UNCTAD, 2007).

Available data on trade in services are very weak compared to those on merchandise. Only a limited number of industrialized countries collect and report statistics on trade in services at a relatively disaggregated level (ten categories or more). Most non-OECD countries only report data on trade in so-called commercial services, broken down into transport (largely freight and passenger transport by sea and air), travel (expenditures by nonresidents—mostly tourists—while staying in a foreign country) and other services. The last category includes items such as brokerage, insurance, communications, leasing and rental of equipment, technical and professional services, and income generated by the temporary movement of labour, as well as property income (royalties).

Global cross-border trade in services stood at US$2.7 trillion in 2006, of which 50 per cent was in the nontravel (tourism) and nontransport categories. Excluding intra-EU cross-border trade, the total is some US$2 trillion. As total trade in merchandise was some US$12.5 trillion in 2006, cross-border trade in services reported in balance-of-payments statistics is a bit over 20 per cent of world trade as measured by the balance of payments. Despite the often expressed view that services trade has been expanding rapidly as a result of services outsourcing and offshoring, the share of services receipts in total trade has remained relatively constant since the 1980s. In part this is because of the dynamic growth that has occurred in merchandise trade—driven by fragmentation and global production sharing intra-industry trade—and in part it reflects the fact that many services remain less or nontradable. The relatively constant share of total services in world trade hides large changes in the composition of trade. Much of the growth in cross-border services trade since 1990 has been in so-called business process outsourcing (BPO) services, which is captured in the balance-of-payments category 'other commercial services'. The rapid growth in trade in such activities has led to a significant decline in the shares of more traditional services—transport and travel (Figure 7.1). Relative to the size of domestic services activities, to date the extent of internationalization of services is still quite limited (Bhagwati, Panagariya and Srinivasan, 2004; Amiti and Wei, 2005).

The relative importance of trade in services (as registered in the balance of payments of a country) as opposed to sales of services by affiliates is not known for the world as a whole. This is because comprehensive data on the latter do not exist given that, once established, foreign firms are considered to be residents of the host country. Data reported by a number of OECD members indicate that 'foreign affiliate trade in services' (FATS)—the value of sales of services by affiliates of multinationals—is roughly 50 per cent greater than cross-border exports of services. In the case of the US, the value of outward FATS is significantly greater than

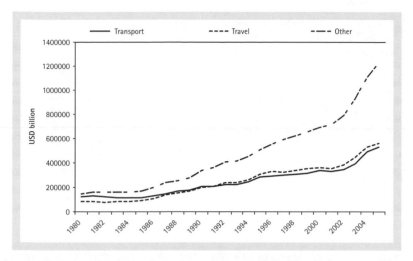

Fig. 7.1. Global cross-border trade in services, 1980–2006

Source: IMF balance of payment statistics.

cross-border trade, a pattern that has held since the mid-1990s (Figure 7.2). It may well be that increased services outsourcing will result in cross-border trade in services coming to dominate the value of FATS at some point in the future, but this is not the case today.

Extrapolating from the fact that FATS is 50 per cent greater than cross-border trade for the countries reporting such data, applying the factor 1.5 to other

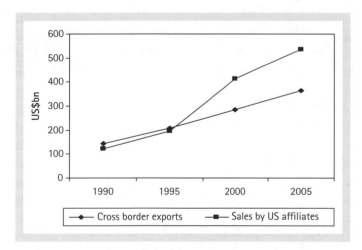

Fig. 7.2. US exports of services and sales of services by US foreign affiliates

Source: US Department of Commerce, Bureau of Economic Analysis.

Table 7.1. Trade in services by mode of supply, 2006

Mode of supply	Category	Value (US$ billion)	Share (%)
Cross-border	Transport and other commercial services	2,000	41.2
Consumer movement	Travel	750	15.5
Commercial presence	Sales by foreign affiliates	2,000	41.2
Temporary entry	Compensation of employees	100	2.1
Total		4,850	100.0

Source: Author's estimates, based on WTO (2007).

commercial services trade of about US$1.4 trillion gives a 'guesstimate' of the total value of FATS of some US$2 trillion.[1] That in turn suggests that aggregate international transactions in services are almost US$5 trillion (Table 7.1). Note that payments associated with the temporary entry of service providers is of trivial quantitative importance. Although probably an underestimate, the low figure reflects the stringent barriers that affect this mode of supply—the potential for greater trade in services through temporary movement of natural persons is very large.

Although in aggregate value terms global trade in services is dominated by OECD countries—which account for about 80 per cent of the total—many developing countries are relatively specialized in exporting services. Small developing countries in particular (defined as those with less than one million people) often derive a large proportion of total foreign exchange revenues from the sale of services. In many cases this reflects mostly tourism. However, a number of developing countries have also become large exporters of transactions processing and related back-office services and information and software development services. The best known example is India, which has become increasingly specialized in services. But many other countries have also registered double-digit export growth rates (Figure 7.3). The high business service export growth rates for developing countries increased their share of global trade to 22 per cent in 2006. Most of this increase reflects expanding exports of Asian countries, which doubled their global market share to 15 per cent.

---

[1] An alternative way of guestimating the total value of FATS is to use the information on global stocks of FDI. For the US, the stock of outward FDI in 2003 was some US$1.8 trillion, of which US$1.3 trillion was in services (UNCTAD 2005). Given FATS of US$477 billion in 2003, this gives a sales/stock ratio of 0.35 for the US. Assuming this applies more generally, given that the total stock of FDI in services was some US$6 trillion in 2006, this generates a global FATS guesstimate of US$2 trillion.

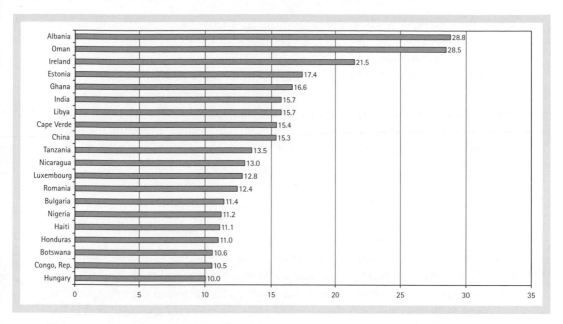

Fig. 7.3. Average growth rate of commercial service exports, 1990–2005

7.2. BARRIERS AND POTENTIAL GAINS FROM POLICY REFORMS

Cross-country data on the magnitude of barriers to trade in services do not exist. Because services are generally intangible and nonstorable, barriers to trade do not take the form of import tariffs. Instead, trade barriers take the form of prohibitions, QRs and government regulation. Quantitative restrictions may limit the quantity or value of imports of specific products for a given time period, or restrict the number or market share of foreign providers of services that are allowed to establish. Such discriminatory QRs are often complemented by nondiscriminatory measures applying equally to foreign and domestic providers. These may consist of limitations on the number of firms allowed to contest a market, or on the nature of their operations. Frequently, this involves either a monopoly (telecommunications) or an oligopolistic market structure (insurance). Considerations relating to consumer protection, prudential supervision and regulatory oversight often induce governments to require establishment by foreign providers or to reserve activities for government-owned or controlled entities.

A distinction needs to be made between policies that discriminate on the basis of nationality of ownership of factors of production, and whether policies affect entry into a market—through whatever mode of supply, including establishment/FDI—and/or the operation of firms (see, e.g. Deardorff and Stern, 2008). This can alternatively be thought about in terms of whether policies affect fixed or variable costs, and whether they create rents for incumbent (domestic) firms. Table 7.2 illustrates the various possibilities.

Two different approaches have been taken to assess the magnitude and impact of policy barriers to trade. The first involves collection of information on applied policies, converting these into coverage/frequency indicators and using the resulting indices as explanatory variables in a statistical analysis to explain observed measures of prices or costs. The second approach is to rely on indirect methods such as calculation of price–cost margins by sector across countries or gravity regressions to estimate what trade flows 'should be' and back out an estimate of the tariff equivalent of policies from the difference between estimated and observed flows. A well-known problem with indirect approaches is that it is not possible to attribute price–cost margins or differences in trade volumes to specific policies— other factors such as the business cycle and natural barriers to trade/contestability will also play a role. Most of the literature has therefore pursued the first approach.

Efforts to directly measure the extent of policy barriers on a sectoral and cross-country basis employ a policy index of some kind that is used to estimate the price, cost or quantity effects of policies. The policy indices are constructed by identifying existing policies towards entry/establishment and seeking to determine if policies differentiate between domestic and foreign firms. For example, in the case of distribution services, a country may have restrictions on nationality of workers, limits on operating hours, restrictions on size and location, rules that prevent advertising through specific types of product promotions, product carve outs for state monopolies and limits on the temporary entry of workers (engineers, executives, etc.). What is needed is to identify the set of potentially pertinent policies and to assign relative weights to them, something which requires sectoral expertise and is inherently subjective.

Table 7.2. A typology of policies affecting trade in services

	Impact on Entry/Establishment	Impact on Operations
Nondiscriminatory	For example, a limit of two mobile phone providers permitted to operate in the country	For example, all retail banks must have personnel on call to monitor and service ATMs
Discriminatory	For example, nationality requirements for senior managers of affiliates; maximum equity ownership limit for foreign investors	For example, car and fire insurance subject to additional capital requirements; cross-border provision of insurance services subject to price regulation

Once indices of policy have been constructed, these can be used to estimate their price and/or cost effects, controlling for standard determinants of performance for the sector concerned. A problem in doing this is to distinguish the effects of nondiscriminatory regulation from discriminatory policies. Regulations generally will increase fixed and/or variable costs of production for firms, and may result in a *de facto* or *de jure* exclusion of new entry, thereby increasing prices. Insofar as regulation is motivated by market failures created by the characteristics of specific service industries—e.g. network externalities, asymmetric information—such price impacts may be social-welfare-enhancing. A number of the price and cost estimates of the impacts of the restrictiveness indices generated by researchers are reported in Table 7.3. These suggest there is significant variation in the extent of discrimination against foreign providers.

The consensus view is that the tariff equivalents of prevailing restrictions are a multiple of those that restrict merchandise trade (Hoekman, 2007). A recent survey undertaken by the World Bank of the extent of discriminatory policies restricting entry by foreign firms in specific services markets in 56 developing countries found significant heterogeneity (Gootiz and Mattoo, 2008). Many sectors are open, especially for FDI. However, in many sectors various restrictions continue to be imposed, and some sectors remain completely closed. 'Sensitive' sectors vary by country reflecting differences in comparative advantage and the legacy of past policies. Many countries maintain foreign equity or entry restrictions for certain services markets. In India, for example, a number of key 'backbone' services sectors were liberalized in the last decade. Barriers to entry by new private firms have been eliminated in telecommunications and freight transport, and are being phased out in insurance and banking. However, restrictions on foreign ownership remain. Professional services like accountancy and legal, retail distribution, postal and rail transport services are formally closed to foreign participation. Moreover, barriers to entry in a number of services sectors, ranging from telecommunications to professional services, are maintained not only against foreign suppliers but also against new domestic suppliers.

Overall, the literature suggests business services such as consultancy are among the least protected sectors. Barriers to competition are higher in transportation, professional services, finance and fixed-line telecommunications. Policies are generally more restrictive in developing countries (Figure 7.4).

The estimates in the literature suggest that although services trade barriers can be significant, there is generally much variation. This reflects the fact that in the late 1980s and throughout the 1990s many countries took action to increase competition on services markets by liberalizing FDI, opening access to foreign competition in backbone sectors such as transport and telecommunications, and privatizing state-owned or controlled service providers. These developments helped support the observed increase in trade flows—both services and goods—and led to a marked increase in the magnitude of services FDI flows and changes in their composition. UNCTAD (2005) reports that in 1970 finance and trade (distribution)

Table 7.3. Selected estimates of price/cost impacts of services policies

Sector	Source and period covered	Measure	OECD countries			Developing countries		
			Simple average	σ	N	Simple average	σ	N
Maritime shipping	Clark, Dollar and Micco (2001); 2000	Percentage impact on shipping costs of mandatory use of certain port services	2.0	2.6	21	5.6	3.5	32
Air transport: economy fare	Doove et al. (2001); late 1990s	Estimated increase (%) in fares over an estimated 'free trade' level for a set of bilateral routes	30.6	19.5	23	63.9	19.6	12
Air transport: APEX discount fare	Doove et al. (2001); late 1990s	Estimated increase (%) in fares over an estimated 'free trade' level for a set of bilateral routes	8.9	4.4	23	16.8	3.5	12
Retail food distribution	Kalirajan (2000)	Impact on costs of barriers on foreign establishment	2.7	1.7	12	2.3	3.2	6
Retail banking	Kalirajan et al. (2000); 1996-97	Percentage impact on net interest margins of discriminatory policies	11.8	11.6	7 (a)	31.8	19.0	9
Engineering	Nguyen-Hong (2000); 1996	Impact of barriers to FDI on price cost margins (%)	5.2	4.1	14	8.4	4.3	6
Mobile telecom	Doove et al. (2001); 1997	Price impact (%) of regulatory policies relative to a notional benchmark regime	26	27	24	21	15	18
International telecom	Doove et al. (2001); 1997	Price impact (%) of regulatory policies relative to a notional benchmark regime	73	61	24	34	9	18

Notes: (a), includes the EU-15 as one observation; σ, standard deviation; N, number of observations.

Source: Data compiled in part from tables reported in Deardorff and Stern (2008), drawing on Findlay and Warren (2000) and Dee (2005).

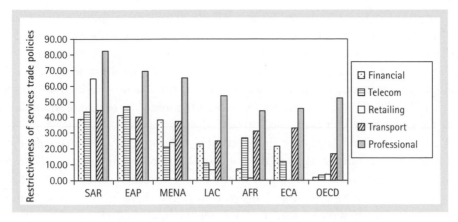

Fig. 7.4. Services trade restrictiveness indices by region and sector

Note: There are in total 76 countries.

Source: Gootiz and Mattoo (2008).

accounted for 65 per cent of the total stock; this dropped to 45 per cent in 2003. Conversely, the share of telecoms, energy, and business services has risen from 17 to 44 per cent. There are significant differences in the composition of FDI inflows into developed and developing countries. Business services accounted for 40 per cent of the total inward FDI stock in developing countries in 2003, compared to only 20 per cent in the OECD.

Gains from policy reform

Services are no different from goods in terms of the economic effects of removing barriers to trade and allowing greater competition from foreign providers. Inefficient firms will be forced to improve their performance or exit the market; more efficient firms will expand and new firms, products and techniques will enter markets. These resource re-allocation effects will improve welfare, although households and communities that were dependent on firms that cannot meet the competition will confront adjustment costs and losses. If there are economies of scale, and greater foreign participation is associated with increased competition, there will be a larger scale of activity, and hence scope for economic growth-enhancing effects as well. There is nothing special about trade here: if greater scale can be achieved merely by eliminating domestic barriers to entry and attracting domestic resources from other sectors this would also generate larger endogenous growth. However, a key difference between trade in goods and services in terms of their growth impact is that 'imports' of services often must be locally produced. If foreign participation merely substitutes for domestic production and the sector does not expand, i.e. the degree of competition remains unchanged, then there may be no positive growth impacts. More generally, if greater technology and knowledge transfer accompanies services liberalization—either embodied in FDI or disembodied—this will stimulate the potential growth impact of pro-competitive policy reforms. There is substantial empirical evidence demonstrating that technology diffuses through trade in goods and affects total factor productivity growth (see e.g. Hoekman and Javorcik 2006). At least theoretically, the same should hold true for technology that is diffused through flows of services.

Compared to the literature on the effects of liberalization of trade in goods, there is much less research focusing on the impacts of services trade reforms. To a large extent this is due to the weaknesses of the data on both policies and outcomes (performance of firms). Bearing that caveat in mind, there has been a significant amount of research in recent years that documents that the effects of policy reforms in services can be significant. In a cross-section, cross-country regression analysis, Mattoo, Rathindran and Subramanian (2006) find that controlling for other determinants of growth, countries with open financial and telecommunications sectors grew, on average, about one percentage point faster than other countries. Fully liberalizing both the telecommunications and the financial services sectors was associated with an average growth rate 1.5 percentage points above that of other countries. Eschenbach and Hoekman (2006a) utilize three indicators of the 'quality' of policy in banking, nonbank financial services and infrastructure, constructed by the European Bank for Reconstruction and Development (EBRD) spanning the period 1990–2004 to investigate the impact of changes in services policy, including liberalization, on economic performance over this period for a sample of 20 transition economies. They find that changes in policies towards financial and infrastructure services, including telecommunications, power and transport, are highly correlated with inward FDI. Services policy reforms are statistically significant explanatory variables for the post-1990 economic performance of the transition economies in their sample.

The positive association between policy reforms in services and inward FDI in services, and between total factor productivity growth performance of firms that use services and this FDI is perhaps the most robust finding to emerge from the limited empirical research on the impacts of services reforms. For example, Arnold, Javorcik and Mattoo (2007) analyse the effects of allowing foreign providers greater access to services industries on the productivity of manufacturing industries relying on services inputs. The results, based on firm-level data from the Czech Republic for the period 1998–2003, show a positive relationship between FDI in services and the performance of domestic firms in manufacturing. In related research focusing on Africa that uses data from over 1,000 firms in ten Sub-Saharan African economies, Arnold, Mattoo and Narciso (2006) find a statistically significant positive relationship between firm performance and the performance of three service input industries for which data were collected through enterprise surveys (access to communications, electricity and financial services). Arnold,

Javorcik, Lipscomb and Mattoo (2008), using panel data for 10,000 Indian firms for the 1990–2005 period, focus on the link between services sector reforms and manufacturing productivity and export propensity. The reforms are associated with a significant increase of FDI into services, outpacing FDI into goods. They find a significant positive relationship between policy reforms in banking, tele-communications and transport and the productivity of Indian firms in manufac-turing industries. Enterprises that rely more intensively on services such as banking and telecommunications have higher total factor productivity growth rates. Although services reforms benefit both foreign and locally owned manufacturing firms, the effects on foreign firms tend to be stronger.

The trade literature has devoted much attention to the effects of 'trade costs'—the nontariff-related costs that are incurred in getting goods from point of pro-duction to point of consumption. Many of the determinants of trade costs are services-related. The most obvious source of such costs is infrastructure-related services. Limão and Venables (2001) estimate that poor infrastructure accounts for 40 per cent of predicted transport costs for coastal countries and up to 60 per cent for landlocked countries. Francois and Manchin (2007) conclude that infrastruc-ture is a significant determinant not only of export levels, but also of the likelihood exports will take place at all. They find that basic infrastructure (communications and transportation) explains substantially more of the overall sample variation in exports than do the trade barriers faced by developing countries.

Such cost factors reflect the specific role of 'transport' services—they are inter-mediates that help determine the costs of trade in goods and thus the producer prices received by firms. The impact on trade (and welfare) of lowering transport-related costs may be much larger proportionately than those that can be obtained from merchandise trade liberalization because transport costs generate real resource costs as opposed to rents (Deardorff, 2001). Insofar as policy generates redundant procedures and duplication of fixed costs, the potential gains from liberalization of 'trade services' are likely to be large.

Francois and Wooton (2007) note that trade in goods may depend on the degree of market power exercised by the domestic trade and distribution sectors. An absence of competition in the domestic distribution service sector can serve as an effective import barrier against goods. Their econometric results point to statistically sign-ificant linkages between effective market access conditions for goods and the struc-ture of the domestic service sector. An implication is that services liberalization can boost trade in goods. More important, by ignoring the structure of the domestic service sector, the benefits of tariff reductions may be overstated. They also find that competition in distribution and related sectors matters more for poorer and smaller exporting countries than for others. This is intuitive, in that small players will have less, if any, ability to counteract the exercise of market power they confront.

Other research has illustrated the interdependence between the efficiency of available domestic service sectors and trade in goods. For example, Francois and

Reinert (1996) document that the importance of services for export performance rises with per capita incomes—business, distribution and communications services become the most important sectoral elements of overall exports in terms of inter-industry linkages. Fink, Mattoo and Neagu (2005) show that international communication costs are a determinant of export performance for higher value, differentiated products, whereas they matter less for more homogenous, bulk-type commodity trade.

Numerous 'services inputs' therefore affect the volume and composition of trade, whether in goods or services. Many of these input costs will factor into the overall level of trade costs confronting firms. Actions to reduce these excess costs and improve quality will enhance the competitiveness of firms located in the markets concerned, with an aggregate effect that is akin to a depreciation of the real exchange rate. Which factors are more important than others will vary across countries. Wilson, Mann and Otsuki (2005) use a gravity model to estimate the effects of four 'trade cost' variables, two of which are services-related: port efficiency, customs clearance, the regulatory environment more broadly and service sector infrastructure (telecommunications, e-business) across 75 countries for the 2000–1 period. The total potential expansion in trade in manufactures from trade facilitation improvements in all the four areas—raising performance of 'underperformers' to the average in the sample—is estimated to be US$377 billion. On average, their port efficiency variable—which includes both maritime transport and airports—account for more than half of the trade costs imposed by policies in their four areas.

The political economy of services liberalization

Depending on local circumstances and political constellations, governments may face more or less opposition to reforms that aim at increasing competition in service markets. Although often supported by other economic sectors, which have an interest in having access to a wide array of efficiently produced service inputs, final consumers may oppose liberalization because of concerns about a reduction in the frequency, quality or geographical coverage of services (e.g. telecommunications, transport, health, education). Labour unions may be concerned about the potential for large-scale layoffs by incumbent firms, and those in society who have benefitted from subsidized access to services may resist a change in the status quo that is expected to raise prices or restrict supply.

Thus, governments may be constrained in implementing reforms that would benefit society at large because of the opposition of politically powerful vested interests. International trade agreements offer a potential way for breaking domestic deadlocks by mobilizing groups to support reform. The traditional *raison d'être* of the GATT—that groups that would benefit from better access to export markets are induced to throw their weight behind import liberalization—should also apply in the services context, as long as export interests exist. Often, however, export interests in services are weaker than in manufacturing or agriculture because services are more difficult to trade. In OECD countries, for example, the ratio of exports to output is on average over six times less for services than for goods. In many instances, potentially tradable services are simply not traded at all; the barriers—whether natural or man-made—are prohibitive. As a result, the number and political weight of import-competing sectors may greatly exceed that of export-oriented service sectors interested in obtaining access to foreign markets. If so, there is greater need to mobilize support from exporters of merchandise that require access to competitively priced and high-quality service inputs if they are to be able to contest global markets. This in turn puts a high premium on the availability of information and analysis of the economic impact of status quo services policies. As important, the required cross-issue linkages may greatly complicate negotiations.

Given that FDI is a significant mode of supplying nontradable services, potential direct investors may have a strong 'export' interest and supply the traditional political economy dynamics that have driven negotiations. Moreover, opposition by domestic firms and labour to the prospect of increased competition from foreign firms may not be as strong in services as in goods. As already mentioned, the gross negative impact on labour employed in services is likely to be lower (given that foreign entrants will often use FDI and employ mostly nationals). The net impact on labour is more likely to be perceived to be positive (as total employment opportunities can be expected to expand). And support for reform by businesses that would benefit from higher quality and lower prices services is more likely to be stronger. Indeed, those that liberalize first may have a strategic advantage—creating further incentives to pursue domestic reforms. Narrow reciprocity, in the form of 'equivalent' concessions being offered by trading partners, is therefore likely to be less of a priority for countries than has been the case for merchandise trade liberalization (Hoekman and Messerlin, 2000).

Blanchard (2007) develops a formal model that provides insights into one possible channel that explains why unilateral reforms have been pursued and that provides an explanation for the lack of strong support by lobbies for the GATS process. She argues that the existence of investment flows (FDI) attenuates the need to use trade agreements to deal with terms of trade externalities. If firms are able to engage in FDI and do so, as more firms originating in any country-pair invest in each other's markets, governments will have less incentive to manipulate tariffs and other policies in an effort to improve their terms of trade. The reason is that doing so, assuming it is feasible and effective, will benefit the foreign firms located in a host market as well as domestic firms. The greater the foreign (FDI) share, the lower the incentive of the government to use border policies, and the less need to use the reciprocity mechanism in trade negotiations. An implication is that the larger are two-way FDI stocks, the more inclined governments are likely to be to lock these in: there is little, if any, downside to doing so. The GATS schedules are on average most far-reaching and comprehensive for mode 3, consistent with the analytical framework developed by Blanchard—presumably reflecting at least in part the large two-way FDI flows among the OECD countries, complemented by the desire on the part of many developing countries to attract FDI.

International agreements can also be helpful in providing focal points for regulatory reform, providing templates for domestic policy measures that are welfare-enhancing. An example is supporting the implementation of pro-competitive regulatory regimes. This is particularly important in the case of network-type services (such as financial and telecom services), where there is a need to deal with problems of asymmetric information (moral hazard, adverse selection) or to ensure universal service. One of the beneficial 'didactic' outcomes of the negotiations on financial services (discussed below) was that it helped educate decision-makers on the importance of distinguishing between liberalization and (de-) regulation. Liberalization involves the elimination of discrimination in the treatment of foreign and national services providers and removal of market access barriers—to both cross-border provision and establishment. But this does not restrict the government's ability to enforce regulatory regimes, undertake prudential supervision, conduct monetary policy or manage external capital flows (Key, 1997). The same applies to other sectors. In all cases, however, the required regulatory capacity must be there, if needed. In principle, multilateral negotiations can help by identifying good regulatory practices and principles that governments should consider adopting, as well as criteria or necessary conditions that must be met before certain reforms should be undertaken.

Another important potential beneficial role multilateral agreements can play is to enhance the credibility of a government's economic policy stance. This can be very important for countries where there is a history of policy reversal. The WTO offers mechanisms for governments to pre-commit to a reform path and to lock-in reforms that have already been achieved. However, the credibility impact of WTO commitments depends on the probability that export interests will contest violations of an agreement. As discussed in Chapter 3, the credibility payoff for small countries may be limited, as exporters in large nations may have little interest in 'suing' such countries.

Many service activities are highly regulated. The regulatory agencies involved have a vested interest in defending their turf, complicating the needed interagency coordination and cooperation in a negotiating context (Feketekuty, 1988). At the same time, there is frequently a need for appropriate regulation. Regulators may have greater objections to liberalization of cross-border exchange than to FDI, as it is more difficult for them to control industries located in foreign jurisdictions. They may prefer that establishment is required as a mode, as this ensures that they will maintain their control of the activity involved. Whatever their preferences may be, trade negotiators on services must interact and consult with the relevant regulatory authorities, which makes it more complex to engage in negotiations. Such complexity is made worse in the case of federal states where the central government often does not have the authority to make commitments on behalf of lower level governments.

Another variable that distinguishes services from goods liberalization is that if FDI is the preferred mode of supply, adjustment will be associated with transfers of ownership of industry. Opposition from affected bureaucracies and from groups with noneconomic concerns (such as the impact of 'denationalization' on national culture) may further increase the complexity of liberalization efforts with respect to services. The challenge for policymakers is to enhance foreign competition while ensuring that the need for regulation of service providers is satisfied. This requires that the case for liberalization be distinguished from the need for regulation or regulatory reform. Regulation to achieve fiduciary, public health or cultural objectives should be in place and strengthened where necessary, and should apply equally to domestic and foreign providers.

Although there are substantial potential benefits from liberalizing key services sectors, these gains cannot be realized by a mechanical opening up of services markets. Governments have an important role to play in putting in place the pre-conditions for an efficient set of service industries, bolstering the case for focusing on key inputs like education and (institutional) infrastructure. Also important is the design of reform programmes. A flawed reform programme can undermine the benefits of liberalization. For example, if privatization of state monopolies is conducted without taking actions to foster greater competition, the result may be merely transfers of monopoly rents to private owners (possibly foreigners). Similarly, if increased entry into financial sectors is not accompanied by adequate prudential supervision, the result may be insider lending and poor investment decisions. Also, if policies to ensure wider access to services are not put in place, liberalization need not improve access to essential services for the poor. Managing reforms of services markets therefore requires integrating trade opening with a careful combination of competition and regulation. Doing so will often be critical to mobilize the political support needed to launch and to sustain efficiency-enhancing policy reforms.

7.3. THE GATS

As an integral part of the WTO, the GATS entered into force on 1 January 1995. A major innovation for the global trading system, which until 1995 covered only trade in goods, the GATS was the result of a 15-year discussion that commenced in the early 1980s. As mentioned in the introduction to this chapter, services were put on the GATT agenda in the early 1980s by the US. Before and during the 1986 ministerial meeting in Punta del Este, Uruguay many developing countries defended the view that new negotiations should not address services. This position was defended most vigorously by the so-called G10—a group of ten developing countries (Argentina, Brazil, Cuba, Egypt, India, Nicaragua, Nigeria, Peru, Tanzania and Yugoslavia)—which rejected launching talks on services, as well as trade-related aspects of intellectual property rights and TRIMs. In the event the majority prevailed, adopting a draft text proposed by Colombia and Switzerland. The main concession to the G10 was agreement that the services negotiations would proceed on a parallel track from talks on goods. Notwithstanding this procedural agreement, it was agreed that the negotiations were to be a 'single undertaking'.

The nonexistence of a common set of border barriers such as tariffs greatly complicated the life of negotiators seeking to agree to incrementally reduce barriers to services trade. As discussed in Chapter 4, negotiators require a focal point—some tangible variable enabling parties to set objectives and assess negotiating progress. Lack of data on trade and the complexities associated with identifying and quantifying barriers to trade made a GATT-type approach—exchanging equivalent 'amounts' of trade liberalization—impossible to emulate. Rather than focusing on the identification, quantification and reduction of barriers, subjective notions of sectoral reciprocity became the focal point of negotiations. This contrasts with the 'first-difference' approach to reciprocity used in tariff negotiations (Bhagwati, 1988).

Thinking on services evolved considerably over the course of the negotiations. Early in the negotiations, many developing countries argued that the lack of data on services trade justified excluding service transactions involving establishment by foreign providers from any agreement. In this they were supported by UNCTAD, which proposed that trade in services be defined to occur only when the majority of value added was produced by nonresidents (UNCTAD, 1985). This definition excluded virtually all transactions through FDI, as foreign factors of production that relocate are generally considered to become residents of the host country for economic accounting purposes. Great emphasis was put on the need for governments to be able to impose conditions on inward FDI and support domestic industries. This implied that a generally applicable national treatment obligation of the type found in the GATT was unacceptable.

The US went into the negotiations with the most liberal proposal: MFN was to apply to all signatories and national treatment was to be a binding, general obligation. Trade was to be defined broadly, including FDI (commercial presence). All measures limiting market access were to be put on the table. The EU also entered into the negotiations with the view that trade in services should be defined so as to include all types of transactions required to achieve effective market access. The EU proposed establishing a committee to determine the 'appropriateness' of regulations, with inappropriate measures to become the subject of liberalization negotiations and commitments on a sector-by-sector basis for all participating countries. Any framework agreement for trade in services was to involve only limited obligations of a generally binding nature. National treatment was to be negotiated on a sector-by-sector basis.

Thus, both the EU and major developing countries expressed an early preference for an agreement with relatively soft obligations—the EU arguing that national treatment should only apply to specific sectors, major developing countries opposing even that. Only the US and a number of small open economies—both OECD members and newly industrialized countries like Singapore—were in favour of a 'hard' agreement along GATT lines from the start, with generally binding obligations and universal sectoral coverage. At the end of the day, the EU-developing country preference for a relatively soft framework agreement prevailed. In return for acceptance that trade in services be defined to include all four possible modes of supply and that certain nondiscriminatory measures restricting market access were in principle negotiable, national treatment became a sector-specific commitment. It was also agreed that scheduling of specific commitments would be on both a sector-by-sector and mode-of-supply basis.

Throughout the negotiations lobbies played an important role. The inclusion of services on the Uruguay Round agenda was due in no small part to the efforts of a number of large, mostly American, service companies to get the topic on the table. Leading players in this effort included financial institutions such as American Express and American International Group and professional services firms such as Arthur Anderson (Heeter, 1997). As discussed below, a major difference between the Uruguay and Doha Rounds was the visibility and level of lobbying activity by the private sector in support of an ambitious outcome.

The basic rules

The GATS consists of four main elements.[2]
    (1) a set of general concepts, principles and rules that apply to all measures affecting trade in services;
    (2) specific commitments that apply only to service sectors and subsectors listed in a member's schedule;
    (3) an understanding that periodic negotiations will be undertaken to progressively liberalize trade in services; and
    (4) a set of attachments, protocols and annexes that set out sector-specific disciplines and ministerial decisions that relate to the implementation of the agreement.

[2] Parts of this section draw on Hoekman and Mattoo (2007).

Instead of attempting to define what a service is—long inconclusive debates had rapidly made clear that this would be an unproductive endeavour—GATS negotiators simply adopted a list of services that is based on the UN Central Product Classification:

<table>
<tr><td>1. Business services</td><td>7. Financial services</td></tr>
<tr><td>2. Communication services</td><td>8. Health-related and social services</td></tr>
<tr><td>3. Construction services</td><td>9. Tourism and travel-related services</td></tr>
<tr><td>4. Distribution services</td><td>10. Recreational, cultural and sporting services</td></tr>
<tr><td>5. Educational services</td><td>11. Transport services</td></tr>
<tr><td>6. Environmental services</td><td>12. Other services not elsewhere included.</td></tr>
</table>

Each of these sectors is further subdivided into a total of over 150 activities. Trade is defined (in Article I) to include four modes of supply:

- *Mode 1—Cross-border*: services supplied from the territory of one member into the territory of another. An example is software services supplied by a supplier in one country through mail or electronic means to consumers in another country.
- *Mode 2—Consumption abroad*: services supplied in the territory of one member to the consumers of another. Examples are where the consumer moves, e.g. to consume tourism or education services in another country. Also covered are activities such as ship repair abroad, where only the property of the consumer moves.
- *Mode 3—Commercial presence*: services supplied through any type of business or professional establishment of one member in the territory of another. An example is an insurance company owned by citizens of one country establishing a branch in another country.
- *Mode 4—Presence of natural persons*: services supplied by nationals of one member in the territory of another. This mode includes both independent service suppliers, and employees of the services supplier of another member. Examples are a doctor of one country supplying through his physical presence services in another country, or the foreign employees of a foreign bank.

Any measure affecting the supply of services through any of these modes is covered by the GATS. However, the agreement does not apply to services supplied in the exercise of governmental functions, to measures affecting natural persons seeking access to the employment market of a member, or to measures regarding citizenship, residence or employment on a permanent basis. The inclusion of commercial presence as a mode extends the reach of the agreement to measures affecting FDI, and the inclusion of presence of natural persons to measures affecting the entry of foreign nationals, both of which have traditionally been a tightly controlled province of national government.

The dispute regarding the EU regime for the importation, sale and distribution of bananas (the *Bananas* case.[3] clarified that a broad interpretation of the term 'affecting' is implied in the GATS. That is, measures need not affect trade in services as such but could also be measures taken in other areas that affect services—such as measures in respect of the purchase of goods. In *Bananas* the complainants argued that the EU method of distributing import licences violated the GATS because ACP bananas were largely distributed by EU-based entities. The EU argued that a number of non-EU distributors were allocated quotas for these bananas and that there was therefore no violation of national treatment in distribution. The panel decided to focus not on the nationality of providers, but on the question of allocation of licences. It recognized that '[t]he operator category rules apply to service suppliers regardless of their nationality, ownership or control' (para. 7.324), but concluded that the allocation scheme nonetheless affected the conditions of competition. Thus, the focus was on outcomes (the 'market share' held by EU firms), and not on discrimination per se. The Canada *Autopact* panel, brought by the EU and Japan, was asked whether a duty exemption scheme constitutes a measure affecting trade in services. It concluded, based on the *Bananas* panel, that no measures can be excluded a priori, and that the exemption scheme affected wholesale distribution services. The Appellate Body disagreed stating that this should be determined through an investigation of who supplies wholesale services and how such services are applied (DS139/AB/R, 31 May 2000, para. 165).

The major provisions of the GATS are summarized in Table 7.4. The GATS is overseen by the Council for Trade in Services, and a number of subsidiary bodies—including a Committee on Specific Commitments, charged with monitoring implementation of commitments and addressing technical scheduling questions, and a Committee on Trade in Financial Services. In addition, two working parties have been created, one on domestic regulation and another on GATS rules.

General Agreement on Trade in Services rules can be seen as operating at two levels. First, there is a set of general rules that apply across the board to measures affecting trade in services, of which the most important are *transparency* and the *most-favoured nation* (MFN) principle. Then there are sector-specific commitments made by members on *market access* and *national treatment* that are the core of the GATS, and determine the liberalizing impact of the agreement.

[3] See European Communities: Regime for the Importation, Sale and Distribution of Bananas, Report of the Panel, WT/DS27/R/USA, 22 May 1997, and European Communities: Regime for the Importation, Sale and Distribution of Bananas, Report of the Appellate Body, WT/DS27/AB/R, 9 September 1997.

Table 7.4. Major provisions of the GATS

Article	Subject Matter
I	Definition. Trade in services covers all four modes of supply.
II	General MFN obligation, subject to possibility of scheduling exemptions on a one-time basis.
III	Notification and publication. Obligation to create an enquiry point.
IV	Increasing participation of developing countries. High-income countries to take measures to facilitate trade of developing nations.
V	Economic integration. Allows for free trade and similar agreements.
VI	Allows for domestic regulation. Requirements concerning the design and implementation of service sector regulation, including in particular qualification requirements.
VII	Recognition of qualifications, standards and certification of suppliers.
VIII	Monopolies and exclusive suppliers. Requires that such entities abide by MFN and specific commitments (Articles XVI and XVII) and do not abuse their dominant position.
IX	Business practices. Recognition that business practices may restrict trade. Call for consultations between members on request.
XIV	General exceptions. Allows measures to achieve noneconomic objectives.
XVI	Market access. Defines a set of policies that may only be used to restrict market access for a scheduled sector if they are listed in a member's specific commitments.
XVII	National treatment. Applies in a sector if a commitment to that effect is made and no limitations or exceptions are listed in a member's schedule.
XVIII	Additional commitments. Allows for any other specific commitment to be made on a sector-by-sector basis. To date these have been limited primarily to telecommunications, through the so-called Reference Paper (discussed below).
XIX	Calls for successive negotiations to expand coverage of specific commitments (Articles XVI and XVII).
XXIX	States that annexes are an integral part of the GATS. There are annexes allowing for one-time MFN exemptions, excluding air transport services, and clarifying the potential coverage of maritime transport commitments. The GATS also has four additional protocols, two on financial services (the Second and Fifth), basic telecommunications services (the Fourth) and the movement of natural persons (the Third). Somewhat confusingly, there is no First Protocol.

MFN and transparency

As in the GATT, the core principle of the GATS is MFN treatment. This constitutes a general obligation that in principle is applicable to all covered measures maintained by members for any services sector. Article II:1 of GATS states:

With respect to any measure covered by this Agreement, each Member shall accord immediately and unconditionally to services and service suppliers of any other Member treatment no less favorable than that it accords to like services and service suppliers of any other country.

Although the MFN obligation under GATT 1994 is concerned with measures affecting products, the GATS also pertains to measures affecting service suppliers (that is, producers, legal persons). It thus has a wider reach. Although MFN is a general obligation (Article II), an annex to the GATS allows members to list MFN exemptions upon entry into force of the agreement. Once a member, further exemptions require a waiver from the ministerial conference of the WTO (which must be approved by three-quarters of the members). Most favoured nation exemptions are in principle to last no longer than ten years (that is, until end 2004) and are subject to negotiation in future MTNs, the first of which was to occur within five years of the entry into force of the agreement—i.e. in 2000 (Article XIX).

The need for an annex on MFN exceptions arose from concerns on the part of some members that an unconditional MFN rule would allow competitors located in countries with relatively restrictive policies to benefit from maintaining sheltered markets while enjoying a free ride in less restrictive export markets. This concern was expressed most vividly in GATS discussions on financial services and telecommunications, prompting industry representatives in relatively open countries to lobby for MFN exemptions as a way to force sectoral reciprocity.

Over 60 WTO members submitted MFN exemptions in 1994, with three sectors dominating: audiovisual services, financial services and transportation (road, air and maritime). Exemptions in the audiovisual area tend to be justified on the basis of cultural objectives, often aiming at safeguarding preferential co-production or distribution arrangements with certain countries. Exemptions for financial services were generally driven by reciprocity concerns: countries sought to retain the ability to discriminate against members that do not offer reciprocal access to financial service markets. The goal of many members in this connection was to maintain some leverage vis-à-vis the US. Exemptions in the transport area by developing countries often were motivated by the UNCTAD Liner Code—under which they may reserve up to 40 per cent of liner shipping routes for national flag vessels.

Apart from services specified in individual MFN exemption lists, the only permitted departure from MFN is for economic integration agreements between subsets of WTO members (Article V). As discussed in Chapter 10, this is similar to the provision found in the GATT. In addition, the GATS makes allowance for agreements on the movement of natural persons (Article V *bis*), which permits members to fully integrate their labour markets. The only such agreement notified so far is the one involving Denmark, Finland, Iceland, Norway and Sweden.

Article III (Transparency) requires all members to establish enquiry points to provide, on request, specific information concerning any laws, regulations and administrative practices affecting services covered by the agreement. In addition, members must establish enquiry points to provide, on request, specific information concerning any laws, regulations and administrative practices affecting services covered by the GATS.

National treatment and market access

National treatment (Article XVII GATS) is a so-called *specific* commitment. It is defined as treatment no less favourable than that accorded to like domestic services and service providers. Such treatment may or may not be identical to that applying to domestic firms, in recognition of the fact that identical treatment may actually worsen the conditions of competition for foreign-based firms (for example, a requirement for insurance firms that reserves be held locally). National treatment applies only to those services inscribed in a member's schedule, and then only to the extent no qualifications or conditions are listed in the schedule (see below). As is the case in the GATT, Article XVII applies to both *de jure* and *de facto* discrimination.

Consider some examples of limitations on national treatment. If domestic suppliers of audiovisual services are given preference in the allocation of frequencies for transmission within the national territory, such a measure discriminates explicitly on the basis of origin of the service supplier and thus constitutes formal or *de jure* denial of national treatment. Similarly, the WTO Panel in the Autopact dispute between the EU and Canada (*Canada—Certain Measures Affecting the Automotive Industry*) found that a local content requirement that could be fulfilled by the use of certain locally produced services discriminated against cross-border trade in the same services. Alternatively, consider a measure stipulating that prior residency is required for obtaining a licence permitting a provider to supply a service. Although the measure does not formally distinguish between service suppliers on the basis of national origin, it *de facto* offers less favourable treatment for foreign suppliers because they are less likely to be able to meet a prior residency requirement than like service suppliers of national origin.

In addition to national treatment, the GATS introduced a second specific commitment: a market access obligation (Article XVI GATS). Six types of market access restrictions are in principle prohibited for sectors a country chooses to schedule. These comprise limitations on the:
(1) number of service suppliers allowed;
(2) value of transactions or assets;
(3) total quantity of service output;
(4) number of natural persons that may be employed;
(5) type of legal entity through which a service supplier is permitted to supply a service (for example, branches vs. subsidiaries for banking); and
(6) participation of foreign capital in terms of limits on foreign equity or the absolute value of foreign investment.

Although in principle prohibited, if a member desires to maintain one or more of these six measures for a scheduled sector, it may do so as long as it lists them in its schedule. The introduction of a market access commitment in the GATS reflected the fact that the contestability of service markets is frequently restricted by measures that apply to both foreign and domestic entities. The market access article explicitly covers a number of such measures that were felt to be of particular importance. It can be regarded as the equivalent of GATT Article XI (which prohibits the use of quotas) as all the measures listed except for item 5 are quantitative in nature. In practice, however, it differs in that the market access obligation overlaps with the national treatment requirement, as prohibited market access-restricting measures may also violate national treatment (Hoekman, 1996).

The market access provision is clearly not comprehensive in that it does not deal with nondiscriminatory policies that have the effect of restricting competition generally, in the process blocking market access (e.g. because the fixed costs for foreign firms of satisfying the measure are higher than for local firms). Whether the limitations of Article XVI GATS are relevant for foreign suppliers only or for foreign *and* domestic suppliers; and whether national treatment applies to any Article XVI GATS restriction, are questions that are somewhat ambiguous. The *US—Gambling* panel found (and the Appellate Body concurred) that a series of US federal and state measures which ban the supply of services by foreign and domestic suppliers alike, violated Article XVI GATS because the US had not scheduled and market access exceptions for the relevant sector. An example of such laws was the Federal Wire Act, which states that persons that knowingly use a wire communication facility for the transmission in interstate or foreign commerce of bets and wagers or information assisting in the placing of bets or wagers or any sporting event or contest shall be subject to a fine, imprisoned for up to two years, or both. The Illegal Gambling Act calls for fines and/or prison terms for anyone engaging in an illegal gambling business.

It can be argued that the approach of the panel and AB was misconceived. As the GATS is a trade agreement, it should not regulate the conditions of access to a market for the citizens of a state making a liberalization commitment. All that is required is that the measure be transparent. To this effect, Article III GATS obliges WTO members to '...publish promptly... all relevant measures of general application which pertain to or affect the operation of this Agreement'. This provision leaves some discretion to governments to determine what is covered by this obligation. It is also possible for a WTO member to *cross-notify* (under Article III.5 GATS): laws of general application, even if not notified to the WTO, will become public because of domestic law constraints.

From a policy-perspective, trade liberalization would appear to be served if the applicability of Article XVI GATS was restricted to foreign services and services suppliers only (Hoekman and Mavroidis, 2007). As the GATS involves scheduling of domestic regulation, it would seem most appropriate to view Article XVI as a subset of Article XVII. If such a view is taken, the implication is that WTO members must first decide whether or not to accord national treatment to foreign services and services suppliers. If so, they must indicate this in the column for Article XVII GATS (to comply with Article III on transparency). If they do not, the same reporting requirement obtains. Assuming a government decides not to accord national treatment, and that it wants the relatively more onerous market access condition to be expressed in Article XVI GATS terms, it could choose one or more of the instruments mentioned in Article XVI.2 GATS. It should be noted that this construction of Article XVI GATS does not coincide with the understanding of Article XVI GATS by WTO panels and the Appellate Body.

Other provisions

Other GATS articles address matters such as domestic regulation, recognition of licences and certification of service suppliers, exceptions, policies pertaining to payment for services and the behaviour of public monopolies.

Article VI (Domestic Regulation) requires that members ensure that qualification requirements, technical standards and licensing procedures are based on objective and transparent criteria, are no more burdensome than necessary to ensure the quality of the services concerned, and do not constitute a restriction on supply in themselves. It requires countries to apply regulations in a 'reasonable, objective and impartial manner' to avoid undermining commitments to market access and national treatment. Moreover, countries must have in place appropriate legal procedures to review administrative decisions affecting trade in services. Article VI is among the potentially more important provisions in the GATS given that domestic regulations can have the effect of greatly impeding, if not foreclosing completely, the ability of foreign forms to contest a market. Indeed, given the absence of border-type barriers such as tariffs to restrict trade in services, often access to markets will be impeded, if at all, by domestic regulations. This is one reason why the GATS includes specific market access disciplines. Note, however, that these do not extend to domestic regulation more generally. Nor does Article VI envisage any harmonization of national regulatory policies.

A Working Party on Domestic Regulation is mandated to develop disciplines to ensure that licensing and qualification requirements and related standards are not unnecessary barriers to trade in services (the mandate is provided by Article VI:4). A precursor to this working party, the Working Party on Professional Services agreed in 1998 on a set of principles to ensure transparency of regulations pertaining to licensing of accountants and accountancy services. A noteworthy feature of these disciplines was specific language pertaining to a 'necessity test' for prevailing licensing-related requirements (i.e. a commitment to limit trade only to the extent necessary to achieve the regulatory objective). Article VI GATS gave the Working

Party the mandate to negotiate such disciplines, as it calls for the development of specific disciplines to ensure regulations are not more restrictive than necessary. The extension of a necessity test to domestic regulations on services has been a major source of concern for many NGOs and observers, who note that invariably it will be left to dispute settlement to determine whether the test has been violated.

Article VII (Recognition) promotes the establishment of procedures for (mutual) recognition of licences, educational diplomas and experience granted by a particular member. It permits a member to recognize standards of one or more members and not of others, without violating its GATS obligations—even though services and service suppliers of the former group will have better access to its markets than those of the latter group. The remaining paragraphs of Article VII seek to ensure that this freedom is not abused. Article VII:2 requires a member who enters into a mutual recognition agreement (MRA) to afford adequate opportunity to other interested members to negotiate their accession to such an agreement or to negotiate comparable ones. In this respect, Article VII mandates openness vis-à-vis third countries in a way that Article V, dealing with economic integration agreements, does not. Article VII:3 stipulates that a member must not grant recognition in a manner that would constitute a means of discrimination between countries. Members must inform the Council for Trade in Services about existing MRAs and of the opening of negotiations on any future ones. As of 2007, a total of 21 notifications were received under Article VII:4, of which ten from Latin American countries, four from the United States, three from Switzerland, and one each from the EU, Australia, Norway and Macau. All but one pertains to the recognition of educational degrees and professional qualifications obtained abroad.

Article XIV on exceptions is somewhat broader than what is found in the GATT, providing members with the legal cover to take measures to safeguard public morals, order, health, consumer protection and privacy.

Monopoly or oligopoly supply of services is allowed under the GATS, but governments are required to ensure that firms granted exclusive rights by governments do not abuse their market power to nullify any specific commitments relating to activities that fall outside the scope of their exclusive rights. Article IX recognizes that business practices of service suppliers that have not been granted monopoly or exclusive rights may restrain competition and thus trade in services, and requires that members consult with others on request with a view to eliminating such trade-restricting practices. However, no obligations are imposed regarding the scope and enforcement of competition policy rules—Article IX only requires the provision of nonconfidential information. Given the regulatory diversity prevailing across members in the area of competition policy, going beyond an information exchange obligation was not feasible (the issue of multilateral rules for competition law is discussed in Chapter 13).

Many GATS disciplines apply only to the extent specific commitments are made. This is a consequence of the 'positive list' approach to scheduling commitments.

For example, the balance-of-payments provision (Article XII) applies only for services where specific commitments have been undertaken. It requires that such measures be nondiscriminatory, temporary and phased out progressively as the invoking member's balance-of-payments situation improves. As in the GATT context, no recognition is expressed that import restrictions are second-best instruments to deal with balance-of-payments difficulties. Article XI requires members to refrain from applying restrictions on international transfers and payments for current transactions relating to their specific commitments—it also does not apply generally.

The WTO Dispute Settlement Body is responsible for disputes under GATS. Retaliation from goods to services and vice versa is possible if this is necessary (so-called cross-retaliation). Thus, if a country finds it needs to retaliate because of noncompliance with a panel recommendation and does not wish to restrict imports of goods, it may retaliate by not complying with some of its service commitments.

The GATS contains no provisions similar to Part IV of the GATT on special and differential treatment for developing countries or accepting the (unilateral) ar-rangements for tariff preferences that exist for merchandise trade flows (for example, the Generalized System of Preferences). However, Article XIX of the GATS permits developing countries to offer fewer specific commitments than industrialized nations in negotiations, and Article IV calls for special treatment of least developed countries.

The national treatment and market access obligations of the GATS do not extend to government procurement of services or to subsidy policies. The procurement carve-out greatly reduces the coverage of the GATS, as procurement typically represents a significant share of total demand for services such as accounting, consulting engineering and construction. Dealing with procurement and subsidies proved too complicated and Uruguay Round negotiators left these issues for future deliberations. Article X on industry-specific safeguard actions is also largely a shell, with the agreement again calling for continued negotiations on this topic. Discus-sions on all three subjects were held during 1997–2000, with little result. All three topics were on the agenda of the negotiations that were launched to extend the coverage of the GATS in early 2000.

The structure of specific commitments

As described previously, specific commitments on national treatment and market access apply only to service sectors listed by members, subject to whatever qua-lifications, conditions and limitations are maintained. As commitments are sched-uled by mode of supply as well as by sector, these exceptions may apply either across all modes of supply or for a specific mode. Members also make horizontal commitments that apply to modes of supply, rather than sectors. These are often restrictive in nature. A common example is an 'economic needs test'. Finally, members have the option of making additional commitments by listing actions to be taken that do not fall under national treatment or market access.

Table 7.5 illustrates the rather complicated structure of schedules of commitments. A member has three broad choices: it may schedule '*None*', meaning that it does not impose any limitation on a specific mode of supply for a sector; '*Unbound*,' implying it is essentially free to regulate as it deems appropriate; or it may introduce specific language to describe its commitment. According to the terminology used in the WTO's 2001 Scheduling Guidelines, the first category is known as *full commitment*; the second, *no commitment*; and the third, *commitment with limitations*. A consequence of the decisions to distinguish between general and specific obligations, to schedule specific commitments by mode of supply, and to allow for MFN exemptions is that very much depends on the content of the schedules. The GATS is not a particularly transparent or user-friendly instrument.

Virtually all commitments made in the Uruguay Round were of a binding nature, that is a promise not to become more restrictive than specified for each scheduled sector. Table 7.6 reports sectoral coverage indicators for national treatment and market access commitments for three groups of countries: high-income countries—OECD members, Hong Kong and Singapore; all other countries; and a subset of large developing countries. The latter comprises Argentina, Brazil, Chile, China, Colombia, India, Indonesia, Israel, Malaysia, Pakistan, Philippines, Poland, South Africa, Thailand and Venezuela. Three indicators are reported. First, an unweighted average ratio. This is the share of sectors where a commitment of some kind was made. Second, a weighted average ratio. This adjusts for whether qualifications and exceptions to national treatment and market access were made in each commitment. The weighting scheme used allocates a 0 to unbound commitments, a 1 to commitments not to impose any restrictions, and 0.5 to commitments where restrictions were maintained (see Hoekman, 1996, for details). Third, the share of sectors where commitments imply full free trade: that is, no exceptions or qualifications on national treatment or market access are scheduled. The higher the latter number, the more liberal the country. These ratios are conceptually similar to NTB frequency and coverage indices (see e.g. Nogues, Olechowski and Winters, 1986). Although imperfect, they do allow for rough comparisons to be made across countries.

Rich countries made commitments of some kind for 53.3 per cent of all services, as compared to 15.1 per cent for developing countries. Commitments made by large developing countries were substantially higher than the developing country average, accounting for 29.6 per cent of the total possible. Over one-quarter of developing countries scheduled less than 3 per cent of all services. The weighted average coverage of market access commitments—adjusting for whether exemptions are

Table 7.5. Format and example of a schedule of specific commitments

Commitment Type	Mode of Supply	Conditions and Limitations on Market Access	Conditions and Qualifications on National Treatment	Additional Commitments
Horizontal (applying to all sectors)	1. Cross-border	None	None	
	2. Consumption abroad	Unbound	Unbound	
	3. Commercial presence (FDI)	Maximum foreign equity is 49%	Approval required for equity stakes over 25%	
	4. Temporary entry of natural persons	Unbound except for intra-corporate transfer of senior staff	Unbound except for categories listed in the market access column	
Sector-specific	1. Cross-border	Commercial presence required	Unbound	
	2. Consumption abroad	None	None	
	3. Commercial presence (FDI)	25% of management to be nationals	Unbound	Independent telecom regulator
	4. Temporary entry of natural persons	Unbound, except as indicated in Horizontal commitments	Unbound, except as indicated in Horizontal commitments	

Notes: 'None' implies no exceptions are maintained—that is, a bound commitment not to apply any measures that are inconsistent with market access or national treatment. 'Unbound' implies no commitment of any kind has been made.

Table 7.6. Sectoral coverage of specific commitments in 1995 (%)

	High–Income Countries	All Other Countries	Large Developing Countries
Market access			
Weighted average	40.6	9.4	17.1
No restrictions	30.5	6.7	10.9
National treatment			
Weighted average	42.4	10.2	18.8
No restrictions	35.3	8.5	14.6
Memo: unweighted average	53.3	15.1	29.6

Source: Hoekman (1996).

listed and policies are bound—for the high-income group was 40.6 per cent; that for developing countries 9.4 per cent; and that for large developing countries 17.1 per cent. Commitments by high-income members implying no restrictions accounted for 30.5 per cent of the total. For developing countries as a group the figure was 6.7 per cent; for the large developing country group 10.9 per cent. Numbers for national treatment commitments were very similar. Clearly, GATS members were far from attaining free trade in services at the end of the Uruguay Round.

7.4. Sectoral Agreements

In the closing days of the Uruguay Round it became clear that it would be difficult to come to closure on a number of services sectors, including financial services, basic telecommunications, maritime transport, and one important mode of supply: movement of natural persons. (Air transport services are excluded from the ambit of the GATS altogether.) Rather than allow a situation to develop where countries would withdraw already tabled commitments in these areas or exempt them from the MFN obligation, it was agreed that negotiations in these sectors were to continue after the establishment of the WTO. Negotiations on financial services, basic telecommunications, natural persons and maritime transport were restarted in the spring of 1994. Those on financial services were to be concluded by July 1995, the others by mid-1996. The negotiations on financial and basic telecom services were eventually concluded successfully. The two others failed. As a result the GATS does not cover air and maritime transportation. It also essentially does not cover audiovisual services, as this was excluded by many countries through an absence of scheduled commitments and/or MFN exceptions.

The Negotiating Group on Movement of Natural Persons was the first to conclude its work in July 1995. Twenty schedules of commitments resulting from the negotiations were annexed to the GATS, which entered into force one year later. These commitments did not go significantly beyond the status quo. The lack of progress on this issue was due in part to the departure of the Indian ambassador in late 1994, who had up to that point pursued an active linkage strategy, making progress on other service negotiations conditional on attaining concessions on the movement of natural persons. Negotiations on maritime transport services proved very difficult. A large number of countries, including the US, maintain cabotage restrictions—a prohibition on the use of non-national flag vessels to transport cargo within the national jurisdiction. Many developing countries also are signatories to the 1974 UNCTAD Code of Conduct for Liner Conferences, which allows a share of up to 40 per cent of international liner cargoes to be reserved for national carriers. As no progress could be made to liberalize trade in this sector, the negotiating group suspended talks at the end of June 1996.

Financial services

Financial services were of great importance to the US, reflecting the strength of the US lobbies that sought improved access to foreign markets. As a result the US was unwilling to accept commitments that it regarded as inadequate. At the very end of the Uruguay Round, it was agreed to extend talks on financial services by 18 months, with a deadline of end June 1995. Although the US invoked MFN exemptions for this sector, it was understood these would not be applied until negotiations were concluded. As the 1995 deadline approached, the US indicated that it considered the offers of Japan and several southeast Asian and Latin American countries to be inadequate and that it would invoke its MFN exemptions. In an effort to salvage as much as possible from the negotiations, the EU then proposed that all other participants maintain their offers through the end of 1997. Negotiations resumed in 1997 and were finally concluded successfully in December of that year—with the US participating (and thus removing its MFN exemptions for this sector). A total of 56 schedules representing 70 members were annexed to the GATS (Mattoo, 2000b).

Despite the fact that an increasing number of developing countries recognized that a competitive and efficient financial services sector was a condition *sine qua non* for economic development, and that opening markets to foreign financial firms can strengthen domestic financial systems by creating more competitive and efficient host-country markets, agreement proved elusive. One problem concerned fears of the implications of liberalization for weak domestic financial institutions, and a perceived absence of reciprocity given that many developing countries are importers and not exporters of financial services. Another concern revolved around the implications of GATS rules for management of capital flows and prudential regulation and supervision.

The latter problems were addressed by agreeing that liberalization of capital movements per se is beyond the purview of the GATS, although members are restricted from imposing capital controls that interfere with their specific commitments (except if justified for balance-of-payments reasons). More difficult was where to draw the line as regards the types of regulation that are permitted (policies aimed at increasing the strength and quality of prudential regulation and supervision) and those that should be abolished (policies that act as barriers to trade in financial services) (Key, 2003). An Annex on Financial Services contains a so-called prudential carve-out for domestic regulation of financial services. Included at the insistence of financial regulators, the carve-out allows prudential measures to be imposed to protect consumers of financial services and to ensure the integrity and stability of the financial system. It is unclear what the additionality is of the carve-out, as GATS Article VI essentially provides cover for such regulatory intervention as well.

Most commitments made by WTO members were status quo or less than status quo commitments. However, ten countries used the GATS as a mechanism to pre-commit to future liberalization (Mattoo, 2000b), four of which were countries that were seeking to accede to the EU. Most of the others represented relatively large markets—including Brazil, India, Indonesia and the Philippines. Governments of these countries were under substantial pressure to open access to their markets.

Basic telecommunications

Telecommunications services were split between basic and value-added services during the Uruguay Round. By the end of the round, only commitments had been made for value-added services (such as electronic and voice mail or electronic data interchange), and not for basic voice, data transmission, mobile telephony or satellite services. Negotiations on basic telecommunications recommenced in May 1994 with a deadline of 30 April 1996. In the run-up to the deadline, negotiations were deadlocked. As in the financial services talks, the US was of the view that offers on the table were inadequate, in part because the required 'critical mass' of membership (to prevent free riding) had not been achieved. In April the US withdrew its offer of open satellite market access and the negotiations collapsed. Other negotiators regarded the US move as serving narrow, domestic political differences.

In contrast to what happened in the financial services negotiations, the EU or another party to the talks did not take the initiative to extend discussions. Instead, such an initiative was taken by the Director-General of the WTO, who induced the major players to extend the deadline to February 1997. This was accepted, and negotiations were finally concluded successfully in February 1997, with 55 schedules (representing 69 members) annexed to the GATS. The additional time allowed a number of developing countries to improve their offer—with technical assistance from a group of bilateral donors and multilateral organizations. It also allowed the major players to hammer out difficulties related to differences in prevailing market structures. One such problem concerned international resale of switched telecom services. Because the US is an open competitive market, calls switched through the US by foreign carriers cost relatively little, whereas US carriers were forced to pay much higher fees because many foreign markets were not open. An August 1997 US decision to move to cost-based settlement rates for such payments removed this constraint.

The basic telecommunications agreement is noteworthy in the extent to which countries made commitments to engage in future liberalization. Technological developments—the internet, e-commerce—played an important role in the changing attitude towards increasing competition in the telecom sector. Many developing countries used the GATS as a pre-commitment device—they bound themselves to introduce competition in basic telecoms at precise future dates (Table 7.7). This reflected a recognition that liberalization was in their interest, but should be pursued gradually. Committing to do so a fixed date in the future enhances the credibility of the policy, thus encouraging incumbents to prepare for greater competition as opposed to investing resources in lobbying against implementation of the reform. More generally, the pre-commitment strategy was also seen by many of the governments concerned as an important signalling device towards the international investment community and prospective foreign investors. It is noteworthy that in this area there was no shortage of countries willing to make (pre-)commitments, in contrast to the usual reluctance on the part of many developing countries to use the GATT/WTO as an instrument to lock in policy commitments.

The Reference Paper

A key feature of the agreement that emerged was a 'Reference Paper' setting out regulatory principles to which signatories may subscribe. Technically, this involved making so-called additional commitments in the schedules of participating countries, as allowed by Article XVIII GATS. Some 60 members did so. The need for these principles—which draw on elements of the 1996 US Telecommunications Act—arose from a concern that dominant telecom operators might otherwise abuse their market position and restrict competition from new entrants through their control of so-called bottleneck or essential facilities. This could be because

Table 7.7. Examples of pre-commitments in basic telecommunications

Country	Commitment
Antigua & Barbuda	International voice telephony to be opened as of 2012
Argentina	No restrictions as of 8 November 2000
Bolivia	Restrictions on long distance national and international telecom services removed as of 27 November 2001
Grenada	Exclusive supply until 2006, no restrictions thereafter
Jamaica	Exclusive supply until September 2013, no restrictions thereafter
Trinidad & Tobago	Exclusive supply until 2010, no restrictions thereafter (fixed satellite services open as of 2000)
Venezuela	No restrictions as of 27 November 2000
Cote d'Ivoire	Monopoly until 2005, no restrictions thereafter
Mauritius	Monopoly until 2004, no restrictions thereafter
Morocco	Monopoly until 2001, no restrictions thereafter
Senegal	Abolition of monopoly by 1 January 2007
South Africa	Monopoly until December 2003, thereafter duopoly and consideration of more licences
Tunisia	No restrictions on supply of local calls after 2003
Pakistan	Cross-border supply of voice telephony open by 2004, divestiture of 26% of national monopoly to a strategic investor with exclusive licence for basic telephony for seven years
Thailand	Additional commitments for voice telephone and other services to be made in 2006, conditional upon passage of new legislation

Source: Adapted from Mattoo (2000*a*).

this sector has for a long time been monopolized, and despite efforts to break up these monopolies, control over key infrastructural facilities will not immediately be diversified. Or it could be that large fixed costs and economies of scale render some markets inherently incontestable, i.e. given the minimum efficient scale of operation, the market is simply not large enough to accommodate more than one or two suppliers.

The Reference Paper is wider in scope than Article VIII GATS and its domain more clearly defined than the Basic Telecom Annex. It calls for the establishment of an independent regulator for telecoms. Its disciplines apply to any 'major supplier', defined as one who 'has the ability to materially affect the terms of participation (having regard to price and supply) in the relevant market for basic telecommunications services as a result of: (a) control over essential facilities; or (b) use of its position in the market'. Notably, the conditions to qualify as a 'major supplier', and therefore to be subject to the disciplines in the Reference Paper, do not include government responsibility for its existence, unlike in the case of Article VIII monopolies.

The Reference Paper also goes beyond GATS provisions by requiring interconnection on nondiscriminatory, transparent and reasonable terms, conditions (including technical standards and specifications); of a quality no less favourable than that provided to other suppliers, including its own; priced at cost-oriented rates; in a timely fashion; sufficiently unbundled so that a supplier need not pay for network components or facilities it does not require; at any technically feasible point in the network. Competition safeguards oblige members to prevent a major supplier from abusing control over information, or engaging in anticompetitive cross-subsidization.

The Reference Paper is characteristic of the 'WTO approach' in that the primary concern is to ensure effective market access. Wider concerns about consumer interests and how they may be affected by monopolistic behaviour are not addressed, nor is any focal point provided for regulators regarding the need for and modalities of regulation or competition law. Although the paper was a 'standardized text', some countries customized it in their schedules. Many of the terms and disciplines imposed by the paper are not very specific. What the meaning is of 'anticompetitive', 'cost-oriented', 'independence', etc., is not defined precisely—implying that this is something that will be left to case law.

A start down this path was initiated in 2002 with a dispute between Mexico and US (*Mexico—Measures Affecting Telecommunications Services*). The dispute revolved around claims by the US that the Mexican government was not abiding by its commitments under the Reference Paper, in particular the requirement that dominant operators provide (and price) international interconnection services on the basis of cost. The US also claimed that Telmex had established a de facto cartel comprising itself and a 'competitive fringe' that resulted in restricting access of foreign (US) suppliers. The panel concluded that the international settlement rates charged by Telmex to US telecommunications service suppliers were not cost-based and that Mexico did not provide access to and use of public telecommunications transport networks and services (a violation of Sections 5a and b of the Annex on Telecommunications).[4] Mexico was called upon to remove specific restrictions on the commercial negotiation of international settlement rates and shift towards pricing on the basis of long-run average incremental cost. The panel also found that Mexico failed to abide by Section 1.1 of the Reference Paper, which requires signatories to maintain appropriate measures to prevent anticompetitive practices. However, it concluded that Mexico should be permitted to impose restrictions on the resale of international services from Mexico to other countries.

---

[4] *Mexico—Measures Affecting Telecommunications Services*, Report of the Panel, 2 April 2004, WT/DS204/R. For international phone calls to take place, a telecom carrier must be able to connect into the destination country's telecommunications network. This generally either involves a payment to an operator in the destination country for completing the call, or by leasing capacity (lines) in the destination country and routing calls over those lines. The latter is called 'international simple resale'. The latter was also at issue in this case as the US opposed restrictions that were imposed by Mexico on such resale.

This case was the first 'pure' GATS case in that reference was only made to GATS provisions. It also was the first to address a clear competition issue and to require a WTO member to change its domestic law regulating a service sector. Perhaps most noteworthy is that the panel did not limit itself to the international dimension of telecom regulation in Mexico (international settlement rates) but extended its finding to domestic interconnection regulation. Moreover, the case illustrates that although the panel based much of its reasoning on competition policy principles and arguments, at the end of the day the focus was almost exclusively on market access. Sidak and Singer (2004) argue compellingly that from a welfare (consumer) viewpoint, the types of concerns used by the panel to motivate its decision are more appropriately addressed by the two country's competition authorities, and that the panel used the wrong definition of the relevant market.

The panel to some extent 'wrote law' by interpreting the meaning of anticompetitive practices as including horizontal price-fixing and market-sharing agreements—on the basis that these tend to be per se illegal under most competition laws. This is nowhere specified in the GATS, the Annex on Telecoms or the Reference Paper (the latter only mentions a list of anticompetitive practices, including cross-subsidization). Whether one agrees or not that the panel should have interpreted this language, it is noteworthy that the practices that were deemed anticompetitive were mandated by government regulation (law).[5]

7.5. EXPANDING THE GATS: FROM URUGUAY TO DOHA

The GATS has been characterized by almost continuous negotiations and deliberations in committees and working parties focused on expansion of the coverage of the agreement. The post-Uruguay Round sectoral negotiations discussed above are an example, as were efforts to agree on more specific disciplines on domestic regulation under Article VI GATS. As of the second half of the 1990s onward, most of the focus was on unfinished business from the Uruguay Round in

---

[5] In June 2004, the US and Mexico reached an agreement that implements the panel recommendations. The main features of the agreement notified to the WTO Dispute Settlement Body were that Mexico will remove the provisions of the law relating to the proportional return system, uniform tariff system, and the requirement that the carrier with the greatest proportion of outgoing traffic to a country negotiate the settlement rate on behalf of all Mexican carriers for that country. It will also allow the introduction of resale-based international telecommunications services in Mexico by 2005, in a manner consistent with Mexican law. The United States recognized that Mexico will continue to restrict International Simple Resale (use of leased lines to carry cross-border calls) to prevent the unauthorized carriage of telecommunications traffic.

the area of rules, and an effort to expand the specific commitments in the Doha Round.

Emergency safeguards, subsides and procurement

A number of 'outstanding' rule-making issues were left open after the Uruguay Round for further work and discussion. Thus, the GATS has no rules on subsidies, does not cover public procurement and has no emergency safeguard mechanism. A Working Party on GATS Rules was tasked with negotiating disciplines in these areas. After more than ten years of discussions, agreement on such disciplines remains to be obtained. This may appear rather surprising, considering that subsidies are widely used by governments for a variety of reasons; that public purchases of services can account for 5 per cent of GDP or more; and that governments invariably insist on the inclusion of emergency safeguards in any trade agreement they negotiate. In our view the explanation for the persistence of these lacunae is that the economic case for GATS-specific disciplines in any of these areas is weak.

There is nothing services-specific about procurement: in principle any multilateral disciplines should cover goods and services—as is the case under the plurilateral Agreement on Government Procurement (see Chapter 11). Of primary importance for foreign firms is to have access to procurement markets, and frequently this can only be achieved if they can establish a commercial presence in a country. If the sectoral coverage of the GATS is expanded and foreign providers are able to access markets, the contestability of procurement markets will be enhanced at the same time (Evenett and Hoekman, 2005).

In the services context any disciplines on subsidies will have to focus primarily on domestic production or operating subsidies—the distinction between export and production subsidies found in the GATT is much harder, if not impossible, to make in practice. It is also much harder to envisage emulation of the main GATT discipline—countervailing duties. This implies a need to agree to substantive rules (harmonization) if members want to discipline the use of subsidies, including tax incentives. Difficulties will immediately arise in defining and distinguishing between what is 'legitimate' and what is not. Although there are clearly potential sources of gain for WTO members associated with a set of subsidy disciplines (insofar as subsidies impose negative external effects), subsidies will frequently be the most efficient instrument to pursue specific objectives or to address market failures. Examples could be to ensure universal access to services, promote regional development, or to redistribute income. Cross-subsidies may also sometimes be an appropriate second-best instrument for developing country governments (Laffont and N'Gbo, 2000).

The negotiating history and experience under the GATT-1947 illustrates that agreement on subsidy-related disciplines is difficult to obtain, and that any disciplines may easily be circumvented. Even the EU—which goes much further than the WTO in this area—has encountered recurrent difficulties in enforcing restrictions on the use of state aids. The North American Free Trade Agreement does not even try to tackle this issue. Given there is a rationale for subsidies in many contexts and the revealed preference of many governments to use subsidies, it would appear more effective to seek to extend the reach of the national treatment principle to subsidy policies. Given national treatment, there should be less concern about the impact of subsidy policies, allowing the principle of 'subsidy freedom' to prevail. As in the procurement case, what matters most is market access and national treatment and the current structure of the GATS is geared precisely towards those commitments.

The economic case for an ESM is also weak. One reason for this is again the structure of the GATS. The positive list approach to scheduling commitments allows governments to maintain a variety of discriminatory or market access restricting measures. In addition, the ability (right) to regulate also ensures that governments retain the capacity to intervene to achieve social objectives. Both factors attenuate the need for safeguards. Moreover, insofar as governments do make commitments and come under pressure to re-impose protection (discrimination), they may invoke the re-negotiation modalities that are built into the GATS.

More specifically, a GATT-type ESM is difficult to rationalize (and design) in the services context because of the various modes of supply that can be used for service providers. Given that mode 3 will often be used, a safeguard would require taking action against foreign firms that have established a commercial presence. Why a government would want to do this is unclear, as it is likely to have a major chilling effect on FDI, and, as important from a political economy perspective, will affect negatively the national employees of the targeted foreign-owned firms. These considerations suggest that if a safeguard measure was to be considered, it would most likely exempt mode 3. A consequence could then be to make an ESM a tool to distort the choice of mode of supply (i.e. an instrument of industrial policy): it could create incentives to choose FDI as a mode of supply even if other modes are more efficient (leading away from the principle or objective of modal neutrality).

There is, however, one potentially compelling argument for seeking to develop an emergency safeguard mechanism. A case could be made that the extremely limited nature of liberalization commitments to date on movement of natural persons (mode 4) is in part due to the nonexistence of safeguard instruments. As this is a mode of supply that is of major interest to developing countries and one on which almost all countries maintain stringent restrictions, one could envisage a safeguard instrument that is linked to mode 4 liberalization commitments. The rationale would be to provide liberalizing governments with an insurance mechanism that can be invoked if there are unexpected detrimental impacts on their societies.

Article XIX GATS negotiations and the Doha Round

Article XIX GATS required members to launch new negotiations on services no later than 2000, and periodically thereafter. Initial talks were launched in 2000, and later became part of the 2001 Doha Development Agenda. Much of the pre-Doha talks centred on sector-specific questions, including the need to add new sectors not defined in the GATS classification list, such as energy services, and on an assessment of trade in services. Developing countries were insistent that members abide by Article XIX:3, which states that in establishing the negotiating guidelines and procedures, the Council on Trade in Services is to carry out an assessment of trade in services in overall terms and on a sectoral basis with reference to the objectives of the agreement, including those set out in Article IV:1 (on increasing participation of developing countries in world trade through specific, negotiated commitments). One dimension of this pertained to obtaining credit for autonomous liberalization Many governments had undertaken autonomous reforms and did not want the status quo set of policies to be the baseline for new negotiations—they wanted to have 'credit' for what they had already done. Specific proposals were also put forward on GATS rules. As of the launch of Doha, some 70 proposals on approaches, issues and sectors by more than 40 members had already been tabled.

In March 2001, a set of modalities and guidelines for market access negotiations was agreed. These specified that negotiations would proceed on the basis of requests and offers. The Doha declaration built on this, stating that:

The negotiations on trade in services shall be conducted with a view to promoting the economic growth of all trading partners and the development of developing and least-developed countries. We recognize the work already undertaken in the negotiations, initiated in January 2000...and the large number of proposals submitted...We reaffirm the Guidelines and Procedures for the Negotiations adopted by the Council for Trade in Services...as the basis for continuing the negotiations, with a view to achieving the objectives of the GATS...Participants shall submit initial requests for specific commitments by 30 June 2002 and initial offers by 31 March 2003. (para. 15)

The negotiations were conducted in Special Sessions of the Council for Trade in Services. The 2002 and 2003 deadlines for initial requests and offers laid out in the Doha declaration were missed, as were virtually all subsequent deadlines, reflecting not only the difficulties specific to the services talks but also, as, if not more, importantly, the lack of progress on agriculture and NAMA. Independent of the need for cross-issue linkages, many developing countries resisted making additional commitments on services unless there was a significant quid pro quo within services, in particular better access for mode 4. There was also active opposition to the services talks by a number of NGOs of various stripes, some of which opposed liberalization generally, with many especially concerned with access to health, water and educational services and worried that commitments in these areas would result in inequitable outcomes. Although many high-income countries argued that these concerns were misplaced, given that nothing in the GATS constrains the right of governments to regulate sectors, they did not do enough to address them in a credible manner—e.g. by explicitly linking GATS commitments to the need to put in place appropriate regulation and assist partner countries to improve their regulatory enforcement capacity. A major factor underlying the lack of progress in negotiations was the marked absence of OECD services industries seeking better access to export markets.

Between 2000 and the end of 2005, WTO members pursued a bilateral approach to negotiations, submitting requests to others and making (conditional) offers. Requests tended to be highly ambitious and offers mostly minimalist, especially if compared to actual, applied policies. Adlung and Roy (2005) compared the offers as of 2005 with then existing specific commitments of WTO members. For many countries the coverage of specific commitments was well below 50 per cent of all services and modes of supply. Adlung and Roy conclude that not only did the requests and offers made in the six years following the launch of negotiations imply little if any liberalization of policies; but also most countries were not even willing to use the GATS as a vehicle to 'lock in' existing levels of openness. A number of studies have shown that there is often a major gap between the actual level of openness of sectors and the level of commitments in the GATS. For example, Barth, Caprio and Levine (2006) compare data on specific GATS commitments for financial services with measures of actual policy in this sector for 123 countries. They conclude that, in practice, applied policy is much more liberal than what was committed to in the GATS.

Political economy factors

Why so little movement? Is there a fundamental problem that is specific to services/ GATS? Although the services agenda is more complex than the goods trade, it has been more than ten years since the GATS entered into force, and policymakers have been dealing with services in a trade-negotiating context now for over 20 years. Thus, complexity—although a factor (see e.g. Adlung, 2006)—can only be part of the explanation. A key factor in our view was that there was simply too little private sector engagement and lobbying in support of the GATS process to overcome resistance from those that perceive GATS commitments as being (potentially) costly.

One reason for this may be that markets had already become much more open. The boom in trade in services summarized earlier in this chapter was driven in part by policy reforms and decisions by governments around the world to relax restrictions on foreign provision of services, including through FDI. These reforms in conjunction with booming world trade and investment in services clearly will reduce the incentives of firms to invest resources in supporting multilateral efforts to further open markets—times were good. This is not to say there were no incentives left—both the negotiating requests and the literature on services clearly document that significant barriers to trade and investment continue to prevail. But on the margin it appears to have been the case that services exporters did not perceive there to be a high enough return to actively supporting the Doha talks. One factor underlying this perception may have been the more high-profile opposition to services commitments of NGOs (discussed below). Another may be the incentive effects identified by Blanchard (2007) for mode 3 that were discussed above.

In the case of developing countries—the majority of the WTO membership— most are small and therefore not of great interest to the large players in the WTO, constraining their prospects of negotiating significant additional access to major markets. Moreover, many developing countries are not, or do not, perceive themselves to be (potential) services exporters. Although many poor countries are significant exporters of services, in that services generate a substantial share of their total foreign exchange earnings, often this is derived from activities where the relevant policies are under the control of the exporting government itself, not its trading partner. The most important such service is tourism, where the export revenue generated depends primarily on measures that the tourism destination country puts in place itself.

As far as mode 1 services trade is concerned, developing countries are exporters, but this is often not constrained at all, with the exception of services such as gambling where importing countries may reserve the activity to the state or ban it altogether. But most of the business process outsourcing, call centres, etc. that are growth areas for many countries are not constrained by trade policy measures in the destination or importing country. Although there is certainly increasing opposition against such trade in high-income countries, outside of government contracts there is little that is currently done to restrict such activities from being 'offshored'. Turning to mode 3, most developing countries do not have significant 'offensive' interests, in contrast to high-income economies.

The one mode that is of great relevance to potential exporters from developing countries is mode 4. Figure 7.5 presents data drawn from Gootiz and Mattoo (2008), which shows that all countries impose high barriers to mode 4 trade. It is unlikely however that much can be achieved on mode 4 access to high-income country markets, especially for less skilled services activities. In the case of the EU, for example, the initial offers made during the Doha Round were most limited in the areas that were of greatest interest to developing countries—in particular mode 4, but also mode 1 (see Table 7.8). In part this is a reflection of the difficulties EU members have in liberalizing these modes within the EU context (Hoekman, Mattoo and Sapir, 2007), which reflect regulatory policies and not the absence of

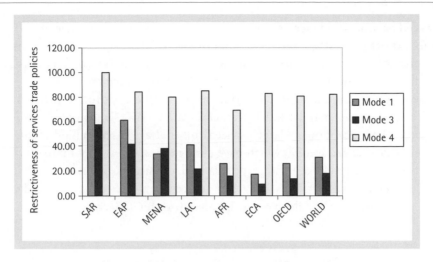

Fig. 7.5. Services trade restrictiveness indices by mode

Source: Gootiz and Mattoo (2008).

national treatment. Mode 4 is very politically sensitive and in practice, insofar as importing countries are willing to consider relaxing barriers, experience suggests they will do so only on a bilateral basis in a bilateral setting. The lack of serious prospects for mode 4 liberalization in the GATS framework effectively removes many potential export interests in many poor developing countries from the process.

A related factor that may help explain the very limited progress that has been made to date is that the GATS has a strong sectoral focus. Its coverage is determined by a positive list, with governments scheduling commitments on a sector-by-sector basis. Given that most countries will not be significant (potential) net exporters in most sectors, reciprocity requires that countries find the required

Table 7.8. EU–15 commitment index in services (per cent)

Mode of Supply	Pre-Doha (1994)	April 2003 Offer	Difference (% Points)
Mode 1	50.5	57.2	6.7
Mode 2	66.9	88.2	21.3
Mode 3	63.0	82.9	19.9
Mode 4	3.5	4.5	1.0
Total	46.0	58.2	12.2

balanced of concessions across different services sectors, or, if countries do not have strong export interests in any services, in other WTO areas. Even if one abstracts from the latter set of countries, crafting a series of bilateral deals on services among the subset of countries with services interests may be difficult.

The forgoing implies that a key dimension of the reciprocity mechanism—services exporters—may be much weaker in many WTO members than is true for goods. The exception are large service firms that are based in high-income and emerging market economies, which have clear interests in selling more services to each other. The result is a rather unbalanced picture as far as export interests are concerned—in effect, if exchanges of 'concessions' are to be restricted within the services arena, it would have to be an intra-OECD/large emerging markets affair.

Regulatory considerations and concerns

If pro-liberalization forces are relatively weak, certainly compared to the Uruguay Round, resistance to enhancing the GATS became stronger over time. Opposition came from two groups. The first is familiar from the goods context: import-competing firms/incumbents, workers, unions—those who stand to lose from liberalization. Second, distinct from the goods context, sectoral regulators may resist international cooperation on regulatory measures that is anchored in a binding trade agreement or is motivated by trade concerns.

In both OECD and developing countries there are incumbent firms and workers with firm-specific skills that may lose from liberalization. The offers that have been tabled in the Doha Round reveal that OECD countries are most willing to make concessions in modes 2 and 3, where the levels of commitment were already fairly substantial prior to Doha. The markets of all of the more advanced industrialized economies tend to be relatively open, helping to explain the fact that these countries account for some 75 per cent of global trade in services—both cross-border and FATS. Although there is political resistance to mode 1 trade driven by worries about the employment impacts of offshoring and greater use of business process outsourcing to locations in developing countries, policies that restrict such trade are primarily regulatory in nature, and not affected by the WTO talks. The mode that is most affected by outright barriers, mode 4, and that is of great interest to many developing countries, is the mode OECD countries are least willing to open.

Resistance to liberalization in developing countries varies across sectors and modes (Hoekman, Mattoo and Sapir, 2007; Gootiz and Mattoo, 2008). Differences in policy stance across sectors are driven by the differential impacts of technology and the legacy of past structures. In telecommunications, many countries have exploited new technological possibilities by directly introducing competition, especially in mobile communications. Adjustments by public sector incumbents were facilitated by the fact that telecom markets have been growing rapidly, with overall sectoral employment expanding. Other technology-dependent sectors such as IT-enabled business services never confronted pressure for protection of the domestic market—there were no incumbents. In other sectors where restrictions continue to prevail this is often driven by the legacies of past policies that limit the ability of domestic firms to confront competition. For example, in countries dominated by public sector banks with excessive staffing levels and weak balance sheets as a result of directed lending at nonmarket rates, large displacements will result from full liberalization. Adjustment and employment concerns therefore may be an important factor impeding liberalization.

The intangible nature of most services makes it hard for buyers of services to investigate or test their quality prior to purchase. The extent of asymmetric information often creates a necessity to regulate services in order to protect consumers. Regulating services may also be desirable in order to remedy other types of market failures, including imperfect competition, which is often present in network services such as telecommunications where the number of providers is limited. Externalities may cause a problem if there is also imperfect information—e.g. in the case of financial services, where the failure of one institution may cause problems to the entire sector. For all these reasons, activities tend to be highly regulated.

Although consumers should, in principle, favour reforms that increase the number of suppliers and, in principle, lower prices and/or increase the range of services offered, they may in fact oppose them for fear that reforms will lower service quality and/or increase the market power of (foreign) firms. Regulators may be concerned that trade liberalization will impede their ability to enforce domestic regulatory standards. Trade will bring with it regulatory competition if services suppliers are only subject to the norms and standards that apply in their home markets. A case in point was the dispute between Antigua and Barbuda and the US on gambling services. Thus, if trade is permitted to occur on the basis of the qualifications and certifications obtained in the home country of providers, there may be concerns regarding whether host country norms are met.

The scope for traditional reciprocity-driven negotiations in services is inherently more limited than for goods because of concerns relating to regulatory autonomy. The prevalence of regulation complicates and constrains use of the reciprocity mechanism for services because it is very difficult to design multilateral rules and national commitments in a way that clearly separates or distinguishes between measures that are protectionist and measures that have a good domestic efficiency or social equity rationale. A critical challenge then is how to differentiate between legitimate concerns relating to quality and performance, and regulatory require-ments that simply constitute barriers to entry, creating rents for incumbents by raising prices. Marginal 'quid pro quo' changes to domestic regulatory policies may not enhance welfare—indeed, they could easily lower it. Regulators may therefore be concerned that market access negotiating dynamics could adversely affect their ability to design and implement regulatory norms that maximize national welfare.

An additional regulation-related complicating factor is that successful liberalization in developing countries will often require substantial strengthening of domestic regulatory institutions and related infrastructure. The impacts of more competitive market structures following liberalization on access to services by poorer households in developing countries have been mixed. In cases like mobile telecommunications, a positive relationship has been observed in many developing countries because initial conditions were bad—few households had access. However, in other areas, like financial services, unless improved regulatory measures are put in place, liberalization may have an adverse effect on access to credit for rural areas and the poor (Mattoo and Payton, 2007). Putting in place mechanisms to ensure better access to services post-liberalization is important from an equity perspective. It is also important from a political economy perspective to bolster support for implementing efficiency-enhancing policy reforms and sustaining them over time. Absent actions to address regulatory weaknesses, countries may not be in a position to fully realize the potential benefits of trade reforms in services (*or* goods) (Hoekman and Mattoo, 2007).

A shift in approach: the 2005 Hong Kong ministerial

The December 2005 WTO ministerial meeting in Hong Kong appeared to recognize that the status quo approach, bilateral request–offer negotiations, was not generating the desired results. Annex C of the Hong Kong Ministerial Declaration endorsed a shift towards plurilateral or collective negotiations among subsets of members. The idea was to limit talks to a critical mass of countries, so as to reduce transactions costs while still ensuring that most of the gains from agreement would be internalized among those participating. The pursuit of what Schelling (1978) has called a 'k-group strategy'—the minimum number of countries ('K') out of a larger set ('N') that internalizes enough of the total potential gains from cooperation to make free riding by the remaining $N\text{-}K$ players feasible—is easier to implement in the WTO setting for services than it is for goods trade because of the way the GATS is structured. Article XIX GATS mentions plurilateral negotiations as modality that could be used by members. The positive list approach to define the country coverage of specific commitments on a sector-by-sector basis already requires that negotiations be sectoral.

The decision to move to negotiations among subsets of countries and focus on agreeing to a set of 'minimum standards' for liberalizing commitments—thus shifting the burden on a member to justify its refusal to concede the threshold level rather than on other members to extract the minimum concessions—implied a move away from first difference reciprocity. Instead, the focus becomes achieving a common set of policies that apply to all signatories, while allowing for de facto differentiation between WTO members in terms of participation. Countries that have little to offer for a specific sector or mode are effectively exempted from participation—they can free ride on the outcome of negotiations between the principal stakeholders.

Plurilateral talks were pursued among some 30–40 countries, basically OECD members and the larger developing economies, starting in early 2006.[6] Requests were tabled for legal; architecture/engineering; computer-related; postal/courier; telecommunications; audiovisual; construction; distribution; education; environmental; financial; maritime; air transport; and energy services; as well as cross-border trade; mode 3; mode 4; and MFN exemptions. Requests were generally less ambitious than those made in the earlier bilateral request–offer process, which often called for full market access and national treatment in sectors of export interest to the *demandeur*. Although progress was made as a result of the shift in negotiating modalities, the inability to move forward on agriculture and nonagricultural market access dominated the efforts of negotiators. This shift illustrated the more general trend towards limiting negotiations to a critical mass of countries.

Although WTO members clearly recognized a change in tack was needed to deal with the problem of asymmetric interests, the shift towards small(er) group negotiations does not address the regulatory constraints identified above: worries about regulatory autonomy (which apply as much to the large players involved in the plurilateral talks as to the countries that are permitted to free ride) and limitations in the capacity of poor countries to put in place and enforce regulatory measures to complement liberalization. Indeed, by effectively excluding the majority of the WTO membership from negotiations, the plurilateral approach creates a new problem: exempted countries may not be confronted with a need to liberalize, but they also are excluded from the potential gains associated with undertaking domestic policy reforms themselves. Moreover, insofar as such reforms are needed to exploit export opportunities, they may also lose out on that front. The first problem can be resolved through explicit measures that guarantee to regulators that their autonomy will not be constrained by the GATS. Mattoo (2005) argues that making national treatment the primary objective of negotiations would do much to provide such assurances. The second problem requires actions to assist developing countries to improve domestic regulatory capacities. Despite increasing recognition among WTO members that more

---

[6] As noted in earlier chapters, past practice suggests that for sectoral liberalization agreements to be applied on a MFN basis the 'internalization' ratio needs to be on the order of 90 per cent of total trade. This was the focal point used in the negotiations on the Information Technology Agreement (see Chapter 6).

needs to be done to provide assistance to developing countries to bolster trade capacity—exemplified by the creation in Hong Kong of an 'Aid for Trade' taskforce—to date services have not attracted much attention in aid for trade deliberations.

7.6 FUTURE CHALLENGES

Whatever the outcome of the Doha Round talks, experience to date suggests that WTO members confront a number of challenges relating to both the architecture of the GATS and the balance of benefits and costs associated with GATS membership.

National treatment and market access. On the architectural front, a priority area for action is to clarify the relationship between national treatment and market access obligations. As argued previously, there is overlap between the two disciplines—some (many) market access limitations are discriminatory, and thus would also violate national treatment. It would have been far clearer to make national treatment the primary discipline covering all forms of *de jure* and *de facto* discrimination (Hoekman and Mattoo, 2007). Arguably the bulk of empirically important restrictions today are discriminatory measures. Nondiscriminatory measures are less of an economic problem and likely to be more of a political issue—because multilateral disciplines in this area are more likely to be seen as intrusive.

Sectoral coverage. Important sectors including maritime transport, air transport services and audiovisual services have all been excluded from key GATS disciplines. Although interests in the latter tend to be highly concentrated and countries have a variety of noneconomic objectives that may motivate restrictive policies, exclusion of the transport sectors significantly reduces the relevance of the GATS. In addition the limited use that has been made to date by members to lock in applied policies also limits the relevance of the agreement.

Domestic regulation. A major question confronting members is whether it is desirable to develop horizontal disciplines for domestic regulations, and, if so, whether it is feasible. Although it is certainly the case that domestic regulation can be a major trade barrier, it is not clear to us that seeking to agree on disciplines on nondiscriminatory regulation is a particularly useful endeavour. Going further down the path of defining criteria for a 'necessity test' approach—putting the burden of proof on governments to show that a particular regulation which has detrimental effects on foreign providers is necessary to achieve an objective—will be difficult to apply in the WTO. The much weaker integration ambitions that prevail among WTO members and the absence of supranational enforcement can easily lead to disputes regarding what is 'necessary' and put an excessive burden on the dispute settlement system. Attention might more productively focus on expanding the reach of the national treatment principle, abolishing MFN exemptions, and ensuring that MFN applies in the area of standards and mutual recognition. Given the limited reach of existing national treatment commitments and prevalence of discriminatory policies, a focus on national treatment is both less intrusive and conceptually much more straightforward than seeking to move further into the domain of domestic regulation. This is not to deny that there is not potentially a high rate of return on efforts to agree on common norms on a sectoral basis—but this may be better done outside the WTO by specialized bodies that bring together the competent regulators and decision-makers. We return to the broader question of where to draw the boundaries of the WTO in the penultimate chapter.

Aid for trade. The focus of the WTO is on market access. Policy advice and assistance for regulatory reform and public investments in services infrastructure are provided by international financial institutions and specialized agencies. There is virtually no link between the two processes. This disconnect persists even though improved regulation—ranging from prudential regulation in financial services to pro-competitive regulation in a variety of network-based services— will be critical to realizing the benefits of services liberalization in many sectors. Policy intervention will also be necessary to ensure universal service because liberalization by itself may not improve access for the poor. There may be good reasons to defer liberalization and/or not to make binding commitments if there are weaknesses in prudential or pro-competitive regulation, or if adjustment costs are likely to be severe and affect the feasibility/sustainability of reform. More important than rules on domestic regulation, especially for developing countries, is to focus on complementary initiatives such as regulatory transparency, improving domestic regulatory capacity and clarification of issues like applicable jurisdiction. This implies that the Aid for Trade agenda in services needs to go far beyond technical assistance to help countries make market access commitments— the focus of the language on technical assistance for services negotiations in the 2005 Hong Kong Ministerial Declaration. Regulation-related assistance will need to be supplied by the appropriate international development agencies and specialized professional and sectoral entities. We return to this subject in Chapter 12.

Modal or technological neutrality. The current approach to scheduling specific commitments distinguishes between the four modes of supply that define trade (Article I GATS). As a result, national schedules may distort incentives to use the most efficient mode, while also creating uncertainty regarding the rules that prevail in instances where more than one mode is used to service a market. Such uncertainty can also create difficulties in predicting how a panel will interpret the schedules, and thus reduces the perceived benefits from initiating dispute settlement procedures. One way to reduce potential inconsistencies in commitments across modes within a specific sector is to require one-to-one mappings between commitments on modes ('nondiscrimination across modes') (Feketekuty, 1998). Such a technological neutrality principle was embodied in the Agreement on Basic Telecommunications. Modal neutrality is an objective worth pursuing because, as is often emphasized in the literature, trade and investment have increasingly become complementary. It is also frequently noted that it will become more difficult to maintain a clear distinction between trade in goods and trade in services, as technology may give producers the choice of delivering their products in tangible or in disembodied (digitized) form. A priori, it would appear that any multilateral disciplines should apply equally to international transactions regardless of the mode of supply.

Some fundamental 'architectural' issues arise here. For example, a case can be made that WTO members should consider developing disciplines that distinguish between trade and investment, with trade in goods or services being subject to a set of common rules, and movement of factors of production being subject to another set of rules. This in effect has been the approach taken in the NAFTA, which includes a separate chapter on investment (in goods or services), which is distinct from the rules relating to cross-border trade (in goods and services). This approach results in much greater consistency and clarity of the applicable rules and disciplines than the current WTO structure. These are longer run questions that must be addressed at some point. For the time being, within the GATS setting, a focus on modal neutrality can be a useful halfway house.

Achieving greater transparency. It is widely recognized that the 'scheduling technology' used in the GATS does not greatly promote transparency. A fundamental need is to improve the available information on status quo policies. This will facilitate national reform efforts and help identify where the multilateral process can support such efforts. Unfortunately, there is nothing in the GATS or the WTO that encourages and assists countries in generating comprehensive information on applied policies and evaluating the impact of these policies. Some progress was made in the Uruguay Round with the creation of the Trade Policy Review Mechanism, but more can and should be done. Priority should be given to greatly improving statistics and data on trade barriers and entry-cum-operating restrictions in services. Analogous to the role played by the OECD secretariat in compiling information on agricultural policies in the 1980s, international organizations and policy institutes should devote the resources required to document the status quo and to put this information in the public domain.

The importance of strengthening capacity to collect and analyse information cannot be overemphasized. A common mistake made by governments involved in regulatory reform is to reduce the ability of agencies to compile the information needed to monitor the impact of reforms. Better information on status quo policies, their effects, and the impact of GATS-based liberalization agreements will assist governments to make policy and provide stakeholders (business, civil society) with the information needed to engage in the domestic policy formation process. One option that deserves serious consideration in this connection is to resurrect an Australian proposal made at the 1996 WTO ministerial meeting to engage in a negative list *reporting* exercise of prevailing policies in services for transparency purposes. This should be accompanied with adequate technical and financial assistance to help developing countries, in particular LDCs, participate in the transparency exercise.

7.7. CONCLUSION

There is widespread recognition among governments and civil society that pursuit of regulatory reforms in the services area can have large payoffs. In this respect the political context today is quite different from that prevailing in 1986 when the Uruguay Round was launched. Opposition to liberalization certainly exists in many countries, and nations differ on the desirable modalities and speed with which to pursue reforms. There are also valid concerns regarding the need to put in place the appropriate regulatory policies and strengthen regulatory institutions before certain types of liberalization are undertaken. But the thrust of policy in the majority of nations is towards a more market-oriented stance, as is reflected in widespread privatization of utilities, telecom operators, airlines and so forth. The success of the financial and basic telecom sectoral talks was largely due to the fact that most of the governments involved were convinced of the need to pursue regulatory reforms in these sectors, including liberalization and elimination of entry barriers. This was a pre-condition for both agreements to materialize—it was clear that the associated regulatory reforms did not go beyond what had already been accomplished or decided in the national (unilateral) context.

A significant expansion of the coverage of national treatment and market access commitments is needed to make the GATS more relevant. The potential scope for tradeoffs in the GATS context is quite large, and there should be no need to rely on cross-issue linkages if a critical mass approach is taken by WTO members. An obvious linkage strategy *within* services would be an exchange of mode 3 for mode 4, with developing countries making greater national treatment and market access commitments on FDI across a wide range of sectors, in return for significant expansion of access to high-income markets through movement of natural persons. Although reform in services has been and will continue to be primarily driven by domestic priorities, the challenge is to make the GATS a more effective device to support domestic reforms. One way to do that began to emerge in Hong Kong in 2005 in the shape of an Aid for Trade initiative, and the strengthening of the Integrated Framework for Trade-related technical assistance (see Chapter 12). Using the GATS more as a lock-in device, as a mechanism to commit to future reforms at specified dates, greater efforts to ensure that developing country service suppliers are granted better access to the larger markets, especially through mode 4, and a willingness to put sectors such as air and maritime transport on the negotiating table would go far towards making the GATS a more relevant instrument.

7.9. FURTHER READING

Geza Feketekuty, *International Trade in Services: An Overview and Blueprint for Negotiations* (Cambridge: Ballinger, 1988) offers a comprehensive contemporary discussion of why services were put on the agenda in the Uruguay Round. See Julian Arkell, 'Lobbying for Market Access for Professional Services', in Michel Kostecki (ed.), *Marketing Strategies for Services* (Oxford: Pergamon Press, 1994) for an insider's account of lobbying and marketing strategies employed by service sectors in the GATS negotiations and in other fora to enhance access to foreign markets.

The economics of services and services negotiations are discussed in Aaditya Mattoo, Robert M. Stern and Gianni Zannini (eds), *A Handbook on International Trade in Services* (Oxford: Oxford University Press, 2008). Bernard Hoekman, 'Liberalizing Trade in Services: A Survey,' *Policy Research Working Paper No. 4030* (World Bank, 2006) provides a comprehensive survey of the economic literature.

Various GATS-related topics are discussed in depth in Patrick Messerlin and Karl Sauvant, *The Uruguay Round: Services in the World Economy* (Washington, DC: World Bank, 1990), which also includes a number of country-specific viewpoints. UNCTAD and the World Bank, *Liberalizing International Transactions in Services: A Handbook* (Geneva: United Nations, 1994) discusses many of the policy issues that arise in liberalizing services, focusing on all four modes of supply. Sumantha Chaudhuri, Aaditya Mattoo and Richard Self discuss options and challenges in making progress on Mode 4 in 'Moving People to Deliver Services: How Can the WTO Help?' *Journal of World Trade* 38 (3) (2004): 363–93.

John Croome, *Reshaping the World Trading System: A History of the Uruguay Round* (Deventer: Kluwer Law International, 1999) provides a comprehensive discussion of the services negotiations. Jagdish Bhagwati, 'Trade in Services and the Multilateral Trade Negotiations', *World Bank Economic Review* 1 (1987): 549–69 is an excellent contemporary discussion of the issues from a developing country point of view. Bernard Hoekman, 'Assessing the General Agreement on Trade in Services', in Will Martin and L. Alan Winters (eds), *The Uruguay Round and the Developing Economies* (Cambridge: Cambridge University Press, 1996) offers a detailed analysis of the GATS and the commitments made by WTO members. Rudolf Adlung and Martin Roy assess the coverage of specific GATS commitments of WTO members in 'Turning Hills into Mountains? Current Commitments under the General Agreement on Trade in Services and Prospects for Change,' *Journal of World Trade*, 39 (2005): 1161–94.

Gary Hufbauer and Erika Wada, *Unfinished Business: Telecommunications After the Uruguay Round* (Washington, DC: Institute for International Economics, 1997) and Wendy Dobson and Pierre Jacquet, *Financial Services Liberalization in the WTO* (Washington, DC: Institute for International Economics, 1998) describe and assess the post-Uruguay Round basic telecom and financial services negotiations. Priorities and alternative options to extend the GATS are discussed in Pierre Sauvé and Robert Stern (eds), *GATS 2000: New Directions in Services Trade Liberalization* (Washington, DC: Brookings Institution, 2000).

CHAPTER 8

PROTECTION OF INTELLECTUAL PROPERTY

MULTILATERAL cooperation in the field of intellectual property rights (IPRs) dates back more than a century. Although certain IPR-related issues were a matter of long standing concern under the GATT—in particular trade in counterfeit goods—it was not until the creation of the WTO that enforceable rules regarding ownership rights to intellectual property were embedded in the trading system. The Agreement on Trade-related Intellectual Property Rights (TRIPS) is unique in the WTO-context in that it imposes obligations upon governments to adopt a set of substantive rules in an area that traditionally has been the purview of domestic regulation. It is an example of what Tinbergen (1954) has called positive integration. This contrasts with the 'negative' integration that is the basic principle underlying GATT disciplines, which involves agreement not to use certain policies that directly affect (distort) trade flows—such as export subsidies or quotas—or if used, imposes constraints on when and how they may be applied.

This chapter provides an overview of the economic rationale for protection of IPRs and the forces behind moves to bring IPRs into the trading regime, the basic elements of the substantive disciplines imposed by TRIPS, and implementation-related questions and conflicts to date.

8.1. INTELLECTUAL PROPERTY RIGHTS AND INTERNATIONAL TRADE

Intellectual property can be defined as information that has economic value when put into use in the marketplace (Maskus, 2000). Ownership rights to intellectual assets span those ideas, inventions and creative expression on which there is a public willingness to bestow the status of property (Sherwood, 1990). Examples of legal expressions of IPRs include industrial property, copyrights and so-called neighbouring or related rights. Industrial property principally concerns protection of inventions through patents and trademarks. The subject matter of copyright is usually described as literary and artistic works. All these ownership rights are territorial in nature, so that the level and conditions of protection are a function of national laws and enforcement institutions.

The rationale for government protection of IPRs depends considerably on the characteristics of the knowledge that is involved. As a first cut, it can be noted that patents, copyrights and neighbouring rights, industrial secrets and industrial designs have one broad commonality: they all fall within the broad category of knowledge goods. They are the result of research and development (R&D)—invention and innovation. In contrast, trademarks and marks of origin are not knowledge goods. Instead, their aim is to allow product differentiation through the creation of brands and to provide information to consumers. Although not knowledge goods, the importance of trademarks and geographic indications of origin in trade—and as potential protectionist devices—is significant. The issues that arise from an economic perspective are analogous to those that result from the use of technical barriers to trade (see Chapter 5). The following discussion therefore focuses primarily on IPRs for knowledge goods.

Knowledge has the characteristics of a public good in that the stock of knowledge does not diminish with consumption: the marginal cost of distributing an additional unit of a knowledge good is zero. Consequently, from a static efficiency perspective the optimal allocation of resources requires that such goods have a zero price. However, this does not take into consideration that inventions have to be produced and that technological innovation can require considerable investment. With a zero price for knowledge goods, investors have no pecuniary incentive to invest in R&D activities. A zero price is therefore socially suboptimal in a dynamic sense, as it discourages innovation and technological progress. Of course, in practice many types of knowledge cannot be diffused at zero cost. Moreover, investments may need to be made to use and adapt knowledge to fit local circumstances. There are costs to imitation, including fixed costs, and many production techniques require tacit knowledge (knowhow) that is difficult to obtain. Thus, creators of many types of inventions are often able to benefit even in the absence of legal IPRs. The empirical evidence suggests that IPRs are needed not so much to promote inventions (many of which would occur anyway) but to provide an incentive to engage in costly R&D activities, which turn inventions (pure knowledge) into innovations (products or production processes that can be used in industry). The degree of protection afforded to innovations has an impact on inventor's profits and therefore on investment in R&D.

Patents or copyrights grant an inventor or author a temporary monopoly over the use of the invention or the reproduction of a work. They prevent competitors from using their knowledge without permission and/or payment. The rents resulting from the reduction in competition (and thus the ability to charge prices that exceed marginal costs) enable the owners to recoup their investments in R&D and profit from their creation, thus creating an incentive for the production of knowledge. Intellectual property rights also contribute to more rapid public disclosure of inventions, as a necessary condition for the grant of a patent is full disclosure and description of the technology for which protection is being sought. This provides competitors with useful information that can be employed in an effort to 'invent around the patent'—in practice a major source of innovation and technological progress (Maskus, 2000). In the absence of IPRs certain types of industrial inventions and the associated technical information would be kept secret much longer, with detrimental consequences for diffusion.

Governments are generally concerned with establishing an optimal mix between the need for a temporary monopoly to create incentives for the innovation needed to realize dynamic gains (growth driven by technical progress) and the benefits of free access to knowledge. In formulating their IPR policies they must reconcile static efficiency considerations (which imply that knowledge goods should be free or available at very low cost) with the longer term objectives of encouraging innovation and technological progress. There is no unique solution to this problem. Whether a given regime is optimal depends on the objectives and circumstances of countries and the economic sectors involved. Conflicts of interest between countries can easily occur. A priori, the case for harmonization of intellectual property regimes is weak—the type of regime that is most appropriate will vary with the level of development of a country.

Intellectual property rights became a trade issue for a number of reasons. Knowledge-based industries in industrialized countries have grown in relative importance. International trade in goods embodying IPRs increased substantially in recent decades as the share of manufactures in total merchandise trade has expanded, and within manufactures, the share of 'high-technology' goods has increased. Starting in the 1980s, a number of industrialized country governments began to perceive that inadequate enforcement of IPRs in importing countries reduced the competitive advantage of their exporting firms. Although trade in counterfeit goods had been an irritant for the multilateral trading system for a long time, as technologies for duplication became both more advanced and cheaper, trade in goods embodying 'stolen' knowledge became an increasingly contentious issue.

Examples of counterfeit include imitations of premium goods such as 'replica' Cartier or Rolex watches available on numerous Internet sites, Lego toys and Dunhill handbags, as well as pirate copies of compact discs, software and video films. Resulting disputes were frequently addressed through bilateral channels, with the threat of trade sanctions to induce action by importing country governments. The US played a prominent role in using unilateral threats of trade sanctions to deal with alleged IPR infringements in foreign countries. The two main instruments employed were Section 337 of the 1930 US Tariff Act, and Section 301 of the 1974 Trade Act, as amended by the 1988 Omnibus Trade and Competitiveness Act. The former was used against imports into the US, the latter against foreign governments (Box 8.1.).

The EU has instruments similar to those used by the US to address foreign trade practices, but has traditionally been much less activist than the US (Blakeney, 2004). In part, the recourse to unilateral 'self-help' instruments by major traders reflected the fact that the International Court of Justice, the main dispute settlement forum in this area prior to the creation of the WTO, requires agreement between the interested parties to submit a case to it. Moreover, many of the countries targeted under instruments such as Special 301 were not signatories of the relevant international conventions in this field, so that recourse to international dispute settlement was simply not available. Of course, these reasons did not justify the use of unilateral, threat-based approaches. The appropriate response to the problem would be to seek to negotiate a multilateral agreement that would make all parties better off. Eventually this was attempted in the Uruguay Round.

The use of US trade law provisions was challenged under GATT dispute settlement provisions on a number of occasions. In a 1981 case concerning invocation of Section 337 against Canadian exports of certain automotive springs assemblies, the dispute settlement panel found that the application of US law could be justified under GATT Article XX:*d* (General Exceptions—see Chapter 9). The panel's findings were endorsed by the GATT Council on the understanding that this did not preclude future examinations of the use of Section 337. A subsequent panel considered an EEC complaint concerning a Section 337 action against exports of Aramid fibres by Akzo, a Dutch chemical firm. This panel concluded that Section 337 was inconsistent with Article III:4 (national treatment), because it discriminated against imported products alleged to infringe US patents. Another GATT case was initiated by Brazil, after a decision by the US—following a Section 301 investigation—to increase tariffs on a range of Brazilian products in retaliation against perceived inadequate patent protection

Box 8.1. Sections 301 and 337 of US trade law

Section 301 of the US Trade Act of 1974 gives the President authority to retaliate against foreign trade practices that are deemed to restrict US exports. What such practices were was not spelled out and it was left to the discretion of the President whether or not to retaliate. A Section 301 action is initiated by private parties (in the US), and initially involves pressure being exerted on the foreign government to adopt different policies. If the response is deemed to be insufficient, attempts to negotiate agreements may be made. If negotiations fail, the US may retaliate by restricting access to its market.

The Omnibus Trade and Competitiveness Act of 1988 introduced changes to 301, rendering it much more threatening for foreign countries. Because Congress perceived the President to be insufficiently vigorous in pursuing foreign unfair trading practices, the 1988 Act called for formal investigations of private complaints. It created a new procedure—'Super 301'—that required the US Trade Representative (USTR) to create an inventory of unfair practices in foreign countries, to select priority targets from that list, set deadlines for action to be taken and to restrict the exports of these countries if the governments concerned did not act. Super 301 was complemented by a new 'Special' 301 provision that pertained to the identification of countries where protection of IPRs was deemed to be inadequate. It is Special 301 that is relevant to this chapter.

Section 337 of the US Tariff Act of 1930 allows for investigations to be initiated to determine whether foreign producers of goods imported into the US are supported by unfair trade practices and are injuring an efficiently operating US industry, act to prevent the establishment of such an industry or are anticompetitive (restrain trade). What these practices are is again not defined precisely, but many of the cases brought against imports under Section 337 have involved claims of infringement of US-held IPRs. The Omnibus Trade and Competitiveness Act of 1988, subsequently renewed in 1991 and 1999, eliminated the need to demonstrate that the unfair practice had injured a domestic industry if the allegation concerned a violation of IPRs.

The successful negotiation of the TRIPS Agreement precludes such unilateral action, as allegations of violations of the agreement must be pursued through WTO dispute settlement mechanisms. Requiring the US to use a multilateral rather than a bilateral approach to conflict resolution constituted an important motivation for developing countries to agree to the creation of TRIPS. However, Section 301 is still relevant as it is the instrument through which the US may retaliate if authorized to do so by the Dispute Settlement Body in the case of dispute that has gone through the WTO process.[1]

for pharmaceuticals and fine chemicals in Brazil (see Hudec, 1993, for more on these cases).

Business communities in OECD countries maintained that infringements of IPRs constituted a straightforward matter of piracy and theft, and called for

[1] In November 1998, Sections 301–10 of the US Trade Act of 1974 were the basis of a dispute settlement case in the WTO. The panel concluded these provisions of US trade law were not inconsistent with the GATT because of US undertakings—articulated in the Statement of Administrative Action approved by the US Congress at the time it implemented the Uruguay Round agreements—that it would abide by its obligations under the WTO in the invocation of the law. The DSB adopted the report in January 2000.

multilateral rules and enforcement of IPRs. Many developing countries opposed this strongly, arguing that protection of IPRs was a domestic policy matter, that lack of protection of IPRs on their part had a negligible impact on producers in OECD countries, and that adoption of stronger IPRs would be detrimental to their welfare and development prospects. For example, patent protection was held to be potentially detrimental to food security by raising the costs of inputs (seeds, fertilizers) and to the health of poor segments of the population (which would have to pay more for patent-protected pharmaceutical products). However, opposition was not universal. Some interest groups in developing countries favoured stronger IPRs. Examples were industries that depend on inward FDI and licensing for technology, and producers of indigenous and traditional knowledge.

The eventual acceptance of TRIPS in the Uruguay Round by developing countries reflected a package deal of sorts, comprising a mix of carrots and sticks. The stick was represented by the fear that if they did not agree they would be increasingly vulnerable to unilateral arm-twisting by the US and the EU. Carrots included the (implicit) quid pro quo that was offered by OECD countries in the form of agreeing to the phase-out of the MFA, agreeing to outlaw VERs and to bring agriculture back into the GATT. A growing perception that IPRs could be beneficial also played a role. Examples included protection of indigenous knowledge and cultural heritage, fostering innovation, and giving domestic industries better access to new technologies.

8.2. International Conventions and the GATT

Several international conventions exist that lay down standards for protection of intellectual property. These include the Paris Convention (on patents), the Berne Convention (on copyright), the Rome Convention (on sound recordings and music), the Performance and Phonograms Treaty and the Treaty on Intellectual Property in Respect of Integrated Circuits (Table 8.1). These and other conventions are administered by the World Intellectual Property Organization (WIPO), a Geneva-based UN body. Both the Paris and Berne Conventions were first negotiated over a century ago, and have been periodically updated and expanded. The need for international cooperation on IPRs arose over a century ago because IPRs are country-specific, created by national legislation. As creators of innovations must file for IPRs in each jurisdiction where they want protection, they have an incentive to push governments to adopt similar procedures and standards. Little

Table 8.1. IPRs: instruments and related international agreements

Type of IPR	Instruments of Protection	Subject Matter	Main Fields of Application	Major International Agreements
Industrial property	Patents, utility models	New, nonobvious inventions capable of industrial application	Manufacturing, agriculture	Paris Convention, Patent Cooperation Treaty (PCT), Budapest Treaty, Strasbourg Agreement, TRIPS
	Industrial designs	Ornamental designs	Manufacturing, clothing, automobiles, electronics, etc.	Hague Agreement, Locarno Agreement, TRIPS
	Trademarks	Signs or symbols to identify goods and services	All industries	Madrid Agreement, Nice Agreement, Vienna Agreement, TRIPS
	Geographical indications	Product names related to a specific region or country	Agricultural products, foodstuffs, etc.	Lisbon Agreement, TRIPS
Literary and artistic property	Copyrights and neighbouring rights	Original works of authorship	Printing, entertainment (audio, video, motion pictures), software, broadcasting	Berne Convention, Rome Convention, Geneva Convention, Brussels Convention, WIPO Copyright Treaty 1996, WIPO Performances and Phonograms Treaty, Universal Copyright Convention, TRIPS
Sui generis protection	Plant breeders' rights	New, stable homogenous, distinguishable plant varieties	Agriculture and food industry	Convention on New Varieties of Plants (UPOV), TRIPS
	Database protection	Electronic databases	Information processing industry	European Council directive 96/9/EC
	Integrated circuits	Original layout designs of semiconductors	Microelectronics industry	Washington Treaty, TRIPS
Trade secrets		Secret business information	All industries	TRIPS

Notes: All international treaties except TRIPS, the Universal Copyright Convention and the European Council Directive 96/9/EC are administered by WIPO. Indices calculated using the Hoekman (1996) methodology; see Section 7.3 above.

Source: Braga, Fink and Sepulveda (2000).

harmonization occurred, however, and many international conventions did not go much beyond agreement to apply the national treatment principle.

Most net exporters of knowledge-intensive goods were not fully satisfied with the existing conventions and sought to fill certain gaps through the GATT. For example, the Paris Convention does not stipulate the minimum duration of patents or define what should be patentable. No international agreements existed on proprietary business information (trade secrets). Standards of protection for computer software and sound recordings were deemed to be too weak by the industries concerned. Many countries considered that existing agreements dealt inadequately with counterfeiting and that national laws on trademarks were often too weak or poorly enforced. Finally, producers sought an effective multilateral dispute settlement mechanism to deal with IPR-related issues. Existing conventions did not contain binding, effective procedures in this regard. A major attraction of the GATT was that it had an enforcement mechanism.

The General Agreement on Tariffs and Trade 1947 provisions related to IPRs were quite limited. Among the GATT provisions referring specifically to IPRs are those on marks of origin (Article IX)—which require that these not be used to restrict trade—and Articles XII:3 and XVIII:10, which state that a condition for using QRs for BOP purposes is that these not violate IPRs legislation. The general exceptions provision of the GATT (Article XX:d) states that measures necessary to protect IPRs are not subject to GATT as long as they are nondiscriminatory (see Chapter 9). Although GATT rules such as national treatment (Article III), MFN (Article I), transparency (Article X) and nullification and impairment (Article XXIII) applied to actions taken in connection with national enforcement of IPRs, the general relevance of GATT for IPR regulations was limited. In effect, no substantive disciplines applied in this area. Moreover, GATT rules such as national treatment related to products, whereas those of the IPR conventions also concern persons.

Intellectual property rights-related matters raised in the GATT before the Uruguay Round mainly concerned trade in counterfeit goods, and involved trademark and design infringement, access to and misuse of certification marks, appraisal of the value of IPRs in connection with goods being imported, and use of marks of origin. Informal negotiations on trade in counterfeit goods were held during the Tokyo Round, and led to the tabling of a draft code on the subject by the United States. However, no agreement proved possible on this question (Winham, 1986). The subject was first put formally on the GATT agenda in November 1982, when ministers asked the Council to determine whether it would be appropriate to take joint action in the GATT framework on trade in counterfeit goods and, if so, what this action should be. In 1985, a Group of Experts established to advise the Council concluded that trade in counterfeit goods was a growing problem that needed multilateral action, but could not agree on whether the GATT was the right forum for this. This question was resolved at the 1986 ministerial meeting at Punta del Este that launched the Uruguay Round.

8.3. THE URUGUAY ROUND NEGOTIATIONS

The negotiation on TRIPS was one of the more difficult of the Uruguay Round, both politically and technically. The issue was relatively new to GATT and involved a North–South split. Industrial countries, led by the US, sought an ambitious and comprehensive agreement on standards for protection of IPRs of all kinds. They argued that negotiations should consider a wide range of IPRs and that enforcement through the dispute settlement system as well as through domestic laws and customs procedures was a necessity. Led by the same countries that opposed comprehensive discussions on services—India, Brazil, Egypt, Argentina and Yugoslavia—developing countries sought to draw a firm distinction between work on trade in counterfeit goods and IPRs more broadly defined. They were willing to cooperate on the former, but opposed the latter. The first order of priority for poor countries was to ensure that unilateral measures to protect IPRs did not cause barriers to legitimate trade. There was a general concern that greater protection of IPRs would strengthen the monopoly power of multinational companies, and detrimentally affect poor populations by raising the price of medicines and food.

The first two years of negotiations were dominated by disagreements over the mandate of the negotiating group. Areas of disagreement included standards of protection, use of unilateral sanctions, the reach of competition law, and the need for—and length of—transitional periods. One of the most difficult questions was how far new rules could go to protect intellectual property. Was it acceptable for GATT contracting parties to draft substantive standards on intellectual property and embody them in an international agreement? Some developing countries, led by India, argued that GATT or its successor organization was not the right place for setting and enforcing IPR standards. They felt that this was a task for WIPO—which already administered some 20 multilateral conventions—and for individual governments themselves. As far as unilateral sanctions were concerned, developing countries wanted industrialized nations to renounce the option of unilateral trade sanctions. They called for a credible commitment to multilateral dispute settlement procedures. This aspect of the negotiations was complicated by the initial US refusal to change its legislation (Section 337), which a GATT panel had found to be discriminatory in nature (see above). The US linked modifying its laws to conform with the panel recommendations to satisfactory progress in the TRIPS discussions. In the event, at the end of the day the US agreed to comply with the panel's findings, although implementation was problematical (Hudec, 1993).

In contrast to the rest of the Uruguay Round, the TRIPS negotiations were not about freeing trade, but about getting developing countries to implement existing international IPR conventions (and in a number of areas, to go beyond them). The agenda essentially centred on the establishment of minimum standards for IPRs in all countries. The talks divided developed countries—the major net exporters of knowledge and knowledge-intensive products with high levels of IPR protection that would find it easy to meet whatever minimum standards were adopted—from many developing countries, invariably net importers, many of which did not have IPR legislation. Although the final outcome went beyond existing international conventions in a number of respects, the major implications were for developing countries.

As discussed further below, from an economic perspective a good case can be made that the TRIPS talks were zero-sum in the short run, as stronger enforcement of rights in developing countries could result in large transfers from the South to the North. But gains from trade across IPR issues were clearly available. Developing countries wanted to control US trade policy (301), maintain sufficient discretion to safeguard national interests, and minimize the adjustment costs of strengthening IPRs protection. They were also keen to see stronger disciplines on the use of contingent protection, agricultural support in OECD countries and improved access for exports of labour-intensive manufactures. The objectives of the high-income industrialized countries centred on stronger IPR standards, multilaterally agreed, with multilateral enforcement. Incentive structures also differed over the course of the Uruguay Round.

Important in this connection is that developing countries were not really a cohesive bloc on the TRIPS issue. Some of the poorer nations that had tightened their domestic protection of IPRs unilaterally so as to attract FDI and technology or as a response to the threat of US action, feared being undercut by competitors in other developing countries without legal protection. Many also came to the view that stricter IPR protection was in their interest in the longer run, not only because it was a necessary component of a more general move towards a market economy, but also because of the link between IPRs and FDI and related access to knowledge. But it was the scope for cross-issue tradeoffs that ultimately created the pre-conditions for a successful conclusion of the negotiations. In exchange for agreeing to TRIPS, developing nations obtained the prospect of better market access for their textile, clothing and agricultural exports. Without a deal on IPRs it is unlikely that the Agreements on Textiles and Clothing, on Agriculture and on Safeguards could have been concluded.

8.4. WTO Rules On Intellectual Property Rights

The TRIPS agreement is an integral part of the WTO—its provisions apply to all members. It is a complex agreement—with seven major parts and 73 articles—that covers copyrights and related rights (rights of performers, broadcasters and phono-gram producers), layout-designs of integrated circuits, geographical origin indica-tions, trademarks, industrial designs and patents (Table 8.2). The agreement:

(1) establishes minimum substantive standards of protection for the above rights;
(2) prescribes procedures and remedies that should be available to enforce these rights; and
(3) extends basic GATT principles such as transparency and nondiscrimination to IPRs (although allowance is made for the fact that a number of inter-national conventions permit departures from MFN or national treatment in certain circumstances).

The agreement builds upon the main international conventions administered by the WIPO. In a number of instances TRIPS established disciplines that go beyond existing international norms. With respect to copyrights, WTO members are required to comply with the substantive provisions of the Berne Convention for the protection of literary and artistic works, except regarding protection of moral rights. Computer software is to be protected as a literary work under the Berne Convention, and copyright is to extend to computerized databases—something that was not part of the Berne Convention. As of 1994, 57 developing countries and two industrialized nations had not provided protection of computer software (Braga, 2004).

Another significant addition to international rules on copyrights are the provi-sions on rental rights, giving authors of computer programs and producers of sound recordings the right to authorize or prohibit the commercial rental of their works to the public. A similar exclusive right is also applicable to films. Performers are to be given protection from unauthorized recording and broadcast of live performances (bootlegging). Here again TRIPS goes beyond existing IPRs discip-lines as the Rome Convention on rights of performers, producers of sound recordings and broadcasters has few signatories, particularly among developing countries. The TRIPS agreement requires governments to allow recording com-panies from one country to attack unauthorized reproduction and sale of its products within another country. The protection for producers of sound record-ings and performers is to be for at least 50 years, whereas broadcasting stations are granted a 20-year period during which use of their programs requires their authorization.

The agreement defines the types of marks eligible for protection as a trademark or service mark. It also specifies the minimum rights that members must grant to mark owners, subject to certain reservations. Marks that have become well known in a particular market enjoy additional protection. For example, owners of foreign marks may not be forced to use their marks in conjunction with local marks. Governments must provide means to prevent the use of any geographical indica-tions that mislead consumers as to the origin of goods and are required to

Table 8.2. Major provisions of the TRIPS agreement

Article Comments	Subject
Cross-cutting provisions	
3. National treatment	Applies to persons
4. Most favoured nation treatment	Reciprocity exemptions for copyright; grandfathering of existing regional and bilateral agreements
6. Exhaustion	No rule imposed except nondiscrimination
Copyright and related rights	
9. Apply Berne Convention	Does not require moral rights
10. Programmes and data	A significant change in global norms; compilations protected as literary works
11. Rental rights	A significant change in global norms
12. Term of protection	Minimum 50-year term. Clarifies corporate rights
14. Neighbouring rights protection for phonogram producers, performers	
Trademarks and related marks	
15. Protectable subject matter	Confirms and clarifies Paris Convention
16. Rights conferred	Deters use of confusing marks and speculative registration; strengthens protection of well-known marks
19. Requirement of use	Clarifies nonuse. Deters use of collateral restrictions to invalidate marks
21. Licensing and assignment of rights	Prohibits compulsory licensing
22–4. Geographical indications	Definitions; additional protection for wines and spirits
Industrial designs	
26. Protection	Minimum term protection: ten years
Patents	
27. Subject matter coverage	Patents to be provided for products and processes in all fields of technology. Biotechnology covered. Exceptions allowed for plants and animals, as long as a system is in place to protect plant varieties
28. Rights conferred	Exclusive rights on sale and importing of patented product or process
30. Exceptions to rights conferred	Allows limited exceptions to patent rights as long as this does not unreasonably prejudice the right holder
31. Other use without authorization of right holder	Specific disciplines on use of compulsory licences
	Domestic production can no longer be required; nonexclusive licenses with adequate compensation
33. Duration of protection	Minimum 20-year patent length from filing date
34. Burden of proof for process patents	Defendants must prove their process differs from the patent
Integrated circuits designs	
36. Scope of protection	Protection extends to articles incorporating infringed design. Significant change in global norms

(cont.)

Table 8.2. (Continued)

Article Comments	Subject
38. Term of protection	Minimum ten years
Protection of undisclosed information	
39. Trade secrets protected against unfair methods of disclosure	New in many developing countries
Abuse of IPRs	
40. Control of anticompetitive practices	Wide latitude for competition policy to control competitive abuses, subject to other WTO disciplines
Enforcement of IPRs	
41–64. Requires civil, criminal enforcement	Detailed provisions on minimum standards for enforcement
	Agreement not to bring nonviolation cases until TRIPS Council determines the scope and modalities for such complaints
Transitional arrangements	
65–6. Transition periods round to 2016	5 years for developing and transition economies; 11 for LDCs, extended during the Doha.
70. Pipeline protection for pharmaceuticals	Not required. Provision for maintaining novelty and exclusive marketing rights
Institutional arrangements	
71. Review and amendment	TRIPS Council to monitor and review the agreement on expiration of the transitional period

Sources: Adapted from WTO (1994); Maskus (2000); and Hoekman, Mattoo and Sapir (2007).

discourage any use that would constitute unfair competition. Trademarks containing a geographical indication that could mislead the public on the true origin of the product are to be refused or invalidated. Geographical indications for wines and spirits are given specific protection. The agreement calls for a multilateral system of registration and notification of geographical indications for wines to be negotiated.

The protection of industrial designs under TRIPS was also strengthened relative to existing international norms. Designs are to be protected for a minimum period of 10 years. Owners of such designs may prevent the importation, sale or production of products bearing a design that is a copy of the protected one. World Trade Organization members must comply with the substantive provisions of the Paris Convention (1967) on patents. At least 20-year patent protection is to be provided for almost all inventions, including both processes and products. The 20-year lower bound implies harmonization toward the standards maintained by industrialized countries. It was an important rule because certain countries, including OECD members, that provided for shorter patent terms had to lengthen that protection—an issue that led to a WTO dispute settlement case brought by the US against

Canada (Box 8.2.). The provisions of the TRIPS Agreement on protection of patents required profound changes in many countries. In 1994 some 25 developing nations and four industrial nations did not recognize patents for pharmaceutical products, and 31 developing and six industrialized countries provided no protection for plant varieties (Braga, 2004).

The permitted exclusions from patentability comprise plants and animals (other than microorganisms), computer programs, and biotechnological processes. However, plant varieties must be given protection, either through patents or a *sui generis* (special or more specific) system. Inventions may be excluded from patentability for reasons of morality, public order or because of therapeutic, diagnostic or surgical usefulness. As a general rule, rights conferred in respect of patents for processes must extend to the products directly obtained by the process.

There is substantial flexibility in defining the conditions for awarding patent protection, including recognition of narrow claims, provision of utility models and pre-grant opposition procedures. Maskus (2000) notes that such elements of IPRs systems helped generate Japanese productivity gains after the Second World War by encouraging local entrepreneurs to pursue process innovations. There are no restrictions on the grounds that may be used to impose compulsory licensing to correct for anticompetitive practices (abuse of IPRs—Article 31 TRIPS) or for reasons of a national emergency. Thus, WTO members retain broad scope for compulsory licensing, including for nonworking of rights (Watal, 2000). This reinforced developing countries bargaining power vis-à-vis large drug suppliers

---

Box 8.2. Do new WTO obligations apply retroactively?

The TRIPS Agreement specifies that patent duration should be at least 20 years. However, Section 45 of Canada's Patent Act provided a 17-year term to patents granted prior to 1 October 1989. The US considered that this violated the TRIPS Agreement (invoking Article 33 TRIPS). Canada held that a WTO member should not be required to extend the duration of protection for existing patents that were granted for a shorter period prior to the existence of TRIPS, invoking the basic principle of nonretroactivity of treaty obligations. Canada referred to Article 28 of the Vienna Convention on the Law of Treaties, which provides that a treaty's provisions do not operate to bind a party in relation to any act, fact or situation which predates the treaty's entry into force for that party. Both the Panel and AB rejected Canada's claim on the basis of the TRIPS Agreement provision (Article 70.2 TRIPS), which created obligations in respect to all existing subject matters and decided that Canada was required to afford the mandated minimum of 20 years protection to patents that existed when TRIPS entered into force. The Appellate Body considered that Canada's interpretation would preclude the application of virtually the whole of the TRIPS Agreement (WT/DS170/AB/R, 18 September 2000).

in international markets, providing them with an additional instrument to lower the cost of medicines.

Once patents approach expiry, generic manufactures can step in and compete for market share. A standard tactic of holders of valuable patents is to try and maximize the length of protection by seeking to make it more difficult for competing firms to ramp up production before the patent expires so that they can flood the market once it has ended. Another early WTO dispute brought by the EC against Canada clarified what type of activities by competitors are permitted before the patent expires. The Canadian law in question allowed generic manufacturers to test patented products before the expiration of the patent. This practice was upheld by a 2000 WTO panel (WT/DS170/AB/R), but a companion provision allowing production and storage of such products before the patent expiration was declared in violation of TRIPS. The panel found that Article 30 TRIPS (allowing limited exceptions to the exclusive patent rights as long as these do not unreasonably prejudice the legitimate interests of patent holders) covered the regulatory excepting for testing but not the storage exception.

The Treaty on Intellectual Property in Respect of Integrated Circuits (1989) provides the basis for the protection of layout designs of integrated circuits. The TRIPS Agreement goes beyond this treaty by requiring a minimum protection period of ten years and extension of rights to products incorporating infringing layout designs.

Trade secrets and know-how of commercial value are protected against acts that conflict with honest commercial practices such as breach of confidence. However, the relevant provision of TRIPS (Article 39), does not define what acts are unfair, leaving governments free to allow for reverse engineering (Maskus, 2000; UNCTAD-ICTSD, 2005). Test data on agricultural or pharmaceutical chemicals submitted to the authorities in order to obtain marketing approval must also be protected against unfair commercial use.

World Trade Organization members are obliged to provide procedures and remedies under their domestic law for effective enforcement of IPRs by right-holders (both foreign and national). Such procedures should be fair and equitable, entail reasonable time limits and not be unnecessarily complicated or costly. Requirements on the civil and administrative procedures and remedies include provisions on evidence of proof, injunctions, damages and other remedies. In cases when delay is likely to result in irreparable harm to the right-holder, prompt and effective provisional measures must be available. The Agreement also deals with measures to be taken at the border by customs authorities against pirated or counterfeit goods.

Article 40 TRIPS recognizes that some licensing practices or conditions pertaining to IPRs may have adverse effects on trade or impede the transfer and dissemination of technology. It allows for members to specify in their legislation practices or conditions that constitute an abuse of IPRs and give rise to intervention by the government. The TRIPS Agreement provides some flexibility by leaving it to the discretion of governments how to regulate 'exhaustion' of IPRs. In legal parlance, IPRs are exhausted once an invention or a product embodying the IPRs has been sold, allowing the purchaser to make fair use of the product for private purposes and to re-sell. Under an international exhaustion rule, a protected product, once introduced in a market anywhere in the world, can be imported into the country without permission of the IPRs holder. Under a national exhaustion rule the goods may only be re-sold to buyers that are resident in the country—that is, 'parallel imports' are prohibited. International exhaustion allows buyers to purchase patented and branded products wherever they find the most favourable prices.[2] An intermediate approach is to apply a regional exhaustion rule—which is the case under EU law. Countries with large knowledge industries tend to apply a national exhaustion rule, reflecting the interests of industry, whereas those that do not frequently adopt international exhaustion.

All members had one year following the date of entry into force of the WTO to implement the agreement. Developing countries were entitled to a delay of an additional four years for all provisions of the agreement with the exception of MFN and national treatment. If a developing country had to extend product patent protection to areas of technology that were not protected before TRIPS (for example, pharmaceuticals or agricultural chemicals), it could delay the application of the provisions on product patents to such areas for an additional five years. Least developed countries were granted a 12-year period to conform to the agreement (until 1 January 2006), with the possibility of requesting a longer period if deemed necessary. They did so during the Doha Round and obtained an extension through 2016.

These transition periods are all rather arbitrary in that they do not reflect careful assessments of likely implementation costs. Instead, they reflect issue linkage considerations: the transition period for the abolition of the MFA was ten years, and liberalization under the ATC was heavily back-loaded. This helps explain why developing countries (non-LDCs) insisted on a ten-year transition for implementation of the key part of the TRIPS agreement—patent protection of pharmaceuticals. Although the TRIPS agreement may be too riddled with holes as far OECD right-holders are concerned, developing countries committed themselves to doing more on the IPRs front than OECD countries did with regard to traditional issues such as contingent protection and market access. Indeed, many TRIPS disciplines applied with immediate effect, including in the patent area the requirement to provide for exclusive marketing rights during the transition period (Watal, 2000). Simulation studies and other types of economic analysis of the outcome of the Uruguay Round discussed later in this chapter suggest that on balance the costs of

---

[2] The term parallel signifies that the transactions take place alongside sales by the IPRs owner through its own distribution channels. See Abbott (2007).

TRIPS for developing countries may have outweighed the benefits obtained in other areas of the negotiation.

8.5. IMPLEMENTATION AND DISPUTES

Implementation of the TRIPS agreement involved substantial adjustments and costs for many developing countries. Bringing legislation into conformity in a way that best reflects the interests of a country takes time and scarce human resources. Creating or strengthening the domestic institutions required to enforce the new laws costs money. Such costs did not need to be incurred by OECD countries, as they were already largely in compliance with TRIPS standards and had the necessary enforcement infrastructure in place. Developing countries had to revise or adopt new legislation, ensure that judges were trained in the application of IPR law, and educate customs and other enforcement authorities so that they understood the new rules and had the tools and resources to apply them. Efforts needed to be made to educate the business community and civil society as well.

Designing an intellectual property regime that is relevant for the situation and characteristics of the economy of a developing country is not straightforward. Simply copying the regime that is in place in an OECD country will not do. The type of intellectual property that needs to be protected varies across countries, as does institutional capacity. Rather than develop a patent office along European or US lines it may be more important to develop mechanisms to protect the fruits of indigenous culture such as music or crafts. How to do this in a cost-effective manner requires research and trial and error experience. At the time the TRIPS agreement was being negotiated, insufficient knowledge existed to allow such concerns to be embodied in the drafting of the agreement.

Finger and Schuler (2000) reviewed World Bank projects in the area of IPRs and concluded that the costs of implementing the TRIPS agreement could be substantial. In large part this is because required reforms go beyond drafting new legislation. What matters are the administrative structures needed to apply the new norms (for example, bolstering the capacity to review applications, including investments in computerized information systems and extensive training for staff) and buttressing enforcement capacity. Although developing countries were granted a transition period to implement the agreement, in many cases the time required for upgrading IPR regimes spans a longer period than was granted. Many countries did not have the resources available to undertake the comprehensive reforms and institutional strengthening that was required. Little analysis exists of the actual costs that are associated with full implementation of TRIPS. However, a feature of IPRs is that they are valuable assets. Thus, firms and investors are therefore ready to pay for the costs of obtaining a right, be it a patent, trademark or copyright. In practice, patent offices—once up and running—can pay for themselves from fees. The implication is that the lion's share of the implementation costs are likely to be associated with training of officials and the potential 'diversion' of scarce administrative capacity to an agenda that is may not be a priority from an economic development perspective.

During the first ten years of the WTO over two dozen cases referring to TRIPS were submitted for dispute settlement. Given that many of the major substantive provisions of the agreement did not yet apply to developing countries, most of these cases involved the major OECD countries. However, India was one of the first countries to be subjected to a complaint, following separate cases filed in 1996 by the US and the EC against Japan's copyright regime for sound recordings (Box 8.3).

The US was the most active early user of dispute settlement, with the majority of cases brought against the EU. It complained, inter alia, of an alleged lack of protection of trademarks and geographical indications for agricultural products and foodstuffs in the EU, failure to grant copyright and neighbouring rights in

Box 8.3. Early TRIPS disputes: music royalties in Japan and the 'mailbox' provision in India

The first dispute settlement cases brought under TRIPS were against Japan, brought by the US and EC (WT/DS28 and WT/DS42). They were similar to the dispute between the US and Canada regarding length of patent protection: Japan did not provide at least 50-year copyright protection for sound recordings. The case never went through the panel process. Japan reached a mutually agreed solution with the complainants, agreeing to revise its legislation to bring it into conformity with TRIPS.

The first case under TRIPS to go through both the panel and AB stages was launched by the US in late 1996 (WT/DS50). (Here again the EU followed the US example, bringing its own case a few months later.) The US challenged India's implementation of the so-called mail box provision (Article 70 TRIPS) with respect to patent protection for pharmaceutical and agricultural chemical products. This specifies that a developing country delaying implementation of TRIPS obligations in an area of technology that was previously unprotected must secure the legal security of patent applications. This was meant to ensure that no subsequent claimant would be able to assert the same patent once the transition period for implementing the TRIPS obligation expired. The panel and AB found that India had failed to establish a mechanism that adequately preserved novelty and priority in respect of applications for product patents for pharmaceutical and agricultural chemical inventions, and was also not in compliance with Article 70.9 of the TRIPS Agreement by failing to establish a system for the grant of exclusive marketing rights. Two related cases were subsequently brought against Argentina.

certain EU member states, nonenforcement of IPRs in Greece (allegations that TV stations in Greece regularly broadcast copyrighted motion pictures and television programmes without the authorization of copyright owners), Denmark's alleged failure to make provisional measures available in the context of civil proceedings involving IPRs, and Portugal's term of patent protection under its Industrial Property Act. The EU in turn has taken the US to task on legislation that precludes registration or renewal in the United States of a trademark if it was previously abandoned by a trademark owner whose business and assets were confiscated under Cuban law (Section 211 of the US Omnibus Appropriations Act) and a law that permitted commercial entities such as bars and restaurants to play music and television without payment of royalties (Section 110:5 of the US Copyright Act). The latter two cases are illustrative of the types of disputes that have been brought under TRIPS: on the one hand addressing a conflict where specific commercial interests are at stake, and on the other seeking to ensure that general legislation complies with TRIPS—even if the law in question appears to be quite reasonable.

At issue in the trademark case (WT/DS/176) were the rights to the name Havana Club. The EU filed the complaint on behalf of a French company, Pernod-Ricard, which sold Cuban-produced rum under the Havana Club trade name (as part of a joint venture with a Cuban state-owned enterprise) but could not do so in the US because Bacardi, a Bermuda-based firm, had obtained the US rights to this name from the original Cuban owners whose assets were nationalized by the Cuban government in 1960.[3] The Cuban family that had the original trademark in the US had let it lapse in 1973, and in 1976 the Cuban state export company registered the name in the US. However, 20 years later, Bacardi sought out the original family members and obtained their agreement to use the name and began to distribute rum in the US market under the Havana Club label. This led Pernod to sue in the US courts. Williams (2005) notes that part of the Bacardi response to the Pernod threat was to lobby successfully to revise existing US law by including specific language on trademarks that had been confiscated by Cuba into the general spending bill that was being considered by the US Congress at the time (the US Omnibus Appropriations Act).

The end result of the WTO panel and AB process was to find that Section 211 of this Act violated national treatment and MFN (because it denied trademark owners access to US courts by not giving them legal standing). However, the US was free under TRIPS to establish the criteria to determine ownership of IPRs such as trademarks and trade names, including the right to refuse registration of confiscated marks. As a result of the case, the US agreed to revise its legislation to bring it into compliance, but the commercial dispute between Bacardi and Pernod on the trade name continued to be pursued in the US courts. As in other, more

---

[3] What follows draws on the discussion in Williams (2005).

high-profile cases such as *Bananas* and *Gambling*, this dispute illustrates that the ultimate or even proximate commercial interests that are at stake may not involve firms headquartered or based in the country that brings it to the WTO.

The second case concerned nonpayment of royalties for music or programmes broadcasted in bars and similar retail spaces (WT/DS160), permitted under Section 110 of the US Copyright Act. This dispute revolved around the 'minor exception' doctrine—that the violating practice only has a minor effect on the rights-holder. The case was brought by the EU on behalf of a complaint lodged by the Irish Music Rights Organization. The genesis of the complaint was an amendment by the US of its copyright law (introduced via the Fairness in Music Licensing Act of 1998) that expanded the coverage of exemptions for certain retail establishments to pay royalties for music.

The 2000 WTO panel distinguished between the 'business exemption' applying to a very large percentage of bars and restaurants and 'home-style exemption' applying to a limited set of cases where the music (not recordings) was being broadcast by means of a single, standard TV set or radio of a kind commonly used in private homes. It concluded that 'business exemption' could not be considered 'defined and limited' in the sense of TRIPS Article 13 because of the large percentage of establishments to which it applied. It considered, however, that the 'home-style exemption', which applied to 13–18 per cent of small establishments, was not a major potential source of royalties and that in any event royalties would be difficult (costly) to collect. Therefore, the 'home-style exemption' was considered not to violate the TRIPS Agreement. The US did not appeal the report.

This case illustrates both how the TRIPS agreement is more intrusive than the traditional GATT disciplines, and how international disciplines pertaining to domestic regulatory regimes may have unintended and unanticipated consequences (the *Gambling* case is another example). Surely US negotiators had not foreseen the implications of TRIPS for the legislation that was contested in this case. In effect, the Irish musicians' organization was able to contest a US domestic political economy equilibrium that was reflected in a US law that balanced the interests of IPRs holders and buyers/users. Given that the practices that the EU complained about were put in place by the legislature of the country with the strongest music and broadcasting industry in the world, presumably the provisions of the US law were acceptable to US producers. After all, the proprietors of the bars and restaurants will have bought or otherwise paid for the music they play in their establishments.

An obvious question is how much was at stake in this case. Because the US was not able to revise its legislation within the reasonable period established by an arbitrator, the US and the EC notified the DSB in 2001 of their agreement to pursue binding arbitration under Article 25.2 of the DSU to determine the magnitude of the loss incurred by the EU rights-holders (the level of nullification or impairment of benefits). The arbitrator determined that the loss amounted to

€1,219,900 per year or US$1.1 million at the then prevailing exchange rate—a rather trivial amount. As part of the Wartime Supplemental Appropriations Act, signed into law on 16 April 2003, the US Congress approved a US$3.3 million appropriation—to cover three years of payments—which was subsequently paid to the European Grouping of Societies of Authors and Composers, at the request of the European Commission. This was the first time that WTO members made use of arbitration (invoked Article 25 of the DSU) to establish the level of compensation to be paid in a case.[4]

Developing countries have also become more active in safeguarding their IPRs interests. For example, in 1998 Thailand asked the US to revoke registration of the 'Jasmati' rice trademark of a US firm. Objections have also been raised to the use of variants of the name Basmati for rice, with India taking steps to protect 'Basmati' as a geographical indication. Tea plantations in the region of Darjeeling launched a campaign to protect the 'Darjeeling' brand from foreign imitations, with a Belgian watchdog agency asked to identify the use of the name 'Darjeeling' in international markets.

8.6. THE DOHA ROUND

In the run-up to—and during—the Doha Round, IPRs continued to remain among the more controversial areas of trade and business regulation, reflecting a sharp North–South divide. Despite their success in putting in place the TRIPS Agreement, IPRs lobbies continued to push for expanding and strengthening rights. They favoured extending the reach of the patent system, reinforcing protection of copyrights and neighbouring rights and extending rules on geographical indications. Advocates of expanding TRIPS pointed to increasing R&D and positive effects of trademarks and geographical indications for value added in developing country business, and noted ways in which the system might be beneficial to developing countries in terms of protection of traditional knowledge and biodiversity. The critics raised concerns about higher prices and access to essential medicines, limited availability of new seed varieties, and risks of abusive licensing practices.

Concerns about the implications of TRIPS became an integral part of the anti-WTO message propounded by many NGOs. The Doha Round offered an opportunity for the two camps to pursue their different visions of what constitutes

---

[4] The funds were used for combating piracy on the Internet and supporting actions for copyright strengthening and enforcement in Europe and the United States. The details of the arbitration award are discussed in Grossman and Mavroidis (2003).

appropriate regulation of IPRs. Proponents of stronger disciplines were mostly on the back foot during the Doha period, devoting much of their energy and resources defending what they had negotiated in the Uruguay Round. Critics conversely were more successful in addressing some of their major concerns as regards the TRIPS agreement, which included access to essential medicines and protecting traditional knowledge and biodiversity.

Essential medicines

Among some 10 million people who pass away each year due to infectious diseases more than 90 per cent live in developing countries (WHO, 2005). The most dangerous infectious diseases in low-income countries of Africa, Asia and Latin America include HIV/AIDS, respiratory infections, malaria and tuberculosis. The TRIPS Agreement (Article 31: f) recognizes that IPRs should not come in the way of action by governments to address pressing public policy needs. Thus, in a case of an important public health emergency, if local drug manufacturers are unable to produce enough to satisfy the demand for the medicines protected by patents, a WTO member government can require the producer to licence the medicine to other firms to address any (expected) shortage. The TRIPS rules negotiated in the Uruguay Round stipulated that production under compulsory licensing must be predominantly for the domestic market. This created a problem for developing countries with no production capacity as they would need to import the drugs.

The question of how to produce 'global public goods' in a world where countries have divergent norms and preferences, in part reflecting differences in economic development, is increasingly prominent on the international policy agenda. The TRIPS Agreement raised concerns regarding at least three public (or quasi-public) goods: the generation of new knowledge, the maintenance of rules fostering open trade and competition, and the provision of public health (Shaffer, 2004). Many developing countries viewed the TRIPS Agreement as an impediment in their efforts to combat public health emergencies by restricting availability of patented medicines and by transferring scarce resources to patent-owners and producers in high-income countries. As developing economies are often overwhelmed by infectious diseases, access to affordable medicines was a vital concern.

The TRIPS Agreement became part of the equation insofar as the relevant drugs were protected by patents. Fixing the imbalance between countries with and without local production capacity as regards their ability to invoke compulsory licences for pharmaceuticals came to be perceived as a test as to whether the WTO could address development concerns.

The most publicized aspect of the debate has been over HIV/AIDS in Africa. As access to low-cost drugs is increasingly recognized as a key component of treatment strategies, the patent status (and resulting high cost) of the new antiretroviral drugs were perceived as a barrier to prevention and treatment.[5] The pharmaceutical industry argued that the HIV/AIDS problem in Africa resulted from poverty and should be treated as such, suggesting for example that the appropriate solution was for high-income governments to provide subsidies to pay for the drugs. They maintained that serious limitations on patent protection would be counterproductive, resulting in less R&D on products of particular interest to the developing world. A leading role in this campaign was assumed by one of the most influential Washington industry associations, representing some 48 pharmaceutical companies: the Pharmaceutical Research and Manufacturers of America (PhRMA).

The industry's stance resulted in severe criticism of the TRIPS Agreement by a broad constellation of nongovernmental groups as well as some governments and international bodies. In August 2000, the UN Sub-Commission for the Protection and Promotion of Human Rights adopted a resolution that recognized 'the apparent conflict' between the TRIPS Agreement and international human rights law. The resolution underlined that the implementation of TRIPS did not adequately reflect the fundamental nature and indivisibility of human rights, including the right of everyone to enjoy the benefits of scientific progress and its applications, the right to health, the right to food, and the right to self-determination (Article 2).

Another influential critical voice was a report by the UK Commission on Intellectual Property Rights, sponsored by the UK Department for International Development (DFID) and chaired by a distinguished Stanford University Law Professor, John Barton. The report expressed serious doubts concerning the benefit of the current IPR regime for the poor segments of world population and pointed to the system's shortcomings in the area of public health and development (Barton et al., 2002). Numerous NGO campaigns echoed such comments and the possible adverse impact of IPRs on access to medicines became a high profile matter of public debate.

At the same time, the pharmaceutical industry sought to enforce TRIPS through action in national courts as well as through their governments in the WTO. The highest profile such effort occurred in South Africa and attracted worldwide attention and opprobrium (Box 8.4). Another instance of such pressure centred on Brazil's decision to increase supplies of generic medicines to address the HIV/AIDS epidemic, which prompted the US to initiate a WTO dispute case in 2000. At issue was a requirement for 'local working' for patents. The US held that the Brazilian law violated TRIPS Articles 27–8 and the national treatment principle by stipulating that a patent was subject to compulsory licensing if the subject matter of the patent was not 'worked' in the territory of Brazil (Abbott, 2002). The

---

[5] In 2003 the triple combination of drugs that was most effective in combating AIDS cost over US$10,000 a year in developed countries, compared to US$200–300 in India, where they were produced without patent protection (Subramanian, 2006). The disparity in prices was even larger in practice if account is taken of the fact that most developing country citizens are not insured and must pay medical expenses privately.

Box 8.4. The South African Medicines Act

Faced with the HIV/AIDS crisis in the early 2000, South Africa passed the Medicines Act, which included a provision that allowed for fast track compulsory licensing of medicines and authorization for parallel importation of drugs. Both provisions were motivated by a desire to give South Africans access to the lowest priced sources of supply of vital pharmaceutical products. The Act permitted the importation of patented medicines that had been commercialized in another market by the patent owner (i.e. South Africa adopted an international exhaustion rule). Pressured by its pharmaceutical industry, the US, with support from the EU, pressed the South African authorities to modify the Act and remove the offending provisions. One of the arguments was that the law breached South Africa's obligations under the TRIPS Agreement. In 2001 a number of major drug corporations brought their case to the Pretoria High Court. Several months later, following a mass media campaign supported by NGOs such as Oxfam and Médecins sans Frontières, the litigation was withdrawn in order not to deteriorate even further the public image of the pharmaceutical companies concerned.

Source: Braithwaite and Drahos (2006). See www.cptech/ip for more on the history of the dispute.

case was settled with an agreement to create a bilateral 'Consultative Mechanism' under which Brazil will notify the US government in advance in the event that it finds it necessary to issue a compulsory licence. There is nothing in the WTO that would require such bilateral notification, and arguably the outcome was a face-saving exercise that is not enforceable.

The widespread criticism of the TRIPS Agreement eventually resulted in the November 2001 Doha Declaration on TRIPS and Public Health. This reaffirmed the right of all countries to protect public health and stated that TRIPS should be implemented in a manner supportive of rights 'to promote access to medicines for all'. The Declaration also recognized the problem confronting countries without industrial or technical capacity to produce drugs in being able to benefit from invoking compulsory licensing provisions and instructed the TRIPS Council 'to find an expeditious solution to the problem of the difficulties that WTO members with insufficient or no manufacturing capacities in the pharmaceutical sector could face in making effective use of compulsory licensing under the TRIPS Agreement' (WTO/MIN(01)/DEC/2) and to do so before the end of 2002.

Several possible solutions were proposed by WTO members: amending the TRIPS agreement; adopting a broader interpretation of Article 30 to authorize third parties to produce and sell drugs without the consent of the rights-holders; promising not to initiate dispute settlement proceedings in case of departure from Article 31(f)—which requires that a compulsory licence must be authorized 'predominantly for the supply of the domestic market of the Member authorizing such use'; and introducing a 'waiver' for Article 31(f) in the sense of Article IX(3) of the WTO (Bourgeois, 2008). It was the latter approach that was eventually adopted following highly contentious negotiations on the scope of—and eligibility for invoking—a provision to facilitate the use of compulsory licensing. A 2003 WTO General Council Decision allowed WTO members to grant compulsory licences with a view to exporting pharmaceutical products to countries with no or insufficient manufacturing capacities (WT/L540). The 2001 Doha Declaration on TRIPS and Public Health, which was outside the single undertaking, was practically the only area in which results had been obtained in time for the review of progress made in the Doha Round during the Cancun ministerial meeting in 2003.

The above process of negotiation was accompanied by significant pressure by the US and a number of other developed countries aimed at minimizing the impact of the 2001 Declaration. There was a strong effort to limit the number of eligible diseases (drugs) and to obtain agreement on a specific list of countries to which the modalities of operationalizing the 2001 Declaration would apply. In the end, the 2003 Council Decision simply states that the drugs concerned address the public health problems, including those mentioned in the 2001 Declaration, which emphasized HIV/AIDS, tuberculosis, malaria and other epidemics, but does not define a limited set of diseases. It also does not limit the country eligibility except through a requirement that the country concerned have insufficient or no manufacturing capacities. In December 2005, at the Hong Kong ministerial meeting, the Decision was made permanent through adoption of an amendment to the TRIPS Agreement that transposes the Decision into an Article 31 *bis* TRIPS. (This was the first ever, and to date only, amendment to a WTO agreement). Under the WTO (see Chapter 2) general entry into force of an amendment requires acceptance by two-thirds of the membership. As of August 2008, counting the EU-27 as one, 18 WTO members had ratified—including the US (the first to have done so).[6]

The Decision (and Article 31 *bis*) waives the obligations of Article 31(f) by allowing WTO members to export pharmaceutical products under a compulsory licence to another country that has invoked the provision to address a public health need (national emergency or other circumstances of extreme urgency or in cases of public noncommercial use are mentioned as examples). It requires importing country governments to put in place mechanisms to prevent re-export and parallel trade—a matter of great concern to the industry. Medicines traded under the regime should be packed, labelled and coloured differently to ensure that they can be identified by Customs if they were to enter into parallel trade, and special reporting requirements are imposed. Over 30 WTO members indicated that they would not use the system set out in the 2003 Decision as importers—the result of efforts by the EU, Japan and the US to limit the extent to which the original TRIPS discipline in this area might be weakened (General Accounting Office, 2007).

---

[6] The 2003 waiver applies to countries that have not yet formally accepted the amendment.

The media debate on patents for medicines contributed significantly to the legitimacy woes of the TRIPS Agreement and the WTO. Concerns by the pharmaceutical companies regarding their public image and support resulted in a change in the hard-line stance taken by the pro-IPR lobby. As a result of the opposition and skilful advocacy by economic development NGOs, patent-holding multinationals began to shift from a strategy that put significant emphasis on litigation to one that began to do more to capture the moral high ground. A number of firms decided to provide developing countries with affordably priced retroviral drugs (that is, engage in differential pricing strategies) or to donate drugs.

The shift coincided with a growing awareness that the drug industry had to rethink its business model, ranging from innovation and patent strategy to marketing and advocacy. A new business model that went beyond the industry's traditional and substantially vertical integration in R&D, production and marketing medicines began to gain popularity. It involved, in particular, a move towards more offshore outsourcing, increased interest in generic drug production, and a convergence of drugs, devices and diagnostics that promised new opportunities for growth and escape from low-margin market segments subject to commodity pricing. The trend towards business modernization combined with public pressure to soften the industry's position with respect to the health matters governed by the TRIPS Agreement resulted in a more flexible approach on these issues by OECD countries. These changes in strategy and positions facilitated agreement on the 2003 Council Decision on TRIPS and Public Health.

How important is the relaxation of the TRIPS disciplines in this area? To date, use of compulsory patent licences by developing countries has been limited. Examples include Taiwan in 2005 for the Avian flu (Tamiflu—a substance owned by Roche),[7] Thailand in 2006 and 2007 for HIV/AIDS and heart disease drugs, and Brazil in 2007 for a HIV/AIDS treatment. The first use of the provision established by the Council by an LDC was a compulsory licence for export of an antiretroviral drug (TriAvir) from Canada to Rwanda in 2007. To implement this Canada issued a compulsory licence allowing a firm based in Canada, Apotex, to use nine patented inventions for manufacturing and exporting TriAvir to Rwanda. Apotex specified that it would sell and export 15.6 million tablets at the cost of its production (about US$0.40 per tablet) and obtained a royalty-free two-year-compulsory licence on the nine Canadian patents to do so in late 2007. Hestermeyer (2007) argues that this was not a good test case as Rwanda could have imported a similar combination drug from India, which was available at US$0.14 per tablet. (Not yet being under patent in India, Rwanda could simply have imported the drug from India.) He also notes that the Canadian firm concluded

---

[7] Other countries such as Indonesia, the Philippines and Thailand threatened to follow suit. Roche responded by stating that these countries are free to manufacture generic versions of Tamiflu because it was not patented in their markets.

that a generic manufacturer has few incentives to go through the WTO process for markets as small as Rwanda and that the two-year maximum term for a compulsory licence in Canada was not enough to recoup the investment associated with producing the drug from scratch (the compound was not sold in Canada).

In practice the compulsory licensing mechanism and the TRIPS flexibilities more generally appear to have had only a limited effect on the availability of medicines for the poor (see e.g. Sihanya, 2005). One reason for this is that many drugs are *not* patented—that is, there are generics already on the market. Another reason is that many developing countries first need to incorporate the possible provisions on compulsory licensing, parallel imports, limits on data protection, use of broad research and other exceptions to patentability into their legislation (Abbott and van Puymbroeck, 2003). Factors such as inadequate distribution systems, the lack of trained personnel to administer the drugs, weak incentives for generic drug manufacturers to supply small quantities to LDCs with no production capacity, and the necessity to use distinctive packaging and notification requirements, all limit the benefits of the compulsory licences (Correa, 2004). According to then-EU trade negotiator, Pascal Lamy, the compulsory licensing arrangement resolved 'about 10% of the problem of access to medicines by developing countries' (*Wall Street Journal*, 2 September 2003). Many public health experts will agree—clearly the public health challenge in poor countries extends far beyond access to low-priced patented drugs. Effective and efficient delivery and distribution mechanisms are also needed, as are infirmaries and hospitals, health-care providers, etc.

Notwithstanding these arguments, the indirect effect of the attention devoted to this matter was undoubtedly significant. Although it is the case that lowering prices of drugs is only part of the answer to public health needs in developing countries, from an economic perspective the approach pursued in the TRIPS and Public Health discussion makes a lot of sense. The countries that cannot afford high-priced drugs are not important in generating the R&D incentives needed to induce investment in the development of new drugs. Thus, pricing drugs at marginal cost in these markets will not have adverse dynamic effects on innovation. As long as re-exports can be precluded, firms—whether generic producers or those that invented the compounds—will be able to cover the costs of servicing these markets by pricing at levels that cover marginal costs while charging higher income markets (much) more, in the process recouping R&D costs. The required market segmentation is critical for developing countries to be able to benefit from this differentiated pricing. The alternative of a uniform pricing rule would be far inferior to low-income markets.

One result of the TRIPS decision was to strengthen the already existing incentive confronting pharmaceutical firms to engage in beneficial price discrimination by establishing a 'price ceiling' for the drugs concerned—defined by the cost of producing and shipping drugs to the markets concerned without having to pay royalties.

The pharmaceutical industry responded by reducing prices for antiretroviral drugs for developing countries, although it should be stressed that this reflected more than just the WTO Decision—the whole episode was a public relations disaster for the industry that it sought to address in part by a willingness to provide drugs at low or zero cost. Greater resources are now also being devoted to accelerate the development and promote the distribution of vaccines for other diseases such as malaria and TB. The fact that these countries are poor means that diseases which predominantly occur there will not be the focus of R&D without public subsidy of some kind. This problem has been recognized by OECD governments and major foundations that are committed to investing substantial resources in such diseases.

That said, conflicts between the industry and governments and regulators will persist, and pharmaceutical companies will continue to defend their rights and base business decisions in part on the strength of IPR enforcement in any given market (Box 8.5).

Traditional knowledge, life forms and biodiversity

Traditional knowledge covers a variety of assets, including genetic resources, indigenous medicinal knowledge and designs. Traditional medicinal knowledge relies on plant treatment, which being obvious or in the public domain, is usually not patented or not patentable. But, a medicine derived from plants that use traditional know-how may be patented by a pharmaceutical company. This raises two types of potential problems for developing countries: (1) IPRs may be acquired by such companies, precluding use by local communities; and (2) holders of the traditional knowledge may not be adequately compensated, if at all.

Finger and Schuler (2004) have noted that TRIPS is mostly about knowledge that rich countries own and want to sell to poor countries. They suggest that the as yet unwritten part of the TRIPS Agreement should be about knowledge that poor people in poor countries generate and might want to benefit from. This in turn suggests asking questions such as: how could one prevent inappropriate patenting of traditional knowledge? What could be done to ensure that providers of traditional knowledge are not excluded from benefits resulting from interventions based on that knowledge? One result of developing country interest in addressing these types of questions was that protection of traditional knowledge became an item on the agenda of a review TRIPS called for in the Doha Ministerial Declaration (para. 19). Technical issues requiring solution included agreeing on an operational definition of traditional knowledge, determination (identification) of 'right-holders' and establishing the legal basis for protection of those forms of traditional knowledge that were in the public domain.

The Doha agenda included a review of TRIPS Article 27.3(b), which allows plants and animals other than microorganisms and essentially biological processes for the

---

Box 8.5. Business interests and patent protection of drugs

The Indian Patent Act prohibits the granting of patent protection to inventions involving a new form of a known substance that does not result in the enhancement of the known efficacy of the substance (Section 3(d)). A Swiss-based multinational company Novartis applied in 2006 for patent protection of its cancer drug Clivec in India. The Indian Patent Office rejected the patent application on the grounds that the subject matter was anticipated and obvious in the light of prior art and that Clivec could not demonstrate sufficient improvement in treatment efficiency over the molecule imatinib, on which the drug was based.

Novartis disagreed with the decision and filed a case with the Madras High Court in Chennai alleging that Section 3(d) of the Indian Patent Act was incompatible with the TRIPS Agreement and the Indian constitution. The court upheld the constitutionality of India's restrictions on 'ever greening' pharmaceutical patents and declined to rule on the compatibility of the Indian national law with the TRIPS Agreement. Novartis decided not to appeal the decision to the Indian Supreme Court. In such circumstances, the only way to determine the compatibility issue would be for Switzerland to initiate a WTO dispute—a move that was unlikely given the political sensitivity of public health issues and patent protection in developing countries. The Novartis court case had already drawn much attention worldwide, with some 420,000 people signing a petition urging the company to drop the case. One of the signatories, Anglican Archbishop Emeritus Desmond Tutu, commented that the court's decision reflected 'what we know in our hearts: that our society's priority must be people's health, not extra profits from patents for rich corporations'. The Paris-based NGO 'Médecins sans Frontières' referred to the High Court's verdict as 'critical for us doctors, who now feel confident that we will be able to continue to rely on India as a source of affordable medicines for our patients'. In August 2007 Novartis announced that it was shelving its investment plans in India, stating that the High Court's ruling was not an invitation to invest in India's R&D. The CEO of the pharmaceutical giant was quoted as saying 'We will invest more in countries where we have protection'.

Source: *Bridges* 11 May (2007); *Financial Times*, 22 August (2007).

---

production of plants and animals (other than nonbiological and microbiological processes) to be excluded from patentability as long as a system was put in place to protect plant varieties. At issue here were questions on such issues as how to define *sui generis* protection of plant varieties and how to deal with ethical questions relating to the patentability of life-forms. Could biological and genetic resources in their natural state be protected by IPRs? Should these resources be protected as intellectual property so that developing country local community or farmers could benefit from their conservation?

The TRIPS Council became the forum for negotiations on the protection of traditional knowledge and folklore as well as the question of the relationship between the TRIPS Agreement and the Convention on Biological Diversity (CBD). A group of developing countries, including Brazil and India, proposed that TRIPS be amended to preclude bio-piracy, i.e. uncompensated and unauthorized appropriation of genetic resources, and to ensure fair and equitable sharing of benefits obtained from traditional knowledge or folklore. A proposed amendment to TRIPS would impose conditions for patents based on biological material or traditional knowledge, including disclosure of their source and evidence of benefit-sharing and prior informed consent. It was also suggested that IPRs could be an instrument for implementing the Convention on Biodiversity, e.g. by providing for sharing of benefits resulting from the use of genetic resources and the disclosure of the geographical source and origin of genetic material (Llewelyn, 2003).

Prior to the July 2008 mini-ministerial meeting in Geneva, proponents of the CBD-related amendment to TRIPS pushed for a disclosure requirement in order for patent applications to be processed, and proposed that members agree to define 'the nature and extent' of prior informed consent and access and benefit-sharing. The biotechnology industry opposed these proposals and raised concerns that the disclosure of origin requirement would result in an undue burden on patent applications, given also that the concept of 'sufficient disclosure' remained subjective. They also considered that any requirements to go ever further in pinpointing the source of genetic material could result in such specificity as to make satisfying the requirement impossible. With respect to biodiversity, the WTO clearly cannot go beyond the creation of rights. This is obviously not sufficient. Maintaining biodiversity requires incentives to ensure that developing country farmers and communities have a self-interest in maintaining diversity stocks. This suggests a need to align the WTO with the CBD to provide a global solution to biodiversity concerns.

Geographical indications

The TRIPS Agreement (Article 22) defines geographical indications (GIs) as '... indications which identify a good as originating in the territory of a Member, or a region or locality in that territory, where a given quality, reputation or other characteristic of the good is essentially attributable to its geographical origin'. It requires GIs to be protected in order to avoid misleading the public and to prevent unfair competition; establishes a higher standard of protection for GIs for wines and spirits (Article 23), and provides for exceptions in instances when a name has become generic (e.g. 'cheddar cheese') or is protected through a trademark.

The TRIPS definition of GIs goes beyond the related and long standing concept of *appellations of origin*. The latter require a quality linkage between the product and its geographical origin to be established, with the geographical name designating the product (e.g. *Bordeaux* or *Jerez*) (Maskus, 2000). Appellations of origin were already incorporated in the Paris and other IPR conventions and thus covered by TRIPS. Geographical indications were a new form of IPR that was embodied in TRIPS, although they had been talked about in the context of the EU and WIPO.

The EU has long favoured stronger global protection of its regional food names by extending the TRIPS rules on GIs to go beyond wines and spirits to include food and other products. In the EU view, 'cheddar' may be generic, but names such as Black Forest ham and Parmesan cheese should be reserved for food products actually produced in those regions of Europe. The EU has implemented a regime within its member countries that does so. For example in 2003, Denmark's cheese producers were required to stop using the Greek name 'feta' for their version of that type of cheese, even though Danish producers supplied more feta cheese to European consumers than did Greece. In line with its own regime, the EU has proposed that the TRIPS Agreement be extended to include a system of 'registered geographical indications' that would require both proof of geographical origin and compliance with applicable product standards.

In response to the EU pressure, the Doha ministerial declaration (para. 18) called for negotiations on the establishment of a multilateral system of notification and registration of GIs for wine and spirits. Two issues were the focus of negotiation: creating a multilateral register for wines and spirits, and strengthening the level of protection for products other than wines and spirits.

The EU efforts to widen the scope of the WTO rules on GIs were actively opposed by a number of countries, including Australia, Brazil, Canada, South Africa and the US as well as other non-European agricultural exporters. These countries took the view that many of the names for which the Europeans wanted protection had become generic. Indeed, many well-known foods have their origin in Europe and many European-origin names have been widely used in the marketing of these foods on world markets. The matter has been a source of conflict for many years, including a number of GATT and WTO disputes (Box 8.6). For example, some US wine producers have used the name 'Champaign' to market sparkling wine—a practice that infuriated the vineyard owners from the Champagne region in France. In the opinion of the opponents of EU strategy, stronger protection of GIs would simply be yet another form of protectionism for the already overprotected EU farm sector.

The subject is not one that divides developed and developing countries—as noted, opponents included the US and other OECD countries such as Australia, and proponents included a number of developing countries such as India, Kenya and Thailand. Proponents regard GIs as an instrument that can be used to help them in marketing their products and to establish and defend market shares and create niches. Opponents take the view that consumers can be informed of the origin of goods through labelling—and already are—and that quality can be assured through trademarks.

The EU made the matter a major negotiating objective in the Doha round, especially after the removal of most of the Singapore issues from the table. There is little doubt that protection through GIs can result in significant increases in profits for producers through premium pricing. Econometric studies have found

Box 8.6. Disputes over food names: scallops and ham

Indications of geographic origin are helpful to both producers and consumers because they reduce information (search) costs. However, national regulations concerning the description or geographic origin of a product may also be used as a protectionist device. A case in point was a 1993 French regulation concerning the description of scallops (a shellfish), which reserved the use of the expression 'Noix de coquille de St. Jacques'— under which scallops are sold in France—to shellfish originating in France. As a result, Canadian scallops—which are identical to French scallops in size, texture and use–could not be labelled as coquille de St. Jacques. Canadian exports of scallops to France dropped, as distributors were confronted with the need to re-label the product under another name. This significantly weakened the competitive position of Canadian scallops on the French market. Canada requested a panel on this issue in 1995 (WT/DS/7), alleging that the nondiscrimination provisions of the WTO had been violated. Peru and Chile, two other producers, followed with a similar case. The panels were suspended after the parties came to a settlement.

Geographical indications are particularly contentious for alcoholic beverages. For example, domestic distributors in Chinese Taipei have sold spirits labelled 'bourbon', 'cognac' or 'scotch', there being no legal framework setting rules for claims concerning content, age or origin. Some consumers also found it difficult to differentiate between brand name products and imitations. Thus, 'Chimas Teacher Extra Old Whisky' produced in India was aimed at those who had heard of Chivas or Teachers, two well-known international brands. Such examples are found in many countries, and have been brought to WTO dispute settlement panels. For example, the EU successfully contested the distribution of 'Chimas Teacher' whisky in India.

Two opponents to the EU approach towards regulation and protection of GIs and marks of origin—the US and Australia—brought a case against the EU in 2003 (WT/DS/174 and WT/DS/290). In its 2005 report, the panel ruled against the EU because it did not allow the registration of non-European food products. The report pointed out that the EU cannot stop producers of Florida oranges or growers of Idaho potatoes from protecting their food names in the EU simply because the US has not put in place a system equivalent to that in Europe for protecting such geographic indications. (The EU refused to recognize such trademarks unless other countries granted similarly broad protection to all European food names—i.e. by seeking such reciprocity it violated the national treatment rule.) The panel finding implied that an EU list of some 600 protected foods and 4,000 wines would have to be opened up to non-European products. However, the ruling partially backed the EU argument that GIs should not be superseded by pre-existing trademarks, and concluded that both forms of IPRs should coexist.

This case has many practical implications. For example, it may be seen as a setback for attempts undertaken by Anheuser-Busch, the US brewery, to ban a Czech beer producer from using the Czech equivalent of the Budvar brand as a rival to the company's trademarked Budweiser beer. However, the ruling also limited the rights of the Czech company, which had registered three geographical indications related to the Budvar name. The Czech company cannot attempt to assert its control over the Budweiser name worldwide, because of another part of the panel report that concluded GIs cannot be extended to include translations into other languages.

Source: WT/DS290/R (2005); *Financial Times* 18 November (2004).

that consumers are willing to pay more for GI products. Fink and Maskus (2006) survey some of the literature, which includes a study of Bordeaux wines that found certain regional designations command a large price premium—as much as US$15 per bottle in the case of the 'Pomerol' designation; a study of the Spanish market for meat products that found products bearing the 'Galician Veal' label commanded a premium of US$0.21 per kilogram; and a study that concluded wines with a 'Napa Valley' designation commanded prices that are 60 per cent higher than wines with simply a 'California' designation. Surveys of consumers have also demonstrated that many buyers—although not necessarily a majority— would pay a premium for origin-guaranteed products. The role of GIs is substantially greater in international trade than in domestic commerce, because informational problems are more pronounced when consumers and producers are located in different countries.

As noted by Maskus (2003), in many respects GIs are similar to trademarks in terms of their economic effects: they increase the incentives to invest in enhancing quality in a region (including control of free riding or shirking by some suppliers in the region, as this would harm the investment in reputation) and reduce consumer search costs and uncertainty regarding the quality or other characteristics of a product by making it more difficult for 'imitators' to sell similar products, which even if not of lower quality have not contributed to the collective investments in creating the 'brand' or market. Geographical indications are also similar to trademarks in that they do not protect the underlying production technology or knowledge used to make the product: Australian wine makers are free to adopt the techniques used in the Bordeaux or Bourgogne regions of France.

The major difference between GIs and trademarks is that the latter are owned by firms, whereas GIs almost by definition will benefit many producers located in a certain area. As a result, exploitation of GIs can be associated with high coordination and other costs. This helps to explain why there are hundreds of thousands of registered trademarks in the world (Baroncelli, Fink and Javorcik, 2005), but fewer than 1,000 registered GIs. An implication is that small regions in low-income countries may not be able to mobilize the resources required to create and exploit GIs as a competitive tool. However, GIs are a potentially useful instrument to define and protect certain forms of traditional knowledge, as GIs can be designed to provide collective right to such knowledge insofar as it is produced or exists in a specific region (Maskus, 2003).

Economic effects of patent protection

In addition to direct administrative compliance costs, implementation of the TRIPS Agreement also gives rise to economic costs and benefits for a country and has cross-country distributional implications. As noted above, IPRs essentially act to create a temporary monopoly for innovators to recoup their investment in inventive activity. As a monopoly, IPR holders can be expected to extract some proportion of consumer surplus by equating marginal revenue to marginal cost. This will generate a static deadweight loss for the products that benefit from protection. Nations that have producers of knowledge will profit, the more so the greater the net export position is. If the industry can exert market power on world markets, not just at home, because of the IPR, the equation becomes even more beneficial. For countries without production, IPRs can only generate a loss. The only source of potential gain for these countries is if global IPR enforcement raises R&D and innovation incentives. This is rather unlikely to be significant given their small markets.

The extent to which prices will rise in response to the exercise of stronger market power is a function of several variables (Maskus, 2000). First, market structure matters crucially. The number of firms (home and foreign) competing with rights-holders, the nature of that competition, the ease of market entry and exit, quality differentiation among products, openness to trade and the feasibility of arbitrage (parallel imports), and wholesale and retail distribution mechanisms are all factors that determine the impact of IPRs. Oversimplifying for purposes of discussion, the more competitive the market for a product before the introduction of IPRs, the lower the substitutability of protected for generic products, and the more concentrated the industry producing protected varieties, the greater the impact of IPRs on prices is likely to be. Second, the less elastic is demand, the greater the price-increasing effect of enhancing market power through IPRs. Third, the strength of competition policy and the willingness to intervene directly through regulation will determine outcomes. For example, policies towards exhaustion of rights (discussed previously) can have a substantial impact. Finally, much depends on the wording of IPRs legislation, including the scope of protection, the provisions for reverse engineering as a means of fair competition and fair-use exemptions in copyright.

In economies that are significant net importers of technologies and knowledge-intensive goods and services, the rents paid by consumers to producers (right-holders) are transferred outside the country. This implies that in an international context, IPRs are not simply a mechanism to redistribute income among different groups in a given society, with an associated static efficiency deadweight loss. They involve significant transfers across countries. Net importers may experience a reduction in national welfare (a terms-of-trade loss) as foreign producers extract rents from domestic consumers.

Maskus and Penubarti (1995) conclude that the strength of national IPRs regimes exerted a statistically significant positive effect on imports of manufactures. That is, stronger protection leads to more trade. Smith (2001) found that strong foreign patent rights increase bilateral exchange on average across all countries, with the positive market expansion effect being particularly pronounced for countries with strong imitative abilities. There is also empirical evidence for US multinationals to suggest that strong foreign patent rights confer a locational advantage that increases affiliate sales and licences relative to exports of goods embodying the IPR-protected knowledge and results in increased flows of knowledge to affiliates of the US multinational corporations (Smith, 2001).

A series of studies, both theoretical and empirical, undertaken after the Uruguay Round generally conclude that the net transfers from South to North will be positive and may be large. Theoretical analyses consistently suggest that incentives and thus optimal policies differ across countries depending on level of development, which in turn affects key variables such as innovative capacity (which affects whether a country is going to focus more on imitation and acquisition of existing knowledge); preferences for types of innovation (e.g. Diwan and Rodrik, 1991, argue that IPRs may be in the interest of developing countries as a way of encouraging investment in technology that that is more relevant to their needs/preferences); and the locational choices of multinationals and the importance of FDI as a channel for knowledge transfer relative to trade or licensing, which in turn depends on many variables, but includes the level of human capital and the strength of IPRs (Yang and Maskus, 2001; Glass and Saggi, 2002). In general, there is a consensus supporting the early conclusion by Deardorff (1992) that uniform standards for IPRs will not maximize world welfare or be in the interest of developing countries. At the same time there is also a consensus that IPR protection will be too weak when policies are set independently by individual governments, because governments will ignore the effects of national IPR policies on consumers and firms in the rest of the world (Grossman and Lai, 2004). Empirical research on the effect of IPRs on economic variables generally finds that stronger IPRs—often measured on the basis of an index of IPRs constructed by Ginarte and Park (1997)—tends to have negative impact on variables such as welfare, growth and innovation in developing countries (e.g. Schneider, 2005; Chaudhari, Goldberg and Jia, 2006; Falvey, Foster and Greenaway, 2006).

A noteworthy attempt to estimate the magnitude of the potential transfers associated with TRIPS is McCalman (2001). He incorporated information on the volume and price of technology transfers through patents, including the likelihood of local imitation across markets, to estimate the net present value of patents if countries were to broaden the coverage and enforce TRIPS-type standards of protection. Estimates of the transfers that could arise are reported in Table 8.3 (results for only a subset of countries are replicated). The first column of Table 8.3 reports estimated net transfers associated with the TRIPS Agreement, which are defined as the increase in the value of patent rights held by residents of a country minus the increase in the value of patent rights granted to nonresidents by that country. (Both figures increase due to the higher patent standards agreed upon in the TRIPS Agreement.) Among the winners are US, Germany, France and Switzerland. Most countries experience a net static loss from (stronger) patent

Table 8.3. Estimated transfers associated with the TRIPS Agreement

	TRIPS Net Transfer (US$ Million) (1)	Net Transfer (% of GDP) (2)	TRIPS Gross Transfer (US$ Million) (3)	% of Gross Transfer Due to Broader Coverage (4)
US	4,553	0.09	73	0.00
Germany	788	0.07	384	0.00
France	568	0.06	0	0.00
Switzerland	22	0.01	288	0.60
Netherlands	−96	−0.04	313	1.00
South Africa	−113	−0.13	123	0.40
Belgium	−224	−0.15	293	0.64
South Korea	−326	−0.18	328	0.92
Spain	−345	−0.10	367	0.45
Japan	−439	−0.02	896	0.00
Mexico	−444	−0.26	445	0.29
India	−526	−0.19	526	0.34
UK	−541	−0.06	1,044	0.00
Brazil	−926	−0.28	930	0.11
Canada	−1,023	−0.21	1,107	0.41

Source: McCalman (2001).

protection. The US stands out as the main winner with benefits that are almost six times greater than those of the second largest beneficiary. Among the most significant predicted losers—some of them unexpected— are Canada, Brazil, the UK, India, Mexico, Japan, Spain and South Korea. Canada's ranking is consistent with the country's alignment with developing countries in the Uruguay Round negotiations on TRIPS. The position of the UK and Japan largely reflects a substantial increase in the value of both countries' patent protection, a rise that is not matched by the increase in value of foreign patents held by the countries' citizens.

The second column puts the size of the net transfer into perspective by comparing it with the country's GDP. It shows, first of all, that the relative size of these transfers is rather small given the size of the national economy. Columns 3 and 4 permit one to distinguish between the transfers associated with a broadening of the sectoral coverage of patent protection and those associated with increasing enforcement effort. They suggest that the transfers from developing countries are mainly due to an increase in enforcement rather than extended coverage of protection, and that for advanced countries the transfer source tends to be equally divided. McCalman points out that this breakdown might imply that, in the future, developing countries will favour the extension of the coverage of patent protection rather than improving enforcement.

Comparing the figures in Table 8.3 with the results of one of the best quantitative assessments of the Uruguay Round commitments to liberalize trade in

goods—Harrison, Rutherford and Tarr (1997)—suggests that the net TRIPS transfers increase the short (long) run gain for US by 40 (20) per cent. Conversely,
developing countries see their net gains diminished as the result of the TRIPS
Agreement, especially in the short run. For some countries, such as Mexico, the
overall net static effect is actually negative—implying a loss from the round,
reflecting not just TRIPS but the loss in preferential access to its major export
market, the US, as a result of the MFN tariff concessions made by the United States.
Of course, all these calculations must be considered illustrative only, as they pertain
only to patents and are dependent on the type of model used for estimation
purposes and the accuracy with which the results of the Uruguay Round commitments, and, more generally, the WTO are captured (Lybbert, 2002). Much of what
the WTO is all about—certainty, rules, tariff bindings, transparency, etc.—is not
captured by the empirical models. However, the model-based analyses do serve to
illustrate that the TRIPS Agreement involves a sizeable transfer to the primary
producers of knowledge—the US and various EU member states in particular.

In the politically sensitive context of medicines, Chaudhari, Goldberg and Jia
(2006) argue that if foreign patents are enforced as required by TRIPS, local producers will exit the market causing large welfare losses on consumers in developing
countries. Using detailed product-level data from India, they estimate that the
withdrawal of the four domestic product groups in the fluoroquinolone subsegment
in India would have inflicted welfare losses of US$305 million upon the Indian
economy, some 80 per cent of which would fall on the shoulders of Indian consumers.

However, Branstetter and colleagues (2007) note that rent transfers and static
welfare losses are only one part of the story. They argue that the level of FDI will
respond to changes in the strength of IPRs protection. Stronger IPRs protection
in developing countries may increase the share of global manufacturing undertaken there as well as the pace at which production of recently invented goods
shifts to them, leading to an overall enhancement of industrial development.
They analyse the response of US multinationals to IPRs reforms in 16 countries in
the 1980s and 1990s and find that these firms expand the scale of their activities in
countries after IPRs reforms. Using industry-level data, they show that industry value
added increases after reforms, particularly in industries that are technology-intensive
and where US FDI is concentrated. Moreover, using an annual count of 'initial
export episodes'—the number of ten-digit products for which US imports from a
given country exceed zero for the first time—as an indicator of the rate at which
production of goods shifts to the reforming countries, they find that this rate of
production transfer increases sharply after IPRs reforms. The Branstetter and
colleagues (2007) analysis illustrates that the possible effects of stronger IPRs on
the global allocation of production, industrial development and longer run global
innovation and growth need to be considered in any assessment of TRIPS. Gould
and Gruben (1996, 2004) discuss the relationship between IPRs, innovation and
economic growth more generally.

Policy implications and options

Given the negative impact effect of TRIPS on importers, very much depends on creating the conditions that maximize the potential for beneficial dynamic effects of IPRs, and on obtaining compensation in other areas that is of sufficient value to offset the short-run loss. The latter is of course what the Uruguay Round was about and the Doha Round might be about. On the former, a variety of policies can be pursued that can reduce the magnitude of the transfer. Examples include taxation of imports of those IPR-intensive goods where foreign producers have significant market (pricing) power, facilitating the absorption and diffusion of know-how, vigorous enforcement of competition law, and direct regulation. The TRIPS Agreement allows significant latitude for governments to draft implementing legislation that attenuates the ability of right-holders to abuse their market power.

Regulation of prices is common in many countries, especially of pharmaceuticals. Although this can result in firms pricing closer to cost, it can have unintended consequences. If prices are set too low, firms may choose not to sell. Firms will also have an incentive to try to circumvent price regulations by inflating costs. One way they may do this is by setting high transfer prices on imported ingredients (Lanjouw, 1998). Another policy option is an active competition regime that ensures that markets are contestable and that there is vigorous inter- as well as intra-brand competition. One element of such a competition policy could be a liberal parallel import regime that limits the ability of right-holders to segment markets.[8] The economics of this issue are complex. Many experts argue that as long as a producer faces competition from other brands, exclusive distribution arrangements do not matter. But in many developing countries inter-brand competition may be weak because only a few distributors control the market. National exhaustion and legally enforceable exclusive distributor arrangements can then have a detrimental impact on welfare.[9] However, preventing parallel imports can also be beneficial if it results in lower prices than would arise under uniform pricing. The decision of whether to adopt international exhaustion is a matter for national authorities to decide independently. Hong Kong's experience illustrates the importance of adopting competition legislation to control 'overshooting' on

[8] As noted above, parallel imports involve traders buying goods protected by IPRs in one market and importing them into another market. Such trade does not involve a violation of IPRs of the type that occurs when goods are counterfeited or copied illegally.

[9] An anecdote recounted to one of the authors in the late 1990s is illustrative. Lebanon has an exclusive distribution ('sole agency') law that gives licence holders (agents) the right to request Customs block entry of goods that have not been authorized by the licence holder (distributor). On a visit to Germany, a businessman buys a batch of second-hand Siemens-made dentist chairs from a university, which had used them for training purposes. On import into Lebanon, clearance of the shipment was blocked because it had not been authorized by the Siemens agent. The businessman was obliged to pay the agent a large fee and was forced to pay customs duty on the chairs on the basis of the value of new chairs, in effect wiping out his anticipated profit.

IPRs. Reportedly, the vigorous enforcement of IPRs has led to the exclusion of grey market, parallel imports and to allegations of abuse of a dominant position, which the Hong Kong government has generally argued to be impossible given its free trade stance. The Director-General of the Department responsible for enforcing IPRs recognized that the absence of a competition law creates problems, but noted that his job was to protect the interests of rights-holders; 'someone else must protect the others' (*Financial Times*, 8 January 1999).

At the end of the day, it is impossible to generalize regarding the effect of the TRIPS Agreement on individual WTO members. The design of the IPR legislation and complementary policies will play an important role. Much depends as well on the impact of IPRs on FDI, on the incentives to innovate, and on the effectiveness of IPR regimes in developing countries in protecting indigenous culture and knowledge. A case study of an Indonesian pharmaceutical firm illustrates that the responses of firms in developing countries will also play a major role (Box 8.7). Konan and La Croix (2006) sum up the basic thrust of the economic literature on

---

Box 8.7. Kalbe Farma of Indonesia

Kalbe Farma PT is an Indonesian pharmaceutical company. The firm produces and markets medicaments for therapeutic use. Under the pre-TRIPS Indonesian patent law the firm was able to copy and sell pharmaceutical products that were protected by international patents. Such products were sold by Kalbe Farma in Indonesia and in other developing country markets, including Bangladesh, Malaysia, Myanmar, Nigeria, Sri Lanka and Vietnam. Once the government began drafting legislation to bring its IPRs regime into conformity with TRIPS, management reviewed its product development strategy. Kalbe Farma production consisted of drugs that were no longer protected internationally as well as pharmaceuticals that were still under patent protection outside the country, but for which a valid patent had never been filed in Indonesia. The company was free to supply the latter to the Indonesian market, but had to exercise restraint in exporting to markets in which the patent protection was still in force. It also imported a range of products, preparations and ingredients from third-party suppliers that were protected. Such imports were expected to become illegal unless acquired from the right-holder or a licensee.

Management decided not to wait for the new TRIPS-consistent law to be passed. Kalbe Farma developed a new marketing and partnership strategy involving both foreign companies and Indonesian firms. It focused on securing marketing rights in Indonesia for foreign patented products and to develop and sell generic drugs no longer under patents. The company also initiated negotiations with international pharmaceutical suppliers to acquire licensing rights for a range of products in Indonesia with a view to establish a leadership position in the domestic market. Kalbe Farma also expanded its R&D, recognizing that competition in the pharmaceutical industry was likely to intensify, including through entry of foreign companies attracted by stronger patent protection. As of 2008 it was the largest publically listed pharmaceutical firm in Indonesia.

Source: Kostecki (2001).

this subject as follows: (1) harmonization is not optimal for the world as a whole—for example, they note that US history provides a clear case of a country that used strong patent rights and weak copyrights in the nineteenth century to enhance its growth prospects; (2) the theoretical literature suggests that there is a strong case for welfare gains to developing countries from patent harmonization (i.e. 'TRIPS') if developed countries pay lump-sums to offset higher royalty payments by developing countries; and (3) although there is a case for IPRs to support innovation, the appropriate scope, depth and enforcement of IPRs will differ across countries according to their economic and political institutions, their per capita income and their capability to engage in and disseminate the fruits of R&D.

These conclusions from the economic literature raise serious concerns about efforts by the EU and US to further strengthen IPRs disciplines in the WTO. Given the difficulty of agreement on these matters in the WTO (in turn a reflection not so much of the arguments of the economists as those of the NGOs!), what is of greater concern are the efforts by OECD nations to introduce 'high standards' of IPR protection in preferential trade agreements with developing countries. As of late 2007 the US had pursued new and expanded (TRIPS-plus) commitments on IPRs in more than 16 bilateral and regional trade treaties, including free trade agreements with Chile, the Dominican Republic and Central American countries (DR-CAFTA), Columbia, Panama and Peru. These treaties, not all of which have been ratified, encompass standards that go beyond the TRIPS Agreement and limit the flexibilities established in that agreement (General Accounting Office, 2007). We discuss these matters further in Chapters 10 and 13.

It should be noted, however, that both the EU and US have at times demonstrated flexibility in this area. Thus, the US has relaxed certain health-related IPRs provisions in some of its PTAs with developing countries, including on technical issues such as patent extension, linking drug approval to patent status and data exclusivity (General Accounting Office, 2007). Similar developments have occurred in the stance taken by the EU in the Economic Partnership Agreements (EPAs) it is negotiating with ACP countries. The European Parliament adopted two resolutions on the matter, expressing concern over the inclusion of TRIPS-plus rules in EU trade agreements stipulating that the European Commission should not include such provisions in EPAs.

8.7. CONCLUSION

The GATT and the GATS are similar in that the focus is primarily on market access liberalization, complemented with general rules and principles relating to the application of trade policies. Both agreements aim at reducing discrimination against foreign suppliers of products. However, as noted previously, the GATS created disciplines on certain domestic regulatory regimes that apply equally to domestic and foreign providers. An example is the requirement that an independent regulatory authority be established for the basic telecommunication industry for signatories of the Reference Paper (see Chapter 7). Similarly, the GATT has also begun to move down this track. An example are the two agreements on product standards, which require WTO members to adopt international standards if these exist and requires a 'defence' in cases where this is not the case. To date, however, the emphasis of multilateral disciplines pertaining to domestic regulatory policies is overwhelmingly on procedure or process—little substantive harmonization is imposed. Insofar as harmonization disciplines apply—as in the case of standards—the substantive norms are not developed by the WTO but by the competent international bodies, such as the UN (e.g. the Food and Agricultural Organization) and the Codex Alimentarius Commission. This is not the case with the TRIPS Agreement, which establishes minimum, common standards for IPRs that must be satisfied in all WTO members. Although many of these standards were developed under WIPO auspices, TRIPS goes beyond existing conventions in a number of important areas.

The approach taken in the TRIPS Agreement is somewhat analogous to a Directive in the EU context: it sets minimum standards, but leaves it to signatories to determine how these requirements will be implemented. Article 1 TRIPS states: 'Members shall be free to determine the appropriate method of implementing the provisions of this Agreement within their own legal system and practice'. Nonetheless, the TRIPS Agreement obliges governments to take positive action to protect IPRs in specific ways. Both the GATT and the GATS are essentially limited to disciplines that apply ten members if they choose to pursue certain policies.

With the TRIPS agreement, OECD-based pharmaceutical, entertainment and software industries, which were largely responsible for getting TRIPS on the agenda, obtained much of what they sought when the negotiations were launched. Their objective was multilaterally agreed minimum standards of IPRs protection in all GATT contracting parties, an obligation to enforce such standards and the creation of an effective multilateral dispute settlement process. It is fair to say that developing countries agreed to substantially more than even an optimist might have predicted in 1986 when the round began.

There are no definitive empirical estimates of the impact of the TRIPS Agreement on developing countries. Although the dynamic effects of the agreement are clearly vital in this regard, the conclusion by Dani Rodrik before the Uruguay Round was finalized continues to hold:

all evidence and arguments . . . point to the conclusion that, to a first-order approximation, TRIPS is a redistributive issue: irrespective of assumptions made with respect to market structure or dynamic response, the impact effect of enhanced IPR protection...will be a transfer of wealth from [developing country] consumers and firms to foreign, mostly industrial-country firms   (Rodrik, 1994: 449).

The estimates of McCalman (2001) cited above suggest that the transfer to OECD countries is not trivial and they show that including TRIPS in the equation significantly reduces the net gains from the Uruguay Round.

The TRIPS agreement was signed because it encompassed a tradeoff between IPRs and the rest of the Uruguay Round agenda. The deal to abolish the MFA and reintegrate agriculture into the trading system, the acceptance of a positive list approach to coverage in the GATS, a stronger dispute settlement mechanism, and the agreement to outlaw VERs were all elements in the final equation. Although it is not possible to identify specific issue linkages, it is very suggestive that the transition period for the phase-out of the MFA was similar to that for developing countries to fully implement the TRIPS Agreement. There was also recognition that without TRIPS, ratification of the Uruguay Round package by the US Congress was unlikely given the political weight of the US industries supporting stronger IPR disciplines. The regime shift that occurred among many developing countries in the 1980s in attitudes towards inward FDI also played a role. Attracting FDI in certain higher tech sectors requires enforcement of IPRs. Finally, there is little doubt that the threat of continued unilateral action on the part of the US (but also the EU) played a role.

Although the US and the EU pushed to enforce the TRIPS Agreement vigorously, including not just against major developing countries, but against each other and other OECD nations, in more recent years they have also demonstrated willingness, especially with respect to LDCs in Africa suffering from the HIV/AIDS epidemic, to show forbearance. The US government issued an Executive Order in May 2000 to help make HIV- and AIDS-related drugs and medical technologies more affordable and accessible in Sub-Saharan African countries. The order prohibits the US government (USTR) from using Section 301 to seek the revocation or revision of IPRs policies of beneficiary Sub-Saharan African countries that regulate HIV or AIDS pharmaceuticals or medical technologies (for example, by allowing parallel imports or regulating prices) if such policies promote access to antiretroviral drugs or medical technologies for affected populations. At about the same time as the Executive Order was issued, the pharmaceutical industry announced an initiative to reduce prices for antiretroviral drugs for developing countries. G8 leaders also announced efforts to devote greater resources to accelerate the development and promote the distribution of vaccines for HIV and AIDS, malaria, TB and other infectious diseases. Developments during the Doha Round negotiations also illustrates a more general acceptance of the need to balance enforcement of private rights with public health objectives and priorities.

8.8. FURTHER READING

A useful guide to the TRIPS Agreement and its negotiating history is provided by UNCTAD-ICTSD in *Resource Book on TRIPS and Development* (Cambridge: Cambridge University Press, 2005). Keith Maskus, *Intellectual Property Rights in the Global Economy* (Washington, DC: Petersen Institute for International Economics, 2000) is a highly recommended book-length survey and analysis of the economic implications of the TRIPS Agreement. A 2002 report by the Commission on Intellectual Property Rights, a high-level group chaired by John Barton, provides an in-depth analysis and a set of policy recommendations to make the prevailing IPR regime more supportive of the needs of developing countries, see *Integrating Intellectual Property Rights and Development Policy*, London, September (2002) (http://www.iprcommission.org/papers/pdfs/final_report/CIPRcoverintrofinal. pdf). The trade policy and broader economic dimensions of the debate on TRIPS and essential medicines is discussed by Kamal Saggi in 'Trade-Related Policy Coherence and Access to Essential Medicines,' *Journal of World Trade*, 42 (2008): 69–39.

Ambassador B. K. Zutshi, India's chief negotiator during the deal-making stages of the Uruguay Round, gives an insiders' view of the TRIPS negotiations from a developing country perspective in 'Bringing TRIPS into the Multilateral Trading System', in J. Bhagwati and M. Hirsch (eds), *The Uruguay Round and Beyond: Essays in Honour of Arthur Dunkel* (Ann Arbor: University of Michigan Press, 1998). Jayashree Watal, *Intellectual Property Rights in the World Trade Organization: The Way Forward for Developing Countries* (New Delhi: Oxford University Press, 2000) provides a comprehensive legal analysis of the TRIPS Agreement, focusing in particular on the options and implications for developing countries.

An excellent resource for IPR-related disputes and policy developments is the Consumer Project on Technology (at www.cptech.org). Other Internet sources that provide information on recent developments concerning TRIPS include the WTO homepage (at www.wto.org); the World Intellectual Property Organisation (at www.wipo.org); the joint International Centre for Trade and Sustainable Development (ICTSD) and UNCTAD site on IPRs (at www.iprsonline.org); and the Consumer Project on Technology (at www.cptech.org/ip).

CHAPTER 9

SAFEGUARDS AND EXCEPTIONS

VIRTUALLY all international trade agreements or arrangements contain safeguard provisions and exceptions. Broadly defined, the term 'safeguard protection' refers to a provision permitting governments under specified circumstances to withdraw—or cease to apply—their normal obligations in order to protect (safeguard) certain overriding interests. Safeguard provisions are critical to the existence and operation of trade-liberalizing agreements, as they function as both insurance mechanisms and safety valves. They provide governments with the means to go back on specific liberalization commitments—subject to certain conditions—should the need for this arise (safety valve). Without them, governments may refrain from signing an agreement that reduces protection substantially (insurance motive). This chapter focuses primarily on the safeguards and exceptions embodied in the GATT. Those of the GATS are either very similar or still in an embryonic stage. Safeguard provisions in the agreement on TRIPS are discussed in Chapter 8.

The various provisions of the WTO in this area can be separated into two categories. The first are those that can be used in the event of the occurrence of a predefined set of circumstances, which legitimize temporary increases in import barriers. The second constitute permanent exceptions to the general obligations. The first category can be further divided into those dealing with so-called unfair trading practices (exports that are dumped or that benefit from actionable subsidies) and those that can be applied without having to demonstrate 'unfairness' on the part of trading partners. For the latter, the trigger solely concerns economic circumstances in the importing country. Many of the provisions allowing for temporary imposition of protection that are not in response to 'unfair' trade can give rise to claims for compensation by affected exporting nations.

Provisions that allow for the *temporary* suspension of obligations include:

Antidumping (AD): measures to offset dumping—pricing of exports below what is charged in the home market; foreign pricing below costs of production; or foreign pricing below what is charged in a third market—that materially injures a domestic industry (Article VI GATT).

Countervailing duties (CVDs): measures to offset the effect of subsidization that materially injures a domestic industry (Article VI GATT).

Balance of payments (BOP): restrictions on imports to safeguard a country's external financial position (Articles XII and XVIII:*b* GATT; Article XII GATS).

Infant industries: governmental assistance for economic development, allowing import restrictions to protect infant industries (Articles XVIII:*a* and XVIII:*c* GATT).

Emergency protection: temporary protection in cases where imports of a product cause or threaten serious injury to domestic producers of directly competitive products (Article XIX GATT).

Special safeguards: provisions embodied in the Agreements on Agriculture and Textiles and Clothing or in protocols of accession (in particular that of China) allowing for actions to be taken to restrict trade.

General waivers: allowing members to ask for permission not to be bound by an obligation (Article IX WTO). In contrast to the other mechanisms, this requires formal approval by the WTO Council.

Provisions allowing for permanent exceptions from general obligations include:

General exceptions: measures to safeguard public morals, health, laws and natural resources, subject to the requirement that such measures are nondiscriminatory and are not a disguised restriction on trade (Articles XX GATT; XIV GATS).

National security: allowing intervention on national security grounds (Articles XXI GATT; XIV*bis* GATS; 73 TRIPS).

Re-negotiation or modification of schedules: allowing for the withdrawal of concessions (bound tariff reductions or specific commitments) if compensation is offered to affected members (Articles XXVIII GATT; XXI GATS).

Only three of these provisions have an economy-wide rationale (balance of payments, general exceptions and national security). All the others are product/industry or issue/agreement-specific. All the industry-specific instruments are imperfect substitutes for each other: they all address the same issue, protecting domestic firms from foreign competition. In practice the balance-of-payments provision was often used by developing countries to protect specific industries, whereas industrialized countries have tended to use AD most frequently.

The GATS does not have provisions on contingent or infant industry protection, and an analogue to GATT Article XIX remains to be drafted (see Chapter 7). In large part this reflects the difficulty of applying these concepts to trade in services. The GATS does contain provisions allowing for actions to safeguard the balance of payments, for general exceptions and for re-negotiation of commitments. These provisions are similar to those of the GATT, except that the language on modification of schedules differs from GATT by calling for mandatory arbitration if no agreement can be reached on compensation.

The rationale for safeguard instruments

The inclusion of some of the above provisions in a trade agreement is straightforward to understand. Government will want to be able to implement policies to achieve national security goals, pursue noneconomic objectives, and re-negotiate a deal *ex post*. They may also consider dumping or export subsidies to be unfair practices—although as discussed below it is not at all clear that these practices are inefficient (lower world welfare). What is perhaps less obvious is why the GATT (and other trade agreements) includes a safeguard provision. After all, if parties can re-negotiate, a safeguard procedure is redundant. In practice in the GATT years it did seem to be redundant as an Article XIX action was not that different from a re-negotiation—imposition of protection had to be accompanied by an offer of compensation for affected exporters. As discussed below, the result was that it was rarely used. Instead, countries used other instruments—including some that clearly violated GATT rules.

The rationale for a safeguard instrument can be understood in the context of the repeated game literature that analyzes the determinants of sustaining cooperation. If the short-term incentives confronting a government to cheat are not too large, but there are time periods where there is a politically driven need to deviate temporarily, a safeguard mechanism permits this to occur in a 'legal' and transparent way without giving rise to tit-for-tat retaliation and a breakdown of cooperation. If the need (incentive) is temporary, it makes little sense to engage in a re-negotiation. A temporary need to protect an industry might arise because governments need to slow down the adjustment to increased import competition to facilitate a more 'orderly' restructuring of an industry. Although the use of trade policy is likely to be inefficient in terms of fostering restructuring, it may be the only instrument to which a government has access.

Bagwell and Staiger (1990) and Horn, Maggi and Staiger (2006) provide another rationale for an escape clause: it provides governments with access to trade policy in periods in which there is high demand for imports, thereby avoiding the use of less efficient domestic instruments. In their analysis the presumed trigger is a (temporary) change in import volume that provides an efficiency (terms of trade) rationale for raising tariffs. Given that the source of the 'problem' is increased imports, a trade measure is most efficient.

Most scholars take the view that the prime reason trade agreements include safeguards is that this provides governments with some flexibility *ex post*, and that this encourages more cooperation in the negotiation phase. That is, they provide insurance to governments—and import-competing industries—that if the result of liberalization is a level of imports that is hard to handle, protection can be re-imposed. In this view, the inclusion of a safety valve supports greater and deeper liberalization. As we will discuss below, there is some evidence for this view.

Use of safeguards and exceptions

The intent of the drafters of the GATT was that re-negotiation would be the primary mechanism to deal with a need for permanent rebalancing of concessions, and that Article XIX GATT would be used to grant temporary protection to industries finding it too difficult to confront increased import competition following negotiated liberalization (an MTN). The AD and CVD provisions were included in large part at the behest of the US, Canada and several European nations, which had such statutes on the books, although they were rarely used.

During the first 20 years of the GATT, re-negotiations and Article XIX were the major instruments used (Figure 9.1). Over time, however, industries in developed countries increasingly lobbied for VERs to obtain relief from import competition. Voluntary export restraints became a major instrument of protection in the 1970s because they provided some compensation for affected exporters, were

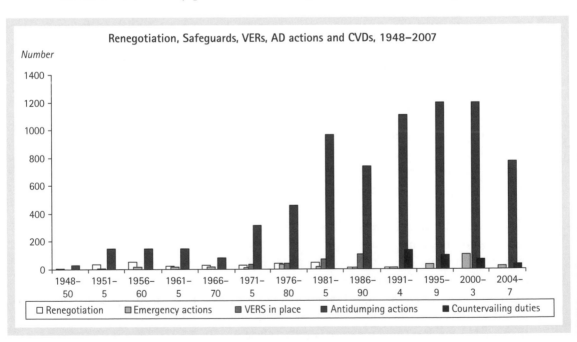

Fig. 9.1. Use of safeguard instruments, 1948–2007

Note: Data for antidumping and countervailing duties refer to investigations launched.

Sources: Finger (2001); Finger and Zlate (2005); Zanardi (2005); www.wto.org.

discriminatory, and were often directed against countries that did not have initial negotiating rights or principal supplier status (see Chapter 4). In the early 1980s, VERs covered some 10 per cent of world trade, with a trade-weighted average tariff equivalent on the order of 15 per cent (Kostecki, 1987). Although in absolute terms the number of VERs was relatively small, they often affected all the major suppliers and covered many product categories.

Starting in the mid-1970s the use of AD expanded substantially. Between 1980 and 1986, the EU imposed 213 AD actions, as compared to only 10 Article XIX measures. In the same period, the US imposed five Article XIX measures, as compared to some 195 AD actions (Finger and Olechowski, 1987). The revealed preference for AD and VERs reflected the fact that the conditions that needed to be satisfied to invoke Article XIX protection were relatively stringent. As discussed below, until this was changed in the Uruguay Round, Article XIX actions had to be nondiscriminatory and affected exporters had the right to compensation (or failing adequate compensation, could seek authorization from the GATT Council to retaliate). Governments preferred VERs and AD, as these instruments allowed them to discriminate across exporting countries and did not require (additional) compensation.

The total number of AD investigations rose steadily starting in the 1980s, with a dip in the late 1980s, reaching an all-time high of 309 in 2002. India, which adopted AD legislation in 1985 but only started to use the instrument in 1992 (following a major trade reform in 1991), initiated the most AD investigations in the 1995–2007 period (508), followed by the 'traditional' users of AD: the US (402), the EU (372), Argentina (222), and South Africa (205).[1] China is the leading target, having been at the receiving end of 597 investigations during this period.

There is often a cyclical aspect to the use of contingent protection. Once the wheels of international trade slow down, measures such as AD tend to increase. To invoke these instruments, business firms must be able to claim that they suffer injury from imports. Rapid economic growth in most parts of the world economy during 2003–6 led to a decline in the use of administered protection. As macro-economic conditions deteriorate, it is safe to predict that an increasing number of AD cases will appear.

Up to the mid-1990s developing countries did not use the 'standard' instruments of contingent protection. Instead, they frequently invoked Article XVIII:*b* of the GATT to justify the use of QRs. If developing countries desired to impose tariffs they usually had significant leeway to do so because most had either not bound their tariffs or had bound them at high ceiling rates. In such cases countries are free to impose higher tariffs—there is no need to use AD or safeguards. Over time the invocation of Article XVIII:*b* as cover for the use of QRs by developing countries

---

[1] South Africa launched 211 cases in the 1948–58 period—by far the most intensive user of AD in the early GATT period (Zanardi, 2005).

declined, in part due to a shift towards more effective and efficient instruments to deal with BOP problems.

Table 9.1 provides a brief summary of the frequency with which various instruments have been invoked. Whatever the political rationale for safeguard instruments, their mere existence may reduce competitive pressure on domestic import-competing firms. They are also all inefficient, in the sense that the costs to

Table 9.1. Frequency of use of safeguard provisions

Instrument and GATT Article	Frequency of Use
Periodic—three year—renegotiations at the initiative of the country desiring to raise a bound tariff rate, Articles XXVIII:1 and XXVIII:5	1955–95: 207 instances 1995–2008: 24 instances (of which 12 re-negotiations still ongoing in October 2008)[a]
'Special circumstances' re-negotiations, Article XXVIII:4	1948–2008: 65 instances[b]
Waivers under GATT Article XXV	113 granted of which 44 still in effect in 1994 Between 1995 and 2007: 123 granted (including extensions)
Waivers under Article IX WTO	83 granted in the 2000–8 period
Withdrawal of a concession for infant industry purposes, Article XVIII:a and c	XVIII(a): 9 through September 2008 XVIII(c): 9 through September 2008
Measures by developing countries for BOP purposes, Article XVIII:b	Used by 16 countries at least once between 1959 and 2008
Emergency protection, Article XIX	1950–94: 150 actions (3.4 per year) 1995–2000: 49 investigations (9 per year) 2000–8 (June): 69 investigations (8.6 per year) 1995–2007: 83 measures imposed
Special safeguards under the ATC	1995–2005: 65 requests
Special safeguards, Agreement on Agriculture	Ten countries imposed actions in one or more years during 1995–2001 covering a total of 757 tariff lines (HS four-digit)[c]
Special safeguards against China under Protocol of Accession	21 investigations between 2002 and 2006;
Countervailing duties, Article VI	1985–2007: 522 initiations 1985–2007: 265 measures As of September 2008, more than 50 measures in force
Antidumping duties, Article VI	1995–2007: 3,200 initiations 1995–2007: 2,049 measures imposed About 1,300 measures in force as of September 2008

[a] Re-negotiations were minimal during 1995–2008 as tariffs were modified under rectification procedures or in the context of adopting the Harmonized System.
[b] Zero instances under the WTO during the 1995–2007 period.
[c] Data from G/AG/NG/S/9/Rev. 1.

Sources: Finger (2002); Bown (2008, 2009); WTO official documents and updates obtained from the WTO secretariat.

consumers are almost invariably larger than the benefits that accrue to the protected industry. In addition, industries can be expected to exploit substitution possibilities across instruments if these exist, making it more difficult for governments to control trade policy.

The various provisions allowing for protection under the GATT can undermine the liberalizing dynamic of the WTO, and limit the usefulness of the WTO to governments that seek insulation from protectionist lobbies. Governments (and their advisors) find it very difficult to sell the argument that it makes no economic sense to draft legislation which allows the various WTO provisions to be invoked. Invariably the response will be to point to the US, Canada or the EU—all active users of contingent protection. 'If they use it, why should we refrain' is a frequently heard argument. As a result, many developing countries have put in place the legal and administrative infrastructure to implement AD investigations. As a group, they have become the leading users of AD.

Views on the impact of contingent protection depend significantly on whether these measures are seen as 'facilitating devices', allowing liberalization to proceed, or as 'loopholes' that allow protectionist lobbies to reduce import competition and manage markets. The debate in this area is analogous to that arising on product standards: do they act more as barriers or are they catalysts for industrial upgrading and improving efficiency? Although there is general recognition that contingent protection plays an important political role, many exporters would argue there are excessive opportunities to re-impose protection. Economists also emphasize that some of the instruments that are legal under the WTO make no economic sense (antidumping in particular) as the underlying behaviour is not 'unfair', and are redundant from the perspective of being able to intervene for insurance or safety valve purposes.

9.1. Re-negotiation of Concessions

The GATT allows governments to re-negotiate tariff concessions and schedules (Article XXVIII). Re-negotiation centres on the compensation that must be offered as a quid pro quo for raising a bound rate. Under GATT rules, modification of schedules takes three basic forms: 'open season', which may be conducted every three years following a binding; 'special circumstances re-negotiations', which may take place when approved by GATT contracting parties; and 'reserved right re-negotiations', which may occur anytime during the three-year period following a binding if a notification is made by interested governments to that end (Dam, 1970).

Developing countries may follow a simplified procedure to modify or withdraw concessions. In negotiating the compensation required, account is taken of the interests of the country with which the concession was originally negotiated (which has so-called initial negotiating rights—INRs), the interest of the country having a 'principal supplying interest', as well as that of countries having a 'substantial interest'. Principal or substantial supplying interest requires a major or a sizeable share, respectively, in the market concerned, determined on the basis of import statistics for the last three years for which information is available.[2]

Countries having a substantial interest in the concession concerned (the negotiated tariff binding) have consultation rights only, whereas countries that have INRs or are principal suppliers, have negotiation rights. In disputed cases it is up to the Council to determine whether a given country is a principal supplier or whether it has a substantial interest. No such cases arose under GATT 1947. The main objective of the principal supplier rule is to provide for the participation in the negotiations, in addition to the country with the INRs, of countries with a larger share in the trade affected by the concession than the country with INRs might have. This allows a balance to be maintained between the old, previously negotiated situation and new trade patterns that emerge over time. Exceptionally, when the concession to be withdrawn affects trade that constitutes a major part of the total exports of a given country, the country may also enjoy principal supplier status (Article XXVIII: 1).

The Uruguay Round Understanding on the Interpretation of Article XXVIII enhanced the opportunities of affected exporters to participate in tariff re-negotiations. The WTO member for which the relative importance of exports of the product on which a tariff is increased is the highest (defined as exports of the product to the market concerned as a proportion of the country's total exports) is considered to have a principal supplying interest if it does not already have so (or an INR) under GATT 1947 procedures. If no agreement is reached on compensation, affected countries may withdraw equivalent concessions.

Article XXI is analogous to the GATT renegotiation provision Article XXVIII, allowing for members to withdraw commitments after a three-year period has elapsed from the time that the commitment entered into force. The intent to modify must be notified to the GATS Council, and gives rise to compensation discussions. If agreement cannot be reached on compensation, the GATS provides for arbitration (no retaliation is allowed until the arbitration process has been completed). If the recommendations resulting from the arbitration are not implemented, affected members that participated in the arbitration may retaliate without needing authorization by the GATS Council. In this respect the GATS goes beyond GATT, which only provides for countries concerned to refer disagreements

---

[2] Principal supplying interest is determined with reference to the share in the export market; substantial supplying interest is determined in relation to a country's total volume of exports.

regarding compensation to the Council for Trade in Goods, who may in turn 'submit their views'.

The mechanisms for—and disciplines on—modification of tariff schedules are important. Before the completion of the Uruguay Round, on average re-negotiation of concessions occurred every year with respect to some 100 items, as compared to some 80,000 tariff lines bound. During the 1955–95 period, over 30 GATT contracting parties utilized the re-negotiation option more than 200 times (Table 9.1). To date, in the WTO period re-negotiations have been limited because adjustments have occurred in the context of adopting and implementing new versions of the Harmonized System (see Chapter 5). There were 24 re-negotiations under GATT Article XXVIII between 1995 and 2008, over half of which were ongoing at the time of writing.

In 2003, the EU indicated its intention to withdraw the tariff commitments listed in the Schedules of its ten new members (G/SECRET/20 and G/SECRET/20/Add.1). The issue was considered by the General Council throughout 2005 and 2006, as a result of the EU's nonrecognition of claims of interest submitted by Honduras and Guatemala in the consultations and negotiation process under Article XXVIII and XXIV GATT, as well as the entry into force of an EC-wide regime for bananas (2006). Consultations were being pursued at the time of writing with the aim of finding a satisfactory solution.[3]

9.2. WAIVERS

Tariff re-negotiations are limited in nature: by definition they only pertain to instances in which a country wants to raise tariffs above previously bound levels. Article XXV:5 GATT allows a member to request a waiver from one or more other obligations. Over 100 waivers were granted in the first 45 years of GATT history (Table 9.1), of which 44 were still in effect in 1994. From a systemic perspective, the waiver option allows members to obtain an exemption from a specific rule in situations where they might otherwise have been forced to withdraw from the agreement because of political imperatives at home. Waivers can be good or bad from an economic perspective. For example, a number of waivers were granted under GATT 1947 to countries allowing them to impose surcharges on imports for BOP purposes. Although this is an inferior instrument to deal with a BOP

---

[3] The status of re-negotiations is reported at www.wto.org/english/tratop_e/schedules_e/goods _schedules_table_e.htm

problem, at least it is better than the instrument called for by the relevant GATT provision—that is, QRs.

By far the most famous waiver was requested by the US in 1955. As noted in Chapter 5, QRs are allowed under Article XI of the GATT for agricultural commodities as long as concurrent measures are taken to restrict domestic production or to remove a temporary domestic surplus. Although it was the US that drafted this rule when negotiating the GATT, it proved too stringent for Congress, which did not wish to be bound by any international agreement and forced the Administration to ask for a waiver of this obligation in 1955. The waiver was necessary as existing US programmes supported domestic industries such as sugar and dairy without incorporating any incentives to reduce output. The root of the problem was Section 22 of the Agricultural Adjustment Act, which states that the Secretary of Agriculture must advise the President if he believes any agricultural commodity is being imported so as to interfere with Department of Agriculture price support programmes. Depending on the finding of an investigation into the matter, tariffs or QRs may be imposed. Because Section 22 violated GATT rules, US Administrations were reluctant to apply it. However, Congress had no such inhibitions, and amended Section 22 in 1951 to require the President to carry out its provisions regardless of international agreements, that is, the GATT (Evans, 1972: 72).

Under the WTO, disciplines on waivers were tightened. Article IX WTO allows waivers to be requested for any obligation imposed under a Multilateral Trade Agreement. Waivers under the WTO are time bound—in contrast to the GATT 1947—and are reviewed annually to determine if the exceptional circumstances requiring the waiver continue to exist. Any waiver in effect at the entry into force of the WTO was to expire by January 1997, unless extended by the WTO ministerial conference. Through 2006, 123 waivers were granted, including waiver extensions subsequent to annual reviews. Most waivers concerned technical issues related to the introduction of changes to WTO Schedules of tariff concessions following the adoption of the 2002 update of the HS. Politically important waivers concerned the nonapplication of Article 70.9 TRIPS to LDCs (see Chapter 8) for pharmaceutical products (until the end of 2015), EU preferences for the former Yugoslav republics (until 2011), the extension of Canada's waiver for its CARIBCAN preferential access programme (2011), the extension of a waiver for the Kimberley process (concerning certification schemes for rough diamonds to prevent trade in diamonds originating in conflict countries (2012) and the waiver for the ACP Cotonou convention (agreed at the Doha ministerial in 2001).[4] In addition, waivers have been granted in response to implementation concerns raised by developing countries, e.g. for customs valuation. As discussed in Chapter 5, a number of implementation matters were addressed by the relevant GATT committees.

---

[4] Information on waivers is reported in the WTO Annual Report (Section IV), which is available on the WTO homepage.

9.3. EMERGENCY PROTECTION (SAFEGUARDS)

Article XIX is GATT's general safety valve. It permits governments to impose measures to protect domestic producers seriously injured by imports. Designing a safeguard mechanism so that a balance is achieved between making it difficult to open the safety valve and avoiding an explosion of the boiler is not easy. The drafters of the GATT chose to be rather strict in this regard. Article XIX GATT states that necessary conditions included: (1) unforeseen developments; (2) resulting from the effects of obligations incurred by a contracting party (e.g. tariff concessions made in a MTN); (3) leading to increased imports; (4) that cause or threaten serious injury to domestic producers.

Safeguard measures were to be imposed on a nondiscriminatory basis. The interests of affected exporting countries were protected by a requirement that they be compensated. If no agreement was reached in consultations on compensation, an exporting country could be authorized to retaliate (suspend equivalent concessions or other obligations) against the safeguard-taking country. The compensation requirement made Article XIX a substitute for Article XXVIII renegotiation, the main difference being that the latter allows for a permanent change. Although Article XIX actions were supposed to be temporary in principle, no formal time limits were imposed. As a result some actions lasted for many years (Sampson, 1987).

The contracting parties to the GATT-1947 took only 150 official safeguard actions during the 1948–94 period (Table 9.1). Of these, only 20 led to (offers of) compensation—mostly in earlier years; retaliation occurred in 13 instances (GATT, 1994b). Article XIX was therefore used relatively infrequently. Reasons for this included the requirement that safeguard actions be nondiscriminatory (affect all exporters), a preference for QRs (much more difficult to implement in a nondiscriminatory manner than a tariff), the need to offer compensation, and the fact that in some jurisdictions (such as the US) granting of emergency protection is subject to the discretion of the President, who is required to take into account the impact of taking action on the economy. The relatively stringent conditions for obtaining Article XIX cover for protection reflected the fact that such protection violates earlier tariff commitments. This is not the case with AD or CVDs. As dumping or subsidization were agreed to be actionable, such measures are not a violation of tariff bindings as long the criteria laid out in the relevant GATT provisions are met. This helps to understand why over time AD came to be used increasingly as a de facto safeguard.

In addition to AD, discussed below, in the 1970s and 1980s VERs were used extensively to restrain exports of steel products and automobiles. Although

GATT-illegal (GATT, 1994b: 434)—with the exception of the MFA restraints, which had been sanctioned by the GATT—VERs did not give rise to formal dispute settlement cases. The reason was that no-one had an incentive to bring cases. Third country exporters, including the principal suppliers with which original tariff concessions on the goods involved had been negotiated, did not oppose VERs restricting their (new) competitors, and affected exporters tended to accept VERs because they allowed them to capture part of the rent that was created.

Instead of being confronted with an import tariff, the revenue of which is captured by the levying government, a VER involves a 'voluntary' cut back in export volume on the part of exporters. This reduction in supply will raise prices—assuming that other exporters do not take up the slack. Exporters therefore may get more per unit sold than they would under an equivalent tariff. Essentially they obtain what would be the quota rents if QRs were to be used (see Annex 2). There is a very large literature on VERs that will not be discussed here as VERs are now mostly of historical interest (see section 9.10).[5] The key points to remember about VERs are that they imply some direct compensation of affected exporters and that they selectively target exporters. Thus, they partially (and implicitly) satisfied GATT 1947 compensation requirements, while allowing for the circumvention of its MFN rule. The fact that VERs did not require import-competing industries to go through a formal process and satisfy the causality and injury standards that applied under Article XIX procedures made them particularly attractive for those seeking protection.

The specific criteria that are imposed in Article XIX were readily interpretable at the time, because the invocation of the instrument was tied to the specific commitments that GATT contracting parties had made in 1947. As argued by Sykes (2003), with the passage of time, the link to recently made concessions and 'unforeseen' developments made increasingly less sense. Implementing legislation in major traders such as the US did not mention the criterion that an import surge be linked to liberalization commitments and in practice countries simply required there to be a link between increased imports and serious injury.

This makes little economic sense. Imports are endogenous: they are determined by other factors and thus cannot be an independent source of injury to an import-competing industry. The quantity of imports will depend on the balance between domestic demand and supply in the importing country, and on the net demand and supply forces in the rest of world—which will determine the world market price for the good concerned. A variety of shocks that affect demand

---

[5] VERs have not disappeared completely. The EU for example, imposed what are effectively VERs in the context of bilateral agreements for steel exports with certain (non-WTO) transition economies, including Russia and the Ukraine, in 2003–4 (see Vermulst et al. 2004). Another example of new VERs was China's negotiated export limits to the US and EU in 2005 following the expiry of the ATC (discussed in Chapter 6).

and supply—such as changes in consumer tastes or the technology available to produce the good—will affect the market clearing world price, which in turn will determine the quantity imported into any given market. Although these considerations do nothing to undermine the political rationale for a safeguards instrument, they make it difficult for a government to determine whether 'imports' are actually the 'cause' of injury. A more economically justified approach would be to focus only the question of whether the import supply schedule has been affected, controlling for variables that affect domestic demand and supply— an approach that has been suggested by a number of economists (see Sykes, 2003). In practice, of course, trade may have little to do with the pressure for protection—generally the source of the problem is a lack of competitiveness of a given industry and a desire by a government to provide it with some 'breathing space'.

By the time the Uruguay Round was launched, the major objective of frequently targeted countries was to constrain the use of AD and VERs and to reassert the dominance of Article XIX in instances where the underlying problem was to address the pressure of import competition: the majority of cases. Two options were available: tighten the disciplines on the use of VERs and AD, or, alternatively, reduce the disincentives to use Article XIX. Both approaches were pursued. Little progress was achieved on the AD front (see below), but agreement was reached to ban the use of VERs and to make Article XIX more attractive to import-competing industries. Progress on the latter front was facilitated because importing country governments increasingly recognized that VERs were costly and not very effective—something that economists did not stop from pointing out in study after study (for example, De Melo and Tarr, 1992). Voluntary export restraints encouraged quality upgrading by affected exporters and entry by new exporters, including affected firms that relocated production facilities to other countries.

The Uruguay Round Agreement on Safeguards

A major achievement of the Uruguay Round Agreement on Safeguards was the prohibition of VERs and similar measures on the export or the import side (such as export moderation, export-price or import-price monitoring systems, export or import surveillance, compulsory import cartels and discretionary export or import licensing schemes). Any such measure in effect as of January 1995 was to be brought into conformity with the new rules or phased out by mid-1999.

The agreement requires that safeguard measures be taken only if an investigation demonstrates that imports have increased so much to have caused or threaten serious injury to an import-competing domestic industry. Investigations must include reasonable public notice to all interested parties and public hearings or other mechanisms through which traders and other affected parties can present their views on whether a safeguard measure would be in the public interest. Investigating authorities must publish a report setting forth their findings and reasoning.

Serious injury is defined as a significant overall impairment in the situation of a domestic industry. In determining injury, the domestic industry is defined as those firms whose collective output constitutes a major share of total domestic output of the product concerned. Factors to determine whether increased imports have caused serious injury include the magnitude of the increase in imports, change in market share, and changes in the level of sales, production, productivity, capacity utilization, profits and employment of the domestic industry. The AB in its case law has made clear all mentioned factors must be examined. A causal link needs to be made between increased imports and serious injury or threat thereof. Imports do not have to be the sole or even the major source of injury, but if factors other than increased imports are also causing injury to the domestic industry, such injury may not be attributed to increased imports.

Protection is limited to what is necessary to prevent or remedy serious injury caused by imports. If a QR is used, it may not reduce imports below the average level of the last three representative years, unless clear justification is given that a lower level is necessary to prevent or remedy serious injury. Although in principle safeguard actions must be nondiscriminatory, QRs may be allocated on a selective basis if the Committee on Safeguards accepts that imports from certain members have increased disproportionately in comparison to the total increase in imports, and the measures imposed are equitable to all suppliers of the product. Such 'quota modulation' may be maintained for four years at the most.

If use is made of QRs, they may be administered by exporters if this is mutually agreed. Thus, although VERs are prohibited, something analogous may be used if implemented as part of a GATT-conform procedure. Safeguard actions based on absolute increases in imports that are consistent with the provisions of the agreement do not require compensation of affected exporting countries for the first three years. In principle, safeguard instruments should be degressive—the level of protection should decline over time—and not last more than four years. All actions are subject to a sunset clause. The maximum total number of years a safeguard may be applied is eight years. If an action is extended beyond four years, a necessary condition is that the industry demonstrates that it is adjusting. If individual market shares of developing countries are less than 3 per cent of total imports, and the aggregate share of such countries less than 9 per cent of total imports, they are exempt from safeguard actions.

Notwithstanding the many procedural requirements, if governments want to they can put in place provisional safeguards virtually immediately. Article XIX is not called 'Emergency Action' for nothing—in 'critical circumstances' the Agreement on Safeguards allows Members to put in place safeguards immediately on a provisional basis (Article 6). As put by Vermulst, Pernaute and Lucenti (2004),

'...the safeguards instrument is an extraordinarily blunt instrument capable of very rapid deployment against imports covering broad categories' (p. 26).

Summing up, the Agreement of Safeguards brought existing practices that were GATT-inconsistent inside the tent, but subjected their use to multilateral surveillance and rules. Thus, VER-type measures came to be permitted under the WTO in certain conditions—in contrast to GATT 1947. Although this implies a move away from economically superior policies in an abstract sense, this is the price that had to be paid to avoid continued circumvention of GATT 1947 disciplines, which had become increasingly irrelevant. In addition, although the new agreement maintained the requirement that governments taking an action should enter into compensation discussions with affected exporters, the latter were not permitted to retaliate during the first three years of a safeguard. This example of creative drafting aimed at making the use of safeguards easier.

The WTO experience with safeguards

In the first 12 years of the WTO, members initiated 118 safeguard investigations, implying an annual average rate that was more than double what had prevailed in the GATT years (Table 9.2). This suggests that the intended weakening of WTO rules had the desired effect, especially as much of the increase reflects greater invocation of the instrument by developing countries—i.e. new users. Although the deal seems to have stuck in the sense that VERs are no longer prevalent, compared with other instruments of contingent protection such as antidumping (see below) safeguard measures continue to be used relatively infrequently.

Reasons for this probably include not only the continued relatively easier access to AD, but also the legal uncertainty that surrounds the use of safeguards. The WTO case law has not been kind to countries using safeguards—every case that has been contested has been lost by the safeguard-invoking country. Indeed, among the three major instruments of contingent protection, use of safeguards has been contested by far the most frequently relative to the total number of times the instrument has been used by WTO members. This is because key terms such as 'unforeseen developments', 'serious injury', 'increased quantities' and 'cause' are

Table 9.2. Safeguard measures (1995–2007)

	1995–9	2000–3	2004–7	Total
OECD countries	8	20	2	28
Developing countries	8	25	22	55
Total	16	45	24	83

Note: Annual data span 1 November to 31 October.
Source: WTO, Safeguards Committee Annual Reports; WTO Annual Reports.

not defined in the agreement. Without clarity regarding the baseline to be applied to imports, how to assess the link between imports and injury, and what constitutes an 'unforeseeable' event that generates an import surge, governments confront great uncertainty on whether the approaches they follow will pass muster.

Sykes (2003) and Grossman and Sykes (2007) argue in some detail that the AB has not done much to clarify matters. Instead it has simply reverted to the language of Article XIX and the Agreement on Safeguards in reviewing panel decisions, without clarifying the meaning of the key terms. Particularly problematical has been the insistence of the AB on applying the 'unforeseen developments' test to safeguard actions. In practice this had ceased to be applied or considered relevant by GATT contracting parties, and for that reason is not included in the Agreement on Safeguards. The re-introduction of this test by the AB effectively reversed the intent of those who had negotiated the Safeguards Agreement. Overall, 'Appellate Body decisions since the inception of the WTO have only made matters worse, to the point that the legal requirements for the use of safeguards are largely incoherent, and no nation can employ them without the near certainty of defeat in the dispute resolution process should they be challenged' (Grossman and Sykes, 2007: 91). Sykes (2003) concludes that the incoherence can only be resolved through a re-negotiation of the agreement or through action by the AB to define key terms. To date it has not been willing or able to do so.

Given the length of the WTO dispute settlement process—some three years on average—in effect WTO members have three years to impose a measure that violates tariff bindings. Perhaps not coincidentally, this is the same period provided under the Safeguard Agreement during which no retaliation may be implemented by affected exporters. The lack of clarity regarding the rules of the game increases the incentives for governments to take actions they deem necessary and wait for dispute settlement to take its course.

Although the absolute number of safeguards has been relatively small, it is important to take into account that safeguards, if they conform to WTO rules, will be nondiscriminatory and thus affect *all* imports. This is not the case with AD. Thus the economic impact of one safeguard can greatly exceed that of a number of AD actions. The 2002 US Steel Safeguard is an example of an action that had a major impact on trade—and that generated a series of disputes (Box 9.1).

Analysis of the impacts of post-Uruguay Round safeguard actions by Bown and McCulloch (2007) suggests that in practice these measures have often not conformed with the MFN principle, due in part to the *de minimis* provisions that are applied to exclude small developing countries from the reach of the measure. Another source of discrimination in the application of safeguards is that PTA partners are often excluded. Bown (2007) finds evidence that Canada's use of trade remedies was structured in a way so as to reinforce the discrimination that underpins the NAFTA.

Box 9.1. The 2001–2 US Steel Safeguards

The steel industry in the United States has a long history of being protected and subsidized. A variety of QRs were put in place starting in the 1970s, as well as hundreds of AD and CVD actions in the course of the 1980s and 1990s. The protection of the industry was costly given that steel is a key input into numerous sectors that together generate much more value added than does the steel industry itself. In 2001, steel users in the US employed 57 workers for every employee in steel (Ikenson, 2002). Moreover, parts of the industry were modern and competitive, in particular the so-called mini-mills that relied on scrap metal as feedstock.

In 2001, the industry sought additional protection once again, this time in the form of an across-the-board safeguard action. The US ended up imposing safeguard tariffs ranging between 8 and 30 per cent on ten steel product groups (a total of 272 ten-digit tariff lines). Steel imports from PTA partners (Canada, Israel, Jordan and Mexico) were excluded from these measures, as were imports from 100 developing countries that fell under the *de minimis* provision. There were also firm-specific 'product exclusions'. These were driven by the needs of steel-using firms, which had been asked by USTR to submit requests for exclusions of products that were critical to their production and that could not be supplied by US firms. The United States Trade Representative granted about 1,000 firm-specific exemptions, permitting continued imports from specified foreign steel-producing firms. (The exclusions were *not* for the specific products concerned—i.e. they were not MFN exclusions, but applied only to specified suppliers.)

The result of these various exemptions was that affected exporters confronted an effective tariff increase that was higher than would have occurred if the safeguard had been truly MFN. Bown (2004d) estimated that overall imports of the affected steel products fell by some 14 per cent in the year following the increase in tariffs; but exports of the nonexempted suppliers dropped by some 30 per cent (or US$1.2 billion). He concludes that the country and product exclusions resulted in an outcome that was akin to what would have been observed if the US had imposed a series of AD and CVD actions—as it had in fact done in the 1990s. The US action illustrated how a safeguard action can be manipulated to provide the same sort of discriminatory treatment as the explicitly discriminatory AD law.

In 2002, nine WTO members—Brazil, China, Chinese Taipei, the EU, Japan, Korea, New Zealand, Norway and Switzerland—challenged the safeguard action in the WTO. The panel found that the safeguards violated Articles 2.1, 4.2(b) and 3.1 of the Agreement of Safeguards by failing to show a 'causal link' between increased imports and serious injury and by failing the 'parallelism' requirement. The latter calls for a country taking an action to base the duties imposed on the injury caused by the countries included in the injury investigation (the US was found not to have done what was needed to exclude the effect of imports from its PTA partners in determining the cause and level of injury). Moreover, the US failed to provide a reasoned and adequate explanation demonstrating the impact of the 'unforeseen developments' it had identified on imports and how the facts supported the US determination of an increase in imports.

The unforeseen developments identified by the US included the Asian financial crisis and the collapse of the Soviet Union, both of which were argued to have led to a collapse in demand, with the resulting excess production of steel directed at the US market.

(cont.)

Box 9.1. *(Continued)*

Although the panel was sympathetic towards this argument the problem for the US was that US law makes no reference to the 'unforeseen developments' test and that it had not been applied in the investigation as a cause of increased imports.

On appeal, the panel's findings were substantially up-held for all products concerned. Given noncompliance by the US, the EU was authorized to raise tariffs amounting to US$2.2 billion on US goods. It targeted products such as citrus fruit and textiles in an effort to mobilize internal political opposition to the US measures in question. The US responded in December 2003 by terminating the safeguard measures.

This safeguard action had several spillover effects. One was that the EU immediately responded to the US action by launching 21 safeguard actions of its own for the steel products concerned—imposing provisional tariff quotas the very same day the US measures were announced for 15 categories of steel products. This was driven by a fear of trade deflection—the EU sought to foreclose its market to the exporters most affected by the US action. The EU motivated its measures as a response to the 'unforeseen' US action. The European measures were removed in December 2003, in parallel with the termination of the safeguard by the US.

Bown and Crowley (2007) present indirect evidence that the EU fears may have been justified. They analyze the impact of US safeguards on Japanese exports. They find that US action led to a decline of 60–70 per cent in the value of Japan's *overall* exports of affected products—in part because excess supply created by the safeguard in other markets prevented Japanese exporters from diverting output elsewhere.

Source: Bown (2004*d*); Vermulst, Pernaute and Lucenti (2004); Grossman and Sykes (2007).

Special safeguards: Textiles and Clothing, Agriculture and Accession Protocols

Special safeguard actions have been included in some WTO agreements, in particular the WTO Agreements on Textiles and Clothing (ATC) and the Agreement on Agriculture, which has a Special Safeguard (SSG) clause. Both of these are discussed in Chapter 6. Special provisions allowing for country-specific safeguards were also included in China's Protocol of Accession—see Chapter 12. Historically, the GATT nonapplication clause was sometimes used in lieu of the type of specific provisions written into China's accession protocol. The best known example occurred in the case of Japan's accession. At the time there was strong pressure from some contracting parties to introduce a new Japan-specific safeguard mechanism. This was rejected, and led to over a dozen contracting parties invoking Article XXXV ('Non-Application of the Agreement between Specific Contracting Parties') when Japan acceded. In a number of cases, Japan subsequently negotiated bilateral agreements containing special safeguard clauses that led to revocation of Article XXXV.

9.4. ANTIDUMPING ACTIONS

Loosely defined, dumping occurs when a firm sells products on an export market for less than what it charges on its home market for the same product. Dumping is also said to occur if the export price of a product is below the cost of production. World Trade Organization rules allow action to be taken against dumped imports if dumping causes or threatens material injury to a domestic import-competing industry. This is a much weaker standard than the serious injury criterion used in the case of safeguards. Antidumping is an option—there is no requirement for members to have an AD mechanism. At the time the GATT was first negotiated, AD was rarely used. It was included in the GATT at the insistence of the US, which starting from the 1930s Reciprocal Trade Agreements Act linked (reciprocal) trade liberalization to the existence of administrative protection mechanisms (Nelson, 2006). In effect, the function of the AD mechanism and other instruments of contingent protection in the US was to replace a system in which specific industries lobbied the US Congress for specific tariffs with one where industries seeking protection had to go through an administrative mechanism (Finger, Hall and Nelson, 1982). In 1950, there were only 37 cases, of which 21 taken by South Africa. Over time it became much more popular: over 4,000 AD investigations have been initiated by WTO members since the late 1970s. Between 1995 and 2007, there were 3,200 investigations by WTO members, of which 2,049 led to AD measures (Table 9.3).

Antidumping became increasingly controversial during the 1980s as its use expanded. Numerous AD actions were challenged during the Uruguay Round, in part reflecting a strategy on the part of targeted countries to use dispute settlement as a vehicle to support positions that were being taken in the negotiations. It remains an area that generates many disputes: 27 panels dealing with AD were established between 1995 and 2008 (WTO, 2008). In almost all cases the panel found against the country that had taken the AD action, and in a number of instances recommended that illegal AD duties be removed and reimbursed (Peters-mann, 1997; Nelson, 2006).

The main users of AD have traditionally been Australia, Canada, the EU and the US. Since the creation of the WTO, the use of AD by developing countries has increased dramatically. The top users of AD in 2005–8 included India, Argentina and South Africa. The frequent users of AD listed in Table 9.3 account for over 95 per cent of investigations and actions imposed, but are the targets for only about two-thirds of all AD measures. China is the most frequent target, followed by the US and the EU.

In recent years, AD measures taken against Chinese exporters have continued to increase both in terms of the number of cases and as a percentage of all AD actions by WTO members. During 1995–2007 over 420 AD actions were imposed against

Table 9.3. Main users of antidumping actions, 1995–2007 (shares in parentheses)

Country	Number of Investigations	Number of Actions Imposed	Number of Times Targeted by Investigations	Number of Times Targeted by Actions
OECD members				
Australia	191 (5.9)	72 (3.5)	20 (0.6)	8 (0.4)
Canada	142 (4.4)	87 (4.2)	32 (1.0)	13 (0.6)
EU	372 (11.6)	244 (11.9)	65 (2.0)	44 (2.1)
Japan	6 (0.2)	3 (0.1)	141 (4.4)	103 (5.0)
Korea	105 (3.3)	54 (2.6)	243 (7.6)	143 (7.0)
Mexico	94 (2.9)	81 (4.0)	40 (1.2)	26 (1.3)
New Zealand	53 (1.6)	22 (1.1)	9 (0.3)	3 (0.1)
Turkey	115 (3.6)	113 (5.5)	39 (1.2)	22 (1.1)
US	402 (12.5)	245 (12.0)	181 (5.6)	108 (5.3)
Developing				
Argentina	222 (6.9)	161 (7.9)	28 (0.9)	15 (0.7)
Brazil	147 (4.6)	75 (0.4)	94 (2.9)	72 (3.5)
China	138 (4.3)	104 (5.1)	597 (18.6)	423 (21.1)
Egypt	61 (1.9)	44 (2.1)	12 (0.4)	4 (0.2)
India	508 (15.8)	355 (17.3)	131 (4.1)	78 (3.8)
Indonesia	66 (2.1)	29 (1.4)	135 (4.2)	76 (3.7)
Malaysia	43 (1.3)	25 (1.2)	81 (2.5)	48 (2.3)
Peru	64 (2.0)	45 (2.2)	2 (0.1)	0 (0.0)
South Africa	205 (6.4)	121 (5.9)	55 (1.7)	34 (1.7)
Thailand	39 (1.2)	28 (1.4)	129 (4.0)	80 (3.9)
Venezuela	31 (1.0)	25 (1.2)	18 (0.6)	12 (0.6)
Other	132 (4.1)	72 (3.5)	1,058 (33.0)	728 (35.5)
Total	3,210 (100)	2,049 (100)	3,210 (100)	2,049 (100)

Source: WTO (2008) AD Initiations and Measures: By Reporting Member and Exporting Country From: 1 January 1995 to 31 December 2007.

China, three times as many as against South Korea, the second largest target (143 cases). This reflects both the dynamism of China's exporters and the terms of the Accession Protocol (the nonmarket economy status of China—Box 9.2). Given the overall decline in numbers of AD actions in the mid-2000s, the increase in China's share as a target implies there is substantial and increasing discrimination against China. More generally, AD is disproportionally used by developing economies against developing economies (Figure 9.2).

The sectoral incidence of AD is highly concentrated. Over 50 per cent of all investigations target steel products or chemicals. Antidumping duties tend to be very high when compared to the average MFN tariff applied on manufactures in OECD nations. Duties against China of over 100 per cent are common: the average duty in the 2002–4 period imposed by the US was 148 per cent (Bown, 2009).

Box 9.2. China and antidumping measures

In the EU and the US, AD rulings against Chinese exporters are often based on a comparison of export prices of Chinese products with prices of the same type of products in a third country. China tends to be detrimentally affected by these practices. In about 40 per cent of all EU preliminary AD investigations against China in 2001–5, the US was used as a 'third country'. This approach is clearly problematic as it is easy to find dumping if prices of Chinese products are compared with those of the same type of products in an advanced country. Conversely, the US often opted to use India for comparison purposes, calculating a 'hypothetical cost' of Chinese products based on the cost of raw materials and publicly regulated charges in India plus a 'hypothetical profit' margin to determine the price used for the comparison. In general, the costs and charges in India were higher than those in China and the method of calculating 'hypothetical profits' was arbitrary, pushing up the prices used for the comparison (Rushford, 2005).

China's accession protocol—see Chapter 12—includes a number of 'WTO-minus' provisions (including special safeguards) that are motivated by the perception that China was not a fully fledged market economy when it acceded. These provisions will cease to apply once a WTO member determines that China is a market economy, or 15 years after China's accession, whichever comes first. China's status as a 'nonmarket economy country' in the WTO allows for highly arbitrary practices to be used in calculating dumping margins. The US uses six factors to determine if a country is a market economy, including the 'extent wage determination is based on labour-management negotiations' and 'the extent to which investment by foreign companies is recognized'. Concrete numerical standards are not specified. The EU's criteria consider to what extent 'prices and costs are determined by the market's demand-supply balance' and if 'corporate financial conditions are not subjected to the effects of serious distortions such as those which occur in a non-market economic system' (Rushford, 2005). According to the Heritage Foundation Index of Economic Freedom (2008 edition), China ranks 126th in the world. However, lower-ranking Ukraine (133rd place) and Russia (134th place) are recognized as 'market economy countries'.

China has engaged in bilateral negotiations with individual WTO members to achieve 'market economy' status. It has also used the WTO dispute settlement mechanism. For example, in September 2008, China filed its third dispute settlement case in the WTO, challenging the legality of American AD and CVD measures imposed on Chinese-made paper. (The first case brought by China was in 2002, when it joined a group of WTO members that contested the US steel safeguard action discussed previously.)

Source: Committee on Anti-dumping Practices, Meeting of 28 April (2008); and Rushford, 2005.

A brief summary of GATT disciplines

The basic GATT provision dealing with AD is Article VI. This does not prohibit dumping, but simply establishes certain rules that apply if governments decide to take actions to offset dumping. Starting in the 1960s, reflecting increasing use of AD, efforts began to be made to further define multilateral disciplines in this area. A code

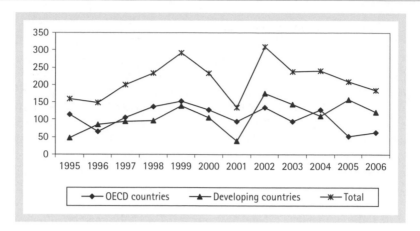

Figure 9.2. Antidumping investigations, 1995–2006

Source: WTO, Antidumping Committee and WTO Annual Reports, 2000–7.

on AD was negotiated in the Kennedy Round. It was opposed by the US Congress, and in practice was only applied insofar as its provisions were consistent with US legislation. In the Tokyo Round, the AD code was re-negotiated. This code—which only bound signatories—became the basis of the Uruguay Round agreement on AD (formally entitled the Agreement on Implementation of Article VI).

Dumping is defined in GATT as offering a product for sale in export markets at a price below normal value. Normal value is defined as the price charged by a firm in its home market, in the ordinary course of trade. Trade is considered not to be ordinary if over an extended period of time (normally one year) a substantial quantity of goods is sold at less than average total costs (the sum of fixed and variable costs of production plus selling, general and administrative costs). If sales on its domestic market are too small to allow price comparisons, the highest comparable price charged in third markets is used. Alternatively, the exporting firm's estimated costs of production plus a reasonable amount for profits, administrative, selling and any other expenses may be used to determine normal value (the so-called constructed value).

In cases where there is no export price or where it appears to the investigating authorities that the export price is unreliable because of a relationship between the parties to a transaction, the export price may also be constructed. Constructed values should be based on the price at which the imported products are first resold to an independent buyer, or if they are not resold to an independent buyer, 'on such reasonable basis as the authorities may determine'. The comparison of the export price and the normal value must be made at the same level of trade (normally ex-factory) and as close as possible to the same time. Allowance is to be made for differences in factors such as the conditions and terms of sale, the quantities involved, physical characteristics, and differences in relevant costs. In an investigation, exporters must be allowed at least 60 days to adjust their export prices to reflect sustained movements in exchange rates during the period of investigation.

Actions against dumping may only be taken if it can be shown that it has caused or threatens material injury of the domestic import-competing industry. Injury determinations must be based on positive evidence and involve an objective examination of the volume of the dumped imports, their effect on prices in the domestic market, and the impact on domestic producers of like products. A significant increase in dumped imports, either in absolute terms or relative to production or consumption in the importing country, is a necessary condition for finding injury. Significant price undercutting of domestic producers, a significant depressing effect on prices, or the level of the dumping margin are other indicators that may be used. The term 'significant' is not defined. Although differences in views as to what is significant might be dealt with through the dispute settlement process, this possibility is limited as panels are constrained in their ability to overrule substantive decisions taken by domestic investigating authorities (see below).

An illustrative list of injury indicators is given in the agreement. These include actual and potential decline in sales, profits, output, market share, productivity, return on investments or utilization of capacity; factors affecting domestic prices; the magnitude of the margin of dumping; actual and potential negative effects on cash flow, inventories, employment, wages, growth, ability to raise capital or investments. This list is not exhaustive, and no single or combination of factors is decisive. Dumped imports must be found to cause injury because of dumping. The necessary causality must be established on the basis of all relevant evidence before the authorities. Any other known factors that are injuring the domestic industry must be taken into account, and may not be attributed to the dumped imports. Factors that may be relevant include the volume and prices of imports not sold at dumping prices, contraction in demand or changes in the patterns of consumption, trade restrictive practices of—and competition between—the foreign and domestic producers, developments in technology, and the export performance and productivity of the domestic industry.

This brief summary of the major elements of the AD Agreement illustrates that it is very technical and complex. Many of its articles are only decipherable for lawyers specialized in this particular area of trade law. The wording of the Agreement reflects numerous compromises reached in the Tokyo and Uruguay Rounds. It is a combination of elements of the domestic laws and practices of major WTO members and periodic attempts by target countries to limit the protectionist biases inherent in the use of AD in most jurisdictions. These biases have proven difficult to eradicate. The reason for this is simple: AD is fundamentally flawed from an economic perspective and cannot be fixed by tinkering with the methodological arcana of investigations. For all practical purposes, there is nothing wrong with dumping. It is a normal business practice. The problem is antidumping. As argued by Finger (1993*a*), disciplining AD requires efforts by negatively affected parties (consumers, users) to alter domestic implementing legislation to allow their interests to be represented in investigations.

What's wrong with dumping?

Why dumping occurs is not considered relevant under GATT rules. From a normative, economic, perspective this is important, however. A typology of business motivations for dumping is presented in Table 9.4.

Sporadic dumping may occur without any deliberate intention if the exporting firm has to decide on how much to produce before demand conditions or exchange rates are known. Sporadic dumping may also arise from a lack of experience in pricing a new product. The trading environment facing a firm is usually uncertain, so dumping will often be beyond the control of a firm. For example, unexpected changes in exchange rates may lead a firm to dump even if it had no intention of doing so. However, in most cases dumping reflects a deliberate business strategy followed by exporting companies and constitutes a conscious, premeditated pricing practice aimed at the accomplishment of specific business objectives.

The best known motivation is simple price discrimination between markets. The wording of GATT rules specifically targets this rationale. A firm having some control over prices and operating in two separate markets may find it advantageous to discriminate in its price formation in favour of foreign consumers in order to maximize profits. Price discrimination across markets will occur whenever demand for a product is more elastic in export markets than at home, that is, for any given change in price, foreign consumers change their demand more than domestic customers. Dumping in the sense of spatial price discrimination requires that

Table 9.4. Motivations for dumping

Type of Dumping	Objectives of the Exporting Firm
Sporadic or random	No deliberate intention to dump
Price discrimination	Maximize profits given differences in demand across markets
Cyclical	Cover at least variable costs and maintain capacity during periods of slack demand
Defensive	Minimize losses due to excess capacity or to deter entry by competitors
Scale economies	Price below cost initially with expectation of recouping investment outlays (fixed costs) over time as sales expand
Market-creating	To establish a new product as the market leader—revenue, not profit maximization
Head-on	To attack a dominant supplier in an export market
Predatory	To establish a monopoly on an export market

there are barriers to re-importation of the dumped product into the exporter's home market. Otherwise, price differentials across markets would tend to be eliminated through arbitrage, allowing for transport and transactions costs. As discussed further below, this suggests that the problem with dumping, if any, are the trade barriers that prevent such arbitrage.

As noted above, selling below average total cost can also constitute dumping, and it is not strictly necessary that prices charged in the export market be below those charged at home. Issues of trade policy and differing price elasticities then become irrelevant.[6] The cost-dumping case is important in practice, because many exporters produce exclusively or predominately for export, or sell only specific products for export. Often it may be in a firm's interest to sell below variable or even marginal costs (the cost of producing an extra unit of output) for a while. Although by doing so the firm will make a loss (because its fixed costs are not recovered), this may be necessary in the short run to establish or increase market share, or to enable the firm to move down its learning curve, thus increasing expected long-run profits.

A firm may engage in cyclical dumping to stabilize its production over the business cycle. Dumping arises as the firm reduces prices to cover only average variable during periods of slack demand. This can be perfectly rational, insofar as the firm expects better times in the future and perceives the costs of laying off workers and reducing capacity to be higher than continuing production without covering all costs. Indeed, differences in labour markets and employment practices of firms across countries are one factor explaining why firms from some countries are more prone to engage in cyclical dumping than others (Ethier, 1982). If it is very costly for a firm to lay off workers—because of high legislated redundancy payments for example—it will continue to produce more than a firm that confronts a very flexible and less regulated labour market.

Certain forms of dumping have a pronounced strategic dimension. Exporting at prices below production cost may help deter entry by potential competitors into a firm's home market. This can be called defensive dumping (Davies and McGuinness, 1982). A firm may also price exports below total production cost on a longer term basis if such a strategy permits it to realize economies of scale (these exist if unit costs decline as output expands). A firm may need to move down its learning curve as fast as possible. As output increases, production workers tend to become more efficient and unit costs of production fall. Dumping in these cases is part of a strategy to attain an optimal scale of production.

A related rationale for dumping arises in cases of new high-technology products (such as video recorders in the 1970s and early 1980s). Here a firm may attempt to

---

[6] The price elasticity of demand for a product is the ratio of the percentage change in the quantity demanded to the percentage change in the price. For example, if prices increase by 5 per cent and the corresponding quantity decreases by more than 5 per cent, demand is price elastic.

discourage domestic firms from engaging in the development of a competing product by establishing a large market share. Products where there is proprietary technology may foster dumping in the early stages of the product cycle. Profitability in such products often depends on consumers choosing a specific standard. In the video case, there were two main competing standards or formats in the 1970s, VHS and Betamax. Both needed to attract enough adherents to form a large enough customer base to recoup investment in R&D. When firms are trying to establish market share quickly, dumping may be part of an effective competitive strategy. A firm may also choose to export at prices that do not cover even marginal cost when, instead of maximizing profit, it prefers to maximize sales. Such 'head-on dumping' may be used as part of an attack on a price leader in a given export market. Head-on dumping was practiced extensively by Japanese semi-conductor and electronics producers in export markets in the 1980s.

The foregoing rationales for dumping are driven by market structures, business cycles, or the characteristics of the products that are produced. Of these deliberate strategies, only one is potentially detrimental to the welfare of the country importing the dumped product: predation. Predation was the original rationale for US AD legislation, passed in 1916. The fear was that a foreign firm (or cartel) could deliberately price products low enough to drive existing domestic firms out of business and establish a monopoly. Once established, the monopolist could more than recoup its losses by exploiting its market power. For predation to work, the monopolist (cartel) must not only eliminate domestic competition, but must also be able to prohibit entry by new competitors. For this to be possible it must either have a global monopoly or it must convince the importing government to impose or tolerate entry restrictions. It is not clear why a government would do this. Not surprisingly, in practice, post-Second-World-War cases of successful predatory dumping are the exception, not the rule. Research by economists has demonstrated that over 90 per cent of all AD investigations in OECD countries would never have been launched if a competition standard—potential threat of injury to competition, as opposed to injury to competitors—had been used as a criterion (Messerlin, 2000). The same has been concluded for AD investigations by developing countries— e.g. in only eight of 223 cases could there conceivably have been a potential predation rationale for AD in India (Aggarwal, 2002). Proponents of AD often have a narrower definition of predation in mind than the economic one described above. The fact that competition from other, outside sources will in most realistic circumstances prevent the formation of a monopoly is considered irrelevant. What matters is the (continued) existence of the domestic industry. But AD will not help in achieving this objective. What is needed is adjustment of the industry, something that AD is unlikely to encourage.

Import-competing firms usually object to underselling, and not to price discrimination or selling below cost. This has been emphasized by de Jong (1968), who noted that popular opinion refers to dumping when foreign producers are able to undersell the domestic supplier in his own market. As described by de Jong, this notion was translated as social dumping in early discussions concerning AD legislation. Although this term was not clearly defined, it was apparent that it referred to underselling by foreign firms in the domestic market, made possible by lower labour costs abroad (that is, comparative advantage). In practice, it is underselling that importing-competing firms consider unfair, reflecting their inability or unwillingness to meet the price set by a foreign competitor.

That predation has very little to do with AD as it is practiced is perhaps best illustrated by the United States, which has two antidumping statutes. One, the Antidumping Act of 1916, maintains a predation standard for antidumping, and is very rarely invoked. The other, the Tariff Act of 1930, as amended, has a price and cost-discrimination standard, and is the one usually invoked by import-competing industries. Interestingly, the 1916 Act was the subject of dispute settlement cases in 1998. The cases, brought by the EU and Japan, alleged that the existence of the 1916 Act violated the national treatment rule and WTO disciplines on AD (which stipulate that the remedy to offset dumping is limited to AD duties and undertakings). Japan objected to the provisions of the Act that the importation or sale of imported goods that is found to be unlawful (predatory) may constitute a criminal offence and give rise to claims for damages. The trigger for bringing the case to the WTO was a court action brought under the 1916 Act against affiliates of Japanese companies. These cases are somewhat ironic, in that there is a valid rationale for imposing civil liabilities or criminal penalties in cases where predation is found to exist, as long as the same disciplines apply to domestic firms. A problem in this instance is that US competition authorities may not intervene against pricing practices of firms that are in violation of the 1916 Act, as competition law enforcement has evolved significantly since that statute was passed.

What's wrong with antidumping?

Antidumping constitutes straightforward protectionism that is packaged to make it look like something different. By calling dumping unfair, the presumption is that AD is fair and thus a good thing. This is good marketing, but bad economics. From an economic perspective there is nothing wrong with most types of dumping. Antidumping is not about fair play. Its goal is to tilt the rules of the game in favour of import-competing industries.

Advocates of AD policies sometimes argue that AD is a justifiable attempt by importing country governments to offset the market access restrictions existing in an exporting firm's home country that underlie the ability of such firms to dump. Such restrictions may consist of import barriers preventing arbitrage, but may also reflect the nonexistence or weak enforcement of competition law by the exporting country. For example, the US has claimed that lax Japanese antitrust enforcement permits Japanese firms to collude, raise prices, and use part of the resulting rents to cross-subsidize (dump) products sold on foreign markets. Antidumping is clearly an inferior instrument to address foreign market closure because it does not deal with the source of the problem—the government policies that artificially segment markets, or allow this to occur. An AD duty may put pressure on affected firms to lobby their government to eliminate such policies—or to abolish private business practices that restrict entry—but does so in a very indirect manner. Once investigations are initiated, any changes in policies or practices cannot have an impact on the finding. In many cases there will not be significant barriers to entry, so there is not much to be done by exporters to improve access to their home markets. Indeed, under current procedures no account is taken of whether price discrimination or selling below cost is the result of market-access restrictions. Building this into the analysis would appear to be a first necessary step.[7]

A more compelling argument for AD is that it is a useful (political) safety valve that allows countries to implement and sustain more general trade liberalization. This is the same argument that is used to justify safeguards—the difference being that AD allows targeting of specific exporters and thus is argued to be less costly for the economy. This is an argument that dates back to Jacob Viner (1923) and that can be (and is) applied to both high-income and developing countries. The hypothesis is difficult to reject given that OECD countries are on average very liberal when it comes to tariffs, despite sometimes intensive use of AD. Finger and Nogues (2006) argue that in Latin America AD was used as a pro-liberalization, safety valve device. This role of AD is also consistent with research that shows a relationship between deterioration in macroeconomic conditions and the use of AD. Thus, for example, Aggarwal (2004) in a cross-country study covering the 1980–2000 period concludes that a 1 per cent deterioration of the trade balance or a 1 per cent increase in the growth rate of imports into a country is associated with a 2 per cent increase in the number of AD investigations. This replicates earlier findings—e.g. Takacs (1981), Leidy (1997) and Knetter and Prusa (2003).

Others argue that the evidence offered in support of the safety valve hypothesis is mostly anecdotal, and that AD constitutes an obstacle to free trade in developing countries (Niels and ten Kate, 2006). One reason for this is that AD may generate incentives for 'retaliation'—tit-for-tat responses by targeted countries. More generally, as countries emulate the OECD countries and adopt and use AD, there may be a general spread of the instrument and an overall reversal of liberalization. It is certainly the case that major users of AD in the 2000s have tended to include countries that in the 1990s were targeted: including China and Brazil. There is some

---

[7] If the purported problem protection abroad and/or a lack of competition in an exporter's home market—as is also the case for the predation argument for AD—the first best option is to replace AD with national competition law enforcement. A second best option is to apply competition principles to AD enforcement—e.g. make AD action conditional on a finding that significant barriers to entry exist in the exporter's home market.

evidence that retaliation threats are one reason for the use of AD by major exporters, and that it has an effect in *restraining* the use of AD by importing countries (Bloningen and Bown, 2003; Feinberg and Olsen, 2004). Thus, the spread of AD is not necessarily bad from an overall, global, liberalization perspective.

Bown (2008) undertakes an econometric investigation of the determinants of AD in developing countries and concludes that the same political economy variables explain the use of AD as in the OECD countries—including macroeconomic conditions, the size of import-competing industries (and thus their political 'influence' and ability to organize), the 'familiarity' of the industry with AD (including having been the target of actions in export markets), the extent of import competition, and their economic performance. However, he finds that the ratio of AD actions imposed to investigations launched is higher than in OECD countries—some 70 per cent compared to about 50 per cent—and that there is significant heterogeneity across developing countries. In India, for example, macroeconomic variables do not play a role, whereas they are important in Argentina.

Even if one accepts that AD is a useful device that supports a general open trade policy, it is costly for affected firms, consumers and third countries. The extensive history with the instrument in OECD countries illustrates that even if it plays a positive role in encouraging or supporting general liberalization, it can be a long-term source of continued trade policy induced distortions. For example, Gallaway and colleagues (1999) estimate that the economy-wide welfare costs (real income losses) from AD and CVDs in the US in 1993 were in the range of US$2–4 billion. Although not trivial, this is not particularly large if compared to the distortions imposed by the Smoot-Halley tariffs of the 1930s. An implication drawn by Nelson (2006) is that the rules that have been put in place do work to constrain protection seeking. Of course, this is not just, or even primarily, due to the rules on AD, but of the overall set of incentives that countries have put in place through the WTO and recurring MTNs.

Although the overall share of affected imports into major markets has been small—no more than a few per cent at most—the impact on affected exporters is often significant. Niels and ten Kate (2006), in an analysis of Mexican AD, find that an investigation reduces imports from targeted countries by over 70 per cent, as their prices are forced up, volumes fall and they lose market share. In their study other exporters did not take up the slack—instead the benefits accrued to Mexican import-competing firms who saw their market shares expand. Bown and Crowley (2007), using data for the 1992–2001 period, find that AD actions against Japan by the US deflected Japanese exports, increasing these by some 5–7 per cent in the average third country market. More interestingly, AD actions against other countries by the US reduced Japanese exports of the same products to those third markets by between 5 and 19 per cent—presumably reflecting greater sales of the products concerned by the exporters on their home markets. They argued that these deflection and trade-suppression effects are an incentive for affected countries to adopt and apply AD laws of their own.

A key problem with AD is the discretion that often is granted to investigating authorities—or, alternatively, the guidelines under which such authorities are forced to operate by law—to follow procedures that can make the instrument blatantly protectionist. In practice methodologies used to determine whether dumping has occurred and calculate the size of the dumping margin are such that high positive margins can be found in many circumstances. An often-used practice is to calculate dumping margins by using methodologies that raise the normal value and lower the average export price, thereby increasing the dumping margin. Normal values can be biased upward by not including sales in the home market made at prices considered to be below cost, and by excluding sales in the export market that are above the calculated normal value. The latter procedure has been justified on the basis that 'sales at a high price should not be allowed to conceal dumped sales' (Hindley, 1994: 97). In cases where the normal value is constructed on the basis of costs, dumping margins can be inflated through the inclusion of high profit and overhead margins in the calculation of the normal value, but not allowing for this in the calculation of the costs of sales for exports.

Another problem is that injury criteria may be manipulated by firms. This is potentially of some importance, as the injury test tends to be the main factor constraining the access of import-competing industries to protection (Finger and Murray, 1990). Indicators of injury include trends in market share, employment, profits, capacity, capacity utilization, import penetration and price underselling (the exporters charging prices below what is charged by the import-competing industry). Many of these variables will not be closely linked to trends in imports, but depend on business cycle influences. Although all of these indicators may to some extent be correlated with injury, many can be manipulated by firms, thus creating an incentive for 'indirect rent seeking' by either feigning that criteria have been met, or by deliberately taking actions that will induce injury as defined in the law (Leidy and Hoekman, 1991; Leidy, 1994a). This enhances the threat effect of AD, and may foster so-called cascading of protection.

Under AD, protection generally follows automatically if the criteria are satisfied. Potential countervailing forces, such as users and consumers, remain outside the administrative process and are effectively neutralized by the law—they do not have legal standing in most jurisdictions.[8] By invoking instruments of contingent protection, an upstream industry that produces an input may significantly injure a downstream industry that uses the input. This increases the

---

[8] A noteworthy exception is the EU, where imposition of an AD action requires approval of the European Council, which is comprised of political representatives (ministers) of the member states. The Council operates on the basis of simple majority voting.

probability that downstream firms will seek and gain protection in turn. Indeed, by initiating and winning an AD action, upstream suppliers may be able to manipulate the health of downstream firms to the advantage of both (Hoekman and Leidy, 1992). As a result, instances of contingent protection may cascade along the chain of production.[9]

This vertical linkage across instances of contingent protection illustrates one way in which AD procedures may facilitate cartelization along the production stream. Antidumping and similar laws may also facilitate tacit or explicit collusion by enforcing existing cartels and substantially reducing price competition in affected markets (Messerlin, 1989, 1990). A credible threat of invocation of unfair-trade laws may provide a means for industries to engage in implicit collusion that could not otherwise be maintained (Leidy, 1994a). Antidumping and similar procedures are initiated by private parties (firms or industry associations). These interested parties are active in pursuing the adoption of more restrictive rules and employing credible threats of invocation of procedures to negotiate VERs. The expansion of the scope and use of unfair-trade laws has been characterized as reflecting the de facto privatization of trade policy (Messerlin, 1990).

Matters are made worse from a competition and transparency perspective by the practice of negotiating price undertakings with exporters that are subject to AD investigations. Once a preliminary dumping or injury margin has been established, exporters will have some sense of the likely magnitude of the final AD duty that could be imposed. This provides them with an incentive to offer to raise their prices (or cut back supply). Offering such undertakings is explicitly allowed for in the EU's AD legislation (EEC Regulation No. 2423/88), and AD investigations frequently result in undertakings being accepted by the European Commission. The US does not accept undertakings, but in practice similar deals are struck, the difference being that US industry is given (informal) assurances by exporters that they will reduce exports or raise prices. Such agreements often explain why US AD petitions are withdrawn at some point after an investigation has been launched (Prusa, 1992).

Undertakings are akin to VERs, and are concluded for the same reasons. Exporters prefer them to the alternative of paying AD duties. With an undertaking they can at least capture some of the rents that are created by reducing supply. The downside of undertakings is similar to the downsides of VERs—they are less transparent to domestic users and consumers. Indeed, often it will not be generally known that there are undertakings in place. They may also hide a variety of collusive practices. Undertakings clearly are more detrimental to the national

[9] Research by Feinberg and Kaplan (1992) provides evidence of cascading. In a statistical analysis of all antidumping and countervailing duty cases during the period 1980–6 brought by US producers and users of metals, they found that user industries tended to file for protection after upstream industries, and that the share of all cases accounted for by downstream industries increased significantly over time. Analysis of cases involving producers and users of chemicals led to the same finding.

welfare of countries using them than duties are, raising the question of why they are used. Possible explanations include transaction costs—it is easier for an administration to rely on industry to carry the burden of monitoring whether a deal is implemented than having customs apply discriminatory tariffs—and foreign policy considerations. By transferring rents abroad, the negative impact on trading partners is reduced. Out of 165 definitive AD measures imposed between July 2005 and June 2006, more than 10 per cent were price undertakings.

It is often pointed out that one way to attenuate the negative effects of AD on national welfare is to impose filters that require determining what the likely impact on the economy would be of imposing AD duties. So-called public interest clauses can be introduced that require the authorities to do this. They have not been very effective in practice, in part because the 'public interest' is not defined clearly enough, and in part because those that will be affected negatively are often not consulted. Although losers may be effectively excluded from the process of determining whether to intervene, they do have access to the political system, and may have a strong enough incentive to seek to change the law so that the interests of users are considered.

Developments in this direction occurred in the EU and the US during the 1990s. In 1996, the US Congress held hearings on possible modifications to US AD law, pressured to do so by influential industries that relied heavily on imports of components. More progress in the direction of considering the interests of users and consumers occurred in the EU. A 1994 case concerning imports of gum rosin is illustrative. The Commission concluded that 'the negative effects of antidumping measures on the users of gum rosin would be overwhelmingly disproportionate to the benefits arising from antidumping measures in favor of the Community industry'.[10] The EU industry's production capacity was limited, so that imposition of duties would substantially increase the costs for industries that use gum rosin as an input. Accordingly, the Commission concluded 'that protective measures would not be appropriate and that it would not be in the Community interest to continue the proceeding'.

There is increasingly a debate and differences in view between EU member states regarding the desirability of imposing AD actions. Such actions must be approved by the European Council on the basis of a simple majority vote. European Union members that do not have a significant domestic industry for a product will not have much incentive to support states that want to protect that industry. Increasingly, as a result of global production sharing and fragmentation of production (specialization in tasks), EU-based firms selling an endproduct in the EU will have sourced much of the labour-intensive part of the production process from non-EU firms. Shoes are an example: most shoes sold by EU firms are fabricated in Asia. But that fabrication process accounts for only a small share of the value of the

---

[10] Official Journal, L 41/54, 12 February 1994.

shoe—most of which is generated by designers, the trademark, branding, marketing and distribution services that are mostly produced in the EU. The result of such changes in the organization of production has been a shift in the balance of interests within the EU on trade policy, which may explain the fall in the number of AD actions that were initiated by the European Commission in the 2000s (Evenett and Vermulst, 2005). Another factor is that the EU became more restrained in taking AD actions against imports from Eastern European nations—historically a major target—as many have now acceded to the EU. The environment in major OECD countries thus may be slowly turning away from the overly enthusiastic use of AD that characterized the late 1990s.

However, as noted, developing countries are stepping into the breach (Table 9.2). What that implies in terms of the global incidence of AD is unclear. On the one hand it suggests that AD use may increase further. On the other hand, it may result in a situation of 'mutual deterrence'—where countries refrain from launching actions for fear of being confronted with 'retaliatory' AD actions. The larger trading countries have implemented AD mechanisms in part so as to be able to respond to AD threats.

The Uruguay Round Agreement

The WTO Antidumping Agreement made some progress in disciplining the use of AD. A sunset clause was added. Antidumping duties must be terminated within five years of imposition, unless a review determines that both dumping and injury caused by dumped imports continues to persist or that removal of the measure would be likely lead to the recurrence of dumping and injury. *De minimis* rules were agreed to. Duties may not be imposed if dumping margins are less than 2 per cent, or the level of injury is negligible, or the market share of a firm is less than 3 per cent and cumulatively less than 7 per cent for all exporters supplying less than 3 per cent. Discretion with respect to methodologies used to determine dumping and injury margins was reduced. In effect, practices such as the biased averaging methodologies described earlier were authorized, but subjected to certain constraints. The agreement also imposed disciplines on the use of 'best information available' procedures to determine dumping margins—under which investigating authorities use data supplied by the petitioning industry rather than the firms alleged to be dumping if these did not (fully) respond to questionnaires.

Although these changes made AD somewhat less protectionist, many of the practices that were identified in the 1980s as leading to significant protectionist biases remained untouched. For example, Moore (2006*a*) concludes that although US authorities lived up to the letter of the agreement's rules on the use of 'best information' or 'facts available' in practice not much changed: average dumping margins in cases where data from questionnaires were deemed to be inadequate actually increased relative to the pre-Uruguay Round period, as did the percentage of cases in which this technique was used. The use of the approach extends to industrialized countries such as Japan—where firms confronted an average 87 per cent AD duty when 'facts available' were used by the US Department of Commerce.

Similarly, despite calls for an 'average-to-average' comparison of home and export prices in the determination of dumping, authorities may compare a normal value that has been calculated on a weighted average basis with the prices of individual transactions (that is, not take into consideration export sales above normal value), if they 'find a pattern of export prices which differ substantially among different purchasers, regions, or time periods and if an explanation is provided why such differences cannot be taken into account appropriately by the use of a weighted average to weighted average or transaction-to-transaction comparison' (Article 2.4.2). The first condition will usually be met, so much depends on the extent to which explanations are demanded. As no objective criteria were established—only an explanation is required—this does not appear to be much of a constraint. However, given that before the Uruguay Round, US investigating authorities consistently refused to use average-to-average comparisons, the requirement under the WTO to do so—even though subject to loopholes—was an improvement (Palmeter, 1995).

Procedural biases and methodological abuses are very difficult, if not impossible to regulate away given the definition of dumping. For example, the requirement that AD duties be terminated within five years would appear to be a major improvement from an economic welfare point of view. In practice this may not be a binding constraint, however, as it is conditional upon whether a review investigation finds that dumping and injury continues (or threatens) to persist. Another example pertains to the definition of an interested party in AD cases. This provides users and final consumers of the import a voice during the investigations, but restricts them to providing evidence that is relevant to the determination of dumping, or injury to domestic firms that compete with the imported product. The fact that a duty or undertaking may injure their proper business is not a factor that can be brought forward. The agreement also does not require any consideration of the economy-wide impact of AD duties, the state of competition in the domestic market, let alone an investigation into the market access conditions prevailing in the exporter's home market.

Although the WTO's general dispute settlement mechanism applies, Article 17.6 of the AD Agreement restricts the ability of panels to focus on the substance of a case, as they are required to accept any 'reasonable interpretation' of the facts put before an AD domestic authority. In cases where the agreement can be interpreted in more than one way, a decision by investigating AD authorities must be accepted if it is based upon one of the permissible interpretations. New information that was not available or used by investigating authorities may not be used by a panel to overturn an AD action. In many cases panels will be limited to determining whether the procedural requirements of the agreement were violated. A major goal of US user industries in the Uruguay Round was to limit the ability of GATT panels to overturn domestic AD decisions (Palmeter, 1995). The standard of review embodied in the agreement reflects the power of the industries supporting AD. This lobby was strong enough to make this specific issue a deal breaker for the US. It obtained most of what it sought.

Little was done in the Uruguay Round negotiations to discipline AD because the talks were essentially conducted between the users of AD measures on the one hand, and the countries that pursued export-oriented development strategies on the other. This meant that the negotiations differed substantially from those in the Tokyo and the Kennedy Rounds, where the negotiating process mainly involved user countries. The user–exporter dichotomy made it difficult to come up with a balanced package deal in the Uruguay Round. Exporting country governments had little to offer in the negotiations. As dumping is a private practice, governments cannot and should not prohibit it. Countries such as Japan, Hong Kong, Korea and Singapore considered that their export trade was detrimentally affected by AD measures, and made many proposals to discipline the use of methodologies that were biased toward finding high dumping and injury margins. In this they had some success, in that practices that were tolerated but not explicitly subject to GATT disciplines became subject to multilateral rules specifying the conditions under which they could be used.

A number of contentious practices could not be resolved in this manner. A good example pertains to so-called anticircumvention measures, which Japan and Korea sought to subject to multilateral rules. Exporting firms may try to circumvent AD actions by establishing assembly plants either in the importing country (where the final product has become subject to AD duties) or in third countries. Anticircumvention became an important issue in AD enforcement as of the late 1980s. In June 1987, the EU adopted legislation allowing measures to be imposed to prevent circumvention of antidumping measures on finished products. Such measures could be applied to products assembled or produced in the EU, using imported materials or parts. In the year following adoption of this regulation, the EU initiated investigations on electronic typewriters, electronic scales, excavators and photocopiers. All of these products were assembled or produced by Japanese-related companies in the EU.

Japan challenged the anticircumvention measures before the GATT, arguing that the existence of dumping and injury related to imports of components was not investigated. It also held that the provision contained GATT-inconsistent local content requirements as it stipulated that duties could be imposed if the value of components originating in the country subject to the initial AD duty exceeded the value of all other parts by a specified margin. Finally, Japan noted that the duties were imposed only on manufacturers associated with foreign companies that were already subject to AD duties. Domestic producers were not affected even if they used the same imported components (discrimination). Australia, Hong Kong and Singapore made detailed submissions critical of the EU circumvention regulation. The EU argued that the anticircumvention provision was adopted after experience had shown that the initiation of AD action was frequently followed by the estab-lishment of assembly operations in the EU motivated by a desire to circumvent AD duties. The US supported the EU's objective of combating circumvention of AD duties, it having similar concerns.

The GATT panel that considered the case concluded that the anticircumvention duties on the finished products, being levied on products manufactured within the EU, were not customs duties but internal taxes. Because these were levied on a discriminatory basis, they were inconsistent with national treatment. The EU was requested to bring the application of its anticircumvention mechanism into con-formity with GATT obligations. Although Japan won this battle, as adopted panel reports become part of the GATT case law, it did not win the war. No agreement emerged on anticircumvention in the Uruguay Round, as negotiators could not agree on a specific text. The matter was referred back to the Committee on Antidumping Practices.

The use of AD to arrive at VER-type undertakings is particularly troublesome. Threat effects can also arise under Article XIX-type safeguard protection, but these will generally be less distorting. Safeguards are more transparent, nondiscrimina-tory, less arbitrary and less prone to capture. Antidumping mechanisms are an option allowed under the WTO; they are not required. The best option for governments concerned with equity and efficiency is not to pass AD legislation, and to abolish it if it exists. Safeguards are a much better and more honest instrument to address the problem AD is used for, providing import-competing industries with time to adjust to increased foreign competition.

Given that current AD procedures make no attempt to determine whether markets are uncontestable, one way to reduce the protectionist bias that is inherent in the status quo is for governments to put greater effort into determining whether the conditions alleged to give rise to 'unfair trade' actually exist. Suggestions that have been made in this regard include making antidumping conditional on a determination that the exporters home market is not contestable, and shifting away from an 'injury to competitors' standard towards an 'injury to competition standard' (Hoekman and Mavroidis, 1996; Messerlin, 2000). Greater efforts should also be made to consider the economy-wide effects of taking action by giving users the legal standing to defend their interests. The basic problem is a political economy one: there are powerful vested interests that are in favour of AD. This suggests that a necessary condition for AD reform is greater mobilization of countervailing forces in the domestic political arena. In addition to users, one group that may see its incentives to push for AD reforms increase is the exporter community. The more that developing countries start to use AD against high-income country exporters, the less inclined such firms may be to accept the ongoing geographic spread of this instrument.

AD disputes

Numerous disputes have been brought to the WTO regarding the imposition of AD measures. Recent cases have included *US—zeroing* (a complaint by Japan in 2007); *Mexico—Steel Pipes and Tubes* (a complaint by Guatemala in 2007); *Korea—Certain paper* (a complaint by Indonesia in 2005 and 2007); *EU—Tube or Pipe Fittings* (a complaint by Brazil in 2003); *EU—Bed Linen* (a complaint by India in 2003); and *Argentina—Poultry Antidumping Duties* (a complaint by Brazil in 2003). As the agreement's procedural rules are complex, investigating authorities, especially those in developing countries, may find it difficult to jump through all the hoops that are established by the WTO. One can speculate that to some extent the strategy that was pursued in the Uruguay Round was to make it more costly for industry and government agencies to undertake AD actions. Such costs impact disproportionately on developing countries, both as respondents and as users of AD.

Space constraints prohibit a detailed discussion of the numerous AD disputes. Interested readers are referred to the homepage of the WTO and the sources mentioned in Section 9.10 below. Most disputes have revolved around allegations that specific provisions of the AD Agreement were violated. A number of the cases were discussed above and others are mentioned below. There have been two disputes that address AD legislation as opposed to specific cases of implementation of national laws and regulations. Both cases concerned the US. The first pertained to a 1916 vintage AD law and has already been discussed. The second dealt with the Continued Dumping and Subsidy Offset Act of 2000—commonly referred to as the Byrd Amendment, after the Senator who introduced the provision as an amendment to an agricultural funding bill.

The Byrd Amendment provided that if AD duties (or CVDs) were imposed by the US government, the collected revenues were to be distributed to the firms that had supported bringing the case. Between 2001, when the amendment went into effect and October 2007, when the US Treasury ceased to disburse duties, over $1.5 billion was transferred to US enterprises. Sectors that received the most included steel producers, candle and pasta makers. Clearly, the amendment increased the incentives for industries to file cases as it substantially increased the 'return' on investing in a case. It also increased incentives for firms that might not have supported an AD action to join a case, as only those that did so could claim a share of the collected revenues. From an economic perspective the main effect of the provision was to increase the rents associated with AD for import-competing firms. In an empirical assessment of the effects of the amendment, Olson (2004) finds that it resulted in more AD petitions. However, she does not find that it led to more firms petitioning. Thus, it does not appear to have played the role that some observers argued it had: helping firms in an industry satisfy the requirement that a majority of firms (measured by size) must support bringing a case. Olson and Liebman (2005) provide evidence that potential beneficiaries of the amendment made larger political campaign contributions to lawmakers that might sponsor it. This was a classic example of 'protection for sale'—although the financial transfers made by the firms to lawmakers' campaigns were swamped by the actual AD revenues that were collected and disbursed to the industries concerned. The lobbying had a very high rate of return.

Not surprisingly, the Byrd Amendment was not to the liking of other WTO members, ten of which joined together in contesting it. The WTO question was whether the transfer of tariff revenues violated the AD Agreement. The panel and AB ruled that the transfer of revenues constituted a type of action against AD that was not allowed under the AD Agreement—which speaks only of AD duties, provisional measures or price undertakings. Article 18.1 AD states that no specific actions against AD may be taken other than those conforming to GATT 1994. The Byrd revenue transfers were deemed specific actions, and therefore in violation of the Agreement. The US did not revise its legislation within the reasonable period of time, with the result that in 2005 the EU, Canada and Mexico retaliated. Canada targeted US live swine, cigarettes, oysters and certain specialty fish; whereas the EU imposed what it termed 'smart sanctions': a set of tariffs that generated the same amount of revenue as the US collected on EU exports that were subjected to AD duties. These retaliatory tariffs would continue to be levied until such time as the US stopped disbursing revenues.[11]

Horn and Mavroidis (2005) analyse the AB report on this case and argue that it is a prime example of incoherence and inconsistency, as well as being economically wrong in major respects. An important part of the reasoning of the panel and the AB was that the transfer of revenues would increase competitive pressure on exporters in the US market. However, there is no presumption that the firms would invest their windfalls into enhanced productivity—economic theory suggests that if additional investments were expected to be profitable, then firms would undertake them without needing a subsidy. What the impacts of the subsidies would be on competition is contingent of what is done with the revenues. Horn and Mavroidis note that the rents might facilitate exit of firms. If so, it might just as well result in less competition (and have the effect of encouraging rather than discouraging dumping). They also point out that an alternative line of argument against disbursements of duties would have been to claim that this constituted an illegal subsidy insofar as it did more than offset the injurious effect of dumped imports.

---

[11] See http://ec.europa.eu/trade/issues/respectrules/dispute/pr170407_en.htm

The Doha Round negotiations

In the Doha Round AD figured prominently in the Negotiating Group on WTO Rules. The US, with powerful lobbies that sought to retain the status quo, initially resisted efforts to launch negotiations on AD. Washington relented, however, when it became evident that a new round could not succeed without some concessions on antidumping. The compromise that emerged was that the Doha Development Agenda should aim at 'clarifying and improving disciplines'. The gap between the US and other countries seeking to impose stronger disciplines was wide.

Prior to the Doha ministerial conference, a coalition of developed and developing WTO countries called the 'Friends of Antidumping' (the EU, Brazil, China, India, Japan, Korea and ten other members) pushed for new trade remedy rules. The EU, having become a leading target of AD measures, was concerned by the significant differences in national trade remedy procedures and the diverse interpretation and application of the WTO rules across countries. Developing members of the group felt that they were disproportionately affected by AD actions and sought some form of 'special and differential treatment' under the AD agreement. In response, the US decided to push an 'offensive agenda' to address the increasing 'misuse' of trade remedies. Given the frequency with which WTO dispute panels ruled against the US in trade remedy cases, Washington was particularly keen to tighten the 'standard of review' provisions to preclude that panels or decisions by the AB could change the balance of AD-related rights and obligations.

The negotiations occurred in three overlapping phases. First, members presented over 140 papers specifying the general areas in which they desired new AD rules. Second, (following the Cancun ministerial), positions were considered in more detail, often involving legal drafting, to get a clearer idea of the various proposals and a 'realistic' view of what might attract broader support. Finally, the last phase focused on drafting a standardized questionnaire to be used in AD investigations to reduce costs and increase transparency (WTO, 2005). Thus, negotiations dealt with a very large number of highly specific issues rather than with the 'big picture'. Several discussion threads that emerged during 2002–8 are briefly considered in what follows.

Dumping margins. Numerous WTO members considered that the methodology used by some countries to calculate dumping margins led to highly inflated duties that were disproportionate to the amount needed to mitigate the injury to the domestic industry or the level of dumping. Particularly criticized was the US methodology, which typically resulted in average margins between 60 and 70 per cent. Proposals that drew broad support included a ban on 'zeroing', a mandatory 'lesser duty' rule, and increased use of price undertakings.

Zeroing. In the US, AD orders imposed on imported products must be equal to the dumping margin or 'the amount by which the normal value exceeds the export price or constructed export price of the subject merchandise (19 USlC. 1677(35)(A)).

The margin is usually computed by first identifying, to the extent possible, all US transactions, sale prices and levels of trade for each model or type of product concerned sold by each company in the exporting country. These model types are then aggregated into subcategories, known as 'averaging groups', which are used to calculate the 'weighted average export price'. The export prices for each subgroup are then compared to the corresponding agency-calculated 'weighted average normal value' (Jones, 2006). Finally, the results of these comparisons are summed up to determine the overall dumping margin of the imported product concerned.

When the US Department of Commerce adds up the dumping margins of each of the subgroups to determine an overall margin it sometimes encounters negative margins in a subgroup, an indicator that the items in that category are not being dumped. However, rather than including the negative margins in their calculations (which might result in a lesser overall margin) the Department factors in the results of that subgroup as a zero. A similar approach is used when re-calculating dumping margins in administrative reviews of AD orders or suspension agreements. One justification for the zeroing practice is that the dumping margin could be skewed if, when determining the weighted average dumping margin, the subgroup that has the negative dumping margin represents a substantial percentage of export sales.

The US 'zeroing' practice has been challenged repeatedly. In February 2004, the EU requested the establishment of a dispute settlement panel on zeroing, citing 31 US AD cases targeting European products. The EU considered that in these cases the dumping margin would have been minimal, or even negative, in the absence of zeroing. The October 2004 panel report ruled against zeroing in *de novo* AD investigations but concluded that the US might use zeroing in administrative reviews of existing AD orders (WTO, 2005). In part, the panel concluded that the denial of offsets when calculating the weighted average dumping margin using the 'average-to-average' comparison method when conducting the original investigation violated provisions of Article 2.4.2 of the Antidumping Agreement—an aspect of the ruling that Washington did not appeal. In April 2006, the AB overturned the panel's conclusion that 'zeroing' was permissible in administrative reviews (WT/DS294/AB/R). In a subsequent case brought by Mexico, the AB reversed the panel's finding that simple zeroing in periodic reviews is not, as such, inconsistent with WTO rules (WT/DS344/AB/R).

Lesser Duty Rule. Article 9.1 of the Antidumping Agreement encourages the imposition of an AD duty that is lower than the full dumping margin if investigating authorities determine that the lesser amount is sufficient to offset the injury suffered or threatened to the domestic industry. Numerous WTO countries favour amending the Antidumping Agreement to require a mandatory, rather than discretionary, 'lesser duty rule'. Developing countries were particularly interested in ensuring that a mandatory rule applied to their exports, and have proposed this measure as part of a 'special and differential treatment' provisions that would apply to developed nations.

Injury determinations. A number of WTO members argued that the guidelines and definitions to assess injury in the agreement were too subjective and that national procedures often lacked transparency. Several proposals involved more specificity on the criteria for making injury determinations and a more precise definition for the terms such as 'material injury', 'material retardation', or 'threat of material injury'. In particular it was stressed that in many circumstances factors other than dumping were to blame for industry declines and consequently it was preferable to introduce more objective criteria for establishing the existence of a clear and substantial link to dumping before determining injury.

Price undertakings. Article 8 of the AD Agreement permits the use of 'voluntary undertakings from any exporter to revise its prices or to cease exports to the area in question at dumped prices' provided that investigating authorities are satisfied that the injurious effect of the dumping is eliminated. Several members favoured increased use of 'price undertakings,' because they believed that the practice was less damaging to exporters while still mitigating the injury to domestic producers. Some developing countries favoured mandatory use of price undertakings in AD actions taken by developed countries. This was ironic in that these measures are essentially equivalent to VERs—which explicitly were outlawed in the Uruguay Round. US antidumping law allows for these types of alternative arrangements, known in US law as 'suspension agreements', but in practice the Department of Commerce used this option infrequently. As of 2007 there were only six US suspension agreements in place, in comparison to more than 260 active AD orders.

Mandatory Sunset of AD Orders. Article 11 of the AD Agreement requires that each AD order be terminated after five years unless authorities determine in a review that it would be likely to lead to a recurrence of dumping and subsequent injury. In practice this turned out to have little effect in markets such as the US, as reviews generally resulted in extension of the measures (Moore, 2006*b*; Cadot, De Melo and Tumurchudur, 2007). In practice US AD orders were likely to remain in place as long as the domestic industry opposed their removal. There was little that could be done in this area without stronger explicit rules, as the AD Agreement only has very cursory language on how reviews should be done. Four disputes on this specific issue went through the WTO process between 1995 and 2005, none of which did much for the complainants.

The basic problem was that Article 11.3 AD Agreement only lays out two principles: AD should be terminated after five years; but may be extended if a review determines that removal of the AD duty would be likely to lead to continuation or recurrence of injurious dumping. Whether and how this should be determined is left for the country taking action to determine. The AB has taken a strictly 'textual' approach here, as in other areas of WTO law: as there is no specific discipline in Article 11.3, there is nothing to rule on and thus members are free to pretty much do as they please. This can lead to situations where AD duties are extended even if there are no imports, as was the case in the 2005 dispute *US—AD*

Measures on Oil Country Tubular Goods (WT/DS282). This affected Mexican steel exports. After being hit by AD duties the Mexican firms stopped exporting altogether. Nonetheless, after five years the duties were extended, which led to the dispute being brought.

There was strong support for a mandatory termination of AD orders within five years—among such major traders as China, Japan or Brazil. Another group of countries favoured a more moderate approach that would list specific circumstances or definitive factors that authorities must consider before extending AD orders. Finally, still others criticized the length of time that sunset review procedures take to complete and favoured a mandatory 12-month time limit. The basic issue was largely ignored: that what is required is a specific mechanism which recognizes that in reviews the issue is to determine whether injurious dumping may emerge. That is, the focus of reviews must be prospective, not retrospective. All the rules of the AD Agreement are retrospective: did dumping actually occur and did it cause material injury?

Special and differential treatment. Many developing countries complained that AD actions affected them disproportionately. The Antidumping Agreement (Article 15) recommends that developed countries show 'special regard' for the economic situation of least developed and developing nations, and suggests that 'constructive remedies' be used instead of assessing AD duties. However, the agreement does not require or specify a particular course of action in AD proceedings. The 'Friends of Antidumping' and others suggested that specific provisions were needed to offer to developing countries 'meaningful special and differential treatment' when facing AD action in developed countries. It was suggested that 'special regard' should mean requiring developed countries to negotiate/accept mandatory price undertakings (suspension agreements) when investigating products of developing countries, and raising the *de minimis* threshold.

Conclusion

To recap, dumping is rarely an anticompetitive practice. Predatory pricing is possible, but will not be profitable as long as governments ensure that markets remain contestable. At the same time, AD creates a large number of distortions. The existence of AD induces rent-seeking behaviour on the part of import-competing firms, and leads exporting firms to alter production, allocation, and production-location decisions in ways that can easily reduce welfare at home and abroad. The threat effects of AD are important and insufficiently recognized. Antidumping can imply substantial uncertainty regarding the conditions of market access facing exporters and increase the costs of goods for importers. The chilling effect on imports of AD threats can be great. The start of an investigation is a signal to importers to diversify away from targeted suppliers. This signal is strengthened once provisional findings have been issued. These create incentives for the conclusion of agreements with affected exporters.

The experience with both the use of—and expansion in the number of—AD actions, and the lack of success in legislating stronger disciplines that are effective in controlling the use of AD, is rather disheartening to those, like us, who are concerned about the discriminatory and trade distorting effects this instrument has. Seeking to control the use of AD through the WTO is not likely to be very productive. The EU experience illustrates that what matters in ensuring a greater recognition of the costs of AD in the decision-making process is to give those who benefit from 'dumped' imports a voice. In the EU this voice can be—and is—expressed by the member states that do not have significant production capacity and are basically importers. More generally, as firms engage in ever greater specialization and slicing up of the value chain the costs of AD for one part of that chain become more transparent and more likely to give rise to opposition by firms that specialize in other parts of the chain—and find themselves confronted with higher costs. The solution therefore is greater voice: political mobilization by users of imports to defend their interests.

9.5. MEASURES TO COUNTERVAIL SUBSIDIZED IMPORTS

Countervailing duty or antisubsidy procedures, similar to AD, are allowed under Article VI of the GATT. The objective is again to ensure 'fair competition'. In contrast to AD, the language in this case makes more sense as firms cannot compete against state treasuries. An implication is that CVDs have a stronger economic rationale than AD, insofar as subsidies distort competition, a measure to countervail them—if effective in restraining the use of subsidies—may make sense. However, as discussed below, this will not always be the case.

As noted in Chapter 5, although the GATT prohibits export subsidies on manufactures, and agreement in principle was reached at the 2005 ministerial in Hong Kong to ban the use of agricultural export subsidies by 2013, the WTO permits other types of subsidies. However, unless a subsidy is in the 'green box' (the set of permitted and nonactionable measures), governments which consider that their industries are adversely affected by subsidized imports may impose CVDs. A necessary condition is that an investigation determines that imports have been subsidized and have caused material injury to domestic industry.

The procedures to be followed in subsidy and injury investigations are described in detail in the Agreement on Subsidies and Countervailing Measures (SCM), which in turn build on the Tokyo Round Subsidies Code. As in the case of AD disciplines, the injury test is the key element underlying the agreement's implicit objective of reconciling legitimate national government subsidy policies with the interests of nations affected by those policies. That is, the focus is on dealing with the externality created by foreign government policies.

The US has been the largest user of CVDs, initiating over 100 investigations between 1985 and 2008. A substantial number of these CVD cases were not brought to a conclusion, reflecting the introduction of trade-restricting bilateral agreements for steel products in the 1980s. Other major players such as the EU and Japan have made relatively little use of CVDs. In part this is because other policies for safeguarding producers' interests are available and easier to implement (AD), and in part because many countries fear that initiation of CVD investigations could lead to retaliatory investigations. As the US does not devote many resources to explicit subsidization of manufacturing, its government has never felt constrained in using CVDs. The use of CVDs has been on a declining trend (Table 9.5). (It should be noted that the data are incomplete due to significant numbers of missing notifications—see WTO, 2004.)

One reason for the increase in CVDs in the early 2000s was a more active stance on the part of the EU and Canada. Asian exporters such as India, Korea and Taiwan were among the main targets of CVDs. One could observe a decline in the incidence of CVDs during the first five years following the Uruguay Round due to the six-year peace clause contained in the Agriculture Agreement and the greater clarity provided by the SCM Agreement regarding what types of subsidies are countervailable.

Political economy of countervailing duties

There are two possible rationales for responding to foreign subsidy policies via import restrictions. The first is to offset the injurious effect of such policies on domestic industries. The second is to induce the foreign government to change its policy. The first rationale has little economic merit, as the imposition of import

Table 9.5. Countervailing duties (1995–2007)

	1995–9	2000–3	2004–7
Investigations launched	99	69	34
Total measures in force	47	53	19
Of which: OECD nations	30	45	15
Developing countries	17	8	4

Source: WTO, Committee Annual Reports; and WTO Annual Reports.

barriers (CVDs) distorts the decisions of consumers, and will generally reduce the welfare of the country taking action. A subsidy granted to a foreign firm will generally only be one aspect of the industrial policy that is applied by a foreign government. Such governments may also pursue direct and indirect tax policies, engage in investments in infrastructure, and so forth. Given the difficulty of determining the real (general equilibrium) effect of any kind of foreign industrial policy, it will always be very difficult, if not impossible, to determine the appropriate counteraction.

The argument that restricting imports of products which have benefitted from unfair government assistance can be justified as a means of inhibiting the use of such measures has greater economic merit (Deardorff and Stern, 1987). It may be the case that even though a CVD is welfare-reducing in the short run, the threat of CVDs induces foreign governments to refrain from subsidizing. The relevance of this argument depends on whether the cost to the foreign country of a CVD is greater than the benefit it realizes from the subsidy policy. This may not be the case, especially if the policy aims to offset a market failure or is driven by noneconomic considerations. As important, even if the subsidy cannot be justified by market failure or public good considerations, the effectiveness of CVDs depend on the ability of the country imposing them to affect the terms of trade of the country granting the subsidy. Small countries are unlikely to be able to have an impact on the subsidizer's exporters that are large enough to induce them to pressure their governments not to impose the subsidy. A better option is to engage in discussions with the subsidizing country and seek compensation. This is an option that in principle is available under the WTO (see below).

Countervailing duties are superior to AD in that the instrument is better targeted at the source of the perceived externality: foreign government intervention. In contrast to the case of dumping by firms, in the subsidy context it is possible to build a case for 'unfair competition'. However, for most countries countervailing subsidies will rarely make economic sense, unless the subsidy is expected to be temporary. In the case of agricultural subsidization by OECD countries, for example, the policy could be regarded as structural, so that affected producers are well advised to adjust to the situation. Governments can provide their producers with income support if they desire, but imposition of CVDs is equivalent to throwing good money after bad. After all, the subsidy is equivalent to a transfer from a foreign government to the consumers of the importing country. If a tariff is imposed on these imports, the economy will be worse off than if nothing is done. Imposition of a CVD may benefit the domestic industry, but is equivalent to a tax on the rest of the economy. Consumers lose the benefit of the foreign subsidy as prices are forced up, and at best the country ends up with an additional deadweight loss. However, this loss is smaller than is the case under a regular tariff, as there is no production distortion (see Annex 2).

WTO disciplines

The GATT history on CVDs revolves around the use made by the US of this instrument, it being the primary user. When the US acceded to GATT, it grand-fathered its existing CVD legislation. The negotiation of a Code on Subsidies and Countervailing Measures in the Tokyo Round was driven by a desire by targeted countries to see the US adopt an injury test (which was not required under its law). This attempt was somewhat successful, in that the US signed an agreement that required an injury test. However, in practice, the US made this conditional upon bilateral commitments with respect to subsidy policies. US CVD policies therefore continued to be a source of controversy.

In the Uruguay Round the issue of subsidies and CVDs was substantially clarified. The WTO makes a distinction between different types of subsidies, depending on their trade impact and their objective (see Chapter 5). Subsidies that have an economy-wide impact and are not specific (education, general infrastructure, basic R&D) or have a noneconomic rationale (regional disparities, income support) are permitted and not subject to the threat of CVDs (nonaction-able). For subsidies that are not in this 'green box' and that have adverse effects on trade, WTO members have the choice of initiating CVD investigations or invoking dispute settlement procedures. Both routes may be pursued simultaneously. How-ever, only one remedy may be applied.

As noted in Chapter 5, adverse effects include injury to a domestic industry, nullification or impairment of tariff concessions, or serious prejudice or threat thereof to the country's interests. Serious prejudice is deemed to exist if the total *ad valorem* subsidization of a product exceeds 5 per cent, subsidies cover operating losses of an industry or enterprise, or there is forgiveness of government-held debt. Serious prejudice may arise if the subsidy displaces imports of like products on either the subsidizing or third country markets. If actionable subsidies have an adverse effect on a WTO member, it may ask for consultations with the country maintaining the subsidy program. If consultations fail to settle matter within 60 days, the WTO's dispute settlement provisions may be invoked. If a panel deems adverse effects to exist, the subsidy programme must be revoked, or the affected country otherwise compensated. If the panel's recommendations are not imple-mented within six months, the affected country can retaliate by withdrawing equivalent concessions.

Necessary conditions for imposition of CVDs include demonstration of the existence of a subsidy, a finding that a domestic industry producing similar (like) products is materially injured, and establishment of a causal link between the subsidization and injury. Injury requires that the volume of subsidized imports has increased, that this has had an impact on price levels or is reflected in price undercutting of domestic firms and that this in turn has had a detrimental effect on the domestic industry. At least 25 per cent of the firms in the domestic industry must support the launching of a CVD investigation. Recall that the export subsidy dispute between Brazil and Canada revealed that in the case of an illegal (prohibited) subsidy these rules do not apply. Canada was authorized to retaliate (countervail) up to the amount of the subsidy (as determined by the arbitrators), independently of the injury suffered by the Canadian industry (see Chapter 5). Interpreted in dispute settlement (the *Brazil—Aircraft* case), the rules on export subsidies in the SCM Agreement appeared to limit the capacity of developing countries to ensure trade financing for exports, based on market benchmarks devised for and by developed nations in the OECD Arrangement. Consideration should be given to an alternative method, which would take into account, the structural differences of financial markets in developing countries as well as the challenges of nations that have been confronted by financial crises in depending on private capital markets for the financing of export trade (Howse, 2008).

Detailed requirements and deadlines are established regarding the different phases of investigations, including the collection of evidence, the rights of interested parties, the calculation of the extent to which a subsidy benefits the recipient, the determination of injury, possible remedies, and access to judicial review of the CVD decision. As is true for AD, a sunset provision of five years applies, unless a review determines that the abolition of protection would likely lead to the continuation or recurrence of injury. When confronted with CVD investigations, developing countries benefit from *de minimis* thresholds. If the subsidy is less than 2 per cent of the per unit value of products exported, developing countries are exempt from countervail (for LDCs the threshold is 3 per cent). An exemption also applies if the import market share of a developing country is below 4 per cent, and the aggregate share of all such countries is below 9 per cent of total imports. In the Doha Round, a number of countries suggested a mandatory 'lesser duty rule', which would prevent authorities in importing countries from offsetting the full calculated amount of subsidies.

As noted previously, CVDs are used substantially less frequently than AD, and average tariffs imposed are relatively low. Disputes have arisen on the use of subsidies, some of them very high-profile cases (see Chapter 3) but these have not extended to the use of CVDs. This may change in the future. The US Commerce Department broke new ground in 2007 by launching a CVD case against China—a country it does not deem to be a 'market economy'—claiming that exports of glossy paper used in packaging had benefitted from production subsidies. The International Trade Commission (ITC) found that US industry was not materially injured by the imports, and the temporary CVDs were lifted. Now that the US has started to use CVDs, pressures may rise to invoke the provisions of the SCM Agreement against China. In 2007 the US launched 14 CVD investigations against Chinese exports of steel products, chemicals, paper, tyres and magnets.[12]

[12] http://www.usitc.gov/trade_remedy/731_ad_701_cvd/investigations/active/index.htm

9.6. TRADE RESTRICTIONS FOR BALANCE-OF-PAYMENTS PURPOSES

The GATT permits the imposition of trade restrictions to safeguard a country's external financial position (Articles XII and XVIII:*b*). The inclusion of such provisions reflects the fact that when the GATT was created, a system of fixed exchange rates prevailed (the so-called Bretton Woods system). Fixed exchange rates remove an instrument through which governments can seek to address balance-of-payments (BOP) disequilibria. If a country with a deficit cannot devalue and if wages are relatively inflexible as well, there is a case for imposing temporary import restrictions. An across-the-board tariff in conjunction with a subsidy to exports is under certain conditions exactly equivalent to a nominal devaluation of the currency.

The BOP provisions of the GATT were widely used by both industrialized and developing countries. The former used Article XII as cover, the latter Article XVIII:*b*. Use of QRs for BOP purposes by developed, mostly European, countries occurred mostly in the 1950s when many currencies were not convertible. In contrast, developing country use of Article XVIII:*b* was fairly constant until the 1990s (Table 9.1). Most developing countries had no need to use Article XIX safeguard actions to protect their industries if needed, as their tariffs were generally not bound or bound at high levels. They did need GATT cover to use QRs, however, and this was the role of Article XVIII—it permits, indeed encourages, the use of QRs for BOP purposes. This was an idiosyncrasy of the GATT 1947, and contradicted the general preference for price-based instruments such as tariffs. In general, an import surcharge would be less distortionary than QRs (see Annex 2).

The challenge to OECD negotiators in the Uruguay Round was to close the BOP loophole, which in practice was simply an avenue to legally impose QRs, albeit subject to GATT surveillance. Closing the loophole should have been facilitated by the move away from the fixed exchange rate system that had occurred in the 1970s. The move towards flexible (more easily adjustable) exchange rates reduces the rationale for resorting to trade restrictions to safeguard a country's external financial position. Exchange rate adjustment provides an automatic and effective mechanism for adjustment of current account imbalances if complemented by supporting measures (fiscal and monetary discipline). Experience clearly demonstrates that QRs are not the right instrument to deal with BOP problems. The IMF and World Bank routinely obtained agreements with borrowing governments not to introduce import restrictions for BOP purposes in their adjustment lending to developing countries (Finch and Michalopoulos, 1988).

Most developing countries responded to this line of argument by emphasizing that their foreign exchange shortages did not stem so much from their own policies as from protectionist policies of their trading partners. Although this was a disingenuous argument at best, given that overvalued exchange rates were usually a major cause of foreign exchange shortages and rationing, it was against this background that the issue of BOP escape clauses was considered in the Tokyo Round. A 1979 Declaration on Trade Measures Taken for Balance-of-Payments Purposes reinforced scrutiny over the trade and adjustment policies of industrial countries, but asserted that developing countries should be allowed greater latitude in safeguarding their foreign exchange reserves. During the 1980s, industrialized countries argued increasingly that the clause rendered the participation of developing countries in GATT to a large extent meaningless. This damaged both the trading system (because it undermined adherence to the principles on which the system rests) and developing countries, as the latter had no effective means within the GATT context to counter powerful protectionist interests at home. The measures imposed tended to be permanent, whereas BOP difficulties are mainly of a cyclical nature. The trade restrictions were also often imposed on selected products, rather than being applied across the board as would be necessary for BOP purposes.

WTO disciplines

In the Uruguay Round, new language on Article XVIII was agreed that reduced the scope to use QRs, and strengthened surveillance of BOP actions. The contracting parties to the GATT-1947 committed themselves to publicly announce time-schedules for the removal of restrictive import measures taken for BOP purposes. They also agreed to give preference to those measures that have the least disruptive effect on trade. Such measures include import surcharges, import deposit requirements or other equivalent trade measures with an impact on the price of imported goods. The use of new QRs for BOP purposes requires a justification why price-based measures cannot arrest the deterioration in the external accounts. Only one type of restrictive import measure may be applied on a product. The emphasis on the use of price-based measures was a significant improvement over the old GATT.

Surcharges or similar measures must be applied on an across-the-board basis. However, exemptions may be made for certain essential products, necessary to meet basic consumption needs or which help improve the BOP situation, such as capital goods or inputs needed for production. A WTO member applying new restrictions or raising the general level of its existing restrictions must consult with the BOP Committee within four months of the adoption of such measures. Each year a member taking BOP actions must provide the WTO Secretariat with a consolidated notification providing information at the tariff line level on the type of measures applied, the criteria used for their administration, product coverage and trade flows affected. Countries applying BOP measures must engage in periodic consultations with the BOP Committee. The report prepared for such meetings must include an overview of the BOP situation and the policy measures that have been taken to restore equilibrium, a description of the restrictions that are applied, progress towards removing the restrictions, and a plan for the elimination and progressive relaxation of remaining barriers. The WTO Secretariat also prepares a report, using data obtained from the IMF, regarding the macroeconomic situation in the country concerned. The IMF is represented at all BOP committee meetings.

There is therefore in principle rather close surveillance of BOP actions. Very much depends, however, on the willingness of the BOP Committee to insist that measures are no longer or not justified. Under the GATT 1947 not much could be expected from this committee (Eglin, 1987). In practice the main source of discipline came from the international capital markets, from international financial institutions and from bilateral pressure by WTO members to stop invoking Article XVIII as cover for trade restrictions. A total of ten developing countries revoked Article XVIII during the 1980s and early 1990s, largely following the adoption of more appropriate macroeconomic policies and unilateral liberalization efforts. Multilateral surveillance exercised by the BOP Committee played only a minimal role in this. The GATT dispute settlement system had more teeth. For example, Korea's use of Article XVIII:b was challenged in the 1980s by beef exporters, who alleged that Korea no longer had a BOP problem and that restrictions on beef could therefore not be justified by this Article, as claimed by Korea. The panel that dealt with this case found in favour of the petitioners and recommended that Korea be required to eliminate its import restrictions on beef.

Disciplines under the WTO are more binding. The difference between GATT and the WTO was illustrated by a case brought against India in 1997 by the United States. The US claimed that QRs maintained by India—a long standing user of Article XVIII:b—on importation of a large number of products, covering more than 2,700 agricultural and industrial product tariff lines, were inconsistent with GATT Articles XI:1 and XVIII:11 as well as other provisions of the WTO. The panel that considered the allegations found that the measures violated India's WTO obligations and nullified or impaired benefits accruing to the US under the Agreement on Agriculture. The AB upheld the report, and the panel and AB reports were adopted in September 1999. Noteworthy is that the AB rejected India's argument that the panel had no jurisdiction given that the BOP Committee had not pronounced on the matter.

India stated its intention to comply with the recommendations and rulings of the DSB, and drew attention to the panel's suggestion that the reasonable period of time for implementation in this case could exceed 15 months in view of India's status as a developing country. After consultations, the US and India agreed most changes would be made by April 2000, with the remainder to be implemented by

April 2001. This case would not have been possible under GATT. It signaled the end of decades of invocation by India of Article XVIII as a cover for QRs.

The Doha Round negotiations concerning BOP measures mainly occurred in the working group on investment and in the context of discussions on special and differential treatment. Early papers submitted by Canada, Taiwan, Japan and Korea acknowledged that a possible WTO investment agreement would need to contain exceptions from disciplines when the host country faces a BOP problem. The US argued that the right of free transfer of capital was crucial and that BOP restrictions were a 'self-defeating strategy' in the long term (*Bridges*, 31 September 2002). Developing countries stressed that they needed 'safety valves' during financial crises, and suggested addressing this matter in the new WTO Working Group on Trade and Finance. They also argued that Article XVIII:B was not serving the objective of economic development (see Chapter 12 and the next section).

A related debate concerned the role of the IMF in the WTO Committee on Balance-of-Payments Restrictions—with developing countries expressing concern that the IMF was encroaching on the Committee's work by offering increasingly prescriptive rather than analytical views. The IMF has a formal role and input into deliberations on BOP matters—as was illustrated in the discussion of *Dominican Republic—Cigarettes* dispute discussed in Chapter 5.

9.7. INFANT INDUSTRY PROTECTION

Article XVIII:*a* GATT allows for the removal of tariff concessions if necessary to establish an industry in a developing country. It does not differ much in substance from Article XXVIII (re-negotiation of tariffs), as compensation negotiations must be initiated. Article XVIII:*c* permits the use of QRs or other nontariff measures by developing countries for infant industry purposes. This provision requires the approval of WTO members, and compensation may also be requested. At the end of the Tokyo Round, the GATT infant industry exception was widened considerably to allow for measures intended to develop, modify or extend production structures more generally, in accordance with a country's economic development priorities. These exceptions have rarely been invoked as a cover for the use of import quotas, probably due to the fact that the BOP loophole embodied in Article XVIII:*b* was preferred. In comparison to the latter, surveillance and approval procedures under the infant industry provisions are more strict, and the possibility of retaliation more likely.

In most circumstances the economic rationale for invocation of Article XVIII:*c* is weak, as a QR in itself will do very little to stimulate the establishment of a competitive industry (this question is discussed at greater length in Chapter 12). Any justification for a government to help in the establishment of an industry must be based on market failure. Even if it is assumed that a government can correctly identify the market failure, a QR will never be an appropriate instrument to offset the source of the distortion. Usually a subsidy of some type will be a less inefficient instrument to promote the establishment of an industry. From an economic viewpoint, the drafters of the GATT were therefore justified in placing relatively stringent conditions on the use of infant industry protection. But, as has been the case with other GATT disciplines as well, the result of this was to induce a shift towards invoking substitute GATT cover: the BOP route and TRIMs (see Chapter 5). Given that a number of countries have used TRIMs for industrial development purposes, as the TRIMs Agreement becomes a binding constraint on developing countries, an increase in the invocation of Article XVIII may occur for infant industry purposes. However, enough scope exists to intervene in ways that make more economic sense, through use of subsidies, public investment and the use of safeguard protection if deemed necessary.

In the Doha Round negotiations many developing countries argued that the various provisions of Article XVIII were not serving their original objective. In support, they noted the rare usage of certain sections of the Article, especially Section C, and outlined (or re-outlined in India's case, see WT/GC/W/363) the need to make the Article more 'user-friendly'. In that regard, the WTO Secretariat circulated two papers on the usage of XVIII:*c* (WT/ COMTD/W/39 & 39/Add.1). The main objectives of developing countries in the Doha Round was to gain additional flexibility in using Articles XVIII:*a* and XVIII:*c* to raise tariffs or impose quotas to protect infant industries. However, there was no agreement on whether the Article could or should be modified. Those opposing revision of existing disciplines noted that infant industry protection had a poor record of encouraging the growth of competitive sectors and initiating broader industrial development. On the contrary it often created vested interests that aimed at prolonging protection, imposing costs on the domestic economy. Moreover, infant industry safeguards put the government in the position of 'picking winners', requiring that government administration be prepared to follow a clear timetable for reduction of infant industry protection and to allow business firms that cannot become viable within that time period to fail.

For infant industry protection to work, a strong framework of accountable, stable, and sufficiently autonomous institutions is required, a particular challenge for many of the countries pushing for more flexibility under Article XVIII:*c*. There is a large literature on the rationale for active industrial policy, much of which is surveyed in Pack and Saggi (2005). Given the complexity and uncertainty associated with picking sectors (or firms) or managing a process of 'self-discovery' supporting firms to identify their own competitive advantage (advocated by Rodrik, 2004), it seems much more efficient in the current state of intensifying world competition and the growing importance of extensive and complex supply networks to remove policies that prevent foreign firms from offering goods and services in developing countries.

This does not imply that governments should not seek to use domestic regulation and tax/subsidies to encourage local learning, protect the environment, etc. But, the case for trade policy to address market failures is particularly weak. Using trade policy to promote industrial development is an outdated and self-defeating strategy in a world of tradable services, increased FDI flows, and global production chains and trade in tasks (Hoekman, Michalopoulos and Winters, 2004).

9.8. General Exceptions

Both the GATT and the GATS contain provisions entitled 'General Exceptions' allowing members to take measures that violate a rule or discipline if necessary to achieve noneconomic objectives (GATT Article XX; GATS Article XIV). Such objectives include protection of public morals (XX:*a*), the health and safety of human, plant or animal life (XX:*b*) and to secure compliance with other GATT rules (XX:*d*). GATT Article XX also allows controls to prevent imports of goods produced with prison labour (XX:*e*), to protect cultural heritage (XX:*f*), to conserve natural exhaustible resources (as long as the same measures are applied to domestic production or consumption as well, XX:*g*), and to control exports of goods in short supply or subject to public intervention (XX:*i* and *j*).

Both GATT and GATS allow for measures to be imposed to secure compliance with laws or regulations that are not inconsistent with multilateral rules (examples mentioned include prevention of deceptive and fraudulent practices, and protection of privacy of individuals). A necessary condition for the invocation of the exception provisions of the WTO is that measures do not result in 'arbitrary or unjustifiable' discrimination between countries (i.e. MFN), and are not a disguised restriction on international trade. In addition to exceptions that focus on the attainment of noneconomic objectives, all three multilateral trade agreements have a national security exception (GATT Article XXI, GATS Article XIV *bis* and TRIPS Article 73).

The general exceptions articles are purposely worded in rather broad and vague terms. There are no compensation or approval requirements. There is also no notification requirement—it is up to affected parties to raise a measure they perceive to be discriminatory and detrimental to their interests with the member applying them. If that member defends the measure under the exceptions provisions of the WTO, the only recourse is the dispute settlement mechanism.

Article XX GATT disputes generally revolve around a two-tiered test. First, is a contested measure one that is listed in the Article's subparagraphs *a* through *j*? If so, does it satisfy the nondiscrimination requirement and constitute the least trade restrictive means to achieve the specific objective listed in the subparagraphs? This latter condition requires a panel to decide if the trade-restricting measure in question is necessary to achieve the government's purported objective. Together with nondiscrimination, this 'necessity test' is the main discipline on invocation of Article XX GATT (and Article XIV GATS). It is sometimes argued that the 'necessity test' involves a balancing test: are the benefits of a trade-restricting measure in achieving a goal greater than the costs in terms of lower trade? This is not the case. Although the AB has discussed such an approach it has not applied it—limiting itself instead to a determination whether the level of protection a member desires to achieve through a measure is the least trade-restrictive one available (Regan, 2007).[13]

For example, in *Korea—Beef* the AB ruled that a requirement that foreign beef be sold through a separate parallel retail system to prevent unfair competition (fraudulent sales of foreign beef as high-quality Korean nondairy beef) was not necessary because other, less trade-restrictive policies were available. In a case concerning a policy imposed in Thailand prohibiting imports of cigarettes, the panel found that this violated Article XI (prohibition on QRs). An argument by the Thai government that an import ban was justified under Article XX because it was necessary to control smoking was rejected, because other less trade-restrictive instruments were available (so the QR was not necessary). Another example of the necessity rule in action was a 2008 decision regarding a US policy requiring Thai and Indian shrimp exporters to post a bond to guarantee payment of retroactively imposed increases in AD duties if a review found higher AD margins. The US argued that its 'Enhanced Continuous Bond Directive' was justified under Article XX:*d* because it was necessary to secure compliance with a GATT consistent discipline. The AB rejected this because the US had not shown there was a significant risk that Thai and Indian exports of shrimp would be sold at prices implying higher AD margins and thus greater AD duty liabilities. That is, the measure was not necessary.

Many disputes in this area revolve around discrimination rather than the necessity test. In the Thai cigarettes case just mentioned, as domestic production was unconstrained, the import ban violated national treatment (which also implied, of course, that the ban could not be effective in achieving the purported objective). In a dispute concerning a ban by Brazil on imports of retreaded tires from the EU (DS332, December 2007) motivated by health and environmental concerns, the AB ruled against Brazil because it allowed retreaded tyres to come in from Mercosur

---

[13] To date there have been four disputes in which the AB interpreted the word 'necessary': *Korea—Beef* (2001); *EC—Asbestos* (2001); *US—Gambling* (2005); and *Dominican Republic—Cigarettes* (2005). Regan (2007) discusses the apparent inconsistencies of the arguments made in these cases regarding the interpretation given to 'necessity' at some length.

partners—and thus fell foul of the nondiscrimination rule. This was a rather ironic case as the discrimination arose as a result of a dispute between Brazil and its Mercosur partners following the implementation of a general ban by Brazil. After losing the Mercosur dispute and being forced to exempt its partners, the resulting discrimination led to a violation of the WTO rules. The fact that intra-Mercosur trade was small was not relevant. Similar reasoning has applied in other Article XX cases.

In practice, governments have great leeway in arguing that trade measures are necessary, as long as nondiscrimination is respected (Box 9.3). This also applies to remedies and retaliation. The *US—Gambling* case provides an example. After the US failed to implement the ruling (see Chapter 7), arbitrators determined in 2008 that Antigua was allowed to impose US$21 million in retaliation—the amount that Antigua and Barbuda could have earned if they had been able to contest the segment of the Internet gambling market that was legal in the US (horse racing). The arbitrators rejected the argument of Antigua that its loss equalled US$3.4

Box 9.3. EC—Asbestos

Chrysotile asbestos is considered to be a highly toxic material, possessing significant threats to human health. However, due to its resistance to very high temperature, that type of asbestos has been widely used in various industrial sectors. To control the health risks associated with asbestos, France, which had previously been an importer of large quantities of chrysotile asbestos, imposed a ban on the substance. The WTO panel and the Appellate Body both rejected Canada's challenge to the import ban on asbestos and asbestos-containing products, reinforcing the view that the WTO Agreements allow members to define their own levels of protection of human health and safety.

Canada argued that a distinction should be made between chrysotile fibres and chrysotile encapsulated in a cement matrix. The latter, in Canada's opinion, prevented release of fibres and did not endanger human health. Canada also argued that the substances France was using as substitutes for asbestos had not been sufficiently studied and could themselves be harmful to human health. It considered that the French ban violated GATT Articles III:4 and XI, and Articles 2.1, 2.2, 2.4 and 2.8 of the TBT Agreement. The EU, who represented France in the case, justified the prohibition on the grounds of human health protection, arguing that asbestos was hazardous not only to the health of construction workers subject to prolonged exposure, but also to anyone subject to occasional exposure. Brussels argued that the ban was not covered by the TBT Agreement and with regard to GATT 1994, it requested the panel confirm that the ban was either compatible with Article III:4 or necessary to protect human health within the meaning of Article XX(b). Despite finding a violation of Article III, the Panel ruled in favour of the EU in that the ban could be justified under Article XX(b). In other words, the ban was 'necessary to protect animal, human, plant life or health'. It also met the conditions of the chapeau of Article XX. On appeal, the AB upheld the panel's ruling in favour of the EC, while modifying its reasoning on a number of issues.

billion—the value of potential sales of internet gambling services more generally. Although this may well have been a reasonable estimate, this market did not really exist in legal terms, as the US banned US firms as well as foreign ones from providing such services. The only type of gambling permitted to US firms was on horse racing.

Pressure has increased substantially on WTO members to extend and clarify the limits of the exceptions provisions of the WTO. These pressures are coming from two directions. On one side, various interest groups in OECD countries have sought to induce their governments to invoke the provisions as cover for the imposition of trade barriers motivated by environmental or social concerns. On the other hand, exporting countries are concerned that the exceptions articles not become loopholes importing country governments can use to argue that a particular trade restriction is 'necessary' to achieve a noneconomic objective. Clearly, a critical issue is the application of the criterion of whether a measure that discriminates against imported products is necessary to achieve the public policy objective. The AB to date has made it clear that members have freedom to use trade measures to achieve the regulatory objectives listed in the exceptions articles. What matters in this connection (in addition to satisfying MFN) is whether there is a less trade-restrictive feasible measure—i.e. one that can be used without incurring significantly greater administrative costs.

National security

The national security exemptions are particularly ill-suited for dispute settlement, as in such cases panels would have to judge whether trade restrictions are necessary to protect national security. This can obviously be a very sensitive issue, especially as the language of the national security exceptions are particularly vague. Article XXI GATT allows measures to be imposed whenever a government considers this 'necessary for the protection of its essential security interests' both in time of war or 'other emergency in international relations'. Sometimes efforts to invoke a national security rationale are blatantly spurious. When Sweden imposed import quotas on footwear in 1975, it argued that this was motivated by 'national security' concerns because it needed to have a domestic industry to guarantee the country would not be short of army boots in time of war. This argument did go over well with Sweden's trading partners.

Not surprisingly, GATT was rarely used as an instrument to contest economic sanctions imposed for foreign policy reasons. A US embargo against Nicaragua in 1985 was contested by the Nicaraguan government, but the panel ruled that it did not violate the GATT. It also noted that it was precluded from judging the validity of—or the motivation for—the US action (Jackson, 1997). More recently, a dispute between the EU and the US has tested the limits of the national security exception (Box 9.4).

Box 9.4. National security and the US Helms–Burton Act

The US Cuban Liberty and Democratic Solidarity (LIBERTAD) Act of 1996, more commonly known for the legislators that drafted it, Messrs Helms and Burton, calls for trade restrictions on goods of Cuban origin, as well as possible refusal of entry visas and work permits for non-US nationals who have (or whose employers have) economic activities in Cuba. Thus, the bill banned visits to the US by directors of foreign firms doing business in Cuba. The EU argued that this violated numerous WTO rules, including the basic principles of MFN and national treatment. The US responded that its actions were justified under the national security exceptions of the GATT and the GATS. The EU requested a panel in October 1996. The panel, comprised of three venerable men, including the former GATT Director-General Mr Arthur Dunkel, faced a very difficult task. On the one hand, a whitewash would threaten the credibility of the WTO. On the other hand, the US would have found it virtually impossible to accept an adverse ruling, which would have stirred up large-scale opposition to membership of the WTO. If, as was very probable, the US would have ignored an adverse finding by the panel, it might have encouraged other countries to follow the US example. In the event cooler heads prevailed, and the panel suspended its work at the request of the EU in April 1997 after a bilateral resolution to the conflict was concluded.

9.9. CONCLUSION

Political realities, especially in countries in the process of moving from highly distorted trade regimes to a more neutral policy stance, often dictate that there be mechanisms allowing for the temporary re-imposition of protection in instances where competition from imports proves to be too fierce. Safeguard mechanisms are therefore likely to be a pre-condition for far-reaching liberalization to be politically feasible. Governments need loopholes that permit 'backsliding' for a variety of reasons. One that has not been discussed so far is a sympathy motive. Societies tend to have sympathy for groups severely affected by large, exogenous shocks. They support granting assistance to such groups because they too may be affected some day. This insurance motive is complemented by what Corden (1974) has called the conservative social welfare function (see Deardorff, 1987). Governments tend to oppose large absolute reductions in real incomes of any significant portion of society.

Trade policy is generally an inefficient instrument in that it tends to create more distortions than it solves. Indeed, Deardorff and Stern (1987) have likened trade policy to doing acupuncture with a two-pronged fork; even if one of the prongs finds the right spot, the other prong can only do harm. This applies to protection in response to market disruption as well. Protection is a very costly form of intervention, both in a static sense (as demonstrated by studies of costs per job saved such as Hufbauer and Elliot, 1994, and Messerlin, 2001), and in a dynamic sense (due to the distortions that reduce economic growth). In practical terms, however, given a sociopolitical need to address market disturbance, temporary contingent protection may be the best response in situations where import penetration has increased substantially. The issue then is to design and implement procedures that are effective, equitable and minimize distortions. The WTO does little in terms of providing guidance to policymakers wishing to rationalize or create an economically sound system to deal with market disruption caused by imports. Allowing for the possibility of emergency protection sends a signal to firms that the government cannot or will not commit itself to a given level of intervention or support. This can negatively influence the performance of particular firms—who may build this insurance into their management decisions. This can in turn give rise to so-called time-inconsistency problems. If a government is pursuing a liberalization programme, but firms do not adjust because they expect to be able to obtain protection in the future, it may not be optimal (politically) for the government not to grant such protection (or alternatively, to remove the temporary, emergency protection). The design of the mechanism and the rules and criteria that apply are therefore important. External obligations—such as those applying under the WTO—can help in reducing possible time inconsistency problems, but cannot eliminate them.

In practice the WTO arguably allows for too many escape valves, some of which make no economic sense. This has given rise to a form of Gresham's Law, in that bad provisions (such as AD) have driven out good provisions (safeguards). Countries in the process of developing or reforming their trade laws are well advised not to implement all the options allowed under the WTO to impose trade barriers, as it can make it much more difficult to control the trade policy formation process. All that is really required to help manage the adjustment of domestic industries to vigorous import competition is the general GATT safeguard mechanism. Countervailing duties have a rationale even for countries that cannot realistically affect the behaviour of the countries that are engaging in subsidization, as they allow a government to take action when it deems that the interests of domestic producers outweigh those of consumers. Antidumping and the use of trade measures for BOP reasons are best avoided. The many countries already caught in the AD morass are well advised to put in place mechanisms that ensure the economic costs of AD are considered in the decision-making process. Providing groups that will lose from AD protection legal standing to defend their interests is the most direct way of doing so.

Finally, it should be kept in mind that provisions such as Articles XIX and XXVIII GATT (or Article XXI GATS) are only relevant if tariffs have been bound (specific commitments have been made). If this is not the case, countries will have the latitude to simply raise tariffs if the political need for this arises. For the GATT rules to fully bite, tariffs must be bound. For GATS to bind, specific commitments must be made. As discussed in Chapters 4, 5 and 7, on both the goods and services front much still remains to be done to achieve full binding of applied tariffs and services policies.

9.10. FURTHER READING

Safeguard protection for import-competing industries has been analysed extensively in the economic literature. Robert Baldwin, 'Assessing the Fair Trade and Safeguards Laws in Terms of Modern Trade and Political Economy Analysis', *The World Economy*, 15 (1992): 185–202, discusses the (political economy) issues and surveys some of the literature. Gary Sampson, 'Safeguards', in J. M. Finger and A. Olechowski (eds), *The Uruguay Round: A Handbook* (Washington, DC: The World Bank, 1987) reviews the history of Article XIX in the GATT through 1986. Alan Deardorff, 'Safeguards Policy and the Conservative Social Welfare Function', in Henryk Kierzkowski (ed.), *Protection and Competition in International Trade* (Oxford: Basil Blackwell, 1987) discusses why governments need safeguard instruments. Brian Hindley, 'GATT Safeguards and Voluntary Export Restraints: What are the Interests of the Developing Countries?' *World Bank Economic Review*, 1 (1987): 689–705, discusses the incentive effects of VERs. A classic paper on VERs is Richard Harris's, 'Why Voluntary Export Restraints are "Voluntary"', *Canadian Journal of Economics*, 18 (1985): 799–809. Patrick Low, *Trading Free: The GATT and US Trade Policy* (New York: Twentieth Century Fund, 1993) discusses in some detail the political economy of the US shift towards the use of VERs, as well as the evolution of US trade policy thinking and practice.

Richard Eglin, 'Surveillance of Balance-of-Payments Measures in the GATT', *The World Economy*, 10 (1987): 1–26, reviews the GATT experience with Article XVIII actions and multilateral surveillance. The contributions by Finger, Hindley and L. Alan Winters in *The New World Trading System* (Paris: OECD, 1994) are good summaries of what was agreed on contingent protection in the Uruguay Round. J. Michael Finger, 'Legalized Backsliding: Safeguard Provisions in the GATT', in Will Martin and Alan Winters (eds), *The Uruguay Round and the Developing Economies* (Cambridge: Cambridge University Press, 1996) presents a comprehensive discussion of the various loopholes in the GATT that allow for backsliding. Michael Finger and Ludger Schuknecht, 'Market Access Advances and Retreats: The Uruguay Round and Beyond', in Bernard Hoekman and

Will Martin (eds), *Developing Countries and the WTO* (Oxford: Basil Blackwell, 2000) summarize the first five years of WTO members' use of safeguards and exceptions. An overview of the legal and economic issues related to safeguards in the WTO is provided by Alan Sykes, *The WTO Agreement on Safeguards: A Commentary* (Oxford: Oxford University Press, 2006). Chad Bown and Rachel McCulloch, 'Trade Adjustment in the WTO System: Are More Safeguards the Answer?', *Oxford Review of Economic Policy*, 23 (2007): 415–39, discuss the rationales for safeguards and the effectiveness of the instruments provided for under the WTO to address them.

There is a huge literature on antidumping, both legal and economic. Much of the economic literature is summarized in Douglas Nelson, 'The Political Economy of Antidumping: A Survey', *European Journal of Political Economy*, 22 (2006): 554–90. That journal issue includes numerous articles that review the 'state of the art' of our knowledge of the effects and incidence of AD. J. Michael Finger (ed.), *Antidumping: How it Works and Who Gets Hurt* (Ann Arbor: University of Michigan Press, 1993) provides an excellent set of papers that analyse AD at the country level and conclude that these often make little economic sense. J. M. Finger and Julio Nogues, *Safeguards and Antidumping in Latin American Trade Liberalization: Fighting Fire With Fire* (Washington, DC: World Bank, 2006) offer a more recent collection of country case studies that comes to a more positive assessment of the political utility of AD and safeguards.

Patrick Messerlin, 'Antidumping Regulations or Pro-cartel Law? The EC Chemical Cases', *The World Economy*, 13 (1990): 465–92, documents how an industry can capture AD procedures to enhance its market power. P. K. M. Tharakan, 'The Political Economy of Price-Undertakings', *European Economic Review*, 35 (1991): 1341–59, analyses the use of and motivations for undertakings in EU application of AD. For a comprehensive, insider account of the Uruguay Round AD Agreement, see Mark Koulen, 'The New Antidumping Code Through its Negotiating History', in J. Bourgeois, F. Berrod and E. Fouvier (eds), *The Uruguay Round Results: A European Lawyer's Perspective* (Brussels: European Interuniversity Press, 1995).

A database on global AD and safeguards activity is available (at: http://people. brandeis.edu/~cbown/global_ad). This website hosts a detailed database on 19 different national governments' use of AD, as well as all WTO members' use of safeguard measures. A good source of up-to-date policy-oriented papers on contingent protection and related issues is *The Journal of World Trade* (Kluwer). Douglas Nelson and Hylke Vandenbussche, *The WTO and Anti-Dumping: Critical Perspectives on the Global Trading System and the WTO* (Edward Elgar, 2005) present a collection of the major contributions that have been made to the AD literature.

An overview of the use of WTO waivers is offered by James Harrison, 'Legal and Political Oversight of WTO Waivers', *Journal of International Economic Law*, 11 (2) (2008): 411–25. The issue of re-negotiation of concessions is extensively discussed in Anwarul Hoda, *Tariff Negotiations and Renegotiations under the GATT and the WTO: Procedures and Practices* (Cambridge: Cambridge University Press, 2001).

CHAPTER 10

PREFERENTIAL TRADE AGREEMENTS AND REGIONAL INTEGRATION

Both the GATT and the GATS make explicit allowance for preferential trade agreements among a subset of members. Such agreements can be of two types: reciprocal and nonreciprocal. This chapter deals with the former; the latter are discussed in Chapter 12 as they arise in trade relations between industrialized and developing countries. Both types of preferential trade are inconsistent with the MFN principle and are therefore subject to multilateral disciplines that define minimum conditions that must be met for an agreement. The WTO also provides for multilateral scrutiny of such agreements. This chapter discusses the rationales for preferential trade agreements (PTAs) between WTO members, the WTO rules and their application in practice, and the economic literature exploring the relationship between PTAs and multilateralism (the trading system)—both theoretical and empirical. Given the steadily expanding number of PTAs, a critical question for the WTO is whether the network of PTAs create incentives to lower trade barriers on a MFN basis and thus help achieve a major objective of the drafters of the GATT.

Reciprocal trade agreements among subsets of the WTO membership have become a prominent part of the trade landscape. As of late 2007, 380 PTAs had been notified to the GATT/WTO. Of that number, 300 agreements were notified under Article XXIV of the GATT, 22 agreements involving developing countries

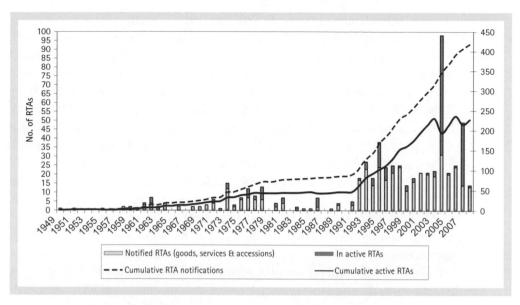

Fig. 10.1. Number of preferential trade agreements (1948–2007)

Source: WTO.

were notified under the Enabling Clause, and 58 under Article V of the GATS. Although these numbers are suggestive of a proliferation of PTAs, it is important to recognize that a large number of the PTAs notified to the GATT and WTO have involved prospective members of the EU and became irrelevant once the countries acceded to the EU.[1] About 200 PTAs were in force at the end of 2007 (Figure 10.1). Of these PTAs, customs unions account for less than 10 per cent. Many of the PTAs involve contiguous countries but many do not. In this chapter we reserve the term 'regional integration' for PTAs limited to neighbouring countries.

Since the late 1950s, the EC has been the market leader in the PTA business. European countries account for more than half of all PTAs notified to the WTO and that were still in force in 2008. The major regional grouping in Europe is the European Union, with 27 members in 2008. Other European PTAs include the European Free Trade Association (EFTA, Iceland, Lichtenstein, Norway and Switzerland).[2] and the Central European Free Trade Agreement. The EU has concluded

[1] As noted by Pomfret (2007), after the expansion of the EU by ten new members in 2004, some 65 PTAs between these countries and the EU became redundant. Note also that the numbers overstate the prevalence of PTAs because separate notifications are required under the GATT and the GATS for agreements that cover both goods and services—as many PTAs now do.

[2] At varying points in time EFTA also included Austria, Denmark, Finland, Portugal, Sweden and the UK, all of which left to become members of the EU. The European Free Trade Association has a very close economic relationship with the EU, governed by the European Economic Area Agreement.

Stability and Association Agreements with countries in south-eastern Europe, has PTAs with almost all Mediterranean nations, Chile, Mexico and South Africa, and a series of Economic Partnership Agreements (EPAs) with African, Caribbean and Pacific (ACP) countries. The EU has expressed interest in negotiating agreements with India, Korea, and the members of the Association of South-East Asian Nations (ASEAN), and the Central American Common Market, among others (WTO, 2007).

The US became a proponent of PTAs in the 1980s, starting with agreements with Israel (in 1985) and Canada (1988), followed in 1992 by the North American Free Trade Agreement (NAFTA) with Canada and Mexico. Since the mid-1990s, the US has concluded PTAs with Australia, Bahrain, Chile, four Central American countries (El Salvador, Guatemala, Honduras and Nicaragua) and the Dominican Republic (DR-CAFTA), Jordan, Morocco and Singapore. As of mid-2008, PTAs with Peru and Oman had been ratified but were pending implementation, whereas PTAs with Colombia, Panama and South Korea were awaiting approval by the Congress.

Virtually all OECD nations are now a member of one or more PTAs. Examples include the Australia and New Zealand Closer Economic Relations PTA and EFTA, as well as bilateral agreements involving members of these agreements. The long standing exception among OECD countries used to be Japan. This changed starting in 2000, with a PTA with Singapore. Since then Japan concluded bilateral deals with other trading partners in Asia (Malaysia, Indonesia, the Philippines and Thailand) as well as Chile and Mexico. An agreement with ASEAN was signed in April 2008, and talks initiated with Australia, India, Switzerland and Vietnam.

As can be inferred from the above, developing countries have been active participants in the expansion of PTAs. Often they are the '*demandeurs*' for agreements with the EU and the US, as well as using PTAs as mechanisms to create larger regional markets. The Association of South-East Asian Nations and Mercosur (the Southern Common Market) spanning Argentina, Brazil, Paraguay and Uruguay are just two examples of PTAs between developing countries.

Pomfret (2007) distinguishes between three waves of preferential trade activity. The first was in the 1960s, following the creation of the EEC, which induced other European countries to create EFTA, and many developing countries to form blocs of their own—many of which were unsuccessful and collapsed. The second was initiated in the 1980s with the decision of the US to negotiate PTAs and the move by the EU to deepen its integration process through the Single Market programme and widen its membership to 15 countries (achieved in 1995). This was complemented by the negotiation or revitalization of PTAs between developing countries that were more outward oriented—indeed, preferential liberalization went hand-in-hand with (or followed) unilateral liberalization. In the early 2000s, a third wave started, led by East Asian countries, partly as a response to the financial crisis of the late 1990s and partly a reaction to the rapid increase in China's economic power.

The specifics of each PTA vary greatly from case to case, but they all generally have one thing in common: discrimination against other countries. Preferential trade agreements take many forms. At their simplest they lower or remove tariffs on imports originating in partner countries. Many go beyond tariffs to also cover NTMs. More recent vintage PTAs often include services trade and investment. At their most far-reaching, PTAs encompass instruments of domestic economic regulation and political cooperation, and may represent a step towards nation-building or international federalism.

The economic literature distinguishes between different types of PTAs. The most 'shallow' form is a bilateral trade agreement. This may do nothing more than grant a country MFN and national treatment. These types of agreement can be relevant for non-WTO countries—an example is a 2005 agreement between Laos and the US. More generally the term bilateral trade agreement covers deals where the parties involved do not go to free trade but only cut tariffs by a certain percentage. Such agreements are illegal under the WTO for industrialized nations but may be concluded by developing countries (Chapter 12). More far-reaching is a free trade agreement (FTA), which removes tariffs on trade between member countries, with each country retaining its own tariff structure against outsiders. A customs union is a free trade area with common external trade policies. A common market is a customs union that also integrates factor markets, allowing for the free movement of labour (workers) and capital. Finally, an economic union is a common market that includes some degree of harmonization of national economic policies of member states. In practice, PTAs are often a combination of these ideal types. Many (indeed most) tend to fail to conform to these ideal types. For example, contingent protection often remains applicable to intra-bloc trade in PTAs, implying that internal trade is not truly free. Many PTAs have not lead to internal free trade because certain sectors or industries are excluded and because differences in the external tariffs across members imply the need to enforce rules of origin to prevent arbitrage activity between low and high tariff members. Many customs unions fail to put in place a common external trade policy, resulting in continued border controls that impede trade flows between PTA members. And numerous agreements give rise to cooperation on matters of economic policy, regulation or factor markets without ever having achieved free trade between the participating members.

10.1. MOTIVATIONS FOR PREFERENTIAL TRADE AGREEMENTS

In one form or another, PTAs have been around for hundreds of years. There were proposals for the provinces of France to establish a customs union in 1664.

Customs unions were precursors to the creation of new states in, for example Germany (the Zollverein) and Italy. Although nation-building objectives have been a spur to regional integration, historically, as discussed in Chapter 1, the exercise of power has been much more important in this regard. The primary driving force behind PTAs has been mercantilist: access to export markets. Negotiation of PTAs also has had a cyclical dimension. The 1930s saw great fragmentation of the world trading system as governments sought to shelter domestic industries and safeguard access to supplies. Preferential trade agreements were pursued as an instrument through which to undo some of the costs of unilateral protectionism and currency blocs. After the Second World War, regional integration contributed to the political reconstruction of Europe through the implementation of the Benelux Customs Union (1947), the creation of the European Coal and Steel Community in 1952 and the more far-reaching EEC (in 1957).

The creation of the EEC stimulated 'copy cat' regionalism among developing countries in 1960s. The associated PTAs were mostly driven by a desire to apply import-substitution industrialization strategies within a larger economic area to realize scale economies and to achieve political objectives. The agreements tended to be very protectionist (with high external barriers) and interventionist (with governments pursuing industrial policies and influencing the location of specific industries within the territory of the PTA). They were generally failures. By the late 1970s the ineffectiveness of most of these PTAs had become evident. None seemed to have contributed much to economic development, some had collapsed and the strains of the debt crisis in the 1980s made many of those that survived largely moribund.

In the mid-1980s a change in attitudes towards international trade and competition began to occur. Unilateral liberalization decisions by many governments were complemented by a new wave of more open PTAs. The EU played a major role in the resurgence of PTAs by negotiating agreements with Central and Eastern European and Mediterranean nations, as well as continuing to expand its membership, starting with Portugal and Spain in 1986. In the Americas, the Canadian–US FTA of 1988 was extended to Mexico through NAFTA in 1994, Mercosur was formed in 1991. In Asia, ASEAN members extended 25 years of political and economic cooperation with a formal free trade agreement in 1992 and admitted new members, including Vietnam (1995), Laos and Myanmar (1997) and Cambodia (1999). In Africa, a number of initiatives were launched, including the Common Market for Eastern and Southern Africa (COMESA)—which extends as far north as Egypt—and the Southern African Development Community (SADC). Members of the Arab League revitalized their long standing but stalled integration efforts by creating a Pan-Arab Free Trade Agreement (PAFTA) to remove tariffs on intra-regional trade, which was implemented ahead of schedule in 2005.

Why go preferential?

Chapter 1 has already discussed the rationales that may induce governments to negotiate trade agreements. Recall that the two major explanations offered by economists revolve around improving market access for exporters (the terms of trade argument) and credibility (time consistency)—trade agreements may be used by governments as a commitment device. In principle a multilateral agreement that includes all countries should dominate one that is limited to only one or several partner countries: better access to the world market dominates what can be offered by just a few countries, and a multilateral set of disciplines should do more for credibility than a PTA. After all, having more countries to hold the government to account would seem to be a more powerful source of discipline than one that involves only a few countries.

So why engage in PTAs? How might these arrangements do a better job in delivering market access and credibility? An extensive literature has suggested numerous possibilities. The arguments can be split along three lines, two building on the 'standard' economic rationales, and one focused more on noneconomic factors, such as foreign policy and national security motivations.

'Better' market access. The WTO does not offer free trade. A FTA with a major trading partner does and on a *preferential basis.* Such preferred access is valuable, the more so the larger the partner market and the higher the barriers the partner maintains on imports from competing suppliers. It may be easier to get if a country is small and thus not perceived as much of a threat by import-competing firms in the partner country (countries). Moreover, as tariffs fall—whether because of unilateral decisions or trade agreements—the relative importance of NTMs as barriers to trade and market integration rise (Baldwin, 1970). Preferential trade agreements may offer better instruments than the WTO for traders to get governments to *deal with market segmenting nontariff policies* that prevent the benefits of tariff removal from being (fully) realized. This can include the removal of the threat of contingent protection, on a *de facto* if not *de jure* basis (Prusa, 2006). In addition to issues that are covered by the WTO, a PTA may also offer the opportunity to negotiate disciplines on policies is areas that are not (yet) included in the WTO. Thus, PTAs offer the possibility of *deeper integration of product markets* than may be on offer in the WTO.

Preferential trade agreements may also help *put pressure on members of the WTO* to do more or to do it faster. The US moved from active hostility to a proponent of PTAs in the mid-1980s in part because of dissatisfaction with the 1982 refusal of GATT partners to initiate a MTN that covered services trade (Schott, 1989). Another factor was the end of the Cold War, which reduced American willingness to accept the *opportunity cost of free riding* by other countries in the WTO and the costs to the US of preferential liberalization elsewhere in the world. Finally, there are so-called *domino effects* (Baldwin, 1995): as major trading powers create trade blocs, incentives for excluded countries to seek similar trading relationships increase, because the costs of being a nonmember rise. Exclusion from a major PTA market (or confronting higher barriers and costs than do 'insiders') can change the political economy equilibrium in the excluded country—increasing the incentives for exporters to mobilize and pressure their governments to seek accession or negotiate a PTA with the large blocs.

Focal points for—and greater credibility of—domestic reform. In principle a trade agreement can be used as a commitment and signalling device by governments seeking to change expectations and lobbying behaviour of firms and interest groups. As discussed in Chapter 1, the theoretical (and practical) arguments for using trade agreements as a commitment device depend on there being a credible enforcement mechanism. In the WTO context this may not exist, especially for small countries that cannot affect the terms of trade and are too small to make it worthwhile to bring to the WTO court. Preferential trade agreements may offer stronger enforcement mechanisms, especially if private interests have direct access to courts or other tribunals and mechanisms, and thus create alternatives to the WTO to bring cases (Piérola and Horlick, 2007). A few PTAs have supranational enforcement mechanisms, the EU being the primary example, which can reduce uncertainty regarding implementation of the agreement. Enforcement is obviously also relevant for the market access incentives to negotiate a PTA—if seen as more effective, there is less uncertainty associated with the PTA than there is with the WTO. This is especially the case if the available remedies are stronger. Preferential trade agreements may also allow more credible commitments to be made if proximity of member countries reduces monitoring costs and similarity with partners—in terms of per capita income, etc.—reduces implementation costs.

Political objectives, regional cooperation and club goods. In addition to these rationales there may be 'noneconomic' foreign policy and national security objectives driving PTAs. Indeed, these often predominate in public discussion and debates, with any economic costs being argued to be the price of achieving the noneconomic objectives. Some problems or issues may be shared by only a limited number of (often neighbouring) countries, and therefore call for cooperation that is limited to the countries that will benefit from cooperation. Regional infrastructure such as bridges, railways and roads, power pools and electricity grid interconnection are examples of such 'club goods'. Interest in cooperation may extend to a willingness to engage in provision of financial transfers to support the delivery of regional public goods or achieve other objectives such as regional economic development. More ambitious forms of cooperation may extend to seeking to create a larger political entity. The German Zollverein—see Chapter 1—is a prominent historical example; the EU may become another. The collapse of Soviet hegemony allowed the countries of Eastern Europe and the Baltic to embrace democracy and market-based economic systems. Accession to the EU was seen by them as a tool to counter Russia's aspirations of a regional power, cement the transition to a market economy and revive the common European cultural heritage. Less positively, PTAs may offer convenient 'displacement activity' for governments—providing an opportunity for photo opportunities and the appearance of strengthening relationships with partner countries without doing much if anything to liberalize trade. The activity may help achieve foreign policy objectives but has no economic meaning.

Other objectives that reflect a mix of market access and political goals are *precedent-setting and first-mover* objectives. Bilateral trade negotiations give the major trading powers an opportunity to establish certain rules of the game in areas that are not (yet) covered by the WTO, especially nontrade areas of policy, or to go beyond what is feasible multilaterally. Examples include IPRs, competition and investment policies, and disciplines relating to labour standards and environmental norms. Related is the *laboratory* rationale: countries may be able to experiment in a PTA context and 'discover' what works and what does not in ways that may not be possible in the WTO.

As discussed in Chapter 1, at any point in time a certain level of market access restrictions emerges as an equilibrium outcome of interactions between different groups in the political market of a country. In seeking better market access, export-oriented firms can push for liberalization at home (which will help exports as a result of the so-called Lerner symmetry proposition: a tax on imports is a tax on exports); try to convince foreign governments to liberalize (by forming coalitions with interests in the foreign country that would benefit from opening); push for multilateral liberalization (a MTN, or a sectoral deal such as the ITA—see Chapter 6); or push for a PTA.

A PTA by definition involves substantially fewer countries than a MTN. Indeed, many PTAs involve only two countries. This may make them easier to negotiate. In part this is because obtaining agreement to exclude certain sensitive policy areas may be more feasible than in a multilateral negotiation—especially if the PTA countries share similar 'sensitivities'. In part it may be because the set of possible policy packages that could make all parties better off is larger under a PTA, encompassing issues that could not appear on the negotiating agenda of a MTN. Issue linkage or side-payments therefore may be more feasible as the negotiation set expands, facilitating agreement. The side-payments may include mechanisms to transfer income from one member to another; in the MTN-context this is rarely possible.[3] Many PTAs involve relatively similar countries. The more similar are countries in their endowments and income levels, the likelier it is that intra-industry trade will be significant. This may facilitate preferential liberalization (Box 10.1).

---

[3] Although some steps in this direction were taken in the Doha Round with the Aid for Trade initiative—see Chapter 12.

Box 10.1. Intra-industry trade and PTAs

Increased internationalization of markets and technological advances put pressure on firms to seek greater efficiency through larger markets and improved access to foreign technologies and investment. Preferential trade agreements can help realize these objectives by providing cheaper access to intermediate inputs and facilitating the two-way cross-border movement of parts of a product for further processing. Such intra-industry trade may give rise to less adjustment pressures than inter-industry trade because jobs lost due to customers shifting to more efficient foreign suppliers may to a large extent be offset by the job-enhancing expansion in foreign demand for similar, differentiated goods produced domestically. The political opposition to liberalization that expands inter-industry trade may be stronger because industries that are less competitive than those abroad will generally be forced to contract substantially. This is not to say that intra-industry trade will not lead to adjustment and thus pressure for protection. Specialized and relatively immobile factors of production injured by import competition can be expected to seek protection. But the injury in this case is more at the firm than at the industry level. Other firms in the industry will expand. This makes it more difficult to maintain protection, as there will be conflicting interests within industries.

The relevance of this for PTAs is that intra-industry trade tends to be high among countries with similar endowments and relatively high per capita income levels—nations that have tended to form PTAs in the post-Second World War period. Levels of intra-industry trade between the members of the most successful PTAs—the EU, EFTA, NAFTA and the Australia–New Zealand Closer Economic Relations (CER) agreement—are high, both for trade in goods and trade in services (Egger, Egger and Greenaway, 2006).

Intra-industry trade has grown rapidly since the 1980s and is part and parcel of the global production sharing and specialization that was discussed in Chapter 1. It may also generate pressures on PTA member governments to liberalize more generally to facilitate the participation of national firms to slice up their production chains. As discussed later in this chapter, over time, once tariffs are removed on a preferential basis, the net benefits of a PTA may fall for firms, especially if the rules of origin constrain (raise the costs of) global sourcing. This may lead firms to support external liberalization (Baldwin, 2006a).

Much attention has been devoted by researchers to identifying the impacts of PTAs on members and nonmembers. Of obvious interest is whether PTAs are detrimental to world welfare, both in the short run (their impact effects) and in the longer run (taking induced growth effects into account), and whether they are building or stumbling blocks for multilateral cooperation in the WTO. The latter question—first posed in this way by Bhagwati (1991)—has generated numerous papers by economists, and is a question to which we return in Section 10.3.

The economic impact of PTAs on member and nonmember countries will depend on the type of agreement concerned (FTA, customs union or common market) and on the degree to which intra-regional trade is liberalized. The more extensive is internal liberalization, the greater the resulting increase in competition on regional markets. Although this is welfare-enhancing for member countries—and presumably the object of economic integration—it may also be associated with greater adjustment pressures for inefficient industries located in member countries. The latter may attempt to shift some of the adjustment burden onto third countries by seeking increases in external barriers.

Regional integration can be detrimental to members and nonmembers by inducing a shift away from the most efficient supplier of goods or services. The formation of a trading bloc can give rise to so-called trade diversion (a shift from an efficient outside supplier to a higher cost regional one, induced by the elimination of tariffs on partner country producers that are higher cost than competitors on the world market, see Annex 2). Early observers of PTAs such as Hirschman (1981) and Tumlir (1983) pointed out that a PTA is likely to require trade diversion for political reasons, as this is an effective mechanism for compensating lobbies that oppose liberalization. Nonmembers may be harmed through investment diversion as well as trade diversion if enterprises decide to invest inside PTAs and produce locally, rather than export to the PTA. The prospect of EU enlargements, for example, has resulted in substantial increases in FDI into accession countries by both EU and non-European companies that are interested in serving the EU market. Thus, the 2004 enlargement of the EU to include Hungary, Poland, the Czech Republic, Slovakia, Slovenia and the Baltic States, followed by Bulgaria and Romania in 2007, encouraged investment by non-European firms as well as EU-based multinationals in both manufacturing and services sectors in these Eastern European countries.

Such investment responses may also arise in response to deepening of PTAs. Baldwin, Forslid and Haaland (1996) studied the effect of the announcement of the Single Market programme in the EU in the late 1980s, and concluded that this had a significant negative impact on inward FDI flows into EFTA countries. Foreign direct investment only recovered after the EFTA members applied for EU membership and the remaining EFTA countries concluded the European Economic Area agreement with the EU.

10.2. WTO Disciplines

The rules of the WTO do relatively little to limit the potential for trade and investment diversion. The WTO is somewhat schizophrenic about PTAs—permitting them subject to satisfaction of specific disciplines that, in principle, make things worse for nonmembers. The major provisions are Articles XXIV GATT and V GATS, complemented by multilateral surveillance of PTAs.

GATT Article XXIV: customs unions and FTAs

Article XXIV of the GATT allows FTAs and customs unions if:

(1) trade barriers after formation of the PTA do not rise on average (Article XXIV:5);

(2) all tariffs and other regulations of commerce are removed on substantially all intra-PTA exchanges of goods within a reasonable length of time (Article XXIV:8); and

(3) they are notified to the WTO Council.

The rationales for the first and last criteria are obvious. World Trade Organization members should be told when countries decide to pursue a PTA as otherwise the PTA members open themselves to dispute settlement and retaliation for violating the nondiscrimination rules. Nonmembers will not want to allow those forming a PTA use it as a means of raising protection against them. If restrictions on imports from nonmember economies are no higher than before, the extent of possible reductions in imports from nonmembers is reduced (although clearly not zero—the higher are external barriers, the greater the likely trade diversion). A practical problem faced by the drafters of Article XXIV was that the formation of a customs union by necessity requires changes in the external tariffs of some PTA members as they adopt a common external tariff. The rule that applies to customs unions is that duties and other barriers to imports from outside the union may not be on the whole higher or more restrictive than those preceding the establishment of the customs union (Article XXIV:5*a*). The interpretation of this phrase became a source of much disagreement among GATT contracting parties in the pre-WTO period. The rule for FTAs was unambiguous, however. Duties applied by each individual PTA member may not be raised (Article XXIV:5*b*).

The second condition imposed by Article XXIV is somewhat counterintuitive in that maximum preferential liberalization in itself is likely to be more detrimental to nonmembers than partial liberalization. Requiring it, however, ensures that countries are limited in their ability to violate the MFN obligation selectively. As noted by Finger (1993*b*), the rationale behind the second condition is a public choice one: it is an attempt to ensure that participants in PTAs go all the way and not to use the PTA as a mechanism to selectively pick and choose sectors. The determination of whether PTAs satisfy Article XXIV is the responsibility of the WTO Council. In the GATT period, the Council generally created a working party to establish if the conditions were satisfied by a notified PTA. Under the WTO, a Committee on Regional Trade Agreements (CRTA) has taken over this task.

The GATT experience in testing FTAs and customs unions against Article XXIV was very discouraging. Various aspects of the rules and their application, including enforcement of the requirement that PTAs be approved by the CONTRACTING PARTIES *before* they entered into force, proved unsatisfactory. Starting with the Treaty of Rome establishing the EEC in 1957, almost no examination of

PTAs notified under Article XXIV led to a unanimous conclusion or specific endorsement that all the agreements met the GATT requirements. As noted by the chairman of the working party on the 1989 Canada–United States Free Trade Agreement, commenting on the inability to reach a consensus, 'Over fifty previous working parties on individual customs unions or free trade areas have been unable to reach unanimous conclusions on the compatibility of these agreements with the GATT—on the other hand, no such agreement has been explicitly disapproved' (*GATT Focus*, December 1991). Only four GATT-era working parties were able to agree that a PTA satisfied the requirements of Article XXIV (Schott, 1989). Thus, GATT rules largely were a dead letter, although the consultations that occurred allowed interested nonmembers to express their concerns.

The reasons underlying this impotence go back to the creation of the EEC. A conscious decision was made by GATT contracting parties in the late 1950s not to closely scrutinize the formation of the EEC. The reason was that it was made clear by the EEC member states that a finding that the Treaty of Rome was inconsistent with Article XXIV would result in their withdrawal from GATT (Snape, 1993). Whether or not a serious threat, the consensus rule of the GATT ensured that even if a working party had concluded that the EEC did not satisfy Article XXIV, the EC members could block adoption of the report. In any event, to paraphrase Finger (1993*b*), at the end of the day the other GATT signatories blinked, establishing a precedent that was often followed subsequently. Many if not most of the PTAs notified to GATT embodied many holes and loopholes (Hoekman and Leidy, 1993).

A contributing factor impeding the ability of working parties to agree was that the wording in Article XXIV is not precise. Legitimate differences of opinion could exist on how to define 'substantially all trade', how to determine whether the external trade policy of a customs union has become more restrictive on average, and what is a reasonable length of time for the transition towards full implementation of a PTA. The 'substantially all trade' test was particularly important. Does this permit the wholesale exclusion of one or more major sectors—as was the case in the EEC, where agriculture was subject to a managed trade regime (the CAP)? In the GATT period, the EC argued in favour of at least 80 per cent coverage of pre-PTA trade flows; others argued in favour of a more comprehensive coverage test. Currently, the de facto focal point appears to be somewhere around 90 per cent. This can be inferred, for example, from the view taken by the EU that in its EPA negotiations with ACP countries Article XXIV would be satisfied if the EU included all its imports from ACP partners, while the latter could limit their commitment to liberalization of 80 per cent of their imports from the EU (Stevens and Kennan, 2005).

Another ambiguous dimension of the language in Article XXIV:8 is that it is not clear what 'other regulations of commerce' covers, and in particular whether it includes the preferential rules of origin used by PTA members and instruments of contingent protection. Article XXIV is entirely silent on rules of origin, which is rather surprising given that they have an important bearing on the effects of a PTA. The WTO membership have not been able to agree on the rules of origin question although debates in GATT working parties during the 1970s illustrate that officials were well aware that such rules can have important implications for the trade effects of PTAs (Box 10.2).

Can members of FTAs still use antidumping or safeguard measures against each other, or conversely, may they exempt each other if they apply such instruments to their external trade? Case law has concluded that contingent protection may be used by PTA members as long as the rules of the relevant WTO agreements are satisfied and as long as they do not use total imports—including from PTA partners—as the basis on which to determine if (serious) injury has occurred. This so-called parallelism requirement was confirmed by two dispute settlement cases, one involving Argentina, a member of Mercosur and one against the US (a NAFTA member): if PTA partner imports are considered in determining injury, they also need to subject a safeguard action if one is imposed.[4]

An effort was made in the Uruguay Round to make some of the criteria more precise, thereby removing one excuse for a working party not to come to a firm conclusion on a PTA. The GATT 1994 Understanding on the Interpretation of Article XXIV recognizes that the effectiveness of the role of the Council for Trade in Goods in reviewing agreements notified under Article XXIV needed to be enhanced. This was to be pursued in part by clarifying the criteria and procedures for the assessment of new or enlarged agreements, and by improving the transparency of all agreements notified to GATT under Article XXIV. The Understanding reaffirms that PTAs should facilitate trade between members—but did not define what is meant with 'substantially all trade'. Parties to a PTA are called upon 'to the greatest possible extent avoid creating adverse effects on the trade of other members' (GATT, 1994a: 31).

Greater specificity proved possible on the evaluation of the general incidence of the duties and other regulations of commerce applicable before and after the formation of a customs union. This must be based upon 'an overall assessment of weighted average tariff rates and of customs duties collected' by the WTO Secretariat, based on import statistics for a previous representative period (to be supplied by the customs union) on a tariff line basis broken down by WTO member country of origin.

Article XXIV:6 requires members seeking to increase bound tariff rates upon joining a customs union to enter into negotiations—under Article XXVIII (Modification of Schedules, see Chapter 9)—on compensatory adjustment. In doing this, reductions in duties on the same tariff line made by other members of the customs union must be taken into account. If such reductions are insufficient compensation, the Understanding requires the customs union to offer to reduce

---

[4] *Argentina—Footwear* (WT/DS/121) and *US—Wheat Gluten* (WT/DS/166).

Box 10.2. Rules of origin in free trade agreements

The extent of intra-regional trade liberalization under a FTA depends on its rules of origin. Upon the formation of a FTA, nonmember countries may not only be confronted with trade diversion due to the preferential nature of the abolition of barriers to trade, but also because of an effective increase in protection due to the choice of rules of origin. Assume an intermediate product enters a country free of duty and that this country accedes to a FTA. Industries using this input that export to FTA members may then have an incentive to shift to higher cost PTA-based producers of intermediates in order to satisfy the rules of origin for their product. In effect, the rule of origin may become the equivalent to a prohibitive tariff for the original third country suppliers of components, thus generating trade diversion (Krueger, 1997a). Research suggests that the tariff equivalent of NAFTA rules of origin is 3–4 per cent (Anson et al., 2005).

An important factor is whether the rule allows for cumulation. Suppose a product is imported that has been processed in at least two countries, both of which have preferential status. An origin system is cumulative if the importing country only requires that sufficient processing of the product has occurred in any of the countries to which the PTA applies. That is, it allows the exporting country of the final product to add (cumulate) the value added in other member countries to that added by itself. If the valued added criterion is 40 per cent, and 30 per cent was added in Country 1 and 20 per cent in Country 2, the product would meet the criterion under a cumulative origin system. Under a noncumulative system of origin 40 per cent would have to be added in each country. Noncumulative rules of origin are much more restrictive than rules that allow cumulation.

The more restrictive the rules of origin, the more they will reduce the extent of liberalization implied by the FTA. In an empirical analysis of trade between the EU and individual EFTA countries—each of which in principle had duty-free access to the EU—Herin (1986) found that the costs associated with satisfying the rules of origin imposed by the EU were high enough to induce 25 per cent of EFTA exports to enter the EU by paying the applicable MFN tariff.

GATT-1947 working parties were not able agree whether rules of origin are covered by Article XXIV:8. For example, in the context of the 1972 FTA between the EEC and EFTA States, the US argued that the rules of origin would generate

...trade diversion by raising barriers to third countries' exports of intermediate manufactured products and raw materials. This resulted from unnecessarily high requirements for value originating within the area. In certain cases...the rules disqualify goods with value originating within the area as high as 96 per cent. The rules of origin limited non-originating components to just five per cent of the value of a finished product of the same tariff heading [for] nearly one-fifth of all industrial tariff headings. In many other cases a 20 per cent rule applied.   (GATT, 1974: 152–3)

Although it would appear that rules of origin are unambiguously detrimental to the welfare of participating countries, this is not necessarily the case. Duttagupta and Panagariya (2007) demonstrate that restrictive rules of origin can raise welfare by reducing the magnitude of trade diversion in trade in final goods. However, intuition suggests that in most cases, restrictive rules such as the triple transformation or yarn-forward rules used for textile products in NAFTA (products must be made from cloth embodying yarn

(cont.)

> **Box 10.2. (Continued)**
>
> originating within the region) will be costly to consumers (Krueger, 1999). The obvious solution is to pursue harmonization—e.g. for WTO members to agree to use the (non-preferential) WCO rules (see Chapter 5). Alternatively, they could lower external MFN tariffs to zero as this would remove the need for rules of origin! As discussed below, in practice the EU has pursued a regional harmonization strategy and has put in place a system under which there is cumulation to reduce the costs of rules of origin.

duties on other tariff lines, or to otherwise provide compensation. Where agreement on compensatory adjustment cannot be reached within a reasonable period from the initiation of negotiations, the customs union is free to modify or withdraw the concessions and affected members are free to withdraw substantially equivalent concessions (to retaliate).

The 1994 Understanding established a ten-year maximum for the transition period for implementation of an agreement, although allowance is made for exceptional circumstances (to be defended in the Council for Trade in Goods). Working parties are called upon to make appropriate recommendations concerning interim agreements—PTAs with a transitional implementation period—as regards the proposed time period and the measures required to complete the formation of the PTA. If an interim agreement does not include a plan and schedule, the working party must recommend one. Parties to a PTA may not implement it if they are not prepared to modify it in accordance with the recommendations. Implementation of the recommendations is subject to subsequent review.

Developing countries are not bound by Article XXIV as a result of the 1979 Decision on Differential and More Favorable Treatment of Developing Countries (the so-called Enabling Clause—see Chapter 12). This essentially removes the 'substantially all trade' test and allows for preferences between developing country PTA members (that is, the full removal of internal barriers—free trade—is not required). For example, Mercosur (a customs union) was notified to GATT under the Enabling Clause, not under Article XXIV.

GATS Article V: Economic Integration

The GATS is similar to the GATT in allowing for PTAs that liberalize trade in services on a discriminatory basis, subject to conditions and surveillance. The relevant provision, Article V GATS, is entitled Economic Integration, not Free Trade Areas and Customs Unions (as is Article XXIV GATT), reflecting the fact that the GATS covers not only cross-border trade in services but also the three other modes of supply. Article V GATS imposes three conditions on economic integration agreements. First, such agreements must have substantial sectoral coverage, in terms of the number of sectors, volume of trade affected and modes of supply. Preferential trade agreements may not provide for the a priori exclusion of any mode of supply. Second, PTAs must provide for the absence or elimination of substantially all measures violating national treatment in sectors where specific commitments were made in the GATS. This must be achieved at the entry into force of the agreement or within a reasonable time frame. Third, PTAs may not result in higher trade barriers against third countries.

The substantial sectoral coverage requirement is weaker than the 'substantially all trade' criterion of Article XXIV. The same conclusion applies regarding the criteria on the magnitude of liberalization required and the external policy stance of the PTA, as the benchmark is not free trade among PTA members, but the specific commitments made under the GATS by the PTA members. As discussed in Chapter 7, most of these are far from implying free trade. Those members of the WTO engaged in economic integration efforts intending to withdraw or modify specific market access or national treatment commitments (raise external barriers) must follow the re-negotiation procedures set out in Article XXI GATS (Modification of Schedules—see Chapter 9).

There are a number of loopholes allowing for the formation of agreements that do not fully comply with multilateral disciplines. For example, Article V:2 of the GATS allows for consideration to be given to the relationship between a particular PTA and the wider process of economic integration among member countries. Article V:3 gives developing countries involved in a PTA flexibility regarding the realization of the internal liberalization requirements and allows them to give more favourable treatment to firms that originate in PTA members. That is, it allows for discrimination against firms originating in nonmembers, even if the latter are established within the area. These special and differential treatment type of provisions are unlikely to be very effective in achieving their presumed objective: attracting FDI. More importantly, they weaken the scope of multilateral disciplines, giving governments (interest groups) an opportunity to pursue agreements that are more detrimental to nonmembers.

Effectiveness of WTO disciplines

As mentioned, GATT experience in enforcing Article XXIV was disappointing, to put it mildly. Although Article XXIV is far from perfect from an economic perspective—more on this in the next section—in principle it imposes serious discipline, especially after the Uruguay Round Understanding. Despite the replacement of working parties by a single Committee on Regional Trade Agreements to review the compliance of PTAs, as under GATT 1947, agreement on whether a PTA satisfied Article XXIV and Article V proved impossible during the 1995–2007 period. The only exception was the customs union between the Czech and Slovak

Republics—not surprising given that the two countries were a federation prior to their 'velvet divorce' in January 1993. (As both countries are now EU members, this customs union no longer applies.) As under GATT, the reason for this impotence is the consensus rule.

In December 2006 the WTO General Council established a new transparency mechanism for PTAs. The mechanism—a product of the Doha Round Negotiating Group on Rules—imposes the obligation on members to inform the WTO Secretariat on newly launched negotiations as well as newly signed PTAs. Notified PTAs will be considered on the basis of a factual presentation by the WTO Secretariat, with the process to be concluded within one year of notification. Any member of the WTO may ask questions or make comments concerning factual presentations of PTAs and the implementation of the liberalization commitments relating to PTAs should be notified to the WTO Secretariat. Agreements falling under Article XXIV of GATT and GATS Article V will be considered by the Committee on Regional Trade Agreements (CRTA). Trade arrangements between developing countries falling under the Enabling Clause will be reviewed by the Committee on Trade and Development. The transparency mechanism was implemented on a provisional basis in 2007 and was expected to be reviewed and adopted on a permanent basis as part of the overall results of the Doha Round (WT/L/671, 18 December 2006).

The transparency mechanism for PTAs may help move the balance of assessments of PTAs back towards what was intended by the drafters of the GATT—*ex ante* review and engagement by the collective membership on the design of a PTA, as opposed to what gradually emerged over time: ineffectual *ex post* assessments (Mavroidis, 2007). However, the track record to date suggests that multilateral scrutiny is unlikely to be an effective source of discipline on PTAs. The Doha Round transparency mechanism does not have any teeth, and it was clear from the deliberations that preceded the creation of the mechanism that many WTO members do not intend to use it as a means of exerting greater pressure on countries to abide by the rules. The fact that they call the process 'consideration' of a PTA as opposed to 'examination' of a PTA is quite revealing in this regard.

That said, greater transparency may have an indirect effect by supporting greater scrutiny of PTAs by citizens of the countries concerned. It may also facilitate greater use of the WTO dispute settlement mechanism to contest specific aspects of PTAs. It is rather puzzling that relatively little use has been made of dispute settlement procedures to contest the operation or design of PTAs after 1995. In principle nothing constrains a WTO member from invoking Article XXIV or Article V—it is not necessary that the CRTA has come to a conclusion on whether a PTA complies with the WTO rules to contest the operation of a PTA. During the GATT period the incentive to bring a case was greatly reduced by the consensus rule that applied to both the establishment of a panel and the adoption of panel reports. But this constraint disappeared with the establishment of the WTO.

To date, there have been two disputes where conformity with Article XXIV was a factor. The first was a 1996 case brought by India against Turkey, regarding Turkey's imposition of quantitative restrictions on imports of textile and clothing products. These were imposed by Turkey as a result of a customs union agreement with the EU—the restrictions were applied by the EU so that Turkey had no choice but to apply them too. The DSB established a panel, which found that Turkey's measures were inconsistent with Articles XI and XIII GATT—the ban on quantitative restrictions. Of interest to this chapter, the panel rejected Turkey's assertion that its measures were justified by Article XXIV GATT. On appeal, the Appellate Body upheld the panel's conclusion that Article XXIV of GATT 1994 does not allow Turkey to adopt, upon the formation of a customs union with other WTO members, measures that are inconsistent with other WTO disciplines. However, the Appellate Body also concluded that the legal interpretation of Article XXIV by the panel was erroneous, and determined that a panel should *first* ascertain whether a PTA complies with Article XXIV before considering other GATT provisions. This appears to opens a rather large door to disputes.

A second case was brought in 2001 by Korea against the US, which had imposed safeguard measures on imports of circular welded carbon quality line pipe (steel products) but exempted its NAFTA partners. As in the India–Turkey dispute, the case was decided on the basis of other WTO provisions—in this case the Agreement on Safeguards—but of interest is the discussion of the Article XXIV defence invoked by the US. In *US—Line Pipes* Korea maintained that a PTA must be presumed inconsistent with Article XXIV until the CRTA makes a determination to the contrary (which of course it never has). However, the Panel held that because Korea did not refute the evidence provided by the US to the CRTA when it notified NAFTA, there was a prima facie case of consistency of NAFTA with Article XXIV. In the report on NAFTA submitted by the US to the CRTA, the US stated that duties on 97 per cent of the NAFTA-parties' tariff lines would be eliminated within 10 years. With respect to other regulations of commerce—which include safeguards—the report made a reference to the principle of national treatment, transparency and a variety of other market access rules (WT/DS34/AB/R, October 2001).

Mavroidis (2006) has argued that there is great scope to use dispute settlement to directly address instances where PTAs do not comply with Article XXIV GATT and/or Article V GATS. The additional transparency that will be generated as a result of the 2006 transparency mechanism may facilitate moving down this track. But Mavroidis also notes that the spread of PTAs is now such that virtually all WTO members are implicated and are thus likely to worry about the potential adverse consequences of using the DSU to attack a specific PTA. Fundamentally, the problem of using the DSU to deal with perceived nonconforming PTAs is the fact that disputes must be brought by a specific WTO member, i.e. the multilateral enforcement that is in principle needed given the resulting collective action problem simply does not exist.

Experience to date suggests that multilateral surveillance will only have a limited impact on the design and content of PTAs. An implication is that the payoff to efforts to strengthen specific WTO disciplines on PTAs is likely to be low, even if agreement could be attained. More fundamentally, it has been argued that efforts to devise a realistic rule that will ensure the trade policy stance of a PTA will be welfare-improving for members *and* the rest of the world are doomed to failure (Winters, 1999). There is simply no way to square the circle. As has been noted by many observers, the proliferation of PTAs extant clearly illustrates that WTO members regard PTAs as being in their interest. Thus, what matters is the economics—the incentives that are created by the proliferation of PTAs as regards the average level of MFN protection. That said, the rules are not irrelevant. In particular, they have had a major impact on the trade relations of a significant number of developing countries with the EU. As discussed in Chapter 12, an important reason why the EU concluded EPAs with ACP countries was to replace a system of unilateral preferences that violated GATT rules (and thus required a waiver) with a set of reciprocal trade agreements that satisfied Article XXIV. Interestingly, given the long history of nonenforcement of WTO rules in this area, it was the EU itself that was the 'enforcer' of Article XXIV, in that the desired trade coverage ratio of the EPAs was determined by the EU's view of what is the minimum required by Article XXIV.

10.3. TRADING BLOCS AND THE TRADING SYSTEM

A key factor determining the importance of the effective absence of multilateral disciplines is the extent to which PTAs have detrimental effects on nonmembers and how they react. For the trading system what matters are the dynamic forces that are created by PTAs—do they create incentives that lead to a reduction in the external barriers of PTAs and nonmembers? As is the case for trade policy more generally, the most powerful pressures for reform are almost invariably domestic, not external, although external forces can help support domestic constituencies that favour a more liberal trade regime. That suggests a focus on the economic impacts of PTAs on interest groups.

What follows briefly considers three relevant questions in this regard. First, what is the impact of PTAs on trade and welfare of members? Second, what are the consequences for nonmembers? Third, what are the incentives created by PTAs once they have been formed for both members and nonmembers in terms of their trade policy strategies?

Impacts of PTAs on members

The effects of a PTA are determined by their coverage and design and on whether and how they are implemented. If a PTA is not implemented it cannot have an effect. Many of the PTAs negotiated since the 1960s were only partially implemented, if at all, or else excluded so many industries and tariff lines that their trade effects could only be minimal. The more recent vintage PTAs are generally implemented, and as mentioned tend to have more substantial coverage of merchandise trade flows.

Empirical research assessing the magnitude of the trade impacts shows, not surprisingly, that PTAs increase trade between members. That is, after the PTA is implemented, one observes greater trade flows between members. The difficulty for researchers, however, is to establish whether there is a causal effect. In a world where countries and thus trade is growing one would expect more intra-PTA trade without a PTA. Matters are compounded by countries also undertaking unilateral liberalization at the same time or before they engage in PTAs—what then is driving increased intra-PTA trade?

This suggests that empirical evaluations of PTA impacts must compare outcomes to what would have happened absent the PTA (the counterfactual). This is very difficult if not impossible as the PTA exists after all. What can be done, however, is to control for other factors and variables that affect trade flows. The basic workhorse tool that tends to be used to assess the effects of PTAs is the gravity model. This is a model that has been shown to be very effective at explaining trade volumes between country pairs, and that is consistent with what economic theory predicts are the determinants of trade. In a nutshell it postulates that trade between two countries is a function of their size, their wealth, their distance from each other, whether they are contiguous and speak the same language, and policy variables. The latter include the existence of a PTA.

Much of the literature on this subject is summarized by Schiff and Winters (2003). Surprisingly, there is no agreement on whether PTAs lead to more intra-PTA trade—indeed some studies find a negative effect. More recent research using the gravity model by Baier and Bergstrand (2007) argues that the findings of much of this literature greatly understate the trade effects of PTAs because they ignore the political economy of trade policy, i.e. why the PTA was negotiated in the first place. Technically, what researchers often assume is that the formation of a PTA is exogenous. In practice it is not likely to be—instead the level of trade can be expected to determine whether or not to join a PTA. If account is taken of this endogeneity, the impact of PTAs on trade volumes with partner countries rises significantly. On average PTAs do have a significant effect on intra-PTA trade: according to Baier and Bergstrand (2007) on average a FTA doubles trade between two members after ten years.

Of course, more trade is not necessarily good from a welfare perspective. What matters is how much of what is observed is trade creation and how much is diversion. Not surprisingly, empirical assessments of the impact of PTAs do not come to uniform conclusions. Much depends on the structure of trade before and after the formation of the PTA, on the pattern of comparative advantage, the size and composition of the PTA, etc. That said, many PTAs have been found to generate trade diversion. For example, in a study of eight major PTAs over the 1970–92 period, Frankel, Wei and Stein (1997) found that increases in intra-bloc trade were accompanied by reductions in trade with nonmembers, i.e. generated trade diversion. Similarly, Soloaga and Winters (2001), focusing on nine major PTAs over the period 1980–96, found trade diversion in European PTAs (explained by the fact that little external liberalization occurred during this period relative to intra-PTA liberalization), whereas PTAs among developing countries saw trade increase with both members and nonmembers. The explanation for this is that trade policies were reformed by the developing countries more generally, i.e. reforms were not limited to preferential liberalization. Controlling for developments in general (MFN) trade policies, the non-European PTAs had no independent effect on intra-PTA trade flows (Schiff and Winters, 2003: 42–3).

Very detailed analysis at the HS six-digit level of disaggregation (some 5,000 products) of the impact of the FTA between Canada and the US and the subsequent NAFTA by Romalis (2005) provides clear evidence of trade diversion. He shows that the greatest increases in US imports from Mexico occurred in items on which the US imposes the highest MFN tariffs, i.e. those goods where NAFTA provides Mexico with the highest preferential tariff margins. A similar result obtains for Canada. Although overall welfare effects of NAFTA for the US are small, one reason for this is the trade diversion, which results in higher prices of protected goods. Romalis (2005) also finds that volume effects are significant: NAFTA increases trade between Mexico and both Canada and the US by almost 25 per cent. Thus, studies suggest that there may well be significant market access and terms of trade benefits for countries joining a PTA, as well as distributional effects—with consumers paying the costs of any trade diversion.

Clearly, a narrow focus on merchandise trade is inadequate to assess the effects of PTAs. As, if not more, important, are the impacts on investment and FDI, and the associated potential for the acquisition and diffusion of technology, and the extent and implications of the 'deeper integration' dimensions of PTAs. Many studies have found that 'serious' PTAs may encourage FDI inflows and that these in turn can generate positive productivity spillovers (Schiff and Winters, 2003). There is nothing automatic about such investment and spillover effects, however. The experience of some 20 developing countries between 1980 and 2000 illustrates that many PTAs have not led to significant new FDI inflows (World Bank, 2005).

Impacts of PTAs on nonmembers

From the perspective of the trading system, the impacts of PTAs on nonmembers is the relevant question. Economists sometimes argue that a necessary condition for PTAs not to be detrimental to nonmembers is that the volume of imports by member countries from the rest of the world not decline on a product-by-product basis after the implementation of the agreement (McMillan, 1993). The empirical literature suggests that the trade volume test has been met in the past. Although the intensity of intra-regional trade increased in the second half of the twentieth century, the propensity of regions to trade with the rest of the world, expressed as a percentage of their GDP, has also expanded (Anderson and Norheim, 1993). Global integration—as measured by trade flows and capital flows—does not appear to have been affected negatively by PTAs.

As pointed out by Winters (1997), the 'trade volume test' is a flawed one in that it does not guarantee that nonmembers are not hurt by a PTA. For the welfare of nonmembers what matters is the impact of a PTA on trade flows and the associated change in prices. Even if the Article XXIV conditions are met, and even if the net aggregate imports of PTA members do not contract, imports of particular products by the region may decline *ex post*, or prices received by exporters may fall, harming producers in the rest of the world.

The converse of the trade diversion discussed above is that it implies a decline in exports for nonmember countries to a PTA, and perhaps an overall decline in aggregate exports if the diverted trade cannot be redirected to other markets and sold at the same price. Schiff and Winters (2003) discuss much of the literature, which finds that nonmembers have at times experienced significant reductions in exports. In the case of NAFTA, Romalis (2005) concludes that every 1 per cent reduction in intra-NAFTA tariffs causes a decline in exports to NAFTA from the rest of the world ranging from 1.3 to 3.9 per cent. Although such findings are suggestive, a more appropriate measure of the welfare impact of a PTA on nonmembers is to focus on what happens to their export prices in PTA markets after the agreement is formed. Chang and Winters (2002) show that Brazil's membership of Mercosur was accompanied by a improvement in Brazil's external terms of trade. Exporters based in the US, EU, Japan and Korea all saw the relative prices of many of their goods on the Brazilian market fall. There is also some evidence of negative investment effects (Baldwin, Forslid and Haaland, 1996).

Limão (2006) and Karacaovali and Limão (2008) have shown that in the case of both the EU and the US, PTAs may be a force working against nonmembers: they find that both the EU and the US made fewer (shallower) multilateral (MFN) liberalization commitments in the Uruguay Round on tariff lines where there were significant preference margins for imports from their preferential trading partners. Limão (2007) hypothesizes that this may reflect the use of market access as 'payment' for concessions by PTA partners in nontrade areas. Whatever the rationale, this is evidence that PTAs can have stumbling block effects.

Thus, notwithstanding the fact that there is little evidence of large-scale negative effects of the spread of PTAs—as reflected in the steady increase in world trade and openness discussed in Chapter 1—the economic literature suggests that there is no justification for complacency regarding the effects of PTAs. Preferential trade agreements impose costs on nonmembers even if they do not raise external levels of protection. Nonmember suppliers become less competitive because they continue to pay tariffs, whereas competing producers from member countries do not. Where there are economies of scale, PTAs may help lower member country firms' costs by expanding their home market. Conversely, they may restrain the ability of firms in nonmembers from realizing economies of scale.

There are various ways through which PTAs may constrain national interest groups and thus foster a more liberal external trade policy (De Melo, Panagariya and Rodrik, 1993). A first can be called the preference-dilution effect: because the region implies a larger political community, each of the politically important interest groups in member countries will have less influence on the design of common policies. The second is a preference-asymmetry effect: because preferences on specific issues are likely to differ across member countries, the resulting need for compromises may increase the probability of more efficient outcomes. The creation of PTAs may also disrupt the formation of rent-seeking interest groups, as these have to reorganize at the regional level, establishing an institutional structure that allows them to agree on a common position. But, PTAs may also facilitate the adoption of less liberal policies. Consumer interests may be harder to defend in a PTA than at the national level, whereas producer interests are more likely to be strengthened than weakened (Tumlir, 1983). Each national producer group may face less opposition when seeking price-increasing policies, and may indeed find support from other producer groups in other countries that pursue their own interests. The need for striking compromises may then result in a less liberal regulatory regime. Moreover, it may be in the interest of national politicians to let a regional organization satisfy national pressure groups as this is less transparent for domestic voters and can be justified as being necessary to maintain the agreement.

Much will generally depend on the type of PTA that is involved, FTA, customs union or hub-and-spoke system. The first two types differ from the last in that they imply nondiscrimination between the members of the agreement: any benefit granted to member country B by member country A is also available to member country C. Under a hub-and-spoke system this is not necessarily the case: each country negotiates a separate agreement with the hub country, and perhaps with other spoke partner countries as well. A major difference between a FTA and a customs union or common market is that the latter implies a common external trade policy. Whatever the extent of internal liberalization of trade and competition, implementation of a common external trade policy can give rise to an upward bias in the level of external protection over time if import-competing industries pursue instruments of contingent protection such as antidumping actions. Thus, there may be no net increase in external trade barriers at the formation of a customs union, but there can easily be an upward trend if contingent protection is maintained. In contrast, FTAs have a different dynamic, as members in some sense compete in their external trade policies. Although the political economy of FTAs versus customs unions is complex, on balance, FTAs are likely to be more liberal than customs unions (Box 10.3).

Box 10.3. Pressures for protection: FTAs and customs unions

Under a customs union or common market the potential returns to protection-seeking will be higher than under a FTA: the expected payoff for a unit of lobbying effort increases because the size of the protected market is bigger. Moreover, liberal-minded governments that join a customs union may find it impossible to prevent domestic industries from seeking protection or to block the imposition of protection. For example, it may be the case that certain countries did not use (or make available) contingent protection before joining a customs union. However, once a member country, any domestic firm has access to the central trade policy authority and will be able to petition for AD. Indeed, the welfare gains to liberal countries from joining a customs union that employs contingent protection are reduced, as consumers are faced with higher expected levels of protection without knowing which industries will be affected (Hoekman and Leidy, 1993).

More generally, once a common external trade policy applies, decision-making structures may be biased toward more rather than less protection because of the so-called restaurant bill problem. If a group goes to a restaurant and shares the cost of the bill, each has an incentive to order more expensive dishes than they would if they ate on their own, as to some extent the others are expected to pick up part of the cost. The same is true in the EU (Winters, 1994b). The costs of protection are borne by all EU consumers, and are roughly proportional to each country's GDP. Benefits accruing to producers are proportional to the share of each country in total EU production of the good concerned. This establishes an incentive for each government to pursue protection for those products where their share of total EU production exceeds their country's share of EU GDP. Thus, the Netherlands may not like the EU-wide protection for cars sought by France and Italy, but may accept it if other policies are adopted for products in which it is relatively specialized (such as agriculture). Indeed, if larger countries are able to get the Commission to propose protectionist policies in specific areas, all EU member states have an incentive to ensure that some of their producers also obtain protection.

The external trade policy bias towards protection that may arise under a customs union will be weaker in a FTA. Because there is no common external trade policy, member countries compete in their external trade policies. Industries cannot lobby for area-wide protection. Although import-competing firms in member countries may have an incentive to obtain such protection, each industry will have to approach its own government. The required coordination and cooperation may be more difficult to sustain than in a customs union where the centralization of trade policy requires firms to present a common front. In any particular instance, some member country governments will award protection, whereas others will not. If industries in member countries are all

(cont.)

Box 10.3. (*Continued*)

competing against third suppliers, protection by one member may benefit industries in other member states. Such free riding can result in less protection than in the absence of the FTA (Deardorff, 1994). This benefit may be offset by other aspects of FTAs, in particular the need for rules of origin, which may allow industries to limit the extent of intra-area liberalization and can be detrimental to nonmembers (see Box 10.2 above).

Some evidence is beginning to emerge that supports these theoretical considerations on the likely dynamics of FTAs versus customs unions. Rigorous empirical research on the relationship between preferential and MFN tariffs over time is sparse as a result of data constraints—information on the implementation of PTAs and the sequencing over time between unilateral and preferential tariff reduction is not available for many PTAs. In the case of Latin America, however, a study by Estevadeordal, Freund and Ornelas (2008) concludes that the preferential tariff reduction following PTA formation in Latin America promotes subsequent external tariff reduction for those PTAs that are not customs unions. Bohara, Gawande and Sanguinetti (2004), focusing on the impact of preferential trade flows from Brazil to Argentina, find that greater imports from Brazil led to lower MFN tariffs in Argentina, especially in sectors where trade diversion occurred as a result of Mercosur. As the potential for trade diversion is especially great for South-South PTAs—because developing countries tend to have relatively high external trade barriers—the associated costs provide a powerful force for multilateralization: lowering external barriers to trade will reduce such costs.

Responses by nonmembers to PTA proliferation

As stressed by Bhagwati (1991), from the perspective of the WTO a key question is whether PTAs are a stepping stone or a stumbling block for multilateral liberalization. There is no consensus on the answer. Indeed, given that PTAs differ so much, there is no reason to expect a single, simple answer, especially as this is inherently a dynamic question—the answer depends critically on how PTAs affect the incentives of pro- and antitrade forces in both PTAs and excluded countries.

The most obvious reaction of third countries to the formation of a PTA is to seek a reduction in the bloc's external trade barriers through a MTN. As noted, this arguably has been a key role of the WTO in practice, with regional integration in Europe becoming a recurrent reason for MTNs under GATT auspices. Much of the Dillon Round (1960–1; see Chapter 4), was devoted to renegotiating a balance of concessions subsequent to the implementation of the EEC's common external tariff.

The same type of objectives played a role in the Kennedy and Tokyo Rounds. At the time of the Kennedy Round, the margins of preference for EEC members had increased substantially, as most of the internal elimination of tariffs had been achieved. 'The record leaves no doubt that a compelling factor in the decision of Congress to pass legislation authorizing a 50 per cent linear cut in tariffs [in the Kennedy Round, see Chapter 4] ... was the belief that the Common Market posed a potentially serious threat to the growth, and perhaps even maintenance of American exports' (Patterson, 1966: 176). Thus, 'the task of the Kennedy Round...was to attempt to mitigate [the] disruptive trade effects of European economic integration' (Preeg, 1970: 29). Some success was achieved, as the Kennedy Round reportedly prevented one-third to one-half of the trade diversion that might have occurred from European integration (ibid.: 220).

The first enlargement of the EEC in 1973—to include Denmark, Ireland and the UK—was a factor behind the launching of the Tokyo Round. The CAP also played a role. A major objective of the US was to improve its market access for agricultural products and to curb the EU's use of export subsidies. Links between regional integration and the Uruguay Round included the adoption of the Single European Act (the 1992 programme), the implementation of the Canada–US FTA, the negotiations on the NAFTA, and the continuing distortions of world agricultural trade induced by the CAP. The foregoing is not to say that PTAs are good because they give countries an incentive to pursue concurrent MTN-based liberalization. Without the EEC, much more progress might have been made towards multilateral liberalization (Winters, 1994b).

Another policy option is to seek to join existing PTAs. The primary example here is again the EU, which expanded from six to 27 member states between 1957 and 2007. In North America, Mexico was induced to seek accession to a Canada-US FTA, with the result being a re-negotiated trilateral FTA, the NAFTA. Other nations have negotiated FTAs with each of the NAFTA members in turn. One motivation for this is market access 'insurance'. The goal is not necessarily so much to obtain duty-free access to the regional market, as average MFN tariffs are relatively low for most products, and many potential members tend to be treated preferentially in any event. More important is the elimination of uncertainty, including the threat of contingent protection. This may be complemented by a desire to enhance the credibility of recently undertaken unilateral liberalization and structural reform efforts. However, particularly important are likely to be the firms in nonmember states that see their competitors get access to an ever larger internal market, allowing them to realize economies of scale and benefit from a reduction in real trade costs. This may well give rise to the 'domino effects' that have been observed in the case of the EU and NAFTA (Baldwin, 1995). Examples of such domino effects abound, especially in the European context. As mentioned at the beginning of this chapter, the EU has numerous PTAs with third countries.

The creation of a PTA may also generate incentives for third countries to pursue PTAs in turn. This may be a defensive rationale, reflecting a desire to strengthen their bargaining position vis-à-vis major trading partners and allow them to 'better defend themselves against discriminatory effects of other regional groups' (Patterson 1966: 147). The formation of EFTA is an example. It was established in 1960 in reaction to the formation of the EEC. Its membership consisted of European countries that did not want to join the EEC because of concerns relating to the supranational aspects of the EEC and the likely level of the common external tariff (most EFTA countries tended to be relatively liberal). The EFTA reaction to the formation of the EEC was not unique. Japan informally proposed a Pacific Free Trade Area with the US, Canada, Australia and New Zealand in the mid-1960s for the same reason (De Melo and Panagariya, 1993). More recently, Pacific nations agreed to pursue regional free trade under auspices of the Asian-Pacific Economic Cooperation (APEC) framework. This is an example of so-called open regionalism, where PTAs are used as a focal point for concerted liberalization. Essentially this involves the formation of a privileged group (see Chapter 4). Free riding problems can be expected to be important in such efforts—it is unlikely that APEC will realize the stated goal of free trade by 2020 given the shift by many of the East Asian economies towards the negotiation of formal PTAs. However, as discussed by Baldwin (2006b), the resulting 'noodle bowl' may generate incentives for firms in the region to push more actively for regional, if not global, free trade.

Arguments suggesting PTAs may be detrimental to the trading system often revolve around some variant of the optimal tariff argument. As trade blocs expand, so does their market power and, at least in principle, their ability to influence the terms of trade in their favour. If successful, this is detrimental to the rest of the world. Although possibly true in some cases, it is not a well-founded generalization that PTAs will have an incentive to increase their tariffs against the rest of the world. For one thing, there are big differences between FTAs and customs unions. As already discussed, members of FTAs may have good reasons for lowering tariffs on nonmembers, as this reduces trade diversion.

Baldwin (2006a, b) argues that there may well be positive incentive dynamics resulting from hub-and-spoke PTAs. The domino effects noted previously may move more countries to lower trade barriers, as over time the 'balance of power' between export- and import-competing interests shifts in favour of those bene-fitting from a more open trade regime. Baldwin's theory of how this may play out starts from the premise that at a given point in time export interests see benefit in expanding access to locations where they can undertake parts of their product process and can get their government to negotiate a PTA. Another important part of the story is that the major players are the big markets—such as the EU—so that one result of the process is a hub-and-spoke system of PTAs. This essentially consists of a set of bilateral trade agreements. Because a hub-and-spoke system involves separate agreements between the hub (e.g. the EU) and the spoke countries, there is much scope to exclude 'sensitive sectors' from the coverage of each bilateral agreement (Snape, Adams and Morgan, 1993). Each spoke is likely to have comparative advantage in a somewhat different set of such sectors. If each country maintains contingent protection options (AD, safeguards) against member countries, powerful import-competing industries in the hub country will have an interest in including wide-ranging safeguard clauses and relatively stringent rules of origin.

This was the case in the Association Agreements negotiated between the EU and various Eastern neighbours in 1992 (Winters, 1995). By allowing bilateral deals regarding sectoral coverage and the depth of the agreement, vested interests could be assuaged through specific rules of origin as well as safeguard provisions. The nature of these types of PTAs were such that they allowed for significant internalization of benefits by producers who wanted to restrict as much as possible the (new) regional market for themselves. Such groups also opposed broader multilateral reform. As summarized by Bhagwati (1993), such groups took the view 'the region is our market', and that 'our markets are large enough'.

In the event, however, the political economy equilibrium that underpinned the hub-and-spoke model of major 'systems' of PTAs began to break down. In part as a result of continuous technological change and in part as a result from increasing competition by China firms in Europe began to see an interest in further reducing the cost of production. One way this could be achieved was through reduction of the administrative costs of the hub-and-spoke system, in particular the associated rules of origin. One result was the adoption of the pan-European Cumulation System in 1997, under which any inputs sourced from *any* of the spokes or the EU member states counts for purposes of determining origin, and thus eligibility for duty-free treatment. This is an example of how regionalism may generate forces through which the objective of a multilateral, nondiscriminatory, trade regime might emerge endogenously.

The Baldwin (2006*a*) story is comforting for those who have been worrying about the systemic implications of PTAs. Saggi and Yildiz (2008) offer another, more theoretical, argument for the positive systemic effects of PTAs. They note that the voluminous literature on PTAs and regional integration ignores a key question: would the WTO serve the cause of global free trade more effectively if it did not include the exception to MFN provided by Article XXIV? Would global free trade be easier to achieve if all WTO members were somehow constrained to pursue trade liberalization on only a multilateral basis? The relationship between preferential and multilateral liberalization has been the subject of much theoretical analysis, but Saggi and Yildiz are among the first to treat both bilateral and multilateral liberalization as endogenous and to allow for the fact that countries are not symmetric in size. A central result is that bilateralism can provide an impetus to multilateral trade liberalization. The insight underlying this result is that a country that is choosing whether or not to participate in global free trade must consider how it would fare under the agreement that would emerge in the absence of its participation. Their model has the reasonable feature that a nonparticipating country is worse off under a bilateral trade agreement than under a multilateral agreement—this is because a preferential agreement discriminates against the outsider whereas a multilateral agreement does not. As a result, a country's incentive to opt for free trade is stronger when the alternative to free trade is a bilateral agreement between the other two countries as opposed to a multilateral one. It is noteworthy that this result obtains in their model despite the fact that the formation of a PTA induces its members to impose lower tariffs on the nonmember relative to their Nash equilibrium tariffs, a result referred to as the tariff complementarity effect in the literature. In fact, even though a preferential agreement leads to more trade liberalization than a multilateral agreement in which all countries do not participate, it harms the outsider relatively more precisely due to the discrimination that is inherent to it.

The analysis of Saggi and Yildiz makes two additional points. First, they demonstrate that the debate regarding preferential versus multilateral liberalization is moot in the absence of some type of asymmetry across countries, which in their model implies that the gains generated by a shift from the status quo of noncooperative tariffs to free trade are unequally split across countries.[5] Indeed, they show that under sufficient symmetry, both the preferential and the multilateral route lead to global free trade. A second important insight provided by their analysis is that to properly address the issue of how preferential trade liberalization interacts with multilateral trade liberalization, we need to better understand when and why countries choose to pursue the preferential route given that the multilateral route is available. Only a model in which both types of liberalization are fully endogenous can shed real light on this question.

Deeper integration and PTAs

So-called deep integration has become an increasingly important feature of PTAs over the last decade and a half as border barriers decline. This spans many aspects of product and market regulation, including standards, government procurement, services, investment, competition, labour and environmental policies, as well as IPRs and protection of other intangible and tangible assets.

As is illustrated by Figures 10.2 and 10.3, there is enormous variance across recent PTAs in the scope and depth of these policy areas, with PTAs that involve the United States generally having the broadest coverage. There is evidence that PTAs include more service sectors than countries have scheduled at the WTO, but the available research also suggests that their clauses do not move much beyond those in the WTO (Fink and Molinuevo, 2007; Roy, Marchetti and Lim, 2007). This

---

[5] In a model with repeated interaction, Saggi (2006) had shown that when countries are asymmetric, the exogenous formation of a preferential trade agreement may facilitate multilateral tariff cooperation whereas such a result does not obtain under symmetry.

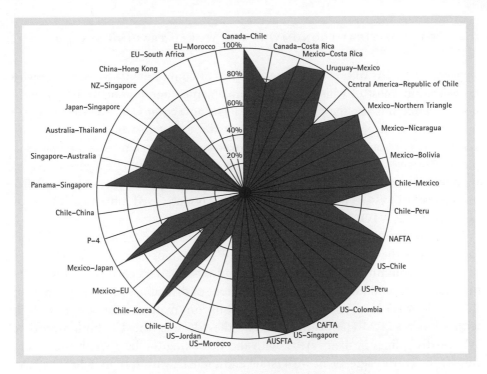

Fig. 10.2. Coverage of 17 investment provisions in selected PTAs

Source: Estavadeordal, Shearer and Suominen 2007.

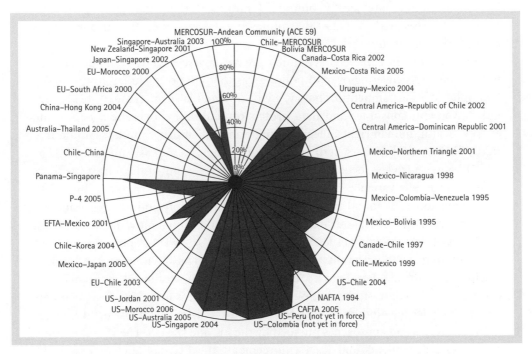

Fig. 10.3. Coverage of 29 services provisions in selected PTAs

Source: Estavadeordal, Shearer and Suominen (2007).

suggests that PTAs may broaden the coverage of commitments to lock-in service liberalization, most of which has been implemented autonomously, but they do not deepen it. It is also the case that many PTAs now cover FDI, whereas the WTO does not. But here again one can question the extent to which disciplines are additional. For example, there are already over 3,000 bilateral investment treaties in place. Moreover, in areas of key importance to the developing countries such as mobility of labour or constraints on the ability of OECD partner countries to offer incentives to investors the bilateral routes have not achieved more than what was possible in the WTO.

How much further than the WTO do PTAs go? Horn, Mavroidis and Sapir (2008) assess the coverage of 14 US and 14 EU PTAs, focusing on the prevalence of WTO+ commitments (provisions that address matters covered by the WTO but that go beyond the WTO in terms of extent of disciplines imposed) and what they call WTO-X commitments: provisions on matters that are not dealt with in the WTO. They conclude that the EU and the US both negotiate WTO+ disciplines in many areas, with the US taking the lead. With the exception of the (early) agreement with Israel and the PTA with Jordan, US PTAs have additional disciplines in almost all the categories distinguished by the authors: industrial market access; agriculture; customs; export taxes; SPS; TBT; STEs: AD; CVDs: subsidies; procurement; TRIMs; services and IPRs. Moreover, these WTO+ disciplines are legally binding (enforceable). In the case of the EU PTAs, the areas with WTO+ disciplines are fewer, in particular for export taxes, SPS, TRIMs and services.

The EU PTAs in contrast have much greater coverage of WTO-X provisions, with some PTAs covering over 30 policy areas that are not included in the WTO. Examples include competition policy, environmental laws, investment, IPRs, capital movement, consumer and data protection, cultural cooperation, education, energy, health, human rights, illegal immigration, illicit drugs, money laundering, R&D, SMEs, social matters, statistics, taxation, and visa and asylum policies. The US PTAs are much less focused on WTO-X policy areas, but at the same time there is also much less variance in the subjects that are covered. They are limited to anticorruption (not found in any EU PTA), competition policy, environmental laws, investment, IPRs, labour market regulation and capital movement. Although the EU is clearly the 'market leader' when it comes to WTO-X provisions, about three-quarters of the relevant articles in the EU PTAs do not impose binding disciplines. Instead, they tend to constitute soft law—technical assistance and cooperation. In contrast, the disciplines in WTO-X areas found in US agreements are generally legally binding (that is, enforceable). This reflects a distinct difference in the strategies and approaches pursued by the EU and the US. The US relies more on binding agreements and legal enforcement, the EU has tended to put the emphasis on embedding technical assistance and other forms of cooperation in its PTAs, and supplementing this with financial aid and policy/political dialogue.

This 'softer' approach is a basic premise of the EU's European Neighbourhood Policy, for example (Hoekman, 2007). Which approach will prove to be more influential in setting standards remains to be seen.

From the perspective of members a key question is whether 'deeper integration' provisions are beneficial in and of themselves, or simply a cost that must be paid to obtain preferential access to major markets. We return to that question in Chapter 13 as it is one that obtains in the WTO context as well. From the perspective of nonmembers and the trading system the basic question is the same as discussed above: what is the impact on them of deeper integration among subsets of countries in PTAs? This depends both on the extent of discrimination that is implied and on the scope for cooperation in a PTA context to increase the likelihood that the norms set by PTAs become the de facto standard or the focal point for subsequent multilateral cooperation in the WTO (or elsewhere).

The prospects for the 'multilateralization' of PTA commitments in these areas may be significant. In many cases regulation is quite naturally applied in a nondiscriminatory fashion, treating domestic and all overseas suppliers or firms equally—where 'domesticity' is defined more frequently in terms of location of production than ownership. This is quite different from tariffs and NTBs affecting trade in goods, where domestic/foreign and intra-foreign discrimination is the objective. From the perspective of achieving regulatory objectives, nationality often will (and should) not matter. But even if regulation applies to all sources of supply, it can still have the effect of segmenting markets and reducing competition.

If liberalization—defined as taking actions to enhance the contestability of a market—is more likely to be nondiscriminatory for regulations than for merchandise trade barriers, it is, equally, less likely to come about at all. This is because it is inherently more far-reaching and because it is simultaneously necessary and very difficult to distinguish between regulations that are genuinely needed for the achievement of domestic objectives and those that are oriented towards segmenting markets and protecting domestic incumbents. In practice it is certainly not inevitable that regulations are applied on a nationality-blind basis—insofar as protectionism is an objective of policymakers, regulation can be (and is) used to achieve this. One reason is that the legitimate, nonprotectionist class of regulation frequently requires the acquiescence of domestic firms if it is to be implemented effectively and almost always entails consulting those firms about any reforms. With the complex and subtle nature of many regulations, incumbents (and national regulators) will have a great deal of influence over regulatory structures and details, and may well have veto power over policymakers.

For cooperation on product market regulation and domestic policies in PTAs one can envisage three different processes of multilateralization (Hoekman and Winters, 2009). First, hegemonic multilateralization: a hegemonic economic power is essentially able to impose its own model on its partners, not necessarily coercively but by the force of its market size. As different partners adopt the hegemon's approach over their own local one, a degree of multilateralism is achieved. And it is possible that as the partners enter further bilateral or regional arrangements with other partners the model is extended. As Schiff and Winters (2003) observe, the accretion of two different groups of supporters around two different models—say a US and a EU model—could make the final multilateral step (harmonization or recognition of equivalence) less rather than more likely. But, if a high degree of similarity or consistency is achieved, goods and services designed for one market can be sold elsewhere, greatly increasing the contestability of markets. Examples of the hegemonic model abound in 'deep integration'. The US requires partners in Bilateral Investment Treaties (BITs) to conform to an identical template and imposes its own intellectual property right (IPR) protection provisions in its PTAs—World Bank (2005). Another example is the EU interest in extending its system of geographical indications through its PTAs (see Chapter 8).

The second route to multilateralism is a convergence route. This operates within a PTA where the erosion of barriers to trade increases the pressure to harmonize regulations because they start to have greater impact on trade patterns, competitiveness and profitability. This is essentially the 'competition between rules' that featured in the EU's Single Market programme, which applies equally to goods and services. It depended, in the case of goods, not only on the removal of traditional barriers to intra-EU trade (tariffs, quotas, etc.) but on the aggressive policy of the European Commission and European Court of Justice towards other limitations on the freedom of movement of goods such as product standards (where the principle of mutual recognition was applied). In services the political sensitivity of the convergence route is evident in the constrained liberalization of cross-border services espoused by the recent Services Directive in the EU and the difficulties that have affected efforts by the EU and the US to make progress in moving towards accepting each other's regulatory norms for specific services as being effectively 'equivalent'. Note that the convergence route also spans a frequently mentioned rationale for PTA-based cooperation in 'non-WTO' areas: PTAs may be a useful forum for experimentation and learning. Successful examples of cooperation between members of a PTA may be adopted in other PTAs (or unilaterally), thus promoting multilateralization over time.

In general, the larger the region or the more important it is as a trading partner, the greater the incentives for a country to adopt the regulatory standards of the PTA. There will often be a link, implicit or explicit, between harmonization of regulatory regimes and the threat of contingent protection. One factor driving harmonization is to reduce the possibility of being confronted with contingent protection. As PTAs increasingly are instruments for such regulatory harmonization, or for the adoption of mutual recognition procedures, the potential cause for concern on the part of nonmembers is obvious. As discussed in Chapter 13, one size fits all is not necessarily optimal.

The third route to multilateralism is the one identified by Baldwin (2006a) for trade in goods—what could be called a political evolution route. Here, changes in the political weight of different parties or in the relative importance of different costs change the political economy so that groups which once sought to segment markets now seek to integrate them. This route is, of course, premised on policies being applied in a discriminatory manner vis-à-vis nonmembers of a PTA and thus will not apply (and will not be needed) if policies are applied on an MFN basis. One difference for deep integration is that, compared with restrictions on goods trade, regulations are complex and require greater complicity from the relevant industry. The strong position of incumbents may make liberalization more difficult; in particular, it is difficult to envisage incumbents in a sector seeking the liberalization of that sector. However, offsetting this is that downstream (using) sectors may have stronger incentives to oppose policies that raise the costs of services than is the case with goods.

Hoekman and Winters (2009) argue that when it comes to 'deeper integration' in PTAs, to date most reform is unilateral. There is very little direct evidence that PTAs do a lot to drive reform. One problem is to determine the direction of causality. One cannot infer from the spread of specific PTA disciplines ('templates') that PTAs are driving reforms beyond what governments had already decided was beneficial autonomously. Most research in this area focuses on legal texts, not on extent to which PTAs imply/require or result in changes in national legislation. It may well be that the source for reform has primarily been knowledge and information—the demonstration effects of successful countries or the general focus of academia and the international community on the benefits of deregulation, competition, etc. Maybe the IMF, World Bank, OECD, APEC, etc., which have been advocating for better policies and more transparency for years are the key: the World Bank's *Doing Business* report may well have been a more potent driver of reforms than the PTAs of which countries were members.

Even if developing countries are adopting disciplines in PTAs and applying them on a MFN basis, this does not imply that the norms concerned are beneficial for them. The content of the norms that are included in PTAs obviously matter. Whether these are autonomously decided or externally imposed, they need to benefit the countries that adopt them and the countries affected by them (the nonmembers). From this perspective, another important priority is the establishment of institutions or other means to help developing countries take an informed view of what they are asked to do in PTA negotiations and how neighbours' PTAs impact upon them. The pressure by high-income countries for developing country PTA partners to adopt TRIPS-plus disciplines is an example.

Finally, the opportunity costs of PTAs in terms of taking up scarce administrative capacity of developing country governments needs to be recognized. One can question whether the negotiation of PTAs is the best use of the limited policy attention and human resources that are available in many low-income countries (Schiff and Winters, 2003). Much depends on the content of a PTA and the strategic use that is made of it. Preferential trade agreements that are not implemented or not used as instruments to realize substantial economic benefits can have a significant opportunity cost in terms of diversion of policy attention and capacity.

10.4. Conclusion

Always a central element of the trade policy strategy of European countries, 'regionalism' has become an important form of international cooperation on trade policy for virtually all the members of the WTO, developed and developing. Although subject to conditions contained in Articles XXIV GATT and V GATS, multilateral disciplines are not enforced. On a number of dimensions they are also weak. An example is the absence of any disciplines with respect to preferential rules of origin in the WTO (Box 10.3). Another is the absence of a requirement that PTAs be open to new members (Bhagwati, 1993). Multilateral surveillance is limited— even if the CRTA were effective, the focus is on WTO tests and not on the economic effects of PTAs. The WTO Secretariat has no mandate to monitor the trade value or terms-of-trade effects of PTAs. Developing countries can opt out of WTO disciplines on PTAs altogether by invoking the Enabling Clause.

Most of the economic literature on PTAs has been theoretical or policy-focused. Rigorous empirical research on the effects of PTAs has been limited until recently. The weight of the empirical analyses of PTAs suggests that if one abstracts from the many PTAs that were never implemented or were designed to have no effect in opening up economies, overall the benefits outweigh the costs, especially if the focus of attention is on the dynamic effects over time. Preferential trade agreements may lead or retard nondiscriminatory reductions in tariffs, but the evidence that is now emerging suggests that PTAs have complemented multilateralism in the sense of promoting lower barriers against the rest of the world.

The proliferation of PTAs has been accompanied by steadily declining barriers to trade generally and high growth rates in world trade. The uniform tariff equivalent of all applied most-favoured-nation tariffs of high-income OECD countries in 2005 was 4.8 per cent. Excluding agricultural products, the figure drops to 2.7 per cent (Kee, Nicita and Olarreaga, 2008). For the developing countries, applied MFN tariffs have also fallen substantially; Kee and colleagues estimate that the median average overall trade restrictiveness index was 7.5 per cent for the 57 countries for which data are available in 2005, compared with 12.3 per cent ten years earlier. Much of this liberalization trend is not due to PTAs. The fact that MFN tariffs have fallen significantly in almost all countries, whatever their participation in PTAs, suggests that unilateral decisions to liberalize have been paramount (Martin and Messerlin, 2007).

Whatever the overall impact of individual PTAs on trade in goods, prices and welfare, to date they do not appear to have had a serious negative effect on the overall trend towards greater openness of economies around the globe. Indeed, a good case can be made that the spread of PTAs has done little to substantially reduce the extent to which trade flows are distorted by preferences, as most of the recent PTAs are (a) between small countries; (b) between countries that have (very) low external protection and many zero-rated MFN duties; and/or (c) exclude those sectors where there is significant protection, e.g. agriculture (Pomfret, 2007).

Restrictive rules of origin and cumulation criteria further reduce the impact of many PTAs. The combination of the exclusion of agriculture and restrictive rules of origin is particularly important in EU PTAs with countries that are not accession candidates. The large export supply response following the implementation of preferential access agreements between the US and some African and Middle Eastern countries—e.g. Lesotho and Jordan—illustrates the importance of including agriculture and using liberal rules of origin for labour-intensive manufactures such as apparel. Both Lesotho and Jordan have preferential access agreements with the EU but have not seen exports to the EU expand because of more restrictive rules of origin than are applied by the US to these two countries.

There is a good case to be made that when it comes to tariffs the evidence is beginning to support those who argue that on net the recent vintages of PTAs have been building blocks. But tariffs increasingly are not at the core of the PTA action, given that average MFN duties have fallen to low levels in major markets. Preferential trade agreements may embody many good practices and some go far beyond the WTO in terms of liberalizing markets. Thus, in the EU there are no tariffs, no safeguard mechanisms and full binding of policies. To a large extent the current benchmark for good practice in trade policy is the set of policies and rules that apply to movement of goods, services, labour and capital inside the EU. The challenge is to pursue multilaterally what the serious PTAs are implementing internally. This has been the trend. Indeed, it appears that developments in PTAs are frequently reflected in analogous developments on the multilateral front. Differences between the PTAs and the multilateral trading system at any point in time have been limited in part because efforts to negotiate PTAs have stimulated concurrent, and largely successful, efforts to achieve further multilateral trade liberalization. Indeed, the multilateral system often leads (Hoekman and Leidy, 1993; Pomfret, 2007).

Preferential trade agreements represent a challenge and an opportunity for the multilateral trading system. The opportunity is to use them as experimental laboratories for cooperation on issues that have not (yet) been addressed multilaterally, especially issues where the outcome is applied on a MFN basis. The challenge is to control the discrimination that is inherent in any PTA. The inability of the CRTA to come to decisions on whether PTAs satisfy Articles XXIV and V is a problem in this regard. Absent such determinations, transparency—through multilateral surveillance—is important, as this helps mobilize domestic and regional groups who are negatively affected by PTA policies.

Both the GATT and GATS contain provisions relating to transparency and multilateral surveillance. Countries intending to form, join or modify a PTA must notify this, and make available relevant information requested by WTO members. Although CRTA efforts to determine the consistency of the agreement with multilateral rules are not effective, they do generate information, especially since 2006 when a new transparency mechanism was established by the WTO General Council. The key need may not be more multilateral disciplines, but greater internal scrutiny by stakeholders in member countries of regional trade policy to ensure that the interests of all groups in society are considered. Although multilateral surveillance can be helpful as an objective source of information and analysis, ultimately, domestic transparency requires domestic political will. Multilateral trade negotiations can and should play a complementary role. At the end of the day, the more successful the WTO is in reducing external barriers of members through MTNs, the less problematical PTAs will be from a systemic and non-member perspective. Attempts to impose stricter rules on PTAs, or to use the dispute settlement system, are unlikely to be fruitful strategies.

10.5. FURTHER READING

The classic original treatment of the economics of regional integration is Jacob Viner, *The Customs Union Issue* (New York: Carnegie Endowment for World Peace, 1953). For an excellent historical discussion of the issue of regionalism and preferential liberalization in the GATT context, see Gardner Patterson, *Discrimination in International Trade: The Policy Issues, 1945–1965* (Princeton: Princeton University Press, 1966).

The literature on the economics of regional integration is surveyed by Richard Baldwin and Anthony Venables, 'International Economic Integration', in Gene Grossman and Kenneth Rogoff (eds), *Handbook of International Economics, vol.3* (Amsterdam: North Holland, 1997) and by Arvind Panagariya, 'Preferential Trade Liberalisation: The Traditional Theory and New Developments', *Journal of Economic Literature*, 37 (June 2000): 287–331. WTO, *Changing Landscape of Regional Trade Agreements* (Geneva: WTO, 2007) surveys the content and coverage of PTAs and provides a number of relevant quantitative and qualitative indicators.

The relationship between regionalism and multilateralism is the subject of L. Alan Winters', 'Regionalism Versus Multilateralism', in Richard Baldwin, Daniel Cohen, André Sapir and Anthony Venables (eds), *Market Integration, Regionalism and the Global Economy* (London: CEPR, 1999). Maurice Schiff and L. Alan Winters, *Regional Integration and Development* (Washington, DC: World Bank, 2003) offer a thoughtful and in-depth assessment of the impact of PTAs on developing countries and the policy options confronting developing country governments.

For a characteristically insightful analysis of the implications of the increasing emphasis on PTAs by governments, see Jagdish Bhagwati, *Termites in the Trade System: How PTAs Undermine Free Trade* (Oxford: Oxford University Press, 2008).

CHAPTER 11

PLURILATERAL AGREEMENTS

THE GATT 1947, a treaty between contracting parties that functioned on the basis of consensus, was very difficult to amend and expand. As discussed in Chapters 1 and 2, in an effort to circumvent this problem, in the 1960s and 1970s groups of like-minded countries that sought to agree on more specific rules for policies covered by the GATT negotiated so-called codes of conduct. These codes bound only signatories, and were mostly applied on a MFN basis. Most of the existing codes were mapped into the WTO during the Uruguay Round, and their disciplines became binding upon all WTO members. They are discussed in Chapters 5 and 9. However, four Tokyo Round codes were not converted into multilateral agreements. Instead they became so-called plurilateral agreements. These bind only signatories and do not have to be applied on a MFN basis. As the WTO has no general MFN obligation—nondiscrimination requirements are contained in each of the various multilateral trade agreements—the plurilateral agreements contained in Annex 4 of the WTO are examples of what has been termed conditional MFN agreements.

Although members are free to discriminate against nonsignatories of a plurilateral agreement, subsets of WTO members cannot simply get together and form a club without the permission of other members. A plurilateral agreement can only be appended to the WTO on the basis of consensus (Article X:9 WTO). The plurilateral option therefore offers a mechanism for groups of WTO members to agree to rules in a policy area that is not covered by the WTO or goes beyond existing disciplines, as long as the membership as a whole perceives this not to be detrimental to their interests.

Of the four Tokyo Round agreements included in Annex 4 of the WTO in 1995, two ceased to apply in September 1997. The International Bovine Meat Agreement and the International Dairy Agreement were terminated after their governing bodies decided that the objectives of the agreements could more effectively be pursued through other WTO bodies, including the Committees on Agriculture and Sanitary and Phytosanitary Measures (they are discussed in Hoekman and Kostecki, 1995). As of 2008, only two plurilateral agreements were operational, the Agreement on Government Procurement and the Agreement on Trade in Civil Aircraft. Of the two, the government procurement agreement is by far the more important.

11.1. Government Procurement

All over the world government agencies procure goods and services as inputs into the production of public goods and services—education, defence, utilities, infrastructure, health and so forth. The size of the associated public procurement market is often very large, depending on the economic system of a nation and its GDP. Governments concerned with maximizing the use of scarce financial resources have developed procedures and mechanisms to attempt to ensure that public entities procure goods and services efficiently. A common element is to mimic the working of the market by requiring that public entities seek competitive bids from potential suppliers of goods and services.

Starting in the 1980s, many governments began to pursue more far-reaching efforts to enhance the efficiency of public services by directly subjecting production units to competitive forces. Examples include privatization of state-owned enterprises, permitting entry of privately owned firms into sectors traditionally reserved for public entities (such as utilities) and contracting out activities to independent suppliers. These developments changed the public procurement market significantly. What was once produced 'in-house' by government entities began to be supplied by private operators—shrinking the public procurement market. But at the same time the overall market for goods and services did not decline—there was simply a shift towards real market-based contracting as opposed to one where the focus was on mimicking the role of the market through competitive bidding for government contracts.

The cost-minimizing goal underlying competitive bidding requirements for purchases by public entities is frequently not attained because legislation requires procuring entities to pursue other objectives as well. These may include a desire to promote the development of domestic industry or technology, to support particular types of firms (such as small- and medium-sized enterprises) and to safeguard national security. Often, such objectives are pursued by requiring procurement practices to be used that discriminate against foreign suppliers. Examples of discriminatory policies pursued by governments include outright prohibitions on foreign sourcing (civil servants must fly national airlines), threshold criteria for foreign sourcing to be permitted (minimum cost or price differentials compared to local suppliers), or satisfaction of offset or local content requirements.

As a result, government procurement policies are often a somewhat schizophrenic exercise in 'constrained cost minimization'. The basic goal is value for money, subject to the other policy goals that need to be taken into account. In practice, these other goals often imply that for all, or part, of any contract the scope of competition is reduced to the set of firms that meet specific criteria laid out in legislation or procurement regulations. In some instances there may not be any competition at all. Governments may use selective or single tendering procedures under which a procuring entity directly approaches a specific firm for a bid. Discriminatory public procurement practices are a major market access issue on the WTO agenda, given that procurement markets account for 5–10 per cent of GDP in most WTO members.

If many countries pursue discriminatory procurement practices, the end result for the world as a whole is likely to be inferior in welfare terms to a cooperative outcome where governments agree to refrain from using procurement as a tool to protect national industries or to pursue noneconomic objectives. After all, governments have other policies that can achieve the other objectives that are pursued through procurement policy—such as subsidies and the tax system. Recognizing this, governments have attempted to negotiate multilateral rules of the game for public procurement. The Tokyo Round Government Procurement Agreement (GPA) was the reflection of such an effort. Liberalization of procurement markets has also been pursued in a regional context. Procurement disciplines are prominent in the EU, where member states are prohibited from discriminating against tenders from foreign firms (be they located in other EU member states or outside Europe). As is the case with IPRs, international cooperation has been driven in part by bilateral pressures. A number of US laws require USTR to monitor foreign procurement policies that impact negatively on US firms, and foreign government procurement figures prominently in the USTR's annual Trade Practices report (see the USTR homepage). The same is true for similar reports issued by the EU (under the Trade Barriers Regulation), Japan and other countries. This pressure is not only focused on discriminatory practices; the US in particular has stressed issues related to transparency and corruption.

Discriminatory procurement policies are often considered prima facie evidence of protectionism—governments explicitly favour domestic suppliers of goods and services. However, procurement policy that gives a price preference of 10 per cent to a local industry or to firms from a specific region or below a certain size is not equivalent to a 10 per cent tariff. This is because demand by the private sector for imports may not be affected by the preference policy. As long as the government market is only a fraction of total demand for a product, as is often the case, the tariff equivalent will only be a fraction of 10 per cent. Indeed, as pointed out by Baldwin and Richardson (1972) in a seminal analysis, if domestic and foreign products are good substitutes and government demand is less than the initial domestic supply capacity, discrimination will have no effect on prices, overall output and welfare. The increased demand by the government for domestic output will be exactly offset by greater private sector imports, so that the policy has no effect on equilibrium prices and production of the domestic industry.

This result continues to obtain if there is imperfect competition (oligopoly) as long as goods are perfect substitutes.[1] Imports might actually increase as a result of discriminatory policy if domestic firms are induced to cut back sales to the private sector in an attempt to raise prices. However, if government demand exceeds local production, discrimination will result in domestic prices being bid up, and output of the domestic industry will expand to meet demand. If allowance is made for the fact that in the longer run firms will enter into markets where there are excess profits, over time prices will fall and at the end of the day the discrimination policy may again have no negative implications for welfare (see Annex 2).

Matters are different if the procurement is for products for which there are just a few suppliers. In such situations there may be potential economic rationale for discrimination. McAffee and McMillan (1989) show that if domestic firms have a competitive disadvantage in producing the product (are higher cost producers compared to foreign firms), and only a limited number of firms (foreign and domestic) bid for the contract, a price preference policy may induce foreign firms to lower their bids. If the products procured are intangible (services) or there are problems in monitoring and enforcing contract compliance, discrimination can increase the likelihood of performance. Problems of asymmetric information and contract compliance may give entities a natural preference to choose suppliers located within their jurisdictions as this can reduce monitoring costs. Such proximity incentives will make it more difficult for foreign firms to bid successfully, even in the absence of formal discrimination. The policy issue that then arises is whether there are barriers against establishment (FDI) by foreign suppliers (Evenett and Hoekman, 2005).

Although discriminatory procurement may enhance national welfare by lowering procurement costs in small numbers settings, simulation studies suggest that welfare gains are likely to be modest at best. Greater profits of domestic firms or cost-savings to public entities will tend to offset by increased prices. As a result, the potential cost-savings are reduced (Deltas and Evenett, 1997). Given that in most

---

[1] As noted by Deardorff and Stern (1998), domestic middlemen will always have an incentive to import a good and resell it to the government after processing it enough to qualify as domestic. The same forces therefore apply if goods are imperfect substitutes. Difficulties in determining the origin of products will always reduce the effectiveness of discriminatory policies, such as procurement preferences, that are not enforced by customs officials. The level of tariffs and NTBs applied at the border will be the main constraint on such arbitrage activities.

instances the optimal discriminatory policy will be difficult to determine (it generally will vary depending on the specifics of the situation), in practice favouritism can be expected to be more costly than a policy of nondiscrimination. In many situations the information required to judge if diverging from nondiscrimination is beneficial will not be available. Nondiscrimination has therefore been argued to be a good rule of thumb (Hoekman, 1998).

If account is taken of the rent-seeking distortions that may be induced by discriminatory policies and the social cost of corruption and bribery, the case for nondiscrimination is substantially strengthened. All of the above arguments regarding the economic pros and cons of discrimination cease to apply if government entities do not maximize social welfare. Nondiscrimination will generally reduce discretion and enhance transparency of the procurement process and thus reduce the scope for rent-seeking. Most important in this connection is transparency and a system of rules to impede corruption. Open and competitive bidding, whether or not there are preferences for domestic industry, is a key instrument in this regard.

The WTO Government Procurement Agreement

As noted in Chapter 5, Article III:8 GATT excludes procurement from the national treatment obligation. Article XIII GATS does the same for services. The 1979 Tokyo Round GPA extended basic GATT obligations such as nondiscrimination and transparency to the purchases of goods by selected government entities. The GPA has been re-negotiated three times. The second, 1996 version of the Agreement, extended its reach to services. The most recent revision of the GPA was provisionally agreed in December 2006 (GPA/W/297). The periodic re-negotiations are mandated by the Agreement itself. Although they have coincided with the Uruguay and Doha Rounds, as a plurilateral agreement, the (re-)negotiations were not formally part of the rounds.

The aim of the latest revision—which significantly re-wrote and re-organized the 1996 version—was to make the GPA more attractive to nonsignatories by simplifying the rules, to reflect advances in information technology and to expand the coverage of the agreement (Anderson, 2007). Final agreement on the 2006 text is conditional on a mutually satisfactory outcome of parallel (and ongoing) negotiations to open up additional government procurement to international competition. A purported objective of the re-organization and redrafting of the text of the GPA was simplification and making it reflect better the process that procuring entities go through. It is not clear that this objective was achieved—in our view in some respects the 1996 text was more transparent and easier to understand.

As a result of the periodic re-negotiations, the coverage of the GPA has expanded substantially over time to include services and more government entities, and its

disciplines clarified and updated to reflect new technologies and procurement practices. Membership of the GPA is limited to mostly OECD countries. As of 2008 it
comprised Canada, the European Communities, the 27 EU member states, the
Netherlands with respect to Aruba, Hong Kong, Iceland, Israel, Japan, Liechten-
stein, Norway, the Republic of Korea, Singapore, Switzerland and the United States.[2]

The GPA applies to 'any measure regarding covered procurement, whether or not
it is conducted exclusively or partially by electronic means' (Article II:1). The concept
of procurement covers all contractual options, including purchase, leasing, rental
and hire purchase, with or without the option to buy.[3] A positive list is used to
determine what procurement is covered. The GPA applies *only* to entities listed in
Appendix I of the agreement. There are three 'entity annexes': Annex 1 lists covered
central government entities; Annex 2 lists subcentral government entities; and Annex
3 lists all other entities that procure 'in accordance with the provisions of this
Agreement'. Annex 3 is a catch-all category that includes bodies such as utilities.
Entities listed in Annex 3 may be partially or totally private. What constitutes a
government entity is nowhere defined in the agreement, reflecting a lack of consensus on what constitutes a public undertaking—more specifically, whether a former
state-owned or controlled enterprise that has been privatized or that is subject to
competition should be required to follow GPA procurement practices. Instead a
pragmatic approach is taken—governments negotiate which entities are listed.

The entities listed in the three annexes are subject to the rules and disciplines
of the GPA with respect to their procurement of goods and services if the value of
the procurement exceeds certain specified thresholds (see Table 11.1) and the
goods or services involved are not exempted from the coverage of the agreement.
As far as goods are concerned, in principle all procurement is covered, unless
specified otherwise in an annex. Procurement of services is subject to a positive
list: only the procurement by covered entities of services explicitly scheduled in
Annexes 4 and 5 are subject to the GPA's rules, and then only insofar as no
qualifications or limitations are maintained in the relevant annexes. To give an
indication of the orders of magnitude involved in the 1995 extension of the GPA's
coverage to subcentral entities and services—the offers made by the US and the
EU covered some US$100 billion of purchases, with care being taken to maintain
reciprocity through addition of removal of specific entities and sub-national
authorities (Schott and Buurman, 1994: 74).

The primary obligation imposed by the GPA on covered entities is nondiscrimination—national treatment and MFN (Article V). This extends not only to

[2] The European Communities refers to the Community's institutions. Formally, there were 40 signatories to the GPA in 2008, as each EU member state has signed the agreement individually
in addition to the European Communities. This is because in some dimensions of procurement EU
member states retain competence.

[3] The GPA applies to purchases of goods and services that are not intended for resale. If government
entities engage in trade (buying and selling) Article XVII GATT applies (see Chapter 5).

Table 11.1. GPA thresholds for coverage of procurement contracts (SDRs)

Category of Procurement	Threshold
Central government entities	
Goods	130,000
Services except construction services	130,000
Construction services	5,000,000[†]
Annex 2: Subcentral government entities	
Goods	200,000[‡]
Services except construction services	200,000[‡]
Construction services	5,000,000[§]
Annex 3: All other entities whose procurement is covered by the Agreement	
Goods	400,000[¶]
Services except construction services	400,000[¶]
Construction services	5,000,000[§]

In general public enterprises or public authorities such as utilities.
[†] Israel: 8.5 million; Japan 4.5 million (with architecture services: 450,000).
[‡] US and Canada: 355,000; Israel: 250,000.
[§] Israel: 8.5 million; Japan and Korea: 15 million.
[¶] Canada and Israel: 355,000; Japan: 130,000.

Source: WTO Government Procurement Agreement.

imports but also to subsidiaries of locally established foreign firms. The GPA thus goes beyond the GATT, which does not extend national treatment to foreign affiliates, and the GATS, which does so only if specific commitments to that effect have been made. Under the GPA all foreign affiliates established in the country are to be treated the same as national firms. Local content, price preferences and similar discriminatory policies are prohibited. Moreover, signatories may not discriminate against foreign suppliers by applying rules of origin that differ from those they apply in general to MFN-based trade.

Most of the provisions of the GPA concern transparency broadly defined. Thus, much attention is given to requiring signatories to specify where information on procurement systems and opportunities will be published (including through electronic means). These must be listed in Appendices II through IV to the GPA. There are detailed requirements for publication of notices of intended procurement, the conditions for participation and permitted systems to ascertain that suppliers are qualified, technical specifications and tender documentation, minimum time periods to allow bids to occur and regular reporting of statistics on procurement activities of covered entities.

The GPA does not explicitly require that procurement be competitive or that certain procurement methods be used. In this regard it is quite different from the procurement guidelines that other international organizations and national governments apply. Regarding conduct of procurement, signatories are simply required to '... conduct covered procurement in a transparent and impartial manner that is consistent with this Agreement, using methods such as open tendering, selective tendering and limited tendering; avoids conflicts of interest and prevents corrupts practices' (Article V:4). Open tendering is any method that allows any supplier to bid (i.e. competitive tendering). Selective tendering is a method where only suppliers that satisfy specific criteria for participation may bid (usually prequalified suppliers). Limited tendering is noncompetitive and usually involves a procuring entity approaching one or more potential supplier of its choice.

The rules in the GPA regarding selective tendering are basically aimed at ensuring that foreign suppliers can demonstrate they qualify and are not discriminated against in this regard (e.g. have the information needed). Limited tendering may only be used if no tenders were received or they were not responsive, only one supplier can provide the good or service (e.g. artwork, products protected by IPRs), for additional, follow-on deliveries, in situations of extreme urgency, for commodities (the presumption being that there is a world price for standardized, homogenous goods) or for prototypes.

There is no explicit hierarchy of the three tendering methods mentioned in Article V and governments are free to use others. The preference for competitive procurement methods is implicit in the agreement, reflected in requirements that notices of intended or planned procurement be published (including information on the mode of procurement, its nature and quantity, dates of delivery, economic and technical requirements, and amounts and terms of payment), in the conditions that must be satisfied if governments use limited tendering, and in the disciplines on treatment of tenders and contract awards. Article XIII on limited tendering makes it clear that competition is preferred by making use of this method conditional on it not being used to avoid competition among suppliers, to discriminate or protect domestic suppliers. Article XV requires that entities award contracts to the supplier 'determined to be fully capable of undertaking the contract' and who is either the lowest tender (if price is the sole criterion) or the tender that is most advantageous (in terms of the evaluation criteria set out in the notices or tender documentation). It is rather surprising that the objective of competitive procurement is not embedded in the preamble of the agreement. The 'fuzziness' as regards the preference for competitive bidding may reflect the desire of signatories to see membership of the GPA expand to include developing countries.

Price-preference policies, offsets and similar policies that are widely used by governments are in principle prohibited for covered procurement as a result of the national treatment rule (Article V). This has been a problem for developing countries, as these countries use procurement as an instrument to achieve objectives other than 'value for money'. Article IV of the 2006 GPA permits developing countries to negotiate the right to adopt or retain price preference policies and offset requirements on a transitional basis, and delay the implementation of any and all provisions other than MFN for up to three years (five years for a LDC). Moreover, after accession the GPA Committee may extend the transition periods or approve the use of new transitional price preferences or offsets if there are 'special circumstances that were unforeseen during the accession process' (Article IV:7). Existing signatories also commit themselves to 'give due consideration to any request by a developing country for technical cooperation and capacity building' (Article IV:8). Some scope therefore exists for maintaining a price preference or offset policy—but it is time-limited.

The nature of procurement is such that most of the time, unless rapid action can be taken, firms will not have an interest in bringing cases contesting violations of the rules of the game. Accordingly, the GPA supplements the right of signatories to invoke the WTO DSU—which is too slow to be relevant for many real-world procurement situations—with a requirement that members establish domestic review procedures. These bid-protest or -challenge mechanisms should provide for rapid interim measures to correct breaches of the agreement or a failure of a government entity to comply with the measures implementing the GPA (Article XVIII). Measures to preserve commercial opportunities may involve suspension of the procurement process, or compensation for the loss or damages suffered. This may be limited to the costs for preparing the tender or the costs relating to the challenge, or both.

Articles IX and XVII GPA require each signatory, on request from another party, to promptly provide pertinent information concerning the reasons why the supplier's application to qualify was rejected, why an existing qualification was terminated, and information necessary to determine whether a procurement was conducted in accordance with the GPA, including pertinent information on the characteristics and relative advantages of the tender that was selected. The 2006 provisions in this area are weaker than those in the 1996 agreement.

Operation of the GPA

The GPA requires signatories to report annual statistics on procurement by covered entities to the Committee on Government Procurement. Such data reporting was intended to help parties determine how well the agreement was functioning, in part by providing comparable cross-country information on sourcing practices. Signatories began reporting statistics for the year 1983. Unfortunately, there has been very little empirical research using these data, and it does not appear that signatories to the GPA have used the statistics as a way of monitoring the operation of the agreement.

Data reported in Hoekman (1998) for the 1983–92 period—when only central government procurement of goods was covered by the GPA—revealed that the largest procurement market, by a substantial margin, opened up under the GPA was that of the United States, which accounted for almost half of the total procurement reported. Smaller countries, on average, procured much more on international markets than did large countries. If Canada, the EU, Japan and the US were excluded, about 60 per cent of purchases by covered entities exceeding the threshold went to national suppliers. This compared to more than 90 per cent for the large players. As EU statistics defined 'domestic' as including intra-EU sourcing, reported self-sufficiency ratios for the EU-12 were above 90 per cent on average. In interpreting these statistics it should be noted that no distinction is made between domestic firms proper and foreign firms that have established a local presence. To the extent that large countries attract a greater amount of FDI, higher self-sufficiency ratios are not indicative of discriminatory policies.

In the EU, Japan and the US, the share of domestic firms in total above threshold procurement by covered entities remained virtually unchanged during 1983–92. For the smaller countries, however, with the exception of Singapore and Switzerland, the share of procurement from national sources declined over time. It is impossible to attribute such changes in sourcing patterns to the GPA—regional developments also played a role, such as the NAFTA in North America and efforts to liberalize EU procurement markets. Unilateral deregulation and privatization policies also must have had an impact. Nonetheless, the finding that smaller GPA members became less nationalistic in their purchasing decisions suggests that practices did become more open.

During the same period, the share of contracts that exceeded the threshold tended to increase. In 1983–5, some 39 per cent of all procurement by covered entities fell above the threshold. By 1991–2, it had risen to 49 per cent. This can be explained in part by a reduction in the threshold in 1988, from SDR150,000 to SDR130,000. As of the early 1990s, the share of above threshold contracts for both EU and US entities averaged around 60 per cent.

Under the GPA, open competitive tendering procedures are, in principle, to be used for all contracts that exceed the relevant threshold. As noted earlier, limited tendering procedures involving an entity negotiating with potential suppliers individually is only allowed under certain conditions and members are required to report data on their use of this method. The issue became important in US–Japan trade relations in the 1980s, following US complaints that the use of limited tendering was excessive (Stern and Hoekman, 1987). In the period investigated by Hoekman (1998), the use of limited tendering varied from a reported low of zero (Singapore) to a high of over 30 per cent on average for France, Italy, Switzerland and Hong Kong. Across all signatories the average share of limited tendering was about 13 per cent. As of 1992, both the EU and the US used limited tendering for about 10 per cent of contracts. Japan's use of limited tendering rose from around 12 per cent during 1983–5 to 21 per cent during 1990–2.

Choi (2003) and Evenett and Shingal (2006) have undertaken country-specific studies of the operation and impact of the GPA, focusing on Korea and Japan respectively. Choi finds that accession to the agreement by Korea was followed by a reduction in the share of procurement using limited tendering (which fell from 27 per cent in 1993–5 to 22.5 per cent in 1996–8. However, the share of foreign supplied goods during this period fell. Evenett and Shingal conclude that in 1999 in Japan more contracts fell below the GPA thresholds than in earlier years, and that of the contracts that exceeded the threshold—and thus were covered by the GPA—a smaller share was awarded to foreign suppliers in 1998–9 than in 1990–1. Thus, during the 1990s, it appears that the GPA did nothing to increase the market access for foreign suppliers.

The data reporting requirements of the GPA are not as useful or informative as they might be because most signatories do not report on a timely or comprehensive basis. One reason the studies just mentioned focus on Korea and Japan is that these countries report regularly. More regular reporting—and analysis of the reports by the WTO Secretariat—would do much to improve knowledge regarding implementation of the agreement. That said, what matters from an economic point of view is primarily the size of government demand for a good or service relative to total domestic supply. As discussed previously, it is particularly in cases where the government is a big player relative to domestic supply that there can be significant effects on national welfare and foreign suppliers. Multilateral scrutiny will have potentially the largest payoff if it focuses on such situations. As the GPA reporting requirements are quite burdensome, an added benefit of a more focused approach to data collection would be a reduction in the costs of surveillance.

There have been only three disputes under the WTO on procurement that have led to invocation of the DSU. All have involved the EU or the US. In 1996, the EU objected to a law of the Commonwealth of Massachusetts that prohibited public authorities in Massachusetts from procuring goods or services from persons who do business with Myanmar. The EU (joined in 1997 by Japan) argued that this violated the GPA, as Massachusetts is covered under the US schedule to the GPA. A panel was established, but proceedings were suspended at the request of the complainants, following a US Supreme Court decision that struck down the ban as being unconstitutional because it infringed upon the authority of the President of the United States to set foreign policy. In 1997, the EU raised the procurement of a navigation satellite by the Japanese Ministry of Transport, arguing that the technical specifications in the tender were not neutral because they referred explicitly to US specifications. Here also a MAS was found (a panel was never established).

A third case concerned US allegations that the Korean Airport Construction Authority's practices relating to qualification for bidding as a prime contractor, domestic partnering and the absence of access to challenge procedures violated the GPA. In the Inchon airport dispute the US argued that Korea had failed to comply with the GPA by imposing bid deadlines and domestic partnerships and by awarding the construction contract to the Korean Airport Authority. The WTO panel ruled that the Korean Airport Authority was not covered by the GPA (it was not listed in Korea's annexes) and therefore was outside the scope of the agreement (Matsushita, 2006).

There have also been cases involving developing countries that are not members of the GPA. For example, in 1991, two Brazilian firms won an international tender for electric power transformers issued by the Federal Electricity Commission of Mexico. Subsequently, three of the Mexican firms that lost the tender brought an antidumping petition against the Brazilian firms. Antidumping duties ranging from 26 to 35 per cent were imposed in September 1993. Brazil requested the GATT Antidumping Committee to conciliate, arguing that the AD duty was calculated by comparing prices bid by the different firms for the original tender, and not by comparing prices charged in the home and the export market. This dispute was also resolved bilaterally (Hoekman and Kostecki, 1995).

As is the case regarding trends in procurement sourcing by signatories, little is known about the extent to which the GPA domestic challenge mechanisms have been used in practice. Matsushita (2006) discusses one instance that arose in Japan. In this case, Motorola, a US company, brought a complaint against a Japan Railway procurement tender, arguing that it did not use an ISO standard whose enactment was imminent. The review body ruled that the GPA did not require procuring entities to take such expected changes in international norms into account—what matters are the standards that prevail at the time a tender is issued.

The challenge of expanding membership

Public procurement markets are too big to be left beyond the reach of the multilateral trading system. As mentioned above, membership of the GPA is quite limited. Indeed, not all OECD countries have signed it, e.g. Australia and New Zealand are not members. The US has made expansion of membership a priority issue, linking this to the broader issue of combating corruption.[4] Despite long standing efforts to expand the number of signatories, very little progress in that direction has been achieved in the 30 years that the GPA has existed. The increase in membership since the early 1980s has predominantly been driven by the expansion of the EU from 12 to 27 members. Given that the EU is a signatory to the GPA and imposes procurement disciplines that are much more detailed and

---

[4] This has mostly been reflected in unilateral decisions to make bribery and corrupt procurement a criminal offence in the United States and efforts to obtain agreement from OECD members to do the same. In April 1996, largely at the insistence of the US, OECD members agreed not to allow firms to write off bribes against tax obligations (Oxford Analytica, 18 April 1996). In 1997 the OECD adopted the Convention on Combating Bribery of Foreign Public Officials in International Business Transactions, which made bribery a criminal offence and required all signatories to pass legislation to that effect.

prescriptive than those of the GPA, the expansion of membership to date does not reflect very well on the agreement.

A number of countries that have acceded to the WTO since 1995 made commitments to negotiate accession to the GPA, with China being the most notable and important economy to have done so. Time will tell whether these accession promises will be realized. China has a clear interest insofar as membership of the GPA will give it access to markets of signatories. One reason low-income countries have been reluctant to accede to the GPA is that they do not see reciprocal concessions from GPA members as having value. Negotiating leverage is a function of the size of the incremental market access that aspiring members can offer, and for most developing countries this tends to be small. Moreover, many developing countries are not players on the international procurement market, implying that the standard mercantilist bargain is not available to move things along.

Even if one abstracts from the skewed nature of the bargain from a (political) mercantilist perspective, what matters is whether adherence to the rules of the GPA will improve welfare. Taking a more 'rational' economic perspective, the question confronting developing countries is whether the eventual loss of the ability to use procurement policy as an instrument of industrial, regional or social policy is a good or bad thing. And, if it is a bad thing, whether there are other sources of gain that offset the loss. There is not a lot of empirical research on the effectiveness of procurement discrimination in achieving the industrial and other policy objectives. Tax/subsidy instruments are likely to be more efficient in assisting domestic target groups than procurement favouritism, but governments may confront fiscal constraints that impede the use of such policies. Moreover, an advantage of procurement that favours specific domestic groups is that it can help the most efficient firms in that group (as they must compete for the contracts) (Watermeyer, 2004), whereas a subsidy to a region or a minority will be less selective. This is a policy area that should be the focus of much more targeted research in developing countries—most of the literature pertains to the OECD countries. Whatever the case may be, in practice a large share of the procurement market where discrimination is now used to pursue equity and social objectives is unlikely to be of great interest to foreign suppliers: the average size of contracts is likely to be relatively small.

Price preferences have the advantage of being transparent and less distortive than other types of discriminatory policies that are often pursued (such as bans on participation by foreign bidders or local content and offset requirements). Tariffying such policies through an agreement permitting the maintenance of price preference schemes by developing countries would provide a focal point for future multilateral negotiations to reduce discrimination. Such preferences are allowed subject to certain conditions and limits by multilateral development banks. Provisions for their use are also included in the UNCITRAL Model Law on Procurement. Many developing countries have incorporated such preferences into their legislation. Recognition of the legitimacy of price preferences and offsets for developing countries—without time limits and transition periods—could help alter the incentives for accession.

Many of the purchases by government entities comprise services or products where economic forces favour procuring from local suppliers. In such cases, procurement preferences will only be binding if foreign firms cannot contest the market through FDI, or if government entities differentiate across firms on the basis of their nationality. Outright market access restrictions that take the form of a ban on FDI are costly to the economy as a whole, and policy efforts that focus on elimination of such bans are likely to have a greater payoff than attempting to outlaw discrimination.

The Working Group on Transparency in Procurement

Discrimination is just one, albeit important, dimension of possible multilateral disciplines for government procurement. It is widely believed that there are significant potential gains from disciplines that promote transparent procurement mechanisms, thereby reducing the scope for corruption and rent seeking. The 1996 WTO Singapore ministerial conference established a working group to study 'transparency in government procurement practices' and ways to develop 'elements for inclusion in an appropriate agreement'. Many developing countries perceived this to be a Trojan horse (a vehicle to start discussing discrimination and extend the coverage of GPA disciplines). However, given that discrimination is probably a second-order issue in comparison with corruption, there was a strong prima facie case to focus on transparency first and foremost.

The WTO working group proceeded by addressing the 'Items on the Chairman's Checklist of Issues' relating to a potential agreement on transparency in government procurement. The checklist comprised such broad issues as the definition of government procurement and the scope and coverage of a potential agreement, the substantive elements of a potential agreement on transparency, including various aspects of access to general and specific procurement-related information and procedural matters, as well as compliance mechanisms of a potential agreement and issues relating to developing countries, including the role of SDT and technical assistance and capacity-building. Signatories of the GPA not surprisingly strongly supported negotiations on transparency, as did a number of non-GPA countries such as Australia. Several draft proposals for an agreement were submitted in November 1999, including by the EU, Japan, Australia and a joint submission by Hungary, Korea, Singapore and the US. These countries sought to conclude an agreement at the Seattle ministerial. Many developing countries emphasized that much more discussion was needed on the implications of transparency obligations in the procurement area.

At the Doha ministerial conference in 2001, ministers agreed that negotiations of transparency in procurement would take place after the fifth ministerial conference 'on the basis of a decision to be taken, by explicit consensus, at that Session on modalities of negotiations'. The ministerial declaration emphasized that 'negotiations shall be limited to the transparency aspects and therefore will not restrict the scope for countries to give preferences to domestic supplies and suppliers'. In line with the Doha Ministerial Declaration, which highlighted the need to 'take into account participants' development priorities, especially those of least-developed country participants', the Working Group on Transparency in Government Procurement discussed extensively the development implications of a possible agreement in this area. The Doha mandate also recognized the need for enhanced technical assistance and capacity-building and contained a commitment to provide such assistance both during any negotiations and after their conclusion.

No agreement on modalities for negotiations could be reached at the fifth ministerial conference, held in Cancun in September 2003. On 1 August 2004, the WTO General Council adopted a decision that removed this subject, as well as competition and investment, from the Doha Work Programme. The decision did not indicate what might occur, if anything, following the completion of the Doha Round. It is difficult to understand why there was resistance to negotiating an agreement on transparency in procurement. The most compelling explanation is that many developing countries were not convinced that this would not end in a future discussion on market access. From a systemic perspective that is indeed what would be logical—given the size of procurement markets this is clearly an area where there is a rationale for WTO members to agree to mutual disarmament. In the absence of market access incentives and disciplines it is also not obvious what the rationale is for discussing transparency in the WTO. Some of the economic dimensions of enhancing transparency of procurement processes are discussed in Annex 2. It is shown that there is not necessarily a one-to-one mapping between more transparency and more market access.

11.2. THE CIVIL AIRCRAFT AGREEMENT

The Agreement on Trade in Civil Aircraft aims to reduce both tariffs and trade-distorting NTMs affecting production and trade in civil aircraft. It was the only sector-specific agreement covering a manufactured product that was successfully negotiated in the Tokyo Round. Members to the agreement include most leading civil aircraft exporters (the Russian Federation, not a WTO member, is an exception). A Committee on Civil Aircraft oversees the agreement.

The agreement is to a large extent a zero-for-zero tariff agreement, as signatories agree to eliminate import duties on civil aircraft and the bulk of aircraft parts. The agreement also includes disciplines on TBT and subsidies. A major reason it was negotiated was because little progress could be made during the Tokyo Round on subsidies. The *demandeur* for the agreement was the US, which sought to constrain the ability of European governments to subsidize Airbus, as it was increasingly becoming a competitor for US companies producing large civil aircraft (Boeing, Lockheed, McDonnell Douglas). US efforts to ban the use of subsidies failed, however, and no binding disciplines were introduced that went beyond then-prevailing rules on subsidies—which were quite weak (see Chapter 5).

Disputes regarding trade in civil aircraft have been a recurring element of trade relations between the US and the EU, reflecting the battle for market share fought between Boeing and McDonnell Douglas on the one hand (now merged), and Airbus on the other. The Civil Aircraft Agreement has not succeeded in reducing the sources of tension between these two dominant players, nor has it been effective in addressing conflicts between smaller aircraft producing nations such as Canada and Brazil. The latter became embroiled in disputes regarding the alleged use of export subsidies in the late 1990s, but the Agreement on Civil Aircraft did not play a role in the various panel cases, which are discussed in Chapter 3.[5]

The EU and the US instead pursued a bilateral track. In the mid- to late 1980s tensions flared up between the US and the EU following a decision by Air India to cancel an order for Boeing 757 jets after Airbus offered big discounts on its new A320 plane. This led to the negotiation of a bilateral agreement between the two parties that incorporated more specific disciplines. The 1992 EU–US Agreement on Trade in Large Civil Aircraft (defined as planes with a capacity of 100 seats or more) required that the parties provide each other with data on financing of new aircraft; banned new production subsidies outright; limited the amount of so-called launch aid (support for the development of a new type of aircraft) to one-third of total development costs; and constrained indirect support (such as R&D funding) to 4 per cent of any recipient firm's annual turnover and 3 per cent for the industry as a whole. Moreover, launch aid must be fully repaid within 17 years with an interest rate that reflects the government's costs of funds.

These disciplines, although still permitting a significant amount of support to be given to airplane producers, did bite: Airbus had received assistance that exceeded the limits laid out in the 1992 agreement. Irwin and Pavcnik (2004) estimate that implementation of the agreement increased global aircraft prices by some 4 per cent, and the marginal costs of production by 5 per cent. But the agreement did not result in a cessation of the commercial rivalry between the EU and the US. Matters

[5] *Canada—Measures Affecting the Export of Civilian Aircraft*, complaint by Brazil (WT/DS70, WT/DS71); *Brazil—Export Financing Programme for Aircraft*, complaint by Canada (WT/DS46).

came to a head in 2004 as a result of US objections to what it regarded as excessive launch aid and other support that the EU agreed to provide Airbus for the development of the A380, the double-decker jumbo jet. The US withdrew from the agreement and initiated DS proceedings in the WTO. The EU immediately retaliated by bringing a case of its own, alleging that Boeing was benefitting from large-scale subsidies in the form of investment incentives (including tax concessions and infrastructure) provided by state-level governments in the US, as well as prohibited export subsidies and excessive R&D financing (much of which was for military contracts but benefitted the civilian production lines). The US invoked the SCM Agreement, arguing serious prejudice and adverse effects (loss of markets, price suppression, etc.). The EU argued before the panel that the Civil Aircraft Agreement and the subsequent bilateral extension should be applied, and that many of the measures the US had challenged were not subsidies as defined in the SCM Agreement (because they were repaid by Airbus).

An interesting feature of this case is that until 2004 neither party had invoked WTO mechanisms, not just DS but also CVDs. One reason for the absence of CVDs was that the US industry did not want to bring cases forward for fear of retaliation. As in other areas this is one where the changing structure of the global production process has greatly affected the incentives confronting both the aircraft producers and their governments. An increasing share of the components that make up an airplane are produced outside the EU and US respectively. Airbus sources from US suppliers and Boeing from EU-based firms. Both source from the rest of the world.

How the dispute will be resolved remains to be determined. Given the long standing pattern of recurring intervention by both parties in the industry, the linkages to national security and the high-tech nature of aircraft production, the very large fixed costs of aircraft development and the effective duopoly nature of the global industry, it is very unlikely that any WTO ruling will be implemented. It is also clear that neither party will be found to be in compliance with WTO rules. What will be required is a new agreement that imposes stricter disciplines but recognizes that governments will continue to support the industry. Hufbauer (2007) recommends re-negotiating the plurilateral agreement, building on the OECD experience with disciplining export credit subsidies. This could involve a mix of minimum standards for subsidies, combined with a 'peace clause' (agreement not to file cases—as was done in the Uruguay Round Agreement on Agriculture for subsidy disputes for a period of time—see Chapter 6) and effective notification, monitoring and surveillance by a WTO body.

Economists differ in their view of whether the EU decision to support the entry of Airbus was beneficial for the EU or for the world as a whole. Early analysts emphasized that there was most likely a good case to be made for the EU policy as it increased competition on a highly concentrated market—in effect the US had a monopoly on wide-body civil aircraft. But the increased (subsidized) competition also led to substantially greater concentration of the US industry, with Lockheed-Martin exiting the sector and McDonnell Douglas taken over by Boeing. Although a textbook example of 'strategic trade policy', whether or not the EU subsidy policies have improved welfare remains an open question.

11.3. TOWARDS MORE CLUBS IN THE WTO?

Plurilateral agreements are outliers in the WTO system. Although there are presently only two such agreements, only one of which has proven to be robust and fully effective, the fact that the WTO offers the flexibility of negotiating such agreements may prove important in the future. One of the benefits of the Tokyo Round 'codes approach' was that it allowed for a 'variable geometry'. The downside of the codes was that they addressed GATT issues and it was not completely clear whether the MFN rule applied to them. This was important because the codes dealt with matters that were subject to the GATT—in effect they were used to overcome the immense difficulty that existed in obtaining the required agreement to revise existing disciplines (amend the GATT). There also was no unified dispute settlement system, creating the potential for forum shopping and the development of diverging case law.

With the creation of the WTO and the DSU there is, in principle, greater scope for subsets of WTO members to use plurilateral agreements to move forward on specific topics. Such agreements are a vehicle for like-minded countries to cooperate in areas not (yet) addressed by the WTO. They allow countries not willing to consider disciplines in a policy area to opt out. Given that the Doha Round clearly revealed that it may not be possible to get consensus on launching a negotiation on a subject, let alone conclude the negotiation successfully, the plurilateral route offers a mechanism to introduce areas into the WTO without the disciplines applying to all members. Accommodating diversity in interests through greater use of plurilaterals was one of the recommendations of the Sutherland Report (Sutherland et al., 2004). Fears that a move down this road would result in a potential repeat of the Uruguay Round TRIPS experience—where negotiators started with a limited agenda centring on trade in counterfeit goods but ended up with an agreement that harmonized elements of domestic intellectual property legislation—has been a factor underlying resistance by many developing countries to this idea. Their concern is that accepting a plurilateral agreement to be brought into the WTO sets a precedent that they will be confronted with subsequently. However, the GPA illustrates that there is no presumption that nonsignatories will be 'forced' to sign a plurilateral deal as time goes by—the GPA has been in existence for decades and membership remains very limited.

Lawrence (2006) discusses what he calls the club-of-clubs option and argues that this approach can help the WTO address the diverging interests of its members in an efficient way. He suggests a number of criteria, including that: clubs be restricted to subjects that are clearly trade-related, any new agreement is open to all members in the negotiation stage, i.e. participation in the development of rules should not be limited to likely signatories; and that club members be required to use the DSU to settle disputes, with eventual retaliation being restricted to the area covered by the agreement (as is the case under the GPA). Although greater use of plurilateral agreements will result in a multi-tier system with differentiated commitments and some erosion of the MFN principle—as club members would have the right to restrict benefits to other members—there is already significant differentiation in the level of obligations across countries.

11.4. FURTHER READING

Little has been written on how plurilateral agreements fit into the WTO framework. The trade policy-oriented literature on government procurement and civil aircraft is also relatively sparse. Many of the contributions in Bernard Hoekman and Petros C. Mavroidis (eds), *Law and Policy in Public Purchasing: The WTO Agreement on Government Procurement* (Ann Arbor: University of Michigan Press, 1997) discuss the genesis, operation and relevance of the GPA to countries at differing levels of development. Contributions also cover the UNICITRAL model law for procurement and procurement regimes of non-GPA members such as India and New Zealand. Sue Arrowsmith, *Government Procurement in the WTO* (London: Kluwer Law International, 2003) provides a comprehensive discussion of the GPA from a mostly legal perspective.

A classic study of the economics of discrimination in procurement is Robert Baldwin and J. David Richardson, 'Government Purchasing Policies, Other NTBs, and the International Monetary Crisis', in H. English and K. Hay (eds), *Obstacles to Trade in the Pacific Area* (Ottawa: Carleton School of International Affairs, 1972). R. Preston McAfee and John McMillan, 'Government Procurement and International Trade', *Journal of International Economics*, 26 (1989): 291–308, make the theoretical case for discrimination in markets characterized by imperfect competition and small numbers of bidders. Albert Breton and Pierre Salmon review the literature and question some of the conventional wisdom regarding the rationales for procurement policies in 'Are Discriminatory Procurement Policies Motivated By Protectionism?', *Kyklos*, 49 (1995): 47–68.

The role of the Civil Aircraft Agreement and the rivalry between the EU and US is discussed in Steve McGuire, *Airbus Industrie* (London: McMillan, 1997) and Nina Pavcnik, 'Trade Disputes in the Commercial Aircraft Industry,' *The World Economy* (2002): 733–51.

Robert Lawrence, 'Rulemaking Amidst Growing Diversity: A Club of Clubs Approach to WTO Reform and New Issue Selection,' *Journal of International Economic Law* (2006) suggests that greater use be made of plurilateral agreements in the WTO.

CHAPTER 12

....

DEVELOPING COUNTRIES AND ECONOMIES IN TRANSITION

....

FOR a long time, the GATT was a club that was primarily of relevance to OECD countries. Developing countries did not participate fully in the exchange of concessions in negotiations, although they benefitted from generally applicable national treatment and MFN disciplines. With the creation of the WTO this changed. Developing countries became subject to a large number of obligations— some newly negotiated in the Uruguay Round, others originally negotiated during earlier rounds among industrialized nations. The resulting implementation 'overhang' had significant repercussions for the organization, resulting in 'development concerns' becoming a more prominent agenda item and the creation of mechanisms to provide assistance to developing country members. The implementation problems are part of the broader challenge of integrating developing and transition economies into the global trading system. Almost all countries have become much more open to trade and FDI, but a large subset have not sustained high growth or diversified their economies.

Although differences in view persist on the appropriate role of government intervention to support or restrain trade (see Chapters 1 and 9), there is general agreement on the strong positive association between economic development and trade expansion. The WTO promotes trade, and in that sense could be expected to be seen as an institution that promotes development. However, despite the boom in world trade that has occurred in the last 30+ years—in part under the stewardship of the GATT/WTO—and the increasing participation of many developing countries in world trade, many observers have been concerned about the impact of the GATT/WTO on the economic development prospects of poor countries (see e.g. Stiglitz, 2000; Oxfam, 2002).

These concerns often boil down to two specific problems. First, the focus of the institution on negotiating market access 'concessions' on a reciprocal basis. Here, the problem is that in the case of small developing countries which are of only limited interest from an export perspective, the system of reciprocity does not 'work'. Political scientists would characterize this as a reflection of the huge asymmetries in power between WTO members. Being price-takers on world markets, such countries cannot offer enough to induce larger traders—the most interesting markets—to improve access. This also reduces the value of the WTO as a commitment mechanism as it implies fewer enforcement incentives (see Chapters 1 and 3).

Second, common policy disciplines may not be appropriate for all countries. For example, taxing trade may be the most effective method for a government of a developing country to raise revenue, implying that reducing tariffs, even if in principle seen as desirable by a government, only becomes feasible once the capacity exists to reliably tap domestic tax bases. Increasingly, the ambit of the WTO extends beyond trade policy. Although harmonization of regulatory policies may reduce negative spillovers on foreign firms, there may be strong economic efficiency rationales for regulatory diversity. Even where harmonization is welfare-enhancing, it may give rise to asymmetric implementation costs, in that the burden may fall disproportionately on poorer countries (Finger and Schuler, 2000).

This chapter discusses developing country participation in the GATT/WTO, efforts in the Doha Round to address developing countries' concerns, and the ongoing debate regarding the appropriate role of the WTO in helping its poorer members to more fully use trade opportunities to increase economic growth and welfare. The chapter also discusses the experience with accession to the WTO by developing and transition economies, including by China in 2001.

12.1 DEVELOPING COUNTRY PARTICIPATION

The terms of developing country participation in the multilateral trading system have oscillated between reciprocity and disengagement. A timeline of major highlights is summarized in Table 12.1. Four stages can be identified:

Table 12.1. Developing countries and the trading system

Date	Event
1947	Twelve of what would now be called low-income countries accede to the GATT on essentially the same terms as developed countries. An infant-industry protection clause (Article XVIII) is the main development-specific provision in GATT.
1954–5	Article XVIII is modified to include XVIII:*b* allowing for QRs to be used for BOP purposes whenever foreign-exchange reserves are below what is considered necessary for economic development. This vague test constitutes much weaker discipline than Article XII. It has been invoked extensively (see Chapter 9).
1964	Establishment of UNCTAD. A Committee for Trade and Development is created in the GATT to address development-related concerns.
	The International Trade Centre (ITC)—a technical cooperation agency in the area of trade promotion—is created by GATT contracting parties charged with assisting developing countries to promote exports.
1965	A new Part IV on Trade and Development is added to the GATT, establishing the principle of nonreciprocity for developing countries. However, Part IV contains no legally binding obligations, other than to consult.
1968	The US accepts the Generalized System of Preferences (GSP)—as called for by UNCTAD—under which industrialized countries voluntarily grant tariff preferences to developing countries.
	The ITC becomes a joint venture between GATT and UNCTAD.
1971	A GATT waiver is granted authorizing tariff preferences under the GSP. Another waiver is adopted for the Protocol on Trade Negotiations among Developing Countries (Geneva Protocol).
1973–9	More than 70 developing countries participate in the Tokyo Round. The Enabling Clause is adopted. It formalizes the concept of 'special and differential treatment' (SDT), makes the 1971 waivers permanent and includes language on graduation. Most developing countries abstain from signing the various Tokyo Round codes.
1986	Developing countries participate in the preparation for a new round. The Punta del Este ministerial declaration launching the Uruguay Round contains numerous references to SDT.
1994	All developing country GATT contracting parties join the WTO, adopting the results of the Uruguay Round as a Single Undertaking.
1997	The Integrated Framework for Trade-related Technical Assistance for Least Developed Countries is created at the Singapore ministerial.
1999	Developing countries put forward more than half of all the submissions for the Seattle ministerial meeting.
2000	US passes the African Growth and Opportunity Act (AGOA), granting duty- and quota-free market access to African countries.
2001	Doha Development Agenda launched; ministerial declaration calls for 'strengthening of SDT provisions and making them more precise, effective and operational' (para. 44).
	EU 'Everything But Arms' duty- and quota-free initiative for LDCs adopted.
	China accedes to the WTO.
2002	WTO Global Trust Fund established to help developing countries participate in and benefit from negotiations.
2003	Creation of the G20, a coalition of developing countries including Brazil, China, India and South Africa; Brazil launches disputes against US cotton subsidies and EU sugar subsidies.
	Four LDCs, Benin, Burkina Faso, Chad and Mali—the so-called cotton four—push for a Doha Round accelerated initiative on cotton (see Chapter 6).

Table 12.1. *(Continued)*

Date	Event
2005	Agreement at the Hong Kong ministerial for high-income countries to provide LDCs with duty- and quota-free access for at least 97% of trade.
	The hundredth dispute is initiated by a developing country.
2006	WTO taskforce calls for an Aid for Trade initiative.
2008	Donors and LDCs put in place the Enhanced Integrated Framework.
	Expiry of the WTO waiver for EU–ACP preferences on 1 January.

(1) limited membership of low-income countries in GATT (12 of the original 23 signatories were developing economies) based on a formal parity of obligations (1947–64);

(2) substantial expansion of developing country membership, based on the concept of more favourable and differential treatment (1965–86);

(3) deepening integration of developing countries into the GATT-WTO system, with a return to greater reciprocity (1987–97); and

(4) a shift back to an emphasis on special and differential treatment (SDT), especially for LDCs, increasing de facto differentiation and heterogeneity of views (1998–present).

The initial premise underlying GATT 1947 was essentially parity of obligations—making no distinction between rich and poor trading nations, despite arguments by India and other countries that provisions were needed to allow developing countries to protect industries (Hudec, 1987). A number of provisions allowing for such measures to be applied were included in the GATT, but they implied reciprocity in that their invocation was subject to disciplines (see Chapter 9). In the mid-1950s, with a large number of colonies approaching independence, the concept of giving SDT to developing countries arose. The underlying justification for this reflected development thinking at the time—most notably work by Raúl Prebisch and Hans Singer—which was premised on the argument that developing countries needed to foster industrial capacity both to reduce import dependence and to diversify away from traditional commodities. Diversification was needed in part because commodities were held to be subject to long-term declining terms of trade (because of low income elasticity of demand) as well as detrimental short-term price volatility (Singer, 1950; Prebisch, 1952). This gave rise to the policy prescription of high trade barriers so as to protect infant industries—i.e. import-substitution industrialization—and a call for exemptions from the GATT negotiating principle of reciprocity in the exchange of market access commitments.

At the same time it was recognized that exports were important as a source of foreign exchange and that the local market might be too small for a protected local industry to be able to realize economies of scale. The second plank of the SDT agenda therefore revolved around calls for preferential access to export markets—a general system of preferences that would give developing countries better than most-favoured-nation (MFN) treatment in the major markets of the world—the industrialized countries. A final plank of SDT was development assistance targeted towards helping developing countries penetrate export markets. This was the rationale for the creation of the ITC in 1964 by the GATT CONTRACTING PARTIES. Despite an effort to improve 'coherence' by making the ITC a joint body of the GATT and UNCTAD in 1968, this plank of the response to developing country concerns became a bit of an orphan in subsequent years. It was somewhat ironic that renewed recognition of the need for proactive assistance came back to the fore in the Doha Round, resulting in the creation of an 'enhanced integrated framework' to assist LDCs to benefit from trade opportunities.

All three types of preferential treatment were justified in various ways. One argument was so-called export pessimism. The fear was that if developing countries relied upon exports for growth, their supply of commodities would exceed what could be absorbed by the world. The resulting excess supply and consequent decline in world prices justified trade restrictions by developing countries—in effect, they should impose tariffs to improve their terms of trade (Prebisch, 1952; Bhagwati, 1988). Given their reliance on exports of commodities, export pessimism was complemented by the view that developing countries needed protection to achieve industrialization and economic development, and that a 'new world trade order' was required to break the vicious circle of underdevelopment. It was also argued that developing countries suffered from foreign exchange shortages and that protectionist policies were needed to protect their balance of payments. International trade was seen by some as an instrument of exploitation and self-sufficiency as an appropriate objective for policy.

Part IV of the GATT and the Enabling Clause

The institutional expression of this line of thinking was embodied in the creation of UNCTAD in 1964, and the formation of a political bloc of developing countries in the UN called the 'Group of 77' (G77). In 1965, developing country demands for special status in the multilateral trading system led to the drafting of a new Part IV of the GATT. This formalized the concept of SDT for developing countries. To a large extent the adoption of Part IV can be seen as a reaction of GATT contracting parties to the creation of UNCTAD and the generalized system of preferences (GSP) established under UNCTAD auspices.[1] As of that moment, SDT was a core component of the trading system.

---

[1] UNCTAD was founded in 1964, with Raúl Prebisch, an Argentine national, as the first Secretary-General.

Special and differential treatment implied that developing countries were not expected to grant reciprocal tariff concessions and bind tariffs.[2] For example, the 1973 ministerial meeting that launched the Tokyo Round stated that the negotiations should secure additional benefits for developing countries in order to achieve a substantial increase in their foreign exchange earnings, diversification of their exports and an acceleration of the rate of growth of their trade. It confirmed that developed nations should not expect reciprocal concessions from developing economies. The inconsistency between these goals and the policy of allowing developing countries to maintain protection and GATT-inconsistent trade regimes was not openly remarked upon. However, during the negotiations, high-income countries repeatedly voiced their dissatisfaction with the reluctance of developing countries to agree to expand GATT disciplines. This found its expression in the negotiation of codes on various issues in which membership was voluntary, see Chapters 5 and 11, thus avoiding the veto that was likely by developing countries if an attempt was made to amend the GATT to include new obligations.

One result of the Tokyo Round was the 1979 Framework Agreement, which included the so-called Enabling Clause. Officially called Differential and More Favorable Treatment, Reciprocity and Fuller Participation of Developing Countries, it provided for departures from MFN and other GATT rules. The Enabling Clause created a permanent legal basis for the operation of the GSP. It codified principles, practices and procedures regarding the use of trade measures for BOP purposes (Articles XII and XVIII), and made GATT's Article XIX redundant for developing countries by giving them flexibility in applying trade measures to meet their 'essential development needs'. It also weakened the reach of Article XXIV on regional integration by eliminating the 'substantially all trade' requirement and the provision prohibiting an increase in the average level of external protection for customs unions.

The quid pro quo for the codification of these exemptions was the inclusion of a graduation principle. This was vaguely worded, however, and was more in the nature of a statement of principle. An important reason for this fuzziness was that most of the SDT provisions were (and remain) 'best endeavour' commitments—they are not binding. No dispute settlement cases can be launched by a developing country government on the basis that a high-income country is not delivering on the promises that are made in the various agreements.

---

[2] Much depended here on how a country acceded to the GATT. Most developing countries acceded under Article XXVI:5c, under which former colonies could undertake to accept the obligations initially negotiated by the metropolitan government. As these had generally not established separate tariff schedules for their colonies, newly independent states were able to accede without submitting a schedule. Countries that were not ex-colonies were generally required to negotiate accession under Article XXXIII GATT, a tougher proposition that required establishment of a tariff schedule.

The idea that the most successful developing trading nations should begin to move back towards a parity of obligations first appeared in the late 1970s. The basic objective of OECD countries was to progressively integrate into the GATT system developing countries with large markets or substantial trade levels and growth. This strategy was not so much inspired by growing evidence that economic development required liberal trade and pro-market policies—which was being compiled under the leadership of scholars such as Jagdish Bhagwati and Anne Krueger—but because a number of countries had managed to grow sufficiently to become attractive markets. The fact that many such countries often had large positive trade balances with industrialized countries provided an additional incentive to try to impose graduation criteria. Conversely, the developing countries concerned had more of an incentive to play the reciprocity game to improve and defend their access to export markets.

A problem with graduation was that no agreement existed on what constituted a developing country. Indeed, the issue was carefully avoided. For example, when Portugal and Israel claimed developing country status in the GATT Balance-of-Payments Committee so as to be able to invoke Article XVIII:*b*, the committee avoided pronouncing itself on the matter. It was left to countries to self-declare their status, usually upon accession to the GATT. Individual contracting parties could also decide for themselves whether to treat a particular trading partner as a developing country. This continues to be the case under the WTO. An exception concerns the group of 49 least-developed countries, where the UN definition is used. In practice, therefore, graduation was and is left to bilateral interaction and tends to be limited to obvious candidates. The decision by Korea to cease invocation of Article XVIII to justify trade restrictions (discussed in Chapter 9) is an example. However, to this day countries such as Singapore and South Korea continue to define themselves as developing countries in the WTO—'graduation' happens *de facto* not *de jure*, and often on an issue or agreement-specific basis.[3]

Although the rationale for SDT was based on prevalent theories that import substitution was a necessary element in effective development strategies, as mentioned previously, the GATT reciprocity dynamic was less effective in a developing economy context. A necessary condition for reciprocity to work is that decision-makers confront lobbies that seek better access to foreign markets. A problem was that potential gainers from such greater access, export industries, often did not exist or were small in developing countries. Moreover, those that might have favoured domestic liberalization as a quid pro quo for better access to foreign markets often benefitted from preferential (GSP) treatment, reducing their incentive to go head-to-head with domestic import-competing industries. Frequently,

---

[3] In the case of nonreciprocal preference programmes (GSP or GSP+), the donor country defines what the eligibility and graduation criteria are. These vary widely across OECD countries.

export industries were also granted exemptions from tariffs on their imported inputs, further reducing incentives to oppose protection at home.

Policymakers in many developing countries were also highly sceptical of the benefits of full participation in the GATT. Although the key problem from a development perspective was not GATT and its reliance on reciprocity, but the pursuit of inappropriate economic policies, GATT did little to help convince governments to adopt more liberal trade policies. Only if a country managed through its own efforts to grow, run a trade surplus, and become a potentially attractive export market, were pressures exerted to bring the country into the GATT fold. Finally, global foreign policy considerations also played a role in the acceptance of SDT. Some high-income countries believed that an insistence on reciprocal obligations might help push poor nations to join the Soviet bloc (Kostecki, 1979). A concerted decision by major developing countries not to participate in the GATT would have been contrary to Western interests.

Increasing pursuit of economic self-interest

Developing country stances towards trade policy changed in the early 1980s, reflecting the debt crisis and the associated need to generate more foreign exchange and improve economic performance, the demonstration effect of the benefits of the export-oriented policy stance taken by the dynamic economies of South-East Asia, and the gradual collapse of central planning. As national trade policies became more neutral and export industries grew, interest in the GATT increased. Preferences and free riding were less beneficial to developing countries than they had expected. One reason was that MTNs were essentially conducted among developed trading nations, which concentrated on their own trade interests. As discussed in Chapter 4, the principal supplier rule used in MTNs helps ensure that free riding is minimized (Finger, 1974, 1979). Products of major importance to developing countries such as agriculture or textiles and clothing were either excluded from GATT or granted protectionist treatment on an ad hoc basis. Indeed, as noted in earlier chapters, the fact that developing countries were not playing the GATT game is one explanation for the continued existence of protectionist policies on textiles and clothing, footwear and other 'sensitive' labour-intensive sectors in OECD countries in the 1980s. Once developing country governments started to pursue unilateral liberalization and export-oriented strategies, the existence of high market access barriers in these sectors mobilized export lobbies to support more active participation in the GATT.

Unilateral changes in national policy stances led to a major shift in both the strategy and the tactics of developing countries in the GATT. They participated actively in the Uruguay Round, including the reciprocal exchange of 'concessions', and had a significant impact on the design of the GATS, and the Agreements on Textiles and Clothing, Safeguards and Agriculture. This influence was manifest from the very start of the talks. At the 1986 Punta del Este ministerial meeting, a group of smaller developing and developed economies (the Swiss-Colombian coalition) played an important mediating role between the US, the EU, and large developing countries such as Brazil and India. This marked a sea change not just in terms of increased participation, but also because it became obvious that it was no longer appropriate to regard developing countries as a bloc. (This had never been the case but it became increasingly obvious in the Uruguay Round.) Instead, countries pursued their self-interest in a much more open way than in the past. This included teaming up with high-income countries if this was appropriate. The Cairns Group, discussed in Chapter 6, was a prominent example of a North-South coalition of countries that sought to liberalize world trade in agricultural products.

In contrast to the Kennedy and Tokyo Rounds, the Uruguay Round was a single undertaking: all agreements were to apply to all members, and all members were to submit schedules of concessions and commitments. With the Uruguay Round an important step was taken towards ending the dichotomy that had characterized the GATT for several decades. The primary reflection of SDT in the Uruguay Round were the various transition periods for the different agreements and the more limited extent of tariff cuts that needed to be made by developing countries. But the key change relative to the GATT years was that all the agreements applied to all developing countries.

Although the single undertaking implied a dramatic change for developing countries, the creation of the WTO did not mean SDT is dead. Ending SDT was not on the Uruguay Round agenda. Indeed, the Punta del Este Ministerial Declaration explicitly stated that

CONTRACTING PARTIES agree that the principle of differential and more favourable treatment embodied in Part IV and other relevant provisions of the General Agreement... applies to the negotiations... [D]eveloped countries do not expect reciprocity for commitments made by them in trade negotiations to reduce or remove tariffs and other barriers to trade of developing countries.   (p. 7)

Thus, SDT remained embedded in the WTO. Special provisions for developing and least developed countries can be grouped under five headings: lower level of obligations, more flexible implementation timetables, commitments by developed countries to take into account developing country interests, more favourable treatment for LDCs, and promises of technical assistance and training. With the exception of the Agreement on Subsidies and Countervailing Measures, no criteria for 'graduation' were agreed to. As mentioned in Chapter 5, the SCM agreement has *de minimis* provisions for developing countries and exempts nations with per capita incomes below US$1,000 from CVDs on export subsidies as long as global market shares do not exceed 3.5 per cent for a product. Although BOP rules and procedures were tightened, revocation of Article XVIII remains an issue that is effectively negotiated on an ad hoc basis.

Developing countries play an active role in the WTO, although there is enormous variation across countries in terms of participation in the WTO committee structure, dispute settlement and MTNs. Large countries such as Brazil and India are very active, as are many middle-income countries in Latin America and Asia. They increasingly take a leadership role and collaborate on an issue-by-issue basis. As discussed in Chapter 4, the creation of negotiating coalitions such as the G20 and G33 has had a major impact on the dynamics of negotiations. The number of submissions made to WTO bodies by developing countries has expanded steadily. In the run-up to the Seattle ministerial meeting, for example, developing countries submitted close to 100 proposals on topics ranging from traditional market access issues to 'second generation' topics such as competition and investment policy (WTO, 2000).

During the Doha Round negotiations developing countries submitted many hundreds of proposals and defended their trade interests actively. For example, in the nonagricultural market access (NAMA) negotiations, ministers agreed in Doha 'to reduce or as appropriate eliminate tariffs, including the reduction or elimination of tariff peaks, high tariffs, and tariff escalation, as well as non-tariff barriers, in particular on products of export interest to developing countries' (Article 49). Much of talks revolved around the so-called exchange rate or balance of concessions between agriculture and NAMA negotiations. In this, as in other areas of the negotiations, SDT objectives were pursued vigorously. For example, the G33 group of developing countries proposed that up to 20 per cent of their agricultural tariff lines be defined as 'special' and that up to half of these would be exempted from tariff cuts, with the rest being subjected to only modest reductions (see also Chapter 4).

Another proposal tabled by the Mercosur members—Argentina, Brazil, Paraguay and Uruguay—called for developing country customs unions to be granted additional opportunities to shield products from tariff cuts, in order to preserve their common external tariff. Specifically, they proposed subjecting up to 16 per cent of industrial products to tariff cuts half as deep as those that would normally be required by the Swiss formula, with no cap on the share of imports involved. The argument for additional flexibility was that customs union members have only restricted ability to use flexibilities, as the common external tariff requires shielding the same products from tariff reduction resulting from the application of the 'Swiss formula' and the set of sensitive products differed across members of Mercosur. Although strongly opposed by other WTO members, in 2008 negotiators were more open to the idea of granting a limited measure of special consideration to the Southern African Customs Union (SACU), reflecting the fact that SACU includes two LDCs (Swaziland and Lesotho) and two countries that account for only a very small fraction of world trade (Namibia and Botswana).

More active participation extended to the poorest countries, even those without representation in Geneva, who formed into regional or issue-specific negotiating groups. Examples are the Africa group and the LDC group, which developed collective positions in the Doha Round in separate ministerial level meetings before major WTO conferences. These groups were supported by regional institutions— such as the African Union in case of Africa countries—as well as organizations such as the Agency for International Trade Information and Cooperation (AITIC), established in 2004, the International Centre for Trade and Sustainable Development (ICTSD), and International Lawyers and Economists Against Poverty (ILEAP). The latter are sources of advice, assistance and analysis and have done much to complement the activities of larger entities such as UNCTAD and the ITC to increase awareness and knowledge of the topics on the negotiating table. Although it remains the case that huge disparities exist in the ability of countries to participate in the WTO processes—many LDCs still do not have offices in Geneva for example—limited involvement may also be rational in that the payoff to participation may be limited for poor countries.

Developing countries are active users of the dispute settlement system, accounting for about 40 per cent of all complaints between 1995 and 2007, up from around one-third during the GATT years, and increasingly use WTO procedures against each other (Box 12.1; see also the discussion in Chapter 3). Particularly striking is the growth of cases against developing countries during the WTO period. Developing countries were defendants in only 8 per cent of all the cases brought during the GATT years (Busch and Reinhardt, 2002); in the 1995–2007 period this rose to 40 per cent. This is in part a reflection of the fact that GATT rules often did not bind and the increase in both coverage of multilateral disciplines and membership of developing countries.

The increased use of DS clearly illustrates the tendency for developing countries to defend their national economic interests. Despite the fact that many countries actively participated in negotiating coalitions, this has not impeded them from using the DS system against each other to enforce WTO agreements. The tendency to pursue self-interest is even more clearly illustrated by the use of DS to attack unilateral preference programmes that benefit only subsets of developing countries. Starting in the late 1990s more advanced and larger developing countries began to contest preference programmes that did not comply with WTO rules (the Enabling Clause requirement that preferences be 'generalized, non-reciprocal and nondiscriminatory').

An example was the December 1998 decision by Brazil to contest the EU GSP scheme as inconsistent with the Enabling Clause and the MFN rule and resulting in the impairment of benefits accruing to Brazil. This request for consultations, joined by a number of other Latin American nations, led to a six-year waiver being negotiated for the EU ACP preferences in Doha in 2001, and the launch of the EPA negotiations between the EU and ACP countries. As discussed in Chapter 3, the agreement on the waiver was also part of the MAS negotiated in *Bananas-III*, another example of a distributional conflict between groups of developing countries.

Box 12.1. Developing countries and dispute settlement

Developing countries have begun to use multilateral procedures to settle disputes much more than in the past. These go beyond the high-profile cases discussed in Chapter 3 (such as *Bananas*). A random selection of cases provides an indication of the types of disputes that have been brought.

- Singapore versus Malaysia (1994). The first case brought to the WTO. Singapore objected to Malaysian import procedures for plastic resins, alleging discrimination. The case was settled bilaterally in 1995.
- Brazil versus Peru (1997). Brazil objects to a countervailing duty investigation being carried out by Peru against imports of buses from Brazil.
- Chile versus US (1997). Chile contests a CVD investigation on imports of salmon, claiming insufficient evidence of injury.
- Colombia versus US (1997). Colombia argues that US safeguard measure against imports of broom-corn brooms violates the Agreement on Safeguards.
- India, Malaysia, Pakistan and Thailand versus US (1996). Contest a ban on import-ation of shrimp and shrimp products by the US under Section 609 of US Public Law 101–162 arguing violation of MFN and use of QRs (see Chapter 13).
- Brazil versus EU (1998). Contests the EU GSP regime as inconsistent with the Enabling Clause.
- Honduras and Colombia versus Nicaragua (1999). Claim Nicaragua's Law 325 of 1999, which provides for the imposition of charges on goods and services from Honduras and Colombia, violates MFN and tariff concessions.
- Argentina versus Chile (2000). Claim against Chilean price band system for safeguard actions.
- India versus Argentina (2001). Measures preventing imports of medicines.
- India versus EU (2003). Claim that the EU GSP+ scheme violates Enabling Clause.
- Antigua and Barbuda versus US (2003). Measures against cross-border supply of gambling services (mode 1).
- Brazil, Thailand and Australia versus EU (2003). Alleged violations of disciplines on export subsidies for sugar.
- Brazil versus US (2003). Contests US subsidy programmes assisting upland cotton producers.
- Bangladesh versus India (2004). Imposition of antidumping duties.
- Pakistan versus Egypt (2005). Measures against imports of safety matches.
- Panama versus Colombia (2006). Customs measures against certain imports.

A case brought by India against the EU GSP+ programme in 2003 is another example. This programme gave additional preferences to countries satisfying specific nontrade policy-related criteria (implementation of measures to combat the production and trade of narcotics). *EC—Tariff Preferences* was an important case because the 2004 Appellate Body ruling clarified what is permitted under the Enabling Clause. It concluded, somewhat surprisingly, that in principle WTO members *are* permitted to grant preferences to specific groups of developing countries as long as the targeted (preferred) group shares the same 'development, financial or trade need' as defined by an objective standard or set of criteria, *and* the need can be effectively addressed by granting preferences. Thus, differentiation is permitted as long as any developing country that meets the specified standard or norm is eligible for the preference. What constitutes 'objective criteria' is left to the donor country to determine—what matters is that there is no exclusion of countries that satisfy whatever criteria are established. Following the dispute, the EU changed the GSP+ programme, extending eligibility criteria (conditionality) to span compliance with (adoption of) 27 international conventions pertaining to labour standards, and making eligibility conditional on not exceeding certain trade performance thresholds.[4]

A final example is the case brought by Brazil in 2003 against EU export subsidies for sugar that was discussed in Chapter 6. Although ostensibly directed at EU violation of its export subsidy commitments for sugar, the case had major implications for ACP countries that had benefitted from guaranteed access to the EU market. The result of the case was that the EU was obliged to cut back exports of sugar significantly, with direct consequences for ACP producers. The reforms to CAP—in part to bring the EU into compliance with WTO commitments—lowered intervention prices, reduced EU output and substantially diminished rents for ACP sugar producers, generating adjustment costs in these countries as well as for EU producers. The fact that the EC did not ring fence the ACP sugar export volume in the reform of its sugar regime was an exogenous shock for the ACP that they could not have foreseen, even though it had been clear for some time that the EU would change the programme in the context of its decision to negotiate reciprocal trade agreements to replace the Cotonou Convention, and that there would also be some 'erosion' of rents as a result of the EBA initiative to grant duty-free, quota-free access to LDC exports of sugar as of 2009 (Hoekman and Howse, 2008).

[4] Trade criteria are a common feature of all preferential access programmes. For example, under the US GSP countries may lose eligibility for a specific product if exports exceed a 'competitive need limit' (US$110 million per tariff line in 2005) or account for more than 50 per cent of total US imports in that category. An inter-agency committee makes eligibility and graduation decisions after reviewing petitions from interested parties. Hudec (1987) concludes that a consequence is that import-competing lobby groups have made GSP a bastion of unregulated protectionism in the United States. Since the programme first entered into force in 1976, some 40 countries have 'graduated' from the GSP programme. Country eligibility for the EU GSP is determined by 'indices' that combine the development and specialization level of the country: $I=0.5[\ln(Y_i/Y_{EU})+\ln((X_i/X_{EU})]$, where Y_i (Y_{EU}) is the GDP per capita in the beneficiary country (EU) and X_i (X_{EU}) is the manufactured exports of the beneficiary country (EU) to the EU (beneficiary country). The index increases in value as the beneficiary country becomes more developed and/or runs a surplus in manufactured goods trade with the EU. A second graduation criterion is the ratio of imports from a given country to total EU imports of a product and this country's share of total EU imports. See Hoekman and Ozden (2005).

Post-Uruguay Round implementation concerns

A subsidiary body of the WTO General Council, the Committee on Trade and Development is the focal point for trade-related concerns of developing countries. A Subcommittee on Least Developed Countries focuses on issues of interest to the poorest WTO members. A frequent agenda item for these committees after the Uruguay Round was implementation and participation-related concerns, in particular the need for technical assistance and improving the effectiveness and application of the almost 100 SDT provisions found in WTO agreements.[5]

Implementation concerns were of three types. One was to ensure that high-income WTO members would deliver on their market access commitments. A second related to the ability of developing countries to implement the many Uruguay Round agreements before the various transition periods expired. Here a problem was that implementation of agreements had not been made conditional on obtaining adequate financial and technical assistance. The third was to question whether the substantive disciplines of some of the WTO agreements were compatible with national development priorities.

Many developing countries were concerned about the way the US and the EU had implemented the first stage of integrating textiles and clothing products into the GATT. As discussed in Chapter 6, the first tranches of liberalization essentially excluded any product of significant export interest. The use of transitional safeguards under the ATC by the US also did little to encourage developing countries. As mentioned, two dispute-settlement cases were brought regarding such measures. Although both were won, the signal that was being received was worrisome.

The Uruguay Round and the establishment of the WTO changed the character of the trading system. The GATT was very much a market access-oriented institution—its function was to harness the dynamics of reciprocity for the global good. Negotiators could be left to follow mercantilist logic—the end result would be beneficial to all contracting parties. This dynamic worked less well for developing countries, for reasons explained above. For these countries the burden of liberalization rested much more heavily on the shoulders of governments—even if they wanted to, the scope to use the GATT was often limited because exporters had fewer incentives and were less powerful than in OECD countries. The reciprocal, negotiation-driven dynamic also worked much less well for issues that were 'lumpy' and where the terms of the debate revolved around what rules to adopt, not around how much of a marginal change was appropriate. Once discussions centre on rules, especially disciplines on domestic policy and regulations, it is more difficult to define intra-issue compromises that make economic sense. Cross-issue linkage becomes necessary.

---

[5] The various provisions are identified and discussed in a secretariat document prepared for the Committee on Trade and Development (WT/COMTD/W/66), available on the WTO website.

Views on whether the package that emerged from the round was a balanced one differ widely. Studies of the Uruguay Round suggest all regions gained, with the magnitude of the gains depending importantly on the extent to which governments reduced barriers to trade (see Martin and Winters, 1996). Others argue that the models miss many of the important dimensions of the WTO agreements, especially the rent transfers associated with the TRIPS agreement and the implementation costs generated by the various agreements (Srinivasan, 1998; Finger and Schuler, 2000; Ostry, 2002). Whatever one's view, it is clear that the approach taken towards ensuring and supporting implementation of WTO agreements by developing countries was not an effective one. Limiting recognition of this problem to the setting of uniform transition periods was clearly inadequate. Many would argue that what is needed is greater willingness to allow more flexibility in determining whether all rules should apply to all countries. The case for uniform application of agreements that involve reducing trade barriers—tariffs, NTBs—is very strong. But in other areas requiring minimum levels of institutional capacity—such as customs valuation—'one size fits all' is a bad rule of thumb.

In the run-up to the Seattle ministerial in 1999, both types of implementation concerns—holding high-income countries to their promises and dealing with the problems of complying with Uruguay Round agreements—were put forward by developing countries as priorities to be addressed. The ministerial virtually coincided with the five-year mark after which most transition periods were to expire for developing countries (non-LDCs). By then it had become clear that many countries were struggling to implement agreements such as customs valuation, standards and TRIPS.

Numerous submissions were made, both with respect to old issues and suggestions for topics to be negotiated during the first year of a new round. Developing countries sought immediate action to tighten antidumping rules and expand *de minimis* provisions, and relaxation of subsidy rules to allow for export-promoting policies. On SPS and TBT, it was proposed to make technical assistance mandatory and to devise mechanisms to ensure that the views of countries at differing levels of development would be heard in international standards-setting bodies. On clothing, commitments were sought by importing countries to accelerate the elimination of the MFA, and commitments that antidumping would not be applied on goods that were subject to QRs. On TRIMs many countries sought extension of transition periods, an opportunity for governments that had not notified illegal TRIMs to do so and to be granted a transition period to phase them out, and an exemption from the ban on domestic content requirements. On IPRs, the demands included acceptance that the TRIPS agreement does not prevent developing countries from issuing compulsory licences for drugs listed by the WHO as essential, an extension of transition periods, a prohibition on patenting of plant and animal life, and operationalization of TRIPS provisions for transfer of technology on fair and mutually advantageous terms.

Most of these demands were opposed by the US and many other OECD countries, who did not wish to reopen Uruguay Round agreements. Given the debacle in Seattle, no concrete results emerged from the ministerial meeting. However, it was clear to WTO members that absent progress on implementation concerns it would be very difficult to launch a new round. In the aftermath of Seattle, the Quad put together a 'confidence-building package'. They proposed a case-by-case consideration of requests for extension of transition periods, improved market access for LDCs (but allowing for exceptions, and without mention of antidumping), and a promise 'to undertake to work to devote adequate resources' for technical assistance efforts. All in all, this package did little, if anything, to 'build confidence' that implementation concerns were being taken seriously. The market access offer did not go much beyond the status quo, the technical assistance language was vague, and the case-by-case approach to requests for extension was already largely provided for in the various WTO agreements. Indeed, developing countries had already been seeking, and obtaining, extensions under certain agreements, in particular that on customs valuation.

In May 2000 the WTO General Council adopted a work programme to review implementation-related concerns. Although little resulted from this process, the implementation agenda and work programme was part of a pre-negotiation process, akin to what occurred after the failed 1982 ministerial in the area of services. The various questions and concerns became prominent agenda items in the Doha Round.

12.2. DOHA: SPECIAL AND DIFFERENTIAL TREATMENT REVISITED

The Doha Ministerial Declaration reaffirmed the importance of SDT, stating that provisions for SDT were an integral part of the WTO agreements and that negotiations were to 'take fully into account the principle of [SDT...] embodied in Part IV of the GATT 1994...and all other relevant WTO provisions' (para. 50). It also called for a review of WTO SDT provisions with the objective of 'strengthening them and making them more precise, effective and operational' (para. 44). Modalities for further commitments, including provisions for SDT were to be established no later than 31 March 2003 (para. 14). On implementation, para. 12 of the Doha Decision on Implementation-related Issues and Concerns instructed the CTD to provide a report to the WTO General Council 'with clear recommendations for a decision'.

Years of negotiation followed, revealing deep divisions between WTO members on the appropriate scope of SDT and how to achieve the Doha mandate.

Box 12.2. Summary of main SDT Doha proposals by WTO agreement

- GATT Article XVIII: greater freedom to restrict trade for infant industry protection/ meeting development needs.
- GATT Article II: allow duties for fiscal purposes notwithstanding tariff bindings.
- GATT Article XVII: recognize importance of state-trading for developing countries.
- Part IV GATT: make improved market access (preferences) mandatory; hold developed countries responsible for achievement of Part IV objectives (e.g. growth in exports; diversification).
- WTO Article IX (waivers): commitment not to question benefits sought by developing countries and to grant LDC requests expeditiously or automatically.
- Agriculture: permanent exemptions in the calculation of the AMS for capital and input subsidies to resource poor farmers; raising the *de minimis* level of exempt AMS.
- Decision on Net Food Importers: developed countries to make specific, binding commitments to a revolving fund to provide grant aid.
- SPS: actions to reduce market access impediments, extension of transition periods, mandatory technical assistance.
- ATC: accelerated quota growth.
- TBT: create implementation fund; longer transition periods; impact assessments.
- TRIMs: longer transition periods for developing countries; exemption for LDCs.
- Antidumping: limit use by developed countries against developing economies; prohibition on use of duties as a remedy.
- Customs valuation: automatic extension of transition periods; right to use minimum prices for valuation purposes; mandatory provision of technical assistance for LDCs.
- Pre-shipment inspection: mandatory cooperation between customs authorities; technical assistance for price verification and fraud.
- Rules of origin: financial support for participation in WCO and WTO Origin Committee.
- Import licensing: preferential treatment for LDCs/developing countries; exemptions from reporting requirements.
- SCM: greater subsidy freedom.
- Safeguards: *de minimis* 3 per cent market share for every developing country; greater freedom to extend and repeat safeguards.
- GATS: establish and monitor benchmarks for technical assistance and market access; phase-out of mode 4 restrictions by developed countries; WTO to conclude agreements with other organization to address supply side constraints.
- TRIPS: increased flexibility in implementing the agreement as it concerns pharmaceuticals needed for eradication of endemic diseases; extension of transitional period; implementation of developed country commitments on technology transfer; increased technical assistance; compensation for indigenous knowledge; reconciliation of TRIPS with UN Convention on Biological Diversity.
- DSU: monetary compensation for losses to developing countries due to WTO illegal acts; panels to assess how developing country concerns and SDT requirements were addressed; longer time periods if defendant.
- Uruguay Round Decision on Measures in favour of LDCs: compliance with WTO to be at discretion of LDC; mandatory requirement that developed countries grant duty/ quota free access and address SPS and rules of origin constraints.

Box 12.2. (*Continued*)

- Tokyo Round (1979) Enabling Clause: all LDCs to be given full duty-/quota-free access before Cancun ministerial; LDCs to be compensated for preference erosion through elimination of all NTBs on their exports, debt relief and financial compensation for erosion for products accounting for more than 50% of export earnings; credit for unilateral liberalization; reiteration of principle of nonreciprocity.
- Accession of LDCs: reduce requirements and burdensome processes.
- Transparency: establishment of a mechanism to monitor the implementation of SDT provisions; greater accountability of high-income nations in delivering SDT.

Some 88 proposals were made by developing countries, many of them by the African, LDC and 'Like-minded' groups. They break down into demands for: (1) better preferential access to markets; (2) greater freedom to use trade restrictions; (3) greater freedom to delay or refrain from adoption of WTO rules or policy principles; (4) proposals relating to development aid and technical assistance for implementation; and (5) calls for greater transparency and accountability on the part of the industrialized country membership of the WTO for achieving SDT objectives. Box 12.2 classifies proposals by major WTO agreement.

The discussion on SDT was plagued by procedural and substantive disagreements. In an effort to break the impasse in the run-up to the Cancun ministerial meeting, the Chair of the General Council suggested classifying proposals into three categories: a set to be agreed before or at Cancun (38 mostly agreement-specific proposals); another group of 38 proposals that should be addressed in negotiating groups dealing with the substantive issues in question as part of the Doha Round; and a residual set of 12 proposals where it was clear that consensus would be very difficult to reach.[6] The 'early harvest' set included 12 proposals on which agreement had already been reached during deliberations in 2002—mostly technical assistance and information/transparency-related—as well as a group that in the Chair's view were important in terms of having a development impact and in which agreement appeared possible. These included proposals relating to balance-of-payments and infant industry protection, monitoring of actions by developed countries, waivers and transition periods, notification requirements, transfer of technology and simplification of rules of origin. The Chair's Category 2 proposals spanned antidumping, subsidies, agriculture, GATS, dispute settlement, SPS, TRIMs, safeguards and TRIPS.

The proposals were of two main types: replacing the best-endeavours language of SDT provisions calling on actions by developed countries with binding obligations requiring them 'to deliver'; and weakening the reach of substantive WTO

[6] See *Bridges Weekly Trade News Digest* (2003: 7, (13 and 17); www.ictsd.org).

disciplines. Given that much of what is embodied in Part IV is outside the control of industrialized countries, it is not surprising that they objected to suggestions that SDT become a binding obligation. Economists could (and did) argue that insofar as the economics of the disciplines embodied in many WTO agreements are sound, many of the proposals to weaken their reach are unlikely to benefit developing countries. The substance and economics of the disciplines in each of these areas are discussed in other chapters of this book.

Economic arguments were not very prominent in the negotiations, however. From a development standpoint, the discussions on SDT were striking in that the focus was not on whether a particular proposal had developmental merit. Proposals were not objected to so much because they would not do much good to the country or group proposing them, but because they would impose negative externalities. This was perhaps clearest with respect to proposals for deeper preferences for LDCs. For example, Paraguay argued that waivers from Article I GATT (MFN) should not be used to accord advantages or privileges to developing countries where they clearly discriminate against other developing countries. Instead, privileges granted should abide by the spirit and the letter of the Enabling Clause and its provisions, i.e. apply to all developing countries. In cases where this is not done, Paraguay suggested that the preference-granting country provide excluded developing countries with compensation.[7] Insofar as little in the way of a negative spillover would result from a proposal, other members tended to be relaxed. Thus, in practice, industrialized countries are prepared to accept export subsidies from LDCs almost indefinitely because such subsidies are unlikely to cause serious problems to their own domestic industries (and because LDCs do not have the financial wherewithal to undertake significant subsidy programmes in any event), not because there is a strong belief that this makes sense from a development perspective.

To many observers the SDT negotiations pointed to a need for: (1) greater differentiation between developing countries; and (2) greater emphasis on economic analysis and argument of why and how a specific proposal would be beneficial from a development perspective (Stevens, 2002; Hoekman, 2005; Page and Kleen, 2005). Part of the problem was arguably the Doha ministerial mandate, which made it difficult to more fundamentally rethink the framework for SDT in the WTO. The suggestion by the Chair to address most of the substantive SDT proposals in specific negotiating groups made sense in terms of pragmatism. It also has an opportunity cost: if a good framework for SDT had been in place which ensured that poor and/or small countries would not be subject to significant downside risks from accepting to negotiate on the Singapore issues, the Cancun meeting might have ended more successfully.

---

[7] TN/CTD/W/5, /Add.1, /Add.2.

Several options have been proposed in the literature for a different approach to SDT (see Hoekman, 2005, for references to the literature):

- acceptance of the principle of 'policy space': flexibility for all developing countries as currently (self-)defined in the WTO whether to implement a specific set of (new) rules, as long as this does not impose significant negative (pecuniary) spillovers.[8]
- a simple rule-of-thumb approach: allow opt-outs for agreements that require significant investment to implement for all countries satisfying broad threshold criteria such as minimum level of per capita income, institutional capacity or economic scale. As countries come to surpass thresholds over time, disciplines automatically would become applicable;
- an agreement-specific approach: this would involve the *ex ante* setting of specific criteria on an agreement-by-agreement basis to determine whether countries could opt out of the application of negotiated disciplines for a limited time period. Criteria could include indicators of administrative capacity, country size and level of development, and implementation could be made conditional upon adequate financial and technical assistance being offered;
- a country-specific approach: this would make implementation of new rules a function of national priorities. World Trade Organization disciplines implying significant resources would be implemented only when this conforms with or supports the attainment of national development strategies. A process of multilateral monitoring and surveillance, with input by international development agencies, would be established to ensure that decisions are subject to scrutiny and debate;
- a combination of country- and agreement-specific approaches: conditional on acceptance of certain binding core rules (e.g. MFN, the ban on quotas and tariff concessions), countries would be able to invoke a consultative, 'pre-panel' mechanism if they did not implement an agreement (or are challenged to that effect). This would focus not just on the legality of a policy instrument but on assisting governments to attain their objectives through the use of more efficient instruments than trade policies, including development assistance and other forms of cooperation.

A common element of all these proposals is that implicit or explicit use is made of economic criteria to determine the applicability of resource-intensive rules. This is controversial, as it implies differentiation among countries, something that continues to be rejected by many developing countries in the WTO. As discussed above, whether SDT is invoked is left to individual members (i.e. whether or not to self-declare as a developing country) and a mix of unilateral action and bargaining by developed country members whether to accept this and provide SDT. Country

---

[8] As noted in Chapters 1 and 3, in practice small countries are less likely to be confronted with disputes, so the proposal would to some extent simply formalize the prevailing status quo.

classification inevitably creates tensions among governments as to which countries would be counted in and which out. Although a major advantage of simple criteria is that it is 'clean'—there is no need for additional negotiation—the disadvantage is that criteria imply *ex ante* differentiation, which is not acceptable to many countries in the WTO (notwithstanding that it is standard practice in other international organizations). The alternative case-by-case approach is more 'resource-intensive', but experience shows that agreeing on a rule- or agreement-specific set of criteria is feasible—witness the Subsidies Agreement per capita income threshold for the use of export subsidies or the net food importers group in the Agreement on Agriculture.

Proposals revolving around full 'policy space' (free discretion as long as it does not injure other developing countries) or the application of specific criteria—be it by country (e.g. per capita income) or agreement—do little if anything to engage governments and stakeholders, or to help them identify better policies or areas where complementary actions/investments are needed. Instead, the focus is purely 'legalistic': SDT is needed as a mechanism to prevent countries from undertaking investments or implementing rules they do not wish to and to avoid being confronted by the threat of DS. A more country-specific approach that involves a process that encourages policy dialogue and accountability on all sides could do much to enhance the development relevance of the WTO, while at the same time reducing the perceived downside risk of undertaking new commitments for developing countries.

Potential advantages include: (1) it would bolster the engagement with developing country governments on their policies—complementing the Trade Policy Review (which is arguably under-utilized because the WTO Secretariat is not permitted to form judgements regarding the WTO consistency of observed policies or their impacts within and across countries); (2) generate assessments of whether policy instruments are achieving development objectives; (3) allow discussion/identification of less trade-distorting instruments; (4) allow for inputs from other entities, including national think-tanks and the private sector; and (5) help improve communication/interaction between the development and trade communities.

The fundamental problem with SDT in the WTO is that the only instrument on which members focus is the one that they negotiate on: trade policy broadly defined. The approach taken by the GATT/WTO to address development concerns can be characterized as an effort to use 'trade as aid'. Although this is understandable, it is fundamentally incoherent. Whereas trade is better than aid—indeed, trade is a necessary condition for development—the problem with the WTO approach to SDT is that it distorts incentives; is often ineffective; if effective, is inefficient and inequitable; and has significant negative repercussions on the realization of a nondiscriminatory multilateral trading system. As discussed in the next two subsections, using trade policy as an instrument to promote industrial development has not had much success. There is also substantial evidence that trade preferences are costly instruments, not just for excluded countries and the trading system as a whole, but also for the donor and recipient countries. But, most fundamentally, preferences do little to help countries deal with the domestic distortions that impede their competitiveness.

Infant industry protection

Industrial development is an integral part of any economy's development strategy.[9] The manufacturing sector is often viewed as the leading edge of modernization and skilled job creation, as well as a fundamental source of various positive spillovers. Accordingly, although many developing countries have scaled back trade barriers over the past 20 years, the industrial sector remains relatively protected, in part as a result of special tax concessions and relatively low tariff rates for importers of manufacturing machinery and equipment. Even when policies do not explicitly favour large firms, they may benefit relatively more from trade protection, both because their products compete more directly with imports, and because sectors with large, capital-intensive firms lobby the government more effectively. The bias against small entrepreneurs is exacerbated when financial repression is a problem, as credit rationing typically excludes the smallest borrowers first.

The infant industry argument, based on the existence of some type of market failure and dynamic positive externalities, is the main rationale underlying most advocacy of industrial policy. Kemp (1964) provides the first careful statement of the argument, identifying processes such as worker learning-by-doing as the source of the social benefits from intervention and distinguishing between learning processes that are internal to the firm and those that are external. As the former are appropriable by the firm, only the latter warrant government intervention, and then only if the reductions in cost over time compensate for the higher costs incurred during the period of assistance.

This argument does not provide a justification for blanket assistance to all firms in an industry or even a subindustry: the existence of an externality and the required cost-saving must be demonstrated in every case. Moreover, the tax-subsidy to be provided to firms should be temporary. Baldwin (1969) pointed out that a tariff or subsidy provides no incentive per se for a firm to acquire more knowledge. Because tariffs or subsidies are output-based (provide incentives for greater production), a firm will increase output by the least costly method, not necessarily by acquiring more technology. In theory, to capture the learning-related spillovers a subsidy related to knowledge creation is called for; e.g. a subsidy to those workers who learn by doing. Most knowledge or skill acquisition is

[9] For a more extensive discussion see Bora, Lloyd and Pangestu (2000) and Pack and Saggi (2005).

process-, job- or product-specific, so that the corrective subsidy should be targeted to the process, job or product.

These qualifications are examples of a more general conclusion emerging from the literature on government intervention. Any externality or market failure calls for a tax-subsidy, the base of which is the variable that generates the externality or failure, and the tax-subsidy rate will be that rate which gives the optimal effect (Bhagwati, 1971). Any policy other than the optimal tax-subsidy causes by-product distortions that will impose costs on the economy (Corden, 1974). In principle the tax-subsidy rate will vary across firms in an industry if the strength of the effect justifying intervention varies across firms. Even when an intervention is called for, a choice of a suboptimal instrument with by-product effects reduces the net benefits obtainable from the optimal instrument and may in fact be welfare-reducing. Finally, the economy-wide effects of intervention in one industry also need to be borne in mind—a tariff on an input will cause the effective protection of down-stream users to decline.

A recent argument for 'infant industry' type intervention has been offered by Hausmann and Rodrik (2003), who emphasizes a specific type of learning externality: providing incentives for firms to invest resources so as to help discover where a country has a comparative advantage. The argument they make is that in the process of transformation investments need to be made in new activities. The private payoffs to successful investments are much lower than the social benefit because the private gains may get eroded very rapidly in those cases where investments prove to be profitable—through new entry into what has been revealed to be profitable businesses. Thus, there is a nonappropriability problem. Their analysis suggests a role for government to increase the incentive to undertake 'exploratory' investments in new (nontraditional) activities—in addition to standard public goods such as property rights, as well as a liberal trade regime that allows access to inputs and technologies. At the same time, appropriate policies to foster investment (self-discovery) must be complemented by policies which ensure that failed experiments result in the exit of firms that entered into activities where there is no comparative advantage. What is needed, therefore, is a mix of promotion and discipline. Although learning externalities certainly exist, achieving such a balance is a major challenge.

A more general argument for policies to support industry (entry into nontraditional economic activities) revolves around enhancing the competitiveness of firms. To a large extent arguments along these lines are second-best type arguments—other policies and/or the institutional environment are such as to impose extra costs on firms located in the developing country, direct action to remove these excess costs is not feasible, giving rise to a need for policies aimed at compensating for these costs. But, there are also market failure aspects of 'competitiveness' arguments for intervention. Often these revolve around credit constraints for small- and medium-sized firms—e.g. absence of financing for investment in new technology or new business lines—that prevent upgrading and the production of higher value-added products, information asymmetries or externalities related to training to personnel. Insofar as such market failures exist, policy interventions need to be targeted at their source. In the case described above, moreover, the intervention will be horizontal or cross-cutting in scope, not sector-specific.

As mentioned, infant industry arguments may also be based on the presence of policies that are used to attain specific objectives—such as revenue collection—but which give rise to distortions in the economy. Assuming that the underlying policies cannot be changed in the short to medium term, this gives rise to the so-called theory of the second-best. In the context of international trade, there may be a second-best case for trade restrictions. For example, if imports of certain goods are subject to tariffs, welfare can be improved if tariffs or subsidies are levied on some or all of the remaining goods. Second-best rationales for protection are not a strong foundation for intervention as it is often not clear why in practice the policies that cause distortions cannot be changed. Moreover, determining the second-best policy requires a great deal of knowledge on the determinants of the behaviour of agents in the economy, which often does not exist. Third-best interventions made in ignorance of the true values of some behavioural parameters may be welfare-reducing.

There are also political economy and moral hazard problems associated with protection of infant industries. The prospect of protection can give rise to rent-seeking behaviour with associated scope for (legal) lobbying and (illegal) corruption. Moral hazard problems can easily arise as the reward for doing well is the removal of protection. This can generate perverse incentives for firms never to perform 'too well' so as to retain protection. In practice there are many examples of 'infants' that never 'grow up' and become able to compete internationally (Pack and Saggi, 2005).

Changes in the preferential trade landscape

The inability to conclude the SDT negotiations did not mean that nothing happened during the Doha Round in this area. One result of the insistence on SDT and the need to address Uruguay Round implementation concerns was that LDCs were not expected to make any market access commitments in the Doha Round. This 'Doha Round for free' decision was formalized at the Hong Kong ministerial in 2005. In addition, LDCs were granted better preferential access to major OECD markets. The EU's 'Everything But Arms' duty- and quota-free initiative for LDCs, the US African Growth and Opportunity Act, and the 2003 duty-/quota-free access programme for LDCs implemented by Canada, as well as similar schemes adopted by other OECD members, all provide better access than their GSP programmes by expanding product coverage and completely removing tariffs. Moreover, at the

Hong Kong ministerial agreement was reached to extend such duty-free access as a permanent WTO commitment for at least 97 per cent of the exports of LDCs. In addition to better access for LDCs, initiatives were launched to do more to assist countries to improve their competitiveness in export markets (the latter are discussed below).

The deepening of preference regimes for LDCs can in part be seen as a response to the increasing pressure being exerted by Latin American and Asian countries that did not benefit from the EU's ACP regime to reduce the extent to which they confronted trade diversion costs. As the WTO allows deeper preferences for LDCs, and almost by definition these are countries with limited supply capacity and thus not a major threat as competitors, other developing countries supported these LDC initiatives.[10] A corollary of deeper preferences for LDCs is that preferences for other developing countries are eroded. As already mentioned, such erosion was particularly significant for countries and products that had benefitted from guaranteed access to the EU market.

Much of the extensive economic literature on this subject concludes that preferences do little good to recipients and may do harm (Grossman and Sykes, 2005; Hoekman and Ozden, 2006). The reasons for this include the following:

The rules determining eligibility are defined by granting countries. Such criteria include rules of origin and product coverage. Rules of origin may be so strict (constraining) that it is cheaper for countries to pay the MFN tariff. Research suggests that the 'tariff equivalent' of rules of origin averages between 3 and 5 per cent (Francois, Hoekman and Manchin, 2006). This figure has remained remarkably constant over time—the first quantitative estimate ever made in the literature for EEC-EFTA trade in the early 1980s by Herin (1986) concluded that the 'tariff equivalent was in the 5 per cent range.

The importance of rules of origin as a constraint to utilization of preferences was revealed by the export supply response to AGOA. A number of African countries saw exports to the US explode in product categories in which they already had duty-free access to the EU. The more liberal rules of origin under AGOA allowed imports of yarn and fabric from anywhere in the world, whereas the EU did not. Given the absence of an efficient textile industry in African countries, they were unable to utilize the EU preferences (Brenton and Hoppe, 2006). Exports of apparel from African LDCs to the EU and US were almost equal in 2000, but the value of exports to the US in 2004 was almost four times greater than the value of exports to the EU (Figure 12.1). In the context of the 2007 Economic Partnership Agreements the EU relaxed its rules of origin for textiles and clothing significantly,

---

[10] An exception is Bangladesh, a significant exporter of textiles and clothing. The fact that Bangladesh is an LDC does much to explain why in Hong Kong it was not possible to obtain agreement to grant LDCs duty- and quota-free access for 100 per cent of LDC exports.

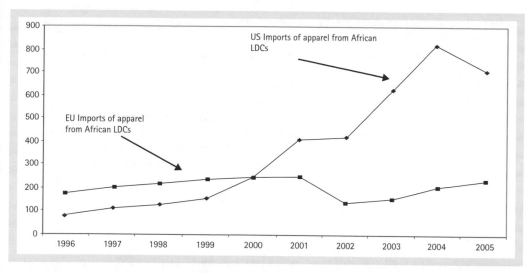

Fig. 12.1. Liberal rules of origin matter: EU and US imports of apparel from African LDCs (US$ million)

Source: Brenton and Hoppe (2006).

adopting a 'single transformation' rule (as in AGOA). However, this only applies to partners that have signed EPAs—it does not apply to countries with GSP or EBA status.

Product eligibility. Often goods in which developing countries have a comparative advantage are 'sensitive' products that have the highest tariffs. Preferences for these products have frequently been limited. Related to this is that recipients may not produce the relevant goods. The low level of industrialization and diversification in many low-income countries has contributed to low utilization.

Preferences are uncertain. The granting country is free to change eligibility, the administrative rules, and can erode the value of preferences granted by engaging in unilateral liberalization, undertaking MFN liberalization as a result of a MTN, or, as is increasingly the case, conclude PTAs with countries that compete directly with those who have preferential access (Box 12.3). One reason for the decline in exports to the US in 2004 shown in Figure 12.1 was that there was uncertainty regarding renewal of the liberal AGOA rules of origin in 2004 (they ended up being extended). There is very little scope to use WTO litigation to reduce the extent of uncertainty as granting countries are permitted to determine the rules of the game. In any event, recipients are unlikely to see it in their interest to litigate as that may increase the prospects of being excluded from benefits altogether.

Box 12.3. Unilateral preferences are uncertain

To benefit from preferential access, exporters must be able to document that products originate in countries that have been granted preferences. The rules of origin applied by a donor country can easily greatly reduce or nullify the benefits of preferences. To give an example, in 1983, the US adopted the Caribbean Basin Initiative, which granted Caribbean countries duty-free access to the US for many products. To determine whether a product was eligible for preferential treatment, at least 35 per cent of the value of the good imported into the US must have been generated in the Caribbean. The preference scheme induced foreign investment in the Caribbean, including companies that established operations in Costa Rica and Jamaica to convert surplus European wine into ethanol, which was then exported to the US. This production process met the 35 per cent value-added test. Two years later, with production and exports doing well, the exporters were hit with a rule change: a US congressman introduced an amendment to a tax bill raising the value-added requirement for ethanol to 70 per cent—an impossible requirement to meet for the Caribbean producers. The US industry that had lobbied for this rule change was never threatened by the imports, which never exceeded 3 per cent of US consumption (Bovard, 1991: 22).

The repercussions of the changes that have been implemented over time by the EU with respect to the preferences granted to ACP countries for sugar and bananas also illustrate that preference programmes are subject to exogenous shocks—in this case stemming from other countries invoking their WTO rights.

Nontrade conditionality. Preferences may be subject to (nontrade) conditionality (satisfaction of labour rights, environmental requirements, etc.). That is, there may in fact be significant reciprocity, but in areas not subject to WTO disciplines.

Importers will capture part of the benefits. Even in cases where preferences have value (are used), applying to highly protected sectors in donor countries and thereby generate rents, in practice these rents will not accrue completely to the recipient country. Instead, a share of the rents will be captured by importers (distributors, retailers). Ozden and Sharma (2006) estimate that Caribbean exporters capture only two-thirds of preference margin in the US market, whereas Olarreaga and Ozden (2005) conclude that the share of rents captured by exporters under AGOA are even lower.

Perverse specialization. If the sectors for which preferences are granted are not the ones in which a country has a comparative advantage, firms may be induced to invest in activities that can only survive *because* of the preference. If the preference induces such investment—that is, it is effective—it automatically creates a future adjustment burden as well as current resource misallocation distortions. Moreover, the preferences can result in countries not exiting a sector or not upgrading facilities and improving productivity because they have no need to.

Perverse political economy effects. Ozden and Reinhardt (2005) find that US GSP recipients implement more protectionist trade policies than countries that are removed from the GSP programme. They explain this apparently perverse effect of preferences by noting that preferences decrease the incentives for domestic export-ers to mobilize in favour of more liberal trade policies. As own trade policies are more important for developing countries' growth prospects than barriers in export markets, the perverse incentive effect of unilateral preferences may be quite dam-aging. This last line of argument has not gone unchallenged (see Box 12.4). If a (transitional) SDT regime is required to help developing countries to successfully liberalize their economies, Ozden and Reinhardt may be finding evidence that preference programmes are working as intended. Clearly for some countries—the

Box 12.4. A theoretical foundation for preferences?

Conconi and Perroni (2004) develop a theoretical framework that provides a possible economic rationale for what is observed by Ozden and Reinhardt. They argue that preferences are premised on inter-temporal reciprocity, and that the fact that recipients lower their trade barriers once they have graduated from GSP may simply reflect a temporal lag between reciprocal concessions, rather than GSP graduation directly inducing countries to liberalize.

The stylized facts that inform their analysis are: LDCs get deeper preferences than other developing countries; as (very) small price takers LDCs should in principle pursue unilateral liberalization, but do not; and preferences are granted on an explicitly temporary basis. These stylized facts are argued to indicate that the (political) con-straints on trade liberalization faced by LDC governments are viewed by all parties as transitory, and that the apparent gap between short-run protection incentives and long-run liberalization incentives reflects a commitment problem for LDC governments. This time-consistency problem reflects the power of import-competing lobbies. This com-mitment problem can then explain both the scope for SDT-based trade cooperation with a large developed country, and the temporary nature of SDT.

Given the commitment problem and allowing for adjustment costs, a self-enforcing dynamic agreement will necessarily feature higher protection in the small country in comparison with the long-run equilibrium tariff (i.e. delayed implementation); and, lower protection by the large country (i.e. temporary GSP concessions). In the Conconi and Perroni model, the market access (to the North) and the protection component of SDT (in the South), even though not formally tied, are linked by conditionality both within and across periods. In each period, cooperative policies are sustained by the threat of future punishment; at the same time, concessions are exchanged across different time periods—with the large country offering temporary preferences in ex-change for future market access, and the small country's determination to disentangle itself from its commitment problem being shored up by the prospect of facing future punishment by the large country for failing to succeed.

Whatever the case may be regarding the rationale for preferences, what matters is that the domestic economy 'works'—that there are no major distortions. In practice, as has been documented extensively, and as discussed in other chapters, domestic distortions are the major bottleneck impeding efficient production and economic growth.

successful ones that were 'graduated'—GSP may have played a role in generating the initial export expansion and then breaking a domestic political deadlock that precluded opening up the economy. Major exporters such as Hong Kong, Taiwan, South Korea and Singapore all benefitted from US and EU preferences in the 1970s, and subsequently to being removed from eligibility continued to do very well on the export front.

The duty- and quota-free initiatives put in place since 2000 help address only some of the problems that affect preference programmes. A key remaining factor is the rules of origin, which are still at the discretion of granting countries. The basic problem of supply capacity and lack of competitiveness of firms in the LDCs remains, as do the political economy downsides just noted. Finally, it is important to recognize the systemic effects of the continued use of preferences. These include trade diversion and the eventual adjustment costs as preferences are eroded. Preferences can give rise to detrimental trade diversion as the set of goods that beneficiary developing countries produce and trade will tend to overlap with other developing countries that are not beneficiaries. Borchert (2008) finds that the absolute magnitude of diversion caused by the EU GSP programme is economically significant, affecting large Asian countries in particular. Prospective adjustment costs may be particularly important in that they can impede further multilateral liberalization by creating a bootlegger-Baptist situation: beneficiaries are induced to support trade-distorting policies in donor countries that primarily benefit domestic producers in those countries—at the expense of the rest of the world (nonpreferred exporters) and domestic consumers/taxpayers. It is not surprising that many ACP countries often supported the EU in the Doha agricultural talks.

Some of the downsides of preference programmes for beneficiaries identified above can be addressed, but only at the cost of potentially making matters worse for excluded countries. For example, in 2008 the EU had plans to replace the different rules of origin that applied in its trade agreements—based on value added, change of tariff classification, or technical requirements—with a single criterion referred to as a maximum foreign content. This would define the degree of transformation required to confer origin to a product in terms of the maximum amount of value that can come from the use of imported parts or materials. The principal advantage of applying a 'maximum foreign content' principle is that it is transparent and can readily be applied across products. The adoption of such an approach would be somewhat akin to the tariffication of NTMs in the agriculture negotiations in the Uruguay Round. Future WTO negotiations could then focus on gradually reducing the restrictiveness of the rule (Cadot and De Melo, 2007). From a SDT perspective, an advantage is that it would allow for maximum foreign content levels to be set lower for LDCs, helping these countries to utilize duty-free access.

However, making preferences more effective will at the same time increase the costs of trade diversion and raise the incentives to oppose further MFN liberalization because of fears of preference erosion. The research by Nuno Limão (see Chapter 10) demonstrates that such diversion effects prevail in the US and the EU—both liberalize less in products that are important for preferred partners. The significance of erosion as a constraint on further liberalization depends very much on how large the benefits of preferences are (see Annex 2 for an illustration of the economics of preferential trade and erosion). Research on this question has shown that preferences are most valuable when they guarantee access through quota-like policies. Increasingly, that type of preferential access has disappeared in favour of tariff preferences only. An implication is that much of the erosion that could occur has already taken place—examples are the implementation of the ATC, which removed rents for less efficient exporters that had specific quota-protected access to major markets, and the unilateral reforms that were implemented by the EU for sugar and bananas.

Although there is a case to be made in favour of complete duty-free and quota-free access to major markets for the poorest countries, with liberal rules of origin that allow inputs to be imported from the most competitive sources of supply, such preferences should be seen as a transitional instrument. One rationale is that such preferences can help offset some of the competitive disadvantages firms LDCs operate under, and may help focus attention on the supply capacity and infrastructure investments that are needed in order to engage in global production networks (Hoekman, Ng and Olarreaga, 2002). That said, in absolute terms, most poor households in the world do not live in the poorest countries; preferences for some come at the cost of poor people in nonpreferred developing countries.

A large body of research has shown that discriminatory trade policies have been of limited use to many developing countries. Although a number of countries benefitted from such programmes as a result of being granted quota rents on traditional commodities such as sugar and bananas, this arguably has worked against their export diversification. Moreover, the plethora of preferential access programmes has encouraged the proliferation of reciprocal trade agreements, further distorting world trade flows and moving the trading system away from nondiscrimination. The fact is that despite preferences and SDT, many of the poorest WTO members have seen their share of world trade stagnate or decline since the 1970s.

All in all, both experience and extensive research suggests that shifting away from SDT as traditionally pursued in the WTO, in favour of an approach that focuses directly on the reasons developing countries cannot compete on world markets would have much higher payoffs. This is mostly a domestic reform agenda that revolves around facilitating trade, lowering trade and operating costs, and improving the productivity of firms and farmers. Shifting to other instruments that provide more direct assistance to realize these objectives would improve policy coherence by marrying greater overall *nondiscriminatory* access to markets to an enhanced ability on the part of low-income countries to exploit such access (Hoekman, 2002). Aid for trade also offers a potential mechanism for addressing preference erosion. For example, Limão and Olarreaga (2006) show that shifting from tariff preferences to a system of equivalent import subsidies (i.e. a form of development assistance) in OECD countries might encourage additional tariff liberalization and reduce distortions created by preferential trade.

As discussed further below, such considerations helped to put aid for trade on the agenda of international policymaking and the WTO.

12.3. BEYOND SDT: AID FOR TRADE (REFORM)

From the very beginning the third plank of SDT has been technical assistance to help firms exploit export opportunities—this motivated the establishment of the ITC in 1964. Over time, the connection between the ITC and its parents (UNCTAD and GATT/WTO) became rather weak. The WTO itself had virtually no capacity to assist its members. In 1999, when developing countries had raised the profile of implementation as a priority matter of concern, the WTO budget provided for only US$470,000 for technical cooperation activities by the secretariat. All of this was used for travel and subsistence expenses of staff, mostly in connection with training seminars and workshops.

At the 1996 Singapore ministerial conference, ministers committed themselves to addressing the problem of increasing marginalization of LDCs in world trade, and to work towards greater coherence in international economic policymaking and improved cooperation among agencies in providing technical assistance. Ministers agreed to a Plan of Action for LDCs. It envisaged closer cooperation among the WTO and multilateral agencies assisting LDCs in the area of trade.

To implement the plan, an Integrated Framework (IF) for trade-related technical assistance for LDCs was established. The Framework was endorsed in October 1997, at a WTO High Level Meeting for LDCs, where it was decided that six agencies—ITC, IMF, UNCTAD, United Nations Development Programme (UNDP), World Bank and WTO—would take joint responsibility for the implementation of the framework for identifying trade-related technical assistance to LDCs (Box 12.5). The idea was that needs would be addressed as part of the regular delivery of assistance by the agencies and/or bilateral donors. Essentially an unfunded mandate established by trade ministers, the IF achieved little in its early years. Over time its functioning was improved as the development community (see below) began to devote greater attention to the trade agenda.

Box 12.5. The Integrated Framework for technical assistance for LDCs

The primary rationale for the IF was to address the concerns expressed by developing countries regarding inadequacies of the implementation assistance provisions in the Uruguay Round agreements, which were of a best-endeavours nature. The WTO itself did not have the budget or the expertise to provide assistance to LDCs on the scale that was needed. Industrialized countries were not willing to transfer the resources required to either the WTO or on a bilateral basis. Nor were they willing to revisit the substantive obligations that had been negotiated in the Uruguay Round with which LDCs were to comply after transition periods had expired. The IF was an attempt to square the circle by shifting the problem to development-oriented agencies that had access to resources. Proponents also argued the IF would help to reduce duplication of effort among the agencies, and generate information on specific needs in trade-related areas.

The IF involved the preparation of 'needs assessments' by LDCs, followed by so-called integrated responses by the six agencies, indicating in which areas they could or were providing assistance. Gaps were to be filled by donor country pledges at 'round tables' that were to be organized for each of the LDCs by the agencies. Needs assessments were produced for 40 LDCs in the two-year period following the 1997 High Level Meeting. The responses indicated little in the way of overlap or lack of coordination among agencies, but did reveal significant demand for additional grant assistance. In mid-2000, an independent review of the IF concluded the process had not been effective because needs assessments were not sufficiently embedded in the development plans and strategies of recipient countries, and because inadequate funding had been provided to meet LDC needs. The IF also did little to address the underlying causes of the implementation problems of LDCs. In part this was because it did not address the disconnect between a number of the WTO agreements and the development priorities of low-income countries (Finger and Schuler, 2000), and in part it reflected the lack of adequate funding.

In response to the review, the six agencies proposed that greater stress be placed on ensuring that trade policy, trade-related technical assistance, and capacity-building needs are articulated in a broader development context to ensure that trade-related assistance needs are assessed alongside a country's other priorities. Insofar as trade concerns were identified as a priority area, it was expected that this would increase the chances that the necessary resources would be made available to LDCs. The agencies also proposed that donor support be sought for the creation of a trust fund dedicated to helping LDCs to develop the necessary analytical and policy framework for mainstreaming trade into national development strategies, for developing programmes and projects, and for training and capacity-building.

A subsequent taskforce recommended in 2005 that an Enhanced Integrated Framework (EIF) be established, with an independent secretariat and Executive Director. Progress in setting up the EIF was slow, reflecting in part the need to establish governance structures and put in place a mechanism to manage the dedicated fund that was recommended by the taskforce to provide additional financing to support trade activities in LDCs. In 2008 a Trust Fund Manager and an Executive Director were appointed and the new executive secretariat was ready to commence operations. Allocation decisions are taken by a new EIF board, comprising voting representatives of three bilateral donors and three LDCs. As of end 2008, over US$200 million had been pledged by bilateral donors to the EIF trust fund. Challenges that remain include providing adequate in-country support to the IF process, linking the WTO-based EIF secretariat to national capitals, and monitoring and evaluation of EIF programs.

One important change was the creation in 2001 of a dedicated trust fund to finance diagnostic activities—which extended far beyond WTO implementation issues—and small technical assistance projects. Although this helped to cover the costs of identifying trade-related priorities in LDCs, financing of these priorities was left to existing mechanisms for the allocation of development assistance. A perception on the part of LDCs that the IF was primarily a mechanism for studies and analysis as opposed to an instrument to deliver more aid resources to deal with identified priorities led to calls on their part for strengthening the mechanism and giving it substantially greater resources. A 2006 taskforce recommended that the IF be bolstered by creating a dedicated secretariat and a funding mechanism for its work programme (to be undertaken by the agencies and contractors). This fund was recommended to be on the order of US$200–400 million. At the time of writing the process of establishing this 'Enhanced IF' is ongoing.

The IF was the first formal effort to bring development agencies into the trade (WTO) picture. It was an initiative that came from the trade community, not the development community. The same was true of another initiative that was launched around the same time as the IF—the Joint Integrated Trade Assistance Programme (JITAP). This was a joint venture between the ITC, UNCTAD and the WTO, and was more narrowly focused on the delivery of trade-related technical assistance. The Joint Integrated Trade Assistance Programme was more limited in terms of its country coverage (16 beneficiary countries), but in contrast to the IF was not restricted to LDCs. The projects that were supported by JITAP were also more narrowly targeted, Programme interventions aimed primarily at trade ministries and their immediate constituencies.

Support for integration into the world economy through liberalization of trade-related policies was a major aspect of the programmes and activities of the IMF and World Bank in the 1980s. In the 1990s there was a significant shift in the focus of development institutions towards reducing poverty more directly, and working with governments to implement national poverty reduction strategies. A result of this shift in focus and modus operandi was that a larger share of development assistance was directed towards health, education and public expenditure management, with less resources going to infrastructure, agriculture and trade. In the late 1990s, governments of many developing countries perceived a need to focus more on stimulating higher economic growth rates. This view was supported by several taskforce reports. Thus, the UN Millennium Taskforce on Trade stressed that trade could do much to help achieve the Millennium Development Goal of halving poverty by generating higher growth rates (UN Millennium Project, 2005). The same message came from the Commission for Africa (2005).

The ability of poor countries to harness trade opportunities to promote development depend on policies that encourage new job creation, increase productivity, raise wages and move producers out of subsistence agriculture. Global trade reform, although important in and of itself, will not ensure these outcomes. Domestic supply constraints are the main reason for the lack of trade growth and diversification in many of the poorest developing countries. Without action to improve supply capacity, reduce transport costs from remote areas, increase farm productivity through extension services and improve the invest-ment climate, trade opportunities cannot be fully exploited and the potential gains from trade will not be maximized. Although the specific interventions that will generate the largest payoffs will differ between countries, the implication is that there is a case for additional 'aid for trade' as a complement to global trade reform (Prowse, 2006).

The agenda is huge. Poor roads and ports, poorly performing customs, weak-nesses in regulatory capacity, and limited access to finance and business services are all factors determining trade performance. They are all also areas where develop-ment assistance can help support reform efforts of governments and enhance the capacity to trade. For example, enterprises in Tanzania report that on average it takes about 12 days for exports and 19 days for imports to clear customs.[11] In comparison, it takes only two and three days for exports and imports to clear customs in the Philippines. It takes 116 days to move an export container from the factory/farm in Bangui (Central African Republic) to the nearest port and fulfil all the customs, administrative, and port requirements to load the cargo onto a ship. It takes 71 days to do so from Ouagadougou (Burkina Faso). In contrast, it takes only 20 days in China, Malaysia or Chile. On average it takes three times as many days, nearly twice as many documents and six times as many signatures to trade in a poor country as it does in rich countries (Figure 12.2).

Much of the behind the border competitiveness agenda is services-related and goes beyond transport. Power outages cost the median firm in Tanzania 5 per cent of sales. Firms try to cope by providing their own infrastructure: in Nigeria, over 90 per cent of firms with more than 20 employees have generators. But the marginal cost of such power is about two and half times higher than power from the grid, and the capital cost of a generator is equal to about 20 per cent of the total cost of machinery and equipment. Unreliable infrastructure can be most problematic for small firms, who are less likely to be able to cope.

An important step towards mobilizing additional resources to bolster trade cap-acity was the commitment by the G8 heads of government in May 2005 to increase aid to developing countries to build physical, human and institutional capacity for trade, and to grant additional support to build developing countries' capacity to take advantage of the new opportunities for trade that would result from a positive conclusion of the Doha Round.[12] The 2005 Hong Kong WTO ministerial meeting

---

[11] All data are from World Bank, *Doing Business 2006.*
[12] See G8 Declaration, Gleneagles (2005, Africa text: para. 22 (a)).

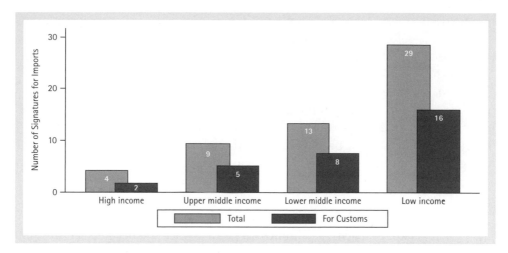

Figure 12.2. More complex and costly procedures in the poorest countries

Source: Doing Business.

established a task force on aid for trade to recommend how to move forward in operationalizing this agenda. In its report the taskforce sketched out a number of the key elements of operationalizing a concerted effort to expand aid to strengthen trade capacity and performance (WTO, 2006). This includes mechanisms to better define priorities and to ensure that funds and expertise will be made available to address demands. The taskforce also stressed the importance of more regular monitoring of the development assistance for trade that is provided to developing countries.

Much remains to be done to define and put in place the modalities for moving forward on aid for trade, especially for non-LDCs (Page, 2006). This is important whatever the ultimate outcome of the Doha Round. More effective mechanisms through which additional resources can be made available to developing countries to help them implement their trade strategies and benefit from trade opportunities will have a high return independent of the WTO process. Indeed, in the event of a Doha failure, a very similar trade agenda is likely to be pursued by many WTO members in the context of PTAs.

The challenges revolve around three broad questions: identification of the trade agenda at the national and regional level; providing assistance and financing; and effective monitoring and evaluation of both process and outcomes (Njinkeu and Cameron, 2008). An important question will be to determine the appropriate role of the different international agencies in this process and ensure coherence and coordination. As aid for trade is mostly a national and regional agenda that revolves around trade facilitation, improving regulatory regimes and hard infra-structure, delivery must involve primarily the development agencies with a country presence, working together with national governments and the private sector. These are not areas in which the WTO has a comparative advantage or capacity.

12.4. EXPANDING MEMBERSHIP: WTO ACCESSION

Despite the vigorous debates and numerous concerns expressed by developing countries and NGOs about the development relevance of the WTO, it is often pointed out that there is a long queue of countries seeking the accede to the organization. As noted in Chapter 2, there were 27 countries in the accession queue as of mid-2008, and 24 countries have joined since the WTO was established—all of them developing and transition economies. As discussed briefly in Chapter 2, the accession process is resource-intensive and complex. The major challenges confronting existing WTO members in terms of managing accessions are twofold. One is to integrate large, resource-rich countries such as China, Russia and Saudi Arabia. The first and last of these succeeded in joining, in 2001 and 2005, respectively, whereas Russia has yet to do so. A second challenge is to deal with resource poor LDCs in an appropriate manner. What follows briefly discusses both the challenges and the way they have been addressed, and the recent literature that attempts to assess impacts of WTO accession on trade of the new members.

China

China was a founding member of the GATT in 1947 but ceased to participate soon thereafter, once the Communist party took power. China was a signatory of the Uruguay Round agreements, reflecting the fact that negotiations on the country's accession to GATT were initiated during the round. The accession negotiations were difficult and lasted for over 14 years. The long drawn-out negotiation process had several reasons.

First, China's export growth performance and potential. China is a major trading nation. For many WTO members, China is the main source of labour-intensive imports that are putting considerable pressure on domestic producers. As a result, China is often the target of antidumping and safeguard measures. Because China was not a WTO member, such contingency protection did not have to conform to the usual WTO rules. Given the command nature of China's economy in the early years of accession negotiations, many WTO members were only willing to accept China after its economy had become more market-based. Representatives of the business community were of the view that the WTO accession should be used as an instrument to open the Chinese market to exports, and as a mechanism for achieving substantial reforms. Much of the negotiations therefore involved not just market access issues, but efforts to change basic legislation, enforce property rights, increase transparency and generally ensure that a 'level playing field' prevailed on the Chinese market. Given that the Chinese government was pursuing reforms throughout the period of negotiations, the regulatory situation was a moving target, further complicating the accession process.

Second, China sought to be treated as a developing country. It demanded long transition periods as well as special and differential treatment. In the earlier stages of the accession talks, it also opposed committing to significant liberalization, in part in an effort to keep bargaining chips and to protect inefficient state industries. China's negotiators also sought to keep tariff bindings significantly above applied rates. This was not acceptable to the major WTO players.

Third, noneconomic considerations played an important role in the accession negotiations. As with other transition economies, there was a close link between trade and foreign policy stances of developed countries, especially in the case of the US. Washington did not provide China with unconditional MFN status, as the Jackson-Vanik amendment to the 1974 Trade Act prohibited the US from granting unconditional MFN treatment to nonmarket economies that did not allow free emigration.[13] Until the US Congress approved 'permanent normal trade relations status' in September 2000, MFN status had to be renewed annually by the President, and was subject to congressional approval. This usually was a tough battle, as MFN was made conditional on China's human rights record and other foreign policy considerations (such as relations with China Taipei). Old-fashioned protectionism also played a role. The Democratic party, with strong ties to trade unions, feared being accused of generating employment losses as a result of stronger Chinese competition. The Republican party was highly critical of China's birth control policies and lack of religious freedoms. Thus, elements of both the right and the left in the US were hesitant to support treating China on a MFN basis. The decision by the US Congress to grant China permanent MFN status in 2000 was therefore a major breakthrough, particularly as it followed the debacle of the Seattle ministerial conference and the failure of the US government to obtain 'fast track' negotiating authority.

In the autumn of 2000, China's accession negotiations entered their final phase. The progress reflected the willingness by China to make far-reaching commitments. In principle, all enterprises located in China were granted the right to trade all goods throughout the country (with the exception of those subject to state trading). The WTO accession protocol contained extensive pre-commitments by China to liberalization, including in many services sectors, with most restrictions to be phased out by 2005. China also cut tariffs significantly, reducing average MFN rates for agricultural products to 15.4 per cent (down from 35.6 per cent), and tariffs for nonagricultural goods to 9.1 per cent (down from 21.9 per cent) (Table 12.2). Moreover, it essentially bound all its tariffs at levels at or close to its applied rates.

---

[13] This was a major reason why the US invoked Article XIII WTO, the nonapplication clause, in a number of WTO accessions (see Chapter 2).

Table 12.2. Tariff commitments of selected acceding countries (%)

Member	Year of Accession	Agriculture			Nonagricultural Products		
		Bound Tariff	Initial MFN Tariff	Post MFN Tariff	Bound Tariff	Initial MFN Tariff	Post MFN Tariff
Ecuador	1996	25.0	14.4	14.4	21.3	11.5	11.5
Bulgaria	1996	36.0	na	18.4	23.1	na	8.7
Mongolia	1997	18.9	na	na	17.3	na	na
Panama	1997	27.7	20.2	na	22.9	11.0	na
Kyrgyz Republic	1998	12.3	na	7.01	6.8	na	4.7
Latvia	1999	8.8	8.2	8.2	9.4	2.8	2.3
Estonia	1999	17.3	0.2	0.2	7.3	0.05	0.0
Jordan	2000	23.7	25.7	20.6	15.1	21.6	14.4
Georgia	2000	11.7	11.9	10.6	6.5	10.4	6.4
Albania	2000	9.4	15.3	9.3	6.6	16.0	6.6
Oman	2000	28.0	3.4	3.4	11.6	4.9	4.7
Croatia	2000	9.4	13.9	9.5	5.5	4	3.9
Lithuania	2001	15.2	9.4	8.6	8.3	2.62	2.3
Moldova	2001	12.2	13.2	na	6.0	4.2	na
China	2001	15.8	35.6	15.4	9.1	21.9	9.1
Chinese Taipei	2002	15.3	16.7	na	4.8	6.6	na
Armenia	2003	14.7	7.0	7.0	7.5	2.3	2.2
Macedonia, FYR	2003	20.9	11.3	na	6.2	13.4	na
Nepal	2004	41.4	13.2	na	23.5	13.2	na
Cambodia	2004	28.1	19.5	19.5	17.7	15.9	15.9
Saudi Arabia	2005	12.4	11.3	11.0	10.5	12.0	na
Average		19.2	13.9	10.9	11.8	9.7	6.6

Note: All data are simple (unweighted) averages of tariff lines.

Source: Martin (2005).

The Chinese accession is distinctive in that it embodies certain 'WTO-minus' provisions. In contrast to so-called WTO-plus commitments which may be—and often have been—demanded from accession countries (relating to matters not required by the WTO, such as privatization), WTO-minus provisions imply that an acceding members agrees to forgo or abstain from rights that other WTO members have under the multilateral agreements. In the case of China, WTO-minus commitments were needed because a number of WTO members insisted on being able to impose contingent protection on imports from China in a non-WTO consistent way. Thus, China's protocol of accession allows WTO members to take product-specific safeguard actions on the basis of 'market disruption' rather than the more constraining 'serious injury' criterion required by the WTO for a 12-year period. As regards antidumping and countervailing duties, the protocol put the burden of proof on Chinese exporters to demonstrate that 'market economy conditions' prevailed. If importing country authorities decided such proof was insufficient, nonmarket methodologies could be used to determine the extent of dumping. These WTO-minus provisions will cease to apply once each WTO member determines that China is a market economy, or 15 years after China's accession, whichever comes first. The textiles and clothing industry was a major player in this debate, given concerns about the strength of China's comparative advantage and the Uruguay Round ATC, which required all import quotas to be removed by the end of 2005 (Box 12.6).

Martin (2005) notes that these WTO-minus provisions are made worse as a result of the MFN principle: the result was that concerns of a few WTO members which led to product-specific safeguards being negotiated in bilaterals with China ended up being multilateralized. The same occurred with respect to provisions allowing some WTO members to extend ATC quotas on Chinese imports through 2008, which implied that countries that had not previously imposed quotas under the MFA could do so. Although these special safeguards are unfortunate and unnecessary given that the existing provisions in the WTO are wide enough to address import competition, they illustrate the nature of the bargaining process that is associated with accession. From an economic perspective it should be borne in mind that China managed to become a major trading nation despite being treated on a discriminatory basis before its accession, so that these provisions simply reduce the benefits of membership for a period of time. Much more important for China was that the process of accession was used strategically to pursue and support a broad range of domestic policy reforms that helped China to continue its high rate of growth.

Russia and the trading system

The relationship between Russia and the GATT has a long history with strong political overtones. The Soviet delegation took active part in the Bretton Woods

Box 12.6. Cotton, clothing and China's accession

The prospect of China's accession to the WTO had many ramifications for the global textile and clothing industry. For example, China is the world's second largest producer of cotton, after the United States. Much of the world's trade in cotton is governed by the so-called Liverpool rules, established in Liverpool a century ago when the UK port dominated the trade. The Liverpool Cotton Association (LCA), a body that sets product standards and oversees the trade, feared that once China became a WTO member and rules restricting trade were abolished, private entrepreneurs in China would be able to deal directly with foreign buyers. Given that most of China's output has been directed to the local market by the entities that controlled the distribution of cotton on the Chinese market, and that there was a large stockpile of cotton available in the country, there were concerns that the global market might be flooded with cotton after China joined the WTO and the liberalization of trading rights was implemented.

At the same time firms operating in the textile and clothing sector around the world were concerned that 'their' markets would be flooded by Chinese exports after China's accession once their governments were obliged to follow WTO rules on contingent protection. Fears were greatly compounded by the prospect of the end of import quotas mandated by the ATC (see Chapter 6).

The fears of the cotton traders and those of garment producers were not consistent— for Chinese garment exports to increase presumably they would need to consume more cotton. In the event China did not flood the market with cotton. Instead, China became a net importer of cotton as it expanded garment production and exports. Imports of cotton grew rapidly even as domestic production of cotton continued to expand to supply the domestic industry. This in turn explains the special safeguards imposed on China in its accession. The average export tax equivalent of import quota restrictions on Chinese exports of textiles and clothing was 20 and 36 per cent respectively. The removal of barriers associated with full implementation of the ATC clearly eliminated a major constraint on Chinese export potential in this sector.

Source: Financial Times, 17 August (2000: 6); Martin (2008).

Conference (1944) preceding the creation of the IMF and the International Bank for Reconstruction and Development (World Bank). Moscow was expected to participate in the two Bretton Woods institutions and in the future arrangements for the multilateral trading system (Mikesell, 1951). At that time the United States favoured Soviet participation. The American 'Suggested Charter' that was to provide a basic document for discussions at the London Conference (1946) on the ITO took the monopoly of foreign trade in the Soviet Union for granted and offered technical arrangements to render it more consistent with nondiscrimination.

In the event, the Soviets refused to accept the Bretton Woods agreements, absented themselves from the London and Havana conferences and also stayed away from the Geneva negotiations on the GATT. At the time, Moscow believed that participation in the post-war economic order carried with it a danger that the

United States might expand economically and politically into the Soviet sphere of influence. The Soviet expectation of economic crises in the post-war Western world also contributed to the decision to put off economic cooperation. In spite of the *rapprochement* that occurred between certain COMECON countries and the GATT in the 1960s and early 1970s, the USSR continued to remain outside the trading system. Moscow's reluctance was largely motivated by political considerations. The Soviet Union was not a trading power and the GATT—a technical rules-based entity—was not regarded as an appropriate framework for exercising Soviet influence in the trade area. Instead, Moscow pressed for the creation of a comprehensive trade organization under UN auspices, with effective links to UN political organs, and universal membership (Kostecki, 1979).

With the fall of Communism in the late 1080s, accession to the GATT and later the WTO began to be perceived as a necessary element of Russia's integration in the world economy. Organization for Economic Cooperation and Development members welcomed and encouraged the change in attitude. Russia applied for accession to the GATT in 1993. A memorandum on the foreign trade regime was submitted in March 1994. With the establishment of the WTO in 1995, the accession discussions were expanded to include services and IPRs. Although there was extensive discussion of many aspects of Russian trade policy over the years—in part driven by recurrent changes in this regime—many issues proved difficult to resolve. This included legislation affecting FDI in services, protection of IPRs, the jurisdiction between federal and local authorities in the area of standards, and issues related to Russia's PTAs with neighbouring countries (former members of the Soviet Union).

Key decisions Russia had to make included determining the level at which to bind tariffs, the support provided to agriculture and the coverage of specific commitments on services. The government felt that significant levels of protection were necessary during the transition to a market economy to allow restructuring of inefficient state enterprises. Accordingly, the Russian delegation presented initial offers to bind tariffs at rates much higher than those actually applied and proposed to leave a number of tariffs unbound. This strategy was also motivated by tactical considerations. Because applicants cannot typically negotiate improvements in access to markets of WTO members, it was deemed desirable to keep bargaining chips to obtain improved access in future negotiating rounds. As in the case of China, this did not serve to help move talks forward.

The accession process was not pursued vigorously. Political struggles between the executive and the Duma over legislation, frequent changes in governments, the rising influence of economic elites in the energy and service sectors—whose interests might adversely be affected by a liberal service offer—and continued uncertainty regarding the relations between the central government and the regions impeded the process (Aslund, 2007). As in the case of China, a number of concerns prevailing in major OECD countries also made the process more difficult. To some extent the issues were similar, including the reach of state-trading and nonmarket economy status and, for the US, the provisions of the Jackson-Vanik amendment. The latter was important, as on conclusion of the accession negotiations of the Kyrgyz Republic and Mongolia, the US had been forced to invoke the WTO nonapplication clause (Article XIII WTO).

By the spring of 2007, Russia had negotiated MFN status or better with all its significant trading partners and successfully concluded bilateral accession agreements with all but two recently acceded WTO members (Cambodia and Vietnam) and Georgia.[14] Russia agreed to reduce its bound MFN tariffs to about 8 per cent on average and to commitments to liberalize trade in key services sectors (that is, to go beyond binding the status quo). For example, the prohibition on foreign participation in mandatory insurance lines, as well as limits on the number of licences granted to foreign life insurance firms, were to be phased out five years after the date of accession. However, in certain key areas for Russia negotiators succeeded in avoiding liberalization. An example was refusal to allow branch banking by foreign suppliers, the first instance of a non-LDC acceding country to avoid such a commitment. At the time of writing the conflict with Georgia—which was already a major factor holding up conclusion of the accession talks in 2007—is likely to further delay accession prospects.

Accession of LDCs and other low-income countries

A number of early efforts by LDCs to join the WTO were not happy experiences. Nepal and Cambodia were the first LDCs seeking accession to join the WTO in 2004. In the case of Cambodia the process took almost 10 years. This compares to the accession at a stroke of a pen that applied to former colonies when they acceded to GATT upon independence—this was possible as result of Article XXVI:5(c) GATT, a provision that expired with the creation of the WTO. Vanuatu, which sought accession in 1995, suspended accession talks in 2001. Reasons included perceptions that too much was being asked and a general lack of ownership and understanding of the (net) benefits that would accrue to the country. As discussed in Gay (2005), one reason was a disconnect between the development concerns and objectives of the Vanuatu government and the hard-nosed negotiating stances that were taken by major WTO members, which applied the whole panoply of WTO rules to Vanuatu's trade regime without consideration of the specific circumstances that prevailed.[15] Another factor was the lack of adequate impartial technical assistance.

[14] What follows draws on Tarr (2007).
[15] Indeed, demands went beyond the WTO agreement. For example, the US reportedly sought revision of land ownership laws to allow foreign freehold ownership, a very sensitive political issue: the Vanuatu constitution prohibits freehold ownership of land. As a result of the inability to accede to the US request, concessions had to be made elsewhere (Gay, 2005).

The problems incurred by LDCs in acceding to the WTO reflected badly on its members. Least developed countries were held to standards that were higher than those applicable to many incumbents, and the negotiations were perceived by many as highly skewed against the LDCs. Some countries joined after making commitments that they were unlikely to be able to implement, let alone benefit from. A result of the Vanuatu decision to suspend accession talks was a December 2002 decision by the General Council that calls for the exercise of restraint by WTO members in seeking concessions and commitments from acceding LDCs and calling on them to ensure some parity between what was sought of new LDC members and those that had joined in the GATT years.

What is the value of accession and WTO membership?

The process of accession to the WTO is a long hard road for most countries, requiring major policy changes, adoption of new legislation and establishment or strengthening of domestic institutions. Despite arguments that are sometimes made by critics that accession involves a very asymmetric process in which accession candidates end up making commitments that reduce their welfare (Jawara and Kwa, 2003), the revealed preference of governments is to go through the process. This suggests that they perceive the return on their investment to be positive.

The most obvious source of benefits is associated with the MFN rules and the other WTO disciplines that preclude discrimination against the new entrants. Examples include pressures to accept voluntary export restraints of the type that have tended to be imposed by OECD countries on transition economies, or discrimination in the application of instruments of contingent protection. An illustration of the latter was shown by Francois and Niels (2004) who found that in the application of AD actions countries that were not WTO members were much more likely to be subjected to duties or price/quantity undertakings than WTO members.

The accession experiences reveal that the countries using them as a mechanism to pursue domestic reforms, at the same time as bringing their trade policies into line with WTO requirements, got the most out of the process in terms of enhanced economic growth performance. Examples include Cambodia, China and Vietnam. Perhaps surprisingly, however, there is little empirical analysis of the source and value of the associated benefits. In part this is because many of the benefits of the WTO are difficult to quantify—e.g. the security offered by MFN and the tariff bindings that have been made by WTO trading partners, and the possibility of invoking the DSU. In part it reflects the fact that WTO accession generally is accompanied by a broader set of domestic policy reforms and it is difficult, if not impossible, to attribute these to WTO accession. Indeed, the most successful accession countries use the process as a mechanism to overcome political economy resistance to opening the economy—China is perhaps the best example.

A first step in assessing the effects of accession is to determine how policies change. This is most easily done for tariffs. Table 12.2 reports average applied tariffs pre- and post-WTO accession for a selected group of countries, as well as the average level at which tariffs are bound, for agriculture and nonagricultural products. It is evident that there is significant heterogeneity. Many countries did very little if anything in reducing applied levels of agricultural protection. Many of the markets concerned are small. China is the exception, making very significant reduction commitments. More liberalization is apparent for nonagricultural goods, with China again doing the most. However, the general picture that emerges is one of limited liberalization, perhaps in part a reflection of the relatively low levels of protection prevailing in many of the countries concerned. A similar pattern obtains for services, where the stylized facts are that accession countries make a significant number of commitments—more than incumbents have made on average—but these are mostly of a binding nature, rather than imposing actual (additional) liberalization (see Chapter 7). Here again China is an outlier, having made extensive pre-commitments to liberalize services trade in its Protocol of Accession (Mattoo, 2004).

The limited extent of liberalization commitments by accession countries suggests that the impact of accession on trade should not be very large. This indeed is what research by Rose (2004) suggests is the case. Rose undertakes a gravity model analysis of the determinants of bilateral trade flows of GATT/WTO members for a 50-year period and fails to find a distinct impact associated with GATT/WTO membership. In related research, Gowa and Kim (2005) argue that the GATT had a (statistically) significant positive effect on trade between only five contracting parties: Canada, France, Germany, the UK and the US. Similarly, Subramanian and Wei (2007) argue that WTO membership increases trade—by some 40 per cent on average—but only for those countries that participated in the process of reciprocal exchange of trade policy commitments. Not surprisingly, given the emphasis put on SDT, they do not find a positive trade effect for developing country membership in GATT. Tomz, Goldstein and Rivers (2007) come to the same conclusion on the basis of a broader assessment of the impacts of trade agreements: countries with 'institutional' standing—i.e. that accepted the obligations associated with agreements—experienced an increase in bilateral trade.

More to the point from the perspective of the accession question, Rose (2005) and Subramanian and Wei (2007) find that there is a positive trade impact for developing countries that joined the WTO after 1995. Kennett, Evenett and Gage (2005) undertake detailed country-specific analysis of two accession cases and find that, once other determinants of market entry were controlled for, sales of long standing products to existing foreign markets rose after WTO accession. They estimate that just under a fifth of Bulgaria's recent export growth is attributable to its WTO accession. No such result is found for Ecuador, which can be explained by a significant *increase* in protection post accession. Tang and Wei (2006) assess accessions between 1990 and 2001 and conclude that when this sample is compared to nonacceding, non-WTO members there is a significant positive impact on both economic growth and on the investment-to-GDP ratio. Fink and Marchetti (2008) undertake a similar exercise and conclude that there is a positive FDI effect following accession.

These positive findings create a bit of puzzle in that it seems difficult to square significant trade or FDI effects with the limited extent of actual liberalization that seems to occur, especially if account is also taken of the fact that in general there is no liberalization at all associated with accession in the relevant export markets. This brings us back to the fact that much of the action is not with respect to tariffs, but other dimensions of WTO membership—such as transparency, reduced uncertainty, etc.—and the effects of complementary (and parallel) efforts at domestic reform. A plethora of empirical research using a variety of methodologies has shown that at the end of the day 'what you do is what you get' (Winters, 1999): the real income gains and poverty reduction resulting from better trade opportunities (market access—the focus of the WTO) depend on the domestic business environment confronting firms.[16]

The benefits that stem from the accession process are determined not just by the reforms that are implemented and the extent to which it is used 'strategically' by governments. As important is sustaining the reforms and addressing supply side constraints. As has been discussed in other parts of this book, the utility and effectiveness of WTO mechanisms in helping governments stay the course is affected by market size. Small, remote countries are simply not of great interest to exporters, so they are much less likely to contest policies that violate WTO commitments. Location also matters a lot in this regard—being close to a large, wealthy market will help attract FDI, with investors that have an interest in ensuring that policy conforms to WTO disciplines. Eschenbach and Hoekman (2006b) note that many of the transition economies that acceded to the WTO after 1995 made far-reaching commitments to open services markets. However, those located in Central Asia did not see the steady improvement in the quality and efficiency of services regulation—which in turn supported large inflows of FDI—that was observed in the countries geographically closer to the EU, including those that were not EU accession candidates.

12.5. CONCLUSION

For a long time, developing countries were effectively second-class members of the multilateral trading system. The insistence on SDT and the refusal to engage in

---

[16] See, for example, the contributions to Hertel and Winters (2006) and Hoekman and Olarreaga (2007).

reciprocal negotiations meant that the benefits of GATT membership were sub-stantially diminished. As argued repeatedly throughout this book, the main value of the GATT and the WTO is as an instrument that helps governments maintain a liberal and transparent trade policy, and as a mechanism to open and maintain access to foreign markets. By excluding themselves from the progressive liberaliza-tion induced by the dynamics of reciprocity, developing countries greatly reduced the relevance of GATT membership. The end result was that throughout the 1960s and 1970s, levels of protection in developing countries remained much higher than in OECD countries, and that the latter kept higher trade barriers on the goods of primary interest to developing countries.

Three decades of experience with the SDT strategy revealed it to be ill-advised. The fundamental dynamic of the trading system was and remains reciprocity. Those not willing to play this game found the benefits of free riding to be small. Indeed, from an economic perspective, the strategy was particularly counter-productive, as import substitution proved to be a very costly and ineffective development strategy (Bhagwati, 1988). External events and the lessons of experience gradually changed the attitude of many countries towards trade policy in the 1980s. The debt crisis induced many nations to adopt a more liberal and neutral policy stance. As important was the demonstration effect of the successful export-based economies of East Asia, and the collapse of Communism in Eastern Europe and the former Soviet Union. The internal political balance of power changed in many developing countries, as export interests became more sign-ificant. The GATT played a role in this process, but it was a minor one. The major force was unilateral reform and the shift to outward-oriented development strategies. In contrast to OECD countries, the mercantilist dynamics of trade reform were not important in the liberalization that occurred in most developing countries.

As new centres of economic activity emerged—in South-East Asia in particu-lar—these countries became subject to increasing pressure to 'graduate'. In the Uruguay Round 'graduation big time' occurred for all developing countries. In return for participating in the Uruguay Round 'grand bargain'—which included signing on to the TRIPS Agreement, the GATS, agreeing to the multilateralization of the Tokyo Round codes, binding of all agricultural tariffs and a significant increase in binding of industrial tariffs—developing countries helped realize a substantial strengthening of the rule-based multilateral trading system. The quid pro quo they obtained included the abolition of VERs (as part of the Agreement on Safeguards), the progressive elimination of the MFA and the re-integration of agriculture into the GATT.

Developing countries also benefitted from the increased security of trade rela-tions under the WTO, given the strengthened and unified dispute settlement mechanism. With the inclusion of services and IPRs in the WTO, unilateral threats and actions in these areas can only be taken by industrialized countries after a dispute settlement panel has found a violation and retaliation for noncompliance with panel recommendations has been authorized by the WTO. Finally, membership of the WTO may increase the credibility of domestic economic reforms in developing nations by reducing the uncertainty of trade regimes. This last possibility is potentially quite important, although much depends on the decisions of governments to exploit the opportunities offered by the WTO by binding tariffs at applied rates and making specific commitments for services. In practice, accession to the WTO is likely to deliver more in the way of commitment than is the case for incumbents.

The Uruguay Round left an implementation hangover for many developing countries, generating a renewed emphasis on SDT. At the same time, more advanced and 'less-preferred' developing country governments began to put more pressure on high-income countries to abide by the WTO rules, which require that all developing countries benefit from preferences and that better treatment be limited to the LDCs. This is arguably a positive development in principle, although it had significant implications for the countries that benefitted from special treatment, such as the ACP. The ultimate impact on the ACP countries will depend on the economic impacts of the Economic Partnership Agreements that have replaced the EU unilateral preference regime for non-LDCs. Many have argued that from a development perspective the design of the EPAs leaves much to be desired, not least as there is significant scope for welfare-reducing trade diversion. Much will be determined by what ACP countries do on behind the border policies as well as the extent to which they will extend liberalization on a MFN basis instead of limiting it to the EU (Hinkle et al., 2008).

It is easy to question the economic value of the SDT that was sought in the Doha Round, both in terms of revisiting existing WTO disciplines and in terms of exemptions and exclusions in the market access and rules related negotiations. Whatever one's conclusions—and in our view much of what was sought is not in the economic interest of the countries concerned—the de facto decision to pursue SDT on an agreement-by-agreement basis is a positive development. This is because the differential treatment is made explicit and transparent, and is (would be) part of a binding deal.

Many have argued that making 'development' a prominent objective of the Doha Round—starting with calling the negotiation the Doha Development Agenda—was a mistake. After all, there is no way that the WTO can deliver 'development' and making this the focal point creates the risk that the round would be seen as a failure no matter what the outcome. Indeed, as argued in this chapter, it may have made matters worse by stimulating more intensive reliance of instruments that have been shown to be costly and often ineffective. The problem of development lies at the centre of deeply rooted and complex country-specific economic, social and political processes (Srinivasan, 2007). Trade policy is only a small part of the set of instruments that matter.

The emergence of aid for trade on the agenda is a positive development in this regard. It suggests that WTO members recognize that trade liberalization alone is not enough to benefit poor countries, and that promises to provide technical assistance are an inadequate response to concerns regarding adjustment and implementation costs. A lesson from post Uruguay Round experience is that there is a need to bring trade policy more centrally into the development process and development strategies. This is required at two levels. At the national level, it is necessary in order to ensure that governments have a basis on which to negotiate agreements in an area. They must be able to identify what types of rules will promote development and what type would entail an inappropriate use of scarce resources. At the international level, it is necessary in order to enhance the communication between trade and development assistance bodies in member countries (see also Chapter 14). One reason for the implementation assistance problems that were encountered was that the best-endeavours commitments on assistance that were made by OECD trade negotiators were not 'owned' by counterpart agencies in their governments that controlled the money (development assistance).

Although the substance of the 'aid for trade' agenda is certainly not a new one—indeed, all of the areas for potential intervention have been pursued by developing country governments and donors over many years—the recognition that this is a matter that concerns both the international trade and development communities may help at the margin to shift the focus of policy away from SDT and towards domestic factors that inhibit investment and export growth. Looking forward, the challenge will be to apply the principle of comparative advantage in defining the respective roles of the trade and development communities in the delivery of aid for trade and supporting policy reforms. Designing and assisting in the implementation of aid projects is what the development agencies were created for. It would be an example of policy *in*coherence if the WTO were to get in the business of defining and delivering aid. Although there will be—and are—specific trade areas where the WTO membership may agree that there needs to be an explicit linkage between aid and implementation/enforcement of agreements, delivery of assistance in such areas should be left to the private sector and the development agencies.

12.6. FURTHER READING

Much has been written about the role of developing countries in the trading system, and the impact of the free riding strategy that was pursued in the 1960–80 period. Robert Hudec provides an excellent analysis of the issue, as well as a review of the relevant GATT history in *Developing Countries in the GATT Legal System* (London: Trade Policy Research Centre, 1987). An accessible account of the effects of the inward looking, import-substituting development strategies popular in the 1960s and 1970s, as well as the shift towards more outward-looking policies in the 1980s is given by Jagdish Bhagwati in *Protectionism* (Cambridge, MA: MIT Press, 1988). T. N. Srinivasan, *Developing Countries and the Multilateral Trading System: From GATT to the Uruguay Round and the Future* (Westview Press, 1999) provides a detailed analysis of the developing country dimensions of multilateral trading rules and the strategies pursued by developing countries in the GATT and the Uruguay Round.

Brian Hindley, 'Different and More Favorable Treatment—and Graduation', in J. M. Finger and A. Olechowski (eds), *The Uruguay Round: A Handbook for the Multilateral Trade Negotiations* (Washington, DC: World Bank, 1987) offers a short, perceptive review of SDT-related issues written at the start of the Uruguay Round. Bernard Hoekman and Caglar Ozden collect and summarize many of the key contributions to the literature analysing the economic effects of GSP schemes and SDT in *Trade Preferences and Differential Treatment of Developing Countries* (London: Edward Elgar, 2006). The contributions in Jagdish Bhagwati and John Ruggie (eds), *Power, Passions and Purpose: Prospects for North-South Negotiations* (Cambridge: MIT Press, 1984) discuss strategies followed by developing countries regarding international cooperation and global negotiations on economic matters during the 1970s and early 1980s. The contribution by Martin Wolf in that volume ('Two-Edged Sword: Demands of Developing Countries and the Trading System') offers a critical analysis of the impact of developing countries' insistence on nonreciprocity in the GATT.

Rubens Ricupero, the former Secretary-General of UNCTAD and trade negotiator for Brazil discusses developing country strategies and concerns during the Uruguay Round in 'Integration of Developing Countries into the Multilateral Trading System', in J. Bhagwati and M. Hirsch (eds), *The Uruguay Round and Beyond: Essays in Honor of Arthur Dunkel* (Ann Arbor: University of Michigan Press, 1998). Gilbert Winham, 'Explanations of Developing Country Behavior in the GATT Uruguay Round Negotiation', *World Competition Law and Economics Review*, 21 (3) (1998): 109–34, analyses the negotiating positions taken by developing countries in the Uruguay Round. J. Michael Finger and Philip Schuler, 'Implementation of Uruguay Round Commitments: The Development Challenge', *The World Economy*, 23 (2000): 511–26, discuss the implementation challenges, including likely resource costs, that confront developing countries as a result of the Uruguay Round, and argue that in a number of areas implementation may make little sense from a development perspective. Richard Blackhurst, William Lyakurwa and Ademola Oyejide assess the challenges and opportunities for enhancing the ability of African countries to benefit from the WTO in 'Options for Improving Africa's Participation in the WTO', *The World Economy*, 23 (2000): 491–510.

Readings on Doha and developing countries include Richard Newfarmer (ed.), *Trade, Doha, and Development: A Window into the Issues* (Washington, DC: World Bank, 2005); Simon Evenett and Bernard Hoekman (eds), *Economic Development and Multilateral Trade Cooperation* (Basingstoke, UK: Palgrave Macmillan, 2006); Gary P. Sampson and W. Bradnee Chambers (eds), *Developing Countries and the WTO: Policy Approaches* (New York: United Nations University Press, 2008); and Basudeb Guha-Khasnobis (ed.), *The WTO, Developing Countries, and the Doha Development Agenda: Prospects and Challenges for Trade-Led Growth* (London: Palgrave-McMillan, 2004). The papers collected by Dominique Njinkeu and Hugo Cameron (eds), *in Aid for Trade and Development* (Cambridge: Cambridge University Press, 2007) provide a discussion the genesis of the revival of aid for trade and how to move forward.

China's accession is discussed and analysed comprehensively in the contributions to Deepak Bhattasali, Shantong Li and Will Martin (eds), *China and the WTO: Accession, Policy Reform and Poverty Reduction Strategies* (Washington, DC: World Bank, 2004). For a detailed discussion of Russia's relations with the GATT and in the early WTO years, see Peter Naray, *Russia and the World Trade Organization* (Basingstoke and New York: Palgrave, 2000). David Tarr discusses the experience with and status of Russia's bid to accede to the WTO in 'Russian WTO Accession: What Has Been Accomplished, What Can Be Expected,' *Policy Research Working Paper 4428* (World Bank, 2007).

CHAPTER 13

....

TOWARDS DEEPER INTEGRATION? THE 'TRADE AND' AGENDA

....

STARTING with the Kennedy Round, MTNs began to focus on domestic regulatory policies and administrative procedures that have an impact on trade. This trend shows no sign of abating. In the Doha Round competition law and investment policy was discussed, and there are long standing proposals and pressures to incorporate disciplines on labour standards and environmental policy. The focus of the GATT was largely limited to the reduction or abolition of discrimination against foreign products. The approach was one of negative or shallow integration: agreement not to do specific things (for example, raise tariffs above bound levels, use indirect taxes to discriminate against foreign products, or to use QRs) or to do things in a certain way *if* a government decided to pursue a policy (for example, make a determination of injury caused by dumping a pre-condition for the imposition of an AD action). Shallow integration has been (and continues to be) the bedrock of the trading system. But this approach is more difficult to use to address differences in domestic regulatory regimes. Positive or deep integration may be required: agreement to pursue common policies, to harmonize (Tinbergen, 1954; Lawrence and Litan, 1991).

Deep integration became more prominent on the WTO agenda because the liberalization of traditional trade policy instruments increased the visibility of differences in national regulatory regimes. The memorable analogy made by Baldwin (1970) illustrates the underlying dynamic. He compared trade liberalization to draining a swamp: as the water recedes, a variety of tree stumps and other obstacles (nontariff measures) are revealed that must be removed before the land can be used. Calls for deeper integration at the multilateral level range from coordinated application of national policies to the harmonization of regulatory regimes. Such harmonization is sometimes held to be necessary to ensure 'fair trade' or equality of competitive opportunities for foreign and domestic firms.

This chapter discusses the general subject of dealing with 'behind the border' regulation in the WTO context, and provides an introduction to the main issues that are likely to be prominent on the multilateral negotiating agenda in the coming decades. A key question is to identify the rationale for—and objectives behind—proposals to address a specific matter in the WTO, and determine what type of cooperation is appropriate, if any. In many areas, both old and new, there is still great scope for shallow integration (the elimination of discrimination). In others deeper integration is required in order to realize benefits from cooperation. Independent of the type of cooperation that will generate the greatest gains, it is important to determine whether the WTO is the appropriate forum to address a specific subject. To date, a key criterion for inclusion has been that the issue is be trade-related. This explains why new topics are often discussed in the WTO under the heading of trade and the environment, trade and labour, trade and competition, trade and investment, trade and human rights, and so forth. A major challenge for the WTO members is to determine where to draw the line: how trade-related should a regulatory area be to be considered in the WTO?

13.1. CONTESTABILITY OF MARKETS AS A CRITERION

Sovereign states have pursued a sequential approach to economic integration of markets in the multilateral context. They first focused on reducing barriers to market access, initially border measures such as tariffs and quotas, later domestic policies with a potential trade impact such as subsidies and product standards. More recently efforts have also turned to areas where domestic regulatory regimes are directly at issue—such as services. The objective has generally been to enhance the contestability of markets for foreign products. Although the Uruguay Round mostly continued to revolve around shallow integration, a number of the agreements that emerged involved limited harmonization. Examples are the requirement to value goods on the basis of invoices (transaction values), the call to use international standards where these exist in the area of SPS and TBT, and, most notably, the TRIPS Agreement. After the Uruguay Round was concluded, the 'Reference Paper' defining minimum standards of regulation for basic telecom service providers continued the trend.

One reason for increasing pressures for deep integration is that this may be a necessary condition for governments to fully commit themselves not to use trade policy anymore—that is, to accept free trade. Another reason is the globalization of production. Firms are centred less and less on purely national markets. The managerial and technological innovations of the last decades of the twentieth century—such as just-in-time inventory management and the increased tradability of services resulting from declining transport, telecommunications and information technology costs—allow greater specialization and geographic diversification of production. This in turn makes differences in national regulations pertaining to services, FDI, transfer of technology and protection of intangible assets more costly for firms. Enterprises consequently seek to minimize the regulatory constraints to enter, operate in, and exit from markets. Harmonization can be one way to achieve the desired reduction in costs and uncertainty.

Market access has been the *raison d'être* of the GATT trading system. Should it remain the basic objective of the WTO? The TRIPS Agreement, Doha Round efforts to negotiate rules for antitrust, investment and procurement policies, and the calls to extend the WTO to cover labour standards suggests that many WTO members and interest groups do not think so. A good case can be made that the focus of the attention of the WTO should extend beyond market access narrowly defined. After all, if there are gains from cooperation on regulatory policies, these should be pursued. However, what should be included and what should be kept off the agenda? One criterion could be whether there is a link to the contestability of markets for goods, services and factors. If policy areas have a direct bearing on the conditions of competition prevailing on markets, they have a potential place under the WTO.

There are many policies that may affect the contestability of markets for foreign providers. They include traditional trade policies (tariffs, quotas, contingent protection), restrictions on FDI (prohibitions or discriminatory treatment), preferential government procurement policies, subsidies and other policies that treat foreign products or producers in a discriminatory manner. They may also span *nondiscriminatory* policies insofar as these have a differential impact on foreign firms. Examples include competition law and enforcement, product standards and service sector regulation. A first step for policymakers is to classify policies in terms of their impact on the contestability of markets and the type of cooperation that is required. The more that can be done through shallow integration, the likelier that agreement is feasible and that the WTO reciprocity-based negotiating mechanisms can help. Major areas where great progress can still be achieved via the traditional GATT approach of mutual disarmament are tariffs (still very high for agriculture and 'sensitive' industries), discriminatory government procurement, FDI and regulatory policies for services. In all these areas what is needed in the first instance is agreement to allow foreign firms to contest domestic markets and for governments to refrain from discrimination—that is, to apply the principles of national treatment and MFN.

What about generally applicable regulation of competition and government policies to attain noneconomic objectives? These may affect competition on markets. But cooperation on such policy areas will inherently be difficult to achieve. The payoffs of proposals on domestic regulations that apply on a nondiscriminatory basis are less clear, in part because harmonization may not be appropriate from an economic welfare perspective. In contrast to trade policy, when it comes to regulation there are few hard and fast rules of thumb that governments can rely on to ensure that agreements enhance welfare. In part this is because different interests are affected when it comes to regulation, including many issue-specific groups— environmental lobbies, consumer organizations, human rights activists and so forth. Preferences across societies will differ across countries depending on local circumstances, tastes and conditions.

Many NGOs have objectives that are not related to the market access goal of the WTO. Environmental groups are concerned with improving and safeguarding the environment, both at home and abroad. Other groups are concerned with social standards, or human and animal rights. The aim of these groups is often to export national standards to other countries. In this they may be supported by industries who are worried about their competitiveness vis-à-vis firms located in countries that have low environmental or labour standards, or are interested in selling their know-how in meeting standards to foreign enterprises. Such industries may push for import barriers as a way of offsetting the resulting 'unfair competition' or as an instrument to pressure foreign governments to adopt higher standards. Trade policy is rarely an appropriate instrument for attaining environmental or other noneconomic objectives. Efficiency considerations require that policy instruments are used which target perceived problems at the source. Trade policy cannot do this (see Annex 2). Indeed, in a number of areas it is not even clear that there is scope for gains to be realized from deep integration efforts—the issues are zero-sum.

Figure 13.1 provides a framework for thinking about whether deep integration is called for on an issue, and how useful and feasible efforts in this direction are likely to be in the WTO. Issues are plotted along three dimensions. The horizontal axis depicts the efficiency rationale for favouring diversity or uniformity in norms. The vertical axis plots the degree to which there are distributional tensions and differences associated with outcomes. In addition, issues are characterized by how trade-related they are— either strongly, weakly or not at all. In principle the latter should not be in the WTO.

Economic forces favouring global norms include uniformity of consumer preferences across nations, economies of scale and scope (including network externalities), or the fact that a particular issue involves a global externality and requires concerted action (for example, ozone depletion). Support for norm diversity, on the other hand, will be stronger the greater are national differences in preferences, the willingness to pay for particular standards, consumption patterns, and legal and political institutions. The smaller are the physical spillovers caused by production or consumption in one nation on another, the stronger the case for uniformity.

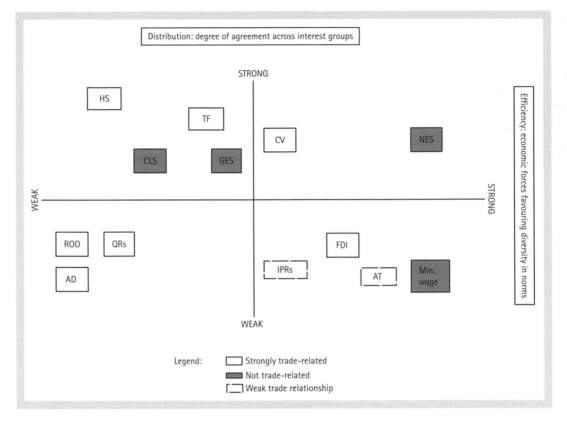

Fig. 13.1. Diversity versus uniformity in rules

Note: ROO=rules of origin; GES, (NES)=global (national) environmental standards; CV=customs valuation; AT=antitrust; TF=trade facilitation; CP=contingent protection; CLS=Core Labor standards.

For example, in principle there is a strong case for the adoption of a common system to classify goods. Classification is strongly trade-related and there are positive externalities from adopting common rules. This also applies to QRs—there is virtual unanimity that this is an economically inferior instrument of protection. A uniform rule, a prohibition, is therefore appropriate. The same applies to rules of origin (ROO) (harmonize), and antidumping (AD) (abolish). At the other end of the spectrum are issues where differences in national preferences, or absence of cross-border spillovers call for diversity in rules. Examples are national environmental standards (NES in Figure 13.1), which must by necessity reflect local circumstances and preferences or the existence and level of the minimum wage. Many of the issues mapped on the horizontal axis are multidimensional. For example, in the area of labour market regulation and standards there is a much stronger rationale for uniform rules for core labour standards such as a prohibition on slavery than there is for minimum wage legislation—most will agree that slavery should be outlawed, but such agreement does not exist on the need for a legislated minimum wage, let alone its appropriate level.

Although it is relatively straightforward to map issues on to the horizontal axis, whether countries will be able to cooperate—pursue common policies or accept diversity—depends on political forces. A major determinant of outcomes is the extent to which interest groups push or oppose a specific outcome. In the case of the HS classification system, for example, there were no powerful groups that opposed it, although agreeing to the classification took a lot of effort given that customs administrations had different views and concerns. In the case of AD, as discussed in Chapter 9, there are vocal and powerful interest groups that oppose introduction of the economically preferable uniform rule—a ban. A good deal of diversity can be expected to continue to prevail. The converse may also arise—a uniform rule is imposed where it may not be optimal (for example, TRIPS).

Some of the issues plotted in Figure 13.1 are not trade-related. Examples are environmental norms and national labour market regulations. As discussed further below, these have little direct bearing on trade, and trade policy is not an effective instrument to enforce whatever norms might be agreed. In some of these instances there is a good case for international harmonization (core labour standards, global environmental spillovers)—but a strong case can be made that the WTO should not be the forum for such cooperation.

Maskus (2002) develops a somewhat different approach to the question of what types of policy areas should be covered by the WTO. He uses four specific criteria: how trade-related they are (are there trade impacts?), the importance of international externalities that trade rules might overcome, existence of policy coordination failures of countries to enforce collective interests through stronger standards, and the ability of WTO dispute settlement (that is, using the threat of trade sanctions) to deal with them effectively.

13.2. FOREIGN DIRECT INVESTMENT POLICIES

With the exception of the general rules and specific commitments of the GATS, there are no disciplines in the WTO regarding policies towards international labour or capital movement. The GATT rules pertain to trade or trade-related policies—they do not extend to the policies used by governments to restrict or attract FDI. The GATT also has nothing to say about policies that affect the operations of firms that are established in a particular country—such as requirements concerning the employment of nationals, limitations on operations by branches and affiliates, restrictions on the number or location of establishments, and so forth. As long as a policy does not lead to discriminatory treatment of products, a WTO member is free to pursue any policies it pleases with respect to FDI in nonservice industries.

Some WTO members have argued that there is a need to negotiate multilateral rules for investment policies, such as the right of establishment and national treatment for foreign investors. These arguments largely revolve around market access objectives. In many sectors the preferred mode of supplying a market may be through FDI, not exports.

More generally, trade and investment are increasingly complementary—an ever larger share of global trade is intra-firm, involving exchanges between related enterprises (see Chapter 1). For example, US Department of Commerce data indicate that two-thirds of US trade involves US multinationals, of which about half is intra-firm (Schatz and Venables, 2000). Cross-border investment flows tripled during 1995–2005 and foreign capital stocks are now twice the size of global GDP. Much of the FDI that occurs today involves trade. Globalization of production—with firms sourcing from least-cost producers all over the world—makes investment regulations more important to enterprises because such geographic splintering often requires that the firm establish joint ventures or affiliates in various locations to ensure quality, or because technologies are proprietary. At the same time governments seeking to attract FDI may compete with one another—offering subsidies, tax concessions and so on to investors. Such competition is expensive and inefficient from a world welfare point of view because the total amount of FDI is not influenced by tax incentives—only its location. The end result of competition for FDI may be a suboptimal level of taxation of capital relative to other factors of production. Insofar as governments are playing a zero-sum game, they have an incentive to agree to mutual disarmament.

Many countries apply licensing and approval regimes and impose related red tape costs on foreign investors. They may also impose equity ownership restrictions. Such policies may reflect welfare-enhancing attempts to shift foreign profits to the domestic economy or welfare-reducing rent-seeking activities by bureaucrats and their constituents. Sometimes the effect of policies is simply to waste real resources (so-called frictional costs—see Baldwin, 1994 and Annex 2). Various arguments have been suggested as to why WTO members should consider the creation of a multilateral agreement on investment:

- national policies to encourage (subsidize) FDI may impose negative spillovers on other countries leading to an inefficient outcome for the world as a whole. An often mentioned example is tax competition between governments (Moran, 1998);
- an international agreement may serve as a mechanism through which governments can reduce investor uncertainty and reduce risk premia by making irrevocable policy commitments (Francois, 1997; Fernandez and Portes, 1998);

- trade and investment are closely interlinked, and many national rules overlap, so it makes sense to link the international rules governing them;
- given that the GATS covers FDI, it makes no sense not to have similar rules for nonservices FDI. General rules are required to ensure that investment policies do not distort the mode of supply choice of foreign firms (Feketekuty, 1998);
- an agreement can be a valuable tool for governments that are hostage to local incumbents that oppose foreign entry by being part of a 'grand bargain'. As FDI and trade are increasingly two sides of the same coin, rules should focus on the full set of policies that affect actors' decisions—both trade and investment-related regulations;
- given some 3,000 bilateral investment treaties (BITs), there are potentially large savings in transactions costs and reduction in overlaps and differences in coverage that could be eliminated by a multilateral agreement;
- finally, investment rules under the WTO umbrella would benefit from its institutional framework, in particular the strong WTO Dispute Settlement System.

The various arguments for an investment agreement in the WTO can be classified into four types of rationales: negative spillovers created by competition for FDI; policy credibility; completing the WTO architecture; and issue linkage (Hoekman and Saggi, 2002). What follows briefly discusses these.

(1) *International spillovers.* From an individual country's perspective, incentives to attract FDI may be justified if there exist externalities from FDI. For example, developing countries may hope that FDI will generate technological spillovers for local firms, thereby making more efficient use of existing resources. Spillovers may arise by local firms adopting technologies introduced by the multinational through imitation or reverse-engineering, by workers trained by the multinational transferring information to local firms or starting their own firms, and through derived demand by multinationals for local provision of services that can also be used by local firms. There exists a large literature that tries to determine whether or not host countries enjoy 'spillovers' (positive externalities) from FDI and what forms of domestic regulation will maximize the positive impact of FDI on the host country's economic growth (Busse and Groizard, 2008). The empirical support for positive spillover effects is mixed, with a number of studies using firm level data concluding that FDI has a negative effect on the performance of domestically owned firms and others finding positive effects. In practice much depends on the time period considered and whether the focus is on horizontal or vertical spillovers. There is more robust evidence of positive spillovers towards local suppliers to foreign firms (vertical spillovers) (Hoekman and Javorcik, 2006).

If governments believe that there exists a solid economic case for promoting inward FDI via incentives because of positive externalities, countries may find themselves in a bidding war for FDI. This can be to the detriment of the parties involved if it leads to excessive payment to the investor. The proliferation in the use of incentives to FDI suggests that this is an important possibility, and that there may be a case for international cooperation to ban or discipline the use of fiscal incentives. A key issue here is whether fiscal incentives are effective. If not, there is no argument for international cooperation on efficiency grounds as the incentives basically end up as transfers to multinationals. On the other hand, it is precisely when such incentives fail to attract FDI that countries have the most to gain from committing to not using them. The evidence on this issue is far from clear. Many studies conclude that incentives do not play an important role in altering the global distribution of FDI. What matters instead are fundamentals (market size, human capital, trade facilitation, labour market regulation, protection of property rights and enforcement of contracts, etc. Others conclude that incentives do have an effect on location decisions, especially for export-oriented FDI (Caves, 2007).

Even if incentives affect FDI, the efficiency case against competition for FDI is not clear-cut. Incentives may actually help ensure that FDI goes to those locations where it is most highly valued. Policy may act as an efficient signalling device that improves the allocation of investment across jurisdictions by ensuring that FDI moves to where it has the highest social return. In practice, however, locational competition is generally not driven by information asymmetries. This is the case in particular for efforts by high-income countries to retain or attract FDI that would be more efficiently employed in developing countries. Labour unions and groups representing the interests of local communities may oppose plant closures and efforts by firms to transplant facilities. Similar motivations underlie the use of trade policy instruments such as antidumping by OECD countries. It is important therefore to distinguish between locational incentives employed by developing countries and investment policies used by industrialized nations. The latter are much more likely to be inefficient and focus on attracting industries that otherwise would not have come or would have left. Investment incentives, as well as complementary policies that protect industries that cannot compete and should either exit or relocate (examples are rules of origin in regional agreements and antidumping) are prime candidates for international negotiations (Moran, 1998).

As in the case of subsidies affecting trade, obtaining agreement on what type of incentives should be permitted and what types should be constrained is likely to be difficult. Even if no financial incentives are granted, a country can offer a regulatory environment that may enhance its attractiveness to investors. Some of those regulatory incentives may in turn be considered 'unfair' (for example, low labour or environmental standards). Any type of industrial policy if applied on a national treatment basis may affect the location decision of a firm. As mentioned, the empirical literature on this topic suggests that foreign investors give little weight to fiscal incentives; what matters for them are factors such as the quality of infrastructure, political stability, and labour costs and available skills (Wheeler and Mody, 1992). The pressure on rational governments to engage in investment incentive competitions may therefore be lower than is sometimes assumed. In practice, incentives are likely to be most important, and most expensive, for countries that are attempting to offset policy-induced distortions which reduce their attractiveness for FDI. The solution in these cases is to deal with the distortions—bad infrastructure, political instability, etc.— directly. For these reasons, focusing on extending the fundamental disciplines of the WTO—transparency, national treatment, MFN and binding of policies— to the investment policy area may be much more productive than focusing on subsidy policy disciplines.

(2) *Credibility*. It is sometimes argued that a multilateral investment agreement may help countries enhance the perceived credibility of their FDI policies. In order to assess the relevance of the credibility argument for an investment agreement, it is necessary to identify how much of what might be embodied in such an agreement can be pursued and implemented unilaterally. The experience of transition economies re-confirms that economic fundamentals are the crucial determinants of FDI (Campos and Kinoshita, 2003). Some countries that concluded Association Agreements with the EU attracted very little FDI (e.g. Bulgaria in the late nineties) in large part because at that time privatization was not pursued with any vigour, the political environment was uncertain, and the macroeconomic policy such that inflation attained triple digits. The Czech Republic, Hungary and Poland did attract significant FDI inflows, but it is unclear what role the investment provisions of the Association Agreements played. Fundamentals, including privatization, re-establishment of private property rights, and geographic proximity to Europe (especially Germany) clearly played an important role.

Many countries that are looking for FDI have made use of a variety of existing, non-WTO credibility-enhancing institutions. These include accepting arbitration of disputes under the Convention on the Settlement of Investment Disputes between States and Nationals of Other States, by the International Chamber of Commerce (ICC), or by the UN Committee on International Trade Law (UNCITRAL),[1] depending on the preferences of the investor. Sometimes such commitments are embedded in BITs. Countries that are in the market for credibility can also use existing WTO disciplines to schedule market access opening policies for services (including granting of the right of establishment), and choose to lock in low-tariff regimes by binding these under GATT rules. There is still huge scope for developing countries to use the WTO as a credibility-enhancing instrument—as noted in Chapter 7, the coverage of services commitments is very limited, and tariff

---

[1] The International Centre for the Settlement of Investment Disputes (ICSID) operates under the aegis of the World Bank to apply the Convention. The ICC has a Court of Arbitration. UNCITRAL has adopted a set of Arbitration and Conciliation Rules that can be used in the settlement of commercial disputes.

bindings for merchandise imports are often significantly higher than applied rates. Although credibility with respect to investment-related policies can certainly be pursued via a multilateral investment agreement, those governments that are convinced they have a need to use external instruments to achieve such objectives could start by exploiting existing instruments much more fully. The same argument applies to PTAs—most do not go very far on the FDI front.

(3) *The architectural argument.* The current architecture of the WTO is quite messy: the WTO is an apex institution that embodies three major multilateral agreements. Of these, one incorporates FDI as a mode of supply and another protects IPRs. Given that trade and investment are increasingly complementary, it is difficult to maintain a clear distinction between trade in goods and trade in services, as technology may give producers the choice of delivering their products in tangible form or in disembodied form. A priori, it would appear that any multilateral disciplines should apply equally to international transactions regardless of the mode of delivery. This suggests that WTO members should consider developing disciplines that distinguish between trade and investment, with trade in goods or services being subject to a set of common rules, and movement of factors of production being subject to another set of rules. This, in effect, has been the approach taken in the NAFTA, which includes a separate chapter on investment (in goods or services), which is distinct from the rules relating to cross-border trade (in goods and services). Emulating this approach would result in much greater consistency and clarity of the applicable rules and disciplines.

This is a compelling rationale for discussing FDI-related policies in the WTO. After all, the WTO deals with trade, and there is no reason why this should not extend to trade in capital, especially as FDI in services is already covered by the GATS.

(4) *The grand bargain.* The OECD's failure in the late 1990s to negotiate a Multilateral Agreement on Investment (MAI) among supposedly like-minded countries (see Henderson, 1999) suggests that limiting attention to investment policies is a recipe for failure—the agenda needs to be broader to allow tradeoffs and issue linkages. Although a multilateral agreement might prove valuable to developing countries that confront difficulties in removing red tape unilaterally, the negotiation process must allow issues to be brought to the table that are of sufficient interest to domestic constituencies so that they will invest resources to fight for a better investment regime. Foreign pressure for market access may be enough in itself, but generally source country interest groups seeking such access will have to bring something to the table to motivate constituencies in host countries to assist them. More generally, FDI liberalization may be used as a negotiating chip to obtain concessions in other areas. One possibility would be to focus on the broader nexus of policies that affect location decisions by firms, as this could allow tradeoffs between trade and investment policies. There are a large

number of issue linkages that would improve global welfare—for example, disciplines on OECD investment incentives for reductions in developing country tariffs.

Logic suggests that if this path is followed movement of labour should be put on the table as well. Purely from an economic viewpoint, the argument for free movement of labour is no weaker than that for the free movement of capital (Panagariya, 2000). Clearly, countries that play the role of source countries in the movement of capital are likely to play the role of host countries for labour. However, it is unlikely that governments will be prepared to go far down this path anytime soon. The issues involved become considerably more thorny once labour mobility is introduced into the mix, and a complete revamping of the trading system may be required. Account must also be taken of the potential downside—issue linkage can be a two-edged sword. Efforts to expand the agenda to investment may allow groups in society to seek cross-issue linkages in areas such as the environment or labour standards that could be detrimental to the original *raison d'être* of the WTO: to progressively liberalize international trade.

From an economic perspective, the payoff to eliminating entry restrictions facing multinational firms producing nontradables (that is, services) is likely to be greatest, as FDI is the main mode of supply (Chapter 7). Similarly, if red tape on inward FDI is motivated in part by the existence of high trade barriers, priority should be given to trade liberalization to facilitate imports. Both can be pursued independently of FDI talks through continued multilateral liberalization of trade in goods and services. The GATS in particular has an important role to play in this connection as it already covers FDI in the sectors where it is most important as an instrument to contest markets—in services industries. The fact that the GATS allows commitments on establishment as a mode of supply weakens the case for making a stand-alone investment agreement in the WTO a negotiating priority. Once substantial further progress has been made to liberalize trade in goods and services on a nondiscriminatory basis, including national treatment and market access through establishment in service activities, it will become much clearer whether the potential benefits of seeking general rules on investment policies are large enough to justify launching a multilateral negotiation in this area.

The working group on trade and investment

The 1996 WTO ministerial meeting in Singapore established a working group to examine the relationship between trade and investment policies. This group did little to span the differences in view regarding the appropriateness of the WTO as an instrument to enforce disciplines on investment policies. Proponents of multilateral rules included most OECD countries and a number of middle-income developing economies such as Costa Rica and Chile. A large number of developing countries opposed launching investment negotiations, however. Many

NGOs—especially environment and development-oriented groups—were also active opponents of negotiating rules in this area. Their concerns were articulated at some length during the attempt by the OECD to establish a MAI in the late 1990s. Nongovernmental organizations opposed the draft MAI text as unbalanced, giving investors too much scope to oppose and circumvent government regulation aimed at social or environmental objectives through provisions on investor-state dispute resolution.[2] Although NGO opposition played a role in the demise of the MAI, lack of strong business support was also a major factor. Countries submitted long lists of derogations and exceptions to the general provisions of the proposed MAI, reducing business interest in the negotiation. The MAI illustrated that OECD countries were not ready to agree to disciplines regarding the use of investment incentives, an area of great importance to developing countries.

Efforts to launch negotiations on investment policies in the Doha Round did not fare much better. The reasons for the failure are discussed in depth by Evenett (2007a). In principle, the investment area could have been helpful to balance the negotiating agenda, as it was of interest to the EU in particular. In practice, however, at the end of the day many countries either saw the subjects as not being in their interest—i.e. moving them away from their status quo level of welfare (insistence by the US that any negotiation should include portfolio investments did not help) and (or) were of the view that even if they agreed to negotiate, it would not do much to generate additional movement towards liberalization of agriculture by the EU. Arguments that investment rules would benefit those who applied them did not cut much ice, not least because OECD countries did not want to discuss disciplines on investment incentives, a major source of international externalities. The end result was that investment became one of the three Singapore issues taken off the Doha agenda in July 2004.

13.3. COMPETITION POLICY

Competition law (antitrust in US parlance) is increasingly attracting the attention of trade policy officials. This is driven by export interests who argue that anticompetitive practices impede their ability to sell goods and services in foreign markets, and by concerns that 'mega-mergers' between firms located in different jurisdictions can have anticompetitive effects. National competition law comprises the set of rules and disciplines maintained by governments relating either to agreements between firms that restrict competition or to the abuse of a dominant

---

[2] See Henderson (1999) for a comprehensive description and assessment of the MAI story.

position (including attempts to create a dominant position through merger). A major objective in most jurisdictions is efficient resource allocation, and thereby the maximization of national welfare, by ensuring that firms do not abuse a dominant position or negotiate competition-restricting agreements that are detrimental to social welfare. The focus of competition laws is on competition, reflecting the belief that this is a powerful force for economic efficiency. However, many laws recognize that specific agreements between firms that may reduce competition can be efficiency enhancing, and make allowance for such agreements. Countries vary in the emphasis that is placed on efficiency—many also include social objectives and 'fairness' considerations in their legislation.

Competition policy has a much broader domain than competition law. It comprises the set of measures and instruments used by governments that determine the conditions of competition that reign on their markets. Antitrust or competition law is a component of competition policy. Other components can include actions to privatize state-owned enterprises, deregulate activities, cut firm-specific subsidy programmes, and reduce the extent of policies that discriminate against foreign products or producers. A key distinction between competition law and competition policy is that the latter pertains to both private behaviour and government policy, whereas antitrust rules pertain only to the behaviour of firms.

Many dimensions of competition policy are already on the WTO agenda. Examples include trade policy, subsidies, IPRs and market access in services. The focus of the debate in the WTO is therefore on whether there should be specific rules pertaining to national competition law and its enforcement—one specific element of a nation's competition policy. The WTO is not starting completely from scratch. Three WTO agreements contain provisions on or related to competition law: TRIMs, TRIPS and the GATS. The TRIMs Agreement is limited to a call to consider the need for possible disciplines in this area in the future. The TRIPS Agreement allows governments to take measures to control anticompetitive practices in contractual licences that adversely affect trade and may impede the transfer and dissemination of technology. The GATS recognizes that business practices may restrain competition and thus trade in services, but no obligations are imposed on members regarding either the scope or the enforcement of competition law. Members are only obliged, on request, to enter into consultations with a view to eliminating business practices that are claimed to restrict trade in services. The member addressed 'shall accord full and sympathetic consideration to such a request and shall cooperate through the supply of publicly available nonconfidential information of relevance to the matter in question' (Article IX). There is no requirement to act, only an obligation to provide information. It is therefore unclear how a restrictive practice is to be eliminated, or what constitutes a restrictive business practice. Indeed, members remain free not to apply competition law to services.

As in the case of the environment or labour standards (see below), a nation's choice regarding the existence and substance of its competition laws is currently its own affair. What matters for the WTO is whether such laws—or their absence—have implications for trade. In the case of competition rules the answer is clearly yes. In 1996, the WTO created a working group to investigate the relationship between trade and competition policies. Views on whether competition law disciplines should be incorporated into the multilateral trading system vary widely in both the policy and academic communities. Despite an ever-expanding literature on the subject, the debate remains contentious; there is no emerging consensus regarding whether and how to address competition issues in the WTO. This was reflected in the first report issued by the working group in late 1998, which simply recommended that discussions in the group be continued.

Competition policy has been on the international agenda for many years. The draft of the ITO charter included a chapter dealing with restrictive business practices, reflecting concerns—driven by German cartels and Japanese zaibatsu in the pre-war period—that international cartels and restrictive business practices can block market access. In the 1970s an active discussion took place in the UN-context on the need to discipline restrictive business practices by multinational enterprises—this resulted in a best-endeavours set of principles that was adopted by the United Nations in 1980.[3] Renewed attention emerged in the 1980s due to perceptions that restrictive distribution practices and conglomerates in Japan (keiretsu) impeded access to markets. The US argued for many years that keiretsu foreclosed markets for foreign suppliers by buying predominantly from each other and retaining close vertical linkages between manufacturers, wholesalers and retailers. The Kodak-Fuji dispute (see Chapter 3) was a noteworthy example of the US concerns. In the second half of the 1990s, the EU was in the forefront, arguing that all WTO members should be required to adopt and enforce competition laws. Disputes between competition authorities on 'mega-mergers', e.g. Boeing-McDonnell Douglas, Worldcom-Sprint, GE-Honeywell, as well as a resurgent interest in combating cartels reinvigorated calls for multilateral disciplines on competition policy—one reflection of which was a 1998 OECD Recommendation on Hard Core Cartels.

US authorities recognized the need for international cooperation, but were not willing to allow their rules to be subordinated to an international regime. US competition authorities did not want to change their laws in any way or to find themselves fighting market access battles, although US law had begun to provide for this in certain circumstances (Fox, 1997). Proponents of introducing international competition rules in the WTO initially had a predominantly market access-driven agenda. Nonexistent or poorly enforced competition laws were argued to hinder access by allowing domestic firms to foreclose or greatly increase the cost of entry. Japan and other Asian WTO members, most vocally Hong Kong,

---

[3] Formally, the Set of Multilaterally Agreed Equitable Principles and Rules for the Control of Restrictive Business Practices.

argued that the main issue from a WTO perspective is not competition law but the use of traditional instruments of contingent protection such as antidumping to restrict access to markets.

Smaller countries, especially developing ones, expressed concern about possible anticompetitive behaviour by large (dominant) multinationals. Both the EU and the US are large economic entities, with domestic competition authorities that are well equipped to address anticompetitive behaviour that has detrimental consequences for consumers located in their jurisdiction. Developing countries have less capacity to discipline possible anticompetitive abuses by foreign multinational firms on their markets. Perhaps the most obvious example is an export cartel designed to exploit market power on foreign markets. Such cartels benefit home countries if any detrimental effect on home consumers is more than offset by the gains to producers associated with their ability to raise prices on foreign markets. The latter will be to the detriment of foreign welfare if the costs to consumers there outweigh the increase in domestic producer surplus.

This brief introduction illustrates that there is significant variation in the interests of different countries regarding the type of multilateral competition disciplines that might be considered beneficial (acceptable). The main interest of the EU and US is to use competition law disciplines as an export-promoting device and to reduce the scope for conflict in the approval of mergers between large firms; they are less interested in subjecting the behaviour of their firms in foreign markets to international disciplines. Market access is also of interest to small countries, but they may be concerned as well with being able to invoke assistance in disciplining anticompetitive behaviour of firms located in foreign jurisdictions.

Much of world trade does not occur between independent firms operating on textbook-type perfectly competitive markets. Instead, competition is imperfect in that firms have some power to influence prices on markets, pursue collaborative ventures, or engage in intra-firm trade (see Figure 13.2). Such interactions are by no means an indication that competition is weak, and that there is a need to enforce competition rules. What matters is that markets are contestable. In many of the specific examples mentioned in Figure 13.2, government policy plays a role in reducing the contestability of the market, either through specific actions (such as STEs, allowing international cartels, or discriminatory government procurement) or through more general policy. In principle, there is therefore a good case to be made for focusing on the competitive implications of existing WTO rules.

There are a number of holes in the WTO as far as competition law is concerned. First, purely private business practices restricting access to markets that are not supported by the government cannot be attacked under GATT or GATS. Second, there is no requirement that WTO members have a competition law, let alone that it meet certain minimum standards. Many members have a competition law of some kind, but there are significant differences in norms and their enforcement. Third, the reach of WTO is currently restricted to measures by governments that

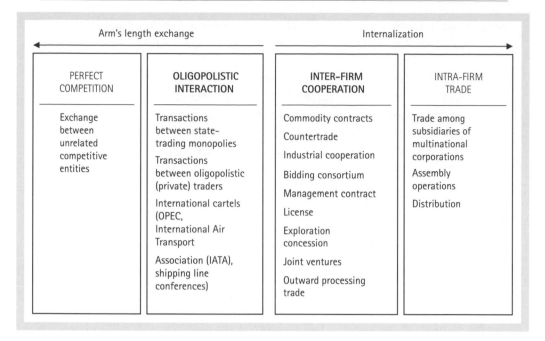

Fig. 13.2. Interactions in international trade

affect the conditions of competition in their territory. Practices by firms on export markets or tolerance by governments of anticompetitive behaviour on export markets by firms headquartered in their territory cannot be addressed. Finally, in a number of areas covered by the WTO—TRIPS being the foremost example— competition law has an important role to play in the implementation of the agreement, but there is no agreement on substantive standards, giving rise to potential for nonviolation disputes.

One problem confronting developing countries is anticompetitive behaviour— by foreign governments or firms—that they cannot address. Examples are export cartels and export taxes. Although export prohibitions or QRs and export subsidies are prohibited (see Chapter 5), current GATT rules basically give members the freedom to impose tariffs on exports. They also allow for export monopolies. This implies that members remain substantially free to attempt to raise the relative price of their exports, to the detriment of the rest of the world and that efforts to agree to multilateral disciplines regarding the treatment of export cartels in domestic competition law, if successful, will have to be complemented by analogous tightening of the rules regarding the scope for governments to pursue strategic trade policies more generally.

Over the last two decades, concerns regarding export behaviour have been complemented by problems arising in multijurisdictional merger cases. Competition authorities want effective leverage over mergers that may have cross-border effects, whereas firms want to minimize the number of agencies to which they are accountable. In principle, mergers between firms that will have a very high combined market share in markets where they are not domiciled can be a serious source of concern for a competition authority. Although many global mergers and alliances have been approved without disputes by the major affected jurisdictions, a number of cases in the late 1990s and in the 2000s led to tensions. One example was the merger between Boeing and McDonnell Douglas (MDD), where the US and the EU took different views, and only a last minute compromise prevented a serious trade conflict from erupting. The EU was concerned that certain of Boeing's long-term sole-sourcing contractual arrangements with airlines risked permanently excluding Airbus if they were not challenged. Thus, the concern was not only that the merger might result in higher prices for aircraft, but to protect the interests of the only EU competitor of Boeing-MDD (Airbus Industrie). The EU refused to approve the merger unless Boeing agreed not to enforce the sole-sourcing contracts, which in the end it accepted. The contested arrangements were actually unrelated to the merger as they involved Boeing and some of its customers—if they were bad for the EU, they were bad independent of the merger (Mavroidis and Neven, 1999). This raises the question of why objections were not raised earlier by the EU (or by MDD in the pre-merger period).

This case illustrated that interests of different jurisdictions can diverge considerably in merger cases. It suggests there may be value to adoption of rules to foster transparency such as harmonization of notification procedures. Less clear is how to address the problem of national authorities making mutually exclusive demands on a merging entity. For an international agreement to have prevented a similar dispute or the eventual negotiated outcome, it would have to impose clear standards for examination and review of mergers. The EU and the US already cooperate on antitrust matters under the auspices of a bilateral agreement that includes so-called positive comity language. This was not sufficient to prevent the dispute. One can question whether international rules could be devised that would be effective in requiring any one jurisdiction to back off in such cases.

How likely is it that countries will use antitrust strategically? Horn and Levinsohn (2001) conclude that this is not very likely, even in areas where it would seem most easily applied—merger policies and export cartels. However, Bond (1997) builds a model that gives rise to strategic behaviour by antitrust jurisdictions, and uses this to explain a late nineteenth century 'race to the bottom' in US merger standards (Box 13.1). Whether or not there are serious spillovers associated with merger standards, mergers are often politically sensitive, with national legislatures and governments resisting takeovers by foreign firms. EU decisions to oppose a merger between MCI Worldcom and Sprint, two US-based telecommunications providers, and a joint venture between Time Warner and EMI, led the US Senate antitrust subcommittee to express concerns that EU competition policy enforcement was influenced by a desire to protect EU-based firms (*Washington Post*,

Box 13.1. US state–level regulatory competition

Technological changes in the late nineteenth and early twentieth century led to a decline in transportation costs (railways, telegraph) and increased competition on many markets in the US. Federal law at the time focused on combating anticompetitive practices of large 'trusts' engaged in inter-state commerce. As the federal statute (the Sherman Act) banned price-fixing agreements, this gave firms an incentive to merge. State, not federal, authorities were responsible for approving mergers and granting corporate charters. This allowed states that were willing to have lax merger standards to pass laws that encouraged firms to merge and incorporate in their states. The most liberal state, New Jersey, managed to attract more than half of all corporations with a capitalization of US$10 million or more. By 1902 New Jersey was able to pay off the entire state debt from the tax it imposed on the capital stock of merging firms, and abolish property taxes. Other states tried to follow New Jersey's lead and a 'race to the bottom' ensued. Eventually 42 states adopted laws similar to New Jersey's, although with only limited effect—firms stayed in New Jersey.

The analysis of this episode by Bond (1997) illustrates that incentives to restrict mergers and price-fixing agreements across countries will vary with their endowments and political organization. Differences in the power of interest groups will determine the national antitrust stance. If more weight is put on the profits of merging firms, it is more likely to be permissive; conversely, if consumers are powerful it will be restrictive. If disciplines on antitrust are not harmonized, a race to the bottom can ensue. Centralization of antitrust at a higher level may allow a better cooperative outcome to result.

This analysis can be contrasted with state-level policies aimed at attracting investment. In a recent empirical analysis of the effect of US state policies on the location of manufacturing, Holmes (1998) finds that the share of manufacturing in employment in states with pro-business regulatory environments increases by one-third compared to a bordering state without such policies. This result is noteworthy not only in indicating that policies matter, but also in suggesting that differences across states are relatively stable. The measure of policy chosen (whether a state had a law banning requirements that all employees of a firm join a union) has not changed significantly since 1958: in the last two decades only two states passed such laws, while none repealed them. Here there was no race to the bottom. In general, there is little evidence for such 'races' (Vogel, 1995).

6 October 2000: E3). Conversely, there was substantial congressional hostility to a proposed takeover by Deutsche Telekom of Voicestream Communications in the summer of 2000, on the basis that the German state owned the majority of Deutsche Telekom shares.

The political economy of cooperation on competition law is very different from more traditional trade liberalization. Competition law does not lend itself very easily to incremental changes (the exchange of concessions). Moreover, specific policies that are pursued by governments may be in the national interest. Thus, any agreement to make binding commitments to follow a positive comity rule in mergers (let alone agree on common standards of review) and to prohibit export cartels (or even to agree to provide information) will imply costs for countries that benefit from the exploitation of market power. They can therefore be expected to demand a quid pro quo. A problem from a practical perspective is that for the WTO's traditional public choice dynamics (reciprocity) to work, antitrust-related market access barriers affecting a country's exporters must be large enough to offset the gains accruing to industries benefitting from national competition law exemptions. This suggests that a linkage strategy may well be necessary to make progress in this area.

What about the political economy argument that international competition disciplines might prove helpful to overcome domestic opposition to the implementation of pro-competitive policies? The foundation of the GATT and the WTO is that in the pursuit of a market access agenda, the national welfare is promoted. National antitrust has a very different focus from national trade policy in that the emphasis should be on welfare and the competitive process. This implies that the economic rationale for putting it on the WTO agenda is much weaker than for trade policy—national authorities should already be engaged in combating anticompetitive business practices. The pursuit of a market access agenda may result in outcomes that are detrimental from a welfare point of view (the latter possibility is a major reason some competition authorities are leery of putting antitrust on the WTO agenda). For the WTO dynamic to work, one must start from the presumption that competition law has been or will be captured by domestic producer lobbies, and therefore does not focus on welfare maximization. If so, and this may indeed be the case in some countries, there would be a rationale for pursuing international competition disciplines in the WTO. The problem remains, however, that the WTO process is driven by export interests (market access), not national welfare considerations. There is no assurance the rules that will emerge will be welfare-enhancing. Doubts can therefore be expressed regarding the ability of a WTO-based process to play as constructive a role in the area of competition law as it has in the area of trade policy.

Seeking substantive harmonization of antitrust rules is clearly a nonstarter. There is too much variance across jurisdictions. Even if similar multilateral rules can be agreed upon, national competition authorities will often weight aspects of a case differently. Optimal policy depends on many national (idiosyncratic) variables. For example, whether a country is better off allowing parallel imports or restricting it depends on the situation—no generalization is possible (Maskus and Chen, 2004). Competition law is an area where 'one size fits all' does not apply. Instead, shallow integration would appear a more fruitful approach towards cooperation—including application of the principle of national treatment and increasing the transparency of competition law enforcement. The WTO could also play a beneficial role in areas that are most trade-related—such as export cartel exemptions—and increasing the competition scrutiny of the trade policies that are permitted under existing multilateral rules.

The Doha Round failure

In 1997 a Working Group was established in the WTO to investigate the relationship between trade and competition policies. The 2001 WTO ministerial meeting in Doha agreed that negotiations on this subject were to be launched at the fifth WTO ministerial in 2003 on the basis of modalities to be agreed by consensus. At the 2003 Cancun meeting no such consensus emerged, reflecting continued differences in views on the merits of introducing binding competition law disciplines into the WTO, and in July 2004 the General Council agreed that competition would be excluded from the Doha Round. This despite some seven years of discussion and exchange of views in the Working Group, deliberations that had greatly changed the substance of what was being proposed by proponents.[4]

As discussions progressed over the 1996–2003 period, the emphasis that was put on spillover rationales for cooperation was gradually reduced. Instead, increasingly stress was put on 'systemic' or self-interest type arguments for antitrust disciplines—that legislation in this area was beneficial from a national perspective and would strengthen the global trading system (by complementing trade policy disciplines). On the market access front—among the most prominent of the initial rationales—efforts to put competition-related issues on the WTO agenda were driven primarily by producer interests. In effect, the governments concerned were pursuing a traditional 'export-promotion' objective, not welfare or efficiency—the major focus of many national antitrust regimes. Hence, a basic tension existed regarding the consistency of an international agreement on competition policy geared towards dealing with market access pressures (specific producer interests) and the focus of antitrust on national welfare (dynamic efficiency).

In the case of trade policy, the pursuit of mercantilist objectives by trade negotiators leads to an outcome that is welfare-improving (unambiguously for small economies that are price takers on world markets). In the case of competition policy this cannot be said—trading commitments on competition policy motivated by market access objectives could have negative implications for the enforcement of competition law more generally. Not surprisingly, it was therefore resisted by a number of competition authorities (e.g. Klein, 1996), and this part of the agenda was largely taken off the table in the course of Working Group deliberations. Instead, the focus shifted to support for a more general approach involving strengthening of national competition authorities in developing countries.

A problem with this shift was that a major potential source of benefit for smaller and poorer countries was not on the table. Levenstein, Oswald and Suslow (2002) analyze the purchases of developing countries of sixteen goods whose supply was

---

[4] Annual reports prepared by the WTO Secretariat on the deliberations of the WTO Working Group on the Interaction between Trade and Competition Policy for the years 1998–2003 provide a good synthesis of the issues discussed. See WT/WGTCP/2 through WT/WGTCP/7.

found to be internationally cartelized by European and/or American enterprises at some point during the 1990s. They found that in 1997 developing countries imported US$36.4 billion of goods from a set of 10 industries that had seen a price-fixing conspiracy during the 1990s. This represented 2.9 per cent of developing country imports and 0.7 per cent of their GDP. Such cartels are generally illegal under domestic antitrust laws. Other cartel-type arrangements have been shown to have serious detrimental effects on developing countries—examples include international air and maritime transport cartels, which impact on enterprise-level competitiveness. These are legal in that the arrangements are (inter-)governmental, but can raise prices significantly for developing country shippers and consumers. Fink, Mattoo and Neagu (2002) estimate that restrictive trade and anticompetitive practices raise maritime liner transport costs by up to $3 billion on goods carried to the US alone.

In principle, national competition authorities can use domestic antitrust law against cartels that have effects in their territory—whether domestic or international. However, many developing countries have limited ability to do so (Bhattachareja, 2004). The obvious solution is technical assistance and capacity-building, which became a major focus of the deliberations of the Working Group. However, an alternative approach would be for developed WTO members to discipline the ability of their own firms to collude to raise prices in developing countries (Hoekman and Mavroidis, 2003). This would avoid implementation costs for developing country governments while addressing the negative spillover. Hoekman and Saggi (2007) investigate the feasibility of a deal involving linkage between specific antirust disciplines of interest to poor countries—a ban on export cartels enforced by high-income countries—and market access commitments. They show that 'buying' competition enforcement from the trading partner through a mix of transfers of some kind and market access concessions maximizes the scope for cooperation. This suggests a rationale for countries to link binding of tariffs to an agreement to ban export cartels and 'outsource' the enforcement. However, no move in this direction proved possible in the WTO.

A number of conclusions can be drawn from the experience to date in the WTO:

• the focus of discussions and potential negotiations was not clearly on negative spillovers and/or market access constraints. The arguments that were made by proponents that competition policies are important for 'development' were not compelling because governments can and do adopt national competition policies without the WTO. International cooperation to address negative spillovers caused by national competition policy enforcement—e.g. to deal with international cartels (including export cartels)—was to be on a voluntary basis. But this did little to benefit small developing countries. It certainly did not help them deal with their concerns about international cartels and exemptions for export cartels in OECD competition laws;

604 THE POLITICAL ECONOMY OF THE WORLD TRADING SYSTEM

- given that the primary rationale offered for launching negotiations was that common competition principles would be in the interest of all developing countries, there needed to be significant domestic political economy problems in those countries that impeded unilateral action. How valuable internationally binding commitments are in this type of situation depends on the circumstances of individual countries. In the run-up to Cancun, many countries appear to have concluded that the payoff was small. Many of those countries already had antitrust legislation at the time (Epstein and Greve, 2004);
- a necessary condition for undertaking binding commitments is that countries have experience with the policy area. Countries need to be 'comfortable' with an issue and knowledgeable about the implications of proposed rule-making. In the competition case this minimum comfort level often did not exist;
- mechanisms involving voluntary exchange of information, peer review, etc., may be a pre-condition for governments to identify where formal cooperation (rules) is beneficial. Indeed, this may be a more effective and efficient vehicle for cooperation. One result of the WTO Working Group discussions was that voluntary fora for cooperation were either established or strengthened. The primary example is the International Competition Network—a forum for competition enforcers and lawyers to collaborate on guidelines for, and assessments of, national competition regimes. Other examples of such fora are the OECD, APEC and UNCTAD.

13.4. TRADE FACILITATION

Reliable, high-speed delivery systems are essential in today's global business environment where supply chain management is undergoing rapid changes due to the IT advances and the growing reliance of many sectors on outsourcing and partnerships. Leading car producers now purchase some 95 per cent of the value of their final product as parts sourced outside their workshops. The associated just-in-time international supply chains and subcontracting arrangements are critically dependent on getting goods and people to where they are needed when they are needed. Border controls and related administrative and documentary requirements can create significant delays in crossing frontiers and may impose significant costs on businesses that are part of integrated global production networks. Such firms do not maintain large (and thus costly) inventories—they rely on obtaining components from partners.

Trade facilitation may be defined as the simplification and harmonization of international procedures affecting trade flows. It focuses in particular on the

activities, practices and formalities involved in collecting, presenting, communi-
cating and processing data required for the movement of goods and services across
national borders. That means notably import and export procedures, payments,
insurance and transportation. The documents required in most export transactions include the commercial invoice, the packing list, a certificate of origin, an
insurance certificate, the carrier's declaration (or consignment note), letter of
credit or bill of exchange, certification of conformity for product standards and,
in some cases, a hazardous cargo certificate. Customs-related transaction costs—
not including the opportunity costs of delays—can represent between 3 and 10 per
cent of a shipment's value (Walsh, 2006). This implies that the cost to firms of
satisfying customs clearance and related requirements will often exceed the duties
paid on their exports. Costs are compounded if there is corruption. Case studies in
a number of developing countries and transition economies suggest that unofficial
payments may raise the marginal tax rate on imported products by more than 25
per cent (Kostecki, 2000).

   Border controls and associated costs and delays are particularly important for
express carrier companies, who generally invest significant resources in dealing with
documentary requirements (Box 13.2). E-commerce is playing an increasingly
important role in this connection by fragmenting containers of goods that could
have been cleared on a single entry into dozens of individual shipments that each
require separate customs documents and clearance procedures. Paper-based and
outdated customs procedures are still rife in much of the world. The same documentation may be required for a small package, a lorry or a ship. Some examples are
illustrative. Certified photocopies are often refused in developing countries, although their use is the norm in many high-income countries. Shipments may be
delayed because rubber stamps on documents are not pressed hard enough or put in
the wrong place. Customs authorities may refuse documents because they are
signed in black rather than blue ink (blue being viewed as an indication that a
document is original). In a series of case studies undertaken by Kostecki (2001) in
Eastern Europe, wine was denied entry because the corks in the bottles were not
considered to be in conformity with technical requirements, differences in date
indications on the packaging of chocolates in a shipment led to a clearance delay of
three weeks, and a British firm had its shipment of cider delayed because customs
had no product code for it and refused to label it an 'apple drink'.

   International traders have been quicker to apply new information technologies
than customs authorities in many countries. Technology now provides traders with
the facilities to develop cost effective international systems that employ a 'one stop'
data capture facility. The electronic transfer of data between parties involved in
trade transactions, including banks, insurers, transport companies, importers and
exporters, or forwarders permits the use of comprehensive transaction data files
that can also be used for customs and related control purposes. Technology-driven
trading systems render conventional paper-based export and import declarations

---

Box 13.2. DHL and customs procedures

Handling international shipments is not a trivial matter. Such shipments have to conform to specific shipping and packaging guidelines, and comply with special requests and documentary requirements. If a given shipment is customs-dutiable, it needs to be accompanied by an invoice at all times. If it is a noncommercial shipment, such as a sample, faulty part or a gift it calls for a pro-forma or nonbusiness use invoice. And so forth. Time-sensitive shipments are often handled by international express couriers such as DHL.

DHL, owned by Deutche Post, is the global market leader of the international express and logistics industry, with a 40 per cent market share. DHL offers expertise in express, air and ocean freight, overland transport, contract logistics solutions as well as international mail services, combined with worldwide coverage and an in-depth understanding of local customs procedures. The company's 2008 international network linked more than 220 countries and territories worldwide and was employing about 300,000 people. In addition to transporting documents, it handles parcels and larger shipments. The range of core and supplementary activities comprise order taking, pickup, documentation, real-time tracking of shipments, packaging, transportation and delivery. DHL also provides advice and information to clients and partners. The most important factor causing chinks in DHL's delivery process is customs-related controls and red tape. Getting parcels through the border and ensuring the necessary documentation is in place is an important element of the DHL service chain. DHL's strategic advantage (speed) is directly dependent on the efficiency of customs administration and the skill of DHL staff in developing mechanisms to satisfy customs requirements. The company therefore closely monitors customs administrations around the globe and maintains a high level of in-house customs expertise.

One element allowing rapid delivery is that shipments are often sent before all paperwork has been checked and cleared. In such cases, the DHL customs services staff sort things out after shipment has started. DHL personnel in the field and shippers are contacted 'en route' and informed about customs issues they must deal with urgently. If changes in invoicing are required, these are forwarded to the manager of the customs services unit in the importing country who will take the steps needed to ensure rapid clearance. An Electronic Database Interlink system plays a key role in maintaining continuous communication between local and centralized units, complemented with direct contacts with customs administrations.

Source: Kostecki (2000) and www.dhl.com.

---

and traditional customs control points redundant as far as revenue assessment and data capture is concerned. As a result, in OECD countries, customs is increasingly becoming a regulatory and standards-related enforcement body. Access to advanced consignment data enable customs to use profiling techniques to identify high-risk consignments and to concentrate on problem-solving rather than on traditional border control.

More efficient procedures and minimizing redundancy can provide important benefits. Because the costs involved are often frictional, the gains to traders and society can easily exceed those associated with trade liberalization. Red tape does not create rents or revenues as do tariffs or QRs. Instead, it simply generates waste (see Annex 2). Trade facilitation issues such as customs modernization, trade-related infrastructure, inland transit, logistics services, information systems and port efficiency are particularly important for developing countries. Numerous studies have shown that trade facilitation is a 'win-win game': more transparency and procedural uniformity in customs can lower trade costs significantly (Table 13.1).

In 2007 it took 10 weeks and about US$6,500 to ship a 20-foot container from Shanghai (China) to landlocked Chad, whereas it would take four weeks and less than US$3,000 to bring the same container to a landlocked place in Europe. Singapore, with only four documents and at most five days required to clear goods through the customs at an average cost of around US$400 per container, was the world champion of trade facilitation. Many African countries are at the other end of the scale, with six to eight weeks required and average costs of above US$2,000 per container. Landlocked countries face particular difficulties because of transit costs and delays.

Many of the policies concerned require harmonization of norms if costs are to be reduced. Thus, trade facilitation is one of the subjects on the regulatory trade agenda where deep integration is required if gains are to be maximized. Multilateral cooperation between states in trade-related standard setting and regulation dates back more than a century. For example, over 30 inter-governmental organizations were created during the 1860–1914 period motivated in part by trade facilitation (Box 13.3). By far the most frequent covered infrastructure: mail (1863), marine signalling (1864), technical railway standards (1883), ocean telegraphy (1897) and aerial navigation (1910). Multilateral cooperation supported the emergence of a Europe-wide market for industrial goods. International interconnection norms agreed under auspices of the International Telecommunications Union eliminated the need for telegrams to be printed at each border post, walked across and retyped. The Radiotelegraph Union aimed to prevent a global radio monopoly by requiring interconnection across different technologies. International railway unions

Table 13.1. The burden of customs clearance

	Exports			Imports		
	Number of Documents	Time (Days)	Cost (US$/Day)	Number of Documents	Time (Days)	Cost (US$/Day)
OECD average	4.5	9.8	905	5	10.4	986
East Asia and Pacific	6.9	24.5	885	7.5	25.8	1,014
Latin America and	6.7	22.6	1,095	7.7	24.0	1,208
Sub-Saharan Africa	8.1	35.6	1,660	9.0	43.7	1,986

Source: World Bank, *Doing Business* (2008).

Box 13.3. Pre-1914 trade-related inter-governmental organizations

---

Infrastructure and related 'software'

International Telegraph Union (1865)

Universal Postal Union (1874)

International Railway Congress Association (1884)

Central Office for International Railway Transport (1890)

Diplomatic Conference on International Maritime Law (1905)

Universal Radiotelegraph Union (1906)

Permanent International Association of Road Congresses (International Automobile Convention) (1909)

Standards

International Bureau of Weights and Measures (1875)

Metric Union (1877)

International Bureau of Analytical Chemistry of Human & Animal Food (1912)

Intellectual property

International Union for the Protection of Industrial Property (1883) (Paris Convention)

International Union for the Protection of Literary and Artistic Works (1886) (Berne Convention)

Trade

Brussels Tariff Union (International Union for the Publication of Customs Tariffs) (1890)

Hague Conference on Private International Law (1893)

International Bureau of Commercial Statistics (1913)

Dispute settlement

Permanent Court of Arbitration (1899)

International Court of Prize (1907; never ratified)

Source: Adapted from Murphy (1994: 48–9).

---

promoted networks by standardizing rolling stock, allowing companies to use each other's rolling stock, and enforcing a single bill of lading—so that a single document could be used for all trans-European shipments. European countries (except for Russia and Spain) adopted the same rail gauge, drove on the left, and aligned signals, brakes and timetables (Pollard, 1974: 50–1). All this was largely driven by the private sector—business can often achieve cooperation more readily than governments. The uniform bill of lading predates the introduction of the Single Administrative Document used by EU member states for customs clearance by almost a century. The Rail Union of 1890 played a significant role in dismantling protectionism in the late nineteenth century by prohibiting transit duties on goods shipped by rail. The Brussels Tariff Union made the remaining restrictions transparent by publishing lists of tariffs in five languages. Inter-governmental organizations proliferated after the Second World War with the formation of the UN system. Many of these bodies aim to foster economic growth by developing norms and cooperating to facilitate the expansion of international markets and manage conflicts between jurisdictions. Fora in which governments cooperate in developing standards range from technical requirements for maritime and air transport (International Maritime Organization, ICAO) to customs procedures (WCO).

Cooperation continues to be pursued to facilitate trade in numerous bodies, most of which have little to do with the WTO. The Centre for Facilitation of Procedures and Practices for Administration, Commerce and Transportation is an example. This evolved from the United Nations Economic Commission for Europe's Working Party on the Facilitation of International Trade Procedures. Since 1960, this organization has pursued the harmonization and automation of customs procedures and information requirements, and has issued the internationally recognized Trade Facilitation Recommendations (Staples, 2002). This body also worked extensively on standards for electronic data interchange, developing the United Nations Electronic Data Interchange for Administration Commerce and Transport. These standards facilitate the exchange of trade-related information between parties that typically handle international trade transactions.

Industry groups are active proponents of trade facilitation. The International Express Carriers Conference—now the Global Express Association—sponsored by FedEx, UPS, TNT and DHL among others; the International Chamber of Shipping; the International Road Transport Union; the International Federation of Freight Forwarders Associations; the International Association of Ports and Harbours; and the International Federation of Customs Brokers Association are some examples. The ICC is also very active, having been instrumental in putting the subject of trade facilitation on the agenda of the 1996 WTO ministerial conference in Singapore.

The Doha trade facilitation negotiations

The WTO has no provisions dealing explicitly with trade facilitation. Instead, as discussed in Chapter 5, it has specific provisions dealing with aspects of the customs clearance process: Article VII and the Uruguay Round agreement on customs valuation, Article VIII on fees and formalities; Article V on the treatment of goods in transit; and Article X requiring transparency of national trade regulations. In response to the demand by business to develop more comprehensive rules to facilitate trade, WTO members put trade facilitation on the agenda at the Singapore ministerial meeting in 1996. Although there was a general agreement on the importance of trade facilitation, developing countries were initially not very enthusiastic about negotiating on the subject in the WTO. Part of the concern related to potential implementation costs. Governments were also reluctant to take on additional obligations that might increase their exposure to WTO disputes.

After years of exploratory discussions, WTO members finally agreed to launch negotiations on trade facilitation in July 2004, on the basis of modalities contained in Annex D of the so-called July package (see Chapter 4). A two-track approach to negotiations was suggested; nations would work toward implementing current standards and requirements while creating the next generation of facilitation measures that would satisfy the needs of global corporations. Under the July package mandate, governments were expected to clarify and improve GATT Articles V (Freedom of Transit), VIII (Fees and Formalities connected with Importation and Exportation) and X (Publication and Administration of Trade Regulations). The negotiations also aimed to enhance technical assistance and capacity-building in this area and to improve effective cooperation between customs and other branches of government on trade facilitation and customs compliance matters.

The negotiation process was characterized by a positive engagement by all countries (including LDCs). Negotiations progressed in a constructive manner, in part because of general agreement that developing countries should be given assistance to conceive and implement better trade facilitation practices. Joint sponsoring of proposals with OECD governments testified to a clear sense of common purpose. Negotiations followed a bottom-up approach with no tendency for small group negotiations or need for a chair's text as in other negotiating groups of the Doha Round. Progress was facilitated by national needs assessments in capitals supported by the World Bank and bilateral donors to assist countries to determine where customs practices could be improved, and what technical and financial support was required to implement improvements. Another factor was that the negotiating group was able to finance the participation of capital-based customs officials from African countries.

Proposals referred to matters such as fees and formalities, transparency, questions of transit, implementation, SDT and technical assistance. With respect to the fees and formalities, they called for a greater predictability and reliability of procedures, suggested cost-based fees and charges and aimed at simplified formalities and documentation. The proposals also suggested greater use of international standards, adoption of a single window for traders, and elimination of pre-shipment inspection, mandatory customs brokers and consular fees. The main objective was to ensure expedited release and clearance of goods, wider use of risk assessment techniques and authorized traders, and better post-clearance audits. The suggested transparency provisions required better access to information for traders, wider use of modern technology (Internet publication and management by customs), establishment of enquiry points and prior publication and consultation of advance rulings and right of appeal for traders.

Improving transit access was particularly important for landlocked countries. The latter sought strengthened nondiscrimination provisions, predictable and reduced fees and charges, transparent transit formalities and documentation for traders. They also favoured use of international standards, promotion of regional transit arrangements and suggested new limitations on inspections and controls (e.g. for bonded transport) as well as quota-free transit. A noteworthy feature of the negotiations was acceptance of the principle that implementation by developing countries would be conditional on (linked to) receipt of development assistance to implement trade facilitation reforms (see Chapter 12).

The contours of a possible deal had emerged by 2008. This included an emerging consensus that a single and binding agreement was needed and that a plurilateral approach was not desirable. It was expected that all WTO members would sign an agreement, with specific commitments detailed in an implementation plan (with varying timelines) based on three specific categories of commitments: those taking effect immediately; those requiring a transition period; and those requiring both additional time and technical assistance and capacity-building support before entering into force. Examples of what might be embodied in an agreement include establishment of an enquiry point for information on trade regulations; a requirement to provide advance rulings on tariff classification and valuation; creation of a formal border agency 'cooperation mechanism' for the exchange of information among members; limits on inspection of goods in transit; and elimination of proscribed transit routes.[5]

The trade facilitation agenda goes far beyond the subjects that are the focus at the WTO, which is constrained by the Doha ministerial mandate to Articles V, VIII and X. Other relevant GATT disciplines—for example, on customs valuation, pre-shipment inspection and product standards—also have a direct bearing on the costs associated with getting goods across borders. The same is true of the GATS—which offers the opportunity to make specific commitments on important logistics-related services such as transport, distribution, warehousing, etc. This points to the need to view the trade facilitation agenda at both the national and regional, and multilateral levels broadly.

For example, consider the effects of rules of origin (Staples, 2002). These rules have become extremely cumbersome, especially in the context of preferential trade. The origin audit manual that applies to intra-NAFTA trade in goods runs to approximately 800 pages, reflecting both the need to prevent trade deflection and the capture of rules of origin by special interest lobbies. The NAFTA value content rules require companies to maintain detailed records, to require information from suppliers that they do not need for any business purpose and to provide certifications about the origin and regional content of goods shipped to customers. Even after the greatest care, companies, their suppliers and their customers may all have to undergo a long and arduous audit by any one—or more than one—of the three NAFTA

---

[5] See 'WTO Negotiations on Trade Facilitation: Compilation of Members Textual Proposals,' WTO, TN/TF/W/43/Rev.14, 12 March (2008).

governments. The NAFTA is not an outlier—similar situations prevail in other PTAs. One solution to the protectionist use (capture) of rules of origin would be to make the nonpreferential rules of origin that are being developed by the WCO mandatory in new PTAs. Given the impotence of the CRTA, see Chapter 10, embedding such a rule in an agreement on trade facilitation might be a more effective source of discipline.

Thus, trade facilitation is multidimensional. The WTO has a role to play, as do many other organizations, both public and private. Guidance on good customs and trade facilitation practices has been developed by a variety of specialized bodies, including the WCO and World Bank. These entities have developed 'tool-kits' to determine how efficient national practices in this area are, and what should be

Box 13.4. The revised Kyoto Convention

The Kyoto Convention comprises a set of principles and detailed annexes that lay out standards and recommended best practices for customs procedures and related administrative practices. Originally drafted in 1973, efforts to revise the Convention to reflect the dramatic changes that had occurred in technology and trade practices were concluded in 1998. The new Convention entered into force in 2000. It embodied a comprehensive set of good administrative practices in the area import and export procedures, transit arrangements, and warehousing based on the experience in various countries on a variety of customs-related procedures. The revised Convention is a 'blueprint' for modern and efficient customs procedures. Governing principles include transparency, simplicity and predictability of customs procedures, providing a system to appeal customs matters, greater use of risk management techniques (including risk assessment and selectivity of controls) and information technologies (including the use of pre-arrival information to drive programmes of selectivity), greater reliance on partnerships with national trade communities, and coordinated intervention with other national agencies. As of mid-2008, 58 countries had signed the revised Kyoto Convention—slightly more than one-third of the WTO membership.

The impact of the convention depends on whether it is implemented by WCO members. In contrast to the WTO, the WCO does not have any enforcement mechanisms. This has led representatives of the international express industry (which comprises firms such as DHL and FedEx) and the ICC to suggest that efforts be made to make implementation of the new Kyoto Convention mandatory for WTO members. Some WTO members have argued that the WTO should not be used to enforce an instrument that has been developed by another organization. A counterargument to this view is that WTO members have already given the WCO the responsibility for developing the rules of origin for nonpreferential trade, as well as responsibility for promoting the WTO Agreement on Customs Valuations (including providing technical assistance to those countries in transition from the old GATT valuation system). Cooperation between the WCO and the WTO in implementing and enforcing the new Kyoto Convention could help encourage a move towards greater harmonization of customs practices among WTO members.

considered as part of an overall reform strategy. In the 1990s, WCO members negotiated a revision of the 1974 International Convention on the Simplification and Harmonization of Customs Procedures, which had become outdated. For example, there was no recognition of modern techniques of risk assessment, the importance of computerization and electronic data interchange, or the use of *ex post*, audit-based systems of control. An updated and completely revamped Kyoto Convention establishing 'international standards and facilitative customs procedures for the twenty-first century' was completed in 1999 (WCO, 1999). Implementing and enforcing the revised Kyoto Convention will require substantial effort and resources (Box 13.4).

A key question is whether instruments such as the WCO Kyoto convention should be made enforceable under the WTO—the same way that many of the provisions of the WIPO conventions on IPRs were made enforceable. Developing countries were struggling for many years to implement the WTO customs valuation agreement. Given weak institutional structures, lack of modern communications and information systems, inadequately trained staff, and so forth, even if trade facilitation is an area where in principle 'one size fits all', it will take poorer countries much longer to attain the good practices that are enumerated in the Kyoto convention, and significant technical and financial assistance will be needed.

13.5. ENVIRONMENTAL POLICIES

The impact of environmental regulation on trade became the subject of discussions in the GATT in the late 1960s. This was a period when fears arose about the limits to growth and the rapid depletion of global natural resources. Environmental policies began to be pursued with greater vigour in OECD countries, leading to complaints by affected industries that the costs of these regulations reduced their ability to compete on world markets. A Working Group on Environmental Measures and International Trade was established by GATT contracting parties in 1971. However, it never met, as interest in the subject waned following the recurrent oil price shocks and the economic turmoil that followed. In 1991, after a period when environmental issues had again attained a high profile on the international policy agenda, the Working Group was re-activated. In the WTO it was transformed into a Committee on Trade and the Environment, with the mandate to investigate the relationship between environmental and trade policies.

Factors that drove environmental issues onto the agenda included increasing recognition of the existence of cross-border environmental spillovers, perceptions that national environmental policies were inadequate, concerns that trade was bad for the environment, fears that national environmental policy would reduce the competitiveness of domestic firms, and a perception that environmental policies were increasingly being used for protectionist purposes.

Cross-border spillovers. Production and consumption activities in one country may have detrimental impacts on other countries. Such negative spillovers or externalities may be physical (air and water pollution, acid rain) or intangible (animal rights, consumption of ivory). In such cases there is a basis for cooperation and negotiation. However, (unilateral) trade policy will not be the appropriate instrument to deal with the externality. Standard economic theory requires that externalities be addressed at their source. This implies that either the production or the consumption activity be curtailed directly by confronting the producer or consumer with the real costs of the activity, or that property rights be assigned that give owners an incentive to manage and price resources appropriately. For an externality to arise there must be a market failure that results in prices of the resources used being too low—marginal private costs of an activity are lower than the true marginal social costs (see Annex 2). Trade sanctions cannot offset an environmental externality efficiently, because they affect both consumers and producers of a good, and usually impact on only a part of total production or consumption.

Although this is often recognized, trade policy is attractive to environmentalists because it can be used to induce countries to apply environmental policies that are in principle targeted at the source of the problem. The issue here is to determine the appropriate standard of protection and the feasibility of enforcing it. Countries may have very different preferences regarding environmental protection, reflecting differences in the absorptive capacity of their ecosystems, differences in income levels (wealth) and differences in culture. Insofar as there are cross-country spillovers—physical or psychological—the appropriate policies will need to be negotiated. What matters from a trading system point of view is that the choice of environmental policy in cases where there are spillovers is not an issue that is appropriately dealt with in the WTO. International agreements on the matter are required, negotiated by the competent authorities (not trade officials). Trade policy might be agreed to be an instrument to enforce internationally agreed obligations. As long as there is consensus on this between WTO members, no legal problem arises. There may well be economic problems, however. The effectiveness of trade sanctions will be limited if the targeted nation does not have the resources to enforce appropriate environmental regulations. In such cases the sanction may make it harder for the country to achieve environmental improvements because the trade barriers reduce income.

'Inadequate' national policies. The same conclusion with respect to trade policy applies if there are no cross-border spillovers. In that case each country must determine for itself what are appropriate environmental policies. The WTO does not impose any constraints on a government regarding pursuit of environmental

policies on its territory. If it seeks to prevent the consumption of particular products, it may restrict imports, as long as the ban, tax or product standard is also imposed on domestic goods (recall that GATT Article XX makes allowance for general exceptions, see Chapter 9). However, the GATT does prevent the extraterritorial enforcement of national standards. Thus, a WTO member cannot use trade policies to force another member to enforce different (stronger) environmental standards on its territory. Efforts to do so have taken the form of attempts to require foreign firms to use specific production processes. A famous example was a US ban on tuna imports from Mexico, justified by the fact that Mexican fishing boats did not use the dolphin-friendly nets required under US regulations. A GATT panel ruled against the US in this case, greatly enhancing the perception of environmentalists that substantial 'greening of the GATT' was required (Esty, 1994). An important subsequent case (shrimp-turtles) is discussed later in this section. In such instances there is a clear-cut case for compensation if a trading partner seeks to impose standards that are higher and more costly than what is optimal for a country to implement. Using coercive trade sanctions is inappropriate.

Trade and the environment. A perception that trade is bad for the environment also played a role in bringing environmental issues to the WTO. It has been argued that freeing trade will lead to expansion of production and thus pollution, that liberalization will facilitate relocation of firms to countries with lax regulatory environments, that greater trade implies the need for greater transport, leading to more degradation, and so forth. All of these arguments are weak at best. Although trade and liberalization may give rise to such effects, this is negative from a social welfare viewpoint only if appropriate environmental policies are not pursued. If such policies are in place, producers and consumers will take into account the cost to the environment, and this will be reflected in the price of goods and services. As greater trade and specialization subsequent to liberalization will lead to greater wealth, the capacity and willingness of voters to devote more resources to the environment will also increase.

Trade policy may sometimes have adverse consequences on the environment. For example, agricultural support programmes have led to the use of production methods that are excessively polluting; fish subsidies have helped lead to depletion of ocean fish stocks, and by restricting imports of the most environmentally efficient biofuels and subsidizing consumption of less efficient local output consumers are prevented from switching towards less polluting types of energy that originate in parts of the world where the environmental costs of extraction are lower.

Similar considerations apply to proposals to penalize or avoid consumption of lower-cost imported food products that can be produced locally. Often this will not make any sense from an environmental perspective—in that even with the transport-related emissions and other costs the net impact of imports on the environment may well be much less than if similar products are raised locally. As important, there is a significant danger that use of trade policy for environmental reasons will be captured by protectionist interests, result in retaliation and further weaken the rules-based multilateral trading system. Proposals to adopt labelling systems that provide consumers with information on the carbon footprint of a product may be better solutions than the use of explicit trade sanctions but they run the risk of arbitrariness, discrimination, and unintended consequences if not designed carefully (Brenton, Edwards-Jones and Jensen, 2008).

Carbon labelling offers consumers and companies the opportunity to judge products on the basis of the greenhouse gas emissions that a given product generates. However, it is clearly critical that the methodology used is accurate and spans the whole supply chain. For example, developing country workers may walk to work or use communal transport, whereas in developed countries people often drive in their cars. In agriculture, many developing countries use much fewer inputs like nitrogen-based fertilizer (which cause emissions of one of the most harmful greenhouse gases) and fuel (with associated emissions of carbon dioxide). However, these countries are often located far from major export markets and thus require more fuel-consuming transportation. Emission-efficient supply chains demand that the advantages of labour-intensive techniques and sunshine (as opposed to developed country mechanization and heated greenhouses) outweigh the disadvantage of transport-related emissions. Such differences need to be reflected in carbon labelling. Decisions about which activities in the production chain to include in the analysis are, therefore, crucial from both a scientific and development perspective. Schemes that concentrate on only specific parts of the production chain will generally be very misleading.

Using trade policy to restrict trade so as to reduce environmental degradation is inappropriate. Indeed, often protection will have adverse consequences on the environment. Thus, agricultural support programmes have led to the use of production methods that are excessively polluting. Coal subsidies in the EU encourage the use of inputs that are much more detrimental to the environment than imports would be (Anderson, 1992). By restricting imports and subsidizing consumption of local output, consumers are prevented from switching towards less polluting types of energy that originate in other parts of the world—areas where the environmental costs of extraction are often lower as well.

Competitiveness. Environmental policies may reduce the ability of enterprises located in countries with high standards to compete with those that operate in nations with low standards. This is exactly what the policy aims at. If high standards are what a society wants, then the result should be that the affected activities contract. Restricting imports makes no sense, as it promotes the activities that the environmental policy is attempting to constrain. This, of course, is one reason why domestic industries may seek to 'level the playing field' through trade policy—it is one way to avoiding part of the impact of environmental regulation. More generally, if there is a preference for more environmentally friendly goods on the part of consumers, there should be a willingness to pay for them.

Environmental protectionism. Environmental policies may unnecessarily (or de-liberately) be used to restrict trade. This has been a major concern of many WTO members, and has been an important factor for considering environmental policy in the WTO. Environmental policies have often been of the command and control type rather than more efficient price-based instruments such as taxes. The reason is that such instruments may create rents that can be captured by the industries which are affected by the environmental regulations. Industry then has an incentive to push for inefficient policies in situations where environmental groups are suffi-ciently powerful to get environmental standards adopted (see Annex 2). Environ-mental policies that are based on regulation rather than taxation may easily have trade-restricting effects because the trade equivalent may be a ban on imports. The US tuna-dolphin case noted earlier is a case in point.

The challenge is to determine whether the market access effect of a domestic measure is necessary to achieve underlying policy objectives. Mechanisms to decide what is legitimate are therefore vital (Box 13.5). There is great danger in acceding to pressure for import barriers that are ostensibly justified on level playing field

---

Box 13.5. Economic effects of recycling requirements

A number of US states have passed mandatory recycling laws that require a minimum percentage of the content of newsprint be recycled material, motivated by a desire to reduce the rate at which old newsprint fills up dumps and landfills. These laws were detrimental to Canadian producers of pulp and newsprint, who use virgin wood (forestry products are a major Canadian export and source of comparative advantage). Some Canadian producers found it prohibitively expensive to import old newsprint to combine with new pulp and paper. The result was a 10 per cent reduction in their US sales.

Similar types of regulations have been a prominent source of market access disputes in the EU. A 1981 Danish bottle recycling law required that all beer and soft drinks be packaged in reusable containers and that retailers take back all containers sold. Metal containers were banned. Other EU producers contended that the law imposed discrim-inatory costs on them. Although the law was nondiscriminatory, two-way transporta-tion costs for bottles were prohibitive beyond a distance of 300 kilometres. The EU Commission challenged the law, arguing that less trade-restrictive instruments could attain the government's objectives. However, the European Court of Justice found the disposal and re-use requirements to be legal, and only required that Denmark accept metal containers as long as producers could meet the re-use requirements.

These examples illustrate that although domestic policies can restrict market access, this may be tolerated if it can be justified on the basis of overriding noneconomic objectives. But they also illustrate that WTO members need to develop clear rules of the game and establish credible dispute settlement systems to determine when these rules have been violated.

Source: Vogel (1995).

grounds. The prospect of protection may induce import-competing firms to support environmental groups in their pursuit of regulation. This increases the likelihood of inefficient instruments being chosen, as these generate greater rents.

An example of possible process standards is illustrative. Suppose that environmentalists are concerned with excessive killing of turtles by shrimp fishermen and have convinced the government that domestic fishermen must use nets that incorporate effective turtle-exclusion devices. The domestic industry may then argue that as a result of this policy they face unfair competition from foreign sources not subject to this regulation. Moreover, environmental groups can be expected to insist that foreign imports of shrimp meet the same standards, not because of any concern for the plight of domestic fishermen, but because of their concern for turtles. A tariff on imports is unlikely to be acceptable to the environmental group. Instead, they are likely to demand a ban on imports.

Although there might be a stated willingness on the part of environmentalists to exempt those foreign sources that can prove they do not kill turtles (perhaps because there are no turtles in their waters), in practice this may be very difficult to establish. It involves not only allowing inspection of trawlers, but also providing assurance that no mixing of sources occurs. Even if this can be done by foreign suppliers, establishing the turtle friendliness of their products will take time and be costly, so that the environmental policy will make it more attractive to shift to third markets or to substitute products. Domestic fishermen will not care whether there are turtles in foreign waters. For them what counts is the playing field—domestic regulations raise costs and they would like to be compensated for this. The uniform application of the process standard will both have significant trade-distorting effects and is very likely to increase the level of protection (see Annex 2).

As in other areas, greater transparency and more objective analysis of the impact of environmental policies on trade, and vice versa, is required. This is the mandate that was given to the Committee on Trade and the Environment (CTE) at the end of the Uruguay Round. As mentioned above, the CTE was a continuation of a working group that was originally formed in 1971, but had been dormant until 1991. Reviving the group was a reaction by GATT contracting parties to the controversy caused by the tuna-dolphin dispute. This had caused NGOs to consider the GATT anti-environment, and developing countries to worry about environmental norms being used to restrict trade. The CTE focused its work primarily on the trade and trade policy aspects of environmental policy, including the trade effects of eco-labelling, provisions in multilateral environmental agreements (MEAs) to use trade sanctions or bans as enforcement or implementation instruments, the environmental effects of agricultural support policies, and trade in domestically prohibited goods. The CTE's report to the first WTO ministerial conference in a 1996 report was a disappointment to NGOs, who had lobbied for specific recommendations to make WTO rules more 'environmentally friendly'.

The CTE played a useful role in educating trade officials on international efforts to cooperate on environmental matters—including treaties and conventions. It also played a beneficial role in educating the environmental community regarding the limits of WTO rules. Dialogue between the various communities became more constructive in the second half of the 1990s, and greater transparency played a key role in this process. One illustration of this was that in the run-up to the Seattle ministerial, environmental concerns were prominent in proposals that sought significant reductions in subsidies for fisheries, forestry and agriculture. Many WTO members regarded this as a rare potential 'win-win' situation where two objectives could be attained with one instrument.

Through the work of the CTE, trade and environment issues have been explored at great length. One result has been that there is widespread recognition that trade policy has little, if any, role to play in the pursuit of environmental objectives, that the WTO does not restrict the use of green policies by members, that MEAs are the appropriate instrument to address global environmental problems, and that carrots, not sticks, are called for if a country seeks to induce another to adopt stricter environmental norms. The shrimp-turtles dispute between the US and a number of Asian countries illustrated these principles (Box 13.6). In many of these cases, a more appropriate approach by concerned NGOs is to push for voluntary labelling or to pursue a consumer boycott. Such approaches allow consumers to make informed choices regarding the products they buy, and create incentives for producers to adopt new technologies and incur the labelling costs by increasing the price of goods that are preferred by concerned segments of the population.

International trade can play a role in the reduction of greenhouse gases and the use of more energy-efficient production technologies by allowing firms to import environmentally friendly technology embodied in equipment, thus allowing more efficient production and consumption.[6] Trade can also help with adaptation, by enhancing access to relevant technologies—such as genetically modified seeds and efficient irrigation methods—and by encouraging technology transfer and dissemination of knowledge and know-how on available techniques. An important first step toward the adoption of more environmental friendly technologies would be to reduce trade restrictions on imports of environmental goods and services—products that result in less use of energy or generate energy in more environmentally efficient ways. Many such products face relatively high trade barriers, both when measured in terms of the tariff trade restrictiveness index or the overall trade restrictiveness index (tariffs and NTMs), especially in developing countries (Figure 13.3).[7] The negative spillovers associated with policies that restrict trade in such technologies increase their welfare cost. Reducing barriers that have protection of

---

[6] The following paragraphs draw on World Bank and IMF (2008).

[7] These indices measure the uniform tariff equivalent of applicable trade policies.

Box 13.6. The Shrimp–Turtles Case

Sea turtles are an endangered species, protected under multilateral environmental agreements. They are often caught by fishermen harvesting shrimp. To reduce the incidence of turtle deaths, the US National Marine Fisheries Service designed a so-called turtle exclusion device (TED) to reduce the likelihood of turtles becoming trapped in the nets of shrimp trawlers. In 1987, the use of such TEDs became mandatory for the US shrimp fishing fleet. Reflecting pressure by US environmental groups concerned with global conservation of sea turtles and the fishing industry, concerned about 'unfair competition', the US Congress adopted legislation in 1989 (ESA, 1973: Section 609) prohibiting the importation of shrimp products from countries that do not use TEDs or similar devices, unless the US certifies them as having US-equivalent programmes to prevent sea turtle mortality. Initially, the US issued guidelines stipulating that the law would only apply to countries in the Caribbean and the Western Atlantic Ocean where the US was negotiating a regional agreement for the protection of sea turtles. In 1995, the US Court of International Trade ruled that the law should be applied to all imports. In 1997, India, Malaysia, Pakistan and Thailand requested the DSB establish a panel. The US defended its programme under Article XX GATT.

In principle, WTO rules only allow production process standards like the TED to be applied to imports if it can be shown that the processes targeted have repercussions for the physical characteristics (quality) of the product concerned. An example would be a requirement that shrimp be washed in water of a certain level of purity. In many cases process standards cannot be justified under this criterion, requiring countries to invoke Article XX—GATT's exception provision. In the shrimp-turtles case, the relevant provision was Article XX:g—which allows for trade-restrictive measures if necessary for the 'conservation of exhaustible natural resources'.

The panel did not discuss whether and how Section 609 related to the environmental exceptions of Article XX, but focused on the general provision of Article XX stating that measures may not 'constitute...arbitrary or unjustifiable discrimination' nor be a 'disguised restriction on international trade'. The panel found against the US on this basis. On appeal, the Appellate Body reversed the panel by concluding that Section 609 was aimed at the protection of a natural resource and was therefore covered by (legal under) Article XX:g. However, it agreed with the panel that the way Section 609 was applied resulted in arbitrary and unjustifiable discrimination because insufficient efforts had been made to negotiate arrangements to protect sea turtles similar to what had been negotiated with countries in the Western Hemisphere (Latin American countries had been granted three years to comply, Asian economies only four months). The Appellate Body also criticized the coercive nature of the measure, arguing that it is 'not acceptable in international trade relations for one WTO Member to use an economic embargo to require other Members to adopt essentially the same... program,... without taking into consideration different conditions which may occur in the territories of those other Members'.

US environmental groups had feared the panel ruling would lead to renewed political pressure to weaken or repeal the US TED requirements. However, the Appellate Body finding only required that the US find ways to implement Section 609 in a nondiscriminatory manner and make a serious effort to negotiate. Recognizing the political sensitivity of the case, the Appellate Body stressed that 'we have not decided that the ... Members of the WTO cannot adopt effective measures to protect endangered species, such as sea turtles'. Moreover, 'we have not decided that sovereign states should not act together bilaterally, plurilaterally or multilaterally... to protect endangered species or otherwise protect the environment'. Thus, it emphasized that these types of cases are best addressed through international agreements and negotiation.

Summing up, the Appellate Body decision in the shrimp case signalled that extraterritorial application of national norms can be legal under the WTO (Article XX GATT) and that there is some leeway for countries to use trade policy to enforce norms relating to production process methods (PPMs) that do not have implications for the characteristics of traded products. The fact that the Appellate Body did not explicitly address the PPM issue was attacked by developing countries such as Thailand, who argued that this sent a dangerous signal, potentially opening the door for countries to apply PPM norms in other areas as well (such as labour). However, as Article XX makes no mention of labour standards, this would not be possible.

domestic industry as their main objective would help encourage the adoption of more efficient technologies and more environmental friendly forms of energy.

Tariffs and NTMs are significant impediments to the diffusion of clean energy technologies in developing countries. Liberalizing global trade in four such technology groups—high efficiency and clean coal technologies, efficient lighting, solar photovoltaics and wind power—could result in large increases in trade volumes (Table 13.2).

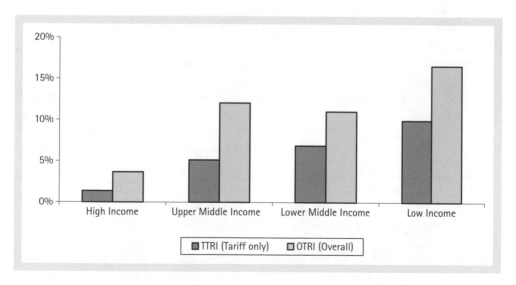

Figure 13.3. Environmental goods confront significant trade restrictiveness

Source: World Bank and IMF (2008).

Table 13.2. Increase in trade from liberalizing clean energy technologies (%)

Technology Option	Scenario 1 Eliminating Tariffs Only	Scenario 2 Eliminating Tariffs and NTMs
Clean coal technology	3.6	4.6
Wind power generation	12.6	22.6
Solar power generation	6.4	13.5
Efficient lighting technology	15.4	63.6
All four technologies	7.2	13.5

Source: World Bank (2007).

The Doha talks

The jurisprudence that has emerged under the WTO has made clear that the trade rules do not take precedence over environmental concerns. WTO members have long recognized the need for coherence amongst international institutions in addressing global environmental challenges, but the Doha Round was the first time that the issue of trade and environment featured explicitly in a MTN. The principal objective of the Round in this area was to enhance the mutual supportiveness of trade and environment. The 2001 Doha Ministerial Declaration (Paragraph 31 (iii)) called for negotiations on 'the reduction or, as appropriate, elimination of tariff and nontariff barriers to environmental goods and services', with a view to enhancing the mutual supportiveness of trade, environment and development. The focus was on effects of environmental policies on market access, the relevant provisions of the TRIPS agreement, labelling requirements for environmental reasons, technical assistance and sharing expertise for national environmental reviews.

Limited progress was made in achieving these goals as a result of disagreements on how to define 'environmental goods and services' and how to design liberalization commitments in a way that appropriately differentiates developed from developing countries. Developed nations supported a positive list approach: identifying specific lists of goods and then negotiating the elimination or reduction of bound tariffs and NTMs on an MFN basis. A number of developing countries preferred a 'project' approach, under which liberalization would be only for the duration of environmental projects. Building on the list approach, a 2007 US-EU proposal suggested that WTO members start with agreeing to eliminate tariffs and NTBs for specific environmentally friendly products, with SDT for developing countries, including longer phase-in periods. The objective was to have a zero tariff environment for these products and technologies by 2013 at the latest. This proposal generated some controversy—including whether ethanol and other bio-fuels should be included in the list of climate-friendly technologies.[8]

The negotiations on the relationship between WTO and the MEA provided a unique opportunity for creating positive synergies between the trade and environment agendas at the international level. Whatever the outcome of the Doha Round, there is regular and routine contact between the WTO Secretariat and the secretariats of the MEAs. Other subjects on the Doha agenda were also highly relevant from an environment perspective, in particular the negotiations on strengthened disciplines for fisheries subsidies.

A number of WTO countries consider environmental reviews to be useful tools for trade agreements. The purpose is to ensure closer links between environmental and trade policies and to identify actions that would enhance positive environmental impacts. The Doha Declaration took note of 'the efforts by Members to conduct national environmental assessments of trade policies on a voluntary basis'. However, countries continue to have different approaches to environmental reviews. The EU has carried out sustainability impact assessments on trade negotiations; Canada undertook an environmental assessment of the WTO negotiations; and the US conducted an environmental review of the Doha Development Agenda. Numerous developing country members stressed that any such environmental reviews should remain voluntary.

Whether trade policy should be part of the answer to the problem of supporting international cooperation to reduce greenhouse gas emissions is a long standing matter of debate. With the increased focus on global climate change in the second half of the 2000s, proposals were made that trade policy should be used to raise the cost of imported products that are deemed to have been produced with environmentally inefficient technologies and as a means of 'encouraging' countries to participate in international agreements from which they may otherwise abstain.[9] Much of these discussions were a rehash of debates that had played out in the 1970s and 1980s and the analytical frameworks that were developed then to determine appropriate trade policy responses could be applied directly to the new concerns about global warming and climate change (e.g. Blackhurst, 1977; Anderson and Blackhurst, 1993).

Trade policy has a role to play in instances where governments (or a group of signatories to an environmental agreement) impose carbon taxes or equivalent instruments on domestic production to reduce greenhouse gas emissions. An equivalent tax on imports of the products that are subject to the carbon tax regime will ensure that local output is treated the same as foreign products. Such

---

[8] In the HS, ethanol is classified as an agricultural product (independent of its end use); bio-diesel is classified as an industrial product. See Howse, van Bork and Hebefrand (2006).

[9] Draft climate change legislation in both the EU and US have included proposals to impose restrictions on imports unless an international agreement subjecting all industrialized countries to similar climate change mitigation measures is reached (Brewer, 2008).

border tax adjustments can, in principle, help mitigation efforts without impacting international competitiveness while encouraging participation by others. However, border tax adjustments by themselves are second-best instruments—the first-best policy is to levy an environmental tax at the origin. Determining the appropriate (equivalent) tax for a given product is not straightforward. Taxes should accurately reflect the production process used by the exporting firm, and information on this may not be available. Border tax adjustments also give rise to risks of hiding tariffs or export subsidies and may be inconsistent with WTO regulations.

Using trade policy to take action against countries that have not signed a MEA in an effort to induce them to do so is periodically advocated by analysts, NGOs or policymakers. In principle this might be argued to be WTO-legal as a result of Shrimp-Turtles: importing countries can argue that the measures they impose on domestic production under the MEA allow them to take action against products using PPMs that damage the environment. This would need to take the form of new tariffs or taxes on the products produced with the violating PPMs—the action could not take the form of a CVD as nonapplication of a MEA is not a subsidy as defined by the SCM Agreement. Although a feasible legal strategy, the use of trade measures is costly to the importing country and is unlikely to result in a change in behaviour by a country like the US (which was the target of those advocating the strategy) (Bhagwati and Mavroidis, 2007).

Trade liberalization is just one aspect of enhancing access to cleaner technology by rapidly growing developing economies. Trade serves as a major channel for international technology transfer to developing countries, but in many cases FDI may be more important. Many developing countries also have weak environmental standards, low pollution charges and weak enforcement capacity. This reduces the incentives to acquire and apply more sophisticated clean energy technologies.

13.6. SOCIAL POLICIES AND LABOUR STANDARDS

Discussions relating to workers' rights and trade have a long history. Indeed, they predate discussions on IPRs, going back at least 150 years. In the nineteenth century, the question was one of improving working conditions. Trade entered the picture because of concerns expressed by industries that domestic legislation prohibiting child labour or limiting the working week would put them at a competitive disadvantage (Leary, 1996). Recurring international discussions starting in the late nineteenth century led to the creation of the ILO in 1919. The ILO is a unique body, insofar as it is tripartite—bringing together employers, labour unions and governments. The ILO has passed numerous conventions dealing with various aspects of working conditions. Governments adopt (ratify) these on a voluntary basis.

The ILO has no binding enforcement mechanism, although it does monitor compliance by member states. The constitution of the ILO provided that a member could initiate a complaint that a government was not implementing a convention it had ratified. This could give rise to the establishment of a commission to investigate the case and recommend a remedy, including 'measures of an economic character', that is, sanctions. As noted by Charnovitz (2002), this procedure was never used. As is the case with IPRs, the primary reason proponents are seeking to introduce labour standards into the WTO is because the WTO has a functioning dispute settlement and enforcement system. A complementary factor (as with the environment) is a fear that liberalization of trade and closer integration of the world economy may lead to a race to the bottom, with countries that have high standards being forced to lower them if they want their firms to remain competitive with industrializing countries.[10]

At the insistence of the US and France, labour standards were introduced on the WTO agenda in the final stage of the Uruguay Round. The objective of these countries was to initiate discussions on the introduction of a Social Clause specifying minimum standards in this area, presumably as a pre-condition for market access. This was not the first attempt to introduce the issue. The US and other OECD countries had made efforts in this area periodically since the 1950s. Although the attempt to establish a committee or working party failed in 1994, calls for linking the benefits of WTO membership, or even membership itself, to the adoption and enforcement of minimum labour standards continued to be heard. Three months after the creation of the WTO, the Director-General of the ILO wrote to the WTO urging that members should be required to ratify ILO conventions on so-called core labour standards, including the prohibition of forced labour and the right for workers to form unions and engage in collective wage bargaining (*Financial Times*, 9 March, 1995: 9).

Populist calls to reduce differences in labour costs across countries are not at the core of the issue in the WTO context. Labour costs reflect the income and productivity of a country. Insisting that liberalization of trade be made conditional upon convergence in labour costs makes absolutely no sense, and would constitute blatant protectionism. The gains from trade result precisely from differences in costs, which are due to differences in endowments, technological capacities and output per worker. The focus of attention in the WTO is primarily on so-called

[10] This concern is not just a 'developed versus developing country' issue. It also played a role in European integration. See Sapir (1995).

core labour standards and basic workers' rights, not the minimum wage. In practice, proponents are seeking the recognition and enforcement of five general rights: banning exploitative use of child workers, eliminating forced labour, preventing discrimination in the workplace, allowing free association of workers, and permitting workers to bargain collectively (Maskus, 1997). Supporters of a social clause in the WTO seek the latitude to impose (multilateral) trade sanctions against countries that do not protect these rights.

Two issues arise. First, is there a link between labour standards and trade—that is, are trade flows distorted because of differences in standards? More specifically, is there a competitiveness issue? Second, are trade sanctions a useful (efficient) tool to enforce core labour standards?

The impact of labour standards on competitiveness of firms depends on the circumstances (Ehrenberg, 1994). It is not necessarily the case that high standards—with respect to social security, for example—will reduce the ability of firms to compete on world markets. If firms can ensure that the incidence of the implicit tax is borne by workers—that is, that the work force pays for the resulting benefits through lower wages—labour costs may be unaffected. Moreover, insofar as the cost-raising effects of workers' rights cannot be fully shifted to workers, the resulting increase in product prices (due to higher costs) will put pressure on the exchange rate (because foreign demand for exports falls as prices increase, all other things equal). The resulting depreciation will lower the standard of living by raising the cost of imports. Although the whole economy thus bears the burden of the higher standards, the exchange rate adjustment allows firms to continue to compete on world markets. As in the case of environmental policies, as long as the labour standards in force reflect the desires of voters, the costs of implementation simply reflect the tradeoff between monetary and nonmonetary wealth that society has made. However, if standards are unilaterally imposed on a country, it is very unlikely that they will reflect the preferences of the population. Imposing a tariff or other trade barriers to offset the cost disadvantage for domestic firms is not necessary to 'level the playing field' and will distort resource allocation. Account should also be taken of the substantial danger that such instruments will be captured by protectionist interests, seeking to limit imports from labour-abundant developing countries. Contrary to what might be expected, however, it is not necessarily the case that labour unions in OECD countries will be the main lobby for protection (Box 13.7).

Trade policy is an inefficient tool to enforce labour standards, assuming agreement could be reached on what the relevant standards should be. Trade restrictions will generally have a detrimental effect on the realization of the noneconomic objectives that are pursued by pro-labour standards groups. Trade restrictions raise the prices of imports, thus imposing a welfare cost at home, while at the same time worsening the labour situation in the target country. Demand for labour services will fall, and plants will downsize or close. Trade sanctions are akin to a tax on

Box 13.7. Labour standards and US labour unions

One might expect that support for international labour standards by OECD unions and NGOs reflects protectionist interests. Empirical studies have failed to find compelling evidence suggesting that lack of compliance with core labour standards has an impact on trade (Kucera and Sarna, 2006). If so, they do not affect production and employment, so that protectionism seems an unlikely motivation for pushing labour standards. However, van Beers (1998) finds that labour standards do influence trade within the OECD.

Krueger (1997b) analysed the determinants of support in the US House of Representatives for the Child Labour Deterrence Act of 1995. Although the proposed law was not passed, it was intended to prohibit imports of goods produced abroad by children under 15 years old, and would subject child labour practices to a review by the US Secretary of Labor. Krueger found that: '... Congressmen from districts with a high concentration of high school dropouts are less likely to cosponsor the Child Labor Deterrence Act' (p. 289), and that higher rates of unionization were not associated with support for the Act. She postulated that an explanation for this result was that unionized workers tend to be more highly skilled, therefore not benefitting directly from a ban on imported goods made with child labour. The implication is that, in seeking to strengthen workers' rights abroad, unions are not pursuing their narrow self-interest. Her results are only suggestive, as legislators may have chosen not to sponsor the legislation even though they were supportive of it (Srinivasan, 1998). Less educated and less skilled individuals tend to vote less and to work in nontradable service industries, therefore possibly carrying less weight in a congressman's decision whether to be a cosponsor.

Whatever the case may be, much of the concern regarding labour standards in developing countries reflects a genuine concern about the labour situation in low-income economies. This concern has been captured in part by import-competing interests (firms), who would like to see competitive pressures reduced. A major problem then is to enhance the understanding of the electorate in OECD countries that linking trade and labour standards is an inappropriate and counterproductive strategy.

Source: Adapted from Stern (2000).

employment of low-skilled workers. Using trade remedies to enforce labour standards would worsen the problems at which they are aimed (by forcing workers in targeted countries into informal or illegal activities). Unemployment will rise and, given the absence or weakness of social safety nets (unemployment insurance), can be expected to have a detrimental impact on poverty. It should come as no surprise, therefore, that developing countries oppose any attempt to link market access to labour standards.

Developing countries in particular are very hesitant to consider even the least controversial norms for fear that this would be the thin end of the wedge. They note that Article XX:e GATT already contains a provision permitting import restrictions against goods produced by prison labour, that Article XXI:c GATT allows for UN-mandated sanctions, and that this is all that is required in the WTO.

There is considerable international agreement that certain core labour rights should be globally recognized and protected, but this is seen to be the task of the ILO.

Rather than use threats, attainment of core labour standards can be pursued more effectively through instruments that are targeted directly at improving outcomes. For example, efforts could be made to improve the quality of, and access to, primary education for poor children in order to reduce child labour exploitation, via programmes to subsidize the purchase of school supplies, provide transportation and reduce the costs of schooling (Maskus, 1997). It is important to avoid a confrontational approach to this issue and to pursue collaborative solutions that help developing countries improve labour standards. Attempts to force countries to adopt standards that do not reflect national preferences and conditions should be rejected (Bhagwati and Srinivasan, 1996). Gains from trade arise in large part because countries differ, and national social policies are simply one determinant of these differences. They do not constitute barriers to trade, or give rise to 'unfair' trade.

As mentioned, proposals to ensure that basic labour standards would apply in all WTO members made no headway during the Uruguay Round. The issue was put on the agenda of the 1996 Singapore WTO ministerial conference by the US, France and Canada. These countries called for the recognition of such standards and suggested that WTO members work with the ILO to ensure that they are observed. This attempt failed. No agreement proved possible on even the most minimalist approach that is generally taken towards new issues: the establishment of a working group to investigate the link between trade and labour standards. The Singapore ministerial declaration rejected the use of labour standards for protectionist purposes, and stated that the comparative advantage of countries, particularly low-wage developing countries, must in no way be put into question; that WTO members were committed to the observance of internationally recognized core labour standards; that the ILO is the competent body to set and deal with labour standards; and that economic growth and development fostered by increased trade and further trade liberalization contributes to the promotion of these standards.

In the run-up to the 1999 Seattle ministerial the issue was again put forward by the US, which tabled a formal proposal on trade and labour in October 1999. The US called for the creation of a working group on trade and labour to examine the effects of trade on employment, the impact of greater openness on the scope and structure of basic social protections and safety nets in WTO members, the relationship between trade, development and core labour standards, the scope for trade incentives to promote implementation of standards, the magnitude of forced or exploitative child labour engaged in export production, and the impact of derogations from national labour legislation, including in export processing zones, on trade and development.

A statement by US President Clinton during Seattle that he would favour the use of sanctions against violations of trade agreements, including labour provisions, hardened the resolve of developing countries to resist the US proposal (Odell, 2002). The focus of the working group was less on labour conditions than the impact of labour regulations (or the lack thereof) on export competition. This emphasis on labour standards in production for export illustrates that developing countries have cause for concern regarding the push to incorporate labour standards in the WTO. After all, there is nothing special about exports. Presumably any concern regarding core labour standards should extend to all production, including production that is not for export. Conversely, labour standards can affect export competition without being specific to the export industry. The export industry is typically only singled out when it comes to EPZs, the argument often being that countries apply different ('more lenient') labour laws there than in the rest of the country.

Whether or not the WTO should favour a multilateral agreement on labour standards continues to be a controversial matter. The WTO does not name violation of core labour rights as a basis upon which trading nations may impose barriers to trade against an offending country, although Article XX GATT might justify trade sanctions on the basis that inadequate labour standards threaten 'public morals' and 'human life and health' or give rise to 'social dumping'. However, it is generally accepted that there is no framework for enforcing core labour standards in the WTO (Stern and Terrell, 2003). Given the strong differences in views there was no possibility of the proponents to put labour standards on the Doha Round agenda.

Human rights

The labour norms discussed above are often regarded as part of a broader set of human rights. Despite controversy surrounding the question of whether specific human rights should be embedded in the WTO, members have introduced such rights into specific dimensions of the WTO. Article XX GATT is one example of a provision allowing for trade action to be taken—an example was its invocation to allow trade sanctions against apartheid South Africa, justified on the basis of violations of human rights by that government. Invocation of the nonapplication provision against accession candidates on the basis of human rights violations is another example (see Chapter 2). The waiver that runs through 2012 for the use of trade measures (licensing and certification) to enforce the Kimberley Agreement on conflict diamonds is another. The EU GSP+ programme is yet another (Chapter 12). Finally, human rights have figured prominently in several accession negotiations. Aaronson (2007) discusses the various points of entry through which human rights have been put on the table in the WTO.

13.7. DOMESTIC REGULATION

The rhetoric of policymakers and their advisors often suggests that deeper integration is necessary to attain free trade. During the period leading to the creation of the EEC, Jelle Zijlstra, the Dutch Minister of Economic Affairs, argued that credible tariff removal required 'common policies on taxes, wages, prices and employment policy' (Milward, 1992: 188). Similarly, the Belgian government felt that policy harmonization was required to equalize costs, and that without it a customs union would not be feasible because countries would impose new forms of protectionist policies. The Belgian coal mining industry argued in the late 1940s that a common market could only be accepted if German wage and social security costs were raised to Belgian levels. French officials persistently demanded policy harmonization in the social area—equal pay for both sexes, a uniform working week—as a pre-condition for trade liberalization (French standards in this area were higher than in other countries).

Although governments may seek to agree on common regulatory principles to govern the behaviour of public entities or restrict the use of domestic policies, this is best done directly and should not be made a pre-condition for trade liberalization. A strategy that seeks to link trade policy to regulatory reform in foreign countries will generally be quite costly, given the welfare losses from protection. For small countries, it will also be ineffective. Foreign economic policies are best regarded as part of the environment—they may be detrimental to some groups in society, but this does not offset the gains that can be obtained from trade liberalization. Deep integration based on international standards applied on a nondiscriminatory basis to all traders may enhance global welfare. But, the need for deeper integration on most issues, old, new or new-new, is limited. Frequently, shallow integration is a more powerful instrument, as it involves competition between regulatory regimes that reflect national circumstances.

The WTO rules are directed towards market access and trade in products. How goods and services are produced has traditionally been irrelevant under GATT, with the exception of situations listed in Article XX GATT (such as prison labour). With the WTO this changed: the norms embodied in the TRIPS agreement relate directly to production processes by requiring IPRs to be enforced. The shrimp-turtle and asbestos cases suggest countries may impose process standards for environmental reasons if this can be motivated on global public good grounds. These developments suggest there is a need to determine the extent to which deeper policy integration should be pursued in the WTO. Where to draw the line has become an area of vigorous debate among policy officials, analysts and civil society.

One option for rule-making on regulatory issues is to become more prescriptive regarding the types of instruments government should use to offset market failure in those instances where society decides the benefits of intervention outweigh the costs. A basic rule of thumb that is suggested by the economic literature is that price-based instruments dominate so-called command and control type of regulation. The latter result in inefficiency for the same reason that quotas are less efficient than tariffs (see Annex 2). This suggests that countries should apply regulatory instruments which use the market to encourage flexibility and choice both of products and production techniques: taxes or tradable quotas to deal with environmental externalities, labelling to deal with information asymmetries including risk, and liability insurance to encourage product safety (Rollo and Winters, 2000). However, requiring such economic criteria in the application of regulatory policy as an enforceable WTO rule would involve potentially far-reaching second-guessing of governments by WTO panels. Societies have different tastes, cultures, governmental and legal systems, endowments, and so forth. Regulatory decisions will reflect these different circumstances. Here again, one size does not fit all.

If there are cross-border externalities or global public goods, international regulation should be nondiscriminatory, restricted in geographical coverage to the scope of the spillovers, and implemented locally, in line with local circumstances and tastes—that is, the regulatory agency should be accountable to the relevant communities (Rollo and Winters, 2000). For the WTO to be the locus of international regulatory efforts, the spillover or market failure that is involved should have a direct bearing on the conditions of competition prevailing on a market.

The discussion in this chapter suggests that there is little scope for the WTO to expand its reach significantly beyond the status quo through deeper integration. The main beneficial role it might play in most areas calling for national regulation is ensuring transparency. Most cross-border spillovers arise in areas in which the WTO has no expertise—they are generally only weakly trade-related, if at all. Allowing for the use of trade sanctions to enforce whatever regulatory norms are adopted will generally be counterproductive in terms of the (noneconomic) objectives that the regulation seeks to attain.

At the national level, the clearest role for the WTO in terms of regulatory regimes concerns those policies that directly affect the ability of foreign providers of goods and services to contest a market. As discussed in Chapter 7, nonrecognition of professional certification and qualifications is a major barrier to trade. Similarly, de facto discrimination across countries and suppliers due to MRAs for product standards and conformity assessment regimes has a direct effect on trade. These are regulatory areas where deep integration is not necessarily required. Shallow integration—extending the reach of the national treatment and MFN principles, and bolstering the information collection and analysis functions of the WTO, including the TPRM—can do much to reduce the associated cost differentials for traders.

13.8. Conclusion

The WTO faces a daunting agenda. A true test of the organization in the coming years will be the extent to which members prove willing and able to increase the contestability of markets by sweeping away policies that imply discrimination against foreign firms and products. Much still needs to be done in the traditional market access domain of the WTO. Services, agriculture and textiles and clothing continue to be heavily protected in many countries. Tariffs on merchandise imports in developing countries are still relatively high. There is also much that needs to be done to control the use of contingent protection, especially antidumping. The new, 'regulatory trade agenda' is by no means necessarily the area where the greatest welfare gains from reform are to be realized. One important reason is that in many of the 'new' areas one size fits all is not the right prescription.

There is substantial scope for governments to accede to pressures from lobbies to impose regulatory policies that have the effect of restricting trade. Such policies are most likely in environment and health-related areas. Many of the more controversial issues that are giving rise to disputes and tensions concern the use of biotechnology, genetically modified organisms (GMOs), patenting of life forms, the use of health and safety standards based on the 'precautionary principle', and the regulation of drugs (pharmaceuticals) and medical service providers. Currently, these issues are addressed in a variety of WTO bodies, including the SPS and TBT committees, the Committee on Trade and Environment, the Dispute Settlement Body, and the TRIPS, GATT and GATS councils. Much of the discussion concerns whether there are (or should be) international standards, and whether specific measures that have a trade-restricting effect are necessary to attain a given regulatory objective. Deep integration in this area will probably prove difficult to achieve. If pursued, the WTO is often not the right forum—other specialized bodies and mechanisms exist that can and should be used, not least because they allow the discussion to extend beyond governments (Box 13.8).

Significant further shallow integration of the type that has traditionally been pursued by the WTO remains possible. This may include efforts to increase the presumption that governments should use price- and market-based instruments where possible, and avoid the use of direct ('command and control') regulation. This would help reduce the scope for protectionist capture of regulatory regimes. However, moving towards formal multilateral rules that require 'market-friendly intervention' is unlikely to be feasible, nor is it necessarily Pareto optimal given differences in institutional environments and circumstances across countries. A basic element of any approach towards reducing regulatory tensions is greater transparency regarding the rationale for, and analysis of the effect of, intervention. As with antidumping, the focus should be to ensure that domestic groups have access to the information they need to determine the implications of status quo

Box 13.8. GMOs and the Biosafety Protocol

How to treat GMOs is a question of great concern to NGOs and civil society. The financial stakes are huge, as are the economic development and environmental dimensions of the debate. Opposition to trade in products embodying GMOs is mainly driven by fears among consumers and environmental groups that it poses serious risks to public health and biodiversity. The GMO industry insists that bio-engineered products are safe for consumers and represent no danger to the environment. In the US, producers and industrial users point to the fact that their products have been approved by the US Food and Drug Administration (FDA).

'Traditional' farmers in Europe and in developing countries have also opposed the use of GMOs. EU farmers fear the competitive implications of US dominance in this industry, and the effects of greatly expanded crop yields on prices of their harvests. Developing country farmers are concerned about the potential dependence on bio-engineered seeds and technology, especially given the development of so-called terminator genes in GMO-enhanced seeds, which cannot be replanted.

The GMO issue created serious transatlantic tensions in the late 1990s. Calls for labelling of genetically modified grains by the EU, and general opposition by NGOs and consumers in the EU to the use of GMOs, led a number of US producers to withdraw from the market through divestitures. Firms that either produce or use GMOs supported the strict scientific evidence line taken in the WTO SPS agreement, and suggested that labelling should be enough to enable consumers to make their own buying decisions. In the WTO context, the US and Canada proposed the establishment of a working group to review the adequacy of existing rules concerning the use of GMOs. This was opposed by environmental NGOs such as Greenpeace and consumer groups in Europe, who favoured an international convention - outside the WTO - that would permit the application of the precautionary principle, and saw this as an attempt to block efforts to negotiate a convention on bio-safety by the UN Environment Programme (UNEP).

Here, as in other standards-related areas where there are potentially serious spillovers, international cooperation is the appropriate way forward. In January 2000, a treaty was concluded as an annex to the UN Convention on Biological Diversity. The so-called Biosafety Protocol supported the view of NGOs favouring the precautionary principle by allowing countries to restrict imports of GMOs even if scientific evidence regarding their danger remains uncertain. The Protocol embodies a provision stating that 'it shall not be interpreted as implying an incompatibility with the rights and obligations of a Party under any existing international agreements [i.e. the WTO] applying to the transboundary movements of living modified organisms'. The US (and Canada) accepted this in part because North American consumers had begun to share European concerns about the risks of genetically modified crops. Nongovernmental organizations such as Greenpeace and the Transatlantic Consumers' Dialogue played a role in that shift in public opinion, having created an international coalition of organizations that opposed the use of GMOs.

policies, so that they can determine if the benefits of regulatory regimes outweigh the costs.

As far as the 'new' issues are concerned that have been discussed in this chapter, investment policies are perhaps the most important in terms of market access and being trade-related. This is an issue area where a classic GATT approach (shallow integration) can work quite well. However, given the enormous agenda that confronts members in liberalizing trade and investment in services, any effort to establish rules on FDI policies in the near future must be part of a grand bargain that significantly improves welfare for all WTO members. Many of the existing investment-related policies that have negative effects on other countries have proven very difficult to address in PTAs and were excluded from the stillborn MAI.

Harmonization of competition laws is both highly unlikely and undesirable. The types of agreements that would be unambiguously welfare-improving for the world as a whole imply potentially significant redistribution of resources (profits) across countries, and losses to concentrated interests in OECD countries. Here again potential gains exist, but there will be a need for linkage. In general, investment regimes and competition law are policy areas where many countries need to take actions at the national level, and where there is a great need for technical and financial assistance. Thus, there is certainly a case to be made for cooperation in terms of designing and implementing domestic policies and strengthening national institutions. However, putting these issues on the WTO agenda before substantial national experience has been obtained is putting the cart before the horse.

Although in principle investment policies and competition law 'fit' into the WTO, as policies can have cross-border spillover effects on conditions of competition (the terms of trade), this is not the case with environmental and labour policies. While there are certainly potential benefits from global cooperation, in the latter areas, the WTO is not the appropriate forum. This is not to say these subjects are not relevant from a WTO perspective. An important challenge for the future will be to contain the threat of protectionist capture of the environment and labour standards issues. But reciprocal negotiations on standards in these areas—especially in instances where there are no cross-border spillovers—is clearly inappropriate. In addition to the many reasons discussed in this chapter, it must also be recognized that pursuit of this route would give rise to the possibility that labour and environmental policies become an instrument to retaliate or to seek trade concessions (Roessler, 1998). This would result in the noneconomic objectives that underlie the use of standards in these areas not being realized.

The need for deep integration in most of the 'new' areas is limited at best. Abstracting from a grand bargain, the only example discussed in this chapter where it could have large payoffs is trade facilitation. This is cause for optimism, as the traditional GATT reciprocity dynamics do not work when it comes to deeper integration. Shallow integration remains a powerful source of discipline that can have a significant effect in enhancing the contestability of markets. For example, extending its reach to factor markets would have enormous effects. Although this is still a long way in the future, traditional mechanisms such as transparency, exchange of information, surveillance and analysis of the effects of policies can play a major role in helping WTO members adopt more efficient and effective forms of regulation. As argued elsewhere in this book, civil society has a major role to play in this connection. The agenda is to a large extent domestic, implying that domestic actors must determine what are the appropriate policies. Relying on the WTO to identify 'best practices' is unlikely to be a fruitful strategy.

13.9. FURTHER READING

On the general theme of deep integration and the problems of dealing with domestic policy differences, see Jagdish Bhagwati and Robert Hudec (eds), *Harmonization and Fair Trade: Prerequisite for Free Trade?* (Cambridge, MA: MIT Press, 1996); G. Burtless et al., *Gobaphobia* (Washington, DC: Brookings, 1998); and R. Lawrence, A. Bressand and T. Ito, *A Vision for the World Economy* (Washington, DC: Brookings, 1996). John Braithwaite and Peter Drahos discuss international efforts to cooperate on regulation in *Global Business Regulation* (Cambridge: Cambridge University Press, 2000).

SECO and Simon Evenett 'The Singapore Issues and the World Trading System: The Road to Cancun and Beyond,' (Swiss State Secretariat for Economic Affairs, 2003) is an exhaustive analysis and discussion of the proposals that were made in the Doha Round and their merits.

Rachel McCulloch, 'Investment Policy in the GATT', *The World Economy*, 13 (1990); 541–53, and DeAnne Julius, 'International Direct Investment: Strengthening the Policy Regime', in *Managing the World Economy: Lessons from the First 50 Years After Bretton Woods* (Washington, DC: Institute for International Economics, 1995) discuss the need for—and possible elements of—multilateral rules on investment. David Henderson, 'The MAI Affair; A Story and Its Lessons' (London: The Royal Institute of International Affairs, 1999) provides a description and critical assessment of the attempt to negotiate a multilateral agreement on investment in the OECD. UNCTAD's annual *World Investment Report* is the standard source of global data on FDI trends.

F. M. Scherer, *Competition Policies for an Integrated World Economy* (Washington, DC: Brookings Institution, 1994) provides an introduction to the linkages between competition and trade policies. A. Auquier and R. Caves, 'Monopolistic Export Industries, Trade Taxes, and Optimal Competition Policy', *Economic Journal*, 89 (1979): 559–81, analyse many of the questions that arise in dealing with export monopolies and cartels—this is not a new issue. Bernard Hoekman and Petros C.

Mavroidis, 'Competition, Competition Policy, and the GATT', *The World Economy*, 17 (1994): 121–50, question the need to give priority to attempting to establish global competition rules in the WTO. Merger-related disputes between the EU and the US are discussed in Simon Evenett, Alexander Lehman and Benn Steil (eds), *Antitrust Goes Global: What Future for Transatlantic Cooperation?* (Washington, DC: Brookings Institution, 2000).

A managerial perspective on trade facilitation is presented by Michel Kostecki, *International Marketing and the Trading System* (Geneva: ITC, 2000). The amended Kyoto Convention 'On the Simplification and Harmonization of Customs Procedures' can be downloaded from the World Customs Organization's homepage (www.wcoomd.org). An overview of the Doha Round negotiations on trade facilitation is presented in J. M. Finger and J. S. Wilson, 'Implementing a WTO Agreement on Trade Facilitation: What Makes Sense?' *World Bank Policy Research Paper 3971* (2006).

Kym Anderson and Richard Blackhurst (eds), *The Greening of World Trade Issues* (London: Harvester Wheatsheaf, 1992) have collected papers written mostly by trade economists exploring the linkages between trade and the environment. Daniel Esty, *Greening the GATT: Trade, Environment and the Future* (Washington, DC: Institute for International Economics, 1994) provides a balanced and comprehensive treatment of the issues written more from an environmental perspective. Håkan Nordström and Scott Vaughan discuss the trade-environment nexus from a WTO perspective in *Trade and Environment* (Geneva: WTO, 1999). Scott Barrett, *Environment and Statecraft* (Oxford: Oxford University Press, 2002) provides an in-depth treatment of the need for and challenge of international cooperation in this area. Alice Palmer and Richard Tarasofsky, 'The Doha Round and Beyond: Towards a Lasting Relationship Between the WTO and the International Environmental Regime' (London: Chatham House, 2007) discuss multilateral environmental agreements in general and their interactions with the WTO.

Ronald Ehrenberg, *Labor Markets and Integrating National Economies* (Washington, DC: Brookings Institution, 1994) discusses the economics of labour market regulation and the need for convergence in labour standards in an integrating world economy. Gabrielle Marceau provides a comprehensive overview of the legal debates regarding WTO agreements and case law and labour standards in D. Bethlehem, D. McRae, R. Neufeld and I. Van Damme (eds), *The Oxford Handbook of International Trade Law* (Oxford: Oxford University Press, 2008). Keith Maskus, 'Should Core Labor Standards Be Imposed Through International Trade Policy?' *Policy Research Working Paper 1817* (World Bank, 1997) surveys and assesses the various arguments that have been made for putting labour standards on the WTO agenda. For an excellent review of the labour standards question in the context of the WTO, see Robert Stern and Katherine Terrell, 'Labor Standards and the World Trade Organization: A Position Paper,' (Michigan: University of Michigan, August 2003).

Pietro Nivola (ed.), *Comparative Disadvantages? Social Regulations and the Global Economy* (Washington, DC: Brookings, 1997) presents an in-depth discussion of the tensions that arise between national regulatory regimes and 'competitiveness'. David Vogel, *Trading Up: Consumer and Environmental Regulation in a Global Economy* (Cambridge, MA: Harvard University Press, 1995) provides an excellent treatment of the relationship between trade, trade policy and regulatory regimes that discusses a number of cases in depth.

Catherine Mann, Tsunehiro Otsuki and John Wilson investigate the potential impact of improving trade facilitation and reducing trade costs in 'Assessing the Benefits of Trade Facilitation: A Global Perspective,' *World Economy*, 28 (6): 841–71. James Anderson and Eric van Wincoop, 'Trade Costs,' *Journal of Economic Literature* 42 (3) (2004): 691–751, survey the empirical literature on the magnitude of trade costs.

CHAPTER 14

LEGITIMACY, COHERENCE AND GOVERNANCE

TRADE policy in a pluralistic society is made through a complex process of decision-making involving government, political parties, business interests, trade unions, consumer organizations and other members of civil society. In a changing world, rules and procedures affecting trade age quickly. New technologies and new business needs emerge, changing lobbying incentives with respect to trade policy, and altering the need for regulation and associated administrative procedures. Trade rules are therefore subject to continuous pressure for change. This pressure occurs mostly at the national level, but is also reflected at the WTO level. Delegations and the secretariat may be lobbied by interest groups, and are influenced indirectly through research or demonstrations on the streets.

Negotiating power and resources differ dramatically across countries, and across groups within countries. Having a large stake in trade policy, industrial and agricultural interests are often very actively involved in lobbying for or against trade policies at both the domestic and international levels. Small and medium-sized enterprises (SMEs) and NGOs of various kinds generally play much less of a role in national trade policy debates. This started to change in the 1990s. One reason for the increased activism was a perception that 'big business' dominated the process, reducing the perceived legitimacy of the trading system. Many developing countries also regarded the Uruguay Round negotiation outcomes as unbalanced, reducing their sense of 'ownership' of WTO rules and provisions.

An active debate was initiated towards the end of the 1990s on the legitimacy, governance and coherence of the multilateral trading system. This debate was part of a much larger discussion on the (distribution of the) costs and benefits of globalization, and on whether and how to 'manage' the process of international economic integration. After the 1999 Seattle ministerial conference many NGOs came to be of the view that the WTO was not inclusive and did not allow them to express their views. Faced with the NGO criticism, WTO members countered that the WTO is an inter-governmental organization, and that NGOs have to play by the rules that all interest groups have to play by—that is, use domestic advocacy and consultative processes to get their views reflected in national policies. Of course, a necessary condition for this to be feasible is that such mechanisms exist at the national level. The legitimacy of the WTO is to a large extent dependent on the national processes through which trade policy is formulated and changed, as the WTO is a member-driven organization that operates on the basis of consensus.

This chapter discusses the role of industry groups and NGOs in the formulation of trade policies at the national and global level, and the importance of transparency and openness in policy formation to ensure that governments are accountable. Information is a necessary condition for the 'contestability' of policy in national political markets, which in turn is a necessary condition for the 'coherence' of such policies, as well as the legitimacy of whatever multilateral rules are negotiated.

14.1. INDUSTRY AND TRADE POLICY FORMATION

Firms may lobby for policies that shelter them from foreign competition, generate monopoly rights, or exempt them from taxes. They may also ask their governments to push for better access to foreign markets and may develop strategies to work with foreign counterparts (customers, local governments) to directly lobby for policy changes abroad. The task of policymakers, legislators and civil society is to ensure to the greatest extent possible that such lobbying is controlled and filtered through institutions that limit the risk of capture by the powerful. As a general rule, trade policy is the responsibility of the legislative and executive branches. The latter comprise the ensemble of government departments and agencies that are responsible for implementation and often also play a major role in defining and setting policy. The relevant agencies include not only the ministry of trade, but also the ministries of foreign affairs, economy and finance, as well as specialized bodies dealing with agriculture, technical standards, intellectual property, transportation, construction, telecommunications, justice, education and so forth. The consistency of domestic and external policies is typically a matter that is addressed at the cabinet with the assistance of advisory committees and organizations. Important trade policy decisions frequently require legislative changes and therefore parliamentary approval.

Conflicts are inherent in the process of defining trade policies because almost invariably trade policy involves the redistribution of income across groups in society. Some will gain and others lose from any policy that changes the tax or regulatory regime affecting imports or exports. Tensions (turf fights) between various government departments are likely to occur as well. The required compromise has to be reached though bargaining and decisions by the higher political authorities. For example, the ministry of finance may want to tax foreign trade to generate revenue and oppose liberalization. It may be supported by government departments that confront lobbying for protection by declining industries, but resisted by the ministry of economy, which may seek to use liberalization and tariff exemptions as an instrument of investment and export promotion. The ministry of labour may favour trade barriers to safeguard employment in uncompetitive industries, whereas the ministry of foreign affairs may favour more open policies as part of a foreign policy strategy. As discussed in Chapter 4, interest group preferences can be expected to play an important role in determining the stance taken by sectoral and economic ministries.

Differences in the institutional structure for trade policymaking generally reflect differences in economic and political systems, especially the role of the state in the economy, the importance of market forces and the strength of private property rights, and the power structure that has emerged over time. To prevent the regulatory capture of sectoral agencies and the policy formation process, there is a need for openness—transparency and consultation. Public participation is an efficient mechanism to help decision-makers identify stakeholders and the social benefits and costs of a policy. The objective of consultation mechanisms is to improve both the quality of trade policy and to ensure that it is acceptable to voters or the political support base of the government. Many countries have created a formal structure of general and issue-specific advisory bodies that institutionalize the exchange of information between the business community, other interest groups and the government (Box 14.1). In other nations, business and government rarely meet, or the interaction is limited to a small elite with preferential access.

The formal institutional mechanisms that are found in many countries to encourage public participation in trade policymaking may not reflect the reality of how policy is actually made. What matters is how different interests are balanced, and whether all interests have access to the system. The greater the role of the state, the less market-oriented the economy, the less business interests are likely to be consulted. As economies open up and political systems become more pluralistic, business interests will have greater incentives and opportunities

Box 14.1. Government–business interaction in selected countries

In Canada, an extensive programme of consultations and outreach with all stakeholders including business organizations, NGOs and consumer interest groups is pursued throughout the process of defining Canada's trade policy. As part of this effort, the Trade Negotiations and Agreements' website offers detailed information on trade policy matters and invites comments on negotiating priorities and objectives from NGOs, business organizations and the public at large. The Federal Government also maintains a close relationship with the governments of provinces and territories by means of a variety of different mechanisms. Provincial authorities are consulted on the identification of priority trade-policy issues, design of negotiating strategies and positions during the preparations for, and course of international trade negotiations. In addition to comments and proposals solicited from Canadians at large, there are 10 active Sectoral Advisory Groups on International Trade that offer the Minister for International Trade strategic advice on sector-specific issues. An Academic Advisory Council provides the Deputy Minister for International Trade with an additional venue to review and identify knowledge gaps and research priorities.

In India, the Ministry of Commerce is assisted in trade policy formulation by advisory bodies participating in the Board of Trade. The Indian Institute of Foreign Trade conducts research and training in international trade. Several sectoral institutes dealing with packaging, diamonds, textiles and chemicals concentrate on industry-specific issues. Statutory commodity boards advise on trade policies for tea, coffee, rubber, spices and tobacco. Industry associations such as the Confederation of Indian Industries, the Federation of India Exporter's Organization, the Federation of Indian Chambers of Commerce, and think-tanks such as the Indian Center Research on International Economic Relations also contribute to policy proposals.

In Morocco, the National Foreign Trade Council, comprising 30 government officials and 36 business representatives, is responsible for preparing advisory opinions on foreign trade issues and new legislative proposals. The private sector of the Dominican Republic is represented in the Commission for the Follow-up of Integration Schemes, the Foreign Trade Commission, the Lomé IV Commission, the National Free Zones Council, and in the national commissions dealing with trade in bananas, coffee and cocoa. The Joint Public-Private Consultative Committee constitutes the main formal government-business forum in Thailand. The Committee, which deals extensively with trade policy issues, is chaired by the Prime Minister and includes several cabinet ministers. The private sector has established the Joint Standing Committee on Commerce, Industry and Banking whose members include the Board of Trade (a private body comprising business associations), the Thai Chamber of Commerce, the Foreign Trade Chamber of Commerce, the Federation of Thai Industries and the Thai Bankers' Association. The Joint Committee is a forum for discussion and coalition-building and an important player in the trade policy formation process.

Source: WTO, Trade Policy Reviews (various years).

to express their views. States that emphasize the virtue of entrepreneurship and the allocative role of markets are more prone to accept private business input into trade policymaking. These dynamics can be observed in many countries. For example, following the autonomous reforms in Latin America in the 1980s, export interests became a factor in trade policy. They played a role in the subsequent push to pursue regional integration. The FTAA initiative, launched in 1994, led to the creation of the Business Network of Hemispheric Integration—with a membership of 400 organizations—the Americas Business Forum and the APEC Business Advisory Council (Ostry, 2000). Smaller firms frequently perceive that their interests are neglected in such bodies, spawning the creation of specialized associations.

An example is Philfoodex, an umbrella organization of mainly small and medium-sized food processing firms in the Philippines. The organization was established in 1986 to defend the interests of food processors. As the food processing industry developed in the 1980s, smaller firms realized that the Chamber of Food Manufacturers—at the time the major food manufacturers association in the Philippines—was dominated by large sugar producers that had an interest in high prices for sugar. The trade liberalization approach followed by the Philippines in the 1980s involved reducing tariffs on processed food while maintaining sugar prices above the world market level. As a result, local factories producing sugar-intensive goods such as candies and chocolate had a hard time meeting competition from imports. The industry suffered from negative effective protection (see Chapter 4). Starting in the late 1990s, Philfoodex became actively involved in lobbying legislators and government officials for cheaper sugar (see Kostecki, 2001, and www.philfoodex.com).

Corporate interests at the WTO level

Numerous industry associations, business coalitions and multinational companies are active in Geneva as well as in national fora. Among the more visible business groups are the European Round Table of Industrialists (Brussels), the Geneva Association (a think-tank of some 80 insurance companies), the World Business Council for Sustainable Development and the US Coalition of Service Industries (CSI) and its counterpart, the European Community Services Group. The Paris-based International Chamber of Commerce (ICC) maintains a permanent representative in Geneva, largely to follow WTO developments (Box 14.2). The US National Association of Manufacturers coordinates North American business interests through the 'US Alliance for Trade Expansion' and initiates and supports many US trade liberalization proposals. It played an important role in the TRIPS negotiation. The CSI and British Invisibles—a UK-based association of service firms—were important actors mobilizing support for inclusion of services in the

---

Box 14.2. The International Chamber of Commerce and the WTO

The International Chamber of Commerce (ICC), a Paris-based nongovernmental organization linking thousands of companies and business associations around the globe, is an active player in providing a business view on matters its members want to see addressed by the WTO. The ICC has called for less diverse, complex and opaque rules of origin, modernized and simplified customs procedures and action to combat extortion and bribery in international business. The ICC favours the establishment of a global WTO framework of rules governing cross-border investment, greater disciplines on subsidies and expanded membership of the WTO plurilateral agreement on government procurement. It has also called for lower customs tariffs, and liberalization of trade in financial services, basic telecommunications, maritime transport, professional services and cross-border movement of professional, technical and managerial personnel.

The ICC periodically prepares and distributes position papers on such trade policy issues and meets with WTO delegations in Geneva. The Chamber is accredited as a NGO at WTO ministerial meetings and its documents and position papers were available at the WTO webpage during the last three ministerial conferences in Hong Kong, Cancun and Seattle, along with documentation submitted by other NGOs.

Uruguay Round. Specialized associations such as the US Dairy Foods Association, the Pork Producers Council, the American Sugar Alliance or the Council of Bars and Law Societies of Europe were also active during the Uruguay Round (Arkell, 1994).

Individual multinational enterprises were also active in the background during the Uruguay Round. Global firms such American Express, American International Group, Citibank and Arthur Andersen provided important intellectual inputs and exercised influence during the preparatory phase of the negotiations that led to the conclusion of GATS. The objective of these firms was generally to improve access to export markets. Certain companies have particularly important stakes in the WTO. Examples are inspection and trade facilitation firms such as Société Générale de Surveillance (SGS), and international express and courier companies such as DHL and Federal Express. Société Générale de Surveillance maintained a senior position to follow GATT-related matters during the Uruguay Round and assumed a leadership role within the International Federation of Inspection Agencies, the body that represents the interests of pre-shipment inspection firms.

In the 2000s corporate interest in and engagement with the WTO declined. To some extent this probably was a reflection of the economic situation: times were good—world trade was expanding rapidly for most of the Doha Round (see Chapter 1). Many governments had pursued economic policy reforms, including with respect to FDI, driven in part by the ongoing process of economic fragmentation and specialization and in turn allowing this to proceed. The accession of China in 2001 and the boom in China created major opportunities for multinational businesses, not least as it also induced further reforms in other countries. There also appeared to be a perception on the part of business that reforms were unlikely to be reversed, reducing the value associated with binding of liberalization initiatives in the WTO. Some industries were also less proactive in the Doha Round because of concerns to safeguard what had been achieved in the Uruguay Round. This was the case for example for IPRs and the TRIPS Agreement, against which a strong backlash emerged in the late 1990s and early 2000s. Finally, it may have been that there was an increasing realization that the WTO was perhaps not the most effective institution through which to push for better access to specific markets or to enforce specific commitments. Alternatives included PTAs and BITs—which proliferated further during the Doha Round. Whatever the reasons, the lack of vigorous support by business for the Doha Round was a significant factor in the lack of progress that was achieved.

Increased openness and internationalization of production has led to changes in business-government dialogue. There has been something of a paradigm shift in the approach taken by business in advocacy on trade policy. This is summarized in Table 14.1. The trends are towards cooperation with other interest groups, working through and with networks and increasing engagement of smaller firms as opposed to only the largest corporations.

14.2. NGOs and Civil Society

Industry lobbies play a major role in the formulation of trade policy, both at the national and the international level. That business interests dominate the WTO is not very surprising—after all, business has the largest stake in trade. However, other groups also play a role, especially at the national level. Unions have traditionally been a major political force in many countries, and influence trade policy stances. Environmental and human rights groups are also important players, especially on specific policies that directly affect their interests. Business groups are increasingly complemented by (and sometimes face competition and opposition from) NGOs in the trade policy formation process, at the national level, and, more visibly, at the international level.

Nongovernmental organizations are generally nonprofit entities with voluntary membership that pursue noneconomic objectives. They are a relatively large industry in their own right. Larger NGOs may have annual budgets in the hundreds of millions of US dollars coming from private sources, government donations and sales of goods and services. Nonprofit groups (mostly NGOs) provide over 8 per cent of all jobs in North America and 6 per cent in the UK

Table 14.1. Advocacy in trade policy: a paradigm shift?

New approach	Traditional approach
Great emphasis on a structured and formal consultation process. Bureaucracy is seen more as a facilitator rather than decision-maker.	Nontransparent, informal consultations drive the formal consultation process. Bureaucracy dominates the decision-making.
Emphasis on transparency. Policy proposals are subjected to public scrutiny through public hearings, debate and Internet sites.	Lack of transparency. Hidden deals at a political level or within bureaucracy are possible.
Consultations comprise all major stakeholders: industry associations, regional interest groups, consumers, trade unions, NGOs, etc.	Decision process is dominated by a limited number of large companies and the most powerful industries with links to the government.
International orientation, with regional and bilateral trade arrangements gaining in importance. The influence of foreign investors is strongly felt.	Domestic (nationalistic) orientation. Trade policy is largely formulated keeping in mind the interests of major domestic industries.
Important role of networks (and online Internet communities) in coalition-building and issue management.	Coalition-building and issue management are centralized in the hands of bureaucracy, politicians and powerful economic actors.
Advocacy focuses on issues requiring technical expertise. Skills to communicate in simple terms with government and public at large are needed.	Advocacy focuses on market access issues and on the related redistribution of income.
Smaller business organizations and organizations based in developing countries are more active on the international level.	Advocacy on the international level is rather limited and is mainly conducted by large multinational companies.

Source: Hocking and McGuire (2004); Kostecki (2005, 2007).

(*The Economist*, 29 January 2000). None of the largest NGOs focus predominantly on trade matters, however.[1]

A common denominator underlying the objectives of many NGOs that are active on the trade front is sustainable development: ensuring that social and ecological objectives are considered in addition to economic ones. In the 1990s, the umbrella concept of sustainable development brought together a large number of diverse groups that pursue environmental, social, human rights and cultural objectives. These groups are often multinational in nature, linking national organizations in a loose network, increasingly connected to each other through the Internet. In contrast to industry lobbies, many NGOs seek the limelight and are adept at using the media to attract attention to their views. An example was provided at the Seattle ministerial by Greenpeace handing out green condoms to delegates as a way of bringing across their message that in their view what was required was a set of principles to make trade 'safe for the environment'. Non-governmental organizations are also more inclined to complement activities at the national level with actions that centre on global issues and the activities of international organizations.

Declining confidence in political institutions, pressure for decentralization and calls for new forms of direct democracy have been factors leading to NGOs becoming 'mainstream' institutions. Relationships with industry have gradually moved away from purely adversarial to include partnerships aimed at creating 'win-win' situations between sustainability and efficiency. An example was a joint Oxfam-Unilever project in Indonesia that aimed to identify how to improve the potential of distribution chains to generate employment and income. This joint research effort found that for every direct employee there were many more jobs in distribution chains, suggesting that for NGOs seeking to improve conditions for producers and other workers within supply chains, it is important to analyse the policies of multinationals towards the distribution and retail aspect of their value chains (Clay, 2005). To the extent that any neat division existed between the corporate and the NGO worlds, by the mid-1990s it was long gone. Today corporate work provides a non-negligible share of NGO financing.

Governments have also responded to the emergence of NGOs. For example, in the 1990s a Transatlantic Consumer Dialogue (TACD) mechanism was created to allow for NGO input into trade and related policies to complement the Transatlantic Business Dialogue (TABD). Not surprisingly, given the disparity in interests, 'levelling the playing field' is not straightforward. Public Citizen, a US-based NGO, noted that the US Administration did not adopt any TACD recommendations, while accepting 50 per cent of TABD proposals (www.citizen.org/pctrade September 2000).

---

[1] Of those that have been active on trade, the largest is probably Oxfam, which had an annual budget of over US$500 million in 2007.

NGOs and the WTO

Although NGOs have been a noticeable element in the UN system and other international bodies for many years, their influence in MTNs and the GATT was minimal until the late 1980s. This changed fundamentally in the Uruguay Round, when environmental groups became concerned that trade liberalization might have detrimental consequences for the environment. It was largely at the behest of NGOs that the Committee on Trade and the Environment was resuscitated in 1991. After the creation of the WTO in 1995, NGOs remained active. Largely because of concerns about the impacts and consequences of globalization—and the 'marketing' efforts of the then Director-General Ruggiero, who maintained in speech after speech that the WTO was a central player in, and pillar of, the globalization process—NGOs opposing global economic integration began to perceive the WTO as an appropriate target. Groups opposing globalization marched against the organization at the 1998 ministerial meeting in Geneva, and dominated the press coverage of the ministerial meetings in Seattle (1999) and Cancun (2003).

Three broad categories of NGOs can be distinguished in terms of their general approach to the WTO: 'conformers', 'reformers' and 'radicals' (Scholte, O'Brien and Williams, 1999). The 'conformers' endorse the activities and objectives of the WTO system, accept the premise that global integration and a reliance on the market provides the best prospects for economic growth and development. 'Reformers' comprise entities that recognize the value of a rules-based multilateral trade system that is based on open markets and nondiscrimination, but are concerned that existing procedures or rules result in inefficient outcomes. The reformers want to modify the system. Finally, the 'radicals' seek to abolish the WTO or to substantially reduce its powers and competence.

The vast majority of NGOs are either reformers or radicals. They tend to be active in five areas: labour rights, human rights, environment, consumer protection and economic development. Most NGOs pursue goals that are only marginally trade-related. Traditionally, the labour movement has been most active in trade policy. The largest US trade union federation, the AFL-CIO, is a major player, as is the International Federation of Free Trade Unions (Brussels), which claims to represent 124 million members in 143 countries. Both support the introduction of core labour standards in the WTO.

A number of the major nonlabour NGOs that concentrate on global economic issues and focus on the WTO are listed in Table 14.2. Although most NGOs that are active with respect to international trade are based in high-income countries, the number of Southern NGOs is non-negligible. Among the more prominent, the Third World Network (TWN) is a NGO based in Asia that is generally critical of trade liberalization. The Consumer Unity and Trust Society (CUTS) is a joint venture between African and Asian NGOs that has a consumer interest perspective.

Table 14.2. Examples of NGOs engaged on WTO-related issues

NGO (Home Base)	Objective and Type of Activity
ActionAid International (UK)	Making the trading system more development friendly
Consumers International (UK)	Global network of organizations that defend consumer interests
Consumer Unity & Trust Society (CUTS) International (India)	Research and advocacy concerning trade and sustainable development both at the multilateral and regional level
Evian Group (Switzerland)	A global network that promotes an open, inclusive and global market economy through a dialogue between corporate, government and opinion leaders
IDEAS (Geneva)	Assist low-income countries to integrate into the world trading system in a way that supports poverty reduction and economic development efforts
Institute of Agriculture and Trade Policy (US)	Support efforts to forge stronger and fairer multilateral trade rules
InterAction (US)	A network of 150 organizations actively working on trade and development issues, including fair trade
International Chamber of Commerce (Paris)	Promotes cross-border trade and investment
International Centre for Trade and Sustainable Development (Geneva)	Support more sustainable trade and development through information, analysis, networking/dialogue and training
The International Federation of Free Trade Unions (Brussels)	Promotion of labour and human rights issues in the context of trade policy
International Institute for Sustainable Development (Canada)	Policy analysis and recommendations for sustainable development in a number of areas including international trade and investment
International Policy Network (UK)	Improve public understanding of the role of trade liberalization
One World (Global)	Network of 1,600 NGOs that promotes sustainable development, social justice and human rights
OXFAM International (Oxford)	Advocate design and implementation of more development-friendly trade rules that will have a greater impact on reducing poverty
Public Citizen Global Trade Watch (US)	Challenges corporate globalization, arguing that the globalization model is neither a random inevitability nor 'free trade'
Third World Network (Malaysia)	Focuses on trade, social and environmental issues pertaining to the South; advocates for greater policy space and flexibility

The South Centre is an entity created by the G77 to defend developing country interests in the WTO. The International Centre for Trade and Sustainable Development (ICTSD), also based in Geneva, publishes an informative newsletter on trade developments in and outside the WTO called *Bridges* (downloadable from www.ictsd.org), undertakes analysis of trade negotiating issues and organizes frequent meetings between practitioners, analysts and stakeholders. A competitive advantage of many NGOs is that they are not obliged to work with governments—as many international organizations are.

All of the NGOs listed in Table 14.2, as well as many others, closely followed the Doha trade negotiations. Indeed, NGOs were much more visible and influential than the business community. Many of the developing country-centred NGOs focusing on the WTO are of recent vintage, and some were created as a response to the establishment of the WTO. In contrast, the Northern NGOs that have been active on WTO issues tend to be well established. Nongovernmental organizations such as the Sierra Club, the Worldwide Fund for Nature and Greenpeace have favoured the imposition of trade restrictions on products that are deemed to have been manufactured using environmentally damaging production methods, to preserve biodiversity or forestry stocks, and so forth. Most environmental NGOs tend to be critical of the WTO, reflecting their lack of enthusiasm about globalization. They often argue that WTO-supported liberalization weakens health and environmental standards in the global economy.

Consumer organizations became more active in the world trading system in the 1990s. Their interests include issues related to basic consumer rights (safety, information, choice), as well as the right to an environment that enhances the quality of life. Consumer interests are represented at the international level by networks of consumer organizations such as Consumers International and the Transatlantic Consumer Dialogue. The latter played a major role in mobilizing public opposition to hormone-based meat production. Major development-oriented NGOs include Christian Aid, the World Development Movement and Oxfam. All three have developed positions on a wide range of trade-related issues, including market access and ensuring fair terms of trade for developing countries.

Many of the NGO argue that:

- the WTO is dominated by—and is an instrument of—industry lobbyists and multinational corporations, resulting in the neglect of environmental, labour, consumer and sustainable development issues, as well as social cohesion and equity;
- the WTO needs to move to a more participatory approach through the creation of consultation mechanisms and advisory bodies if it is to generate greater trust and mobilize civic engagement and 'ownership'; and
- countervailing power is needed to increase government accountability in trade negotiations and this is best achieved by granting the NGO community direct access to the WTO.

Article V.2 WTO specifies that the WTO General Council may make appropriate arrangements for consultation and cooperation with NGOs. When the General Council approved the use of the WTO website for publishing WTO documents and information, it reserved a section of the site for information specifically for NGOs. It also encouraged the Secretariat to work more closely with NGOs to exchange views on topics related to WTO Agreements (WT/L/162). Procedures to do so were established in 2001 in a Secretariat paper (WT/INF/30). Interactions with NGOs have taken on different formats, ranging from briefings to public symposia. The General Council recognized that the coordinators of the work of WTO councils and committees might participate in events promoted by NGOs as long as this was done in a personal capacity. An annual Public Forum has become one of the platforms for dialogue with NGOs. However, WTO member governments are not open to any suggestion for a direct involvement of NGOs in the WTO fora. Interactions with NGOs continue to occur mostly on an ad hoc basis. Moreover, this takes place primarily in Geneva, limiting the engagement with NGOs to those with sufficient resources to set up shop in Geneva or to incur the cost of regular visits there. Nongovernmental organizations were also offered an opportunity to submit position papers directly to the WTO Secretariat, which posted them on the NGO section of the WTO website and prepared a monthly list of all the submitted material.

In the 2000s, the NGOs continued to pressure for the right to access the WTO council and committee meetings, to be heard at these meetings (at least at some of them) and to have the opportunity to submit written documents. Informal proposals have been made to create a single and transparent procedure to enable participation by any and all NGOs wishing to do so. Willets (2002), for example, has suggested that the WTO begin by accepting those NGOs that enjoy consultative status in the UN Social and Economic Council and that a commission comprised of NGO representatives define a Code of Conduct for NGOs participating in WTO bodies. Other proposals are to make a distinction between NGOs directly engaged in trade issues and those that are not, with only the former qualifying for participation. Another idea is to differentiate between organizations that pursue commercial interests (industry representatives, trade associations, etc.) and those that are noncommercial (Ratton Sanchez, 2006). Director-Generals of the WTO have established what can be seen as NGO/WTO cooperation mechanisms in the form of Advisory Bodies. The first of these was set up by Mike Moore (in 2001) and was followed by two more during the term of Supachai Panitchpakdi (in 2003). Oxfam International and Friends of the Earth, who were invited to participate, refused to do so on the grounds that they were not representative enough of civil society.

An important policy shift was marked in a 1996 Singapore ministerial decision to permit participation by NGO representatives in the plenary sessions of ministerial conferences. However, NGOs do not have the right to a voice in the sessions. Since 1998, the General Council has allowed the WTO Secretariat to organize informative meetings (or briefings) for NGOs during the ministerial conferences on the progress of the negotiations, and after 1999 additional measures were adopted in response to the intensified demands for NGO participation. These included: (1) briefings, in Geneva by the Secretariat after meetings between members; (2) debate panels; (3) the organization of working sessions; and (4) allowing the Secretariat to accept written position papers by NGOs. These developments prompted new activities surrounding the ministerial conferences, including panels and seminars. In addition, there are symposia organized by the WTO that are open to the general public. As of 2008, more than a dozen such events have been held. Since 2005, the public fora are managed in partnership with NGOs responsible for organizing the panel debates and choosing the general theme of the forum.

In spite of these initiatives to enhance the interactions with NGOs, the primary channel for NGO influence remains informal. One mechanism used by some NGOs is to participate as a member of the official national delegation to a WTO meeting. Some NGOs, particularly those with representation in Geneva, even managed to get informal access to specific WTO council and committee meetings. Equally import- ant indirect forms of NGO influence were the research reports they prepared on the application of commitments assumed within the WTO and their high-exposure campaigns. There is no doubt that the daily contact with the WTO Secretariat, the debates held by the organization (in symposia and working groups) and the work of the Advisory Bodies were useful mechanisms for the NGO indirect involvement.

Since 1998, NGOs have been permitted to submit to the panels or to the Appellate Body, amicus curiae briefs. The first such opportunity presented itself in relation to the Shrimp-Turtles case. However, procedures for the acceptances of amicus curiae briefs have swung back and forth, generating insecurity among NGOs over whether or not their contributions would be accepted in the DSB. The number of amicus curiae briefs submitted before the DSB has increased over the years prompting the development of specific procedures for their acceptance. Panels, for example, have adopted as a rule that they would accept positions submitted prior to the hearing with the parties. The Appellate Body even went so far as to define procedure in detail, on deadlines and methods, for the acceptance of amicus curiae briefs in its analysis of the dispute against the EC concerning measures affecting asbestos and asbestos-containing products (WT/DS135). In September 2005, in the *Hormones* disputes (WT/DS320, WT/DS321), the panel decided even to publicly broadcast the audience with the parties to the dispute, in accordance with previously defined proceedings. In the Doha Round process of reviewing the dispute settlement system, demands have been made either for expressly permitting the submission of amicus curiae briefs and establishing a specific procedure for doing so (Article 13) or limiting NGO participation.

The premise of WTO members essentially remains that democratically elected governments which negotiate trade deals represent their citizens—if they do not, they can and should be voted out of office. If necessary, any deal can then be re-negotiated using the mechanisms that have been built into the WTO for that purpose. The primary responsibility for taking into account the different interests of NGOs in trade policymaking is considered to lie at the national level. Efforts to actively engage NGOs directly in the work of the WTO or its meetings are therefore generally rejected by most WTO members. However, NGOs have valid cause for concern if they do not have adequate opportunities to feed their views into the national political and institutional processes through which trade policy positions are formulated. At present, there is little the WTO can do to require members to implement mechanisms that give NGOs access to the policymaking process. Some NGOs (such as Consumer International) have therefore proposed that WTO members develop guidelines for national consultation mechanisms and encourage members to adopt and implement them with a view to allowing civil society to participate in national (or regional) trade policymaking. Absent a move in this direction, which would be a major step for the WTO, the main need is to ensure that the operations of the WTO are transparent and that there is 'full information' so that member governments can be held accountable in domestic political fora.

In democracies, all interested groups have the opportunity to express their views on trade and related policy issues to representatives in the legislature and the government. Given the need to be elected, politicians will be responsive to those interests, as they must mobilize votes come election time. In centralized systems power tends to be more concentrated, and many groups will find it more difficult to express their views and influence the process. Whatever the political system, information is a key ingredient in good policymaking and holding governments and legislatures accountable. Nongovernmental organizations and other interest groups can play a valuable role in providing information and collecting data. A major focus of many of the Southern NGOs mentioned above is to provide information, to undertake analysis, and to help build capacity in developing countries to defend their interests. There is empirical evidence to suggest that government responsiveness to interest group pressures in trade policymaking increases with the growth of independent and effective business organizations (Kostecki, 2007). Business engagement was an important factor in shifting US trade policy from a foreign-policy to a commercially driven stance.

14.3. GOVERNANCE OF THE WTO

The WTO operates on the basis of consensus. As noted in previous chapters, the decision-making mechanics of the WTO were subject to severe criticism in the run-up and aftermath of major ministerial meetings, especially Seattle and Cancun.

Many low-income and small WTO members expressed great frustration regarding the difficulty of keeping abreast of developments, and objected to being excluded from the consultations and meetings where compromises are struck and deals are made. In early 2000, the WTO Council identified this as a priority matter to be addressed in order to re-establish confidence in the WTO. More generally, the inability of WTO members to close a Doha deal has led to increasing calls that a new approach towards decision-making is required.

Two types of proposals have attracted most attention. The first is to move away from consensus and create a decision-making and management structure that relies on an Executive Board or Committee of the type found in the World Bank or IMF. Membership would be based on 'economic weight' (e.g. trade shares), with some permanent representatives and others rotating. Those on the Board would speak on behalf of groups of countries that they were chosen to represent. The second is to provide much greater scope for civil society and nonexecutive branch bodies to participate in WTO processes.

Most developing countries object strongly to an IMF or World Bank model, as they believe that the consensus principle maximizes their ability to safeguard their interests. An alternative, less ambitious change would be to give a Board/Steering Committee the task of hammering out a proposed consensus on issues, which would then need to be ratified by all WTO members (Schott and Watal, 2000). Rather than pursue major structural reforms, Schott and Watal propose instead that the focus be on procedural improvements to ensure that small group meetings (such as the Green Room) are transparent. This could involve agreeing that consultations be open-ended, that all members are informed that Green Room Meetings are being pursued, that all members be given an opportunity to state their views, and that the outcome is reported in a timely fashion to those WTO members not present (Luke, 2000).

Efforts in this direction were largely implemented by the WTO Secretariat in the post-2000 period under the general heading of improving internal transparency (Pedersen, 2006). Following the Seattle ministerial meeting the Chairman of the General Council launched a process of consultations that generated some 20 'nonpapers' that fed into a report by the Chairman. Although most members were of the view that transparency and consultative processes could be improved, there was strong support for a number of basic principles and conclusions: there was no need for radical reform of the WTO; the WTO consensus practice should be maintained; and the system of informal consultations was a fundamental element of the WTO process. What was needed was to ensure that any member could make their views known and that the outcome of consultations be reported back to the full membership, in particular at ministerial conferences. Compared to Seattle, subsequent ministerial meetings were organized in a way that greatly increased transparency. They included informal briefings of heads of delegations by ministers who were appointed to be 'Friends of the Chair' on various negotiating issues and a decision to keep two hours at the end of each day meeting-free to allow interaction between delegations.

The Sutherland Report, prepared by an advisory body at the request of the WTO Director-General Panichpakdi in 2005, proposed the establishment of a senior official level Consultative Group of no more than 30 members, in which some members would have permanent membership and others would rotate. The purpose of this group—which would be limited to officials based in capitals and could meet at ministerial level when necessary—would be to give political guidance to negotiators 'when appropriate' and map out possible areas of agreement/proposals for moving forward on WTO business. Meetings of the group at the senior official level would occur before every ministerial meeting to prepare the ground/agenda, etc. One rationale for the creation of such a group was that it would formalize the ad hoc 'mini-ministerial meetings' that had frequently been called by subsets of WTO members to deal with Doha Round questions. The report argued that formalization of what was emerging on an informal, ad hoc basis would help enhance the effectiveness of a smaller group interaction. The Sutherland Report also proposed increased high-level participation in Geneva talks by capital-based policymakers; annual meetings of the WTO ministerial Conference (as opposed to every two years); and a WTO summit of the heads of state of members every five years.

The suggestion to establish a consultative body was not aimed at replacing the consensus-based mode of operation of the WTO. It was not intended to be a decision-making body, and thus differed from the 'international financial institution' model. However, the report did suggest that some actions be taken to weaken the 'consensus constraint' to decision-making. Concretely, it proposed requiring every WTO member that refused to agree to a measure or proposal that had widespread support to specify that the reason for doing so was that a vital national interest was at stake. The idea was to raise the threshold (cost) for members to use blocking consensus as part of a logrolling strategy. None of these proposals generated any traction among the WTO membership.

Blackhurst and Hartridge (2005) agree that a focus on transparency is not sufficient. Instead they argue that the WTO needs an 'efficient-size sub-group of members for the purpose of discussing, debating and negotiating draft decisions that can be put to the entire membership for adoption'. Importantly, they argue that participation in this group needs to be 'fully transparent, predictable, equitable and legitimate in the eyes of all WTO members'.

An alternative approach, supported by many NGOs, is to open access to the deliberations of the WTO to civil society representatives. Nongovernmental organizations have noted repeatedly that they can obtain observer status at UN meetings, but are excluded from the WTO. This exclusion pertains not just to negotiation and dispute settlement sessions, but also to regular committee and council meetings. The nature of the process of cooperation makes it difficult, if not impossible, to accommodate private participation in negotiations. The wide range of issues involved and numerous linkages that may be made render the negotiating process complex. Allowing single-issue groups to have a voice in negotiations would preclude many of the needed tradeoffs and bargains. This is a task for governments who have been entrusted with the task of safeguarding the public interest. The required deal-making and posturing cannot be done in the open. Negotiators will not agree to open their back-room bargaining to the continuous scrutiny of groups with vested interests that will immediately publicize all instances where their preferences are not being defended by negotiators. Complete transparency of negotiations will result in deadlock—officials will not be able to make tradeoffs that result in a welfare-enhancing outcome. To put it in Prince Bismarck's words: 'citizens should not be permitted to observe how laws or sausages are made'.

What matters then is accountability *ex post* and access to policymakers *ex ante*. As noted in Chapter 4, stakeholders must be able to inform their government representatives of their preferences and interests. Better access at the domestic level should do much to improve the representativeness of positions taken at the WTO by members. Greater transparency at the WTO level can help ensure that governments are held accountable. Decisions by WTO members to de-restrict many nonconfidential documents more rapidly and to make them accessible to the public through the Internet have done a lot to improve transparency relative to the GATT.

Granting major NGOs with a global reach access to formal, non-negotiating sessions of WTO bodies as observers could help improve transparency. Article V:2 WTO—which allows the General Council to make appropriate arrangements for cooperation with NGOs on matters related to the WTO—provides a vehicle for putting in place mechanisms to achieve this if WTO members want to. Many of the demands of the NGO community in this regard deserve support. For example, Consumer International has proposed that the WTO introduce accreditation of international NGOs to grant them observer status, following the example of other international organizations, develop criteria for confidentiality to allow automatic de-restriction of nonconfidential documents, and require the immediate release of draft agendas to facilitate national consultation. The major problem that arises in implementing the proposal to grant observer status is to determine who gets accredited. Given the huge number of meetings that take place every year and the costs of participation, only the largest NGOs are likely to take up the option. One solution to this problem is to require cooperation between NGOs, or to devise a rotation rule. Given the existence of joint ventures such as the ICTSD it would appear relatively straightforward to accredit a small number of NGOs as observers, and require them to provide all interested actors with their reports on WTO meetings. A necessary condition for moving down this path will be to address the question of criteria for observer status more generally, including for international organizations. This has been a matter of contention between WTO members, reflecting foreign policy considerations (in particular, concerning a request by the League of Arab States to become an observer).

The most far-reaching version of proposals in the direction of expanding the set of actors in the WTO is to create a legislative assembly to complement the current exclusive presence of the 'executive branch' of members in WTO fora. Making this operational could help ensure greater engagement by countries in the WTO and 'ownership' of the institution. For example, Bellmann and Gerster (1996) have argued for the creation of a 'WTO Parliament' with representatives from all member states. The objective would be to strengthen links with national legislatures and enhance understanding of and input into negotiations and the regular work programmes of the WTO. Representatives of legislatures can and do participate in WTO ministerial conferences and may be represented in national delegations that participate in the various WTO councils—see Chapter 2). However, there is no formal mechanism for regular engagement by legislators in the WTO (Skaggs, 2004). The idea has been strongly opposed by WTO members, in particular developing countries. Their view is that the WTO is an inter-governmental institution and that negotiating trade policy is a matter that falls in the purview of governments, with the role of national legislatures being to provide the mandate for, and approval of, what is negotiated. However, greater engagement with and by legislatures would seem to be a useful mechanism to increase public participation with the WTO.

Starting in 2001, international parliamentary conferences on the WTO have been organized by the Inter-Parliamentary Union in cooperation with the European Parliament, both in Geneva and at ministerial conferences. One argument used by parliamentarians in favour of greater engagement in the WTO is that they are elected, in contrast to NGOs, and that regular interaction will enhance the quality of their (national) oversight of their executive branches.

What about the dispute settlement process? As noted in Chapter 3, many NGOs have been eager to obtain access to panels in order to defend environmental and other interests. The Appellate Body has already taken the decision to accept amicus briefs. Going further and allowing observers into the room as observers would require changes in the dispute settlement mechanism—including professionalization of panels. However, as was discussed in Chapter 3, there are strong arguments against granting the private sector—be it business or civil society groups—standing to take cases to the WTO.

Greater efforts to ensure transparency do not necessarily have to involve the WTO itself. Another option that might be considered is the creation of an international public interest body that would act as a forum to explore the technical (economic, scientific) and social aspects of specific contentious issues or proposed areas for action at the WTO (Hoekman and Mavroidis, 2000). If this is made independent of the WTO, it could allow for direct access by nongovernmental bodies. A transparency body might help shed light and build consensus by identifying whether there are cross-border spillovers, their size, the economic or environmental impact of policies, including their distributional effects within and across countries, and whether alternative instruments exist that could attain governmental or societal objectives (more) efficiently. Such an entity could be used as a discovery mechanism through which greater understanding could be obtained regarding the effects of national policies on various constituencies and stakeholders, both within and across economies. It could play a constructive role by acting as a focal point for exploring the pros and cons of potential multilateral rules in new areas, and a forum to analyse the economic and development impact of specific policy measures that have been taken or are proposed. Such an entity could also be a forum to determine the scientific basis—or lack thereof—of regulatory policies in sensitive areas (biotech, GMOs). Such policies are rapidly becoming a major source of tension and controversy, and developing countries in particular could benefit from a neutral and objective forum in which standards-related policies and issues are analysed.

The need for (value of) such a mechanism was revealed by a number of the major disputes that have been adjudicated. As mentioned in Chapter 6, an important consequence of the cotton dispute was that it made clear how much the US was subsidizing cotton production. This type of 'discovery' requires resources and detailed analysis—without this it will not be known who is doing what to whom. In short, a transparency entity could help ensure that the development dimension of current and proposed multilateral rules be considered. In principle it could be a public–private partnership, including industry associations, think-tanks and NGOs among its members, with part of the funding being generated by public institutions. Of great importance is that it has the resources required to perform quality work, and be independent of governments and the WTO Secretariat. Independence and separation will minimize the extent to which discussions and analysis are influenced by strategic negotiating considerations and specific concerns of the individual member states. The latter have a long history of constraining the ability of the WTO Secretariat to assess the impacts of national policies. The latest example of this constraining influence was the transparency initiative on regional trade agreements discussed in Chapter 10—which was limited to a strictly factual documentation of PTAs.

14.4. COHERENCE OF NATIONAL POLICIES

The 'coherence' of policies pursued by international economic organizations was one of the subjects on the agenda of the Uruguay Round negotiating group on the Functioning of the GATT System (FOGS), Box 14.3. Ensuring coherence

Box 14.3. The Uruguay Round FOGS negotiation

The launch of the Uruguay Round in 1986 included establishment of a negotiating group on the Functioning of the GATT System (FOGS). The mandate of this group was to strengthen the trading system through better monitoring of trade policies, improving the effectiveness and decision-making of the institution, and increasing GATT's contribution to the coherence of global economic policies. Better surveillance had been strongly endorsed by a group of wise men (the so-called Leutwiler report—GATT, 1985). At the time there was no analogue to the Article IV consultations of the IMF with its members, the country economic memoranda prepared by the World Bank, or the national economic surveys published by the OECD. A motivation for creating the FOGS group included the very large macroeconomic imbalances that had emerged in the 1980s and the developing country debt crisis. Both generated pressures for protection and in both cases trade barriers impeded the process of adjustment (for example, by limiting the export growth opportunities of highly indebted countries).

The FOGS group agreed to the creation of the TPRM, but made less progress on the other two issues. The group discussed several areas where trade and macro policies were at odds, but revealed serious disagreements on the economic issues (for example, the US disagreed with the EU that exchange rate instability had a disruptive effect on trade). In the run-up to the 1988 mid-term ministerial meeting in Montreal it became apparent that little could be done on the broader 'coherence' front. In the end the only coherence-related outcome of the FOGS discussions was the ministerial declaration on the contribution of the WTO to Achieving Greater Coherence in Global Economic Policy Making. This instructed the WTO to 'pursue and develop cooperation' with the Bretton Woods organizations and called on the Director-General to review with the heads of the IMF and the World Bank the implications of WTO's responsibilities for cooperation and the forms such cooperation might take' (GATT, 1994a: 442). In addition, cooperation with the Bretton Woods institutions was defined as one of the WTO's five explicit functions (Article III:5 WTO).

Source: Croome (1999).

with the Bretton Woods institutions (the IMF and the World Bank) is one of five specified functions of the WTO (Article III:5). The rationale for this was that macroeconomic or exchange rate policies pursued by WTO members could serve to create pressures for protection and offset trade liberalization.

What coherence means is not defined in the Uruguay Round declaration. A good case can be made that the concept makes little sense in that it focuses on the wrong set of actors. International organizations represent the interests of their owners—member countries. It is up to the governing boards of these organizations to ensure that the mandates that are given to the organizations are 'coherent'. This is not to deny that policy advice or activities may sometimes be overlapping or inconsistent. The former requires coordination and regular communication between the staff of organizations. The latter is not necessarily a problem as ultimately it is the responsibility of governments to define priorities and the policy instruments used to pursue national objectives.

Important problems of 'incoherence' arise primarily at the national level. Given that sovereign governments have the responsibility to design economic, social and other policies to achieve the objectives of the electorate (society), it is up to governments to construct policy packages that do the job. If they do not, they will face the consequences at the next election. Clearly, in many cases 'incoherent' national policies can have spillovers in the sense of having offsetting effects on the attainment of a particular objective. Thus, trade barriers that restrict exports of developing countries may help domestic industries, but they work to nullify the development assistance that is provided by the development ministry and NGOs. Incoherence of this type is the natural state of the world, as different groups in society invariably will have different preferences and objectives, and will have different views regarding the policies that should be used in any given situation (Winters, 2007). Such incoherence is another example of the need for information and analysis of policies, and is an issue where NGOs could potentially play a constructive role. In practice, NGOs often ignore the negative implications of trade and industrial policies on the achievement of their objectives.

The emphasis that is put on the World Bank and IMF in the WTO provision on coherence does not mean that policymakers did not recognize that the coherence problem is generally a national one. Winters (2000) speculates that trade ministers hoped through the coherence mandate to discipline the activities of other ministers that have a detrimental effect on trade—such as macroeconomic policies that lead to real exchange rate appreciation. Another possible explanation is that the trade community (trade ministries) attempted to create a mechanism to induce ministries of finance, development and planning in both OECD and developing countries to allocate resources for the implementation of WTO disciplines. Winters (2007) revisits his analysis of the desirability and feasibility of coherence, and concludes that in the course of the Doha Round some progress was made in recognizing the importance of complementing trade negotiations and liberalization with other forms of cooperation, but concludes that little concrete progress has been achieved to date (see also Chapter 12).

Towards greater national coherence

Trade policy affects the whole economy: policy decisions should therefore be made in a context that allows not only the interests of all potentially affected actors to be considered, but also the efficacy of the set of policies that are pursued by the government. This will not be done unless an explicit attempt is made to design institutions such that an economy-wide focus is indeed taken. In the legislative context, the coherence of national policies will depend in part on how representatives are elected. If they represent distinct geographic regions, lobbies will seek to influence their representatives, who in turn will seek the support of other representatives. The resulting logrolling can lead not only to highly protectionist outcomes, but also to situations where policies work at cross-purposes.

Many parts of the government are involved in trade policy especially now that the trade agenda increasingly spans services, IPRs, investment and regulatory policies. Trade ministries tend to represent their countries in trade negotiations, but often will need to cooperate with other ministries, ranging from finance and foreign affairs to sectoral ministries (transport, telecommunications, etc.) and regulatory agencies (SPS, patent office, etc.). Thus, in both the process of formulating and implementing policy there is a need for coordination and a common understanding of the overall objectives of the government and the implications of trade agreements for national policy. Many countries have established national councils for consultations and interaction with citizens and specific interest groups, as well as inter-ministerial bodies that promote information exchange and inter-governmental coordination.

A fundamental objective of the design of trade policy institutions should be to ensure that affected groups can express their views and engage in the policy formation process while limiting the extent to which lobbies are able to capture the policymaking process. Achieving this is difficult, and will depend on the specifics of individual countries. However, some general principles are by now well known. Assuming for purposes of discussion that trade taxes are not a necessary revenue-generating instrument, good practices should build upon the recognition that trade policy is an inefficient redistributive instrument. A first requirement then is that the net cost to the economy of a policy is estimated *ex ante* and monitored *ex post*, and the incidence of any implicit tax is identified.

One way this can be done is by an agency that has a statutory mandate to determine the impact of a trade policy on the economy, both in terms of efficiency (resource cost) and equity (income redistribution). Such a body should have a pure transparency function: advising the government on the effects and incidence of the trade and investment policy stance that is maintained, as well as the 'coherence' of the trade policy stance with official objectives in other areas—development assistance, for example. Such institutions should have a purely advisory role vis-à-vis the government: the task is to shed light. Institutions of this type have been created in a number of countries (Spriggs, 1991). Many of the proposals for establishment of such bodies have been inspired by the Australian Industries Assistance Commission, currently called the Productivity Commission (for a history, see Rattigan, 1986).

Coherence in trade policy cannot be addressed in isolation. Indeed, the reason that trade policies are used may be that more efficient instruments are not available. As discussed in Chapter 12, one area in which some progress is being made towards greater coherence is in development assistance policy (aid for trade). Giving developing countries financial assistance on the one hand while restricting their exports on the other is an example of 'incoherent' policy—in the sense that they work against each other. A number of OECD governments have recognized that this is a problem. For example, the government of Sweden's development policy stresses the importance of coherence, noting that many other policy instruments may be more effective in reducing poverty than the instruments available in development cooperation (www.sweden.gov.se/sb/d/3102).

14.5. CONCLUSION

A necessary condition for 'ownership' of the WTO by civil society in member countries is that they perceive that multilateral cooperation helps attain national objectives (and does not work against the attainment of objectives they have a strong interest in). Both business and NGOs have a role to play in attempting to influence policies at home as well as the multilateral rules of the game. A precondition for constructive engagement is a better understanding on the part of NGOs and civil society of what the WTO does and does not do, what it can do, and what it should not be asked to do. This requires intellectual honesty and a good faith effort to identify and use efficient policy instruments to pursue objectives.

Legitimacy and coherence start at home. What matters is that society has a say in the process through which policies are negotiated at the WTO by ensuring that there are mechanisms for expressing views to their governments. Such views can be aggregated and expressed directly at WTO meetings, using the media and the Internet as dissemination vehicles. This is an option that NGOs pursued effectively in the late 1990s and 2000s, attracting global attention for their points of view. But leveraging this attention into policy change requires effective engagement with the national governments that are the members of the WTO, and a willingness to consider the magnitude and incidence of the costs and benefits of alternative policy options that are proposed to attain specific objectives.

A number of the concerns that were expressed by the NGO community regarding the WTO over the last decade were valid. Many were not. Compared to most international organizations the WTO does not have a serious 'democratic deficit'. The consensus rule ensures that each member has a voice, and that groups of like-minded countries can block efforts to move in a direction they oppose. There is a need to improve the functioning of the WTO, but this does not require major structural changes in the governance of the institution. The WTO plays a valuable role in forcing NGOs to push for more efficient instruments to pursue their noneconomic objectives. The fact that the scope to use trade restrictions as a unilateral instrument to push through specific environmental or social standards is circumscribed is beneficial to world welfare. At the same time NGOs (and business) can play a valuable role in ensuring that civil society perceives the WTO to be of value. Maximizing the two-way flow of information can only be beneficial. This will help identify national and international policy 'coherence' problems and facilitate the accountability of governments. Enhancing access to information on the regular meetings of the WTO, including timely publication of the agenda and outcomes, would be beneficial. Greater transparency and objective analysis of issues and proposals is a key input into better policymaking, and NGOs have an important role to play in that regard.

14.6. FURTHER READING

J. Scholte et al., 'The World Trade Organization and Civil Society', in Brian Hocking and Steven McGuire (eds), *Trade Politics: International, Domestic and Regional Perspectives* (London: Routledge, 2004) and D. Esty, 'Non-governmental Organizations at the World Trade Organization: Cooperation, Competition, or Exclusion', *Journal of International Economic Law* 1, (1998), discuss the WTO's early relationship with civil society. For an extensive analysis of the influence of NGOs on the creation and application of international rules, see also P. Kohona, 'The Role of Non-state Entities in the Making and Implementation of International Norms,' *The Journal of World Investment*, 2 (3) (2001): 537–78.

On NGO participation in the WTO, see F. Roessler, 'The Institutional Balance between the Judicial and Political Organs of the WTO,' in M. Bronckers and R. Quick (eds), *New Directions in International Economic Law: Essays in Honor of John H. Jackson*, (Boston: Kluwer Law International, 2001); Michelle Ratton Sanchez, 'Brief Observations of the Mechanisms for NGO Participation in the WTO,' *International Journal on Human Rights*, 3 (4) (2006): 103–25, and Silvia Ostry 'Civil Society: Consultation in Negotiations and Implementation of Trade Liberalization and Integrated Agreements: An Overview of the Issue' (mimeo, 2003) (available at www.iadb.org). Steve Charnovitz and J. Wickham, 'Non-governmental Organizations and the Original International Trade Regime', *Journal of World Trade*, 29 (1995): 111–22, discuss the role of NGOs in the drafting of the ITO charter.

Richard Blackhurst and David Hartridge, 'Improving the Capacity of WTO Institutions to Fulfill Their Mandate,' in E.-U.Petersmann (ed.), *Reforming the World Trading System: Legitimacy, Efficiency and Democratic Governance* (Oxford: Oxford University Press, 2005) discuss approaches towards improving the governance of the WTO. Gregory Shaffer, 'Parliamentary Oversight of WTO Rule-Making: The Political, Normative, and Practical Contexts,' *Journal of International Economic Law*, 7 (3) (2004) provides a comprehensive analysis of the case for and options for increasing participation of parliamentary representatives in the WTO. Peter Pedersen, 'The WTO Decision-making Process and Internal Transparency,' *World Trade Review*, 5 (2006): 103–31, summarizes the developments that occurred in the WTO to enhance internal transparency after the Seattle ministerial meeting.

An overview of advocacy issues in trade policymaking from a lobbyist's perspective is presented in M. Kostecki 'Business Advocacy in the Global Trading System: How Business Organizations May Shape Trade Policy' (Geneva: International Trade Centre, 2005). Valentin Zahrnt, 'Domestic Constituents and the Formulation of WTO Negotiating Positions: What the Delegates Say,' *World Trade Review*, 7 (2) (2008): 393–421, reports on a survey of WTO delegations that explores the impact of national stakeholders on negotiations. One of the best NGO websites on the WTO and trade policy matters is that of the International Centre for Trade and Sustainable Development (www.ictsd.org), which provides links to all the major NGOs, and publishes the very informative newsletter *Bridges*.

CHAPTER 15

···

WHERE TO FROM HERE?

···

THE GATT was created by governments with a clear vision of the cooperation that was needed to foster economic growth and reconstruction after the Second World War. Although the vision called for an ITO, the GATT managed to fulfil the objectives of the original signatories quite well. It proved a very successful instrument to liberalize trade. High-income country tariffs were reduced very substantially under its auspices. As a result, trade-distorting aspects of domestic policies increasingly became the focus of attention. To return to Professor Robert Baldwin's analogy, trade liberalization can be likened to the draining of a swamp: as the water level (average tariff levels) falls due to successful pumping efforts, rocks, stumps and all manner of other obstacles (NTBs) become visible (Baldwin, 1970). The GATT 1947 did much to drain the swamp for industrialized countries. It was much less successful in inducing developing countries to reduce tariffs—unilateral actions by governments many of such economies in the 1980s and 1990s also did much to drain the swamp there. The GATT was also less successful in clearing the drained land (eliminating NTBs) and keeping the water from flooding back (in the form of contingent protection and VERs). Removing the tree stumps and rocks was difficult in part because some of the policies concerned were of regulatory nature. Reciprocal exchange of concessions is far more difficult when it comes to regulatory policies than it is for tariffs and quotas.

The Uruguay Round was a landmark in the history of the trading system. Agriculture and textiles and clothing, two sectors that for all intents and purposes had been removed from the ambit of the GATT, were brought back into the fold. The system of multilateral rules was extended to include IPRs and trade in services. Moreover, because of the Single Undertaking rule, all countries desiring to become a member of the new WTO were forced to accept a variety of disciplines in areas ranging from customs valuation to subsidies. Under the GATT countries were free not to sign on to these disciplines, and most developing countries did so. The Uruguay Round was widely seen to be a major step forward in strengthening the trading system. Although it was recognized that certain agreements—most notably TRIPS—were not necessarily in the interest of low-income countries and would give rise to asymmetric implementation costs, proponents argued that this was more than offset by the inclusion of agriculture, the commitment to phase out the MFA, and the creation of the WTO—an organization with a much stronger dispute settlement mechanism than the GATT, which was widely held to be beneficial to small and poorer countries.

As discussed in Chapter 1, the WTO has two primary functions—it is a market for the exchange of trade policy 'concessions' and it is a mechanism through which the resulting set of commitments (the code of conduct) is enforced. Since its creation in 1995, the members have not proven very successful in using the WTO market to expand the coverage of the institution. Successes in concluding agreements on telecommunications, financial services and information technology products in the late 1990s could not be replicated in later years. Efforts to negotiate rules on competition, investment and transparency in government procurement failed. Even when stripped of new issues, negotiators could not get to 'yes' in the Doha Round. As of early 2009, when we write this, the Doha Round remains to be completed. At the same time, the code of conduct has worked remarkably well. Disputes are brought and mostly settled in conformity with panel/AB findings. The numerous WTO bodies and committees meet regularly and do their business, acting as focal points for the relevant government officials to exchange information and raise and address questions in a cooperative manner. The lack of progress in the Doha Round and the small number of high profile disputes that do not get resolved—such as *EC—Hormones*—tend to obscure the many ways in which the WTO works well in implementing the code of conduct. Perhaps the best—and most important— examples of this in the last decade were the 1997–8 East Asian financial crisis and the global financial meltdown that began in the summer of 2007. Although the repercussions of the 2008–9 global recession have yet to play themselves out, both in 1997–8 and during 2008–9 there was relatively little resort to traditional trade policy instruments to protect domestic import-competing industries.

What explains the disconnect between the lack of progress on negotiating new commitments and the relatively robust operation of the negotiated code of conduct? What are the implications for WTO members and the institution? Much has been written on the Doha Round, with many observers taking the view that the funda- mental reason for deadlock was that there was not enough on the table that truly mattered to politically powerful constituencies in member countries. Mattoo and Subramanian (2008*b*, 2009), for example, suggest that as of 2008 the Doha Round had become a distraction, focusing on marginal issues. They argue that the market access agenda being negotiated had little economic relevance—a case also made by other economists, e.g. Evenett (2007*b*), who noted that global simulation models suggested that a failed Doha Round would cost China the equivalent of only three days of growth. Moreover, the critics point out that key national policies that impose large negative spillovers on other countries were not on the Doha agenda. Examples are the lack of environmental policies to reduce carbon emissions; export restrictions on food crops by major producers in times of shortage (as happened in 2007–8); the cartelization of the world oil market and resulting policy responses by importers (e.g. subsidization of inefficient bio-fuel production, with unanticipated knock-on effects on global food prices); allegations of manipulation of exchange rates to enhance the competitiveness of exports, especially by China (a matter that is in the purview of the IMF but that proved too politically sensitive to address in that institution); and the rise of sovereign wealth funds and the prospects that invest-ment decisions by large surplus countries could destabilize financial markets or give rise to a protectionist response by capital importing countries seeking to keep 'sensitive' asserts in national hands and control. Mattoo and Subramanian conclude that what is needed is a new round of Bretton Woods talks (referring to the original negotiations at the town of Bretton Woods in the US that led to the formation of the IMF and the World Bank) between the major economic powers.

While the Doha Round clearly did not address many of the important sources of policy-induced negative spillovers that call for multilateral cooperation, this line of critique is not very helpful in identifying what the WTO should do or why the Doha Round failed to come to closure. Would a significant expansion of the WTO negotiating agenda facilitate reaching agreement on the market access issues that were the focal point of the Doha Round? Is the WTO the appropriate venue for discussing the economic issues just mentioned? Whatever one's views, the real question is whether abandoning the Doha Round would help move forward the cooperation that is required on the various (new) matters that were not on the Doha agenda. This appears quite unlikely. Without denying that the 'missing' policy areas identified above are important and should be the focus of cooperation and possible concerted action, the negotiating failures of the WTO should not be overly dramatized. The negative views ignore the code-of-conduct side of the institution, which works well, and the fact that historically the major outcome of negotiations has been 'lock-in' rather than large-scale liberalization of applied trade policies. Before going down the track of greatly expanding the WTO negotiating agenda, it is necessary to assess whether a grand issue-linkage strategy will have better prospects of success—and as important, not give rise to serious downside risks in terms of unravelling the trade policy disciplines that have been built up over many decades. An overemphasis on the need to negotiate new disciplines in areas that are 'missing' risks throwing out the baby with the bathwater. It is worth recalling the difficulties that were created by efforts to launch negotiations on the Singapore issues—which would appear less contentious and difficult to agree on than some of the topics just mentioned. Moreover, as discussed in Chapter 4, establishing the agenda of an MTN takes a lot of time. Indeed, the critics of Doha can be seen as engaging in the 'vision' and agenda-setting pre-negotiation formation stages of an MTN.

As already noted, there was relatively little serious protectionist backsliding during the global recession of 2008–9, This can certainly be attributed in part to the WTO system. But it must also be recognized that the political economy of trade policy has changed as a result of the great expansion in trade integration that has occurred since the early 1980s. The qualitative change in the nature of cross-border exchange that has occurred in recent decades may prove to be a game changer. In the 1950s, international trade was relatively simple: a product was made in country X and shipped to an importer in country Y. Interactions between producer and buyer were superficial. Foreign direct investment was generally a substitute for trade—a way to jump over high tariff walls. This has changed fundamentally. The service intensity of production and consumption increased significantly. Many firms now sell intangibles—processes, performance, information, a lifestyle image—that may or may not be bundled with tangible products. In the current economy, value tends to be closely associated with the performance and utilization of systems composed of material products, services, information of commercial value (trademarks, patents) and client–producer relations.

Establishment of a relationship with clients is often crucial, as is ensuring that customers have access to complementary products, services, upgrades and maintenance. What counts is performance in meeting the customer's needs. More often than not this implies custom tailoring of solutions. Strategic partnerships and networking are frequently necessary to provide the solution to a client's problem. Firms increasingly need to enter into ad hoc or more formal relationships with other firms. Production and consumption has become more and more a joint process, requiring inputs and feedback from the customer.

Managing the intangible aspects of the production process often requires establishment in a foreign market and access to telecommunications networks and global databases. Foreign direct investment and trade are more and more complementary, reflected in the steady increase in global production sharing discussed in Chapter 1. One implication is that the incentive structure of firms towards trade policy changes. As discussed in Chapter 7, the greater the share of FDI in an industry, and the more international the production chain becomes, the less incentive governments have to use trade policies. Multinationals need to be able to buy from the lowest cost source to stay competitive, whereas local export interests need to ensure that the regulatory regime allows them to compete for contracts with globally diversified firms. Both have incentives to push for a liberal FDI environment. These changes in incentives help explain the liberalization observed in many countries starting in the 1980s and suggest that the shift in policy will be robust.

In our view the difficulties in bringing Doha to closure are in part a reflection of the fact that there is less left to negotiate on market access because of the developments that were just discussed. But it is also important to recognize that, as has been shown in this book, there are still significant tariff peaks, large-scale agricultural protection, and barriers to services trade and investment. Moreover, given that the WTO is primarily a lock-in mechanism and rule-setting body—a facet of the institution that is too frequently ignored by lobbies, the press and academia— what was on the table in Doha arguably was significant from an 'insurance' perspective (Hoekman and Vines, 2007; Messerlin 2008a). This applies not just to tariff bindings in agriculture and NAMA but to the proposed capping of agricultural subsidies at close to applied levels. Claims of the Doha Round's marginality also ignore the rule-setting dimensions. For example, fishing subsidy disciplines, a ban on agricultural export subsidies, and an agreement on trade facilitation would all be of significant value. All this suggests that arguments there was little on the table of economic relevance overstate matters. Whatever the fate of the Round, an important question for WTO members and analysts is to determine whether and how the way the Doha negotiations were pursued were a factor in the lack of progress. The Doha Round was characterized by the use of formula approaches in the market access negotiations, the single undertaking principle (nothing is agreed until everything is agreed), and 'universality'—all WTO members participated and needed to agree to the outcome. All three factors arguably played a role in impeding progress.

As noted several times in this book, in the Doha Round WTO members reverted to the Tokyo Round practice of relying on a formula approach to determine tariff cuts and reductions in permitted agricultural subsidies. A consequence of the participation in the negotiations by all WTO members was that the formula approach gave rise to extensive efforts by groups of countries to obtain exemptions from the full force of the formula. Matters were compounded by many OECD negotiators applying a narrow interpretation of tariff binding principle, equating liberalization with a change in which all post-Doha bound tariffs should be lower than pre-Doha applied tariffs. This led to 'overshooting' in the proposed coefficients—i.e. very ambitious proposals that would have eliminated prevailing differences between bound and applied rates in non-LDCs and lowered average applied rates. The result was a push by developing countries for large-scale exceptions. Matters were compounded by specific groups of countries arguing for special treatment reflecting their situation or circumstances—small and vulnerable economies (SVEs), recently acceded members (RAMs), etc. As noted by Messerlin (2008b), less ambition in terms of the coefficient coupled with more transparent and noncountry-specific exceptions to the formula offers the potential of greater success over time—recognizing that MTNs recur and that progress will be incremental. Similar observations apply to agriculture where the 2003 Harbinson proposal (drafted by the then Chairman of the Agricultural negotiating group) appeared to largely (pre-)define the outcome of negotiations. While what was on the table in 2008 did not diverge very significantly in broad outline and approach from what was suggested by Harbinson as a good focal point of the negotiations, progress might have been more rapid if the draft modalities proposed by the Chair had been less prescriptive/ambitious, thereby avoiding several years of effort by WTO members that protect the sector to water down the suggested modalities.

As discussed in Chapter 13, the Doha Round experience suggests that greater reliance and use of plurilateralism could have beneficial effects. It is not at all clear that one of the premises of the single undertaking—that it will foster issue linkages and thus increase the overall gains from cooperation by expanding the negotiation set—holds water. The issue linkage that characterized the Uruguay Round may have been possible only because there was a regime change—countries had to decide whether or not the join the WTO. This was a one time event. An explicit shift to a club-type approach in considering new rules for new areas would offer the opportunity for a critical mass of members to move forward on an issue, while allowing others to abstain. The rationale for this is most clear for subjects where the gains from cooperation may not be substantial, or where benefits and costs are distributed very asymmetrically. If so, a small group approach to negotiating agreements would allow progress to occur among those who perceive benefits from cooperation.

The traditional market access agenda that remains to be addressed by the WTO—reducing the level of border barriers, abolishing discriminatory policies—remains quite large. The potential gains from further liberalization and binding of policies affecting trade in goods and services is still substantial. More-over, much of the research that has been done on the economics of new issue areas suggests that in some cases the WTO is not the right forum for cooperation in that binding, enforceable rules may be inappropriate and/or that the subjects are only weakly trade-related, if at all. This suggests that attention should focus on the traditional 'shallow integration' agenda of the GATT/WTO, leaving it to other international bodies and conventions to address nontrade issues that give rise to global spillovers.

Multilateral negotiations on nonborder policies, administrative procedures and domestic legal regimes have proven to be much more complex than traditional trade policy talks. It is difficult, if not impossible, to trade 'concessions'—instead the focus revolves around the identification of specific rules that should be adopted. The disciplines that are proposed by some countries may not be in the interest of others. Given disparities in economic power and resources, to a large extent negotiations on rules can be expected to reflect the agenda of high-income countries (and specific interest groups in these countries). In contrast to traditional trade liberalization, the rules that emerge in a given area may not be consistent with the development priorities of low-income countries. No longer is it the case that 'one size fits all' is necessarily a good rule. With the gradual demise of tariffs and the ever greater prominence of nontariff, domestic regulatory policies—standards, investment regulations, environmental, social, or competition norms—there is a danger of moving away from positive sum ('win-win') games towards zero sum situations.

The basic rules of the GATT—progressive liberalization of bound tariffs, MFN, national treatment—worked in the interest of all. Any reduction in trade protection achieved by negotiators through the reciprocal exchange of market access 'concessions' was in their own and partner countries' interests. Negotiators could safely be delegated the task of negotiating trade barrier reductions. Although the outcome was by no means optimal, there was little need for economic policymakers or civil society to be concerned about the potential for negative aggregate welfare outcomes resulting from a negatiation. The core GATT rules were unambiguously good rules for all members, whether developing or industrialized. The reason was that tariffs do not make much economic sense for small economies and reduce welfare for the world as a whole. This is not the case when it comes to national regulatory regimes. Such regimes may well (and certainly should) be welfare-enhancing. Thus, the probability of a potential downside from multilateral negotiations materializes. This is particularly important for developing countries, and points to the importance of a greater reliance on plurilateral approaches and financial and technical assistance in addition to traditional transition periods.

The anatomy of influence in the WTO/GATT system has evolved significantly over the last decade or so. The stalemate in the Doha Round can be partly attributed to the significant shift in economic power away from a US-EU dominated trading system towards a multipolar one in which countries such as China, India, Brazil and other emerging economies assume an increasingly important role. Between 1980 and 2008 China's GDP (in purchasing power terms) grew to attain 50 per cent of the levels of that of the EU and the US, making China the third largest economy in the world. Some of the problems in the negotiations reflect the fact that many interest groups in high-income countries are unable to consider that rules of economic behaviour should be redefined to reflect the new anatomy of influence in the trading system. Although this shift renders WTO bargaining more complex—reflected in the rise of developing country coalitions—it does not mean that the basic aspects of the WTO are any less relevant; to the contrary.

ANNEX 1

GATT/WTO
MEMBERSHIP, 2008

Table A1.1

Member Country	Year of Joining GATT/ WTO	Share in World Trade (%)	Average MFN Applied Tariff	Average Bound Tariff	Type of Delegation in Geneva	Size of Geneva Mission
Albania	2000	0.22	5.4	7.0	UN	2
Angola	1994	0.16	7.3	59.2	UN	4
Antigua and Barbuda	1987	0.00	9.7	58.7	UN	0
Argentina	1967	0.32	12.0	31.9	UN	10
Armenia	2003	0.01	2.9	8.5	UN	1
Australia*	1948	1.09	3.5	9.9	WTO	9
Austria	1951	6.31			UN	4
Bahrain	1993	0.08	5.0	34.4	UN	4
Bangladesh	1972	0.10	14.6	169.2	UN	5
Barbados	1967	0.01	13.5	78.1	UN	7
Belgium*	1948	2.60			UN	10
Belize	1983	0.00	10.8	58.2	None	0
Benin	1963	0.01	11.9	28.3	UN	7
Bolivia	1990	0.3	8.3	40.0	UN	3
Botswana	1987	0.3	7.8	18.8	UN	8
Brazil*	1948	0.93	12.2	31.4	UN	21
Brunei Darussalam	1993	0.03	3.6	25.3	UN	5
Bulgaria	1996	0.18			WTO	3
Burkina Faso	1963	0.01	11.9	41.8	UN	7
Burundi	1965	0.00	12.7	68.2	UN	2
Cambodia	2004	0.03	14.2	19.0	UN	6

(cont.)

Table A1.1.   (*Continued*)

Member Country	Year of Joining GATT/ WTO	Share in World Trade (%)	Average MFN Applied Tariff	Average Bound Tariff	Type of Delegation in Geneva	Size of Geneva Mission
Cameroon	1963	0.02	17.9	79.9	UN	9
Canada	1948	2.93	5.5	6.5	WTO	13
Cape Verde	2008	0.00	10.4		UN	1
Central African Rep.	1963	0.00	17.9	36.2	None	0
Chad	1963	0.02	17.9	79.9	UN	4
Chile*	1949	0.38	6.0	25.1	WTO	7
China*	2001	6.53	9.9	10.0	WTO	18
Chinese Taipei	2002	1.63	6.3	6.6	WTO	16
Colombia	1981	0.20	12.5	42.9	WTO	6
Congo, Dem. Rep. (Zaire)	1971	0.02	12.0	96.2	UN	3
Costa Rica	1990	0.08	5.5	42.8	WTO	4
Côte d'Ivoire	1963	0.05	11.9	11.1	UN	5
Croatia	2000	0.14	5	6.3	UN	2
Cuba*	1948	0.06	10.8	21.3	UN	5
Cyprus	1963	0.08			UN	3
Czech Republic (Czechoslovakia)*	1993	0.84			UN	6
Denmark	1950	0.76			UN	4
Djibouti	1994	0.00	27.8	41.0	UN	2
Dominica	1993	0.00	9.9	58.7	None	0
Dominican Republic	1950	0.08	8.5	34.9	UN	11
Ecuador	1996	0.09	11.7	21.8	WTO	5
Egypt	1970	0.20	16.7	36.8	UN	10
El Salvador	1991	0.05	6.7	36.6	WTO	5
Estonia	1999	0.08			UN	4
European Communities		39.18	5.2	5.4	UN	15
Fiji	1993	0.01	9.6	41.9	UN	5
Finland	1950	0.54			UN	6
France*	1948	3.86			WTO	6
Gabon	1963	0.02	17.9	21.4	UN	8
The Gambia	1965	0.00	19.0	102.0	None	0
Germany	1951	8.05			UN	8
Ghana	1957	0.04	13.0	92.5	UN	4
Georgia	2000	0.02	1.4	7.5	UN	3
Greece	1950	0.45			UN	5
Grenada	1994	0.00	10.2	56.7	None	0
Guatemala	1991	0.07	5.6	42.2	WTO	6
Guinea Bissau	1994	0.00	11.9	48.6	None	0
Guinea, Rep. of	1994	0.01	11.8	20.1	UN	4
Guyana	1966	0.01	11.1	56.6	None	0
Haiti	1950	0.01	2.8	18.7	WTO	6
Honduras	1994	0.03	5.6	32.6	WTO	5

Table A1.1. *(Continued)*

Member Country	Year of Joining GATT/ WTO	Share in World Trade (%)	Average MFN Applied Tariff	Average Bound Tariff	Type of Delegation in Geneva	Size of Geneva Mission
Hong Kong, China	1986	2.57	0	0	WTO	7
Hungary	1973	0.59			WTO	4
India*	1948	1.48	14.5	50.2	WTO	10
Indonesia	1950	0.61	6.9	37.1	UN	8
Ireland	1967	1.10			UN	4
Israel	1962	0.44	6.5	22.2	UN	3
Italy	1950	3.49			UN	5
Jamaica	1963	0.04	7.3	49.6	UN	6
Japan	1955	5.00	5.1	5.1	UN	19
Jordan	2000	0.07	11.2	16.3	UN	3
Kenya	1964	0.04	12.7	95.7	UN	6
Korea, Rep. of	1967	2.53	12.2	17.0	UN	20
Kuwait	1963	0.29	4.6	100.0	UN	4
Kyrgyz Republic	1998	0.01	4.8	7.5	UN	4
Latvia	1999	0.07			UN	3
Lesotho	1988	0.01	7.8	78.5	UN	4
Liechtenstein	1994				UN	4
Lithuania	2001	0.13			UN	4
Luxembourg*	1948	0.44			UN	2
Macao, China	1991	0.06	0	0	UN	5
Macedonia	2003	0.39	7.8	7.2	UN	3
Madagascar	1963	0.01	12.4	27.4	UN	3
Malawi	1964	0.01	13.5	75.9	None	0
Malaysia	1957	1.12	8.4	24.5	WTO	7
Maldives	1983	0.01	20.2	36.9	UN	0
Mali	1993	0.01	11.9	28.5	UN	4
Malta	1964	0.03			UN	3
Mauritania	1963	0.01	11.9	19.6	UN	5
Mauritius	1970	0.03	3.5	93.7	UN	7
Mexico	1986	1.87	12.6	36.1	WTO	7
Moldova	2001	0.02	5.2	6.9	UN	2
Mongolia	1997	0.01	5.0	17.6	UN	4
Morocco	1987	0.16	23.0	41.3	UN	8
Mozambique	1992	0.02	10.3	97.4	UN	4
Myanmar (Burma)*	1948	0.02	5.6	83.0	UN	4
Namibia	1992	0.02	7.8	19.1	UN	1
Nepal	2004	0.01	12.6	26.0	UN	4
Netherlands*	1948	3.48			UN	6
New Zealand*	1948	0.22	3.0	9.9	WTO	6
Nicaragua	1950	0.02	5.6	41.7	UN	5
Niger	1963	0.00	11.9	44.3	UN	3
Nigeria	1960	0.25	12.0	118.3	UN	6

(cont.)

Table A1.1. (*Continued*)

Member Country	Year of Joining GATT/ WTO	Share in World Trade (%)	Average MFN Applied Tariff	Average Bound Tariff	Type of Delegation in Geneva	Size of Geneva Mission
Norway*	1948	0.83	8.1	20.7	WTO	8
Oman	2000	0.11	5.5	13.8	UN	2
Pakistan*	1948	0.19	14.1	59.9	WTO	6
Panama	1997	0.04	7.2	23.5	WTO	3
Papua New Guinea	1994	0.03	5.3	32.4	None	0
Paraguay	1992	0.03	10.4	33.4	UN	4
Peru	1951	0.15	10.2	30.1	UN	7
Philippines	1979	0.03	6.3	25.6	WTO	9
Poland	1967	0.92			UN	5
Portugal	1962	0.46			UN	3
Qatar	1994	0.17	4.9	16.0	UN	4
Romania	1971	0.32			UN	4
Rwanda	1966	0.00	18.7	89.5	UN	3
Saint Kitts and Nevis	1994	0.00	9.2	75.9	None	0
Saint Lucia	1993	0.00	8.9	61.9	None	0
Saint Vincent & Grenadines	1993	0.00	9.9	62.5	None	0
Saudi Arabia	2005	1.00	5.0	11.7	UN	3
Senegal	1963	0.02	11.9	30.0	UN	5
Sierra Leone	1961	0.09	13.6	47.4	None	0
Singapore	1973	2.10	0.0	12.1	WTO	6
Slovak Republic (Czechoslovakia)*	1993	0.33			UN	3
Slovenia	1994	0.18			UN	3
Solomon Islands	1994	0.00	10.3	79.1	None	0
South Africa*	1998	0.54	7.8	19.1	UN	8
Spain	1963	2.36			UN	11
Sri Lanka (Ceylon)*	1948	0.07	11.0	30.3	UN	2
Suriname	1978			18.5	None	0
Swaziland	1993	0.02	7.8	19.1	UN	6
Sweden	1950	1.21			UN	4
Switzerland	1966	1.23	7.5	9.3	WTO	7
Tanzania	1961	0.03	12.7	120.0	UN	9
Thailand	1961	1.05	10.0	28.1	WTO	13
Togo	1964	0.01	11.9	80.0	None	0
Tonga	2007	0.00	15.6	17.6	UN	3
Trinidad and Tobago	1962	0.07	7.5	55.7	UN	5
Tunisia	1990	0.11	26.8	57.9	UN	4
Turkey	1951	0.86	10.0	28.3	WTO	10
Uganda	1962	0.01	12.6	73.4	UN	4
Ukraine	2008	0.34	6.9	5.8	UN	3
United Arab Emirates	1994	0.79	5.0	14.7	UN	4

Table A1.1. (*Continued*)

Member Country	Year of joining GATT/ WTO	Share in World Trade (%)	Average MFN Applied Tariff	Average Bound Tariff	Type of Delegation in Geneva	Size of Geneva Mission
United Kingdom*	1948	4.91			UN	9
United States of America*	1948	12.22	3.5	3.5	WTO	16
Uruguay	1953	0.04	10.6	31.6	UN	4
Venezuela	1990		13.2	36.5	UN	5
Vietnam	2007	0.32	16.8	11.4	UN	18
Zambia	1982	0.02	13.9	106.4	UN	8
Zimbabwe (Southern Rhodesia)*	1948	0.01	20	91.6	UN	11

Notes: Asterisks indicate founding members of the GATT. Names in parentheses indicate the country names in 1947. Three founding members subsequently withdrew: China, Lebanon and Syria. China joined the WTO in 2001. During 1995-2008 the following countries also joined: Ecuador, Bulgaria, Mongolia, Panama, Kyrgyz Republic, Latvia, Estonia, Jordan, Georgia, Albania, Oman, Croatia and Lithuania, Moldova, Chinese Taipei, Macedonia, Armenia, Cambodia, Nepal, Saudi Arabia, Viet Nam, Tonga, Cape Verde and Ukraine (in chronological order).

Share of world trade: calculations are based on official 2006 WTO statistics (imports and exports of merchandise and services by country. Hong Kong and Singapore re-exports are included. Year of MFN applied average tariff is 2007 except for Fiji, Guyana, Israel, Jamaica, Malawi, Moldova, Nigeria, Rwanda, Sierra Leone, Tonga, Tunisia and Ukraine where the figure is for 2006.

Source: VanGrasstek (2007) and WTO.

THE ECONOMICS OF TRADE POLICY—BASIC CONCEPTS

1. Why trade?

A simple framework for understanding the gains from trade is laid out in Figure 2.1. This represents the economy of a country X that can produce two types of products, computers (C) and apples (A) in various combinations or proportions. If it specializes completely in one of these two products, it can produce either P worth of computers or P_1 of apples. More realistically, it will produce some combination. If the country X uses all of its productive resources efficiently, the production possibilities are represented by the curve PP_1. All points above and to the right of PP_1 represent combinations of quantities of computers and apples that are beyond the reach of the country's productive capacity. Points to the left of the PP_1 curve involve either unused capacity or the use of inefficient production techniques.

The production-possibility curve PP_1 represents the supply side of the economy. Consumer preferences (demand) determine the specific combination of computers and apples that will be produced. A useful device to characterize consumer preferences is the community indifference curve, represented by U_1 and U_2 in Figure A2.1. Consumption of C and A yields satisfaction or utility to consumers. Each social indifference curve represents bundles of C and A that generate the same level of utility. Bundles located on a higher indifference curve (U_2) yield greater utility (welfare) than those located on a lower curve (U_1). Indifference curves bend in toward the origin because as consumption of computers falls, more and more

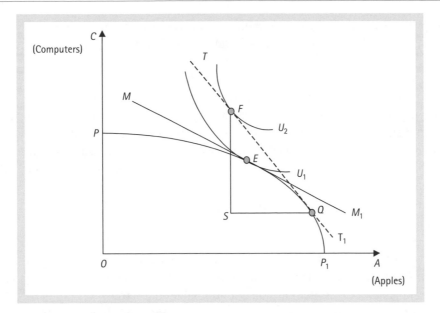

Fig. A2.1. The gains from trade

apples must be consumed to maintain the same level of satisfaction. There is a diminishing marginal rate of substitution between products—consumers prefer combinations of products to extremes: gin and tonic is better than only gin or only tonic.

With no international trade (that is, in autarchy) and assuming that markets are competitive, the economy will be in equilibrium at point E. At this point the highest possible indifference curve (level of welfare) is attained, given available resources. Point E is the point of tangency between the production possibility curve (PP_1) and the highest community indifference curve (U_1). Thus, at E the slopes of the two curves are equal. In technical terms, at E the marginal rate of transformation in production (which reflects the amount of resources that must be released from production of apples to produce an additional computer) is equal to the community's marginal rate of substitution (the rate at which the representative consumer is willing to substitute apples for computers in consumption). This common ratio determines the price of computers relative to apples (say, two tons of apples for one additional computer).

If account is taken of the opportunity to engage in trade, the country can achieve a higher level of welfare by specializing in production. What the country specializes in will depend on how relative prices at home (opportunity costs) compare to those prevailing in foreign markets. Assume the relative price for apples is higher in the world market. Producers in X will find it profitable to shift resources from the computer to the apple industry. This is represented by the move along the production possibility curve from E to Q. Output expands in the industry with a comparative advantage (apples), pulling resources away from the industry which has a comparative disadvantage (computers) (see Chapter 1 for a definition of the term comparative advantage).

The shift in resources involved (structural adjustment) is driven by the difference in domestic and world relative prices. As resources move into the industry in which the country has a comparative advantage, marginal opportunity costs increase in that industry (this is because as production of a good increases it generally becomes harder to find factors of production that are as efficient as those already in use, or it may be that each industry uses capital and labour in different proportions). The shift in resources will stop when the domestic cost ratio becomes equal to the world exchange ratio (TT_1 in Figure A2.1). As in the autarchy case, equilibrium requires the marginal rate of transformation in production to equal the marginal rate of substitution in consumption. Moreover, both of these must equal the world relative price (or terms of trade). In Figure A2.1, this is the case if X produces at point Q and consumes at point F. Trade allows the country to attain a higher level of welfare: U_2 represents a level of utility that was not attainable in autarchy.

Although the country gains from trade, the concept of a community indifference curve hides the fact that some segments of society may lose from the shift to trade. Workers and owners of computer companies will incur costs as demand for their output falls. The concept of the community indifference curve also presupposes interpersonal comparability of utility: one unit of utility taken away from person A may be compensated by an additional unit of utility obtained by person B so that the total community's utility remains unchanged. What the theorems on the gains from international trade imply is that the gains to those who benefit are larger than the losses incurred by those who lose. That is, the *net* benefits are positive. In principle, those who gain have enough to compensate the losers and still come out ahead. In practice, compensation mechanisms or social safety nets may not exist, or they may be inadequate. This helps explain the resistance that often arises against liberalization of trade. There are also structural adjustment costs. This takes time to work through and is associated with social and psychological, as well as economic costs. Workers may have to be retrained and must find alternative employment.

2. Import tariffs

What follows illustrates the effects of an import tariff on a single commodity in a small country. A 'small' country is one whose supply and demand decisions do not influence international prices. Figure A2.2 shows the country's domestic supply (S) and demand (D) curves for a particular commodity. As the importing country is small, it faces a horizontal international supply curve S_I, that is, the world price P_w for its imports is constant—no matter how large imports are, there is no effect on the world price. At that price the country's consumption is OQ_4, production is OQ_1 and imports make up the difference equal Q_2Q_3.

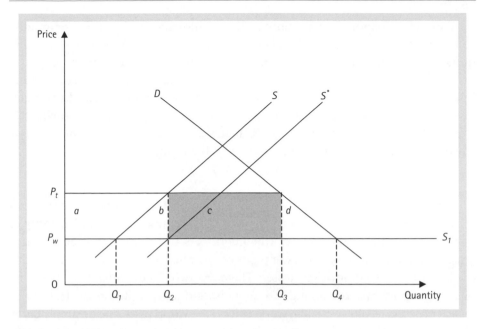

Fig. A2.2. Effect of trade policy in a small economy

Assume that the country M imposes an *ad valorem* tariff of 20 per cent. As a result, the domestic price increases by 20 per cent (to P_t) and imports fall by $Q_1Q_2 + Q_3Q_4$. The higher domestic price induces consumers to buy less (Q_3Q_4) and domestic producers to produce more (Q_1Q_2).

The area under the domestic demand curve in Figure A2.2 measures the total welfare that the consumers obtain from consumption of the commodity considered. As consumers pay an amount equal to the price times the quantity consumed, the triangular area under the demand curve and above the horizontal line at the going price level represents 'consumer surplus'—the difference between the value in use and the price paid.

An import tariff reduces the consumer surplus by the quadrilateral area $a+b+c+d$. However, domestic producers gain area a and the government collects tariff revenue equal to the shaded rectangle c (which equals the tariff times the quantity of imports). From the national point of view, therefore, areas c and a are not losses. They represent the transfers that are induced by the tariff, resources being transferred from consumers (reduction in consumer surplus) to government and producers. The increase in producer surplus (area a) constitutes rents. Consumer surplus is the difference between value in use and value in exchange and can be graphically presented by the area below the demand curve (D) and above the international offer curve (S).

The net welfare loss resulting from the import tariff is represented in Figure A2.2 by the areas b and d. Area d can be thought of as the loss incurred by consumers from losing the opportunity to consume the additional quantity of the commodity at the pre-tariff price p_w. Area b represents the loss resulting from the fact that domestic production expands beyond the optimal level—the extra output is produced at a cost higher than the world price. Areas b and d represent the net losses to society from imposing an import tariff. These are called 'deadweight' losses—they represent pure waste. If demand and supply are approximately straight lines in the relevant range, then the deadweight loss is approximately equal to the decline in imports times one-half the tariff.

3. Quantitative restrictions

The foregoing setup is also useful to analyse the impact of quantitative restrictions (QRs). In the case of a QR, the line segment Q_2Q_3 represents the total quantity of imports allowed into the country (the quota). As in the case of a tariff, area a represents the increase in domestic producer surplus (rents for domestic producers) and $b+d$ are deadweight losses. There are two major differences, however. First, an important shortcoming of a quota is its rigidity. If, for example, technological progress results in a fall in world prices (the world price line or supply curve shifts downward), the only effect is to increase rents. In the case of a tariff this does not occur. Second, area c no longer equals tariff revenue. Under a quota, the increase in the domestic price generated by the QR creates so-called quota rents. These rents go to whoever owns the quota rights. If importers get the quota rights, they receive the windfall profit. In the case of a VER, the rents go to the exporters. If the government auctions the quota to the highest bidder, it will capture the rents. The magnitude of the rents that accrue to rights-holders depends in part on the extent to which lobbying expenses are incurred in obtaining import or export licences. It is quite possible that competition for licences results in significant dissipation of rents. Magee, Brock and Young (1989) analyse the determinants of lobbying expenditures and conclude that in general only a fraction of the rents available will be spent on lobbying.

4. Rent seeking

One of the negative effects of trade controls is that it gives rise to so-called rent seeking behaviour. Rent seeking (or directly unproductive profit-seeking (DUP) activities—Bhagwati, 1982) involves resources being diverted from productive activity and towards efforts to obtain special benefits such as monopoly status, import licences, or bureaucratic preferences that generate economic rents (Tullock, 1967; Krueger, 1974; Bhagwati and Srinivasan, 1980; Messerlin, 1981). Substantial resources may be devoted to lobbying to obtain quota and similar rights. Profit-oriented firms will use resources in lobbying for monopoly (protection), up to the point where an extra dollar invested in lobbying equals the expected value of the resulting trade protection. Numerous players may enter the rent seeking market, but only some will be successful. The resources invested in rent seeking generally constitute economic waste and may give rise to 'political corruption' (Tullock, 1988). 'Rent avoidance' activities, that is, actions by other groups in society to oppose rent seeking, increase waste further—such counterlobbying would not take place in the absence of rent seeking. Incentives to seek and oppose rents are distributed unequally across society. Concentrated interests, such as producers or large firms, have stronger individual incentives to organize and lobby than more dispersed consumers or taxpayers who tend to be much more marginally affected and are concerned by a large number of issues (Downs, 1954).

The analysis of 'rent seeking' changed perceptions of the cost of protection. Traditionally, economists considered only the deadweight costs of the distortions introduced by trade restrictions. The realization that the actual social cost of protection may be much greater provides an additional argument against protectionism. As is always the case when it comes to so-called second-best situations (Bhagwati, 1971), one cannot say with certitude that rent seeking will always be welfare-reducing, nor is it possible to determine to what extent competition for rents will dissipate them. If lobbying resources are pulled away from activities that are characterized by distortions (market failures leading to prices not reflecting true opportunity costs) lobbying may actually increase welfare.

5. Subsidies

Domestic production may expand as a result of a subsidy, in the process reducing imports by lowering the cost (price) of domestic output. The effect of subsidy can also be analysed in the framework of Figure A2.2, which illustrates a small country case where the country in question is a price taker. Assume away tariffs or QRs. The effect of a subsidy (a monetary payment per unit of production) to domestic producers is to shift the domestic supply curve down vertically from S to S^*. For any level of output, average and marginal production costs are reduced by the amount of the subsidy. Domestic production expands from oQ_1 to oQ_2 and imports fall. However, the domestic price remains equal to the world price and total domestic consumption remains unchanged. Imports are reduced by less than under a tariff or quota, and national welfare consequently falls less because there is no consumer deadweight loss (d).[1] The total amount of subsidy (the transfer payment from government to producers) is measured in Figure A2.2 by area $a+b$. Area a is a pure governmental transfer, whereas area b involves the same inefficiency in resources use as in the case of a tariff or quota and constitutes therefore a deadweight loss.

Although subsidies are a less inefficient means of protection of domestic industry than border measures, they tend to be unpopular for political reasons. Domestic

---

[1] Note that the converse of this is that offsetting a subsidy on imported goods through a countervailing duty, see Chapter 9, is less distortionary than the imposition of regular tariff. The CVD will impose a deadweight consumption loss, by raising domestic prices above the world price, but does not create a production distortion.

producers prefer quotas or tariffs to an equivalent subsidy because the latter are more visible, perceived as public handouts and are therefore less secure, being subject to periodic approval by the budgetary authorities.

6. Real trade costs

Assume country N imposes a variety of duplicative inspection requirements on imports that do not add any social value. For example, customs may require that importers provide data that is not relevant for duty calculation purposes. Goods may be subject to conformity assessment procedures at the border that are equivalent to those undertaken at the point of production or shipment. Such redundant 'processing' requirements raise the costs of trading. Assume the cost per unit of imports of such requirements is equivalent to the tariff depicted in Figure A2.3. The result is then that imports equal Q_2Q_3. Assume further that the government decides to remove the requirement for country B, say because of a mutual recognition agreement. Domestic prices fall, domestic producer surplus falls, and consumer surplus increases by area $a+b+c+d$. The net gain for the country is $b+c+d$. This is much larger than what arises if a tariff were to be removed because there is no tariff revenue to be lost—the policies that are removed generated pure social waste. In general, the rectangles that represent revenues, rents or frictional costs are larger than the triangles that reflect efficiency losses. Although tariff revenues or quota rents imply transfers across different groups—and thus do not contribute to welfare improvements when policies are changed—when wasteful (frictional) policies are removed, society gains the associated rectangles. This explains why

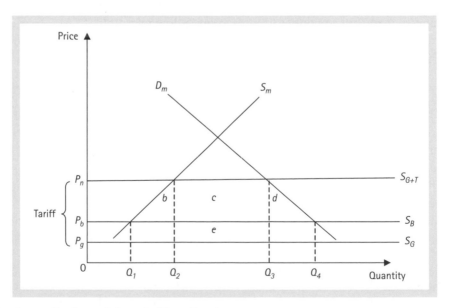

Fig. A2.3. Preferential trade liberalization

estimates of the welfare gains from eliminating frictional costs are much higher than the gains from abolishing tariffs.

7. Preferential trade: trade creation, trade diversion and consumption effects

Preferential trading arrangements such as free trade areas, customs unions or common markets imply a partial movement towards free trade and therefore greater economic efficiency. Whether a particular regional (discriminatory) trading arrangement raises or lowers welfare depends on a number of factors, in particular the relative magnitude of trade creation and trade diversion.

Assume country N trades with two partners B and G. Domestic demand and supply curves are represented by D_N and S_N respectively. Assume all three countries produce steel, and that G is a lower cost supplier than B. Let country N impose a nondiscriminatory *ad valorem* tariff on imports of steel. This is shown in Figure A2.3 as the vertical distance between S_G and S_{G+T}. As G's steel is cheaper than B's, N imports only from G, total imports being Q_2Q_3 and domestic producers selling $0Q_2$. Assume now that N and B create a customs union. The tariff continues to apply to imports from G, but not to imports from country B. The elimination of tariffs on B makes the S_B the relevant supply function for domestic consumption. Country G loses all its export sales. As B is a higher cost supplier, the resulting efficiency loss equals the rectangle e (the cost difference between G and B times the quantity of steel which is diverted). As the domestic price of steel declines in N from P_n to P_b, consumption expands from $0Q_3$ to $0Q_4$, production declines from $0Q_2$ to $0Q_1$ and imports increase from Q_2Q_3 to Q_1Q_4. The net welfare gain for N is equal to areas b and d minus area e (the loss in producer surplus, area a, is 'transferred' to consumers, as is the loss in tariff revenue that used to be collected, area c). Whether welfare in N increases or declines as a result of the customs union depends therefore on whether areas $b+d$ (efficiency gains) are greater than area e (a welfare loss as this is a part of the initial tariff revenue loss that is not offset). Steel producers see output fall as consumers switch to cheaper steel from B. This is trade creation, and improves welfare. However, N no longer imports from the most efficient supplier and this creates an efficiency loss, equal to area e. There is trade diversion. Steel producers in B are happy because they gain export markets. However, country G loses the export market to B and is therefore negatively affected in market N (but may not lose if it shifts supplies to the rest of the world). Moreover, N may also be a net loser if trade diversion is greater than trade creation.

8. Basic analytics of preferences and preference erosion

A simple measure of the effects of unilateral trade preferences is the difference between the applied tariffs facing a country and the MFN tariffs that would otherwise apply: the 'margin of preference'. Figure A2.4, from Francois, Hoekman and Manchin (2006) characterizes the import market for a particular product, where a high-income country imports varieties of good X from two suppliers, indicated as S_{LDC} and $S_{non-LDC}$. The effect of granting tariff preferences to the LDC is represented in the top left panel of Figure A2.4 by a shift of the LDC supply curve, with exports by the LDC expanding from $X_{LDC, 0}$ to $X_{LDC, 1}$. The benefit for the LDC exporter is represented by area A. Because the LDC supplier is now cheaper for consumers, demand shifts away from the nonpreferential supplier. This is shown in the upper right panel of Figure A2.1 and results in a loss in the exporter's surplus equal to area B.

Thus, trade preferences involve benefits for preferred exporters and costs for excluded exporters of identical products or close substitutes. The size of the costs and benefits for affected exporters depends on the responsiveness (elasticity) of export supply and import demand to price changes, and the degree of substitution between preferential and other suppliers. The less the varieties are good substitutes, the smaller the reduction in demand for the non-LDC supplier following the implementation of preferences for the LDC. If either the supply or the demand curve for the products being considered were perfectly elastic, then the gain to the exporting country with preferences would be much bigger than that illustrated in Figure A2.4: it would equal the area of the rectangle defined by the tariff (or preference margin) times the quantity exported (as the increase in the price received by the exporter would equal the preference margin).

The case of horizontal supply curves seems quite appropriate for situations where small countries are supplying relatively homogenous products to much larger economies—as in the case of LDCs supplying raw agricultural products to the US or the EU. In practice a crude measure of the value of preferences defined as the product of the preference margin and the quantity exported provides an upper limit on the potential losses from preference erosion.

Preference erosion involves the reduction or elimination of tariffs on the non-preferential supplier. This is illustrated in the bottom two panels of Figure A2.4. Removing the tariff on other suppliers means that third country exporters see their exports increase from $X_{non-LDC, 1}$ to $X_{non-LDC, 2}$. In the new equilibrium, there is a gain in exporter surplus of area E, which may be greater or less than the original loss of exporter surplus resulting from the preferences, area B. The LDC experiences a drop in demand from $D_{LDC, 1}$ to $D_{LDC, 2}$. This results in a partial, though generally not full, loss of the benefits from the original preference scheme. This is represented by area C, which is shown as being less than area A. The reason the loss is not complete is that preferences include, in part, the benefits relative to the original tariff-ridden equilibrium from a nondiscriminatory tariff reduction by the importer. At the same time, third countries recover some of the costs originally imposed by the preference scheme.

If buyers or intermediaries in the importing country have market power the benefits of the preferential tariff reductions may be captured, at least in part, by them rather than the exporters. In addition, administration costs related to the

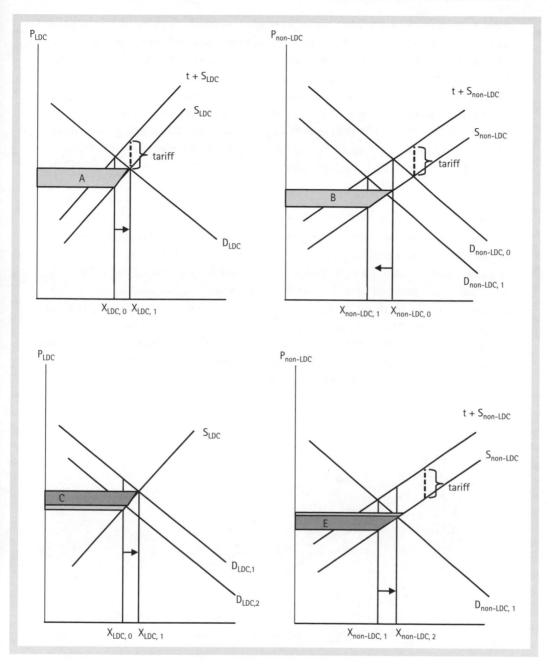

Fig. A2.4. The mechanics of preferences and preference erosion

implementation of preferential trade programmes—such as rules of origin—will eat up some of the benefits. The empirical literature assessing the magnitude of the costs associated with rules of origin and other administrative requirements concludes that on average such costs are on the order of 3–4 per cent (Francois, Hoekman and Manchin, 2006). Although not shown in Figure A2.4, this implies deadweight losses involving parts of areas A and C. In the case of market power, the result is a redistribution of the benefits of preferences to importers. With administration costs, the share of the gains that is lost is not redistributed, but is a deadweight loss. In both cases, the trade effects of preference programmes will be less as well.

9. Dumping (price discrimination) and profit maximization

Dumping occurs when a firm sells a good in an export market at a price below that charged in the home market (see Chapter 9 for a detailed discussion). Assume for simplicity that the firm is a monopolist and that initially there is no trade. The firm will produce Q_1 and sell this at price P_1 in the home market (Figure A2.5). This strategy is dictated by profit maximization, which requires that the firm equates its marginal revenue (MR) with marginal cost (MC).

Now suppose that the firm has the option to export. The world price is P_2—the firm is too small to affect world prices. Assume further that the domestic and the international markets are segmented—there are tariffs or other barriers to trade

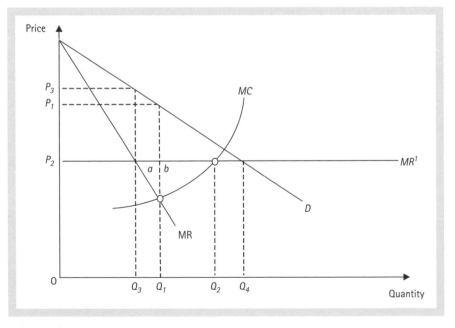

Fig. A2.5. Dumping

which prevent any of the firm's exports from coming back into the domestic market. Being able to sell on the world market alters the firm's marginal revenue curve. In effect, the firm confronts two marginal revenue curves. Up to quantity oQ_1 marginal revenue (MR) at home exceeds that on the world market—thereafter MR from selling in the world market is higher. In this new situation the firm will reduce its domestic supply to oQ_3 (the point at which MR at home equals MR abroad), in the process raising the domestic price to P_3 (technically, the reason for this is that marginal costs rise as output expands). Given that profit maximization requires that marginal revenue equal marginal costs, the firm will export quantity Q_3Q_2 at the international price P_2 The option of exporting at (the lower) international price increases the firm's profits by an amount equivalent to areas $a+b$ in Figure A2.5, the difference between MR and MC for the exported quantity. The differences in elasticities in demand in the two markets induce the firm to implement a price discrimination strategy: it engages in dumping.

Is dumping bad from a welfare point of view? Clearly, it has no impact on the welfare of foreign consumers or firms—the exporting firm simply prices to market: the world price is given and remains unaffected. However, domestic consumers lose (as the price goes up at home).

10. Trade liberalization as a pro-competitive device

The situation in Figure A2.5 is one where home prices are significantly above world prices. It is assumed that the economy is small—world prices are taken as given. If the country were to liberalize, the monopolist would confront import competition, with goods priced at P_2 The monopoly would immediately become unsustainable and the firm would be forced to price output at P_2 as well, increasing national welfare. Free trade would result in the domestic firm selling oQ_2 into the domestic market (all its output), and the country importing an additional quantity Q_2Q_4 from the rest of the world. Insofar as dumping is facilitated by the existence of barriers to trade that protect the dumper's home market, the appropriate policy response is not for the importing country to impose antidumping duties, but for the home country to eliminate the barriers to arbitrage that prevent traders from re-exporting the product into the home market. As mentioned in Chapter 9, in practice there is no effort in the antidumping context to determine whether there are barriers to arbitrage.

Of course, there may be other factors that allow the exporting firm(s) to exercise market power on the home market. If so, there is cause for the application of domestic competition law to determine whether there are anticompetitive practices that are detrimental to national welfare. Trade policy is part of the competition policy toolkit. The classic case of a monopoly is illustrated in Figure A2.6. Absent trade—say as a result of a prohibitive tariff or an import ban, the domestic monopoly price is far above the world price. Opening up the economy would drive the domestic price down to the world price, expand domestic output and

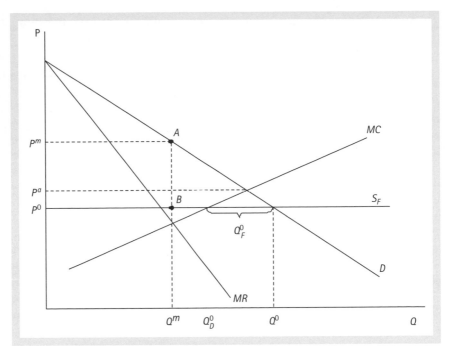

Fig. A2.6. Domestic monopoly and trade

generate imports of Q_F^o. A barrier that limits entry (starting from free trade) allows foreign firms to stay in market until S_F rises to P^a.

11. Discriminatory government procurement

Many governments discriminate in favour of domestic firms when they buy goods and services. The effect of such discrimination depends on market structure and on the size of government demand. In a competitive market, Baldwin (1970) and Baldwin and Richardson (1972) showed that a procurement ban on foreign purchases from foreign car producers by the government will affect output levels, imports and prices *only* if government demand exceeds domestic supply at the moment the ban was imposed. If government demand was less than or equal to domestic private sector supply, the imposition of a procurement ban for a given industry would have *no effect* on imports, output or national welfare. This is because the ban merely reshuffles demand between foreign suppliers and the domestic producers of cars. To see why, suppose originally the government bought five cars from abroad. After the ban these five cars must be supplied by domestic firms, which in turn would have five fewer cars to supply domestic private consumers. However, foreign firms have exactly five unsold cars which they can now supply to domestic consumers, making up any apparent shortfall. Therefore, when government demand is relatively small, a procurement ban merely reshuffles

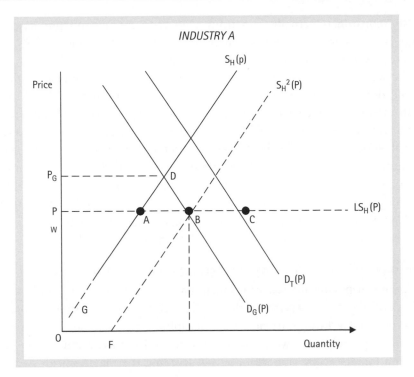

Fig. A2.7. Procurement discrimination in a competitive market

sales between domestic and foreign firms, with no effect on overall imports (market access), output or prices.

If, however, government demand exceeded domestic supply at the prices that prevailed before the ban was imposed, the price of cars for the government must increase to encourage domestic supply to expand to meet government demand. The end result is that government demand falls, domestic sales to the government rise, and imports fall (Figure A2.7).[2] If the world price determined the pre-ban price for domestic private consumers, they will be unaffected by the procurement ban. After all, domestic consumers can buy all the cars they want on world markets at the world price. In contrast, if foreign producers customize their cars to the domestic market, the procurement ban leaves foreign producers with at least 15 cars which they used to sell to the domestic government but are now prevented from doing so. As these cars were customized for a specific market (suppose they have steering wheels on the left hand side), then the possibility of selling these cars on the world market is remote. The foreign car suppliers are left with little choice but to offer additional cars to domestic consumers at lower prices. In this case,

---

[2] Figures A2.7–A2.9 are drawn from Evenett and Hoekman (2005).

domestic consumers actually gain from a government ban on purchases from foreign cars—as the ban creates a temporary surplus of foreign goods, which results in lower prices being paid by domestic consumers.

In the case where procurement discrimination raises the price paid by the government, domestic firms expand output and see their profits rise. New firms will want to enter this protected industry, driving down the price paid by the government until the incentive to enter this market (the higher-than-usual profits) has gone. The principal consequence of allowing free entry into the market is that the price paid by the government may fall to equal the world price—potentially eliminating any price wedge between that paid by private consumers and the government. Whether entry occurs depends on the prevalence of natural—and policy-induced—barriers to entry. Therefore, the long-term consequences of a procurement ban are determined in part by domestic competition policies and restrictions on FDI.

12. Corruption and transparency in government procurement

Corrupt government officials can solicit payments from actual and potential suppliers of goods and services to the public sector. A major rationale for efforts during the Doha Round to negotiate disciplines to increase transparency of government procurement was to reduce the scope for corruption, in the process increasing market access opportunities by 'levelling the playing field'. A growing body of evidence suggests that corrupt officials deliberately expand expenditures on goods and projects—such as aircraft and construction—which are highly differentiated and for which there are few, if any, comparable reference prices in world markets. Put simply, officials with an interest in personal rents will employ nontransparent procurement procedures to expand government spending where the opportunities for self-enrichment are greatest. Another consequence of having to pay bribes to bid for government contracts is to reduce the number of domestic bidders. That is, the result can be thought of as shifting outward the government demand curve for products where there are opportunities for corruption, and at the same time shifting in the supply curve of firms.

To determine the maximum possible effect on foreign market access of improving the transparency of a procurement regime, assume that initially foreign firms found it so costly to overcome the opaque contracting procedures that none of them willingly supply the domestic government. Figure A2.8 represents the short-run domestic supply and demand curves for a good. With an opaque procurement system, foreigners do not supply anything to the government and domestic firms sell output Q_2 at price P_2 to the state. Now suppose that, following a multilateral agreement, a transparent procurement procedure is imposed and corruption ceases. This reform has two effects: the first is to reallocate government spending away from goods that were more prone to bribery and the second is to allow foreigners to sell to the government. In terms of Figure A2.8, the first effect shifts the government's demand curve from D_g to D_{g1}. The government takes advantage

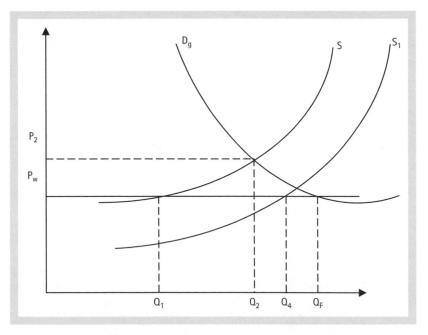

Fig. A2.8. Nontransparent procurement and market access (1)

of its new access to world prices and buys quantity Q_3, which is less than if the demand curve had remained at D_g. The quantity imported rises from zero to (Q_3-Q_1). However, the case represented in Figure 8 is not the only relevant one: if the fall in government demand is large enough so that domestic firms can now entirely supply the government's demand (at world prices), market access may not improve at all. In fact, it is possible for improvements in transparency to raise welfare without enhancing market access.

Elimination of a nontransparent procurement procedure will have another effect, namely expanding the number of domestic firms willing to sell to the government. This case is shown in Figure A2.9. The starting point is the same as in Figure A2.8: in the presence of a nontransparent procurement procedure, the equilibrium price P_2 prevails and domestic firms supply quantity Q_2. Ignoring the effect of transparency reform on the government's demand curve, such reform results in more domestic firms entering the market (as these firms no longer have to spend time and money on payments to officials), which shifts the domestic supply curve to S_1. With the government now able to buy at world price P_W, domestic firms supply Q_4 and imports expand to (Q_F-Q_4). For a sufficiently large outward shift of the domestic supply curve, there may be no market access improvement at all. Overall then, there is no guarantee that improving transparency will increase both welfare and market access simultaneously.

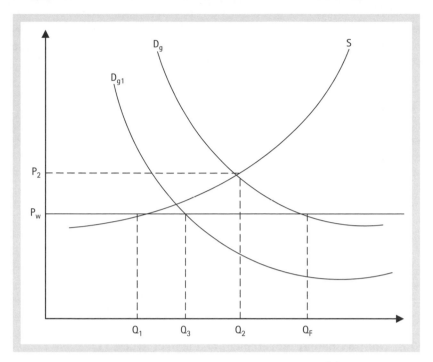

Fig. A2.9. Nontransparent procurement and market access (2)

13. Dealing with domestic market failure and externalitie[3]

Markets may fail to allocate resources efficiently for a number of reasons. There may be information asymmetries, property rights may not exist, or there may be externalities. In presence of distortions, intervention by the government may be called for. As distortions seldom directly involve trade, the general conclusion that emerges from the literature is that trade policy should not be used as an instrument to offset distortions. These should be corrected with domestic policies.

Using taxes to correct for externalities

As in previous examples, assume perfect competition. In the absence of external- ities, the supply curve, S, measures (vertically) both the marginal private cost (MPC) and the marginal social cost (MSC) of producing a good (Figure A2.10). The market equilibrium at quantity Q_e equates the quantities supplied and demanded. The effect of a negative externality (producers do not take into account

---

[3] What follows draws on Alan Deardorff, 'Lecture Notes on the Economics of Government Intervention', World Bank Institute, 1998 (see www.worldbank.org/trade).

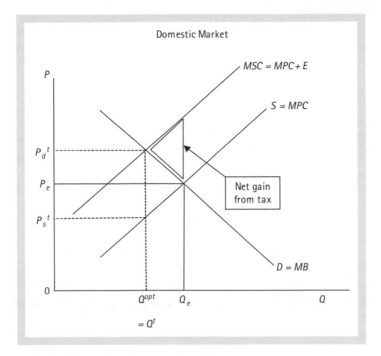

Domestic Market

$MSC = MPC + E$

$S = MPC$

$P_d{}^t$

P_e

Net gain
from tax

$P_s{}^t$

$D = MB$

0

Q^{opt} Q_e

$= Q^t$

Fig. A2.10. Domestic market failure: the tax case

the impact of their actions on other groups in society) is to make MSC exceed MPC by the amount of the externality, E. Thus, Q_e does not equate the marginal benefit and marginal social cost of producing the good.

This means that this output is not optimal. From a social point of view there is too much production. Because of the negative externality, the optimum is where $MSC = MB$, at the intersection of the demand curve with the MSC curve (which lies a distance E above the supply curve). A tax equal to E will reduce output to the optimal level. The welfare benefit of the reduced externality is equal to E times one-half the drop in output. In the figure, this is the triangle of 'net gain from tax' that is shown. Note that the incidence of the tax is shared between producers and consumers. Producers see the price they receive fall, whereas consumers see the price they pay increase.

A regulation that limits output to Q^{opt} accomplishes the same purpose as a tax in dealing with a domestic externality, and has the same positive effect on national welfare. However, the amount that the government would have collected in tax revenue goes instead to the producers as increased profits, or rent, from the regulation (their costs go down, whereas their price goes up). Although the tax hurts producers and will be resisted by them if instead of a tax the government uses a regulation, this will be less detrimental to producers and therefore be welcomed by them. Both hurt consumers equally.

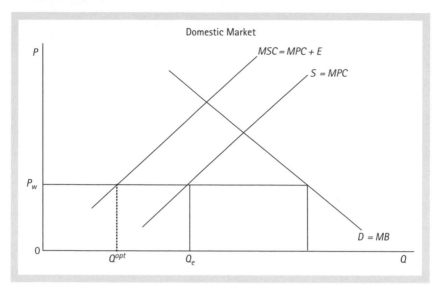

Fig. A2.11. **Offsetting domestic externalities in a small trading economy**

Allowing for trade

The foregoing assumed there was no trade. If we now allow for trade in the product concerned and consider again a small open economy that cannot affect the terms of trade but is confronted with an externality, the optimum output after imposition of the appropriate tax or regulation is determined by the world price P_w. Domestic output is Q^{opt}, which is less than Q_e. However, by fixing the price to demanders, trade causes producers to bear the whole cost of the tax—the incidence of the tax cannot be shifted in part to consumers (Figure A2.11). Conversely, if a regulation is used, domestic producers will lose the rents they used to capture. They can be expected to blame this 'loss' on trade, perceiving it as unfair, and they may lobby for some sort of protection, such as a tariff equal to the tax. This is likely to be motivated on the basis of some version of 'levelling the playing field'.

This framework is directly relevant to the debates and conflicts that arise in the WTO context regarding the use of regulations requiring (or prohibiting) the use of specific production or processing techniques. These impose additional costs on producers, shifting the supply curve up. The cost of attaining the optimal level of output is borne completely by domestic producers, who then have an incentive to lobby to have imports subject to the same processing requirement to 'level the playing field'. If foreign production generates the same negative externality for the domestic country as domestic production, then this is appropriate. However, if,

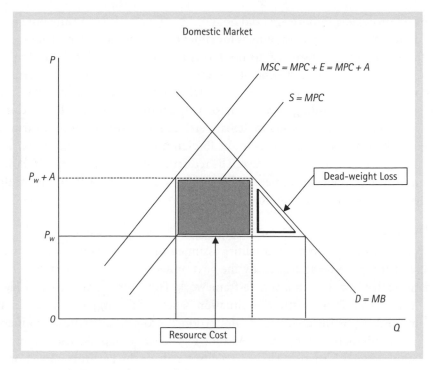

Fig. A2.12. Leveling the playing field

more realistically, foreign production generates no domestic externality, there is no justification for any burden being imposed on imports. Suppose foreign production occurs in a location where pollution is more readily dissipated, per capita incomes are too low to allow abatement technologies to be used, there is less risk aversion, or there is no concern regarding local environmental spillovers (see Chapter 13). In all such cases, a requirement that imports also be processed identically to domestic production (use a particular technology, etc.), simply adds to their cost without generating any social benefit in either the domestic or the foreign country.

The processing requirement on imports is akin to a tariff or quota in that it increases production costs and shifts the foreign supply curve up by the amount A, raising the price of imports from the world market to $P_w + A$ (Figure A2.12). In the new equilibrium domestic output rises and becomes the same as it was without any policy at all, whereas consumption and imports are both reduced. Domestic producers are indifferent, as their cost and price have both risen by the same amount. Domestic consumers are worse off as their surplus has declined. Part of that loss is payment for the elimination of the externality, which is a benefit and therefore cancels out. But the rest—the shaded areas in Figure A2.12, are net losses for the country and the world. The triangle is the usual deadweight loss of raising the price to consumers above the true marginal cost. The rectangle is an additional social cost, in that real resources are wasted on processing imports that did not need it. These costs constitute pure waste. They do not generate rents or revenues for either interest groups or the state.

Although there is a clear case to use tariffs rather than regulation to 'level the playing field', as this at least generates revenue for the government, a tariff will again negate the benefit from the tax in reducing the externality, as it will result in domestic output expanding beyond the socially optimal level. It will also cause a deadweight loss by raising prices to demanders. In both cases, whatever instrument is used, if there are no externalities in the foreign market, intervention to raise the price of imports is counterproductive. The reduction in domestic output following the imposition of the environment policy is appropriate—there is no justification for imposing the same costs on foreign production.

14. The inefficiency of a trade ban to address cross-border spillover[4]

The foregoing discussion of externalities assumed the market failure was domestic and could therefore be addressed by the government. Cross-border spillovers are more difficult to address in a simple framework. However, an analogue to Figure A2.10 can be used to illustrate a situation where exporting countries do not consume and importing countries do not produce a commodity whose production gives rise to international spillovers. Assume Figure A2.13 maps African supply and East Asian demand for ivory. The externality E reflects the negative impact on the utility of conservationists in other parts of the world that is caused by the slaughter of elephants—that is, the value they put on reducing this slaughter from $0Q_e$ to $0Q_t$.[5] Production (and trade) equal to $0Q_e$ induces a loss for the conservationists equal to the triangle ecj. If they can impose a complete ban on ivory trade, conservationists increase their welfare by this amount, at the cost of total producer and consumer surplus forgone equal to area ace. The latter is clearly much greater than the former, so that the ban is inefficient. In practice, conservationists will not compensate the losers—so that the ban implies a large implicit transfer.

A more efficient solution would be to reduce trade through a tax that equates the global marginal benefit of restricting output to the global marginal cost. Such a tax would reduce welfare in Africa and East Asia, but this would be offset to a large extent by tax revenue (equal to $bdfh$). As is always the case, the tax generates two 'loss triangles' for producers and consumers, but these are offset by equivalent gains for conservationists (reflecting the reduction in the externality). In fact, as conservationists gain area $cdbj$, global welfare increases by bcj (the net gain from the tax). Equity requires that conservationists compensate losers, in particular poor African producers—so that the tax revenue and the value of area bcj should be transferred to these countries. If this is done, conservationists are forced to pay for

---

[4] This example is drawn from Anderson (1992: 40 ff).
[5] The supply curves in Figure A2.12 are not parallel because we assume that the externality (and the associated tax) is proportional to output produced.

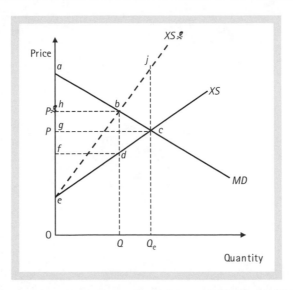

Fig. A2.13. Using taxes and trade bans to offset global externalities

what they want to achieve, and African producers can be more than compensated for their loss. The problem of generating such outcomes in practice is that those who benefit from the alleviation of global externalities are rarely willing to pay. Thus, the needed transfers do not occur, even if tax instruments are employed (which generally is not the case).

15. Trade in services

The analytics of trade in services is analogous to trade in goods if production takes place wholly within one country and is then 'shipped' to an importing country through telecommunications networks or the mail (mode 1 under the GATS). As discussed in Chapter 7, often trade in services will involve the movement of providers. The simplest analytical framework to understand the effects of trade that involves movement of providers across borders is laid out in Figure A2.14. This assumes there are two countries endowed with OL^1 and L^1O^* workers respectively. The marginal product of labour in each country is downward sloping as a result of diminishing returns. Each country produces the same good—assume further that this is a nontradable service. In the absence of trade the wage in the home country—endowed with the most labour—is L^1C, in the foreign country it is L^1B. Thus $W < W^*$. Assume now that trade becomes feasible—workers are allowed to move (mode 4) or it can now occur through telecom networks (mode 1). Trade then equalizes wages, with L^1–L^2 home workers working in/for foreign. Global welfare increases by the area ABC (note that in this simple model GDP equals the area under each MPL curve, with capital receiving the area above the rectangles defined by the product of the wage and the workforce employed in each country).

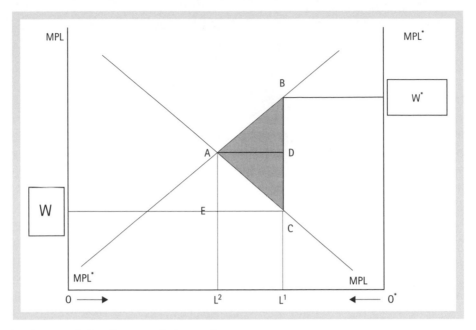

Fig. A2.14. Gains from trade in services

The trade results in both internal and international redistribution. Wages rise at home as workers leave, but this reduces returns to domestic capital. Wages fall in the foreign country as workers arrive; this increases returns to domestic capital. If the movement of workers (service providers) is permanent, home loses ACL^2L^1; the foreign country gets all the extra output and all of the net gains from trade (ABC). If migration is temporary, and all the income received by domestic workers that moves is remitted back the gains will be shared equally: the gain to home is ACD (net gain given the capital loss); the gain to foreign is ADB (where capital gains more than outweigh labour losses).

FURTHER READING

An excellent discussion of the economics of nontariff policies can be found in Alan Deardorff and Robert Stern, *Measurement of Non-Tariff Barriers* (Ann Arbor: University of Michigan Press, 1998). Alan Deardorff's homepage on the Internet provides a very useful glossary of trade policy terms, including definitions of the many types of policy instruments that are used to restrict or expand trade (see www.econ.lsa.umich.edu/~alandear). The economics of the interaction between environmental and trade policies are discussed in some detail in the contributions to Kym Anderson and Richard Blackhurst (eds), *The Greening of World Trade Issues* (Hempstead: Harvester Wheatsheaf, 1992). Aaditya Mattoo, Robert Stern and Gianni Zannini (eds), *Trade in Services: A Handbook* (Oxford: Oxford University Press, 2007) do the same for trade in services.

BIBLIOGRAPHY

AARONSON, S. (2007), 'Seeping in Slowly: How Human Rights Concerns are Penetrating the WTO', *World Trade Review*, 6 (3): 413–49.

ABBOTT, F. M. (2002), 'The Doha Decision on the TRIPS Agreement and Public Health: Lighting a Dark Corner at the WTO', *Journal of International Economic Law*, 5: 2.

ABBOTT, F. (2007), 'Parallel Importation: Economic and Social Welfare Dimensions', mimeo.

—— and VAN PUYMBROECK, R. (2003), *Compulsory Licensing for Public Health: A Guide and Model Documents for Implementation of the Doha Declaration Paragraph 6 Decision* (eBookMall, Inc.).

ADAMS, C. (1993), *For Good and Evil: The Impact of Taxes on the Course of Civilization* (Lanham: Madison Books).

ADLUNG, R. (2006), 'Services Negotiations in the Doha Round: Lost in Flexibility?', *Journal of International Economic Law*, 9 (4): 865–93.

—— and MARTIN, R. (2005), 'Turning Hills into Mountains? Current Commitments under the General Agreement on Trade in Services and Prospects for Change', *Journal of World Trade*, 39: 1161–94.

AGGARWAL, A. (2002), 'Antidumping Law and Practice: An Indian Perspective', ICRIER Working Paper No. 85.

—— (2004), 'Macroeconomic Determinants of Antidumping', *World Development*, 32: 1043–57.

ALLEN, D. (1979), 'Tariff Games', in S. Brams, A. Schotter and G. Schwoediauer (eds), *Applied Game Theory* (Wuerzburg: Physica-Verlag).

ALSTON, J., SUMNER, D. and BUNCKE, H. (2007), 'Impacts of Reductions in US Cotton Subsidies on West African Producers', Oxfam America, mimeo.

AMINIAN, N., FUNG, K. C. and NG, F. (2007), 'A Comparative Analysis of Trade and Economic Integration in East Asia and Latin America', *Economic Change and Restructuring*, 42 (1): 105–37.

AMITI, M. and WEI, S. (2005), 'Fear of Service Outsourcing: Is It Justified?', *Economic Policy*, 20 (42): 308–47.

ANDERS, S. and CASWELL, J. (2007), 'Standards-as-Barriers versus Standards-as-Catalysts: Assessing the Impact of HCAAP Implementation on US Seafood Imports', University of Massachusetts Working Paper 2007-7.

ANDERSON, J. (1992), 'Effects on the Environment and Welfare of Liberalizing World Trade: The Cases of Coal and Food', in K. Anderson and R. Blackhurst (eds), *The Greening of World Trade Issues* (London: Harvester-Wheatsheaf).

—— and VAN WINCOOP, E. (2004), 'Trade Costs', *Journal of Economic Literature*, 42 (3): 691–751.

ANDERSON, K. (1995), 'Lobbying Incentives and the Pattern of Protection in Rich and Poor Countries', *Economic Development and Cultural Change*, 43: 401–23 (January).

—— (2008), *Distortions to Agricultural Incentives: A Global Perspective* (London and Washington, DC: Palgrave-Macmillan and World Bank).

—— and BLACKHURST. R. (eds) (1993), *The Greening of World Trade Issues* (London: Harvester-Wheatsheaf).

—— and HAYAMI, Y. (1986), *The Political Economy of Agricultural Protection* (Sydney: Allen and Unwin).

—— and NORHEIM, H. (1993), 'History, Geography and Regional Integration', in K. Anderson and R. Blackhurst (eds), *Regional Integration and the Global Trading System* (London: Harvester-Wheatsheaf).

—— and VALENZUELA, E. (2008), 'Estimates of Distortions to Agricultural Incentives, 1955–2007', at http://go.worldbank.org/YAO39F35E0

—— and WINTERS, A. (2008), 'The Challenge of Reducing International Trade and Migration Barriers', University of Adelaide, mimeo.

—— MARTIN, W. and VALENZUELA, E. (2006), 'The Relative Importance of Global Agricultural Subsidies and Market Access', *World Trade Review*, 5 (3): 357–76.

—— —— and van der MENSBRUGGHE, D. (2006), 'Global Impacts of the Doha Scenarios on Poverty', in Hertel, T. and WINTERS, L. A. (eds), *Poverty and the WTO: Impacts of the Doha Development Agenda* (New York and Washington, DC: Palgrave-Macmillan and the World Bank).

ANDERSON, R. (2007), 'Renewing the WTO Agreement on Government Procurement: Progress to Date and Ongoing Negotiations', *Public Procurement Law Review*, 16 (5): 325–51.

ANSON, J., CADOT, O., ESTEVADEORDAL, A., DE MELO, J., SUWA-EISENMANN, A. and TUMURCHUDUR, B. (2005), 'Assessing the Costs of Rules of Origin in North-South PTAs with an Application to NAFTA', *Review of International Economics*, 13 (3): 501–17.

ARKELL, J. (1994), 'Lobbying for Market Access for Professional Services: Accounting, Architecture, Engineering, and Legal Services', in M. Kostecki (ed.), *Marketing Strategy for Services* (Oxford: Pergamon Press).

ARNOLD, J., MATTOO, A. and NARCISO, G. (2006), 'Services Inputs and Firm Productivity in Sub-Saharan Africa: Evidence from Firm-Level Data', World Bank Policy Research Working Paper No. 4038.

—— JAVORCIK, B. and MATTOO, A. (2007), 'The Productivity Effects of Services Liberalization: Evidence from the Czech Republic,' World Bank Policy Research Working Paper No. 4109.

—— —— LIPSCOMB, M. and MATTOO, A. (2008), 'Services Reform and Manufacturing Performance: Evidence from India', World Bank, mimeo.

ASLUND, A. (2007), 'Russia's Policy on Accession to the World Trade Organization', *Eurasian Economics and Geography*, 48 (3) (May–June).

ATKINS, C. (2005), 'FSC/ETI Transition Relief in the New JOBS Act: Does the US Have to Quit Cold Turkey?', Special Report—Tax Foundation (March).

BACCHETTA, M. and BORA, B. (2004), 'Industrial tariffs, LDCs and the Doha Development Agenda', in B. Guha-Khasnobis (ed.), *The WTO, Developing Countries and the Doha Development Agenda: Prospects and Challenges for Trade-Led Growth* (Basingstoke, United Kingdom: Palgrave Macmillan).

BAFFES, J. (2005), 'Cotton: Market Setting, Trade Policies, and Issues', in A. Aksoy and J. Beghin (eds), *Global Agricultural Trade and Developing Countries* (Washington, DC: World Bank).

BAGWELL, K. and STAIGER, R. (1990), 'A Theory of Managed Trade', *American Economic Review*, 80: 779–95.

—— (2002), *The Economics of the World Trading System* Cambridge, MA: The MIT Press.

—— (2004), 'Multilateral Trade Negotiations, Bilateral Opportunism and the Rules of the GATT/WTO', *Journal of International Economics*, 63: 1–29.

—— MAVROIDIS, P., and STAIGER, R. (2006), 'The Case for Tradable Remedies in WTO Dispute Settlement', in S. Evenett and B. Hoekman (eds), *Economic Development and Multilateral Cooperation* (London: Palgrave-McMillan).

BAIER, S. and BERGSTRAND, J. (2007), 'Do Free Trade Agreements Actually Increase Members' International Trade?', *Journal of International Economics* 71: 72–95.

BAILEY, S. (1932), 'The Political Aspect of Discrimination in International Economic Relations', *Economica*, 12: 96–115.

BALDWIN, R. (1994), *Towards an Integrated Europe* (London: CEPR).

—— (1995), 'A Domino Theory of Regionalism', in R. Baldwin, P. Haaparanta, and J. Kiander (eds), *Expanding European Regionalism: The EU's New Members* (Cambridge University Press).

—— (2000), 'Regulatory Protectionism, Developing Countries and a Two Tier Trading System,' in Susan Collins and Dani Rodrik (eds), *Brookings Trade Forum 2000* (Washington, DC: Brookings Institution).

—— (2006a), 'Multilateralising Regionalism: Spaghetti Bowls as Building Blocs on the Path to Global Free Trade', *The World Economy*, 29 (11): 1451–518.

—— (2006b), 'Managing the Noodle Bowl: The Fragility of East Asian Regionalism', CEPR Discussion Paper No. 5561.

—— and VENABLES, A. (1997), 'International Economic Integration,' in G. Grossman and K. Rogoff (eds), *Handbook of International Economics, iii* (Amsterdam: North Holland).

—— FORSLID, R. and HAALAND, J. (1996), 'Investment Creation and Diversion in Europe,' *The World Economy*, 19 (6): 635–59.

—— EVENETT, S. and Low, P. (2007), 'Beyond Tariffs: Multilateralising Deeper RTA Commitments,' presented at the conference 'Multilateralising Regionalism', 10–12 September, Geneva.

BALDWIN, R. E. (1969), 'The Case Against Infant Industry Protection', *Journal of Political Economy*, 77: 295–305.

—— (1970), *Non-Tariff Distortions in International Trade* (Washington, DC: Brookings Institution).

—— (1986), 'Toward More Efficient Procedures for Multilateral Trade Negotiations', *Aussenwirtschaft*, 41: 379–94.

—— and CLARKE, R. (1987), 'Game Modeling the Tokyo Round of Tariff Negotiations', *Journal of Policy Modeling*, 9: 257–84.

—— and RICHARDSON, J. D. (1972), 'Government Purchasing Policies, Other NTBs, and the International Monetary Crisis', in H. English, and K. Hay (eds), *Obstacles to Trade in the Pacific Area* (Ottawa: Carleton School of International Affairs).

BANKS, G. (1983), 'The Economics and Politics of Counter-trade', *The World Economy*, 6: 159–82.

BARFIELD, C. (2001), *Free Trade, Sovereignty and Democracy: The Future of the World Trade Organization* (Washington, DC: AEI Press).

BARONCELLI, E., FINK, C. and JAVORCIK, B. (2005), 'The Global Distribution of Trademarks: Some Stylised Facts', *The World Economy*, 28 (6): 765–82.

BARTH, J., CAPRIO, G. and LEVINE, R. (2006), *Rethinking Bank Regulation: Till Angels Govern* (Cambridge and New York: Cambridge University Press).

BARTON J. *et al.* (2002), 'Integrating Intellectual Property Rights and Development Policy', Report of the Commission on Intellectual Property Rights (Chaired by John Barton), London, September.

BAUMOL, W. (1967), 'Macroeconomics of Unbalanced Growth', *American Economic Review* 57: 415–26.

BEERS, C. VAN (1998), 'Labour Standards and Trade Flows of OECD Countries', *World Economy*, 21 (1): 57–73.

BELLMANN, C. and GERSTER, R. (1996), 'Accountability in the World Trade Organization', *Journal of World Trade*, 30 (6): 31–74.

BEN-DAVID, D. and LOEWEY, M. (1997), 'Free Trade, Growth, and Convergence', NBER Working Paper No. 6095.

—— and PAPPELL, D. (1998), 'Slowdowns and Meltdowns: Post-war Growth Evidence from 74 Countries', *Review of Economics and Statistics*, 80: 561–71.

BERNARD, A., JENSEN, B., REDDING, S., and SCHOTT, P. (2007), 'Firms in International Trade', *Journal of Economic Perspectives*, 21: 105–30.

BHAGWATI, J. N. (1971), 'The Generalized Theory of Distortions and Welfare', in J. Bhagwati *et al.* (eds), *Trade, Balance of Payments and Growth: Papers in Honor of Charles P. Kindleberger* (Amsterdam: North-Holland).

—— (1982), 'Directly Unproductive, Profit-seeking (DUP) Activities', *Journal of Political Economy*, 90: 988–1002.

—— (1984), 'Splintering and Disembodiment of Services and Developing Nations, *The World Economy*, 7: 133–44.

—— (1987), 'Trade in Services and the Multilateral Trade Negotiations', *World Bank Economic Review*, 1: 549–69.

—— (1988), *Protectionism* (Cambridge, MA: MIT Press).

—— (1991), *The World Trading System at Risk* (Princeton, NJ: Princeton University Press).

—— (1993), 'Regionalism and Multilateralism: An Overview', in J. De Melo and A. Panagariya (eds), *New Dimensions in Regional Integration* (Cambridge, MA: Cambridge University Press).

—— (1994), 'Fair Trade, Reciprocity and Harmonization: The New Challenge to the Theory and Policy of Free Trade', in A. Deardorff, and R. Stern (eds), *Analytical and Negotiating Issues in the Global Trading System* (Ann Arbor, MI: University of Michigan Press).

—— (1998), *A Stream of Windows: Unsettling Reflections on Trade, Immigration and Democracy* (Cambridge, MA: MIT Press).

—— (2004), *In Defense of Globalization* (New York: Oxford University Press).

—— and IRWIN, D. (1987), 'The Return of the Reciprocitarians: US Trade Policy Today', *The World Economy*, 10: 109–30.

—— and MAVROIDIS, P. (2007), 'Is Action Against US Exports for Failure to Sign Kyoto Protocol WTO-legal?', *World Trade Review*, 6 (2): 299–310.

—— and PATRICK, H. (eds) (1990), *Aggressive Unilateralism: America's 301 Trade Policy and the World Trading System* (Ann Arbor: University of Michigan Press).

BHAGWATI, J. N. and SRINIVASAN, T. N. (1980), 'Revenue Seeking: A Generalization of the Theory of Tariffs', *Journal of Political Economy*, 88: 1069–87.

BHAGWATI, J. and SRINIVASAN, T. N. (1996), 'Trade and the Environment: Does Environmental Diversity Detract From the Case for Free Trade?', in J. Bhagwati, and R. Hudec (eds), *Harmonization and Fair Trade: Prerequisite for Free Trade?* (Cambridge, MA: MIT Press).

—— PANAGARIYA, A. and SRINIVASAN, T. N. (2004), 'The Muddles over Outsourcing', *Journal of Economic Perspectives*, 18 (4): 93–114.

BLACK, A. (1999), Globalization and Restructuring in the South African Automotive Industry, *Journal of International Development*, 13 (6), 779–96.

BLACKHURST, R. (1977), 'International Trade and Domestic Environmental Policies', in *Les Relations Internationales dans une Monde en Mutation* (Geneva: Institut Universitaire de Hautes Etudes Internationales).

—— (1998), The Capacity of the WTO to Fulfil Its Mandate', in A. Krueger (ed.), *The WTO as an International Organization* (Chicago: University of Chicago Press).

—— and HARTRIDGE, D. (2005), 'Improving the Capacity of WTO Institutions to Fulfill Their Mandate,' in E. U. Petersmann (ed.), *Reforming the World Trading System: Legitimacy, Efficiency and Democratic Governance* (Oxford: Oxford University Press).

BLAKENEY, M. (2004), 'International Intellectual Property Jurisprudence after TRIPs', in D. Vaver and L. Bently (eds), *Intellectual Property in the New Millennium.* (Cambridge, Cambridge University Press).

BLANCHARD, E. (2007), 'Reevaluating the Role of Trade Agreements: Does Investment Globalization Make the WTO Obsolete?', University of Virginia, mimeo.

BLANDFORD, D. and JOSLING, T. (2008), 'The WTO May 19th Agricultural Modalities Proposals and their Impact on Domestic Support in the EU and the US', World Bank, mimeo.

BLONINGEN, B. and BOWN, C. (2003), 'Antidumping and Retaliation Threats', *Journal of International Economics*, 60: 249–73.

BOHARA, A., GAWANDE, K. and SANGUIETTI, P. (2004), 'Trade Diversion and Declining Tariffs: Evidence from Mercosur', *Journal of International Economics* 64: 65–88.

BOLAKY, B. and FREUND, C. (2008), 'Trade, Regulations, and Income', *Journal of Development Economics*, 87 (2): 309–21.

BOND, E. (1997), 'Competition Policy in Customs Unions: Theory and an Example from US History', Penn State University, mimeo.

BORA, B. (2001), *Trade Related Investment Measures and the WTO: 1995–2001* (Geneva: United Nations Conference on Trade and DEVELOPMENT, UNCTAD).

—— LLOYD, P. J. and PANGESTU, M. (2000), 'Industrial Policy and the WTO', *The World Economy*, 23: 543–60.

BORCHERT, I. (2008), 'Trade Diversion Under Selective Preferential Market Access', World Bank, mimeo.

BORRELL, B. (1996), 'Policy-making in the EU: The Banana Story, the WTO and Policy Transparency', *Australian Journal of Agricultural and Resource Economics*, 41 (2): 263–76.

BOURGEOIS, J. H. J. (2008), 'Post Cancún WTO TRIPs—A Bumpy Road', in Stefan Griller (ed.), *At the Crossroads: The World Trading System and the Doha Round*, pp. 380–405 (Vienna and New York: Springer).

BOVARD, J. (1991), *The Fair Trade Fraud* (New York: St. Martin's Press).

BOWN, C. (2004*a*), 'On the Economic Success of GATT/WTO Dispute Settlement', *Review of Economics and Statistics*, 37: 678–720.

—— (2004*b*), 'Developing Countries as Plaintiffs and Defendants in GATT/WTO Trade Disputes', *The World Economy*, 27: 59–80.

—— (2004*c*), 'Trade Policy under the GATT/WTO: Empirical Evidence of the Equal Treatment Rule', *Canadian Journal of Economics*, 37 (3): 678–720.

—— (2004*d*), 'How Different Are Safeguards from Antidumping? Evidence from US Trade Policies Towards Steel', Brandeis University, mimeo.

—— (2005), 'Participation in WTO Dispute Settlement: Complainants, Interested Parties and Free Riders', *World Bank Economic Review*, 19 (2): 287–310.

—— (2007), 'Canada's Anti-dumping and Safeguard Policies: Overt and Subtle Forms of Discrimination', *The World Economy*, 30 (9): 1457–76.

—— (2008), 'Global Antidumping Database, Version 3.0', Department of Economics and International Business School, Brandeis University.

—— (2009), 'China's WTO Entry: Antidumping, Safeguards, and Dispute Settlement,' in Robert Feenstra and Shang-Jin Wei (eds), *China's Growing Role in World Trade* (Chicago: University of Chicago Press).

—— and CROWLEY, M. (2006), 'Policy Externalities: How US Antidumping Affects Japanese Exports to the EU', *European Journal of Political Economy*, 22 (3): 696–714.

—————— (2007), 'Trade Deflection and Trade Depression', *Journal of International Economics*, 72 (1): 176–201.

—— and HOEKMAN, B. (2005), 'WTO Dispute Settlement and the Missing Developing Country Cases: Engaging the Private Sector', *Journal of International Economic Law*, 4: 861–90.

—————— (2008), 'Developing Countries and Enforcement of Trade Agreements: Why Dispute Settlement Is Not Enough', *Journal of World Trade*, 42 (1): 177–203.

—— and McCULLOCH, R. (2007), 'Trade Adjustment in the WTO System: Are More Safeguards the Answer?', *Oxford Review of Economic Policy*, 23 (3): 415–39.

BRAGA, C. (2004), 'Trade-Related Intellectual Property Issues: The Uruguay Round Agreement and its Economic Implications', in K. Maskus (ed.), *The WTO, Intellectual Property Rights and the Knowledge Economy* (Cheltenham and Northampton: Edward Elgar).

BRAGA, C. P., FINK, C. and SEPULVEDA, C. P. (2000), "Intellectual Property Rights and Economic Development", World Bank Working Paper No. 412.

BRAITHWAITE, J. and DRAHOS, P. (2000), *Global Business Regulation* (Cambridge: Cambridge University Press).

—————— (2006), *Information Feudalism: Who Owns the Knowledge Economy?* (London: The New Press).

BRAMBILLA, I., KANDELWAL, A. and SCHOTT, P. (2007), 'China's Experience under the MFA and the ATC', NBER Working Paper No. 13346.

BRANSTETTER, L., FISMAN, R., FOLEY, F. and SAGGI, K. (2007), 'Intellectual Property Rights, Imitation, and Foreign Direct Investment: Theory and Evidence', NBER Working Paper No. 13033.

BRENTON, P. and HOPPE, M. (2006), 'The African Growth and Opportunity Act, Exports, and Development in Sub-Saharan Africa', The World Bank Policy Research Working Paper No. 3996.

BRENTON, P., EDWARDS-JONES, G. and JENSEN, M. (2008), 'Carbon Labeling and Low Income Country Exports: A Look at the Issues', World Bank, mimeo.

BREWER, T. (2007), 'US Climate Change Policies and International Trade Policies: Intersections and Implications for International Negotiations', Georgetown University, mimeo.

BRODA, C., LIMÃO, N. and WEINSTEIN D. (2006), 'Optimal Tariffs: The Evidence', CEPR Discussion Paper No. 5540.

BRONCKERS, M. and VAN DEN BROEK, N. (2005), 'Financial Compensation in the WTO', *Journal of International Economic Law*, 8 (1), 101–26.

BROWN, W. (1950), *The United States and the Restoration of World Trade* (Washington, DC: The Brookings Institution).

BROWN, F. and WHALLEY, J. (1980), 'General Equilibrium Evaluations of Tariff-Cutting Proposals in the Uruguay Round', *Economic Journal*, December: 838–66.

BUSCH, M. and REINHARDT, E. (2001), 'Bargaining in the Shadow of Law: Early Settlements in GATT/WTO Disputes', *Fordham International Law Journal*, 24: 158–72.

———— (2002), 'Testing International Trade Law: Empirical Studies of GATT/WTO Dispute Settlement', in D. Kennedy and James Southwick (eds), *The Political Economy of International Trade Law: Essays in Honor of Robert Hudec* (Cambridge: Cambridge University Press).

———— (2006a), 'Three's a Crowd: Third Parties and WTO Dispute Settlement', *World Politics* 58: 446–77.

———— (2006b), 'Fixing What Ain't Broke: Third Party Rights, Consultations and the DSU', in K. Van der Borght and D. Georgiev (eds), *Reform and Development of the WTO Dispute Settlement System* (London: Cameron May).

———— and SHAFFER, G. (2008), 'Does Legal Capacity Matter? Explaining Patterns of Protectionism in the Shadow of WTO Litigation', mimeo.

BUSSE, M. and GROIZARD, J. (2008), 'FDI, Regulations and Growth', *The World Economy*, 31 (7): 861–86.

CADOT, O. and DE MELO, J. (2007), 'Rules of Origin: The Case of a Single Set Criteria,' *Focus* (Geneva: ICTSD).

———— and TUMURCHUDUR, B. (2007), 'Anti-Dumping Sunset Reviews: The Uneven Reach of WTO Disciplines', CEPR Discussion Paper No. 6502.

CALVIN, L. and KRISSOFF, B. (2005), 'Resolution of the US–Japan Apple Dispute', Report FTS31801, US Department of Agriculture, Economic Research Service, October.

CAENEGEM, W. (2003), 'Registered Geographical Indications. Between Intellectual Property and Rural Policy', *The Journal of World Intellectual Property*, 5: 699–719.

CAMPOS, N. F. and KINOSHITA, Y. (2003), 'Why Does FDI Go Where It Goes? New Evidence from Transition Economies', IMF Working Paper No. 03/228.

CAVES, R. (2007), *Multinational Enterprise and Economic Analysis* (Cambridge: Cambridge University Press).

CHAN, K. (1985), 'The International Negotiation Game: Some Evidence from the Tokyo Round', *Review of Economics and Statistics*, 67: 56–64.

CHANG, W. and WINTERS, L. A. (2002), 'How Regional Blocs Affect Excluded Countries: The Price Effects of MERCOSUR', *American Economic Review*, 92 (4): 889–904.

CHARNOVITZ, S. (2002), 'Should the Teeth Be Pulled? An Analysis of WTO Sanctions', in D. L. M. Kennedy and J. D. Southwick (eds), *The Political Economy of International Trade Law* (Cambridge: Cambridge University Press).

—— and WICKHAM, J. (1995), 'Non-Governmental Organizations and the Original International Trade Regime', *Journal of World Trade*, 29 (5): 111–22.

CHAUDHARI, S., P. GOLDBERG, P. and JIA, P. (2006), 'Estimating the Effects of Global Patent Protection in Pharmaceuticals: A Case Study of Quinolones in India', *American Economic Review*, 96 (5), 1477–514.

CHAUFFOUR, J. P. (2008), *Global Food Price Crisis: Trade Policy Origins and Options* (Washington, DC: World Bank).

CHEN, M. and MATTOO, A. (2008), 'Regionalism in Standards: Good or Bad for Trade?' *Canadian Journal of Economics*, 41 (3): 838–63.

CHEN, C., YANG, J. and FINDLAY, C. (2008), 'Measuring the Effect of Food Safety Standards on China's Agricultural Exports', *Review of World Economics*, 144 (1): 83–106.

CHING, LIM LI and LIN, LIM LI (2006), *Historical Agreement on Documentation for GMO Shipments*, South–North Development Monitor, Penang, Malaysia, March.

CHOI, I. (2003), 'The Long and Winding Road to the Government Procurement Agreement: Korea's Accession Experience', in W. Martin and M. Pangestu (eds), *Options for Global Trade Reform: A View from the Asia Pacific* (Cambridge: Cambridge University Press).

CLAY, J. (2005), *Exploring the Links Between International Business and Poverty Reduction* (Oxford: Oxfam).

CONCONI, P. and PERRONI, C. (2004), 'The Economics of Special and Differential Trade Regimes', CEPR Discussion Paper No. 4508.

CONSTANTINI, V., CRESCENZI, R., DE FILIPPIS, F. and SALVATICI, L. (2007), 'Bargaining Coalitions in the WTO Agricultural Negotiations', *World Economy*, 30: 863–91.

CONYBEARE, J. (1987), *Trade Wars* (Princeton, NJ: Princeton University Press).

CORDEN, M. (1974), *Trade Policy and Economic Welfare*, first edition (Oxford: Oxford University Press).

CORREA, C. (2004), 'Access to Drugs Under TRIPs: A Not So Expeditious Solution', *Bridges* (Geneva: ICTSD, January).

CROOME, J. (1999), *Reshaping the World Trading System: A History of the Uruguay Round* (The Hague: Kluwer Law International).

CURZON, G. (1965), *Multilateral Commercial Diplomacy* (London: Michael Joseph).

—— (1973), *Multilateral Commercial Diplomacy* (Leiden: Sijthoff).

—— and CURZON, V. (1973), 'GATT: Traders' Club', in R. Cox, and H. Jacobson (eds), *The Anatomy of Influence: Decision Making in International Organizations* (New Haven: Yale University Press).

—— —— (1976), 'The Management of Trade Relations in the GATT', *International Economic Relations of the Western World, 1959–71* (London: Random House).

CZUBALA, W., SHEPHERD, B. and WILSON, J.S. (2007), 'Help or Hindrance? The Impact of Harmonized Standards on African Exports', World Bank Policy Research Working Paper No. 4400.

DAM, K. (1970), *The GATT: Law and International Economic Organization* (Chicago: University of Chicago Press).

DAVEY, W. (2005), 'The WTO Dispute Settlement System: The First Decade', *Journal of International Economic Law*, 8: 17–50.

DAVIES, N. (1997), *Europe: A History* (London: Random House).

DAVIES, A. (2008), 'The WTO and Government Procurement', *European Journal of International Law*, 19: 617–20.

DAVIES, S. and MCUINNESS, A. (1982), 'Dumping at Less than Marginal Cost', *Journal of International Economics*, 12: 169–82.

DAYARATNA-BANDA, O. and WHALLEY, J. (2007), 'After the Multifibre Arrangement, the China Containment Agreements', *Asia-Pacific Trade and Investment Review*, 3 (1): 29–54.

DE GORTER, H. and SWINNEN, J. (2002), 'Political Economy of Agricultural Policy', in B. Gardner and G. Rausser (eds), *Handbook of Agricultural Economics*, 2B: 1893–1943 (Amsterdam: Elsevier).

—— JUST, D. and KROPP, J. (2008), 'Cross-Subsidization Due to Infra-Marginal Support in Agriculture: A General Theory and Empirical Evidence', *American Journal of Agricultural Economics*, 90 (1): 42–54.

DE JONG, H. (1968), 'The Significance of Dumping in International Trade', *Journal of World Trade Law*, 2: 162–88.

DE MELO, J. and PANAGARIYA, A. (1993), 'Regionalism and Multilateralism: An Overview', in De Melo, J. and Panagariya, A. (eds), *New Dimensions in Regional Integration* (London: CEPR).

—— and TARR, D. (1992), *A General Equilibrium Analysis of US Foreign Trade Policy* (Cambridge, MA: MIT Press).

—— PANAGARIYA, A. and RODRIK, D. (1993), 'Regional Integration: An Analytical and Empirical Overview', in J. De Melo and A. Panagariya (eds), *New Dimensions in Regional Integration* (Cambridge, MA: Cambridge University Press).

DEARDORFF, A. (1987), 'Safeguards Policy and the Conservative Social Welfare Function', in H. Kierzkowski (ed.), *Protection and Competition in International Trade* (Oxford: Basil Blackwell).

—— (1992), 'Welfare Effects of Global Patent Protection', *Economica* 59 (233): 35–51

—— (1994), 'Third-Country Effects of a Discriminatory Tariff', *The World Economy*, 17: 75–86.

—— (2001), 'International Provision of Trade Services, Trade and Fragmentation', *Review of International Economics*, 9: 233–48.

—— and STERN, R. (1987), 'Current Issues in Trade Policy: An Overview', in Robert Stern (ed.), *US Trade Polices in a Changing World Economy* (Cambridge, MA: MIT Press).

—— and STERN, R. M. (1998), *Measurement of Non-Tariff Barriers* (Ann Arbor, MI: University of Michigan Press).

—— —— (2008), 'Empirical Analysis of Barriers to International Services Transactions and the Consequences of Liberalization', in A. Mattoo, R. M. Stern and G. Zannini (eds), *A Handbook on International Trade in Services* (Oxford: Oxford University Press).

DEBAERE, P. (2005), 'Small Fish—Big Issues: The Effect of Trade Policy on the Global Shrimp Market', CEPR Discussion Paper No. 5254.

DEE, P. (2005), 'A Compendium of Barriers to Trade in Services', Australian National University, mimeo.

DELTAS, G. and EVENETT, S. (1997), 'Quantitative Estimates of the Effects of Preference Policies', in B. Hoekman, and P. Mavroidis (eds), *Law and Policy in Public Purchasing: The WTO Agreement on Government Procurement* (Ann Arbor, MI: University of Michigan Press).

DESTLER, I. M. (2005), *American Trade Politics* (Washington, DC: Institute for International Economics).

DEVEREAUX, C., LAWRENCE, R. and WATKINS, M. (2006), *Case Studies in US Trade Negotiation: Making the Rules*. Washington, DC: Institute for International Economics.

DICKEN, P. (1998), *Global Shift: Transforming the World Economy* (London: Paul Chapman).

DIEBOLD, W. (1952), *The End of the ITO* (Princeton, NJ: Princeton University Press).

DISDIER, A., FONTAGNÉ, L. and MIMOUNI, M. (2007), 'The Impact of Regulations on Agricultural Trade: Evidence from SPS and TBT Agreements', Working Paper No. 2007–04, CEPII.

DIWAN, I. and RODRIK, D. (1991), 'Patents, Appropriate Technology, and North–South Trade', *Journal of International Economics*, 30: 27–47.

DJANKOV, S., FREUND, C. and PHAM, C. (2006), 'Trading on Time', World Bank Policy Research Working Paper 3909.

DOLLAR, D. and KRAAY, A. (2002), 'Growth is Good for the Poor', *Journal of Economic Growth*, 7 (3): 195–225.

—————— (2004), 'Trade, Growth, and Poverty', *Economic Journal*, 114 (493): F22–F49.

DOLZER, R. and SCHREUER, C. (2008), *Principles of International Investment Law* (Oxford: Oxord University Press).

DOWNS, A. (1954), *An Economic Theory of Democracy* (New York: Harper & Row).

DOYLE, M. (1986), *Empires* (Ithaca, NY: Cornell University Press).

DUTTAGUPTA, R. and PANAGARIYA, A. (2007), 'Free Trade Areas and Rules of Origin: Economics and Politics', *Economics and Politics*, 19 (2): 169–90.

EGGER, H., EGGER, P. and GREENAWAY, D. (2006), 'The Structure and Effects of Endogenous Regional Trade Agreements', University of Nottingham Research Paper No. 2006/14.

EGLIN, R. (1987), 'Surveillance of Balance-of-Payments Measures in the GATT', *The World Economy*, 10: 1–26.

EHRENBERG, R. (1994), *Labor Markets and Integrating National Economies* (Washington, DC: Brookings Institution).

ESCHENBACH, F. and HOEKMAN, B. (2006a), 'Services Policy Reform and Economic Growth in Transition Economies, 1990–2004', *Review of World Economics*, 142 (4): 746–64.

—————— (2006b), 'Services Policies in Transition Economies: On the EU and WTO as Commitment Mechanisms', *World Trade Review*, 5 (3): 415–43.

ESTEVADEORDAL, A., FREUND, C. and ORNELAS, E. (2008), 'Does Regionalism Affect Trade Liberalization Towards Non-Members?', *Quarterly Journal of Economics*, 123 (4): 1531–75.

ESTY, D. (1994), *Greening the GATT: Trade, Environment and the Future* (Washington, DC: Institute for International Economics).

ETHIER, W. (1982), 'Dumping', *Journal of Political Economy*, 90: 487–506.

—— (2001a), 'Punishments and Dispute Settlement in Trade Agreements', University of Pennsylvania PIER Working Paper No. 01–021.

—— (2001b), Theoretical Problems in Negotiating Trade Liberalization, *European Journal of Political Economy*, 17, 209–32

—— (2004), 'Political Externalities, Nondiscrimination and a Multilateral World', *Review of International Economics*, 12: 303–20.

—— (2007), 'The Theory of Trade Policy and Trade Agreements: A Critique', *European Journal of Political Economy*, 23: 605–23.

EVANS, J. (1972), *The Kennedy Round in American Trade Policy* (Cambridge, MA: Harvard University Press).

EVENETT, S. (2007*a*), 'Five Hypotheses Concerning the Fate of the Singapore Issues in the Doha Round', *Oxford Review of Economic Policy*, 23 (3): 392–414.

—— (2007*b*), 'Reciprocity and the Doha Round Impasse: Lessons for the Near-Term and After', CEPR Policy Insight No. 11 (London: CEPR, September).

—— and HOEKMAN, B. (2005), 'Government Procurement: Market Access, Transparency and Multilateral Trade Rules', *European Journal of Political Economy*, 21 (1): 163–83.

—— and SHINGAL, A. (2006), 'Monitoring Implementatiom: Japan and the WTO Agreement on Government Procurement', in S. Evenett, and B. Hoekman (eds), *Economic Development and Multilateral Trade Cooperation* (Basingstoke, UK: Palgrave-Macmillan).

—— and VERMULST, E. (2005), 'The Politicisation of EC Anti-Dumping Policy: Member States, Their Votes, and the European Commission', *The World Economy*, 28 (5): 701–17.

—— LEHMAN, A. and STEIL, B. (eds) (2000), *Antitrust Goes Global: What Future for Transatlantic Cooperation?* (Washington, DC: Brookings Institution).

FALVEY, R., FOSTER, N. and GREENAWAY, D. (2006), 'Intellectual Property Rights and Economic Growth', *Review of Development Economics*, 10 (4): 700–19.

FEENSTRA, R. and KAPLAN, S. (1993), 'Fishing Downstream: The Political Economy of Effective Protection', *Canadian Journal of Economics*, 26: 150–8.

—— and KEE, H. (2004), 'On the Measurement of Product Variety in Trade', *American Economic Review*, 94 (2): 145–9.

—— and OLSEN, K. (2004), 'The Spread of Antidumping and the Role of Retaliation in Filings', *Southern Economic Journal*, 72: 877–90.

FEKETEKUTY, G. (1988), *International Trade in Services: An Overview and Blueprint for Negotiations* (Cambridge, MA: Ballinger Publications).

—— (1998), 'Setting the Agenda for Services 2000: The Next Round of Negotiations on Trade in Services', in J. Schott (ed.), *Launching New Global Trade Talks: An Action Agenda* (Washington, DC: Institute for International Economics).

FELBERMAYR, G. and KOHLER, W. (2007), 'Does WTO Membership Make a Difference at the Extensive Margin of World Trade?', CESifo Working Paper No. 1898.

FERNANDEZ, R. and PORTES, J. (1998), 'Returns to Regionalism: An Analysis of the Non-Traditional Gains from Regional Trade Agreements', *World Bank Economic Review*, 12: 197–220.

FINCH, D. and MICHALOPOULOS, C. (1988). 'Development, Trade, and International Organizations', in A. Krueger (ed.), *Development with Trade: LDCs and the International Economy* (San Francisco: Institute for Contemporary Studies).

FINDLAY, R. and O'ROURKE, K. (2007), *Power and Plenty: Trade, War and the World Economy in Second Millennium* (Princeton University Press).

FINDLAY, C. and WARREN, T. (eds) (2000), *Impediments to Trade in Services: Measurement and Policy Implications* (Routledge: Sydney).

FINGER, J. M. (1974), 'Tariff Concessions and the Exports of Developing Countries', *Economic Journal*, 335: 566–75.

—— (1979), 'Trade Liberalization: A Public Choice Perspective', in R. Amacher, G. Haberler, and T. Willett (eds), *Challenges to a Liberal International Economic Order* (Washington, DC: American Enterprise Institute).

—— (1982), 'Incorporating the Gains from Trade into Policy', *World Economy*, 5: 367–77.

—— (1991), 'The GATT as International Discipline Over Trade Restrictions: A Public Choice Approach', in R. Vaubel, and T. Willett (eds), *The Political Economy of International Organizations: A Public Choice Approach* (Boulder, CO: Westview Press).

—— (ed.) (1993a), *Antidumping: How it Works and Who Gets Hurt* (Ann Arbor, MI: University of Michigan Press).

—— (1993b), 'GATT's Influence on Regional Agreements', in J. De Melo, and A. Panagariya (eds), *New Dimensions in Regional Integration* (Cambridge: Cambridge University Press).

—— (2002), 'GATT Experience With Safeguards: Making Economic and Political Sense of the Possibilities that the GATT Allows to Restrict Imports', in B. Hoekman, A. Mattoo, and P. English (eds), *Development, Trade and the WTO: A Handbook* (Washington, DC: The World Bank).

—— and MURRAY, T. (1990), 'Policing Unfair Imports: The United States Example', *Journal of World Trade*, 24: 39–55.

—— and SCHULER, P. (eds) (2004), *Poor People's Knowledge: Promoting Intellectual Property in Developing Countries* (Washington, DC: World Bank).

—— HALL, K. and NELSON, D. (1982), 'The Political Economy of Administered Protection', *American Economic Review*, 72: 452–66.

—— and OLECHOWSKI, A. (eds) (1987), *The Uruguay Round: A Handbook for the Multilateral Trade Negotiations* (Washington, DC: The World Bank).

FINGER, J. and NOGUES, J. (eds) (2006), *Safeguards and Antidumping in Latin American Trade Liberalization: Fighting Fire with Fire* (Washington, DC: World Bank).

—— and SCHULER, P. (2000), 'Implementation of Uruguay Round Commitments: The Development Challenge', *The World Economy*, 23: 511–25.

FINK, C. and MARCHETTI, J. (2008), 'Does WTO Membership Promote FDI?', University of St. Gallen, mimeo.

—— and MASKUS, K. (2006), 'The Debate on Geographical Indications in the WTO,' in R. Newfarmer (ed.), *Trade, Doha, and Development: A Window into the Issues* (Washington, DC: World Bank).

—— and MATTOO, A. (2004), 'Regional Agreements and Trade in Services,' *Journal of Economic Integration*, 19 (4): 742–79

—— and MOLINUEVO, M. (2007), *East Asian Free Trade Agreements in Services: Roaring Tigers or Timid Pandas?* (Washington, DC: World Bank).

—— MATTOO, A. and NEAGU, C. (2001), 'Trade in International Maritime Services: How Much Does Policy Matter?', *World Bank Economic Review*, 16 (1): 81–108.

—— —— and RATHINDRAN, R. (2003), 'An Assessment of Telecommunications Reform in Developing Countries', *Information Economics and Policy*, 15 (4): 443–66.

—— —— —— (2005), 'Assessing the Impact of Communication Costs on International Trade', *Journal of International Economics*, 67 (2): 428–45.

FITCHETT, D. (1987), 'Agriculture', in J. M. Finger and A. Olechowski (eds), *The Uruguay Round: A Handbook on the Multilateral Trade Negotiations* (Washington, DC: The World Bank).

FLIESS, B. and SAUVÉ, P. (1998), 'Of Chips, Floppy Disks and Great Timing: Assessing the WTO Information Technology Agreement' (Paris: Institut Français des Relations Internationales).

FONTAGNÉ, L., VON KIRCHBACH, F. and MIMOUNI, M. (2005), 'An Assessment of Environmentally-Related Non-tariff Measures', *The World Economy*, 28 (10): 1417–39.

Fox, E. (1998), 'International Antitrust: Against Minimum Rules; For Cosmopolitan Principles', *The Antitrust Bulletin*, 43: 5–20.

Francois, J. (1997), 'External Bindings and the Credibility of Reform', in A. Galal and B. Hoekman (eds), *Regional Partners in Global Markets* (London: Centre for Economic Policy Research).

—— (2001), 'Maximizing the Benefits of the Trade Policy Review Mechanism for Developing Countries', in B. Hoekman and W. Martin (eds), *Developing Countries and the WTO* (Oxford: Blackwell).

—— and Manchin, M. (2007), 'Institutions, infrastructure, and trade', World Bank Policy Research Paper 4152.

—— and Martin, W. (2004), 'Commercial policy, bindings and market access' *European Economic Review*, 48: 665–79.

—— and Niels, G. (2004), 'Political Influence in a New Antidumping Regime: Evidence from Mexico', CEPR Discussion Paper 4297.

—— and Reinert, K. (1996), 'The Role of Services in the Structure of Production and Trade: Stylized facts from Cross-Country Analysis', *Asia-Pacific Economic Review*, 2: 35–43.

—— and Rose, A. (2002), 'An Estimate of the Effect of Common Currencies on Trade and Income', *Quarterly Journal of Economics* 117: 437–66.

—— and Wooton, I. (2007), 'Market Structure and Market Access', World Bank Policy Research Working Paper No. 4151.

—— and Wörz, J. (2006), 'MPEC-based panel estimation of non-tariff barriers', University of Linz, mimeo.

—— Wei, S. and Stein, E. (1997), *Regional trading blocs in the world economic system* (Washington, DC: Instititute for International Economics).

—— Hoekman, B. and Manchin, M. (2006), 'Preference Erosion and Multilateral Trade Liberalization', *World Bank Economic Review*, 20 (2): 197–216.

—— —— and Wörz, J. (2008), 'Does Gravity Apply to Intangibles? Trade and FDI in Services', mimeo.

—— Horn, H. and Kaunitz, N. (2008), 'Trading Profiles and Developing Country Participation in the Dispute Settlement System', IFN Working Paper 730 (Stockholm: Research Institute of Industrial Economics).

Fuchs, V. (1968), *The Service Economy* (New York: Columbia University Press).

Gallagher, J. and Robinson, R. (1953), 'The Imperialism of Free Trade', *Economic History Review*, 6: 1–15.

Gallaway, M., Bloningen, B. and Flynn, J. (1999), 'Welfare Cost of the US Antidumping and Countervailing Duty Laws', *Journal of International Economics*, 49: 211–44.

Gardner, B. (1987), 'Causes of US Farm Commodity Programs', *Journal of Political Economy*, 97: 290–310.

Gardner, R. (1969), *Sterling-Dollar Diplomacy: The Origins and the Prospects of Our International Economic Order, second edition* (New York: McGraw-Hill).

Garrett, G. (1992), 'International Cooperation and Institutional Choice: The European Community's Internal Market', *International Organization*, 46: 543–60.

GATT (1974), *Basic Instruments and Selected Documents* (Geneva: GATT).

—— (1985), *Trade Policies for a Better Future* (Leutwiler Report) (Geneva: GATT).

—— (1994*a*), *The Results of the Uruguay Round of Multilateral Trade Negotiations: The Legal Texts* (Geneva: GATT).

—— (1994*b*), *Analytical Index* (Geneva: GATT).

—— (1994*c*), 'The Results of the Uruguay Round: Market Access for Goods and Services' (Geneva: GATT).

GAWANDE, K. and HOEKMAN, B. (2006), 'Lobbying and US Agricultural Policy,' *International Organization*, 60: 527–61 (Summer).

—— and KRISHNA, P. (2004), 'The Political Economy of Trade Policy: Empirical Approaches', in J. Harrigan and E. Kwan Choi (eds), *Handbook of International Trade* (Oxford and MALDEN, MA: Blackwell).

—— —— and ROBBINS, M. (2004), 'Foreign Lobbies and US Trade Policy,' NBER Working Paper No. 10205.

—— —— and OLARREAGA, M. (2005), 'Lobbying Competition over Trade Policy', NBER Working Paper No. 11371.

GAY, D. (2005), 'Vanuatu's Suspended Accession Bid: Second Thoughts?', in P. Gallagher, P. Low, and A. Stoler (eds), *Managing the Challenges of WTO Participation* (Cambridge: Cambridge University Press).

GENERAL ACCOUNTING OFFICE (2007), 'Intellectual Property: US Trade Policy Guidance on WTO Declaration on Access to Medicines May Need Clarification', GAO-07-1198 (28 September).

GIBBON, E. (1776), *The Decline and Fall of the Roman Empire*, 1977 edition (Harmondsworth: Penguin Books).

GINARTE, J. and PARK, W. (1997), 'Intellectual Property Rights and Economic Growth', *Contemporary Economic Policy*, 15 (3): 51–61 (July).

GLASS, A. and SAGGI, K. (2002), 'Intellectual Property Rights and FDI', *Journal of International Economics*, 56: 387–410.

GOLDIN, I., and VAN DER MENSBRUGGHE, D. (1996), 'Agricultural Tariffication under the Uruguay Round', in W. Martin and L.A. Winters (eds), *The Uruguay Round and the Developing Countries* (Cambridge: Cambridge University Press).

GOOTIZ, B. and MATTOO, A. (2008), 'Restrictions on Services Trade and FDI in OECD and Developing Countries', World Bank, mimeo.

GOULD, D. and GRUBEN, W. (1996), 'The Role of Intellectual Property Rights in Economic Growth', *Journal of Development Economics*, 48: 323–50.

—— —— (2004), 'The Role of Property Rights in Economic Growth', in K. Maskus (ed.), *The WTO, Intellectual Property Rights and the Knowledge Economy* (Cheltenham, Northampton: Edward Elgar).

GOWA, J. and KIM, S.-Y. (2005), 'An Exclusive Country Club: The Effects of the GATT on Trade, 1950–1994'. *World Politics*, 57: 453–78.

GREENAWAY, D., MORGAN, W. and WRIGHT, P. (2002), 'Trade Liberalization and Growth in Developing Countries', *Journal of Development Economics*, 67: 229–44.

GREIF, A. (1993), 'Contract Enforceability and Economic Institutions in Early Trade: The Maghribi Traders Coalition', *American Economic Review*, 83: 857–82.

GRINOLS, E. and PERRELLI, R. (2006), 'The WTO Impact on International Trade Disputes: An Event History Analysis', *The Review of Economics and Statistics*, 88 (4): 615–24.

GROSSMAN, G. (1981), 'The Theory of Domestic Content Protection and Content Preference', *Quarterly Journal of Economics*, 96: 583–603.

—— and HELPMAN, E. (1994), 'Protection for Sale', *American Economic Review*, 84: 833–50.

—— —— (2002), *Interest Groups and Trade Policy* (Princeton, NJ: Princeton University Press).

GROSSMAN, G. and LAI, E. (2004), 'International Protection of Intellectual Property', *American Economic Review*, 94 (5): 1635–53 (December).

—— and MAVROIDIS, P. (2003), 'United States—Section 110(5) of the US Copyright Act, Recourse to Arbitration under Article 25 of the DSU', *World Trade Review*, 2 (2): 233–49

—— and SYKES, A. (2005), 'A Preference for Development: The Law and Economics of GSP', *World Trade Review*, 4: 41–68.

———— (2007), 'United States: Definitive Safeguard Measures on Imports of Certain Steel Products', *World Trade Review*, 6 (1): 89–122.

GROUPE-MAC (1988), *Technical Barriers in the EC: An Illustration by Six Industries*, Research on the Costs of Non-Europe, vol. 6 (Brussels: Commission of the European Communities).

GUZMAN, A. and SIMMONS, B. (2005). 'Power Plays and Capacity Constraints: Selection of Defendants in WTO Disputes', *Journal of Legal Studies*, 34: 557–98.

HAMILTON, C. and WHALLEY, J. (1989), 'Coalitions in the Uruguay Round', *Weltwirtschaftliches Archiv*, 125: 547–62.

HARRIGAN, J. and BARROWS, G. (2006), 'Testing the Theory of Trade Policy: Evidence from the Abrupt End of the Multifibre Arrangement', NBER Working Paper No. 12579.

HARRIS, R. (1985), 'Why Voluntary Export Restraints are "Voluntary"', *Canadian Journal of Economics*, 18: 799–809.

HARRISON, G. W., RUTHERFORD, T. F. and TARR, D. G. (1997), 'Quantifying the Uruguay Round', *Economic Journal*, 107: 1405–30.

HAUSMANN, R. and RODRIK, D. (2003), 'Economic Development as Self-Discovery', *Journal of Development Economics*, 72 (2): 603–33.

HEETER, C. (1997), 'Lobbying for Trade Liberalization in Professional Services: The Case of Andersen Worldwide', University of Neuchâtel, mimeo.

HENDERSON, D. (1986), *Innocence and Design: The Influence of Economic Ideas on Policy* (New York: Basil Blackwell).

—— (1999), *The MAI Affair, A Story and Its Lessons* (London: The Royal Institute of International Affairs).

HERIN, J. (1986), 'Rules of Origin and Differences between Tariff Levels in EFTA and in the EC', Occasional Paper No. 13 (Geneva: EFTA).

HERTEL, T. W. and KEENEY, R. (2006), 'What is at Stake: The Relative Importance of Import Barriers, Export Subsidies, and Domestic Support', in K. Anderson and W. Martin (eds), *Agricultural Trade Reform and the Doha Development Agenda* (Basingstoke, UK: Palgrave Macmillan).

HERTEL, T. and WINTERS, A. (eds) (2006), *Poverty and the WTO: Impacts of the Doha Development Agenda* (Basingstoke, UK: Palgrave Macmillan).

HESTERMEYER, H. (2007), *Human Rights and the WTO: The Case of Patents and Access to Medicines* (Oxford: Oxford University Press).

HILLMAN, A. and MOSER, P. (1996), 'Trade Liberalization as Politically Optimal Exchange of Market Access', in M. Canzoneri, W. Ethier, and V. Grilli (eds), *The New Transatlantic Economy* (New York: Cambridge University Press).

HINDLEY, B. (1994), 'Safeguards, VERs and Anti-Dumping Action', in *The New World Trading System: Readings* (Paris: OECD).

HIRSCHMAN, A. (1969), *National Power and the Structure of Foreign Trade* (Berkeley: University of California Press).

—— (1981), *Essays in Trespassing* (London: Cambridge University Press).

HOCKING, B. (1989), 'Determining the Need for Issue-Linkages in Multilateral Trade Negotiations', *International Organization*, 43: 693–714.

—— (1996), 'Assessing the Uruguay Round Agreement on Services', in W. Martin and L. A. Winters (eds), *The Uruguay Round and the Developing Economies* (Cambridge, MA: Cambridge University Press).

—— (1998), 'Using International Institutions to Improve Public Procurement', *World Bank Research Observer*, 13 (2): 249–69.

—— (2002), 'Strengthening the Global Trade Architecture for Development: The Post-Doha Agenda', *World Trade Review*, 1 (1): 23–46.

—— (2005), 'Operationalizing the Concept of Policy Space in the WTO: Beyond Special and Differential Treatment', *Journal of International Economic Law*, 8 (2): 405–24.

—— (2006), 'Liberalizing Trade in Services: A Survey', Policy Research Working Paper No. 4030.

—— (2007), 'Regionalism and Development: The European Neighbourhood Policy and Integration à la Carte', *Journal of International Trade and Diplomacy*, 1 (1): 1–55.

—— and HOWSE, R. (2008), 'EC-Sugar: Cross-Subsidization and the World Trade Organization', *World Trade Review*, 7 (1): 149–78.

—— and JAVORCIK, B. (eds) (2006), *Global Integration and Technology Transfer* (Washington, DC: Palgrave/McMilllan and World Bank).

—— and KOSTECKI, M. (1995), *The Political Economy of the World Trading System: From GATT to WTO* (Oxford: Oxford University Press).

—— and LEIDY, M. (1992), 'Cascading Contingent Protection', *European Economic Review*, 36: 883–92.

—— —— (1993), 'Holes and Loopholes in Integration Agreements: History and Prospects', in K. Anderson, and R. Blackhurst (eds), *Regional Integration and the Global Trading System* (London: Harvester-Wheatsheaf).

—— and MATTOO, A. (2007), 'International Trade: Multilateral Disciplines on Trade in Services', in Andrew Guzman and Alan Sykes (eds), *The Handbook of International Economic Law* (Chicago: University of Chicago Press).

—— and MAVROIDIS, P. (1994), 'Competition, Competition Policy and the GATT', *The World Economy*, 17: 121–50.

—— —— (1996), 'Dumping, Antidumping and Antitrust', *Journal of World Trade*, 30: 27–52.

—— —— (eds) (1997), *Law and Policy in Public Purchasing: The WTO Agreement on Government Procurement* (Ann Arbor, MI: University of Michigan Press).

—— —— (2000), 'WTO Dispute Settlement, Transparency and Surveillance', *The World Economy*, 23: 527–42.

—— —— (2003), 'Economic Development, Competition Policy and the WTO', *Journal of World Trade*, 37 (1): 1–28

—— and MAVROIDIS, P. C. (2007), *The World Trade Organization: Law, Economics and Politics* (London: Routledge).

—— and MCUIRE, S. (eds) (2004), *Trade Politics* (London and New York: Routledge).

—— and MESSERLIN, P. (2000), 'Liberalizing Trade in Services: Reciprocal Negotiations and Regulatory Reform', in P. Sauvé, and R. Stern (eds), *Services 2000: New Directions in Services Trade Liberalization* (Washington, DC: Brookings Institution).

HOCKING, B. and NICITA, A. (2008), 'Trade Policy, Trade Costs and Developing Country Trade', World Bank, mimeo.

——and OLARREAGA, M. (eds) (2007), *Global Trade and Poor Nations: Impacts and Implications of Trade Reform on Poverty* (Washington, DC: Brookings Institution).

——and OZDEN, C. (eds) (2006), *Trade Preferences and Differential Treatment of Developing Countries* (Cheltenham/Northampton: Edward Elgar).

——and SAGGI, K. (2000), 'Assessing the Case for Extending WTO Disciplines on Investment Related Policies', *Journal of Economic Integration*, 15: 588–610.

————(2007), 'Tariff Bindings and Bilateral Cooperation on Export Cartels', *Journal of Development Economics*, 83: 141–56.

——and TRACHTMAN, J. (2008), 'Canada-Wheat: Discrimination, Non-Commercial Considerations and the Right to Regulate Through State Trading Enterprises', *World Trade Review*, 7 (1): 45–66.

——and VINES, D. (2007), 'Multilateral Trade Cooperation: What Next?', *Oxford Review of Economic Policy*, 23 (3): 311–34.

HOEKMAN, B. and WINTERS, L. A. (2007), 'Trade and Employment: Stylized Facts and Research Findings,' in A. Ocampo, K. S. Jomo and S. Khan (eds), *Policy Matters: Economic and Social Policies to Sustain Equitable Development* (New York: Zed Books).

——and WINTERS, A. (2009), 'Multilateralizing Preferential Trade Agreements: A Developing Country Perspective', in R. Baldwin and P. Low (eds), *Multilateralizing Regionalism: Challenges for the Global Trading System* (Cambridge: Cambridge University Press).

——NG, F. and OLARREAGA, M. (2002), 'Eliminating Excessive Tariffs on Exports of Least Developed Countries', *World Bank Economic Review*, 16 (1): 1–22.

——————(2004), 'Reducing Agricultural Tariffs versus Domestic Support: What is More Important for Developing Countries?', *World Bank Economic Review*, 18 (2): 175–204.

——MICHALOPOULOS, C. and WINTERS, L. A. (2004), 'Special and Differential Treatment of Developing Countries: Moving Forward After Cancún', *The World Economy*, 27: 481–506.

——MATTOO, A. and SAPIR, A. (2007), 'The Political Economy of Services Trade Liberalization: A Case for International Regulatory Cooperation?', *Oxford Review of Economic Policy*, 23 (3): 367–91.

——HORN, H. and MAVROIDIS, P. C. (2008), 'Winners and Losers in the WTO Dispute Settlement System', IFN Working Paper No. 769 (Stockholm: Research Institute of Industrial Economics).

HOLMES, T. (1998), 'The Effect of State Policies on the Location of Manufacturing: Evidence from State Borders', *Journal of Political Economy*, 106: 667–705.

HONMA, M. (1993), 'Japan's Agricultural Policy and Protection Growth', in T. Ito and A. O. Krueger (eds), *Trade and Protectionism* (Chicago: University of Chicago Press).

HORN, H. (2006), 'National Treatment in the GATT', *American Economic Review*, 96 (1): 394–404.

——and HOWSE, R. (2008), 'EC—Customs Classification of Frozen Boneless Chicken Cuts', *World Trade Review*, 7 (1): 9–38.

——and LEVINSOHN, J. (2001), 'Merger Policy and Trade Liberalization', *Economic Journal*, 111 (470): 244–76.

—— and MAVROIDIS, P. C. (2001), 'Economic Aspects of the Most-Favored Nation Clause', *European Journal of Political Economy*, 17 (2): 233–79.

—— —— (2004), 'Still Hazy After All These Years: The Interpretation of National Treatment in the GATT/WTO Case Law on Tax Discrimination', *European Journal of International Law*, 15: 39–69.

—— —— (2005), 'United States: Continued Dumping and Subsidy Offset Act of 2000', *World Trade Review*, 4 (3): 525–50.

—— —— (2007), 'A Survey of the Literature on the WTO Dispute Settlement System', CEPR Discussion Paper No. 6020.

—— and MAVROIDIS, P. (2008a), 'The WTO Dispute Settlement Data Set: User's Guide', at www.worldbank.org/trade

—— —— (2008b), 'WTO Dispute Settlement Database', at http://www.worldbank.org/trade/wtodisputes

—— and WEILER, J. (2004), 'European Communities—Measures Affecting Asbestos and Asbestos-Containing Products', in H. Horn and P. Mavroidis (eds), *Principles of International Trade Law: The WTO Case Law of 2001* (Cambridge: Cambridge University Press).

—— MAVROIDIS, P. and NORDSTRÖM, H. (2005), 'Is the Use of the WTO Dispute Settlement System Biased?' in P. Mavroidis and A. Sykes (eds), *The Law and Economics of the WTO Dispute Settlement System* (Edward Elgar Publishing).

—— MAGGI, G. and STAIGER, R. W. (2006), Trade Agreements as Endogenously Incomplete Contracts, NBER Working Paper No. 12745.

—— MAVROIDIS, P., and SAPIR, A. (2008), 'Beyond the WTO: Coverage and Legal Inflation in EU and US Preferential Trade Agreements', Bruegel, mimeo.

HOWSE, R. (2008), 'Pursuing Sustainable Development Startegies: The Case of the Balance of Payment Rules in the WTO', University of Michigan, mimeo.

—— and HORN, H. (2008), 'European Communities—Measures Affecting the Approval and Marketing of Biotech Products', mimeo.

—— and TUERK, E. (2006), 'The WTO Impact on Internal Regulations: A Case Study of the Canada–EC Asbestos Dispute', in G. Bermann and P. Mavroidis (eds), *Trade and Human Health and Safety* (New York: Cambridge University Press).

—— VAN BORK, P. and HEBEFRAND, C. (2006), 'WTO Disciplines and Biofuels' (Washington, DC: International Food and Agricultural Trade Council), at www.agritrade.org

HUDEC, R. (1987), *Developing Countries in the GATT Legal System* (London: Trade Policy Research Centre).

—— (1993), *Enforcing International Trade Law: The Evolution of the Modern GATT Legal System* (New York: Butterworth).

—— (2002), 'The Adequacy of WTO Dispute Settlement Remedies for Developing Country Complainants', in B. Hoekman, A. Mattoo, and P. English (eds), *Development, Trade and the WTO: A Handbook.* (Washington, DC: The World Bank).

HUFBAUER, G. (2007), 'Boeing vs. Airbus: Fighting the Last War', *Handelsblatt* (June 19), at www.iie.com

—— and ADLER, M. (2008), 'The Special Safeguard Mechanism: Possible Solutions to the Impasse', Peterson Institute for International Economics, mimeo.

—— and ELLIOTT, K. A. (1994), *Measuring the Costs of Protection in the Unites States* (Washington, DC: Institute for International Economics).

HULL, C. (1948), *The Memoirs of Cordell Hull*, 2 vols. (New York: Macmillan).

HUNGERFORD, T. (1991), 'GATT: A Cooperative Equilibrium in a Non-Cooperative Trading Regime?', *Journal of International Economics*, 31: 357–69.

IKENSON, D. (2002), 'Steel Trap: How Subsidies and Protectionism Weaken the US Steel Industry', Cato Briefing Paper No. 14.

IMF (2006) 'Article VIII Acceptance by IMF Members: Recent Trends and Implications for the Fund' (Washington, DC: IMF, 26 May).

INGCO, M. (1996), 'Tariffication in the Uruguay Round: How Much Liberalization?', *The World Economy*, 19 (4): 425–47.

IRWIN, D. (1996), *Against the Tide: An Intellectual History of Free Trade* (Princeton, NJ: Princeton University Press).

—— and PAVCNIK, N. (2004), 'Airbus vs. Boeing Revisited: International Competition in the Aircraft Market', *Journal of International Economics*, 64: 223–45.

—— MAVROIDIS, P. and SYKES, A. (2008), *The Genesis of the GATT* (Cambridge: Cambridge University Press).

ISMAIL, F. (2007), *Mainstreaming Development into the WTO: Developing Countries in the Doha Round* (Jaipur: CUTS).

ISO/IES GUIDE 2: (1991), General Terms and Their Definitions Concerning Standardization and Related Activities (Geneva: International Standardization Organization).

IVANIC, M. and MARTIN, W. (2008), 'Implications of Higher Global Food Prices for Poverty in Low-Income Countries', *Agricultural Economics*, December.

JACKSON, J. H. (1969), *World Trade and the Law of GATT* (Indianapolis: Bobbs-Merrill).

—— (1990), *Restructuring the GATT System* (London: Pinter Publishers).

—— (1997), *The World Trading System: Law and Policy of International Economic Relations* (Cambridge, MA: MIT Press).

JAFFEE, S. and HENSON, S. (2004), 'Standards and Agro-Food Exports from Developing Countries: Rebalancing the Debate', World Bank Policy Research Working Paper No. 3348.

JOHNSON, D. G. (1973), *World Agriculture in Disarray* (New York: St. Martin's Press).

JONES, V. (2006), 'WTO: Antidumping Issues in the Doha Development Agenda', Congressional Research Service Report, Washington, DC at: http://www.au.af.mil/au/awc/awc-gate/crs/rl32810.pdf

JOSLING, T. (1977), *Agriculture in the Tokyo Round Negotiations*, Thames Essay no. 10. (Ashford: Headly Brothers for the Trade Policy Research Centre).

—— (1994), 'Agriculture and Natural Resources', in S. Collins, and B. Bosworth (eds), *The New GATT* (Washington, DC: Brookings Institution).

KARACAOVALI, B. and LIMÃO, N. (2008), 'The Clash of Liberalizations: Preferential vs. Multilateral Trade Liberalization in the European Union', *Journal of International Economics*, 74 (2): 299–327.

KEE H., NICITA, A. and OLARREAGA, M. (2008), 'Estimating Trade Restrictiveness Indices', *Economic Journal*, 119 (534): 172–99.

KEESING, D. (1998), *Improving Trade Policy Reviews in the World Trade Organization*, Policy Analyses in International Economics, 52 (Washington, DC: Institute for International Economics, April).

KELLER, W. and SHIUE, C. (2007), 'Tariffs, Trains, and Trade: The Role of Institutions versus Technology in the Expansion of Markets', University of Colorado, mimeo.

KEMP, M. C. (1964), *The Pure Theory of International Trade* (Englewood Cliffs: Prentice-Hall).

KENNETT, M., EVENETT, S. and GAGE, J. (2005), 'Evaluating WTO Accessions: Legal and Economic Perspectives', mimeo.

KEOHANE, R. (1984), *After Hegemony* (Princeton, NJ: Princeton University Press).

—— (1986), 'Reciprocity in International Relations', *International Organization*, 40: 1–27.

KEY, S. (1997), 'Financial Services in the Uruguay Round and the WTO', Occasional Paper No. 54 (Washington, DC: Group of Thirty).

—— (2003), *The Doha Round and Financial Services Negotiations* (Washington, DC: American Enterprise Institute).

KINDLEBERGER, C. (1983), 'Standards as Public, Collective and Private Goods', *Kyklos*, 36: 377–96.

KNETTER, M. and PRUSA, T. (2003), 'Macroeconomic Factors and Antidumping Filings: Evidence from Four Countries', *Journal of International Economics*, 61 (1): 1–17.

KONAN, D. and LA CROIX, S. (2006), 'Have Developing Countries Gained From the Marriage Between Trade Agreements and Intellectual Property Rights?', University of Hawaii-Manoa Economics Working Paper No. 06–5.

—— and MASKUS, K. (2006), 'Quantifying the Impact of Services Liberalization in a Developing Country', *Journal of Development Economics*, 81: 142–62.

KOSTECKI, M. (1979), *East–West Trade and the GATT System* (London: Macmillan Press for the Trade Policy Research Centre).

—— (1982), *State Trading in International Markets* (New York: St. Martin's Press).

—— (1987), 'Export Restraint Agreements and Trade Liberalization', *World Economy*, 10: 425–53.

—— (2000), 'DHL Worldwide Express: Providing Just-in-time Services Across Customs Borders in Central and Eastern Europe', in Y. Aharoni, and L. Nachum (eds), *The Globalization of Services: Some Implications for Theory and Practice* (London and New York: Routledge).

—— (2001), *International Marketing and the Trading System* (Geneva: ITC).

—— (2007), 'Vested Interests and Trade Policy-Making: The Influence of Business and NGOs in Transition and Developing Economies', *Argumenta Oeconomica*, 19 (1): 97–124.

—— and TYMOWSKI, M. J. (1985), 'Customs Duties versus Other Import Charges in the Developing Countries', *Journal of World Trade Law*, 19: 269–86.

KOSTECKI, M. M. (2005), *Business Advocacy in the Global Trading System: How Business Organizations May Shape Trade Policy* (Geneva: International Trade Centre).

KRASNER, S. (1983), 'Structural Causes and Regime Consequences: Regimes as Intervening Variables', in S. Krasner (ed.), *International Regimes* (Ithaca, NY: Cornell University Press).

KRUEGER, A. (1974), 'The Political Economy of the Rent-Seeking Society', *American Economic Review*, 64: 291–303.

—— (1997*a*), 'Free Trade Agreements as Protectionist Devices: Rules of Origin', in J. Melvin, J. Moore, and R. Riezman (eds), *Trade, Theory and Econometrics: Essays in Honor of John S. Chipman* (London: Routledge).

—— (1997*b*), 'International Labor Standards and Trade', in *Annual Bank Conference on Development Economics* (Washington, DC: The World Bank).

—— (1999), 'Trade Creation and Trade Diversion under NAFTA', NBER Working Paper No. 7429.

KRUEGER, A., SCHIFF, M. and VALDES, A. (1988), 'Agricultural Incentives in Developing Countries: Measuring the Effects of Sectoral and Economy-Wide Policies', *World Bank Economic Review*, 2 (3): 255–71.

KUCERA, D. and SARNA, R. (2006), 'Trade Union Rights, Democracy, and Exports: A Gravity Model Approach', *Review of International Economics*, 14 (5): 859–82.

LAFFONT, J. and N'GBO, A. (2000), 'Cross-Subsidies and Network Expansion in Developing Countries', *European Economic Review*, 44: 797–805.

LANJOUW, J. (1998), 'The Introduction of Pharmaceutical Product Patents in India: 'Heartless Exploitation of the Poor and Suffering'?', NBER Working Paper No. 6366.

LAWRENCE, R. (2003), *Crimes and Punishment: Retaliation under the WTO* (Washington, DC: Institute for International Economics).

—— (2006), 'Rulemaking Amidst Growing Diversity: A "Club of Clubs" Approach to WTO Reform and New Issue Selection', *Journal of International Economic Law*, 9(4): 823–35.

—— and LITAN, R. (1991), 'The World Trading System After the Uruguay Round', *Boston University International Law Journal*, 8: 247–76.

LEARY, V. (1996), 'Worker's Rights and International Trade: The Social Clause', in J. Bhagwati and R. Hudec (eds), *Harmonization and Fair Trade: Prerequisite for Free Trade?* (Cambridge, MA: MIT Press).

LEE, D. (2007), 'The Cotton Club: The Africa Group in the Doha Development Agenda,' in Donna Lee and Rorden Wilkinson (eds), *The WTO After Hong Kong* (London: Routledge).

LEIDY, M. (1994a), 'Trade Policy and Indirect Rent-Seeking: A Synthesis of Recent Work', *Economics and Politics*, 6: 97–118.

—— (1994b), 'Quid Pro Quo Restraint and Spurious Injury: Subsidies and the Prospect of CVDs', in A. Deardorff, and R. Stern (eds), *Analytical and Negotiating Issues in the Global Trading System* (Ann Arbor, MI: University of Michigan Press).

—— (1997), 'Macroeconomic Conditions and Pressures for Protection Under Antidumping and Countervailing Duty Laws: Empirical Evidence from the United States', *IMF Staff Papers*, 44 (1): 132–45.

—— and HOEKMAN, B. (1991), 'Spurious Injury as Indirect Rent Seeking: Free Trade under the Prospect of Protection', *Economics and Politics*, 3: 111–37.

—— —— (1993), 'What to Expect from Regional and Multilateral Trade Negotiations: A Public Choice Perspective', in K. Anderson and R. Blackhurst (eds), *Regional Integration and the Global Trading System* (New York: Harvester-Wheatsheaf).

LEVY, P. and SRINIVASAN, T. N. (1996), 'Regionalism and the (Dis)advantage of Dispute Settlement Access', *American Economic Review*, May: 93–8.

LIMÃO, N. (2006), 'Preferential Trade Agreements as Stumbling Blocks for Multilateral Trade Liberalization: Evidence for the United States', *American Economic Review*, 96: 896–914.

—— (2007), 'Are Preferential Trade Agreements with Non-Trade Objectives a Stumbling Block for Multilateral Liberalization?', *Review of Economic Studies*, 74 (3): 821–55.

—— and OLARREAGA, M. (2006), 'Trade Preferences to Small Developing Countries and the Welfare Costs of Lost Multilateral Liberalization', *World Bank Economic Review*, 20 (2): 217–40.

—— and SAGGI, K. (2008a), 'Tariff Retaliation Versus Financial Compensation in the Enforcement of International Trade Agreements', *Journal of International Economics*, 76 (1): 48–60.

—— —— (2008b), 'Asymmetries of Country Size and the Role of Financial Compensation in the Enforcement of International Trade Agreements', mimeo.

—— and VENABLES, A. (2001), 'Infrastructure, Geographical Disadvantage and Transport Costs', *World Bank Economic Review*, 15: 315–43.

LINDERT, P. H. (1991), 'Historical Patterns of Agricultural Policy' in C. P. Timmer (ed.), *Agriculture and the State: Growth, Employment and Poverty* (Ithaca: Cornell University Press).

LLEWELYN, M. (2003), 'Which Rules in World Trade Law—Patents or Plant Variety Protection?', in Thomas Cottier and Petros Mavroidis (eds), *Intellectual Property, Trade, Competition and Sustainable Development* (Ann Arbor, MI: The University of Michigan Press).

LLOYD, PETER (1982), 'State Trading and the Theory of International Trade', in Michel Kostecki (ed.), *State Trading in International Markets*, pp. 117–41 (London: Macmillan).

LOW, P. (1993), *Trading Free: The GATT and US Trade Policy* (New York: Twentieth Century Fund).

—— (1995), *Pre-Shipment Inspection Services* (Washington, DC: The World Bank).

LUKE, D. (2000), 'African Countries and the Seattle Ministerial Meeting: A Personal Reflection', *Journal of World Trade Law*, 34: 39–46.

LYBBERT, T. (2002), 'On Assessing the Cost of TRIPS Implementation', *World Trade Review*, 1: 309–21.

MAERTENS, M. and SWINNEN, J. (2009), 'Trade, Standards, and Poverty: Evidence from Senegal', *World Development*, 37 (1): 161–78.

MAGEE, S., BROCK, W. and YOUNG, L. (1989), *Black Hole Tariffs and Endogenous Policy Theory* (Cambridge: Cambridge University Press).

MAGGI, G. (1999). 'The Role of Multilateral Institutions in International Trade Cooperation', *American Economic Review*, 89 (1): 190–214

—— and RODRIGUEZ-CLARE, A. (1998), 'The Value of Trade Agreements in the Presence of Political Pressures', *Journal of Political Economy*, 106 (3): 574–601.

—— —— (2008), 'A Political Economy Theory of Trade Agreements', *American Economic Review*, 97 (4): 1374–406.

MANN, C. and LIU, X. (2009), 'The Information Technology Agreement: Sui Generis or Model Stepping Stone?', in R. Baldwin and Patrick Low (eds), *Multilateralizing Regionalism* (Cambridge: Cambridge University Press).

MANSFIELD, D. (1994), *Power, Trade and War* (Princeton, NJ: Princeton University Press).

MARCEAU, G. (2009), 'Trade and Labour: Rematching an Old Divorced Couple?', in D. Bethlehem, D. McRae, R. Neufeld, and I. Van Damme (eds), *The Oxford Handbook of International Trade Law* (Oxford: Oxford University Press).

MARTIN, W. (2002), 'Regulatory Standards in the WTO: Comparing Intellectual Property Rights with Competition Policy, Environmental Protection, and Core Labor Standards', *World Trade Review*, 1 (2): 135–52.

—— (2003), 'Observations on the Development Potential of Geographical Indications', Yale University, mimeo.

—— (2005), 'Some Development Implications of WTO Accession Procedures', World Bank, mimeo.

—— (2008), 'Some Support Policy Options for Cotton in China', World Bank, mimeo.

—— and CHEN, Y. (2004), 'Vertical Price Control and Parallel Imports: Theory and Evidence', *Review of International Economics*, 12 (4): 551–70.

—— and MATTOO, A. (2008), 'The Doha Development Agenda: What's on the Table?', Policy Research Working Paper No. 4672.

MARTIN, W. and MESSERLIN, P. (2007), 'Why Is It So Difficult? Trade Liberalization Under the Doha Agenda', *Oxford Review of Economic Policy*, 23 (3): 347–66.

——and PENUBARTI, M. (1995), 'How Trade-Related Are Intellectual Property Rights?', *Journal of International Economics*, 39: 227–48.

——OTSUKI, T. and WILSON, J. (2005), 'The Cost of Compliance with Product Standards for Firms in Developing Countries: An Econometric Study', World Bank Policy Research Working Paper No. 3590.

MASKUS, K. (1997), 'Should Core Labor Standards Be Imposed Through International Trade Policy?', Policy Research Working Paper No. 1817 (Washington, DC: The World Bank).

——(2000), *Intellectual Property Rights in the Global Economy* (Washington, DC: Institute for International Economics).

MASKUS, K. E., WILSON, J. S. and OTSUKI, T. (2001), 'An Empirical Framework for Analyzing Technical Regulations and Trade', in K. E. Maskus and J. S. Wilson (eds), *Quantifying Trade Effect of Technical Barriers: Can It Be Done?* (Ann. Arbor, MI: University of Michigan Press).

MATSUSHITA, M. (2006), 'Major WTO Dispute Cases Concerning Government Procurement', *Asian Journal of WTO & International Health Law and Policy*, 1 (2): 299–316.

MATTOO, A. (2000a), 'Developing Countries in the New Round of GATS Negotiations: Towards a Proactive Role', *The World Economy*, 23 (4): 471–90.

——(2000b), 'Financial Services and the WTO', *The World Economy*, 23 (3): 351–86.

——(2004), 'The Services Dimension of China's Accession to the WTO', in D. Bhattasali, S. Li, and W. Martin (eds), *China and the WTO: Accession, Policy Reform and Poverty Reduction Strategies* (Washington, DC: World Bank).

——(2005), 'Services in a Development Round: Three Goals and Three Proposals', *Journal of World Trade*, 39 1223–38.

——and PAYTON, L. (eds) (2007), *Services Trade and Development: The Experience of Zambia* (Washington D.C.: Palgrave and World Bank).

——and SUBRAMANIAN, A. (2008a), 'Currency Undervaluation and Sovereign Wealth Funds: A New Role for the World Trade Organization', World Bank Policy Research Working Paper No. 4668.

————(2008b), 'Multilateralism Beyond Doha', World Bank Policy Research Working Paper No. 4735.

————(2009), 'From Doha to the Next Bretton Woods: A New Multilateral Trade Agenda', *Foreign Affairs*, 88 (1): 15–26.

——RATHINDRAN, R. and SUBRAMANIAN, A. (2006), 'Measuring Services Trade Liberalization and its Impact on Economic Growth: An Illustration', *Journal of Economic Integration*, 21: 64–98.

MAVROIDIS, P. C. (2000), 'Remedies in the WTO: Between a Rock and a Hard Place', *European Journal of International Law*, 11 (4): 763–813.

——(2006), 'If I Don't Do It Somebody Else Will (or Won't)', *Journal of World Trade*, 40: 187–214.

——and NEVEN, D. (1999), 'Some Reflections on Extraterritoriality in International Economic Law', in *Mélanges offerts à Michel Waelbroeck, Vol 1: International Law* (Brussels: Presse Universitaire de Bruxelles).

MAVROIDIS, P. (2007), *Trade in Goods* (Oxford: Oxford University Press).

McAFFEE, R. P. and McMILLAN, J. (1989), 'Government Procurement and International Trade', *Journal of International Economics*, 26: 291–308.

McCALMAN, P. (2001), 'Reaping What You Sow: An Empirical Analysis of International Patent Harmonization', *Journal of International Economics*, 55: 161–86.

McMILLAN, J. (1988), 'A Game-Theoretic View of International Trade Negotiations', in J. Whalley (ed.), *Rules Power and Credibility* (London: University of Western Ontario).

—— (1993), 'Does Regional Integration Foster Open Trade? Economic Theory and GATT's Article XXIV', in K. Anderson and R. Blackhurst (eds), *Regional Integration and the Global Trading System* (London: Harvester-Wheatsheaf).

MEADE, J. (1940), *The Economic Basis of Durable Peace* (London: G. Allen & Unwin Ltd).

MELITZ, M. (2003), 'The Impact of Trade on Intraindustry Reallocations and Aggregate Industry Productivity', *Econometrica* 71: 1695–725.

MESSERLIN, P. (1981), 'The Political Economy of Protection: The Bureaucratic Case', *Weltwirtschaftliches Archiv*, 117: 469–96.

—— (1989), 'The EC Antidumping Regulations: A First Economic Appraisal, 1980–85', *Weltwirtschaftliches Archiv*, 125: 563–87.

—— (1990), 'Antidumping Regulations or Pro-Cartel Law? The EC Chemical Cases', *The World Economy*, 13: 465–92.

—— (1998), 'Technical Regulations and Standards in the EU', World Bank, Memo.

—— (2000), 'Antidumping and Safeguards', in J. Schott (ed.), *The WTO After Seattle* (Washington, DC: Institute for International Economics).

—— (2001), *Measuring the Costs of Protection in Europe* (Washington, DC: Institute for International Economics).

—— (2008*a*), 'Walking a Tightrope: World Trade in Manufacturing and the Benefits of Binding', GMF Policy Brief.

—— (2008*b*), 'Reviving the Doha Round: The Agenda for the Developed Countries,' in A. Deardorff, P. Dee, P. Messerlin, C. Findlay, R. Stern, and J. Whalley, *Monitoring International Trade Policy: A New Agenda for Reviving the Doha Round* (London: CEPR and Kiel Institute).

—— and NOGUCHI, Y. (1991), 'The EC Antidumping and Anti-Circumvention Regulations: A Costly Exercise in Futility', Institut d'Etudes Politiques, mimeo.

—— and ZARROUK, J. (2000), 'Trade Facilitation: Technical Regulations and Customs Procedures', *The World Economy*, 23: 577–94.

MICHALOPOULOS, C. (2001), *Developing Countries in the WTO* (Houndmills, Basingstoke: Palgrave).

MIKESELL, R. F. (1951), 'Negotiating at Bretton Woods, 1944', in R. Dennett, and J. Jonson (eds), *Negotiating with the Russians* (Boston: Princeton University Press).

MILGROM, P. D. N. and WEINGAST, B. (1990), 'The Role of Institutions in the Revival of Trade: The Law Merchant, Private Judges, and the Champagne Fairs', *Economics and Politics*, 2: 1–23.

MILL, J. S. (1848), *Principles of Political Economy, With Some of Their Applications to Social Philosophy*, W. J. Ashley (ed.) (1961) (New York: Kelley).

MILWARD, A. (1992), *The European Rescue of the Nation State* (Berkeley: University of California Press).

MITCHELL, D. (2005), 'Sugar Policies: An Opportunity for Change', in A. Aksoy and J. Beghin (eds), *Global Agricultural Trade and Developing Countries* (Washington, DC: The World Bank).

—— (2008), 'A Note on Rising Food Prices', Policy Research Working Paper No. 4682 (Washington, DC: World Bank).

MITCHELL, D. (1969), *An Essay on the Early History of the Law Merchant* (New York: Burt Franklin Press).

MOENIUS, J. (2004), 'Information versus Product Adaptation: The Role of Standards in Trade', International Business and Markets Research Center Working Paper, Northwestern University.

MOORE, M. (2006*a*), 'US Facts-Available Antidumoing Decisions: An Empirical Analysis', *European Journal of Political Economy*, 22: 639–52.

—— (2006*b*), 'An Econometric Analysis of US Antidumping Sunset Review Decisions', *Weltwirtschaftliches Archiv*, 142: 122–50.

MORAN, T. (1998), *Foreign Direct Investment and Development* (Washington, DC: Institute for International Economics).

—— (2002), *Strategy and Tactics for the Doha Round: Capturing the Benefits of Foreign Direct Investment* (Manila, Asian Development Bank).

MURPHY, C. (1994), *International Organization and Industrial Change: Global Governance Since 1850* (New York: Oxford University Press).

NARLIKAR, A. and ODELL, J. (2006), 'The Strict Distributive Strategy for a Bargaining Coalition: The Like Minded Group in the WTO, 1998–2001', in J. Odell (ed.), *Negotiating Trade: Developing Countries in the WTO and NAFTA* (Cambridge: Cambridge University Press).

—— and TUSSIE, D. (2004), 'The G20 at the Cancun Ministerial: Developing Countries and their Evolving Coalition in the WTO', *The World Economy*, 27 (7): 947–66.

NELSON, D. (2006), 'The Political Economy of Antidumping: A Survey', *European Journal of Political Economy*, 22: 554–90.

NEVEN, D. (2001), 'How Should Protection Be Evaluated In Article III GATT Disputes?', *European Journal of Political Economy*, 17: 421–44.

NG, F. and YEATS, A. (1999), 'Production Sharing in East Asia: Who Does What for Whom and Why?', World Bank Policy Research Working Paper No. 2197, Washington, DC

—— —— (2003), 'Major Trade Trends in East Asia: Implications for Regional Cooperation and Growth', World Bank Policy Research Working Paper No. 3084.

NIELS, G. and TEN KATE, A. (2006), 'Antidumping Policy in Developing Countries: Safety Valve or Obstacle to Free Trade?', *European Journal of Political Economy*, 22: 618–38.

NJINKEU, D. and CAMERON, H. (eds) (2008), *Aid for Trade and Development* (Cambridge: Cambridge University Press).

NOGUES, J. (1998), 'The Linkages of the World Bank with the GATT/WTO', in A. Krueger (ed.), *The WTO as an International Organization* (Chicago: University of Chicago Press).

—— OLECHOWSKI, A. and WINTERS, L.A. (1986), 'Extent of Nontariff Barriers to Industrial Countries' Imports', *World Bank Economic Review*, 1: 181–99.

NORDSTROM, H. and SHAFFER, G. (2007), 'Access to Justice in the WTO: The Case for a Small Claims Procedure', ICTSD Issue Paper, Geneva.

NORDSTRÖM, H. and S. VAUGHAN (1999), *Trade and Environment* (Geneva: WTO).

NORTH, D. (1990), *Institutions, Institutional Change and Economic Performance* (Cambridge: Cambridge University Press).

ODELL, J. (2002), 'The Seattle Impasse and its Implications for the WTO', in Daniel L. M. Kennedy and James D. Southwick (eds), *The Political Economy of International Trade Law: Essays in Honor of Robert Hudec* (Cambridge: Cambridge University Press).

—— (2005), 'Chairing a WTO Negotiation', *Journal of International Economic Law*, 8 (2): 425–48.

——(ed.) (2006), *Negotiating Trade: Developing Countries in the WTO and NAFTA* (Cambridge: Cambridge University Press).

——(2007), 'Growing Power Meets Frustration in the Doha Round's First Four Years', in L. Crump and S. J. Maswood (eds), *Developing Countries and Global Trade Negotiations* (London: Routledge).

——(2009), 'Breaking Deadlocks in International Regime Negotiations: The WTO, Seattle and Doha', *International Studies Quarterly,* forthcoming.

OECD (1993), 'Industrial Policy in OECD Countries', *Annual Review 1992* (Paris: OECD).

OLARREAGA, M. and Ç. OZDEN (2005), 'AGOA and Apparel: Who Captures the Tariff Rent in the Presence of Preferential Market Access?', *The World Economy,* 28 (1): 63–77.

OLSON, M. (1965), *The Logic of Collective Action: Public Goods and the Theory of Groups* (Cambridge, MA: Harvard University Press).

OLSON, K. (2004), 'Subsidizing Rent Seeking: Antidumping Protection and the Byrd Amendment', American University, mimeo.

——and LIEBMAN, B. (2005), 'The Returns to Rent-Seeking: Campaign Contributions, Firm Subsidies and the Byrd Amendment', mimeo.

O'ROURKE, K. and WILLIAMSON, J. (1999), *Globalization and History: The Evolution of a 19th Century Mid-Atlantic Economy* (Cambridge, MA: MIT Press).

OSTRY, S. (2002), 'The Uruguay Round North–South Bargain: Implications for Future Negotiations', in D. Kennedy and J. Southwick (eds), *The Political Economy of International Trade Law: Essays in honor of Robert E. Hudec* (Cambridge: Cambridge University Press).

OTSUKI, T., WILSON, J. and SEWADEH, M. (2001), 'What Price Precaution? European Harmonization of Aflatoxin Regulations and African Groundnut Exports', *European Review of Agricultural Economics,* 28 (3), 263–84.

OYE, K. (1992), *Economic Discrimination and Political Exchange: World Political Economy in the 1930s and 1980s* (Princeton, NJ: Princeton University Press).

PAARLBERG, R. L. (1997), 'Agricultural Policy Reform and the Uruguay Round: Synergistic Linkage in a Two-Level Game?', *International Organization,* 51: 413–44.

PACK, H. and SAGGI, K. (2005), 'The Case for Industrial Policy: A Critical Survey', *World Bank Research Observer,* 21 (2): 267–97.

PAGE, S. (ed.) (2006), *Trade and Aid: Partners or Rivals in Development Policy?* (London: Cameron May).

——and KLEEN, P. (2005), 'Special and Differential Treatment of Developing Countries in the World Trade Organization', *Global Development Studies No. 2* (Stockholm: Report for the Ministry of Foreign Affairs, Sweden).

PAJUNEN, K. (2008), 'Institutions and Inflow of Foreign Direct Investment: A Fuzzy-Set Analysis', *Journal of International Business Studies,* 39 (4): 652–69.

PALMETER, N. D. (1995), 'United States Implementation of the Uruguay Round Antidumping Code', *Journal of World Trade,* 29 (3).

——and MAVROIDIS, P. C. (2004), *Dispute Settlement In The WTO, Practice And Procedure,* second edition (Cambridge: Cambridge University Press).

PANAGARIYA, A. (2000), 'Preferential trade liberalization: the traditional theory and new developments', *Journal of Economic Literature,* 37 (June): 287–331

——(2002), 'Developing Countries at Doha: A Political Economy Analysis', *The World Economy,* 25 (9): 1205–33.

PATTERSON, G. (1966), *Discrimination in International Trade: The Policy Issues, 1945–1965* (Princeton, NJ: Princeton University Press).

PAUWELYN, J. (2005), 'Enforcement and Countermeasures in the WTO: Rules are Rules—Towards a More Collective Approach', *American Journal of International Law*, 94: 335–47.

PAVCNIK, N. (2002), 'Trade Liberalization, Exit, and Productivity Improvements: Evidence from Chilean Plants', *The Review of Economic Studies*, 69: 245–76.

PEDERSEN, P. (2006), 'The WTO Decision-Making Process and Internal Transparency', *World Trade Review*, 5 (1): 103–31.

PELKMANS, J. (2007), 'Mutual Recognition in Goods. On Promises and Disillusions', *Journal of European Public Policy*, 14 (5): 699–716.

PENROSE, E. (1953), *Economic Planning for the Peace* (Princeton, NJ: Princeton University Press).

PETERS, G. (1995), *The Politics of Bureaucracy* (London: Longman Publishers).

PETERSMANN, E. (1997), *The GATT/WTO Dispute Settlement System* (Kluwer: Deventer).

PETERSON, E. and ORDEN, D. (2005), 'Effects of Tariffs and Sanitary Barriers on High- and Low-Value Poultry Trade', *Journal of Agricultural and Resource Economics*, 30 (1): 109–27.

————(2007), 'Avocado Pests and Avocado Trade', *American Journal of Agricultural Economics*, 90 (2): 321–35.

PHILBRICK, M. (2008), 'Risk Assessment and the SPS Agreement: A Case for Bounded Objectivity, Risk/Benefit Analysis, and Normative Subsidiarity', mimeo.

PIÉROLA, F. and HORLICK, G. (2007), 'WTO Dispute Settlement and Dispute Settlement in the 'North–South' Agreements of the Americas: Considerations for Choice of Forum', *Journal of World Trade*, 41 (5): 885–908.

POLLARD, S. (1974), *European Economic Integration, 1815–1970* (London: Thames and Hudson).

POMFRET, R. (2007), 'Is Regionalism an Increasing Feature of the World Economy?', *World Economy*, 30: 923–47.

PORGES, A. (2000), 'The Banana War: Whose Market Access?', The World Bank, Washington, DC, mimeo.

PREBISCH, R. (1952), 'The Economic Development of Latin America and Its Principal Problems', *Economic Bulletin for Latin America*, 7: 1–22.

PREEG, E. (1970), *Traders and Diplomats* (Washington, DC: Brookings Institution).

PROWSE, S. (2006), 'Aid for Trade—Increasing Support for Trade Adjustment and Integration: A Proposal', in S. Evenett and B. Hoekman (eds), *Economic Development and Multilateral Cooperation* (Washington, DC: Palgrave-MacMillan and World Bank).

PRUSA, T. (1992), 'Why Are So Many Antidumping Petitions Withdrawn?', *Journal of International Economics*, 33: 1–20.

————(2006), 'Preferential Trade Agreements and the Incidence of Antidumping Disputes', Rutgers University, mimeo.

PUTNAM, R. D. (1988), 'Diplomacy and Domestic Politics: The Logic of Two-Level Games', *International Organization*, 42: 427–60.

RAIFFA, H. (1983), *The Art and Science of Negotiation* (Cambridge, MA: Harvard University Press).

RAMSEY, F. (1927), 'A Contribution to the Theory of Taxation', *Economic Journal*, March.

RATTIGAN, A. (1986), *Industry Assistance: The Inside Story* (Melbourne: Melbourne University Press).

RATTON SANCHEZ, M. (2006), 'Brief Observations of the Mechanisms for NGO Participation in the WTO', *International Journal on Human Rights*, 3 (4): 103–25.

REDDY, R. (2000), 'The Meaning of Seattle', *The Hindu*, at www.indiaserver.com

REGAN, D. (2006), 'What are Trade Agreements For?', *Journal of International Economic Law*, 9 (4): 951–88.

—— (2007). 'The Meaning of 'Necessary' in GATT Article XX and GATS Article XIV: The Myth of Cost–Benefit Balancing', *World Trade Review*, 6: 347–69.

REGE, V. (1999), 'Developing Country Participation in Negotiations Leading to the Adoption of WTO Agreement on Customs Evaluation', *World Competition*, 22 (1) (March).

REINHARDT, E. (2000), 'Aggressive Multilateralism: The Determinants of GATT/WTO Dispute Initiation 1948–1998', Emory University, mimeo.

—— (2001), 'Adjudication Without Enforcement', *Journal of Conflict Resolution*, 45: 174–95.

RICUPERO, R. (1998), 'Integration of Developing Countries into the Multilateral Trading System', J. Bhagwati and A. Hirsch (eds), *The Uruguay Round and Beyond: Essays in Honor of Arthur Dunkel* (Ann Arbor, MI: University of Michigan Press).

RODRIGUEZ, F. and RODRIK, D. (2001), 'Trade Policy and Economic Growth: A Skeptic's Guide to the Cross-National Evidence', *NBER Macroeconomics Annual 2000*, 261–324 (Cambridge, MA: MIT Press).

RODRIK, D. (1987), 'The Economics of Export-Performance Requirements', *Quarterly Journal of Economics*, 102: 633–50.

—— (1994), 'Comments on Maskus and Eby-Konan', in A. Deardorff, and R. Stern (eds), *Analytical and Negotiating Issues in the Global Trading System* (Ann Arbor, MI: University of Michigan Press).

—— (1995), 'The Political Economy of Trade Policy', in G. Grossman, and K. Rogoff (eds), *Handbook of International Economics, Vol III* (Amsterdam: North Holland).

—— (1997), 'TFPG Controversies, Institutions and Economic Performance in East Asia', CEPR Discussion Paper No. 1587 (May).

—— (2004), 'Industrial Policy for the Twenty-First Century', CEPR Discussion Paper No. 4767.

—— (2005), 'The Global Governance of Trade as if Development Really Mattered', in P. King and S. King (eds), *International Economics and International Economic Policy* (New York: McGraw-Hill).

ROESSLER, F. (1985), 'The Scope, Limits and Function of the GATT Legal System', *The World Economy*, 8: 289–98.

—— (1998), 'Domestic Policy Objectives and the Multilateral Trade Order', in A. Krueger (ed.), *The WTO as an International Organization* (Chicago: University of Chicago Press).

ROLLO, J. (2007), 'The Challenge of Negotiating RTA's for Developing Countries: What Could the WTO do to Help?', in R. Baldwin and P. Low (eds), *Multilateralising Regionalism* (Cambridge: Cambridge University Press).

—— and WINTERS, L. A. (2000), 'Subsidiarity and Governance Challenges for the WTO: The Examples of Environmental and Labour Standards', *The World Economy* (April).

ROMALIS, J. (2005), 'NAFTA's and CUSFTA's Impact on International Trade', NBER Working Paper No. 11059.

ROSE, A. (2004), 'Do We Really Know That the WTO Increases Trade?', *American Economic Review*, 94 (1): 98–114.

Rose, A. (2005), 'Which International Institutions Promote International Trade?', *Review of International Economics*, 13 (4): 682–98.

Roy, M., Marchetti, J. and Lim, H. (2007), 'Services Liberalization in the New Generation of Preferential Trade Agreements: How Much Further than the GATS?', *World Trade Review*, 6 (2): 1455–93.

Runge, F. and von Witzke, H. (1990), 'European Community Enlargement and Institutional Choice in the Common Agricultural Policy', *American Journal of Political Science*, 34 (1): 254–68.

Rushford, G. (2005), 'America Dumps on Free Trade', *Far Eastern Economic Review*, 168.

Sachs, J. and Warner, A. (1995), 'Economic Reform and the Process of Global Integration', *Brookings Papers on Economic Activity*, 1: 1–95.

Sadikov, A. (2007), 'Border and Behind-the-Border Trade Barriers and Country Exports,' IMF Working Paper No. 07/292.

Saggi, K. (2002), 'Trade, Foreign Direct Investment, and International Technology Transfer: A Survey', *World Bank Research Observer*, 17 (2): 191–235.

—— (2009), 'The MFN Clause, Welfare, and Multilateral Cooperation between Countries of Unequal Size', *Journal of Development Economics*, 88 (1): 132–43.

—— and Sara, N. (2008), 'National Treatment at the WTO: The Roles of Product and Country Heterogeneity', *International Economic Review*, 49: 1367–96.

—— and Sengul, F. (2008), 'On the Emergence of an MFN Club: Equal Treatment in an Unequal World', *Canadian Journal of Economics*, 42 (1): 267–99.

—— and Yildiz, H.M. (2005), 'An Analysis of the MFN Clause under Asymmetries of Cost and Market Structure', *Canadian Journal of Economics*, 38 (1): 242–54.

—— and Yildiz, H. (2008), 'Bilateralism, multilateralism, and the quest for global free trade', Southern Methodist University, mimeo.

Sampson, G. (1987), 'Safeguards', in J. M. Finger, and A. Olechowski (eds), *The Uruguay Round: A Handbook for the Multilateral Trade Negotiations* (Washington, DC: The World Bank).

—— and Snape, R. (1985), 'Identifying the Issues in Trade in Services', *The World Economy*, 8: 171–81.

Samuelson, W. (1985), 'A Comment on the Coase Theorem', in Alvin Roth (ed.), *Game Theoretic Models of Bargaining* (Cambridge, MA: Cambridge University Press).

Sapir, A. (1995), 'Trade Liberalization and the Harmonization of Social Policies: Lessons from European Integration', in J. Bhagwati and R. Hudec (eds), *Fair Trade and Harmonization: Prerequisites for Free Trade?, Vol. 1 Economic Analysis* (Cambridge, MA: MIT Press).

—— and Trachtman, J. (2008), 'Subsidization, Price Suppression and Expertise: Causation and Precision in Upland Cotton', *World Trade Review*, 7 (1): 183–209.

Schattschneider, E. (1935), *Politics, Pressures, and the Tariff* (New York: Arno Press).

Schatz, H. and Venables, A. (2000), 'The Geography of International Investment', Policy Research Paper No. 2338 (Washington, DC: World Bank).

Schelling, T. (1978), *Micromotives and Macrobehaviour* (New York: W.W. Norton).

Schiff, M. and Winters, L. A. (2003), *Regional Integration and Development* (Washington, DC: World Bank).

Schmitz, J. A. Jr. (1996), 'The Role of Public Enterprises: How Much Does It Differ Across Countries?', *Federal Reserve Bank of Minneapolis Quarterly Review*, 20: 2–15.

SCHNEIDER, P. (2005), 'International Trade, Economic Growth and Intellectual Property Rights: A Panel Data Study of Developed and Developing Countries', *Journal of Development Economics*, 78 (2): 529–47.

SCHNEPF, R. (2008), 'Brazil's WTO Case Against the US Cotton Program', *CRS Report* RS22187, Order Code RL32571, Washington, DC.

SCHOLTE, J., O'BRIEN, A. and WILLIAMS, M. (2004), 'The World Trade Organization and Civil Society', in B. Hocking, and S. McGuire (eds), *Trade Politics* (London and New York: Routledge).

SCHOTT, J. (ed.) (1989), *Free Trade Areas and US Trade Policy* (Washington, DC: Institute for International Economics).

—— and BUURMAN, J. (1994), *The Uruguay Round: An Assessment* (Washington, DC: Institute for International Economics).

—— and WATAL, J. (2000), 'Decision-Making in the WTO', *International Economic Policy Brief 00-2* (Washington, DC: Institute for International Economics).

SCHWARTZ, W. and SYKES, A. (1997). 'The Economics of the Most Favored Nation Clause,' in J. Bhandani and A. Sykes (eds), *Economic Dimensions in International Law* (Cambridge: Cambridge University Press).

SCOTT, J. (2006), 'Cooperative Regulation in the WTO: The SPS Committee,' Global Law WP 03/06, New York University.

SECO and S. EVENETT (eds) (2003), 'The Singapore Issues and the World Trading System: The Road to Cancun and Beyond', Swiss State Secretariat for Economic Affairs, June.

SELL, S. (2007), 'Intellectual Property and the Doha Development Agenda', in D. Lee and R. Wilkinson (eds), *The WTO After Hong Kong* (London: Routledge).

SEMERJIAN, H. and BEARY, E. (2001), 'Mutual Recognition of Measurements: Potential Impact on International Trade in IVDs', *IVD Technology*, May.

SHAFFER, G. (2003), *Defending Interest: Public–Private Partnerships in WTO Litigation* (Washington, DC: Brookings).

—— (2004), 'Recognizing Public Goods in WTO Dispute Settlement: Who Decides Who Decides? The Case of TRIPS and Pharmaceutical Patent Protection', *Journal of International Economic Law*, 7 (2): 459–82.

—— (2006), 'The Challenges of WTO Law: Strategies for Developing Country Adaptation', *World Trade Review*, 5 (2): 177–98.

SHEPHERD, B. (2007), 'Product Standards, Harmonization, and Trade: Evidence from the Extensive Margin', World Bank Policy Research Working Paper No. 4390.

SHERWOOD, R. (1990), *Intellectual Property and Economic Development* (Boulder, CO: Westview Press).

SIDAK, J. G. and SINGER, H. (2004), 'Uberregulation Without Economics: The World Trade Organization's Decision in the US–Mexico Arbitration on Telecommunications Services', *Fed Comm LJ* 57: 1–61.

SIHANYA, B. (2005), 'Patents, Parallel Imports and Compulsory Licensing of HIV/AIDS Drugs: Experience of Kenya', in P. Gallagher, P. Low and A. Stoler (eds) *Managing the Challenges of WTO Participation*, pp. 284–99 (Cambridge: Cambridge University Press).

SINGER, H. (1950), 'US Foreign Investment in Underdeveloped Areas, the Distribution of Gains Between Investing and Borrowing Countries', *American Economic Review*, 40: 473–85.

SKAGGS, D. (2004), 'How Can Parliamentary Participation in WTO Rule-Making and Democratic Control be Made More Effective in the WTO?', *Journal of International Economic Law*, 7 (3): 656–85.

SMITH, P. (2001), 'How Do Foreign Patent Rights Affect US Exports, Affiliate Sales, and Licenses?', *Journal of International Economics*, 55 (2): 411–39 (December).

SNAPE, R. (1987), 'The Importance of Frontier Barriers', in H. Kierzkowski (ed.), *Protection and Competition in International Trade* (London: Basil Blackwell).

—— (1991), 'International Regulation of Subsidies', *The World Economy*, 14: 139–64.

—— (1993), 'History and Economics of GATT's Article XXIV', in K. Anderson, and R. Blackhurst (eds), *Regional Integration and the Global Trading System* (London: Harvester-Wheatsheaf).

—— ADAMS, J. and MORGAN, D. (1993), *Regional Trading Arrangements: Implications and Options for Australia* (Canberra: Australian Government Publishing Service).

SOLOAGA, I. and WINTERS, L.A. (2001), 'Regionalism in the Nineties: What Effect on Trade?', *North American Journal of Economics and Finance*, 12: 1–29.

SPINANGER, D. (1999), 'Faking Liberalization and Finagling Protection: The ATC at its Best' (Washington, DC: The World Bank) at www.worldbank.org/trade

SPRIGGS, J. (1991), 'Towards an International Transparency Institution: Australian Style', *The World Economy*, 14: 165–80.

SRINIVASAN, T. N. (1998), *Developing Countries and the Multilateral Trading System: From GATT to the Uruguay Round and Beyond* (New York: Harper Collins).

—— (2007), 'Saving Doha or Saving the WTO?', Yale University, mimeo.

STAIGER, R. W. and TABELLINI, G. (1987), 'Discretionary Trade Policy and Excessive Protection', *American Economic Review*, 77 (5): 823–37.

STAPLES, B. R. (2002), 'Trade Facilitation: Improving the Invisible Infrastructure', in B. Hoekman, A. Mattoo and P. English (eds), *Development, Trade and the WTO: A Handbook* (Washington, DC: The World Bank)

STERN, R. M. (2000), 'Labor Standards and Trade', in M. Bronckers and R. Quick (eds), *World Trade Law: Essays in Honor of John Jackson* (The Hague: Kluwer Law International).

STERN, R. and HOEKMAN, B. (1987), 'The Codes Approach', in J. M. Finger, and A. Olechowski (eds), *The Uruguay Round: A Handbook for the Multilateral Trade Negotiations* (Washington, DC: The World Bank).

—— and TERRELL, K. (2003), 'Labor Standards and the World Trade Organization: A Position Paper', University of Michigan, August.

STEVENS, C. (2002), 'The Future of SDT for Developing Countries in the WTO,' Institute for Development Studies, Sussex, mimeo (May).

—— and KENNAN, J. (2005), 'EU–ACP Economic Partnership Agreements: The Effects of Reciprocity', Institute for Development Studies briefing paper.

STIGLITZ, J. (2000), 'Two Principles for the Next Round, or, How to Bring Developing Countries in from the Cold', *The World Economy*, 23: 437–54.

SUBRAMANIAN, A. (2006), 'TRIPs, Medicines and Patents', mimeo.

—— and WEI, S. (2007), 'The WTO Promotes Trade, Strongly but Unevenly', *Journal of International Economics*, 72 (1): 151–75

SUMNER, D. A. (2006), 'Reducing Cotton Subsidies: The DDA Cotton Initiative', in K. Anderson and W. Martin (eds) *Agricultural Trade Reform and the Doha Round Agenda* (New York: Palgrave Macmillan).

SUTHERLAND, P., SEWELL, J. and WEINER, D. (2001), 'Challenges Facing the WTO and Policies to Address Global Governance', in G. Sampson (ed.) *The Role of the World Trade Organization in Global Governance*, pp. 81–112 (New York: United Nations University Press).

—— *et al.* (2004), 'The Future of the WTO: Addressing Institutional Challenges in the New Millennium' (Geneva: WTO).

SYKES, A. (1995), *Product Standards for Internationally Integrated Goods Markets* (Washington, DC: Brookings Institution).

—— (2003), 'The Safeguards Mess: A Critique of the WTO Jurisprudence', *World Trade Review*, 2: 261–304.

TAKACS, W. E. (1981), 'Pressures for Protectionism: An Empirical Analysis', *Economic Inquiry*, 19: 687–93.

TANG, M. and WEI, S. (2006), 'Is Bitter Medicine Good for You? The Economic. Consequences of WTO/GATT Accessions', IMF, mimeo.

TARR, D. (2007), 'Russian WTO Accession: What Has Been Accomplished, What Can Be Expected', Policy Research Working Paper No. 4428, The World Bank.

TASLIM, M. A. (2006), 'Dispute Settlement in the WTO and Least Developed Countries: The Case of India's Antidumping Duties on Lead Acid Battery Imports from Bangladesh', ICTSD, mimeo.

TINBERGEN, J. (1954), *International Economic Integration* (Amsterdam: Elsevier).

TOLLISON, R. and WILLETT, T. (1979), 'An Economic Theory of Mutually Advantageous Issue Linkages in International Negotiations', *International Organization*, 33: 425–49.

TOMZ, M., GOLDSTEIN, J. and RIVERS, D. (2007), 'Membership Has Its Privileges: The Impact of the GATT on International Trade', *American Economic Review*, 97 (5): 2005–18.

TREBILCOCK, M. and HOWSE, R. (2005), *The Regulation of International Trade*, third edition (London: Routledge).

—— and SOLOWAY, J. (2000), 'International Trade Policy and Domestic Food Regulation: The Case for Substantial Deference by the WTO Dispute Settlement Body under the SPS Agreement', in D. Kennedy and J. Southwick (eds), *The Political Economy of International Trade Law: Essays in Honor of Robert Hudec* (Cambridge: Cambridge University Press).

—— —— (2002), 'International Trade Policy and Domestic Food Safety Regulation', in D. Kennedy and J. Southwick (eds), *The Political Economy of International Trade* (Cambridge: Cambridge University Press).

TULLOCK, G. (1967), 'The Welfare Costs of Tariffs, Monopolies and Theft', *Western Economic Journal*, 5: 224–32.

—— (1988), 'Rent Seeking', in J. Eatwell, M. Milgate and P. Newman (eds), *The New Palgrave: A Dictionary of Economics*, 4: 147–9 (London: Macmillan).

TUMLIR, J. (1983), 'Strong and Weak Elements in the Concept of European Integration', in F. Machlup, G. Fels and H. Müller-Groeling (eds), *Reflections on a Troubled World Economy* (London: Macmillan).

—— (1985), *Protectionism: Trade Policy in Democratic Societies* (Washington, DC: American Enterprise Institute).

—— (2003), 'Plant- and Firm-level Evidence on the "New" Trade Theories', in E. Kwan Choi and J. Harrigan (ed.), *Handbook of International Trade* (Oxford: Basil Blackwell).

ULLRICH, H. (2004), 'Comparing EU Free Trade Agreements: Services', *ECDPM Brief*. European Centre for Development Policy Management, at www.ecdpm.org

UN Millennium Project (2005), 'Trade for Development'. Task Force on Trade (New York: United Nations Development Programme).

UNCTAD (1985), 'Services and the Development Process', TD/B/1008/Rev. 1. (Geneva: United Nations).

UNCTAD (1994), *The Outcome of the Uruguay Round: Supporting Papers to the Trade and Development Report, 1994* (Geneva: United Nations).

——(2005), *World Investment Report: The Shift towards Services* (Geneva: United Nations).

——(2007), *World Investment Report* (Geneva: United Nations).

——(2008), *UNCTAD Investment Brief, No.1* (Geneva: United Nations).

UNCTAD-ICTSD (2005), *Resource Book on TRIPs and Development* (Geneva UNCTAD-ICTSD).

UNCTC (1991) *The Impact of Trade-Related Investment Measures on Trade and Development: Theory, Evidence and Policy Implications* (Geneva: United Nations Conference on Trade and Development, UNCTAD).

UNTER, B. (1998), 'Maximizing Custom Benefits: A Global Model for Regulatory Reform', Presented at the US-China Standards, Testing and Certification Workshop, Washington, DC, 17–18 February.

USTR (2004), '2004 National Trade Estimate Report on Foreign Trade Barriers', Washington, DC Office of the United States Trade Representative, at www.ustr.gov/Document_Library/Section_Index.html

VANRASSTEK, C. (2007), 'The Challenges of Trade Policymaking: Analysis, Communication and Representation', UNCTAD, mimeo.

VERDIER, T. (2005), 'Socially Responsible Trade Integration: A Political Economy Perspective', in F. Borguignon, B. Pleskovic and A. Sapir (eds), *Are We on Track to Achieve the Millennium Development Goals?* (Washington, DC: World Bank).

VERMULST, E., PERNAUTE, M. and LUCENTI, K. (2004), 'Recent EC Safeguards Policy: "Kill Them All and Let God Sort Them Out"', mimeo.

VINER, J. (1923), *Dumping: A Problem in International Trade* (Chicago: University of Chicago Press).

VOGEL, D. (1995), *Trading Up: Consumer and Environmental Regulation in a Global Economy* (Cambridge, MA: Harvard University Press).

WACZIARG, R. and WELCH, K.H. (2008), 'Trade Liberalization and Growth: New Evidence', *World Bank Economic Review*, 22 (2): 187–231.

WALSH, J. (2006), 'New Customs', *Finance and Development*, 43(1), at http://www.imf.org/external/pubs/ft/fandd/2006/03/walsh.htm

WARLEY, T. (1976), 'Western Trade in Agricultural Products', in *International Economic Relations in the Western World 1959–71* (London: Royal Institute of International Affairs).

WATAL, J. (2000), *Intellectual Property Rights in the World Trade Organization: The Way Forward for Developing Countries* (New Delhi: Oxford University Press, India, and London: Kluwer Law International).

WATERMEYER, R. (2004), 'Facilitating Sustainable Development through Public and Donor Procurement Regimes: Tools and Techniques', *Public Procurement Law Review*, 13 (1): 30–55.

WCO (1999), *International Convention on the Simplification and Harmonization of Customs Procedures (Amended)* (Brussels: WCO).

WESTON, A. and DELICH, V. (1999), 'Settling Trade Disputes after the Uruguay Round: Options for the Western Hemisphere', Latin American Trade Network Discussion Paper No. 10 (June).

WHALLEY, J. (1988), *The Uruguay Round and Beyond* (London: Macmillan).

—— (1996), 'Developing Countries and System Strengthening in the Uruguay Round', in W. Martin, and L. A. Winters (eds), *The Uruguay Round and the Developing Countries* (Cambridge, MA: Cambridge University Press).

WHEELER, D. and MODY, A. (1992), 'International Investment Location Decisions: The Case of US Firms', *Journal of International Economics*, 33: 57–76.

WHO (2005), *The World Health Report* (Geneva: World Health Organization).

WILCOX, C. (1949), *A Charter for World Trade* (New York: Macmillan).

WILLIAMS, I. (2005), 'The Secret History of Rum', *The Nation* (22 November), at http://www.thenation.com/doc/20051205/secret_history_of_rum

WILSON, J. S. (1998), *Standards and APEC: An Action Agenda* (Washington, DC: Institute for International Economics).

—— and OTSUKI, T. (2004), 'To Spray or Not to Spray: Pesticides, Banana Exports, and Food Safety', *Food Policy*, 29 (2): 131–46.

—— MANN, C. and OTSUKI, T. (2003), 'Trade Facilitation and Economic Development: A New Approach to Quantifying the Impact', *World Bank Economic Review*, 17 (3): 367–89.

—— —— —— (2005), 'Assessing the Benefits of Trade Facilitation: A Global Perspective', *World Economy*, 28 (6): 841–71.

WINHAM, G. R. (1986), *International Trade and the Tokyo Round Negotiation* (Princeton, NJ: Princeton University Press).

WINTERS, L. A. (1987a), 'Reciprocity', in J. M. Finger and A. Olechowski (eds), *The Uruguay Round: A Handbook for the Multilateral Trade Negotiations* (Washington, DC: The World Bank).

—— (1987b), 'The Political Economy of the Agricultural Policy of Industrialized Countries', *European Review of Agricultural Economics*, 14: 285–304.

—— (1989), 'The So-called Noneconomic Objectives of Agricultural Support', *OECD Economic Studies*, 13: 238–66.

—— (1990), 'The Road to Uruguay', *Economic Journal*, 100: 1288–1303.

—— (1994a), 'Subsidies', in *The New World Trading System: Readings* (Paris: OECD).

—— (1994b), 'The EC and Protection: The Political Economy', *European Economic Review*, 38 (3–4), 596–603.

—— (ed.) (1995), *Foundations of an Open Economy: Trade Laws and Institutions for Eastern Europe* (London: Centre for Economic Policy Research).

—— (1997), 'Regionalism and the Rest of the World: The Irrelevance of the Kemp-Wan Theorem', *Oxford Economic Papers*, 49: 228–34.

—— (1998), 'Regionalism versus Multilateralism', in R. Baldwin *et al.* (eds), *Market Integration, Regionalism and the Global Economy* (London: CEPR).

—— (1999), 'Regionalism vs. Multilateralism,' in R. Baldwin *et al.* (eds) *Market Integration, Regionalism and the Global Economy* (London: CEPR).

—— (2000), 'Coherence With No 'Here': WTO Co-operation with the World Bank and the IMF', University of Sussex, mimeo.

—— (2004), 'Trade Liberalisation and Economic Performance: An Overview', *Economic Journal*, 114: F4–21.

—— (2007), 'Coherence and the WTO', *Oxford Review of Economic Policy*, 23: 461–80.

WOLF, M. (1984), 'Two-Edged Sword: Demands of Developing Countries and the Trading System', in J. Bhagwati and G. Ruggie (eds), *Power, Passions and Purpose: Prospects for North–South Negotiations* (Cambridge, MA: MIT Press).

WOLF, M. (1999), 'Uncivil Society', *Financial Times*, 1: September 12.

World Bank (1986), *World Development Report* (Washington, DC: The World Bank).

—— (2004), *Trade Policies in South Asia* (Washington, DC: World Bank).

—— (2005), *Global Economic Prospects: Trade, Regionalism, and Development* (Washington, DC: World Bank).

—— (2007), *International Trade and Climate Change: Economic, Legal, and Institutional Perspectives* (Washington, DC: World Bank).

—— (2008), *Doing Business 2007* (Washington, DC: World Bank).

World Bank and IMF (2008) *Global Monitoring Report* (Washington, DC: World Bank).

WTO (1998*b*), *Trade Policy Review: Indonesia*, WT/TPR/S/117 (Geneva: World Trade Organization).

—— (2004), *World Trade Report 2004* (Geneva: WTO).

—— (2005), Trade Standards and the WTO: The Economics of Standards and Trade, *World Trade Report 2005* (Geneva: WTO).

—— (2006), 'Recommendations of the Taskforce on Aid for Trade', WT/AFT/1, 27 July (Geneva: WTO).

—— (2007), *World Trade Report 2007: Six Decades of Multilateral Trade Cooperation* (Geneva: WTO).

—— (2008), *World Trade Report 2008: Trade in a Globalizing World* (Geneva: WTO).

YANG, G. and MASKUS, K. E. (2001), 'Intellectual Property Rights, Licensing, and Innovation in an Endogenous Product-Cycle Model', *Journal of International Economics*, 53 (1): 169–87.

ZEDILLO, E. (2007), 'Surviving the Doha Round', in B. Hoekman and M. Olarreaga (eds), *Impacts and Implications of Global Trade Reform on Poverty* (Washington, DC: Brookings Institution).

—— *et al.* (2005), 'Strengthening the Global Trade Architecture for Economic Development: An Agenda for Action', at www.ycsg.yale.edu

ZIMMERMAN, T. (2006), The DSU Review (1998–2004) 'Negotiations, Problems and Perspectives', in K. van der Borght and D. Georgiev (eds), *Reform and Development of the WTO Dispute Settlement System*, pp. 445–72 (London: Cameron May).

INDEX